THE NEW
WEBSTER'S
CROSSWORD
DICTIONARY

THE NEW WEBSTER'S CROSSWORD DICTIONARY

Donald O. Bolander, M.A., Litt. D.

Previously published in hardcover as
The New Webster's Crossword Puzzle Dictionary.

BERKLEY BOOKS, NEW YORK

THE BERKLEY PUBLISHING GROUP
Published by the Penguin Group
Penguin Group (USA) Inc.
375 Hudson Street, New York, New York 10014, USA
Penguin Group (Canada), 90 Eglinton Avenue East, Suite 700, Toronto, Ontario M4P 2Y3, Canada
(a division of Pearson Penguin Canada Inc.)
Penguin Books Ltd., 80 Strand, London WC2R 0RL, England
Penguin Group Ireland, 25 St. Stephen's Green, Dublin 2, Ireland (a division of Penguin Books Ltd.)
Penguin Group (Australia), 250 Camberwell Road, Camberwell, Victoria 3124, Australia
(a division of Pearson Australia Group Pty. Ltd.)
Penguin Books India Pvt. Ltd., 11 Community Centre, Panchsheel Park, New Delhi—110 017, India
Penguin Group (NZ), 67 Apollo Drive, Rosedale, North Shore 0632, New Zealand
(a division of Pearson New Zealand Ltd.)
Penguin Books (South Africa) (Pty.) Ltd., 24 Sturdee Avenue, Rosebank, Johannesburg 2196,
South Africa

Penguin Books Ltd., Registered Offices: 80 Strand, London WC2R 0RL, England

THE NEW WEBSTER'S CROSSWORD DICTIONARY

A Berkley Book / published by arrangement with Lexicon Publications, Inc.

PRINTING HISTORY
Lexicon Publications edition published 1991
Berkley mass-market edition / November 1991

Copyright © 1991 by Lexicon Publications, Inc.

Visit our website at www.penguin.com.

ISBN: 978-0-425-12882-4

BERKLEY®
Berkley Books are published by The Berkley Publishing Group,
a division of Penguin Group (USA) Inc.,
375 Hudson Street, New York, New York 10014.
BERKLEY® is a registered trademark of Penguin Group (USA) Inc.
The "B" design is a trademark belonging to Penguin Group (USA) Inc.

PRINTED IN THE UNITED STATES OF AMERICA

40 39 38 37 36 35 34 33

A

A, a: ... AN, AY, PER, EACH
   Greek: .... ALPHA
   Hebrew: .... ALEPH
aa: .... LAVA
aardvark: ...... ANTEATER,
              ENDENTATE
Aaron: *ally:* .... HUR
   brother: .... MOSES
   burial place: ...... HOR
   father: .... ARAM
   rod: .... MULLEIN
   sister: .... MIRIAM
   son: .... NADAB, ABIHU,
      ELEAZAR, ITHAMAR
abaca: ...... HEMP, FIBER,
     LINAGA, LUPIS
aback, taken: ... SURPRISED,
   STARTLED, CONFUSED,
     DISCONCERTED
Abaddon: ..... HELL, HADES
abaft: ... AFT, BACK, ASTERN,
     BEHIND, REAR
abalone: .... ORMER, AWABI,
   EARSHELL, ASSEIR, MOLLUSK
abandon: .. LEAVE, DISCARD,
   JUNK, VACATE, FORSAKE,
   DESERT, ABDICATE, RENOUNCE
abandoned: .... LEFT, LOST,
   DESOLATE, DERELICT,
   FORSAKEN, DISSOLUTE
abase: ..... DEMEAN, LOWER,
   MORTIFY, HUMBLE, DEGRADE,
     DEPRECIATE
abash: ...... AWE, SHAME,
   EMBARRASS, HUMILIATE,
   CONFOUND, DISCOMFIT,
   INTIMIDATE, DISCONCERT
abate: ... EBB, END, SUBSIDE,
   LESSEN, SLOW, REDUCE,
   DECREASE, DIMINISH, SLACKEN,
     WANE, EASE
abatis: .... OBSTACLE,
     BARRICADE
abbe: ...... ABBOT, CLERIC,
     MONK, PRIEST
abbess: ... AMMA, PRELATESS

abbey: ... PRIORY, CONVENT,
   MONASTERY, SANCTUARY
abbot: ..... ABBAS, COARB
   assistant: ...... PRIOR
abbreviate: .. CUT, ABRIDGE,
   SHORTEN, CONTRACT,
   CONDENSE, TRUNCATE
abdicate: .... RENOUNCE,
   RESIGN, VACATE, SURRENDER,
     RELINQUISH
abdomen: .... BELLY,
   STOMACH, PAUNCH, VENTER
abduct: ...... TAKE, STEAL,
   KIDNAP, SHANGHAI
Abel: *brother:* .. CAIN, SETH
   parents: .... ADAM, EVE
aberration: ..... DELUSION,
   DEVIATION, DERANGEMENT,
   DELIRIUM, HALLUCINATION
abet: ... AID, HELP, FOMENT,
   INCITE, ASSIST, SUPPORT,
     ENCOURAGE
abeyance: ..... SUSPENSION,
   SUPPRESSION, CESSATION,
     PENDENCY
abhor: ..... DETEST, HATE,
   DISLIKE, EXECRATE, LOATHE
abide: ... LIVE, STAY, AWAIT,
   RESIDE, SOJOURN, REMAIN,
   ENDURE, TOLERATE
ability: ..... SKILL, FLAIR,
   POWER, APTITUDE, TALENT,
   CALIBER, COMPETENCE,
   CAPABILITY, FACULTY
abject: .. LOW, BASE, PITIFUL,
   MEAN, PALTRY, WRETCHED,
   GROVELING, SLAVISH
abjure: ...... DENY, SPURN,
   REJECT, RECANT, REPUDIATE,
   RENOUNCE, DISAVOW
able: ..... APT, FIT, ADEPT,
   CAPABLE, SKILLFUL,
   COMPETENT, QUALIFIED,
     TALENTED
ablution: .... BATH(ING),
   WASHING, CLEANSING
abnegate: ... DENY, ABJURE,
   REFUSE, DISAVOW, FORSWEAR,
     REJECT

abnormal: .... ODD, QUEER, IRREGULAR, ABBERANT, UNNATURAL, EXTRAORDINARY

abode: ..... NEST, HABITAT, DOMICILE, RESIDENCE, HABITATION, HOME

of animals: ... STY, LAIR, DEN, WARREN, HUTCH, ZOO, MENAGERIE

of birds: .... COTE, NEST, AERIE, AVIARY

of gods: . MERU, ASGARD, ASGARTH, OLYMPUS

of dead: ... DAR, ARALU, ORCUS, HADES, SHEOL, HEAVEN, PURGATORY

abolish: . END, KILL, ANNUL, CANCEL, NULLIFY, REPEAL, REVOKE, DISCARD, DISCONTINUE

abominable: .... VILE, ATROCIOUS, LOATHSOME, DETESTABLE, EXECRABLE, HATEFUL

Snowman: .... YETI, MONSTER

abominate: .. HATE, ABHOR, DETEST, LOATHE, EXECRATE

aboriginal: ... FIRST, NATAL, ORIGINAL, PRIMITIVE, INDIGENOUS

aborigine: .... NATIVE, SAVAGE, INDIAN, INDIGENE

abortion: ...... MISBIRTH, MISCARRIAGE, FETICIDE, FOETICIDE, MISCONCEPTION

abortive: .... VAIN, FUTILE, FRUITLESS, UNSUCCESSFUL

abounding: .... RIFE, FLUSH, REPLETE, ABUNDANT, PLENTIFUL, TEEMING

about: ..... RE, OF, ANENT, NEAR, SOME, ALMOST, CIRCA, REGARDING, CONCERNING, APPROXIMATELY

above: . ON, UP, ATOP, OVER, ALOFT, HIGHER, UPON, PAST, EXCEEDING, SUPERIOR

abrade: ...... RUB, CHAFE, GRATE, RASP, SCRAPE, IRRITATE

Abraham: *birthplace:* ... UR

brother: . HARAN, NAHOR

father: .... TERAH

grandfather: .... NAHOR

nephew: .... LOT

son: ..... ISAAC, MEDAN, MIDIAN, SHUAH, ISHMAEL, ZIMRAN

wife: .... SARA, HAGAR, SARAH, SARAI, KETURAH

abramis: ...... CARP, FISH, BREAM

abrasive: .. EMERY, ERODENT, QUARTZ, SAND(PAPER), CORUNDUM

abridge: .... CUT, SHORTEN, CURTAIL, CONDENSE, ABBREVIATE

abridgment: .... SUMMARY, SYNOPSIS, DIGEST, EPITOME

abrogate: .. ANNUL, CANCEL, REVOKE, REPEAL, ABOLISH, RESCIND

abrupt: .. CURT, RUDE, STEEP, HASTY, BRUSQUE, SUDDEN, UNEXPECTED, PRECIPITATE

Absalom: *captain:* .. AMASA

father: .... DAVID

sister: .... TAMAR

slayer: .... JOAB

abscess: .... PUSTULE, BOIL, ULCER

abscond: ..... ELOPE, FLEE, DECAMP, LEVANT, ESCAPE, ELOINE

absence: ...... LACK, VOID, LEAVE, VACUUM, DEFICIENCY, NONAPPEARANCE

absent: .. OUT, AWAY, GONE, LACKING, ABSORBED, ABSTRACTED

absolute: ...... DEAD, PURE, TOTAL, ENTIRE, STARK, SHEER, COMPLETE, CERTAIN, DEFINITE, ULTRA, CLEARANCE

absolve: ..... FREE, CLEAR, PARDON, REMIT, ACQUIT, RELEASE, EXONERATE

absorb: . . SOP, TAKE, MERGE, ENGROSS, UNITE, COMBINE, ENGULF, DRINK, SWALLOW, ASSIMILATE

abstain: . . . . . . DENY, FAST, WAIVE, ESCHEW, REFRAIN, FOREGO, REFUSE

abstinence: . . . . SELF-RESTRAINT, SELF-DENIAL, CHASTITY, CELIBACY, TEMPERANCE, TEETOTALISM

abstract: . . . . . . CULL, TAKE, REMOVE, BRIEF, DEDUCT, PRECIS, COMPEND, ABRIDGE, EPITOME, SUMMARY

abstruse: . . . . . DARK, DEEP, RECONDITE, SUBTLE, OBSCURE, ESOTERIC

absurd: . . . . . . INANE, SILLY, RIDICULOUS, LUDICROUS, NONSENSICAL, FOOLISH, PREPOSTEROUS

abundant: . . . . . LUSH, RIFE, AMPLE, PLENTIFUL, PROFUSE, TEEMING, AFFLUENT, NUMEROUS

abuse: . HARM, HURT, MAUL, MISTREAT, INJURE, MISUSE, VIOLATE, MALTREAT

abut: . . . . . ADJOIN, BORDER

abyss: . . . . PIT, GULF, CHASM, HOLE, GORGE, DEPTH

Abyssinia: . . . . see **Ethiopia**

acacia: . . . . . TREE, LOCUST, BABUL, MIMOSA, SHITTAH, ARABIC, COOBAH, MYALL

academic: . . . . CLASSIC, ERUDITE, SCHOLASTIC, SCHOLARLY, LEARNED, PEDANTIC

academy: . . . . SCHOOL, LYCEUM, SEMINARY, ANNAPOLIS, WEST POINT, USMA, USNA

acarid: . . MITE, TICK, INSECT, ARACHNID

accede: . . . . . AGREE, GRANT, ALLOW, CONSENT, ASSENT, ACQUIESCE

accelerate: . . . . RACE, URGE, SPEED, HASTEN, ADVANCE, INCREASE, STIMULATE

accent: . . . . . . TONE, STRESS, BROGUE, RHYTHM, ICTUS, EMPHASIS, MARK

accentuate: . . . . STRESS, INTENSIFY, EMPHASIZE

accept: . . . . . . TAKE, ADOPT, AGREE, ADMIT, ALLOW RECEIVE, ACQUIESCE

access: . . WAY, DOOR, GATE, ROAD, ENTRY, ENTRANCE, INCREASE, ADMISSION, APPROACH, PASSAGEWAY

accessory: . . . . . AIDE, ALLY, TOOL, EXTRA, ADJUNCT, HELPER, ASSISTANT, APPURTENANT, ACCOMPLICE, ADDITIONAL

accident: . . . . CHANCE, CASUALTY, MISHAP, CALAMITY, DISASTER

acclaim: . . . . . . HAIL, LAUD, PRAISE, CHEER, EXTOL, APPLAUD

acclimate: . . INURE, HARDEN, HABITUATE, ACCUSTOM

acclivity: . . . . . . BANK, HILL, SLOPE

accommodate: . . . . AID, FIT, HELP, ADAPT, OBLIGE, GRANT, ADJUST, YIELD, RECONCILE, LODGE

accompany: . . ESCORT, PILOT, CONDUCT, CONVOY, CHAPERON(E)

accomplish: . . . . DO, ATTAIN, EFFECT, FINISH, FULFILL, ACHIEVE, CONSUMATE

accomplished: . . . . . . ABLE, ADEPT, EXPERT, SKILLED, PROFICIENT, TALENTED

accomplishment: . . . . FEAT, DEED, SKILL, TALENT, ACHIEVEMENT, ATTAINMENT

accord: . . . . . . UNITY, GIVE, SETTLE, UNISON, HARMONY, CONCURRENCE

accost: .. HAIL, GREET, CALL, MEET, ADDRESS, SALUTE, APPROACH, WAYLAY

account: ... TAB, BILL, ITEM, TALE, SAKE, STATEMENT, EXPLAIN, COMPUTE, STORY, REPORT, RECORD, EXPLANATION

accountant: .... CPA, AUDITOR, BOOKKEEPER, CALCULATOR

accouter: . ARM, RIG, DRESS, EQUIP, CLOTHE, ARRAY, OUTFIT

accredit: .... APPOINT, APPROVE, DEPUTE, AUTHORIZE, CERTIFY

accrue: .. EARN, GAIN, ENSUE, RESULT, ACQUIRE, INCREASE, ACCUMULATE

accumulate: .... AMASS, ACCRUE, GARNER, COLLECT, GATHER, AGGREGATE

accurate: .... TRUE, EXACT, RIGHT, PRECISE, CORRECT

accuse: .... CHARGE, BLAME, ATTACK, INDICT, ARRAIGN, IMPEACH, DENOUNCE

accustom: ... ADAPT, TRAIN, INURE, ENURE, ACCLIMATE, HABITUATE, TOUGHEN

ace: ..... ONE, TOPS, STAR, HERO, EXPERT, AVIATOR

acerbate: ... VEX, EMBITTER, IRRITATE, EXASPERATE

acetic acid: ...... ACETATE, VINEGAR

acetone: . ACETOL, KEYSTONE

acetose: ...... ACID, SOUR

acetum: .... VINEGAR

acetylene: .... GAS, TOLANE, ETHIN(E)

ache: ... PAIN, PANG, YEARN, THROB, PINE, DESIRE

achieve: ... DO, WIN, REACH, ATTAIN, SUCCEED, FULFILL, REALIZE, ACCOMPLISH

achievement: .... FEAT, EXPLOIT, ACCOMPLISHMENT, ATTAINMENT

Achilles: .... PELIDES

advisor: .... NESTOR
friend: ..... PATROCLUS
horse: .... XANTHUS
parents: .. PELEUS, THETIS
slayer: .... PARIS
teacher: ...... CHIRON, CENTAUR
victim: .... HECTOR
vulnerable spot: .... HEEL

acid: .... SOUR, TART, ACRID, SHARP, BITING, ACETOUS

acidity: .... ACOR, ACERBITY

acknowledge: . OWN, ADMIT, ALLOW, GRANT, AVOW, SIGN, RECOGNIZE, ANSWER, CONFESS, CONCEDE

acme: .... TOP, PEAK, APEX, PINNACLE, SUMMIT, ZENITH

acolyte: .... ALTARBOY, NOVICE, HELPER

acomia: .... BALDNESS

acorn: .. NUT, OVEST, MAST, CAMATA, BALLOTE

acquaint: .... TELL, TEACH, APPRISE, INFORM, NOTIFY, FAMILIARIZE

acquainted: .... KNOWN, FAMILIAR, (CON)VERSANT

acquiesce: .. AGREE, ACCEDE, ASSENT, COMPLY, CONFORM, CONSENT

acquire: ... GET, WIN, EARN, GAIN, OBTAIN, LEARN, PROCURE, ATTAIN

acquit: ...... FREE, CLEAR, ABSOLVE, EXCUSE, RELEASE, EXONERATE, EXCULPATE

acrid: ... ACID, SHARP, SOUR, BITING, CAUSTIC, PUNGENT, BITTER, HARSH

acrimonious: ...... ANGRY, GRUFF, BITTER, STINGING, CAUSTIC, HARSH

acrobat: .... GYMNAST, TUMBLER, CONTORTIONIST, AERIALIST

acrogen: ...... MOSS, FERN

acropolis: ..... FORT, HILL, CITADEL

across: ... OVER, TRAVERSE, OPPOSITE, ATHWART, ASTRADDLE

acrostic: ..... AGLA, GAME, PUZZLE, CROSSWISE

act: .. DO, LAW, BILL, DEED, FEAT, EMOTE, PLAY, STUNT, DECREE, PERFORM, EDICT, BEHAVE, PORTRAY

action: ... CASE, STEP, DEED, LAWSUIT, FUNCTION, ACTIVITY, COMBAT, BEHAVIOR, PERFORMANCE

field of: .. BOWL, ARENA, STAGE, COURT, DIAMOND, STADIUM

put into: ...... ACTUATE, ACTIVATE

to recover: .... TROVER, REPLEVIN

word: .... VERB

active: .. BUSY, ASTIR, SPRY, AGILE, ALERT, LIVELY, BRISK, WORKING, MOVING, PRODUCTIVE

activity: ..... ADO, STIR, OPERATION, MOVEMENT

actor: ... LEAD, STAR, EXTRA, THESPIAN, MIME, HISTRIO(N), PLAYER, PERFORMER, TROUPER, ENTERTAINER

actress (see actor): ... DIVA, STAR, INGENUE

actual: .... TRUE, REAL, FACTUAL, GENUINE, EXISTING, TANGIBLE, VERITABLE

actuality: .... FACT, BEING, TRUTH, VERITY, REALITY, SUBSTANCE

actuate: ..... URGE, MOVE, ROUSE, IMPEL, INCITE, STIR, MOTIVATE, ANIMATE, ACTIVATE

acumen: ..... WIT, INSIGHT, KEENNESS, SHREWDNESS, ACUTENESS

acute: .... CUTE, FINE, KEEN, SHREWD, ASTUTE, INTENSE, SEVERE, CRITICAL, URGENT

A.D.: .... ANNO DOMINI

ad: .... ADVERTISEMENT, NOTICE, INSERTION, ENDLESSLY, FOREVER

adage: ...... SAW, AXIOM, MAXIM, SAYING, PROVERB, BROMIDE

Adam: first wife: .... LILITH

needle: .... YUCCA

second wife: ...... EVE

son: ... ABEL, CAIN, SETH

adamant: . HARD, FIRM, SET, OBDURATE, UNYIELDING, IMMOVABLE

adapt: .... FIT, SUIT, APPLY, INURE, ADJUST, CONFORM, COMPLY, CHANGE, ORIENT, ACCLIMATE

add: ...... SAY, SUM, JOIN, AFFIX, ANNEX, TOTAL, ATTACH, AUGMENT, COMBINE, COMPUTE, INCREASE, SUPPLEMENT

added: ..... AND, EKE, PLUS

addict: ... FAN, BUFF, USER, DEVOTEE, FIEND, HOPHEAD, POTHEAD, ACIDHEAD, MAINLINER, ENTHUSIAST

addiction: .... HABIT, INCLINATION, ATTACHMENT, HABITUATION

addition: ... AND, ELL, ALSO, PLUS, RIDER, ANNEX, ADJUNCT, CODICIL, ADDENDUM, AMENDMENT, APPENDAGE

additional: .... NEW, MORE, EXTRA, OTHER, FURTHER, AUXILIARY

addle: ... MIRE, SPOIL, RIPEN, MUDDLE, CONFUSE, BEWILDER, CONFOUND

address: ...... CALL, HAIL, SPEECH, TALK, HOME, ABODE, ACCOST, GREET, POISE, DIRECT, MANNER, LECTURE, CONSIGN, PETITION

adduce: ...... CITE, NAME, OFFER, ALLEGE, INFER, QUOTE, ADVANCE, MENTION

adept: . . APT, ABLE, SKILLED, HANDY, CAPABLE, EXPERT, DEFT, PROFICIENT

adequate: . . . AMPLE, EQUAL, ENOUGH, SATISFACTORY, SUFFICIENT, SUITABLE

adhere: . . . . GLUE, HOLD, CLING, STICK, UNITE, CLEAVE, PERSIST

adherent: . . . . . . FOLLOWER, DISCIPLE, ZEALOT, VOTARY, ITE, IST, DEVOTEE, STICKING, RETAINER, PARTISAN

adhesive: . . . . . GUM, GLUE, PASTE, MASTIC, MUCILAGE, CEMENT, EPOXY

adjacent: . . . . . NEAR, NEXT, CLOSE, BESIDE, ADJOINING, CONTIGUOUS, NEIGHBORING

adjoin: . . . . . . ABUT, TOUCH, ATTACH, BORDER, CONTACT, NEIGHBOR

adjourn: . . . . . . END, CEASE, STAY, CLOSE, DISSOLVE, DISCONTINUE, SUSPEND, RETIRE, RECESS

adjudge: . . . . . . DEEM, FIND, AWARD, CONDEMN, DECREE, DECIDE, SENTENCE, SETTLE, SENTENCE, DETERMINE

adjudicate: . . . . TRY, HEAR, RULE, SENTENCE, DECIDE

adjust: . . FIT, FIX, TRIM, SIZE, ADAPT, ALIGN, ATTUNE, ORIENT, ARRANGE, RECTIFY

adjutant: . . . . . AIDE, ALLY, HELPER, ASSISTANT

ad-lib: . . . . . . EXTEMPORIZE, IMPROVISE

administer: . . . . . RUN, GIVE, MANAGE, CONDUCT, GOVERN, HUSBAND, DISPENSE

admire: . . . . . . LIKE, LOVE, VALUE, ESTEEM, REGARD

admit: . . . . . . OWN, ALLOW, GRANT, ACCEPT, CONFESS, PROFESS, CONCEDE, RECEIVE, ACKNOWLEDGE, INTROMIT

admonish: . . . . WARN, CHIDE, ADVISE, REBUKE, REPROVE, CAUTION, COUNSEL, SERMON(IZE)

adobe: . . . MUD, CLAY, BRICK

adolescence: . . . . TEENS, YOUTH, TEENAGE, PUBERTY

adopt: . . . . . TAKE, ACCEPT, ESPOUSE, EMBRACE, CHOOSE, FOLLOW, MAINTAIN

adore: . . . . . . DOTE, LOVE, ADMIRE, WORSHIP, IDOLIZE, REVERE

adorn: . . . DECK, GILD, TRIM, DRESS, ARRAY, BEDECK, DECORATE, GARNISH, ORNAMENT, BEAUTIFY, EMBELLISH

adrift: . . ASEA, LOST, LOOSE, DERELICT, AFLOAT, UNTIED

adroit: . . . . . . DEFT, ADEPT, HABILE, SKILLFUL, CLEVER, DEXTROUS

adulate: . . . LAUD, FLATTER, PRAISE, COMPLIMENT

adult: . . GROWN(UP), MATURE, OF AGE

person: . . . . MAN, WOMAN

insect: . . . . IMAGO

tadpole: . . . . FROG

wriggler: . . . . . MOSQUITO

adulterate: . . CUT, MIX, ALTER, DEBASE, DEFILE, DENATURE, CORRUPT, CONTAMINATE

adulterated: . . . . . . IMPURE, COUNTERFEIT

adust: . . . BURNT, SCORCHED, PARCHED, SUNBURNT

advance: . . . AID, PAY, GAIN, MOVE, MARCH, BOOST, RAISE, PROGRESS, PROMOTE, PROPOSE, ACCELERATE

slowly: . . . . CREEP, INCH, WORM

advanced: . . . . . FAR(GONE), ENLIGHTENED, PROGRESSIVE

advantage: . . . . GAIN, EDGE, PROFIT, ODDS, BENEFIT, LEVERAGE, OPPORTUNITY

advent: ... COMING, ARRIVAL, APPROACH

adventure: .... LARK, RISK, PERIL, GEST(E), QUEST, ENTERPRISE, VENTURE, ESCAPADE, EXPERIENCE

adventurous: .... RASH, DARING, RECKLESS, AUDACIOUS, FOOLHARDY, COURAGEOUS

adversary: .... FOE, ENEMY, RIVAL, OPPONENT, ANTAGONIST

adverse: .. HOSTILE, OPPOSED, CONTRARY, UNFAVORABLE, INIMICAL

adversity: ... WOE, DISTRESS, MISFORTUNE, POVERTY, CALAMITY

advertisement: .... AD, BILL, SIGN, NOTICE, ORBIT, HANDBILL, BLURB, POSTER, BILLBOARD, NEON, COMMERCIAL

advice: ..... NEWS, NOTICE, COUNSEL, OPINION, REPORT, MESSAGE, RECOMMENDATION, ADMONITION

advise: ...... TELL, WARN, INFORM, APPRISE, CAUTION, ACQUAINT, RECOMMEND

adviser: .... MONITOR, COUNSELOR, MENTOR

advocate: . FAVOR, ENDORSE, ESPOUSE, SUPPORT, RECOMMEND, LAWYER, ABETTOR, DEFENDER

adz: ...... AX(E), HATCHET, CUTTING TOOL

aegis: .... SHIELD, AUSPICES, PROTECTION, SPONSORSHIP

Aeneas: ....
great grandson: ... BRUT
parents: ..... ANCHISES, VENUS
son: .... IULUS, ASCANIUS
wife: .. CREUSA, LAVINIA

Aeneid: author: .... VERGIL, VIRGIL

aeonian: .. ETERNAL, LASTING

aerial: ...... AIRY, LOFTY, UNREAL, ANTENNA, ETHEREAL, IMAGINARY

aeronautics: ..... SCIENCE, AVIATION

aerostat: ... BALLOON, BLIMP, DIRIGIBLE, ZEPPELIN

aerugo: ...... RUST, PATINA, VERDIGRIS

aes: .... COIN, BRONZE

aesthetic: .... ARTISTIC, TASTEFUL

Aether's father: .... EREBUS

Aetolian prince: .... TYDEUS

afar: ... AWAY, OFF, DISTANT

affable: ... SUAVE, POLITE, AMIABLE, FRIENDLY, SOCIABLE

affair: .... CASE, EVENT, BUSINESS, MATTER, ROMANCE, TRANSACTION

affect: .. MOVE, STIR, ALTER, IMPEL, CHANGE, PRETEND, FEIGN, IMPRESS, INFLUENCE, TOUCH, IMPRESS

affectation: ...... AIR, POSE, PRETENSE, PRETENSION, MANNERISM
of elegance: .... FRIPPERY

affection: ... LOVE, AMOUR, REGARD, FONDNESS, AILMENT, DISEASE, FEELING

affiance: ..... FAITH, TRUST, BETROTH, ENGAGE, PLEDGE

affidavit: .... OATH, STATEMENT, DEPOSITION, DECLARATION

affiliate: .. ALLY, UNIT, JOIN, ASSOCIATE, MERGE, BRANCH

affinity: ... LIKING, KINSHIP, RELATION, CONNECTION

affirm: ..... AVER, AVOW, ATTEST, ASSERT, SWEAR, VOUCH, RATIFY

affirmation: .... AFFIDAVIT, CONFIRMATION, DECLARATION, DEPOSITION

affix: ... FIX, JOIN, ATTACH, FASTEN, STAMP

afflict: . AIL, TRY, VEX, PAIN, BESET, DISTRESS, TROUBLE

affluence: . . RICHES, WEALTH, ABUNDANCE, OPULENCE, PROSPERITY

afford: . . GIVE, LEND, SPARE, YIELD, SUPPLY, FURNISH

affray: . . . . . . RIOT, MELEE, BRAWL, FIGHT, STRIFE

afloat: . . . . . . ASEA, ADRIFT, CURRENT, SEABORNE, FLOATING

afoot: . . . . . . ABOUT, ASTIR, ABROAD, MOVING, WALKING

aforesaid: . . PRIOR, PREVIOUS, FOREGOING, ANTECEDENT

aforethought: . . . PREPENSE, DELIBERATE, PREMEDITATED

afraid: . . . AGHAST, SCARED, FEARFUL, ALARMED, TERRIFIED, FRIGHTENED, TIMOROUS

Africa: old name: . . . LIBYA

African: . . NEGRO, NEGROID, BLACK

antelope: . . . . . GNU, KOB, KUDU, ADDAX, GONGO, ELAND, ORIBI, PEELE, DUIKER, IMPALA, KOODOO, BLESBOK, BOSHBOK, GEMSBOK, BLESBUCK, BONTEBOK, DUICKERBUCK, HARTEBEEST

aunt: . . . . TANTA

bat: . . . . . . HAMMERHEAD

burrowing animal: . . . . . . GERBIL, SURICATE, AARDVARK

caffeine tree: . . . . . KOLA, COLA

carnivore: . . LION, RATEL, HYENA, CHEETAH, LEOPARD

colonist: . . . . BOER

desert: . . . IGIDI, LIBYAN, SAHARA, KALAHARI

garment: . . . . HAIK, TOBE, KAROSS

gold district: . . . . . RAND

grassland: . . . . . . VELD(T)

Hottentot: . . . . . . NAMA

hunting party: . . . . SAFARI

hut: . . . . . KRAAL, TEMBE

lake: . . . . NYAS(S)A, T(S)ANA, VICTORIA, CHAD

language: . . . . TAAL, BANTU, HAUSA, HAMITE, SWAHILI

Moslem Muslim: . . BERBER

mountain: . . . . . . ATLAS, KENIA, NATAL, CATHKIM, CAMERON, DRAKENBERG, KILIMANJARO

Portuguese colony: . . . . . . ANGOLA

region: . . CONGO, NUBIA, SUDAN, SOUDAN

river: . . . . . . NILE, TANA, BINUE, CONGO, SHARI, VOLTA, GAMBIA, UBANGI, CALABAR, SENEGAL, ZAMBESI

tree: . . AKEE, BANU, COLA, KOLA, MOLI, SHEA, ABURA, ARTAR, SASSY, SIRIS, BAOBAB, ASSAGAI, COPAIBA

valley: . . . . DAAL, WADI, WADY, KLOOF

wood: . . . . . . TEAK, EBONY

Afrikaans: . . . . BOER, TAAL

aft: . . . . BACK, REAR, ABAFT, (A)STERN, POSTERIOR

after: . . ANON, NEXT, LATER, BEHIND, FOLLOW, SUBSEQUENT, SUCCEEDING

aftermath: . EFFECT, ROWEN, RESULT, SEQUEL, CONSEQUENCE

afterthought: . . . . . . REGRET, REMORSE, RECONSIDERATION

in letter: . . . . . . POSTSCRIPT

afterward: . . . THEN, LATER, THEREAFTER, SUBSEQUENTLY

again: . . ANEW, ANON, MORE, OVER, RECUR, REPEAT, ENCOURE, BESIDES, FURTHER

against: . . . CON, NON, ANTI, CONTRA, VERSUS, OPPOSED, ADVERSE

agama: . . . . LIZARD, IGUANA, CHAMELEON

Agamemnon:
brother: . . . . . MENELAUS
children: . . . . . IPHIGENIA, ELECTRA, ORESTES

father: . . . . ATREUS

agate: . . . . ONYX, RUBY, MARBLE, ACHATE, QUARTZ, TYPE

agave: . . ALOE, PITA, AMOLE, ISTLE, SISAL, DATIL, MESCAL, MAGUEY, PULQUE

juice drink: . . . . PULQUE, MESCAL

age: . . . . . . ERA, EON, TIME, CYCLE, RIPEN, MELLOW, CENTURY, MATURE, LIFETIME, GENERATION, ADOLESCENCE, PUBERTY

aged: . RIPE, OLD(EN), ANILE, INFIRM, MATURE, SENILE, ELDERLY

agency: . . . . . . HAND, FORCE, LEVER, MEANS, MEDIUM, OPERATION

agendum: . . . . RECORD, PROGRAM, RITUAL

agent: . . SPY, CAUSE, ENVOY, FACTOR, MEANS, DEALER, BROKER, PROXY, DEPUTY, EMISSARY, REPRESENTATIVE, MIDDLEMAN, PROCTOR

insurance: . . UNDERWRITER

agglomerate: . . . HEAP, MASS, LUMP, CLUSTER, GATHER, COLLECTION

aggravate: . . . . IRK, VEX, ANNOY, WORSEN, IRRITATE, INTENSIFY

aggregate: . . . . . . ALL, SUM, MASS, TOTAL, GATHER, COMPOSITE

aggressive: . . . . . MILITANT, ASSERTIVE, PUSHING, ENTERPRISING

aggressor: . . . . . . ATTACKER, ASSAILANT

aggrieve: . . . . HARM, HURT, OFFEND, INJURE, WRONG

aghast: . . AMAZED, SHOCKED, STUNNED, TERRIFIED, HORRIFIED

agile: . . . DEFT, SPRY, LITHE, NIMBLE, DEXTROUS, ACTIVE, QUICK

agitate: . . . . VEX, RILE, STIR, ALARM, HARRY, CHURN, ROUSE, EXCITE, AROUSE, DISTURB, FLUSTER, FOMENT, PERTURB, ACTIVATE

agnate: . . . . KIN, ALLIED, COGNATE

agnomen: . . . . . NAME, ALIAS

agnostic: . . . . ATHEIST, DOUBTER, SKEPTIC, NESCIENT

Agnus Dei: . . . . BELL, LAMB, PRAYER

ago: . . . . . PAST, ERST, GONE, YORE, SINCE

agog: . . . AVID, KEEN, EAGER, EXCITED, EXPECTANT

agonize: . . . . RACK, SUFFER, STRAIN, WRITHE, STRUGGLE

agony: . . PANG, PAIN, THROE, TRIAL, ANGUISH, DISTRESS, TORMENT, SUFFERING

agouti: . . . . . PACA, RODENT

Agra: tomb: . . . TAJ MAHAL

agree: . . . . . . FIT, JIBE, SUIT, ADMIT, GRANT, CONCUR, MATCH, TALLY, ASSENT, ACCEDE, APPROVE, COINCIDE, CORRESPOND

agreeable: . . . . EASY, GOOD, NICE, COMELY, SAVORY, AMIABLE, WELCOME, PLEASING, SUITABLE, PLEASANT, ACCEPTABLE, WILLING AMENABLE

agreement: . . . . DEAL, PACT, TREATY, ASSENT, CARTEL, ACCORD, BARGAIN, CONCORD, CONTRACT, COVENANT, CONSENSUS, CONSPIRACY

Agrippa: temple: . . . . PANTHEON

Agrippina's son: . . . . NERO

ague: . . . . FEVER, CHILL, MALARIA

ahead: . . . . . FORE, BEFORE, ONWARD, LEADING, FORWARD, PRECEDING

aheuhuete: . CEDAR, CYPRESS
aid: .... ABET, BACK, HELP,
ASSIST, RESCUE, SUCCOR,
FURTHER
Aida: *composer:*..... VERDI
lover: .... RADAMES
rival: .... AMNERIS
aide: .... DEPUTY, ORDERLY,
ASSISTANT, ADJUTANT,
SUBORDINATE
ail: ..... FAIL, PAIN, FALTER,
SUFFER, DECLINE
ailment: .... ILLNESS,
DISORDER, DISEASE, MALADY,
COMPLAINT, INFIRMITY
aim: ..... END, GOAL, PLAN,
SIGHT, DESIGN, OBJECT,
TARGET, INTENT, PURPOSE,
AMBITION
aimless: .... IDLE, RANDOM,
DESULTORY, HAPHAZARD,
PURPOSELESS
air: . SKY, ARIA, MEIN, TUNE,
SONG, VENT, OZONE, ETHER,
MANNER, CARRIAGE,
VENTILATE, ATMOSPHERE
element: .. ARGON, XENON,
OXYGEN, NITROGEN
aircraft: .... BLIMP, PLANE,
COPTER, GLIDER, AIRPLANE,
BALLOON, DIRIGIBLE,
AUTOGIRO, HELICOPTER,
FUSELAGE
airport: . DROME, AIRDROME,
AIRFIELD, AERODROME
airtight: .. SEALED, HERMETIC
airy: ..... GAY, COOL, THIN,
ETHEREAL, LIGHT, JAUNTY,
BREEZY, DELICATE
aisle: .. NAVE, WALK, ALLEY,
CORRIDOR, PASSAGEWAY
akin: ..... SIB, LIKE, NEAR,
CLOSE, AGNATE, GERMANE,
RELATED
alabaster: .... GYPSUM
alacrity: ..... HASTE, SPEED,
CELERITY, RAPIDITY,
READINESS, QUICKNESS
Aladdin's spirit: .... GENIE,
JINNI

Alamo: .... FORT, TREE,
BATTLE, POPLAR, SHRINE,
MISSION
hero: .. BOWIE, CROCKETT
alar: ...... PETRIC, WINGED,
AXILLARY, WINGLIKE,
WINGSHAPED
alarm: . BELL, NOISE, SCARE,
PANIC, SIREN, AROUSE,
DISMAY, FRIGHT, SIGNAL,
TERROR, TOCSIN, WARN(ING),
FRIGHTEN
albacore: ... TUNA, TUNNY,
BONITO
alcohol: ... ETHYL, METHYL,
ETHANOL, METHANOL,
INTOXICANT, SPIRITS, LIQUOR
alcoholic: ..... DRUNKARD,
DIPSOMANIAC
drink:.... ALE, GIN, RUM,
BEER, WINE, GROG, LAGER,
VODKA, BRANDY, LIQUOR,
WHISKY
Alcoran: .... KORAN
Alcott herione: ... JO, MEG,
AMY, BETH
alcove: .. BAY, NOOK, NICHE,
RECESS, ORIEL, BOWER,
CUBICLE
ale: .... MUM, BOCK, BREW,
BEER, ALEGAR, LAGER,
PORTER, HAPPY, STOUT, STINGO
alembic: .... STILL, RETORT,
VESSEL, DISTILLER
alert: .. GLEG, WARY, AGILE,
ALARM, AWAKE, AWARE,
EAGER, SHARP, READY, ACTIVE,
LIVELY, WARNING, VIGILANT,
WATCHFUL, OBSERVANT
alewife: ..... FISH, WALLEYE,
POMPANO, HERRING
Alexander:
battlesite: ...... GRANICUS
conquests: .... ISSUS,
ARBELA, PARTHIA
horse: ...... BUCEPHALUS
kingdom: .... MACEDONIA
mathematician: ....
PTOLEMY

patriarch: .... PAPA
theologian: ...... ARIUS
writer: .... ORIGEN
alfalfa: .... HAY, LUCERN(E),
FODDER
alforja: ...... BAG, POUCH,
SADDLEBAG
alga: ...... NORI, DIATOM,
DESMID, NOSTOC, ANABAENA,
CONFERVA, SPYROGYRA,
SEAWEED
algae genus: ...... ALARIA
like: .... ALGOID
algarroba: .... TREE, CAROB,
MESQUITE, CALDEN, LOCUST
algesia: .... ACHE, PAIN,
ALGESIS
algid: .. COLD, COOL, CHILLY
Algonquian Indian: ... SAC,
CREE, LENAPE, OTTAWA,
MIAMI, SHAWNEE, ARAPAHO(E)
friend: .... NETOP
Indian money: ....
SE(A)WAN, SEWANT
Ali Baba: .... WOODCUTTER
brother: .... CASSIM
word: .... (OPEN) SESAME
alias: .. NAME, TITLE, OTHER,
PSEUDONYM, PEN NAME,
SOBRIQUET
alibi: ...... PLEA, EXCUSE,
PRETEXT
alien: .... METIC, REMOTE,
EXOTIC, ADVERSE,
FOREIGN(ER), IMMIGRANT,
STRANGER, OUTSIDER
alienate: ..... PART, WEAN,
ESTRANGE, SEPARATE,
TRANSFER
alienist: ..... PSYCHIATRIST
alight: . LAND, STOP, ARRIVE,
DESCEND, DISMOUNT
alike: .... AKIN, LIKE, SAME,
EQUAL, UNIFORM, IDENTICAL,
MATCHED
aliment: ... FOOD, ALIMONY,
RATIONS, NOURISHMENT
alimony: .... AILMENT,
ALLOWANCE, MAINTENANCE

alive: ... BUSY, VIVE, ALERT,
VITAL, QUICK, EXTANT,
EXISTENT
alkali: .... LYE, SALT, SODA,
BORAX, POTASH, ANTACID
alkaloid: .... ARICIN,
CAFFEIN(E), ESERIN(E),
ARABINE, CODEIN(E), DITAMIN,
QUININ(E), MESCALINE,
BERBERIN(E), MORPHINE
all: ... SUM, TOTAL, ENTIRE,
WHOLE, EVERY(ONE),
AGGREGATE, COMPLETELY
allay: .... AID, CALM, EASE,
HELP, QUIET, COMFORT,
ASSUAGE, ASSURE, APPEASE,
MOLLIFY, SLAKE, ALLEVIATE
allege: ...... AVER, CLAIM,
ASSERT, STATE, SWEAR,
CHARGE
allegiance: ... DUTY, HONOR,
FEALTY, FIDELITY, LOYALTY,
DEVOTION
allegory: .... FABLE, STORY,
PARABLE, METAPHOR
alleviate: ...... EASE, HELP,
ABATE, ALLAY, ESSEN,
ASSUAGE, RELIEVE, DIMINISH,
MITIGATE
alley: ... WAY, PATH, LANE,
PASSAGE, STREET, WALK
alliance: ..... PACT, UNION,
TREATY, LEAGUE, COALITION,
FEDERATION, CONFEDERACY
allied: ...... AKIN, SIMILAR,
LINKED, JOINED, RELATED,
UNITED, ASSOCIATED
allium: ...... LEEK, ONION,
GARLIC
allocate: ... FIX, DEAL, METE,
ASSIGN, GRANT, DISTRIBUTE,
ALLOT, ASSIGN, AWARD,
SHARE, SPECIFY, APPORTION
allow: ... LET, GRANT, ADMIT,
ACCEPT, PERMIT, PROVIDE,
CONCEDE, AUTHORIZE,
TOLERATE
allowance: .... GIFT, SHARE,
MARGIN, RATION, PORTION,

SUPPORT, SANCTION, PERMISSION, REDUCTION, TOLERANCE

alloy: . . . . MIX, METAL, MIXTURE, ADMIXTURE, AMALGAM

allude: . HINT, IMPLY, REFER, MENTION, INSINUATE, INTIMATE

allure: . LURE, BAIT, CHARM, SEDUCE, ENTICE, ATTRACT

allusion: . . . . HINT, INKLING, INNUENDO, REFERENCE, INTIMATION

ally: . . . . AIDE, JOIN, HELPER, PARTNER, ASSOCIATE, CONFEDERATE

almighty: . GREAT, EXTREME, OMNIPOTENT, ALL-POWERFUL

alms: . . . . . DOLE, CHARITY, HANDOUT, TUITION

aloe: . . PITA, AGAVE, MAGUEY

aloft: . . . . UP, HIGH, ABOVE, SKYWARD, OVERHEAD

aloha: . . . . . LOVE, GREETING, FAREWELL, WELCOME, AFFECTION

alone: . . . . BARE, SOLE, SOLO, ONLY, SINGLE, SOLITARY

aloof: . . . . COLD, APART, RESERVED, REMOTE, DISTANT

alopecia: . . . . BALDNESS

aloud: . . . . AUDIBLE

alpaca: . . . . . WOOL, CLOTH, LLAMA, VICUNA, RUMINANT

Alpine: . . . . HAT, STICK, ALPESTRAL

dress: . . . . DIRNDL

goat: . . . . IBEX, STEINBOK

herdsman: . . . . SENN

dwelling: . . . . CHALET

pass: . (MONT)CENIS, COL, SIMPLON

primrose: . . . . AURIOULA

wind: . . FOEHN, BISE, BORA

Alps: . . . . . TIROL, TYROL, DOLOMITES, MATTERHORN, BLANC, BERHINA, JUNGFRAU

also: . . AND, TOO, YET, MORE, LIKEWISE, BESIDES, FURTHER

altar: . . . . . . TABLE, SHRINE, CHANCEL

area: . . . . APSE

boy: . . . . ACOLYTE

carpet: . . . . PEDALE

cloth: . . . COSTER, DOSSAL

enclosure: . . . . . . BEMA

platform: . . . . . . PREDELLA

rail: . . . . SEPTUM

top: . . . . MENSA

table: . . . . CREDENCE

alter: . . TURN, VARY, ADAPT, CHANGE, ADJUST, MUTATE, MODIFY, PERMUTE

altercation: . . . . SPAT, BRAWL, FIGHT, QUARREL, DISPUTE, ARGUMENT

alternate: . . . . VARY, OTHER, ROTATE, SUBSTITUTE, STAND-IN, RECIPROCATE

alternative: . . . . CHOICE, EITHER, AND/OR, OPTION

although: . . . . EVEN, WHILE, DESPITE, NOTWITHSTANDING

altogether: . . . . IN ALL, WHOLLY, QUITE

alum: . . STYPTIC, ASTRINGENT

aluminum: . . . .

ore: . . . . BAUXITE

oxide: . . . . ALUMINA

alumnus: . . . . GRAD(UATE)

alveolate: . . . . PITTED, HONEYCOMBED

always: . . . . E'ER, EVER, FOREVER, ETERNALLY, INVARIABLY, PERPETUALLY

ama: . CUP, CRUET, CHALICE, VESSEL

amah: . . . . NURSE, SERVANT

amalgamate: . . . MIX, BLEND, FUSE, MERGE, COMBINE, CONSOLIDATE

amanuensis: . . . . . . SCRIBE, TYPIST, SECRETARY, SCRIVENER

amass: . . . HEAP, PILE, SAVE, GATHER, COLLECT, ACCUMULATE

amateur: . . . . . . HAM, TYRO, NOVICE, DABBLER, NEOPHYTE, GREENHORN, NONPROFESSIONAL

amaze: . . . . AWE, STUN, ASTOUND, SURPRISE, ASTONISH

Amazon: . . . . RIVER, WOMAN, WARRIOR

ambassador: . . . . . . AGENT, DEPUTY, ENVOY, DIPLOMATE, MINISTER, EMISSARY

papal: . . NUNCIO, LEGATE

amber: . . . . . RESIN, YELLOW

ambience: . . . . MILIEU, ENVIRONMENT, SURROUNDINGS

ambiguous: . . DARK, VAGUE, DOUBTFUL, INDEFINITE, UNCERTAIN, OBSCURE

ambit: . . . . . . LIMIT, SCOPE, CIRCUIT, BOUNDS, EXTENT

ambition: . . . . . GOAL, HOPE, WISH, DESIRE, ASPIRATION

amble: . . MEANDER, SAUNTER

ambo: . . . . DESK, PULPIT, STAND, LECTERN

ambrosia: . . . HONEY, NECTAR

ambry: . . . . . . SAFE, CHEST, NICHE, CUPBOARD, LOCKER, CLOSET, PANTRY

ambush: . . . . . TRAP, AWAIT, WAYLAY, AMBUSCADE

ameliorate: . . . . EASE, HELP, IMPROVE, BETTER, RELIEVE, ALLEVIATE

amenable: . . . . PLIANT, OBEDIENT, AGREEABLE, RECEPTIVE

amend: . . . . . ALTER, REVISE, REFORM, CHANGE, MODIFY

amends: . . . . APOLOGY, REDRESS, PAYMENT, ATONEMENT, COMPENSATION

amenity: . . . . CIVILITY, COURTESY

amerce: . . . . . PUNISH, FINE, PENALIZE

America: . . . .
see **Countries of the World;
United States**

American: . . . . GRINGO, YANQUI, YANK(EE), AMERICANO

amethyst: . . . GEM, QUARTZ, PURPLE, ONEGITE

amiable: . . . . WARM, GENIAL, AFFABLE, FRIENDLY, AGREEABLE

amicable: . . . . . . FRIENDLY, PEACEABLE

amice: . . CAPE, HOOD, COWL, TIPPET, ALMUCE

amid(st): . . . . AMONG, MIDST

amigo: . . . . FRIEND

amiss: . . . . . . AWRY, ASKEW, WRONG, FAULTY, INCORRECT

amity: . . . . PEACE, ACCORD, HARMONY, FRIENDSHIP

ammunition: . . AMMO, SHOT, SHELLS, BULLETS, POWDER, GRENADES, ORDNANCE, MUNITIONS

amnesia: . . . . FUGUE, LAPSE, BLACKOUT, FORGETFULNESS

amnesty: . . . . PARDON, OVERLOOKING

among: . . IN, WITH, AMID(ST), MID(ST), BETWEEN

amor: . . . . LOVE, EROS

amorous: . . EROTIC, ARDENT, LOVING, FERVENT, PASSIONATE

amorphous: . . . . VAGUE, IRREGULAR, FORMLESS, SHAPELESS

amount: . . SUM, DOSE, UNIT, PRICE, TOTAL, WHOLE, DEGREE, EXTENT, NUMBER, QUANTITY, AGGREGATE

small: . . . BIT, DASH, WISP, PINCH, SHRED, TRACE, TRIFLE, FRAGMENT

amphibian: . . . . FROG, TOAD, NEWT, ANURA, CAUDATE, SALAMANDER

amphitheater: . . . . . . BOWL, ARENA, GALLERY, STADIUM, AUDITORIUM

amphora: . . JAR, URN, VASE

ample: . . . . . . FULL, MUCH, BROAD, GREAT, ENOUGH, PLENTY, SPACIOUS, ABUNDANT, SUFFICIENT

amplify: . . . . . . MU, SWELL, EXPAND, INCREASE, AUGMENT, ELABORATE

amputate: . . LOP, CUT, SEVER

amuse: . . . . DIVERT, ENGAGE, PLEASE, DISTRACT, TICKLE, ENTERTAIN

amusement: . . . . FUN, PLAY, GAME, SPORT, DIVERSION, RECREATION, ENTERTAINMENT

amusing: . . . . DROLL, FUNNY, COMICAL, HUMOROUS, LAUGHABLE

amygdala: . . ALMOND, TONSIL

Amy's sisters: . . . . JO, MEG, BETH

an: . . . . . . EACH, ONE, PER, ANYONE, ARTICLE

anaconda: . . . . . BOA, SNAKE, CONSTRICTOR

anadem: . . CROWN, WREATH, GARLAND

an(a)esthetic: . . GAS, OPIATE, SEDATIVE, ANALGESIC

analogy: . . . . LIKENESS, COMPARISON, SIMILARITY, RESEMBLANCE

analysis: . . . . . TEST, STUDY, REDUCTION, INVESTIGATION

analyze: . . . . ASSAY, STUDY, DISSECT, EXAMINE, DIAGNOSE, DETERMINE

anarchy: . . . . . RIOT, CHAOS, REVOLT, DISORDER, VIOLENCE, LAWLESSNESS

anathema: . . . . OATH, CURSE, BLASPHEMY, DENUNCIATION

anatomy: . . . BODY, SCIENCE, SKELETON, STRUCTURE

ancestor: . . . . . SIRE, ELDER, FOREBEAR, FAMILY, RELATIVE, FOREFATHER, PREDECESSOR

ancestry: . . . . RACE, FAMILY, LINEAGE, PEDIGREE, ANTECEDENTS

anchor: . . . . . TIE, FIX, MOOR, AFFIX, KEDGE, BERTH, HOOK, BOWER, ATTACH, FASTEN

hoist: . . . . CAPSTAN, WINDLASS

parts: . . . . . ARM, FLUKE, RING, CROWN, SHANK, STOCK, PALM

anchorite: . . MONK, ASCETIC, HERMIT, RECLUSE

ancient: . . . . . . OLD, AGED, BYGONE, HOARY, ANTIQUE, ARCHAIC, HISTORIC, PRIMEVAL

ancillary: . . . . SUBORDINATE, AUXILIARY, SUBSIDIARY

ancon: . . . . ELBOW, CONSOLE

and: . . . . . TOO, PLUS, ALSO, BESIDES, FURTHER, MOREOVER, AMPERSAND

Andes: . . . . MOUNTAIN

camel-like animal: . . . . . . GUANACO, LLAMA, VICUNA, ALPACA

grass: . . . . ICHU

plain: . . . PARAMO, LLANO

plateau: . . . . PUNA

anele: . . . . . . BLESS, ANOINT

anemic: . . LOW, WAN, PALE, WEAK, LIFELESS, BLOODLESS

anent: . . . . . . ON, RE, ABOUT, REGARDING, CONCERNING

anesthetic: . . . . GAS, ETHER, DULLING, SEDATIVE, OPIATE, COCAIN(E), NOVACAINE, CHLOROFORM

anew: . . . . OVER, AGAIN, AFRESH

angel: . . . . DEVA, SERAF, YAKSA, BACKER, SPIRIT, CHERUB, SERAPH(IM), MESSENGER, SPONSOR

angelic: . . . . SAINTLY, CHERUBIC, HEAVENLY, CELESTIAL

angels collectively: . . . . HIERARCHY

angelus: . PRAYER, DEVOTION

anger: . . . . IRE, FURY, RAGE, WRATH, RANCOR, RILE, ENRAGE, EMOTION, PASSION, ANTAGONISM, INDIGNATION

Anglo-Saxon: . . . . . ENGLISH

Angora: . . CAT, GOAT, YARN, WOOL, HAIR, RABBIT

angry: . . MAD, SORE, IRATE, CROSS, FUMING, WROTH, FURIOUS

anguish: ...... PANG, PAIN, AGONY, GRIEF, MISERY, DOLOR, DISTRESS, TORMENT

ani: ... CUCKOO, BLACKBIRD

anil: .... SHRUB INDIGO

anile: ... OLD, FEEBLE, INFIRM, SENILE, SIMPLE, FOOLISH

animal: ...... BIPED, BRUTE, BEAST, BESTIAL, CARNAL, MAMMAL, RODENT, SENSUAL, CARNIVORE, MARSUPIAL, QUADRUPED

animate: .. FIRE, MOVE, STIR, DRIVE, IMBUE, IMPEL, INCITE, QUICKEN, INSPIRE, STIMULATE, ACTUATE, ACTIVATE, ENCOURAGE, (EN)LIVEN, VIVIFY

animosity: ... HATE, HATRED, ENMITY, MALICE, RANCOR, HOSTILITY, ANTAGONISM, MALEVOLENCE

animus: ...... MIND, WILL, SPIRIT, ATTITUDE, INTENTION, INCLINATION

anise: ... ANET, DILL, CUMEN, FENNEL, FLAVOR

anisette: ... CORDIAL, LIQUOR

ankle: ... CUIT, HOCK, TALUS, TARSI, JOINT, TARSUS

annal: ... RECORD, ARCHIVE, HISTORY, REGISTER, CHRONICLE

Annapolis: ..... ACADEMY, USNA

    student: ... PLEB, PLEBE, CADET, MIDSHIPMAN

anneal: .. BAKE, FUZE, HEAT, SMELT, GLAZE, TEMPER

annex: .... ADD, ELL, WING, JOIN, SEIZE, APPEND, ADDITION, ATTACH(MENT)

annihilate: ..... END, KILL, SLAY, RAZE, WRECK, DESTROY, DEMOLISH, EXPUNGE, ERADICATE, EXTERMINATE

annotation: .... NOTE, COMMENT, REMARK, REFERENCE, FOOTNOTE

announce: .... TELL, ASSERT, INFORM, REPORT, STATE, DECLARE, PROCLAIM, HERALD, ADVERTISE, BROADCAST

announcement: .. AD, EDICT, NOTICE, BLURB, BULLETIN, PROCLAMATION

annoy: ..... IRK, VEX, TRY, GALL, RILE, HARRY, PEAVE, TEASE, MOLEST, DISTURB, PESTER, HECKLE, IRRITATE, AGGRAVATE, (BE)DEVIL, EXASPERATE

annual: ...... BOOK, PLANT, FLOWER, YEARLY, YEARBOOK, ETESIAN, PUBLICATION

annuity: ... INCOME, PENSION

annul: .... UNDO, VOID, CANCEL, REVOKE, RECALL, VACATE, ABOLISH, RESCIND

annular: ... ROUND, BANDED, RINGED, CIRCULAR

annum: .... YEAR

annunciate: ..... ANNOUNCE

anodyne: .... BALM, OPIATE, REMEDY, SEDATIVE, PAINKILLER, PALLATIVE

anoint: ... OIL, BALM, ENOIL, ANELE, CROWN, SMEAR, SPREAD, BLESS, MOISTEN, CONSECRATE

anomalous: .. ODD, STRANGE, PECULIAR, IRREGULAR, ABNORMAL

anon: .... SOON, LATER, AFRESH, SHORTLY, THENCE, IMMEDIATELY, PRESENTLY

anonymous: .... NAMELESS, UNKNOWN, UNSIGNED, INCOGNITO

another: .... NEW, SECOND, FURTHER, DIFFERENT, ADDITIONAL

anserine: ..... DULL, STUIPD, STOLID, FOOLISH, GOOSELIKE

answer: ... DO, ECHO, PLEA, REPLY, RESULT, RETORT, RESPOND, RESPONSE, REBUTTAL, REJOIN(DER), DEFENSE

ant: .... ANAI, ANAY, MIRE, PISMIRE, EMMET, TERMITE, INSECT
cow:. . . . . APHID
eater: . . . TAPIR, ECHIDNA, TAMANDU, AARDVARK
nest: . . . . HILL, FORMICARY

anta: . . . . . . PIER, COLUMN, PEDESTAL, PILASTER

antagonism: . . . . . . ENMITY, ANIMOSITY, HOSTILITY, OPPOSITION

antagonist: . . . . FOE, RIVAL, ENEMY, OPPONENT, ADVERSARY

Antarctic: . . . . OCEAN, CONTINENT, CIRCLE

ante: . . PAY, STAKE, RAISE, PRICE, BEFORE, PRIOR

antecedent: . . . FORE, CAUSE, PRIOR, FORMER, ANCESTOR, PRECEDING

antedate: . . . . PREDATE, PRECEDE

antenna: . . . . . . PALP, HORN, AERIAL, FEELER, LEAD-IN

anterior: . . . . . FRONT, PRIOR, BEFORE, PREVIOUS, PRECEDING

anteroom: . . . . HALL, FOYER, LOBBY, VESTIBULE, ANTECHAMBER

anthem: . . . . . SONG, HYMN, PSALM, MOTET, AGNUS DEI

anther: . . . . TIP, STAMEN

anthesis: . . BLOOM, BLOSSOM

anthology: . . . . ANA, COLLECTION, POTPOURRI, COMPILATION

anthozoan: . . POLYP, CORAL, ANEMONE

anthropoid: . . . . . APE, LAR, GIBBON, SIMIAN, MONKEY, GORILLA, CHIMPANZEE, ORANG(UTAN), TROGLODYTE

anti: . . . . CON, CONTRA, AGAINST, OPPOSED, HOSTILE

antic: . . DIDO, CAPER, STUNT, PRANK, CLOWN, CAPRICE

anticipate: . . . HOPE, EXPECT, FORESEE, PORTEND

antidote: . . . . . . CURE, SODA, EMETIC, SERUM, REMEDY

antimacassar: . . TIDY, DOILY

antipathy: . . . . DISGUST, DISLIKE, RANCOR, ENMITY, DISTASTE, AVERSION, REPUGNANCE

antiquated: . . . . OLD, AGED, FOSSIL, OBSOLETE, PASSE, ANCIENT, OUTMODED, ARCHAIC

antitoxin: . . . . SERUM, ANTIVENIN

antler: . . . . HORN, SPINE
branch: . . . . . . BAY, BEY, PRONG, BROW, TINE
main stem: . . . . . . BEAM
unbranched: . . . . . HORN, SPIKE, DAG(UE)

antrum: . . . . SINUS, CAVERN, CAVITY

anurous: . . . . TAILLESS, ACAUDAL, ACAUDATE

anvil: . . INCUS, BLOCK, TEEST, STITHY, BEAKIRON

anxiety: . . . . . . FEAR, CARE, DREAD, WORRY, MISGIVING, CONCERN, APPREHENSION

any: . . AN, PART, ALL, SOME, WHICHEVER

anything: . . . . AUGHT

aoristic: . . . . INDEFINITE

aorta: . . . . . . ARTERY, TRUNK

apace: . FAST, QUICK, RAPID, SWIFT(LY), SPEEDY

Apache: . . . . YUMA, INDIAN

apart: . . . . ASIDE, AWAY, ALONE, SPLIT, ASUNDER, SEPARATE

apartment: . . . FLAT, ROOM, SUITE, ABODE, BUILDING, DWELLING

apathetic: . . . . . COLD, DULL, PASSIVE, INDIFFERENT, LISTLESS, UNMOVED

apathy: . . . . INDIFFERENCE, COOLNESS, DISINTEREST

ape: . . . . COPY, MIME, MIMIC, BABOON, MONKEY, SIMIAN, IMITATE, PRIMATE, SIMULATE, ANTHROPOID, IMPERSONATE

apercu: . . . . GLANCE, DIGEST, OUTLINE, INSIGHT

aperitif: . . DRINK, APPETIZER

aperture: . . . . . . GAP, VENT, LEAK, HOLE, SLOT, STOMA, MOUTH, OPENING, ORIFICE

apetalous: . . . . . . PETALLESS

apex: . . . . . TIP, TOP, ACME, CREST, PEAK, VERTEX, CLIMAX, ZENITH, SUMMIT, PINNACLE

aphid: . . . . . INSECT, LOUSE

aphorism: . . . . SAW, MAXIM, AXIOM, ADAGE, SAYING, PROVERB, APOTHEGM

Aphrodite: . . . . VENUS, URANIA, GODDESS, BUTTERFLY

Aphrodite: . . . .
consort: . . ADONIS, ARES
mother: . . . . DIONE
priestess: . . . . HERO
son: . . . . . . EROS, ENEAS
temple site: . . . . . PAPHOS

apiece: . . . . PER, EACH

aplomb: . . . . . TACT, NERVE, POISE, ASSURANCE, CONFIDENCE

apnea: . . . . ASPHYXIA

apocopate: . . ELIDE, SHORTEN

apocryphal: . . . SHAM, FALSE, SPURIOUS, COUNTERFEIT

apodal: . . . . FOOTLESS

apogee: . . ACME, APEX, PEAK, CLIMAX, ZENITH

Apollo: . . SUNGOD, PHOEBUS, DELIUS
birthplace: . . . . DELOS
father: . . . . ZEUS, JUPITER
instrument: . . LUTE, LYRE, BOW
mother: . . . LETO, LATONA
oracle site: . . . . . DELPHI
priest: . . . . ABARIS, CALCHAS
sister: . . . ARTEMIS, DIANA
son: . . . . ION, IAMUS

apologue: . . MYTH, PARABLE, FABLE, ALLEGORY

apology: . . . . ALIBI, EXCUSE, REGRETS, EXPLANATION, JUSTIFICATION

apoplexy: . . . . STROKE, PARALYSIS

apostate: . . . . HERETIC, RENEGADE, DESERTER, RECREANT, FAITHLESS, TURNCOAT

apostle: . . . . DISCIPLE, PREACHER, MISSIONARY

apothegm: . . . . SAW, MAXIM, AXIOM, ADAGE, SAYING, APHORISM, DICTUM

apotheosize: . . DIEFY, EXALT, GLORIFY, CONSECRATE

Appalachian range: . . . . RAMAPO

appal(l): . . . . . STUN, SHOCK, DISMAY, ASTONISH, FRIGHTEN, HORRIFY, TERRIFY

appanage: . . . . ADJUNCT, PREQUISITE, PRIVILEGE, ALLOWANCE, DEPENDENCY, ENDOWMENT, PEROGATIVE

apparatus: . . . . GEAR, TOOL, DEVICE, MACHINE, EQUIPMENT, MECHANISM, INSTRUMENT, CONTRIVANCE

apparel: . . . . . GARB, DRESS, OUTFIT, ATTIRE, COSTUME, GARMENT, CLOTHING, RAIMENT, VESTMENT

apparent: . . . CLEAR, OVERT, PLAIN, VISIBLE, EVIDENT, OBVIOUS, PATENT, MANIFEST

apparition: . . DREAM, SPIRIT, GHOST, SPRITE, PHANTOM, SPECTER, FANTASY, SPECTRE, WRAITH, EIDOLON

appeal: . . . ASK, BEG, CALL, PRAY, PLEA, INVOKE, ENTREAT, PLEAD, PETITION, ATTRACTION

appear: . . . . . . COME, DAWN, SEEM, LOOK, ISSUE OCCUR, ARRIVE, EMERGE

appearance: . . . . AIR, MIEN, LOOK, VIEW, ASPECT, MANNER, SEMBLANCE, PRESENCE

appease: . . . . . . EASE, CALM, SOOTH, QUIET, PLACATE,

ALLAY, PACIFY, CONTENT, SATISFY, MOLLIFY

appellation: . . . NAME, TERM, SURNAME, COGNOMEN, SOBRIQUET, TITLE, DESIGNATION

append: . . . . . . ADD, AFFIX, ATTACH

appendage: . . . . . LEG, TAIL, ARM, LIMB, ADDITION, ADJUNCT

appendix: . . . . ORGAN, ADDENDUM, SUPPLEMENT, OUTGROWTH

appertain: . . BELONG, RELATE

appetite: . . . . YEN, LUST, HUNGER, DESIRE, CRAVING, LONGING, THIRST, APPETENCE

appetizer: . . CANAPE, RELISH, APERITIF, ANTIPASTO, HORS D'OEUVRE

applaud: . . . . . . CLAP, LAUD, ROOT, CHEER, PRAISE, EXTOL, ACCLAIM, COMMEND

apple: . . . CRAB, POME, PIPPIN, RUSSET, WINESAP, ROME, YORK, GOLDEN, McINTOSH, JONATHAN, BALDWIN, DELICIOUS, GREENING, GRIMES, YELLOW, GRAVENSTEIN, QUEENING

acid: . . . . MALIC

juice: . . CIDER, APPLEJACK

pulp: . . . . POMACE

applicable: . . . APT, USEFUL, RELATIVE, RELEVANT, PERTINENT

application: . . . . USE, FORM, BLANK, REQUEST, PRACTICE, REMEDY, DILIGENCE, RELEVANCE

apply: . . . . . . ASK, USE, PUT, PLACE, DEVOTE, REQUEST, EMPLOY

force: . . . . . EXERT, PRESS

friction: . . . . RUB, GRATE, RASP

pressure: . . . . INFLUENCE, COERCE

appoint: . . . . NAME, ASSIGN, ELECT, AWARD, DETAIL, ORDAIN, CHOOSE, DESIGNATE, DELEGATE, NOMINATE

appointment: . . DATE, BERTH, TRYST, POSITION, NOMINATION, ENGAGEMENT, DESIGNATION, EMPLOYMENT

apportion: . . . . . DEAL, METE, ALLOT, SHARE, DIVIDE, DISTRIBUTE, ALLOCATE

apposite: . . . . . APT, TIMELY, RELEVANT, APPROPRIATE

appraise: . . . . RATE, ASSAY, JUDGE, ASSESS, ESTIMATE, EVALUATE

appreciate: . . . . LOVE, PRIZE, VALUE, ENJOY, CHERISH, ESTEEM, UNDERSTAND

apprehend: . . . . . NAB, SEE, KNOW, FEAR, GRASP, ARREST, REALIZE, PERCEIVE, UNDERSTAND, COMPREHEND

apprehension: . . . . . . FEAR, DOUBT, DREAD, ALARM, WORRY, ARREST, ANXIETY, CAPTURE, PERCEPTION, FOREBODING

apprentice: . . . . . . TRAINEE, HELPER, LEARNER, NOVICE, BEGINNER

approach: . . . . COME, ROAD, NEAR, ACCESS, ACCOST, BROACH, ADVANCE, APPROXIMATE

appropriate: . . . . ADD, APT, FIT, MEET, TAKE, STEAL, RIGHT, PROPER, USURP, PREEMPT, GERMANE, SUITABLE, APPLICABLE, CONFISCATE

approve: . . . . LIKE, PASS, AGREE, ALLOW, FAVOR, RATIFY, CONSENT, CERTIFY, CONFIRM, ENDORSE, ACCREDIT, SANCTION, AUTHORIZE

approximate: . . NEAR, CLOSE, ABOUT, CIRCA, ESTIMATE, APPROACH

appurtence: . . . . ANNEX, ADJUNCT, APPANAGE, ACCESSORY, BELONGING

apron: . . . BIB, BOOT, COVER, PINAFORE, SHIELD, RUNWAY, TARMAC

apropos: . . . . APT, FIT, RELEVANT, APPORTUNE, FITTING, APPROPRIATE

apt: . . . . ABLE, DEFT, ADEPT, PRONE, QUICK, CLEVER, APTOPOS, FITTING, RELEVANT, SUITED, INCLINED, APPROPRIATE

aptitude: . . . . . . GIFT, FLAIR, KNACK, TALENT, ABILITY, FACULTY, CAPACITY, INCLINATION

aqua: . . . . . . WATER, LIQUID

aquarium: . . . . BOWL, POOL, POND, TANK

aqueduct: . . . . . PIPE, DUCT, CANAL, CHANNEL, CONDUIT, PASSAGE

arable: . . FERTILE, PLOWABLE, TILLABLE

arachnid: . . . . . CRAB, TICK, MITE, SPIDER, ACARUS, SCORPION, TARANTULA

arbiter: . . . . . JUDGE, UMPIRE, REFEREE, ARBITRATOR, MEDIATOR, OVERMAN

arbitrary: . . . . SEVERE, ABSOLUTE, DESPOTIC, CAPRICIOUS, DICTATORIAL, TRYANNICAL

arc: . . . . BOW, ARCH, BEND, CURVE, SPARK, QUADRANT, RAINBOW

arcade: . . . AVENUE, LOGGIA, STREET, PORTICO, GALLERY, ARCATURE

arcane: . . . . SECRET, HIDDEN, MYSTERIOUS

arch: . . . . . ARC, BOW, SLY, BEND, CHIEF, MAIN, CURVE, CRAFTY, CLEVER, CUNNING, PRINCIPAL

archaic: . . . OLD, OBSOLETE, ANCIENT, ANTIQUATED

archangel: . . . SATAN, URIEL, ANGELICA, GABRIEL, MICHAEL, RAPHAEL

archbishop: . . . . . . PRELATE, PRIMATE

archetype: . . . . IDEA, MODEL, SAMPLE, PATTERN, EXAMPLE, PROTOTYPE

architect: . . MAKER, ARTIST, AUTHOR, DESIGNER, BUILDER, CREATOR

Arctic: . . . ICY, COLD, POLAR, FRIGID, NORTH(ERN)

arcuate: . . . . BENT, BOWED, CURVED, ARCHED

ardent: . . HOT, AVID, EAGER, FERVID, FERVENT, INTENSE, ZEALOUS, DESIROUS, ENTHUSIASTIC

ardor: . . . FIRE, LOVE, ZEST, ZEAL, VERVE, ELAN, DESIRE, FERVOR, PASSION, ENTHUSIASM

arduous: . . . HARD, ONEROUS, LABORIOUS, DIFFICULT, STRENUOUS

area: . . ZONE, SCENE, TRACT, SCOPE, RANGE, ENVIRON, EXTENT, DISTRICT, REGION; TERRITORY

arena: . . . . PIT, OVAL, RING, RINK, FIELD, COURT, SCENE, SPHERE, STADIUM, GRIDIRON, DIAMOND, HIPPODROME, AMPITHEATER

Ares: . . . . MARS
parents: . . . . ZEUS, HERA
sister: . . . . ERIS

argent: . . . . . . COIN, MONEY, SHINING, SILVER(Y)

argosy: . . BOAT, CRAFT, SHIP, FLEET, VESSEL, GALLEON

argot: . . . . . . CANT, JARGON, SLANG, LINGO, DIALECT, PATOIS

argue: . . . . PLEAD, REASON, DISPUTE, BARGAIN, OBJECT, DEBATE, DISCUSS, CONTEST, DEFEND, CONTEND, WRANGLE

aria: . . . . . AIR, SONG, SOLO, TUNE, MELODY, ARIETTA

arid:: . . . DRY, BARE, BARREN, DESERT, MEAGER, UNFERTILE, JEJUNE, PARCHED, STERILE, WITHERED, WATERLESS

ariel: . . . . SPIRIT, SATELLITE, GAZELLE

ariose: . . MELODIC, SONGLIKE

arise: . . . . . LIFT, REAR, RISE, SOAR, ISSUE, ASCEND, EMANATE, DEVELOP, ORIGINATE

aristocracy: . . . . ELITE, NOBILITY, OLIGARCHY

aristocrat: . . . . CLASS, ELITE, NOBILITY, NOBLEMAN, GOVERNMENT

Aristotle: . . . . GREEK, PHILOSOPHER

birthplace: . . . . . STAGIRA

disciple: . . . . PERIPATETIC

logic: . . . . . . DEDUCTIVE, SYLLOGISM

teacher: . . . . PLATO

ark: . . . . BOAT, SHIP, BARGE, CHEST, COFFER, SHELTER, REFUGE

builder: . . . . NOE, NOAH

landing place: . . . . (MT)ARRAT

arm: . . . LIMB, BOUGH, EQUIP, BRANCH, MEMBER, FORTIFY, PREPARE, FURNISH, TENTACLE, WEAPON, APPENDAGE, PROJECTION

bone: . . . . ULNA, RADIUS, HUMERUS

joint: . . . . . ARES, ELBOW, WRIST

of the sea: . . . BAY, INLET, FIRTH, FIORD, FJORD

pertaining to: . . . BRACHIAL

armada: . . . . . NAVY, FLEET, FLOTILLA, WARSHIPS

armament: . . . . ARMS, ARSENAL, WEAPONRY, EQUIPMENT, ORDNANCE

armet: . . . . HELMET

armistice: . . . . LULL, PEASE, TRUCE, CEASE-FIRE, CESSATION, SUSPENSION

armoire: . . . . CABINET, CUPBOARD, WARDROBE

armor: . . . . . . MAIL, SHIELD, PLATE, DEFENSE, ORDNANCE, PROTECTION

armpit: . . . . . AXILLA, OXTER

army: . . . . . . HOST, CROWD, FORCE, MILITIA, TROOPS, HORDE, LEGION, NUMBER, THRONG, SOLDIERS

group: . . . CORPS, SQUAD, TROOP, COMPANY, REGIMENT, BRIGADE, DIVISION, PLATOON, BATTALION

rank: . . . . GENERAL, COLONEL, CAPTAIN, LIEUTENANT, SERGEANT, CORPORAL, PRIVATE, MAJOR

aroma: . . . . . . ODOR, SCENT, SMELL, SAVOR, FLAVOR, BOUQUET, PERFUME, FRAGRANCE

aromatic: . . . . SPICY, SWEET, PUNGENT, PIQUANT, FRAGRANT, ODOROUS

around: . . . NEARBY, ABOUT, CIRCA, ENCIRCLING, ENVELOPING

arouse: . . . CALL, SPUR, STIR, FIRE, WAKE, ALARM, EXCITE, ANIMATE, INCITE, INFLAME, ACTUATE, FOMENT, PIQUE, STIMULATE

arraign: . . . INDICT, ACCUSE, CHARGE, SUMMON, IMPEACH

arrange: . . . FIX, SET, FORM, PLAN, SORT, ADAPT, ARRAY, PREPARE, GRADE, SPACE, CLASSIFY, ADJUST, ORGANIZE

arrangement: . DEAL, INDEX, ORDER, PLAN, AGREEMENT, SCHEME, SYSTEM, CONTRACT, SET-UP, SETTLEMENT

arrant: . . . . THIEF, OUTLAW, VAGRANT, NOTORIOUS, UNMITIGATED, OUT AND OUT, BOLD

array: . . . DECK, ROBE, DRESS, ADORN, ATTIRE, CLOTHE, APPAREL, ORDER, FURNISH, MARSHAL

arrest: . . . FIX, NAB, ARREST, HALT, STEM, CHECK, STOP, HOLD, SEIZE, PINCH, DETAIN, RESTRAIN, APPREHEND

arrive: . . . . . . COME, LAND, REACH, ATTAIN, APPEAR

arrogance: . . PRIDE, HUBRIS, CONCEIT, EGOTISM, HAUTEUR

arrogant: . . . . BOLD, PROUD, HAUGHTY, LOFTY, IMPUDENT, CAVALIER, IMPERTINENT, OVERBEARING

arroyo: . . . . . . WADI, GULLY, GULCH, HONDO, RAVINE, CHANNEL, STREAMBED

arson: . . . . . . FIRE, BURNING, INCENDIARISM, PYROMANIAC

art: . . . CRAFT, TRADE, SKILL, ARTIFICE, FINESSE, INGENUITY, PAINTING, MUSIC, DRAMA, DANCE

style: . . . . DADA, GENRE, BAROQUE, CUBISM, IMPRESSIONISM, SURREALISM, OBJECTIVISM, PRIMITIVISM, ABSTRACTIONISM

Artemis: . . . . . UPIS, DIANA, DELIA, PHOEBE

birthplace: . . . . . . DELOS

mother: . . . LETO, LATONA

twin: . . . . APOLLO

victim: . . . . ORION

artery: . . WAY, ROAD, ICTUS, AORTA, ROUTE, VESSEL, CONDUIT, CARATOID, STREET, MAXILLARY, HIGHWAY

article: . . . . . AN, ONE, THE, ESSAY, PAPER, ITEM, REPORT, THING, OBJECT, FEATURE, COMPOSITION

articulate: . . . CLEAR, SPEAK, VOCAL, FLUENT, VERBAL, DISTINCT, JOINTED, PRONOUNCE, ENUNCIATE

artifice: . . ART, CRAFT, RUSE, GUILE, WILE, PLAN, HOAX, FRAUD, DODGE, DEVICE, TRICK(ERY), DECEPTION, STRATEGEM

artificial: . . . . FALSE, SHAM, ERSATZ, FORCED, SPURIOUS, SIMULATED, SYNTHETIC, COUNTERFIET, FICTITIOUS

artisan: . . . . . ARTIST, SMITH, MECHANIC, ARTIFICER, CRAFTSMAN, TRADESMAN, OPERATIVE

artist: . . . . . . ACTOR, SINGER, PERFORMER, PAINTER, MUSICIAN, PIANIST, ETCHER, DANCER, SCULPTOR

artless: . . . . . . OPEN, FRANK, NAIVE, CANDID, RUSTIC, SIMPLE, NATURAL, INGENUOUS, UNSOPHISTICATED

Aryan: . . . . . . MEDE, SLAV, CAUCASIAN

as: . . FOR, QUA, THAT, THUS, WHILE, WHEN, EQUAL, SINCE, BECAUSE, THOUGH, SIMILAR, THEREFORE

asafetida: . . . . HING, LASER, RESIN, FERULA

ascend: . . . . RISE, SOAR, MOUNT, CLIMB, SCALE, CLAMBER, PROGRESS

ascendancy: . . . . . . POWER, CONTROL, PRESTIGE, DOMINATION, CLAMBER, PROGRESS

ascertain: . . . . . . GET, FIND, PROVE, LEARN, VERIFY, ASSURE, DETERMINE

ascetic: . . MONK, YOGI, STOIC, FRIAR, AUSTERE, HERMIT, ESSENE, RECLUSE, ANCHORITE, EREMITE, STYLITE

ascot: . . . . SCARF, (NECK)TIE, CRAVAT, RACETRACK

ascribe: . . . BLAME, ASSIGN, CHARGE, IMPUTE, CREDIT, ASSIGN, ACCREDIT, ATTRIBUTE

aseptic: .... CLEAN, BARREN, STERILE

ash: ... COKE, TREE, EMBER, POWDER, PALLOR

ashen: ... WAN, GRAY, PALE, WHITE, PALLID, GHASTLY

ashore: .... AGROUND, BEACHED, STRANDED

aside: .... OFF, AWAY, GONE, APART, SEPARATE

asinine: ...... DULL, CRASS, SILLY, INANE, IDIOTIC, STUPID, ABSURD, FOOLISH

ask: .. BEG, SUE, PRAY, QUIZ, DEMAND, INQUIRE, SOLICIT, INVITE, QUESTION, BESEECH, ENTREAT, IMPLORE, SOLICIT, REQUEST, INTERROGATE

asleep: .... DEAD, IDLE, LATENT, DOZING, DORMANT, INACTIVE, NAPPING, SLUMBERING

asp: ... VIPER, SNAKE, ADDER

aspect: ... FACE, MIEN, VIEW, LOOK, SIGHT, MANNER, VISAGE, PHASE, OUTLOOK, FEATURE, APPEARANCE

aspen: ..... TREE, POPLAR, FLUTTERING, TREMBLING, QUIVERING

asperse: ..... SLUR, ABUSE, LIBEL, DEFAME, VILIFY, REVILE, SLANDER

aspersion: .... SLUR, INNUENDO, SLANDER, CALUMNY, BAPTISM

asphyxia: .... APNEA, ACROTISM, SUFFOCATION

aspic: ... MOLD, GELATIN(E), JELLY, RELISH, LAVENDER

aspirant: ...... CONTENDER, CANDIDATE

aspiration: ... GOAL, IDEAL, DESIRE, BREATH, AMBITION

aspire: .. HOPE, LONG, SEEK, WISH, TOWER, YEARN, BREATHE

aspirin: .... TABLET

ass: .. DOLT, FOOL, DONKEY, BURRO, DUNCE, CHUMP, IMBECILE, SIMPLETON, ONAGER, JACK, JENNY

assail: .. PELT, BESET, STONE, ACCUSE, ATTACK, INVADE, IMPUGN, ASSAULT

assailant: ...... ATTACKER, AGGRESSOR

assassin: ...... THUG, KILLER, BRAVO, SLAYER, CUTTHROAT

assault: ... BEAT, RAID, RAPE, POUND, STORM, ASSAIL, ATTACK, CHARGE, INVADE, BOMBARD, AGGRESSION

assaulter: .... MUGGER

assay: .... TEST, PROVE, EXAMINE, ANALYZE, ANALYSIS, APPRAISE, DETERMINE

assemble: ..... MASS, MEET, RALLY, GATHER, MUSTER, COLLECT, CONVENE, CONGREGATE, RALLY

assent: ..... AGREE, YIELD, ACCEDE, CONSENT, COMPLY, SUBMIT, APPROVE, ACQUIESCE, CONCUR(RENCE)

assert: .... OKAY, YES, SAY, AVER, STATE, SWEAR, ALLEGE, DECLARE, AFFIRM, ADVANCE, CONTEND, MAINTAIN

assess: ... RATE, TAX, LEVY, FINE, CHARGE, IMPOSE, APPRISE, APPORTION

asset: ..... GOODS, MONEY, WEALTH, CAPITAL, EFFECTS, PROPERTY, POSSESSION, ESTATE, RESOURCE, VALUABLES

assiduous: ... BUSY, ACTIVE, DILIGENT, SEDULOUS, ATTENTIVE, INDUSTRIOUS, PERSEVERING

assign: .... FIX, GIVE, METE, ALLOW, ALLOT, DESIGNATE, ALLOCATE, SPECIFY, APPOINT, TRANSFER, RELEGATE

assimilate: ..... MIX, ADAPT, BLEND, MERGE, ABSORB, LEARN, DIGEST, INCORPORATE

assist: . . . . . AID, ABET, HELP, FAVOR, NURSE, RELIEVE, SUPPORT, ATTEND, SUSTAIN

assistant: . . . . . AIDE, HAND, DEPUTY, ADJUTANT, ASSOCIATE, AUXILIARY, ACCOMPLICE, SUBORDINATE

associate: . . PAL, AIDE, ALLY, CHUM, JOIN, LINK, COHORT, HELPER, COLLEAGUE, CONNECT, PARTNER, COMRADE, AFFILIATE

association: . . . BODY, CLUB, GUILD, UNION, CARTEL, LEAGUE, LODGE, SOCIETY, SYNDICATE, ORGANIZATION

assortment: . . . . . . LOT, SET, OLIO, BATCH, GROUP, VARIETY, MIXTURE, COLLECTION, MISCELLANY

assuage: . . . . . . EASE, CALM, ALLAY, PACIFY, SOOTHE, SOLACE, RELIEVE, MITIGATE, DIMINISH

assume: . . . . . . DON, TAKE, ADOPT, INFER, FEIGN, AFFECT, CLOTHE, SUPPOSE, UNDERTAKE, SURMISE, PRETEND, SIMULATE, ARROGATE

assurance: . . . FAITH, NERVE, TRUST, APLOMB, SAFETY, PROMISE, SECURITY, CONFIDENCE, CERTAINTY, GUARANTEE

assuredly: . . SURELY, VERILY, TRUTHFULLY, INDUBITABLY, CERTAINLY, DECIDEDLY, UNDOUBTEDLY

astern: . . . AFT, BAFT, ABAFT, REAR, BEHIND, BACKWARD

astir: . . . . . . ALERT, ABOUT, ACTIVE, MOVING, AWAKE, ROUSED

astonish: . . . . . . AWE, DAZE, AMAZE, ASTOUND, STARTLE, CONFOUND, SURPRISE

astound: . . . . . STUN, AMAZE, SHOCK, APPAL, STAGGER, BEWILDER, ASTONISH, OVERWHELM

astrakhan: . . . . APPLE, EARACUL, KARAKUL, CLOTH

astral: . . . REMOTE, STELLAR, STARRY, STARLIKE

astray: . . . . . . LOST, AMISS, WRONG, ABROAD, ERRANT, FAULTY, WANDERING

astringent: . . . . ACID, ALUM, ACERB, STYPTIC(AL), HARSH, STERN, SEVERE, TANNIN, ACRIMONIOUS

astronaut: . . . . . . SPACEMAN, COSMONAUT

American: . . . . . . GLENN, SCOTT, WHITE, YOUNG, ALDRIN, ANDERS, BORMAN, CERNAN, CONRAD, LOWELL, SCHIRRA, GRISSOM, COLLINS, SHEPHARD, MITCHELL, McDIVITT, STAFFORD, CUNNINGHAM, ARMSTRONG

Russian: . . . . . GAGARIN, KOMAROV

astronomical: . . FAR, GREAT, HUGE, DISTANT, IMMENSE, COLOSSAL

astute: . . . . SLY, KEE, WILY, ACUTE, SHREWD, CRAFTY, CANNY, SMART, CLEVER, CUNNING, DISCERNING

asunder: . . . . . APART, SPLIT, SEPARATED

asylum: . . . . HOME, HAVEN, HARBOR, RETREAT, REFUGE, SANCTUARY, SHELTER, INSTITUTION

at: . . . . . BY, ON, TO, THERE

all: . . . . ANY, AUGHT

all times: . EVER, ALWAYS

hand: . . . BY, NIGH, HERE, NEAR, PRESENT

large: . . . . . FREE, LOOSE, ABROAD

last: . . . . FINALLY, ULTIMATELY

no time: . . . . NEVER

odds: . . . . . OUT, HOSTILE

once: . . . . NOW, PRONTO, IMMEDIATELY

that time: . . . . . . THEN, WHEREAT, THEREAT, THEREUPON
variance: . . . . DIFFERENT
atelier: . . STUDIO, WORKSHOP
athanasia: . . . . IMMORTALITY
atheist: . . . . . . DOUBTER, AGNOSTIC, INFIDEL, NONBELIEVER
Athens: . . . . ATTIC
astronomer: . . . . MECTON
citadel/hill: . . . ACROPOLIS
clan: . . . . OBE
coin: . . . OBOLI, CHALCUS
founder: . . . . . . CECROPS
law-giver: . . . . . . SOLON, DRACO
philosopher: . . . . PLATO, SOCRATES, ARISTOTLE
sculptor: . . . . . . PHIDIAS
statesman: . . . . ARISTIDES, PERICLES, CIMON
temple: . . . . . NIKE, ZEUS, PARTHENON
athletic: . . . . . AGILE, VITAL, BRAWNY, ROBUST, STRONG, MUSCULAR, VIGOROUS, ACROBATIC, ENERGETIC
athletics: . . SPORTS, GAMES, EXERCISES, GYMNASTICS
atmosphere: . . . . AIR, TONE, AURA, ETHER, MIASMA, FEELING, BACKGROUND, ENVIRONMENT
atoll: . . REEF, ISLAND, BIKINI
atom: . . . BIT, JOT, IOTA, ION, MITE, MONAD, PROTON, NEUTRON, MOLECULE, PARTICLE
atomic: . . . . . TINY, MINUTE, NUCLEAR, MOLECULAR, INFINTESIMAL
atomize: . . SPRAY, PULVERIZE
atone: . . . . . EXPIATE, AMEND, REDEEM, RESTORE
atonement: . . . . . . PENANCE, REDRESS, REDEMPTION, REPARATION
atrium: . . . . . . HALL, COURT, CAVITY, AURICLE, ENTRANCE

atrocious: . . . . VILE, AWFUL, CRUEL, BRUTAL, SAVAGE, HORRIBLE, ABOMINABLE, HEINOUS
atrophy: . . . . RUST, SHRINK, WITHER, EMACIATION
attach: . . . ADD, JOIN, AFFIX, ANNEX, ADHERE, APPEND, CONNECT, FASTEN
attaché: . . . AIDE, DIPLOMAT
attack: . . . FIT, BOUT, RAID, ASSAIL, ASSAULT, CHARGE, INVADE, STRIKE, OFFENSIVE, ONSLAUGHT, AGGRESSION
attain: . . . GET, WIN, EARN, GAIN, REACH, ARRIVE, OBTAIN, ACHIEVE, SUCCEED, ACCOMPLISH
attar: . . . . . . OIL, PERFUME, (ROSE)EXTRACT
attempt: . . . . . . TRY, ESSAY, EFFORT, ATTACK, ENDEAVOR, UNDERTAKE, EXPERIMENT
attend: . . . SEE, MIND, HEED, SERVE, ASSIST, LISTEN, FOLLOW, ESCORT, ACCOMPANY
attendant: . . . . . MAID, PAGE, GUIDE, USHER, NURSE, VALET, ESCORT, FRIEND, PORTER, WAITER, ORDERLY, SERVER, SERVANT, RETAINER, SERVITOR, ASSISTANT, CONSEQUENT, CONCOMITANT
attention: . . . . . . EAR, HEED, CARE, STUDY, REGARD, DILIGENCE, NOTICE, CONSIDERATION, VIGILANCE, CONCENTRATION
attest: . . . . SEAL, SWEAR, VOUCH, CERTIFY, CONFIRM, TESTIFY, AFFIRM, DEMONSTRATE
Attica, capital of: . . . ATHENS
Attila: . . . HUN, ETZEL, ATLI
attitude: . . . AIR, BIAS, POSE, MOOD, SLANT, STAND, ASPECT, BEARING, FEELING, POSITION, OPINION, POSTURE, DISPOSITION

attract: . . . . . . DRAW, LURE, COURT, TEMPT, ALLURE, ENTICE, CHARM, SEDUCE, INTEREST, FASCINATE, CAPTIVATE

attribute: . . ASSIGN, BLAME, IMPUTE, ASCRIBE, QUALITY, CHARACTERISTIC

attrition: . . . . . WEAR, GRIEF, ABRASION, FRICTION, EROSION, REPENTANCE

battle of: . . . . SIEGE

attune: . . KEY, TUNE, ADJUST, TEMPER, PREPARE, HARMONIZE, RECONCILE

audacious: . . . BOLD, BRASH, SAUCY, DARING, BRAZEN, ARROGANT, IMPUDENT, RECKLESS, INSOLENT

audacity: . . . CHEEK, CRUST, NERVE, BRASS, COURAGE, DARING, INSOLENCE, TEMERITY, IMPUDENCE, IMPERTINENCE

audiphone: . . . . HEARING AID

audition: . . . . TEST, TRIAL, HEARING, TRY-OUT

auditor: . . . . CPA, HEARER, LISTENER, ACCOUNTANT, COMPTROLLER

auditory: . . . . . ORAL, OTIC, AURAL, ACOUSTIC, AURICULAR

augment: . . . . . ADD, GROW, SWELL, APPEND, EXPAND, EXTEND, AMPLIFY, ENLARGE, INCREASE, MULTIPLY

augur: . . BODE, OMEN, SEER, DIVINE, FORESEE, INDICATE, AUSPEX, PORTEND, PROPHET, SOOTHSAYER

august: . . . . . GRAND, NOBLE, SOLEMN, STATELY, IMPOSING, MAJECTIC, DIGNIFIED, VENERABLE

aura: . . . . AIR, HALO, ODOR, SAVOR, FEELING, EMANATION, ATMOSPHERE

of splendor: . . . . . NIMBUS

aural: . . . . . . OTIC, AUDIBLE, AURICULAR

aureole: . . . . HALO, CROWN, LIGHT, NIMBUS, GLORY, CORONA

auricle: . . . . EAR, PINNA, ATRIAM

Aurora: . . . . . . EOS, DAWN, MORNING, BOREALIS, AUSTRALIS

auroral: . . BRIGHT, RADIANT, ROSEATE, EOAN

auspex: . . . . . . AUGER, SEER

auspice: . CARE, EGIS, OMEN, AEGIS, PORTENT, DIVINATION, PROPHECY, INDICATION, PATRONAGE

auspicious: . . . . FAVORABLE, PROPITIOUS, ADVANTAGEOUS

austere: . . . . °. COLD, STERN, HARSH, RIGID, FORMAL, SOMBER, SEVERE, ASCETIC, UNSMILING, RIGOROUS, FORBIDDING

authentic: . . . . . PURE, REAL, TRUE, VALID, CORRECT, GENUINE, ORIGINAL, BONAFIDE, VERITABLE, AUTHORITATIVE

author: . . . . MAKER, PARENT, SOURCE, CREATOR, WRITER, COMPOSER, PRODUCER, ORIGINATOR

authoritative: . . . . OFFICIAL, CONCLUSIVE, LEGITIMATE, MAGISTERIAL

authority: . . . BOARD, POWER, RIGHT, EXPERT, REGIME, COMMAND, WARRENT, SANCTION, INFLUENCE, LICENSE, JURISDICTION, AUTHORIZATION

authorize: . . ALLOW, PERMIT, APPROVE, LICENSE, LEGALIZE, EMPOWER, ACCREDIT, DEPUTE, COMMISSION

autochthon: . . . . . . NATIVE, ENDEMIC, ABORIGINE, INDIGENE

autocrat: . . . . DESPOT, DICTATOR, TSAR, MOGUL

automation: . . . . . . ROBOT, GOLEM, ANDROID, MACHINE

automobile:..... BUS, JEEP, COUPE, CRATE, SEDAN, JALOPY, FLIVVER, ROADSTER, CONVERTIBLE, (MOTOR)CAR

autopsy:.... POST-MORTEM, DISSECTION, EXAMINATION, NECROPSY

auxiliary:..... SUBSTITUTE, AIDE, ALLY, BRANCH, HELPER, ADJUNCT, ANCILLARY, ADDITIONAL, SUBSIDIARY, SUBORDINATE, COADJUTOR

avail:... USE, HELP, PROFIT, UTILIZE, ASSISTANCE

available:..... FREE, OPEN, HANDY, READY, PRESENT, ACCESSIBLE, CONVENIENT, OBTAINABLE

avarice:.. GREED, CUPIDITY, RAPACITY

avaricious:...... GREEDY, HUNGRY, STINGY, MISERLY, GRASPING

avenge:..... REPAY, PUNISH, REQUITE, RETALIATE, REVENGE, VINDICATE

avenue:...... MALL, ROAD, ALLEY, DRIVE, STREET, ARCADE, ROADWAY, BOULEVARD, PROMENADE, THOROUGHFARE

aver:....... CLAIM, SWEAR, ASSERT, AFFIRM, DECLARE

average:.... MEAN, USUAL, RATIO, MEDIAN, ORDINARY, NORM(AL), PROPORTION

averse:.... LOATH, AGAINST, OPPOSED, RELUCTANT, UNWILLING

aversion:.... HATE, DISGUST, DISLIKE, ANTIPATHY, REPUGNANCE, REVULSION

avert:.. FEND, WARD, AVOID, THWART, DEFLECT, PREVENT, FRUSTRATE

Avesta language:.... ZEND

avid:....... KEEN, EAGER, GREEDY, ARDENT, DESIROUS

avocation:... WORK, TRADE, HOBBY, PASTIME, DIVERSION

avoid:... QUIT, SHUN, SHIRK, DODGE, ELUDE, ESCAPE, SIDESTEP, ABSTAIN

avow:.. AVER, STATE, ADMIT, CONFESS, MAINTAIN, ACKNOWLEDGE

await:....... BIDE, TARRY, EXPECT, ATTEND, WATCH

awake:..... ALERT, ROUSE, ACTIVE, ACTIVATE, ATTENTIVE

award:..... PRIZE, MEDAL, GRANT, BESTOW, ADJUDGE, DECISION

aware:... ALERT, KNOWING, INFORMED, CONSCIOUS, COGNIZANT, SENSIBLE

away:..... GONE, OFF, OUT, ABSENT, ABROAD, DISTANT

awe:....... AMAZE, DAUNT, WONDER, BEWILDER, REVERENCE, INTIMIDATE, VENERATION

awful:....... UGLY, HORRID, ADVERSE, APPALLING, DREADFUL, TERRIBLE

awkward:... INEPT, CLUMSY, BUNGLING, UNGAINLY, UNWIELDY, GAUCHE, MALADROIT, UNGRACEFUL

awning:.. CANVAS, SHELTER, CANOPY, MARQUEE, SUNSHADE

awry:.. BIAS, ASKEW, AMISS, WRONG, OBLIQUE, CROOKED

ax(e):...... ADZ, HATCHET, CLEAVER, TOMAHAWK

axilla:... ARMPIT, SHOULDER

axiom:...... SAW, ADAGE, MAXIM, PRINCIPLE, PROVERB, APOTHEGM

axle:... SPINDLE, ARBOR, ROD

ayah:.. AMAH, MAID, NURSE, NURSEMAID

ay(e):..... YES, YEA, EVER, ALWAYS, AFFIRMATIVE

Azores island:...... PICO, FAYAL, FLORES, TERCERIA

port:......... HORTA

volcano: .... Pico
Aztec:. . . . .
  emperor:. . . . Montezuma
  god: . . . . . Xipe, Eecatl,
               Xipetotic
  myth: . . . . . Nata, Nana
  language: . . . . . Nahuatl
  temple: . . . . Teopan,
               Teocalli
azure:. . . . . (SKY)BLUE,
    CERULEAN, CLOUDLESS,
               UNCLOUDED
azygous: . . . . . . ODD, SINGLE
               MATELESS

B

B: . . . . Greek: BETA
  Hebrew: . . . . BETH
Baal: . . . . GOD, IDOL, DIETY
babble: . . . . . BLAB, GABBLE,
  BLABBER, CHATTER, PRATTLE,
               MURMUR, JABBER
babel: . . . . DIN, TOWER,
  TUMULT, JARGON, CONFUSION
baboon: . . . . APE, CHACMA,
               (MAN)DRILL
babushka: . . SCARF, KERCHIEF
baby: . . . BABE, DOLL, CHILD,
  PAMPER, CODDLE, INFANT,
  MOPPET, BAMBINO, PAPOOSE,
               YOUNGSTER
  carriage: . . PRAM, BUGGY,
    GOCART, STROLLER,
               PERAMBULATOR
Babylonian: . . . . . . WICKED
  abode of dead: . . . ARALU
  city: . . . . AKKAD, CALNEH,
    CUNAXA, CUTHAH
  hero: . . . . ADAPA, ETANA
  king: . . . NEBUCHADNEZZAR
  mountain: . . . . . . ARARAT
  people: . . . . ELAMITE,
               SUMERIAN
  river: . . . . TIGRIS,
               EUPHRATES
  tower: . . . . . . ZIGGURAT

bacchanal: . . . . ORGY,
               CAROUSER
bacillus: . . . . . GERM, VIRUS,
               MICROBE
back: . . . . . AID, REAR, HIND,
  ABET, TAIL, ASSIST, REVERSE,
  SPONSOR, VERIFY, SUPPORT,
  SECOND, FINANCE, ENDORSE,
  TERGUM, DORSUM, POSTERIOR,
               REINFORCE
backbone: . . . . . GRIT, GUTS,
  NERVE, PLUCK, SPINE, METTLE,
  COURAGE, VERTEBRA
backer: . . . . ANGEL, PATRON,
  SPONSOR, SUGAR DADDY
backlog: . . . . RESERVE,
  SURPLUS, ACCUMULATION
backslide: . . . FALL, REVERT,
  RELAPSE, DETERIORATE
backward: . . . . . SHY, DULL,
  SLOW, LOATH, STUPID,
  REVERSE, LAGGING, PERVERSE,
  BASHFUL, RETARDED,
  BEHINDHAND, UNPROGRESSIVE
bactrian: . . . . CAMEL
bad: . . ILL, EVIL, UNFIT, VILE,
  WRONG, ROTTEN, SINFUL,
  WICKED, HARMFUL, SPOILED,
  INFERIOR, DEFECTIVE
badge: . . . . PIN, SIGN, MARK,
  EMBLEM, SYMBOL, INSIGNIA
badger: . . . . . NAG, TORMENT,
  ANNOY, HARASS, PESTER,
  HECKLE, HARRY, WORRY,
               TEASE
  animal: . . . . BROCK,
    WOMBAT, CARCAJOU,
    HAWKER, BANDICOOT
badinage: . . FOOL, CHATTER,
  BANTER, RAILLERY
baffle: . . BALK, FOIL, ELUDE,
  STUMP, PUZZLE, DELUDE,
  OUTWIT, CONFUSE, MYSTIFY,
  CONFOUND, BEWILDER,
               FRUSTRATE
bag: . . . . . SAC, POKE, SACK,
  TRAP, CATCH, SNARE, PURSE,
  DUFFEL, LUGGAGE, SATCHEL,

HANDBAG, RETICLE, SUITCASE,
UDDER, CAPTURE
baggy: .... LOOSE, FLABBY,
PUFFED, UNPRESSED
bagnio: ... PRISON, BROTHEL,
CABANA, BATHHOUSE
bagpipe: .. DRONE, MUSETTE,
DOODLESACK, SORDELLINA
pipe: .. DRONES, CHANTER
sound: .... SKIRL
Bahama Islands: ... ABACO,
ANDROS, BIMINI, ELEUTHERA
capital:........ NASSAU
bail: ... BOND, LADE, SCOOP,
RELEASE, SURETY, BUCKET,
PALISADES, FORTIFICATION
bailiff: ..... AGENT, REEVE,
OVERSEER, STEWARD, SHERIFF,
CONSTABLE
bailiwick: ... AREA, DOMAIN,
SPHERE, PROVINCE,
HOMEGROUND, JURISDICTION
bait: .... LURE, TRAP, TEMPT,
BADGER, HECKLE, DECOY,
TORMENT, PROVOKE,
ENTICE(MENT), GUDGEON
bake: .... DRY, COOK, FIRE,
ROAST, GRILL, BROIL, ANNEAL
baking: *chamber:* .... OAST,
OVEN, KILN
dish: .... COCOTTE,
RAMEKIN, CASSEROLE
soda: .... SALERATUS
baksheesh: ..... TIP, ALMS,
GRATUITY
balance: . EVEN, REST, POISE,
ADJUST, EQUATE, OFFSET,
SCALES, REMAINDER,
STABILITY, EQUILIBRIUM
balcony: .... PORCH, PIAZZA,
TERRACE, GALLERY, GAZEBO,
VERANDA
bald: .. BARE, PLAIN, CRUDE,
FRANK, HAIRLESS, GLABROUS
balderdash:....... TRASH,
DRIVEL, NONSENSE, PALAVER,
RIGMAROLE
baldness: .... ACOMIA,
ALOPECIA, CALVITIES

baldric: ..... BELT, GIRDLE
bale:.... WOE, EVIL, CRATE,
DEATH, BUNDLE, DISASTER,
PACKAGE, SORROW
baleen: .... WHALEBONE
baleful:........ BAD, EVIL,
DEADLY, SINISTER
balk: .. JIB, SHY, FOIL, SKIP,
STOP, REVEL, OBSTRUCT,
BLUNDER, OUTWIT, THWART,
FRUSTRATE
Balkan: .. SLAV, SERB(IAN),
ALBAN(IAN), BULGAR(IAN),
RUMAN(IAN), YUGOSLAV,
SLOVENE
balky:... MULISH, STUBBORN,
CONTRARY, OBSTINATE
ball: .... ORB, BEAD, GLOBE,
IVORY, DANCE, SPHERE,
PELLET, BULLET, SPHEROID
ballad: ...... SONG, POEM,
SONNET, DERRY, CALYPSO
ballast: ...... LOAD, TRIM,
WEIGHT, BALANCE,
STABILIZE(R)
ballet: ... DANCE, ADAGIO,
CHOREOGRAPH, MASQUE,
PANTOMINE
dancer:..... BALLERINA,
DANSEUSE
skirt: .... TUTU
jump: ... JETE, ENTRECHAT
posture: .... ARABESQUE
ballot: ...... POLL, ELECT,
VOTING, TICKET, SLATE,
CHOICE
balm: .. OIL, SALVE, BALSAM,
LOTION, RELIEF, SOOTHE,
COMFORT, OINTMENT,
FRAGRANCE, PERFUME,
UNGUENT, ANODYNE
balmy: .. MILD, SOFT, SUNNY,
FRAGRANT, SOOTHING, INSANE,
CRAZY, FOOLISH, IDIOTIC
balneal: .... BATH(ING)
baloney: ... BUNK, HUMBUG,
NONSENSE, BUNCOMBE,
BOLOGNA

balsam: ... FIR, GUM, RESIN, BALM, RIGA, TOLU, IMPATIENS, COPAIBA

Baltic: *gulf:* .... RIGA
city: ...... RIGA, DANZIG
island: ... ALSEN, DAGO, FARO, OS(S)EL
river: .... ODER
state: .... LATVIA, LITHUANIA, ESTONIA, FINLAND

balustrade: ...... RAILING, PARAPET, BAN(N)ISTER

bamboo: ..... CANE, GRASS, REED, TONKIN

bamboozle: ... DUPE, TRICK, CHEAT, DEFRAUD, PUZZLE, BUFFALO

ban: ..... BAR, VETO, TABU, TABOO, OUTLAW, FORBID, PROHIBIT, EXCLUDE, PROCLAMATION

banal: .... INANE, TRITE, CORNY, VAPID, SILLY, HACKNEYED, TRIVIAL

banana: . PLANTAIN, PESANG, MUSA, ENSETE

band: ..... BAR, TIE, CORD, RING, TAPE, BELT, STRIP, ZONE, COPULA, BINDING, COLLAR, COMPANY, FILLET, FETTER, FASCIA, GATHER, GROUP, GIRDLE

bandage: ...... BIND, TAPE, DRESS, GAUZE, FASCIA, SPICA, LIGATE, LIGATURE, SWATH(E)

bandeau: .... BAND, STRIP, RIBBON

bandicoot: .... RAT, BADGER

bandit: .... THIEF, OUTLAW, ROBBER, BRIGAND, LADRONE, HIGHWAYMAN
more than one: .. BANDITTI

bandleader: ..... MAESTRO, CHORAGUS, CONDUCTOR

bandy: ...... SWAP, TRADE, DISCUSS, EXCHANGE, CHAFFER, BOWED

bane: .... EVIL, PEST, RUIN, CURSE, DEATH, MURDER, POISON, NUISANCE

baneful: .... BAD, EVIL, HARMFUL, DEADLY, PERNICIOUS, VENOMOUS, RUINOUS

bangle: .... TRINKET, BRACELET, ORNAMENT

banish: ...... EJECT, EXPEL, EXILE, DISMISS, DEPORT, PROSCRIBE, RELEGATE, EXPATRIATE

banister: .... RAILING, BALUSTER, BALUSTRADE

bank: .... DIKE, EDGE, RELY, DEPEND, MOUND, MARGIN, RIDGE, SHOAL, SHORE

bankrupt: .. BROKE, RUINED, INSOLVENT, DEPLETED, FAILURE, PENNILESS

banner: ... PENNANT, FLAG, ENSIGN, BANDEROLE, FOREMOST, LEADING, PENNON, STREAMER, GONFALON

banquet: ..... MEAL, FEAST, DINNER, REPAST, FESTIVAL

banquette: .... BENCH, SIDEWALK

banter: ... FOOL, JEST, JOSH, TEASE, PERSIFLAGE, RAILLERY, BADINAGE, PLEASANTRY

baptism: ... RITE, ASPERSION, IMMERSION, CHRISTENING
basin: .... FONT, FONTAL
robe: .... CHRISOM
water: .... LAVER

baptize: . DIP, NAME, PURIFY, CLEANSE, CHRISTEN, INITIATE

bar: .. BAN, ROD, DAM, LOCK, PUB, SHUT, STOP, BENCH, BLOCK, COURT, ESTOP, LEVER, STRIPE, GRILLE, EXCLUDE, PRECLUDE, LAWYERS, BARRIER, COUNTER, BISTRO, DRAMSHOP, OBSTRUCT, PROHIBIT

barbarian: .... HUN, BOOR, GOTH, WILD, BRUTE, SAVAGE, BEAST, UNCIVILIZED

barbarity: . . . . CRUELTY, RUDENESS, SAVAGERY, BRUTALITY, INHUMANITY

barbarous: . . . . RUDE, WILD, BRUTAL, CRUEL, PRIMITIVE, INHUMAN, UNCIVILIZED

Barbary: *ape:* . . . . . MAGOT, SIMIAN

states: . . ALGIERS, TUNIS, TRIPOLI, MOROCCO

barbed: . . . . STINGING, CUTTING, HOOKED, UNCINATE

barber: . . TONSOR, SHAVE(R), HAIRCUTTER

bard: . . POET, RUNER, DRUID, SCOP, SINGER, MUSICIAN

of Avon: . . . SHAKESPEARE

bare: . . . BALD, NUDE, MERE, EMPTY, STRIP, NAKED, EXPOSE, REVEAL, DENUDE, STARK, DIVULGE, BARREN, UNCOVERED

barely: . . . . . . ONLY, FAINT, HARDLY, MERELY, SLIGHTLY, SCARCELY, MEAGERLY, SCANTILY

bargain: . . DEAL, PACT, SALE, CHEAP, CONTRACT, DICKER, HAGGLE, TRADE, BARTER, NEGOTIATE

barge: . . . TUB, TOW, SCOW, KEEL, BOAT, COLLIDE, WHERRY, LIGHTER, TENDER, GONDOLA, INTERFERE

barn: . . . BYRE, STALL, LOFT, SHED, STABLE, STOREHOUSE, HAYLOFT

barnstorm: . . . . TOUR, CAMPAIGN

barometer: . . . . . . ANEROID, OROMETER, STATOSCOPE

barometric: . . . . BARIC

line: . . . . ISOBAR

baron: . . . . PEER, MAGNATE, NOBLEMAN

baroque: . . ROCOCO, ORNATE, IRREGULAR, EXTRAVAGANT

barracks: . . . CAMP, CASERN, QUARTERS, GARRISON

barrage: . . ATTACK, VOLLEY, BARRIER, BOMBARD, CANNONADE

barranca: . . . RAVINE, GORGE

barrel: . . . . KEG, TUN, BUTT, CASK, DRUM, CYLINDER, TIERCE, SPEED UP, CONTAINER, KILDERKIN

barren: . . . DRY, ARID, BARE, EMPTY, STARK, DESERT, STERILE, DEVOID, EFFETE, IMPOTENT, INFERTILE, UNFRUITFUL, JEJUNE

barricade: . . . . . BAR, BLOCK, BARRIER, ABAT(T)IS, PALISADE, OBSTACLE, ROADBLOCK, STOCKADE, OBSTRUCTION

barrio: . . . . . SLUM, GHETTO, VILLAGE

barrister: . . . . LAWYER, ADVOCATE, ATTORNEY, COUNSELOR

bartender: . . . . . . BARMAN, BARKEEP(ER), TAPSTER

barter: . . . . . . SWAP, TRADE, TRUCK, DICKER, BARGAIN, EXCHANGE

bartizan: . . TURRET, LOOKOUT

basal: . . BASIC, FUNDAMENTAL

basalt: . . . MARBLE, POTTERY

base: . . . . . BED, EVIL, FOOT, POOR, MEAN, ROOT, VILE, BASIS, DIRTY, ABJECT, BOTTOM, MENIAL, GROUND, IMPURE, IGNOBILE, DEGRADING, CONTEMPTIBLE, FOUNDATION, HEADQUARTERS

architectural: . . . . SOCLE, PLINTH

baseless: . . IDLE, UNFOUNDED, GROUNDLESS

bashful: . . SHY, COY, TIMID, MODEST, SHEEPISH, RETIRING

basic: . . . . . . BASAL, VITAL, ESSENTIAL, PRIMARY, ELEMENTAL, FUNDAMENTAL

basilica: . . . CHURCH, SHRINE, TEMPLE, LATERAN

basin: . . . . PAN, DISH, BOWL, FONT, SINK, POND, LAVER,

PISCINA, STOUP, DOCK,
MARINA, VESSEL, RESERVOIR
altar: .... PISCINA
basis: .... BASE, ROOT,
BOTTOM, GROUND, SUPPORT,
PREMISE, FOUNDATION
bask: ... SUN, WARM, BATHE,
ENJOY, LUXURITATE
basket: ..... CHEST, CRATE,
HAMPER, GABION, DOSSER,
SCUTTLE, PANNIER
Basque: .... IBERIAN
bassinet: ...... (BABY)BED,
BASKET, CRADLE
bastard: ...... BASE, FALSE,
IMPURE, HYBRID, MONGREL,
INFERIOR, COUNTERFEIT,
ILLEGITIMATE
wing of bird: .... ALULA
baste: .... SEW, BEAT, TACK,
CUDGEL, MOISTEN, STRIKE,
THRASH
bastille: ... PRISON, TOWER,
FORTRESS
bastion: ... FORT, BULWARK,
DEFENSE
bat: ...... HIT, BEAT, CLUB,
STICK, CUDGEL, STRIKE, WINK,
BLINK, VAMPIRE
batch: ..... LOT, SET, MASS,
GROUP, MIXTURE, QUANTITY
bateau: .... BOAT
bath: .... DIP, WASH, SOAK,
STEEP, PLUNGE, SHOWER,
ABLUTION
bathe: ...... LAVE, WASH,
MOISTEN, SUFFUSE, IMMERSE
bathhouse: .... BAGNIO,
CABANA, SAUNA
Bathsheba: husband: ......
DAVID, URIAH
son: .... SOLOMON
baton: .. ROD, STAFF, STICK,
WAND, SCEPTER, TRUNCHEON
batrachian: .... TOAD, FROG
batten: .... THRIVE, FATTEN,
WOODSTRIP, FASTEN
batter: ... RAM, DENT, BEAT,
MAIM, POUND, HAMMER,
SHATTER, BATSMAN

battle: . WAR, DUEL, ACTION,
FIGHT, CONTEST, COMBAT,
CONFLICT, STRUGGLE,
COMPETITION
batty: ...... CRAZY, SILLY,
ECCENTRIC
bauble: ...... TOY, BEAD,
BUTTON, TRIFLE, TRINKET,
GIMCRACK, GEWGAW, DOODAD
bawdy: ...... LEWD, DIRTY,
OBSCENE, INDECENT
house: . BROTHEL, BAGNIO
bawl: .... CRY, YELL, WEEP,
HOWL, SHOUT, BELLOW,
VOCIFERATE
out: .... SCOLD, REPROVE,
REPRIMAND
bay: .... COVE, GULF, HOWL,
BIGHT, BARK, FIORD, FJORD,
INLET, WING, HORSE, HAVEN,
RECESS, WINDOW, ESTUARY,
ULULATE, INDENTATION
bayou: ..... BROOK, CREEK,
INLET, RIVER, STREAM,
BACKWATER, EVERGLADES
bazaar: .... SHOP, FAIR
be: ...... ARE, LIVE, ABIDE,
EXIST, OCCUR, HAPPEN,
BELONG, CONTINUE
beach: .. BANK, MOOR, SAND,
COAST, SHORE, STRAND,
GROUND, SEASIDE
beacon: ..... GUIDE, SIGNAL,
PHAROS, CRESSET, WARNING,
LANTERN, LIGHTHOUSE, PIKE
bead: ...... DROP, BUBBLE,
BAUBLE, GLOBULE
beam: .... BAR, RAY, GLOW,
FLASH, GLEAM, LIGHT, SHINE,
SIGNAL, SMILE, DIRECT,
GIRDER, TIMBER, RAFTER,
RADIATE, CROSSBAR, SUPPORT
beaming: ... GAY, RADIANT,
SMILING, HAPPY
bear: ..... CUB, LUG, TOTE,
BEGET, BREED, BRING, BRUIN,
CARRY, KOALA, POLAR,
ENDURE, KODIAK, STAND,
SUFFER, GRIZZLY, SUPPORT,

SUSTAIN, TOLERATE, TRANSPORT

beard: . . AWN, BARB, ARISTA, WHISKERS, BARBEL, BURNSIDES, GOATEE, VANDYKE

bearing: . . AIR, MIEN, POISE, ASPECT, COURSE, RELATION, CARRIAGE, POSTURE, MANNER, DEMEANOR, PRESENCE, CARRYING, SIGNIFICANCE

beast: . . . . . BRUTE, ANIMAL, MONSTER, QUADRUPED

of burden: . . . . . OX, ASS, YAK, MULE, BURRO, CARABAO, CAMEL, HORSE, LLAMA, DONKEY, ONAGER

beastly: . . . . GROSS, BRUTAL, BESTIAL, THEROID, INHUMAN, DISGUSTING

beat: . . . . MIX, BANG, BASH, BELT, CANE, CLUB, FLOG, LASH, WHIP, DRUB, PULSE, REPEL, FLAIL, TROUNCE, POMMEL, RHYTHM, CADENCE, POUND, DEFEAT, FORGE, THRASH, SURPASS, PUMMEL, LAMBASTE

beatific: . . JOYFUL, BLISSFUL, BLESSED

beatify: . . . . BLESS, HALLOW, GLORIFY, SANCTIFY

beau: . . . . . . FLAME, DANDY, SUITOR, LOVER, ESCORT, STEADY, COURTER, FELLOW

beautician: . . . . MANICURIST, COIFFURIST, HAIRDRESSER, COSMETICIAN

beautiful: . . . FAIR, COMELY, LOVELY, PRETTY, HANDSOME, GORGEOUS, EXQUISITE

because: . . . . . . AS, SO, FOR, THAT, SINCE, INASMUCH

beck: . . . . STREAM, SUMMON, BECKON, NOD

beckon: . . . . . CALL, WAVE, SUMMON, COMMAND

becloud: . . . . DARKEN, OBSCURE, CONFUSE, MUDDLE

become: . . GET, GROW, SUIT, BEFIT, CHANGE, DEVELOP

bed: . . . . . . COT, PAD, BASE, BUNK, BERTH, COUCH, LAYER, PALLET, BOTTOM, CHANNEL, STRATUM, FOUNDATION

bedeck: . . . . . TRIM, ADORN, ARRAY, ORNAMENT, EMBELLISH

bedevil: . . . . ABUSE, ANNOY, HARASS, PLAGUE, PESTER, WORRY, TORMENT

bedlam: . . . . . . RIOT, NOISE, UPROAR, CONFUSION, MADHOUSE, TUMULT, TURMOIL

Bedouin: . . . ARAB, NOMAD, MOOR, BERBER, WANDERER

bee: . . . APIS, PARTY, SOCIAL, INSECT, MEETING, ANDRENID, HYMENOPTER

structure: . . . HONEYCOMB
colony: . . . . HIVE
female: . . . . QUEEN
glue: . . . . PROPOLIS
house: . . . . HIVE, APIARY, SKEP
keeper: . . . . . . APIARIAN, APIARIST, SKEPPIST
male: . . . . DRONE
pollen brush: . . . . SCOPA, SAROTHRUM

beebread: . . . . . . AMBROSIA

beefy: . . . . . HEFTY, BRAWNY, FLESHY, MUSCULAR

Beelzebub: . . . DEVIL, SATAN

beer: . . . . ALE, MUM, BOCK, MALT, SUDS, BREW, LAGER, KVAS(S), WEISS, PORTER, STOUT, STINGO

cask: . . TUNG, KEG, BUTT, PUNCHEON
mug: . . . . . TOBY, STEIN, SEIDEL, FLAGON, TANKER, SCHOONER

beet: . . ROOT, SUGAR, CHARD, MANGEL

Beethoven's birthplace: . . . . BONN
opera: . . . . FIDELIO
symphony: . . . . . . EROICA, PASTORAL, FIRST TO EIGHTH

befall: . . HAP, COME, HAPPEN, OCCUR, BECHANCE

befitting: . . . . PROPER, SUITABLE, APPROPRIATE

before: . . . . ERE, AHEAD, FRONT, PRIOR, EARLIER, PREVIOUS, PRECEDING FORMERLY

long: . . . . . SOON, ANON, SHORTLY, PRESENTLY

befoul: . . . . SOIL, DIRTY, POLLUTE, ENTANGLE, CONTAMINATE

befriend: . . . . AID, HELP, ASSIST, SUCCOR, SUPPORT, SUSTAIN

beg: . . . . . ASK, WOO, COAX, PRAY, MOOCH, PLEAD, IMPLORE, BESEECH, REQUEST, ENTREAT, IMPORTUNE, PANHANDLE, SUPPLICATE

beget: . . BEAR, SIRE, FATHER, CREATE, PRODUCE, PROCREATE

beggarly: . . . . POOR, MEAN, PETTY, CHEAP, ABJECT, PALTRY, INDIGENT, DESPICABLE

begin: . . OPEN, START, ENTER, INITIATE, COMMENCE, INSTITUTE, ORIGINATE

beginner: . . . . . BOOT, TYRO, NOVICE, ROOKIE, RECRUIT, TRAINEE, NEOPHYTE, APPRENTICE, GREENHORN

beginning: . . . DAWN, ROOT, SEED, GERM, START, ONSET, ORIGIN, BIRTH, GENESIS, INITIAL, OUTSET, COMMENCEMENT

beguile: . . . . . LURE, AMUZE, DECEIVE, DELUDE, CHEAT, CHARM, ENSNARE, COZEN, MISLEAD, ENTERTAIN

behave: . . . . ACT, WORK, REACT, DEPORT, CONDUCT, COMPORT, FUNCTION

behavior: . . . MIEN, ACTION, CONDUCT, COMPORT, DECORUM, MANNER, DEPORTMENT

behind: . . . . AFT, PAST, REAR, RUMP, LATE, PASSE, ABAFT, ASTERN, (A)REAR, TARDY, ARREAR, POSTERIOR

being: . . . . SELF, HUMAN, ENTITY, LIVING, MORTAL, PERSON, EXISTENCE, CREATURE, ACTUALITY

belabor: . . PLY, BEAT, WHIP, ASSAIL, ATTACK, POUND, THRASH

belated: . . TARDY, DELAYED, OVERDUE

beleaguer: . . BESET, BESIEGE, ASSAULT, BLOCKADE, SURROUND

belief: . . . . . ISM, MIND, SECT, CREED, DOGMA, FAITH, TRUST, OPINION, DOCTRINE, CREDENCE, CONVICTION, PERSUASION

belittle: . . . . . DECRY, SNEER, SLIGHT, MINIMIZE, DENIGRATE, DEMEAN, KNOCK, DEPRECIATE, DISPARAGE

bell: . . . . GONG, RING, CHIME, BELLOW, TOCSIN, CAMPANA, CARILLON

jar: . . . . CLOCHE

belladonna: . . . . . . REMEDY, NARCOTIC, MANICON, NIGHTSHADE

bellicose: . . . IRATE, HOSTILE, WARLIKE, BELLIGERENT

belligerent: . . . . . . HOSTILE, WARLIKE, BELLICOSE, PUGNACIOUS, COMBATIVE, CONTENTIOUS, LITIGIOUS, AGGRESSIVE, QUARRELSOME

bellow: . . . CRY, BAWL, ROAR, WAIL, YELL, SHOUT

bellwether: . . SHEEP, LEADER

belly: . . . . BAG, GUT, BULGE, PAUNCH, ABDOMEN, STOMACH

belong: . . . . . . BEAR, APPLY, RELATE, PERTAIN, APPERTAIN

belongings: . . . GEAR, GOODS, ASSETS, ESTATE, CHATTELS, POSSESSIONS, PROPERTY

below: ...... ALOW, DOWN, UNDER, (BE)NEATH, INFERIOR, (UNDER)NEATH

belt: .... AREA, BAND, BEAT, SASH, ZONE, STRIP, BLOW, GIRDLE, CORDON, STRAP, CESTUS, REGION, BALDRIC, CINGULUM, CINCTURE, ZOSTER

bemoan: .... WAIL, GRIEVE, LAMENT, DEPLORE

bench: .. PEW, SEAT, SETTEE, WORKTABLE, COURT

bend: .... BOW, SAG, ARCH, FLEX, TURN, ANGLE, CROOK, CURVE, TWIST, KINK, BUCKLE, REFRACT, STOOP, YIELD, GENUFLECT

beneath: .... BELOW, UNDER, LOWER, UNDERNEATH, UNDERGROUND

benediction: ..... PRAYER, BLESSING, INVOCATION, BENISON

benefactor: .. AGENT, ANGEL, DONOR, PATRON, SAVIOR, PHILANTHROPIST

beneficial: ... GOOD, USEFUL, SALUTARY, BENIGN, HEALTHFUL, WHOLESOME, LUCRATIVE, SALUBRIOUS, PROFITABLE, BENEFICIENT

benevolent: .. KIND, HUMANE, LOVING, LIBERAL, GENEROUS, CHARITABLE, MUNIFICIENT, PHILANTHROPIC

benign: .... GOOD, KIND, BLAND, GENTLE, SALUTARY, FAVORABLE, BENEFICIAL, WHOLESOME

benison: .... BLESSING, INVOCATION, BENEDICTION

Benjamin's father: ... JACOB

bent: .... AIM, SET, BOWED, FLAIR, TASTE, CROOKED, CURVED, BOUND, TALENT, PENCHANT, APTITUDE, INCLINATION, PROPENSITY

bequeath: ..... GIVE, WILL, ENDOW, LEAVE, BESTOW, DEMISE, TRANSMIT

bequest: .... LEGACY, HERITAGE, ENDOWMENT, INHERITANCE

berate: .... SCOLD, REBUKE, REPROVE, UPBRAID, CENSURE

bereave: ...... ROB, STRIP, SADDEN, DEPRIVE, DISPOSSES

bereft: .. LORN, LOST, POOR, DEPRIVED FORLORN, DESTITUTE

berserk: ...... MAD, AMOK, AMUCK, ENRAGED, MANIACAL

berth: ..... BED, JOB, DOCK, SLIP, BUNK, PLACE, BILLET, MOORING, ANCHORAGE

beryl: .... JEWEL, EMERALD, AQUAMARINE

beseech: ... ASK, BEG, PRAY, ENTREAT, APPEAL, SOLICIT, PLEAD, IMPLORE, SUPPLICATE

beside: ... BY, NEAR, CLOSE, ALONGSIDE, ADJACENT

besides: ... AND, TOO, ALSO, ELSE, MOREOVER, EXCEPT, FURTHERMORE

besiege: ..... BESET, SEIGE, STORM, ATTACK, CROWD, HARASS, PESTER, BELEAGUER

besmirch: ..... SOIL, STAIN, TARNISH, SULLY, DIRTY, DEFAME, BESMIRCH

best: ..... ACE, BEAT, TOPS, CHOICE, FINEST, UTMOST, GREATEST, DEFEAT, OUTWIT, OUTSTRIP, TOPFLIGHT

bestial: .... VILE, WILD, BRUTISH, BRUTAL, SAVAGE, ANIMAL, INHUMAN

bestow: ..... GIVE, AWARD, ALLOT, GRANT, CONFER, DEVOTE, DONATE, PRESENT, BEQUEATH

bet: ... ANTE, RISK, WAGER, STAKE, GAMBLE, PARLAY, PLEDGE

bete noire: . . . HATE, DREAD, OUTCAST, PARIAH, BUGBEAR, BUGABOO

betide: . . . . OCCUR, CHANCE, BEFALL, HAPPEN

betoken: . . . . SHOW, AUGUR, DENOTE, PORTEND, FORESHOW, INDICATE

betray: . . . . SELL, TELL, DECEIVE, REVEAL, DISCLOSE, VICTIMIZE

betrayer: . . . . TRAITOR, SEDUCER, DECEIVER

betroth: . . PLEDGE, ENGAGE, PLIGHT, PROMISE, AFFIANCE

better: . . . . . . MEND, EXCEL, REFORM, OUTDO, SAFER, AMEND, SURPASS, IMPROVE, RELIEVE

between: . . . . AMID, AMONG, BETWIXT, MIDDLE, INTERMEDIATE

bevel: . . . CANT, EDGE, BEZEL, SLANT, INCLINE, OBLIQUE

beverage: . . . ADE, ALE, TEA, WINE, BEER, GROG, MILK, SAKE, COCOA, LAGER, LEBAN, DRINK, COFFEE, EGGNOG, LIQUOR, COCKTAIL

bevy: . . HERD, PACK, DROVE, FLOCK, COVEY, FLIGHT, COLLECTION

bewail: . . . . CRY, WEEP, BEMOAN, MOURN, LAMENT, GRIEVE, DEPLORE, COMPLAIN

bewilder: . . . . DAZE, AMAZE, BAFFLE, PUZZLE, MYSTIFY, STUPEFY, CONFUSE, PERPLEX, ASTONISH

bewitch: . . . . . HEX, CHARM, ENTICE, ENAMOUR, ENCHANT, FASCINATE, CAPTIVATE, ENTRANCE

beyond: . . . . . OVER, ABOVE, PAST, YONDER, FURTHER, EXCEEDING

bezel: . . . . RIM, EDGE, FACET, FLANGE, CROWN, TEMPLATE

bias: . . . . BENT, SLANT, BIGOTRY, OBLIQUE, PARTIALITY, PREJUDICE, DIAGONAL, INFLUENCE, TENDENCY, PREDILECTION

biased: . . . . . PARTIAL, ONE-SIDED, NARROW-MINDED, PREJUDICED

bibelot: . . . . . CURIO, BRIC-A-BRAC, TRINKET, ORNAMENT

bicker: . . . SPAR, TIFF, FIGHT, CAVIL, ARGUE, DISPUTE, WRANGLE, QUARREL, SQUABBLE

bid: . . . CALL, OFFER, ORDER, INVITE, DIRECT, TENDER, DECLARE, COMMAND, PROPOSAL, OVERTURE

bide: . . STAY, WAIT, DWELL, RESIDE, REMAIN, CONTINUE, TOLERATE

bier: . . PYRE, GRAVE, COFFIN, HEARSE, LITTER, CATAFALQUE

bifurcate: . . . SPLIT, FORKED, BRANCHED

big: . . . HUGE, VAST, GREAT, LARGE, MIGHTY, LEADING, IMPRESSIVE, POMPOUS, MASSIVE, ENORMOUS, GIGANTIC, TREMENDOUS

bighead: . . CONCEIT, EGOTISM

bighorn: . . . . SHEEP, ARGALI

bight: . . . . BAY, BEND, COIL, LOOP, GULF, CORNER, NOOSE, CURVE, HOLLOW

bigot: . . . . ZEALOT, FANATIC, HYPOCRITE

bijou: . . . . . . JEWEL, TRINKET

bile: . . GALL, CHOLER, ANGER, VENOM, BITTERNESS

bilk: . . . . GYP, HOAX, CHEAT, DEFRAUD, DECEIVE, SWINDLE

bill: . . . ACT, DUN, LAW, TAB, NOTE, BEAK, CHARGE, POSTER, INVOICE, STATUTE, STATEMENT

foot the: . . . . PAY

of exchange: . . . . . DRAFT

of fare: . . . . CARD, MENU, CARTE

of lading: . . . CARGO LIST

of Rights: . . . . . . MAGNA
CHARTA
billet: . . . NOTE, POST, BERTH,
LETTER, HARBOR, NOTICE,
QUARTER(S), LODGING,
POSITION
billow: . . . . . . ROLL, WAVE,
BULGE, SURGE, SWELL,
ROLLER, BREAKER
bimonthly: . . . . . . BIMENSAL
bin: . . . . BOX, CRIB, BASKET,
BUNK, HAMPER, RECEPTACLE
binate: . . . . . DUAL, DOUBLE,
PAIRED, TWOFOLD
bind: . JAM, TIE, TAPE, ROPE,
HOLD, GIRD, CONFINE, ATTACH,
SECURE, BANDAGE
binder: . . BAND, CORD, ROPE,
COVER, BALER, FOLDER
binge: . . . LARK, ORGY, SPREE,
BENDER, CAROUSAL
biographical sketch: . . . .
PROFILE
biography: . . VITA, MEMOIR,
HISTORY, LIFE(STORY)
biology: . . . . ECOLOGY,
GENETICS
biped: . . . . MAN, TWO-FOOTED
bird: . . . . see special section
Birds
biretta: . . . . CAP, BIRET,
SKULLCAP, BERRETTA
birl: . . . . SPIN, WHIR(R),
ROTATE, REVOLVE
birth: . . . . . . BEAR, GENESIS,
ORIGIN, DESCENT, LINEAGE,
NATIVITY, BEGINNING,
PARENTAGE, EXTRACTION
after: . . . . . . POSTNATAL
before: . . . . . . PRENATAL
birthright: . . . . HERITAGE,
PATRIMONY, INHERITANCE
bis: . . AGAIN, TWICE, REPEAT,
ENCORE, DUPLICATE
biscuit: . . . BUN, ROLL, SNAP,
SCONE, WAFER, CRACKER,
COOKY, PRETZEL, POPOVER,
HARDTACK, ZWIEBACK,
MACAROON

bisect: . . . . . . FORK, HALVE,
CROSS, SPLIT, DIVIDE,
SEPARATE
bishop: . . . . . . POPE, PRIEST,
PRELATE, PONTIFF, PRIMATE,
CLERGYMAN
assistant: . . . . COADJUTOR,
VERGER
cap: . . . . . . HURA, MITRE,
MITER, BIRETTA
jurisdiction: . . . . SEE,
DIOCESE
lap cloth: . . . . . GREMIAL
staff: . . CROSIER, CROZIER
throne: . . APSE, CATHEDRA
vestment: . . . . ALB, COPE,
CHIMER, ROCHET, GREMIAL,
TUNICLE, SURPLICE
bison: . . . . BOVINE, BUFFALO,
BONASUS, AUROCHS
bisque: . . . SOUP, ICE CREAM,
BISCUIT
bissextile: . . . . . . LEAP YEAR
bistort: . . . . ASTRINGENT
bistro: . . . . . . BAR, TAVERN,
WINESHOP, NIGHTCLUB,
RESTAURANT
bit: . . . JOT, WEE, CURB, IOTA,
ITEM, MITE, MOTE, TOOL,
WHIT, COIN, CHECK, SPECK,
SCRAP, SHRED, PIECE, MOMENT,
TRIFLE, SMALL, BLADE, NIPPED,
MORSEL, FRAGMENT
bite: . . . . . . EAT, NIP, CHEW,
GNAW, STING, SNACK, MORSEL,
NIBBLE, MOUTHFUL, MASTICATE
biting: . . . . . ACRID, SHARP,
CAUSTIC, CUTTING, STINGING,
MORDANT, NIPPY, SCATHING,
SARCASTIC
bitter: . . GALL, SOUR, ACERB,
ACRID, BITING, GRIEVOUS,
HARSH, CAUSTIC, VIRULENT,
PAINFUL, ACRIMONIOUS
bitterness: . . . . . . ACRIMONY,
BILE, HATE, ENMITY, MALICE,
RANCOR, ACERBITY
bitumen: . . . . . . TAR, PITCH,
ASPHALT, ALCHITRAN

bivalve: .... CLAM COCKLE, MUSSEL, SCALLOP, OYSTER, QUAHOG, MOLLUSK

bivouac: ..... ETAPE, CAMP, ENCAMP(MENT)

bizarre: ..... ODD, QUEER, FANTASTIC, OUTRE, GROTESQUE

black: .... JET, DARK, EBON, INKY, NEGRO, RAVEN, SOOTY, WICKED, FORBIDDING

blackamoor: .... NEGRO

blackbird: ...... ANI, DAW, CROW, RAVEN, OUSEL, OUZEL, MERL(E), GRACKLE, COWBIRD, STARLING, JACKDAW

blacken: ... INK, TAR, SOOT, SOIL, CLOUD, SULLY, JAPAN, SMEAR, MALIGN, SLANDER, DARKEN, DENIGRATE

blackguard: .. CAD, VILLAIN, VAGRANT, CRIMINAL, SCOUNDREL

blackhearted: ..... CRUEL, WICKED, MALEVOLENT

blacklist: ... BAN, OSTRACIZE

blackmail: ... BRIBE, COERSE, TRIBUTE, EXTORTION

blackout: ... FAINT, SWOON, DARKEN, CENSORSHIP

bladder: ..... AIR BAG, SAC, INFLATE, VESICLE

blade: .... OAR, BONE, EDGE, LEAF, VANE, DANDY, KNIFE, SWORD, SPEAR, TOLEDO, PROPELLER

blame: ...... ONUS, FAULT, GUILT, ACCUSE, CHARGE, CONDEMN, CENSURE, REPROOF, REPROACH, CRITICIZE, ACCUSATION

blameless: .. CLEAN, PERFECT, SPOTLESS, INNOCENT, IRREPROACHABLE

blanch: .. FADE, PALE, SCALD, WHITEN, BLEACH, ETIOLATE

bland: ... KIND, MILD, SOFT, GENTLE, AFFABLE, SUAVE, SMOOTH, SOOTHING, TEMPERATE

blank: .. BARE, FORM, VOID, CLEAN, EMPTY, WHITE, BARREN, VACANT, UNFILLED

blanket: .... WRAP, COVER, SHEET, QUILT, THROW, MANTA, SERAPE, AFGHAN, PONCHO, COVERLET

blase: ...... BORED, WEARY, SATED, SATIATED

blasphemy: ...... IMPIETY, CALUMNY, SACRILEGE, PROFANITY, IRREVERENCE

blast: .... GALE, GUST, DISCHARGE, BLIGHT, EXPLODE, EXPLOSION, DETONATION, ERUPTION

blatant: ..... LOUD, GROSS, NOISY, FLASHY, SHOWY, VULGAR, VOCIFEROUS, LOUDMOUTHED

blaze: ... BURN, FIRE, FLARE, FLAME, FLASH, SHINE, TORCH, CONFLAGRATION

blazon: ... BLARE, DECLARE, DISPLAY, PROCLAIM, EXHIBIT, EMBLEM

bleach: ... WHITEN, BLANCH, PURIFY, ETIOLATE, CHLORE, DECOLOR

bleed: .. FLOW, LEAK, SUFFER, OOZE, AGONIZE, EXTORT

blemish: .. MAR, DENT, BLOT, FLAW, MARK, SCAR, DEFECT, FAULT, STAIN, MACULATE, TARNISH, IMPERFECTION

blench: ..... SHRINK, QUAIL, BLEACH, RECOIL, FLINCH

blend: ... FUSE, JOIN, MELD, MERGE, COMBINE, MINGLE, MIX(TURE), HARMONIZE

bless: .... HALLOW, BEATIFY, ENDOW, GLORIFY, SANCTIFY, CONSECRATE

against evil: .... SAIN

blessed: .... HOLY, SACRED, DIVINE, BLISSFUL, BEATIFIED

blight: .... DESTROY, FRUSTRATE, SEAR, RUST, SMUT, MILDEW, NIP, BLAST, RUIN

blind: . . . . HOOD, SHADE,
SECRET, DAZZLE, SHUTTER,
EYELESS, SIGHTLESS,
CONCEALED
blink: . . . . WINK, FLASH,
IGNORE, FLUTTER, GLIMPSE,
TWINKLE, NICTATE
bliss: . . . . . . JOY, RAPTURE,
DELIGHT, ECSTASY, FELICITY,
CONTENTMENT
blister: . . BLOB, BLEB, BLAIN,
BULLA, BUBBLE, VESICATE,
VESICLE
blithe: . . . . GAY, HAPPY,
MERRY, CHEERFUL, SPRIGHTLY
bloat: . . . . PUFF, SWELL,
EXPAND, DISTEND, INFLATE,
DRUNKARD
block: . . . . . BAR, DAM, NOG,
CLOG, CUBE, FOIL, STOP,
IMPEDE, HINDER, OPPOSE,
SQUARE, THWART, PULLEY,
OBSTACLE, OBSTRUCTION
blockade: . . . . . DAM, SEIGE,
ISOLATE, EMBARGO,
OBSTRUCTION, BOTTLE-UP,
ROADBLOCK
blockhead: . . . . . . ASS, OAF,
DOLT, FOOL, CHUMP, IDIOT,
NINNY, NITWIT, HALFWIT,
NUM(B)SKULL
blood: . . . . . SAP, GORE, LIFE,
RACE, FLUID, LINEAGE,
KINSHIP, PEDIGREE
cancer: . . . . LEUKEMIA
cell: . . . . MONOCYTE
clot: . . . . THROMBOSIS
deficiency: . . . . . . ANEMIA,
ANAEMIA
disease: . . . . . . LEUKEMIA
fluid part: . . . . . PLASMA,
SERUM, OPSONIN
pertaining to: . . . HEMATIC
poisoning: . . . . PY(A)EMIA,
SAPR(A)EMIA, SEPTICEMIA,
TOXEMIA
study of: . . . HEMATOLOGY
vessel: . . . . VEIN, AORTA,
ARTERY, CAPILLARY

bloodbath: . . . . . . PURGE,
MASSACRE
bloodcurdling: . . . FRIGHTFUL,
HORRIBLE, TERRIBLE,
HORRIFYING
bloodline: . . . . . ANCESTRY,
LINEAGE, PEDIGREE, DESCENT
bloodshed: . . . . . . DEATH,
KILLING, CARNAGE, SLAUGHTER
bloodthirsty: . . . . . . CRUEL,
CARNEL, PITILESS, MURDEROUS,
SANGUINARY
bloom: . . FLOWER, BLOSSOM,
FLOURISH, FLOREATE
blot: . . . . MAR, DAUB, SPOT,
STAIN, SULLY, EFFACE,
SMUDGE, STIGMA, MACULA,
DISGRACE, EXPUNGE
blow: . . . . . JAB, TAP, BANG,
BASH, BELT, BRAG, BUMP,
CONK, CUFF, DRUB, HUFF,
LASH, PUFF, SLAM, SLAP, SLUG,
SOCK, SWAT, BLAST, BURST,
CLOUT, KNOCK, SOUND, SPEND,
STORM, WHACK, BUFFET,
DEPART, WALLOP, ASSAULT,
INFLATE, CALAMITY,
MISFORTUNE
blowup: . . . SCENE, EXPLODE,
INFLATE, OUTBURST, EXPLOSION
bludgeon: . . BAT, HIT, CLUB,
BILLY, COERCE, CUDGEL
blue: . . . . . LOW, SAD, SKY,
AQUA, GLUM, AZURE, PERSE,
COBALT, LIVID, GLOOMY,
CELESTE, GENTIAN, DEJECTED,
TURQUOISE
bluepoint: . . . . OYSTER
blueprint: . . . . . . MAP, PLAN,
PLOT, TRACE, DRAFT, SKETCH,
OUTLINE, DIAGRAM,
CYANOTYPE
blues: . . . . . . SONG, MEGRIM,
DUMPS, DOLDRUMS,
DESPONDENCY
bluff: . . . BANK, BRAG, CURT,
BLUNT, CLIFF, GRUFF, ABRUPT,
MISLEAD, BLUSTER, DECEIVE,
BRAVADO, BRUSQUE,

HOODWINK, PRECIPICE,
BAMBOOZLE
in poker: . . . . RAISE,
COUNTER-RAISE
rounded: . . . . MORRO
blunder: . . . ERR, FLUB, SLIP,
BLOTCH, ERROR, GAFFE,
STUMBLE, MISTAKE, BUNGLE,
FLOUNDER, FAUX PAS
blunt: . . . CURT, DULL, TERSE,
BLUFF, OBTUSE, BRUSQUE,
GRUFF OBTUND
blur: . . . . . DIM, MIST, SPOT,
BLOT, STAIN, CLOUD, HAZE,
MACULATE, MACKLE, OBSCURE
on film/photo: . . . . . FOG
bluster: . . . . . . BLOW, RAGE,
RANT, BULLY, THREATEN,
BELLOW, STORM, BRAVADO
boa: . . . . ABOMA, SCARF,
SNAKE, ANACONDA,
CONSTRICTOR, PYTHON
board: . . . EATS, FARE, KEEP,
LATH, SLAT, FOUND, MEALS,
PANEL, PLANK, FOOD, COUNCIL,
PLANCH(E)
boast: . . BLOW, BRAG, CROW,
VAUNT, EXTOL, FLAUNT,
GLORIFY, GASCONADE
boat: . ARK, TUB, GIG, BARK,
DORY, JUNK, SCOW, SHIP,
YAWL, BARGE, CANOE, CHOW,
DINGY, FERRY, KETCH, LINER,
SHELL, SKIFF, SMACK, BATEAU,
CUTTER, DINGHY, DUGOUT,
PACKET, VESSEL, GONDOLA,
LIGHTER, STEAMER, SCHOONER,
SAMPAN
bobbin: . . . . PIN, CORD, REEL,
SPOOL, PIRN, SPINDLE
bobby: . COP, BULL, OFFICER,
POLICEMAN
bobcat: . . . . . LYNX, WILDCAT
Boccaccio's work: . . . .
DECAMERON
bode: . . . . . OMEN, PRESAGE,
AUGUR, PORTEND, FORETELL,
PROGNOSTICATE

bodice: . . VEST, JUPE, CHOLI,
BASQUE, CHOLL, WAIST,
CORSAGE
bodkin: . . . . . . PIN, HAIRPIN,
NEEDLE, DAGGER, STILETTO,
PONIARD, EYELETEER
body: . . . BOLE, BULK, FORM,
MASS, SOMA, TRUNK, TORSO,
FLESH, CHASSIS, CORPSE,
PERSON, CARCASS, SUBSTANCE
heavenly: . . . . SUN, STAR,
MOON, COMET, PLANET,
METEOR, ASTEROID,
SATELLITE
of advisers: . . . . . CABINET
of assistants: . . . . . STAFF
of persons: . . . . . . POSSE,
ARMY, CORPS, TROOP
of the: . . . . SOMATIC,
CORPOR(E)AL
bodyguard: . . . . ESCORT,
RETINUE, LIFEGUARD,
PROTECTOR
bog: . . . . . FEN, MIRE, MOOR,
QUAG, SINK, MOSS, MARSH,
OOZE, SWAMP, MUSKEG,
QUAGMIRE
boggy: . . . . . MIRY, SWAMPY,
MARSHY, QUAGGY
bogus: . . FAKE, SHAM, FALSE,
PHONY, SPURIOUS,
COUNTERFEIT
Bohemian: . . . ARTY, GYPSY,
ARTIST, DILETTANTE
boil: . . . . . STY, RAGE, STEW,
SEETHE, CHURN, BUBBLE,
SIMMER, ANGER, PUSTULE,
CARBUNCLE, FURUNCLE
boiler: . . . . COPPER, KETTLE,
RETORT, FURNACE, CA(U)LDRON
boisterous: . . . LOUD, RUDE,
NOISY, ROUGH, UNRULY,
VIOLENT, TURBULENT,
VOCIFEROUS
bold: . . . BIG, LARGE, NERVY,
FRESH, BRAVE, AUDACIOUS,
DARING, FEARLESS, FORWARD,
PROMINENT, COURAGEOUS

bole: . . . CLAY, STEM, BOLUS, CRYPT, TRUNK, OPENING

bolero: . . . . . WAIST, JACKET, VEST, DANCE

composer: . . . . RAVEL

boll: . . . POD, KNOB, BUBBLE, WEEVIL, CAPSULE, PROTUBERANCE

bolster: . . . . . CUSHION, PAD, PILLOW, PROP, SUPPORT

bolt: . . . BAR, PIN, ROD, RUN, FLEE, GULP, LOCK, PAWL, ARROW, COTTER, CLOSE, LATCH, SHAFT, RIVET, DECAMP, DESERT, SECURE, SHACKLE, LIGHTNING

fastener: . . . . NUT

pivot: . . . . PINTLE

turner: . . . . SPANNER

bolus: . . . . PILL, BOLE, LUMP, MASS

bomb: . . . . . . ATOM, SHELL, MISSLE, ATTACK, BOMBARD, EXPLOSIVE, GRENADE, PROJECTILE

bombard: . . . . BOMB, SHELL, BATTER, STRAFE

bombastic: . . TURGID, TUMID, FUSTIAN, FLOWERY, POMPOUS, OROTUND, GRANDIOSE, RANTING, FLAMBOYANT, PLETHORIC

bon ami: . . . . LOVER, FRIEND, SWEETHEART

bona fide: . . . REAL, GENUINE, AUTHENTIC

bond: . . . . . TIE, VOW, BAIL, LINK, DUTY, GLUE, KNOT, CHAIN, CEMENT, PLEDGE, ADHESIVE, SECURITY, COVENANT, GUARANTEE, AGREEMENT

bone: . . . . . . OS, RIB, OSSA, BLADE, TIBIA, DICE, CUBE, FEMUR, SKULL, STERNUM, HUMERUS, FIBULA, VERTEBRA, CLAVICLE, SCAPULA

boner: . . . ERROR, BLUNDER, MISTAKE

bonnet: . . . . HAT, CAP, HOOD, CHAPEAU, HEDDRESS

folding: . . . . CALECHE, CALASH

projecting rim: . . . . . BRIM

woman's: . . . . . . CAPOTE

bonnie/bonny: . . . GAY, FINE, PRETTY, BEAUTIFUL, HANDSOME

bonus: . . TIP, GIFT, BOUNTY, AWARD, PREMIUM, DIVIDEND

book: . . . . LOG, TEXT, TOME, LIBER, DIARY, ENTER, ENGAGE, PRIMER, READER, REGISTER, RECORD, VOLUME, MANUAL, CATALOG, SCHEDULE

bookkeeper: . . . . . . CLERK, AUDITOR, ACCOUNTANT

boom: . . . . . JIB, SPAR, POLE, GROW, SPRIT, BARRIER, RESOUND, FLOURISH, SUPPORT, PROSPERITY

boomerang: . . . KILEY, KYLIE, KALIE, REBOUND, KICKBACK, RICOCHET, BACKFIRE

boon: . . . . . GAY, BENE, GIFT, FAVOR, MERRY, BENEFIT, PRESENT, REQUEST, BLESSING, PLEASANT

boondocks: . . . . STICKS, BACKWOODS, WILDERNESS, HINTERLAND

boor: . . . . . CAD, OAF, LOUT, CHURL, RUSTIC, CLOD, CLOWN, LUMMOX, PLEASANT

boorish: . . . . RUDE, CLUMSY, AWKWARD, UNCOUTH, ILL-MANNERED, UNCULTURED

boost: . . . . HELP, LIFT, PUSH, HEIST, RAISE, INCREASE, ELEVATE, ENDORSE

booth: . . SHED, SHOP, SOOK, STALL, STAND, KIOSK(O)

bootleg: . . . ILLEGAL, ILLICIT, SMUGGLE, ILLEGITIMATE, SURREPTITIOUS

booty: . . LOOT, PRIZE, GRAFT, SPOILS, SWAG, PELF, PLUNDER

border: . . . . HEM, RIM, BRIM, EAVE, DADO, EDGE, SIDE,

RAND, TRIM, BRINK, FRAME,
FLANK, FRINGE, MARGIN,
FRONTIER, BOUNDRY,
PERIPHERY

borderline: ..... DOUBTFUL,
INDEFINITE

bore: ..... BIT, HOLE, PALL,
TIRE, REAM, ANNOY, AUGUR,
GIMLET, GAUGE, DRILL,
WEARY, CALIBER, TUNNEL,
PENETRATE

boreal: .... NORTHERN,
NORTHWIND

boredom: ... ENNUI, TEDIUM

boring: .... DRY, DULL,
TIRESOME, TEDIOUS,
UNINTERESTING

borough: ..... BURG, TOWN,
BURGH, VILLAGE, TOWNSHIP

borrow: ...... COPY, TAKE,
LOAN, ADOPT, STEAL, PLEDGE

boscage: .... WOOD, GROVE,
THICKET

bosom: ...... CLOSE, MIDST,
BREAST, INTIMATE, BELOVED

boss: .... PAD, BURR, KNOB,
STUD, CHIEF, MASTER, SACHEM,
OWNER, MANAGER, OVERSEER,
FOREMAN, EMPLOYER,
SUPERVISOR

bosun: .... BOATSWAIN

botch: .... MAR, MESS, FLUB,
FAIL, SPOIL, GOOF, MUFF,
FUMBLE, BUNGLE

both: .... TWO, ALIKE,
TOGETHER, EQUALLY

bother: ..... AIL, NAG, VEX,
ANNOY, WORRY, HARASS,
MOLEST, TROUBLE, PESTER,
DISTURB, IRRITATE

bottle: ... JUG, VIAL, FLASK,
CRUET, PHIAL, CARAFE,
DECANTER, CARBOY, COSTREL,
FLAGON, MAGNUM, DEMIJOHN

bottleneck: .. SNAG, BARRIER,
BLOCKADE, HINDRANCE

bottom: .. BED, BASE, ROOT,
BASIS, FLOOR, DREGS, GROUND,
SOURCE, LOWEST, FOUNDATION

boudoir: .. ROOM, BEDROOM,
CABINET

bouffant: .... FULL, PUFFED,
BULGING

bough: .... ARM, LEG, TWIG,
LIMB, SPRIG, BRANCH

bougie: ...... WAX, CANDLE

boullabaisse: ... SOUP, STEW,
CHOWDER

boulevard: .... STREET,
AVENUE, CONCOURSE,
PROMENADE, THOROUGHFARE

bounce: ..... BANG, BLOW,
BUMP, THUMP, JUMP, EJECT,
SPIRIT, EXPEL, DISMISS, SPRING,
REBOUND, RICOCHET

bouncing: ..... BIG, BUXOM,
LUSTY, HEALTHY

bound: .... HOP, LEAP, TIED,
JUMP, SKIP, SWORN, LIMIT,
BORDER, DEFINE, PLEDGED,
HURDLE, CONFINED, SECURED,
DESTINED, OBLIGED, ENCLOSED,
HEADED, CONSTRAINED

boundary: .. END, RIM, EDGE,
LINE, MERE, METE, AMBIT,
LIMIT, VERGE, BORDER,
BUTTING, TERMINUS,
PERIMETER, CIRCUMFIRENCE

boundless: ... VAST, UNTOLD,
ENDLESS, INFINITE, UNLIMITED

bounteous: .... GOOD, RICH,
AMPLE, LIBERAL, PROFUSE,
GENEROUS, ABUNDANT,
PLENTIFUL, MUNIFICENT

bounty: .... BONUS, AWARD,
REWARD, PREMIUM, GRATUITY,
ALLOWANCE, GENEROSITY,
LARGESSE

bouquet: ..... ODOR, AURA,
AROMA, SPRAY, NOSEGAY,
CORSAGE, FRAGRANCE,
COMPLIMENT

bourgeois: .... STUPID,
COMMON, MEDIOCRE,
MIDDLECLASS, RESPECTABLE,
COMMONPLACE, CAPATALISTIC

bourn(e): ... GOAL, BOUND, BROOK, REALM, DOMAIN, STREAM, BOUNDRY, OBJECTIVE

boutique: ..... STORE, SHOP

bovine: .... OX, COW, CALF, BULL, DULL, SLOW, STOLID, STEER, BISON, CATTLE, PATIENT, TAURINE

bow: .... NOD, BEND, STOOP, SUBMIT, DEFER, CURVE, YIELD, STOOP

bowdlerize: ...... CENSOR, EXPURGATE

bowel: . GUT, BELLY, COLON, INTESTINE, ENTRAIL, INTERIOR

bower: ..... NOOK, ARBOR, RETREAT, COTTAGE, ANCHOR, ALCOVE, SHELTER, PERGOLA

bowl: ..... CUP, PAN, ROLL, DISH, ARENA, BASIN, CRATER, VESSEL, STADIUM

bowling: .... TENPINS, DUCKPINS

term: ..... SPLIT, SPARE, STRIKE

box: .. BIN, CAGE, CRIB, CUFF, CASE, SPAR, SEAT, SLUG, CHEST, CADDY, CRATE, TRUNK, CARTON, CASKET, COFFIN, CONFINE, ENCLOSE, RECEPTACLE

boxer: .... DOG, PUG(ILIST), FIGHTER, BRUISER, PRIZEFIGHTER

boy: ...... LAD, TAD, CHAP, CHILD, YOUTH, SHAVER, URCHIN, MAN-CHILD, YOUNGSTER, STRIPLING

brace: .. LEG, TWO, TIE, PAIR, PROP, BIND, COUPLE, CRUTCH, SPLINT, TIGHTEN, STIFFEN, SUPPORT, STIMULATE, FASTENER, REINFORCE

bracelet: ...... BAND, RING, CHAIN, ARMIL, WRISTLET, BANGLE, MANACLE, HANDCUFF

bracing: .... INVIGORATING, STIMULATING, REFRESHING

bracket: .... CLASS, LEVEL, STRUT, CONSOLE, CORBEL, GROUP, FIXTURE, CATEGORY, CLASSIFICATION

brackish: ... SALTY, BRINY, SALINE, NAUSEOUS

brag: .. BLOW, CROW, BOAST, STRUT, VAUNT, BRAGGART, PRETENSE, GASCONADE

braggadocio: .... BRAGGART, BOASTING, PRETENSION

braid: .... LACE, TRIM, PLAT, TRESS, BAND, PLAIT, QUEUE, LACET, WEAVE, ENTWINE, INTERLACE

brain: ... BEAN, WITS, MIND, INTELLECT, CEREBRUM

brainless: ... SILLY, STUPID, FOOLISH, IDIOTIC, THOUGHTLESS

brainpan: .. SKULL, CRANIUM

brake: .. CAGE, CURB, SLOW, FERN, BLOCK, CHECK, DELAY, COPSE, HARROW, HINDER, RETARD, SLOWDOWN, THICKET

bramble: .... BRIER, THORN, RASPBERRY, DEWBERRY, BLACKBERRY

brambly: . PRICKLY, THORNY

branch: .. ARM, BOW, FORK, SPUR, STEM, TWIG, LIMB, BOUGH, BROOK, RIVULET, OFFSHOOT, MEMBER, DIVERGE, DIVISION, RAMIFY, TENDRIL, RAMUS, FURCATE

brand: .. BURN, SEAR, KIND, MARK, STAMP, LABEL, DISGRACE, STIGMA(TIZE), TRADEMARK

brandish: ... WAVE, SHAKE, HURTLE, FLOURISH, SWING

brash: . BOLD, RASH, HASTY, FORWARD, BRITTLE, INSOLENT, FRAGILE, IMPUDENT

brass: ...... METAL, ALLOY, NERVE, MONEY, BRAZEN, OFFICER, IMPUDENCE

brassard: . BADGE, ARMBAND

brassy: . . . . . BOLD, BRAZEN, IMPUDENT, INSOLENT

brat: . . . IMP, CHILD, APRON, CLOAK, URCHIN, INFANT, CLOTHING

bravado: . . . BLUFF, BLUSTER, BOMBAST, SWAGGER

brave: . . BOLD, FACE, DARE, GAME, DEFY, MANLY, STOUT, HEROIC, PLUCKY, VALIANT, DAUNTLESS, COURAGEOUS

brawl: . . ROW, MELEE, FRAY, RIOT, FIGHT, UPROAR, BROIL, FRACAS, STRIFE, ALTERCATION

brawny: . . . FLESHY, STURDY, STRONG, STRAPPING, MUSCULAR

braze: . . . . SOLDER

brazen: . . . . BOLD, FORWARD, BRASSY, IMPUDENT, IMMODEST, SHAMELESS

breach: . . . GAP, RIFT, BREAK, CRACK, SPLIT, HERNIA, RUPTURE, FISSURE, FRACTURE, VIOLATION, DISRUPTION

bread: . . . BUN, ROLL, LOAF, FOOD, PONE, RUSK, MUFFIN, LIVELIHOOD, SUSTENANCE

break: . . . GAP, BUST, REND, SNAP, CLEFT, PAUSE, HIATUS, SEVER, SMASH, CRACK, DEMOTE, SHATTER, RUPTURE, FRACTURE, SURPASS, SEPARATE, DISCLOSE

down: . . . . ANALYZE, ITEMIZE, DEMOLISH, DEBACLE, COLLAPSE, FAILURE

in: . . . ENTER, INTERRUPT, INTRUDE

of day: . . . . DAWN, MORN, SUNUP, DAYBREAK

off: . . . . . . SEVER, STOP, SEPARATE, DISCONTINUE

out: . . . . . ERUPT, ESCAPE

through: . . . . PIERCE, PENETRATE

up: . . . . END, SPLIT, DISPERSE, DISBAND, DISSOLVE, SEPARATE

breaker: . . . . WAVE, SURF, COMBER, BILLOW

breakneck: . . . . FAST, DANGEROUS

breakthrough: . . . . BREACH, INFILTRATION

breakwater: . . . DAM, DIKE, MOLE, PIER, PILE, QUAY, JETTY, BULWARK

breast: . . . . . . BUST, BOSOM, CHEST, OPPOSE, THORAX

breath: . . . . AIR, GASP, PANT, ODOR, WHIFF, PUFF, SIGH, LIFE, WIND, VAPOR, BREEZE, WHISPER, HALITUS, RESPIRATION, EXHALATION, MOMENT

breathe: . . GASP, LIVE, PANT, PUFF, EXIST, ASPIRE, INHALE, EXHALE, WHEEZE, RESPIRE, SUSPIRE

breather: . . . . REST, PAUSE, BREAK, RECESS, ARMISTICE

breech: . . RUMP, BORE, BUTT, BLOCK, BUTTOCKS, DERRIERE, POSTERIOR

breed: . . . . ILK, RACE, KIND, REAR, BEGET, CLASS, CASTE, HATCH, RAISE, STOCK, STRAIN, CREATE, PRODUCE, VARIETY, SPECIES, PROPAGATE, ORIGINATE, REPRODUCE

breeding: . . . . REARING, UPBRINGING, EXTRACTION

breeze: . . . AIR, BLOW, GUST, GALE, WIND, BREATH, WHISPER, ZEPHYR

breve: . . . NOTE, WRIT, BRIEF, ORDER, LETTER

brevet: . . . . CONFER, PROMOTION, COMMISSION

brevity: . . . . BRIEFNESS, SHORTNESS, CONCISENESS, TERSENESS

brew: . . . . . ALE, BEER, TEA, MAKE, PLOT, LAGER, FOMENT, CONCOCT, LIQUOR, PREPARE, BEVERAGE

bribe: . . . FEE, TIP, SOP, GIFT, HIRE, GRAFT, TEMPT, PAYOLA, GREASE, BOODLE, SUBORN, CORRUPT, GRATUITY

bric-a-brac: . . . . CURIO, BIBELOT, KNACKKNACK

bridal: . . NUPITAL, MARITAL, WEDDING

bridge: . . . WAY, GAME, LINK, SPAN, PONTOON, TRESTLE, CONNECT, CATWALK, VIADUCT, CANTILEVER

bridle: . . REIN, CURB, BRAKE, CHECK, GUIDE, HALTER, SUDUE, HARNESS, CONTROL, RESTRAIN, SUPPRESS

brief: . . CURT, SHORT, TERSE, QUICK, PITHY, CONCISE, COMPACT, SUMMARY

brier: . . . . PIPE, BARB, BUSH, BRAMBLE, HEATH, THORN

brig: . . . . . SHIP, JAIL, PRISON, GUARDHOUSE

brigand: . . . BANDIT, PIRATE, ROBBER, SOLDIER, LADRONE, HIGHWAYMAN

bright: . . . . APT, GAY, ROSY, ACUTE, ALERT, CLEAR, LUCID, QUICK, SMART, VIVID, SUNNY, CLEVER, RADIENT, SHINING, CHEERFUL, GLEAMING, LUSTROUS, LUMINOUS, SPARKLING

brightness: . . ECLAT, GLOSS, SHEEN, SPARKLE, LUSTER, RADIANCE, BRILLIANCE

brilliant: . . . . . . SAGE, WISE, BRIGHT, CLEVER, VIVID, RADIENT, SHINING, SPARKLING, PRISMATIC, TALENTED

brim: . . . . . . LIP, RIM, EDGE, BRINK, VERGE

brindled: . TAWNY, FLECKED, STREAKED

brine: . . . SEA, OCEAN, TEARS, SALTY, MARINADE

bring: . . . BEAR, TAKE, FETCH, CARRY, IMPORT, CONVEY, PRODUCE TRANSPORT

brink: . . . . . END, LIP, EDGE, VERGE, MARGIN

brisk: . . . FAST, SPRY, ALERT, QUICK, LIVELY, SHARP, ACTIVE, ENERGETIC, VIVACIOUS

brittle: . . . . . WEAK, BRASH, CRISP, CANDY, FRAIL, CRISPY, FRAGILE, CRACKLY, DELICATE, BREAKABLE

broach: . . . . AWL, ROD, TAP, OPEN, VENT, SPIT, BEGIN, PRICK, CHISEL, RIMER, REAMER, SKEWER, VIOLATE, INTRODUCE

broad: . . VAST, WIDE, LARGE, AMPLE, ROOMY, WOMAN, GENERAL, SPACIOUS, EXTENSIVE, COMPREHENSIVE

broadcast: . . . . . SOW, SEED, SEND, SPREAD, SCATTER, ANNOUNCE, TRANSMIT, TELEVISE

broaden: . . . WIDEN, EXPAND, EXTEND, SPREAD

broadminded: . . . . LIBERAL, TOLERANT, UNDERSTANDING

broadside: . . . . BILL, TRACT, SALVO, CIRCULAR, PAMPHLET

Brobdingnagian: . . . . HUGE, GIANT, GIANTIC, COLOSSAL

brocade: . . . CLOTH, BROCHE, BALDACHIN, BAUDEKIN

brochure: . . . . TRACT, CIRCULAR, PAMPHLET

brogan: . . . . . . BOOT, SHOE, BROGUE

brogue: . . . . SHOE, HOSE, ACCENT, DIALECT, TROUSERS

broil: . . BURN, CHAR, ROAST, BRAWL, GRILL, BRAISE, BARBECUE, ALTERCATION

broke: . . . . PENNILESS, INSOLVENT, BANKRUPT

broken: . . . . BURST, TAMED, SMASHED, RUPTURED, SPLINTERED, VIOLATED, INTERRUPTED, INTERMITTANT

broker:.... AGENT, FACTOR, DEALER, JOBBER, REALTOR, MIDDLEMAN

bromide:... TRITE, SEDATIVE, PLATITUDE

bronco:...... PONY, HORSE, CAYUSE, MUSTANG

bronze:.. TAN, BUST, BROWN, ALLOY, STATUE, COPPER, AENEOUS

brooch:.... BAR, PIN, OUCH, CLIP, CLASP, CAMEO

brood: .... SIT, SULK, MOPE, THINK, COVEY, FLOCK, HATCH, PONDER, YOUNG, FAMILY, LITTER, CLUTCH, PROGENY, COGITATE, OFFSPRING

brook: .. BEAR, GILL, CREEK, STREAM, BAYOU, RILL(ET), RIVULET, RUNNEL, ENDURE, TOLERATE

brooklime: ..... VERONICA

broom:...... SWAB, BRUSH, SWEEP, WHISK, SHRUB, BESOM, CLEANER

broth:.... SOUP, CONSOMME, BOUILLON, POTAGE, BROO, BREE

brothel: .. BORDEL(LO), CRIB, BAGNIO, BAWDYHOUSE

brotherhood:....... GUILD, LODGE, FRIARY, UNION, SODALITY, FRATERNITY, ASSOCIATION, COMPANIONSHIP

brouhaha:....... UPROAR, HUBBUB, COMMOTION

brow:.... TOP, EDGE, BRAE, CREST, EYEBROW, FOREHEAD

brown:.... DUN, TAN, SEPIA, UMBER, DUSKY, BEIGE, RUSSET, SORREL, TAWNY, KAHKI, SIENNA, TOAST, TANNED

browse: ...... CROP, FEED, NIBBLE, GRAZE, FORAGE, GLANCE

bruin:............. BEAR

bruise: .. BASH, DENT, MAUL, MAIM, CRUSH, POUND, BATTER, CONTUSE, DISCOLORATION

bruit:........ TELL, NOISE, CLAMOR, RUMOR, REPORT, SPREAD, GOSSIP, HEARSAY

brumous: ... FOGGY, MISTY, SLEETY, HIEMAL, WINTERY

brunt: ... JAR, JOLT, BLOW, IMPACT, SHOCK

brush: ..... SKIM, DUSTER, BROOM, SWEEP, TOUCH, CLEAN, GRAZE, POLISH, PAINT, FIGHT, STROKE, SKIRMISH, THICKET

brushwood:........ COPSE, THICKET, COPPICE, SCRUB, BRAKE

brusque:...... CURT, RUDE, ABRUPT, BLUNT, IMPOLITE, SHORT, BLUFF, GRUFF

brutal: .... CRUEL, SAVAGE, BESTIAL, BRUTISH, COARSE, INHUMAN, BARBAROUS

bubble:.. BALL, BLOB, BLEB, BEAD, BOIL, FOAM, EMPTY, BLISTER, GLOBULE

bubbling: ..... GAY, FIZZY, EFFUSIVE, SPARKLING, EFFERVESCENT

buccaneer: .. PIRATE, VIKING, MARINER, ROBBER, CORSAIR, FREEBOOTER

buck: .... RAM, DEER, GOAT, MALE, REAR, STAG, DOLLAR, RESIST, DANDY, SAWHORSE

buckaroo:....... COWBOY, HORSEMAN

bucket:.... TUB, BAIL, PAIL, SKEEL, SCOOP, VESSEL, SCUTTLE, CANNIKIN

buckle:... BOW, CURL, KINK, BEND, JOIN, WARP, CLASP, CATCH, TWIST, YIELD, GRAPPLE, FASTENER, COLLAPSE

bucolic: .... RURAL, SIMPLE, RUSTIC, PASTORAL

Buddha: .... FO, GAUTAMA, SHAKYAMUNI

Buddhist: ....
church:... TERA, PAGODA
fate:.......... KARMA
final release: ... NIRVANA

gateway: . . . . TORAN
hatred: . . . . DOSA
hell: . . . . NARAKA
holy city: . . LHASA, LASSA
language: . . . . PALI
literature: . . . . SUTRA
paradise: . . . . JODO
priest: . . LAMA, MAHATMA
scripture: . . SUTRA, SUTTA
budget: . . . . . . BAG, POUCH,
STOCK, BUNDLE, PARCEL,
PROGRAM, SCHEDULE,
APPROPRIATION
buff: . . . . . FAN, TAN, BLOW,
SHINE, BUFFET, POLISH,
LEATHER, SPINDLE, DEVOTEE,
ENTHUSIAST
buffer: . . . . . . PAD, FENDER,
BUMPER, CUSHION, ABSORBER
buffet: . . . BAR, BLOW, CUFF,
TOSS, STRIKE, TABLE,
CREDENZA, COUNTER,
CUPBOARD, SIDEBOARD
buffoon: . . . WAG, WIT, FOOL,
MIME, CLOWN, COMIC, DROLL,
JESTER, HUMORIST, HARLIQUIN,
PUNCHINELLO
bug: . . . . GERM, FLAW, MITE,
ROACH, BEETLE, INSECT,
ANNOY, IRRITATE
buggy: . . PRAM, CART, SHAY,
TRAP, NUTTY, CARRIAGE,
PERAMBULATOR
build: . . FORM, REAR, ERECT,
SHAPE, RAISE, CREATE,
CONSTRUCT, ASSEMBLE,
FABRICATE, STATURE, PHYSIQUE
building: . . CHURCH, EDIFICE,
MANSION, PAVILION,
DWELLING, STRUCTURE
bulb: . . . BUD, LAMP, CORM,
ROOT, KNOB, TUBER, GLOBE,
PROTUBERANCE
bulge: . . . BUMP, HUMP, LAMP,
BLOAT, POUCH, SWELL,
EXTEND, SWELLING, PROTRUDE,
PROJECTION, PROTUBERANCE
bulk: . . . . SIZE, MASS, BODY,
GROSS, TOTAL, VOLUME,

EXTENT, QUANTITY, WHOLE
MAJORITY
bulky: . . . . . . BIG, LARGE,
MASSIVE, PONDEROUS
bulldoze: . . RAM, DIG, FORCE,
SCOOP, COERCE, BULLY,
FRIGHTEN, BROWBEAT
bulletin: . . . . MEMO, REPORT,
NOTICE, STATEMENT,
PUBLICATION, ANNOUNCEMENT
bullfighter: . . . . . . MATADOR,
TOREADOR, PICADOR
bullheaded: . . . . STUPID,
STUBBORN, OBSTINATE,
HEADSTRONG
bullion: . . BAR, INGOT, GOLD,
SILVER, BILLOT
bully: . . BOSS, GOOD, GREAT,
THUG, HECTOR, HARASS,
TYRANT, BRUISER, CORNED
BEEF, RUFFIAN, BROWBEAT,
DOMINEER, BULLDOZE,
INTIMIDATE
bulwark: . . . . . . FORT, WALL,
DEFENSE, RAMPART,
BREAKWATER, EARTHWORK
bump: . . . . HIT, JOLT, LUMP,
BULGE, COLLIDE, JOSTLE,
SWELLING
off: . . . . . . KILL, MURDER
slang: . . . . REPLACE
bumptious: . . . . . . PUSHING,
CONCEITED, INSOLENT,
ARROGANT
bunch: . . HERD, PACK, TUFT,
FLOCK, CLUMP, CLUSTER,
BUNDLE, COLLECTION
buncombe: . . . . ROT, BUNK,
DRIVEL, HUMBUG, POPPYCOCK,
TWADDLE, MALARKEY
bundle: . . BALE, ROLL, PACK,
PARCEL, BUNCH, SHEAF,
GROUP, PACKAGE
bungalow: . . HOUSE, COTTAGE
bungle: . . GOOF, MUFF, MESS,
BOTCH, SPOIL, FOOZLE,
BLUNDER, FUMBLE
bunk: . . . . BED, COT, BERTH,
HOKUM, HOOEY, LODGE, SLEEP,
NONSENSE

bunker: ... BOX, BIN, TANK, CHEST, SANDTRAP

buoyant: ...... GAY, HAPPY, LIGHT, ELASTIC, ANIMATED, FLOATABLE, CHEERFUL, RESILIENT, VIVACIOUS

burden: .. TAX, LOAD, DUTY, ONUS, IMPOSE, OPPRESS, TROUBLE, CUMBER, ENCUMBER

bureau: ..... CHEST, DESK, OFFICE, AGENCY, DRESSER, HIGHBOY, DEPARTMENT, CHIFFONIER

burgeon: ...... BUD, GROW, SHOOT, SPROUT

burglar: ..... YEGG, THIEF, ROBBER

burial: .... INTERMENT

burl: .... KNOT, VENEER

burlesque: .... COPY, FARCE, PARODY, COMEDY, CARICATURE

burly: .. FAT, HEAVY, LARGE, HUSKY, STOUT, CORPULENT, MUSCULAR

burn: .... SEAR, CHAR, FIRE, BROIL, BLAZE, FLAME, SINGE, BRAND, SCORCH, CREMEATE, COMBUST, SMOLDER, INCINERATE

burning: ...... HOT, AFIRE, AFLAME, ANGRY, FIERY, ABLAZE, EAGER, TORRID, GLOWING, FEVERISH

burnish: ...... RUB, GLAZE, POLISH, GLOSS, SHINE, FURBISH

burnsides: .... BEARD, WHISKERS

burro: ...... ASS, DONKEY

burrow: ... DIG, DEN, HOLE, TUNNEL, EXCAVATE

bursa: . SAC, POUCH, CAVITY

bursar: ... PURSER, CASHIER, TREASURER

burst: .. BUST, BLOW, BLAST, ERUPT, BREAK, SPLIT, SALVO, EXPLODE, RUPTURE

bury: ... SINK, HIDE, COVER, INURN, INTER, INHUME, ENTOMB, IMMERSE, CONCEAL, SECRETE, SUBMERGE

bush: ...... CLUMP, GROVE, SHRUB, BRIER, BRANCH, THICKET

bushing: ... LINING, PADDING

bushmaster: .. VIPER, SNAKE

business: .... ART, JOB, LINE, TASK, FIRM, WORK, CAUSE, TRADE, STORE, OFFICE, AFFAIR, CALLING, CONCERN, VOCATION, PROFESSION, INDUSTRY, COMPANY, OCCUPATION, ENTERPRISE, COMMERCE, ESTABLISHMENT

bust: ..... RAIN, FAIL, BOSOM, BREAST, DEMOTE, BREAK, BURST, FAILURE, BANKRUPT

bustle: .... ADO, STIR, FUSS, FLURRY, HUSTLE, POTHER, HURRY, ACTIVITY

busy: ..... ACTIVE, OCCUPY, LIVELY, DILIGENT, EMPLOYED, OCCUPIED, ASSIDUOUS, INDUSTRIOUS

but: ..... YET, ONLY, SAVE, STILL, UNLESS, EXCEPT, HOWEVER, MERELY, NEVERTHELESS

butcher: ...... KILL, SPOIL, BUNGLE, MURDER, MEAT-SELLER, SLAUGHTER

butler: .. SERVANT, STEWARD, MAJORDOMO, MAITRE D'HOTEL

butt: ...... JUT, RAM, CASK, GOAT, JOINT, BREECH, TARGET, BARREL, BUTTOCKS

in: .. MEDDLE, INTERFERE, INTERVENE, INTRUDE

butte: .... HILL, MESA, MOUNTAIN

butterfly: .. IO, KIHO, SATYR, URSULA, IDALIA, ADMIRAL, VANESSA, VICEROY, GRAYLING, SKIPPER, MONARCH, ARTHEMIS, FRITILLARY, SWALLOWTAIL

buttery: .. LARDER, PANTRY, SPENCE, STOREROOM

button: .. KNOB, KNOP, HOOK, STUD, CATCH, BADGE, EMBLEM, BUCKLE, FASTEN

buttress: . . . PIER, PILE, PROP, STAY, BRACE, SUPPORT, BOLSTER, REINFORCE

buxom: . . . . . JOLLY, PLUMP, COMELY, FLORID, OBEDIENT, HEALTHY

buy: . . . . GAIN, SHOP, TRADE, BRIBE, SECURE, RANSOM, ACQUIRE, PURCHASE

buyer: . . . . AGENT, EMPTOR, SHOPPER, PURCHASER, CONSUMER

buzz: . . . . HUM, CALL, RING, WHIR, GOSSIP, SIGNAL, DRONE, WHISPER

by: . . . . AT, AGO, PER, NEAR, PAST, APART, CLOSE, BESIDE, THROUGH

bygone: . . . . . . PAST, YORE, FORMER, ELAPSED

byname: . . . . SURNAME, COGHOME, NICKNAME, SOBRIQUET

byre: . . . . . . BARN, STABLE, COWBARN

bystander: . . . . SPECTATOR, ONLOOKER

byway: . . PATH, LANE, ALLEY, SIDEROAD

byword: . . . AXIOM, SAYING, PROVERB, CATCHWORD

C

C: . . . . HUNDRED, 100
Greek: . . . . GAMMA
symbol for: . . . CONSTANT
Caaba: . . . . SHRINE
cab: . . TAXI, HACK, HANSOM, CARRIAGE
cabal: . . . RING, PLOT, JUNTA, CLIQUE, FACTION INTRIGUE
cabalistic: . . . SECRET, MYSTIC
caballero: . . . . KNIGHT, CAVALIER, HORSEMAN, GENTLEMAN
cabana: . . COTTAGE, BAGNIO, BATHHOUSE

cabaret: . . . . CAFE, TAVERN, BARROOM, NIGHTCLUB, RESTAURANT

cabin: . . . HUT, SHED, LODGE, SHACK, CHALET, COTTAGE, CABANA, LOGHOUSE, STATEROOM

cabinet: . . BOX, CASE, BUHL, CHEST, BUREAU, CLOSET, ADVISORS, CONSOLE, ALMIRAH, CUPBOARD, ARMOIRE, CHIFFONIER

cabochon: . . . . . GEM, STONE, ORNAMENT

cacao: . . . . BEAN, COCOA, CHOCOLATE
seed powder: . . . . BROMA

cache: . . . HIDE, BURY, STORE, CONCEAL, SECRETE, STOREHOUSE

cachet: . . . . . SEAL, CAPSULE, STOREHOUSE, STAMP, WAFER

cackle: . . . . CLACK, LAUGH, BABBLE, GOSSIP, CHATTER, PRATTLE

cacophonous: . . . . . HARSH, RAUCOUS, DISSONANT, DISCORDANT, UNMELODIOUS

cactus: . . . . . DILDO, NOPAL, CHOLLA, CEREUS, CHAUTE, MESCAL, SAGUARO, PEYOTE

cad: . . . . . CUR, HEEL, BOOR, RASCAL, BOUNDER, SCOUNDREL

cadaver: . . . . . . BODY, STIFF, CORPSE, CARCASS, REMAINS

cadence: . . LILT, PACE, BEAT, METER, RHYTHM, CADENZA, MODULATION

cadet: . . SON, PLEBE, JUNIOR, MIDSHIPMAN

cadge: . . . . . . BEG, MOOCH, SPONGE, PEDDLE

cadre: . . . . CELL, FRAME, GROUP, SCHEME, FRAMEWORK

caduceus: . . . . STAFF, WAND, SCEPTER

Caesar: . . . SALAD, EMPEROR, DICTATOR
assassin of: . . . . CASCA, CASSIUS, BRUTUS

country conquered: . . . . . .
GAUL
fatal day: . . . . IDES
caesura: . . . . . REST, BREAK,
PAUSE
cafe: . . . . . . BISTRO, SALOON,
CABERET, RESTAURANT,
TEAHOUSE, COFFEEHOUSE
cage: . BOX, PEN, COOP, JAIL,
AVIARY, PRISON, CONFINE,
IMPRISON, ENCLOSURE
cagey: . . SLY, WARY, TRICKY,
CUNNING
cahoots, in: . . . . . . LEAGUE,
PARTNERSHIP, CONNIVANCE,
CONSPIRACY
caiman: . . JACARE, CAYMAN,
ALLIGATOR
Cain: . . . . MURDERER,
FRATRICIDE
brother: . . . . ABEL
land of: . . . . NOD
parents: . . . . ADAM, EVE
son: . . . . ENOCH
caisson: . . . . . BOX, WAGON,
CHEST, TUMBREL, PONTOON,
SANDHOG
caitiff: . . . EVIL, MEAN, VILE,
CRAVEN, CAPTIVE, COWARDLY
cajole: . . . . . . COAX, JOLLY,
CHEAT, DELUDE, FLATTER,
WHEEDLE, BLANDISH
cake: . . . . BUN, LUMP, TART,
MASS, SCONE, TORTE, PASTRY,
WAFER, FRITTER, HARDEN,
CIMBAL, MERINGUE, SOLIDIFY
calabash: . . . . GOURD, SHELL
calaboose: . . JUG, BRIG, JAIL,
PRISON, GAOL
calamitous: . . . . . SAD, EVIL,
FATAL, TRAGIC, RUINOUS,
DISASTROUS
calamity: . . . . . BLOW, EVIL,
RUIN, MISERY, REVERSE,
ACCIDENT, DISASTER,
CATASTROPHE
calcium: . . . . TUFA, CALCITE,
GYPSUM, PLASTER, QUICKLIME
calculate: . . . . . . AIM, PLAN,
GUESS, THINK, COUNT,

COMPUTE, ESTIMATE,
CONSIDER, RECKON, FIGURE,
DETERMINE
calculating: . . . . . . CRAFTY,
CUNNING, SHREWD, CAUTIOUS
calculation: . . . . SHARE,
ACCOUNT, FORECAST,
PRUDENCE, LOGISTICS,
COMPUTATION
calderite: . . . . GARNET
caldron, cauldron: . . . . POT,
VAT, BOILER, KETTLE
calendar: . . . . . LIST, DIARY,
REGISTER, AGENDA, DOCKET,
SCHEDULE, ALMANAC
caliber: . . . . . . BORE, RANK,
DEGREE, QUALITY, ABILITY,
GAUGE, METTLE, TALENT,
DIAMETER
caliph: . . . ALI, ABU, IMAM,
OMAR, OTHMAN, CALIPHATE
calix: . . . . . . CUP, CHALICE
calk: . . . STOP, SEAL, CLOSE,
OCCLUDE
call: . . DUB, CRY, DIAL, PAGE,
NAME, YELL, DRAFT, SHOUT,
VISIT, AROUSE, ANNOUNCE,
SUMMON, ADDRESS, CONVOKE,
(TELE)PHONE, CHALLENGE
calligrapher: . . . . . . WRITER,
COPYIST, PENMAN, ENGROSSER
calling: . . . . JOB, TRADE,
CAREER, METIER, VOCATION,
PURSUIT, BUSINESS, FUNCTION,
PROFESSION, OCCUPATION,
EMPLOYMENT
callous: . . . . . HARD, TOUGH,
HORNY, OBDURATE, UNFEELING,
PITILESS, HARDHEARTED,
INDIFFERENT
callow: . . . . . . BARE, GREEN,
IMMATURE, YOUTHFUL,
UNFLEDGED, INEXPERIENCED
calm: . . . COOL, LULL, MILD,
STILL, SOBER, ALLAY, ABATE,
QUIET, PACIFY, PACIFIC,
PLACID, IMPASSIVE, MOLLIFY,
PLACATE, SERENE, SMOOTH,

SOOTHE, IMPASSIVE, TEMPERATE, COMPLACENT
before the:...... STORM
caloric:..... HEAT, THERMAL
calorie, calory: ... THERM(E)
calumniate: .... SLUR, LIBEL, MALIGN, DEFAME, VILIFY, ASPERSE, SLANDER
calyx: ... LEAF, SEPAL, PETAL
cam:... COG, CATCH, WIPER, TAPPET, TRIPPET, TRIPPER
camalig: .... HUT, GRANARY, STOREHOUSE
camarilla: ... CABAL, CLIQUE, JUNTA, COMBINATION
cambogia:..... (GUM)RESIN
cambrai: .... BATISTE, LINEN
cambric:... LAWN, PERCALE, COTTON, BATISTE, LINEN
camel: ... DELOUL, MEHARI, RUMINANT, GUANACO, DROMEDARY, BACTRIAN
camellia:........ JAPONICA
camelopard: ...... GIRAFFE
Camelot:........ ARTHUR, MERLIN, ROUND TABLE, KNIGHTS
cameo:..... GEM, CARVING, SCULPTURE, ANAGLYPH
camion: ...... BUS, DRAY, WAGON, TRUCK
camisole:........ JACKET
Camorra:....... (SECRET) SOCIETY
like group: .... MAF(F)IA
camouflage: ... FAKE, HIDE, SCREEN, CONCEAL, DISGUISE, DECEPTION
camp:... BASE, TENT, TABOR, BIVOUAC, QUARTERS, SHELTER
campaign:... DRIVE, SOLICIT, CANVASS, CRUSADE, BARNSTORM
campus: ..... QUAD, FIELD, YARD, GROUNDS
can: .... JUG, TIN, FIRE, JAIL, DISMISS, PRISON, CONSERVE, CONTAINER, DISCHARGE
canal:.... CUT, TUBE, DUCT, DRAIN, DITCH, TRENCH,

CHANNEL, CONDUIT, PASSAGE, AQUEDUCT, WATERWAY
canape:.. RELISH, APPETIZER, HORS D'OEUVRE
canard:..... DUCK, RUMOR, HOAX, FABRICATION
cancel:..... OMIT, ANNUL, ERASE, REMIT, DELETE, EXPUNGE, ABOLISH, SCRATCH, RESCIND, REVOKE, RECALL, OBLITERATE
cancer:..... CRAB, TUMOR, BENIGN, CARCINOMA, LEUKEMIA, MALIGNANT
like:........ CANCROID
candent:.... GLOWING, HOT
candescent:..... GLOWING, LUMINESCENT
candid:... PURE, OPEN, FAIR, FRANK, BLUNT, HONEST, SINCERE, OUTSPOKEN, IMPARTIAL
candidate:....... NOMINEE, ASPIRANT, APPLICANT, PROSPECT
list: .... TICKET, ROSTER, SLATE, BALLOT
candle: ... WAX, DIP, TAPER, CIERGE, BOUGIE, CHANDELLE
holder: .. SCONCE, HEARST, CANDELABRA, CHANDELIER, CANDLESTICK, GIRANDOLE
candor:........ FAIRNESS, KINDNESS, SINERITY, FRANKNESS, IMPARTIALITY
candy: .. KISS, SWEET, TAFFY, FUDGE, BONBON, COMFIT, SWEETMEAT, LOLLYPOP, CARMEL, BRITTLE, FONDANT, LOZENGE, CONFECTION
cane: .... ROD, BEAT, STEM, REED, WHIP, FLAY, FLOG, STICK, STAFF, HICKORY, BAMBOO, RATTAN, MALACCA
canine (see dog): ..... DOG, CUR, PUP, FOX, WOLF, JACKAL
canister:....... BOX, CAN, CONTAINER
canker:... ROT, SORE, RUST, INFECT, DECAY, CORRODE

cannibal: . . . SAVAGE, MAN-
EATER, CANIVORE
cannikin: . . CUP, CAN, PAIL,
BUCKET
cannon: . . . . GUN, MORTAR,
HOWITZER, ORDNANCE,
ARTILLERY
shot: . MISSLE, PROJECTILE
cannular: . . . . HOLLOW,
TUBULAR
canny: . . . SLY, WARY, WILY,
CAREFUL, CAUTIOUS, SHREWD
canoe: . . . . . . BOAT, BIRCH,
KAYAK, DUGOUT, PITPAN,
PIROQUE
canon: . . . LAW, CODE, RULE,
DECREE, PRECEPT, STATUTE,
CRITERION, CLERGYMAN,
REGULATION
canonical: . . . . . . ACCEPTED,
ORTHODOX, AUTHORITATIVE
canopy: . . COPE, CIEL, HOOD,
DAIS, COVER, SHADE, AWNING,
TESTER, MARQUEE
canorous: . . . . CLEAR,
MELODIOUS, MUSICAL
cant: . . . . . TIP, LEAN, TURN,
TILT, SING, ARGOT, LINGO,
SLANG, SLANT, DIALECT,
PATOIS, JARGON, INCLINE,
SINGING
cantankerous: . . . . ORNERY,
PERVERSE, IRRITABLE, BAD-
TEMPERED, CONTENTIOUS,
QUARRELSOME
canteen: . . P.X., BAR, SHOP,
FLASK, CANTINA,
POST EXCHANGE
canter: . . . . JOG, RUN, GAIT,
LOPE, GALLOP
canticle: . ODE, SONG, HYMN,
CHANT, PSALM, ANTHEM,
BRAVURA
cantina: . . . STORE, SALOON,
CANTEEN
cantle: . . . . PIECE, SLICE
cantor: . . . . LEADER, SINGER,
SOLOIST, PRECENTOR
cantus: . . . . . . SONG, CHANT

Canuck: . . . . CANADIAN
canvas: . . . . DUCK, TARP,
SAIL(S), TENT(S), PICTURE,
PAINTING, TARPAULIN
canvass: . POLL, SIFT, STUDY,
SEARCH, SOLICIT, EXAMINE,
DISCUSS, ELECTIONEER
canyon: . . . . GORGE, CHASM,
GULCH, VALLEY, RAVINE,
ARROYO
cap: . . . . FEZ, LID, HAT, TOP,
TAM, COIL, COIF, DOME, HOOD,
BERET, BEANY, COVER, CROWN,
EXCEL, OUTDO, HELMET,
BONNET, TURBIN, SURPASS,
HEADGEAR, TARBOOSH,
MORTARBOARD, DETONATOR,
YARMULKA
capable: . . . . APT, ABLE,
EXPERT, ADEPT, SKILLED,
EFFICIENT, COMPETENT,
QUALIFIED, PROFICIENT
capacious: . . . . . FULL, WIDE,
AMPLE, SPACIOUS, LARGE,
ROOMY, EXTENSIVE,
COMMODIOUS
capacity: . . . . . SIZE, POWER,
SPACE, SKILL, EXTENT,
CONTENT, VOLUME, ABILITY,
STRENGTH, APTITUDE,
POSITION, CAPABILITY
cape: . . . . COPE, HEAD, NESS,
CLOAK, STOLE, TALMA,
MANTA, AMICE, SERAPE,
MANTLE, HEADLAND,
MANTILLA, FORELAND,
MANTELET, PROMONTORY
caper: . . . . HOP, LEAP, ROMP,
ANTIC, DIDO, JUMP, SKIP,
DANCE, FRISK, GAMBOL,
PRANK, CAVORT, FROLIC,
PRANCE, CAPRIOLE
capillary: . . . . HAIRLIKE,
MINUTE, SLENDER
capital: . . . CITY, CASH, SEAT,
MAIN, CHIEF, MONEY, ASSETS,
WEALTH, LEADING, PRINCIPAL,
EXCELLENT

capitulate:... AGREE, YIELD, SUBMIT, SURRENDER, ENUMERATE

capote:..... HOOD, CLOAK, COVER, BONNET, MANTLE, OVERCOAT

caprice:.... WHIM, FANCY, HUMOR, ANTIC, NOTION, VAGARY, FREAK, WHIMSY, IMPULSE

capricious:.... WHIMSICAL, FICKLE, MOODY, ECCENTRIC, ERRATIC, COMICAL, FLIGHTY, FANTASY, INCONSTANT, WAYWARD

Capricorn:........ GOAT, CONSTELLATION

capriole:...... LEAP, CAPER

capsize:.. TIP, KEEL, UPSET, OVERTURN

capstan:..... DRUM, HOIST, WINDLASS

capsule:... POD, CAP, SEAL, CASE, PILL, BOLL, WAFER, CACHET, AMPULE, CONTAINER

captain:..... HEAD, CHIEF, LEAD(ER), MASTER, SKIPPER, COMMANDER

caption:.... TITLE, LEADER, LEGEND, HEADING, SUBTITLE, HEADLINE

captious:... SEVERE, CRAFTY, CYNICAL, TRICKY, CRITICAL, CONTRARY, IRASCIBLE, FAULT FINDING

captivate:...... WIN, TAKE, CATCH, ENAMOR, CHARM, SUBDUE, CAPTURE, FASCINATE, ATTRACT, INFATUATE, ENTHRALL, ENCHANT

captive:... SLAVE, ENAMOR, CAITIFF, PRISONER

captivity:....... SLAVERY, SERFDOM, BONDAGE, CONFINEMENT, IMPRISONMENT

capture:.... GET, WIN, NET, NAB, BAG, TAKE, TRAP, LAND, HOOK, CATCH, SEIZE, SEIZURE, COLLAR, ARREST, OBTAIN, APPREHEND

car:.. BUS, BOX, AUTO, JEEP, SEDAN, COACH, TRAIN, JALOPY, HOTROD, CHARIOT, VEHICLE, AUTOMOBILE, CONVERTIBLE, ARMORED

carapace:... SHELL, LORICA
animal with:..... CRAB, TURTLE, TORTOISE, TERRAPIN, ARMADILLO

caravan:... VAN, TRIP, TREK, TRAIN, CONVOY, SAFARI

carbine:...... GUN, RIFLE, MUSKET, WEAPON, ESCOPET

carbohydrate:..... SUGAR, STARCH, PECTIN, DEXTROSE, CELLULOSE

carbon:.. LEAD, SOOT, COKE, COPY, CRAYON, REPLICA, GRAPHITE

carborundum:..... EMERY, ABRASIVE

carboy:....... JUG, BOTTLE

carbuncle:.... BOIL, PIMPLE, GARNET, ABSCESS

carcass:.... BODY, CORPSE, FRAMEWORK, SKELETON

card:..... ACE, WAG, LIST, PLAN, MENU, COMB, JOKER, CHART, TICKET, PROGRAM, SCHEDULE, ECCENTRIC, PASTEBOARD

cardigan:.. FABRIC, JACKET, SWEATER, WAMPUS

cardinal:...... BIRD, MAIN, BASIC, CHIEF, VITAL, PRINCIPAL, FUNDAMENTAL

care:... DUTY, HEAD, FRET, MIND, WISH, TEND, NURSE, WORRY, ANXIETY, BURDEN, REGARD, CUSTODY, CHARGE, CHERISH, CONCERN, CAUTION, ATTENTION, RESPONSIBILITY

careen:.... TIP, CANT, LIST, LEAN, TILT, HEEL, LURCH, INCLINE

career: .... TRADE, CALLING, PURSUIT, VOCATION, PROFESSION, OCCUPATION

careful: ..... WARY, EXACT, CHARY, FRUGAL, PRUDENT, DISCREET, CAUTIOUS, THRIFTY, WATCHFUL, VIGILANT, METICULOUS

careless: ...... LAX, RASH, SLACK, CASUAL, UNTIDY, HEEDLESS, RECKLESS, SLOPPY, SLIPSHOD, SLOVENLY, NEGLIGENT, INATTENTIVE, THOUGHTLESS

caress: ..... HUG, PET, PAT, KISS, NECK, FONDLE, STROKE, EMBRACE, CUDDLE

caretaker: .... KEEPER, JANITOR, TRUSTEE, CUSTODIAN, CONCIERGE

cargo: ...... LOAD, BURDEN, FREIGHT, LADING, SHIPMENT

caribou: ... DEER, REINDEER

caricature: .... APE, MOCK, COPY, MIMIC, FARCE, PARODY, SATIRE, TRAVESTY, CARTOON, DISTORTION, BURLESQUE

carillon: ..... PEAL, BELLS, CHIMES, GLOCKENSPEIL

carl: ..... CHURL, BONDMAN, VILLEIN

carmine: .... RED, CRIMSON, SCARLET

carnage: .. POGRAM, MURDER, SLAUGHTER, MASSACRE, BLOODSHED, BUTCHERY

carnal: ...... LEWD, BODILY, SENSUAL, SEXUAL, EARTHLY, SECULAR, TEMPORAL, CORPORAL, WORLDLY

carnauba: .... PALM

carnival: .. FAIR, FETE, GALA, FESTIVAL, REVELRY, MERRYMAKING, EXHIBITION

carol: .... SING, SONG, NOEL, YODEL, WARBLE, MADRIGAL

carom: ..... SHOT, GLANCE, RICOCHET, REBOUND

carousal: ...... LARK, RIOT, ORGY, BINGE, SPREE, REVEL, FROLIC, REVELRY, WASSAIL, FESTIVAL, JAMBOREE

carousel: .. MERRY-GO-ROUND

carp: . CAVIL, SCOLD, PRATE, CENSURE, CRITICIZE, COMPLAIN, GOLDFISH

carpenter: .... ANT, WRIGHT, JOINER, WOODWORKER, CABINETMAKER

carpus: .... WRIST

carriage: .. GIG, MIEN, SHAY, PRAM, BUGGY, COACH, WAGON, POISE, BEARING, VEHICLE, CARIOLE, CHAISE, LANDAU, SURRY, MANNER, CONDUCT, PHAETON, BEHAVIOR, CONVEYANCE, PERAMBULATOR

carried: .... BORNE, TOTED, LUGGED, WAFTED, TRANSPORTED

carrier: ... HOD, SHIP, PLANE, PORTER, BEARER, TOTER, FLATTOP, POSTMAN, RAILROAD, TEAMSTER, MESSENGER

carrion: ..... VILE, CORPSE, REFUSE, FILTHY, ROTTEN, CARCASS, DECAYING

carrot: ..... ROOT, FENNEL, PLANT, ENTICEMENT

carry: .... LUG, CART, BEAR, TAKE, TOTE, LEAD, TRANSPORT, CONVEY, CONVOY, EXTEND, TRANSMIT, TRANSFER, SUSTAIN, SUPPORT

cart: ..... VAN, HAUL, DRAY, BOGY, BOGIE, SULKY, LORRY, CARRY, WAGON, CONVEY, CARIOLE, VEHICLE, TRUNDLE

cartel: .. PACT, POOL, TRUST, TREATY, CONTRACT, CHALLENGE, AGREEMENT, MONOPOLY, SYNDICATE

cartilage: ... TISSUE, GRISTLE

cartograph: ..... MAP, PLAT, CHART

carton: .... BOX, CASE, CONTAINER

cartoon: . . . DRAWING, COMIC STRIP, SKETCH, CARICATURE

carve: . . . CUT, CHISEL, SLICE, INCISE, SCULPT, ENGRAVE

cascade: . . . . . . FALL, LINN, WATERFALL

case: . . . . . . BOX, BAG, POD, CRATE, EVENT, AFFAIR, CARTON, MATTER, INSTANCE, EXAMINE, EXAMPLE, SITUATION, LAWSUIT, SHEATH, CAPSULE, CONTAINER, QUESTION

casement: . . WINDOW, FRAME, COVERING

cash: . . COINS, JAKE, BRASS, DOUGH, FUNDS, MONEY, SPECIE, CAPITAL, CURRENCY

cashier: . . . . TELLER, DISCHARGE, DISMISS, BURSAR, PURSER

casing: . SHOE, HULL, COVER, SHEATH, FRAME

cask: . KEG, VAT, TUN, BUTT, BARECA, TIERCE, BARREL, FIRKIN, PUNCHEON, HOGSHEAD

casket: . . . BOX, CASK, CASE, CHEST, COFFIN, COFFER, RELIQUARY

Cassandra: . . . . . . SEERESS, PROPHETESS

cassock: . . . . GOWN, PRIEST, VESTMENT, SOUTANE, CLERGYMAN

cast: . . . . HURL, SHED, MOLD, TOSS, FOUND, FLING, THROW, SLING, HEAVE

castaway: . . WAIF, OUTCAST, REJECT, DERELICT, STRANDED

caste: . . . . RANK, BREED, GRADE, CLASS, STATUS

caster: . VIAL, PHIAL, CRUET, ROLLER, CASTOR, BOTTLE, STAND, TRUNDLE

castigate: . . . . BERATE, CHASTISE, REBUKE, REPROVE, CENSURE, PUNISH, CRITICIZE

castle: . . FORT, ROOK, ABODE, CITADEL, CHATEAU, STRONGHOLD

castrate: . . . . . . GELD, SPAY, ALTER, NEUTER, EUNUCH, MUTILATE, CAPONIZE, STERILIZE, EMASCULATE

casual: . . . . . . IDLE, STRAY, CHANCE, INFORMAL, RANDOM, PASSING, OFFHAND, INCIDENTAL, ACCIDENTAL, NONCHALANT, CURSORY

casualty: . . . . . LOSS, DEATH, VICTIM, INJURY, ACCIDENT, DISASTER, FATALITY

cat: . . . . LION, LYNX, PUMA, PUSS, CIVET, TIGER, FELID, TABBY, ANGORA, OCELOT, COUGAR, LEOPARD, JAGUAR, BAUDRONS, MALKIN, MAWKIN, WILDCAT, PANTHER, CARNIVORE

cataclysm: . . FLOOD, DELUGE, DEBACLE, DISASTER, UPHEAVAL, CATASTROPHE

catacomb: . . . . TOMB, CRYPT, CEMETERY

catafalque: . . . . BIER, COFFIN

catalog, catalogue: . . . BOOK, ROLL, LIST, INDEX, RECORD, SCHEDULE, REGISTER, ARRANGE, CLASSIFY, INVENTORY

catalyst: . . . . REAGENT, ACTIVATOR

catamaran: . . . RAFT, BALSA, BOAT, FLOAT

catapult: . . . . HURL, THROW, LAUNCH, BRICOLE, ONAGER, BALLISTA, SLINGSHOT

cataract: . . . . . . LINN, FALLS, CASCADE, DELUGE, DOWNPOUR, WATERFALL

catch: . . BAG, GET, NET, NAB, COP, HOOK, LAND, TRAP, SNARE, SEIZE, DETECT, CORNER, ENMESH, CAPTURE, ENTANGLE, SURPRISE

catching: . . . . . . FETCHING, ALLURING, CONTAGIOUS, INFECTIOUS, ATTRACTIVE

catchy: . . TRICKY, APPEALING, DECEIVING

catechism: . . GUIDE, MANUAL, HANDBOOK

categorical: . . . . . ABSOLUTE, POSITIVE, EXPLICIT, UNEQUIVOCAL

category: . . . . RANK, CLASS, GENRE, DIVISION, SPECIES, CLASSIFICATION

cater: . . . . FEED, SERVE, PANDER, PURVEY, PROVIDE, SUPPLY

caterwaul: . . . . WAIL, MIAUL, HOWL, SCREECH

cathartic: . . . . . . LAXATIVE, CLEANSING, PURGING, PURGATIVE

Cathay: . . . . CHINA

Catholic: . . . . BROAD, PAPAL, GENERAL, UNIVERSAL, TOLERANT, LIBERAL, ECUMENICAL

catlike: . . FELINE, NOISELESS, STEALTHY

catnap: . . . . DOZE

cattle: . . . COWS, KINE, OXEN, BULLS, BEEVES, STEERS, BOVINES

cattleman: . . . . COWBOY, DROVER, HERDER, RANCHER, STOCKMAN

catty: . . . . . MEAN, SPITEFUL, MALICIOUS

catwalk: . . . . BRIDGE, WALKWAY, FOOTWAY

caucus: . . COUNCIL, MEETING, CONFAB, ELECTION

caulis: . . . . STEM, STALK

caulk, calk: . . STOP UP, SEAL, CHINSE

cause: . . . . AIM, ROOT, BASIS, AGENT, REASON, MOTIVE, CREATE, ORIGIN, OBJECT, INDUCE, GROUND, MOVEMENT, OCCASION, ENGENDER

caustic: . . . . LYE, LIME, TART, ACRID, BITING, CORROSIVE, CUTTING, SNAPPISH, VITRIOLIC, MORDANT, MORDACIOUS, SARDONIC, STINGING, SARCASTIC, ACRIMONIOUS

cauterize: . . . . . BURN, SEAR, CHAR, SINGE, STERILIZE

caution: . . . . . . CARE, HEED, WARN, ADVICE, COUNSEL, ADMONISH, PRUDENCE, WARINESS, ADMONITION, WATCHFULNESS

cautious: . . . . WARY, ALERT, GUARDED, PRUDENT, CHARY, CAREFUL, VIGILANT, CIRCUMSPECT

cavalcade: . . . . PARADE, JOURNEY, PAGEANT, PROCESSION

cavalier: . . . . . GAY, BRAVE, PROUD, KNIGHT, GALLANT, HAUGHTY, GENTLEMAN, ARROGANT

cavalry: . . . TROOPS, HORSES, HORSEMEN

cavalryman: . . . . . LANCER, HUSSAR, DRAGOON, TROOPER, GENDARME

cave: . . . . DEN, HOLE, LAIR, COVE, HOLLOW, CRYPT, GROTTO, ANTRE, ANTRUM, CAVERN, CAVITY, COLLAPSE

caveat: . . . NOTICE, CAUTION, BEWARE, WARNING

caviar: . . . ROE, EGGS, RELISH

cavil: . . . . . . CARP, QUIBBLE, OBJECT, BICKER, CRITICISE

cavity: . . . . PIT, CAVE, DENT, HOLE, CELL, VOID, FOSSA, SINUS, ANTRUM, CAVERN, HOLLOW, VACUUM, FOLLICLE, EXCAVATION

cavort: . . PLAY, LEAP, CAPER, PRANCE, GAMBOL

cayenne: . . . PEPPER, CANARY, CAPSICUM

cayman: . . . ALLIGATOR, YAKI

cayuse: . . . . . PONY, BRONCO

cease: .... END, HALT, STOP, REST, PAUSE, DESIST, FINISH, DISCONTINUE, REFRAIN, TERMINATE, DISCONTINUE

ceaseless: ... EVER, ENDLESS, CONTINUAL, INCESSANT, CONTINUOUS

cecum: ... PIT, PORE, POUCH, CAVITY

cede: .. GIVE, AWARD, YIELD, GRANT, TRANSFER, SURRENDER

cedula: .. PERMIT, DOCUMENT, CERTIFICATE

celebrate: .... SING, REVEL, HONOR, PRAISE, OBSERVE, GLORIFY, SOLEMNIZE, COMMEMORATE

celebrated: .. FAMED, NOTED, EMINENT, OBSERVED, FAMOUS, RENOWNED, SOLEMNIZED

celebrity: ..... HERO, STAR, IDOL, LION, FAME, RENOWN

celerity: .... HASTE, SPEED, QUICKNESS, DISPATCH, SWIFTNESS

celestial: ..... HOLY, DIVINE, URANIC, ANGELIC, ETHEREAL, HEAVENLY

celibacy: .... CHASTITY, BACHELORHOOD

celibate: ... CHASTE, SINGLE, BACHELOR, SPINSTER, UNMARRIED

cell: ...... EGG, GERM, JAIL, CRYPT, GROUP, VAULT, PRISON, CHAMBER, BATTERY
cavity: .... VACUOLE
center: .... NUCLEUS
division: .... SPIREME
generative: ..... GAMETE
study of: ..... CYTOLOGY

cellar: ..... PANTRY, WINE-STOCK, BASEMENT, STOREROOM

cement: .. GLUE, JOIN, KNIT, PASTE, STICK, UNITE, PUTTY, COHERE, MORTAR, SOLDER, MASTIC, ADHESIVE, MUCILAGE

cemetery: ..... GRAVEYARD, BONEYARD, ACROPOLIS, CATACOMB

cenobite: ...... NUN, MONK, RECLUSE, ESSENE, ANCHORITE

censor: ... CRITIC, RESTRICT, SUPPRESS, REVIEWER

censure: ..... FLAY, BLAME, CHIDE, DECRY, ACCUSE, BERATE, REBUKE, CONDEMN, REPROVE, REPROACH, CRITICIZE, REPRIMEND

cent: ... COIN, PENNY, COPPER

center: .... HUB, MID, AXIS, CORE, FOCUS, HEART, PIVOT, NUCLEUS, HEADQUARTERS, MIDDLE

central: ... MID, BASIC, CHIEF, FOCAL, MAIN, MIDDLE, LEADING, PRIMARY, PIVOTAL

Central America: ....
PANAMA, HONDURAS, SALVADOR, GUATEMALA, NICARAGUA, COSTA RICA

centrifugal: ...... INERTIA, EFFERENT, RADIATING

centripetal: ...... AFFERENT

century: ...... AGE, SIECLE, HUNDRED

cephalopod: .... SQUID, OCTOPUS, CUTTLE(FISH), INKFISH

ceramics: .. TILES, POTTERY, PORCELAIN, EARTHENWARE

cereal: ... RYE, BRAN, CORN, MUSH, GRITS, OATS, RICE, GRAIN, MAIZE, WHEAT, BARLEY, FARINA, HOMINY, MILLET, OATMEAL, SOYBEAN, PORRIGE, BUCKWHEAT

cerebral: .... MENTAL, INTELLECTUAL

cerebrate: .. THINK, PONDER, COGITATE

ceremonious: ...... GRAND, LOFTY, FORMAL, SOLEMN, STATELY

ceremony: ...... FETE, RITE, POMP, PARADE, RITUAL, PAGENT, OCCASION, FORMALITY, CELEBRATION

certain: . . . REAL, SURE, TRUE, EXACT, FIXED, ACTUAL, ASSURED, PRECISE, ABSOLUTE, OFFICIAL, POSITIVE, CONFIDENT, DEPENDABLE, INFALLIBLE, INDUBITABLE

certificate: . . . BOND, CHECK, SCRIP, TICKET, DIPLOMA, VOUCHER, STATEMENT, CREDENTIAL, DECLARATION

certify: . . . . SWEAR, AFFIRM, ATTEST, VOUCH, VERIFY, DEPOSE, ASSURE, TESTIFY, GUARANTEE, NOTARIZE

cervine: . . ELK, DEER, STAG, CERVID, MOOSE, REINDEER

cervix: . . . . NECK

cespitose: . MATTED, TUFTED, TANGLED

cessation: . . . . . END, HALT, STOP(PAGE), PAUSE, CEASING, LETUP, SURCEASE, DISCONTINUANCE

cession: . . . CEDING, YIELDING, SURRENDER, CONCESSION

cetacean: . . WHALE, BELUGA, DOLPHIN, GAMPUS, PORPOISE, NARWHAL(E)

chafe: . . IRK, RUB, VEX, FRET, FUME, GALL, HEAT, WEAR, ANNOY, GRIND, ABRADE, HARASS, NETTLE, FRICTION, IRRITATE

chaffer: . . . HAGGLE, HIGGLE, BANDY, DICKER, BARGAIN(ING), NEGOTIATE

chagrin: . . . EMBARRASMENT, DISCOMFITURE, MORTIFICATION

chain: . . . . . TIE, BIND, BOND, JOIN, LINK, CABLE, CATENA, FASTEN, RANGE, FETTER, SHACKLE, SECURE, SERIES, NETWORK, CONSTRAIN

chair: . . SEAT, STOOL, SEDAN, OFFICE, BENCH, CENTER, ROCKER, POSITION, PRESIDE

chalcedony: . . . OPAL, ONYX, AGATE, QUARTZ, JASPER, CARNELIAN, CHRYSOPRASE, CAT'S-EYE, OPALINE

chalet: . . HUT, CABIN, HOUSE, COTTAGE

chalice: . . . AMA, CUP, BOWL, GRAIL, CALIX, GOBLET

challenge: . . . . . DARE, DEFY, CALL, BLAME, BRAVE, CLAIM, IMPUNG, INVITE, DEMAND, PROVOKE, EXCEPTION, QUESTION

chamber: . . . . . CELL, FLAT, HALL, (BED)ROOM, CAMERA, CUBICLE, APARTMENT, CAMARILLA, COMPARTMENT

chamberlain: . . . . . FACTOR, SERVANT, OFFICER, STEWARD, ATTENDANT, TREASURER

chambray: . . . . FABRIC, GINGHAM

chamfer: . . . BEVEL, GROOVE, FURROW, FLUTING

champion: . . . . . . AID, BACK, HERO, DEFEND, VICTOR, ADVOCATE, PROTECT, ESPOUSE, WINNER, DEFEND(ER), UNEXCELLED

chance: . . . . HAP, LOT, FATE, LUCK, ODDS, RISK, CASUAL, GAMBLE, HAPPEN, FORTUNE, ACCIDENT, RANDOM, HAZARD, OPPORTUNITY

cancre: . . . . . . SORE, ULCER, LESION

change: . . . . . . MOVE, VARY, ADAPT, ALTER, AMEND, SHIFT, MODIFY, REVAMP, REVISE, SWITCH, MUTATE, CONVERT, TRANSFER, REARRANGE, TRANSFORM, ALTERATION, CORRECTION, TRANSITION

changeable: . . . FLUID, GIDDY, FICKLE, MOBILE, ERRATIC, VARIANT, PROTEAN, MUTABLE, VOLATILE, UNSTABLE, IRREGULAR, UNCERTAIN, INCONSTANT, CAPRICIOUS

changeling: . . . . . . OAF, DOLT, IDIOT, CHILD, TURNCOAT

channel: . . . RUT, DUCT, PIPE, VEIN, CANAL, DITCH, CHUTE, FLUME, FLUTE, RIVER, SHOOT, STRAIT, COURSE, ARTERY, FURROW, GROOVE, MEDIUM, RUNNEL, SLUICE, STREAM, CONDUIT, PASSAGE, RUNWAY

channeled: . . . . . GROOVED, FLUTED, COURSED, ROUTED, VOLUTED, FURROWED

chanson: . . . . . SONG, LYRIC, BALLAD, MELODY

chant: . . . . CANT, SING, SONG, PSALM, CAROL, MELODY, ANTHEM, INTONE, WORSHIP

poetic: . . . . WARBLE

chantage: . . . . . BLACKMAIL, EXTORTION

chanteuse: . . . . SINGER

chantey: . . . . (SAILOR)SONG

chanticleer: . . COCK, ROOSTER

chantilly: . . . . LACE

chantry: . . . . ALTAR, CHAPEL

chaos: . . . MESS, VOID, BABEL, ABYSS, MIXTURE, JUMBLE, DISORDER, SHAMBLES, CONFUSION

chaotic: . . . . MUDDLED, CONFUSED, DISORDERLY

chapel: . . . . CLOAK, CHURCH, SHRINE, CHANTRY, VESTRY, SANCTUARY

chaperon: . . . . ESCORT, DUENNA, ATTEND, GUARDIAN, ACCOMPANY

strict: . . . . DRAGON

chapman: . . BUYER, TRADER, DEALER, PEDDLER, HAWKER, CUSTOMER, MERCHANT

chapter: . . . . . CELL, LODGE, LOCAL, BRANCH, EPISODE, SECTION

character: . . . . . BENT, KIND, MARK, CODE, ROLE, PART, SIGN, SORT, TRAIT, BRAND, CIPHER, EMBLEM, FIGURE, LETTER, NATURE, SYMBOL, REPUTE, QUALITY, REPUTATION

characteristic: . . . . . . TRAIT, NATURE, FEATURE, QUALITY, TYPICAL, DISTINCTIVE, PROPERTY, ATTRIBUTE, PECULIARITY

charade: . . . ENIGMA, PUZZLE, RIDDLE, TABLEAU

charcoal: . CARBON, LIGNITE, BONEBLACK

chard: . . . . LEAFSTALK, BEET

chare: . . . . CHORE

charge: . . . . FEE, BILL, COST, DUTY, TOLL, RATE, LIE, TOTAL, DEBIT, PRICE, ACCUSE, INSTRUCT, ALLEGE, IMPUTE, INDICT, TARRIFF, ASSAULT, ATTRIBUTE, COMMAND, EXPENSE, MANDATE, ACCUSATION, INCRIMINATE

charisma: . . CHARM, APPEAL, POWER, GRACE, IMPACT

charity: . . ALMS, DOLE, GIFT, MERCY, HANDOUT, LARGESS, LIENIENCE, GENEROSITY, PHILANTROPHY, BENEVOLENCE

charlatan: . . . CHEAT, FAKER, FRAUD, QUACK, IMPOSTOR, EMPIRIC, MAGICIAN, MOUNTEBANK

charm: . . . . . ALLAY, GRACE, MAGIC, SPELL, ALLURE, AMULET, BEAUTY, ENAMOR, ENCHANT, ENTICE, FETISH, PLEASE, ATTRACT, BEGUILE, BEWITCH, DELIGHT, INCANTATION, FASCINATE, CAPTIVATE

charming: . . . . AMIABLE, WINSOME, WINNING, ADORABLE, AGREEABLE, BEAUTIFUL, GLAMOROUS

chart: . . . . MAP, PLAT, PLAN, PLOT, GRAPH, SCHEME, RECORD, LAYOUT, OUTLINE, DIAGRAM

charter: . . . LET, RENT, HIRE, LEASE, FRANCHISE, COMMISSION

chary: . . . . SHY, WARY, FRUGAL, CAREFUL, CAUTIOUS, HESITANT, VIGILANT

chase: . . HUNT, SHAG, CATCH, CHEVY, HARRY, PURSUE, FOLLOW, PURSUIT, FRIEZE, GROOVE, CHANNEL, ENGRAVE, ORNAMENT

chasm: . . . . . GAP, PIT, GULF, RIFT, ABYSS, CLEFT, GORGE, HIATUS, FISSURE, CREVASSE

chassis: . . . . . . FRAME, BODY

chaste: . . . . . . PURE, CLEAN, MODEST, VESTAL DECENT, VIRGIN, VIRTUOUS, CELIBATE

chasten: . . . . SMITE, PUNISH, CHASTISE, SUBDUE, HUMBLE, CORRECT, REPRIMAND

chastise: . . BEAT, FLOG, SLAP, WHIP, BLAME, SCOLD, BERATE, SPANK, PUNISH, REBUKE, THRASH

chastity: . . . PURITY, VIRTUE, CELIBACY, VIRGINITY, DECENCY

chateau: . . . HOUSE, CASTLE, MANSION, FORTRESS

chatelaine: . . . . ETUI, CHAIN, BROOCH, CLASP, MISTRESS

chattels: . . . GOODS, MONEY, WARES, SLAVES, CAPITAL, PROPERTY, LIVESTOCK

chatter: . . . . GAB, JAW, YAP, CHAT, BLAB, PRATE, CLACK, CACKLE, PRATTLE, GOSSIP, BABBLE, GIBBER

chaussure: . . . . SHOE, BOOT, SLIPPER, FOOTWEAR

chauvinism: . . . . . JINGOISM, PATRIOTISM

cheap: . . BASE, POOR, MEAN, ABJECT, SHODDY, STINGY, TAWDRY, BARGAIN, COMMON, INEXPENSIVE, PICAYUNE

cheat: . . . . . . CON, FOB, GYP, BILK, CLIP, CRIB, FOIL, DUPE, FAKE, HOAX, SHAM, SKIN, BUNCO, COZEN, FRAUD, GOUGE, TRICK, WELSH, MULET, CHISEL, DELUDE, FLEECE, HUMBUG, OUTWIT, DECEIVE, DEFRAUD, MISLEAD, SWINDLE,

SCOUNDREL, VICTIMIZE, MOUNTEBANK

check: . . . . . BIT, DAM, NIP, BALK, CURB, REIN, SNUB, STEM, STOP, TEST, BLOCK, BRAKE, CHOKE, DELAY, DETER, LIMIT, REPELL, STALL, STUNT, TALLY, TOKEN, BRIDLE, DEFEAT, DETAIN, HINDER, IMPEDE, OPPOSE, REBUFF, STIFLE, TICKET, VERIFY, CONTROL, INHIBIT, MONITOR, REPRESS, REPULSE, OBSTRUCT, RESTRAIN, FRUSTRATE, SUPERVISE, ASCERTAIN, EXAMINATION

checkered: . . . . PIED, DICED, PLAID, MOTTLED, VARIGATED, TATTERSALL

checkmate: . . . . LICK, STOP, STYMIE, BAFFLE, DEFEAT, THWART, OUTWIT, CORNER, FRUSTRATE

Cheddar: . . . . CHEESE

cheddite: . . . . EXPLOSIVE

cheek: . . . JAW, CHAP, GALL, JOWL, SASS, NERVE, AUDACITY, TEMERITY, IMPUDENCE, INSOLENCE

cheer: . . . . RAH, YELL, ROOT, BRAVO, SHOUT, MIRTH, ELATE, GAIETY, GLADDEN, COMFORT, HEARTEN, APPLAUD, BRIGHTEN, ENLIVEN, ENCOURAGE, HOSPITALITY

cheerful: . . . . . . GAY, GLAD, JOLLY, BLITHE, MERRY, SUNNY

cheerless: . . . . . . SAD, DRAB, BLEAK, DISMAL, DREARY, JOYLESS

cheesy: . . . . CHEAP, SHABBY, CASEOUS

chela: . . . . . . CLAW, PINCER, NOVICE, DISCIPLE

chelonian: . . . . . . TORTOISE, TURTLE

chemise: . . SLIP, SHIRT, SHIFT, SMOCK, LINGERIE

chemist: . . . . ANALYST,
DRUGGIST, PHARMACIST,
APOTHECARY
cherish: . . . . . LOVE, ADORE,
ENJOY, PRIZE, VALUE,
NURTURE, ESTEEM, REVERE,
FOSTER, TREASURE, APPRECIATE
cherub: . . . ANGEL, SERAPH,
SERAPHIM
chess: *castle:* . . . . ROOK
finish: . . . . STALEMATE
opening: . . . . GAMBIT
piece: . . . . . PAWN, ROOK,
CASTLE, KING, QUEEN,
BISHOP, KNIGHT
chest: . . . . BOX, BUST, FUND,
SAFE, ARCA, TRUNK, CASKET,
COFFER, BREAST, BUREAU,
LOCKER, BOSOM, THORAX,
CUPBOARD, TREASURY,
COMMODE
chesterfield: . . . COAT, SOFA,
DIVAN, TOPCOAT, DAVENPORT
chevron: . . . . . . BAR, STRIPE
chew: . . . . . CUD, BITE, CHAW,
GNAW, GRIND, CHAMP, MUNCH,
CRUNCH, MANDUCATE,
MEDITATE, MASTICATE,
RUMINATE
chic: . . . . POSH, SMART,
STYLISH, MODISH, ELEGANT,
FASHIONABLE
Chicago: . . . . . . WINDY CITY
chicanery: . . . . ARTIFICE,
INTRIGUE, TRICKERY,
DECEPTION
chickadee: . . . . . TITMOUSE,
TOMTIT
chicken: . . HEN, COCK, FOWL,
BIDDY, CAPON, PULLET,
BANTAM, POULTRY, ROOSTER,
COCKEREL
chicken hearted: . . . TIMID,
YELLOW, COWARDLY
chide: . . . . . SCOLD, UPBRAID,
CENSURE, REBUKE, BERATE,
BLAME, REPROACH, REPROVE
chief: . . . . AGA, BOSS, HEAD,
ARCH, MAIN, FIRST, MAJOR,

LEADER, PRINCIPAL, FOREMOST,
CAPTAIN, PREMIER,
PREDOMINANT
chiffonier: . . . . BUREAU,
CABINET, COMMODE
chigger: . . . . . . FLEA, MITE,
CHIGOE
child: . . . BOY, IMP, KID, SON,
TAD, TOT, BABE, BABY, BRAT,
CHIT, GIRL, WAIF, TYKE,
CHICK, GAMIN, CHERUB,
INFANT, MOPPET, URCHIN,
TODDLER, PROGENY,
YOUNGSTER
childbirth: . . LABOR, LYING-
IN, TRAVAIL, DELIVERY,
CONFINEMENT, PARTURATION
childish: . . . . . NAIVE, PETTY,
SILLY, SIMPLE, IMMATURE,
ASININE, FOOLISH, PUERILE,
JUVENILE, INFANTILE
children: . . . . ISSUE, BROOD,
PROGENY, OFFSPRING
chill: . . . RAW, AGUE, COLD,
COOL, ALGOR, SHAKE, FROST,
FREEZE, FRIGID, SHIVER,
DEPRESS, MALARIA,
REFRIGERATE
chilly: . . . . RAW, COOL, COLD,
ALGID, BLEAK, ARCTIC, FROSTY
chime: . . . . RIM, BELL, RING,
PEAL, AGREE, CYMBAL,
HARMONY, CARILLON
chimera: . . . FANCY, MIRAGE,
ILLUSION
chemerical: . . . . WILD,
FANCIFUL, ROMANTIC,
IMAGINARY, FANTASTIC,
VISIONARY, UNFOUNDED
chimney: . . FLUE, PIPE, VENT,
TEWEL, FUNNEL, (SMOKE)STACK
chimpanzee: . . . . APE,
ANTHROPOID, TROGLODYTE
chinaware: . . . . DISHES,
CERAMIC, PORCELAIN,
CROCKERY, EARTHENWARE
chink: . . . . . GAP, RENT, RIFT,
RIME, CLEFT, CRACK, CRANNY,

CREVICE, FISSURE, APERTURE,
INTERSTICE

Chinook: . . . WIND, INDIAN,
SALMON, FLATHEAD

chip: . . BIT, CUT, HEW, CLIP,
NICK, CHOP, SLICE, SCRAP,
FLAKE, CHISEL, FRAGMENT,
SPLINTER

chipper: . . GAY, SPRY, PERT,
PERKY, LIVELY, TWITTER,
CHATTER, CHEERFUL

chirography: . . . . . . SCRIPT,
WRITING, ENGROSSING,
HANDWRITING

chirp: . . PEEP, CHEEP, TWEET,
TWITTER

chisel: . . . . . CUT, CHIP, PARE,
CARVE, CHEAT, GOUGE,
HAGGLE, BARGAIN, ENGRAVE,
BURIN, HARDY, SCULPT,
SWINDLE, QUARREL

chit: . . TAB, IOU, BILL, GIRL,
MEMO, NOTE, CHILD, SHOOT,
SPROUT, VOUCHER

chitchat: . . . . . TALK, GOSSIP,
CONVERSATION

chivalrous: . . BRAVE, NOBLE,
POLITE, GALLANT, VALIANT,
COURTEOUS, HONORABLE

chloroform: . . . . KILL,
ANESTHETIC

chock: . . . . . BLOCK, WEDGE,
CLEAT, CHUCK

chocolate: . . . DRINK, CANDY,
COCA, BEVERAGE

choice: . . . . BEST, FINE, PICK,
WILL, CREAM, ELITE, PRIME,
SELECT, ELECTION, VOLITION,
EXCELLENT, PREFERENCE,
SELECTION, ALTERNATIVE

choke: . . . DAM, GAG, CLOG,
PLUG, CLOSE, IMPEDE, STIFLE,
SILENCE, STRANGLE, SMOTHER,
SUFFOCATE, OBSTRUCT,
CONSTRICT, THROTTLE

choler: . . . . IRE, BILE, RAGE,
ANGER, WRATH, SPLEEN

choleric: . . . . ANGRY, CROSS,
ENRAGED, IRATE, TESTY,
IRRITABLE, IRASCIBLE

cholla: . . . . CACTUS

choose: . . . . OPT, CULL, PICK,
ADOPT, ELECT, PREFER,
SELECT, EMBRACE

chop: . . CUT, LOP, AXE, HEW,
JAW, DICE, FELL, HACK, JOWL,
CARVE, MINCE, SLASH, CLEAVE

chord: . CORD, TONE, NERVE,
STRING, TENDON, HARMONY,
FILAMENT

chordate: . . . . . VERTEBRATE

chore: . . . . JOB, CHAR, DUTY,
TASK, STINT, CHARE, ERRAND

chortle: . . . . . LAUGH, SNORT,
CHUCKLE

chorus: . . . . . . SONG, CHOIR,
ACCORD, UNISON, REFRAIN,
SINGERS

girl: . . . CHORINE, DANCER,
SINGER

leader: . . . . . . CHORAGUS,
CONDUCTOR

christen: . . . . NAME, BAPTIZE

Christian: . . . . GENTILE,
DECENT, HUMAN

Christmas: . . . . NOEL,
NATIVITY, YULE(TIDE)

chronic: . . SEVERE, INTENSE,
CONSTANT, RECURRING,
CONTINUAL, HABITUAL,
CONFIRMED

chronicle: . . . ANNAL, DIARY,
ACCOUNT, HISTORY, RECORD,
NARRATIVE

chronicler: . . . . WRITER,
HISTORIAN, ANNALIST,
RECORDER

chrysalis: . . . PUPA, COCOON

chubby: . . . . PLUMP, ROTUND

chuck: . . TOSS, FOOD, HURL,
THROW, DISCARD

chum: . . . . PAL, BAIT, BUDDY,
CRONY, ROOMMATE, FRIEND

chump: . . . ASS, DOLT, BOOB,
FOOL

chunky: . . . STOUT, STOCKY,
CORPULENT

church: . . . . SECT, TEMPLE, CHAPEL, EDIFICE, SANCTUARY, DENOMINATION

churchman: . . . . . MINISTER, PRIEST, ELDER, PASTOR, BISHOP, CLERGY, CARDINAL, ECCLESIASTIC

churl: . . . . CAD, BOOR, LOUT, SERF, KNAVE, RUSTIC, VASSAL, PEASANT, FREEMAN, VILLEIN

churlish: . . . . RUSTIC, SURLY, ROUGH, BOORISH, SULLEN, UNCIVIL

churn: . . STIR, BEAT, SHAKE, AGITATE

chute: . . . . . . TUBE, FLUME, SHOOT, SLIDE, RAPIDS, HOPPER, TROUGH, RUNWAY, DECLINE

cicada: . . . . LOCUST, CIGALA

cicatrix: . . . . . SCAR, SCAB

cicerone: . . . . . GUIDE, PILOT, MENTOR, CONDUCTOR

cigar: . . . . . SMOKE, HAVANA, CORONA, STOGIE, CHEROOT, TOBACCO, PANATEL(L)A, PERFECTO

cigarette: . . . . . . FAG, PILL, SMOKE, CUBEB, GASPER, REEFER

cilium: . . . . . HAIR, EYELASH

cinch: . . . BELT, GIRD, GIRTH, FASTEN, CERTAINTY

cincture: . . BELT, GIRD, RING, GIRTH, GIRDLE, WAISTBAND, ENCIRCLE, ENVIRONMENT

cinder: . . ASH, SLAG, EMBER, CLINKER, RESIDUE

cinema: . . . . . . FILM, SHOW, MOVIE, THEATER, MOTION PICTURE

cingulum: . . . . BELT, GIRDLE

cinnabar: . . . ORE, PIGMENT, VERMILION

cinnamon: . . . . SPICE, BARK, CANELLA

cinquefoil: . . . . CLOVER

cipher: . . . KEY, CODE, ZERO, AUGHT, OUGHT, LETTER, SYMBOL, NAUGHT, NONENTITY

circa: . . . . . ABOUT, AROUND

Circe: . . . . SIREN, SORCERESS, ENCHANTRESS

circle: . . . DISK, HALO, HOOP, LOOP, RING, RINK, CROWN, CYCLE, ROUND, GROUP, ORBIT, CLIQUE, WHIRL, COTERIE, CIRQUE, REVOLVE, ENCOMPASS, SURROUND

circuit: . . . LAP, LOOP, TOUR, ZONE, AMBIT, ROUTE, CYCLE, ORBIT, DISTRICT

circuitous: . . . . CURVED, CROOKED, DEVIOUS, WINDING, INDIRECT, ROUNDABOUT, LABYRINTHINE

circular: . . . . . BILL, ROUND, DISCOID, GLOBULAR, PAMPHLET, CIRCUITOUS, ROUNDABOUT, ADVERTISEMENT

circulate: . . . . . . MIX, MOVE, TURN, ROTATE, SPREAD, DIFFUSE, PUBLISH, PROPAGATE

circumference: . . . . . . ARC, AMBIT, GIRTH, CIRCUIT, BOUNDRY, PERIPHERY

circumlocution: . . . AMBAGE, PERIPHRASE, VERBIAGE, ROUNDABOUT

circumscribe: . . . . . BOUND, LIMIT, DEFINE, ENCIRCLE, CONFINE, ENCOMPASS

circumspect: . . WARY, WISE, CAUTIOUS, CAREFUL, DISCREET, PRUDENT

circumstance: . . FACT, ITEM, EVENT, STATE, DETAIL, AFFAIR, FACTOR, EPISODE, CONDITION, SITUATION, OCCURRENCE

circumvent: . . . . BALK, DUPE, FOIL, EVADE, TRICK, SKIRT, OUTWIT, THWART, DECEIVE, FRUSTRATE

circus: . . . . ARENA, CIRQUE, SHOW, SPECTACLE, HIPPODROME, AMPITHEATRE

cirque: . . . . . . RING, CIRCLE, CIRCUS, RECESS

cirrus: . . . TENDRIL, CLOUDS, FILAMENT

cist: . . . . TOMB, CHEST

cistern: . . . . . SAC, TUB, VAT, WELL, TANK, CAVITY, RESERVOIR

citadel: . | . . . FORT, CASTLE, REFUGE, TOWER, FORTRESS, STRONGHOLD

cital: . . . . SUMMONS

citation: . . NOTICE, MENTION, SUMMONS, QUOTATION, REFERENCE

cite: . . . . CALL, TELL, REFER, QUOTE, SUMMON, MENTION, ACCUSE, ARRAIGN, EXCERPT

citizen: . . . . . VOTER, NATIVE, DENIZEN, ELECTOR, FREEMAN, BURGESS, RESIDENT, SUBJECT, NATIONAL, INHABITANT

citrus fruit: . . . LIME, LEMON, ORANGE, CITRON, MANDARIN, KUMQUAT, TANGELO, GRAPEFRUIT, TANGERINE

city: . . . . BURG, TOWN, COMMUNITY, METROPOLIS, MUNICIPALITY

civil: . . . . . AFFABLE, POLITE, URBANE, POLITIC, GRACIOUS, CIVILIZED, COURTEOUS, RESPECTFUL

civilization: . . . . . . CULTURE, REFINEMENT, CULTIVATION

civilize: . . . . . LEACH, TRAIN, POLISH, REFINE, EDUCATE, CULTIVATE, DOMESTICATE

clad: . . . . . . ROBED, DRESSED, ARRAYED, CLOTHED, ATTIRED

claim: . . . . . ASK, AVER, LIEN, EXACT, RIGHT, TITLE, ASSERT, DEMAND, PROFESS, ALLEGE, MAINTAIN

claivoyance: . . . . . INSIGHT, SAGACITY, DIVINATION, DISCERNMENT

clairvoyant: . . SEER, PROPHET

clamber: . . . . . CLIMB, SCALE

clamor: . . . . CRY, DIN, WAIL, RIOT, NOISE, UPROAR, OUTCRY, RACKET

clamorous: . . . LOUD, NOISY, TURBULENT, BOISTEROUS, VOCIFEROUS

clamp: . . . . . PIN, GRIP, VISE, CLASP, FASTENER

clan: . . . . . SET, CULT, RACE, TRIBE, GROUP, CLIQUE, FAMILY, SOCIETY

clandestine: . . . SLY, COVERT, SECRET, FURTIVE, ILLICIT, HIDDEN, CONCEALED, SURREPTITIOUS

clangor: . . DIN, ROAR, PEAL, HUBBUB, UPROAR

clap: . . . . PEAL, SLAP, BLOW, CRACK, STROKE, APPLAUD

clarify: . . . . . CLEAR, CLEAN, PURIFY, DEFINE, EXPLAIN, ELUCIDATE, ILLUMINATE

clarity: . . . . CLEARNESS, LUCIDITY, BRIGHTNESS, BRILLIANCE

clash: . . BANG, SLAM, BRAWL, CRASH, FIGHT, IMPACT, STRIFE, COLLIDE, CONFLICT, DISAGREE, ARGUMENT

clasp: . . . . HUG, HASP, HOOK, GRAB, HOLD, GRASP, SEIZE, BROOCH, FASTEN, BUCKLE, ENFOLD, CINCH, ENBRACE, FASTNER, BARRETTE

class: . . . . . ILK, CLAN, KIND, RACE, RANK, SORT, KIND, CASTE, GRADE, BREED, GROUP, GENUS, ORDER, SPECIES, VARIETY, CATEGORY

classify: . . RANK, RATE, SIZE, LIST, SORT, GRADE, GROUP, ASSORT, ARRANGE, CATEGORIZE, CATALOG(UE)

classy: . . . . . NIFTY, SMART, ELEGANT, STYLISH

clatter: . . . . DIN, NOISE, HUBBUB, RATTLE, COMMOTION

clavicle: . . . . COLLARBONE

claw: . . . . DIG, HAND, HOOK, NAIL, TEAR, TALON, CHELA, PINCER, SCRATCH, SCRAPE, UNGULA, SCRATCH, LACERATE

clay: . . . . . BOLE, TILE, LOAM,
LUTE, MARL, ADOBE, LOESS,
ARGIL, BRICK, OCHRE,
LATERITE, SAGGER, KAOLIN(E)

clean: . . . . MOP, DUST, SWAB,
WASH, PURE, CLEAR, EMPTY,
SCOUR, SCRUB, PURIFY,
CHASTE, FURBISH, SINLESS,
UNSOILED, SPOTLESS,
ABSTERGE, UNDEFILED,
IMMACULATE

clear: . . . . . . NET, RID, FREE,
GAIN, OPEN, PURE, CLEAN,
LUCID, PRUNE, VIVID, BRIGHT,
EXEMPT, LIMPID, LUCENT,
PATENT, ACQUIT, SETTLE,
ABSOLVE, CLARIFY, CRYSTAL,
EVIDENT, GRAPHIC, OBVIOUS,
APPARENT, DISTINCT, EXPLICIT,
CLOUDLESS, DISENGAGE,
EXONERATE, VINDICATE,
TRANSPARENT

cleat: . . BITT, BLOCK, CHOCK,
KEVEL, BATTEN, PITON,
WEDGE, BOLLARD

cleavage: . . . . . . GULF, RIFT,
CLEFT, DIVISION, FISSION,
SEPARATION

cleave: . . . . CUT, RIP, CHOP,
HOLD, JOIN, PART, REND, RIVE,
SLIT, SPLIT, DIVIDE, SEVER,
CARVE, STICK, CLING, SUNDER,
ADHERE, SEPARATE

clemency: . . . . PITY, GRACE,
MERCY, QUARTER, KINDNESS,
LENIENCY, COMPASSION

clement: . . . . . . MILD, SOFT,
WARM, GENTLE, LENIENT,
MERCIFUL, COMPASSIONATE

Cleopatra's domain: . . . .
EGYPT, NILE

killer: . . . . ASP

lover: . . ANTONY, (JULIUS)
CAESAR

needle: . . . . . . OBELISK

clergyman: . . . . ABBE, DEAN,
CANON, PADRE, PRIOR, RABBI,
VICAR, PRIEST, BISHOP,
CURATE, DEACON, CURATE,
CLERIC, PARSON, PASTOR,
RECTOR, DIVINE, PRELATE,
CARDINAL, CHAPLIN, MINISTER,
PREACHER, REVEREND,
ECCLESIASTIC

clerk: . . . . . . MONK, AGENT,
PRIEST, SCRIBE, TELLER,
SCHOLAR, EMPLOYEE,
SALESMAN, ASSISTANT,
ACCOUNTANT, SCRIVENER,
OFFICE WORKER

clever: . . . . APT, SLY, ABLE,
DEFT, KEEN, AGILE, ADEPT,
ADROIT, HANDY, TALENTED,
BRIGHT, QUICK, SLICK, EXPERT,
CUNNING, SMART, HABILE,
SHREWD, CUNNING, DEXTROUS,
SKILLFUL, INGENIOUS

cliche: . . . TRUISM, BROMIDE,
BANALITY, PLATITUDE

client: . . . . PATRON, PATIENT,
DEPENDENT, CUSTOMER,
RETAINER

cliff: . . . . CRAG, HILL, ROCK,
BLUFF, SCARP, HEIGHT,
PALISADE, PRECIPICE,
ESCARPMENT

climate: . . . . MOOD, REGION,
TEMPER, ATTITUDE, WEATHER,
CONDITION

climax: . . . . CAP, TOP, ACME,
APEX, PEAK, SCALE, APOGEE,
FINISH, SUMMIT, ZENITH,
CULMINATION

climb: . . . RAMP, RISE, SCALE,
ASCEND, MOUNT, ASCENT,
CLAMBER

clinch: . . . . FIX, HUG, BIND,
SEAL, NAIL, GRIP, CLAMP,
GRASP, RIVET, CLUTCH, FASTEN,
SECURE, GRAPPLE, EMBRACE,
CONCLUDE

cling: . . . HANG, HOLD, RELY,
STICK, DEPEND, FASTEN,
ADHERE, COHERE, CHERISH,
EMBRACE, PERSEVERE

clink: . . . . BEAT, BRIG, COIN,
JAIL, RING, PRISON, STRIKE,
TINKLE

clinker: . . . . . SLAG, WASTE

clip: . . . BOB, CUT, LOP, MOW, NIP, CHIP, CROP, DOCK, PARE, SNIP, TRIM, CLASP, PRUNE, SHEAR, HOLDER, CURTAIL, SHORTEN, SWINDLE, DIMINISH, ABBREVIATE

clique: . . . . MOB, SET, BLOC, CLAN, CLUB, GANG, RING, GROUP, CIRCLE, COTERIE, FACTION

cloak: . . . . ABA, CAPA, CAPE, HIDE, MASK, PALL, ROBE, VEIL, WRAP, COVER, GUISE, MANTA, DISGUISE, GARMENT, CAPOTE, CONCEAL, MANTUA, MANTLE, SCREEN, SHROUD, CHLAMYS, PRETEXT, MANTILLA

clobber: . . HIT, BEAT, MAUL, POUND, SMEAR, STRIKE, DEFEAT

cloche: . . . . JAR, HAT, COVER

clod: . . . . . SOD, CLOT, TURF, DOLT, LUMP, EARTH, DIVOT, YOKEL, STUPID

clodhopper: . . . BOOR, CLOD, SHOE, RUSTIC, PLOWMAN

clog: . . . . . GUM, JAM, CLAM, CLOY, CURB, LOAD, SHOE, STOP, CHOKE, SABOT, IMPEDE, SANDAL, GALOSH, BLOCK, DANCE, HAMPER, ENCUMBER, OBSTRUCT

cloister: . . . . . . HALL, STOA, ABBEY, ARCADE, FRIARY, PRIORY, CONVENT, NUNNERY, MONASTERY, SANCTUARY

close: . . BY, CAP, END, HIDE, NEAR, LOCK, NIGH, SEAL, SHUT, STOP, BLOCK, CEASE, DENSE, MUGGY, THICK, TIGHT, CLINCH, FINISH, COMPACT, FINALE, CONCLUDE, NARROW, OCCLUDE, NEARBY, INTIMATE, SULTRY, STINGY, ADJORN, SIMILAR, ADJACENT, CONCLUDE, IMMINENT, FAMILIAR, TERMINATE, PARSIMONIOUS

closeness: . . . . SECRECY, INTIMACY, PARSIMONY, PROXIMITY, STINGINESS, STRICTNESS, CONCISENESS, OPPRESSIVENESS

closet: . . . . ROOM, SAFE, AMBRY, LOCKER, PANTRY, TOILET, CUDDY, PRIVY, CABINET, WARDROBE, CUPBOARD

closure: . . . END, GAG, LIMIT, CLOTURE, STOPPAGE, ENCLOSURE, CONCLUSION

clot: . . . . . . GEL, CLOD, JELL, LUMP, MASS, GRUME, EMBOLUS, THICKEN, SOLIDIFY, COAGULATE

cloth: . . RAG, TWEED, TWILL, CANVAS, CALICO, CHINTZ, SATIN, FABRIC, SERGE, DENIM, LINEN, BURLAP, TAFFETA, MUSLIN, NAPKIN, DRAPERY, GINGHAM, TEXTILE, GARMENT, RAIMENT, RATTEEN, WORSTED, MATERIAL, CORDUROY

material: . . . BARK, WOOL, SILK, HAIR, SKIN, FLAX, HEMP, FIBER, COTTON, ACETATE, SYNTHETIC

clothe: . . . . . DON, RIG, TOG, DECK, GARB, GOWN, ROBE, ADORN, ARRAY, DRESS, FROCK, ATTIRE, INVEST, SWATHE, ACCOUTER

clothes: . . DUDS, TOGS, GARB, GEAR, SUIT, WEAR, DRESS, HABIT, ATTIRE, APPAREL, COUSTUME, RAIMENT, TOGGERY, VESTURE, CLOTHING, HABILIMENTS

cloud: . . . . FOG, BLUR, DUST, HAZE, MIST, GLOOM, STAIN, SWARM, TAINT, VAPOR, CIRRUS, DARKEN, NEBULA, NIMBUS, SCREEN, SHADOW, STIGMA, CONFUSE, CUMULUS, STRATUS, OBSCURE, OVERCAST

clough: . . . . . CLEFT, GORGE, RAVINE, VALLEY

clout: . . . . . BAT, HIT, BEAT, CLUB, CUFF, SLAP, SLUG, SWAT, SMITE, STRIKE, THRASH, INFLUENCE

cloven: . . . . . . CLEFT, SPLIT, DIVIDED, BISULCATE

clown: . . . OAF, BOOR, LOUT, FOOL, MIME, ZANY, APER, JESTER, COMIC, CUTUP, BUFFOON, HARLEQUIN, PUNCHINELLO

cloy: . . . . CLOG, GLUT, PALL, SATE, SURFEIT, SATIATE, SATISFY

club: . . . . . BAT, HIT, BEAT, CANE, MAUL, TEAM, MACE, BILLY, CLOUT, LODGE, STAFF, STICK, CUDGEL, CLIQUE, WEAPON, BLUDGEON, SORORITY, TRUNCHEON, FRATERNITY

clubfoot: . . . . TALIPES, DEFORMITY

clue: . . KEY, TIP, IDEA, CLEW, HINT, POINTER, INDICATION

clump: . . BUSH, HEAP, LUMP, TUFT, MASS, BUNCH, PATCH, CLUSTER, THICKET

clumsy: . . . . . BULKY, LUMPY, INAPT, INEPT, GAWKY, INELEGANT, GAUCHE, UNGAINLY, AWKWARD, BOORISH, UNWIELDY, MALADROIT

cluster: . . BUSH, TUFT, KNOT, BUNCH, CLUMP, GROUP, AGGREGATION, GLOMERATION

clutch: . . GRAB, GRIP, HOLD, GRASP, SEIZE, SNATCH

clutter: . . . . . MESS, JUMBLE, LITTER, BUSTLE, DISORDER, CONFUSION

coach: . . . . BUS, CAR, HELP, TEACH, TRAIN, TUTOR, ADVISE, DIRECT, PREPARE, TRAINER, CARRIAGE

coagulate: . . GEL, SET, CAKE, CLOD, CLOT, CURD, JELL, CURDLE, CONGEAL, THICKEN, SOLIDIFY

coal: . . . FUEL, EMBER, STOKE, CARBON, LIGNITE, ANTHRACITE, BITUMINOUS

size: . . . . . COB, NUT, PEA, EGG, LUMP, STOVE, WALLSEND, CHESTNUT

coal mine: . . . . PIT, COLLIERY

bed: . . . . . SEAM, WINNING

gas: . . . . METHANE, FIREDAMP

coal miner: . . . . . PITMAN, COLLIER

coal miner's disease: . . . . . ANTHRACOSIS

coalesce: . . . MIX, FUSE, JOIN, MERGE, UNITE, BLEND, COMBINE, AMALGAMATE

coalescence: . . . . . MERGER, UNION, FUSION, COMBINATION

coalition: . . . TRUST, UNION, LEAGUE, FUSION, MERGER, ENTENTE, ALLIANCE, CONFEDERATION

coarse: . . . LOW, RAW, HARD, LEWD, RANK, RUDE, CRASS, GROSS, CRUDE, HARSH, THICK, RIBALD, ROUGH, COMMON, VULGAR, OBSCENE, RAUCOUS, INDECENT, UNREFINED, INDELICATE

coast: . . BANK, LAND, BEACH, SLIDE, SHORE, SEASIDE, BORDER, RIVAGE, SEASHORE

coastal: . . LITTORAL, RIPARIAN

coat: . . . . BARK, DAUB, GILD, GILT, HUSK, RIND, CLOAK, COVER, CRUST, GLAZE, HABIT, LAYER, PAINT, PLATE, ENAMEL, JACKET, MANTLE, VENEER, GARMENT, PLASTER, COVERING, MEMBRANE

animal: . . FUR, SKIN, HAIR, HIDE, WOOL, PELAGE

coating: . . . . . FILM, GLAZE, PATINA, VENEER, COVERING

coax: .... BEG, DUPE, LURE, URGE, TEASE, ENTICE, CAJOLE, IMPLORE, WHEEDLE, PERSUADE

cobble: .. DARN, MAKE, PAVE, MEND, STONE, PATCH, REPAIR

cobweb: .. NET, TRAP, SNARE, FLIMSY, GOSSAMER

cocaine: .. SNOW, NARCOTIC, ALKALOID, ANESTHETIC

cock: .... TAP, FOWL, HEAP, PILE, STACK, STRUT, VALVE, FAUCET, LEADER, CHICKEN, ROOSTER, CHANTICLEER

cockade: ..... KNOT, BADGE, ROSETTE

cockatoo: .. PARROT, ARARA, MACAW

cockatrice: ..... SERPENT, BASILISK

cockeyed: ... AWRY, DRUNK, ABSURD, SCREWY, CROOKED

cockle: ...... BOAT, WEED, BULGE, STOVE, DARNEL, PUCKER, MOLLUSK, WRINKLE, SHELLFISH

cockpit: .... RING, ARENA, CABIN

cocktail: ... DRINK, APERTIF, DAIQUIRI, MARTINI, APPETIZER, MANHATTAN

cocky: ...... VAIN, SAUCY, ARROGANT, CONCEITED

cod: ...... BAG, POD, AXLE, CUSK, FISH, HOAX, HUSK, BELLY, POUCH, SCROD, BURBOT, BOCACCIO, PILLOW, CUSHION, GLASHAN, WHITING

coda: .... PART, FINALE, CONCLUSION

coddle: ... PET, BABY, COOK, HUMOR, SPOIL, FONDLE, PAMPER, PARBOIL, SPOONFEED

code: .. LAW, CANON, CODEX, CIPHER, SECRET, SIGNAL, PRECEPT

codicil: .... RIDER, APPENDIX

coerce: ..... MAKE, BULLY, DRIVE, COMPEL, FORCE, ENFORCE, BLACKMAIL, CONSTRAIN, INTIMIDATE

coercion: .... FORCE, DURESS, COMPULSION

coffer: .... ARK, BOX, CHEST, HUTCH, TRUNK, CASKET, STRONGBOX

coffin: . BIER, CASE, BASKET, CASKET, LITTER, SARCOPHAGUS

cog: .... CAM, GEAR, PAWL, CATCH, CHEAT, TOOTH, WHEEL, WEDGE, DECEIVE, (COCK)BOAT, SWINDLE

cogent: ..... VALID, POTENT, TELLING, POWERFUL, CONVINCING, CONCLUSIVE, COMPELLING

cogitate: ...... MULL, PLAN, THINK, CONSIDER, PONDER, MEDITATE, CEREBRATE

cognate: ..... AKIN, ALIKE, ALLIED, RELATED, SIMILAR

cognizance: .. HEED, EMBLEM, NOTICE, KNOWLEDGE, RECOGNITION, PERCEPTION

cognomen: .... NAME, SURNAME, NICKNAME, APPELATION

coheir: .... PARCENER

cohere: ...... GLUE, AGREE, CLING, STICK, UNITE, ADHERE, CONNECT

coherence: .... UNION, COHESION, CONNECTION, CONTINUITY, CONSISTENCY

coiffure: .... HAIRDO, HEADDRESS

coil: .... CLEW, WIND, CURL, LOOP, ROLL, HELIX, TWIST, WHORL, SPIRAL, RINGLET, ENCIRCLE, CONVOLVE

coin: .... CASH, MAKE, MINT, INVENT, DEVISE, MONEY, METAL, CREATE, SPECIE, CURRENCY

collector: .. NUMISMATIST

coincide: ...... JIBE, AGREE, CONCUR, HARMONIZE, CORRESPOND

coincident: . . . . . TOGETHER, CONSONANT, CONCURRENT, CONTEMPORARY

colander: . . . . . PAN, SIEVE, STRAINER

cold: . . . . . . ICY, FLU, DEAD, DULL, ALGID, BLEAK, GELID, RHEUM, VIRUS, ARCTIC, CHILLY, FRIGID, FROSTY, WINTRY, CATARRH, DISTANT, GLACIAL, UNHEATED, APATHETIC, INSENSIBLE, UNEMOTIONAL, UNRESPONSIVE

blooded: . . . . . . CALLOUS, PITILESS, UNFEELING

feet: . . . . . FEAR, DOUBT, COWARDICE, APPREHENSION

shoulder: . SNUB, REBUFF, IGNORE, BRUSH-OFF

coliseum: . . HALL, STADIUM, THEATER, AMPHITHEATER

collaborate: . . . . AID, ASSIST, COOPERATE

collapse: . . . . . . CAVE, FALL, FOLD, CRASH, SLUMP, CRUMPLE, DEBACLE, DEFLATE, FAILURE, CONTRACT, DOWNFALL, BREAKDOWN, PROSTRATION

collar: . . . NAB, BAND, GRAB, RING, RUFF, CHAIN, FICHU, RUCHE, SEIZE, GORGET, FLANGE, RABATO, TORQUE, CAPTURE, CHOKER, CHIGNON, CIRCLET, NECKBAND, NECKLACE

collarbone: . . . . . . CLAVICLE

collate: . . . VERIFY, COMPILE, COMPARE

collateral: . . . . INDIRECT, SECURITY, PARALLEL, ANCILLARY, CONCOMITANT

collation: . . . . . TEA, MEAL, SERMON, TREATISE, COLLECTION, CONSULTATION

colleague: . . . . . AIDE, ALLY, DEPUTY, ADJUNCT, PARTNER, ASSISTANT, ASSOCIATE, CONFRERE

collect: . . . CALL, HEAP, PILE, REAP, SAVE, AMASS, GLEAN, HOARD, RAISE, ACCRUE, CONFER, GARNER, GATHER, COMPILE, IMPOUND, ASSEMBLE, AGGREGATE, ACCUMULATE, CONGREGATE

collected: . . . . COOL, CALM, SOBER, SERENE, AMASSED, COMPOSED, CLUSTERED, AGGLOMERATE

collection: . . . . BEVY, BATCH, GROUP, BUNCH, STORE, BUNDLE, ASSEMBLY, REPERTORY, ANTHOLOGY, ASSORTMENT

colleen: . . . . . . GIRL, LASS, DANSEL, MAIDEN

college: . . SCHOOL, ACADEMY, SEMINARY, UNIVERSITY, INSTITUTION, ORGANIZATION

collide: . . . . HIT, RAM, BUMP, CLASH, CRASH, HURTLE, STRIKE

collier: . . SHIP, (COAL)MINER, PITMAN, TENDER

collision: . . . . CLASH, CRASH, IMPACT, SHOCK, SMASHUP, ENCOUNTER, PERCUSSION

colloquial: . . . . . . FAMILIAR, INFORMAL, CONVERSATIONAL

colloquialism: . . . . . . IDIOM, SLANG, PATOIS

colloquy: . . . . TALK, PARLEY, CONVERSATION, CONFERENCE

collude: . . . . PLOT, SCHEME, CONNIVE, CONSPIRE

collusion: . . . . DECEIT, CAHOOTS, SECRECY, AGREEMENT, CONNIVANCE

colonist: . SETTLER, PLANTER, PIONEER, EMIGRANT

colony: . . . . SWARM, COMMUNITY, DEPENDENCY, SETTLEMENT

colophony: . . . . RESIN, ROSIN

color: . . . . . DYE, HUE, FLAG, TINT, TONE, BLUSH, FLUSH, PAINT, SHADE, STAIN, TINGE, BANNER, ENSIGN, DISTORT,

PIGMENT, TINCTURE, COMPLEXION

animal: . . . . ROAN, FAWN, PINTO, TAWNY, DAPPLE, TAUPE, BRINDLE

blindness: . . . . DALTONISM

primary: . . . . . RED, BLUE, BLACK, GREEN, WHITE, YELLOW

secondary: . . . . . . GREEN, ORANGE, PURPLE

colored: . . . . BIASED, DISTORTED, PRISMATIC, MISREPRESENTED

colorful: . . . . . GAY, BRIGHT, VIVID, BRILLIANT

colorless: . . . . . WAN, DRAB, DULL, PALE, BLANK, PLAIN, PALLID, NEUTRAL, BLANCHED, TRANSPARENT, UNINTERESTING

colossal: . . BIG, HUGE, VAST, LARGE, IMMENSE, GIGANTIC, ENORMOUS

colossus: . . . . . GIANT, TITAN, STATUE, MONSTER

Columbus:
birthplace: . . . . . . GENOA
burial place: . . . . SEVILLE
patrons: . . . . . ISABELLA, FERDINAND
ship: . . . . . NINA, PINTA, SANTA MARIA
starting point: . . . . PALOS

column: . . . ROW, FILE, LINE, POST, SHAFT, STELE, PILLAR, PILASTER
base: . . . . PLINTH, STYLOBATE
figure, female: . . . . CARYATID
figure, male: . . . TELAMON, ATLANTES
shaft: . . . . SCAPE
support: . . . . BASE, PEDESTAL, PLINTH
top: . . . . CAPITAL
type: . . . . . DORIC, IONIC, CORINTHIAN

coma: . . . . . . SLEEP, STUPOR, TORPOR, TRANCE, CATALEPSY, COMATOSE, INSENSIBILITY

comb: . . CARD, RAKE, BRUSH, CLEAN, CREST, CURRY, TEASE, SMOOTH, STRAIGHTEN, DISENTANGLE, CARUNCLE

combat: . . WAR, BOUT, COPE, DUEL, TILT, FRAY, CLASH, FIGHT, JOUST, ACTION, BATTLE, OPPOSE, RESIST, STRIFE, CONTEND, COUNTER, SCUFFLE, CONFLICT, STRUGGLE, ENCOUNTER, CONTENTION

combative: . . . . . MILITANT, PUGNACIOUS, BELLIGERANT, QUARRELSOME

combination: . . . KEY, BLOC, GANG, POOL, RING, CABAL, JUNTO, TRUST, UNION, ALLOY, BLEND, CARTEL, CLIQUE, MERGER, FACTION, AMALGAM, MIXTURE, ALLIANCE, COALITION, ASSOCIATION, CONFEDERACY, SYNDICATE

combine: . . . ADD, MIX, WED, BLOC, JOIN, BLEND, MERGE, UNITE, ABSORB, MINGLE, SPLICE, COALESCE, COOPERATE, AMALGAMATE, CONSOILDATE

combustible: . . . . FIERY, EXCITABLE, IRASCIBLE, IMFLAMMABLE

combustion: . . . FIRE, HEAT, BURNING, AGITATION, CONSUMING, CREMATION, INFLAMMATION, CONFLAGRATION

come: . . ARISE, ISSUE, OCCUR, REACH, ARRIVE, APPEAR, RESULT, EMERGE, HAPPEN, DEVELOP, EMANATE, APPROACH
across: . . FIND, GIVE, PAY UP, MEET, CONTRIBUTE
back: . . . . RECUR, RETURN
before: . . . . PRECEDE, ANTECEDE
between: . . . . DIVIDE, INTERVENE, ALIENATE

by: . . GET, GAIN, ACQUIRE, OBTAIN

forth: . . APPEAR, EMERGE, APPROACH

into view: . . . . LOOM, APPEAR, EMERGE

to terms: . . . . AGREE, SETTLE, APPROVE, CONSENT, ACQUIESCE

together: . . . . JOIN, MEET, COLLIDE, GATHER, CONVENE, ASSEMBLE, CONVERGE

up: . . . . . . ARISE, OCCUR, APPEAR

comeback: . RALLY, RETORT, ANSWER, RETURN, REBOUND, RIPOSTE, REPARTEE, REJOINDER

comely: . . . . . . FAIR, LOVELY PRETTY, HANDSOME, DECOROUS, PLEASING, BEAUTIFUL, PERSONABLE

comfort: . . . . . . EASE, REST, CHEER, RELIEF, CONSOLE, SOOTHE, SUCCOR, SOLACE, ASSUAGE, RELIEVE, SUSTAIN, REASSURE, ENCOURAGE

comic: . . . . . DROLL, FUNNY, AMUSING, COMEDIAN, HUMOROUS, LAUGHABLE

coming: . . . . . . DUE, NEXT, FUTURE, ADVENT, APPROACH, ARRIVAL, IMPENDING

command: . . BID, CALL, FIAT, RULE, EDICT, FORCE, ORDER, ADJURE, BEHEST, ENJOIN, DICTATE, CHARGE, CONTROL, DIRECT, GOVERN, MANDATE, REQUIRE, AUTHORITY, ORDINANCE

commander: . . HEAD, CHIEF, LEADER, MASTER, CAPTAIN, GENERAL, OFFICER, PRESIDENT

commanding: . . . IMPOSING, IMPERIOUS, MASTERFUL, IMPRESSIVE, DOMINATING, AUTHORITATIVE

commemoration: . . . AWARD, MEDAL, MEMORIAL, CELEBRATION

commence: . . . OPEN, ARISE, BEGIN, START, FOUND INCEPT, INITIATE, INSTITUTE, ORIGINATE

commend: . . . . . CITE, LAUD, BOOST, EXTOL, BESTOW, PRAISE, APPLAUD, APPROVE, ENTRUST, RECOMMEND, COMPLIMENT

commensurate: . . . . . EVEN, EQUAL, ADEQUATE, APPROPRIATE, PROPORTIONATE

comment: . . . . . NOTE, TALK, NOTATE, REMARK, DISCUSS, EXPLAIN, EXPOUND, CRITICISE, ANNOTATION, COMMENTARY

commerce: . TRADE, BARTER, TRAFFIC, BUSINESS, EXCHANGE, INTERCHANGE

commercial: . . MERCANTILE, ADVERTISEMENT

commingle: . . . . . MIX, JOIN, BLEND, MERGE, UNITE, COMBINE, AMALGAMATE

comminute: . . . MILL, GRIND, CRUSH, PULVERIZE

commiseration: . . . . . . PITY, EMPATHY, COMPASSION, CONDOLENCE

commission: . . TASK, BOARD, TRUST, CHARGE, DEPUTE, ORDAIN, PERMIT, COMMAND, ENPOWER, MANDATE, WARRENT, DELEGATE, ALLOWANCE, AUTHORITY, AUTHORIZE, BROKERAGE, CONSTITUTE, COMPENSATION, PERPETRATION

commit: . . . . . BIND, ALLOT, ASSIGN, REMAND, COMMAND, CONFIDE, CONSIGN, ENGAGE, ENTRUST, DEPOSIT, DELEGATE, IMPRISON, RELEGATE, MEMORIZE, PERPETRATE

commode: . . . CHEST, TOILET, BUREAU, CHIFFONIER,

WASHSTAND, CUPBOARD, CHIFFONIER

commodious: ...... AMPLE, ROOMY, SPACIOUS, CAPACIOUS, BENEFICIAL

commodity: .... WARE, ARTICLE, GOODS, STAPLE

common: ..... LOW, BASE, BANAL, CHEAP, JOINT, USUAL, COARSE, MUTUAL, PUBLIC, VULGAR, AVERAGE, GENERAL, NATURAL, PLEBIAN, POPULAR, REGULAR, FAMILIAR, HABITUAL, ORDINARY, BOURGEOIS, CUSTOMARY, PREVALENT

commonplace: ...... DULL, BANAL, DAILY, PLAIN, STALE, TRITE, USUAL, ORDINARY, PROSAIC, HUMDRUM, UNIMPORTANT

commotion: ..... ADO, DIN, FRAY, FUSS, RIOT, STIR, TO-DO, ALARM, BUSTLE, TURMOIL, HUBBUB, POTHER, UPROAR, FLURRY, BROUHAHA, DISTURBANCE, MUSS

commune: ..... AREA, TALK, ARGUE, ADVISE, CONFER, DEBATE, PARLEY, REVEAL, CONSULT, DISCUSS, DIVULGE, CONVERSE, COMMUNICATE

communicate: ...... TELL, CONVEY, IMPART, INFORM, REVEAL, SIGNAL, DECLARE, DIVULGE, CONVERSE, TRANSMIT

communique: ..... REPORT, MESSAGE, BULLETIN, STATEMENT, ANNOUNCEMENT

community: ... BODY, BURG, CITY, TOWN, STATE, COLONY, HAMLET, NATION, POLITY, PUBLIC, SOCIETY, VILLAGE, DISTRICT, PROVINCE, TOWNSHIP, NEIGHBORHOOD, SIMILARITY

commute: .. ALTER, CHANGE, TRAVEL, CONVERT, EXCHANGE, SUBSTITUTE

compact: ...... BOND, FIRM, HARD, PACT, PLOT, SNUG, TRIM, BRIEF, TERSE, DENSE, SOLID, THICK, TREATY, SERRIED, CONCISE, ALLIANCE, CONDENSE, SUCCINCT, AGREEMENT

companion: .... PAL, CHUM, FERE, MATE, TWIN, WIFE, BUDDY, CRONY, ESCORT, FRIEND, SPOUSE, COMRADE, CONSORT, HUSBAND, PARTNER, COMPADRE, ACCOMPANY, ASSOCIATE, ATTENDANT, COMPEER

company: .. MOB, SET, BAND, BODY, CREW, FERE, FIRM, GANG, HOST, TEAM, CROWD, GROUP, GUEST, HORDE, PARTY, SQUAD, TROOP, ACTORS, CIRCLE, CLIQUE, TROUPE, CONSORT, SOCIETY, VISITOR, ASSEMBLY, ASSOCIATION, CORPORATION

compare: .... EVEN, APPLY, LIKEN, MATCH, CONFER, RELATE, COLLATE, CONTRAST

compartment: .... BAY, BIN, CELL, STALL, BOOTH, ALCOVE, BUNKER, CHAMBER, LOCKER, CAPSULE, SECTION, DIVISION, PIGEONHOLE

compass: .. GAIN, AREA, SIZE, FIELD, GAMUT, RANGE, REACH, SCOPE, ATTAIN, BOUNDS, CIRCLE, EXTENT, CONFINE, ENCLOSE, PELORUS, BOUNDRY, SURROUND, ACCOMPLISH

beam: .... TRAMMEL
case: .... BINNACLE
dial: .... CARD
housing: .... BINNACLE
sight: .... VANE

compassion: .. PITY, MERCY, GRACE, CLEMENCY, SYMPATHY

compatible: ..... SUITABLE, ACCORDANT, AGREEABLE, CONGRUOUS, HARMONIOUS

compel: . . . . . MAKE, MOVE, CAUSE, DRIVE, FORCE, IMPEL, COERCE, EXTORT, INCITE, OBLIGE, ACTUATE, COMMAND, CONSTRAIN, INSTIGATE, INTIMIDATE

compendium: . . LIST, BRIEF, DIGEST, PRECIS, OUTLINE, SUMMARY, SYLLABUS, ABSTRACT, SYNOPSIS, COMPILATION

compensation: . . . . FEE, PAY, BONUS, WAGES, AMENDS, OFFSET, REWARD, SALARY, DAMAGES, PAYMENT, REDRESS, STIPEND, EMOLUMENT, INDEMNITY, RECOMPENSE, RESTITUTION, REMUNERATION

competent: . . . . . . APT, ABLE, SANE, ADEPT, WORTHY, CAPABLE, SKILLED, ADEQUATE, EFFECTIVE, QUALIFIED

competitor: . . . . FOE, ENEMY, RIVAL, OPPONENT, ADVERSARY, COMBATANT, ANTAGONIST, CONTESTANT, CONTENDER

complain: . . . . . BEEF, CARP, CRAB, FRET, FUSS, KICK, MOAN, WAIL, CROAK, GRIPE, WHINE, ACCUSE, BEWAIL, CHARGE, GRIEVE, GROUSE, MURMER, DEPLORE, GRUMBLE, PROTEST, BELLYACHE

complaint: . . KICK, LAMENT, MALADY, CHARGE, PROTEST, SQUAWK, AILMENT, ILLNESS, DISORDER, DISEASE, ACCUSATION, GRIEVANCE

complaisant: . . . EASY, KIND, POLITE, AMIABLE, GRACIOUS, OBLIGING

complete: . . ALL, END, DEAD, FULL, EVERY, ENTIRE, WHOLE, TOTAL, INTACT, UTTER, OUTRIGHT, MATURE, FINISH, ACHIEVE, PERFECT, ABSOLUTE, CONCLUDE, TERMINATE, ACCOMPLISH

complex: . . . . . HARD, MIXED, KNOTTY, NETWORK, TANGLED, TWISTED, MANIFOLD, INTRICATE, SYNDROME, ELABORATE, INVOLVED, DIFFICULT, COMPLICATED, NETWORK

complexion: . . LOOK, COLOR, ASPECT, APPEARANCE, TEMPERAMENT

compliant: . . . . SUBMISSIVE, DUCTILE, WILLING, OBEDIENT, TRACTABLE

complicated: . . . seecomplex

compliment: . . LAUD, EXTOL, EULOGY, PRAISE, TOAST, ADULATE, APPLAUD, COMMEND, FLATTER, TRIBUTE, COMMENDATION, CONGRATULATE

comply: . . . . . OBEY, ABIDE, AGREE, YIELD, ACCEDE, ASSENT, SUBMIT, CONFORM, ACQUIESCE

component: . . . . PART, ITEM, UNIT, MEMBER, ELEMENT, INGREDIENT CONSTITUENT

comport: . . . . . ACT, BEHAVE

compose: . . . . . CALM, LULL, ALLAY, WRITE, CREATE, SOOTHE, FRAME, ADJUST, ARRANGE, CONSTRUCT, CONSTITUTE

composed: . . . . COOL, CALM, WROTE, SERENE, TRANQUIL

composition: . . WORK, OPUS, DRAMA, PIECE, THEME, THESIS, ARTICLE, ESSAY, WRITING, FORMATION, MANUSCRIPT

composure: . . . QUIET, POISE, REPOSE, BALANCE, CALMNESS, SERENITY, EQUANIMITY, SANG-FROID, TRANQUILITY

compound: . . . . . MIX, JOIN, ALLOY, BLEND, UNITE, MEDLEY, COMBINE, CONCOCT, AMALGAM, COMPOSITE, ENCLOSURE

comprehend: . . . SEE, KNOW, GRASP, SEIZE, SENSE, ATTAIN, DIGEST, FATHOM, DISCERN, EMBRACE, REALIZE, INCLUDE, CONCEIVE, PERCEIVE, UNDERSTAND

comprehension: . . . . GRASP, NOESIS, KNOWING, INCLUSION, CONCEPTION, CONNOTATION

comprehensive: . . . . BROAD, CONCISE, ENCYCLIC, SPACIOUS, EXTENSIVE, COMPENDIOUS

compress: . . . . . . PAD, BALE, BIND, CRAMP, CRUSH, PRESS, SHRINK, COMPACT, FLATTEN, SQUEEZE, CONDENSE, CONTRACT, CONSOLIDATE

comprise: . . . . INCLUDE, CONTAIN

compulsion: . . . NEED, URGE, FORCE, DURESS, CONSTRAINT, COACTION, IMPULSE, COERCION

compulsory: . . . . COERCIVE, FORCIBLE, OBLIGATORY, MANDATORY

compunction: . . . . . QUALM, REGRET, REMORSE, SCRUPLE, MISGIVING, PENITENCE

computation: . . CALCULATION

compute: . . . COUNT, TALLY, RECKON, FIGURE, ESTIMATE, CALCULATE, ENUMERATE

computer: . . . . IBM, McINTOSH, ANALOG, DIGITAL, UNIVAC

comrade: . . . . seechum

con: . . . . . ANTI, LEAD, READ, CHEAT, GUIDE, STEER, STUDY, AGAINST, PERUSE, DIRECT, DECEIVE, EXAMINE, SWINDLE, UNDERSTAND

conceal: . BURY, HIDE, MASK, VEIL, CACHE, CLOAK, COVER, SCREEN, SHROUD, SECRETE, DISGUISE, CAMOUFLAGE

concede: . . . . . CEDE, ADMIT, AGREE, EGO, PRIDE, EGOISM, YIELD, GRANT, WAIVE, ASSENT, SURRENDER

conceit: . . . . . . EGO, PRIDE, EGOISM, VANITY, TYMPANY, ARROGANCE

conceited: . . . . VAIN, PROUD, ARROGANT, SNOBBISH, EGOTISTICAL

conceive: . . . . PLAN, BEGIN, FANCY, THINK, IDEATE, DEVISE, IMAGINE, CONTRIVE

concentrate: . . . . FIX, MASS, PILE, FOCUS, COLLECT, COMPACT, CONDENSE, CONSOLIDATE

concept: . . . . . IDEA, NOTION, OPINION, THOUGHT

concern: . . . . . . CARE, FIRM, GRIEF, WORRY, AFFAIR, EMPLOY, REGARD, ANXIETY, COMPANY, INVOLVE, TROUBLE, BUSINESS, SOLICITUDE

concerning: . . . . RE, ABOUT, ANENT, REGARDING

concession: . . FAVOR, GRANT, RIGHT, ADMISSION, PRIVILEGE, FRANCHISE, COMPROMISE

concierge: . . . . PORTER, JANITOR, DOORKEEPER, CARETAKER

conciliate: . . . . PACIFY, APPEASE, SOOTHE, MOLLIFY, PLACATE, SATISFY

concise: . . . . . BRIEF, TERSE, PITHY, COMPACT, SUCCINCT, LACONIC

conclude: . . . . . END, CLOSE, JUDGE, DEDUCE, INFER, FINISH, COMPLETE, TERMINATE

conclusion: . . . . . END, FINIS, FINALE, FINISH, OUTCOME, RESULT, DECISION, JUDGMENT, TERMINATION

concoct: . . . . . . MIX, COOK, DEVISE, PLAN, BREW, HATCH, PREPARE, COMPOUND

concomitant: . . . . ASSOCIATE, ATTENDANT, COINCIDENT, CONCURRENT

concord: . . . . ONENESS, HARMONY, GRAPE, UNISON, TREATY

concrete: . . . . . FIRM, REAL, BETON, SOLID, ACTUAL, SPECIFIC, TANGIBLE

concur: . . . . AGREE, ACCEDE, APPROVE, ASSENT, CONSENT, COINCIDE

condemn: . . . . . BAN, DOOM, BLAME, DECRY, CENSURE, CONVICT, DENOUNCE, SENTENCE

condense: . . . . CUT, DIGEST, REDUCE, SHRINK, ABRIDGE, COMPACT, SHORTEN, COMPRESS, CONTRACT

condescend: . DEIGN, STOOP, FAVOR, PATRONIZE

condign: . . . . FAIR, WORTHY, DESERVED, FITTING, SUITABLE, APPROPRIATE

condition: . . IF, CASE, MODE, TERM, CAUSE, CLASS, HEALTH, STATE, STATUS, ARTICLE, PROVISO, ACCUSTOM, EXCEPTION, PROVISION, LIMITATION, STIPULATION

condone: . . EXCUSE, FORGIVE, PARDON, OVERLOOK

conduce: . . . AID, HELP, TEND, LEAD, GUIDE, CONFER, CONDUCT, CONTRIBUTE

conduct: . . . ACT, RUN, LEAD, RULE, WAGE, GUIDE, ACTION, CONVEY, ESCORT, MANAGE, CHANNEL CONDUIT, OPERATE, BEHAVIOR, TRANSACT, ADMINISTRATE

conductor: . . ESCORT, GUIDE, LEADER, MAESTRO, AQUEDUCT, CONVEYOR, BANDLEADER

conduit: . . DUCT, MAIN, PIPE, TUBE, CABLE, CANAL, SEWER, CHANNEL, CULVERT

confab: . . . . TALK, CHAT, POWWOW, CONFERENCE

confection: . . CANDY, SWEET, BONBON, COMFIT, NOUGAT, CARAMEL, PRALINE, SHERBERT, CONFITURE, SWEETMEAT

confederate: . . . . AID, ALLY, REBEL, UNITE, PARTNER, ASSOCIATE, ACCOMPLICE

confer: . . . GIVE, MEET, TALK, AWARD, ENDOW, BESTOW, PARLEY, CONSULT, DISCUSS, CONVERSE, DELIBERATE

conference: . . . TALK, SYNOD, CONFAB, PARLEY, CAUCUS, PALAVER, POWWOW, COUNCIL, MEETING, DISCUSSION, ASSOCIATION

confess: . . . . . ADMIT, OWN, AVOW, SING, REVEAL, SQUEAL, DIVULGE, DISCLOSE

confession: . . CREED, CREDO, AVOWAL, ADMISSION, REVELATION

confide: . . . . TELL, ENTRUST

confidence: . . . FAITH, TRUST, SECRET, BELIEF, MORALE, COURAGE, ASSURANCE

game: . . . . BUNCO, BUNKO, FRAUD, SWINDLE

confident: . . . . . BOLD, SURE, SECURE, ASSURED, CERTAIN, CONSTANT, FEARLESS

confidential: . . . . . COVERT, SECRET, PRIVATE, ESOTERIC

confine: . . . BOX, DAM, HEM, PEN, CAGE, JAIL, LOCK, LIMIT, RESTRICT, IMMURE, FETTER, IMPRISON, INCARCERATE

confirm: . . . . PROVE, AFFIRM, ATTEST, VERIFY, RATIFY, VALIDATE, CORROBORATE, SUBSTANTIATE

confiscate: . . . . SIEZE, USURP, ESCHEAT, APPROPRIATE

conflict: . . WAR, DUEL, FRAY, CLASH, FIGHT, BATTLE, COMBAT, MUTINY, STRIFE, DISCORD, CONTEST, STRUGGLE, REBELLION

conform: . . . . . OBEY, ADAPT, AGREE, YIELD, COMPLY, ACCOMODATE

confound: ... ABASH, AMAZE, STUMP, CONFUSE, ASTOUND, BEWILDER, PUZZLE, PERPLEX, DISCONCERT

confront: .... FACE, STAND, MEET

confuse: .... MIX, DAZE, ABASH, BEFOG, CLOUD, MUDDLE, DISCONCERT, PUZZLE, FLUMMOX, PERPLEX, FLABBERGAST, BEWILDER, CONFOUND

confusion: ..... FUSS, MESS, MOIL, RIOT, CHAOS, MIX-UP, BEDLAM, DISORDER, DISARRAY, HUBBUB, JUMBLE, MUDDLE, RUMPUS, RUCKUS, WELTER, TANGLE, TURMOIL, COMMOTION

congeal: ..... GEL, SET, ICE, JELL, FREEZE, THICKEN, SOLIDIFY, CURDLE, COAGULATE

congenial: .... BOON, FRIENDLY, COMPATIBLE, AGREEABLE

congratulate: ... LAUD, HAIL, SALUTE, COMMEND, COMPLIMENT, FELICITATE

congregate: ... MEET, GROUP, SWARM, COLLECT, GATHER, ASSEMBLE

congress: . SYNOD, COUNCIL, MEETING, ASSEMBLY, CONCLAVE, CONFERENCE, LEGISLATURE

congruity: .... ACCORD, FITNESS, HARMONY, AGREEMENT, CONSISTENCY

conifer: ..... YEW, FIR, PINE, CEDAR, SPRUCE, LARCH

conjecture: .. FANCY, GUESS, OPINE, SURMISE, THEORY, IMAGINE, SPECULATE, SUSPICION

conjoint: ... LINKED, UNITED, TOUCHING COMCOMITANT

conjugal: .... MARITAL, MATRIMONIAL, CONNUBIAL

conjure: .... PRAY, CHARM, INVENT, SUMMON, INVOKE, IMAGINE, CONSPIRE, EXORCISE

connate: .... AKIN, INBORN, INNATE, CONGENITAL

connect: ... TIE, ALLY, BIND, LINK, JOIN, CHAIN, UNITE, COUPLE, FASTEN, COMBINE, ASSOCIATE

connection: ..... TIE, BOND, LINK, UNION, NEXUS, KINSHIP, RELATION, CONTACT, ALLIANCE, JUNCTION, RELEVANCE

connive: .... PLOT, FOMENT, CONSPIRE, COOPERATE

conquer: ... GET, WIN, BEAT, GAIN, LICK, ROUT, CRUSH, DEFEAT, SUBDUE, MASTER, TRIUMPH, OVERCOME, VANQUISH, SUBJUGATE

consanguinity: .... KINSHIP, AFFINITY, RELATIONSHIP

conscience: ...... QUALM, REMORSE, SCRUPLE, COMPUNCTION

conscious: ... ALIVE, AWARE, AWAKE, FEELING, KNOWING, SENSIBLE, COGNIZANT, SENTIENT, PERCEPTIVE

conscript: .. DRAFT, ENROLL, FORCE, ENLIST, RECRUIT, MUSTER

consecrate: ... BLESS, DEIFY, DEVOTE, ANOINT, ORDAIN, DEDICATE, HALLOW, SANCTIFY

consent: .... AGREE, ALLOW, GRANT, ASSENT, CONCUR, ACCEDE, AGREEMENT, PERMISSION

consequence: .. END, RESULT, EFFECT, OUTCOME, SEQUAL, AFTERMATH, IMPORTANCE

consequently: ... SO, ERGO, THEN, THUS, HENCE, THEREFORE, SUBSEQUENTLY

conservative: .... STAID, STABLE, MODERATE, PRUDENT RIGHT(IST), REACTIONARY

consider: . . . . DEEM, MULL, HEED, JUDGE, THINK, STUDY, WEIGH, PONDER, REGARD, EXAMINE, INSPECT, REFLECT, COGITATE, MEDITATE, SPECULATE, CONTEMPLATE

consideration: . . . FEE, PRICE, TOPIC, ASPECT, ESTEEM, MOTIVE, REASON, REGARD, RESPECT, DEFERENCE, INCENTIVE, RECOMPENSE

consign: . . . . . . GIVE, SEND, ALLOT, AWARD, ASSIGN, COMMIT, DEVOTE, ADDRESS, ENTRUST, DELIVER, RELEGATE

consistent: . . FIRM, DURABLE, LOGICAL, UNIFORM, COHERENT, ENDURING ACCORDANT, CONGRUOUS, CHANGELESS, COMPATIBLE

console: . . . . CALM, ALLAY, ANCON, CHEER, ORGAN, SOLACE, SOOTHE, COMFORT, BRACKET, CABINET, RELIEVE, ALLEVIATE, ENCOURAGE

consolidate: . . . . KNIT, POOL, BLEND, UNITE, MERGE, COMBINE, COALESCE, CONDENSE, SOLIDIFY, STRENGTHEN, AMALGAMATE

conspicuous: . . CLEAR, PLAIN, EXTANT, FAMOUS, PATENT, EMINENT, GLARING, OBVIOUS, SALIENT, APPARENT, MANIFEST, PROMINENT, NOTICEABLE, DISTINCTIVE, OUTSTANDING

conspiracy: . . . . PLAN, PLOT, RING, CABAL, SCHEME, INTRIGUE, CONNIVANCE, AGREEMENT

constant: . . . . . . EVEN, FIRM, TRUE, FIXED, SOLID, STABLE, STEADY, CERTAIN, FAITHFUL, CHRONIC, FOREVER, LASTING, UNIFORM, ENDURING, CONTINUAL, PERMANENT, PERPETUAL, UNVARYING, UNWAVERING

constellation: . . . . . . GROUP, DIPPER, GATHERING, CONFIGURATION

consternation: . . . . . . FEAR, ALARM, DISMAY, FRIGHT, TERROR, AMAZEMENT, TREPIDATION

constituent: . . . . ITEM, PART, PIECE, VOTER, MEMBER, ELECTOR, ELEMENT, COMPONENT, INGREDIENT

constitution: . . . LAW, CODE, BEING, CANON, STATE, HEALTH, CHARTER, PHYSIQUE, MAKE-UP, ORDINANCE, STRUCTURE, COMPOSITION, ORGANIZATION

constrain: . . . . . BIND, CURB, CHAIN, DETER, IMPEL, LIMIT, FORCE, COMPEL, COERCE, OBLIGE, CONFINE, ENFORCE, OPPRESS, REPRESS, VIOLATE, RESTRAIN

constrict: . . TIE, BIND, CURB, CHOKE, LIMIT, HAMPER, CONTRACT, SQUEEZE, COMPRESS, CONDENSE, RESTRICT

construct: . . . . FORM, MAKE, REAR, ERECT, BUILD, DEVISE, COMPOSE, FASHION, FABRICATE

construe: . . . . INFER, PARSE, EXPLAIN, ANALYZE, CONSTRUCT, INTERPRET

consult: . . . . . . ASK, CONFER, REFER TO, ADVISE, DISCUSS, CONSIDER

consume: . . EAT, USE, BURN, WEAR, DRINK, SPEND, WASTE, ABSORB, DEVOUR, EXPEND, CORRODE, DESTROY, EXHAUST, DISSIPATE

consummate: . . . . END, FULL, IDEAL, FINISH, ACHIEVE, PERFORM, COMPLETE, PERFECT, CULMINATE

consumption: . . USE, WASTE, DECAY, EXPENSE, DESTRUCTION, TUBERCULOSIS, PHTHISIS

contact: ...... JOIN, MEET, TOUCH, UNION, IMPACT, JUNCTION, CONNECTION, CONTIGUITY

contagious: ..... CATCHING, SPREADING, INFECTIOUS, COMMUNICABLE

contain: . HAVE, HOLD, KEEP, CHECK, ENCLOSE, EMBODY, INCLUDE, COMPRISE

contaminate: ... FOUL, SOIL, STAIN, TAINT, DEFILE, SULLY, INFECT, POISON, CORRUPT, POLLUTE, ADULTERATE

contemn: .. DESPISE, SCORN, SPURN, REJECT

contemplate: ... MUSE, PLAN, SCAN, VIEW, STUDY, THINK, PONDER, REFLECT, CONSIDER, MEDITATE

contemporaneous: . COEVAL, LIVING, EXISTING, CURRENT, SIMULTANEOUS

contempt: .. DISDAIN, SCORN, SNEER, CONTEMN, DISDAIN, DERISION

contemptible: .. BASE, VILE, LOW, MEAN, PETTY, ABJECT, PALTRY, SCURVY, SORDID, WRETCHED, DESPICABLE

contend: .. VIE, COPE, WAGE, FIGHT, ARGUE, CLAIM, ASSERT, COMBAT, STRIVE, COMPLETE, DISPUTE, MAINTAIN

content: ..... CALM, HAPPY, AMOUNT, APPEASE, GRATIFY, SATISFIED, CAPACITY

contention: ...... DISPUTE, STRIFE, DISCORD, QUARREL, ARGUMENT, CONFLICT, STRUGGLE, LITIGATION, CONTROVERSY

contest: ..... SUE, VIE, FEUD, TRIAL, AGON, DISPUTE, FIGHT, OPPOSE, COMPETE, RESIST, TOURNEY

contestant: .. RIVAL, PLAYER, ENTRY, ENTRANT, CANDIDATE, DEFENDANT, PLAINTIFF, COMPETITOR, CONTENDER

contiguous: .. NEXT, NEARBY, ADJACENT, TOUCHING, ADJOINING, NEIGHBORING

continent: .... CHASTE, MAINLAND, TEMPERATE, AFRICA, ANTARCTICA, ASIA, AUSTRALIA, EUROPE, NORTH AMERICA, SOUTH AMERICA

contingency: .... CHANCE, EVENT, POSSIBILITY, UNCERTAINTY, EMERGENCY

continual: .... ENDLESS, REGULAR, UNIFORM, CONSTANT, INCESSANT, UNCEASING, INVARIABLE

continue: . LAST, LIVE, STAY, UNITE, EXTEND, RESUME, PERSIST, PROCEED, SUSTAIN, PERSEVERE

continuous: ...... NONSTOP, UNBROKEN, CONNECTED

contour: ..... FORM, CURVE, SHAPE, FIGURE, OUTLINE, PROFILE, SILHOUTTE, CONFIGURATION

contra: ... OFFSET, AGAINST, COUNTER, OPPOSITE

contract: ...... BAND, PACT, CATCH, INCUR, LEASE, CARTEL, ENGAGE, PLEDGE, REDUCE, COMPACT, ABRIDGE, CURTAIL, PROMISE, NARROW, AGREEMENT, SHRINK, CONDENSE, OBLIGATION

contradict: ... DENY, BELIE, REBUT, REFUTE, GAINSAY, NEGATE, DISPROVE

contradiction: ..... DENIAL, PARADOX, ANTILOGY, INCONSISTENCY

contrary: . AVERSE, CONTRA, BALKY, OPPOSED, REVERSE, OBSTINATE, PERVERSE

contravene: .. DEFY, OPPOSE, DISPUTE, DISAGREE, VIOLATE, DISREGARD

contribute: . . . . . AID, HELP, GIVE, DONATE, BESTOW, ASSIST

contribution: . . . . GIFT, DONATION, SHARE, LARGESS

contrite: . . . . SORRY, REPENTANT, REGRETFUL, PENITENT

contrivance: . . . . . . DEVICE, GADGET, GIMMICK, CONTRAPTION, INVENTION

contrive: . . . . . . PLAN, PLOT, MAKE, DEVISE, INVENT, SCHEME, ACHIEVE, CONCOCT, CONSPIRE

control: . CURB, HOLD, VEIN, RULE, CHECK, GUIDE, POWER, STEER, DIRECT, HANDLE, MANAGE, CONDUCT, RESTRAIN, DOMINATE

controversy: . . SUIT, DEBATE, STRIFE, DISPUTE, QUARREL, ARGUMENT, DIFFERENCE, LITIGATION

contumacious: . . . . UNRULY, INSOLENT, STUBBORN, INSUBORDINATE, DISOBEDIENT

contusion: . . . BLOW, BRUISE, INJURY

convene: . . . SIT, CALL, MEET, GATHER, ASSEMBLE, SUMMON, CONVOKE

convenient: . . . . HANDY, USEFUL, EXPEDIENT, AGREEABLE, ACCESSIBLE

convention: . . . . . . CUSTOM, USAGE, ASSEMBLY, MEETING, PRACTICE, TRADITION, CONFERENCE

man: . . . . DELEGATE

conventional: . . . . . . USUAL, FORMAL, PROPER, CORRECT, ACCEPTED, CUSTOMARY, ORTHODOX

conversant: . . . . EXPERT, SKILLED, FAMILIAR, ACQUAINTED

conversation: . . . CHAT, TALK, PALAVER, DIALOGUE, COLLOQUY

converse: . . . . . CHAT, TALK, SPEAK, CONFER, OPPOSITE, REVERSE, COMMUNE

convert: . . . . ALTER, AMEND, RENEW, CHANGE, RESTORE, REVERSE, PERSUADE, TRANSFORM, PROSELYTE, TRANSLATE

convex: . . . . BOWED, ARCHED, CAMBER, CURVED, ROUNDED

convey: . . BEAR, CEDE, DEED, CARRY, SEND, GUIDE, BRING, ASSIGN, DEMISE, IMPART, CONDUCT, DELIVER, TRANSPORT, TRANSMIT, TRANSFER

convict: . . . . . FIND, FELON, PROVE, ATTAIN, CAPTIVE, CONDEMN, CULPRIT, CRIMINAL, PRISONER, JAILBIRD, SENTENCE

conviction: . . CREED, DOGMA, FAITH, BELIEF, OPINION, SENTENCE

convincing: . . . . VALID, COGENT, TELLING, FORCIBLE, CONCLUSIVE, PERSUASIVE

convivial: . . . . GAY, GENIAL, JOLLY, JOVIAL, FESTIVE, SOCIABLE

convoke: . . . . . . CALL, MEET, GATHER, SUMMON, CONVENE, ASSEMBLE

convolute: . . . . . COIL, WIND, TWIST, WRITHE, CONTORT

convoy: . . . . . . LEAD, GUARD, GUIDE, ESCORT, CONDUCT, ACCOMPANY

convulse: . . . . . FIT, SPASM, THROE, UPHEAVAL, PAROXYSM, AGITATION

cook: . . . . . FRY, BAKE, BOIL, CHEF, SEAR, STEW, BROIL GRILL, POACH, ROAST, BRAISE, SAUTEE, SIMMER, CODDLE, PREPARE, PROCESS

cookie, cooky: . . BUN, CAKE, SNAP, HERMIT, BISCUIT, MACAROON

cooking: . . . .

art: . . CUISINE, CULINARY,
MAGIRICS
device: . . . RANGE, STOVE,
GRILL, BRASIER, GRIDDLE,
ROTISSERIE
odor: . . . . NIDOR
vessel: . . PAN, POT, OLLA,
CHAFER, SPIDER, TUREEN,
BROILER, GRIDDLE,
ROASTER, SKILLET,
COLANDER

cool: . . . . . . FAN, ICE, CALM,
COLD, CHILL, SOBER, CHILLY,
PLACID, QUENCH, SERENE,
UNMOVED, COMPOSED,
MODERATE, TRANQUIL,
COLLECTED, TEMPERATE,
NONCHALANT, REFRIGERATE

cooperate: . . . . HELP, AGREE,
UNITE, COMBINE, CONNIVE,
CONSPIRE, CONTRIBUTE,
COLLABORATE

coordinate: . . ADAPT, EQUAL,
ADJUST, ARRANGE, HARMONIZE

cop: . . BAG, NAB, ROB, BULL,
HEAD, LIFT, CATCH, CREST,
FILCH, STEAL, SWIPE,
POLICEMAN, FLATFOOT

cope: . . . . . VIE, CAPE, FACE,
CLOAK, EQUAL, FIGHT, VAULT,
CANOPY, COMBAT, HANDLE,
MANTEL, STRIVE, CONTEND,
VESTMENT

copious: . . FULL, LUSH, RICH,
AMPLE, LAVISH, FLOWING,
PROFUSE, PLENTIFUL,
ABUNDANT

coppice: . . . . . WOOD, COPSE,
GROVE, FOREST, THICKET

copy: . . . APE, ECHO, IMAGE,
MIMIC, MODEL, ECTYPE
FOLLOW, EMULATE, IMITATE,
REPLICA, TRACING, DUPLICATE,
FACSIMILE, IMITATION,
REPRODUCE, REPRODUCTION

copyright: . . . . PATENT

coquette: . . . . . FLIRT, DALLY,
TRIFLE

coral: . . . . KEY, REEF, ATOLL,
POLYP, SKELETON, ZOOPHYTE,
MADREPORE, POLYPITE

cord: . . . BAND, BOND, ROPE,
TWINE, NERVE, STRING,
TENDON, SENNIT, MEASURE

corded: . . . . . . TIED, POPLIN,
REPPED, RIBBED, WELTED,
TWILLED, CORDUROY

cordial: . . (also see **liqueur**)
WARM, ARDENT, ELIXIR,
GENIAL, HEARTY, FRIENDLY,
AMIABLE, ANISETTE,
HOSPITABLE

cordite: . . . . EXPLOSIVE

cordon: . . . . . CORD, BRAID,
RING, GUARD, RIBBON

core: . . COB, HUB, NUT, GIST,
PITH, FOCUS, HEART, CENTER,
KERNEL, MATRIX, MIDDLE,
ESSENCE, NUCLEUS

corium: . . . . . SKIN, LAYER,
DERMA, DERMIS

cork: . . . . . OAK, TAP, BUNG,
BARK, PLUG, FLOAT, SHIVE,
STOPPER, STOPPLE

corm: . . . . BULB, TUBER

corn: . . SALT, MAIZE, GRAIN,
KERNEL, HELOMA, CALLUS,
PAPILLOMA
bread: . . . PONE, TORTILLA
meal/food: . . MASA, SAMP,
MUSH, GRITS, SCRAPPLE,
HOECAKE, HOMINY,
SUCCOTASH

corned: . . . . SALTED

corner: . . GET, BLEND, NOOK,
TRAP, TREE, ANGLE, BIGHT,
CATCH, COIGN, ELBOW, NICHE,
CRANNY, RECESS, MONOPOLY,
REGION

cornice: . . BAND, DRIP, EAVE,
CROWN, MOLDING

cornucopia: . . . . HORN

corny: . . . . . TRITE, BANAL,
STALE, SENTIMENTAL

corollary: . . RESULT, TRUISM,
THEOREM, INFERENCE,
DEDUCTION, CONSEQUENCE

corona: . . . . . . AURA, HALO,
CIGAR, CROWN, AUREOLE,
WREATH, GARLAND

coronet: . . . . CROWN, TIARA,
ANADEM, DIADEM, WREATH

corporal: . . . . BODILY,
PERSONAL

punishment: . . . . . DEATH,
FLOGGING, WHIPPING

corporate: . . . . UNITED,
COMMON, COMBINED,
AGGREGATE

corporation: . . . BODY, FIRM,
TRUST, COMPANY,
FOUNDATION, COMBINATION

corporeal: . . . . REAL, SOMAL,
ACTUAL, BODILY, CARNEL,
SOMATIC, MATERIAL, PHYSICAL

corpse: . . . . . BODY, MUMMY,
STIFF, CADAVER, CARCASS

corpulent: . . . . . FAT, OBESE,
PLUMP, STOUT, FLESHY,
PORTLY, ADIPOSE

corpuscle: . . . . CELL,
LEUCOCYTE, HEMATID

lack of red: . . . . . ANEMIA

correct: . . . . FIT, FIX, CURE,
EDIT, TRUE, AMEND, EXACT,
RIGHT, ADJUST, CHANGE,
PROPER, PUNISH, REBUKE,
REFORM, REMEDY, REPAIR,
REVISE, CHASTEN, PRECISE,
RECTIFY, REPROVE, ACCURATE,
TRUTHFUL, CASTIGATE

correspond: . . . SUIT, MATCH,
AGREE, EQUAL, TALLY, WRITE,
CONCUR, COINCIDE,
COMMUNICATE

correspondence: . . ANALOGY,
LETTERS, TRAFFIC, AGREEMENT,
CONGRUITY, SIMILARITY,
COMMUNICATION

corridor: . . . . . HALL, AISLE,
ARCADE, GALLERY,
PASSAGEWAY

corrigible: . . . . . AMENABLE,
CORRECTIVE, CORRECTABLE

corroborate: . . . . . SUPPORT,
CONFIRM, SUSTAIN,
SUBSTANTIATE

corrode: . . . EAT, BITE, BURN,
ETCH, RUST, GNAW, ERODE,
DECAY, CONSUME

corrosive: . . ACID, MORDANT,
BITING, CAUSTIC, DESTRUCTIVE

corrugate: . . . . CRIMP, PLEAT,
FURROW, CRINKLE, WRINKLE

corrupt: . . . BAD, ROT, EVIL,
VILE, BRIBE, SPOIL, SULLY,
TAINT, DEBASE, DEFILE,
INFECT, IMPURE, POISON,
PUTRID, ROTTEN, CROOKED,
DEFILED, PERVERT, POLLUTE,
PUTREFY, DISHONEST,
ADULTERATE, CONTAMINATE

corsair: . . . . PIRATE, ROBBER,
FREEBOOTER, PRIVATEER

ship: . . . . XEBEC

cortege: . . . . . SUITE, TRAIN,
RETINUE, PARADE, PROCESSION

cortex: . . . . BARK, RIND

corundum: . . . RUBY, SAND,
EMERY, TOPAZ, AMETHYST,
SAPPHIRE

coruscate: . . . FLASH, GLEAM,
SPARKLE, GLITTER

coryza: . . . . . COLD, CATARRH

cosmetic: . . . CREAM, HENNA,
PAINT, ROUGE, ENAMEL,
POWDER, MASCARA, LIPSTICK

cosmic: . . . . VAST, ORDERLY,
INFINITE, UNIVERSAL,
GRANDIOSE

cosmonaut: . . . . ASTRONAUT,
SPACEMAN, ROCKETMAN

cosmos: . . . . REALM, ORDER,
EARTH, GLOBE, WORLD,
THISTLE, HARMONY, UNIVERSE

cosset: . PET, LAMB, PAMPER,
FONDLE, CARESS

cost: . . . LOSS, PRICE, VALUE,
CHARGE, EXPENSE, DAMAGE,
SACRIFICE, EXPENDITURE

costa: . . . . . RIB, SIDE, VEIN,
RIDGE, BORDER

costly: ... DEAR, HIGH, RICH, EXPENSIVE, PRECIOUS, PRICELESS, EXTRAVAGANT

costume: .. RIG, GARB, ROBE, SUIT, DRESS, HABIT, ATTIRE, APPAREL, CLOTHES, RAIMENT, UNIFORM, ENSEMBLE

cot: ... BED, ABODE, COUCH, HOUSE, SHELTER, CHARPAI, CHARPOY, COTTAGE

cote: .... HUT, SHED, HOUSE, SHELTER, COTTAGE

coterie: .... SET, CIRCLE, CLIQUE, JUNTO, CAMARILLA

cotta: .... MANTLE, SURPLICE

cottage: .. COT, HUT, CABIN, LODGE, BOWER, CHALET, CABANA, BUNGALOW

cotter: ... PIN, BOLT, WEDGE

couch: .... BED, COT, LAIR, SOFA, DIVAN, LITTER, PALLET, SETTEE, RECLINE, LOUNGE, DAVENPORT

cougar: .... PUMA, PANTHER, CATAMOUNT

cough: ...... HACK, TUSSIS

coulee: ..... LAVA, RAVINE, GULCH, GORGE

council: ..... DIET, BOARD, CABAL, JUNTA, SYNOD, SENATE, CABINET, MEETING, ASSEMBLY, CONCLAVE, CONGRESS, CONFERENCE, CONSISTORY

counsel: ... ADVICE, ADVISE, CONFER, ADVOCATE, RECOMMEND, CONSULTATION

counselor, counsel: .... ADVISER, LAWYER, MENTOR, PROCTOR, ATTORNEY, BARRISTER

count: .... ADD, EARL, NAME, RELY, TOTE, COMTE, SCORE, TALLY, CENSUS, DEPEND, FIGURE, NUMBER, RECKON, COMPUTE, NUMERATE, ASCERTAIN, CALCULATE, ENUMERATE

countenance: .... AID, ABET, FACE, FAVOR, ASPECT, VISAGE, APPROVE, FEATURE, SUPPORT, ENCOURAGE, APPEARANCE

counter: .. BAR, CHIP, PAWN, SHELF, STAND, TABLE, OPPOSE, ADVERSE, COMPUTER, CONTRARY, OPPOSITE

counteract: . CHECK, OPPOSE, THWART, BALANCE, NULLIFY, ANTIDOTE, FRUSTRATE, NEUTRALIZE

counterfeit: ... FAKE, SHAM, BOGUS, FALSE, FORGE(D), PHONY, PSEUDO, FALSIFY, SIMULATE, IMITATION, SPURIOUS, FRAUDULENT

countermand: ..... ANNUL, CANCEL, RECALL, REVOKE, ABOLISH, RESCIND, REVERSE, OVERRULE

countless: .... INIFINITE, MYRIAD, INCALCULABLE

country: ..... HOME, LAND, REALM, STATE, TRACT, GROUND REGION, RURAL, DISTRICT, TERRITORY, COMMONWEALTH

county: .... SEAT, SHIRE, DISTRICT, BOROUGH, PARISH

law officer: ..... SHERIFF

coup: .. BLOW, SCOOP, UPSET, ATTACK, STRIKE, STROKE, OVERTURN

couple: ... DUO, TWO, BOND, JOIN, LINK, MATE, PAIR, TEAM, TWIN, YOKE, BRACE, MARRY, UNITE, CONNECT

courage: ...... GRIT, GUTS, HEART, NERVE, PLUCK, SPUNK, VALOR, DARING, METTLE, SPIRIT, BRAVERY, BOLDNESS, FORTITUDE, RESOLUTION

course: ... WAY, DISH, MODE, RINK, ROAD, PATH, ROUTE, CYCLE, TRACK, TRAIL, TREND, METHOD, SERIES, STREET, SYSTEM, HIGHWAY, PASSAGE, PROCESS, ROUTINE, SUBJECT,

PROGRESS, DIRECTION, CURRICULUM

court: . . . . BAR, WOO, AREA, BODY, QUAD, SEEK, YARD, ARENA, CURRY, ASSIZE, BENCH, FORUM, JUDGE, PATIO, SPARK, ATRIUM, HOMAGE, INVITE, PALACE, SOLICIT, TRIBUNAL, ENCLOSURE, QUADRANGLE

courteous: . . . . CIVIL, POLITE, URBANE, REFINED, GRACIOUS, CONSIDERATE

courtly: . . . . AULIC, SUAVE, ELEGANT, STATELY, POLISHED, DIGNIFIED

couturier: . . . . . . DESIGNER, DRESSMAKER

covenant: . . . . . BOND, PACT, ACCORD, CARTEL, PLEDGE, TREATY, COMPACT, PROMISE, CONTRACT, AGREEMENT, TESTAMENT

cover: . . TOP, LID, CAP, HIDE, MASK, PAVE, ROOF, VEIL, COAT, SHEATHE ENVELOP(E), DRAPE, MANTLE, SHIELD, OBSCURE, SHELTER

covered: . . . . CLAD, COVERT, HIDDEN, ENCASED, SCREENED, CONCEALED, SHELTERED

covering: . . . . . FUR, BARK, BOOT, CASE, HOOD, HULL, HUSK, MASK, PALL, ROOF, ARMOR, CRUST, QUILT, SHELL, AWNING, CANOPY, SCREEN, SHEATH, SHROUD, CEILING, OVERLAY, WRAPPER, CASEMENT, CLOTHING, OVERCAST, INTEGUMENT, CAMOUFLAGE

coverlet: . . . . QUILT, THROW, AFGAN, SPREAD, BLANKET, COMFORTER, COUNTERPANE

covert: . . . . . . SLY, SECRET, VEILED, HIDDEN, PRIVATE, SUBROSA, CONCEALED

covet: . . . ENVY, WANT, WISH, DESIRE, CRAVE, YEARN, HANKER

covetous: . . EAGER, GREEDY, DESIROUS, AVARICIOUS

covey: . . BEVY, FLOCK, BROOD

cow: . . . . . AWE, BEEF, KINE, VACA, BASH, SCARE, DAUNT, HEIFER, BOVINE, BULLY, FREIGHTEN, THREATEN, INTIMIDATE

barn: . . . . STABLE, BYRE, VACCARY

cud: . . . . RUMEN

gland: . . . . UDDER

sound: . . . . . . LOW, MOO

unbranded: . . . MAVERICK

young: . . . . . CALF, STIRK, HEIFER

cowardly: . . . TIMID, AFRAID, CRAVEN, YELLOW, CHICKEN, CAITIFF, FAINTHEARTED, PUSILLANIMOUS

cowboy: . . GAUCHO, HERDER, VAQUERO, LLANERO, BUCKAROO, WRANGLER, COWPUNCHER

cower: . . . . . CRINGE, QUAIL, STOOP, SHRINK, CROUCH

cowl: . HOOD, CLOAK, AMICE, BONNET

coxa: . . . . HIP

coy: . . . SHY, TIMID, MODEST, BASHFUL, DEMURE, RETIRING, DIFFIDENT

cozen: . . . . . CHEAT, TRICK, DEFRAUD, DECEIVE

cozy: . . SAFE, TOASTY, SNUG, COMFORTABLE, HOMEY

crack: . . . BANG, BLOW, CLAP, FLAW, JEST, JOKE, LEAK, RIFT, SNAP, QUIP, BREAK, SPLIT, CLEFT, CREVICE, CHINK, CLEAVE, FISSURE

cradle: . . . . BED, COT, CRIB, CRATE, CRECHE

craft: . . . . ART, BOAT, GUILE, TRADE, SKILL, DECEIT, TALENT, CUNNING, ARTIFICE, VOCATION, OCCUPATION

craftsman: . ARTIST, WRITER, ARTISAN, MECHANIC, ARTIFICER

crafty: ... SLY, FOXY, WILY, ADROIT, ARTFUL, SHREWD, TRICKY, CUNNING, DECEITFUL, INGENIOUS, INSIDIOUS

crag: .... TOR, ROCK, CLIFF, PRECIPICE

cram: ... BONE, GLUT, PACK, STUFF, FORCE, STUDY

cramp: .. KINK, PAIN, CRICK, CROWD, HAMPER, HINDER, CONFINE, RESTRICT, FRUSTRATE

crane: ...... DAVIT, HERON, STORK, DERRICK

cranial nerve: ...... VAGUS

cranium: ...... PAN, HEAD, SKULL, BRAINPAN

crank: . WHIM, WIND, TWIST, WINCH, GROUCH, HANDLE, QUEER, ECCENTRIC, CAPRICE

cranky: ... CROSS, IRRITABLE, GROUCHY, AILING

cranny: ..... CREVICE, CHINK

crash: ... FAIL, FALL, SHOCK, FIASCO, FAILURE, COLLAPSE, SMASH, COLLISION

crass: .. RUDE, CRUDE, GROSS, STUPID, COARSE, ROUGH

crate: ..... BOX, CAR, CRIB, BASKET, HAMPER, ENCASE, CONTAINER

crater: .. PIT, HOLE, CAVITY, HOLLOW, CALDERA

cravat: .... TIE, SCARF, ASCOT, OVERLAY, NECKERCHIEF

crave: .. BEG, COVET, YEARN, HANKER, HUNGER

craven: .... AFRAID, COWARD(LY), DEFEATED, POLTROON

crawl: ... INCH, SWIM, CREEP, CRINGE, GROVEL, SLITHER

craze: .... FAD, MODE, RAGE, MANIA, FUROR, FASHION, ROGUE, DERANGE

crazy: .... MAD, LOCO, NUTS, WILD, DAFT, ZANY, BATTY, DAFFY, MANIC, NUTTY, POTTY, WACKY, INSANE, LOONY, KOOKY, COOCOO, LUNATIC, BERSERK, CRACKED, DEMENTED, DERANGED

cream: .... BEST, ELITE, COSMETIC, EMULSION

crease: .. FOLD, MUSS, RUCK, RUGA, CRIMP, PLEAT, CRUMPLE, WRINKLE

create: ...... MAKE, BUILD, CAUSE, DESIGN, INVENT, COMPOSE, FASHION, PRODUCE, GENERATE, ORIGINATE

credence: .... FAITH, TRUST, BELIEF, CONFIDENCE

credential: ..... VOUCHER, CREDENCE, CERTIFICATE, TESTIMONIAL

credenza: .... BUFFET, CUPBOARD, SIDEBOARD

credible: .. LIKELY, RELIABLE, PLAUSIBLE, BELIEVABLE

credit: . LOAN, ASSET, FAITH, TRUST, HONOR, REBATE, ASCRIBE, BELIEVE, ATTRIBUTE

credulous: .... GULLIBLE

creed: ... CULT, SECT, CREDO, DOGMA, FAITH, TENET, BELIEF, DOCTRINE

creek: ..... BAY, RIA, COVE, KILL, SLUE, INLET, STREAM, BAYOU, BROOK, INDIAN, SLOUGH, STREAM, ESTUARY

creep: .. INCH, FAWN, CRINGE, CRAWL, SLINK, SLITHER

crepe: .... FABRIC, PANCAKE, CRINKLED, WRINKLED

crepitate: .. SNAP, CRACKLE, RATTLE

crescent: ..... HORN, MOON, CURVE, LUNAR, SEMILUNAR, MENISCUS, SEMICIRCLE

crest: ..... CAP, TOP, ACME, APEX, COMB, PEAK, CROWN, RIDGE, PLUME HELMET, SUMMIT

crested: .... CROWNED, PILEATED, CRISTATE

crestfallen: ..... DEJECTED, DISPIRITED

cretin: .... IDIOT

crevasse: ..... SPLIT, CHASM, FISSURE

crevice:. . . . . . NOOK, SEAM,
CHINK, CLEFT, CRACK, FISSURE,
CREVASSE

crew: . . . MOB, BAND, GANG,
TEAM, SQUAD, STAFF, CROWD,
COMPANY, MEMBERS,
COMPLEMENT

crewel: . . . . . YARN, CADDIS,
CADDICE, EMBROIDERY

crib:. . . BED, BIN, BOX, RACK,
CHEAT, STALL, STEAL, TROUGH,
MANGER, PLAGIARIZE

crick: . . KINK, CRAMP, CREEK,
HITCH, SPASM, TWIST

crime: . . . SIN, EVIL, WRONG,
FELONY, MISDEED, OFFENSE,
VIOLATION, MALEFACTION

criminal:. . . . YEGG, CROOK,
FELON, KILLER, CONVICT,
CULPRIT, ILLEGAL, GANGSTER,
OUTLAW, MALEFACTOR,
MISCREANT, MALFEASANT,
RECIDIVIST

crimp: . . BEND, FOLD, PLEAT,
WAVE, CURL, FRIZZ, FLUTE,
GOFFER, CRINKLE, CORRUGATE

cringe: . . . . . . BEND, QUAIL,
COWER, WINCE, SHRINK,
CROUCH

cripple:. . MAR, HURT, LAME,
MAIM, WING, IMPAIR, DISABLE,
HAMSTRING, MUTILATE,
INCAPACITATE

crisis: . . . ACME, CRUX, TURN,
PANIC, PERIL, JUNCTURE,
EMERGENCY

cristate: . . . . CRESTED

criterion: . LAW, RULE, TEST,
NORM, AXIOM, CANON,
MEASURE, STANDARD

critic: . . . . . . JUDGE, EXPERT,
SLATER, CARPER, CENSOR,
REVIEWER, DETRACTOR,
FAULTFINDER

critical:. . . . . ACUTE, EXACT,
URGENT, EXIGENT, CAPTIOUS,
DECISIVE, CENSORIOUS,
DISCRIMINATING

criticize: . . PAN, RAP, DAMN,
SLAM, SLUR, BLAME, BLAST,
JUDGE, KNOCK, ROAST,
REBUKE, CENSURE, CONDEMN,
COMMENT, DENOUNCE,
ANIMADVERT

critique: . . . . REVIEW,
COMMENTARY

crock:. . . . . JAR, POT, SMUT,
SOOT, POTSHERD

croft: . . FARM, CRYPT, FIELD,
VAULT, CAVERN

crony: . . . . PAL, CHUM

crook: . . . . . . BEND, HOOK,
CURVE, THIEF, SWINDLER

crooked: . . . . . AGEE, AWRY,
BENT, ASKEW, AKIMBO,
CURVED, ZIGZAG, CORRUPT,
TWISTED, DISHONEST,
TORTUOUS, FRAUDULENT

crop: . . . . . CUT, MAW, CLIP,
REAP, TRIM, WHIP, SHEAR,
GATHER, CURTAIL, HARVEST,
PRODUCE

crosier:. . . . . STAFF, CROOK

cross: . . . . MIX, ROOD, SPAN,
ANGRY, TESTY, BISECT,
CRABBY, CRANKY, ATHWART,
PEEVISH, OBLIQUE, CRUCIFIX,
PETULANT, INTERSECT,
IRRITABLE, FRACTIOUS,
HYBRIDIZE, ILL-HUMORED

crossbar: . . . . . AXLE, RUNG

crossbeam: . . TRAVE, GIRDER,
TRANSOM

crossbreed: . . . . HYBRID,
MONGREL, HYBRIDIZE

cross-examine:. . . . . . GRILL,
QUESTION, INTERROGATE

crow: . . . CAW, ROOK, BOAST,
EXULT, BRAG, RAVEN,
(JACK)DAW, BLACKBIRD

crowbar:. . . . . . PRY, LEVER,
JIMMY, JEMMY

crowd: . . . . . JAM, MOB, SET,
CRAM, PACK, PUSH, BUNCH,
CRAMP, CRUSH, DROVE, FLOCK,
GROUP, HORDE, PRESS, SWARM,
WEDGE, CLIQUE, HUDDLE,

JOSTLE, THRONG, SQUEEZE, MULTITUDE

crown: .... CAP, TOP, PATE, PEAK, ADORN, CREST, TIARA, CLIMAX, DIADEM, SUMMIT, WREATH, CORONATE

crucial: ..... ACUTE, SEVERE, DECISIVE, CRITICAL, PIVOTAL

crude: ... RAW, BARE, RUDE, CRASS, ROUGH, VULGAR, COARSE, UNREFINED, UNCOUTH, UNREFINED

cruel: .... HARD, HARSH, BRUTAL, SAVAGE, UNJUST, BESTIAL, INHUMAN, PITILESS, RUTHLESS, SADISTIC, HEARTLESS, MERCILESS

crumb: ... BIT, SCRAP, PIECE, MORSEL, PARTICLE, FRAGMENT

crumble: ...... ROT, BREAK, CRUSH, DECAY, MO(U)LDER, PULVERIZE, DISINTEGRATE

crumple: ..... MUSS, CRUSH, WRINKLE, COLLAPSE, BUCKLE

crusade: ... WAR, CAMPAIGN, MOVEMENT, EXPEDITION

crush: ... JAM, CRAM, MASH, MILL, BREAK, GRIND, QUASH, QUELL, SMASH, BRUISE, CRUNCH, SQUASH, SUBDUE, CRUMPLE, OPPRESS, SQUEEZE, COMPRESS, OVERWHELM, PULVERIZE

crustacean: .... CRAB, FLEA, PRAWN, LOBSTER, SHRIMP, LIMULUS, ISOPOD, SQUILLA, BARNACLE

crux: ..... NUB, GIST, PITH, CROSS, PUZZLE, PROBLEM

cry: ..... HUE, SOB, BAWL, CALL, HOWL, MEWL, PULE, WAIL, WEEP, YELL, SHOUT, UTTER, WHINE, BELLOW, CLAMOR, LAMENT, SCREAM, SNIVEL, SQUEAL, EXCLAIM

crypt: .. PIT, VAULT, CAVERN, GROTTO

cryptic: .... DARK, VAGUE, HIDDEN, SECRET, OCCULT, OBSCURE, ENIGMATIC

cryptogram: .. CODE, CIPHER

crystal: ..... CLEAR, GLASS, LUCID, TRANSPARENT

crystalline: . PURE, CRYSTAL, PELLUCID

crystallize: .. JELL, CONGEAL, SOLIDIFY, GRANULATE

cubage: ... VOLUME, CONTENT

cubicle: .... BAY, DEN, CELL, NOOK, ROOM, BOOTH, ALCOVE, COMPARTMENT

cuckoo: ... ANI, BIRD, GOWK, KOEL, CRAZY, SILLY, FOOLISH

cucullate: .... COWLED, HOODED

cucumber: .... CUKE, PEPO, GOURD, PICKLE, GHERKIN

cool as a: .... CALM, POISED, COMPOSED

cucurbit: .... GOURD, FLASK

cucurbitaceous herb: ..... GOURD, SQUASH, MELON, CUCUMBER

cud: .... CHEW, RUMEN

cuddle: ... PET, HUG, CARESS, FONDLE, EMBRACE, SNUGGLE, NESTLE

cudgel: ... BAT, CANE, CLUB, DRUB, STICK, THRASH, SHILLALAH, TRUNCHEON

cue: ...... TIP, HINT, BRAID, QUEUE, PROMPT, SIGNAL

cuff: ..... BOX, SLAP, BELT, SWAT, CLOUT, STRIKE, HANDCUFF, WRISTBAND

cull: ...... DUPE, PICK, SIFT, SORT, GLEAN, PLUCK, SELECT

culmination: ... END, ACME, APEX, CLIMAX, ZENITH, COMPLETION

culpable: ... FAULTY, GUILTY, CRIMINAL, CENSURABLE

culprit: .... FELON, CONVICT, OFFENDER, CRIMINAL, MALEFACTOR

cultivate: .... GROW, FARM, TILL, PLOW, REAR, NURSE,

RAISE, FOSTER, DEVELOP, EDUCATE
cultivated: .... CIVIL, POLITE, REFINED, TILLED, CULTURED
culture: ...... AGAR, ARTS, TASTE, POLISH, CIVILIZATION, REFINEMENT
culvert: .... DRAIN, CONDUIT, WATERWAY
cummerbund: .. BAND, BELT, SASH
cumshaw: .... TIP, GRATUITY
cunning: .. SLY, CUTE, FOXY, WILY, GUILE, SMART, CLEVER, CRAFTY, SHREWD
cup: .. MUG, BOWL, CHALICE, CALIX, STEIN, BEAKER, GOBLET
cupboard: .. CUDDY, AMBRY, CLOSET, CABINET, PANTRY, ARMOIRE
cupidity: .... GREED, AVARICE
cupola: .... DOME, KILN, VAULT, TURRET, FURNACE
cuprous oxide: .. CHALCOCITE
cuprum: .... COPPER
cur: ..... MUTT, TIKE, TYKE, CANINE, MONGREL
curare: ..... POISON, URARI, OURALI
curate: ...... ABBE, PRIEST, CLERGYMAN, MINISTER
curative: .... HEALING, REMEDIAL, SANATIVE, MEDICINAL, THERAPEUTIC
curator: . KEEPER, MANAGER, GUARDIAN, CUSTODIAN
curb: .. REIN, BRAKE, CHECK, LIMIT, BRIDLE, THWART, INHIBIT, REPRESS, MODERATE, RESTRAIN, RESTRICT, HINDRANCE
curdle: .... SOUR, SPOIL, CLABBER, CONGEAL, COAGULATE
cure: .... DRY, HEAL, HELP, SALT, SMOKE, PRIEST, REMEDY, THERAPY, PRESERVE, SEASON, RESTORE
curio: ..... VIRTU, BIBELOT, KEEPSAKE, SOUVENIR

curious: ...... ODD, NOSY, QUEER, PRYING, STRANGE, UNUSUAL, MEDDLING, PECULIAR, INQUISITIVE
curl: ..... COIL, BEND, KINK, LOCK, RIPPLE, SPIRAL, RINGLET
curlicue: ... CURVE, FLOURISH
curly: .... KINKY, WAVY
curmudgeon: .. CRAB, MISER, GROUCH
currency: ...... CASH, COIN, BILLS, MONEY, SCRIP, SPECIE, GREENBACKS
current: . NOW, FLOW, FLUX, TIDE, GOING, MOVING, RECENT, STREAM, FLOWING, PRESENT, RUNNING, PREVAILING
curry: ... STEW, BEAT, COMB, CLEAN, GROOM, DRESS, DRUB, SEASONING
curse: .... BAN, CUSS, BANE, DAMN, OATH, SPELL, SWEAR, REVILE, MALISON ANATHEMA, IMPRECATION, EXECRATE, BLASPHEME, MARANATHA, MALEDICTION
cursed: .. BAD, EVIL, WICKED, ODIOUS, EXECRABLE
cursive: .... RUNNING
cursory: ..... BRIEF, HASTY, QUICK, SHORT, CASUAL, SUPERFICIAL
curt: ... RUDE, BLUFF, BRIEF, TERSE, BLUNT, SHORT, BRUSQUE, ABRUPT
curtail: .... CUT, CLIP, ABATE, SLASH, LESSEN, REDUCE, SHORTEN, ABBREVIATE
curtain: .. END, MASK, VEIL, DRAPE, SCREEN, SHADE, SHROUD, VALANCE, VEILING, BACKDROP
curve: .... ARC, BOW, BEND, OGEE, ARCH, VEER, CROOK, TWIST, SPIRAL, CIRCUIT, CONCAVE, CONTOUR, ELLIPSE, FLEXURE, HYPERBOLA, CURVATURE

curvet: . . . LEAP, SKIP, FRISK, CAVORT, FROLIC, GAMBOL, VAULT

cushion: . . . . MAT, PAD, BUFFER, PILLOW, ABSORB, HASSOCK, BOLSTER

cusp: . . . APEX, PEAK, POINT, TOOTH, HORN

custodian: . . GUARD, KEEPER, WARDEN, CURATOR, JANITOR, CARETAKER, CONCIERGE, GUARDIAN

custody: . . . . . CARE, TRUST, CHARGE, CONTROL, SAFEKEEPING, GUARDIANSHIP

custom: . . LAW, TAX, DUTY, MODE, RULE, WONT, HABIT, MORES, USAGE, VOGUE, FASHION, PRACTICE, CONVENTION

customary: . . . RULE, USUAL, COMMON, FAMILIAR, HABITUAL, ORTHODOX, TRADITIONAL, CONVENTIONAL

cut: . . BOB, HEW, LOP, MOW, NIP, SAW, CHIP, CHOP, CLIP, CROP, DOCK, GASH, HACK, NICK, PARE, SLIT, SNIP, SNUB, TRIM, CARVE, MINCE, NOTCH, PRUNE, SEVER, SHEAR, SHORN, SLASH, SLICE, SPLIT, BISECT, BROACH, CHISEL, CLEAVE, DIVIDE, IGNORE, INCISE, LESSEN, REDUCE, SLIGHT, CURTAIL, WHITTLE, LACERATE, RETRENCH, INTERSECT, ECONOMIZE

cutaneous: . . . . DERMAL

cute: . . . . . . CLEVER, SHARP, SHREWD, PRETTY, ATTRACTIVE

cuticle: . . . . SKIN, EPIDERMIS

cutpurse: . . . . THIEF, PICKPOCKET

cutter: . . BOAT, SLED, SLOOP, VESSEL, YACHT, SLEIGH

cutthroat: . . THUG, ASSASSIN, RUFFIAN, MURDERER

cutting: . . . CURT, KEEN, SLIP, TART, SCION, SHARP, BITING, BITTER, CAUSTIC, INCISIVE, WOUNDING, SARCASTIC, TRENCHANT

implement: . . . AX(E), BIT, SAW, ADZ(E), KNIFE, LATHE, MOWER, PLANE, RAZOR, CHISEL, CLEAVER, SCYTHE, SHEARS, SCISSORS, SICKLE, MACHETE

cuttlefish: . . . . SEPIA, SQUID, OCTOPUS

cycle: . . AGE, EON, ERA, BIKE, EPOCH, PEDAL, ROUND, SAROS, WHEEL, CIRCLE, PERIOD, BICYCLE, CIRCUIT, TRICYCLE, MOTORCYCLE, REVOLUTION

cyclone: . . . . . . GALE, WIND, BLAST, STORM, TORNADO, TWISTER, TYPHOON, HURRICANE, WINDSTORM

cylinder: . . . . . . DRUM, PIPE, TUBE, BARREL, BOBBIN, PISTON, PLATEN, ROLLER

cylindrical: . . . . ROUND, TERETE, CENTRIC, TUBULAR

cynic: . . . SKEPTIC, DOUBTER, PESSIMIST

cynosure: . . . . . . POLESTAR, LODESTAR, NORTH STAR

cyst: . . . . . . BAG, SAC, WEN, POUCH, RANULA, VESICLE

czar: . . TSAR, TZAR, DESPOT, EMPEROR

D

D: *Greek:* . . . . DELTA
Hebrew: . . . . . . DALETH, DALEDH

dab: . . PAT, TAP, PECK, SPOT, SMEAR, BLOTCH, TOUCH, STRIKE, PAINT, FLATFISH, FLOUNDER

dabble: . . . . DIP, WET, MESS, DALLY, MEDDLE, POTTER

dactyl: . . . . TOE, FINGER

dactylogram: . . . FINGERPRINT

daedal: . . . VARIED, ARTISTIC, INGENIOUS, INTRICATE, ELABORATE

daft: . . . . CRAZY, SILLY, FOOLISH, INSANE, IDIOTIC

dagger: . . . DIRK, KRIS, SNEE, SKEEN, ANLACE, BODKIN, DIESIS, CREESE, PANADE, STYLET, PONIARD, STILETTO

daily: . . DIURNAL, EVERYDAY, QUOTIDIAN, NEWSPAPER

dairy: . . LACTARY, VACCARY, CREAMERY

dias: . . . SEAT, BENCH, TABLE, CANOPY, PODIUM, PLATFORM, ROSTRUM, TERRACE, ESTRADE

daisy: . . . . . GOWAN, OXEYE, SHASTA, MARGUERITE, MOONFLOWER

dale: . . . . DELL, GLEN, VALE, VALLEY, DINGLE, TROUGH

dalliance: . . . . . CHAT, PLAY, TRIFLE, FLIRTATION

dally: . . . . TOY, CHAT, IDLE, PLAY, DELAY, FLIRT, IDLE, LOITER, TRIFLE

dam: . . . . BAR, DIKE, STAY, STEM, STOP, WEIR, BLOCK, CHECK, CHOKE, MOTHER, BARRIER, BLOCKADE, OBSTRUCT, RESTRAIN, MILLPOND

damage: . . MAR, BLOT, COST, HARM, HURT, LOSS, RUIN, BURST, SPOIL, DEFACE, IMPAIR, INJURE, EXPENSE, SCRATCH, ACCIDENT

damask: . . . . . . ROSE, LINEN

dame: . . . . GIRL, LADY, MATRON, WOMAN

damn: . . . . . CURSE, DOOM, CONDEMN

damnation: . . . . . PERDITION

damp: . . WET, DANK, DEWY, MIST, HUMID, MOIST, MUGGY, MUSTY, RAINY, SOGGY, CLAMMY, DEADEN, MUFFLE, MOISTEN

dance: . . . . . JIG, HOP, BALL, CLOG, HOOF, HULU, PROM, SHAG, CAPER, FRISK, RUMBA, TANGO, STOMP, POLKA, TWIST, WALTZ, MINUET, FOXTROT, BALLET, COTILLION, FANDANGO, CHARLESTON

dancer: . . . ARTIST, HOOFER, CHORINE, DANSEUSE, BALLERINA, TERPSICHOREAN

dancing: . . . . SALTANT, CHOREOGRAPHY

danger: . . . . RISK, PERIL, HAZARD, PITFALL, DISTRESS, JEOPARDY

dangerous: . . RISKY, UNSAFE, CRITICAL, INSECURE, PERILOUS, PRECARIOUS

dank: . . . WET, DAMP, MOIST, HUMID, CLAMMY

dapper: . . . . . NEAT, TRIM, SPRUCE, SMART, NATTY

dappled: . . . . DOTTED, MOTTLED, SPOTTED, PIEBALD, FLECKED

dare: . . . . RISK, FACE, DEFY, DAST, BRAVE, ATTEMPT, VENTURE, CHALLENGE

daring: . . . . BOLD, RASH, BRAVE, HARDY, NERVE, HEROIC, COURAGE, BOLDNESS

dark: . . . . . DIM, EBON, EVIL, MIRK, MURK, BLACK, DINGY, DUSKY, MURKY, SOOTY, UNLIT, VAGUE, CLOUDY, DISMAL, GLOOMY, WICKED, OBSCURE, SINISTER, IGNORANT, SWARTHY, ABSTRUSE, SECRETIVE, TENEBROUS, MYSTERIOUS

darkness: . . . . DUSK, MURK, GLOOM, NIGHT, SHADE, SHADOW, DIMNESS, GLOAMING, TWILIGHT, BLACKNESS

darling: . . . . PET, DEAR, BELOVED, CHERI(E), SWEET, FAVORITE

dart: . . . . FLIT, DASH, LEAP, SPURT, SCOOT, BOUND, LANCE,

SPEAR, MISSILE, ARROW, SPRING

dash: . . . DART, ELAN, HURL, LINE, RACE, RUIN, HURL, RUSH, ARDOR, CRASH, FLING, SMASH, SPRINT, THROW, HURTLE, HYPHEN, SPIRIT

dashing: . . . . BOLD, SHOWY, SPIRITED, STYLISH, FASHIONABLE

dastard: . . . . . . CAD, SNEAK, COWARD, CRAVEN, POLTROON,

dastardly: . . . . FOUL, COWARDLY

data: . . . . FACTS, INPUT, FIGURES, INFORMATION

date: . . . . . AGE, DAY, ERA, EPOCH, PERIOD, FRUIT, RENDEZVOUS, ENGAGEMENT, APPOINTMENT

dated: . . . PASSE, OUTMODED, OLD-FASHIONED

daub: . . . BLOB, BLOT, COAT, SOIL, SMEAR, PAINT, GREASE, PLASTER, SPLOTCH

daunt: . . . AWE, COW, DAZE, FAZE, ABASH, DETER, DISMAY, SUBDUE, REPRESS, INTIMIDATE

dauntless: . . . . BOLD, BRAVE, INTREPID

davenport: . . . . SOFA, DESK, COUCH, DIVAN

dawdle: . . . LAG, IDLE, POKE, DALLY, LOITER, LINGER, PIDDLE, PUTTER, POTTER

dawn: . . . . . . MORN, SUNUP, SUNRISE, AURORA, DAYBREAK, BEGINNING

day: . . AGE, ERA, DATE, TIME, EPOCH, PERIOD

daze: . . . FOG, STUN, DAUNT, BENUMB, DAZZLE, MUDDLE, TRANCE, CONFUSE, STUPEFY, BEWILDER(MENT)

dazzle: . DAZE, SHINE, BLIND, IMPRESS, BEWILDER

de facto: . . . ACTUAL, IN FACT

dejure: . . . . BY RIGHT

deluxe: . . . . ELEGANT, SUMPTUOUS

deacon: . . . . CLERIC, DOCTOR, LAYMAN, ADULTERATE

dead: . . COLD, AMORT, INERT, SLAIN, DEFUNCT, EXPIRED, EXTINCT, DECEASED, LIFELESS, COMPLETE, OBSOLETE, DEPARTED, INANIMATE

deaden: . . . . . DULL, NUMB, MUTE, STUN, BLUNT, DAMPEN, OBTUND, MUFFLE, WEAKEN

deadline: . . . LIMIT, BOUNDRY

deadlock: . . . . . . TIE, DRAW, IMPASSE, STALEMATE, STANDSTILL

deadly: . . . . . . DIRE, FATAL, MORTAL, LETHAL, RUINOUS, VIRULENT, PERNICIOUS

deal: . . . DOLE, SALE, ALLOT, SHARE, TRADE, BESTOW, HANDLE, BARGAIN, INFLICT, DISPENSE, DISTRIBUTE, APPORTION, ADMINISTER, NEGOTIATE

dealer: . . . . . AGENT, BUYER, SELLER, TRADER, BROKER, JOBBER, MANAGER, CHAPMAN, MERCHANT, MIDDLEMAN, DISTRIBUTOR

dear: . . . . COSTLY, BELOVED, DARLING, EXPENSIVE, PRECIOUS

dearth: . . . . . . LACK, WANT, PAUCITY, FAMINE, SCARCITY, DEFICIENCY

death: . . . END, DOOM, MORT, DEMISE, PASSING, MURDER, DECEASE, DEPARTURE, EXPIRATION

mercy: . . . . . EUTHANASIA

put to: . . . . . KILL, HANG, SLAY, CHOKE, MURDER, STIFLE, POISON, GAROTTE, STRANGLE, SUFFOCATE, ASSASSINATE, ELECTROCUTE

debacle: . . . ROUT, DISASTER, FAILURE, COLLAPSE, BREAKDOWN, CATACLYSM

debar: . . . . . . DENY, ESTOP, FORBID, REFUSE, HINDER,

EXCLUDE, DEPRIVE, PREVENT, SUSPEND, DISQUALIFY

debase: ..... ALLOY, LOWER, DEFILE, DEMEAN, REVILE, VILIFY, CORRUPT, DEGRADE, PERVERT, VITIATE, ADULTERATE

debate: ... ARGUE, REASON, DISPUTE, CANVASS, CONTEND, CONTEST, DISCUSS, PALAVER, CONTENTION

debauch: .... ORGY, DEBASE, DEFILE, SEDUCE, VILIFY, CORRUPT, DEPRAVE, POLLUTE, VIOLATE, CONTAMINATE

debilitate: ...... WEAKEN, ENFEEBLE, ENERVATE

debilitated: .... WEAK, RUN-DOWN

debonair: .... GAY, POLITE, SUAVE, URBANE, GRACIOUS

debris: ..... TRASH, WASTE, LITTER, REFUSE, RUBBLE, RUBBISH, DETRITUS

debt: ... ACCOUNT LIABILITY, ARREARAGE, OBLIGATION

debut: . OPENING, ENTRANCE, BEGINNING, INTRODUCTION, PRESENTATION

decade: .... TEN, DECENNIUM

decadence: .... DECAY, DECLINE, RETROGRESSION, DETERIORATION

decapitate: .... BEHEAD

decapod: ..... CRAB, SQUID, SHRIMP, PRAWN, LOBSTER, CRUSTACEAN

decay: .... ROT, FADE, FAIL, RUIN, SPOIL, WASTE, CARIES, WITHER, DECLINE, MOLDER, PUTREFY, DECOMPOSE, GANGRENE, DECADENCE

decease: ...... DIE, DEATH, DEMISE, DEPARTURE, DISSOLUTION

deceit: ...... see **deception**

deceitful: ...... WILY, FALSE, TRICKY, CRAFTY, INSINCERE, DISHONEST, DECEPTIVE

deceive: .... CON, LIE, BILK, DUPE, FOOL, GULL, HOAX, JILT,

BLUFF, CHEAT, COZEN, DODGE, TRICK, SPOOF, BAFFLE, BETRAY, DELUDE, HUMBUG, BEGUILE, DEFRAUD, MISLEAD, HOODWINK, BAMBOOZLE, DOUBLECROSS

decency: .... PROPRIETY, DECORUM

decennium: .... DECADE

decent: ...... FAIR, CHASTE, MODEST, HONEST, PROPER, DECOROUS, RESPECTABLE, APPROPRIATE

deception: ...... LIE, RUSE, SHAM, CHEAT, FRAUD, HOAX, GUILE, MAGIC, TRICK, DECEIT, HUMBUG, EVASION, ARTIFICE, INTRIGUE, TRICKERY, IMPOSTURE, CHICANERY, DUPLICITY, FALSEHOOD, CAMOUFLAGE, COUNTERFEIT, DECEITFULNESS

decide: ..... JUDGE, SETTLE, RESOLVE, CONCLUDE

decimate: .... DESTROY, MASSACRE, SLAUGHTER

decision: ..... END, DECREE, RULING, VERDICT, JUDGMENT, SENTENCE, CONCLUSION, RESOLUTION, DETERMINATION

declaim: ...... RAVE, RANT, ORATE, SPOUT, ELOCUTE, RECITE, PERORATE, HARANGUE

declaration: ..... ASSERTION, STATEMENT, ALLEGATION, ANNOUNCEMENT, PROCLAMATION

declare: ... BID, SAY, AVER, STATE, ASSERT, ALLEGE, PROFESS, ANNOUNCE, MAINTAIN, PROCLAIM

decline: ..... DIP, EBB, FADE, FAIL, SINK, WANE, DROOP, LOWER, SLOPE, SLUMP, ABATE, REFUSE, REJECT, SPURN, DESCENT, DWINDLE, DECREASE, DETERIORATE

decoct: . . BOIL, COOK, SMELT, REFINE, EXTRACT, DISTILL, CONDENSE

decode: . . . . DECIPHER

decompose: . . . . ROT, DECAY, PUTREFY, SPOIL

decorate: . . . . . DECK, TRIM, DRESS, ADORN, FESTOON, GARNISH, EMBELLISH

decoration: . . . . MEDAL, GARNISH, ADORNMENT, TRIMMING, ORNAMENT

decorous: . . . . CALM, GOOD, PRIM, PROPER, DEMURE, MODEST, DIGNIFIED, APPROPRIATE

decorum: . . . . DECENCY, PROPRIETY, DIGNITY

decoy: . BAIT, LURE, ALLURE, ENTICE, PLANT, BLIND

decrease: . . . . . . EBB, FALL, WANE, ABATE, LESSEN, REDUCE, TAPER, SHRINK, DECLINE, DWINDLE, SUBSIDE, DIMINISH, MODERATE

decree: . . . . ACT, LAW, FIAT, RULE, CANON, EDICT, ORDER, ARRET, DECISION, FIRMAN, ORDAIN, MANDATE, STATUTE

decrepit: . . . . . . OLD, WEAK, LAME, FEEBLE, WORN, INFIRM, INVALID

decry: . . . ASPERSE, CENSURE, CONDEMN, BELITTLE, DISPARAGE, DISCREDIT, DENOUNCE

dedicate: . . . APPLY, DEVOTE, HALLOW, INSCRIBE, CONSECRATE

deduce: . . . . . INFER, TRACE, DERIVE, GATHER, CONCLUDE

deduct: . . . . . . DOCK, TAKE, REMOVE, DISCOUNT, SUBTRACT

deed: . . . . . ACT, FEAT, GEST, TITLE, CONVEY, CHARTER, ACTION, EXPLOIT

deem: . . . . . . JUDGE, THINK, RECKON, SURMISE, BELIEVE, CONSIDER

deep: . . WISE, ABYSS, GRUFF, OCEAN, ABSTRUSE, INTENSE, SERIOUS, PROFOUND

deer: . . . RED, ROE, ANIMAL, CERVID, FALLOW, BLACKTAIL, WHITETAIL, BARKING, RUMINANT

American: . . . ELK, WAPITI, MOOSE, CARIBOU

antler: . . . . DAG, TAG

female: . . . . DOE, HIND

male: . . . . . . BUCK, STAG, HART, ROEBUCK

tail: . . . . . . FLAG, SCUT

deface: . . . MAR, RUIN, SCAR, SPOIL, DAMAGE, MUTILATE, DISFIGURE

defame: . . . . . ABASE, LIBEL, SMEAR, ACCUSE, MALIGN, VILIFY, BLACKEN, SLANDER, CALUMNIATE

default: . . . . . FAIL, WELSH, FORFEIT, FAILURE, MISTAKE, NEGLECT

defeat: . . . WIN, BEAT, BEST, FOIL, LICK, LOSS, ROUT, WHIP, WORST, CONQUER, CLOBBER, OVERCOME, REVERSE, TROUNCE

defect: . . . BUG, FLEE, FLAW, LACK, FAULT, DAMAGE, DESERT, BLEMISH, FAILING, SHORTCOMING IMPERFECTION

defective: . . . . BAD, FAULTY, FLAWED, DEFICIENT, IMPERFECT

defend: . . . . FEND, HOLD, GUARD, SECURE, JUSTIFY, SHIELD, PROTECT

defendant: . . . . . . ACCUSED, CULPRIT, APPELLEE

defender: . . . . . . CHAMPION, PROTECTOR, ADVOCATE

defense: . . . . . . EGIS, ALIBI, ANSWER, BULWARK, SHELTER, SAFEGUARD, JUSTIFICATION, PROTECTION

defendant's: . . . . ALIBI

kind of: . . . . ORAL, LEGAL, ATTACK

means of: . . . . . . ARMOR, ABATIS, SPINE, SHELL,

PALISADE, SMOKESCREEN, BARRICADE, MUNIMENT

defensible: ...... TENABLE, EXCUSABLE, JUSTIFIABLE

defer: .. WAIT, DELAY, YIELD, RETARD, SHELVE, SUBMIT, POSTPONE

deference: .... REGARD, RESPECT, YIELDING, OBEISANCE

defiant: ..... BOLD, BRAVE, INSOLENT, CHALLENGING, BELLIGERENT

deficiency: ... LACK, WANT, DEFECT, DEFICIT, BLEMISH, FAILING, SCARCITY, SHORTAGE

defile: ... PASS, SOIL, ABUSE, SMEAR, SULLY, DIRTY, TAINT, POLLUTE, CORRUPT, PASSAGE, VALLEY, DESECRATE

define: .. FIX, BOUND, LIMIT, CLARIFY, OUTLINE, EXPLAIN, DEMARCATE

definite: ..... SURE, CLEAR, FINAL, FIXED, CERTAIN, PRECISE, EXPLICIT, POSITIVE, DECISIVE, CONCLUSIVE

deflect: .. BEND, TURN, WARP, PARRY, SWERVE, DIVERT

defraud: ... GYP, BILK, FAKE, CHEAT, COZEN, TRICK, DECEIVE, SWINDLE

deft: .... APT, AGILE, HANDY, ADROIT, CLEVER, EXPERT, SKILLFUL, DEXTEROUS

defy: .. DARE, FACE, BRAVE, REJECT, RESIST, OPPOSE, CHALLENGE

degrade: .... ABASE, LOWER, SHAME, DEBASE, HUMBLE, DEMEAN, VILFY, HUMILIATE, DEPRECIATE

degree: .. HEAT, RANK, RATE, STEP, CLASS, GRADE, HONOR, PITCH, POINT, STAGE, EXTENT, MEASURE, STANDING, GRADATION

deign: ... STOOP, CONDESCEND

deity: .... GOD, DEVA, CREATOR, DEMIGOD, ALMIGHTY, DIVINITY

dejected: .. LOW, SAD, GLUM, GLOOMY, UNHAPPY, WRETCHED, DOWNCAST, CRESTFALLEN, DEPRESSED, DESPONDENT, DOWNHEARTED

delay: .... LAG, WAIT, SLOW, CHECK, DALLY, DEFER, DETER, STALL, TARRY, ARREST, HINDER, IMPEDE, DETAIN, RETARD, LINGER, HESITATE, OBSTRUCT, PROCRASTINATE

delectable: ...... TASTY, PLEASING, DELICIOUS, DELIGHTFUL

delegate: ..... NAME, SEND, ENVOY, ASSIGN, DEPUTE, LEGATE, APPOINT, EMPOWER, DEPUTY, EMISSARY, TRANSFER, AUTHORIZE, REPRESENTATIVE

delete: ...... OMIT, PURGE, ERASE, EXPUNGE, REMOVE, ELIMINATE, ERADICATE

deleterious: .... BAD, HARMFUL, DAMAGING, INJURIOUS, PERNICIOUS, DETRIMENTAL

deliberate: ... SLOW, THINK, ADVISE, DEBATE, STUDY, PONDER, REFLECT, CONSIDER, MEDITATE, PREMEDITATED, UNHURRIED, INTENTIONAL

delicate: ...... FINE, FRAIL, LIGHT, DAINTY, TENDER, PETITE, EXQUISITE, FRAGILE, SUBTLE, TICKLISH, SENSITIVE

delicious: . TASTY, LUSCIOUS, DELIGHTFUL, DELECTABLE, AMBROSIAL, APPETIZING

delight: ... JOY, GLEE, LOVE, MIRTH, LIKING, PLEASE, ECSTASY, ENCHANT, GRATIFY, PLEASURE, ENJOYMENT

delineate: ..... MAP, DRAW, TRACE, DEPICT, SKETCH, OUTLINE, PORTRAY, DESCRIBE

delinquency: . . . . GUILT, MISDEED, FAILURE, OFFENSE, OMISSION, VIOLATION, MISCONDUCT

delirious: . . . . MAD, MANIC, INSANE, RAVING, DERANGED, FRENETIC

delirium: . . MANIA, FRENZY, HALLUCINATION

delitescent: . . . . LATENT, HIDDEN, INACTIVE

deliver: . . . . RID, DEAL, FREE, SAVE, SPEAK, UTTER, CONVEY, RESCUE, PRESENT, RELEASE, DISPATCH, TRANSFER, DISTRIBUTE

delivery: . . . . RESCUE, TRANSFER, SHIPMENT, DISTRIBUTION, CHILDBIRTH, UTTERANCE, PARTURITION

delude: . . . . DUPE, FOOL, CHEAT, TRICK, MISLEAD, BEGUILE, DECEIVE, HOODWINK

deluge: . . . . . FLOOD, SWAMP, INUNDATE, CATACLYSM

delusion: . . . . TRICK, VISION, MIRAGE, ILLUSION, PARANOIA, HALLUCINATION

delve: . . . . DIG, MINE, PROBE, SEARCH, FATHOM, INVESTIGATE

demand: . . . ASK, CRY, NEED, CLAIM, EXACT, ORDER, COMMAND, ULTIMATUM

demarcate: . . . . . . DELIMIT, SEPARATE

demean: . . . . ABASE, LOWER, DEGRADE, HUMBLE, MALTREAT

demeanor: . . MIEN, ACTION, MANNER, CONDUCT, BEARING, BEHAVIOR, CARRIAGE, DEPORTMENT

demented: . . . . . MAD, LUNY, NUTTY, CRAZY, INSANE

demesne: . . REALM, REGION, DOMAIN

demolish: . . . . . RAZE, RUIN, LEVEL, WRECK, DESTROY, DEVASTATE

demon: . . . . IMP, NAT, OGRE, DEVIL, FIEND, GHOUL, GENIE, SATAN

demoniac: . . . . DEVILISH, LUNATIC, DIABOLIC, FIENDISH

demoralize: . . . . . . CONFUSE, WEAKEN, CORRUPT, PERVERT, UNDERMINE, DISCOURAGE, DISHEARTEN

demote: . . . BUST, DEGRADE, LOWER, REDUCE

demur: . . . . . DELAY, DOUBT, OBJECT, HESITATE, PROTEST

demure: . . . COY, SHY, PRIM, STAID, SEDATE, MODEST, DECOROUS

demurrer: . . . . . . OBJECTION, OBJECTOR

den: . . . . . CAVE, DIVE, HOLE, LAIR, ROOM, STUDY, HAUNT, RETREAT, HANGOUT, HIDEOUT

denial: . . . . REFUSAL, ABSTINENCE, REPUDIATION

denigrate: . . DEFAME, VILIFY, BLACKEN

denizen: . . . NATIVE, CITIZEN, RESIDENT, OCCUPANT, INHABITANT

denominate: . . CALL, NAME, TITLE, INDICATE

denomination: . . CULT, SECT, CLASS, APPELLATION

denote: . . . . . . MARK, MEAN, NAME, CONNOTE, INDICATE, SIGNIFY, DESIGNATE

denounce: . . ASSAIL, ACCUSE, DESCRY, EXCORIATE, CONDEMN, CRITICIZE

dense: . . . . . . CLOSE, HEAVY, MURKY, SOLID, THICK, STUPID, OBTUSE, CROWDED, COMPACT, PACKED, POPULOUS

denture: . . . . PLATE, TEETH, BRIDGE

denude: . . . . . . BARE, STRIP, DIVEST

denunciation: . . . . THREAT, DIATRIBE, ACCUSATION

deny: . . . . . DEBAR, NEGATE, ABJURE, DISOWN, FORBID,

REFUTE, REJECT, REFUSE,
DISAVOW, DEPRIVE, WITHOLD,
REPUDIATE, FORSWEAR
depart: . . . . . GO, DIE, QUIT,
VARY, LEAVE, DECAMP, PERISH,
RETIRE, ABSCOND, WITHDRAW
departure: . . . EXIT, DEATH,
EGRESS, EXODUS, LEAVING,
DEVIATION
depend: . RELY, BANK, REST,
COUNT, TRUST, CONFIDE
dependable: . . . . . CERTAIN,
RELIABLE, TRUSTWORTHY
dependent: . . WARD, CLIENT,
SUBJECT, FOLLOWER,
CONTINGENT, SUBORDINATE
depict: . . . . DRAW, PICTURE,
PAINT, PORTRAY, DESCRIBE,
DELINEATE
deplete: . . . . DRAIN, EMPTY,
EXHAUST
deplorable: . . . . . . GRIEVOUS
deplore: . . . . . . RUE, MOAN,
LAMENT, BEWAIL, COMPLAIN
deport: . . . . . . EXPEL, EXILE,
BANISH, BEHAVE, TRANSPORT
deportment: . . . . . MANNER,
BEHAVIOR, DEMEANOR,
BEARING, CONDUCT
depose: . . . . . OUST, DEPONE,
TESTIFY, REMOVE, ASSERT,
DETHRONE
deposition: . . . . BURIAL,
DEPOSIT, TESTIMONY,
STATEMENT, AFFIDAVIT,
ALLEGATION
depot: . . . . . . BASE, STATION,
TERMINAL, MAGAZINE,
STOREHOUSE, WAREHOUSE
deprave: . . . DEBASE, DEFILE,
CORRUPT, PERVERT, DEBAUCH
depraved: . . . . . . EVIL, VILE,
WICKED, IMMORAL, CORRUPT,
DISSOLUTE
depreciate: . . . FALL, ABASE,
SLUMP, LESSEN, SHRINK,
DEPRESS, BELITTLE, DISPARAGE
depredate: . . . . . ROB, PREY,
DESTROY, PLUNDER, PILLAGE

depress: . . . . . . FALL, SINK,
ABASE, SADDEN, LOWER,
SLUMP, DIMINISH, DAMPEN,
DISHEARTEN
depressed: . . . SAD, GLOOMY,
DEJECTED, DOWNCAST,
DOWNHEARTED
depression: . . . DENT, BASIN,
CRATER, SADNESS, DEJECTION,
RECESSION
deprive: . . . BAR, ROB, DENY,
DEBAR, STRIP, DIVEST,
DISPOSSESS
deputation: . . . . DELEGATION
depute: . . . . . . SEND, ALLOT,
APPOINT, DELEGATE
deputy: . . . . . . AIDE, AGENT,
ENVOY, PROXY, VICAR,
LEGATE, BALIFF, DELEGATE,
SURROGATE, SUBSTITUTE
derange: . . . UPSET, DISTURB,
PERTURB, UNSETTLE, DISORDER,
INTERRUPT, DISARRANGE
deranged: . . . CRAZY, INSANE,
DISTRAUGHT, UNBALANCED
derby: . . . HAT, RACE, SHIRE,
BOWLER
derelict: . . . . . REMISS, TRAMP,
WRECK, FAILURE, CASTAWAY,
ABANDONED, NEGLECTFUL
deride: . . . JEER, MOCK, GIBE,
SCORN, SCOFF, TAUNT,
RIDICULE
derive: . . . GET, DRAW, STEM,
INFER, TRACE, DEDUCE,
EVOLVE, ORIGINATE
derogate: . . . DECRY, LESSEN,
REPEAL, DETRACT, SLANDER,
DISPARAGE, DEPRECIATE
derrick: . . RIG, HOIST, DAVIT,
LIFT, BOOM, SPAR
descant: . . . . SING, MELODY,
COMMENT, ACCOMPANIMENT
descendant: . . . HEIR, CHILD,
SCION, OFFSPRING, PROGENY
female: . . . . . . DAUGHTER
male: . . . . SON
descent: . . . . . FALL, BIRTH,
SLOPE, ORIGIN, DECLINE,

LINEAGE, PEDIGREE, DERIVATION, EXTRACTION

describe: . . . . . TELL, DEFINE, DEPICT, REPORT, EXPLAIN, PICTURE, PORTRAY, RECOUNT, CHARACTERIZE

descry: . . . . SEE, SIGHT, BEHOLD, BETRAY, DETECT, REVEAL, DENOUNCE, DISCLOSE

desecrate: . . DEFILE, VIOLATE, POLLUTE, PROFANE

desert: . . . ARID, FLEE, QUIT, SAND, LEAVE, WASTE, BARREN, ABANDON, DEMERIT, FORSAKE, DESOLATE, WILDERNESS

deserted: . . . . LONELY, FORLORN, DESOLATE, FORSAKEN, ABANDONED, UNINHABITED

deserter: . . . RAT, RENEGADE, BOLTER, TURNCOAT, APOSTATE, RUNAWAY, FUGITIVE

deserve: . . . . . . EARN, MERIT

desiccate: . . . . . . DRY, ARID

design: . . . AIM, END, DRAW, GOAL, IDEA, PLAN, PLOT, DECOR, MOTIF, INTENT, LAYOUT, PATTERN, CONTRIVE, PURPOSE, SCHEME

designate: . . . . MARK, NAME, LABEL, DENOTE, ASSIGN, ENTITLE, SPECIFY, INDICATE, APPOINT

designing: . . . . ARTFUL, CRAFTY, CUNNING, SCHEMING

desire: . . . . YEN, ITCH, LUST, WILL, WANT, WISH, ARDOR, COVET, CRAVE, ASPIRE, HUNGER, THIRST, LONGING, PASSION

desist: . . . . HALT, QUIT, STOP, CEASE, ABSTAIN, FORBEAR, DISCONTINUE

desolate: . . SAD, BARE, RUIN, ALONE, BLEAK, LONELY, DREARY, DESTROY, SOLITARY, DESERTED, DESTITUTE, UNINHABITED, (FOR)LORN, FORSAKEN

despair: . . . GLOOM, MISERY, DESPERATION, DESPONDENCY, HOPELESSNESS

desperate: . . . . . MAD, RASH, FRANTIC, HOPELESS, RECKLESS, DANGEROUS, DESPAIRING

despicable: . . . . BASE, VILE, DIRTY, ABJECT, SORDID, PITIFUL, CONTEMPTIBLE

despise: . . . . . HATE, ABHOR, SCORN, DISDAIN, DETEST, LOATHE, CONTEMN

despoil: . . . . ROB, RUIN, RAID, LOOT, RAVAGE, RAVISH, PILLAGE, PLUNDER

despondency: . . . . . MISERY, DESPAIR, DEJECTION, DEPRESSION

despot: . . . . CZAR, TSAR, AUTOCRAT, DICTATOR, TYRANT

destiny: . . LOT, FATE, DOOM, KARMA, KISMET, FORTUNE

destitute: . . . . POOR, NEEDY, BEREFT, DEVOID, LACKING, BANKRUPT, INDIGENT

destitution: . . . . NEED, POVERTY, PENURY

destroy: . . . END, GUT, RAZE, RUIN, SACK, SLAY, ERASE, SMASH, WASTE, WRECK, ERADICATE, RAVAGE, OBLITERATE, EXTERMINATE

destruction: . . . END, HAVOC, RUIN, WASTE, WRACK, WRECK, WRECKAGE, HOLOCAUST, VANDALISM, SLAUGHTER, MASSACRE, DECIMATION

desultory: . . . IDLE, AIMLESS, RANDOM, HAPHAZARD

detach: . . . . . SEVER, DISJOIN, DISUNITE, SEPARATE, UNFASTEN, DISENGAGE

detached: . . . . FREE, ALONE, ALOOF, SEPARATE, INDIFFERENT

detail: . . . . . . ITEM, RELATE, ARTICLE, NARRATE, SPECIFY, PARTICULAR, ASSIGN(MENT)

detain: ... HOLD, KEEP, STOP, CHECK, DELAY, ARREST, RETARD, CONFINE

detect: ..... SEE, SPY, ESPY, SPOT, DESCRY, EXPOSE, DISCERN, UNCOVER, DISCOVER

detective: .. TEC, BULL, DICK, SLEUTH, SPOTTER, OPERATIVE, HAWKSHAW, GUMSHOE

deter: .. BAR, BLOCK, CHECK, DELAY, HINDER, RETARD, PREVENT, RESTRAIN, DISCOURAGE, INTIMIDATE

deteriorate: .. WEAR, DEBASE, DECAY, DECLINE, PERVERT, CORRUPT, WORSEN, DEPRECIATE

determinate: ...... FIXED, CERTAIN, DEFINITE, SPECIFIC, RESOLUTE

determine: ..... FIX, TEST, AWARD, JUDGE, ASSESS, ASSIGN, DECIDE, DEFINE, SETTLE, ANALYZE, ARRANGE, RESOLVE, CONCLUDE, ASCERTAIN, ADJUDICATE

determined: .... SET, FIRM, INTENT, DECIDED, SETTLED, RESOLUTE, RESOLVED, STUBBORN, OBSTINATE, PERSISTENT

detest: ...... HATE, ABHOR, DISLIKE, DISPISE, LOATHE, EXECRATE

detestable: .. FOUL, HORRID, ODIOUS, HATEFUL, EXECRABLE

detonate: ..... FIRE, BLAST, EXPLODE, FULMINATE

detour: ..... TURN, DIVERT, BYPASS, DEVIATION

detract: ... DECRY, DEFAME, DIVERT, VILLIFY, BELITTLE, DEROGATE, DISPARAGE, DEPRECIATE

detriment: ..... COST, HURT, LOSS, HARM, INJURY, DAMAGE

devastate: ..... RAZE, SACK, LEVEL, WASTE, RAVAGE, DESTROY, SCOURGE, DEMOLISH

develop: ..... FORM, GROW, RIPEN, APPEAR, EVOLVE, FLOWER, REVEAL, ENLARGE, EDUCATE, GENERATE, ELABORATE

deviate: .. ERR, YAW, VARY, VEER, LAPSE, SHEER, STRAY, DEPART, DETOUR, SWERVE, DIGRESS, DIVERGE

device: .. GIN, TOOL, METER, MOTTO, TRICK, DESIGN, EMBLEM, GADGET, SCHEME, FICTION, PROJECT, VEHICLE, ARTIFICE, GIMMICK, GIMCRACK, APPARATUS, APPLIANCE, DOOHICKEY, INVENTION, CONTRIVANCE

devil: ... IMP, BRAT, ANNOY, DEMON, FIEND, SATAN, TEASE, DIABLO, PESTER, GREMLIN, DICKENS, TORMENT, WARLOCK, MEPHISTO, LUCIFER, BEELZEBUB

devious: ... SHIFTY, TRICKY, VAGRANT, INDIRECT, CROOKED, WINDING, CIRCUITOUS, TORTUOUS, ROUNDABOUT

devise: ... PLAN, PLOT, WILL, GIFT, INVENT, CONVEY, CONCOCT, SCHEME, CONTRIVE, FABRICATE

devoid: .... EMPTY, BARREN, VACANT, LACKING, DESTITUTE

devote: .. ALLY, GIVE, APPLY, ATTACH, CONSIGN, CONSECRATE, DEDICATE

devoted: ..... TRUE, PIOUS, DEVOUT, LOYAL, FAITHFUL

devotion: .... ZEAL, ARDOR, PIETY, FEALTY, LOYALTY, FIDELITY

devour: ..... EAT, CONSUME, ENGORGE, DESTROY

devout: ...... HOLY, PIOUS, GODLY, DEVOTED, SINCERE, REVERENT, RELIGIOUS, SPIRITUAL

dexterity: ... KNACK, SKILL, ABILITY, AGILITY, APTNESS,

DEFTNESS, ADROITNESS,
CLEVERNESS

dextrose: ... SUGAR, GLUCOSE

diabolic: ... CRUEL, WICKED,
DEMONIC, INHUMAN, SATANIC,
DEVILISH, FIENDISH, INFERNAL

diadem: ... CROWN, TIARA,
CORONET, HEADBAND

diagnose: .... ANALYZE,
IDENTIFY

diagonal: ... BIAS, OBLIQUE,
SLANTING

diagram: .. MAP, PLAN, PLOT,
CHART, GRAPH, DESIGN,
SKETCH, DRAWING, SCHEMA,
SCHEME

dialect: ...... CANT, ARGOT,
IDIOM, LINGO, SLANG, BROGUE,
PATOIS, SPEECH, JARGON,
VERNACULAR

diameter: .... BORE, WIDTH

diamond: .. GEM, ICE, ROCK,
FIELD, JEWEL, STONE,
LOZENGE, PLAYGROUND

diaphanous: .. THIN, SHEER,
TRANSPARENT, TRANSLUCENT

diary: ...... LOG, RECORD,
REGISTER, JOURNAL, DAYBOOK,
EPHEMERIS

diatribe: .... TIRADE,
HARANGUE, PHILIPPIC,
DENUNCIATION

dice: ..... CUT, CHOP, CUBE,
IVORY, CRAP, CHECKER

dicker: ..... SWAP, HAGGLE,
BARTER, BARGAIN

dictate: .. BID, TELL, IMPOSE,
ORDER, REQUIRE, COMMAND

dictatorial: ...... BOSSY,
ARROGANT, DOGMATIC,
DESPOTIC, IMPERIOUS,
ARBITRARY

diction: ...... ENUNCIATION

dictionary: ...... LEXICON,
WORDBOOK, VOCABULARY,
THESAURUS

dictum: ..... ADAGE, AXIOM,
EDICT, SAYING, STATEMENT

didactic: .... PEDANTIC

dido: . ANTIC, CAPER, PRANK,
TRICK

die: .... DICE, FADE, MOLD,
WANE, STAMP, CROAK, EXPIRE,
DECEASE, PERISH, SUCCUMB,
MATRIX

diet: ..... FARE, FAST, FOOD,
REDUCE, REGIMEN, ASSEMBLY,
LEGISLATURE

difference: . CLASH, CHANGE,
DISPUTE, QUARREL, VARIANCE,
DISSENSION, DISCREPANCY,
DISAGREEMENT

different: ..... ELSE, MANY,
OTHER, SUNDRY, UNLIKE,
DIVERSE, SEVERAL, VARIOUS,
SEPARATE, DIVERGENT,
DISSIMILAR, DIVERSIFIED

difficult: ... HARD, ARDUOUS,
LABORED, OBSCURE, PAINFUL,
ABSTRACT, PUZZLING,
STUBBORN, INTRICATE,
COMPLICATED, TROUBLESOME

difficulty: ... BAR, FIX, JAM,
CLOG, SNAG, PICKLE, PLIGHT,
SCRAPE, STRAIT, PROBLEM,
OBSTACLE, HARDSHIP,
TROUBLE, IMPEDIMENT

diffident: .. COY, SHY, TIMID,
MODEST, RESERVED

diffuse: .... DIVIDE, EXPAND,
EXTEND, SPREAD, VERBOSE,
SCATTER, RADIATE, DISPERSE,
PUBLISH, PERMEATE,
PROPAGATE

dig: .... CLAW, GRUB, MINE,
POKE, ROOT, DELVE, GOUGE,
SCOOP, SPADE, BURROW,
EXHUME, EXCAVATE, UNEARTH

digest: . ABSTRACT, EPITOME,
SUMMARY, SYNOPSIS,
ASSIMILATE, ABRIDGMENT

digit: ... TOE, UNIT, FINGER,
CIPHER, NUMBER, INTEGER

dignified: ... GRAND, NOBLE,
STAID, STATELY, SEDATE,
DECOROUS

dignify: ..... EXALT, HONOR,
ENNOBLE, ELEVATE

dignity: . . . . . HONOR, PRIDE, MAJESTY, NOBILITY, STATELINESS, DECORUM

digress: . . . . . VEER, SWERVE, RAMBLE, DEVIATE, DIVAGATE

dike, dyke: . . . . DAM, BANK, DITCH, LEVEE, CAUSEWAY, EMBANKMENT

dilapidated: . . . . RUINED, DECAYED, RAMSHACKLE, RUN-DOWN

dilate: . . . . . . SWELL, WIDEN, DISTEND, ENLARGE, INFLATE, INCREASE

dilatory: . . . . SLOW, TARDY, REMISS, DELAYING

dilemma: . . . . FIX, QUANDRY, PREDICAMENT

diligence: . . . HEED, EFFORT, CAUTION, APPLICATION, INDUSTRY, PERSEVERANCE

diligent: . . . . BUSY, ACTIVE, CAREFUL, EARNEST, CAUTIOUS, SEDULOUS, HARDWORKING

dilute: . . . . . . THIN, WATER, REDUCE, WEAKEN, ATTENUATE

dim: . . . . BLUR, DARK, DULL, HAZY, VAGUE, FAINT, UNCLEAR, OBSCURE, MURKY

dimension: . . . BULK, SIZE, EXTENT, SCOPE, BREADTH, MEASUREMENT

diminish: . . . . . . EBB, EASE, WANE, ABATE, LOWER, PETER, TAPER, REDUCE, LESSEN, DEPLETE, CURTAIL, DECREASE, ALLEVIATE

din: . . . . NOISE, UPROAR, CLAMOUR, RACKET

dingle: . . . . . . RING, QUIVER, TINGLE, THRILL, VIBRATE

dingy: . . . . DARK, DIRTY, GRIMY, DISMAL, SHABBY

diocese: . . . . SEE, DISTRICT, BISHOPRIC

dip: . . . . BAIL, DUNK, LADE, DELVE, LADLE, IMMERSE, CANDLE, PLUNGE, SUBMERGE

diploma: . . . . DEGREE, CHARTER, CERTIFICATE

diplomate: . . . . ENVOY, CONSUL, ATTACHE, NUNCIO, LEGATE, MINISTER, AMBASSADOR

diplomatic: . . . . POLITIC, TACTFUL, ARTFUL

dipper: . . . . . . SCOOP, LADLE

dipsomaniac: . . . SOT, TOPER, ALCHOHOLIC, DRUNKARD

dire: . . . EVIL, AWFUL, FATAL, DISMAL, TRAGIC, DRASTIC, FEARFUL, TERRIBLE, DREADFUL, HORRIBLE

direct: . . . AIM, BOSS, EVEN, FLAT, HEAD, HELM, LEAD, APPLY, COACH, FRANK, GUIDE, ORDER, STEER, TEACH, TRAIN, GOVERN, ADMINISTER, STRAIGHT, CONDUCT, MANAGE

direction: . . . . . WAY, ROAD, RULE, ORDER, ROUTE, TREND, COURSE, BEARING, COMMAND, CONTROL, GUIDANCE, MANAGEMENT

directive: . . . . ORDER, INSTRUCTION

directly: . . SOON, PROMPTLY, INSTANTLY, IMMEDIATELY

director: . . . . . . BOSS, HEAD, GUIDE, LEADER, CONDUCTOR, SUPERVISOR, MANAGER

dirk: . . . . . . SNEE, DAGGER, PONIARD, SWORD

dirt: . . . . MUD, DUST, MUCK, SOIL, EARTH, FILTH, GRIME, GROUND

dirty: . . FOUL, DINGY, GRIMY, SULLY, DEFILE, FILTHY, IMPURE, SORDID, SULLIED, UNCLEAN, OBSCENE, POLLUTE

disable: . . . . . . LAME, MAIM, WRECK, CRIPPLE, DISQUALIFY, HAMSTRING, INCAPACITATE

disadvantage: . . DRAWBACK, HANDICAP, DETRIMENT

disagreeable: . . . VILE, CROSS, NASTY, HATEFUL, TERRIBLE, OFFENSIVE, REPUGNANT, UNPLEASANT, DISTASTEFUL

disagreement: . . . . . CLASH, FIGHT, DISCORD, DISPUTE, DISSENT, VARIANCE, DIFFERENCE, QUARREL

disappear: . . . GO, PASS, FLY, FADE, FLEE, ESCAPE, VANISH, EVANESCE

disappoint: . . . FAIL, DELUDE, THWART, FRUSTRATE, LET DOWN, DISPLEASE

disapproval: . . . . REJECTION, DISLIKE

show of: . . . . . BOO, HISS, SNEER, SNORT, HOOT

disapprove: . . DENY, REJECT, PROTEST, DISALLOW, TURN DOWN, CONDEMN

disarrange: . . . MUSS, MIXUP, RUFFLE, CONFUSE, DISTURB, UNSETTLE, DISLOCATE

disaster: . . BLOW, EVIL, RUIN, ACCIDENT, CASUALTY, CALAMITY, MISFORTUNE, CATASTROPHE

disavow: . . . . DENY, ABJURE, DISCLAIM, RETRACT, DISOWN, REPUDIATE, RENOUNCE

disburse: . . . EXPEND, SPEND, DEFRAY, OUTLAY, DISTRIBUTE

discard: . . CAST, JILT, SCRAP, SHED, JUNK, DROP, CHUCK, SLUFF, DIVEST, ABANDON, ELIMINATE

discern: . . SEE, SPY, BEHOLD, DETECT, NOTICE, PERCEIVE, UNDERSTAND

discernment: . . FLAIR, TASTE, SENSE, INSIGHT, ACUMEN, APPRECIATION, PERCEPTION, UNDERSTANDING

discharge: . . . . . CAN, DUMP, EMIT, FIRE, FREE, POUR, SACK, EJECT, EMPTY, EXPEL, EXUDE, SHOOT, ACQUIT, BOUNCE, UNLOAD, CASHIER, DISMISS, EXHAUST, RELEASE, EVACUATE, EMISSION

discipline: . . . . WHIP, INURE, TEACH, TRAIN, GOVERN, PUNISH, CHASTEN, EDUCATE, CONTROL

disclaim: . . . . . . see **disavow**

disclose: . . BARE, OPEN, TELL, BETRAY, EXPOSE, REVEAL, DIVULGE

discomfit: . . CONFUSE, UPSET, DISCONCERT, JAR, EMBARRASS, ABASH, RUFFLE

discomfort: . . . . ACHE, PAIN, UNEASE, DISTURB, DISTRESS, EMBARRASS, UNEASINESS

discompose: . . . . UPSET, AGITATE, RUFFLE, CONFUSE, FLUSTER, PERTURB, UNSETTLE, DISTURB, DISCONCERT

disconcert: . . . FAZE, ABASH, UPSET, WORRY, RATTLE, CONFUSE, DISTURB, PERTURB, EMBARRASS, DISCOMPOSE

disconnect: . . . UNDO, SEVER, DISJOIN, UNCOUPLE, SEPARATE, DETACH

disconsolate: . . . . SAD, GLOOMY, FORLORN, DEJECTED

discontinue: . . . END, DROP, STOP, QUIT, HALT, CEASE, DESIST, SUSPEND

discord: . . . . . . DIN, CLASH, CONFLICT, DISSENSION, DISAGREEMENT

discount: . . . . AGIO, REBATE, REDUCE, SUBTRACT, ALLOWANCE, DEDUCT(ION)

discourage: . . DAUNT, DETER, DAMPEN, DEJECT, DEPRESS, DISSUADE, DISHEARTEN, DEMORALIZE

discourse: . . . . TALK, SPEAK, ORATE, EULOGY, HOMILY, PREACH, LECTURE, SERMON, DISCUSS, CONVERSE, TREATISE, DISSERT(ATION), CONVERSATION

discover: . . . . . . ESPY, FIND, LEARN, DETECT, DESCRY, INVENT, LOCATE, UNCOVER, UNEARTH

discreet: . . . WARY, PRUDENT, CAREFUL, POLITIC

discrete: . . . . SEPARATE, DISTINCT

discretion: . . . TACT, OPTION, PRUDENCE, JUDGMENT

discriminate: . . . . . . SECERN, DISTINGUISH, DEMARCATE, DIFFERENTIATE

discrimination: . . . . . TASTE, ACUMEN, DISCERNMENT, PERCEPTION

disdain: . . . SNEER, DESPISE, SCORN, SPURN, CONTEMPT

disease: . . ILLNESS, AILMENT, DISTRESS, SICKNESS, MALADY, DISORDER, PESTILENCE

agent: . . . . . GERM, VIRUS, MICROBE, BACILLUS, PATHOGEN, BACTERIUM, CONTAGIUM

disengage: . . . . FREE, CLEAR, UNTIE, DETACH, LOOSEN, RELEASE, UNFASTEN, EXTRICATE, DISENCUMBER, DISENTANGLE

disfigure: . . . . . MAR, BLUR, SCAR, DEFACE, DEFORM, INJURE, MANGLE, BLEMISH, MUTILATE

disgorge: . . . . . . SPEW, VENT, EJECT, VOMIT, EMPTY, DISCHARGE

disgrace: . . . . . . BLOT, SLUR, ABASE, CRIME, ODIUM, SHAME, STAIN, SCANDAL, SLANDER, INFAMY, IGNOMINY, OBLOQUY, DISHONOR

disguise: . . HIDE, MASK, VEIL, CLOAK, COVERT, MASQUE, CONCEAL, OBSCURE, PRETEND, DISSEMBLE, INCOGNITO, CAMOUFLAGE

disgust: . . . . . REPEL, SHOCK, NAUSEA, OFFEND, REVOLT, SICKEN, AVERSION, LOATHING, DISTASTE, REPUGNANCE

dish: . . . . . CUP, BOAT, BOWL, BASIN, PATEN, PLATE, VIAND, COURSE, SAUCER, TUREEN, ENTREE, COMPOTE, EPERGNE, PLATTER, RAMEKIN, SCUTTLE, CASSEROLE

dishearten: . . . . DAUNT, DAMPEN, DEJECT, DEPRESS, UNNERVE, DEMORALIZE, DISCOURAGE

dishevel: . . . . MUSS, TOUSLE, RUFFLE, RUMPLE, DISORDER, DISARRANGE

dishonest: . . . . . . LIE, LIAR, CHEAT, FALSE, CORRUPT, CROOKED, LYING, DECEITFUL, FRAUDULENT, PERFIDIOUS

dishonor: . . . ABASE, ABUSE, DEFAME, DEFILE, SHAME, VIOLATE, DISGRACE, DISCREDIT, DISPARAGE

disinclined: . . . . AVERSE, AGAINST, UNWILLING, RELUCTANT, INDISPOSED

disinfect: . . . . CLEANSE, STERILIZE, FUMIGATE

disingenuous: . . SLY, FALSE, INSINCERE

disintegrate: . . MELT, DECAY, ERODE, CRUMBLE, BREAKUP, DISSOLVE, SEPARATE, DECOMPOSE

disinterested: . . . APATHETIC, UNBIASED, IMPARTIAL, UNCONCERNED

disjoin: . . . . PART, UNDO, SEVER, DETACH, SUNDER, DISSOLVE, DISUNITE, SEPARATE, DISCONNECT

dislike: . . . . LOATH, DETEST, AVERSION, DISTASTE, ANTIPATHY, DISPLEASURE

disloyal: . . . FALSE, UNTRUE, FAITHLESS, INCONSTANT, PERFIDIOUS, UNFAITHFUL, TREACHEROUS

dismal: . . . SAD, DARK, DIRE, GLUM, BLACK, BLEAK, DREARY, GLOOMY, DINGY, JOYLESS, OMINOUS, UNHAPPY, CHEERLESS

dismay: . . . . . FEAR, ALARM, DAUNT, DREAD, TERRIFY,

DISCONCERT, ALARM, APPALL, FRIGHT, TERROR, ABASH, CONFOUND, DISCOURAGE, CONSTERNATION

dismiss: . . . CAN, BOOT, FIRE, OUST, SACK, CHUCK, EJECT, BANISH, BOUNCE, REJECT, REMOVE, CASHIER, DISBAND, DISCHARGE

disobedient: . . . . NAUGHTY, WAYWARD, MUTINOUS, REBELLIOUS, REFRACTORY, INTRACTABLE, INSUBORDINATE

disorder: . . . . . MESS, MUSS, RIOT, CHAOS, JUMBLE, LITTER, MALADY, MUDDLE, TUMULT, AILMENT, CLUTTER, DERANGE, DISTURB, ILLNESS, TROUBLE, DISARRAY, COMMOTION, CONFUSION, DISCOMPOSE, DISORGANIZE, DISTURBANCE

disown: . . . . . DENY, REJECT, DISAVOW, ABDICATE, DISCLAIM, RENOUNCE, REPUDIATE

disparage: . . . . SLUR, ABUSE, DECRY, SLIGHT, DEMEAN, DEGRADE, DETRACT, BELITTLE, DEROGATE, DISHONOR, MINIMIZE, DISCREDIT, DEPRECIATE

disparate: . . . . UNLIKE, SEPARATE, DIFFERENT, DISSIMILAR

dispatch: . . FREE, KILL, MAIL, NOTE, POST, SEND, HASTE, SPEED, DELIVER, DISPOSE, CELERITY, CONCLUDE, MESSAGE, EXPEDITE, ACCELERATE, PROMPTNESS

dispel: . . . BANISH, DISPERSE, SCATTER, DISSIPATE

dispensation: . . . . . . PLAN, SCHEME, ECONOMY, LICENSE, DISTRIBUTION, MANAGEMENT

dispense: . . . . . . DEAL, DOLE, EFFUSE, EXCUSE, EXEMPT, FOREGO, ABSOLVE, DISTRIBUTE

disperse: . . . . . ROUT, STREW, DISPEL, SPREAD, VANISH, DIFFUSE, SCATTER, DISTRIBUTE

display: . . . . . POMP, SHOW, SCENE, SPORT, STAGE, BLAZON, EXPOSE, FLAUNT, PARADE, REVEAL, EXHIBIT, PAGEANT, DISCLOSE, SPECTACLE, EXHIBITION, DEMONSTRATION

displease: . . . . . . VEX, MIFF, ANGER, ANNOY, PIQUE, OFFEND, PROVOKE, IRRITATE

dispose: . . . SET, MIND, SELL, BEND, PLACE, ADJUST, BESTOW, SETTLE, ARRANGE, PREPARE, DETERMINE, DISTRIBUTE, LIQUIDATE, POSIT

disposition: . . . . BEND, BIAS, MOOD, HEALTH, TEMPER, CONCEPT, ATTITUDE, DISPOSAL, POSTURE, MORALE, PROCLIVITY, TENDENCY, ARRANGEMENT

disprove: . . . REBUT, REFUTE, NEGATE, CONFUTE, EXPLODE, DISALLOW

disputable: . . MOOT, VAGUE, UNSURE, DUBIOUS, DOUBTFUL, UNCERTAIN, INDEFINITE

disputation: . . . . . . DEBATE, POLEMIC, DIALECTIC, ARGUMENT

dispute: . . DENY, FEUD, RIOT, SPAT, ARGUE, BRAWL, BROIL, CABAL, BICKER, DEBATE, DIFFER, HAGGLE, CONTEND, CONTEST, DISCUSS, GAINSAY, QUARREL, WRANGLE, ARGUMENT, QUESTION, SQUABBLE, CONTROVERSY, DISAGREEMENT

disquiet: . . . . VEX, FRET, EXCITE, UNREST, AGITATE, ANXIETY, DISTURB, TROUBLE, TURMOIL, UNEASINESS, RESTLESSNESS

disregard: . . . . OMIT, WAIVE, IGNORE, OVERRIDE, OVERRULE

disrespectful: . . . . RUDE, IMPOLITE, INSOLENT, IMPUDENT

dissemble: . . . . . HIDE, MASK, FEIGN, PRETEND, DISGUISE, SIMULATE

disseminate: . . SOW, STREW, SPREAD, PUBLISH, SCATTER, PROPAGATE, DISTRIBUTE, BROADCAST

dissent: . . . . . VARY, DIFFER, DISAGREE, PROTEST, EXCEPTION

dissertation: . . . . . . ESSAY, THESIS, TREATISE, DISCOURSE, LECTURE

dissipate: . . . SPEND, WASTE, DISPEL, SQUANDER, EXPEND, SCATTER, DISPERSE, EVAPORATE

dissolute: . . . . . LAX, LEWD, LOOSE, WANTON, IMMORAL, LAWLESS, DEBAUCHED, PROFLIGATE, LICENTIOUS

dissolve: . . . . . MELT, THAW, LIQUEFY, DISBAND, DISJOIN, SEPARATE

dissonant: . . . . HARSH, GRATING, DISCORDANT, INHARMONIOUS

dissuade: . . DEHORT, DETER, DIVERT, DISCOURAGE

distance: . . . . . SPAN, DEPTH, RANGE, SPACE, FARNESS, MILEAGE, INTERVAL, OUTSTRIP, REMOTENESS

distant: . . . . FAR, OFF, AFAR, AWAY, COLD, ALOOF, REMOTE, FARAWAY, REMOVED, SEPARATED

distaste: . . DISGUST, DISLIKE, AVERSION, DISPLEASURE

distend: . . . . BLOAT, SWELL, DILATE, EXPAND, STRETCH, INFLATE, ENLARGE

distinct: . . . . . CLEAR, PLAIN, VIVID, LEGIBLE, OBVIOUS, SPECIAL, APPARENT, DIFFERENT, SEPARATE, INDIVIDUAL

distinguish: . . . . DEFINE, DISCERN, SECERN, PERCEIVE, SEPARATE, DESIGNATE, DISCRIMINATE, DIFFERENTIATE

distort: . . . . . WARP, SCREW, TWIST, DEFACE, DEFORM, CONTORT, PERVERT, MISREPRESENT

distract: . . DIVERT, CONFUSE, BEMUSE, MADDEN, PUZZLE, HARASS, AGITATE, DISTURB, PERPLEX, BEWILDER, CONFOUND

distraught: . . MAD, CRAZED, FRANTIC, DERANGED, CONFUSED, HARASSED, DISTRACTED, PERPLEXED

distress: . . AIL, HURT, NEED, PAIN, ANGER, AGONY, AFFLICT, ANNOY, WORRY, GRIEF, GRIPE, WOUND, UPSET, DANGER, HARASS, MISERY, SORROW, ANXIETY, DISEASE, PERPLEX, TROUBLE

distribute: . . . . . DOLE, METE, ALLOT, ISSUE, ASSIGN, DIVIDE, EXPEND, IMPART, PARCEL, DISPOSE, ALLOCATE, DISPENSE, DISPERSE, APPORTION, DISSEMINATE

district: . . . . . AREA, WARD, TRACT, ZONE, CIRCUIT, PARISH, REGION, QUARTER, SECTOR, PRECINCT, PROVINCE, TERRITORY

disturb: . VEX, RAIL, ALARM, UPSET, ANNOY, PESTER, HARASS, MOLEST, AGITATE, PERTURB, TROUBLE, DISTRACT, INTERRUPT

disturbance: . . RIOT, ALARM, BRAWL, STORM, FRACAS, DISORDER, HUBBUB, RUMPUS, UPROAR, TUMULT, TROUBLE, DISORDER, COMMOTION

disunite: . . . SEVER, DETACH, DIVIDE, SUNDER, DISBAND, DISJOIN, DISSENT, DIVORCE, ALIENATE, DISSOLVE, SEPARATE, DISCONNECT

ditch: . . . DIKE, DYKE, MOAT, HIDE, JILT, FOSS(E), CANAL, GUTTER, TRENCH, DISCARD, ABANDON

divan:.. CAFE, SOFA, COUCH, SETTEE, CANAPE, LOUNGE, OTTOMAN, DAVENPORT

dive:.... DEN, LEAP, SWOOP, PLUNGE, HONKY-TONK, SUBMERGE

diverge: .... VARY, DIFFER, BRANCH, DIVIDE, SPREAD, DEVIATE, DIGRESS

diverse: .. MOTLEY, SUNDRY, UNLIKE, VARIED, SEVERAL, SEPARATE, DIFFERENT

diversion: .... GAME, PLAY, FEINT, HOBBY, SPORT, PASTIME, DISTRACTION, AMUSEMENT, RECREATION

divert: ... AMUSE, DISTRACT, DEFLECT, ENTERTAIN, ESTRANGE

divest: .... BARE, STRIP, DENUDE, DEPRIVE, DISROBE, UNCOVER, DISPOSSESS

divide: ... CUT, PART, CLEFT, SEVER, SHARE, SLICE, SPLIT, BRANCH, PARCEL, BISECT, APPORTION, SUNDER, SEPARATE, DIVERGE, PRORATE, ALIENATE, TRANSECT

dividend: .. BONUS, INTEREST

divine: ...... HOLY, GUESS, PIOUS, DETECT, SACRED, PREDICT, GODLIKE, HEAVENLY, CONJECTURE

division: ...... PART, RIFT, GROUP, SHARE, SCHISM, SECTOR, SECTION, CATEGORY, FISSION, PARTITION, SCISSION, SEPARATION

divorce: ... SEVER, SUNDER, DISSOLVE, DISUNION, DISUNITE, SEPARATE, DISSOLUTION

divulge: . BARE, SHOW, TELL, IMPART, REVEAL, UNFOLD, DISCLOSE, PROCLAIM, COMMUNICATE

dizzy: ...... CRAZY, FAINT, GIDDY, SILLY, FOOLISH, GROGGY, LIGHTHEADED, VERTIGINOUS

do: ..... MAKE, SUIT, SERVE, RENDER, ACHIEVE, EXECUTE, PERFORM, PRODUCE, SATISFY, SUFFICE, TRANSACT, ACCOMPLISH

docile: .... GENTLE, PLIANT, TRACTABLE, OBEDIENT, TAME

dock: .... BOB, CUT, MOOR, JETTY, PIER, CLIP, BANG, QUAY, LAND, BASIN, WHARF, MARINA, SHORTEN

doctor: .... DOSE, TREAT, TAMPER, FALSIFY, INTERN, SURGEON, PHYSICIAN, OSTEOPATH, CHIROPRACTOR, MEDICINEMAN

doctrine:.. ISM, CULT, DOXY, CREDO, CREED, BELIEF, DOGMA, TENET, GOSPEL, THEORY, PRINCIPLE, PRECEPT

document:.... BILL, BOOK, DEED, WRIT, LEASE, PAPER, PATENT, CONTRACT, MISSIVE, MORTGAGE, MANUSCRIPT

dodge: . DUCK, RUSE, AVOID, ELUDE, EVADE, PARRY, TRICK, ESCAPE, DECEIVE

doff:..... OFF, VAIL, DOUSE, STRIP, DIVEST, REMOVE, UNDRESS

dog: .. CUR, PUG, PUP, MUTT, TYKE, BITCH, POOCH, PUPPY, WHELP, CANINE, MONGREL, HOUND, SPANIEL, TERRIER, MASTIFF

dogma: ..... CREED, TENET, BELIEF, DOCTRINE

dogmatic: .... ASSERTIVE, PRAGMATIC, INTOLERANT, DICTATORIAL, OPINIONATED

doily: .... MAT, NAPKIN

doldrums:... CALM, DUMPS, ENNUI, BLUES, TEDIUM, DEPRESSION, LISTLESSNESS

dole:..... ALMS, GIFT, METE, ALLOT, CHARITY, DISTRIBUTE

doleful:...... SAD, DISMAL, DREARY, MOURNFUL, LUGUBRIOUS

dolly: . . . CART, DOLL, TRAY, TRUCK, CARRIER

dolor: . . . . . GRIEF, SORROW, ANGUISH, SADNESS, MOURNING

dolt: . . . ASS, OAF, SAP, CLOD, FOOL, CHUMP, DUMMY, DUNCE, NINNY, IMBECILE, BLOCKHEAD, NUMSKULL, NITWIT, SIMPLETON, HALFWIT

domain: . . . . STATE, WORLD, REALM, DEMESNE, DEMENE, ESTATE, SPHERE, BAILIWICK, DOMINION

domestic: . . . . MAID, TAME, LOCAL, NATIVE, SERVANT, MENIAL, ENCHORIAL

domicile: . . . . HOME, ABODE, HOUSE, MENAGE, DWELLING, RESIDENCE, HABITATION

dominant: . . . CHIEF, RULING, CENTRAL, SUPREME, SUPERIOR, ASCENDANT, PARAMOUNT, PRINCIPAL, COMMADING, PREVAILING, PRE-EMINENT, PREPONDERANT

dominate: . . . RULE, GOVERN, CONTROL, MASTER, HECTOR, DOMINEER

domineer: . . . . . BOSS, LORD, RULE, BULLY, HENPECK

dominion: . . . . RULE, SWAY, REALM, REIGN, DOMAIN, EMPIRE, CONTROL, AUTHORITY, JURISDICTION

donate: . . . . . GIVE, BESTOW, PRESENT, CONTRIBUTE

done: . . . . . . OVER, BAKED, ENDED, COOKED, THROUGH, FINISHED, COMPLETED, ACCOMPLISHED

donor: . GIVER, BENEFACTOR, CONTRIBUTOR, PHILANTROPIST

doom: . . . DAMN, FATE, RUIN, DEATH, DECREE, DESTINY, CONDEMN, SENTENCE

door: . . EXIT, ENTRY, HATCH, PORTAL, ACCESS, OPENING, PASSAGE, POSTERN, ENTRANCE

dope: . . DRUG, INFO, CRACK, OPIUM, COCAIN, OPIATE, PREDICT, STUPEFY, NARCOTIC, MARIJUANA, INFORMATION

dormant: . . . . STILL, QUIET, ASLEEP, TORPID, LATENT, RESTING, SLEEPING, INACTIVE, QUIESCENT

dose: . . . . . TREAT, DRENCH, POTION, DRAUGHT, QUANTITY

dossier: . . . . . FILE, RECORD

dot: . . . . LUMP, SPOT, MOTE, POINT, SPECK, PERIOD, SPECKLE, STIPPLE, PARTICLE

dotage: . . . . SENILITY, FEEBLENESS, IMBECILTY

dote: . . . . LOVE, ADORE

double: . . DUAL, FOLD, TWIN, BIFOLD, BINARY, TWICE, DUPLEX, TWOFOLD, PAIRED, DUPLICATE

doubt: . . . . . . FEAR, DREAD, WAVER, SCRUPLE, SUSPECT, DISTRUST, HESITATE, MISTRUST, QUESTION, UNCERTAINTY

doubtful: . . . . UNSURE, DUBIOUS, PERILOUS, WAVERING, AMBIGUOUS, UNCERTAIN, SUSPICIOUS

dough: . . . . . CASH, MONEY, PASTE, BATTER, NOODLE

doughty: . . . . . BOLD, BRAVE, VALIANT, INTREPID

dour: . . . GLUM, GRIM, SOUR, STERN, SEVERE, MOROSE, SULLEN

douse: . . BEAT, BLOW, DOFF, DUCK, CEASE, DRENCH, IMMERSE, EXTINGUISH

dowdy: . . . . SHABBY, FRUMP, TACKY, UNTIDY, SLOVENLY

dowel: . . . . PEG, PIN, PINTLE

dower: . . . ENDOW, BEQUEST, TALENT, INHERITANCE

down: . . . ILL, FLOOR, BELOW, PLUMAGE, OVERTHROW

downcast: . . . SAD, GLOOMY, DEPRESSED, DESPONDENT, DOWN HEARTED

downright: ... PURE, BLUNT, PLAIN, FRANK, DIRECT, SHEER, STARK, ABSOLUTE, POSITIVE, THOROUGH

dowry: ...... GIFT, TALENT, PORTION, ENDOWMENT

doxy: .. ISM, CREED, WENCH, DOCTRINE

doze: .... NAP, NOD, SLEEP, DROWSE, SNOOZE, CATNAP, SLUMBER

drab: .. DULL, SLUT, WENCH, COLORLESS, LACKLUSTER

draft: .. DOSE, PLAN, CHECK, POTION, SKETCH, DRAWING, OUTLINE, BEVERAGE, POTATION, CONSCRIPT

drag: .... TOW, TUG, DRAW, HAUL, PULL, BREAK, TRAIL, DRAWL, DREDGE, GRAPNEL

drain: ..... DRY, SAP, LADE, MILK, CANAL, EMPTY, SEWER, GUTTER, EXHAUST, DEPLETE, FILTER

dram: ...... NIP, SLUG, SIP, DRINK, DRAFT

in assaying: .... CENTNER

drama: ...... PLAY, OPERA, COMEDY, HISTORY, THEATER, TRAGEDY, PAGEANT

drape: ..... HANG, ADORN, COVER, CURTAIN, HANGING, VALANCE

drastic: ...... DIRE, SEVERE, HARSH, EXTREME, RADICAL

draw: ..... TIE, TOW, DRAG, HAUL, PULL, DRAFT, LIMN, DEDUCT, DEPICT, SKETCH, ATTRACT, EXTRACT, PORTRAY, STALEMATE, DELINEATE

drawing: .... DRAFT, DESIGN, SKETCH, DIAGRAM, LOTTERY, PULLING, TRACTION

drawn: .... TIRED, HAGGARD

dreadful: .... DIRE, AWFUL, TERRIBLE, HORRID, HIDEOUS

dream: .... HOPE, MUSE, FANCY, VISION, IMAGINE, REVERIE, ILLUSION, FANTASY, NIGHTMARE

dreary: .... DULL, FLAT, BLEAK, DISMAL, LONELY, GLOOMY, CHEERLESS

dredge: ...... SIFT, SCOOP, DEEPEN, EXCAVATE, SPRINKLE

dregs: .... LEES, SCUM, SILT, DRAFT, FECES, MAGMA, GROUT, REFUSE, RESIDUE, GROUNDS, SEDIMENT

drench: .... SOP, WET, DOSE, HOSE, SOAK, SOUSE, DOUSE, SATURATE, SUBMERGE

dress: .... DON, RIG, DECK, GARB, GOWN, ROBE, SUIT, TRIM, ADORN, ATTIRE, CLOTHE, EQUIP, HABIT, OUTFIT, FROCK, DECORATE, APPAREL, RAIMENT, GARMENT, CLOTHING, GARNISH, ACCOUTERMENTS

dresser: ... CHEST, BUREAU, MODISTE, CUPBOARD, ESCRITOIRE

dressing: ... SAUCE, BEATING, SCOLDING, STUFFING, PLEDGET, BANDAGE, OINTMENT

dribble: ...... DRIP, DROP, DROOL, SLAVER, TRICKLE

drift: .... SAG, PILE, FLOAT, TREND, TENOR, INTENT, TENDENCY, MEANING, INCLINATION, DEVIATION

drill: ..... SOW, TAP, AWL, BORE, PIERCE, AUGER, TRAIN, CLOTH, GIMLET, EXERCISE, PRACTICE, DISCIPLINE, PERFORATE

drink: ... ADE, BIB, LAP, SIP, SHOT, SLUG, SODA, SWIG, TIFF, QUAFF, BOOZE, DRAFT, JULEP, PUNCH, SNORT, TODDY, ABSORB, RICKEY, IMBIBE, QUZZLE, TIPPLE, SWALLOW, BEVERAGE, INTOXICANT

drip: .... DROP, LEAK, SEEP, DRIBBLE, TRICKLE

slang: .... CREEP

drive: . . . RIDE, URGE, GOAD, PROD, PUSH, FORCE, IMPEL, PRESS, SWEEP, COMPEL, PROPEL, ENERGY, PRESSURE, CAMPAIGN

droll: . . . ODD, FUNNY, COMIC, JESTER, AMUSING, BUFFOON, HUMOROUS

droop: . . . . LOP, SAG, BEND, DROP, FLAG, SINK, WILT, DANGLE, WEAKEN, NUTATE, SLOUCH, DECLINE, LANGUISH

drop: . . . . BEAD, BLOB, DRIP, FALL, GOUT, OMIT, SINK, DROOP, LOWER, PLOP, PLUNK, SLUMP, PLUNGE, FORSAKE, GLOBULE, DECREASE, DISCONTINUE

drought: . . ARIDITY, DRYNESS

drove: . . . . . HERD, CROWD, FLOCK, HORDE

drown: . . . . FLOOD, DEADEN, MUFFLE, INUNDATE

drowse: . . . NOD, NAP, DOZE, SLEEP, SNOOZE, SLUMBER

drub: . . . . . . BANG, BEAT, CUDGEL, THRASH, DEFEAT

drudge: . GRUB, MOIL, PLOD, TOIL, SLAVE, CHORE, SCRUB, PLODDER

drug: . . . . POT, DOPE, DULL, HEMP, NUMB, CRACK, HEROIN, OPIUM, OPIATE, COCAINE, PEYOTE, MARIJUANA, NARCOTIC, MEDICINE, STUPEFY, BARBITURATE

drum: . . . . . TABOR, BONGO, BARREL, KEETLE, SNARE, TAMBOUR, TYMPAN, TIMBREL, CYLINDER, TAMBOURIN(E)

drunk(ard): . . . . SOT, SOAK, DIPSO, SOUSE, TOPER, POTSHOT, TIPPLER, TOSSPOT, ALCHOHOLIC, INEBRIATE, DIPSOMANIAC

drunken: . . . . . HIGH, FRIED, BLOTTO, TIGHT, TIPSY, PICKLED, LOADED, SOUSED, STEWED, INEBRIATED, COCKEYED, INTOXICATED

dry: . . . . ARID, BAKE, DULL, BRUT, SERE, WIPE, DRAIN, PARCH, VAPID, BARREN, BORING JEJUNE, INSIPID, STERILE, THIRSTY, TIRESOME, DEHYDRATE, WITHERED, DESICCATE, UNINTERESTING

dual: . . . . . . TWIN, BINARY, DOUBLE, TWOFOLD

dubious: . . . . LEERY, SHADY, VAGUE, SKEPTICAL, DOUBTFUL, UNCERTAIN, DISPUTABLE, QUESTIONABLE

duck: . . . . . BOB, BOW, BIRD, DIVE, AVOID, CLOTH, DOUSE, DODGE, SHIRK, DRAKE, PERSON

duct: . . . . . VAS, PIPE, TUBE, CANAL, CHANNEL, CONDUIT, PASSAGE

ductile: . . . . . . SOFT, FACILE, TENSILE, ELASTIC, PLASTIC, PLIANT, PLIABLE, TENSILE, FLEXIBLE, TRACTILE, MALLEABLE

dude: . . . . FOP, DANDY

dudgeon: . . . . . IRE, ANGER, PIQUE, DAGGER, RESENTMENT

due: . . . . . OWE, JUST, DEBT, RIGHT, PAYABLE, OWING FITTING, PROPER, MATURE, UNPAID

duel: . . . TILT, FENCE, JOUST, FIGHT, CONTEST, COMBAT, CONFLICT

duenna: . . . . CHAPERON

dues: . . . . FEE, TAX

duet: . . . . DUO

dugout: . . . . . . BOAT, CANOE, CONGA, PIROGUE, SHELTER, FOXHOLE

dukedom: . . . . DUCHY

dulcet: . . . SWEET, SOOTHING, AGREEABLE, MELODIOUS

dull: . . . . . . DIM, LAX, DRAB, DRUG, DUMB, FLAT, GRAY, LOGY, SLOW, TAME, BLUNT, CRASS, FOGGY, GROSS, MORON,

PROSY, SHADE, SLACK, VAPID, CLOUDY, DEADEN, DISMAL, DREARY, BORING, JEJUNE, OBTUSE, SLEEPY, STODGY, STUPID, BLUNTED, HUMDRUM, STUPEFY, TEDIOUS, HEBETATE, LISTLESS, TIRESOME, APATETIC, COLORLESS, LETHARGIC, TARNISHED, LACKLUSTER, MONOTONOUS

dullard: . . BOOR, DOLT, OAF, LOUT, DUNCE, MORON, STUPID, SIMPLETON, NUMSKULL

duly: . . . . FITLY, PROPERLY, FITTINGLY, REGULARLY

dumb: . . . . . . DULL, MUTE, SILENT, STUPID, SENSELESS, SPEECHLESS, INARTICULATE

dummy: . . . . . . COPY, DOLT, MUTE, SHAM, FRONT, SILENT, IMITATION, FICTITIOUS, FIGUREHEAD, MANNEQUIN

dump: . . . HOLE, HEAP, PILE, LUMP, UNLOAD, EMPTY, CHUCK, DEPOSIT, STORAGE

dun: . . . . . . ASK, TAN, URGE, BROWN, PESTER

dunce: . . OAF, DOLT, BOOBY, IDIOT, MORON, NINNY, DULLARD, HALF-WIT, BLOCKHEAD, NUMSKULL, SIMPLETON, DUNDERHEAD

dune: . . . . BAR, HILL, RIDGE, MOUND

dungeon: . . . . . CELL, HOLE, VAULT, DUNJON, PRISON, OUBLIETTE

duo: . . . . DUET, PAIR, COUPLE

dupe: . . . . . . APE, CON, FOB, COAX, CULL, FOOL, GULL, TOOL, CHEAT, TRICK, CHEAT, DELUDE, SUCKER, VICTIM, CATSPAW, DECEIVE, MISLEAD, SWINDLE

duplex: . . DOUBLE, TWOFOLD, DWELLING

duplicate: . . . . COPY, ALIKE, DITTO, SPARE, REPEAT, REPLICA, ESTREAT, DOUBLE, FACSIMILE, REPRODUCE

duplicity: . . . . DECEIT, TRICKERY, FRAUD, DECEPTION, DOUBLE-DEALING, FALSENESS

durable: . . . . . FIRM, STABLE, LASTING, ENDURING, PERMANENT

duration: . . . . . . AGE, SPAN, TERM, TIME, SPACE, PERIOD, LIFETIME, EXTENSION, CONTINUANCE

duress: . . . . CRUELTY, COERCION, PRESSURE, AFFLICTION, IMPRISONMENT, CONSTRAINT, COMPULSION

during: . . . . . . TIME, WHILE, PENDING, THROUGHOUT

dusk: . . . . EVE, GLOOM, TWILIGHT, DARKNESS, GLOAMING, CREPUSCLE, NIGHTFALL

dusky: . . . . DIM, DARK, SWART(HY), TAWNY

dust: . . . . ASH, DIRT, MOTE, SMUT, CLEAN, STOUR, POLLEN, EARTH, POWDER, SPRINKLE

dutiful: . . . DOCILE, DUTEOUS, OBEDIENT, COMPLIANT, SUBMISSIVE, CONSCIENTIOUS

duty: . . . . . JOB, TAX, ONUS, ROLE, TASK, TOLL, CHORE, BURDEN, EXCISE, IMPOST, TARIFF, FUNCTION, RESPONSIBILITY, OBLIGATION

dwarf: . . ELF, RUNT, GNOME, PIGMY, PYGMY, SCRUB, STUNT, TROLL, BANTAM, MIDGET, MANIKIN, BELITTLE, OUTSHINE, HOMUNCULUS, OVERSHADOW

dwell: . . . . BIDE, LIVE, STAY, ABIDE, DELAY, LODGE, PAUSE, TARRY, REMAIN, RESIDE, INHABIT

on: . . . . HARP

dweller: . TENANT, RESIDENT, HABITANT, OCCUPANT, INHABITANT

dwelling: . . . HUT, DEN, CAVE, FLAT, LAIR, NEST, HOME, TENT, ABODE, CABIN, HOTEL, HOUSE, HOVEL, MOTEL, DUPLEX, SHANTY, TEEPEE, COTTAGE, LODGING, MANSION, TRAILER, BUNGALOW, DOMICILE, TENEMENT, APARTMENT, RESIDENCE, HABITATION

dwindle: . . . . . . MELT, PINE, WANE, ABATE, PETER, TAPER, WASTE, SHRINK, LESSEN, CONSUME, DECLINE, DIMINISH, DECREASE

dye: . . . . . . HUE, ANIL, TINT, COLOR, FUCUS, IMBUE, STAIN, TINGE, ANILINE

dynamic: . . . . POTENT, FORCEFUL, ENERGETIC, VIGOROUS

dynamics: . . . . STATICS, FORCES, KINETICS

dynamite: . . . . BLAST, EXPLOSIVE

dynamo: . . . . . . GENERATOR, MAGNETO

dynasty: . . . . . RACE, REALM, RULER, MONARCH, DOMINION, SUCCESSION

dyspepsia: . . . . . INDIGESTION

dyspeptic: . . . . CRABBY, GLOOMY, GROUCHY

dysphoria: . . . . . . ANXIETY, DISCONTENT, DISCOMFORT

E

E: *Greek:* . . . . EPSILON

each: . . . . . . ALL, ILK, PER, EVERY(ONE), APIECE

eager: . . . . HOT, AVID, KEEN, WARM, AFIRE, ITCHY, READY, ARDENT, INTENT, ANXIOUS, IMPATIENT, EXCITED, FERVANT, EARNEST, DESIROUS, YEARNING, ENTHUSIASTIC

ear: . . . . . LUG, HEAR, HEED, OBEY, LISTEN, SPIKE, LISTEN, AURICLE, HEARING, ATTENTION

earache: . . . . OTALGIA

early: . . . ERE, OLD, FORMER, TIMELY, ANCIENT, FORWARD, PREMATURE

earmark: . . . . SIGN, BRAND, IDENTIFY, RESERVE, IDENTIFICATION

earn: . . EKE, GET, WIN, GAIN, MERIT, OBTAIN, ACHIEVE, ACQUIRE

earnest: . . . . . AVID, GRAVE, SOBER, EAGER, ARDENT, INTENT, SERIOUS, SINCERE, FERVENT, ZEALOUS, DILIGENT

money: . . ARLES, TOKEN, DEPOSIT, SECURITY, ADVANCE

earsplitting: . LOUD, SHRILL, DEAFENING

earth: . . . . ORB, CLAY, DIRT, DUST, GRIT, LAND, LOAM, MARL, MUCK, ROCK, SOIL, GLOBE, GROUND, UNIVERSE, WORLD, TERRA, FIRMA

earthenware: . . . . . . CHINA, DELFT, POTTERY, PORCELAIN, CROCK(ERY), STONEWARE, TERRA-COTTA

earthly: . . . . CARNAL, WORLDLY, TEMPORAL, SECULAR, TERRENE, MUNDANE, TERRESTRIAL

earthquake: . QUAKE, SEISM, TREMOR, TEMBLOR

focus: . . . . EPICENTER

pertaining to: . . . SEISMAL, SEISMIC

science: . . . . SEISMOLOGY

ease: . . . CALM, REST, ALLAY, KNACK, PEACE, QUIET, RELAX, LOOSEN, PACIFY, POISE, REDUCE, RELIEF, REPOSE, SOOTHE, APPEASE, COMFORT, LEISURE, LIGHTEN, RELIEVE, DIMINISH, MITIGATE, MODERATE, PALLIATE

easily: . . . . GENTLY, READILY, SMOOTHLY, DEXTEROUSLY

Easter: . . . . PASCH(A)

easy: ... CALM, COZY, MILD, CUSHY, LIGHT, FACILE, GENTLE, SECURE, SIMPLE, LENIENT, NATURAL, CAREFREE, FAMILIAR, SMOOTH, GRACEFUL, MODERATE, TRANQUIL, EFFORTLESS

eat: .. SUP, BITE, DINE, FARE, FEED, FRET, GULP, WOLF, GORGE, GNAW, GRUB, RUST, ERODE, FEAST, MULCH, TASTE, ABSORB, DEVOUR, INGEST, CONSUME, CORRODE, SWALLOW

eating: .... DINING, CAUSTIC, EROSIVE, CORROSIVE

ebb: ..... FAIL, SINK, WANE, ABATE, RECEDE, RETIRE, DECLINE, REFLUX, SUBSIDE, DECREASE, DIMINISH

ebon: .. DARK, BLACK, SABLE

ebony: ...... WOOD, BLACK

ebullience: .... ELAN, OVERFLOW, EXUBERANCE

ebullient: .... BOILING, BUBBLING, EXUBERANT EFFERVESCENT

eccentric: .... ODD, CRANK, QUEER, BIZARRE, ERRATIC, STRANGE, ABNORMAL, PECULIAR, ANOMALOUS, SCREWBALL, CAPRICIOUS

eccentricity: ...... ODDITY, QUEERNESS, IDIOSYNCRASY

ecclesiastic: ... ABBE, ABBOT, PRIEST, PRELATE, CLERGYMAN

echinate: .... SPINY, BRISTLY, PRICKLY

echo: .... RING, REPEAT, SECOND, PARROT, IMITATE, RESOUND, RESPOND, RESPONSE, REPETITION, REVERBERATE

eclat: .... FAME, GLORY, PRAISE, ACCLAIM, NOTORIETY, RENOWN, SPLENDOR

eclipse: .... DIM, BLOT, HIDE, BLIND, CLOUD, SHADE, DARKEN, EXCEED, OBSCURE, SURPASS, EXTINGUISH, OVERSHADOW

economical: .... CHARY, FRUGAL, SAVING, CAREFUL, PRUDENT, SPARING, THRIFTY, PROVIDENT

economize: ... SAVE, SKIMP, STINT, SCRIMP, HUSBAND, RETRENCH

ecstasy: .... RAPTURE, JOY, BLISS, DELIGHT, EMOTION, HAPPINESS

ecumenical: ...... LIBERAL, CATHOLIC, GENERAL, UNIVERSAL, WORLDWIDE

eczema: .... HERPES, TETTER

edacity: .. GREED, VORACITY, APPETITE, RAVENOUSNESS

eddy: .. SHIFT, SWIRL, WHIRL, VORTEX, WHIRLPOOL

edema: .... TUMOR, DROPSY, SWELLING, PUFFINESS

Eden: ..... HEAVEN, UTOPIA, PARADISE, GARDEN

edentate: .. SLOTH, ANTBEAR, TOOTHLESS, AARDVARK, ANTEATER, ARMADILLO

edge: .. HEM, LIP, RIM, BANK, BRIM, BROW, SIDE, TRIM, BLADE, BRINK, CREST, FRINGE, KNIFE, MARGE, SIDLE, SKIRT, VERGE, BORDER, FLANGE, MARGIN, BOUNDRY, KEENNESS, ADVANTAGE, SHARPNESS

edging: ... HEM, LACE, PICOT, RUCHE, TATTING, FRINGE, TRIMMING

edgy: ..... TENSE, NERVOUS, IRRITABLE, SNAPPISH

edible: . ESCULENT, EATABLE, COMESTIBLE, VEGETABLE

edict: ..... ACT, LAW, BULL, FIAT, ORDER, DECREE, DICTUM, COMMAND, STATUTE, MANDATE, PROCLAMATION

edify: ..... TEACH, IMPROVE, INSTRUCT, ENNOBLE

edit: ...... EMEND, REDACT, REVIEW, REVISE, CORRECT, REWRITE

edition: . . . . . . COPY, ISSUE,
NUMBER, VERSION, PRINTING

editor: . . . . READACTOR,
PUBLISHER, JOURNALIST

educate: . . . . TRAIN, TEACH,
INFORM, DEVELOP, NUTURE,
INSTRUCT, CULTIVATE,
ENLIGHTEN

education: . . . . . . LEARNING,
TEACHING, TRAINING,
ERUDITION, DISCIPLINE,
KNOWLEDGE, SCHOLARSHIP

educator: . . TUTOR, MENTOR,
TEACHER, PROFESSOR,
INSTRUCTOR

educe: . . . . . DRAW, EVOKE,
ELICIT, EVOLVE, DEDUCE,
EXTRACT

eerie (eery): . SCARY, WEIRD,
SPOOKY, UNCANNY, MACABRE,
ELDRITCH

efface: . . BLOT, BLUR, RAZE,
CANCEL, ERASE, EXPUNGE,
DESTROY, OBLITERATE, WIPE
OUT

effect: . . . . . . CAUSE, RESULT,
ACHIEVE, TENOR, MEANING,
EXECUTE, FULFILL, OUTCOME,
PERFORM, COMPLETE,
IMPRESSION, ACCOMPLISH

effective: . . . . ABLE, ACTIVE,
POTENT, CAPABLE, POWERFUL,
COMPETENT, EFFICIENT,
OPERATIVE

effervesce: . . . . . BOIL, FOAM,
FIZZ, FROTH, BUBBLE, SPARKLE

effervescence: . . . . . FOAMING,
VIVACITY, EXUBERANCE,
LIVELINESS, EBULLIENCE

effete: . . . . . . BARREN, ARID,
STERILE, SPENT, EXHAUSTED,
WORN OUT

efficacious: . . VALID, POTENT,
POWERFUL, EFFECTIVE

efficient: . . . ABLE, CAPABLE,
EFFECTIVE, COMPETENT

efflux: . OUTFLOW, EFFUSION,
EFFLUENCE, EMANATION

effort: . . . . TRY, TOIL, DRIVE,
LABOR, NISUS, PAINS, STRAIN,
ATTEMPT, EXERTION,
ENDEAVOR, STRUGGLE

effrontery: . . . . GALL, GUTS,
BRASS, CHEEK, AUDACITY,
TEMERITY, IMPUDENCE,
PRESUMPTION

effulgence: . . BLAZE, GLORY,
LUSTER, RADIANCE, SPLENDOR,
BRILLIANCE

effuse: . . . . SPREAD

effusive: . . GUSHY, GUSHING,
BUBBLING, EXUBERANT,
OVERFLOWING, DEMONSTRATIVE

egg: . . . GOAD, OVUM, PROD,
SEED, SPUR, URGE, INCITE,
SPORE

egis: . . AIGIS, ARMOR, SHIELD,
DEFENSE, AUSPICES,
SPONSORSHIP, PROTECTION

ego: . . . . SELF, CONCEIT,
PERSONALITY, SELFISHNESS

egocentric: . . SELF-CENTERED

egoism: . . . . . . PRIDE, VANITY,
CONCEIT, SELFISHNESS

egregious: . . . . . . BAD, FINE,
GROSS, EMINENT, FLAGRANT,
SHOCKING EXCELLENT

egress: . . . . EXIT, ISSUE,
OUTLET, PASSAGE, DEPARTURE

eider: . . . . DOWN, (SEA)DUCK

eidolon: . . . . . IMAGE, ICON,
PHANTOM

eight-ball: *behind the:* . . FIX,
SPOT, DILEMMA, PREDICAMENT
  group of: . OCTAD, OCTET,
OCTAVE, OCTETTE
  sided figure: . . . OCTAGON

ejaculate: . . . . BLURT, EJECT,
EXCLAIM, DISCHARGE

eject: . . . CAST, OUST, SPEW,
SPIT, VOID, EMIT, EXPEL,
EVICT, ERUPT, SPOUT, SPURT,
VOMIT, BANISH, BOUNCE,
DISLODGE, DISMISS, SQUIRT,
EJACULATE

eke: . . . AUGMENT, ENLARGE,
STRETCH, APPENDIX, INCREASE,

LENGTHEN, LIKEWISE, SUPPLEMENT

el: . . BEND, WING, EXTENSION

elaborate: . . GREAT, ORNATE, REFINE, DEVELOP, ENLARGE, PERFECT, DETAILED, PAINSTAKING, COMPLICATED

elan: . . . DASH, ARDOR, VIGOR, GUSTO, SPIRIT, ENTHUSIASM

elapse: . . GO, DIE, PASS, SLIP, EXPIRE

elastic: . . . . GARTER, SUPPLE, FLEXIBLE, SPRINGY, RESILIENT, BUOYANT, ADAPTABLE

elate: . . . . CHEER, EXALT, EXCITE, PLEASE, GLADDEN, EXHILARATE

elated: . . . . HAPPY, EXCITED, GLEEFUL, JOYFUL, EXHULTANT

elbow: . . . . . ANCON, BEND, JOINT, NUDGE, JOSTLE, SHOVE, CROWD

elder: . . . . . IVA, SIRE, PRIOR, SENIOR, ANCIENT, ANCESTOR, EARLIER, FORMER

elderly: . . OLD, AGED, SENILE, VETERAN

eldritch: . . . . . . EERY, EERIE, WEIRD, FRIGHTFUL

elect: . . . . . OPT, CALL, PICK, ASSUME, CHOOSE, DECIDE, CHOSEN, SELECT

election: . . . . . POLL, CHOICE, BALLOTING, PLEBISCITE, ALTERNATIVE

elective: . . . . OPTIONAL, VOLUNTARY, ELECTORAL

electric: . STATIC, MAGNETIC, EXCITING

appliance: . . . IRON, OVEN, DRYER, MIXER, RANGE, STOVE, HEATER, WASHER, BLENDER, BROILER, FRY PAN, TOASTER, PROCESSOR

electrify: . . . . EXCITE, SHOCK, THRILL, STARTLE

eleemosynary: . . . . . . FREE, DEPENDENT, CHARITABLE, GRATUITOUS

elegance: . . . . . CHIC, GRACE, POLISH, TASTE, LUXURY, GRANDEUR, REFINEMENT, SPLENDOR

elegant: . . CHIC, FINE, POSH, PLUSH, DAINTY, SUPERB, COURTLY, DE LUXE, REFINED, GENTEEL, POLISHED, BEAUTIFUL, EXQUISITE

elegy: . . . POEM, SONG, DIRGE, LAMENT, REQUIEM

element: . . . . . PART, METAL, FACTOR, ESSENCE, RUDIMENT, COMPONENT, INGREDIENT, CONSTITUENT, ENVIRONMENT

elementary: . . . PURE, BASIC, PRIMAL, SIMPLE, INITIAL, PRIMARY, INCHOATE, ELEMENTAL, FUNDAMENTAL, RUDIMENTARY

elephant: . . . ROGUE, HATHI, JUMBO, TUSKER, MASTODON, MAMMOTH, PACHYDERM

elevate: . . LIFT, RAISE, EXALT, ELATE, ERECT, HOIST, UPLIFT, ENHANCE, GLORIFY, PROMOTE, HEIGHTEN

elevation: . . . . . HILL, RISE, MOUND, MOUNT, HEIGHT, EMINENCE, ALTITUDE, PLATEAU

elevator: . . CAGE, LIFT, SILO, HOIST, GRANARY, WAREHOUSE

elf: . . . . FAY, HOB, IMP, PIXY, PERI, PUCK, DWARF, FAIRY, GNOME, PIGMY, PIXIE, GOBLIN, SPRITE, BROWNIE, LEPRECHAUN

elicit: . . DRAW, PUMP, EDUCE, EVOKE, EXACT, WREST, DEMAND, EXTORT, INDUCE, EXTRACT

elide: . . . . OMIT, SKIP, SLUR, ANNUL, IGNORE, DESTROY, SUPPRESS

eligible: . . . FIT, COMPETENT, QUALIFIED, SUITABLE

eliminate: . . . . . . RID, OMIT, EDUCE, ERASE, EXPEL, DELETE, EXCEPT, REMOVE, EXCRETE, EXCLUDE, SEPARATE

elite: . . . . BEST, PICK, CHOICE, SELECT, CREAM, UPPERCRUST, ARISTOCRACY

elixir: . . . CORDIAL, PANACEA, CURE-ALL, ARCANUM, NOSTRUM

ell: . . . . . . WING, EXTENSION

ellipse: . . . . . . OVAL, CURVE, OVATE

elongate: . . . . STRETCH, LENGTHEN, EXTEND, PROTRACT

elongated: . . . LONG, LINEAR, OBLONG, PROLATE, SLENDER, STRETCHED

elope: . . DECAMP, RUN AWAY, ESCAPE, ABSCOND

eloquent: . . FERVID, FLUENT, ORATORICAL, EXPRESSIVE, PERSUASIVE, ARTICULATE

else: . . . OR, OTHER, BESIDES, INSTEAD, OTHERWISE, DIFFERENT, ADDITIONAL

elucidate: . . CLEAR, CLARIFY, EXPLAIN, SIMPLIFY, INTERPRET, ILLUSTRATE

elude: . . . FLEE, FOIL, AVOID, DODGE, EVADE, ESCAPE, BAFFLE, ILLUDE

emancipated: . . . LEAN, THIN, BONY, GAUNT, SKINNY, WASTED

emanate: . . . . . FLOW, EMIT, ARISE, ISSUE, RADIATE, ORIGINATE

emanation(s): . . . . . . NITON, VAPOR, EFFLUX, OUTCOME, EFFLUENCE, EXHALATION

emancipate: . . . . FREE, MANUMIT, RELEASE, LIBERATE, ENFRANCHISE

emancipation: . . . FREEDOM, RELEASE, LIBERATION, DELIVERANCE, MANUMISSION

emasculate: . . . . GELD, WEAKEN, CASTRATE, STERILIZE

embalm: . . . . PRESERVE

embankment: . . DAM, BANK, BUND, DIKE, QUAY, LEVEE, STAITH, MOUND

embargo: . . . EDICT, ORDER, BLOCKADE, RESTRAINT, STOPPAGE, PROHIBITION, RESTRICTION

embarrass: . . ABASH, ANNOY, SHAME, UPSET, CONFUSE, FLUSTER, NONPLUS, DISCONCERT, DISCOMFIT

embellish: . . . . . DECK, GILD, TRIM, ADORN, BEDECK, ENRICH, EMBOSS, POLISH, DECORATE, GARNISH, ORNAMENT, EMBROIDER

ember: . . ASH, COAL, CINDER, SPARK

embezzle: . . . . STEAL, PECULATE, DEFALCATE

embitter: . SOUR, ACERBATE, FESTER, RANKLE, ENVENOM

emblazon: . . . LAUD, ADORN, EXTOL, DISPLAY, DECORATE

emblem: . . . . . . MACE, SIGN, BADGE, DEVICE, FIGURE, SYMBOL, INSIGNE

embody: . . . UNITE, CONTAIN, ORGANIZE, PERSONIFY, INCARNATE, INCORPORATE

embrace: . . . . . HUG, LOVE, ADOPT, CLASP, CLING, ENARM, GRASP, ENARM, ACCEPT, CARESS, CLINCH, CUDDLE, ENFOLD, HUDDLE, INFOLD, CHERISH, ENCLOSE, INCLUDE, ENCLASP, COMPRISE, ENCIRCLE, BEARHUG

embroider: . . . . . TAT, PURL, COUCH, STITCH, DECORATE, ORNAMENT, EMBELLISH, EXAGGERATE

embroil: . . . . TROUBLE, MUDDLE, INVOLVE, ENTANGLE, IMPLICATE

embryo: . . . . . . CELL, GERM, FETUS, OVULE, FOETUS

emend: . . EDIT, MEND, ALTER, REVISE, CORRECT

emerald: . . . . BERYL, GREEN, SMARAGD

emerge: . LOOM, RISE, ISSUE, APPEAR

emery: . . . . ABRASIVE,
CORUNDUM, CARBORUNDUM
emesis: . . . . VOMITING
emetic: . . VOMIT, CATHARTIC,
EVACUANT, EXPECTORANT
eminence: . . . NOTE, ASCENT,
HEIGHT, RENOWN, REPUTE,
ELEVATION, LOFTINESS,
PROMINENCE
eminent: . . . . . . HIGH, CHIEF,
GREAT, LOFTY, NOTED,
FAMOUS, MARKED, RENOWNED,
CELEBRATED
emissary: . . . AGENT, ENVOY,
(DE)LEGATE, MESSENGER
emission: . . . . . . ISSUANCE,
DISCHARGE, RADIATION
emit: . . . . GIVE, POUR, REEK,
SEND, VENT, ERUCT, EXUDE,
ISSUE, UTTER, EXHALE, EXPIRE,
EXHAUST, RADIATE, DISCHARGE
emolument: . . . FEES, WAGES,
INCOME, PROFIT, SALARY,
BENEFIT, STIPEND
emotion: . . . IRE, ENVY, FEAR,
HATE, LOVE, ANGER, GRIEF,
ECSTASY, FEELING, PASSION,
RAPTURE, AFFECTION,
AGITATION, SENTIMENT
emotionless: . . . UNFEELING,
TORPID, APATHETIC, STOICAL,
INSENSATE
empathy: . . . PITY, AFFINITY,
SYMPATHY, UNDERSTANDING
emphasis: . . ACCENT, STRESS,
WEIGHT, SALIENCE
emphatic: . . . . EARNEST,
FORCIBLE, POSITIVE, STRIKING,
ENERGETIC
empire: . . . . . . RULE, SWAY,
POWER, REALM, DOMAIN,
KINGDOM, DOMINION
empiric: . . . . QUACK,
CHARLATAN, MOUNTEBANK
employ: . . USE, HIRE, AVAIL,
PLACE, OCCUPY, DEVOTE,
ENGAGE, UTILIZE
employment: . . . . . JOB, USE,
TASK, TOIL, WORK, TRADE,

CALLING, PURPOSE, BUSINESS,
VOCATION, OCCUPATION,
PROFESSION
emporium: . . . . MART, SHOP,
STORE, BAZAAR, MARKET
empower: . . . VEST, ENABLE,
DEPUTE, ENTITLE, PERMIT,
AUTHORIZE, DELEGATE
empty: . . BARE, DUMP, FREE,
IDLE, POUR, VOID, BLANK,
DRAIN, EXPEL, INANE, FLUSH,
BARREN, DEVOID, HOLLOW,
UNLOAD, VACANT, VACATE,
DEPLETE, EXHAUST, VACUATE,
VACUOUS, DISGORGE,
EVACUATE, DISCHARGE,
UNOCCUPIED
emulate: . . . APE, VIE, COPY,
EQUAL, RIVAL, COMPETE,
IMITATE
enable: . . EMPOWER, ENTITLE,
QUALIFY
enact: . . . . . . PASS, ORDAIN,
DECREE, EFFECT, PERFORM,
PORTRAY, LEGISLATE
enactment: . . . . LAW, EDICT,
DECREE, STATUTE, PASSAGE,
LEGISLATION
enamelware: . . . . . LIMOGES,
CLOISONNE, CERAMICS,
PORCELAIN, DISHES
enamor: . . . . LOVE, CHARM,
CAPTIVATE, FASCINATE
enchant: . . . CHARM, DELUDE,
BEWITCH, CAPTIVATE,
ATTRACT, DELIGHT, ENTHRALL
encircle: . . HEM, GIRD, RING,
ENGIRT, ENLACE, GIRDLE,
ENBRACE, ENCLOSE, CORDON,
ENVIRON, ENCOMPASS,
WREATHE, SURROUND
enclose: . . . BOX, HEM, GIRD,
FENCE, CIRCLE, CORRAL,
ENCASE, ENCYST, CONTAIN,
ENVELOP, SURROUND
enclosure: . . PEN, STY, CAGE,
COOP, COTE, WALL, YARD,
COURT, FENCE, POUND,

CORRAL, KENNEL, PRISON, PADDOCK, CLOISTER, STOCKADE

encompass: .... BELT, GIRD, RING, WALL, ENCIRCLE, ENCLOSE, ENVIRON, INCLUDE, SURROUND, CIRCUMSCRIBE

encore: .... BIS, AGAIN, REPEAT, REPETITION

encounter: .... FACE, MEET, BATTLE, FIGHT, ACCOST, CONTEST, CONFLICT, CONFRONT

encourage: .... ABET, BACK, BOOST, CHEER, ASSURE, FOMENT, FOSTER, INCITE, COMFORT, INSPIRE, EMBOLDEN, HEARTEN, STIMULATE

encroach: .. POACH, INVADE, TRESPASS, INTRUDE, IMPINGE, INFRINGE

encumber: .. LOAD, SADDLE, BURDEN, HAMPER, IMPEDE, HANDICAP, OBSTRUCT

end: .. AIM, TIP, GOAL, LAST, STOP, TAIL, CEASE, CLOSE, DEATH, FINIS, LIMIT, SCRAP, DESIGN, EXPIRE, FINALE, FINISH, OBJECT, RESULT, UPSHOT, WINDUP, ABOLISH, DESTROY, PURPOSE, COMPLETE, CONCLUSION

endanger: .... IMPERIL, COMPROMISE, JEOPARDIZE

endeavor: .... TRY, SEEK, ESSAY, EXERT, TRIAL, EFFORT, STRIVE, ATTEMPT, STRUGGLE, UNDERTAKE

endemic: .... LOCAL, NATIVE, INDIGENOUS

endive: .... CHICKORY, ESCAROLE

endless: .... ETERNAL, FOREVER, IMMORTAL, INFINITE, CEASELESS, PERPETUAL, INTERMINABLE, EVERLASTING

endorse: ...... BACK, SIGN, BOOST, SECOND, APPROVE, CERTIFY, SUPPORT, SANCTION, AUTHORIZE

endow: ...... VEST, DOWER, ENDUE, BESTOW, BEQUEATH

endowment: ... GIFT, BOON, DOWER, GRANT, TALENT, BEQUEST, DONATION

endurable: ...... LIVABLE, BEARABLE, TOLERABLE, SUPPORTABLE

endurance: .... PLUCK, STAMINA, PATIENCE, STRENGTH, FORTITUDE

endure: .. BEAR, LAST, LIVE, ABIDE, ALLOW, BROOK, STAND, SUFFER, PERSIST, UNDERGO, TOLERATE, CONTINUE

enemy: .... FOE, RIVAL, ADVERSARY, OPPONENT, ANTAGONIST

energetic: ..... LIVE, BRISK, ACTIVE, FORCEFUL, VIGOROUS, DYNAMIC

energize: .... ANIMATE, FORTIFY, ACTIVATE

energy: .. ERG, PEP, VIM, ZIP, BIRR, VIGOR, STEAM, FORCE, SPIRIT, STRENGTH

enervate: ...... SAP, DRAIN, WEAKEN, ENFEEBLE, DEBILITATE

enfold: ...... WRAP, CLASP, COVER, COMPLY, EMBRACE, ENLACE, SWATHE, ENVELOP

enforce: ... EXACT, COERCE, COMPEL, IMPOSE, EXECUTE, CONSTRAIN, PROSECUTE

enfranchise: .... FREE, LIBERATE, MANUMIT, EMANCIPATE

engage: ... BOOK, HIRE, JOIN, MESH, RENT, LEASE, TRADE, ENLIST, PLEDGE, BETROTH, EMPLOY, PROMISE, CONTRACT, RESERVE, AFFIANCE, OCCUPY, UNDERTAKE

engaging: .. SAPID, WINSOME, ATTRACTIVE, INTERESTING

engender: ... BEGET, BREED, CAUSE, PRODUCE, DEVELOP,

GENERATE, PROMOTE, PROPAGATE

engine: ... GAS, GIN, MOTOR, DIESEL, STEAM, MACHINE, TURBINE, APPARATUS, LOCOMOTIVE

English: .... ANGLE, ANGELICAN, ANGLO-SAXON, BRITON, BRITISH

engrave: ...... CUT, ETCH, CARVE, PRINT, CHASE, INCISE, IMPRINT, INSCRIBE

engross: .. ABSORB, ENGAGE, FASCINATE, OCCUPY

engrossed: .... RAPT, INTENT, ABSORBED

engulf: .... SWAMP, WHELM, ABSORB, DEVOUR, SWALLOW

enhance: .... IMPROVE, INCREASE, AUGMENT, INTENSIFY, HEIGHTEN

enigma: .... REBUS, PUZZLE, RIDDLE, MYSTERY, PROBLEM, CONUNDRUM

enigmatic: .... CRYPTIC, OBSCURE, BAFFLING, INSCRUTABLE, MYSTIC(AL), PUZZLING

enjoin: .. BID, URGE, ORDER, DECREE, DIRECT, EXHORT, COMMAND, PROHIBIT

enjoyment: ..... FUN, ZEST, LIKING, RELISH, DELIGHT, PLEASURE, HAPPINESS, SATISFACTION, GRATIFICATION

enlarge: ...... ADD, GROW, REAM, SWELL, WIDEN, DILATE, EXPAND, EXTEND, INCREASE, DISTEND, AMPLIFY, AUGMENT, MAGNIFY, ELABORATE, EXPATIATE

enlighten: .... EDIF, TEACH, INFORM, CLARIFY, EDUCATE, ILLUMINE

enlist: .... JOIN, ENROLL, RECRUIT, REGISTER, VOLUNTEER

enliven: .... WARM, CHEER, ANIMATE, INSPIRE, REFRESH, BRIGHTEN

enmity: ...... FEUD, SPITE, HATRED, MALICE, ANIMUS, RANCOR, DISCORD, HOSTILITY, ANTAGONISM, ANIMOSITY, MALEVOLENCE

ennoble: .... EXALT, HONOR, RAISE, DIGNIFY, GLORIFY

ennui: ... TEDIUM, LANGUOR, BOREDOM, WEARINESS

enormous: ...... BIG, HUGE, VAST, IMMENSE, GIGANTIC, COLOSSAL, MAMMOTH, STUPENDOUS

enough: ... AMPLE, PLENTY, QUITE, SUFFICIENT, ADEQUATE

enrage: .... ANGER, MADDEN, INCENSE, INFURIATE

enrapture: .... DELIGHT, RAVISH, ECSTASY, ENTRANCE, ENCHANT, CAPTIVATE, FASCINATE

enroll: ...... JOIN, ENLIST, INDUCT, ENTER, IMPANEL, INSCRIBE, RECORD, REGISTER

ensconce: .... HIDE, SETTLE, CONCEAL, SHELTER, ESTABLISH

ensemble: .... SUIT, WHOLE, COSTUME, COMBINATION

ensign: ..... FLAG, BANNER, OFFICER, STANDARD, GONFALON

enslave: .. CHAIN, DOMINATE, SUBJUGATE, ENTHRALL

ensnare: .... NET, TRAP, CATCH, TREPAN, ALLURE, ENTRAP, TRICK

ensue: ..... FOLLOW, RESULT

entail: .... IMPOSE, INVOLVE, REQUIRE, NECESSITATE

entangle: .. MAT, WEB, FOUL, KNOT, MESH, CATCH, RAVEL, SNARE, SNARL, ENLACE, ENMESH, ENSNARE, CONFUSE, EMBROIL, COMPLICATE

entente: . TREATY, ALLIANCE, AGREEMENT, UNDERSTANDING

enter: .... JOIN, POST, START, APPEAR, RECORD, ENLIST, ENROLL, INSERT, PIERCE, INSERT, PENETRATE

enterprise: . . ACTION, SPIRIT, ATTEMPT, PROJECT, VENTURE, BUSINESS, GUMPTION, INITIATIVE, UNDERTAKING

entertain: . . . . FETE, AMUSE, TREAT, DIVERT, REGALE, CONSIDER, INTEREST

entertainment: . . FETE, PLAY, CHEER, FEAST, OPERA, REVUE, SPORT, BANQUET, CONCERT, PASTIME, MUSICALE, AMUSEMENT, DIVERSION, RECREATION

enthrall: . . CHARM, ENSLAVE, ENCHANT, CAPTIVATE, FASCINATE

enthusiasm: . . . . . PEP, ELAN, FIRE, ZEAL, ARDOR, VERVE, SPIRIT, CRAZE, MANIA, FERVOR, PASSION, EAGERNESS

enthusiast: . . BUG, FAN, NUT, BUFF, ZEALOT, DEVOTEE, FANATIC, ADDICT, ROOTER, AFICIONADO

enthusiastic: . . AVID, WARM, KEEN, EAGER, ARDENT, RABID

entice: . . BAIT, COAX, DRAW, LURE, TOLE, CHARM, TEMPT, ALLURE, INDUCE, SEDUCE, CAJOLE, ATTRACT, INVEIGH, INVEIGLE

entire: . . . ALL, FULL, EVERY, SOUND, TOTAL, WHOLE, COMPLETE, PERFECT, ABSOLUTE, UNDIVIDED

entity: . . . ENS, UNIT, BEING, THING, EXISTENCE

entomb: . . . . . . BURY, INTER

entourage: . TRAIN, RETINUE, ATTENDANTS

entrails: . . . . GUTS, BOWELS, VISCERA, INNARDS, INTESTINES

entrance: . . . . . . ADIT, DOOR, GATE, HALL, DEBUT, ENTRY, FOYER, MOUTH, ACCESS, ENTREE, PORTAL, POSTERN, ADMISSION, CHARM, DELIGHT, ENRAPTURE, FASCINATE

entrant: . . . . ENTRY, PARTICIPANT, CONTESTANT, COMPETITOR

entreat: . . . ASK, BEG, PRAY, PLEAD, BESEECH, IMPLORE, SUPPLICATE

entree: . . . . . . DISH, ENTRY, ENTRANCE, ADMISSION

entrench: . . . . INVADE, TRESPASS, ENCROACH, INFRINGE

entrust: . . . . GIVE, COMMIT, CONFIDE, CONSIGN, DEPOSIT

entry: . . . . DOOR, POST, ITEM, DEBIT, CREDIT, INGRESS, ACCESS, ENTRANCE

enumerate: . . COUNT, DETAIL, RECKON, COMPUTE, NUMBER, ITEMIZE, CALCULATE

enunciate: . . . UTTER, STATE, DECLARE, PROCLAIM, ANNOUNCE, ARTICULATE

enunciation: . . . . . . DICTION

enure: . HARDEN, ACCUSTOM, HABITUATE

enuresis: . . . . URINATION

envelop, envelope: . . . CASE, HUSK, WRAP, COVER, ENFOLD, ENGIRT, ENWRAP, INFOLD, INVEST, SHEATH, SHROUD, SWATHE, ENCLOSE, WRAPPER, SURROUND

envenom: . . . . CORRUPT, POISON, EMBITTER

environ: . . . . . . HEM, LIMIT, GIRDLE, SUBURB, PURLIEU, LOCALE, VICINITY, OUTSKIRT, ENCIRCLE, ENCLOSE, DISTRICT, SURROUND

environment: . . . . . MEDIUM, MILIEU, ELEMENT, HABITAT, AMBIENCE, SETTING

envoy: . . . . AGENT, DEPUTY, LEGATE, EMISSARY, NUNCIO, AMBASSADOR, MESSENGER, REPRESENTATIVE

envy: . . . . . COVET, GRUDGE, BEGRUDGE, JEALOUSY

eon: . . . . AGE, EPOCH

ephemeral: . . BRIEF, VAGUE, PASSING, TEMPORARY,

TRANSITORY, TRANSIENT,
EVANESCENT, MOMENTARY
epic:.... EPOS, SAGA, POEM,
NOBLE, GRAND, HEROIC,
MAJESTIC, NARRATIVE
epicarp: ...... HUSK, RIND
epicure: .... GLUTTON,
GOURMET, SYBARITE,
GOURMAND, GASTRONOME,
CONNOISSEUR
epidemic: .... PLAGUE,
PANDEMIC, PESTILENCE,
WIDESPREAD
epidermis:.... SKIN, CUTICLE
epigram:..... MOT, ADAGE,
SAYING, MONOSTICH
episode: .... EVENT, SCENE,
STORY, INCIDENT, HAPPENING,
INSTALLMENT
epistaxis: ...... NOSEBLEED
epistle: ..... NOTE, LETTER,
BILLET, MISSIVE
epitaph: .... HICJACET,
INSCRIPTION
epithet:...... NAME, OATH,
TERM, TITLE, PHRASE,
AGNOMEN, SOBRIQUET,
APPELATION
epitome: .... BRIEF, DIGEST,
PRECIS, ABSTRACT, SUMMARY,
ABRIDGEMENT
epoch: ..... EON, AGE, ERA,
DATE, TIME, EVENT, PERIOD
equal:...... PAR, TIE, COPE,
EVEN, JUST, LIKE, SAME, PEER,
ALIKE, LEVEL, MATCH, RIVAL,
COMPEER, EMULATE, UNIFORM
equality:... EQUITY, PARITY,
BALANCE, EGALITY, EVENNESS,
FAIRNESS, IMPARTIALITY
equanimity:........ POISE,
CALMNESS, EVENNESS,
COMPOSURE, SERENITY,
TRANQUILITY, SANG-FROID
equatorial: .... TORRID,
TROPICAL
equestrian: .... RIDER,
HORSEMAN
equilibrium: .... POISE,
BALANCE, EQUIPOISE

equip:.. ARM, FIT, RIG, GIRD,
ARRAY, DRESS, TRAIN,
FURNISH, ACCOUTER
equipment: ..... RIG, GEAR,
ATTIRE, OUTFIT, TACKLE,
HARNESS, MATERIAL
equitable: ..... EVEN, FAIR,
JUST, EQUAL, RIGHT, HONEST,
IMPARTIAL, REASONABLE
equivalent: ..... IDENTICAL
SYNONYMOUS, TANTAMOUNT
equivocal:....... DUBIOUS,
DOUBTFUL, ENIGMATIC,
UNCERTAIN, INDEFINITE,
UNDECIDED, AMBIGUOUS,
PERPLEXING
equivocate: .... LIE, DODGE,
EVADE, PALTER, HEDGE,
WEASEL, QUIBBLE
era: .. AGE, EON, DATE, TIME,
EPOCH, PERIOD
eradicate: .... WEED, ERASE,
DELETE, REMOVE, UPROOT,
DESTROY, ANNIHILATE,
EXTERMINATE
erase:.. BLOT, RAZE, ANNUL,
CANCEL, DELETE, EFFACE,
SCRATCH, EXPUNGE,
OBLITERATE, ERADICATE
erect:.. REAR, BUILD, SET-UP,
RAISE, STAND, ELEVATE,
UPRIGHT, VERTICAL, STRAIGHT,
CONSTRUCT
erelong: ...... ANON, SOON
eremite: ... HERMIT, RECLUSE
erenow: ...... HERETOFORE
Erin: ..... EIRE, HIBERNIA,
IRELAND
eristic: .... ARGUMENTATIVE,
CONTROVERSIAL
ermine:........ FUR, WHITE,
STOAT, WEASEL, MINIVER
erode:........ EAT, WEAR,
CORRODE, DESTROY,
UNDERMINE, DISINTEGRATE
erotic: .... SEXY, AMOROUS,
AMATORY
err: .. SIN, MISS, SLIP, STRAY,
BUNGLE, BLUNDER, DEVIATE,
MISTAKE, TRANSGRESS

errand: . . . . CHORE, MISSION

erratic: . . . QUEER, VAGRANT, STRANGE, IRREGULAR, ECCENTRIC, WANDERING, UNSTEADY, CAPRICIOUS

erroneous: . . FALSE, WRONG, UNTRUE, ERRATIC, INCORRECT, MISTAKEN

error: . . . . . SIN, FLUB, GOOF, MUFF, SLIP, BONER, FAULT, FLUFF, LAPSE, FAULT, MISCUE, BLUNDER, ERRATUM, FALLACY, FAUX PAS, MISTAKE, VIOLATION

erstaz: . . . . ARTIFICIAL, SUBSTITUTE

erudite: . . . . LEARNED, SCHOLARLY, WISE

erudition: . . . LORE, WISDOM, LEARNING, KNOWLEDGE, SCHOLARSHIP

erupt: . . . . BURST, EJECT, EXPLODE

eruption: . RASH, OUTBURST, OUTBREAK, EXPLOSION

escapade: . . . CAPER, PRANK, ADVENTURE, EXCURSION

escape: . . . LAM, FLEE, LEAK, VENT, SLIP, ELOPE, EVADE, ELUDE, ISSUE, AVOID, OUTLET, GETAWAY, DISAPPEAR

escheat: . . . . . FALL, LAPSE, FORFEIT, CONFISCATE

eschew: . . . . . . SHUN, AVOID, ESCAPE, ABSTAIN

escort: . . BEAU, LEAD, SHOW, GUARD, ATTEND, CONVOY, RETINUE, CONDUCT, CHAPERON, ACCOMPANY

escritoire: . . . . DESK, TABLE, BUREAU, SECRETARY

escrow: . . . . BOND, DEED

esculent: . . EDIBLE, EATABLE, COMESTIBLE

escutcheon: . . . ARMS, CREST, SHIELD

Eskimo: . . ITA, YUIT, ATKA, ALEUT, HUSKY, INNUIT, ALASKAN, ESQUIMAU

boot: . . . KAMIK, MUKLUK

canoe: . . . KAYAK, UMIAK, OOMIAK, OOMIAC

dog: . . HUSKY, MALEMUTE

garment: . . PARKA, TEMIAK

house: . . . . IGLU, IGLOO, TOPEK, TUPEK

esophagus: . . . . GULLET

esoteric: . . . . INNER, MYSTIC, SECRET, PRIVATE, ABSTRUSE, CONFIDENTIAL

especial: . . . CHIEF, PECULIAR, PARTICULAR, EXCEPTIONAL

espionage: . . . . ESPY, SPYING

esplanade: . . . WALK, DRIVE, PROMENADE

espousal: . . . . . . BETROTHAL, MARRIAGE, WEDDING, ADVOCACY

espouse: . . . . . . WED, MATE, MARRY, ADOPT, SUPPORT, ADVOCATE

esprit de corps: . . . MORALE, SPIRIT, CAMARADERIE

espy: . . . . SEE, SPOT, SIGHT, WATCH, DESCRY, DETECT, DISCERN, DISCOVER, ESPIONAGE

essay: . . . . TRY, SEEK, PAPER, THEME, TRACT, ATTEMPT, ARTICLE, TREATISE, THESIS

essence: . . ENS, CORE, CRUX, GIST, ODOR, PITH, SOUL, ATTAR, BASIC, FLAVOR, HEART, NATURE, ELEMENT, EXTRACT, PERFUME

essential: . . . . . BASIC, VITAL, INHERENT, MATERIAL, REQUISITE, INTRINSIC, NECESSARY, INDISPENSABLE

establish: . . FIX, SET, BUILD, ERECT, FOUND, SETTLE, PROVE, VERIFY, CREATE, LOCATE, INSTITUTE, ORIGINATE

estate: . . FIEF, HOME, ACRES, MANOR, ALLOD, ASSETS, CAPITAL, DOMAIN, GROUND, DEMESNE, FORTUNE, PROPERTY

esteem: . . . . . ADORE, COUNT, FAVOR, HONOR, PRIDE, PRIZE, VALUE, CREDIT, FAVOR,

ADMIRE, RESPECT, REGARD,
REPUTE, VENERATE,
APPRECIATE

esthetic: .... ARTISTIC,
AESTHETIC

estimate: .... SET, RATE,
GUAGE, GUESS, JUDGE, VALUE,
ASSESS, BUDGET, AVERAGE,
MEASURE, FORECAST, APPRAISE,
CALCULATE, EVALUATE

estop: ..... BAR, FILL, PLUG,
STOP, DEBAR, IMPEDE,
PREVENT, PROHIBIT, OBSTRUCT

estrange: ...... PART, WEAN,
DIVERT, ALIENATE, SEPARATE,
DISUNITE

estuary: .. RIA, LOCH, FRITH,
FIRTH, INLET, FIORD

esurient: .. GREEDY, HUNGRY,
VORACIOUS

et: .... AND

al: .... OTHERS

etch: .... CUT, CHISEL,
ENGRAVE, INSCRIBE

eternal: .. AGELESS, ENDLESS,
FOREVER, LASTING, TIMELESS,
EVERLASTING, UNCEASING,
PERPETUAL

eternity: ...... AGE, OLAM,
(A)EON, TIME, INFINITY,
IMMORTALITY, OLAM

etesian: .. ANNUAL, PERIODIC,
SEASONAL

ether: ..... AIR, SKY, ESTER,
SOLVENT, SPACE, ANESTHETIC

ethereal: ...... AIRY, AIRLIKE,
FRAGILE, DELICATE, HEAVENLY,
CELESTIAL, SUPERNAL

ethical: ..... MORAL, RIGHT,
VIRTUOUS

ethics: .. MORALS, HEDONICS

etiolate: .... PALE, BLANCH,
BLEACH

etiquette: .. FORM, MANNER,
DECORUM, PROPRIETY

eulogize: ..... LAUD, EXTOL,
PRAISE, GLORIFY

eulogy: ..... ELOGE, PRAISE,
ORATION, TRIBUTE, ENCOMIUM,
PANEGYRIC

eunuch: .... GELDING,
CASTRATE

euphony: .. METER, MELODY,
HARMONY

euphoria: .. EASE, COMFORT,
WELL-BEING, SMUGNESS,
COMPLACENCY

euripus: .... CANAL, STRAIT,
CHANNEL

evacuant: .... EMETIC,
DIURETIC, EMPTYING,
CATHARTIC, PURGATIVE

evacuate: ..... EMIT, VOID,
EMPTY, EXPEL, VACATE,
REMOVE, EXCRETE, EXHAUST,
NULLIFY, WITHDRAW,
DISCHARGE

evade: .. BILK, FOIL, AVERT,
AVOID, ELUDE, DODGE, SHIRK,
ESCAPE, ILLUDE

evaluate: .... RATE, GUAGE,
ASSAY, ASSESS, APPRAISE,
PONDER, ESTIMATE

evanesce: ... FADE, VANISH,
DISAPPEAR

evanescent: ...... EVASIVE,
EPHEMERAL, TRANSIENT,
FLEETING

evaporate: .... DRY, VANISH,
CONDENSE, VAPORIZE

evasion: ... DODGE, ESCAPE,
AVOIDANCE, ELUSION,
SUBTERFUGE, EQUIVOCATION

evasive: ... DODGY, SHIFTY,
TRICKY, ELUSIVE, DECEITFUL,
EQUIVOCAL

even: . TIE, FAIR, JUST, FLAT,
EQUAL, EXACT, FLUSH, LEVEL,
MATCH, PLACID, SMOOTH,
UNIFORM, SERENE, TOSSUP,
STEADY, EQUABLE, PARALLEL

evening: .... EVE, DUSK,
SUNSET, EVENTIDE, TWILIGHT,
GLOAMING

event: .... CASE, FACT, FEAT,
CAUSUS, DOING, RESULT,
EPISODE, INCIDENT OCCASION,
OCCURRENCE, HAPPENING

eventual: ... FINAL, ULTIMATE

ever: . . . . . . AYE, ALWAYS, FOREVER, CONSTANTLY, CONTINUALLY

every: . . . . . ALL, ILK, EACH, ENTIRE

everyday: . . . DAILY, USUAL, COMMON, PROSAIC, ORDINARY

evict: . . OUST, EJECT, EXPEL, REMOVE, DISPOSSESS

evidence: . . . . . SHOW, SIGN, PROOF, TRACE, ATTEST, REVEAL, EXHIBIT, SUPPORT, TESTIMONY, INDICATION

evident: . . . . . CLEAR, PLAIN, PATENT, GLARING, OBVIOUS, VISIBLE, APPARENT, MANIFEST, PALPABLE

evil: . . . BAD, ILL, SIN, BASE, HARM, VICE, VILE, CRIME, MENACE, WICKED, ADVERSE, CORRUPT, WICKED, INIQUITY, DEPRAVITY, MALICIOUS

evoke: . . . . . . CALL, EDUCE, AROUSE, REMIND, RECALL, ELICIT, SUMMON

evolution: . . . . BIOGENY, GROWTH, MUTATION, DEVELOPMENT

evolve: . . . . . . EMIT, EDUCE, DERIVE, UNFOLD, WORKOUT, DEVELOP

exacerbate: . . . IRK, ENRAGE, EXCITE, WORSEN, PROVOKE, EMBITTER, INCREASE, IRRITATE, AGGRAVATE

exact: . . . . . EVEN, FINE, LEVY, TRUE, WREST, COMPEL, DEMAND, ELICIT, EXTORT, STRICT, CERTAIN, CORRECT, EXTRACT, LITERAL, PRECISE, ACCURATE, EXPLICIT

exaggerate: . . . . . . OVERDO, AMPLIFY, ENHANCE, ENLARGE, MAGNIFY, STRETCH, INCREASE, EMBROIDER, OVERSTATE

exalt: . . . . . . ELATE, EXTOL, HONOR, RAISE, PRAISE, GLORIFY, ELEVATE

examination: . . . QUIZ, TEST, ASSAY, AUDIT, CHECK, TRIAL, REVIEW, SURVEY, INQUEST, AUTOPSY, SCRUTINY, INQUIRY, INSPECTION

examine: . . TRY, FEEL, SCAN, VIEW, ASSAY, PROBE, INSPECT, ANALYZE, TEST, EXPLORE, SCRUTINIZE

example: . . . . . . CASE, TYPE, MODEL, SAMPLE, INSTANCE, PATTERN, SPECIMEN, PARADIGM, ILLUSTRATION

exasperate: . . IRK, TRY, VEX, GALL, ANGER, ANNOY, NETTLE, INFURIATE, INCENSE, IRRITATE, AGGRAVATE

excavate: . . . . . . DIG, MINE, DELVE, SCOOP, UNEARTH, DREDGE, EXHUME

excavation: . . . . . PIT, MINE, HOLE, STOPE, GRAVE, CAVITY, GROOVE, TRENCH, HOLLOW

exceed: . . . . TOP, BEST, PASS, EXCEL, OUTDO, BETTER, ECLIPSE, SURPASS, OUTSTRIP, OUTREACH, TRANSCEND

excellence: . . MERIT, VIRTUE, DIGNITY, GOODNESS, PERFECTION, SUPERIORITY

excellent: . . . . . . BEST, FINE, GOOD, TOPS, GREAT, PRIME, SUPER, CHOICE, SELECT, WORTHY, CAPITAL, SUPERB, SUPERIOR, OUTSTANDING

except: . . . . BAR, BUT, OMIT, ONLY, SAVE, OBJECT, EXEMPT, UNLESS, BESIDES, EXCLUDE, ELIMINATE

exception: . . DEMUR, DISSENT, EXCLUSION, OMISSION, OBJECTION, CHALLENGE

exceptional: . . . . RARE, ESPECIAL, UNUSUAL, ABNORMAL, UNCOMMON, OUTSTANDING

excess: . . OVER, PLUS, EXTRA, PROFUSE, SURFEIT, SURPLUS,

OVERMUCH, PLETHORA, SUPERFLUITY, INTEMPERANCE

excessive: . . . . . TOO, OVER, UNDUE, EXTREME, OVERMUCH, IMMODERATE, EXTRAVAGANT, EXORBITANT, INORDINATE

exchange: . . . . . CASH, CHOP, MART, SELL, SWAP, BANDY, STORE, TRADE, TRUCK, BARTER, MARKET, RIALTO, SWITCH, COMMUTE, TRANSPOSE

excise: . . . TAX, TOLL, DUTY, IMPOST, CUT OUT, REMOVE, EXSCIND, EXTIRPATE

excite: . . . . ROIL, SPUR, STIR, ALARM, ANGER, IMPEL, PIQUE, FOMENT, INCITE, (A)ROUSE, PROVOKE, AGITATE, ANIMATE, STIMULATE, TITILLATE

excitement: . . . . . ADO, STIR, FEVER, FUROR, TIZZY, FLUTTER, COMMOTION, DISTURBANCE

exclamation: . . . AH, HA, HO, OH, OW, SO AHA, BAH, FIE, HEY, HUH, GEE, TUT, UGH, WOW, YOW, ALAS, DRAT, EGAD, HECK, NUTS, OUCH, POOH, PHEW, PISH, RATS, BRAVO, HUMPH, PSHAW, HURRAH, SHUCKS, WHOOPEE, EXPLETIVE, INTERJECTION

exclude: . . . . . . BAR, OMIT, DEBAR, EJECT, EXPEL, BANISH, EXCEPT, EXEMPT, REJECT, BLACKBALL, ELIMINATE, OSTRACIZE

exclusive: . . . . . ONLY, RARE, SOLE, ALONE, ONLY, ELITE, SINGLE, SELECT, ENTIRELY, MONOPOLY

excommunicate: . . . . . . BAN, DAMN, CONDEMN, UNCHURCH

excoriate: . . . FLAY, ABRADE, DENOUNCE

excrement: . . . . DIRT, DUNG, FECES, ORDURE, MANURE, REFUSE

excruciate: . . . PAIN, GRIND, AGONIZE, TORTURE, TORMENT

exculpate: . . . . FREE, CLEAR, ACQUIT, EXCUSE, PARDON, ABSOLVE, FORGIVE, EXONERATE

excursion: . . . . . . RIDE, SAIL, TOUR, TRIP, JAUNT, TRAMP, CRUISE, JUNKET, OUTING, RAMBLE, VOYAGE, JOURNEY, EXPEDITION

excuse: . . PLEA, ALIBI, REMIT, ACQUIT, PARDON, ABSOLVE, APOLOGY, CONDONE, ESSOIGN, RELEASE, PRETEXT, OVERLOOK

execrable: . . . BAD, HATEFUL, DETESTABLE, NEFARIOUS, ABOMINABLE

execrate: . . . . . . BAN, HATE, DETEST, CURSE, ABHOR, LOATHE

execute: . . . DO, ACT, HANG, KILL, OBEY, SLAY, LYNCH, DIRECT, EFFECT, FINISH, CONDUCT, PERFORM, FULFILL, COMPLETE

exemplar: . . . . MODEL, PATTERN, EXAMPLE, ARCHETYPE

exempt: . . . . FREE, EXCUSE, IMMUNE, EXCLUDE, RELEASE

exercise: . . . PLY, USE, DRILL, EXERT, TRAIN, EMPLOY, LESSON, PARADE, PRAXIS, DISPLAY, PROBLEM, ACTIVITY, PRACTICE

exert: . . EMIT, SPEND, STRAIN, ENDEAVOR, EXERCISE

exhalation: . . . FUME, STEAM, BREATH, HALITUS, EXPIRATION, EVAPORATION, EMANATION

exhaust: . . . FAG, SAP, EMIT, FAIL, TIRE, DRAIN, EMPTY, PETER, SPEND, WEARY, DEPLETE, FATIGUE, DISCHARGE

exhibit: . . . . AIR, FAIR, SHOW, STAGE, EXPOSE, PARADE, REVEAL, DISPLAY, PRODUCE, DISCLOSE, EVIDENCE, PRESENTATION

exhilarate: . . . . ELATE,
ENLIVEN, ANIMATE, STIMULATE,
INVIGORATE
exhort: . . URGE, WARN, PROD,
ADVISE, PREACH, CAUTION
exhume: . . . . DIG, DISINTER,
UNEARTH
exigent: . . . . VITAL, URGENT,
CRITICAL, EXACTING, PRESSING
exile: . . . . . . EXPEL, DEPORT,
OUTLAW, OUTCAST, REFUGEE,
FUGITIVE, RELEGATE,
EXPATRIATE, BANISH(MENT)
exist: . . . . . . (A)LIVE, BE, IS
existence: . . ENS, ESSE, LIFE,
BEING, ENTITY, LIVING,
ESSENCE, REALITY, ACTUALITY
existing: . . . . . REAL, ALIVE,
BEING, EXTANT
exit: . . . DOOR, GATE, GOING,
ISSUE, LEAVE, DEPART, EGRESS,
OUTLET, PASSAGE, DEPARTURE
exodus: . . . . HEGIRA, FLIGHT,
MIGRATION, DEPARTURE,
EMIGRATION
exonerate: . . . . FREE, CLEAR,
ACQUIT, ABSOLVE, DISCHARGE,
EXCULPATE, VINDICATE
exorbitant: . . . . UNDUE,
ABNORMAL, EXCESSIVE,
IMMODERATE, OUTRAGEOUS,
UNREASONABLE
exotic: . . . . ALIEN, FOREIGN,
STRANGE, IMPORTED
expand: . . . . . . WAX, BLOW,
GROW, OPEN, SWELL, WIDEN,
DILATE, EXTEND, SPREAD,
AMPLIFY, DISTEND, ENLARGE,
BROADEN, INFLATE, INCREASE,
LENGTHEN, INTUMESCE
expect: . . HOPE, WAIT, AWAIT,
DEMAND, PRESUME, REQUIRE,
SUPPOSE, ANTICIPATE
expedient: . . . . WISE, DEVICE,
POLITIC, STOPGAP, ADVISABLE,
MAKESHIFT, CONVENIENT
expedite: . . . . . . EASY, FREE,
HASTEN, HURRY, SPEED UP,
ACCELERATE, FACILITATE

expel: . . . OUST, EJECT, EVICT,
EXILE, BANISH, DEPORT,
DISLODGE, DISPOSSESS,
EXPATRIATE
expend: . . . . . . USE, SPEND,
WASTE, CONSUME, DISSIPATE,
DISTRIBUTE
expenditure: . . COST, OUTGO,
OUTLAY, DISBURSEMENT
expense: . . . FEE, COST, LOSS,
PRICE, OUTLAY, CHARGE,
OVERHEAD
experience: . . . . SEE, FEEL,
LIVE, TEST, SKILL, TRIAL,
ORDEAL, SUFFER, UNDERGO
experiment: . . . . . TRY, TEST,
TRIAL, ASSAY, ESSAY, ATTEMPT
expert: . . . . ACE, PRO, DEFT,
GOOD, ADEPT, ADROIT, ARTIST,
SHARP, MASTER, CAPABLE,
SKILLED, AUTHORITY,
PROFICIENT
expiate: . . . . ATONE, AVERT,
REPAIR, SATISFY
expire: . . . . . DIE, END, EMIT,
STOP, CEASE, LAPSE, EXHALE,
PERISH, TERMINATE
explain: . . . . SOLVE, DEFINE,
EXPAND, UNFOLD, CLARIFY,
EXPOUND, DESCRIBE,
EXPLICATE, INTERPRET,
ELUCIDATE
explicit: . . . . CLEAR, EXACT,
PLAIN, DEFINITE, EXPRESS,
PRECISE, SPECIFIC, ABSOLUTE
explode: . . . . . . FIRE, BLAST,
BURST, DISCREDIT, DETONATE
exploit: . . . . ACT, DEED,
ACTION, FEAT, GEST(E),
PROMOTE, PERFORM, UTILIZE
explore: . MAP, FEEL, CHART,
EXAMINE, DISCOVER,
INVESTIGATE
exponent: . . . . . . ADVOCATE
expose: . . BARE, OPEN, SHOW,
DISCLOSE, REVEAL, UNMASK,
DISPLAY, EXHIBIT, UNCOVER

expostulate: . . . . ARGUE, DISCUSS, OBJECT, PROTEST, COMPLAIN, REMONSTRATE

expound: . . DEFINE, EXPOSE, DEVELOP, EXPLAIN, CLARIFY, INTERPRET, ELUCIDATE

express: . . . . . VENT, EMOTE, SPEAK, STATE, UTTER, VOICE, REVEAL, DECLARE, DICTATE, EXPOUND, SIGNIFY, EXPLICIT, DEFINITE, DESCRIBE

expression: . . . . FORM, SIGN, TERM, WORD, IDIOM, TOKEN, PHRASE, SAYING, SYMBOL, REPRESENTATION, ARTICULATION

expressive: . . . . . ELOQUENT, EMPHATIC, SIGNIFICANT

action: . . . . GESTURE

expressly: . . . . NAMELY, PLAINLY, ESPECIALLY, DEFINITELY

expropriate: . . . . DISPOSSESS

expulsion: . . . EXILE, OUSTER, BOUNCE, EJECTION

expunge: . . . ERASE, CANCEL, DELETE, EFFACE, WIPEOUT, DESTROY, OBLITERATE

expurgate: . . CENSOR, PURGE

exquisite: . . . RARE, CHOICE, DAINTY, ELEGANT, DELICATE, BEAUTIFUL, DELICIOUS, FASTIDIOUS

extant: . . . . ALIVE, EXISTING

extemporaneous: . . OFFHAND, IMPROMPTU, IMPROVISED

extend: . . . . JUT, RUN, SPAN, COVER, REACH, RENEW, WIDEN, EXPAND, SPREAD, PROTRACT, AMPLIFY, ENLARGE, STRETCH, CONTINUE, PROLONG

extent: . . AREA, BODY, BULK, LIMIT, RANGE, SCOPE, AMOUNT, DEGREE, SPREAD, LENGTH, EXPANSE, COVERAGE, MAGNITUDE

extenuate: . . . THIN, EXCUSE, WEAKEN, LESSEN, DIMINISH, MITIGATE, PALLIATE, ALLEVIATE, DEPRECIATE

exterior: . . . . ECTAL, OUTER, SHELL, OUTSIDE, FOREIGN, SURFACE, EXTERNAL

exterminate: . . . . EXPEL, UPROOT, DESTROY, EXTIRPATE, ERADICATE, ANNIHILATE

external: . . . . OUT, OUTER, OUTSIDE, EXTRINSIC, EXTERIOR, SUPERFICIAL

extinct: . . . . DEAD, DEFUNCT, EXTINGUISHED, QUENCHED, NON-EXISTENT

extinguish: . . CHOKE, DOUSE, QUELL, SNUFF, STIFLE, DESTROY, SMOTHER, ECLIPSE, SUFFOCATE, ANNIHILATE

extirpate: . . . . RAZE, ERASE, EXPEL, EXCISE, UPROOT, DESTROY, ABOLISH, ERADICATE, EXTERMINATE

extol: . PRAISE, LAUD, EXALT, BLESS, GLORIFY, EULOGIZE

extort: . . . . . FORCE, WRING, MILK, SCREW, EXACT, WREST, COMPEL, BLEED, MULCT, EXTRACT, BLACKMAIL

extra: . . . ADD, BONUS, MORE, OVER, PLUS, ADDED, SPARE, EXCESS, SPECIAL, SURPLUS, ADDITIONAL

extract: . . . . . DIG, PRY, CITE, DRAW, PULL, EDUCE, EXACT, QUOTE, STEEP, EVOKE, WRING, DERIVE, DISTIL, ELICIT, EXTORT, REMOVE, ESSENCE, EXCERPT, QUOTATION

extraction: . . BIRTH, STOCK, ORIGIN, LINEAGE, DESCENT, ESSENCE, BREEDING, PARENTAGE

extraneous: . . ALIEN, OUTER, EXOTIC, FOREIGN, EXTRINSIC, ACCIDENTAL

extraordinary: . . ODD, RARE, UNCO, SIGNAL, UNIQUE, STRANGE, UNUSUAL, EXCEPTIONAL, ABNORMAL,

UNCOMMON, REMARKABLE,
MARVELOUS
extravagant: .... WILD,
COSTLY, LAVISH, BAROQUE,
FANATIC, PROFUSE, EXCESSIVE,
RECKLESS, EXORBITANT,
WASTEFUL, PRODIGAL
extreme: ..... LAST, CLOSE,
FINAL, GREAT, LIMIT, ULTRA,
UTTER, DRASTIC, RADICAL
INTENSE, SEVERE, FARTHEST,
DESPERATE, EXCESSIVE,
STRINGENT, IMMODERATE
extremity: ... END, TIP, TOE,
NEED, POLE, TAIL, LIMIT,
DYING, BORDER, DISASTER,
TERMINAL
extricate: .... FREE, CLEAR,
LOOSE, RESCUE, RELEASE,
LIBERATE, UNTANGLE
extrinsic: .. ALIEN, FOREIGN,
EXTERNAL, ACCIDENTAL,
UNESSENTIAL, EXTRANEOUS
extrude: ..... SPEW, EJECT,
EXPEL, PROJECT, PROTRUDE
exuberant: .... LAVISH,
COPIOUS, EFFUSIVE, PLENTIFUL
exudation: ... GUM, SAP, TAR,
PITCH, RESIN, SWEAT,
DISCHARGE, SECRETION,
EMANATION, PERSPIRATION
exult: ...... CROW, BOAST,
GLOAT, GLORY, REJOICE
exultant: .... ELATED
eye: .. BUD, ORB, DISC, GAZE,
GLIM, LOOK, OGLE, SCAN,
VIEW, OPTIC, WATCH, GLANCE,
REGARD, VISION, OCULUS,
OBSERVE, SCRUTINIZE
black: .... MOUSE, SHINER
cavity: .... ORBIT
colored portion: ..... IRIS
defect: ...... CAST, ANOPIA,
MYOPIA, DIPLOPIA, OXYOPIA
disease: .... IRITIS,
CATARACT, GLAUCOMA,
TRACHOMA, CONJUNCTIVITIS
doctor: .... OCULIST,
OPHTHALMOLOGIST

opening: .... PUPIL
eyeglasses: .. SPECS, LENSES,
MONOCLE, PINCE NEZ,
CHEATERS, LORGNETTE,
SPECTACLES
eyelet: .... GROMMET,
PEEPHOLE, LOOPHOLE,
BUTTONHOLE
eyesight: ..... VIEW, VISION,
OBSERVATION
eyesore: .... UGLY, DEFECT,
BLEMISH
eyetooth: .... FANG, CUSPID,
CANINE
eyewash: .... EXCUSE,
NONSENSE, FLATTERY

F

fable: .. MYTH, TALE, STORY,
LEGEND, FICTION, APOLOGUE,
FALSEHOOD, ALLEGORY,
PARABLE
fabric: .... MAT, RUG, WEB,
FELT, KNIT, WARP, WOOF,
BUILD, CLOTH, FRAME, TOWEL,
WEAVE, CARPET, DIAPER,
NAPKIN, CURTAIN, TEXTURE,
DRAPERY, TEXTILE, MATERIAL,
CONSTRUCT, STRUCTURE,
TAPESTRY, UPHOLESTRY
kind/type: .... NET, REP,
CORD, DUCK, LAME, LAWN,
LENO, TAPA, BAIZE, BEIGE,
CRASH, CREPE, DENIM,
DRILL, GAUZE, PIQUE,
PLAID, SATIN, SCRIM,
SERGE, TERRY, TWEED,
TWILL, VOILE, BURLAP,
CALICO, CANVAS, CHINTZ,
DAMASK, MOHAIR, MUSLIN,
POPLIN, SATEEN, TARTAN,
VELURE, VELVET, BROCADE,
BUCKRAM, CHIFFON,
ERAMINE, GINGHAM,
ORGANZA, PAISLEY,
PERCALE, SUITING,
TAFFETA, WOOLEN,

WORSTED, CASHMERE,
CHENILLE, CORDUROY,
CRETONNE, DUNGAREE,
SHANTUNG, SEERSUCKER
synthetic: ...... NYLON,
ORLON, RAYON, DACRON,
ACETATE, ACRILIN, PLASTIC,
POLYESTER

fabricate: .. LIE, COIN, FORM,
MAKE, BUILD, FRAME, DEVISE,
INVENT, CONCOCT, FASHION,
PRODUCE, CONSTRUCT,
MANUFACTURE

fabrication: .... LIE, DECEIT,
FICTION, FORGERY, UNTRUTH,
PRETENSE, FALSEHOOD

fabulous: ...... MYTHICAL,
ROMANTIC, IMAGINARY,
LEGENDARY, INCREDIBLE,
ASTONISHING

face: ...... MAP, MUG, PAN,
DARE, DEFY, DIAL, MEET,
FRONT, COVER, FACADE,
OPPOSE, VENEER, VISAGE,
SURFACE, CONFRONT, ANSWER,
COUNTENANCE

facetious: ... WITTY, JOCOSE,
COMICAL, JOCULAR, HUMOROUS

facile: .... ABLE, DEFT, EASY,
QUICK, EXPERT, FLUENT,
AFFABLE, ADROIT

facilitate: .. AID, EASE, HELP,
SPEED, FURTHER, QUICKEN,
EXPEL.TE

facsimile: .`.`.. COPY, MODEL,
REPLICA, LIKENESS, DUPLICATE,
REPRODUCTION

fact: ... DATA, DEED, DATUM,
TRUTH, EVENT, REALITY,
ACTUALITY, CIRCUMSTANCE

faction: .... BLOC, SET, SIDE,
CABAL, JUNTO, PARTY, CLIQUE,
DISPUTE

factor: ...... GENE, AGENT,
BROKER, DETAIL, BALIFF,
STEWARD, ELEMENT

factory: ...... MILL, SHOP,
PLANT, WORKSHOP

faculty: .. WIT, EASE, KNACK,
TALENT, POWER, ABILITY,
APTITUDE, CAPACITY

fad: .... MODE, RAGE, WHIM,
CRAZE, FANCY, HOBBY,
FASHION

fade: ...... DIE, DIM, PALE,
WANE, WILT, PETER, DROOP,
PERISH, VANISH, WITHER,
DECLINE, DIMINISH, DISAPPEAR

fag: ... TIRE, DROOP, WEARY,
EXHAUST, DRUDGE, FATIGUE,
HOMOSEXUAL, CIGARETTE

fail: ...... EBB, FLAG, FLOP,
FOLD, LOSE, MISS, SINK,
FLUNK, PETER, DESERT, FIZZLE,
COLLAPSE, MISCARRY,
DEFAULT, LANGUISH

failure: ... DUD, BUST, FLOP,
LACK, LOSS, MISS, DECAY,
LAPSE, LEMON, FIASCO, FIZZLE,
DEBACLE, DECLINE, DEFAULT,
NEGLECT, COLLAPSE, OMISSION

faint: .... DIM, WAN, DARK,
PALE, WEAK, SWOON, FEEBLE,
TIMID, UNCLEAR, OBSCURE,
INDISTINCT

fair: .... CALM, EVEN, JUST,
MART, BLOND, CLEAR, RIGHT,
DECENT, HONEST, BAZAAR,
EXHIBIT, KERMIS, MIDDLING,
UNBIASED, FESTIVAL,
CARNIVAL, EXHIBITION,
IMPARTIAL, BEAUTIFUL,
EXPOSITION

fairy: .. ELF, FAY, ELVE, PERI,
PIXY, PIXIE, NYMPH, SPRITE,
LEPRECHAUN

faith: .. CULT, DOXY, CREED,
TROTH, TRUST, BELIEF,
RELIGION, RELIANCE,
CONFIDENCE

faithful: .. FAST, FIRM, TRUE,
EXACT, LOYAL, PIOUS, HONEST,
STEADY, DEVOTED, CONSTANT,
RELIABLE, ACCURATE

faithless: ... FALSE, ATHEIST,
DISLOYAL, PERFIDIOUS,
TRAITOROUS

fake: . . HOAX, SHAM, BOGUS, CHEAT, TRICK, FALSE, FRAUD, PHONEY, PRETEND, SWINDLE, IMITATION, COUNTERFEIT

fakir: . . MONK, YOGI, SWAMI, ASCETIC, MEDICANT

fall: . SAG, DRIP, DROP, PLOP, RUIN, SLIP, ABATE, CRASH, LAPSE, SLUMP, AUTUMN, PERISH, RECEDE, TOPPLE, TUMBLE, DECLINE, DESCEND, CASCADE, PLUNGE, PLUMMET, COLLAPSE

fallacious: . . . . UNTRUE, ERRONEOUS, MISLEADING, DECEPTIVE

fallacy: . . . . . ERROR, IDOLA, IDOLUM, MISTAKE, DECEPTION

false: . . FAKE, SHAM, BOGUS, PHONY, WRONG, UNTRUE, FORGED, PSEUDO, SPURIOUS, INCORRECT, FAITHLESS, MISTAKEN, ARTIFICIAL, MENDACIOUS

falter: . . FAIL, PAUSE, WAVER, TOTTER, STUMBLE, STAMMER, HESITATE

fame: . . . . . . GLORY, HONOR, KUDOS, RENOWN, REPUTE, REPUTATION

famed: . . . NOTED, EMINENT, NOTORIOUS, REPUTED, CELEBRATED

familiar: . . . . . . BOLD, EASY, FREE, USUAL, COMMON, INTIMATE, FRIENDLY, ORDINARY, WELL-KNOWN

family: . . . . . ILK, KIN, CLAN, LINE, RACE, CLASS, BREED, FLESH, GROUP, STOCK, TRIBE, LINEAGE, KINSFOLK, PROGENY, HOUSEHOLD, GENERATION

famine: . . . . DEARTH, HUNGER SCARCITY, STARVATION, DESTITUTION

famous: . . . . GRAND, NOTED, EMINENT, NOTABLE, CELEBRATED, NOTORIOUS, RENOWNED

fan: . . . . BLOW, BUFF, COOL, BLOWER, EXCITE, ROOTER, FOMENT, DEVOTEE

fanatic: . . . MAD, NUT, CRAZY, RABID, BIGOT, ZEALOT, DEVOTEE, PHRENETIC, PARTISAN

fancied: . . . . UNREAL, IMAGINARY, FICTITIOUS

fancy: . . . . FAD, IDEA, LOVE, WEEM, WHIM, DREAM, GUESS, LIKING, MEGRIM, NOTION, ORNATE, VISION, CAPRICE, FANTASY, DELUSION, ILLUSION

fantastic: . . . . OUTLANDISH, ODD, QUEER, UNREAL, BIZARRE, GROTESQUE, ECCENTRIC

fantasy: . . . . . IDEA, DREAM, FANCY, VISION, ILLUSION, CAPRICE, PHANTASM

far: . . . . . . LONG, REMOTE, DISTANT, ADVANCED

farce: . . . . . . MIME, COMEDY, TRAVESTY, MOCKERY, BURLESQUE

farcical: . . . . COMIC, FUNNY, ABSURD, LUDICROUS, RIDICULOUS

fare: . . EAT, PAY, FOOD, DIET, MENU, RATE, PRICE, RESULT, PASSENGER

farewell: . . . . . ADIEU, ADIOS, ALOHA, CONGE, GOODBY, PARTING, VALEDICTION

farfetched: . . . . . . REMOTE, FORCED, DEVIOUS, STRAINED

farm: . . TILL, CROFT, RANCH, RANGE, BARTON, GRANGE, HACIENDA, CULTIVATE

farming: . . . . . . HUSBANDRY, AGRICULTURE

farrier: . . . . SMITH, BLACKSMITH, VETERINARIAN

farrow: . . . . PIG, LITTER

farther: . . LONGER, REMOTER

fascinate: . . CHARM, ALLURE, ENAMOUR, ATTRACT, BEWITCH, ENCHANT, INTRIGUE, CAPTIVATE

fashion: . . . . . . FAD, RAGE, VOGUE, STYLE, CRAZE, KIND,

SORT, MODE, MOLD, SHAPE, DESIGN, CREATE, MANNER, FABRICATE

fashionable: ... CHIC, RITZY, TONEY, SMART, SLEEK, STYLISH, ALAMODE

fast: .... FIRM, AGILE, BRISK, FIXED, FLEET, HASTY, QUICK, RAPID, STUCK, SWIFT, SECURE, SPEEDY, STARVE, FAITHFUL

fasten: .. FIX, PIN, TIE, BIND, BOLT, CLIP, GLUE, LASH, LINK, LOCK, NAIL, SEAL, WIRE, AFFIX, CHAIN, CLAMP, CLASP, LATCH, RIVET, ANCHOR, ATTACH, SECURE, TETHER

fastener: .... BAR, NUT, PEG, PIN, BOLT, CLIP, HASP, LOCK, NAIL, CLAMP, SNAP, STRAP, CLASP, LATCH, RIVET, BUCKLE, STAPLE, BUTTON, ZIPPER

fastidious: ..... NICE, FUSSY, CHOICY, DAINTY, FINICKY, REFINED, PRECISE, CRITICAL, METICULOUS, PARTICULAR

fat: .. OIL, LARD, RICH, SUET, GROSS, OBESE, PLUMP, THICK, STOUT, PORTLY, PORKY, PUDGY, DUMPY, PUFFY, PURSY, FLESHY, GREASE, STOCKY, TALLOW, ADIPOSE, BLUBBER, PIGUID, CORPULENT

fatal: . DIRE, FERAL, DEADLY, DOOMED, FUNEST, FATEFUL, LETHAL, MORTAL, RUINOUS, DISASTROUS

fate: ..... END, LOT, DOOM, KARMA, CHANCE, KISMET, DESTINY, FORTUNE

father: ...... PA, DAD, POP, ABBA, PUPA, SIRE, ADOPT, BEGET, DADDY, PATER, PARENT, PRIEST, CREATOR, GENERATE

fathom: .... DELVE, PROBE, SOLVE, PLUMB, SOUND, MEASURE

fatigue: ... FAG, BORE, JADE, TIRE, EXHAUST, WEARINESS

fatuous: ..... INANE, SILLY, STUPID, SAPPY, IDIOTIC, FOOLISH, ASININE

faucet: .. TAP, COCK, VALVE, SPIGOT, HYDRANT

fault: .... SIN, DEBT, FLAW, LACK, SLIP, VICE, ABUSE, BLAME, ERROR, LAPSE, DEFECT, FAILING, MISDEED, MISTAKE, WEAKNESS, IMPERFECTION

faultless: ..... PURE, IDEAL, RIGHT, CORRECT, PERFECT, PARAGON, FLAWLESS, IMPECCABLE

faux pas: ..... SLIP, BONER, ERROR, GAFFE, LAPSE, MISSTEP, BLUNDER, BLOOPER

favor: ...... AID, FOR, PRO, BOON, HELP, LEAN, BLESS, GRACE, LEAVE, ESTEEM, LETTER, LIKING, ADVANCE, SUPPORT, RESEMBLE

favorable: .... GOOD, ROSY, CLEAR, BENIGN, OPTIMAL, POPULAR, PLEASING, OPPORTUNE, AUSPICIOUS, PROPITIOUS

favorite: .... PET, DARLING, POPULAR, PREFERRED, MINION

fawn: .... DOE, BUCK, DEER, COLOR, CRAWL, KOWTOW, TOADY, CRINGE, FLATTER, GROVEL, SERVILE, INGRATIATE

faze: ...... ANNOY, DAUNT, WORRY, DISTURB, AGITATE, DISCONCERT, EMBARRASS

fealty: ..... DUTY, HOMAGE, LOYALTY, FIDELITY, ALLEGIANCE

fear: ... AWE, PANIC, ALARM, DREAD, DISMAY, FRIGHT, PHOBIA, TERROR, ANXIETY, MISGIVING, APPREHENSION
of animals: ... ZOOPHOBIA
of being alone: ....
    MONOPHOBIA
of enclosed places: ......
    CLAUSTROPHOBIA
of fire: ..... PYROPHOBIA

of heights: . . . ACROPHOBIA
of lightning: . . . TROPHOBIA
of pain: . . . . ALGOPHOBIA
of strangers: . . . .
XENOPHOBIA

fearful: . . DIRE, TIMID, PAVID,
NERVOUS, AFRAID, WORRIED,
DOUBTFUL, TERRIFIED

fearless: . . . . . BOLD, BRAVE,
DARING, HEROIC, IMPAVID,
INTREPID

feasible: . . LIKELY, POSSIBLE,
PROBABLE, REASONABLE,
PRACTICABLE

feast: . . . . . . EAT, SUP, DINE,
REPAST, FESTIVAL, BANQUET,
REGALE

feat: . . . ACT, DEED, EXPLOIT,
STUNT, ACCOMPLISHMENT

feather: . . . . DOWN, PENNA,
PINNA, PLUME, QUILL, PINION,
PLUMAGE

feature: . FACE, PART, TRAIT,
MOTIF, FORM, ASPECT,
CHARACTERISTIC

febrile: . . . . FEVERISH

feces: . . . . . DREGS, EGESTA,
REFUSE, SEDIMENT, EXCREMENT

fecund: . . FERTILE, FRUITFUL,
PROLIFIC, PRODUCTIVE

federation: . UNION, LEAGUE,
NATION, ALLIANCE

fee: . . . . . DUES, RATE, TOLL,
WAGE, PRICE, CHARGE,
GRATUITY, HONORARIUM

feeble: . PUNY, WEAK, FRAIL,
DOTTY, SICKLY, FRAGILE,
INVALID, FLABBY, FLACCID,
RICKETY

feel: . . GROPE, SENSE, SUFFER,
TOUCH, HANDLE, EXAMINE,
APPRECIATE

feeling: . . . SENSITIVITY, PITY,
TACT, TOUCH, MORALE,
EMOTION, OPINION, PASSION,
SENTIMENT, SENSATION,
AWARENESS

feet: . . . . see **foot**

feign: . . . . ACT, FAKE, SHAM,
SHIRK, AFFECT, ASSUME,

INVENT, DISSEMBLE,
FABRICATE, PRETEND,
SIMULATE

feint: . . . RUSE, SHAM, BLIND,
TRICK, DIVERSION, PRETENSE
in fencing: . . . . APPEL

feldspar: . . . . . . ANORTHITE,
ALBITE, ADULARIA,
MOONSTONE, KAOLIN, ODINITE,
SILICATE, LABRADORITE

felicitate: . . . CONGRATULATE

felicitous: . . . . . APPROPRIATE

felicity: . . . . BLISS, HAPPINESS

fell: . . . . . CUT, HEW, DOWN,
MOOR, PELT, RUIN, CRUEL,
FIERCE, SHREWD, TERRIBLE,
CUTDOWN

fellow (see: **person/man**): . . .
EGG, GUY, LAD, MAN, BEAN,
BOZO, CHAP, DICK, DUCK,
JACK, MATE, PEER, BLOKE,
BUGGER, SIRRAH, COMRADE,
PARTNER, ASSOCIATE

fellowship: . . GUILD, UNION,
SODALITY, COMPANY,
ASSOCIATION, ENDOWMENT,
BROTHERHOOD

felon: . . WILD, CRUEL, FIERCE,
CONVICT, CULPRIT, VILLAIN,
CRIMINAL, WICKED, WHITLOW

felony: . . . . . . RAPE, ARSON,
CRIME, MURDER, OFFENSE

felt: . . . . SENSED, FABRIC

female: . . . GIRL, WOMAN(LY),
FEMININE, EFFEMINATE

femur: . . . . THIGHBONE

fen: . . . . BOG MOOR, MORAS,
MARSH, SWAMP

fence: . . . . BAR, DUEL, PALE,
RAIL, WALL, EVADE, PARRY,
GUARD, HEDGE, PICKET,
BARRIER, ENCLOSE, PALISADE,
DEFENSE, SWORDPLAY

fend: . . WARD, AVERT, SHIFT,
DEFEND, RESIST, PARRY

feral: . . . . . . WILD, DEADLY,
BESTIAL, UNTAMED, SAVAGE

ferment: . . . . . . BREW, FRET,
FEVER, YEAST, UNREST,

SEETHE, FOMENT, UPROAR,
LEAVEN, BACTERIA, (EN)ZYME,
AGITATION, COMMOTION

ferocious: . . . . . FELL, WILD,
CRUEL, FERAL, SAVAGE,
BRUTAL, BEASTLY, FIERCE,
INHUMAN, VIOLENT

ferret: . . . WEASEL, SEARCH,
INVESTIGATE

fertile: . . . FAT, RANK, RICH,
FECUND, PINGUID, FRUITFUL,
TEEMING, PROLIFIC,
PRODUCTIVE

fertilize: . . ENRICH, FRUCTIFY,
POLLINATE, IMPREGNATE

fertilizer: . . . MARL, GUANO,
HUMUS, COMPOST, MANURE,
POLLEN, POTASH, NITRATE

ferule: . . ROD, STICK, RULER,
SCEPTER, PUNISHMENT

fervent: . HOT, KEEN, WARM,
EAGER, FIERY, EARNEST,
INTENSE, ARDENT, PASSIONATE

fervor: . . . FIRE, HEAT, ZEAL,
ZEST, ARDOR, PASSION,
ENTHUSIASM

fester: . . . . ROT, DECAY,
RANKLE, ABSCESS, PUSTULE,
ULCERATE, SUPPURATE,
EMBITTER

festival: . . FAIR, FETE, GALA,
FIESTA, FEAST, FERIA,
HOLIDAY, CARNIVAL,
CELEBRATION

festive: . . . . . . GAY, MERRY,
GENIAL, JOYOUS, JOVIAL

fetch: . . . . GET, TAKE, BRING,
ACHIEVE, CHARM, RETRIEVE,
PRODUCE, WRAITH

fetid: . . . FOUL, OLID, RANK,
PUTRID, ROTTEN, RANCID,
STINKING, ODOROUS

fetish: . . . . IDOL, CHARM,
OBEAH, TOTEM, GRIGRIS,
AMULET, SORCERY, TALISMAN,
VOODOO

fetter: . . . BAND, BOND, GYVE,
IRON, CHAIN, IMPEDE, CONFINE,
SHACKLE, HAMPER, HOBBLE,
MANACLE, HANDCUFF

fettle: . . . TIDY, TRIM, DRESS,
GROOM, STATE, CONDITION

fetus: . . . . . BIRTH, EMBRYO,
CONCEPTION

feud: . . . . . . BROIL ENMITY,
STRIFE, DISPUTE, QUARREL,
VENDETTA

fever: . . AGUE, HEAT, FEBRIS,
FEBRILE, DENGUE, MALERIA,
QUARTAN, CALENTURE,
EXCITEMENT, TEMPERATURE,
BRUCELLOSIS

feverish: . . . . FIERY, HECTIC,
EXCITED, FEBRILE, PYRETIC,
FRANTIC

few: . . . . LESS, SOME, SCANT,
SPARSE, LIMITED

fiasco: . . . . . CRASH, FIZZLE,
TURKEY, FAILURE, WASHOUT

fiat: . . . . DECREE, COMMAND,
SANCTION, ORDINANCE

fiber: . . . . . GRAIN, STRAND,
THREAD, NATURE, QUALITY,
FILAMENT

fibula: . . . PIN, BONE, CLASP,
BROOCH, BUCKLE

fickle: . . . . . . FALSE, GIDDY,
SHIFTY, UNSTEADY, VOLATILE,
FLIGHTY, INCONSTANT,
CAPRICIOUS, CHANGEABLE

fiction: . . TALE, YARN, FABLE,
FALSE, NOVEL, FANTASY

fictious: . . . . BOGUS, FALSE,
PHONY, FABULOUS, MYTHICAL,
ASSUMED, SPURIOUS,
IMAGINARY

fidelity: . . . TRUTH, FEALTHY,
LOYALTY, DEVOTION,
ALLEGIANCE, FAITHFULNESS

fidget: . . FRET, FUSS, WORRY,
FIDDLE, JITTER

fidgety: . . . UNEASY, RESTIVE,
NERVOUS, RESTLESS

field: . . . . LOT, ACRE, AREA,
ARENA, GLEBE, PLAIN, CAMPUS,
GROUND, MEADOW, SAVANNA

fiend: . . . . . . DEMON, DEVIL,
ADDICT, ENEMY, SATAN

fierce: . . . GRIM, WILD, CRUEL, ARDENT, SAVAGE, VIOLENT, INTENSE, FERVENT, FEROCIOUS

fiery: . . . HOT, RED, ARDENT, IGNEOUS, SPIRITED, EXCITABLE, GLARING, VIOLENT

fiesta: . . . . . FETE, FESTIVAL, HOLIDAY, CELEBRATION

fife: . . . . PIPE, FLUTE

fig: . . . . . . BIT, FICO, DRESS, SHAPE, TRIFLE, RETUND

fight: . . . . . BOX, ROW, WAR, BOUT, COPE, DUEL, FRAY, TILT, WAGE, BRAWL, CLASH, MELEE, SCRAP, STRIFE, BATTLE, TUSSLE, WARFARE, COMBAT, OPPOSE, CONTEST, QUARREL, CONTEND, CONFLICT, STRUGGLE

fighter: . . . . PUG, BOXER, BATTLER, DUELIST, SOLDIER, WARRIOR, PUGILIST, GUERILLA, WRESTLER, COMBATANT

figuration: . . . FORM, SHAPE, OUTLINE

figurative: . . . . FLORID, FLOWERY, ALLEGORIC, SYMBOLIC

figure: . . FORM, IDEA, DIGIT, IMAGE, SHAPE, EMBLEM, NUMBER, SYMBOL, COMPUTE, NUMERAL, OUTLINE, DIAGRAM, PICTURE, RECKON, CALCULATE

figurine: . . . . TANAGRA, STATUETTE

filament: . . . . . . HAIR, HARL, FIBER, MANTLE, STRAND, THREAD

filch: . . . . . NIM, ROB, BEAT, FAKE, STEAL, PILFER, PURLOIN

file: . ROW, LINE, LIST, RANK, TOOL, INDEX, RECORD, ARRANGE, CABINET, FOLDER, DOSSIER

filet: . . . . NET, LACE

filibuster: . . . . ORATE, OBSTRUCTION

fill: . . . . . . PAD, CRAM, FEED, GLUT, LOAD, PLUG, SATE, GORGE, STUFF, OCCUPY, SUPPLY, EXECUTE, INFLATE, PERVADE, SATISFY, COMPLETE

fille: . . . . . . GIRL, DAUGHTER

fillet: . . . BAND, BONE, ORLO, CROWN, LABEL, SNOOD, STRIP, TIARA, BINDER, FASCIA, RIBBON, TURBAN

fillip: . . . . . TAP, FLIP, SNAP, TONIC, EXCITE, STIMULUS

filly: . . . . . COLT, FOAL, GIRL, MARE, WOMAN

film: . . . . HAZE, MIST, SCUM, VEIL, LAYER, MOVIE, PATINA, COATING NEGATIVE, PHOTOGRAPH

filter: . . . SIFT, OOZE, DRAIN, SIEVE, PURIFY, STRAIN, PERCOLATE

filth: . . . . DIRT, DUNG, DUST, GORE, ORDURE, VERMIN, SQUALOR, OBSCENITY, INDECENCY

filthy: . . . . FOUL, RICH, VILE, DIRTY, LUCRE, IMPURE, SORDID, OBSCENE, SQUALID, UNCLEAN

finagle: . . . . . CHEAT, TRICK, RENEGE, WANGLE, DECEIVE

final: . . . END, LAST, LATTER, DERNIER, EXTREME, DECIDING, EVENTUAL, ULTIMATE, CONCLUSIVE

finances: . . . . FUNDS, PURSE, ASSETS, ACCOUNTS

financial: . . . . FISCAL, MONETARY, PECUNIARY

financier: . . . . BANKER, TYCOON, CAPITALIST

find: . . GET, CATCH, LEARN, DECIDE, LOCATE, DISCOVER

fine: . . . . . TAX, GOOD, JAKE, KEEN, LEVY, NICE, PURE, THIN, BULLY, DANDY, FRAIL, MULET, SHARP, SHEER, SUBTLE, DELICATE, SPLENDID, EXCELLENT

finesse: . . ART, SKILL, PURITY, CUNNING, DELICACY, SUBTLETY, REFINEMENT

finger: .. TOY, DIGIT, INDEX, PINKY, STEAL, TOUCH, HANDLE, PILFER, BETRAY, PURLOIN

fingerprint: .. DACTYLOGRAM

finial: ...... TIP, TOP, APEX, PEAK, SUMMIT, ORNAMENT

finical: .... FUSSY, CHOOSY, PRISSY, PRUDISH, METICULOUS, FASTIDIOUS, PARTICULAR

finis: ... END, GOAL, CLOSE, CONCLUSION

finish: ..... END, KILL, STOP, CLOSE, BOUND, CEASE, WINDUP, POLISH, ACHIEVE, COMPLETE, CONCLUDE, ACCOMPLISH, TERMINATE

fink: .... SPY, INFORMER, SQUEALER, STRIKEBREAKER

fir: .... BALSAM, EVERGREEN

fire: ..... CAN, BURN, HEAT, ZEAL, ARDOR, ARSON, FLAME, SHOOT, AROUSE, KINDLE, DISMISS, IGNITE, EXCITE, ANNEAL, ANIMATE, EXPLODE, INSPIRE, DETONATE, DISCHARGE

alarm: ..... BELL, SIREN, WHISTLE, PYROSTAT

artillery: .... SALVO, BARRAGE

big: .... CONFLAGRATION

firearm: ... GAT, GUN, IRON, PIECE, RIFLE, MUSKET, PISTOL, DERRINGER, REVOLVER

firebug: .... ARSONIST, INCENDIARY, PYROMANIAC

fireman: .... VAMP, STOKER, HAGBUT, FIRE EATER

fireplace: ... FORGE, INGLE, GRATE, HEARTH

fireplug: .... HYDRANT

firm: ... FAST, HARD, SURE, FIXED, LOYAL, RIGID, SOLID, TIGHT, SECURE, STABLE, STANCH, STEADY, STOLID, ADAMANT, CERTAIN, COMPANY, UNMOVED, FAITHFUL, RESOLUTE

firmament: .... SKY, VAULT, ARCH, HEAVENS

first: ... HEAD, MAIN, ALPHA, CHIEF, PRIME, PRIMAL, INITIAL, ORIGINAL, LEADING, PRIMARY, MAIDEN, FOREMOST, EARLIEST, PRINCIPAL

fiscal: .... MONETARY, FINANCIAL

fish: ..... NET, CAST, HAUL, ANGLE, DRAIL, SEINE, TROLL

fisherman: . EELER, ANGLER, SEINER, PRAWNER, TRAWLER, PETERMAN, PISCATOR, HARPOONER

fishy: .... DULL, SHADY, FUNNY, DOUBTFUL, INPROBABLE, SUSPICIOUS, UNRELIABLE

fission: .... BREAKING, CLEAVAGE, CLEAVING, SCISSION, SPLITTING, REPRODUCTION

fissure: ... GAP, FLAW, RENT, RIFT, RIME, SEAM, VEIN, VENT, CHASM, CHINK, CLEFT, CRACK, SPLIT, CRANNY, LESION, CREVICE, OPENING, APERATURE, CREVASSE

fistic: ... PUGILISTIC, BOXING

fisticuffs: .. BOUT, PUNCHES, BOXING

fistula: ... PIPE, TUBE, SINUS, CAVITY

fit: ... APT, RIG, ABLE, GOOD, MEET, SUIT, WELL, ADAPT, ADOPT, EQUIP, READY, RIGHT SPASM, ADJUST, ATTACK, PROPER, SEEMLY, STRONG, KOSHER, CAPABLE, CONFORM, ELIGIBLE, APOPLEXY, PAROXYSM, CONVULSION

fitful: ... FLIGHTY, RESTLESS, UNSTABLE, VARIABLE, IMPULSIVE, IRREGULAR, SPASMODIC

fitly: .... DULY, MEETLY, PROPERLY, SUITABLY

fitness: .. APTNESS, DECENCY, PROPRIETY, COMPETENCE

fitting: .. APT, MEET, PROPER, SUITABLE

Five Nations: . . . . CAYUGAS, ONEIDAS, MOHAWKS, SENECAS, ONONDAGAS

fix: . . SET, GLUE, MEND, NAIL, SEAL, ALLOT, LIMIT, ADJUST, ANCHOR, ARREST, CEMENT, DEFINE, FASTEN, FREEZE, REPAIR, RIVET, SETTLE, ARRANGE, DILEMMA, DETERMINE, ESTABLISH, PREDICAMENT

fixation: . . . . OBSESSION

fixed: . PAT, SET, FAST, FIRM, FROZEN, INTENT, RIGID, STABLE, CERTAIN, ARRANGED, DEFINITE, IMMOBILE, RESOLUTE, IMMOVABLE, STATIONARY

flaccid: . . . . LIMP, WEAK, FLABBY, YIELDING

flag: . . . FAG, SAG, FAIL, PINE, SIGN, TIRE, WILT, DROOP, BANNER, COLORS, ENSIGN, PENNON, SIGNAL, WEAKEN, DECLINE, BUNTING, PENNANT, LANGUISH, STANDARD

flagellate: . . . . . WHIP, FLOG, THRASH, SCOURGE

flagitious: . . . VILE, WICKED, CORRUPT, HEINOUS

flagon: . . JUG, EWER, STOUP, CARAFE, VESSEL

flagrant: . . . . . RANK, GROSS, WANTON, GLARING, HEINOUS, VIOLENT, SHAMEFUL, ATROCIOUS, EGREGIOUS, OUTRAGEOUS, SCANDALOUS, NOTORIOUS

flail: . . . . . BEAT, FLOG, WHIP, THRASH, THRESH

flair: . . BENT, ODOR, TALENT, APTITUDE, KNACK, ABILITY, DISCERNMENT

flake: . . . CHIP, FLAW, RACK, SNOW, FLECK, SCALE, STRIP, LAMINA, FRAGMENT

flam: . . LIE, TRICK, HUMBUG, BLARNEY, DECEPTION

flamboyant: . . . . . ORNATE, SHOWY, FLOWERY, BOMBASTIC, RESPLENDENT

flame: . . FIRE, GLOW, ARDOR, BLAZE, FLARE, FLASH, LIGHT, SPUNK, SWEETHEART

flaneur: . . . LOAFER, TRIFLER

flank: . . . . SIDE, LOIN, THIGH, BORDER

flap: . . ROB, TAB, WAP, BEAT, CLAP, SLAM, SLAT, FLACK, LAPEL, LAPPET, SWING, AILERON, FLUTTER

flare: . . . . . . BLAZE, FLAME, FLASH, FLECK, FUZEE, FLARE, LIGHT, TORCH, SIGNAL, SPREAD, FLICKER, OUTBURST

flash: . . . . . . BLAZE, BURST, FLARE, FLAME, GLEAM, GLINT, SPARK, GLANCE, MOMENT, GLIMMER, GLIMPSE, GLISTEN, GLITTER, SPARKLE, SCINTILLATE

flask: . . . . . . CRUSE, BOTTLE, CARAFE, FLACON, FLAGON, CANTEEN, COSTREL, THERMOS, MATRASS, CUCURBITE

flat: . . . . DEAD, DULL, EVEN, PLAT, ABODE, LEVEL, PLANE, PRONE, STALE, VAPID, BORING, DREARY, INSIPID, UNBROKEN, APARTMENT, PROSTRATE

flatten: . . . . . . EVEN, LEVEL, DEJECT, SMOOTH, DEPRESS, COMPRESS, DISPIRIT, PROSTRATE

flatter: . . . . CHARM, TOADY, BECOME, CAJOLE, PRAISE, PLEASE, BLANDISH, ADULATE, COMPLIMENT

flatulent: . . . . GASSY, WINDY, TURGID, POMPOUS, BOMBASTIC

flaunt: . . . . . WAVE, BOAST, VAUNT, PARADE, DISPLAY, FLUTTER, SHOW(OFF), BRANDISH

flavin: . . . . PIGMENT

flavor: . . ODOR, SALT, TANG, ZEST, AROMA, SAPID, SAPOR, SAUCE, SAVOR, SCENT, TASTE,

RELISH, SEASON, ESSENCE,
PERFUME, FRAGRANCE

flaw: . . GAP, LIE, MAR, HOLE,
RIFT, SPOT, CLEFT, CRACK,
ERROR, FAULT, DEFECT,
BLEMISH, FRACTURE

flawless: . . . SOUND, PERFECT,
FAULTLESS

flax: . . . . LINEN, FIBER

flay: . . . . . ROB, BEAT, CANE,
SKIN, SCOLD, STRIP, FLEECE,
CENSURE, PILLAGE, REPROVE,
CRITICIZE, EXCORIATE

flee: . . FLY, LAM, RUN, BOLT,
SHUN, SKIP, ELOPE, ELUDE,
DESERT, ESCAPE, ABSCOND,
VANISH

fleece: . . . . . ABB, BILK, FELL,
FLAY, GAFF, PILE, WOOL,
CHEAT, MULET, PLUCK, SHEAR,
STEAL, SWINDLE

fleet: . . . . FAST, FLIT, NAVY,
CREEK, INLET, QUICK, RAPID,
SWIFT, ARMADA, NIMBLE,
SPEEDY, ESTUARY, FLOTILLA

fleeting: . . . . . . TRANSIENT,
EPHEMERAL, TRANSITORY

flesh: . . . . KIN, BODY, MEAT,
RACE, STOCK, FAMILY,
KINDRED, MANKIND

fleshy: . . FAT, BEEFY, OBESE,
PLUMP, PULPY, STOUT,
ADIPOSE, CORPULENT

flex: . . . . BEND, CURVE,
CONTRACT

flexible: . . . . . . SOFT, LITHE,
LIMBER, PLIANT, SUPPLE,
ELASTIC, PLASTIC, TENSILE,
DUCTILE, LISSOM(E),
TRACTABLE

flexure: . . BEND, BENT, CURL,
FOLD, CURVE

flick: . . . . . HIT, FLIP, SNAP,
DASH, WHIP, PROPEL, STREAK,
FLUTTER

flicker: . . . FAIL, FLIT, FLARE,
WAVER, FLITTER, FLUTTER,
PALPITATE, WOODPECKER

flight: . . BOLT, ROUT, FLOCK,
EXODUS, HEGIRA, HEJIRA,
FLEEING, STAMPEDE,
SWARMING, MIGRATION

flighty: . . . . . BARMY, GIDDY,
FICKLE, FOOLISH, FRIVOLOUS,
FANCIFUL, TRANSIENT,
CAPRICIOUS

flimflam: . . TRICK, HUMBUG,
TRIFLE, SWINDLE, RUBBISH,
NONSENSE, DECEPTION

flimsy: . . . LIMP, THIN, WEAK,
FRAIL, SHEER, FEEBLE, SLEASY,
FRAGILE, TRIVIAL, SLIGHT,
TENUOUS

flinch: . . . . . COWER, QUAIL,
START, WINCE, RECOIL,
BLENCH, CRINGE, FALTER,
SHRINK

fling: . . . CAST, DART, DASH,
EMIT, HURL, TOSS, PITCH,
SLING, THROW, HURTLE,
SCATTER

flip: . . TAP, FLAP, PERT, SNAP,
TOSS, TRIP, FLICK, SAUCY,
FILLIP, DRINK, FLIPPANT,
SOMERSAULT

flippant: . . . . . . GLIB, PERT,
SAUCY, SASSY

flirt: . . . . . TOY, DART, JOKE,
MASH, PLAY, RAMP, WOLF,
DALLY, TRIFLE, COQUET(TE),
PHILANDER

flit: . . . . FLY, DART, HOVER,
FLUTTER

float: . . . . BOB, BUOY, CORK,
RAFT,, RIDE, SAIL, SELL, SOAR,
WAFT, DRIFT, HOVER, PONTOON

floating: . . . . . FREE, AWASH,
LOOSE, ADRIFT, AWASH,
FLYING, NATANT, DRIFTING,
VARIABLE

flock: . . . . MOB, BEVY, FOLD,
HERD, PACK, BROOD, BUNCH,
COVEY, CROWD, DROVE,
GROUP, SWARM, FLIGHT,
MULTITUDE, CONGRAGATION

flog: . . . . . TAN, BEAT, CANE,
HIDE, LASH, WALE, WHIP,

LARRUP, SWITCH, THRASH, SCOURGE, TROUNCE, FLAGELLATE, SHELLACK

flood: ... FLOW, FLUX, SPATE, SWAMP, DELUGE, EXCESS, FRESHET, CATARACT, TORRENT, INUNDATE, OVERFLOW, OUTPOURING, INUNDATION

florid: ...... ROSY, FRESH, RUDDY, GAUDY, ORNATE, FLOWERY, BLOOMING

flotsam: .... DRIFTAGE, FLOTAGE

flounce: ...... FLAP, SLAM, FLING, FRILL, RUFFLE, FALBALA, FLOUNDER, FURBELOW

flounder: . DAB, ROLL, SOLE, TOSS, BREAM, FLUKE, MUDDLE, TURBOT, WALLOW, FLOUNCE, HALIBUT, STUMBLE, FLATFISH

flour: ..... DURUM, FARINA, BUCKWHEAT

flourish: ..... BOOM, GROW, RISE, SHOW, WAVE, BLOOM, BOAST, SWING, TWIRL, VAUNT, FLAUNT, BLOSSOM, DISPLAY, FANFARE, PROSPER, SUCCEED, BRANDISH, ROULADE, INCREASE

flout: .... GIBE, JEER, MOCK, SCOFF, FLEER, SCORN, SNEER, TAUNT, INSULT

flow: .. EBB, JET, RUN, FLUX, GUSH, OOZE, POUR, TEEM, WELL, DRAIN, EXUDE, GLIDE, ISSUE, SPILL, SPOUT, SPURT, DELUGE, STREAM, CURRENT

flower: .. BUD, POSY, BLOOM, UNFOLD, BLOSSOM, FAIREST, CHOICEST, CMBELLISH

flowery: ... FLORID, ORNATE, FIGURATIVE, BOMBASTIC, FLAMBOYANT

flowing: ..... FLUX, FLUID, TIDAL, AFFLUX, FLUENT, CURRENT, CURSIVE, FLUXION, EMANATING

flu: ...... GRIPPE, INFLUENZA

flub: ... MUF, ERROR, FAILURE

fluctuant: .... VARYING, UNDULATING

fluctuate: .... SWAY, VARY, VEER, SWING, WAVER, UNDULATE, OSCILLATE, VACILLATE, IRRESOLUTE

flue: .... PIPE, FLUFF, FLUKE, SHAFT, FUNNEL, TUNNEL, CHIMNEY, PASSAGE

fluency: .... GLIBNESS, ELOQUENCE, SMOOTHNESS

fluent: . GLIB, FLUID, FACILE, LIQUID, FLOWING, ELOQUENT

fluff: .... NAP, DOWN, FLUE, LINT, PUFF, FLOSS, ERROR, BONER

fluid: ... GAS, INK, OIL, SAP, SERUM, WATER, FLUENT, LIQUID, MOBILE, FLOWING, FLEXILE, PLASTIC

fluke: .... BARB, FISH, FLUE, HOOK, FLOUNDER

flume: ..... CHUTE, GORGE, RAVINE, SLUICE, STREAM, CHANNEL, TROUGH

flurry: .... ADO, GUST, STIR, HASTE, SKIRL, HURRY, BUSTLE, SQUALL, CONFUSE, FLUSTER, COMMOTION, CONFUSION, AGITATION

flush: ... EVEN, FULL, GLOW, BLUSH, EMPTY, EXCITE, LAVISH, REDDEN, PROFUSE, ANIMATE, PROSPEROUS

fluster: ..... SHAKE, EXCITE, POTHER, FUDDLE, MUDDLE, RATTLE, CONFUSE, UNSETTLE, EMBARRASS, DISCOMPOSE

flutter: ...... FLIT, HOVER, WAVER, TREMBLE, QUIVER, BUSTLE, FLICKER, VIBRATE, PALPITATE

flux: .... FLOW, FUSE, MELT, FLOAT, FLOOD, RESIN, ROSIN, SMELT, SOLDER, FLOWING

fly: ...... FLEE, FLIRT, FLAP, GNAT, SOAR, SCUD, SOLO, WHIR, WING, AVIATE, HOVER,

MIDGE, FLUTTER, MOSQUITO, DISAPPEAR

flying: .. VOLANT, VOLITANT

foal: .... COAT, FILLY

foam: ..... SUD, FIZZ, SCUD, SCUM, YEAST, FROTH, SPUME, LATHER, BUBBLE

fob: .... CHEAT, TRICK

focus: .... POINT, TRAIN, CENTER, CONVERGE, CONCENTRATE

fodder: .... FEED, FOOD, FORAGE, SILAGE, PROVENDER

foe: .... ENEMY, RIVAL, OPPONENT, ADVERSARY

fog: ..... DAZE, HAZE, MIST, MURK, SMOG, BRUME, CLOUD, VAPOR, CONFUSE, OBSCURE

foible:.... FAULT, WEAKNESS

foil: ... BULK, BLADE, ELUDE, EVADE, BAFFLE, STOOGE, STUMP, SWORD, THWART, FRUSTRATE

fold:... BOW, LAP, PEN, PLY, BEND, FAIL, FURL, REEF, RUGA, CRIMP, CLASP, DRAPE, PLAIT, LAYER, PLICA, FLOCK, PLEAT, CREASE, EMBRACE, FLEXURE, ENVELOP

folder: ..... COVER, FOLIO, BINDER, PAMPHLET, BOOKLET, LEAFLET

folio: .... CASE, LEAF, PAGE, BOOK, NUMBER

folklore: ... MYTH, CUSTOM, HISTORY, LEGEND, BELIEFS, TRADITION

follow: ... TAG, COPY, HEED, OBEY, TAIL, ADOPT, ENSUE, CHASE, TRACK, TRAIL, PURSUE, ATTEND, RESULT, ACCOMPANY, IMITATE

follower:..... FAN, IST, ITE, BUFF, PARTISAN, VOTARY, DEVOTEE, DISCIPLE, ADHERENT, SUPPORTER

folly: .... SIN, FATUITY, LUNACY, FOOLISHNESS

foment:.. ABET, BREW, SPUR, AROUSE, INCITE, AGITATE, INSTIGATE

fond: .... ARDENT, DOTING, LOVING, TENDER, ATTACHED, AFFECTIONATE

fondle: ...... PET, COSSET, CARESS, CODDLE, STROKE, DANDLE

font:.. BOWL, BASIN, ORIGIN, SPRING, SOURCE, FOUNTAIN

food: .... PAP, CHOW, DIET, EATS, FARE, GRUB, MESS, FODDER, VIANDS, ALIMENT, VICTUAL, NUTRIMENT, PABALUM, NOURISHMENT

fool:...... ASS, OAF, BOOB, DOLT, DUPE, JAPE, JOKE, SIMP, ZANY, IDIOT, CLOWN, CHUMP, DUNCE, NINNY, TRICK, DELUDE, DECEIVE, JESTER, SIMPLETON

foolish:... MAD, DAFT, RASH, ZANY, BALMY, DIZZY, GOOFY, INANE, SAPPY, SILLY, ABSURD, STUPID, UNWISE, ASININE, CUCKOO, IDIOTIC, LUNATIC, IMPRUDENT, LUDICROUS, RIDICULOUS

football: ... RUGBY, SOCCER, ELEVEN, PIGSKIN

footfall: ...... STEP, TREAD

footing:...... PAR, BASIS, POSITION, FOOTHOLD, TOEHOLD

footnote:...... REFERENCE, COMMENTARY, ANNOTATION

footstool: ...... OTTOMAN, CRICKET, HASSOCK

footwear: ...... BOOT, CLOG, SHOE, SOCK, SPAT, SABOT, BROGAN, BROGUE, SKATE, GALOSH, RUBBER, SANDAL, SLIPPER, MOCCASIN, OVERSHOE, STOCKING

fop: .... DUDE, DANDY

for: .... PRO, BECAUSE, FAVORING, CONCERNING

forage: .... FEED, FOOD, FODDER, RAVAGE, PLUNDER, MARAUD

foray: . . . . . . RAID, RAVAGE, MARAUD, PILLAGE, PLUNDER

forbear: . . . . . . SHUN, SIRE, AVOID, SPARE, DESIST, ENDURE, PARENT, ABSTAIN, REFRAIN, ANCESTOR, TOLERATE

forbid: . . . BAN, DENY, STOP, VETO, TABOO, ENJOIN, REFUSE, INHIBIT, PREVENT, PROHIBIT, INTERDICT, PROSCRIBE

forbidding: . . . . GRIM, UGLY, STERN, REPELLANT, DISAGREEABLE

force: . . . . . VIS, BIRR, DINT, MAKE, DRIVE, IMPEL, POWER, COERCE, COMPEL, DURESS, ENERGY, STRAIN, IMPETUS, CONSTRAIN, STRENGTH, VIOLENCE

forced: . . . . LABORED, RELUCTANT, ARTIFICIAL, COMPULSORY

forceful: . . MIGHTY, STRONG, COGENT, DYNAMIC, ELOQUENT, EFFECTIVE, VIGOROUS, ENERGETIC

ford: . . . . WADE, CROSS

forebode: . . . . PREDICT, PORTEND, FORETELL

foreboding: . . . . OMEN, AUGURY, ANXIETY, OMINOUS, PRESENTIMENT

forecast: . . FORESEE, PREDICT, PROPHESY, PROGNOSIS

forefather: . . . . SIRE, ANCESTOR, PROGENITOR

foregoing: . . . . PAST, ABOVE, PRECEDING, PREVIOUS

foreign: . . . . ALIEN, EXOTIC, REMOTE, DISTANT

forelock: . . . . BANG, COTTER, LINCHPIN

foreman: . . . . . . BOSS, CHIEF, GAFFER, LEADER, CAPTAIN, OVERSEER

foremost: . . . . FIRST, HEAD, MAIN, CHIEF, FRONT, PREMIER, LEADING, PRINCIPAL

forerun: . . HERALD, PRECEDE, ANTECEDE, FORESHADOW

foresight: . . . . VISION, PRUDENCE

forest: . . . . . WOOD, GLADE, WASTE, JUNGLE, TIMBER, WOODLAND, WILDERNESS

forestall: . . . AVERT, PREVENT, ANTICIPATE

foretooth: . . CUTTER, INCISOR

forever: . . . . AYE, ETERN(E), ALWAYS, ENDLESS, PERPETUAL, ETERNALLY, EVERLASTING

foreword: . . . . PREFACE, PREAMBLE, INTRODUCTION

forfeit: . . FINE, LOSE, FORGO, PENALTY, DEFAULT

forge: . . FORM, MINT, SMITHY, FALSIFY, FASHION, IMITATE, SHAPE, BLOOMERY, FABRICATE, COUNTERFEIT

forget: . . . . . . OMIT, LAPSE, OVERLOOK, NEGLECT

forgive: . . . . . . REMIT, SPARE, EXCUSE, PARDON, OVERLOOK, ABSOLVE, CONDONE

forgo: . . . . QUIT, WAIVE, ABSTAIN, FORFEIT, REFRAIN

fork: . . TINE, PRONG, BISECT, BRANCH, CROTCH, BIFURCATE

forlorn: . . . ABJECT, BEREFT, DESERTED, MISERABLE, WRETCHED

form: . . . CAST, BODY, MAKE, MOLD, PLAN, BLANK, BUILD, IMAGE, MODEL, SHAPE, CREATE, FASHION, DEVELOP, CONTOUR, FIGURE, PATTERN, RITUAL, OUTLINE, ORGANIZE, CEREMONY

formal: . . PRIM, EXACT, STIFF, FRIGID, ORDERLY, PRECISE, STILTED, CEREMONIOUS, METHODICAL

formation: . . . RANK, ORDER, STRUCTURE, CONSTRUCTION, ARRANGEMENT

former: . . . . . EX, OLD, ERST, LATE, ONCE, PAST, PRIOR,

WHILOM, EARLIER, QUONDAM,
PREVIOUS, ANTECEDANT
formidable:..... AWESOME,
FEARFUL, ALARMING,
DREADFUL, DIFFICULT,
MENACING
formula:...... LAW, RULE,
CREED, RECIPE, THEORY,
RECIPT, SOLUTION, PRESCRIPTION
forsake: . DENY, DROP, FLEE,
QUIT, SHUN, AVOID, LEAVE,
WAIVE, DESERT, ABANDON,
RENOUNCE
forsaken:..... LEFT, LORN,
FORLORN, DESERTED, DESOLATE
forswear: ... DENY, ABJURE,
REJECT, PERJURE, RENOUNCE
fort:... KEEP, POST, CASTLE,
BASTION, CITADEL, GARRISON,
STRONGHOLD
forte:....... LOUD, SKILL,
STRENGTH, SPECIALTY
forthright: .. DIRECT, FRANK
forthwith:..... NOW, ANON,
PRESENTLY, IMMEDIATELY
fortify:........ ARM, MAN,
BARRICADE, STRENGTHEN
fortitude:..... GRIT, GUTS,
PLUCK, METTLE, COURAGE,
PATIENCE, RESOLUTION,
ENDURANCE
fortuitous:....... CHANCE,
RANDOM, ACCIDENTAL,
INCIDENTAL, ADVENTITIOUS
fortunate:.... GOOD, HAPPY,
LUCKY, FAVORABLE,
AUSPICIOUS
fortune: .. LOT, DOOM, FATE,
LUCK, RICHES, CHANCE,
ESTATE, WEALTH, DESTINY
forum: ... COURT, TRIBUNAL,
ASSEMBLY
forward:..... ON, TO, ABET,
BOLD, HELP, PERT, SEND, SHIP,
FRONT, AHEAD, EAGER, EARLY,
FORTH, REMIT, BEFORE,
EXTREME, FURTHER, TRANSMIT,
DISPATCH, ADVANCE(D),
PRECOCIOUS

foster: ... FEED, HELP, REAR,
NURSE, HARBOR, CHERISH,
NOURISH, PROMOTE
foul:.... BASE, VILE, DIRTY,
GRIMY, NASTY, SULLY,
DEFAME, FILTHY, IMPURE,
MALIGN, UNFAIR, PUTRID,
ROTTEN, OBSCENE, SQUALID,
UNCLEAN, ENTANGLE,
WRETCHED, LOATHSOME
found: . BASE, CAST, ENDOW,
ERECT, ESTABLISH, INSTITUTE,
ORIGINATE
foundation:.... BASE, FUND,
BASIS, CORSET, GIRDLE,
RIPRAP, BEDROCK, ENDOWMENT
founder:...... FAIL, FALL,
AUTHOR, STUMBLE, MISCARRY,
COLLAPSE, ESTABLISHER
foundling:.... WAIF, ORPHAN
fountain:..... WELL, FOUNT,
SPRING, SOURCE, BUBBLER
fourflusher:....... PHONY,
BLUFFER, BRAGGART,
PRETENDER
fourth: ... QUART, QUARTER,
QUADRANT
fowl: .. .~. HEN, COCK, DUCK,
CAPON, GOOSE, TURKEY,
CHICKEN, ROOSTER, PHEASANT
foyer:.... LOBBY, VESTIBULE
fracas:..... BRAWL, MELEE,
QUARREL, RUMBLE, UPROAR
fraction:... BIT, PART, PIECE,
SCRAP, BREACH, RUPTURE,
DECIMAL, FRAGMENT
fractious:.... UGLY, CROSS,
UNRULY, PEEVISH, FRETFUL,
PERVERSE
fracture:..... FLAW, REND,
BREAK, CRACK, BREACH,
RUPTURE, SPLIT
fragile:...... WEAK, FRAIL,
FEEBLE, BRITTLE, FLIMSY,
TENDER, DELICATE, FRANGIBLE
fragment: .. BIT, CHIP, PART,
SNIP, CRUMB, FLAKE, PIECE,
SCRAP, SHARD, SHRED, SIPPET,
FRACTION

fragrance: ... ODOR, AROMA, SCENT, SMELL, INCENSE, PERFUME, BOUQUET

fragrant: .... BALMY, OLENT, SWEET, SPICY, ODOROUS, AROMATIC, REDOLENT

frail: .. FINE, WEAK, BASKET, FLIMSY, SLIGHT, FEEBLE, FRAGILE, SLENDER, DELICATE

frame: .. FORM, MOLD, PLAN, PLOT, RACK, SILL, BUILD, EASEL, PANEL, SHAPE, BORDER, DESIGN, DEVISE, COMPOSE, ARRANGE, CHASSIS, FASHION, OUTLINE, CONSTRUCT

frame-up: .... PLOT, CONSPIRACY

framework: .... RACK, SILL, FABRIC, SHELL, TRUSS, CADRE, SKELETON

franchise: ..... SOC, GRANT, RIGHT, PATENT, LICENSE, CHARTER, SUFFRAGE, PRIVILEGE

frangible: .... BRITTLE, FRAGILE, BREAKABLE

frank: ... FREE, OPEN, RANK, BLUFF, BLUNT, PLAIN, CANDID, DIRECT, HONEST, GENUINE, SINCERE, OUTSPOKEN

frankness: .... CANDOR, OPENNESS, CANDIDNESS

frantic: .... MAD, RABID, INSANE, FURIOUS, VIOLENT, FRENETIC, FRENZIED, DESPERATE, DISTRAUGHT

fraternity: .... CLUB, SORORITY, BROTHERHOOD

fraud: ... FAKE, HOAX, GAFF, GULL, JAPE, RUSE, SHAM, BUNCO, CHEAT, GUILE, DECEIT, HUMBUG, SWINDLE, IMPOSTOR, TRICK(ERY), ARTIFICE, DECEPTION

fraught: .... BESET, FILLED, CHARGED, LOADED, LADEN

fray: .... FEUD, RIOT, BRAWL, FIGHT, MELEE, RAVEL, BATTLE, BUSTLE, CONFLICT, FRAZZLE, TUMULT

freak: .... WHIM, FLECK, QUEER, STREAK, VAGARY, CAPRICE, MONSTER, ATROCITY

free: .. LAX, RID, OPEN, VOID, CLEAR, FRANK, LOOSE, READY, UNTIE, ACQUIT, EXEMPT, GRATIS, REMOVE, RESCUE, ABSOLVE, MANNUMIT, RELEASE, DISENGAGE, LIBERATE, FOOTLOOSE, EMANCIPATE

freedom: ... EASE, ABANDON, CONTENT, LEISURE, LIBERTY, LICENSE, RELEASE, IMMUNITY, LATITUDE, OPENNESS, FRANCHISE, LIBERATION, MANUMISSION, EMANCIPATION, INDEPENDENCE

freely: ... GRATIS, FRANKLY, READILY, HEARTILY, BOUNTIFUL, COPIOUSLY, LIBERALLY, VOLUNTARY, WILLINGLY

freeze: ... ICE, RIME, CHILL, HARDEN, CONGEAL, IMPOUND

freight: .... SHIP, LOAD, CARGO, LADING, TRANSPORT

frenetic, phrenetic: ... MAD, WILD, INSANE, FRANTIC, VIOLENT, DELERIOUS

frenzied: .... AMOK, AMUCK, RABID, BESERK, FRANTIC, FURIOUS, FRENETIC, RAVING, ENRAGED, MADDENED

frenzy: .. MAD, AMOK, FURY, RAGE, FURROR, MANIA, MADNESS, ESTRUS, ORGASM, DELIRIUM

frequent: ... HAUNT, OFTEN, USUAL, COMMON, CONSTANT, HABITUAL

fresh: .... NEW, RAW, COOL, PERT, PURE, BRISK, CLEAN, GREEN, SAUCY, VIVID, BRIGHT, LIVELY, RECENT, UNUSED, IMPUDENT

fret: .. NAG, RUB, VEX, FRAY, FUME, FUSS, GALL, GNAW, POUT, STEW, CHAFE, PIQUE,

TEASE, WORRY, HARASS,
NETTLE, RANKLE

fretful: . . PEEVISH, RESTLESS,
IRRITABLE, PETULANT

friar: . . . FRA, MONK, ABBOT,
FRATER, BROTHER, MONASTIC,
SERVITE, CARMELITE,
DOMINICAN, FRANCISCAN,
AUGUSTINIAN

friary: . . . . CLOISTER,
MONASTERY

friction: . . . . ERASURE,
ABRASION, RUB(BING),
DISSENSION, DISAGREEMENT

friend: . . . . AMI, PAL, ALLY,
CHUM, AMIGO, CRONY, BUDDY,
QUAKER, COMRADE,
SUPPORTER, SYMPATHIZER

friendly: . . . . . . GOOD, KIND,
GENIAL, AFFABLE, AMIABLE,
CORDIAL, AMICABLE

fright: . . . AWE, COW, FEAR,
ALARM, PANIC, SCARE, SHOCK,
DISMAY, HORROR, TERROR

frighten: . . . . SCARE, ALARM,
DAUNT, STARTLE, TERRIFY,
TERRORIZE

frigid: . . . . ICY, COLD, STIFF,
BLEAK, ARCTIC, FORMAL,
FREEZING

frill: . . . PURL, JABUT, RUCHE,
RUFFLE, FLOUNCE, FURBELOW,
ADORNMENT

fringe: . . EDGE, LOMA, SKIRT,
BORDER, EDGING, MARGIN

frisk: . . . LEAP, SKIP, CAPER,
DANCE, FROLIC, GAMBOL,
SEARCH

fritter: . . . . . . CAKE, DALLY,
SHRED, PIECE, WASTE, DAWDLE

frivolous: . . . . . . GAY, GIDDY,
INANE, PETTY, SILLY, PALTRY,
SHALLOW, TRIVIAL, TRIFLING,
FLIGHTY, FLIPPANT

frock (also see: dress): . . . . .
COAT, WRAP, ROBE, TUNIC,
GOWN, SMOCK, JERSEY,
MANTLE, SOUTANE

frolic: . . . . FUN, GAY, GAME,
JINK, LARK, PLAY, ROMP,
CAPER, FRISK, MERRY, PRANK,
SPREE, SPORT, CAVORT,
GAMBOL, MERRIMENT

front: . . . . BOW, VAN, BROW,
FACE, FORE, HEAD, PROW,
BEFORE, FACADE, FORWARD,
OBVERSE

frontier: . . BORDER, DEFENSE,
OUTPOST, BOUNDARY

frost: . ICE, NIP, HOAR, RIME,
CHILL

froth: . . BARM, FOAM, SCUM,
SUDS, SUPME, LATHER

frown: . . . . . . LOUR, SCOWL,
(G)LOWER, GRIMACE

frowzy: . . . . MUSTY, UNTIDY,
UNKEMPT, SLOVENLY

frozen: . . . ICY, HARD, FIXED,
GELID, GLACE, CHILLY, FRAPPE,
IMMOBILE, CONGEALED

frugal: . . . . . CHARY, SPARE,
SAVING, CAREFUL, THRIFTY,
SPARING, ECONOMIC(AL),
PARSIMONIOUS

fruit: . . . . . . DRUPE, RESULT,
YIELD, PRODUCT, OFFSPRING,
CONSEQUENCE

fruitful: . . . . . FAT, FECUND,
FERTILE, ABUNDANT, PROLIFIC,
PLENTIFUL, FERACIOUS,
FRUCTUOU3, PRODUCTIVE

fruitless: . . DRY, GELD, VAIN,
BLANK, FUTILE, STERILE,
BARREN, INEFFECTUAL

frustrate: . . . . . BALK, DASH,
FOIL, VOID, BLANK, BLOCK,
CRUSH, BAFFLE, DEFEAT,
OUTWIT, THWART, HINDER,
NULLIFY, PREVENT

frying-pan: . . . . SPIDER,
GRIDDLE, SKILLET

fuel: . . GAS, OIL, COAL, COKE,
PEAT, WOOD, STOKE, PETROL,
ALCOHOL, CHARCOAL,
GASOLINE, KEROSENE,
METHANOL, PETROLEUM,
COMBUSTIBLE

fugacious: . . . . . . FLEETING, VOLATILE, TRANSIENT, EPHEMERAL

fugitive: . . . . EXILE, EMIGRE, OUTLAW, ESCAPEE, FLEEING, REFUGEE, RUNAWAY, DESERTER, FLEETING, RUNAGATE, ABSCONDER

fulfill: . . MEET, OBEY, EFFECT, FINISH, ACHIEVE, EXECUTE, PERFORM, SATISFY, ACCOMPLISH, COMPLETE, IMPLEMENT

full: . . AMPLE, ROUND, SATED, SOLID, TOTAL, ENTIRE, FILLED, CROWDED, OROTUND, REPLETE, COMPLETE

fully: . . . . . AMPLY, WHOLLY, CLEARLY, UTTERLY, ENTIRELY, PERFECTLY, ABUNDANTLY

fulminate: . . . . EXPLODE, THUNDER, INVEIGH, DETONATE

fumble: . . . . . . BOOT, ERROR, GROPE, BOBBLE, BUNGLE

fume: . . . . GAS, FRET, FOAM, ODOR, RANT, RAVE, REEK, SMOKE, STEAM, STORM, VAPOR

fun: . . . . GAG, GAME, HOAX, JEST, JOKE, PLAY, MIRTH, SPORT, GAIETY, AMUSEMENT, MERRIMENT

function: . . . . ACT, RUN, USE, DUTY, RITE, ROLE, WORK, ACTION, OFFICE, PARTY, OPERATE, ACTIVITY, GATHERING

fund: . . .POOL, MONEY, STOCK, STORE, SUPPLY, DEPOSIT, RESERVE, RESOURCE, FOUNDATION

fundamental: . . . . . . BASAL, BASIC, VITAL, PRIMARY, ORIGINAL, ORGANIC, CARDINAL, ELEMENTAL, ESSENTIAL

funeral: . . BURIAL, CORTEGE, EXEQUIES, OBSEQUIES

funereal: . . . . . . SAD, FERAL, DISMAL, SOLEMN, GLOOMY, MOURNFUL

fungus: . . MOLD, RUST, SMUT, WART, ERGOT, MOREL, YEAST, MILDEW, AGARIC, LICHEN, TRUFFLE, AMANITA, PUFFBALL, MUSHROOM, TOADSTOOL

funnel: . . . . . FLUE, HOPPER, CHIMNEY, SMOKESTACK

funny: . ODD, COMIC, DROLL, QUEER, AMUSING, ABSURD, STRANGE, FARCICAL, HUMOROUS, LUDICROUS

fur: . . . . . . BOA, PELT, SKIN, STOLE, PARKA

furbelow: . . . FRILL, RUFFLE, FALBALA, FLOUNCE

furbish: . . . . CLEAN, SCOUR, BRIGHTEN, BURNISH, RENOVATE

furious: . . . . . MAD, ANGRY, IRATE, FRANTIC, VIOLENT, FRENZIED

furnace: . . . . . . KILN, OVEN, BLAST, FORGE, STOVE, CUPOLA, SMELTER, SMITHY, BLOOMERY, CREMATORY, INCINERATOR

furnish: . . ARM, FEED, GIVE, LEND, CATER, ENDOW, EQUIP, SUPPLY, PROVIDE

furniture: . . GOODS, FIXTURE, EQUIPMENT

furor: . . FURY, RAGE, CRAZE, MANIA, FRENZY, FLURRY, TUMULT

furrow: . . RUT, PLOW, CHASE, SCORE, SEAM, STRIA, GROOVE, WRINKLE, TRENCH, SULCUS, CHANNEL

further: . . . . AID, AND, YET, ABET, ALSO, MORE, AGAIN, BEYOND, MOREOVER, PROMOTE, ADVANCE, ADDITIONAL

furtive: . . . . SLY, WARY, COVERT, SNEAKY, SECRET, STEALTHY, SURREPTITIOUS

fury: . . . . IRE, RAGE, ANGER, WRATH, FRENZY

fuse: . . . . FLUX, MELT, WELD, BLEND, MERGE, SMELT, UNITE, ANNEAL, SOLDER, AMALGAMATE

fusee: . . . . . . FLARE, MATCH, TORCH, SIGNAL

fusion: . . MERGER, ALLIANCE, BLENDING, COALITION

fuss: . . . . . . ADO, ROW, FRET, SPAT, STIR, TO DO, WORRY, PREEN, FIDGET, TINKER, BUSTLE, POTHER, BOTHER, DISPUTE

fussy: . . . . FINICKY, FINICAL, FASTIDIOUS, METICULOUS, PERSNICKETY

futile: . . . IDLE, VAIN, OTIOSE, HOPELESS, USELESS, FRUITLESS

future: . . . . LATER, COMING, POSTERITY, HEREAFTER

fuzz: . . . . . NAP, LINT, DOWN, FLUFF, PUFFBALL

fuzzy: . . . UNCLEAR, BLURRED

fylfot: . . . . . CROSS, EMBLEM, SWASTIKA

G

G: *Greek:* . . . . GAMMA
    Hebrew: . . . . GIMEL

gable: . . . . . DORMER, PINION

gad: . . . . ROD, GOAD, ROAM, ROVE, WHIP, PROWL, SPIKE, RAMBLE, TRAIPSE, GALLIVANT

gadget: . . . . . TOOL, DEVICE, DOODAD, GIMMICK, DOOHICKEY, JIGGER, CONTRIVANCE

Gaelic: . . . . ERSE, IRISH, SCOT(CH), CELT(IC), MANX

gaff: . . . . HOAX, HOOK, PICK, SPAR, SPUR, TALK, SPEAR, FLEECE, TRICK, DECEIT

gaffe: . . . BLUNDER, FAUX PAS

gag: . . . . . HOAX, JOKE, QUIP, CHOKE, HEAVE, RETCH, MUFFLE, MUZZLE, PREVENT, SILENCE

gage (also see: **gauge**): . . . . . BET, PAWN, RISK, WAGER, PLEDGE, APPRAISE, SECURITY, CHALLENGE, ESTIMATE

gain: . . BUY, GET, NET, WIN, EARN, REAP, CLEAR, LUCRE, REACH, ATTAIN, INCOME, PROFIT, SECURE, ACHIEVE, ACQUIRE, REALIZE, INCREASE

gainsay: . . . . DENY, REFUTE, OPPOSE, FORBID, IMPUGN, CONTRADICT

gait: . . . . . RUN, PACE, LOPE, WALK, RACK, STEP, STRIDE, CANTER, GALLOP

gala: . . . . GAY, FETE, MERRY, FIESTA, FESTIVAL, FESTIVE, CELEBRATION

galaxy: . . . . . BEVY, NEBULA, COLLECTION

gale: . . . . BLOW, WIND, GUST, BLAST, STORM, BREEZE, TEMPEST, OUTBURST

gall: . . . . . VEX, BILE, FLAW, FRET, NERVE, ANNOY, CHEEK, HARASS, AUDACITY, IMPUDENCE, TEMERITY, IRRITATION, EFFRONTERY

gallant: . . . . . . BEAU, HERO, BRAVE, BULLY, NOBLE, ESCORT, POLITE, STATELY, IMPOSING, CAVALIER

gallery: . . . . LOFT, PORCH, SALON, ARCADE, PIAZZA, BALCONY, TERRACY, VERANDA, MUSEUM, PORTICO, AUDIENCE, CORRIDOR, COLONNADE

gallivant: . GAD, FLIT, ROAM, TRAVEL

gallop: . . . . RUN, GAIT, LOPE, HURRY, CANTER, HASTEN

galluses: . . . . BRACES, SUSPENDERS

gallows: . . . . . TREE, GIBBET, SCAFFOLD, YARDARM

galore: . . . . PROFUSE, PLENTIFUL, ABUNDANT

galvanize: . . . COAT, EXCITE, STARTLE, STIMULATE

gambit: . . . MOVE, COMMENT, OPENING, MANEUVER

gamble: ... BET, DICE, GAFF, GAME, RISK, STAKE, WAGER, CHANCE, HAZARD, SPECULATE

gambol: .. HOP, LEAP, PLAY, ROMP, CAPER, FRISK, FROLIC, CAVORT

game: .... FUN, LAME, LARK, PLAN, PLAY, PREY, BRAVE, SPORT, FROLIC, PLUCKY, QUARRY, SPUNKY, SCHEME, CONTEST, AMUSEMENT, RECREATION

gamut: ..... RANGE, SCALE, EXTENT, SERIES

gang: ..... MOB, SET, BAND, CREW, PACK, ROAD, TEAM, WALK, GROUP, SQUAD, CLIQUE

gangrene: ..... ROT, DECAY, NECROSIS, MORTIFICATION

gangster: ..... MUG, GOON, HOOD, THUG, YEGG, THIEF, ROUGH, RUFFIAN, HOODLUM, GORILLA, MOBSTER, CRIMINAL

gaol: .... BRIG, JAIL, PRISON, BRIDEWELL

gap: .... FLAW, GULF, HOLE, PASS, RENT, BREAK, CHASM, CLEFT, NOTCH, BREACH, HIATUS, LACUNA, FISSURE, OPENING, APERTURE

gape: .... GAUP, GAWK, GAZE, LOOK, OGLE, YAUP, YAWN, YAWP, STARE, RICTUS, DEHISCE

garb (also see: **dress**): ...... ARRAY, HABIT, STYLE, ATTIRE, CLOTHE, APPAREL, COSTUME, RAIMENT, CLOTHING

garbage: .... OFFAL, TRASH, SWILL, REFUSE, SCRAPS

garble: ... JUMBLE, MANGLE, FALSIFY, DISTORT, MUDDLE, PERVERT

garden: ... BED, PARK, PLOT, YARD, ARBOR, PATCH, HERBARY, ORCHARD, TERRARIUM

gargantuan: ... HUGE, VAST, ENORMOUS, GIGANTIC

garish: ...... LOUD, CHEAP, GAUDY, SHOWY, GLARING, TAWDRY, OFFENSIVE

garland: .... LEI, BAND, CROWN, ANADEM, DIADEM, LAUREL, CHAPLET, FESTOON, WREATH

garment: see: . **garb, dress, undergarment**

garner: ..... REAP, STORE, HOARD, GATHER, COLLECT, GRANARY, ACCUMULATE

garnish: ..... TRIM, ADORN, EMBELLISH, DECORATE, ORNAMENT

garret: .... LOFT, ATTIC, SOLAR, ATELIER, MANSARD, COCKLOFT

garrote: .... KILL, EXECUTE, STRANGLE, THROTTLE

garrulous: .... WORDY, TALKATIVE, VOLUBLE, LOQUACIOUS

gas: .... BRAG, FUEL, FUME, TALK, VAPOR, PETROL, BOMBAST, ANESTHETIC

gash: ..... CUT, HEW, BITE, CHOP, HACK, SLIT, SHARP, SLASH, INCISION

gasket: .. RING, SEAL, LINING

gate: ..... BAR, WAY, DOOR, EXIT, PASS, VALVE, PORTAL, WICKET, POSTERN, ENTRANCE

gather: .. CULL, HERD, MEET, REAP, AMASS, BUNCH, FLOCK, GLEAN, GROUP, INFER, PLUCK, SHIRR, BUNDLE, DEDUCE, GARNER, MUSTER, COLLECT, COMPILE, CONVENE, HARVEST, ASSEMBLE, ACCUMULATE

gathering: ... CROWD, RALLY, PARTY, TROOP, ABSCESS, MEET(ING), CONCOURSE, ASSEMBLY, CONVENTION

gaudy: ...... LOUD, CHEAP, SHOWY, FLASHY, GARISH, TAWDRY, FLORID

gauge (also see: **gage**): ..... RATE, TYPE, JUDGE, VALUE,

CAPACITY, MEASURE, APPRAISE, ESTIMATE

gaunt: .. BONY, LANK, LEAN, SLIM, THIN, SPARE, BARREN, HOLLOW, HAGGARD, DESOLATE, EMACIATED

gauze: .. FILM, LENO, CREPE, FABRIC, TISSUE, BANDAGE

gavel: . . . . . MACE, HAMMER, MALLET

gawk: . . . . GAPE, STARE, SIMPLETON

gawky: . . . . CLUMSY, AWKWARD, UNGAINLY

gay: . . . BOON, HAPPY, JOLLY, MERRY, LIVELY, WANTON, BRIGHT, RIANT, FRISKY, FESTIVE, JOVIAL, JOYFUL, JOCUND, CHEERFUL

gaze: . . . . EYE, GAPE, GAWK, LEER, LOOK, OGLE, PEER, SCAN, STARE, GLARE, REGARD

gazebo: . . . . PAVILION, SUMMERHOUSE

gear: . CAM, COG, KIT, GARB, TOOLS, GOODS, TACKLE, THINGS, OUTFIT, MATERIAL, RIG(GING), HARNESS, BAGGAGE

geld: . . . . SPAY, ALTER, CASTRATE, STERILIZE, EMASCULATE

gelid: . . . ICY, COLD, FROSTY, FROZEN

gem: . . . . JADE, ONYX, OPAL, RUBY, SARD, AGATE, BERYL, CAMEO, JEWEL, PEARL, STONE, TOPAZ, AMULET, GARNET, MUFFIN, SCARAB, SPINEL, DIAMOND, EMERALD, PARAGON, SAPPHIRE, TIGEREYE, AMETHYST, MASTERPIECE

Gemini: . . . TWINS, CASTOR, POLLUX

gender: . . . SEX, KIND, MALE, SORT, BEGET, CLASS, GENUS, FEMALE, NEUTER, GENERATE, FEMININE, MASCULINE

genealogy: . . . TREE, DESCENT, HISTORY, LINEAGE, PEDIGREE

general: . . . . BROAD, GROSS, USUAL, COMMON, AVERAGE, GENERIC, OFFICER, CATHOLIC, WIDESPREAD, UNIVERSAL

generate: . . . . MAKE, BEGET, BREED, DEVELOP, PRODUCE, PROCREATE, ORIGINATE

generation: . . . . . AGE, ERA, KIND, PROGENY

generic: . . . . GENERAL, INCLUSIVE, UNIVERSAL

generous: .. AMPLE, LIBERAL, LAVISH, ABUNDANT, GRACIOUS, UNSELFISH, BOUNTIFUL

genesis: . . . . . ORIGIN, BIRTH, CREATION, BEGINNING

genial: . . . . . WARM, BENIGN, JOVIAL, CORDIAL, FRIENDLY, PLEASANT, AMIABLE

genius: . . . ABILITY, TALENT, APTITUDE, INTELLECT

genre: . . . . KIND, SORT, TYPE, CLASS, STYLE, SPECIES, CATEGORY

gentile: . . . PAGAN, HEATHEN, CHRISTIAN

gentle: .. CALM, EASY, KIND, MEEK, MILD, SOFT, TAME, QUIET, BENIGN, DOCILE, REFINED, POLITE, PLACID, TENDER, LENIENT, PEACEFUL

genuflect: . . . . BEND, KNEEL, CURTSY

genuine: .. PURE, REAL, TRUE, FRANK, PUCKA, ACTUAL, HONEST, SINCERE, BONAFIDE, PUREBRED, AUTHENTIC

genus: .. KIND, SORT, CLASS, ORDER, GENDER, VARIETY, CATEGORY, CLASSIFICATION

geode: . . . . . DRUSE, CAVITY, NODULE

geology: . . . . TECTONICS, EARTH SCIENCE

geomancy: . . . . . DIVINATION

geometry: curve: . . . CIRCLE, SPIRAL, ELLIPSE, EVOLUTE, PARABOLA, SINUSOID

figure: . . . . . CONE, CUBE, LUNE, ANGLE, PRISM,

RHOMB, GNOMON, OBLONG,
SQUARE, SPHERE, PYRAMID,
POLYGON, HELICOID,
RHOMBUS, TRIANGLE,
RECTANGLE, QUADANGLE

principle: . . . . . THEOREM

ratio: . . . . PI, SINE

germ: . . . . . BUD, BUG, EGG,
SEED, SPORE, VIRUS, EMBRYO,
SPROUT, MICROBE, BACTERIA,
RUDIMENT

German: . . . . . . HUN, GOTH,
BOCHE, JERRY, SAXON,
TEUTON

germane: . . . . AKIN, ALLIED,
GENUINE, RELATED, RELEVANT,
PERTINENT

gest(e): . . . DEED, FEAT, JEST,
CONDUCT, EXPLOIT, GESTURE,
BEARING, ADVENTURE

gesture: . . . . . . ACT, GESTE,
TOKEN, MOTION, ACTION,
SALUTE, MOVEMENT

get: . WIN, EARN, FIND, GAIN,
TAKE, TRAP, CATCH, FETCH,
LEARN, REACH, SEIZE, ATTAIN,
OBTAIN, SECURE, ACQUIRE,
ACHIEVE, CAPTURE, PROCURE,
REALIZE, RECEIVE, CONTRACT,
DETERMINE

gewgaw: . . BAUBLE, TRINKET,
TRIFLE, GIMCRACK, DOODAD,
KNICKKNACK

ghastly: . . WAN, GRIM, PALE,
LURID, DISMAL, GRISLY,
PALLID, DEATHLY, HIDEOUS,
MACABRE, GRUESOME,
FRIGHTFUL

ghost: . . . . HANT, SHADE,
SPOOK, UMBRA, DEMON, SPIRIT,
LEMUR, EIDOLON, WRAITH,
PHANTOM, SPECTER, SHADOW,
APPARITION

ghoulish: . . . . . . EERY, EERIE,
FIENDISH, LOATHSOME,
HORRIBLE

giant: . . . ETEN, HUGE, OGRE,
JUMBO, TITAN, TROLL,
CYCLOPS, GOLIATH,

BEHEMOTH, MONSTER,
COLUSSUS, GARGANTUAN

gibberish: . . JABBER, JARGON,
CHATTER, MUMBO-JUMBO

gibbet: . GALLOWS, SCAFFOLD

gibe: . . . . RIB, JAPE, JEER,
MOCK, AGREE, TEASE, SNEER,
HECKLE, FLEER, SCOFF, TAUNT,
DERIDE, RIDICULE

giddy: . . . . . . DIZZY, FICKLE,
FLIGHTY, FRIVOLOUS

gift: . . SOP, TIP, ALMS, BOON,
DOLE, BONUS, DOWER, FAVOR,
GRANT, KNACK, TOKE,
BOUNTY, PRESENT, TALENT,
LEGACY, ABILITY, LARGESS,
GRATUITY, DONATION,
ENDOWMENT

gifted: . . . . TALENTED

gigantic: . . . . . . HUGE, VAST,
IMMENSE, MAMMOTH,
COLOSSAL, TITANIC,
ENORMOUS, GARGANTUAN

giggle: . . . . . LAUGH, TITTER,
SNICKER, SNIGGER

gild: . . . . ADORN, TINGE,
OVERLAY, EMBELLISH

gimcrack: . . . . . TOY, CHEAP,
BAUBLE, FLIMSY, GEWGAW,
TRIFLE, DOODAD, TRINKET,
NOVELTY

ginger: . . . . PEP, VIM, SNAPS,
SPICE, VIGOR, SPIRIT

gingerly: . . WARILY, TIMIDLY,
CAREFULLY, CAUTIOUSLY

gipsy: . . . . see **gypsy**

giraffe: . . . . . . CAMELOPARD

gird: . . . . . BELT, BIND, GIBE,
JEER, SCOFF, BRACE, EQUIP,
CLOTHE, ENCIRCLE, FASTEN,
SECURE, ENCLOSE, SURROUND

girdle: . . . BAND, BELT, RING,
SASH, ZONE, BODICE, CESTUS,
CIRCLE, CORSET, CINCTURE,
CINGULUM, ENCIRCLE,
CUMMERBUND

girl: . . . GAL, SIS, BABE, CHIT,
COED, JILL, LASS, MAID, MISS,
MINX, BELLE, FILLE, FILLY,

SKIRT, WENCH, DAMSEL, HUSSY, FEMALE, TOMBOY, COLLEEN, FLAPPER, INGENUE

gist: . . . . . NUB, CORE, CRUX, PITH, HEART, POINT, ESSENCE, SUMMARY, KERNEL, FOUNDATION

give: . . . . CEDE, DOLE, HAND, METE, ENDOW, GRANT, YIELD, BESTOW, IMPART, CONFER, DONATE, RENDER, PRESENT, CONTRIBUTE

given: . . . . . . FIXED, STATED, DONATED, DISPOSED, INCLINED, SPECIFIED, ASSUMED

glacial: . . . ICY, COLD, GELID, ARTIC, FRIGID, FROZEN

glacier: . . . . ICECAP, ICEBERG

glad: . . . . GAY, FAIN, HAPPY, MERRY, BLITHE, BRIGHT, JOYOUS, PLEASED, WILLING, CHEERFUL, DELIGHTED

glade: . . DELL, VALE, MARSH, VALLEY, CLEARING

glamor: . . . CHARM, ALLURE, BEWITCH, MYSTERY, ROMANCE, FASCINATION

glance: . . . LEER, OGLE, PEEK, PEEP, SCAN, SKIM, FLASH, SQUINT, SCANCE, GLIMPSE

gland: . . . . . LIVER, LYMPH, THYMUS, ADRENAL, SPLEEN, PINEAL, THYROID, PAROTID, PANCREAS, FOLLICLE, EXOCRINE, ENDOCRINE

glare: . . GAZE, STARE, BLAZE, LOOK, GLITTER

glaring: . . . . . RANK, CLEAR, GAUDY, GROSS, PLAIN, VIVID, BURNING, EVIDENT, OBVIOUS, GARISH, FLAGRANT

glass: . . LENS, PANE, BEAKER, BOTTLE, CULLET, GOBLET, MIRROR, CRYSTAL, TUMBLER

glaze: . . COAT, COVER, SLEET, FINISH, POLISH, VENEER, WINDOW

gleam: . . RAY, BEAM, GLOW, FLASH, GLINT, SHEEN, SHINE, GLIMMER, GLITTER, SPARKLE

glean: . . . . CULL, REAP, COLLECT, GATHER

glebe: . . . . CLOD, SOIL, LAND, EARTH, LUMP, FIELD

glee: . . . JOY, MIRTH, GAIETY, SPORT, DELIGHT, ELATION, MERRIMENT

glen: . . . . DALE, DELL, VALE, DINGLE, VALLEY

glib: . . . . EASY, OILY, SLICK, FACILE, FLUENT, SMOOTH, VOLUBLE

glide: . . . . FLOW, SAIL, SKIM, SLIP, SCUD, SOAR, SKATE, SLIDE, SLITHER

glimmer: . . . . . FIRE, GLOW, BLINK, FLASH, GLEAM, FLICKER, GLIMPSE

glimpse: . . . . . BLINK, FLASH, TINGE, TRACE, GLANCE, GLIMMER, INKLING

glisten: . . . . . FLASH, GLEAM, SHINE, SPARKLE, GLITTER, CORUSCATE

gloaming: . . DUSK, TWILIGHT

global: . . . . . . WORLD-WIDE, ROUND, SPHERAL

globe: . . . . ORB, BALL, CLEW, EARTH, SPHERE

globule: . . PILL, BEAD, BLOB, DROP, LIQUID, BUBBLE, SPHERULE

gloom: . . . . . . DUSK, MURK, BLUES, CLOUD, DUMPS, FROWN, SADNESS, DIMNESS, DARKNESS, DEPRESSION

gloomy: . . . DIM, SAD, BLUE, DARK, DOUR, GLUM, DREAR(Y), MOROSE, DISMAL, MOODY, SOMBER, STYGIAN, DEPRESSED, SATURNINE, MELANCHOLY

glorify: . . . . . . BLESS, LAUD, ADORE, EXALT, HONOR, PRAISE

glorious: . . . GRAND, BRIGHT, EMINENT, RADIENT, SPLENDID, MAGNIFICENT

glory: . . . . . . FAME, ECLAT, EXHULT, HONOR, KUDOS, PRAISE, REJOICE, RENOWN, SPLENDOR, RADIANCE

gloss: . . GLOW, SHEEN, SHINE, POLISH, ENAMEL, VENEER, LUSTER, ANNOTATE

glossy: . . . . . . SILKY, SLEEK, SLICK, SHINY, SMOOTH, SPECIOUS, LUSTROUS

glove: . . MITT, CUFF, MITTEN, SHEATH, GA(U)NTLET

glow: . . . . . . BEAM, ARDOR, BLUSH, FLAME, GLEAM, RADIATE

glucose: . . . SUGAR, STARCH, RUTIN, SIRUP, SUCROSE, DEXTROSE

glue: . . . . FIX, GUM, MOUNT, PASTE, STICK, CEMENT, FASTEN, GLUTEN, ADHESIVE, MUCILAGE

glum: . . . . . . DOUR, SULLEN, SULKY, GLOOMY, MOROSE

glut: . . . . . CLOY, FILL, SATE, GORGE, EXCESS, SURFEIT, SATIATE, PAMPER

glutinous: . . . . . SIZY, ROPY, VISCID, GLUEY, GUMMY, STICKY

glutton: . . HOG, PIG, LECHER, EPICURE, GO(U)RMAND

gluttonous: . . . . . . GREEDY, HOGGISH, VORACIOUS

gnarl: . . . KNOT, NURL, SNAG, GROWL, SNARL, TWIST, TANGLE, CONTORT

gnaw: . . . . BITE, CHEW, FRET, CORRODE, TORMENT, HARASS, NIBBLE

gnome (see: . . . . . **elf, fairy**)

go: . . . DIE, RUN, MOVE, QUIT, RIDE, WALK, ELOPE, LEAVE, DEPART, EMBARK, ESCAPE, RETIRE, TRAVEL, PROCEED

goad: . . . . EGG, GAD, ROD, MOVE, SPUR, PROD, URGE, IMPEL, INCITE, NEEDLE, PRICK, STING, STICK, IRRITATE, STIMULUS

goal: . . . . . AIM, END, BOURN, FINIS, SCORE, TALLY, OBJECT, PURPOSE, AMBITION, OBJECTIVE, INTENTION

gob: . . . . . TAR, HUNK, MASS, LUMP, SAILOR, QUANTITY

goblet: . . . . CUP, GLASS, CHALICE, CRYSTAL, VESSEL

goblin: . . . . . (see **elf, fairy**)

god: . . (also see: **diety**) IDOL, ALLAH, CREATOR, ALMIGHTY, BRAHMA, JEHOVAH

godfather: . . . . SPONSOR

godforsaken: . . . . DESOLATE, FORLORN, DEPRAVED, NEGLECTED

godless: . . . PAGEN, WICKED, IMPIOUS, PROFANE, ATHEISTIC

godlike: . . . . . HOLY, DIVINE, OLYMPIAN

godliness: . . . . PIETY

godly: . . . . PIOUS, DEVOUT, DIVINE, RELIGIOUS, RIGHTEOUS

going: . . . . . RUNAWAY, EXIT, GATE, PATH, ROAD, EXODUS, WORKING, LEAVING, DEPARTURE

gold: . . . . . ORE, ORO, GILT, AURUM, MONEY, RICHES, WEALTH, BULLION

golf: *aid:* . . . . CADDY, CADDIE

hazard: . . . . POND, (SAND)TRAP, STYME, BUNKER

position: . . . . STANCE

score: . . . . . . PAR, BOGEY, BIRDIE, EAGLE

term: . . . . LIE, CUP, PAR, TEE, BAFF, FORE, HOLE, HOOK, LOFT, PUTT, TRAP, BOGEY, DIVOT, EAGLE, GREEN, ROUGH, SLICE, BIRDIE, DORMIE, HAZARD, STYME, STROKE, FAIRWAY

gondola: . . . . . . CAR, BOAT, BARGE, CABIN, COACH, COALCAR

gone: . . . . . OFF, OUT, LEFT, AWAY, DEAD, LOST, USED, RUINED, ABSORBED, CONSUMED

good: . . . . . BON, FIT, ABLE, BOON, FINE, KIND, REAL, AMPLE, BRAVE, MORAL, NIFTY, SOUND, VALID, BENIGN, DEVOUT, PROPER, COPIOUS, GENUINE, UPRIGHT, SUITABLE, EFFICIENT, UNSPOILED, DECOROUS

goodness: . . . . VIRTUE, KINDNESS

goods: . GEAR, STOCK, WARE, PROPERTY, MERCHANDISE

gore: . . . . MUD, DIRT, STAB, BLOOD, CUROR, FILTH, SLIME, GUSSET, PIERCE

gorge: . . . . GLUT, PASS, SATE, CHASM, GLUCH, GULLY, KLOOF, CANYON, COULEE, DEFILE, RAVINE, VALLEY, SATIATE, COULOIR

gorgeous: . . GRAND, SHOWY, DAZZLING, GLORIOUS, SPLENDID, BEAUTIFUL, RESPLENDENT, MAGNIFICANT

gorse: . . FURZE, WHIN, SHRUB

gory: . . . . BLOODY

gosling: . . . . GOOSE

gospel: . . . . TRUTH, EVANGEL, DOCTRINE, TEACHING

gossamer: . . . . FILM(Y), (COB)WEB

gossip: . . . . CAT, GAB, BLAB, RUMOR, BABBLE, HEARSAY, TATTLE, CHATTER, BLABBER, SCANDAL, BUSYBODY, TALEBEARER, SCUTTLEBUTT

gouge: . . . . . . ROUT, CHEAT, CHISEL, GROOVE, SWINDLE, DEFRAUD, OVERCHARGE

gourd: . . . . . . PEPO, MELON, SQUASH, BOTTLE, CALABASH, PUMPKIN, CURCURBIT

gourmand: . . . . GLUTTON, GOURMET, EPICURE, CONNISSEUR

gout: . . . . . . CLOT, BURSITIS, ARTHRITIS, PODAGRA

govern: . . . RUN, CURB, REIN, RULE, GUIDE, REIGN, STEER, DIRECT, MANAGE, COMMAND, CONTROL

government: . . RULE, POWER, CONDUCT, CONTROL, REGIMEN, MONARCHY, REPUBLIC, AUTOCRACY, DEMOCRACY, HIERARCHY, OLIGARCHY, MANAGEMENT, ARISTOCRACY, DIRECTION

governor: . . . . . BEY, LORD, PILOT, RULER, RECTOR, REGENT, CAPTAIN, MANAGER, VICEROY, DIRECTOR, REGULATOR

gown: . . . . (see: **dress, garb**)

grace: . . . . TACT, ADORN, CHARM, FAVOR, MERCY, ATTEND, BEAUTY, PRAYER, POLISH, DIGNIFY, CHARISMA

graceful: . . GAINLY, ELEGANT, FITTING, TACTFUL, CHARMING, DEBONAIR, BEAUTIFUL

graceless: . . . . CLUMSY, AWKWARD, INELEGANT

gracious: . . . . . . GOOD, KIND, BENIGN, URBANE, POLITE, MERCIFUL

gradation: . . . . RANK, SCALE, STAGE, DEGREE, NUANCE, SUCCESSION

grade: . . . RANK, RATE, SIZE, SORT, CLASS, LEVEL, ORDER, MARK, DEGREE, RATING, INCLINE

grain: . . BIT, JOT, RYE, CORN, GRIT, OATS, RICE, SEED, WALE, FIBER, MAIZE, TRACE, WHEAT, BARLEY, CEREAL, KERNAL, MILLET, TEXTURE, PARTICLE

granary: . . . BIN, GOLA, CRIB, SILO, GRANGE, GARNER, ELEVATOR, REPOSITORY, STOREHOUSE

grand: . . . EPIC, MAIN, CHIEF, GREAT, NOBLE, AUGUST,

SUPERB, IMMENSE, STATELY, MAJESTIC, MAGNIFICENT, IMPOSING

grandeur: .... POMP, STATE, GLORY, MAJESTY, ELEGANCE, EMINENCE, NOBILITY, SPLENDOR

grandiloquent: ..... HEROIC, TURGID, POMPOUS, BOMBASTIC

grandiose: ... EPIC, POMPOUS, IMPOSING, EXPANSIVE, IMPRESSIVE

grant: .... AID, BOON, CEDE, GIFT, GIVE, LOAN, ADMIT, AGREE, ALLOW, AWARD, ACCEDE, ASSENT, BESTOW, CONFER, PATENT, PERMIT, REMISE, CONCEDE, CONSENT, SUBSIDY, DONATION, FRANCHISE

granular: .. SANDY, COARSE, GRAINY

graph: .... CHART, DIAGRAM

graphic: ..... CLEAR, VIVID, LIFELIKE, PICTORIAL

grasp: .... GRAB, GRIP, HENT, HOLD, TAKE, CATCH, CLASP, SEIZE, CLENCH, CLUTCH, SNATCH, EMBRACE, CONTROL, UNDERSTAND

grasping: ... AVID, GREEDY, MISERLY, COVETOUS, AVARICIOUS

grass: ..... (also see: **grain**) LAWN, REED, TURF, HASSOCK, HERBAGE, PASTURE

grasshopper: .... GRIG, LOCUST, KATYDID, CRICKET

grassland: ..... LEA, LAWN, VALE, CAMPO, FIELD, RANGE, VELDT, PAMPA, SWARD, PASTURE, PRAIRIE, SAVANNA(H)

grate: ...... JAR, RUB, FRET, GRID, RASP, ANNOY, GRILL, GRIND, ABRADE, BASKET, SCRAPE, IRRITATE, FIREPLACE

grateful: .... WELCOME, PLEASED, THANKFUL, APPRECIATIVE

gratification: ...... REWARD, GRATUITY, PLEASURE, RECOMPENSE, SATISFACTION

gratify: .... SATE, PLEASE, FLATTER, SATISFY, HUMOR, PAMPER, APPEASE, DELIGHT, INDULGE, REWARD, REMUNERATE

gratuitous: ..... FREE, GRATIS, NEEDLESS, SUPERFLUOUS

gratuity: .... FEE, TIP, BOON, DOLE, GIFT, VAIL, BONUS, BRIBE, PRESENT, CUMSHAW, BAKSHISH, LAGNIAPPE, PERQUISITE

grave: ..... PIT, BIER, BURY, ETCH, TOMB, CARVE, INTER, SOBER, STAID, MOUND, BURIAL, SEDATE, SOLEMN, SERIOUS, WEIGHTY, OMINOUS

gravestone: ... SLAB, STELE, STELA, MARKER, MEMORIAL, MONUMENT

gravid: .... PREGNANT

gravity: .... WEIGHT, IMPORTANCE, SOLEMNITY, SERIOUSNESS, SIGNIFICANCE

gray: ..... DIM, OLD, DULL, ASHEN, ELDERLY, HOARY, DREARY, DISMAL, GRIZZLY

graze: ..... RUB, FEED, NICK, SKIM, BRUSH, SHAVE, TOUCH, BROWSE, SCRAPE, PASTURE, SCRATCH

grease: .... FAT, OIL, DAUB, LARD, BRIBE, SMEAR, LANOLIN, LUBRICANT, LUBRICATE

great: ..... BIG, DEEP, FELL, FINE, HUGE, MUCH, UNCO, VAST, CHIEF, GRAND, LARGE, NOBLE, EMINENT, IMMENSE, IMPOSING, CLEVER, EXPERT, TITANIC

greatest: ...... ARCH, BEST, MOST, UTMOST, EXTREME, SUPREME

greed: ... EDACITY, AVARICE, AVIDITY, CUPIDITY, GLUTTONY, VORACITY

greedy: . . . . . . AVID, EAGER, STINGY, MISERLY, COVETOUS, ESURIENT, GRASPING, VORACIOUS, RAVENOUS, INSATIABLE, AVARICIOUS, ACQUISITIVE

green: . . . . . NEW, RAW, BICE, LIVE, JADE, NILE, CRUDE, FRESH, LEAFY, MOSSY, NAIVE, OLIVE, CALLOW, RECENT, UNRIPE, SIMPLE, VERDANT, EMERALD, GULLIBLE, IMMATURE, BILIOUS, UNTRAINED

greenhorn: . . . . GULL, JAKE, TYRO, NOVICE, ROOKIE, BEGINNER

greet: . . . . CRY, HAIL, MEET, ACCOST, SALUTE, WELCOME, ADDRESS, RECEIVE, SALAAM

gregarious: . . . . . SOCIABLE, OUTGOING

grief: . . . WOE, HARM, HURT, PAIN, TEEN, AGONY, DOLAR, TEARS, TRIAL, MISHAP, REGRET, MISERY, SORROW, ANGUISH, SADNESS

grieve: . . . . CRY, RUE, PAIN, MOURN, WOUND, BEWAIL, LAMENT, DISTRESS, SADDEN

grievous: . . . . . SAD, BITTER, SEVERE, INTENSE, ATROCIOUS, DEPLORABLE, HEINOUS, LAMENTABLE

grim: . . DOUR, CRUEL, STERN, FIERCE, SAVAGE, SULLEN, MACABRE, RESOLUTE, FURIOUS, SINISTER, GHASTLY, OMINOUS, MERCILESS

grimace: . . MOP, MOW, MUG, MOCK, MOUE, POUT, FLEER, SMIRK, SNEER, SCOWL, FROWN, GLOWER

grime: . . . DIRT, SMUT, SOIL, SOOT, COLLY, SULLY

grind: . . . BRAY, CHEW, GRIT, MILL, MULL, HONE, SAND, CHAFE, CRUSH, GNASH, GRATE, ABRADE, CRUNCH, POWDER, SHARPEN, MASTICATE, PULVERIZE

grinder: . . . . . MILL, TOOTH, MOLAR, MORTAR, PESTLE, MILLSTONE, WHETSTONE, ABRASIVE

grip: . . . . BAG, HOLD, CINCH, CLAMP, CLASP, CLEAT, GRASP, SEIZE, CLENCH, CLUTCH, CONTROL, HANDLE, VALISE

gripe: . . . BEEF, GRIP, GRASP, PINCH, DISTRESS, CLINCH, GROUSE, HARASS, CLUTCH, AFFLICT, CONTROL, HANDLE, COMPLAIN, GRUMBLE

grisly: . . . . . . GRIM, MORBID, HORRIBLE, HIDEOUS, GHASTLY, GRUESOME

grit: . . . . SAND, SOIL, EARTH, GRAIN, NERVE, PLUCK, CLENCH, GRAVEL, COURAGE, FORTITUDE

girth: . . . . . MERCY, REFUGE, PEACE, SECURITY, SANCTUARY

groggy: . . . . . SHAKY, DIZZY, TIPSY, UNSTEADY, WAVERING, TOTTERING

groom: . . SYCE, TIDY, BRUSH, CURRY, DRESS, DEVELOP, HOSTLER, PREPARE, COISTREL, ATTENDANT, BRIDEGROOM, MANSERVANT

groove: . . RUT, SLOT, CANAL, CHASE, FLUTE, GLYPH, SCARF, STRIA, CREASE, FURROW, GUTTER, RABBET, SULCUS, CHANNEL, RIFLING

grope: . . FEEL, TEST, PROBE, SOUND, FUMBLE

gross: . . . . . BIG, FAT, BULK, MASS, RANK, RUDE, BULKY, BURLY, CRASS, CRUDE, DENSE, ENTIRE, PLAIN, ROUGH, THICK, TOTAL, BRUTAL, COARSE, FILTHY, VULGAR, CORPULENT, GLARING, OBVIOUS, FLAGRANT

grotesque: . . . . ABSURD, BAROQUE, BIZARRE, FANTASTIC, INCONGRUOUS

grotto: ... DEN, CAVE, HOLE, CRYPT, VAULT, SHRINE, CAVERN

grouch: ... SULK, GRUMBLE(R)

ground: .. BASE, DIRT, LAND, ROOT, SOIL, BASIS, EARTH, FIELD, MOTIVE, REASON, COUNTRY, TERRAIN, ESTABLISH, TERRITORY, FOUNDATION

groundless: .... IDLE, FALSE, BASELESS, UNFOUNDED, UNJUSTIFIED

grounds: ...... LEES, BASIS, DREGS, GROUT, LAWNS, REASON, RESIDUE, GARDENS, CAMPUS, SEDIMENT, COMPOUND

group: .... MOB, SET, BAND, BEVY, BLOC, BODY, CREW, GANG, HERD, MASS, RING, SECT, TEAM, UNIT, BATCH, BROOD, CABAL, CLASS, CLUMP, CADRE, CORPS, COVEY, DROVE, FLOCK, GENUS, HORDE, SQUAD, TRIBE, CLIQUE, GALAXY, SCHOOL, CLUSTER

grouse: ...... CRAB, GRIPE, GROUCH, GRUMBLE, COMPLAIN, SAGE HEN, PTARMIGAN

grout: ... LEES, MEAL, DREGS, GROUNDS, SEDIMENT, PORRIDGE

grove: ... BUSH, TOPE, WOOD, COPSE, BOSKET, BOSCAGE, COPPICE, THICKET

grovel: ...... FAWN, ROLL, CRAWL, CREEP, CRINGE, WALLOW, FLOUNDER,

grow: ..... BUD, WAX, RISE, RAISE, SWELL, ACCRUE, EXPAND, EXTEND, THRIVE, DEVELOP, ENLARGE, IMPROVE, MATURE, INCREASE, SPROUT, ACCRETE, FLOURISH, CULTIVATE

grown: .... ADULT, MATURE, EXPANDED

grudge: .... ENVY, SPITE, PIQUE, PEEVE, ANIMUS, ILLWILL, MALICE

gruesome: ..... GRIM, UGLY, HORRID, MORBID, SORDID, GRISLY, GHASTLY, MACABRE, HORRIBLE, HORRIFYING

gruff: .. RUDE, BLUFF, HARSH, ROUGH, SURLY, BLUNT, HOARSE, SEVERE, SULLEN, BRUSQUE

grumble: ...... CRAB, KICK, GRIPE, GROUCH, GROUSE, GROWL, RUMBLE, MUTTER, REPINE, COMPLAIN

guarantee: .... BAIL, BOND, VOUCH, ASSURE, AFFIRM, ENSURE, INSURE, SURETY, PLEDGE, CERTIFY, ENDORSE, ASSURANCE, WARRANT(Y)

guard: .. CARE, HERD, HOLD, KEEP, TEND, WARD, FENCE, HEDGE, CONVEY, CONVOY, DEFEND, SHIELD, ESCORT, JAILER, KEEPER, PATROL, PROTECT, POLICE, SENTRY, PICKET, CONSERVE, PRESERVE, SENTINAL, CUSTODIAN, PROTECTOR

guardian: .. TUTOR, KEEPER, PARENT, PASTOR, PATRON, WARDEN, CURATOR, TRUSTEE, TUTELAR, DEFENDER, CUSTODIAN, PROTECTOR

guess: ...... FANCY, INFER, DIVINE, THEORY, OPINION, PRESUME, SURMISE, SUSPECT, ESTIMATE, SPECULATE, CONJECTURE

guest: ..... CALLER, INMATE, LODGER, PATRON, ROOMER, VISITOR, BOARDER, COMPANY

guide: .... KEY, BUOY, CLUE, LEAD, POLE, REIN, RULE, SHOW, ORDER, PILOT, SCOUT, STEER, TEACH, TUTOR, USHER, CONVOY, DIRECT, MANAGE, CONDUCT, CONTROL, COURIER, DIRECTOR

guild, gild: .. CRAFT, UNION, SOCIETY, ASSOCIATION

guile: .... CUNNING, DECEIT, WILE, CRAFT, CHEAT, FRAUD,

DECEIT, CUNNING, DUPLICITY, TREACHERY

guileless: . . . . . OPEN, NAIVE, CANDID, HONEST, ARTLESS, FRANK, SINCERE, INGENUOUS

guilt: . . . SIN, CRIME, CULPA, FAULT, OFFENSE, INIQUITY, CULPABILITY

guiltless: . . . . . PURE, CLEAR, INNOCENT, RIGHTEOUS

guilty: . . . NOCENT, CULPABLE

guise: . . . FORM, GARB, MASK, MIEN, CLOAK, COVER, DRESS, SHAPE, ATTIRE, DECEIT, DISGUISE, PRETENSE, SEMBLANCE, APPEARANCE

gulch: . . . . . . CANON, GORGE, GULLY, ARROYO, CANYON, COULEE, RAVINE, VALLEY

gulf: . . . . GAP, EDDY, ABYSS, BIGHT, CHASM, CLEAVAGE, WHIRLPOOL, SEPARATION

gull: . . . . . . (also see: **fraud, swindle**) COB, DUPE, FOOL, TERM, CHEAT, CULLY, TRICK, VICTIM, DECEIVE, DEFRAUD, MISLEAD

gullet: . . . . . . MAW, CRAW, THROAT, ESOPHAGUS

gullible: . . NAIVE, CREDULOUS

gully: . . . (also see: **gorge, gulch**) GUT, SIKE, WADI, DRAIN, RAVINE, CHANNEL, ARROYO, COULOIR

gulp: . . . BOLT, SWIG, SWIPE, GOBBLE, SWALLOW

gum: . . CLOG, GLUE, LATEX, RESIN, STICK, CHICLE, GLUTEN, IMPEDE, RUBBER, ADHESIVE, MUCILAGE

gumption: . . . . . . COURAGE, ENTERPRISE, INITIATIVE

gun: . . . . . . GAT, ROD, COLT, IRON, RIFLE, CANNON, HEATER, PISTOL, WEAPON, MORTAR, MUSKET, CARBINE, SHOTGUN, REVOLVER, BAZOOKA, AUTOMATIC, BLUNDERBUSS

gunfire: . . . . . RAKE, SALVO, STRAFE, VOLLY, BARRAGE, ENFILADE, FUSILLADE

guns: . . . . . ARMS, WEAPONS, BATTERY, FIREARMS, ARTILLERY, ORDNANCE

gush: . . . . JET, FLOW, POUR, ISSUE, SPOUT, SPURT, EFFUSE, STREAM, OUTPOURING

gust: . . . . . GALE, PUFF, RUSH, SCUD, WAFT, WIND, BLAST, DRAFT, GUSTO, STORM, TASTE, WHIFF, FLURRY, RELISH, SQUALL, OUTBURST

gusto: . . . . ELAN, GUST, ZEST, TASTE, LIKING, RELISH, ENJOYMENT, APPRECIATION

gut(s): . . . . . BELLY, GULLY, PLUCK, BOWELS, COURAGE, DESTROY, STAMINA, STOMACH, ENTRAILS, INTESTINE, EVISCERATE

gutter: . . . . . . SINK, BROOK, DITCH, GULLY, GROOVE, TRENCH, TROUGH, VENNEL, CHANNEL, SCUPPER

guy: . . KID, ROD, CHAP, JOSH, ROPE, STAY, CHAIN, GUIDE, TEASE, FELLOW, RIDICULE

gymnast: . . . . ACROBAT, TURNER, TUMBLER, ATHLETE, BALANCER

gyp: . . . . CHEAT, STEAL, SHARPER, SWINDLE(R), OVERCHARGE

gypsum: . . PARGET, SELENITE, ALABASTER

gypsy, gipsy: . . . . . . NOMAD, ROAMER, ROMANY, GITANO, BOHEMIAN, WANDERER

gyrate: . . . GYRE, SPIN, TURN, TWIRL, WHIRL, ROTATE, REVOLVE

gyre: . . . . . . RING, GYRATE, VORTEX, CIRCUIT, REVOLUTION

gyve: . . IRON, CHAIN, FETTER, SHACKLE

H

habeas corpus: . . . . . WRIT, ORDER

habile: . . . . . APT, FIT, ABLE, CLEVER, HANDY, ADROIT, SKILLFUL, SUITABLE

habiliment: . . . . . . (see also **dress, garb**) ATTIRE, HABIT, APPAREL, COSTUME, RAIMENT, GARMENT, CLOTHING

habilitate: . . . . DRESS, EQUIP, OUTFIT, ENTITLE, QUALIFY, PREPARE

habit: . . . . . . (see also **dress, garb, gown**) RUT, USE, VICE, WONT, ARRAY, ATTIRE, GUISE, USAGE, COSTUME, PRACTICE, CUSTOM, ROUTINE, GARMENT, TENDENCY, DISPOSITION

habitant: . . . . RESIDENT, DWELLER

habitation: . . . . HOME, LAIR, TENT, ABODE, HOUSE, HOVEL, IGLOO, HARBOR, WARREN, LODGING, DOMICILE, DWELLING, RESIDENCE

habitual: . . . USUAL, CHRONIC, COMMON, REGULAR, FREQUENT, ORDINARY, INVETERATE, CUSTOMARY

habituate: . . . INURE, ENURE, DRILL, ADDICT, SEASON, ACCUSTOM, FREQUENT, ACCLIMATE, ACCLIMATIZE

hacienda: . . . FARM, ESTATE, RANCH, PLANTATION, ESTABLISHMENT

hack: . . AX, CAB, CUT, HEW, CHOP, TAXI, COACH, COUGH, DRUDGE, MANGLE, BUTCHER, CARRIAGE, MUTILATE

hackneyed: . . . . OLD, WORN, BANAL, STALE, TRITE, STOCK, CLICHE, COMMON, STEREOTYPED

had: . . . . see **have**

Hades: . . . . . DIS, PIT, HELL, ORCUS, PLUTO, SHEOL, ARALU, TARTARUS, AVERNUS, ABADDON

hag: . . WOOD, COPSE, CRONE, DEMON, WITCH, HARPY, GHOST, MARSH, BELDDAM(E), GOBLIN, SPIRIT, HARRIDAN

haggard: . . . . . . WAN, LANK, PALE, THIN, WILD, GAUNT, DRAWN, ANXIOUS, CADAVEROUS

haggle: . . . CUT, CHOP, HACK, CAVIL, BADGER, BANTER, CHISEL, DICKER, DISPUTE, BARGIN, QUIBBLE, MANGLE, WRANGLE

hail: . . . . . AVE, AHOY, CALL, CHEER, GREET, SLEET, SOUND, WHOLE, ACCOST, SALUTE, ADDRESS, GRAUPEL, METEOR, SIGNAL, SHOWER, GREETING

hair: . . . . FUR, NAP, DOWN, MANE, SHAG, CRINE, TRESS, CURL, THATCH, BRISTLE, FILAMENT

hairdresser: . . . . . FRISEUR, COIFFEUR, COIFFUSE

hairy: . . . . PILOSE, BARBATE, COMATE, COMOSE, HIRSUTE, PILAR(Y), CILIATE, PILEOUS, CRINITE, VILLOUS, SHAGGY

halberd: . . . . . . BILL, SPEAR, GLAIVE, PARTISAN, GISARME, SPONTOON

halcyon: . . . . . CALM, HAPPY, TRANQUIL, PEACEFUL

hale: . . . . . . TUG, VEX, WELL, HAUL, HEAL, PULL, ANNOY, SOUND, HARASS, HEALTHY, ROBUST, HEARTY

half: . . . . . DEMI, HEMI, SEMI, MOIETY, PARTIAL, PARTNER

breed: . . MULE, METIS(SE), MESTEE, MUSTEE, MESTIZO, HYBRID, MESTIF(F), MULATTO, OCTAROON, QUADROON

hearted: . . . . RELUCTANT, UNWILLING, SPIRITLESS, LUKEWARM *wit:* . . DOLT, FOOL, IDIOT, DUNCE, BLOCKHEAD

witted: . . . DOTTY, STUPID, SILLY, IMBECILIC, MORONIC, FOOLISH, SENSELESS

halfway: . . . . . MID, PARTIAL, EQUIDISTANT, INCOMPLETE

halitus: . . FOG, AURA, VAPOR, BREATH, EXHALATION

hall: . . . DORM, SAAL, ENTRY, FOYER, LOBBY, MANOR, ODEON, SALLE, ATRIUM, LYCEUM, SALON, SALOON, CHAMBER, GALLERY, PASSAGE, ANTEROOM, CORRIDOR, VESTIBULE

hallow: . . . . . . HOLY, BLESS, DEDICATE, SANCTIFY, CONSECRATE

hallucination: . . . . MIRAGE, DELUSION, DELIRIUM, FANTASY, CHIMERA

halo: . . . ARC, AURA, GLOW, NIMB, GLORY, CIRCLE, CORONA, NIMBUS, AUREOLA, AUREOLE, GLORIA, GLORIOLE

halogen: . . IODINE, BROMINE, CHLORINE, FLUORINE

halt: . . . . LAME, LIMP, STOP, CEASE, PAUSE, STAND, ARREST, DESIST, TERMINATE

halter: . . . . . . ROPE, LEASH, NOOSE, STRAP, BRIDLE, HACKAMORE

hammer: . . . . . . BANG, BEAT, CLAW, JACK, MAUL, TACK, TAMP, GAVEL, POUND, BATTER, BEETLE, MALLET, PUMMEL, SLEDGE, STRIKE, MALLEATE, BALLPEEN

hamper: . . BIN, CLOG, CURB, SLOW, BLOCK, CRAMP, CRATE, BASKET, FETTER, HINDER, HOBBLE, IMPEDE, CONFINE, MANACLE, HANAPER, SHACKLE, ENCUMBER, OBSTRUCT, TRAMMEL, RESTRICT

hamstring: . . . HOCK, LAME, TENDON, CRIPPLE, DISABLE, HINDER

hand: . . . AID, FIN, PAW, PUD, CLAW, FIST, GIVE, HELP, MITT, PLEDGE, WORKER, ABILITY, FLIPPER, PRESENT, HOLDING, LABORER, PROFER, APPLAUSE, POINTER, TRANSMIT, SIGNATURE

handbag: . CASE, ETUI, GRIP, PURSE, VALISE, SATCHEL, RETICULE

handbill: . . . . . LEAF, FLYER, NOTICE, DODGER, ADVERTISEMENT

handicap: . . . . . ODDS, RACE, BURDEN, HINDER, IMPEDE, ENCUMBER, HINDRANCE, (DIS)ADVANTAGE

handle: . . . . . EAR, LUG, NOB, PAW, PLY, USE, ANSA, DEAL, FEEL, GRIP, HAFT, HEFT, HILT, KNOB, GRIPE, GROPE, HELVE, LEVER, SWIPE, TOUCH, TREAT, WIELD, DIRECT, MANAGE, OPERATE, MANIPULATE

handout: . . AID, ALMS, DOLE, GIFT, METE, CHARITY

handsome: . . . . . FAIR, FINE, AMPLE, LARGE, COMELY, BONNY, SHARP, ELEGANT, LIBERAL, BEAUTIFUL

handwriting: . . . FIST, SCRIPT, MANUSCRIPT, PENMANSHIP

handy: . . DEFT, NEAR, ADEPT, READY, ADROIT, CLEVER, ADJACENT, DEXTEROUS, VERSATILE, CONVENIENT

hang: . . . . . SAG, LOLL, REST, DRAPE, DROOP, HOVER, DANGLE, DEPEND, CRUCIFY, STRING, SUSPEND, EXECUTE, EXHIBIT

hangar: . . . . SHED, GARAGE, STABLE, SHELTER

hanger on: . TOADY, HEELER, LEECH, TRENCHER, SYCOPHANT, PARASITE, DEPENDENT

hanging: . . DRAPE, PENDANT, PENSILE, VALANCE, INCLINED, EXECUTION, SUSPENDED, PENDULOUS, UNSETTLED

hangout: . . . . . . DEN, HAUNT, JOINT, RETREAT

hank: . . . COIL, SKEIN, LOOP, BUNDLE

hanker: . . . . . ITCH, CRAVE, LONG, DESIRE, YEARN

hamsom: . . . . CAB, HACK, CARRIAGE

hap: . . . . LOT, LUCK, BEFALL, CHANCE, FORTUNE, OCCURRENCE

haphazard: . . . . . . CASUAL, CHANCE, RANDOM, AIMLESS, CARELESS, ACCIDENTAL

happen: . COME, FALL, FARE, OCCUR, ARRIVE, BEFALL, CHANCE, TRANSPIRE, EVENTUATE

happening: . . . FACT, EVENT, CHANCE, EPISODE, INCIDENT, OCCASION, OCCURRENCE

happily: . . GLADLY, LUCKILY, CONTENTEDLY, FORTUNATELY, OPPORTUNELY, SUCCESSFULLY, APPROPRIATELY

happiness: . . . . . . JOY, BLISS, MIRTH, DELIGHT, ECTASY, RAPTURE, FELICITY, GLADNESS, ENJOYMENT, WELL-BEING

happy: . . . GAY, COSH, GLAD, BLITHE, LUCKY, MERRY, READY, ELATED, CONTENT, JOYOUS, RADIANT, MIRTHFUL, FORTUNATE, FELICITOUS

harangue: . . . . . NAG, RANT, RAVE, ORATE, SPIEL, SCREED, TIRADE, DIATRIBE, PERORATE, EXHORT(ATION)

harass: . . . . . IRK, NAG, VEX, BAIT, FRET, JADE, GALL, HAZE, RAID, RIDE, ANNOY, BESET, BULLY, CHAFE, CHASE, HARRY, TEASE, WORRY, BADGER, BOTHER, HECKLE, MOLEST,

PESTER, PLAQUE, DISTURB, TORMENT, IRRITATE, TROUBLE

harbinger: . . . OMEN, USHER, HERALD, PRESAGE, FORETELL, PRECURSOR, FORERUNNER

harbor: . . . BAY, COVE, PORT, HAVEN, FOSTER, REFUGE, CONCEAL, CHERISH, RETREAT, SHELTER, ANCHORAGE

hard: . . . FIRM, IRON, MEAN, SOUR, CLOSE, CRUEL, HARSH, RIGID, SOLID, STERN, STIFF, COARSE, FROZEN, ROBUST, SEVERE, STRICT, STRONG, ADAMANT, ARDUOUS, CALLOUS, ONEROUS, OBDURATE, RIGOROUS, SCHEROID, DIFFICULT, FATIGUING, INTRICATE, LABORIOUS, STRENUOUS

harden: . . . GEL, SET, BAKE, CAKE, SEAR, ENURE, INURE, STEEL, ENDURE, FREEZE, OSSIFY, TEMPER, CONGEAL, PETRIFY, STIFFEN, THICKEN, TOUGHEN, CONCRETE, CONDENSE, INDURATE, SOLIDIFY, ACCLIMATIZE

hardheaded: . . . . KEEN, SHREWD, STUBBORN, PRACTICAL, SAGACIOUS

hardly: . . . BARELY, FAINTLY, SCARCELY, HARSHLY, UNFAIRLY

hardship: . . . . RIGOR, TRIAL, INJURY, PENALTY, GRIEVANCE, INJUSTICE, PRIVATION, AFFLICTION

hardy: . . BOLD, FIRM, RASH, WIRY, BRAVE, STOUT, TOUGH, CHISEL, DARING, RUGGED, STRONG, STURDY, ROBUST, DURABLE, INTREPID, RESOLUTE, STUBBORN, COURAGEOUS

hark: . . . HEAR, HEED, LISTEN

harlequin: . . . COMIC, CLOWN, LUDICROUS, BUFFOON

harlot: . . . . . . DOXY, LEWD, WHORE, WANTON, STRUMPET, PROSTITUTE

harm: . . . . . ILL, BALE, BANE, EVIL, HURT, PAIN, ABUSE, GRIEF, WOUND, WRONG, DAMAGE, INJURE, SCATHE, DISEASE, MALIGNANT

harmful: . . . . BAD, EVIL, NASTY, NOCENT, BANEFUL, MALEFIC, NOXIOUS, INJURIOUS

harmless: . . . . SAFE, INNOCUOUS, INOFFENSIVE

harmonious: . . . . . DULCET, CORDIAL, MUSICAL, AMICABLE, PEACEFUL, AGREEABLE, CONSONANT, CONGRUOUS, COMPATIBLE

harmony: . . . . TUNE, AMITY, MUSIC, CHIME, CHORD, PEACE, COSMOS, MELODY, UNISON, CONCORD, RAPPORT, BALANCE, SYMMETRY, AGREEMENT, CONSONANCE

harness: . . RIG, GEAR, EQUIP, DRAFT, TACKLE, HITCH-UP, EQUIPMENT, TRAPPINGS

part: . . . BIT, TUG, HAME, REIN, BLIND, TRACE, BRIDLE, COLLAR, SADDLE, TERRET, HALTER, BILLET, BREECHING, SURCINGLE, MARTINGALE

harpoon: . . . . SPEAR, JAVELIN

harridan: . . . . HAG, CRONE, HORSE, SHREW, VIXEN, WOMAN, STRUMPET

harrow: . . VEX, DISK, DRAG, BRAKE, WOUND, OPPRESS, TORMENT, LACERATE, CULTIVATE

harry: . . . . ROB, VEX, RAID, SACK, ANNOY, HOUND, STEAL, WORRY, HARASS, PESTER, PLAGUE, RAVAGE, TORMENT, PILLAGE, PLUNDER

harsh: . . . RAW, GRIM, HARD, ACRID, BRUTE, CRUDE, CRUEL, GRUFF, RASPY, ROUGH, SHARP, STERN, BITTER, COARSE, SEVERE, STRICT, DRASTIC, UNKIND, ACERBATE, STRIDENT, DISCORDANT

harvest: . . BIND, CROP, REAP, YIELD, GATHER

hash: . . . . CHOP, MINCE, BUNGLE, JUMBLE, MIXTURE, HODGEPODGE

hashish: . . . HEMP, B(H)ANG, NARCOTIC, MARIJUANA, CANNABIS

hassle: . . . . . . FRAY, MELEE, BRAWL, RUCKUS, QUARREL, SQUABBLE, DISCUSSION, COMMOTION

hassock: . . . . . . MAT, SEAT, GRASS, SEDGE, CUSHION, FOOTSTOOL, TUSSOCK

haste: . . RUSH, SPEED, HURRY, BUSTLE, FLURRY, URGENCY, RAPIDITY, QUICKNESS

hasten: . . . . HIE, RUN, RACE, RUSH, DRIVE, HURRY, SPEED, SCURRY, SCAMPER, DISPATCH, EXPEDITE, ACCELERATE

hasty: . . . FAST, RASH, BRASH, FLEET, QUICK, SWIFT, ABRUPT, SPEEDY, SUDDEN, CURSORY, HURRIED, IMPETUOUS, IMPATIENT, IMPULSIVE

hat: . . . . CAP, FEZ, LID, TAM, FELT, BEANY, BERET, DERBY, TOPEE, TOQUE, BEAVER, BOATER, BONNET, BOWLER, CLOCHE, FEDORA, PANAMA, TOPPER, TURBAN, CAUBEEN, CHAPEAU, BIRETTA, HEADGEAR, PETASUS, STOVEPIPE

hatch: . . . BREW, DOOR, GATE, PLAN, PLOT, VENT, BREED, DEVISE, CONCOCT, CONTRIVE, TRAPDOOR, FLOODGATE, FISHTRAP

hate: . . . . . ABHOR, DETEST, LOATHE, RANCOR, REVILE, DESPISE, DISLIKE, MALICE, ABOMINATE, AVERSION

hateful: . . . . . FOUL, ODIOUS, HEINOUS, ABHORRENT, INVIDIOUS, LOATHSOME,

MALIGNANT, EXECRABLE,
REVOLTING, REPUGNANT,
OBNOXIOUS, REPULSIVE,
ABOMINABLE

hatred: . . . . ODIUM, ENMITY,
RANCOR, AVERSION,
ANIMOSITY, HOSTILITY,
MALEVOLENCE

haughty: . . . . . BOLD, LOFTY,
NOBLE, PROUD, SNOOTY,
STUCK-UP, SNOTTY, FATUOUS,
STATELY, ARROGANT,
CAVALIER, SUPERCILIOUS

haul: . . . . . LUG, TOW, TUG,
CART, DRAG, DRAW, PULL,
TOTE, SWAG, BOOTY, CATCH,
HEAVE, TRICE, TRANSPORT

haunt: . . . . DEN, DIVE, LAIR,
NEST, GHOST, SPOOK, INFEST,
OBSESS, RESORT, SPIRIT,
TERRIFY, PERVADE, HANG-OUT,
FREQUENT

have: . . . OWN, HOLD, ENJOY,
RETAIN, CONTAIN, POSSESS,
EXPERIENCE

haven: . . . . BAY, LEE, HOPE,
PORT, ASYLUM, HARBOR,
REFUGE, SHELTER, SANCTUARY

havoc: . . . . . . RUIN, WASTE,
DESTROY, DEVASTATE,
DESOLATION, DESTRUCTION,
DEVASTATION

hawk: . . . IO, GOS, KITE, SELL,
VEND, CADGE, RETCH, ELANET,
FALCON, OSPREY, PEDDLE,
TERCEL, BUZZARD, HARRIER,
KESTREL, SPARROW, VULTURE,
CARACARA, ACCIPITER,
MORTARBOARD

hawser: . . . . LINE, ROPE

hayseed: . . . . . HICK, YOKEL,
FARMER, RUSTIC, COUNTRYMAN

hazard: . . . RISK, JUMP, PERIL,
STAKE, CHANCE, DANGER,
GAMBLE, VENTURE, JEOPARDY

hazardous: . RISKY, CHANCY,
UNSAFE, INSECURE, PERILOUS,
DANGEROUS, UNCERTAIN,
PRECARIOUS

haze: . . . . . FOG, FILM, MIST,
PALL, SMOG, VAPOR, SMAZE,
PESTER, FRIGHTEN

hazy: . . . . . . FOGGY, SMOKY,
VAGUE, OBSCURE, INDISTINCT

head: . . . . . . NOB, TOP, VAN,
BEAN, CONK, LEAD, PATE,
POLL, TETE, CAPUT, SKULL,
CHIEF, FIRST, FRONT, DIRECT,
CAPITA, LEADER, MANAGE,
NOGGIN, NOODLE, SCONCE,
SOURCE, SPRING, CRANIUM,
DIRECTOR, FOREMOST,
PRINCIPAL

headdress: . . . (also see **cap**,
hat) WIG, COIF, POUF, HOOD,
CROWN, MITER, MITRE, TIARA,
TOQUE, SHAKO, BONNET,
COIFFE, HELMET, TURBAN,
DIADEM, TOUPEE, CORONET,
COIFFURE, BIRETTA

heading: . . . . . TITLE, TOPIC,
TROPE, CAPTION

headland: . . . . . CAPE, NESS,
PEAK, BLUFF, RIDGE,
PROMONTORY

headline: . . . TITLE, CAPTION,
FEATURE, BANNER, SCREAMER,
STREAMER

headlong: . . . . RASH, HASTY,
ABRUPT, SUDDEN, RECKLESS,
PELLMELL, IMPULSIVE,
PRECIPITOUS

headman: . . . . . BOSS, CHIEF,
LEADER, HETMAN, CAPTAIN,
FOREMAN, RINGLEADER

headstrong: . . . . RASH,
WILLFUL, STUBBORN,
OBSTINATE, SELF-WILLED,
BULLHEADED, CONTUMACIOUS

heal: . . . . CURE, KNIT, MEND,
REMEDY, REPAIR, RESTORE,
RECONCILE, RECUPERATE

healing: . . BALMY, SANATIVE,
CURATIVE, REMEDIAL,
MEDICINAL, THERAPEUTIC

health: . . . . FIT, HALE, WELL-
BEING, SOUNDNESS

healthy: . . . FIT, HALE, WELL, SOUND, HEARTY, ROBUST, VIGOROUS

heap: . . . . COB, BULK, HILL, LUMP, MASS, PILE, RAFT, RUCK, AMASS, CLUMP, STACK, MOUND, PLENTY, CONGERIES

hear: . . . HARK, HEED, OBEY, LISTEN, LEARN, HEARKEN, AJUDICATE

hearing: . . . . SOUND, TRIAL, ASSIZE, REPORT, LECTURE, INQUEST, AUDITION, AUDIENCE, INTERVIEW

hearsay: . . . . TALK, REPORT, RUMOR, GOSSIP

hearse: . . BIER, BURY, TOMB, DIRGE, GRAVE, COFFIN

heart: . . . . CORE, GIST, LOVE, PITH, CHEER, BOSOM, CENTER, DEPTHS, MIDDLE, SPIRIT, TICKER, COURAGE, BREAST, ESSENCE

heartache: . . . GRIEF, SORROW

heartbeat: . . . PULSE, THROB, SYSTOLE, PALPITATION, PULSATION

heartburn: . . . ENVY, EMITY, PYROSIS, JEALOUSY, CARDIALGIA

heartfelt: . . . . . DEEP, REAL, TRUE, GENUINE, SINCERE

heartless: . . . . CRUEL, HOPELESS, PITILESS, SARDONIC, MERCILESS, DESPONDENT, SPIRITLESS

hearty: . . HALE, RICH, WELL, LUSTY, SOUND, CHEERY, ROBUST, SINCERE, EARNEST, HEALTHY, CORDIAL, GENIAL, ABUNDENT, VIGOROUS, ENERGETIC

heat: . . . . . IRE, FIRE, ZEAL, ARDOR, FEVER, ROAST, TEPOR, ANNEAL, CHALOR, HOTNESS, INFLAME, PASSION, INTENSITY, WARM(TH), EXCITEMENT, TEMPERATURE

heated: . . . . . . HOT, ANGRY, EXCITED

heath: . . MOOR, ERICA, PLAIN, WASTELAND

heathen: . . . PAGAN, INFIDEL, GENTILE, ETHNIC, PAYNIM, IRRELIGIOUS

heave: . . CAST, GASP, HAUL, HEFT, HURL, LIFT, PANT, PULL, PUSH, TOSS, FLING, HOIST, PITCH, RAISE, THROW, VOMIT, ELEVATE, STRUGGLE

heaven: . . SKY, ZION, ETHER, GLORY, WELKIN, ZODIAC, PARADISE, ELYSIUM, NIRVANA, OLYMPUS, FIRMAMENT

heavenly: . . . . HOLY, DIVINE, ANGELIC, OLYMPIC, SUBLIME, EDENIC, CELESTIAL, URANIAN, ETHEREAL, SUPERNAL

heavy: . . . SAD, DULL, LOGY, LOUD, BURLY, DENSE, GROSS, HEFTY, THICK, COARSE, GLOOMY, LEADEN, STODGY, SERIOUS, INTENSE, WEIGHTY, PROFOUND, MASSIVE, BURDENSOME, PONDEROUS

Hebrew: . . . . JEW, ZION, SEMITE, SEMITIC, HEBRAEAN, ISRAELITE

heckle: . . . . NAG, BAIT, GIBE, TAUNT, TEASE, ANNOY, HARASS, HECTOR, NEEDLE

hectic: . . EXCITING, FEVERED, FEVERISH, CONSUMPTIVE

hector: . . . . . . NAG, BULLY, HARRY, WORRY, HARASS, HECKLE, PLAGUE, TEASE, PESTER, BROWBEAT

hedge: . . . . HAW, HEM, REW, BOMA, BUSH, BEARD, FENCE, GUARD, HINDER, PRIVET, WAVER, BARRIER, STRADDLE, QUICKSET, THICKET, TEMPORIZE, EQUIVOCATE, SHILLY-SHALLY

heed: . . . CARE, CURE, HARK, HEAR, MIND, NOTE, OBEY,

LISTEN, NOTICE, REGARD,
OBSERVE, RESPECT, ATTENTION

heedful: .... WARY, CHARY,
CAREFUL, MINDFUL, DILIGENT,
VIGILANT, WATCHFUL,
ATTENTIVE, CONSIDERATE

heedless: .... UNWARY,
LANGUID, CARELESS, RECKLESS,
NEGLIGENT, INDISCREET,
REGARDLESS

heel: ... CAD, END, TIP, CALX,
CANT, TILT, LIST, LEAN, SLANT,
CAREEN, LOUSE, BOUNDER

heft: ... BULK, PULL, HEAVE,
RAISE, WEIGHT, EXERTION,
INFLUENCE

hefty: ...... HEAVY, ROUGH,
RUGGED, MASSIVE, WEIGHTY,
POWERFUL

hegemonic: .... RULING,
LEADING

hegira: .... EXODUS, FLIGHT,
JOURNEY

height: ... TOP, ACME, APEX,
CREST, CLIMAX, SUMMIT,
STATURE, EXTREME, ALTITUDE,
ELEVATION, PINNACLE,
EMINENCE

heighten: .... ELATE, RAISE,
AUGMENT, ELEVATE,
INTENSIFY, INCREASE,
ENHANCE, AGGRAVATE

heinous: .... ODIOUS,
ABOMINABLE, WICKED,
HATEFUL, ATROCIOUS,
MALICIOUS, OUTRAGEOUS

heir: .... SON, HERES, SCION,
LEGATEE, (IN)HERITOR,
SUCCESSOR, BENEFICIARY

held: .... (see hold)

helix: ...... COIL, SPIRAL

hell: .... PIT, ABYSS, HADES,
SHEOL, PRISON, DUNGEON,
INFERNO, ABADDON

hellish: ... WICKED, STYGIAN,
DEVILISH, DIABOLIC, INFERNAL,
DETESTABLE

helm: ...... HELVE, STEER,
WHEEL, DIRECT, RUDDER,
TILLER, GUIDANCE

helminth: .... (TAPE)WORM,
(ROUND)WORM, PARASITE

helmsman: .. PILOT, TILLER,
CONNER, STEERSMAN,
COXSWAIN

help: .... AID, ABET, CURE,
LIFT, MEND, AVAIL, ASSIST,
BOOST, FAVOR, SERVE, RELIEF,
REMEDY, REPAIR, SUCCOR,
SECOND, BENEFIT, FURTHER,
IMPROVE, PROMOTE, SUPPORT,
SUSTAIN, ALLEVIATE, SERVANT,
EMPLOYEES

helpless: ..... LOST, NUMB,
WEAK, FEEBLE, UNABLE,
DESTITUTE, IMPOTENT,
INCOMPETENT

hem: .... SEW, EDGE, SEAM,
SHUT, HEDGE, BORDER,
MARGIN, STITCH, CONFINE,
ENCLOSE, ENCIRCLE, SURROUND

hemorrhage: ..... BLEEDING

hemorrhoid: .. PILES, TUMOR

hemp: ..... IFE, TOW, BANG,
FLAX, JUTE, RINE, FIBER,
BHANG, SISAL, FENNEL,
MANILA, HASHISH, MARIJUANA

hence: ...... SO, FRO, OFF,
AWAY, ERGO, THEN, THUS,
SINCE, THITHER, THEREFORE,
ACCORDINGLY

henchman: .... SQUIRE,
ADHERENT, ATTENDANT,
MOBSTER, FOLLOWER,
HANGER-ON

herald: ...... BODE, CRIER,
USHER, BLAZON, DECLARE,
FORERUN, FORETELL,
PROCLAIM, MESSENGER,
FORERUNNER, HARBINGER,
ANNOUNCE(R)

herb: .... ANET, DILL, LEEK,
MINT, MOLY, SAGE, WORT,
ANISE, BASIL, CHIVE, SEDGE,
THYME, TANSY, CATNIP,
FENNEL, GINGER, MUSTARD,

YARROW, CARRAWAY,
OREGANO, PARSLEY, MAJORAM,
TARRAGON, BERGAMOT,
CHERVIL, GINSENG, ROSEMARY,
CARDAMAN

herd: .... MOB, POD, CREW,
BUNCH, CROWD, DROVE,
FLOCK, GROUP, RABBLE

herdsman: ...... COWBOY,
DROVER, GAUCHO, VAQUERO,
RANCHERO, SHEPHERD,
WRANGLER

here: .... ICI, NOW, READY,
HITHER, PRESENT

hereafter: .. LATER, BEYOND,
FUTURE

hereditary: .... LINEAL,
INNATE, GENETIC, ANCESTRAL,
DESCENDED

heredity:... LINE, GENETICS,
INHERITANCE

heres:............ HEIR

heresy:......... DISSENT,
UNORTHODOXY,
NONCONFORMISM

heritage:..... LOT, LEGACY,
BIRTHRIGHT, PATRIMONY

hermetic: .... MAGICAL,
AIRTIGHT, SEALED, ALCHEMIST

hermit:...... CRAB, MONK,
ASCETIC, ERMITE, RECLUSE,
BEDESMAN, ANCHORITE,
SOLITAIRE, MARABOUT

hermitage: ...... RETREAT,
CLOISTER, MONASTERY

hermitic:....... SECLUDED,
SOLITARY

hernia:... RUPTURE, BREACH

hero: ..... ACE, IDOL, STAR,
DEMIGOD, DEFENDER,
CHAMPION, CONQUEROR,
PROTAGONIST

heroic:... BOLD, EPIC, HUGE,
BRAVE, GREAT, LARGE, NOBLE,
DARING, SPARTAN, EXALTED,
INTREPID, COURAGEOUS

hesitant: .... CHARY, LOATH,
TIMID, TIMOROUS, RELUCTANT,

WAVERING, VACILLATING,
UNCERTAIN

hesitate: ..... WAIT, DELAY,
DEMUR, DOUBT, PAUSE, STALL,
WAVER, FALTER, TEETER,
VACILLATE

heterogeneous: .... MIXED,
MOTLEY, UNLIKE, DIVERSE,
VARIED, FOREIGN, DISSIMILAR,
MISCELLANEOUS

hew:...... CUT, CHIP, CHOP,
FELL, GASH, HACK, CARVE,
WOUND, STRIKE

hex: ...... JINX, (BE)WITCH,
HOODOO

hiatus: .... GAP, BREAK,
CHASM, PAUSE, BREACH,
LACUNA, OPENING, INTERVAL,
INTERRUPTION

hibachi: .... GRILL, BRAZIER

Hibernia: ... ERIN, IRELAND

hick: .. JAKE, RUBE, RUSTIC,
HAYSEED, BUMPKIN

hidalgo: .... NOBLEMAN

hidden:....... LOST, INNER,
PERDU, LATENT, COVERT,
CACHED, CLOSED, BURIED,
SECRET, INNATE, ARCANE,
CRYPTIC, MASKED, OBSCURE

hide: ... BURY, FLOG, MASK,
PELT, SKIN, STOW, VEIL,
CACHE, CLOAK, COVER, SKULK,
SCREEN, SHROUD, CONCEAL,
SECRETE, SHELTER, THRASH,
DISGUISE, WITHHOLD,
CAMOUFLAGE

hideous: ...... GRIM, UGLY,
AWFUL, GRISLY, HORRID,
ODIOUS, GASTLY, DREADFUL,
GRUESOME, HORRIBLE,
SHOCKING, TERRIBLE,
REVOLTING, REPULSIVE

hie: .. HASTEN, HURRY, SPEED

hiemal:... WINTRY, HIBERNAL

high: ... ALT, ALOFT, DEAR,
MAIN, TALL, ACUTE, CHIEF,
DRUNK, FIRST, LOFTY, STEEP,
COSTLY, SHRILL, EMINENT,
EXALTED, ELEVATED,

TOWERING, SUPERIOR,
EXPENSIVE

higest point: . . ACME, APEX,
PEAK, NOON, FINIAL, APOGEE,
CLIMAX, ZENITH, VERTEX,
PINNACLE

highhanded: . . . ARROGANT,
OVERBEARING, ARBITRARY

highly: . . . VERY, EXTREMELY

highway: . . ITER, PIKE, ROAD,
ARTERY, FREEWAY, AUTOBAHN,
CAUSEWAY, TURNPIKE,
THOROUGHFARE

hike: . . . JERK, TOSS, WALK,
MARCH, RAISE, BOOST, TRAMP

hilarious: . . . . . . GAY, MAD,
FUNNY, MERRY, JOVIAL,
JOCULAR, LUDICROUS

hilarity: . . JOY, GLEE, MIRTH,
GAIETY, HAPPINESS, JOVIALITY,
MERRIMENT, EXHILARATION

hill: . . . . BANK, DUNE, FELL,
HEAP, MESA, PILE, BUTTE,
CLIFF, MORRO, MOUND,
MOUNT, BARROW, DJEBEL,
ELEVATION

hillock: . . . . TOFT, TUMP,
CROFT, HURST, KNOLL, KOPJE,
MOUND

hilt: . . HAFT, HELVE, HANDLE

hind: . . . . . DOE, ROE, BACK,
DEER, REAR, STAG, TAIL,
RUSTIC, PEASANT, POSTERIOR

hinder: . . BAR, SLOW, BLOCK,
CHECK, DEBAR, DELAY, DETER,
EMBAR, ESTOP, HEDGE,
ARREST, DETAIN, HAMPER,
HARASS, IMPEDE, RETARD,
INHIBIT, PREVENT, ENCUMBER,
HANDICAP, OBSTRUCT

hindrance: . . . . . BAR, RUB,
CLOG, CURB, SNAG, BLOCK,
CHECK, DELAY, HITCH, ARREST,
OBSTACLE, DETERRENT,
RESTRAINT, DIFFICULTY,
IMPEDIMENT

hinge: . . . AXIS, BUTT, HANG,
KNEE, TURN, JOINT, PIVOT,

ELBOW, DEPEND, GIMMER,
PINTLE

hint: . . CUE, TIP, CLUE, CLEW,
IMPLY, TRACE, ALLUDE,
INKLING, MENTION, SUGGEST,
ALLUSION, INTIMATION,
INTIMATE, INNUENDO,
INSINUATE

hip, hip bone: . . ILIA, COXA,
ILIUM, PELVIS, HAUNCH,
HUCKLE

hire: . . . . BUY, FEE, LET, USE,
RENT, SIGN, WAGE, BRIBE,
LEASE, PRICE, EMPLOY,
ENGAGE, RETAIN, SALARY,
CHARTER, STIPEND,
COMPENSATION

hirsute: . . . . . HAIRY, ROUGH,
COARSE, PILOSE, SHAGGY,
BRISTLY

history: . . . LORE, PAST, TALE,
STORY, ANNALS, MEMOIR,
ACCOUNT, RECORD, CHRONICLE,
BIOGRAPHY, NARRATIVE

histrionics: . . . . ACTING,
DRAMATICS, THEATRICALS

hit: . . . . ACE, BAT, BOP, LAM,
LOB, RAM, RAP, TAP, BEAN,
BIFF, BUMP, BUNT, CLUB,
CONK, CUFF, SLUG, SOCK,
SWAT, WHAM, CLOUT, KNOCK,
SMACK, SMITE, ATTAIN,
POMMEL, COLLIDE, SUCCESS,
BLUDGEON, BULL'S-EYE

hitch: . . . . . . TIE, TUG, HALT,
HOOK, JERK, JOIN, KNOT, LIMP,
PULL, SNAG, CATCH, CRICK,
MARRY, UNITE, ATTACH,
FASTEN, HOBBLE, OBSTACLE,
HINDRANCE

hive: . . . BOX, STORE, SWARM,
APIARY

hoard: . . . . . . SAVE, AMASS,
CACHE, STOCK, STORE, SUPPLY,
HUSBAND, RESERVE, TREASURE,
ACCUMULATE

hoarse: . . . . . GRUFF, HARSH,
ROUGH, HUSKY, GRATING,
RAUCOUS

hoary: ... OLD, AGED, GRAY, MOLDY, MUSTY, WHITE, FROSTY, ANCIENT, CANESCENT, VENERABLE

hoax: ... see **fraud, swindle**

hobble: ...... LIMP, HITCH, FETTER, HAMPER, HINDER, SHACKLE

hobby: ...... FAD, HORSE, PASTIME, FALCON, AVOCATION, DIVERSION

hobgoblin: .... see **elf**

hobnob: .... MINGLE, ASSOCIATE

hobo: ..... BO, BUM, STIFF, TRAMP, VAGRANT, VAGABOND

hodgepodge: ... HASH, MESS, OLIO, STEW, CENTO, POTTAGE, MEDLEY, MELANGE, MISHMASH

hogshead: .... CASK, BARREL

hogtie: .... FETTER, HAMPER

hogwash: .. SWILL, BALONEY

hoi polloi: .... MASSES, RABBLE, POPULACE

hoist: ..... CAT, GIN, BOOM, JACK, LIFT, REAR, BOOST, CRANE, DAVIT, HEAVE, RAISE, WINCH, DERRICK, ELEVATE, CAPSTAN, ELEVATOR, WINDLESS

hoity-toity: .. GIDDY, PROUD, SNOOTY, HAUGHTY, PETULANT, ARROGANT, PATRONIZING

hokum: ... BUNK, NONSENSE, HUMBUG, FOOLISHNESS, BALONEY, APPLESAUCE

hold: .... DAM, OWN, BIND, GRIP, HAVE, HOOK, KEEP, STAY, CARRY, GRASP, GUARD, ADHERE, ARREST, CLEAVE, CLINCH, CLUTCH, DEFEND, DETAIN, HARBOR, OCCUPY, RETAIN, SUSTAIN, CONTAIN, MAINTAIN, RESTRAIN

holdings: ... ASSETS, ESTATE, TENURE, PROPERTY, POSSESSIONS

hole: ... BAY, DEN, EYE, GAP, PIT, BORE, CAVE, COVE, DUMP, FLAW, GATE, GULF, LEAK, MINE, RENT, VENT, ABYSS, CHASM, SHAFT, INLET, BURROW, CAVERN, CAVITY, CRATER, GROTTO, HOLLOW, OPENING, ORIFICE, APERATURE, EXCAVATION, PREDICAMENT

holiday: ...... FETE, FERIA, FIESTA, OUTING, RECESS, PLAYDAY, FESTIVAL, VACATION

holiness: ... PIETY, SANCTITY, SAINTLYNESS

hollow: ... DEN, CAVE, COVE, DENT, HOLE, VOID, EMPTY, FALSE, SCOOP, CAVERN, CAVITY, GROOVE, SOCKET, SUNKEN, VACANT, VALLEY, CONCAVE, FOSSETTE, SPECIOUS, CAVERNOUS

holograph: .. HANDWRITTEN, (MANU)SCRIPT

holocaust: ...... SACRIFICE, DESTRUCTION, ERADICATION

holy: ...... PIOUS, CHASTE, DEVOUT, DIVINE, HALLOW, SACRED, SAINTLY, BLESSED, SPIRITUAL, SINLESS

homage: ... HONOR, EULOGY, FEALTY, REGARD, LOYALTY, OVATION, RESPECT, ADORATION, TRIBUTE, REVERENCE

home: ..... DEN, LAIR, NEST, ROOF, ABODE, HOUSE, ASYLUM, ESTATE, HEARTH, HABITAT, HOSPICE, DWELLING, DOMICILE, HOMESTEAD, RESIDENCE, HOUSEHOLD, INSTITUTION

homelike: . COZY, CHEERFUL, FRIENDLY, FAMILIAR, COMFORTABLE

homely: ..... UGLY, CRUDE, PLAIN, KINDLY, SIMPLE, DOMESTIC, FAMILIAR, FRIENDLY, INTIMATE

homesickness: ... NOSTALGIA

homespun: ... RUDE, PLAIN, COARSE, SIMPLE, UNPRETENTIOUS

homily: .... ADAGE, SERMON, LECTURE, DISCOURSE

hone: ... LONG, MOAN, PINE, DRESS, STROP, YEARN, GRIND, LAMENT, GRUMBLE, SHARPEN, WHET(STONE), OILSTONE

honest: ... FAIR, FULL, JUST, OPEN, FRANK, CANDID, PROPER, SQUARE, GENUINE, SINCERE, UPRIGHT, RELIABLE, TRUTHFUL, VERACIOUS

honesty: ... HONOR, EQUITY, JUSTICE, PROBITY, FAIRNESS, FIDELITY, INTEGRITY, VERACITY, TRUTHFULNESS

honor: ...... FAME, ADORE, AWARD, EXALT, GLORY, GRACE, CREDIT, ESTEEM, HOMAGE, PRAISE, REGARD, RESPECT, REVERE, DIGNITY, ENNOBLE, DECORATION, VENERATE, REVERENCE

honors: .... AWARDS, TITLES, DEGREES, DIGNITIES, TRIBUTES, ACCOLADE, COMPLIMENTS, DECORATIONS

hood: .... CAP, COIF, COWL, HIDE, THUG, AMICE, BLIND, BIGGIN, BONNET, CAPOTE, CAMAIL, CANOPY, TIPPET, NACHELLE, COVERING, GANGSTER

hoodlum: .... PUNK, THUG, ROWDY, RUFFIAN, HOOLIGAN, GANGSTER

hoodoo: .... HEX, JINX, VOODOO, BEWITCH, UNLUCKY

hoodwink: ...... see **fraud, swindle**

hooey: .... BUNK, NONSENSE

hook: ... BARB, BEND, GAFF, GORE, CATCH, CROOK, CLEEK, CURVE, HITCH, SEIZE, STEAL, ANCHOR, CLEVIS, PILFER, HAMULUS, GRAMPON, GRAPNEL, CROTCHET

hooligan: .... see **hoodlum**

hoop: .... BAIL, BAND, RING, TIRE, CLASP, GIRTH, CIRCLE, ENCIRCLE, SURROUND

hoosegow: .. JUG, JAIL, BRIG, CLINK, LOCKUP, PRISON, GUARDHOUSE, PENITENTIARY

hop: ..... JUMP, LEAP, SKIP, VINE, CAPER, DANCE, FRISK, BOUND, FLIGHT, GAMBOL, SPRING

hope: ... LONG, WANT, WISH, ASPIRE, DESIRE, EXPECT, PROSPECT, ANTICIPATION

hopeful: ...... ASPIRANT, OPTIMISTIC, CONFIDENT, EXPECTANT, SANGUINE, CANDIDATE

hopeless: ..... VAIN, FUTILE, FORLORN, USELESS, DOWNCAST, DESPERATE, INCURABLE, DESPAIRING, INEFFECTUAL

horde: .. ARMY, HOST, PACK, CROWD, DROVE, GROUP, SWARM, LEGION, THRONG, MULTITUDE

Horeb: .... (MT.) SINAI, MOUNTAIN

horizon: .. RIM, EDGE, GOAL, LIMIT, SKYLINE, PROSPECT

horizontal: ... FLAT, LEVEL, PRONE, PLANE, FLUSH

horn: .. TUBA, BRASS, BUGLE, SIREN, CORNU, PRONG, ANTLER, CORNET, ANTENNA, TRUMPET, CORNUCOPIA

horologist: ... WATCHMAKER

horrendous: ..... FEARFUL, HORRIBLE, FRIGHTFUL

horrible: ...... DIRE, GRIM, UGLY, GRISLY, GHASTLY, HIDEOUS, DREADFUL, GRUESOME, SHOCKING, TERRIBLE, ATROCIOUS

horrid: .... GRIM, UGLY, AWFUL, FRIGHTFUL, HATEFUL, DREADFUL, REVOLTING, REPULSIVE, OBNOXIOUS, OFFENSIVE

horrified: .... AGHAST, APPALLED

horror: ...... FEAR, DREAD, TERROR, AVERSION, LOATHING, ABHORRENCE

horse: ..... COB, NAG, COLT, MARE, PLUG, PRAD, STUD, DRAFT, FILLY, HOBBY, MOUNT, PACER, STEED, DOBBIN, EQUINE, BRONCO, SORREL, GELDING, TROTTER, MUSTANG, BOLLARD, STALLION, BANGTAIL

horseman: .. RIDER, COWBOY, CENTAUR, VAQUERO, BUCKAROO, CHEVALIER, CABALLERO, EQUESTRIAN

horsemanship: .... MANEGE, EQUESTRIAN, EQUITATION

horseplay: ..... FUN, JINKS, PRANK, COMEDY

hose: .. SOCKS, TUBE, WATER, DRENCH, STOCKINGS

hosiery: .. STOCKINGS, SOCKS

hospice: ...... INN, HOUSE, IMARET, REFUGE, ASYLUM

hospitable: ...... CHEERY, CORDIAL, FRIENDLY, RECEPTIVE, ENTERTAINING

hospital: ... CLINIC, CRECHE, INFIRMARY, SANATORIUM, LAZARETTO

host: .... ARMY, CROWD, HORDE, SWARM, LEGION, MYRIAD, THRONG, MULTITUDE, ENTERTAINER, LANDLORD, INNKEEPER

hostage: .... PAWN, PLEDGE, CAPTIVE, SECURITY

hostel(ry): ..... INN, HOTEL, LODGE, TAVERN

hostile: .... FOE, ENEMY, ADVERSE, OPPOSED, WARLIKE, CONTRARY, INIMICAL, BELLICOSE, MALEVOLENT, ANTAGONISTIC

hostility: ... ANIMUS, ENMITY, HATRED, RANCOR, ILL-WILL, ANIMOSITY, BELLICOSITY, ANTAGONISM

hot: .. ACRID, ANGRY, EAGER, FIERY, SPICY, ARDENT, FERVID, HECTIC, HEATED, SULTRY, TORRID, URGENT, BURNING, EXCITED, FLAMING, INTENSE, PEPPERY, PUNGENT, THERMAL, SIZZLING, PASSIONATE

hotel: .... INN, PUB, HAVEN, HOUSE, MOTEL, HOSTEL, IMARET, TAVERN, LODGINGHOUSE

hotheaded: ... RASH, HASTY, RECKLESS, IMPETUOUS

hound: ... DOG, NAG, HUNT, CHASE, HARRY, FOLLOW, PERSECUTE

hour: .... TAPS, NONE, SEXT, MATIN, CURFEW, PERIOD

hourly: ..... BRIEF, HORAL, OFTEN, RECENT, QUICKLY, FREQUENT(LY), CONTINUAL

house: .... HUT, INN, CASA, COTE, DORM, DUMP, FLAT, HOME, ROOF, NEST, ABODE, CABIN, COVER, DACHA, DOMUS, HOVEL, HOSTEL, HOTEL, LODGE, MANOR, SHACK, VILLA, CASINO, DUPLEX, FAMILY, PALACE, SHANTY, TEMPLE, CHURCH, CHATEAU, COTTAGE, MANSION, SHELTER, THEATER, DORMITORY, DOMICILE, APARTMENT, DWELLING, TENEMENT, RESIDENCE, HABITATION

hover: .. FLIT, FLOAT, PAUSE, WAVER, LINGER, FLITTER, FLUTTER

how: ..... METHOD, MANNER

however: .... BUT, THO, YET, STILL, THOUGH, ALTHOUGH, NEVERTHELESS

howl: .... BAY, CRY, BAWL, WAIL, WAUL, YELL, YIPE, LAMENT, ULULATE

hub: ... CORE, NAVE, CENTER, CENTRE

hubbub: .... ADO, DIN, STIR, NOISE, CLAMOR, RACKET,

RUMPUS, TUMULT, UPROAR, TURMOIL, BROUHAHA, COMMOTION, CONFUSION, DISTURBANCE

huckster: .. ADMAN, BROKER, PEDLAR, PEDDLER, HAWKER, TRADESMAN

huddle: ... CAUCUS, JUMBLE, MINGLE, ASSEMBLE, CONFERENCE

hue: ...... CRY, DYE, TINT, COLOR, SHADE, SHOUT, TINGE, CLAMOR, OUTCRY, COMPLEXION

hug: ... CLASP, CLING, PRESS, EMBRACE, CUDDLE, CHERISH, SQUEEZE

huge: ... BIG, VAST, ENORM, GIANT, GREAT, JUMBO, LARGE, IMMENSE, MASSIVE, MONSTER, TITANIC, COLOSSAL, GIGANTIC, ENORMOUS, MAMMOTH, TREMENDOUS, LEVIATHAN

hull: ..... POD, BULK, HULK, HUSK, SHED, SHUCK, SHELL, STRIP, CALYX, COVERING

human: .... MAN, HOMO, HOMINID, BIPED, MORTAL, PERSON, ADAMITE, CREATURE

humane: ... KIND, MERCIFUL, TENDER, FORGIVING, SYMPATHETIC

humanity: ...... MANKIND, PEOPLE, MERCY, KINDNESS

humanize: .. REFINE, CIVILIZE

humble: ...... LOW, MEAN, MEEK, MILD, POOR, ABASE, ABASH, LOWER, PLAIN, STOOP, DEBASE, DEMEAN, DEGRADE, MODEST, REDUCE, MORTIFY, CHASTISE, CONTRITE, HUMILIATE, UNPRETENTIOUS

humbug: ...... BOSH, DUPE, FLAM, GUFF, HOAX, SHAM, CHEAT, FAKER, FRAUD, TRICK, MISLEAD, DECEIVE, GAMMON, HOKUM, BAMBOOZLE, HORNSWOGGLE

humdrum: .... DULL, DRAB, PROSAIC, ROUTINE, MONOTONOUS, COMMONPLACE

humerus: .... BONE

humid: .. WET, DAMP, MOIST, DANK, SULTRY

humiliate: ... ABASE, ABASH, SHAME, DEBASE, HUMBLE, DEGRADE, MORTIFY, BELITTLE, DISGRACE

humility: .... MODESTY, MEEKNESS, DIFFIDENCE

humming: ... BRISK, ACTIVE, BUZZING, DRONING

hummock: .. HUMP, KNOLL, MOUND, HILLOCK

humor: ... WIT, BABY, WHIM, CODDLE, FANCY, LEVITY, CHOLER, MEGRIM, PLEASE, CAPRICE, GRATIFY, INDULGE, DROLLERY, MOISTURE, TEMPERAMENT, DISPOSITION

humorist: .. WIT, WAG, JOKER

humorous: .. COMIC, DROLL, FUNNY, HUMID, MOIST, WITTY, AMUSING, JOCOSE, COMICAL, JOCULAR, FACETIOUS

hunch: .. BALK, BEND, HUNK, HUMP, LUMP, CHUNK, FUDGE, . INTUITION, PREMONITION

hunger: .. YEN, LONG, PINE, WANT, ACORIA, DESIRE, FAMINE, STARVE, BULIMIA, APPETITE, CRAVING, VORACITY, ESURIENCE

hunk: ... CHIP, LUMP, SLICE, SLAB, PIECE

hunt: .... DIG, SEEK, CHASE, CHEVY, DELVE, DRIVE, HOUND, PROVE, QUEST, STALK, SCOUR, TRACK, TRAIL, FERRET, FOLLOW, PURSUE, SEARCH, SHIKAR

hurdle: ...... LEAP, BOUND, BARRIER, OBSTACLE, SURMOUNT

hurl: .... CAST, DASH, PELT, TOSS, FLING, HEAVE, PITCH,

SLING, LAUNCH, HURTLE, THROW, CATAPULT

hurly-burly: . . . . . HUBBUB, TUMULT, UPROAR, TURMOIL, CONFUSION

hurricane: . . . . STORM, CYCLONE, TEMPEST, TORNADO, TYPHOON

hurry: . . . RUN, PASS, RUSH, DASH, RACE, HUSTLE, FLURRY, SPEED, SCURRY, EXPEDITE, HASTE(N), ACCELERATE

hurt: . . . ACHE, HARM, MAIM, PAIN, ABUSE, BLAME, GRIEF, WOUND, DAMAGE, IMPAIR, INJURE, SCATHE, SORROW, OFFEND DISTRESS

hurtle: . . CAST, DASH, HURL, CLASH, FLING, JOSTLE, COLLIDE

husband: . . . . . KEEP, MATE, SAVE, HOARD, STORE, MANAGE, SPOUSE, CONSERVE, GROOM, CONSORT, PLOWMAN, HELPMATE, CULTIVATE, ECONOMIZE

husbandman: . . . GRANGER, FARMER

husbandry: . . . . THRIFT, FARMING, ECONOMY, FRUGALITY, CULTIVATION

hush: . . CALM, LULL, ALLAY, QUIET, STILL, SILENCE, SOOTHE, REPRESS, SUPPRESS

husk: . . . BARK, BRAN, COAT, HULL, SHELL, CHAFF, STRIP, SHUCK

husky: . . . . . . DOG, HOARSE, ESKIMO, BURLY, ROBUST

hustle: . . . . . PUSH, CROWD, DRIVE, HURRY, JOSTLE, SHOVE

hut: . . . . . BARI, COTE, CRIB, SHED, CABIN, HOVEL, HUTCH, SHACK, CABANA, CHALET, SHANTY, COTTAGE

hutch: . BIN, BOX, HUT, PEN, COOP, CHEST, HOVEL, SHANTY, TROUGH, WARREN

hybrid: . . . . . CROSS, BLEND, MONGREL, COMPOSITE, HALFBREED

hydrant: . . . . PLUG, FAUCET, FIREPLUG

hymn: . . ODE, SONG, DIRGE, PSALM, PAEAN, INTROIT, ANTHEM, REQUIEM, CANTICLE, CHORALE, TE DEUM

hyperbole: . . EXAGGERATION

hypnotic: . . ACETAL, OPIATE, NARCOTIC, SOPORIFIC, LUMINAL, MESMERIC, SOMNIFACENT

hypnotism: . . . COMA, SLEEP, TRANCE, MESMERISM

hypnotize: . . . . CHARM, ENTRANCE, MESMERIZE

hypochondria: . . . . HYP, ANXIETY, MEGRIN, MELANCHOLY

hypocrisy: . . . . CANT, PRETENSE, INSINCERITY, SIMULATION

hypocrite: . . . . SHAM, PRETENDER, LEVITE, PHARISEE, TARTUF(F)E

hypostasis: . . . . . SEDIMENT, DEPOSIT, ESSENCE

hypothecate: . . . . . . PLEDGE, MORTGAGE

hypothermal: . . . . . . TEPID, LUKEWARM

hypothesis: . . . ISM, THEORY, POSTULATE, PROPOSITION, SUPPOSITION, ASSUMPTION

hypothesize: . . . . . ASSUME, SUPPOSE

hysteria: . . . . FIT, PANIC, FRENZY, ANXIETY, EXCITABILITY

hysterical: . . . . . . EMOTIONAL, UNCONTROLLED, FRENZIED

I

ibex: . . . . . . GOAT, TUR, ZAC

ice: . . . DESSERT, BERG, COOL, FLOE, HAIL, RIME, CHILL, SLEET, FROST, GLACE, FREEZE, CONGEAL, GLACIER, SHERBET, DIAMOND, HAUTEUR, REFRIGERATE

icing: . . . . FROSTING

icon: . . . . . . IMAGE, FIGURE, SYMBOL, PICTURE

ictus: . . . FIT, BLOW, ACCENT, UPBEAT, STRESS, STROKE

icy: . . . COLD, ALOOF, GELID, FRIGID, ARCTIC

idea: . . . . AIM, PLAN, FANCY, IMAGE, DESIGN, FIGURE, NOTION, CONCEPT, FANTASY, INKLING, OPINION, PROJECT, THOUGHT, COGNITION, IMPRESSION, CONCEPTION

ideal: . . . . . . HERO, DREAM, MODEL, PARAGON, PERFECT, UTOPIAN, ABSTRACT, FANCIFUL, ARCHETYPE, VISIONARY, FAULTLESS

ideate: . . . . . FANCY, THINK, IMAGINE, CONCEIVE, PRECONCEIVE

identical: . ONE, SAME, SELF, VERY, ALIKE, EQUAL, SELFSAME, EQUIVALENT

identify: . . . . . MARK, NAME, BRAND, PROVE, EARMARK, DESIGNATE

identity: . . . . . NAME, UNITY, ONENESS, SAMENESS, EXACTNESS, INDIVIDUALITY

ideologist: . . . . . . VISIONARY, THEORIST, DREAMER

ideology: . . . . . ISM, DOGMA, THEORY, DOCTRINE, PRINCIPLE

idiocy: . . . FOLLY, STUPIDITY, AMENTIA, ANOESIA, MONGOLISM, FATUITY

idiom: . . . . . . CANT, SLANG, ARGOT, PHRASE, DIALECT, LOCUTION

idiosyncrasy: . . . . . . ODDITY, ECCENTRICITY, PECULIARITY

idiot: . . . . OAF, DOLT, FOOL, BOOBY, DUNCE, CRETIN, NITWIT, DULLARD, IMBECILE, SIMPLETON, BLOCKHEAD, DUNDERHEAD, CHANGELING

idle: . . . . LAZE, LAZY, LOAF, VAIN, DALLY, EMPTY, DAWDLE, FUTILE, LOITER, UNUSED, VACANT, AIMLESS, LOAFING, USELESS, POINTLESS, BASELESS, INACTIVE, INDOLENT

idleness: . . . SLOTH, INERTIA, INACTION, LAZINESS, INDOLENCE

idler: . . . . BUM, DRONE, LOAFER, LAZYBONES, ROUNDER, LOUNGER, LOITERER

idol: . . . . GOD, BAAL, HERO, ICON, LION, STAR, IMAGE, EFFIGY, FETISH, EIDOLON, CELEBRITY

idolize: . . . . ADORE, ADMIRE, REVERE, WORSHIP, VENERATE

idyl(l): . . . . POEM, ECLOGUE, PASTORAL

if: . . . GRANTING, PROVIDED, SUPPOSING

ignite: . . . FIRE, BURN, LIGHT, EXCITE, KINDLE

ignoble: . . LOW, BASE, MEAN, VILE, SORDID, SHAMEFUL, DISGRACEFUL, DISHONORABLE

ignominious: . . . . BASE, ODIOUS, INFAMOUS, SHAMEFUL, DEGRADING, DESPICABLE, DISGRACEFUL

ignominy: . . INFAMY, SHAME, DISGRACE

ignoramus: . . . DOLT, DUNCE, NITWIT, KNOW-NOTHING

ignorance: . . . . . INNOCENCE, NESCIENCE

ignorant: . . . GREEN, STUPID, UNAWARE, NESCIENT, UNLETTERED, UNTAUGHT, UNLEARNED, ILLITERATE

ignore: . . . CUT, OMIT, SNUB, ELIDE, SLIGHT, NEGLECT,

OVERLOOK, DISREGARD, ELIMINATE

ilium: . . . . HIPBONE

ilk: . . . . . SAME, KIND, SORT, CLASS, FAMILY, BREED, STRIPE

ill: . . BAD, SICK, EVIL, HARM, AMISS, WRONG, AILING, FAULTY, WICKED, AILMENT, ADVERSE, TROUBLE, ADVERSITY, DEFECTIVE, INDISPOSED

advised: . . . . UNWISE

at ease: . . . . . . UNEASY, RESTIVE, AWKWARD

bred: . . . . RUDE, IMPOLITE

fated: . . . . UNLUCKY, UNFORTUNATE

tempered: . . . . . . CROSS, PEEVISH, SULLEN, CRABBY, SURLY, CRANKY, MOROSE

use: . . . ABUSE, MALTREAT

will: . . . . . . HATE, SPITE, ENMITY, MALICE, DISLIKE, GRUDGE, RANCOR, HOSTILITY, ANIMUS

illation: . . . . INFERENCE, DEDUCTION, CONCLUSION

illegal: . . . . FOUL, BOOTLEG, ILLICIT, UNLAWFUL, CONTRABAND, BLACKMARKET

illegitimate: . . . . . . BASTARD, ILLEGAL, SPURIOUS, WRONGFUL, MISBEGOT(TEN)

illicit: . . . . see **illegal**

illiterate: . . . . UNREAD, IGNORANT, UNLETTERED, UNEDUCATED

illness: . . . DISEASE, MALADY, AILMENT, DISORDER, SICKNESS, AFFLICTION, INDISPOSITION

illogical: . . . . INVALID, INCONSEQUENT

illuminate: . . . FIRE, ADORN, FLARE, LIGHT, EXPLAIN, KINDLE, CLARIFY, BRIGHTEN, ENLIGHTEN, IRRADIATE, ELUCIDATE

illusion: . . . FANCY, MIRAGE, CHIMERA, FALLACY, FANTASY, DELUSION, DECEPTION, HALLUCINATION

illusive: . . . . FALSE, UNREAL, FATUOUS, DECEPTIVE, FALLACIOUS

illustrate: . . . . . CITE, DRAW, ADORN, PICTURE, EXPLAIN, ELUCIDATE, EXEMPLIFY, REPRESENT, ILLUMINATE

illustration: . . . ICON, GRAPH, SAMPLE, EXAMPLE, DRAWING, DIAGRAM, EXEMPLUM, INSTANCE, DEMONSTRATION

illustrious: . . FAMED, GRAND, NOBLE, NOTED, FAMOUS, EMINENT, RENOWNED, CELEBRATED, DISTINGUISHED

image: . . COPY, FORM, ICON, IDEA, IDOL, EIKON, EFFIGY, EMBLEM, FIGURE, IDOLON, REPLICA, LIKENESS, STATUE, SYMBOL, PICTURE, PORTRAY, CONCEPTION, EMBODIMENT

imaginary: . . IDEAL, UNREAL, FANCIED, MYTHICAL, VISIONARY, ARTIFICIAL, CHEMERICAL, FICTITIOUS

imagination: . . IDEA, FANCY, DREAM, NOTION, FANTASY

imagine: . . . . WEEN, DREAM, FANCY, GUESS, SUPPOSE, SURMISE, CONCEIVE, ENVISION, VISUALIZE

imagist: . . . POET, DREAMER, VISIONARY

imam: . . . . . PRIEST, CALIPH

imaret: . . . . . . INN, HOSPICE

imbecile: . . . . see **idiot, ignoramus**

imbibe: . . . SIP, SOAK, DRINK, IMBUE, INHALE, ABSORB, SWALLOW, ASSIMILATE

imbroglio: . . . . . CONFUSION, DISAGREEMENT, ENTANGLEMENT

imbrue: . WET, STAIN, SOAK, STEEP, DRENCH, MOISTEN, SATURATE

imbue: ... DYE, SOAK, STEEP, STAIN, TINGE, IMBIBE, INFUSE, ANIMATE, INGRAIN, INSPIRE, PERVADE, SATURATE, PERMEATE, IMPREGNATE

imitate: ... APE, COPY, ECHO, MIME, MOCK, MIMIC, FOLLOW, REPEAT, EMULATE, SIMULATE, DUPLICATE, COUNTERFEIT

imitation: ..... COPY, FAKE, SHAM, BOGUS, DUMMY, PASTE, PARODY, EMULATION, FACSIMILE, COUNTERFEIT

immaculate: .. PURE, CLEAN, CHASTE, CORRECT, PERFECT, INNOCENT, UNSOILED, FAULTLESS, SPOTLESS, SINLESS, UNDEFILED, PRISTINE

immanent: ..... INHERENT, INTRINSIC, OMNIPRESENT

immaterial: .... SLIGHT, TRIFLING, SPIRITUAL, INSIGNIFICANT

immature: .... RAW, CRUDE, GREEN, YOUNG, CALLOW, UNRIPE, PUERILE, UNDEVELOPED

immeasurable: ...... VAST, IMMENSE, INFINITE, BOUNDLESS, UNLIMITED, INDEFINITE

immediate: ... CLOSE, NEAR, NEXT, DIRECT, INSTANT, ADJACENT, IMMINENT, CONTIGUOUS

immediately: ... NOW, ANON, AT ONCE, DIRECTLY, FORTHWITH, INSTANTLY, PROMPTLY

immense: .... see **huge**

immerse: . DIP, DUCK, DUNK, BATHE, DOUSE, STEEP, ABSORB, PLUNGE, ENGROSS, BAPTIZE, SUBMERGE

immersed: .. RAPT, ABSORBED

imminent: ...... IMPENDING

immobile: ...... SET, FIRM, INERT, FIXED, STILL, STABLE, MOTIONLESS, STATIONARY

immoderate: ...... UNDUE, EXTREME, EXCESSIVE, INORDINATE, EXTRAVAGANT

immodest: ... BOLD, BRAZEN, FORWARD, INDECENT, OBSCENE, SHAMELESS

immoral: ..... EVIL, LEWD, LOOSE, CORRUPT, WICKED, OBSCENE, WANTON, INDECENT, DISSOLUTE

immortal: .... DIVINE, ENDURING, DEATHLESS, ETERNAL, EVERLASTING, PERPETUAL

immune: .... EXEMPT, PROTECTED

immunity: ...... FREEDOM, EXEMPTION

immure: .... CONFINE, CLOISTER, IMPRISON, ISOLATE, SECLUDE

immutable: .. FIRM, ETERNAL, UNCHANGING, CHANGELESS, UNALTERABLE

impact: ...... PACK, SLAM, SHOCK, FORCE, WEDGE, CONTACT, COLLISION

impair: .. MAR, BLOT, HARM, HURT, WEAR, BREAK, SPOIL, WASTE, INJURE, REDUCE, DAMAGE, VITIATE, DECREASE, ENFEEBLE

impale: ...... SPEAR, SPIKE, PIERCE, CONFINE

impart: ... GIVE, LEND, TELL, SHARE, BESTOW, CONFER, COVEY, DIRECT, REVEAL, DIVULGE, DISCLOSE, COMMUNICATE

impartial: ...... FAIR, JUST, UNBIASED, EQUITABLE

impasse: .... DEADLOCK, STALEMATE

impassioned: .... FIERY, ARDENT

impassive: ..... CALM, STOIC, SERENE, PLACID, STOLID, APATHETIC

impatient: ... EAGER, HASTY, FIDGETY, RESTIVE, INTOLERANT, IRRITABLE

impeach: .. ACCUSE, CHARGE, INDICT, IMPUGN, DISCREDIT, CENSURE, DISPARGE, CHALLENGE

impeccable: .... FAULTLESS, FLAWLESS, BLAMELESS

impecunious: .. POOR, BROKE

impede: ..... CLOG, BLOCK, CHECK, DELAY, FETTER, HAMPER, HINDER, RETARD, STYMIE, OBSTRUCT, HANDICAP
legally: .... ESTOP

impediment: ... BAR, SNAG, HITCH, DEFECT, BARRIER, OBSTACLE, DIFFICULTY, HINDRANCE

impel: .. BLOW, GOAD, MOVE, PUSH, SEND, SPUR, URGE, DRIVE, PROPEL, FORCE, INDUCE, INCITE, COMPEL, CONSTRAIN, ACTUATE, MOTIVATE, STIMULATE

impending: ..... IMMINENT, THREATENING, OVERHANGING

impenetrable: ..... DENSE, IMPERVIOUS

imperative: ...... URGENT, IMPERIOUS, MANDATORY, COMPELLING

imperceptible: .... UNSEEN, INVISIBLE, INTANGIBLE

imperfect: .... POOR, ROUGH, FAULTY, FLAWED, DEFECTIVE

imperial: .... REGAL, ROYAL, KINGLY, MAJESTIC, SOVEREIGN

imperil: .... RISK, HAZARD, ENDANGER, JEOPARDIZE

imperious: ...... URGENT, HAUGHTY, ARROGANT, DESPOTIC, PRESSING, DICTATORIAL, TYRANNICAL

impersonal: .... COLD, GENERAL, DETACHED, OBJECTIVE

impertinence: ... AUDACITY, INSOLENCE, IRRELEVANCE, IMPUDENCE

impertinent: .. RUDE, SASSY, SAUCY, IMPUDENT, FLIP(PANT), INSOLENT, DISRESPECTFUL

impetuous: ... RASH, HASTY, ABRUPT, SUDDEN, RUSHING, IMPULSIVE, PRECIPITATE

impetus: ..... DRIFT, DRIVE, FORCE, MOTIVE, IMPULSE, STIMULUS, INCENTIVE, MOMENTUM

impiety: ...... BLASPHEMY, IRREVERENCE, UNGODLINESS

impinge: .... TRESPASS, ENCROACH

impious: .... GODLESS, PROFANE, IRREVERENT, IRRELIGIOUS

implacable: ..... RELENTLESS, INEXORABLE, INFLEXIBLE, IRRECONCILABLE

implant: ..... ROOT, INSET, EMBED, INSTILL, INFUSE, ENROOT, INCULCATE

implement: .. (also see **tool**) GEAR, DEVICE, FULFILL, ENFORCE, UTENSIL, COMPLETE, APPARATUS, APPLIANCE, ACCOMPLISH, EFFECTUATE, INSTRUMENT

implicate: ...... CONCERN, INVOLVE, INCLUDE, ENTANGLE, INCRIMINATE

implicit: .. TACIT, ABSOLUTE, COMPLETE, IMPLIED, INHERENT

implied: .... TACIT, HINTED, INFERENTIAL

implore: .... BEG, PRAY, PLEAD, BESEECH, ENTREAT, SUPPLICATE

imply: .... HINT, INFER, SUGGEST, INTIMATE, CONNOTE, INSINUATE

impolite: ..... RUDE, CRUDE, ILLBRED, UNMANNERLY, DISCOURTEOUS

impolitic: . . . . UNWISE, TACTLESS

import: . . . . . SENSE, TENOR, CONVEY, DENOTE, INTENT, MEANING, SIGNIFY, INDICATE, SUBSTANCE

importance: . . . . . . VALUE, WEIGHT, MOMENT, GRAVITY, PRESTIGE, CONSEQUENCE

important: . . GRAVE, VITAL, URGENT, SERIOUS, MATERIAL, MOMENTOUS, SIGNIFICANT

importune: . . PLEAD, APPEAL, ENTREAT, BESEECH, SUPPLICATE

impose: . . . . . . FOB, LEVY, INFLICT, FORCE, FOIST, ENTAIL, BURDEN, CHARGE, COMMAND, DICTATE

imposing: . . . . . BIG, BURLY, NOBLE, AUGUST, STATELY, GRANDIOSE, IMPRESSIVE

impost: . . . TAX, DUTY, LEVY, TOLL, TARIFF

impostor: . . . SHAM, FRAUD, CHEAT, FAKER, PHONY, QUACK, DECEIVER, CHARLATAN, PRETENDER, MOUNTEBANK

impotent: . . . . BARREN, UNABLE, STERILE, HELPLESS, POWERLESS

impound: . . . . . TAKE, SEIZE, STORE, FREEZE, COLLECT, APPROPRIATE

imprecation: . . . BAN, CURSE, OATH, BLASPHEMY, EXECRATION

impregnate: . . SOAK, INFUSE, PERMEATE, SATURATE, FERTILIZE, FECUNDATE

impresario: . . . . . PROMOTER, CONDUCTOR, ENTREPRENEUR

impress: . . . . . LEVY, MARK, SEAL, AFFIX, BRAND, DRAFT, PRINT, STAMP, AFFECT, ENGRAVE, IMPLANT, INFLUENCE

impression: . . . . IDEA, MARK, STAMP, EFFECT, IMPRINT, REACTION, INKLING, PRINTING, CONCEPTION

imprimatur: . . . . . LICENSE, APPROVAL, SANCTION

imprint: . . FIX, MARK, PRESS, STAMP, ENGRAVE

imprison: . . . . . CAGE, JAIL, ARREST, COMMIT, IMMURE, CONFINE, INCARCERATE

impromptu: . . . . . OFFHAND, IMPROVISED, EXTEMPORE, EXTEMPORANEOUS

improper: . . . . . EVIL, AMISS, UNDUE, UNFIT, WRONG, UNJUST, ILLEGAL, ILLICIT, INDECENT, UNSEEMLY, INACCURATE, INDECOROUS, UNBECOMING

improve: . . . . MEND, AMEND, BETTER, AUGMENT, BENEFIT, CORRECT, ENHANCE, PERFECT, PROMOTE, INTENSIFY

improvise: . . . AD-LIB, VAMP, DEVISE, INVENT, COMPOSE, CONTRIVE, EXTEMPORIZE

imprudent: . . RASH, UNWISE, CARELESS, RECKLESS, INDISCREET

impudence: . . . . . LIP, GALL, BRASS, CHEEK, NERVE, AUDACITY, INSOLENCE

impudent: . . . . . BOLD, PERT, RUDE, BRASH, FRESH, SASSY, SAUCY, SNOTTY, INSOLENT, IMPERTINENT

impugn: . . . . . DENY, FIGHT, BLAME, ASSAIL, ATTACK, RESIST, CRITICIZE, CHALLENGE, CONTRADICT

impulse: . . . . . . URGE, PUSH, FORCE, MOTIVE, IMPETUS, INSTINCT, THRUST

impulsive: . . . . RASH, FITFUL, IMPETUOUS, CAPRICIOUS

impure: . FOUL, VILE, DIRTY, MIXED, FILTHY, DEFILED, OBSCENE, UNCLEAN, ADULTERATED

impute: . . . ASCRIBE, CHARGE, CREDIT, ATTRIBUTE

in: . . . . AT, WITH, AMID, AMONG, ARRIVED, INCUMBENT

inability: . . . . . . IMPOTENCE, INCAPACITY, INCOMPETENCE

inaction: . . IDLENESS, INERTIA

inactive: . . . . . . DEAD, IDLE, INERT, STILL, LATENT, STATIC, PASSIVE, DORMANT

inadequate: . . . . . . MEAGER, SCANTY, LACKING, DEFICIENT, INSUFFICIENT

inane: . . . . EMPTY, SILLY, VAPID, VACANT, PUERILE, FATUOUS, IDIOTIC, FOOLISH, VACUOUS, POINTLESS, SENSELESS

inanimate: . . . . DEAD, DULL, INERT, STOLID, SPIRITLESS, LIFELESS, UNCONCIOUS

inasmuch: . . . SINCE, BECAUSE

inattention: . . . . NEGLIGENCE

inattentive: . . . . REMISS, CARELESS, HEEDLESS, FORGETFUL, NEGLIGENT, UNHEEDING, UNMINDFUL, ABSTRACTED

inaugurate: . . . OPEN, BEGIN, START, INDUCT, INSTALL, INITIATE, INTRODUCE, DEDICATE

inauspicious: . . . . . ILL, BAD, FOUL, ADVERSE, OMINOUS, UNTIMELY, UNLUCKY, ILL-OMENED, UNFAVORABLE, UNPROPITIOUS

inborn: . . . . INBRED, INNATE, NATIVE, CONNATE, NATURAL, ORGANIC, INDIGENOUS, INHERENT, CONGENITAL

incalculable: . . . . . UNTOLD, BOUNDLESS, COUNTLESS, UNCERTAIN, IMMEASURABLE

incandescence: . . . . . . GLOW, HEAT

incantation: . . . . CHANT, CHARM, MAGIC, SPELL, SORCERY, CONJURATION, INVOCATION

incapacitate: . . . . LAME, CRIPPLE, DISABLE, DISQUALIFY

incarcerate: . . . . JAIL, IMMURE, IMPRISON, CONFINE

incarnate: . . . . . . RED, ROSY, PERSONIFIED

incarnation: . . . . . ADVENT, AVATAR, EMBODIMENT

incautious: . RASH, UNWARY, CARELESS, HEEDLESS, RECKLESS, IMPRUDENT

incendiary: . . . . . . FIREBUG, ARSONIST, AGITATOR, PYROMANIAC, SEDITIOUS, INFLAMMATORY

incense: . . . . IRK, ODOR, ENRAGE, ANGER, AROUSE, INCITE, PROVOKE, ENKINDLE, IRRITATE, PERFUME

incentive: . . . . . GOAD, SPUR, MOTIVE, STIMULUS, INDUCEMENT, ENCOURAGEMENT

inception: . . . START, ORIGIN, BEGINNING, INITIATION

incessant: . . . . STEADY, ENDLESS, ETERNAL, CONTINUAL, CONSTANT, CEASELESS, EVERLASTING

incident: . . . EVENT, EPISODE, ACCIDENT, OCCURRENCE, HAPPENING

incidental: . . MINOR, CASUAL, CHANCE, RANDOM, EXTRINSIC, ACCIDENTAL

incinerate: . . . . . CREMATE, BURN (UP)

incinerator: . . . . . . FURNACE, CREMATORY

incise: . . CUT, EDGE, ENGRAVE

incision: . . . CUT, GASH, SLIT, LANCE, LACERATION

incisive: . . . . . ACUTE, KEEN, SHARP, BITING, PIERCING, CUTTING, TRENCHANT

incite: . . . . EGG, ABET, GOAD, PROD, SPUR, URGE, IMPEL, AROUSE, EXHORT, FOMENT, INDUCE, AGITATE, MOTIVATE, ENCOURAGE, INSTIGATE

inclement: .... RAW, ROUGH, HARSH, STORMY, SEVERE, PITILESS, UNMERCIFUL

inclination: .... BENT, BIAS, URGE, GRADE, SLANT, SLOPE, TASTE, TREND, ASCENT, DESCENT, LEANING, PENCHANT, TENDENCY

incline: ... DIP, BEND, CANT, HEEL, LEAN, LIST, RAMP, TEND, TILT, GRADE, SLANT, SLOPE, TREND

inclined: .. APT, WONT, ALIST, ATILT, PRONE, BIASED, LEANING, MINDED, WILLING, DISPOSED, OBLIQUE

inclose: ... HEM, PEN, EMBAR, ENCASE, SURROUND

inclosure: .. PEN, STY, CAGE, WALL, YARD, FENCE, CORRAL

include: .... CONTAIN, EMBRACE, INVOLVE, ENCLOSE, COMPRISE, ENCOMPASS

incognito: ...... UNKNOWN, DISGUISE

incoherent: ...... BROKEN, ILLOGICAL, RAMBLING, DISJOINTED, DISCONNECTED, INCONSISTENT

income: ..... GAIN, PROFIT, RETURN, EARNING, REVENUE, INTEREST, PROCEEDS, RECEIPTS

incomparable: ... PEERLESS, MATCHLESS, UNEQUALLED, SUPERLATIVE

incompatible: .. REPUGNANT, CONFLICTING, INCONGRUOUS, IRRECONCILABLE

incompetence: ...... INEPT, UNFIT, UNABLE, INCAPABLE, UNQUALIFIED

incomplete: .... PART, LACKING, DIVIDED, IMPERFECT, UNFINISHED

inconclusive: .... DOUBTFUL, UNCERTAIN, INDEFINITE

incondite: .... CRUDE, UNPOLISHED

incongruous: .... ALIEN, ABSURD, DISCORDANT, INCOMPATIBLE, INCONSISTENT, INAPPROPRIATE

inconsequential: .. . TRIVIAL, IRRELEVANT

inconsistent: ..... ABSURD, CAPRICIOUS, DISCORDANT, CONTRADICTORY

inconstant: .... FICKLE, DISLOYAL, UNSTABLE, VARIABLE, CAPRICIOUS

inconvenience: .... BOTHER, ANNOY, TROUBLE, INCOMMODE

incorporate: ... MIX, BLEND, MERGE, EMBODY, INCLUDE

incorrect: ... FALSE, WRONG, FAULTY, ERRONEOUS, INACCURATE

increase: .. ADD, WAX, GAIN, GROW, SWELL, ACCRUE, DILATE, EXPAND, EXTEND, ACCRETE, AMPLIFY, ENLARGE, INFLATE, MAGNIFY, AUGMENT, INCREMENT, MULTIPLY, ACCELERATE

incredible: .. UNBELIEVABLE

incredulous: .... DOUBTING, UNBELIEVING, SKEPTICAL

increment: .... see increase

incriminate: ...... ACCUSE, INVOLVE, CHARGE, IMPEACH, IMPLICATE

incubus: .... LOAD, DEMON, SPIRIT, BURDEN, NIGHTMARE

inculcate: ... INBUE, INFUSE, INSTIL, IMPRESS, IMPLANT

incur: .... CONTRACT, ENCOUNTER

incurable: ...... HOPELESS, REMEDILESS, IRREMEDIABLE

incursion: .... RAID, FORAY, INROAD, ASSAULT, INVASION, INTRUSION

indecent: ...... FOUL, RANK, LEWD, NASTY, COARSE, IMPURE, RISQUE, OBSCENE, IMMODEST, IMMORAL

indecision: .... DOUBT, HESITATION, VACILLATION

indecorous: . . RUDE, COARSE, IMPOLITE, IMPROPER, UNSEEMLY

indeed: . . . TRULY, FORSOOTH, REALLY, CERTAINLY

indefatigable: . . . . TIRELESS, UNTIRING

indefensible: . . INEXCUSABLE, UNJUSTIFIABLE, INSUPPORTABLE

indefinite: . . . UNSURE, HAZY, LOOSE, VAGUE, INEXACT, OBSCURE, NEBULOUS, AMBIGUOUS, EQUIVOCAL, INEXPLICIT, INDISTINCT

pronoun: . . . . . ANY, ONE, SOME, ANYONE, SOMEONE

indelible: . . . . . FAST, FIXED, LASTING, PERMANENT

indelicate: . . . . RAW, CRUDE, GROSS, COARSE, ROUGH, IMPOLITE, IMPROPER, OFFENSIVE, UNREFINED

indemnify: . . . PAY, INSURE, REDEEM, REIMBURSE, COMPENSATE

indent: . . JAG, CHASE, INLAY, STAMP, NOTCH, IMPRESS, BRUISE, EMBOSS, DEPRESS

indentation: . . . . BAY, CUT, NICK, BULGE, NOTCH, DIMPLE, MARGIN, RECESS, CRENELET

indenture: . . . . NOTCH, CONTRACT, AGREEMENT

independent: . . FREE, PROUD, SOVERIGN, UNCOERCED, UNCONTROLLED, UNRESTRICTED

indeterminate: . . . . . VAGUE, UNCERTAIN, UNDECIDED, INDEFINITE

index: . . . . FILE, LIST, MARK, SIGN, TABLE, POINTER, INDICATOR, CATALOG(UE)

Indian: . . . RED, BUCK, CHIEF, BRAVE, SQUAW, REDSKIN, PAPOOSE, ABORIGINE

indicate: . . SAY, CITE, MARK, SHOW, POINT, ALLUDE, DENOTE, EVINCE, REVEAL, DECLARE, SIGNIFY, SPECIFY, DISCLOSE, INTIMATE, DESIGNATE

indication(s): . . . CLEW, CLUE, MARK, NOTE, OMEN, SIGN, PROOF, TRACE, TOKEN, SIGNAL, INDICIA, SYMPTOM, EVIDENCE

indicator: . . . . CLUE, DIAL, HAND, SIGN, VANE, ARROW, CLOCK, GAUGE, INDEX, METER, MARKER, POINTER, REGISTER

indict: . . . . . . BILL, ACCUSE, ATTACH, CHARGE, DECREE, ARRAIGN, IMPEACH

indictment: . . . . . . CHARGE, ACCUSATION

indifference: . . . . . APATHY, COLDNESS, ALOOFNESS, LETHARGY, NEGLIGENCE, CARELESSNESS

indifferent: . . . . COLD, COOL, SOSO, ALOOF, BLASE, STOIC, CASUAL, NEUTRAL, LANGUID, AVERAGE, CARELESS, LISTLESS, MEDIOCRE, APATHETIC, DETACHED, UNCONCERNED

indigence: . . . . . LACK, NEED, WANT, PENURY, POVERTY

indigenous: . . . . INBORN, INNATE, NATIVE, ENDEMIC, NATURAL, INHERENT

indigent: . . . . . POOR, NEEDY, DESTITUTE, PENNILESS

indigestion: . . . . . . APEPSIA, DYSPEPSIA

indignant: . . . ANGRY, IRATE, WROTH, ANNOYED, INCENSED

indignation: . . . . IRE, FURY, ANGER, SCORN, WRATH, DISDAIN, CONTEMPT

indignity: . . . . INSULT, AFFRONT, SLIGHT, HUMILIATION

indirect: . . . . SIDE, DEVIOUS, OBLIQUE, CIRCUITOUS, ROUNDABOUT

indiscreet: . . . . RASH, HASTY, UNWISE, CARELESS, HEEDLESS, IMPRUDENT

indispensable: . . . . . BASIC, VITAL, NECESSARY, ESSENTIAL, REQUISITE, IMPERATIVE

indisposition: . . . . MALADY, AILMENT, ILLNESS, MALAISE, DISORDER, SICKNESS, AVERSION, RELUCTANCE

indisputable: . . . . . . SURE, CERTAIN, EVIDENT, POSITIVE, UNDENIABLE, INDUBITABLE, UNQUESTIONABLE

indistinct: . . . . . DIM, HAZY, FAINT, MISTY, VAGUE, CLOUDY, OBSCURE

individual: . . . . . . (also see **person**) ONE, SELF, SOLE, UNIT, SINGLE, SPECIAL, DISTINCT, SOLITARY, PARTICULAR

indoctrinate: . . . . . . IMBUE, TEACH, INSTRUCT, EDUCATE, BRAINWASH

indolence: . . SLOTH, INERTIA, IDLENESS, LAZINESS, LANGUOR

indolent: . . . . . . IDLE, LAZY, OTIOSE, SUPINE, INACTIVE, LISTLESS, SLOTHFUL

indorse: . . (also see **endorse**) attest, sanction, approve

indubitable: . . . . SURE, CERTAIN, EVIDENT, APPARENT, INFALLIBLE, UNDENIABLE, DOUBTLESS, UNQUESTIONABLE

induce: . . DRAW, LURE, URGE, CAUSE, TEMPT, ELICIT, SUBORN, PERSUADE

inducement: . . . BAIT, PRIZE, MOTIVE, REASON, INCENTIVE, ENTICEMENT

induct: . . . . ENLIST, ENROLL, INSTALL, INITIATE, INTRODUCE

indulge: . . PET, BABY, SPOIL, FAVOR, HUMOR, YIELD, CODDLE, PAMPER, PLEASE, GRATIFY, SATISFY

indulgence: . . . . . FAVOR, SPREE, CLEMENCY, PRIVILEGE, TOLERANCE

indulgent: . . . . EASY, GOOD, KIND, LENIENT, TOLERANT

indurate: . . . INURE, HARDEN

industrial: *giant:* . . . . MAGNATE, TYCOON

industrious: . . BUSY, ACTIVE, ZEALOUS, DILIGENT, HARD-WORKING, SEDULOUS, ASSIDUOUS

inebriate: . . . . . . SOT, TOPER, EXCITE, DRUNK(ARD), EXHILARATE(D), INTOXICATE(D)

ineffectual: . . . . IDLE, VAIN, WEAK, FUTILE, USELESS

inelastic: . . . . . . LIMP, STIFF, RIGID, INFLEXIBLE

inelegant: . . CRUDE, COARSE, VULGAR, AWKWARD, GRACELESS

inept: . . . DULL, SLOW, UNFIT, ABSURD, FOOLISH, CLUMSY, AWKWARD, PUERILE

inert: . . . DEAD, DULL, SLOW, STUPID, SUPINE, TORPID, PASSIVE, IMMOBILE, INACTIVE, NEUTRAL, LATENT, LIFELESS

inertia: . . . SLOTH, IDLENESS, INDOLENCE

inevitable: . . . DUE, CERTAIN, FATEFUL, UNAVOIDABLE, INESCAPABLE

inexorable: . . . . GRIM, HARD, STERN, UNBENDING, INFLEXIBLE, UNYIELDING

inexpedient: . . . . . . UNWISE, IMPOLITIC, IMPRUDENT, INADVISABLE

infamous: . . . . ODIOUS, SHAMEFUL, NOTORIOUS, OUTRAGEOUS, SCANDALOUS

infamy: . . . . . ODIUM, SHAME, DISGRACE, DISHONOR, NOTORIETY

infant: . . . TOT, BABY, CHILD, MINOR, BAIRN, BAMBINO, CHRISHOM

infatuate: . CHARM, ENAMOR, CAPITVATE

infatuation: . . . RAVE, CRAZE, FOLLY, CRUSH, PASSION

infect: . . . . . . TAINT, IMBUE, AFFECT, DEFILE, POLLUTE, CORRUPT, CONTAMINATE

infection: . . TAINT, DISEASE, MALADY, PLAGUE, ILLNESS

infer: . . . . . . GUESS, DERIVE, DEDUCE, GATHER, SURMISE, CONCLUDE, PRESUME

inference: . . . . . COROLLARY, DEDUCTION, CONCLUSION

inferior: . . . BAD, LOW, LESS, POOR, BELOW, LOWER, MINOR, PETTY, IMPURE, CHEAPER, UNEQUAL, SHODDY, MEDIOCRE, SUBORDINATE, EXECRABLE

infernal: . . . . HATEFUL, HELLISH, FIENDISH, DEVILISH, SATANIC, DIABOLICAL

inferno: . FIRE, HELL, ABYSS, HADES

infertile: . . . BARREN, STERILE

infest: . . . . VEX, BESET, OVERRUN, SWARM, PLAGUE

infidel: . . . . PAGAN, ATHEIST, SKEPTIC, AGNOSTIC, HEATHEN

infiltrate: . . . . . LEAK, SEEP, FILTER

infinite: . ENDLESS, ETERNAL, BOUNDLESS, IMMENSE

infinitesimal: . . TINY, SMALL, ATOMIC, MINUTE

infirm: . . . . . . LAME, WEAK, ANILE, FRAIL, SENILE, DECREPIT, UNSTABLE, FRAGILE

infirmity: . . . VICE, AILMENT, DISEASE, DEFECT, FRAILTY, DEBILITY, WEAKNESS, FEEBLENESS

inflame: . . FAN, FIRE, GOAD, ANGER, AROUSE, ENRAGE, EXCITE, IGNITE, RANKLE, KINDLE, MADDEN

inflammable: . . . . FIERY, ARDENT, PICEOUS, EXCITABLE, IRRITABLE, COMBUSTIBLE

inflate: . FILL, ELATE, SWELL, DILATE, EXPAND, INCREASE, DISTEND

inflated: . . . ELATED, TURGID, BLOATED, DILATED, POMPOUS, SWOLLEN, BOMBASTIC

inflect: . . . . TURN, BEND, CURVE, DEFLECT, MODULATE

inflexible: . . . . . SET, FIRM, HARD, FIXED, RIGID, STIFF, ADAMANT, OBDURATE, IMMOVABLE, UNSHAKABLE, IMPLACABLE

inflict,: . . . . . DEAL, IMPOSE, WREAK

influence: . . . . . COAX, HEFT, MOVE, PULL, SWAY, BRIBE, FORCE, IMPEL, LOBBY, AFFECT, COMPEL, EFFECT, INDUCE, WEIGHT, POWER, AUTHORITY

influential: . . . . . . POTENT, EFFECTIVE, POWERFUL, IMPORTANT

influx: . . . . INFLOW

inform: . . . . . TELL, WARN, ALERT, ADVICE, NOTIFY, APPRISE, EDUCATE, ACQUAINT, INSTRUCT, ADVERTISE, COMMUNICATE

information: . . . ITEM, DATA, DOPE, NEWS, WORD, AVISO, FACTS, NOTICE, DIRECTION, LEARNING, KNOWLEDGE

informer: . . . RAT, SPY, FINK, TOUT, STOOL, CANARY, GOSSIP, PIGEON, SNITCH, DELATOR, SQUEALER, REPORTER

infraction: . . . TORT, BREACH, TRESPASS, VIOLATION, INFRINGEMENT

infrequent: . . RARE, SCARCE, SPARSE, SPORADIC, OCCASIONAL, SELDOM

infringe: . . . . INTRUDE, TRESPASS, VIOLATE, ENCROACH

infuriate: . ENRAGE, MADDEN

infuse: . . FILL, STEEP, IMBUE, IMPART, ENGRAIN, IMPLANT, INSTILL, INCULCATE

infusion: . . . . TEA, EXTRACT, TINCTURE, ADMIXTURE

ingenious: ... DEDAL, SHARP, SMART, ADROIT, CLEVER, GIFTED, ENGINOUS, SKILLFUL, TALENTED, INVENTIVE

ingenuity: .. SKILL, ARTIFICE, ADROITNESS, CLEVERNESS

ingenuous: ... OPEN, FRANK, NAIVE, NOBLE, CANDID, HONEST, ARTLESS, INNOCENT, GUILELESS

ingest: .... EAT, INCEPT, SWALLOW

ingrain: .... INFUSE, IMBUE

ingratiate: .. FAWN, FLATTER, INSINUATE

ingredient: ...... ELEMENT, COMPONENT, CONSTITUENT

ingress: ...... ADIT, ENTRY, ACCESS, ENTRANCE

inhabit: ..... LIVE, DWELL, OCCUPY, PEOPLE, SETTLE

inhabitant: .... INMATE, NATIVE, TENANT, RESIDENT, DENIZEN, CIT(IZEN), DWELLER

inhale: .. DRAW, SUCK, SNIFF, BREATHE, INSPIRE, RESPIRE

inherent: ... BASIC, INBORN, INNATE, ORGANIC, IMMANENT, ESSENTIAL, INTRINSIC, INDIGENOUS

inheritance: ...... BEQUEST, LEGACY, HERITAGE, BIRTHRIGHT, PATRIMONY

inheritor: ... HEIR, DEVISEE, LEGATEE

inhibit: ...... CURB, CHECK, FORBID, HINDER, WITHHOLD, RESTRAIN, PROHIBIT, SUPPRESS

inhuman: .... FELL, CRUEL, BESTIAL, BRUTAL, SAVAGE

inhume: ...... BURY, INTER

inimical: .. AVERSE, ADVERSE, HOSTILE, UNFRIENDLY, UNFAVORABLE

inimitable: ..... PEERLESS, MATCHLESS, UNEQUALED

iniquitous: ... BAD, WRONG, SINFUL, UNJUST, WICKED, NEFARIOUS

iniquity: ... SIN, EVIL, VICE, CRIME, INJUSTICE, WICKEDNESS

initial: ..... FIRST, LETTER, OPENING, BEGINNING, INCIPIENT, INCEPTIVE, INTRODUCTORY

initiate: ...... OPEN, ADMIT, BEGIN, START, ENROLL, FOUND, INDUCT, INSTALL, INTRODUCE, ORIGINATE, INSTITUTE

initiative: .. GETUP, ENERGY, GUMPTION, ENTERPRISE

injection: ..... SHOT, HYPO, ENEMA, INOCULATION

injunction: ... WRIT, ORDER, COMMAND, ENJOINING, MANDATE

injure: .. MAR, HARM, HURT, MAIM, SPOIL, SALLY, WOUND, WRONG, DAMAGE, IMPAIR, CRIPPLE

injury: .. HARM, HURT, LOSS, SCAR, TORT, WOUND, WRONG, DAMAGE, LESION, TRAUMA, SCRATCH, OFFENSE, CONTUSION, INJUSTICE

injustice: ... WRONG, INJURY, INEQUITY, HARDSHIP, GRIEVANCE

inkling: .... IDEA, HINT, RUMOR, NOTION, GLIMPSE, SUSPICION, INDICATION, INTIMATION

inland: .. DOMESTIC, INTERIOR

inlet: .. ARM, BAY, RIA, ZEE, COVE, SLEW, SLUE, BAYOU, BIGHT, CREEK, FIORD, FIRTH, FJORD, STRAIT, ESTUARY

inmate: ... GUEST, OCCUPANT, PRISONER, INHABITANT

inn: .... PUB, KAHN, FONDA, HOTEL, MOTEL, SERAI, TAMBO, HOSTEL, IMARET, TAVERN, AUBERGE, HOSPICE, WAYHOUSE, HOSPITIUM, ROADHOUSE, CARAVANSARY

innate: .... INBORN, INBRED, NATIVE, NATURAL, INHERENT, INGRAINED, INTRINSIC,

CONGENITAL, INSTINCTIVE,
HEREDITARY

inner: . . . BEN, ENTAL, INSIDE,
INWARD, INTERIOR, INTERNAL

innocence: . . . . PURITY,
NAIVETE, SIMPLICITY,
SINLESSNESS

innocent: . . . . PURE, BLUET,
NAIVE, CHASTE, ARTLESS,
SIMPLE, CHRISOM, BLAMELESS,
GUILELESS, GUILTLESS,
IGNORANT

innocuous: . . . . . HARMLESS,
INNOCENT

innovation: . . . . . . CHANGE,
NOVELTY, IMPROVEMENT

innuendo: . . . . . CLUE, HINT,
SLUR, ALLUSION, ASPERSION,
INSINUATION

inoculate: . . . INJECT, INFECT,
IMMUNE

inopportune: . . . . ILL-TIMED,
UNTIMELY, INAUSPICIOUS,
MALAPROPOS

inordinate: . . . . UNDUE,
EXCESSIVE, IMMODERATE

inquest: . . SEARCH, INQUIRY,
EXAMINATION, INVESTIGATION

inquire: . ASK, SEEK, QUERY,
DEMAND, EXAMINE, QUESTION,
INTERROGATE, INVESTIGATE

inquisitive: . . . . . . NOS(E)Y,
PRYING, SNOOPY, CURIOUS,
MEDDLESOME

inroad: . . . . . . RAID, FORAY,
BREACH, INVASION,
ENCROACHMENT

insane: . . . MAD, BUGS, DAFT,
LUNY, NUTS, BALMY, BATTY,
CRAZY, DAFFY, LOONY, MANIC,
CRAZED, FOOLISH, FRANTIC,
IRRATIONAL, DEMENTED,
SENSELESS, DERANGED,
FRENETIC, DELIRIOUS,
PHRENETIC

insanity: . . . MANIA, FRENZY,
MADNESS, LUNACY, DELIRIUM,
DEMENTIA, PSYCHOSIS

inscribe: . . . . . ETCH, MARK,
ENTER, WRITE, STAMP, ENROLL,
ENGRAVE, DEDICATE

inscrutable: . . . . SECRET,
ABSTRUSE, ENIGMATIC,
MYSTERIOUS, IMPENETRABLE

insect: . ANT, BEE, BUG, FLY,
NIT, FLEA, GNAT, LICE, MITE,
MOTH, TICK, WASP, APHID,
LOUSE, ROACH, BEETLE,
EARWIG, HORNET, MANTIS,
SPIDER, WEEVIL, CRICKET,
KATYDID, LADYBUG, TERMITE,
MOSQUITO, BUMBLEBEE,
CENTIPEDE

insecure: . . . . . LOOSE, RISKY,
SHAKY, UNSAFE, UNSTABLE,
UNCERTAIN, PERILOUS,
UNRELIABLE

insensate: . . . . COLD, HARSH,
BRUTAL, STUPID, FOOLISH,
UNFEELING

insensibility: . . . . COMA,
APATHY, TORPOR, TRANCE,
LETHARGY, ANALGESIA,
ANESTHESIA, INDIFFERENCE

inside: . . . . . INNER, LINING,
WITHIN, INDOOR(S), INTERIOR,
INTERNAL

insidious: . . . . . . SLY, WILY,
CRAFTY, COVERT, CUNNING,
CONCEALED, DECEITFUL,
TREACHEROUS

insight: . . . . . KEN, ACUMEN,
INTUITION, DISCERNMENT,
CLAIRVOYANCE

insignia: . . . . MARK, BADGE,
EMBLEM

insignificant: . . PUNY, DINKY,
PETIT, PETTY, SMALL, MINOR,
PALTRY, TRIVIAL, MINUSCULE

insincere: . . FALSE, UNTRUE,
FEIGNED, HYPOCRITICAL

insinuate: . . . . HINT, IMPLY,
ALLUDE, INTIMATE, SUGGEST,
PENETRATE

insinuation: . . . . HINT,
INNUENDO

insipid: . . . DRY, DULL, FLAT, TAME, BANAL, STALE, TEPID, VAPID, TASTELESS, LIFELESS, JEJUNE, PROSAIC

insist: . . . . . URGE, DEMAND, AFFIRM, PERSIST

insolence: . . . . NERVE, AUDACITY, ARROGANCE, IMPUDENCE, IMPERTINENCE

insolent: . . . . RUDE, DEFIANT, ARROGANT, IMPUDENT, AUDACIOUS

insolvent: . . . . BROKE, BANKRUPT, DESTITUTE

insouciant: . . . COOL, CALM, CAREFREE, INDIFFERENT

inspect: . . . . PRY, SEE, SCAN, VISIT, PERUSE, EXAMINE, SCRUTINIZE

inspire: . . . . . . MOVE, STIR, CAUSE, IMBUE, AROUSE, EXCITE, INHALE, UPLIFT, BREATHE, INFLUENCE, ANIMATE, MOTIVATE, STIMULATE

instability: . . . . FLEXIBILITY, INSECURITY, INCONSTANCY

install: . . . . SEAT, VEST, INSTATE, INVEST, INDUCT, INITIATE, ESTABLISH

instant: . . . TICK, TIME, WINK, FLASH, JIFFY, TRICE, BREATH, MOMENT, SECOND, URGENT, PRESSING, IMMEDIATE, IMMINENT

instigate: . . . . . . EGG, ABET, GOAD, MOVE, PROD, SPUR, URGE, IMPEL, INCITE, CAUSE, COMPEL, EXCITE, FOMENT, PROMPT, PROMOTE, STIMULATE

instill: . . . . . . IMBUE, INFIX, INFUSE, IMPLANT, INCULCATE

instinct: . . . . . . BENT, GIFT, TALENT, KNACK

institute: . . . . BEGIN, FOUND, START, ORDAIN, ACADEMY, ESTABLISH, INITIATE, ORIGINATE

institution: . CLINIC, SCHOOL, CHURCH, ACADEMY, COLLEGE, HOSPITAL, SEMINARY, UNIVERSITY

instruct: . . . . . LEAD, SHOW, BRIEF, COACH, DRILL, EDIFY, GUIDE, TEACH, TRAIN, TUTOR, DIRECT, INFORM, PREACH, COUNSEL, EDUCATE, ENLIGHTEN, INDOCTRINATE

instruction: . . . . ADVISE, ORDER, CHARGE, LESSON, PRECEPT, PRACTICE, TUTORSHIP, TUTELAGE, TUITION, EDUCATION

instructive: . . . . . . DIDACTIC

instructor: . . . DON, COACH, TUTOR, MENTOR, TEACHER, TRAINER, PRECEPTOR, PROFESSOR, PEDAGOGUE

instrument: . . . . . . (also see **apparatus, device, tool**) DEED, WRIT, AGENT, MEANS, MEDIUM, UTENSIL, CONTRACT, APPLIANCE, IMPLEMENT, DOCUMENT

instrumentality: . . . AGENCY, MEANS, MEDIUM

insubordinate: . . . . . REBEL, UNRULY, MUTINOUS, PEVERSE, SEDITIOUS, REFRACTORY, DISOBEDIENT, REBELLIOUS

insufficient: . . . . SHORT, SCANTY, SCARCE, LACKING, WANTING, DEFICIENT, INADEQUATE

insulate: . . . . ISOLATE, SEGREGATE, QURANTINE

insult: . . . SLAP, SLUR, ABUSE, FLOUT, ASSAIL, OFFEND, RUFFLE, OUTRAGE, REVILE, AFFRONT, INDIGNITY

insurance: . . . . . . COVERAGE, GUARANTY, WARRANTY, ASSURANCE, PROTECTION

insure: . . . . (also see **ensure**) SECURE, PROTECT, ASSURE, GUARANTEE, UNDERWRITE

insurgent: . . . . (also see **insubordinate**) REBEL, MUTINEER, REBELLIOUS

insurrection: . . . . . MUTINY, UPRISING, REVOLT, REBELLION, INSURGENCE

intact: . . . . . SOUND, WHOLE, COMPLETE, UNBROKEN

intangible: . . . . VAGUE, IMMATERIAL, INSUBSTANTIAL, INCORPOREAL

integral: . . . WHOLE, ENTIRE, ESSENTIAL, NECESSARY, COMPOSITE

integrate: . MIX, JOIN, UNITE, UNIFY

integrity: . . . . VIRTUE, HONESTY, PROBITY, SINCERITY, UPRIGHTNESS

integument: . . . . ARIL, COAT, DERM, HIDE, HUSK, RIND, SKIN, TESTA, ENVELOP(E), CUTICLE, COVERING, SHELL

intellect: . . WIT, MIND, NOUS, BRAIN, GENIUS, REASON, MENTALITY, INTELLIGENCE

intellectual: . . . . BRAINY, MENTAL, NOETIC, SOPHIC, EGGHEAD, HIGHBROW

intelligence: . . . . . WIT, MIND, NEWS, WORD, SENSE, ACUMEN, BRAINS, ESPRIT, NOTICE, REPORT, WISDOM, TIDINGS, INFORMATION, INTELLECT, LEARNING

intelligent: . . ACUTE, SMART, CLEVER, SHARP, ASTUTE, BRIGHT, SENSIBLE, BRILLIANT

intelligible: . . . CLEAR, PLAIN, COMPREHENSIBLE, UNDERSTANDABLE

intemperate: . . . . . . SEVERE, VIOLENT, EXTREME, EXCESSIVE, IMMODERATE

intend: . . . AIM, PLAN, MEAN, DESIGN, PROPOSE, CONSTRUE

intense: . . . . . . HOT, ACUTE, GREAT, VIVID, ARDENT, SEVERE, STRONG, EARNEST, EXTREME, FERVENT, VIOLENT, ZEALOUS, POWERFUL, VEHEMENT

intensify: . . . . DEEPEN, ENHANCE, INCREASE, HEIGHTEN

intent: . . AIM, RAPT, EAGER, FIXED, DESIGN, OBJECT, EARNEST, ENGROSSED, PURPOSE, DETERMINED, ATTENTIVE

intentional: . . . . DELIBERATE, VOLUNTARY

inter: . . . . . . BURY, INHUME, INURN, ENTOMB

intercede: . . . . MEDIATE, ARBITRATE, INTERVENE, INTERPOSE

intercept: . . . . STOP, CATCH, PREVENT, INTERRUPT

interdict: . . BAN, BAR, VETO, DEBAR, ENJOIN, FORBID, PROHIBIT, RESTRAIN, PROSCRIBE

interest: . . . . . . GOOD, ZEAL, BEHALF, CLAIM, RIGHT, SHARE, STAKE, PROFIT, BENEFIT, CONCERN, ATTRACT, FASCINATE

interfere: . . CLASH, MEDDLE, MOLEST, TAMPER, COLLIDE, DISTURB, INTRUDE, OBSTRUCT, INTERVENE, INTERPOSE

interim: . . . . . . MEANWHILE, INTERVAL, MEANTIME, PROVISIONAL, TEMPORARY

interlace: . . . WEAVE, BRAID, PLEACH, TWINE

interlock: . . . . . KNIT, LINK, UNITE, CLENCH, ENGAGE

interlope: . . INSERT, MEDDLE, INTRUDE, TRESPASS

intermediary: . . . . . AGENT, MEAN, MEDIUM, GO-BETWEEN, MEDIATOR, MIDDLEMAN

intermediate: . . . . . . MESNE, MEDIUM, MIDDLE, BETWEEN

interminable: . . . . ENDLESS, ETERNAL, INFINITE, CEASELESS, LASTING, TIMELESS, UNENDING

intermission: . . . REST, STOP, RECESS, PAUSE, RESPITE,

ENTRACTE, INTERLUDE,
INTERRUPTION

intermittent: ..... BROKEN,
FITFUL, RECURRENT, PERIODIC,
SPASMODIC

internal: ... INNER, INTERIOR,
INWARD, INTRINSIC, DOMESTIC,
MENTAL, SPIRITUAL

interpose: .. INSERT, THRUST,
INTRUDE, MEDIATE, INTERVENE,
INTERCEDE, INTERRUPT

interpret: ..... REDE, READ,
DECODE, DEFINE, RENDER,
EXPLAIN, CONSTRUE,
TRANSLATE, ELUCIDATE

interpretation: .... MEANING,
EXPLANATION, EXPOSITION,
TRANSLATION, RENDITION

interrogate: ..... ASK, QUIZ,
PROBE, QUERY, INQUIRE,
QUESTION, EXAMINE

interrupt: ...... CUT, STOP,
BREAK, BURST, CEASE, CHECK,
ARREST, HINDER, THWART,
DISTURB, SUSPEND, OBSTRUCT

interruption: ... GAP, PAUSE,
BREACH, BREAK, OUTAGE,
HIATUS, CESSATION,
INTERMISSION

intersect: .. CUT, MEET, JOIN,
CROSS, DIVIDE, PIERCE,
DECUSSATE

intertwine: .... KNIT, LACE,
TWIST, WEAVE, PLEACH,
TANGLE

interval: ... GAP, REST, SPAN,
BREAK, SPACE, BREACH,
HIATUS, RECESS, CAESURA,
INTERLUDE, INTERMISSION

intervene: .... see **interpose**

interweave: .... MAT, PLAT,
BRAID, PLAIT, SPLICE, RADDLE,
ENTWINE (INTER)LACE

intestinal: .... ENTERIC

intestine(s): .. GUT(S), COLON,
BOWEL(S), ENTRAILS, VISCERA

intimacy: .... AFFINITY,
CLOSENESS, CONNECTION,
FAMILIARITY

intimate: ...... HINT, NEAR,
CLOSE, IMPLY, CRONY,
ALLUDE, SECRET, FRIEND,
PRIVATE, SUGGEST, PERSONAL

intimation: .... CLUE, HINT,
INKLING, NOTICE, SUGGESTION,
DECLARATION

intimidate: ..... AWE, COW,
ABASH, BULLY, COERCE,
DAUNT, SCARE, TERRIFY,
FRIGHTEN, BUFFALO,
BAMBOOZLE

intolerance: ...... BIGOTRY

intolerant: ...... NARROW,
BIGOTED, DOGMATIC,
IMPATIENT, PREJUDICED

intoxicate: ... ELATE, EXCITE,
INEBRIATE, STIMULATE

intoxicated: ..... LIT, HIGH,
SHOT, DRUNK, FRIED, BOILED,
SOUSED, POTTED, STEWED,
LOADED, GROGGY, ELATED,
EXCITED, BESOTTED,
PLASTERED, INEBRIATED

intractable: .. WILD, UNRULY,
MUTINOUS, OBDURATE,
PERVERSE, OBSTINATE,
STUBBORN, UNMANAGEABLE

intransigent: ...... RADICAL,
STUBBORN, UNCOMPROMISING

intrepid: . , . . . BOLD, BRAVE,
DARING, VALIENT, FEARLESS,
RESOLUTE, COURAGEOUS

intricate: .... DA(E)DAL,
KNOTTY, COMPLEX, INVOLVED,
DIFFICULT, INVOLUTE,
COMPLICATED

intrigue: ...... PLOT, CABAL,
CHARM, BRIGUE, DECEIT,
DESIGN, SCHEME, ARTIFICE,
PERPLEX, FASCINATE,
CONSPIRACY

intrinsic: .... REAL, TRUE,
INBORN, INATE, GENUINE,
NATURAL, INTERNAL,
ESSENTIAL, INHERENT,
NECESSARY

introduce: .... BEGIN, START,
USHER, BROACH, HERALD,

INFUSE, INSERT, LAUNCH,
PRECEDE, PREFACE, PRESENT,
INDUCT, INITIATE, INSTITUTE
introduction: . . . . . . DEBUT,
PROEM, INTROIT, PREFACE,
PRELUDE, ENTRANCE,
FOREWARD, PREAMBLE,
PROLOGUE, PRESENTATION
intrude: . . . . . see **interpose**
intuition: . . HUNCH, INSIGHT,
INSTINCT, PERCEPTION
inundate: . . . FLOW, DROWN,
FLOOD, SWAMP, DELUGE,
OVERFLOW, OVERWHELM
inure: . . . . . (also see **enure**)
HABITUATE, ACCUSTOM
inurn: . . . . . . BURY, ENTOMB,
INTER
invade: . . . . . RAID, ASSAULT,
INTRUDE, VIOLATE, OVERRUN,
ENCROACH, TRESPASS
invalid: . . . NULL, SICK, VOID,
WEAK, FEEBLE, INFIRM,
SICKLY, NUGATORY,
INEFFECTIVE
invalidate: . . . . . UNDO, VOID,
ANNUL, ABOLISH, NULLIFY,
VITIATE
invaluable: . . DEAR, COSTLY,
PRICELESS, PRECIOUS,
INESTIMABLE
invariable: . . SAME, STEADY,
UNIFORM, CONSTANT,
CONTINUAL, UNCHANGING
invariably: . . . . . . ALWAYS,
FOREVER
invasion: . . (also see **invade**)
INROAD, INTRUSION,
INCURSION, INFRINGEMENT
invective: . . . ABUSE, CURSE,
TAUNT, VITUPERATION,
DENUNCIATION
inveigle: . . . . . . COAX, LURE,
TRICK, ALLURE, ENTICE,
CAJOLE, SEDUCE, PERSUADE
invent: . . COIN, FORM, MAKE,
VAMP, CREATE, DESIGN,
DEVISE, CONCOCT, CONTRIVE,
FABRICATE, ORIGINATE

invention: . . . . . LIE, DEVICE,
FICTION, FIGMENT,
FABRICATION, FALSEHOOD,
CONCOCTION
inventor: . . AUTHOR, COINER,
CREATOR, DISCOVERER,
ORIGINATOR
inventory: . . . . . LIST, STOCK,
STORE, ACCOUNT,
CATALOG(UE), REGISTER
inversion: . . . . REVERSAL
invert: . . . . TURN, REVERSE,
HOMOSEXUAL
invertebrate: . . . . . . WORM,
POLYP, INSECT, MOLLUSK,
SPINELESS
invest: . . DON, GOWN, ROBE,
ADORN, ARRAY, COVER,
DROWN, DRESS, ENDOW,
ENDUE, CLOTHE, CONFER,
ORDAIN, ENVELOP, INSTALL,
SURROUND
investigate: . . . . . PRY, NOSE,
PROBE, STUDY, TRACE,
SEARCH, EXAMINE, EXPLORE,
INQUIRE, RESEARCH,
SCRUTINIZE
investor: . . . . . . CAPITALIST,
SHAREOWNER, STOCKHOLDER
inveterate: . . . . . . CHRONIC,
HABITUAL, CONFIRMED,
INGRAINED, OBSTINATE
invidious: . . . . ODIOUS,
HATEFUL, MALIGNANT,
OFFENSIVE
invigorate: . . . . PEP, BRACE,
RENEW, REFRESH, ENLIVEN,
ANIMATE, STRENGTHEN,
EXHILARATE
invincible: . . . . UNBEATABLE,
INDOMITABLE, UNCONQUERABLE
inviolate: . . . HOLY, SACRED,
UNDEFILED, SACROSANCT,
UNBROKEN
invisible: . . . . . HID, UNSEEN,
UNAPPARENT, IMPERCEPTIBLE
invite: . . . . ASK, BID, CALL,
COURT, ALLURE, ENTICE,
PROVOKE, REQUEST, SOLICIT

invocation: .. PLEA, PRAYER, SERMON, ENTREATY, BENEDICTION

invoice: .... BILL, BRIEF, ACCOUNT, MANIFEST, STATEMENT

invoke: .... CALL, PRAY, APPEAL, CONJURE, ENTREAT, IMPLORE, SOLICIT, SUPPLICATE

involuntary: ..... FORCED, RELUCTANT, UNWILLING, INSTINCTIVE, SPONTANEOUS, ACCIDENTAL, AUTOMATIC, UNINTENTIONAL

involute: .. CURLED, ROLLED, INVOLVED, INTRICATE

involve: .. EMPLOY, ENGAGE, ENTAIL, EMBRACE, REQUIRE, INCLUDE, EMBROIL, ENTANGLE, IMPLICATE, COMPLICATE

involved: .... COMPLEX, INVOLUTE, INTRICATE, IMPLICATED, COMPLICATED

ion: *negative:* .... ANION *positive:* . CATION, KATION

iota: ... BIT, DOT, JOT, ATOM, WHIT, TITTLE, PARTICLE

irascible: .... BRASH, CROSS, IRATE, TESTY, TOUCHY, CAPTIOUS, CHOLERIC, PETULANT, IMPATIENT, IRRITABLE, WRATHFUL

irate: . MAD, ANGRY, WROTH, ENRAGED, FURIOUS, INCENSED, WRATHFUL, IRASCIBLE

ire: .... FURY, RAGE, ANGER, WRATH, CHOLER, TEMPER, RESENTMENT, DISPLEASURE

irenic: ..... CALM, SERENE, PACIFIC, PEACEFUL

iridescent: ...... LUSTROUS, OPALESCENT, VERSICOLOR *gem:* .... OPAL

Irish: ...... CELTIC, GAELIC, HIBERNIAN

irk: ..... (also see **ire**) VEX, BORE, ANGER, ANNOY, DISGUST, CHAFE, PEEVE, UPSET, NETTLE, TROUBLE, IRRITATE

irksome: .... DULL, TEDIOUS, TIRESOME, MONOTONOUS

iron: ... FIRM, HARD, POWER, PRESS, TRIVET, STRONG, MANGLE, FERRITE, SMOOTH, HEMATITE

ironclad: .... MONITOR, WARSHIP, MERRIMAC, IRONSIDES, FOOLPROOF, UNBREAKABLE

ironic(al): ..... SATIRIC(AL), SARCASTIC

irony: .... SATIRE, MOCKERY, SARCASM, RIDICULE

irrational: .. INANE, ABSURD, STUPID, BRUTISH, FOOLISH, SENSELESS, W(H)ACKY, RIDICULOUS

irreconcilable: .... DISCORDANT, CONFLICTING, INCOMPATIBLE

irredenta: .... UNREDEEMED

irregular: .... WILD, EROSE, FALSE, FITFUL, RUGGED, SPOTTY, UNEVEN, CROOKED, ERRATIC, ABNORMAL, ATYPICAL, SPORADIC, UNSTEADY, VARIABLE, DESULTORY, ANOMALOUS, ECCENTRIC

irreligious: .... PAGAN, HEATHEN, PROFANE, IMPIOUS, GODLESS

irremediable: ... HELPLESS, HOPELESS, DESPARATE, INCURABLE, IRREPARABLE

irreproachable: . FAULTLESS, BLAMELESS, IMPECCABLE

irresistible: ..... ALMIGHTY, COMPELLING, OVERPOWERING

irresolute: .. FICKEL, UNSURE, HESITANT, DOUBTFUL, WAVERING, UNDECIDED, INDECISIVE

irrespective: ... REGARDLESS

irreverence: ...... IMPIETY, DISRESPECT, IMPUDENCE, PROFANITY

irrevocable:.... FIRM, FINAL, UNALTERABLE

irrigate: .... WATER, SLUICE

irritable:..... EDGY, CROSS, TESTY, CRANKY, TOUCHY, GRUMPY, IRACUND, PEEVISH, IMPATIENT, IRASCIBLE

irritate: .... IRK, NAG, RUB, VEX, FRET, GALL, GOAD, RASP, RILE, ROIL, ITCH, ANGER, ANNOY, CHAFE, CROSS, GRATE, PEEVE, PIQUE, TEASE, ABRADE, BADGER, BOTHER, EXCITE, HARASS, HECTOR, MADDEN, NEEDLE, RANKLE, PROVOKE, EXASPERATE

is: .... EXISTS, REPRESENTS, PERSONIFIES

Islam adherent:... MOSLEM, MUSLIM, MUSLEM

founder: ..... MAHOMET, MOHAMMED

holycity: ... MECCA, MEDINA

scriptures:...... KORAN

supreme deity: ... ALLAH

island: .. AIT, CAY, ILE, KEY, ISLE, ATOLL, ISLET

islands, group: .... FAROE, SAMOA, ANTILLES, CAROLINE, MARSHALL, ARCHIPELAGO

ism: .. DOXY, DOGMA, OLOGY, TENET, BELIEF, THEORY, SYSTEM, DOCTRINE, HYPOTHESIS

isolate: .... DETACH, ENISLE, SECLUDE, IMMURE, INSULATE, SEPARATE, SEGREGATE, QUARANTINE

isolated: ..... SOLE, ALONE, INSULAR, SINGULAR, SOLITARY, SEGREGATED, QUARANTINED

issue: .... END, COME, EMIT, EXIT, FLOW, GUSH, POUR, SEND, ARISE, CHILD, SALLY, SPOUT, TOPIC, UTTER, EGRESS, EMERGE, ESCAPE, POINT, RESULT, SOURCE, UPSHOT, DESCENT, EDITION, EMANATE, OUTCOME, OUTFLOW, PROGENY, PUBLISH, PROBLEM, QUESTION, EFFLUENCE, OFFSPRING

isthmus: ..... NECK, STRAIT, PENINSULA

itch:.. URGE, CRAVE, DESIRE, HANKERING, IRRITATION

item (also see object):... AD, BIT, UNIT, ENTRY, SCRAP, THING, TOPIC, DETAIL, ACCOUNT, ARTICLE, PRODUCT, PARTICULAR

itemize: ... LIST, ENUMERATE

itinerant: ... HOBO, TRAMP, ERRANT, ROVING, MIGRANT, TRAVELER, NOMADIC, VAGRANT, WANDERER, TRANSIENT, UNSETTLED

itinerary: ..... PLAN, TOUR, GUIDE, ROUTE, RECORD, ROADBOOK, GUIDEBOOK

ivory:........ TUSK, TUSH, CREAMY, DENTINE, IVORIDE, RIBZUBA

ivy: ..... TOD, GILL, HOVE, HEDRA

J

jab: .. HIT, DIG, BLOW, POKE, STAB, LUNGE, PUNCH, THRUST

jabber:.. YAP, CHAT, PRATE, BABBLE, GABBLE, CHATTER, GIBBERISH

jabot:....... FRILL, RUFFLE

jack: ..... NOB, CARD, LIFT, MULE, CLOWN, HOIST, KNAVE, MONEY, DONKEY, FELLOW, RABBIT, SAILOR

jackass: ...... DOLT, FOOL, DUNCE, DONKEY, NITWIT, BLOCKHEAD

jacket: .. COAT, ETON, RIND, SACK, SKIN, BLAZER, BOLERO, CASING, REEFER, JERKIN, SAQUE, CASSOCK, DOUBLET, NORFOLK, SPENCER, WRAPPER, CAMISOLE, PEAJACKET, ROUNDABOUT, WINDBREAKER

jade: ..... FAG, NAG, HACK, MARE, MINX, PLUG, SLUT, TIRE, HUSSY, GREEN, WEARY, STONE, HARASS, EXHAUST, FATIGUE, NEPHRITE

jagged: ...... CLEFT, EROSE, ROUGH, SHARP, SERRATED, RAGGED, NOTCHED

jai-alai: ..... GAME, PELOTA
court: .... FRONTON
racquet: .... CESTA

jail: ... CAN, JUG, PEN, BRIG, CAGE, CELL, COOP, GAOL, KEEP, STIR, CLINK, POKEY, COOLER, LOCKUP, PRISON, BASTILLE, HOOSEGOW, CALABOOSE, INCARCERATE, BRIDEWELL

jalousie: ..... BLIND, SCREEN, SHADE, SHUTTER

jam: ... BIND, CRAM, BLOCK, WEDGE, SHOVE, CROWD, SQUEEZE, PRESERVES

jangle: .... RING, BICKER, QUARREL, ALTERCATION

janitor: ..... SUPER, SEXTON, PORTER, DOORMAN, CONCIERGE, CARETAKER

Japan: ... ENAMEL, VARNISH, LACQUER, NIPPON

jape: .... FOOL, GIBE, JEER, JEST, JOKE, MOCK, FRAUD, TRICK, DERIDE

jar: ... JOG, JUG, OLA, URN, EWER, JOLT, OLLA, VASE, BANGA, CLASH, CRUSE, CROCK, CLOCHE, SHAKE, SHOCK, HYDRIA, RATTLE, AGITATE, AMPHORA, DISCORD, VIBRATE, JARDINIERE

jargon: ...... CANT, ARGOT, IDIOM, LINGO, SLANG, PATOIS, PIDGIN, DIALECT, GIBBERISH

jarl: ..... EARL, CHIEFTAIN, HEADMAN, NOBLEMAN

jasper: ..... MICA, QUARTZ, MORLOP, BLOODSTONE

jaundice: ..... BIAS, ENVY, ICTERUS, JEALOUSY, PREJUDICE

jaundiced: .... BIASED, YELLOW, PREJUDICED

jaunt: .... RIDE, TRIP, SALLY, TRAMP, JOURNEY, EXCURSION

jaunty: ..... AIRY, CHICK, COCKY, PERKY, DAPPER, MODISH, STYLISH, SPRUCE, DEBONAIR, SPRIGHTLY

jawbone: .... MAXILLA

jazz: .... SWING, RAG(TIME), BOOGIEWOOGIE, (BE)POP

jealous: .... ENVIOUS, SUSPICIOUS, GREEN(EYED)

jeer: .... BOO, GIBE, HOOT, JAPE, JIBE, MOCK, SCOFF, SNEER, TAUNT, DERIDE, SARCASM, RIDICULE

jejune: ... DRY, ARID, AVID, DULL, FLAT, BANAL, EMPTY, INANE, STALE, TRITE, VAPID, BARREN, INSIPID

jell: .... SET, CONGEAL, SOLIDIFY, COAGULATE, CRYSTALLIZE

jelly: ..... GEL, JAM, ASPIC, PECTIN, SPREAD, GELATIN(E), PRESERVES

jennet: .... ASS, HORSE, DONKEY

jeopardize: .... EXPOSE, IMPERIL, ENDANGER

jeopardy: ..... RISK, PERIL, DANGER, HAZARD, MENACE

jerk: ... BOB, TIC, FLIP, HIKE, YANK, HITCH, TWEAK, TWIST, TWITCH

jerkin: .... see **jacket**

jersey: .... CLOTH, CATTLE, SWEATER

Jerusalem: .... SION, ZION, SALEM, (HOLY) CITY

jest: .... (also see **jape**) FUN, WIT, BULL, FOOL, JOKE, MIME, QUIP, SKIT, FLIRT, BANTER, TRIFLE, BADINAGE, BURLESQUE, WITTICISM

jet: .... GUSH, BLACK, EBON(Y), RAVEN, SPOUT, SPURT, SPRAY, SQUIRT, STREAM, NOZZLE

jetty: ... MOLE, PIER, GROIN, WHARF

Jew: ...... ESSENE, SEMITE, HEBREW, JUDEAN, ISRAELITE

jewel: .... GEM, OPAL, NAIF, RUBY, SARD, BIJOU, BERYL, GARNET, EMERALD, DIAMOND, AMETHYST, ORNAMENT, BRILLIANT

jewelry: .. PIN, RING, TIARA, BROOCH, EARRING, PENDANT, BRACELET, NECKLACE, LAVALIER(E)

jib: ...... BALK, BOOM, SAIL

jibe: ...... (see **jape, jest**)

jiffy: .... HURRY, TRICE, INSTANT, MOMENT, SECOND

jilt: ..... REJECT, ABANDON, DECEIVE, DISCARD

jimmy: .... BAR, PRY, JACK, LEVER, CROWBAR

jinx: .... HEX, HOODOO

jittery: .... JUMPY, NERVOUS

job: .... DUTY, TASK, WORK, CHARE, CHORE, POSITION, SINECURE

jobber: .... DEALER, WHOLESALER

jockey: ..... RIDER, CHEAT, TRICK, OUTWIT, MANEUVER

jocose: ..... MERRY, DROLL, WITTY, HUMOROUS

jocular: .... DROLL, FUNNY, MERRY, WITTY, JOCOSE, JOVIAL, JOYOUS, JESTING, WAGGISH, HUMOROUS, FACETIOUS

jog: ... LOPE, TROT, NUDGE, REMIND, REFRESH

join: .. TIE, WED, ALLY, FUSE, KNIT, KNOT, LINK, MATE, MEET, MELD, WELD, YOKE, BLEND, ENLIST, GRAFT, HITCH, MARRY, MERGE, UNITE, ATTACH, CEMENT, CONCUR, COUPLE, ENROLL, FASTEN, SOLDER, SPLICE, COMBINE, CONNECT, MORTISE, COALESCE, AMALGAMATE

joint: .. ELL, HIP, TEE, BUTT, KNEE, LINK, NODE, SEAM, ANKLE, ELBOW, HINGE, SCARF, TENON, WRIST, MUTUAL, RABBET, KNUCKLE, COUPLING, JUNCTURE, CONCURRENT

joke: .. EGG, FUN, GAG, KID, PUN, RIB, FOOL, GIBE, HOAX, JAPE, JEST, JOSH, QUIP, TWIT, PRANK, SPOOF, TEASE, BANTER, WISECRACK, WITTICISM

joker: .... WAG, WIT, CARD, CLOWN, JESTER, CUTUP, BUFFOON, FARCEUR

jolt: ..... JAR, BLOW, BUMP, BUTT, JERK, SHAKE, SHOCK, JOUNCE, BOUNCE, SURPRISE

josh: .... see **joke**

jostle: ...... JAR, JOG, JOLT, PUSH, CROWD, ELBOW, NUDGE, SHOVE, BUFFET, HUSTLE

jot: .. BIT, ATOM, IOTA, MITE, MOTE, WHIT, GRAIN, TITTLE, MINIM, POINT, SPECK, PARTICLE

jounce: ...... JOLT, SHAKE, BOUNCE

journal: ...... LOG, DIARY, PAPER, ANNALS, RECORD, DAYBOOK, REGISTER, LOGBOOK, MAGAZINE, PERIODICAL, NEWSPAPER

journalist: .. EDITOR, SCRIBE, PUBLICIST, STRINGER, REPORTER, COLUMNIST, NEWSPAPERMAN, CORRESPONDENT

journey: .. FARE, HIKE, RIDE, SAIL, TOUR, TREK, TRIP, JAUNT, ROUTE, TRAVEL, JUNKET, SAFARI, VOYAGE, ODYSSEY, PASSAGE, EXCURSION

joust: .. BOUT, TILT, COMBAT, TOURNEY, TOURNAMENT

jovial: .. GAY, JOLLY, MERRY, GENIAL, JOCOSE, JOCULAR, CONVIVIAL

jowl: .... CHOP, CHEEK, JAW(BONE), DEWLAP, WATTLE

joy: .... GLEE, BLISS, MIRTH, GAIETY, ECSTASY, DELIGHT, ELATION, RAPTURE, PLEASURE, HAPPINESS

joyous: .. GAY, GLAD, MERRY, BLITHE, ELATED, GLEEFUL, FESTAL, FESTIVE, DELIGHTED

jubilant: .... ELATED, EXULTING, REJOICING, TRIUMPHANT

judge: .... TRY, DEEM, GAGE, RATE, COUNT, GUAGE, CRITIC, DECIDE, SETTLE, UMPIRE, ARBITER, REFEREE, SUPPOSE, CONSIDER, ESTIMATE, SENTENCE, CRITICIZE, DETERMINE, AJUDICATE, ARBITRATOR

judgment: .... DEEM, DOOM, VIEW, ARRET, AWARD, SENSE, TASTE, CENSURE, DECISION, OPINION, SENTENCE, VERDICT, CRITICISM

judicious: ... WISE, POLITIC, PRUDENT, SAGACIOUS, DISCERNING

jug: ... (also see *jar*) EWER, JAIL, OLLA, TOBY, FLAGON, LOCKUP, PRISON, PITCHER, THERMOS, CONTAINER

juggle: ...... RIG, WANGLE, SHUFFLE, MANIPULATE

juice: .... JUS, OIL, SAP, GRAVY, FLUID, LIQUID, LIQUOR, ESSENCE, ELECTRICITY

juicy: .. RACY, SPICY, LIVELY, PIQUANT, SUCCULENT

jumble: ... MIX, HASH, HEAP, MESS, BOTCH, SHAKE, BUMBLE, HUDDLE, LITTER, MEDLEY, MUDDLE, AGITATE, MISHMASH, CLUTTER, DISORDER, CONFUSION

jump: ..... HOP, LEAP, SKIP, START, CAPER, BOUND, VAULT, SPRING, PRANCE, BOUNCE

jumpy: ..... EDGY, JITTERY, NERVOUS, SKITTISH

junction: ..... SEAM, JOINT, UNION, SUTURE, CONTACT, CROSSING, MEETING

junk: ... BOAT, BUNK, DOPE, DRUG, SCRAP, TRASH, WASTE, REFUSE, RUBBISH, DISCARD

junta: ... COUNCIL, MEETING, ASSEMBLY, TRIBUNAL, GOVERNMENT

junto: ...... CABAL, CLIQUE, FACTION, COMBINATION

jurisdiction: .... LAW, SEE, SOC, SOKE, VENUE, SPHERE, DOMAIN, BALIWICK

just: ... EVEN, FAIR, ONLY, EQUAL, LEGAL, VALID, HONEST, BARELY, MERELY, SIMPLY, UPRIGHT, RIGHTEOUS, UNBIASED, EQUITABLE, IMPARTIAL

justice: .... LAW, RIGHT, EQUITY, FAIRNESS, HONESTY

justification: ...... EXCUSE, DEFENSE, WARRANT, AUTHORITY, VINDICATION, EXPLANATION

justify: .... ACQUIT, ADJUST, DEFEND, EXCUSE, ABSOLVE, SUPPORT, WARRANT, SANCTION, VINDICATE

jut: ... ABUT, BUTT, BULGE, PROJECT, OVERHANG, PROTRUDE

juvenile: .... CHILD, ACTOR, YOUNG, IMMATURE, YOUTHFUL, INFANTILE, UNDEVELOPED

K

K: *Greek:* .... KAPPA
Hebrew: .... KAPH

kaddish: .... HYMN, PRAYER, DOXOLOGY

kale: ..... GREENS, CABBAGE, COLLARD, COLE(WORT), BROCCOLI

kanaka: .... HAWAIIAN, POLYNESIAN

kangaroo: . . . . . . ROO, JOEY, WALLABY, MARSUPIAL, MACROPODIAN

kaput: . . . BROKEN, RUINED, DEFEATED, DESTROYED

karma: . . . . . FATE, DESTINY

kayak: . . . . . CANOE, UMIAK

kayo: . . . . KNOCKOUT

kedge: . . . . ANCHOR

keel: . . . . . . LIST, SHIP, TILT, CAREEN, CARINA, CAPSIZE

keen: . . INCISIVE, AVID, NICE, TART, WAIL, ACUTE, EAGER, SHARP, ARDENT, ASTUTE, BITING, CLEVER, LAMENT, SEVERE, SHREWD, SUBTLE, INTENSE, PUNGENT, CUTTING, PIERCING, TRENCHANT, PERCEPTIVE, PENETRATING

keenness: . . . EDGE, ACUITY, ACUMEN, GENIUS, TALENT

keep: . . . FORT, HOLD, SAVE, TEND, GUARD, DETAIN, RETAIN, DEFEND, CONCEAL, CONTAIN, CONFINE, CUSTODY, HUSBAND, MAINTAIN, PRESERVE, RESTRAIN, WITHHOLD

keeper: . . WARDEN, CURATOR, GUARD(IAN), PROTECTOR, CUSTODIAN, CARETAKER

keeping: . . . . CARE, AWARD, GUARD, TRUST, CHARGE, CUSTODY, OBSERVANCE, MAINTENANCE

keepsake: . . . RELIC, TOKEN, MEMENTO, SOUVENIR

keg: . . . . . . TUN, VAT, CADE, CASK, FIRKIN, BARREL

kegler: . . . . BOWLER

kelp: . . . . . VAREC, WRACK, SEAWEED

ken: . . . . . SEE, KNOW, VIEW, SIGHT, DESCRY, DISCERN, INSIGHT, KNOWLEDGE, RECOGNIZE, UNDERSTAND

kennel: . . . . . DRAIN, SEWER, GUTTER, STABLE, DOGHOUSE, ENCLOSURE

keratoid: . . HORNY, HORNLIKE

keratosis: . . . . WART

kerchief: . . . . CURCH, SCARF, BABUSHKA, BANDAN(N)A

kerf: . . . . . CUT, SLIT, NOTCH, GROVE, CUTTING

kernel: . . . . PIT, NUT, CORE, GIST, MEAT, PITH, SEED, GRAIN, HEART, ESSENCE, NUCLEUS

ketch: . . . BOAT, SHIP, YAWL, SAILBOAT

kettle: . . . . . POT, VAT, DRUM, BOILER, CA(U)LDRON

kettledrum: . . . . NAKER, TABOR, TIMBAL, TIMPANO, TIMPANI, AT(T)ABAL

key: . . CAY, PIN, BLOT, CLEF, CODE, ISLE, REEF, TONE, PITCH, CLAVIS, ISLAND, OPENER, WEDGE, COTTER, SOLUTION

keyboard: . . . . MANUAL, CLAVIER

keyed up: . . . . AGOG, EAGER, TENSE, EXCITED, STIMULATED

keynote: . . . . TONIC, THEME, TOPIC, FEATURE

keystone: . . . . SAGITTA, SUPPORT, WEDGE

keyway: . . . . SLOT, CHANNEL

kibbutz: . . . . . . SETTLEMENT

kibitzer: . . . . MEDDLER, ONLOOKER, SPECTATOR

kibosh: . . . . VETO, SQUELCH, NONSENSE

kick: . . . . TOE, BOOT, PUNT, OBJECT, RECOIL, THRILL, GRUMBLE, CALCITRATE, COMPLAIN(T), EXCITEMENT, OBJECT(ION), ENTHUSIASM

kickback: . . . BRIBE, PAYOLA, REBATE

kickshaw: . . . . . TOY, TIDBIT, TRIFLE, TRINKET, GEWGAW, BAUBLE

kid: . . RIB, JOSH, JOKE, GOAT, CHILD, TEASE, SUEDE, BANTER, DECEIVE, LEATHER, YOUNGSTER

kidnap: . . . ABDUCT, SNATCH, SHANGHAI

kilderkin: . . . . CASK, BARREL

kill: . . . . HANG, RUIN, SLAY, VETO, CANCEL, CREEK, CROAK, LYNCH, MURDER, STREAM, DESTROY, CHANNEL, EXECUTE, DISPATCH, LAPIDATE, SLAUGHTER, LIQUIDATE, ASSASSINATE

killer: . . . . ASSASSIN, SLAYER, MURDERER

killing: . . . . . FATAL, PURGE, DEADLY, MURDER, POGROM, CARNAGE, SLAYING, HOMICIDE, MASSACRE, GENOCIDE, SLAUGHTER, BUTCHERY, ABORTICIDE, EUTHANASIA, ASSASSINATION

kiln: . . O(A)ST, OVEN, STOVE, TILER, DRYER, FURNACE

kilt: . . . TUCK, PLEAT, SKIRT, FILIBEG

kin: . . . . CLAN, RACE, FLESH, FOLKS, TRIBE, FAMILY, RELATED, AFFINITY, RELATION, RELATIVE

kind: . ILK, KIN, GOOD, KITH, SORT, RACE, TYPE, BREED, CLASS, GENUS, BENIGN, GENDER, GENTLE, TENDER, SPECIES, VARIETY, GENEROUS, BENEVOLENT

kindle: . . FIRE, BURN, LIGHT, AROUSE, IGNITE, EXCITE, ANIMATE, INFLAME, INSPIRE

kindness: . . GRACE, BOUNTY, LENITY, BENIFICE

kindred: . . . . SIB, TIE, KITH, BLOOD, FLESH, ALLIED, FAMILY, COGNATE, AFFINITY, RELATIVES

king: . . REX, REY, ROI, CZAR, TZAR, RULER, REGULUS, MONARCH, SOVEREIGN

kingdom: . . REALM, WORLD, ESTATE, DOMAIN, EMPIRE, REGION, MONARCHY

kingly: . . . . . NOBLE, REGAL, ROYAL, AUGUST, LEONINE, IMPERIAL, MAJESTIC

kink: . . . BEND, CURL, KNOT, LOOP, BUNCH, CRAMP, CRICK, QUIRK, SNARL, TWIST, BUCKLE, TANGLE, PECULIARITY

kinship: . . . see kin, kindred

kiosk: . . . . PAVILION, NEWSSTAND

kirtle: . . COAT, GOWN, DRESS, SKIRT, TUNIC, GARMENT

kismet: . . . . . FATE, DESTINY

kiss: . . . BUSS, PECK, SMACK, CANDY, CARESS, OSCULATE

kit: . . . . BAG, BOX, LOT, SET, TUB, GEAR, PACK, OUTFIT, BUCKET, COLLECTION

kitchen: . . GALLEY, CUISINE, COOKERY, SCULLERY

kitty: . . . . CAT, POT, ANTE, POOL, STAKES, WIDOW

kleptomaniac: . . . . . . THIEF, FILCHER, PILFERER, SHOPLIFTER

knack: . . . . ART, EASE, GIFT, HANG, FLAIR, SKILL, TRICK, TALENT, APTITUDE, FACILITY, INSTINCT, DEXTERITY

knap: . . CUT, RAP, TOP, BITE, BLOW, CHIP, HILL, SNAP, CREST, KNOLL, KNOCK, NIBBLE, STRIKE, SUMMIT

knapsack: . . . . . . KIT, PACK, (DUFFLE)BAG

knave: . . . BOY, FOOL, JACK, CHEAT, CHURL, LOSEL, ROGUE, SCAMP, RASCAL, VARLET, VILLAIN, SCOUNDREL

knead: . . . . . MOLD, MALAX, MASSAGE, MANIPULATE

knee: . . . . JOINT, GENU

kneecap: . . PATELLA, ROTULA

kneel: . . GENUFLECT, KOWTOW

knell: . . . BELL, OMEN, RING, TOLL, PROCLAIM

knickknack: . . TOY, BAUBLE, TRIFLE, GIMCRACK, DOODAD, NOVELTY, TRINKET GEWGAW

knife: . . . . CUT, BOLO, CHIV, SHIV, SNEE, STAB, BOWIE, BLADE, DAGGER, LANCET, SCALPEL, MACHETE, SWITCHBLADE

knight: . . SIR, EQUES, EQUITE, CAVALIER, PALADIN, TEMPLAR, CHAMPION, CABALLERO

knit: . . . . . BIND, HEAL, JOIN, MEND, PURL, PLAIT, UNITE, WOVEN, CEMENT, FASTEN, PUCKER, COUPLE, CROCHET, WRINKLE, INTERLOCK

knob: . . . . NAB, BURR, HILL, KNOT, LUMP, NODE, UMBO, BULGE, KNOLL, FINIAL, HANDLE

knock: . . . . . HIT, RAP, TAP, BEAT, BLOW, PUMP, HILL, JOLT, KNAP, POUND, THUMP, CLASH, BOUNCE, STRIKE, CRITICIZE

knoll: . . . KNAP, KNOB, LUMP, MOUND, HILLOCK, HUMMOCK

knot: . . . . . BOW, TIE, BOND, BURL, KNOB, LOOP, LUMP, NODE, SNAG, GNARL, HITCH, NOOSE, SNARL, NODULE, TANGLE, CLUSTER, COCKADE, PROBLEM, ENTANGLE

know: . . . . KEN, WIS(T), WOT, AWARE, REGARD, REVEAL, REALIZE, PERCEIVE, COMPREHEND

knowledge: . . . . . KEN, LORE, WISDOM, SCIENCE, LEARNING, AWARENESS, EXPERTISE, COGNITION, CONGIZANCE, INFORMATION

knowledgeable: . . . . . WISE, LEARNED, SAPIENT, INFORMED, INTELLIGENT

kosher: . . . FIT, PURE, CLEAN, PROPER, UNDEFILED

kraal: . . . . PEN, CRAWL, VILLAGE, ENCLOSURE

Kremlin: . . . . CITADEL

krimmer: . . . . . . LAMBSKIN

kris: . . . . . . CREESE, DAGGER

kuchen: . . . . . . COFFEECAKE

kudos: . . . . . . FAME, GLORY, CREDIT, PRAISE, RENOWN, PRESTIGE

kulak: . . . FARMER, PEASANT

kumiss: . . . . DRINK, OMEIRIS

kummel: . . . . LIQUEUR

kvass: . . . . BEER

kyphosis: . . . . . HUMPBACK, CURVATURE

L

L: *Greek:* . . . . LAMBDA

label: . . . . . TAB, TAG, BAND, MARK, NAME, BRAND, STAMP, DOCKET, LAPPET, STICKER, CLASSIFY, DESCRIBE, DESIGNATE

labia: . . . . LIPS

labor: . . . . MOIL, TASK, TOIL, WORK, SWEAT, EFFORT, STRESS, STRIVE, TRAVAIL, DRUDGERY, EXERTION, CHILDBIRTH, PARTURATION

labored: . . . . FORCED, STRAINED, DIFFICULT

laborious: . . . HARD, HEAVY, ARDUOUS, TEDIOUS, DILIGENT, ASSIDUOUS, DIFFICULT, PAINSTAKING

labyrinth: . . . MAZE, PUZZLE, CIRCUIT, INTRICATE

lace: . . . GIN, NET, TAT, BAND, BEAT, CORD, LASH, BRAID, LACIS, NOOSE, PLAIT, SNARE, TWINE, UNITE, WEAVE, EDGING, FASTEN, RIBBON, STRING, MACRAME, NETTING, TATTING, FILIGREE, EMBROIDER, INTERTWINE

lacerate: . . . . CUT, RIP, BITE, REND, TEAR, WOUND, MANGLE

lachrymose: . . . SAD, TEARY, WEEPY, TEARFUL, MOURNFUL

laciniate: . . . . FRINGED

lack: . . . NEED, VOID, WANT, FAULT, MINUS, DEARTH, ABSENCE, FAILURE, POVERTY, SCARCITY, SHORTAGE, DEFICIENCY

lackadaisical: . . . . BLAH, LANGUID, LISTLESS, INDOLENT, SPIRITLESS

lackey: . . . . . SLAVE, TOADY, VALET, FLUNKY, FOOTMAN, SERVANT, ATTENDANT

lacking: . . . . . . SHY, SHORT, ABSENT, BARREN, (DE)VOID, WANTING, DESOLATE, DEFICIENT, DESTITUTE

lackluster: . . . . DULL, DRAB

laconic: . . . . . . BRIEF, PITHY, SHORT, TERSE, CONCISE, SUCCIENT

lacquer: . . ENAMEL, SHELLAC, VARNISH

lacuna: . . . . GAP, SPACE, BREAK, CAVITY, HIATUS

lad: . . . . . . BOY, TAD, YOUTH, SHAVER, STRIPLING, YOUNGSTER, ADOLESCENT

ladder: . . . STY, STEE, SCALE, SCALADE

lade: . . . . . . DIP, BAIL, DRAW, LOAD, SHIP, DRAIN, SCOOP, BURDEN, CHARGE, WEIGHT, FREIGHT

ladle: . . . . DIP, BAIL, SCOOP, SERVE, SPOON, DIPPER

lady: . . . . (also see **woman**) BURD, DAME, DONNA, RANI, MADAM, FEMALE, SENORA, MISTRESS, SIGNORA

lag: . . . . . . FLAG, DRAG, IDLE, TIRE, DALLY, DELAY, STAVE, TARRY, TRAIL, WEARY, FALTER, LOITER, LINGER, DILLYDALLY

laggard: . . . . SLOW, REMISS, LOITERER, BACKWARD, SLUGGISH, STRAGGLER

lagn(i)appe: . . . . . . TIP, GIFT, BONUS, PRESENT, GRATUITY

lagoon: . . COVE, HAFF, LAKE, POND, POOL, LIMAN

laic: . . . . . CIVIL, TEMPORAL, LAYMAN, SECULAR

lair: . . . . . . DEN, LIE, CAVE, HAUNT, HANGOUT, HIDEOUT, RETREAT

laity: . . . . . LAYMEN, PEOPLE

lake: . . . LOCH, MEAR, POND, POOL, SHAT, TARN, SHOTT, LAGOON, PIGMENT, RESERVOIR

lam: . . . . BASH, BEAT, FLOG, FLEE, THRASH, FLIGHT, ESCAPE

lamasery: . . . . . MONASTERY

lamb: . . . . . . (Y)EAN, CHILD, SHEEP, COSSET, FATLING, (Y)EANLING

lambast(e): . . BEAT, THRASH, SCOLD

lambent: . . . . GLOWING, RADIANT, WAVERING, FLICKERING

lame: . . . GAME, HALT, MAIM, CRIPPLE(D), DECREPIT, DISABLE(D), HAMSTRING, SPAVINED, INCAPACITATE

lament: . . . . CRY, RUE, CARE, HOWL, KEEN, MOAN, WAIL, WEEP, DIRGE, ELEGY, MOURN, BEMOAN, BEWAIL, DOLOUR, GRIEVE, REGRET, DEPLORE, COMPLAINT

lamentable: . . . . SAD, WRETCHED, DEPLORABLE, DISTRESSING

laminated: . FLAKY, SCALED, LAYERED, SHEETED

lamp: . . . . . GAS, JET, BULB, DAVY, ETNA, LIGHT, TORCH, LANTERN

lampoon: . . . . . SKIT, SQUIB, SATIRE, RIDICULE, PASQUINADE, CARICATURE

lance: . . . . CUT, DART, HURL, SPEAR, LAUNCH, PIERCE, WEAPON, JAVELIN

lancer: . . . HUSSAR, U(H)LAN

lancers: . . . (SQUARE)DANCE, QUADRILLE

lancet: . . . . FLEAM, SCALPEL, (SURGICAL) KNIFE

land: . . SOIL, CATCH, EARTH, REALM, SHORE, TERRA, TRACT, ALIGHT, ARRIVE, DEBARK, ESTATE, GROUND, REGION, COUNTRY, TERRENE, TERRITORY

lane: . . . . WAY, PATH, AISLE, ALLEY, COURSE, BYWAY, STREET, PATHWAY, FOOTPATH, PASSAGEWAY

language: . . . ARGOT, IDIOM, LINGO, SLANG, JARGON, PIDGIN, TONGUE, SPEECH, DIALECT, DICTION, PARLANCE

artificial: . . . OD, RO, IDO, VOLAPUK, ESPERANTO

languid: . WAN, DULL, SLOW, WEAK, DREAMY, LISTLESS, DROOPING, SLUGGISH, LETHARGIC, LACKADAISICAL

languish: . . . DIE, FADE, FAIL, FLAG, LONG, PINE, WILT, DROOP, FAINT, SWOON, WASTE, DECLINE

languor: . . . . . KAIF, BLUES, ENNUI, BOREDOM, WEAKNESS, DULLNESS, HEAVINESS, LETHARGY, LASSITUDE, INDIFFERENCE

laniard, lanyard: . . . . CORD, ROPE, THONG

lank(y): . . LEAN, SLIM, TALL, THIN, GAUNT, SPARE, GANGLY, SLENDER, GANGLING, UNGAINLY

lanyard: . . . . see **laniard**

lap: . . . . FOLD, LICK, WRAP, CIRCLE, DRINK, ENFOLD, CIRCUIT

lapel: . . . . FOLD, FLAP, REVER(S), FACING

lapidary: . . . . ENGRAVER, JEWEL(L)ER, GEM-CUTTER

lapse: . . . . . ERR, FALL, SLIP, BREAK, ERROR, FAULT, EXPIRE, FAILURE, MISSTEP, RELAPSE, INTERVAL, BACKSLIDE

larceny: . . . THEFT, LOOTING, ROBBERY, STEALING, BURGLARY

large: . . . (also see **huge**) BIG, FREE, VAST, AMPLE, BROAD, BULKY, GIANT, GREAT, GOODLY, COPIOUS, LIBERAL, WEIGHTY, CAPACIOUS, EXTENSIVE, PLENTIFUL, CONSIDERABLE, COMPREHENSIVE

largess(e): . . . . GIFT(S), BOUNTY, CHARITY, PRESENT

lariat: . . ROPE, LASSO, NOOSE, RIATA, REATA

lark: . . . . . . FROLIC, PRANK, SPREE, SONGBIRD, ADVENTURE, CAROUSAL

larrup: . . BEAT, BLOW, FLOG, WHIP, THRASH

lascivious: . . LEWD, WANTON, LUSTFUL, LECHEROUS, SEDUCTIVE, LIBIDINOUS, LICENTIOUS

lash: . . . . . . TIE, BEAT, BIND, BLOW, FLOG, WALE, WHIP, QUIRT, SMITE, BERATE, FASTEN, REBUKE, STRIKE, STROKE, SWITCH, SCOURGE, CENSURE

lashing: . . . TYING, REBUKE, SCOLDING, WHIPPING

lass: . . . . . GAL, GIRL, MAID, MISS, TRULL, WOMAN, MAIDEN, COLLEEN, SWEETHEART

lassitude: . . . . . see **languor**

lasso: . . . . see **lariet**

last: . . . . . DURE, END, TAIL, ABIDE, FINAL, OMEGA, ENDURE, FINALE, LATEST, NEWEST, EXTREME, ENDMOST, HINDMOST, REARMOST, ULTIMATE, CONTINUE, CONCLUDING

lasting: . . . STABLE, CHRONIC, ETERNAL, DURABLE, CONSTANT, PERMANENT, STEADFAST

latch: . . HOOK, LOCK, CATCH, FASTEN(ING)

late: . . . . NEW, TARDY, DEAD, RECENT, FORMER, OVERDUE

latent: . . HIDDEN, DORMANT, CONCEALED, QUIESCENT, POTENTIAL, SUSPENDED, UNDEVELOPED

later: . . ANON, SOON, AFTER, NEWER, BEHIND, HEREAFTER, PRESENTLY, SUBSEQUENT(LY)

lateral: . . . . INDIRECT, SIDEWARD, SIDEWAYS, SIDEWISE

latest: . . . . see **last**

lath: . . . SLAT, SPALE, STAVE, SPLINT

lather: . . FOAM, SOAP, SUDS, FROTH, SWEAT, SPUME, FRENZY

Latin: . . . . ROMAN, ITALIAN, ROMANIC, SPANIARD, LANGUAGE

latitude: . . . . SCOPE, WIDTH, EXTENT, BREADTH, FREEDOM, DISTANCE

later: . . (also see **last**) FINAL, LATEST

lattice: . . . . GRILLE, TRELLIS, SCREEN, ESPALIER

laud: . . . . . . EXALT, EXTOL, PRAISE, ADULATE, APPLAUD, GLORIFY, EULOGIZE, COMPLIMENT

laudable: . . . . . EXEMPLARY, PRAISEWORTHY, COMMENDABLE

laugh: . . BRAY, HAHA, TEHEE, FLEER, SNORT, CACKLE, GIGGLE, HAWHAW, HEEHAW, NICKER, TITTER, GUFFAW, CHORTLE, CHUCKLE, SNICKER

laughable: . . . COMIC, DROLL, FUNNY, WITTY, ABSURD, AMUSING, RISABLE, HUMOROUS, BURLESQUE, FACETIOUS, LUDICROUS, RIDICULOUS

laurels: . . . . . . FAME, HONOR

lavalier(e): . . . . . . PENDANT

lavatory: . . . BASIN, LAVABO, RESTROOM, (WASH)BOWL

lave: . . . . . . DIP, BAIL, LADE, POUR, WASH, BATHE, RINSE

lavish: . . FREE, RANK, WILD, SPEND, WASTE, OPULENT, PROFUSE, LIBERAL, GENEROUS, PRODIGAL, RECKLESS, SPLENDID, SQUANDER, UNSPARING, UNSTINTED, EXTRAVAGANT, MAGNIFICENT

law: . . . . ACT, BAR, JUS, LEX, CODE, RULE, CANON, EDICT, CUSTOM, DECREE, COMMON, JUSTICE, STATUTE, ORDINANCE, REGULATION, PRINCIPLE, ENACTMENT, LEGISLATION

lawful: . . JUST, LEGAL, LICIT, VALID, LEGITIMATE

lawless: . . . UNRULY, ILLEGAL, ANARCHIC, DISSOLUTE, DISORDERLY

lawmaker: . . . . SOLON, SENATOR, LEGISLATOR

lawyer: . . . . JURIST, SHYSTER, ATTORNEY, BARRISTER, COUNSELOR, SOLICITOR, ADVOCATE, MOUTHPIECE

lax: . . . . . FREE, LIMP, SLOW, LOOSE, SLACK, TARDY, REMISS, LENIENT, CARELESS, NEGLIGENT

lay: . . . BET, PUT, SET, BURY, POEM, REST, SONG, DITTY, PLACE, STAKE, WAGER, BALLAD, HAZARD, IMPOSE, MELODY, SECULAR, DEPOSIT, ASCRIBE, RECLINE

layer: . . . . . PLY, COAT, FILM, FOLD, SEAM, TIER, VENEER, PATINA, LAMINA, THICKNESS, STRATUM, LAMINATE

layman: . . . . LAIC, AMATEUR

layout: . . . . . . PLAN, DESIGN, MAKE-UP, FORMAT, PATTERN, ARRANGEMENT

lazy: . . . IDLE, INERT, OTIOSE, INDOLENT, SLOTHFUL, SLUGGISH

leach: . . . . . . WET, MOISTEN, EXTRACT, LIXIVIATE, PERCOLATE

lead: . . CON, CUE, VAN, CLUE, HINT, HEAD, STAR, FIRST, GUIDE, PILOT, METAL, STEER, USHER, BULLET, CONVEY, GALENA, DIRECT, ESCORT, INDUCE, MANAGE, PROMPT, COMMAND, CONDUCT, PIONEER, PRECEDE, GRAPHITE, INFLUENCE

leaden: . . . . . . DULL, GRAY, HEAVY, GLOOMY, CLOUDY, SLUGGISH

leader: ... HEAD, LINE, WIRE, CHIEF, COACH, PILOT, SNELL, CAPTAIN, FOREMAN, HEADMAN, CHIEFTAIN, COMMANDER, PRINCIPAL, CONDUCTOR

leading: ..... DUCT, HEAD, MAIN, AHEAD, CHIEF, FIRST, CAPITAL, CENTRAL, PREMIER, STELLAR, PRINCIPAL, FOREMOST

leaf: ...... OLA, PAD, PAGE, BLADE, BRACT, FOLIO, FROND, PETAL, SEPAL, AEROLA, INSERT, LAMINA, SPATHE, TENDRIL

leaflet: ...... PINNA, TRACT, BOOKLET, FOLDER, HANDBILL, PINNULE, PAMPHLET

league: .. BLOC, BOND, BUND, UNION, COMPACT, ALLIANCE, COVENANT, COALITION, FEDERATION, ASSOCIATION, COMBINATION

leak: ..... DRIP, HOLE, LOSS, OOZE, SEEP, CRACK, ESCAPE, CREVICE, FISSURE

lean: .... BEND, BONY, CANT, LANK, POOR, RELY, SLIM, TEND, THIN, TILT, GAUNT, LANKY, SCANT, SLANT, SPARE, DEPEND, MEAGER, SKINNY, HAGGARD, INCLINE, SCRAWNY, SLENDER, DEFICIENT, EMACIATED

leaning: .. BENT, PENCHANT, INCLINATION

leap: ...... HOP, DIVE, JUMP, LOUP, SKIP, BOUND, CAPER, FRISK, LUNGE, VAULT, BOUNCE, BREACH, CAVORT, GAMBOL, HURDLE, HURTLE, SPRING, CAPRIOLE, ENTRECHAT

learn: ..... GET, FIND, HEAR, MASTER, ACQUIRE, REALIZE, UNEARTH, DISCOVER, MEMORIZE, ASCERTAIN

learned: .. READ, SAGE, WISE, ASTUTE, ERUDITE, LETTERED, EDUCATED, INFORMED, LITERATE, SCHOLARLY

man: .... SAGE, PEDANT, PUNDIT, SAVANT, MULLAH, SCHOLAR, TEACHER, PROFESSOR, INTELLECTUAL

learning: .... ART, LORE, WISDOM, CULTURE, PEDANTRY, EDUCATION, ERUDITION, KNOWLEDGE, DISCIPLINE, EXPERIENCE, SCHOLARSHIP

lease: ..... LET, HIRE, RENT, DEMISE, REMISE, ENGAGE, TENURE, CHARTER, CONTRACT

leash: ... BIND, CORD, CURB, JESS, REIN, ROPE, STRAP, THONG, COUPLE, TETHER, CONTROL

least: ..... FEWEST, LITTLE, LOWEST, MINIMAL, MINIMUM, SHORTEST, SMALLEST, SLIGHTEST

leather: ... TAN, TAW, RAND, WELT, STRAP, THONG, THRASH, TANNERY

kind of: .. ELK, KID, CALF, NAPA, ROAN, SEAL, MOCHA, SUEDE, LEVANT, OXHIDE, SKIVER, BUFFALO, COWHIDE, CHAMOIS, MOROCCO, CORDOVAN

leave: .. GO, LAM, LET, EXIT, QUIT, EXEAT, FAVOR, FORGO, SCRAM, DECAMP, DEPART, DESERT, ENTAIL, FOREGO, PERMIT, RETIRE, VACATE, VAMOSE, ABANDON, ENTRUST, FORSAKE, LIBERTY, LICENSE, BEQUEATH, EMIGRATE, FURLOUGH, VACATION, PERMISSION, RELINQUISH

leaves: .... PAGES, DEPARTS, FOLIAGE

leaving(s): .... (also see **rubbish**) CHAFF, DRAFF, DREGS, GROUT, OFFAL, WASTE, BOTTOM, REFUSE, GROUNDS, RESIDUE, REMNANTS, SEDIMENT, SETTLING, EXCREMENT

lecher: . GLUTTON, PARASITE, DEBAUCHEE, LIBERTINE

lecherous: . . . LEWD, RANDY, LUSTFUL, SENSUAL, SALACIOUS

lectern: . . . . . AMBO, DESK, PULPIT, STAND, ESCRITOIRE

lecture: . . . . LESSON, PREACH, SERMON, ADDRESS, HEARING, ORATION, DISCOURSE, SCOLD(ING), PRELECT(ION)

lecturer: . . DOCENT, READER, PRELECTOR, PROFESSOR

ledge: . . . LODE, SILL, BENCH, BERM(E), RIDGE, SHELF, RETABLE

lee: . . . . . HAVEN, SHELTER, PROTECTION

leech: . . . . . WORM, BLEED, ANNELID, PARASITE, BLACKMAIL, BLOODSUCKER

leer: . . . . . EYE, LOOK, LUST, OGLE, FLEER, MOCK, SCOFF, SMIRK, SNEER, STARE, GRIMACE

leery: . . . . WARY, DUBIOUS, DISTRUSTFUL, SUSPICIOUS

lees: . . see **leavings, rubbish**

leeway: . . SAG, ROOM, SPACE, ELBOWROOM

left: . . . . GONE, PORT, WENT, LARBOARD, DEPARTED

leftist: . . . . . . RED, LIBERAL, RADICAL, REVOLUNTIONARY

leftover: . . (also see **leavings, rubbish**) MORSEL, SCRAP

leg: . . GAM, PIN, HOOF, LIMB, PROP, GAMB(E), SHANK

legacy: . . . . . . GIFT, LEGATE, BEQUEST, WINDFALL, PATRIMONY, INHERITANCE

legal: . . (also see **law**) LICIT, VALID, LAWFUL, JURIDICAL, AUTHORIZED, LEGITIMATE

legalize: . . . SIGN, AUTHORIZE

legate: . . . . ENVOY, DEPUTY, LEGACY, NUNCIO, BEQUEATH, DELEGATE, MESSENGER, AMBASSADOR, REPRESENTATIVE

legatee: . . . . HEIR, INHERITOR

legend: . . LORE, MYTH, SAGA, TALE, FABLE, MOTTO, STORY, TITLE, CAPTION, FICTION, PROVERB, TRADITION, INSCRIPTION

legerdemain: . . . . . . MAGIC, DECEIT, TRICKS, CONJURING, HOCUS-POCUS

legging(s): . . . . SPAT, CHAPS, GAITER, PUTTIE, GAMBADO

legible: . . . . DISTINCT, READABLE, UNDERSTANDABLE, DECIPHERABLE

legion: . . . . . . ARMY, HOST, HORDE, MULTITUDE

legislate: . . . . . . ACT, ELECT, ENACT

legislation: . . . ACT, LAW(S), STATUTE

legislative body: . . . . . DAIL, DIET, RADA, HOUSE, JUNTA, SENATE, ALTHING, COUNCIL, CONGRESS, ASSEMBLY, REICHSTAG, PARLIAMENT

legislator: . . . . SOLON, ENACTOR, SENATOR, LAWMAKER, STATESMAN, CONGRESSMAN, REPRESENTATIVE

legitimate: . . . . . FAIR, JUST, REAL, TRUE, LEGAL, LICIT, VALID, COGENT, LAWFUL, GENUINE, ALLOWED, REASONABLE

legume: . . . PEA, POD, BEAN, SEED, SOYA, LENTIL, LOMENT, VEGETABLE

lei: . . . . FLOWERS, GARLAND, WREATH

leisure: . . . EASE, FREE, IDLE, TIME, SPARE, OTIOSE, FREEDOM, RELAXATION

leisurely: . . . . SLOW(LY), GRADUAL, UNHURRIED, DELIBERATELY

leman: . . . LOVER, MISTRESS, PARAMOUR, SWEETHEART

lend: . . . . LOAN, GRANT, AFFORD, IMPART, FURNISH, ADVANCE

length: . . . . PACE, TERM, DURATION, EXTENT, YARDAGE, DIMENSION

lengthen: . . . . EKE, EXPAND, EXTEND, AMPLIFY, DISTEND, PROLONG, STRETCH, ELONGATE, PROTRACT

lenient: . . . LAX, EASY, KIND, MILD, GENTLE, HUMANE, CLEMENT, MERCIFUL, TOLERANT, FORBEARING

lens: . . . . UNAR, TORIC, BIFOCAL, CONVEX, CONCAVE, MENISCUS, ANSTIGMAT

Lenten: . . . . PLAIN, MEAGER, SOMBER, MEATLESS, CHEERLESS

lentigo: . . . . FRECKLE

lentil: . . . . PEA, SEED, PLANT, LEGUME

leopard: . . . . . . CAT, OUNCE, OCELOT, CHEETAH, PANTHER

leprechaun: . . . . . ELF, FAIRY

leprose: . . . . SCALY, SCURFY

leprosy: . . . . LEPRA

lesion: . . CUT, SORE, ULCER, WOUND, INJURY, DAMAGE, FISSURE

less: . . FEWER, MINOR, MINUS, UNDER, SMALLER, INFERIOR

lessee: . . . . RENTER, TENANT, LEASEHOLDER

lessen: . . BATE, EASE, WANE, ABASE, ABATE, LOWER, PETER, TAPER, IMPAIR, REDUCE, SOFTEN, SHRINK, WEAKEN, MITIGATE, DIMINISH, DECREASE, DISPARAGE, MINIMIZE

lesser: . . . . MINOR, SMALLER

lesson: . . . . . . TASK, MORAL, EXAMPLE, PRECEPT, WARNING, EXERCISE, ASSIGNMENT, INSTRUCTION

let: . . . . . HIRE, RENT, ALLOW, LEASE, LEAVE, ASSIGN, HINDER, IMPEDE, PERMIT, SUFFER, ABANDON, PREVENT, OBSTACLE

letdown: . . . . SLUMP, ANTICLIMAX, RELAXATION, SLACKENING, DISAPPOINTMENT

lethal: . . . . . FATAL, DEADLY, MORTAL, POISONOUS

lethargic: . . . . DULL, HEAVY, INERT, DROWSY, SLEEPY, TORPID, COMATOSE, SLUGGISH, APATHETIC

lethargy: . . APATHY, INERTIA, STUPOR, TORPOR, LANGUOR, LASSITUDE, INERTNESS, DROWSINESS, INDIFFERENCE

letter: . . . . BULL, LINE, NOTE, MEMO, BREVE, BRIEF, VOWEL, BILLET, INITIAL, MESSAGE, EPISTLE, MISSIVE, INSCRIBE, CONSONANT, COMMUNICATION

lettered: . . . . LEARNED, EDUCATED, LITERATE, INSCRIBED

letterpress: . . . . TEXT

lettuce: . . . COS, BIBB, SALAD, BUTTER, MINION, ROMAINE, SIMPSON

letup: . . . . . PAUSE, RESPITE, LESSENING, ABATEMENT

levee: . . . . BANK, DIKE, PIER, QUAY, DURBAR, LANDING, RECEPTION, EMBANKMENT

level: . . . . . AIM, PAR, EVEN, FLAT, RASE, RAZE, TRUE, EQUAL, GRADE, PLANE, HEIGHT, DEMOLISH, SMOOTH, FLATTEN, UNIFORM, HORIZONTAL

lever: . . . . . BAR, LAM, PRY, CRANK, JIMMY, PEAVY, PEDAL, PRISE, SWIPE, TAPPET, CROWBAR, TREADLE

leviathan: . . . (also see **huge**) SHIP, TITAN, WHALE, MONSTER

levitate: . . RISE, SOAR, FLOAT

levity: . . . . . HUMOR, GAIETY, BUOYANCY, FRIVOLITY, SILLINESS, FOOLISHNESS

levy: . . . . . TAX, FINE, WAGE, EXACT, ASSESS, IMPOSE, IMPOST, COLLECT, ASSESSMENT, IMPOSITION

lewd: . . . . . . BASE, BAWDY, CARNAL, COARSE, LUSTFUL,

OBSCENE, SENSUAL, INDECENT, UNCHASTE, SALACIOUS, LASCIVIOUS, LIBIDINOUS, PORNOGRAPHIC

lexicographer: .... AUTHOR, WORDMAN, COMPILER, ONOMASTIC

lexicon: ...... WORDBOOK, DICTIONARY, THESAURUS, VOCABULARY

liability: ...... DEBT, DUTY, DEBIT, LOAN, BURDEN, HANDICAP, OBLIGATION, RESPONSIBILITY

liable: ... APT, OPEN, BOUND, LIKELY, SUBJECT, RESPONSIBLE, ANSWERABLE

liaison: ..... BOND, AMOUR, LINKING, MEETING, INTIMACY, INTRIGUE

liar: /...... CHEAT, FIBBER, DECEIVER, DISSEMBLER, FABRICATOR, PREVARICATOR

libel: ... BILL, MUD, MALIGN, DEFAME, VILIFY, CALUMNY, SCANDAL, SLANDER, ROORBACK

liberal: .. FREE, GOOD, OPEN, AMPLE, BROAD, FRANK, LEFTIST, PROFUSE, RADICAL, ECLECTIC, GENEROUS, ABUNDANT, BOUNTIFUL, EXPANSIVE, BENEVOLENT, MUNIFICENT, BROADMINDED, PROGRESSIVE

liberate: .. RID, FREE, CLEAR, LOOSE, REMIT, ACQUIT, REDEEM, RESCUE, RANSOM, RELEASE, MANUMIT, DISCHARGE, EXTRICATE, EMANCIPATE

libertine: ...... RAKE, ROUE, SKEPTIC, DISSOLUTE, LICENTIOUS, DEBAUCHEE

liberty: .. EASE, PLAY, LEAVE, RIGHT, FREEDOM, LICENSE, PRIVILEGE, EXEMPTION, FAMILIARITY, PERMISSION

libidinous: .. LEWD, LUSTFUL, LASCIVIOUS

library: .... MORGUE, BIBLIOTHECA

lice: .... see louse

license: .... TAX, EXEAT, LEAVE, PATENT, PERMIT, LIBERTY, FREEDOM, SANCTION, AUTHORITY, AUTHORIZE, FRANCHISE, PERMISSION

licentious: ...... LAX, FREE, LEWD, LOOSE, IMMORAL, OBSCENE, LIBERTINE, DISSOLUTE, LASCIVIOUS

lichen: ...... ALGA, MOSS, FUNGUS

licit: ..... DUE, JUST, LEGAL, LAWFUL, PERMITTED

lick: .. LAP, WIN, BEAT, WHIP, THRASH, CONQUER, OVERCOME, VANQUISH

lid: ... CAP, HAT, TOP, CURB, SHUTTER, RESTRAINT, COVER

lie: ... FIB, LAY, BASK, HIDE, LOLL, REST, TALE, EXIST, COVERT, REMAIN, REPOSE, DECEIVE, FALSIFY, RECLINE, UNTRUTH, PERJURE, SPRAWL, STRETCH, FABRICATE, FALSEHOOD, MENDACITY, PROSTRATE, EQUIVOCATE, PREVARICATE

lief: ... DEAR, FAIN, FREELY, GLADLY, VALUED, BELOVED, PLEASING, PRECIOUS, WILLING(LY)

liege: .... LORD, LOYAL, VASSAL, FAITHFUL, SUBJECT, DEVOTED, SOVERIGN

lien: ...... CLAIM, CHARGE, MORTGAGE, ENCUMBRANCE

lieu: .... PLACE, STEAD, INSTEAD

life: .... BLOOD, BIOSIS, BREATH, ENERGY, SPIRIT, VITALITY, VIVACITY, ANIMATION, BIOGRAPHY, EXISTENCE

lifeless: .. ARID, DEAD, DULL, FLAT, AMORT, INERT, VAPID,

INACTIVE, INANIMATE, TASTELESS

lift: . PRY, HEFT, HELP, JACK, PERK, REAR, BOOST, EXALT, HEAVE, HOIST, RAISE, STEAL, SWIPE, DERRICK, ELEVATE, ELEVATOR, PLAGIARIZE

ligature: .. TIE, BAND, BOND, TAENIA, THREAD, BANDAGE

light: .... GAY, AIRY, EASY, FAIR, FIRE, GLIM, LAMP, NEON, AGILE, BLOND, FILMY, FLAME, FLARE, KLIEG, TAPER, TORCH, BEACON, CANDLE, GENTLE, IGNITE, KINDLE, LIVELY, LUMINE, TRIVIAL, CHEERFUL, DELICATE, GOSSAMER, ILLUMINE, ILLUMINATION

lighten: .... EASE, FADE, ALLAY, CLEAR, ALIGHT, BLEACH, ILLUME, GLADDEN, RELIEVE, ALLEVIATE, ILLUMINATE

lighter: .. KEEL, SCOW, BARGE

lightheaded: .. DIZZY, GIDDY, FLIGHTY, DELIRIOUS, FRIVOLOUS, DISORDERED

lighthearted: ... GAY, GLAD, CAREFREE, CHEERFUL, VIVACIOUS

lightning: .... BOLT, LEVIN, FLASH, FIREBALL

like: .. AS, AKIN, COPY, LOVE, SAME, ALIKE, ENJOY, EQUAL, ADMIRE, PREFER, RELISH, COGNATE, SIMILAR, ANALOGOUS, RESEMBLING, SYNONOMOUS

likelihood: .... CHANCE, PROBABILITY

likely: .. APT, PRONE, LIABLE, SEEMLY, TENDING, CREDIBLE, FEISABLE, PROBABLE, SUITABLE, PROMISING

likeness: ..... COPY, FORM, ICON, TWIN, GUISE, IMAGE, EFFIGY, FIGURE, STATUE, ANALOGY, PICTURE, REPLICA, PARALLEL, PORTRAIT,

DUPLICATE, FACSIMILE, IMITATION, SEMBLANCE, PHOTOGRAPH, REPRODUCTION

likewise: ... AND, NOR, NOT, TOO, ALSO, DITTO, BESIDES, MOREOVER

liking: ...... LUST, FANCY, GUSTO, TASTE, PALATE, DELIGHT, AFFINITY, APPETITE, FONDNESS, PENCHANT, PLEASURE, AFFECTION, PREFERENCE

lilt: ...... SING, SONG, TUNE, SWING, RHYTHM, CADENCE

limb: . ARM, FIN, LEG, WING, BOUGH, BRANCH, MEMBER, FLIPPER, SUPPORT

limber: ... FLIP, LIMP, AGILE, LITHE, PLIANT, SUPPLE, LISSOM(E), FLEXIBLE, YIELDING

lime: .. CALX, COLOR, FRUIT, CEMENT, CITRUS, LINDEN

limit: ..... END, FIX, CURB, METE, PALE, SPAN, TERM, CHECK, FENCE, STINT, VERGE, BORDER, BOURN(E), CURFEW, DEFINE, EXTENT, FINISH, MARGIN, BARRIER, CLOSURE, CONFINE, EXTREME, BOUND(ARY), CONCLUDE, DEADLINE, RESTRAIN, RESTRICT, TERMINAL, DEMARCATION, CIRCUMSCRIBE

limited: ... FEW, LTD, LOCAL, SCANT, FINITE, NARROW, RESERVED, PAROCHIAL, RESTRICTED, CIRCUMSCRIBED

limitless: .... VAST, INFINITE, BOUNDLESS, UNBOUNDED

limn: . DRAW, DEPICT, PAINT, SKETCH, PORTRAY, DESCRIBE, DELINEATE

limp: .... LAX, HALT, SOFT, HITCH, LOOSE, FLABBY, FLIMSY, HOBBLE, LIMBER, WILTED, FLACCID, FLEXIBLE

limpid: ...... PURE, CLEAR, LUCID, BRIGHT, CRYSTAL, PELLUCID, TRANSPARENT

line: . . . . . . RAY, ROW, AXIS, CORD, DASH, FILE, MARK, RACE, RANK, REIN, ROPE, SEAM, WIRE, CURVE, QUEUE, ROUTE, SERIF, SWATH, TRADE, BORDER, CORDON, HAWSER, STREAK, STRING, STRIPE, SUTURE, VECTOR, BARRIER, RADIANT, SCRATCH, BOUNDRY, BUSINESS, OCCUPATION, DEMARCATION

lineage: . . . . . . RACE, STEM, BIRTH, BLOOD, CASTE, STOCK, TRIBE, FAMILY, DESCENT, STRAIN, ANCESTRY, PEDIGREE, GENEALOGY

lined: . . . RULED, STRIATE(D), CAREWORN, LINEOLATE

linen: . . CRASH, LAWN, TOILE, DAMASK, BATISTE, CAMBRIC, LINGERIE, STATIONERY

linger: . . . LAG, DRAG, STAY, WAIT, DALLY, DELAY, DWELL, HOVER, TARRY, DAWDLE, LOITER, REMAIN

lingerie: . . . . . . SLIP, LINEN, UNDIES, UNDERWEAR, UNDERTHINGS

lingo: . . . . CANT, ARGOT, JARGON, PATOIS, DIALECT, LANGUAGE, VERNACULAR

linguistics: . . . . . . SYNTAX, GRAMMAR, SEMANTICS, PHILOLOGY, MORPHOLOGY, PHONOLOGY

link: . . TIE, JOIN, LOOP, RING, NEXUS, CHAIN, TORCH, UNITE, ATTACH, COPULA, COUPLE, FASTEN, CONNECT(ION), CATENATE

linn: . . . . POOL, LINDEN, RAVINE, CASCADE, WATERFALL

lion: . . . . . . LEO, CAT, PUMA, STAR, IDOL, SIMBA, FELINE, COUGAR, PANTHER, CELEBRITY

lip: . . . RIM, BRIM, EDGE, KISS, BRINK, LABIA, LABIUM, MARGIN, LABELLUM, INSOLENCE, IMPERTINENCE

liparoid: . . . FATTY, FAT-LIKE

liquefy: . . FUSE, MELT, THAW, FUSILE, DISSOLVE

liquid: . . . . . FLUID, FLUENT, WATERY, BEVERAGE

liquidate: . . PAY, CASH, KILL, SETTLE, DISPOSE, AMORTIZE, DISCHARGE

lissom(e): . . . . AGILE, LITHE, LIMBER, SUPPLE, NIMBLE, SVELT

list: . . TIP, BILL, CANT, CAST, FILE, LEAN, ROLL, ROTA, TILT, BRIEF, INDEX, PANEL, SLATE, TABLE, CAREEN, DOCKET, ROSTER, INCLINE, MANIFEST, REGISTER, SCHEDULE, TABULATE, ITEMIZE, SELVAGE, INVENTORY, CATALOG(UE)

listen: . . . . EAR, HARK, HEAR, HEED, OBEY, AUDIT, ATTEND, HARK(EN), HEARKEN, OVERHEAR, EAVESDROP

listless: . . DULL, FAINT, INERT, ABJECT, DROWSY, LANGUID, HEEDLESS, SLUGGISH, APATHETIC, SPIRITLESS, LACKADASICAL

literal: . . BALD, DULL, REAL, EXACT, FACTUAL, PRECISE, PROSAIC, ACCURATE, VERBATIM

literary: . . VERSED, BOOKISH, ERUDITE, LETTERED, LEARNED, SCHOLARLY

literate: . . . READER, WRITER, LEARNED, EDUCATED, CULTURED, LETTERED

literature: . . . . LETTERS, WRITINGS

lithe: . . SLIM, AGILE, CLEVER, LIMBER, PLIANT, SVELTE, SUPPLE, LISSOM(E), SLENDER, FLEXIBLE

litigant: . . . . . SUER, SUITOR, DEFENDANT, COMPLAINANT

litigation: . . . SUIT, CONTEST, DISPUTE, LAWSUIT, CONTENTION, DISCUSSION

litter: . . . . . BED, HAY, BIER, MESS, COUCH, DOOLY, MULCH, STRAW, STREW, TRASH, YOUNG, REFUSE, RUBBISH, CLUTTER, SCATTER, DISORDER, OFFSPRING, STRETCHER

little: . . . . WEE, POCO, PUNY, TINY, BRIEF, CRUMB, SMALL, PALTRY, PETITE, TRIVIAL, YOUNG, MINUTE

littoral: . . . SHORE, COAST(AL)

liturgy: . . . . MASS, RITE, RITUAL, SERVICE

livable: . . . . BEARABLE, HABITABLE, ENDURABLE, TOLERABLE

live: . . . FARE, ROOM, ABIDE, DWELL, EXIST, VITAL, VIVID, ENDURE, RESIDE, ANIMATE, COHABIT, INHABIT, BREATHE, SUBSIST, CONTINUE, ENERGETIC, EXPERIENCE

liveliness: . . SPIRIT, VITALITY, VIVACITY

lively: . . . . GAY, FAST, KEEN, PERT, SPRY, AGILE, ALERT, BRISK, CANTY, FRESH, PEPPY, PERKY, VIVID, ACTIVE, BLITHE, BRIGHT, CHEERY, FRISKY, NIMBLE, SNAPPY, BUOYANT, SPIRITED, ANIMATED, SPRIGHTLY, VIVACIOUS

livery: . . . STABLE, UNIFORM, CLOTHING

livid: . . . . BLUE, BLEAK, DISCOLORED

living: . . KEEP, BEING, QUICK, VIVID, EXTANT, ANIMATE, LIVELIHOOD

llama: . . . . ALPACA, VICUNA, RUMINANT

load: . . . . CLOG, FILL, LADE, ONUS, PACK, STOW, CARGO, BURDEN, CHARGE, LADING, WEIGHT, SADDLE, FREIGHT, ENCUMBER

loaf: . . . . . CAKE, IDLE, LAZE, LOLL, BREAD, LOITER, LOUNGE, GOLDBRICK, DILLY-DALLY

loafer: . . . BUM, HOOD, SHOE, DRONE, HOOLIGAN, IDLER, LOUNGER

loam: . . . CLAY, DIRT, MARL, SILT, SOIL, EARTH, LOESS, REGUR

loan: . . LEND, PREST, TOUCH, ADVANCE, OBLIGATION

loath: . . . . . AVERSE, ODIOUS, HATEFUL, HOSTILE, UNWILLING, RELUCTANT

loathe: . . . . . . HATE, ABHOR, DETEST, ADVERSE, CONDEMN, DESPISE, DISLIKE, ABOMINATE

loathsome: . . . . FOUL, UGLY, VILE, CLOYING, HATEFUL, ABHORRENT, OFFENSIVE, DETESTABLE, DISGUSTING, REPULSIVE

lobby: . . . . . . HALL, FOYER, LOUNGE, ANTEROOM, VESTIBULE

lobbyist: . . . . PROMOTER, PROPAGANDIST

lobe: . . . . ALULA, EARLAP, LOBULE, LAPPET

local: . . . . BRANCH, BUCOLIC, CHAPTER, LIMITED, TOPICAL, REGIONAL, SPECIFIC, RESTRICTED

locality: . . AREA, SEAT, SITE, SPOT, LOCUS, PLACE, SITUS, REGION, LOCALE, HABITAT, DISTRICT, POSITION, NEIGHBORHOOD

locate: . . (also see **place**) SIT, ESPY, FIND, SEAT, SHOW, SITE, SPOT, STAND, TRACE, SETTLE, SITUATE, STATION, DISCOVER, ESTABLISH

loch: . . . . . BAY, LAKE, POND, POOL, LOUGH

lock: . . . . . JAM, BOLT, CURL, HANK, HASP, LINK, TRESS, COTTER, FASTEN, CONFINE, COWLICK, RINGLET

lockup: . . . . see **jail**

loco: . . . . see **crazy**

locus: . . . . see **locality**

locust: . . . . . . TREE, INSECT, ACACIA, CICADA, CICALA

lodge: . . . . . . (also see **hotel, house**) CLUB, BILLET, BOARD, HOGAN, DWELL, ENCAMP, DEPOSIT, QUARTER, CHAPTER, WIGWAM, BROTHERHOOD

loess: . . . . LOAM, SILT

loft: . . . BIN, ATTIC, GARRET, GALLERY

lofty: . . . . AERY, HIGH, TALL, AERIE, GRAND, NOBLE, PROUD, EMINENT, SUBLIME, ARROGANT, HAUGHTY, MAJESTIC, ELEVATED

log: . WOOD, DIARY, RECORD, TIMBER, BILLET, JOURNAL

loge: . . . . BOX, ROOM, BOOTH, STALL, COMPARTMENT

logic: . . . . REASONING

logical: . . . . . . SANE, SOUND, VALID, COHERENT, RATIONAL, CONSISTENT, REASONABLE

logistics: . . . . SUPPLY, MOVEMENT, QUARTERS, TRANSPORTATION

logy: . . . . DULL, HEAVY, DROWSY, SLUGGISH

loiter: . . . . . LAG, IDLE, LOAF, DALLY, DELAY, TARRY, LOUNGE, LINGER, DAWDLE, SAUNTER

loll: . . . LAZE, HANG, DROOP, TARRY, DANGLE, LOUNGE, SPRAWL, RECLINE

lone: . . . SOLE, SOLO, ALONE, APART, SINGLE, RETIRED, SOLITARY, ISOLATED

loneliness: . . . . . . SOLITUDE, DEJECTION, ISOLATION, DEPRESSION, DESOLATION

lonely: . . . . . . LORN, APART, DISMAL, DREARY, FORLORN, DESERTED, DESOLATE, SECLUDED, SOLITARY, ISOLATED, UNFREQUENTED

long: . . . . FAR, ACHE, HOPE, PINE, SLOW, CRAVE, YEARN, ASPIRE, HANKER, HUNGER, PROLIX, THIRST, LENGTHY, EXTENDED, ELONGATED, PROLONGED, PROTRACTED

look: . . CON, EYE, PRY, SEE, GAPE, GAZE, LEER, MIEN, OGLE, PEEK, PEEP, PEER, PORE, SCAN, SEEK, SEEM, SKEW, FLEER, GLARE, GLIME, LOWER, SIGHT, SNOOP, STARE, ASPECT, BEHOLD, GANDER, GLANCE, GLOWER, REGARD, SEARCH, SQUINT, VISAGE, OBSERVE, DEMEANOR, APPEARANCE

lookout: . . . . GUARD, ESPIER, CONNER, SPOTTER, WATCHER, OBSERVER, WATCHTOWER

loom: . . HULK, LOON, WEAVE, APPEAR, EMERGE, MACHINE, IMPLEMENT

loony: . . . . see **crazy**

loop: . . EYE, LAP, TAB, COIL, KINK, KNOT, RING, BIGHT, BRIDE, NOOSE, PICOT, TERRY, CIRCLE, CIRCUIT, EYE(LET), GROMMET

loophole: . . . . . . OUT, MUSE, MEUSE, ESCAPE, EYELET, OPENING, APERATURE, WEAKNESS

loose: . . . . LAX, FREE, LEWD, OPEN, UNITE, BAGGY, RELAX, SLACK, VAGUE, RANDOM, UNBIND, WOBBLY, IMMORAL, MOVABLE, RELEASE, UNBOUND, INEXACT, INSECURE, DISSOLUTE, UNATTACHED, UNFASTENED

loosen: . . . . PRY, EASE, FREE, UNDO, RELAX, UNTIE, RELEASE, SLACKEN, LIBERATE, UNFASTEN

loot: . . . . . ROB, RIFLE, SACK, SWAG, BOOTY, STRIP, PILFER, RAVAGE, SPOILS, DESPOIL, PILLAGE, PLUNDER, RANSACK

lop: . . BOB, CUT, CHOP, CLIP, HANG, SHED, SNIP, TRIM, DROOP, PRUNE, SLIDE, DANGLE, PENDANT

lopsided: . . . . . . ALOP, ALIST, ASKEW, UNEVEN, CROOKED, UNBALANCED

loquacious: . . . . GABBY, VERBAL, PRATING, VOLUBLE, GARRULOUS, TALKATIVE

lord: . . . . AGHA, EARL, PEER, RULE, TSAR, BARON, LEIGE, RULER, MASTER, PRINCE, BISHOP, MARQUIS, DOMINEER, GOVERNOR, NOBLEMAN, SEIGNOR, SEIGNEUR, VISCOUNT

lordly: . . . . . NOBLE, PROUD, ARROGANT, DESPOTIC, HAUGHTY, IMPERIOUS, MASTERFUL, TYRANNICAL, DICTATORIAL, DOMINEERING, OVERBEARING

lore: . . . . . ADVICE, WISDOM, COUNSEL, ERUDITION, LEARNING, KNOWLEDGE, TRADITION, INSTRUCTION

lorn: . . . . . BEREFT, FORLORN, FORSAKEN, DESOLATE, LONESOME, ABANDONED

lose: . . . . FAIL, MISS, WASTE, DEFEAT, MISLAY, MISPLACE, FORFEIT, SQUANDER, DISSIPATE

loss: . . . . . COST, LEAK, RUIN, TOLL, PRICE, WASTE, DAMAGE, DEFEAT, EXPENSE, FAILURE, DECREASE, DECREMENT, FORFEITURE, DEPRIVATION

lost: . . . GONE, LORN, ABSENT, HIDDEN, RUINED, WASTED, FORLORN, MISLAID, MISSING, STRAYED, ABSORBED, CONFUSED, DEFEATED, ENGROSSED, ABANDONED, FORFEITED, BEWILDERED

lot: . . . . . DOOM, FATE, LAND, LUCK, MUCH, PLAT, PLOT, RAFT, SCAD, SLUE, BATCH, FIELD, GRIST, GROUP, BUNCH, SHARE, AMOUNT, BUNDLE, CHANCE, PARCEL, DESTINY, FORTUNE, PORTION, CABOODLE, ALLOTMENT

loth: . . HATE, ABHOR, DETEST

lotion: . . . . . . BALM, WASH, COLOGNE, OINTMENT, ABLATION, LINAMENT, FRESHENER

lots: . . . GOBS, SCADS, MUCH, PLENTY, PILE

lottery: . . . . . GAME, CHANCE, RAFFLE, DRAWING, SWEEPSTAKE

lotto: . . KENO, BINGO, KEENO

loud: . . . . . . GAUDY, NOISY, SHOWY, VIVID, COARSE, FLASHY, VULGAR, BLATANT, RAUCOUS, VEHEMENT, CLAMOROUS, INSISTENT, TURBULENT, UNREFINED

lough: . . . SEA, LAKE, LOCH, POOL, WATER

lounge: . . . LAZE, IDLE, LOAF, LOLL, SOFA, LOBBY, COUCH, DIVAN, RELAX, LOITER, SETTEE

louse, lice: . . . . NIT, APHID, COOTIE, SLATER, INSECT, PARASITE

lousy: . . . BAD, POOR, DIRTY, DISGUSTING, INFERIOR, PEDICULAR, PEDICULOUS

lout: . . . . . OAF, BOOR, CLOD, DOLT, FOOL, GAWK, HULK, CLOWN, YOKEL, LUBBER, BUMPKIN

louver: . . . . . SLAT, TURRET, WINDOW, TRANSOM

love: . . . . . WOO, DEAR, DOTE, LIKE, ADORE, ALOHA, AMOUR, FANCY, ENAMOUR, IDOLIZE, ROMANCE, FONDNESS, ADORATION, AFFECTION, SWEETHEART, ATTACHMENT

lover: . . . . BEAU, FLAME, LEHMAN, ROMEO, SPARK, SWAIN, BONAMI, ADMIRER, DON JUAN, GALLANT, LOTHARIO, PARAMOUR, SWEETHEART, PHILANDERER

loving: . . . . . FOND, DOTING, EROTIC, AMATIVE, AMATORY, AMOROUS, DEVOTED, AFFECTIONATE

low: . . . . . MOO, BASE, BLUE, DEEP, MEAN, POOR, VILE, WEAK, DIRTY, GROSS, SNIDE, COARSE, COMMON, FEEBLE, HUMBLE, MENIAL, SCURVY, SLIGHT, SORDID, VULGAR, IGNOBLE, SHALLOW, DEJECTED, DEPRESSED

lowbred: . . . CRUDE, COARSE, VULGAR, ILL-MANNERED

lower: . . . . . DIP, DROP, LOUR, SINK, VAIL, ABASE, ABATE, BELOW, DEBASE, DEMIT, FROWN, GLARE, SCOWL, UNDER, BEMEAN, DEBASE, DEMOTE, DEEPEN, DEMEAN, GLOWER, HUMBLE, LESSEN, NETHER, REDUCE, BENEATH, DEGRADE, DEPRESS, SUBSIDE, DIMINISH, INFERIOR, DISPARAGE, DEPRECIATE, WEAKEN

lowest: . . . . . . LAST, LEAST, NAIDIR, BOTTOM, BEDROCK, MEANEST, NETHERMOST

lowly: . . . BASE, MEAN, MEEK, HUMBLE, MODEST, IGNOBLE, UNPRETENTIOUS

loyal: . . . . FIRM, LEAL, TRUE, STANCH, DEVOTED, STAUNCH, CONSTANT, FAITHFUL

loyalty: . . . FEALTY, FIDELITY, HOMAGE, ALLEGIANCE

lozenge: . . . . . PILL, CANDY, JUJUBE, PASTIL, TABLET, TROCHE, DIAMOND, PASTILLE

lubricous: . . . LEWD, TRICKY, WANTON, ELUSIVE, SLIPPERY, UNSTABLE, LASCIVIOUS

lucent: . . . . . CLEAR, LUCID, BRIGHT, SHINING

lucid: . . . . SANE, CLEAR, BRIGHT, LUCENT, CRYSTAL, SHINING, RATIONAL, TRANSPARENT

lucidity: . . SANITY, CLARITY, CLEARNESS, TRANSPARENCY

luck: . . . . . HAP, LOT, FATE, CHANCE, FORTUNE, SUCCESS, FORTUITY, MISCHANCE

lucky: . . CANNY, FORTUNATE, PROPITIOUS, PROVIDENTIAL

lucrative: . . . . PAYING, GAINFUL, BENEFICIAL, PRODUCTIVE, PROFITABLE, REMUNERATIVE

lucre: . . . . GAIN, LOOT, PELF, PROFIT, MONEY, RICHES, WEALTH

ludicrous: . . . COMIC, FUNNY, ABSURD, COMICAL, FOOLISH, RISIBLE, FARCICAL, LAUGHABLE, RIDICULOUS

lug: . . . . TOW, DRAG, DRAW, HAUL, PULL, TOTE, WORM, CARRY

lugubrious: . . . SAD, DISMAL, DOLEFUL, MOURNFUL

lukewarm: . . . . TEPID, INDIFFERENT

lull: . . . CALM, HUSH, ALLAY, QUIET, SLACK, STILL, PACIFY, RESPITE, SOOTHE, COMPOSE, MITIGATE, TRANQUILIZE

luminary: . . . . . . SUN, STAR, MOON, LIGHT, ILLUMINATION, INTELLECTUAL

luminous: . . . CLEAR, LUCID, BRIGHT, SHINING, BRILLANT

lummox: . . . . . LOUT, DUNCE, LUBBER, BUMPKIN, BUNGLER, LUNKHEAD, DUMBBELL

lump: . . . . . BAT, GOB, NUB, WAD, BLOB, BURL, CAKE, CLOT, HUNK, KNOB, KNOT, MASS, NODE, BULGE, CLUMP, HUNCH, WEDGE, DOLLOP, GOBBET, NODULE, NUBBIN, NUGGET

lunacy: . . . . see **mania**

lunge: . . . . . JAB, FOIN, LEAP, STAG, LURCH, PITCH, PLUNGE, THRUST

luny: . . . . . (also see **crazy**) LOONY

lupine: . . . FIERCE, WOLFLIKE

lurch: . . . REEL, ROLL, SWAY, CHEAT, LUNGE, PITCH, TRICK, CAREEN, SWERVE, STUMBLE

lure: . . . . BAIT, DRAW, TRAP, DECOY, TEMPT, ALLURE, ENTICE, INDUCE, SEDUCE, ATTRACT, BEGUILE, INVEIGLE

lurid: . . GAUDY, LIVID, VIVID, GARISH, GHASTLY, GLOWING, HIDEOUS, GRUESOME, SHOCKING, STARTLING, SENSATIONAL

lurk: . . HIDE, PROWL, SKULK, SNEAK, SLINK, AMBUSH

luscious: . . . . RICH, RIPE, SWEET, TASTY, CREAMY, CLOYING, DELICIOUS, VOLUPTUOUS

lush: . . . SOFT, DRUNK, JUICY, ALCHOHOLIC, SUCCULENT, LUXURIANT

lust: . . . . DESIRE, LIKING, PASSION, APPETITE

luster: . NAIF, GLAZE, GLOSS, SHEEN, SHINE, POLISH, RADIANCE, SCHILLER, SPLENDOR, BRILLIANCE, DISTINCTION

lusterless: . . . . . . MAT, WAN, DEAD, DRAB, DULL, FADED, TARNISHED

lustrous: . . . . . NITID, SILKY, GLOSSY, SHINING, RADIANT, NACREOUS, BRILLIANT

lusty: . . . . ROBUST, STURDY, STRONG, VIGOROUS

luxuriant: . . . . . LUSH, RANK, RICH, LAVISH, FERTILE, OPULENT, PROFUSE, PROLIFIC

luxuriate: . . . . BASK, REVEL, WALLOW

luxurious: . . . . . POSH, RICH, GAUDY, PLUSH, COSTLY, ELEGANT, OPULENT, GORGEOUS, SUMPTUOUS, EXTRAVAGANT

lycee: . . . . . SCHOOL, LYCEUM

lye: . . . . . POTASH, CAUSTIC, LIXIVIUM

lying: . . FLAT, AWAIT, PRONE, SUPINE, COUCHANT, DECUMBENT, DISHONEST, PROSTRATE, RECLINING, RECUMBENT, MENDACIOUS

lynch: . . . . . HANG, MURDER, EXECUTE

lynx: . . . . BOBCAT, WILDCAT, CARACAL, CARCAJOU, CATAMOUNT

lyre: . . . ASOR, HARP, TRIGON, CITHARA

lyric: . . . . ODE, ALBA, LIED, ODIC, POEM, EPODE, MELIC, POETIC, RONDEL, SONNET, CANZONE

M

M: *Greek:* . . . . MU

macabre: . . . . . GRIM, EERIE, LURID, GHASTLY, GRUESOME, HORRIBLE, DEATHLIKE

macadam: . . . . . TAR, ROAD, STONES, ASPHALT, PAVEMENT

macaque: . . RHESUS, MONKEY

mace: . . . . ROD, CLUB, MAUL, SPICE, STAFF, STICK, MALLET, SCEPTRE

macerate: . . . . . . RET, SOAK, STEEP, SOFTEN

machete: . . . . . . BOLO, KNIFE

Machiavellian: . . . . . . WILY, CRAFTY, CUNNING, DECEITFUL, TREACHEROUS

machination: . . . PLAN, PLOT, CABAL, DESIGN, SCHEME, ARTIFICE, INTRIGUE, CONSPIRACY

machine: . . . . . CAR, AUTO, TOOL, MOTOR, ROBOT, DEVICE, ENGINE, GADGET, APPARATUS, APPLIANCE, AUTOMATIC, AUTOMATION, MECHANISM, AUTOMOBILE, CONTRIVANCE, MACHINATION, ORGANIZATION

macrocosm: . . . . . . WORLD, UNIVERSE

maculate: ... STAIN, DEFILE, BLOTCH, IMPURE, SPECKLE, BESMIRCH

macule: .. BLUR, BLOT, SPOT, STAIN, BLOTCH, BLEMISH

mad: . SORE, ANGRY, CRAZY, IRATE, RABID, VEXED, INSANE, ENRAGED, FURIOUS, FRANTIC, FRENZIED, FRENETIC, DEMENTED, INCENSED, MANIACAL, FANATICAL, PHRENETIC, PSYCHOTIC, INFURIATED

madam: ..... MME., MRS., LADY, DONNA, SENORA, WOMAN, MILADY, MISTRESS, MADONNA, COURTESAN

madcap: ...... RASH, WILD, IMPULSIVE, RECKLESS, HOTSPUR

made: .... INVENTED, PRODUCED, FABRICATED, CONSTRUCTED, MANUFACTURED

mademoiselle: ..... MLLE., GIRL, MISS, LADY, WOMAN

madman: . LUNATIC, MANIAC

madness: .. IRE, FURY, RAGE, FOLLY, MANIA, BEDLAM, FRENZY, LUNACY, RABIES, DELIRIUM, DEMENTIA, INSANITY, DERANGEMENT

madrigal: ...... ODE, GLEE, POEM, SONG, LYRIC, VERSES

maelstrom: ... EDDY, SWIRL, TURMOIL, WHIRLPOOL

maestro: .... MASTER, TEACHER, CONDUCTOR, COMPOSER

magazine: .... DEPOT, CHAMBER, JOURNAL, STOREHOUSE, WAREHOUSE, PERIODICAL, PUBLICATION

magenta: ... FUCHSIA, DYE, RED

maggot: ..... GRUB, LARVA, WHIM, GENTLE, NOTION, CAPRICE

magic: .. ART, RUNE, OBEAH, SPELL, VOODOO, GRAMMARY, SORCERY, DECEPTION, WIZARDRY, THEURGY, WITCHCRAFT, CONJURATION

magician: .... MAGE, MAGI, MAGUS, MERLIN, SHAMAN, WIZARD, HOUDINI, CONJURER, MANDRAKE, SORCERER, ARCHIMAGE, CHARLATAN

magisterial: .. LOFTY, PROUD, AUGUST, LORDLY, HAUGHTY, POMPOUS, STATELY, ARROGANT, DIGNIFIED, IMPERIOUS

magistrate: ... DOGE, JUDGE, JUSTICE, SYNDIC, ACALADE, BALIFF, BURGESS, PRAETOR

magnanimous: ...... FREE, NOBLE, LIBERAL, GENEROUS, HONORABLE, UNSELFISH

magnate: .. MOGUL, BIGWIG, TYCOON, MILLIONAIRE

magnet: ...... LOADSTONE, LODESTONE

magnetic: .... POLAR, MESMERIC, ELECTRIC, ATTRACTIVE

magnific: .... VAST, GRAND, POMPOUS, SUBLIME, IMPOSING

magnificence: ...... STATE, POMP, GLORY, GRANDEUR, SPLENDOR

magnificent: .. RICH, GRAND, GREAT, NOBLE, REGAL, LAVISH, STATELY, SUBLIME, GLORIOUS, GORGEOUS, PALATIAL, SUMPTUOUS, MUNIFICENT

magnify: .. EXALT, ENLARGE, ENHANCE, GLORIFY, INCREASE, AGGRAVATE, OVERSTATE, EXAGGERATE

magnitude: .... BULK, MASS, SIZE, EXTENT, BIGNESS, DIMENSION, GREATNESS

magnum: .... BOTTLE

magus: .... MAGI, SORCERER, MAGICIAN, ASTROLOGER

Mahomet: .... MOHAMMED, PROPHET

mahout: .... DRIVER, KEEPER

maid: . . . . GIRL, HELP, LASS, BONNE, FILLE, DAMSEL, MAIDEN, SLAVEY, VIRGIN, COLLEN, SERVANT, DOMESTIC

maiden: . . . DEB, NEW, GIRL, JILL, LASS, FIRST, FRESH, NYMPH, DAMSEL, VIRGIN, COLLEEN, DEBUTANTE, UNMARRIED, GUILLOTINE

maidenly: . . GENTLE, MODEST

mail: . . . . BAG, POST, SEND, SHIP, ARMOR, LETTERS, DISPATCH

maim: . . . . . . HURT, LAME, MANGLE, CRIPPLE, DISABLE, MUTILATE

main: . . . . SEA, DUCT, HIGH, PIPE, CHIEF, FIRST, OCEAN, CAPITAL, CONDUIT, LEADING, PURPOSE, FOREMOST, PRINCIPAL

maintain: . . . . AVOW, FEND, HOLD, KEEP, ARGUE, CLAIM, AFFIRM, ALLEGE, ASSERT, AVOUCH, DEFEND, RETAIN, UPHOLD, CONTEND, DECLARE, SUPPORT, SUSTAIN, PRESERVE, CONTINUE

maintenance: . . . . . . UPKEEP, SUPPORT, ALIMONY, LIVELIHOOD

majestic: . . . . . EPIC, GRAND, LOFTY, NOBLE, REGAL, ROYAL, AUGUST, KINGLY, STATELY, ELEVATED, IMPERIAL, DIGNIFIED, SOVERIGN, MAGNIFICENT

major: . . . . . . MAIN, CHIEF, CAPITAL, GREATER, OFFICER, PRINCIPAL, SPECIALIZE

majority: . . . . . AGE, BULK, BODY, MORE, MOST, QUORUM, GREATER, ADULTHOOD, SENIORITY, PLURALITY

make: . . . COIN, FORM, BUILD, FORCE, FRAME, SHAPE, STYLE, COMPEL, CREATE, DEVISE, INVENT, RENDER, COMPOSE, FASHION, PREPARE, PRODUCE, CONSTRUCT, FABRICATE, MANUFACTURE

believe: . . . . ACT, SHAM, FEIGN, MAGIC, FICTION, PRETEND, PRETENSE

known: . . IMPART, REVEAL, DIVULGE, PUBLISH, UNCOVER, DISCLOSE, DISCOVER, PROCLAIM, ADVERTIZE, PUBLICIZE

makeshift: . . RUDE, STOPGAP, TEMPORARY, EXPEDIENT, PROVISIONAL

maladroit: . . . . . . CLUMSY, AWKWARD, BUNGLING, INEXPERT

malady: . . (also see **disease**) AILMENT, ILLNESS, DISORDER, SICKNESS, COMPLAINT, AFFLICTION

malaise: . . . . . . DISCOMFORT

malapert: . . . . BOLD, SAUCY, ILL-BRED, IMPUDENT

malapropos: . . INOPPORTUNE, INAPPROPRIATE

malaria: . . . . . AGUE, CHILL, FEVER, MIASMA

malarkey: . . . . . . DRIVEL, NONSENSE, BALONEY

malcontent: . . . . . . REB(EL), UNEASY, AGITATOR, DISCONTENT, DISSIDENT, REBELLIOUS

male: . . . . . HE, MAN, GENT, MANLY, VIRILE, MANNISH, MASCULINE

animal: . . . . . . RAM, TOM, BOAR, BUCK, BULL, LOCK, HART, JACK, STAG, STUD, DRONE, STALLION

malediction: . . . BAN, CURSE, MALISON, SLANDER, ANATHEMA, BLASPHEMY, DAMNATION, IMPRECATION

malefactor: . . . . FELON, CONVICT, CULPRIT, CRIMINAL, EVILDOER, OFFENDER, WRONGDOER

malefic: . . . . EVIL, HARMFUL

malevolence: . . . HATE, SPITE, ENMITY, MALICE, RANCOR, ILL-WILL, ANIMOSITY, HOSTILITY

malevolent: . . EVIL, HATEFUL, HOSTILE, SPITEFUL, VICIOUS, RANCOROUS, MALICIOUS

malfeasance: . . . . . . CRIME, WRONG, TRESPASS, MISCONDUCT, WRONGDOING

malice: . . ENVY, PIQUE, SPITE, VENOM, ENMITY, GRUDGE, ILL-WILL, RANCOR, ANIMOSITY, MALEVOLENCE

malicious: . . . . EVIL, CATTY, NASTY, BITTER, HEINOUS, VICIOUS, SPITEFUL, MALIGNANT, RANCOROUS, RESENTFUL, VINDICTIVE

malign: . . . . . ABUSE, CURSE, LIBEL, DEFAME, ASPERSE, VILIFY, REVILE, BLACKEN, TRADUCE, SLANDER

malignant: . . EVIL, WICKED, HATEFUL, HEINOUS, NOXIOUS, VICIOUS, HARMFUL, VIRULENT, CANCEROUS, INVIDIOUS

malinger: . . . . SHIRK, SKULK

malison: . . . . CURSE, MALEDICTION

mall: . . . . LANE, WALK, AVENUE, ALLEE, ALLEY, PROMENADE

malleable: . . . SOFT, PLIABLE, DUCTILE, TENSILE, AMENABLE

mallet: . . . TUP, CLUB, MACE, MALL, MAUL, GAVEL, MADGE, BEETLE, PESTLE, HAMMER

malm: . . . . . . LOAM, MARL, LIMESTONE

malodorous: . . RANK, FETID, PUTRID, SMELLY, STINKING, ODIFEROUS

malt: . . . . . BARLEY, LIQUOR

liquor: . . . . . . ALE, BEER, LAGER, STOUT, PORTER

maltreat: . . ABUSE, DEMEAN, MISUSE

mammal: . (also see **animal**) BEAST, OVINE, SWINE, BOVINE, EQUINE, FELINE, MONKEY, RODENT, PRIMATE, EDENTATE, RUMINANT, UNGULANT, CARNIVORE, MARSUPIAL

mammock: . . . TEAR, BREAK, SCRAP, SHRED, MANGLE, FRAGMENT

mammoth: . . . . HUGE, ELEPHANT, MASTADON, ENORMOUS, GIGANTIC

man: . . . . . . (also see **male, fellow, person**) GUY, CHAP, HERO, HOMO, BIPED, BLOKE, HOMME, HUMAN, GUARD, STAFF, HOMBRE, MENSCH, COUNTER, FORTIFY, HUSBAND, LABORER, MANKIND, OPERATE, SERVANT, CREATURE, HOMO SAPIENS

manacle: . . . . . . BOND, CUFF, IRON, CHAIN, FETTER, HAMPER, CONFINE, SHACKLE, HANDCUFF, RESTRAINT

manage: . . . MAN, RUN, BOSS, HEAD, LEAD, RULE, TEND, GUIDE, ORDER, STEER, WIELD, DIRECT, GOVERN, CONDUCT, CONTROL, EXECUTE, HUSBAND, OPERATE, OVERSEE, CONTRIVE, SUPERVISE, ADMINISTER

manageable: . . TAME, RULY, DOCILE, GENTLE, WIELDY, DUCTILE, PLIABLE, FLEXIBLE, WORKABLE, COMPLIANT, TRACTABLE, GOVERNABLE

manager: . . GERENT, SYNDIC, CAPTAIN, CURATOR, FOREMAN, STEWARD, OPERATOR, IMPRESARIO, ENTREPRENEUR

mandamus: . . . WRIT, ORDER

mandarin: . . . . COAT, DUCK, ORANGE, CHINESE, TANGERINE

mandate: . . . . WRIT, ORDER, CHARGE, DECREE, DEMAND, BIDDING, COMMAND, PRECEPT, DIRECTION, COMMISSION, INJUNCTION

mandatory: . . . . IMPERATIVE, OBLIGATORY

mandible: . . . . . . JAW, BEAK
mandrel: . . . . . . AXLE, BALL,
PICK, ARBOR, LATHE, SPINDLE
mane: . . . HAIR, JUBA, CREST,
BRUSH
maneuver: . . PLOY, DEPLOY,
TRICK, JOCKEY, TACTIC,
ARTIFICE, CONTRIVE, ENGINEER,
STRATAGEM, MANIPULATE
manger: . . . BIN, CRIB, RACK,
STALL, TROUGH
mangle: . . CUT, MAR, HACK,
MAIM, GARBLE, IRONER,
SMOOTH, CALENDER,
MUTILATE, DISFIGURE,
LACERATE
mangy: . . . . . . MEAN, SCALY,
SEEDY, SCURVY, SHABBY,
SORDID, SQUALID, SCABBY,
SCABROUS
manhandle: . . . . MAUL
mania: . . . . . CRAZE, FUROR,
FRENZY, MADDNESS, PASSION,
DELIRIUM, OBSESSION,
DERANGEMENT
maniac: . . MADMAN, LUNATIC
maniacal: . . . MAD, CRAZED,
INSANE, RAVING, DEMENTED,
DERANGED, PSYCHOTIC,
HYSTERICAL
manifest: . . . . . LIST, OPEN,
SHOW, ARGUE, CLEAR, INDEX,
OVERT, ATTEST, EVINCE, PLAIN,
PATENT, REVEAL, CONFESS,
DECLARE, DISPLAY, EVIDENT,
WAYBILL, EXPLAIN, EXPRESS,
INVOICE, OBVIOUS, SIGNIFY,
VISIBLE, APPARENT, DISCLOSE,
INDICATE
manifesto: . . . . EDICT,
EVIDENCE, STATEMENT,
DECLARATION, PROCLAMATION
manifold: . . . . . . MULTIPLE,
DIFFERENT, MULTIFOLD,
MULTIPLEX, REPLICATE,
MULTIFARIOUS
manikin: . . . DWARF, MODEL,
PYGMY, PHANTOM, MANNEQUIN

manipulate: . . . . . . RIG, USE,
WORK, TREAT, WIELD, HANDLE,
JUGGLE, MANAGE, CONTROL,
OPERATE, MANEUVER
mankind: . . . (also see **man**)
HUMANS, PEOPLE, HUMANITY
manlike: . . . . MASCULINE
manly: . . . . . . BOLD, BRAVE,
NOBLE, DARING, VIRILE,
RESOLUTE, MASCULINE,
COURAGEOUS
manna: . . FOOD, SUSTENANCE
mannequin: . . . . see **manikin**
manner: . . . AIR, WAY, FORM,
MEIN, MODE, SORT, GUISE,
HABIT, TRICK, ASPECT,
METHOD, BEARING, FASHION,
BEHAVIOR, ATTITUDE,
TECHNIQUE, DEPORTMENT
mannerism: . . . MODE, POSE,
TRAIT, BEARING, AFFECTATION,
PECULIARITY
manners: . . . . MORES,
CONDUCT, COURTESY,
BEHAVIOR, AMENITIES,
ETIQUETTE
manor: . . . . . ABODE, HOUSE,
ESTATE, MANSION, DEMESNE
manse: . . . . RECTORY,
PARSONAGE
manslaughter: . . . . MURDER,
KILLING, SLAYING, BUTCHERY,
HOMICIDE
mansuetude: . . . . KINDNESS,
TAMENESS, GENTLENESS
manta: . . RAY, WRAP, CLOAK,
SHAWL, BLANKET, BULWARK,
SHELTER, MANTELET, DEVILFISH
mantel: . . . . . . ARCH, BEAM,
SHELF, LEDGE, LINTEL
mantilla: . . . . . . CAPE, VEIL,
SCARF, CLOAK
mantle: . . CAPE, COAT, HOOD,
ROBE, CLOAK, COVER, FROCK,
PALLIUM, ENVELOPE, MANTILLA
manual: . . . . . . HANDBOOK,
GUIDEBOOK, TEXTBOOK,
CATECHISM

manufacture: ...... MAKE, FORGE, INVENT, CONCOCT, CONFECT, PRODUCE, FABRICATE

manumission: ... FREEDOM, RELEASE, LIBERATION, DELIVERANCE, EMANCIPATION

manure: ..... DUNG, MUCK, ORDURE, GUANO, FERTILIZER

many: ... RAFF, LOTS, LOADS, DIVERS, MYRIAD, SCORES, DIVERSE, SEVERAL, VARIOUS, NUMEROUS, MANIFOLD, DIFFERENT, MULTITUDE, MULTIFARIOUS, INNUMERABLE

map: ... CARD, PLAN, PLAT, CARTE, CHARD, CHART, GRAPH, IMAGE, DESIGN, SKETCH, SURVEY, DIAGRAM, OUTLINE, PICTURE, DELINEATE, CARTOGRAPH

mar: ... BLOT, SCAR, BOTCH, SPOIL, DAMAGE, DEFACE, DEFORM, IMPAIR, INJURE, MANGLE, BLEMISH, DISFIGURE

maranatha: .... CURSE

marasca: .... CHERRY, MARASCHINO

marasmus: .... WASTE, EMACIATION

maraud: ...... LOOT, RAID, FORAY, PLUNDER, PILLAGE

march: ... FILE, HIKE, TREK, WALK, TROOP, BORDER, DEFILE, PARADE, BOUNDRY, FRONTIER, PROGRESS, CAVALCADE, BORDERLAND, PROCESSION

Mardi Gras: .... CARNIVAL, FESTIVAL

marge: .... MARGIN

margin: .... HEM, LIP, RIM, BANK, BRIM, EDGE, RAND, SIDE, BRINK, SHORE, VERGE, BORDER, FRINGE, LEEWAY, MARGENT

marijuana: .. HAY, POT, TEA, HEMP, WEED, GRASS, REEFER, NARCOTIC, HASHEESH

marina: ..... DOCK, BASIN, HARBOR, ESPLANADE

marine: ...... TAR, FLEET, NAVAL, WATER, ACQUATIC, OCEANIC, PELAGIC, NAUTICAL, MARITIME, LEATHERNECK

mariner: ... COB, TAR, SALT, SAILOR, SEAMAN

marionette: ... DOLL, PUPPET

marital: ...... CONNUBIAL, MATRIMONIAL

mark: .... DOT, GOAL, LINE, NOTE, SCAR, SIGN, BADGE, BRAND, GRADE, LABEL, SCORE, STAMP, STAIN, TOKEN, WATCH, ACCENT, DENOTE, TARGET, BLEMISH, IMPRINT, INSIGNIA, VESTIGE, SYMBOL, INDICATION

marked: ... FATED, DISTINCT, OBVIOUS, EMINENT, NOTICEABLE, CONSPICUOUS

marker: . PEG, BUOY, CAIRN, ARROW, SCORER, PYLON, SIGNAL, PICKET, BRANDER, COUNTER, RECORDER, MONUMENT, GRAVESTONE, MILESTONE

market: .. MART, SALE, SELL, SHOP, PLAZA, STORE, BAZAAR, RIALTO, EXCHANGE, EMPORIUM

marksman: ... SHOT, SNIPER, SHARPSHOOTER

marl: .. CLAY, MALM, EARTH, MANURE

marlinspike: .... FID

marmalade: .... JAM, PRESERVE, CONFECTION

maroon: ... ENSILE, STRAND, ISOLATE, REDDISH, PURPLISH

marquee: ... TENT, CANOPY, AWNING, SHELTER

marquetry: .. INLAY, MOSAIC, PARQUETRY

marriage: ... MATCH, SPLICE, WEDLOCK, WEDDING, NUPTIALS, MATRIMONY

married: .... WEDDED, CONJUGAL, CONNUBIAL

marrow: .... PITH, ESSENCE, INMOST, MEDULLA

marry: ... WED, JOIN, MATE, WIVE, YOKE, HITCH, UNITE, COUPLE, ESPOUSE

marsh: .... BOG, FEN, MIRE, QUAG, SLEW, SLUE, OOZE, FLASH, SWALE, SWAMP, MORASS, MUSKEG, SALINA, SLOUGH, WETLAND, QUAGMIRE, EVERGLADE

marshal: ..... LEAD, ALIGN, ARRAY, GROOM, GUIDE, USHER, DIRECT, PARADE, ARRANGE, ASSEMBLE, OFFICER, OFFICIAL

marshy: ..... WET, FENNY, BOGGY, CALLOW, PALUDINE, PALUDAL, PALUDIC

martial: .... WARLIKE, MILITARY, SOLDIERLY

martyr: ... SAINT, SUFFERER

marvel: ... ADMIRE, WONDER, MIRACLE, ASTONISH, PRODIGY

marvelous: ..... SPLENDID, WONDEROUS, EXCELLENT, INCREDIBLE, MIRACULOUS

masculine: .. MALE, MANLY, STRONG, VIRILE, MANNISH

mash: ... PAP, MESS, CREAM, CRUSH, FLIRT, SMASH, MUDDLE, MIXTURE, TROUBLE

mask: .... HIDE, VEIL, LOUP, CLOAK, COVER, GUISE, VISOR, MASQUE, SCREEN, DISGUISE, CONCEAL, CAMOUFLAGE

mass: .... GOB, WAD, BLOB, BODY, BULK, CLOT, HEAP, LUMP, MUSH, SIZE, BATCH, BOLUS, GROSS, GROUP, STORE, GATHER, GOBBET, PRAYER, SERVICE, LITURGY, ASSEMBLE, AGGREGATE, MAGNITUDE, ACCUMULATE

massacre: .... POGROM, CARNAGE, BUTCHERY, SLAUGHTER

massage: ..... RUB, KNEAD, SHAMPOO, RUBDOWN

massive: .... BIG, HUGE, BULKY, GROSS, HEAVY, LARGE, SOLID, HULKING, WEIGHTY, IMPOSING, PONDEROUS

mast: ..... CUE, SPAR, POLE, STICK, (CHEST)NUTS, BEECHNUTS

master: .... DOM, GET, MAN, BOSS, LORD, MAIN, RULE, SIRE, CHIEF, SAHIB, TUTOR, BRIDLE, DEFEAT, EXPERT, GOVERN, HUMBLE, SUBDUE, CAPTAIN, CONQUER, CONTROL, MAESTRO, PADRONE, EFFENDI, OVERCOME, REGULATE, SURMOUNT, VANQUISH, COMMANDER, EMPLOYER

mastery: ...... GRIP, SWAY, SKILL, CONTROL, VICTORY, CONQUEST, FACILITY, INFLUENCE

masticate: .... CHAW, CHEW, GRIND, CRUSH, GNASH, CRUNCH, MANDUCATE

mastodon: .... GIANT, ELEPHANT, MAMMOTH

mat: ... COT, PAD, RUG, FELT, SHAG, DOILY, SNARL, CARPET, TANGLE, CUSHION, INTERWEAVE

matador: .... BULLFIGHTER, TOREADOR

match: ..... FIT, PIT, BOUT, EVEN, MATE, PAIR, PEER, SPAR, SUIT, TEAM, EQUAL, MARRY, RIVAL, TALLY, VESTA, SPOUSE, COMPARE, CONTEST, LUCIFER, VESUVIAN, PARALLEL, MARRIAGE, CORRESPOND, COUNTERPART

matchless: .. ALONE, UNLIKE, PEERLESS, UNEQUALED, INIMITABLE, INCOMPARABLE

mate: . CAP, PAL, WED, FERE, JOIN, PAIR, PEER, WIFE, BUDDY, MARRY, MATCH, COUPLE, FELLOW, SPOUSE, COMRADE, HUSBAND, PARTNER, COMPANION

material: .... (also see **cloth, fabric, substance**) DATA, GEAR, GOODS, STUFF, BODILY,

CARNAL, MATTER, SENSUAL,
WORLDLY, PHYSICAL,
TANGIBLE, SUBSTANCE,
PERTINENT, ESSENTIAL,
CORPOREAL, NONSPIRITUAL

maternal: . . . . . . MOTHERLY

mathematical: . . . . . EXACT,
PRECISE, ACCURATE

mathematics: . . . . . ALGEBRA,
GEODESY, CALCULUS,
GEOMETRY, LOGARITHM,
ARITHMETIC, TRIGONOMETRY

matinee: . . . . LEVEE, PARTY,
SOIREE, RECEPTION,
PERFORMANCE

matriculate: . . . . . . ENTER,
ENROL(L), REGISTER

matrimonial: . . . . . NUPTIAL,
MARITAL, SPOUSAL, CONJUGAL,
CONNUBIAL

matrix: . . . . DIE, MAT, CAST,
FORM, MOLD, WOMB, GANGUE,
PATTERN

matron: . . . . . . DAME, WIFE,
WIDOW, HOUSEKEEPER

matter: . . . PUS, GEAR, MASS,
PITH, SOLID, TOPIC, AFFAIR,
CONTENT, CONCERN, PROBLEM,
TROUBLE, BUSINESS, QUESTION,
MATERIAL, SUBSTANCE

mattock: . . . AX(E), PICK(AX),
TWIBIL(L)

mature: . . . AGE, OLD, AGED,
GROW, RIPE, ADULT, GROWN,
RIPEN, ACCRUE, MELLOW,
SEASON, DEVELOP(ED),
FULL-GROWN

maudlin: . . . . BEERY, CORNY,
MUSHY, TIPSY, TEARFUL,
WEEPING, LACHRYMOSE,
SENTIMENTAL

maul: . . . . PAW, BEAT, CLUB,
MACE, MALL, ABUSE, GAVEL,
BEETLE, BRUISE, HAMMER,
MALLET, MANGLE, CLOBBER

maumet: . . GOD, IDOL, DOLL,
IMAGE, PUPPET

maverick: . . . . . CALF, WAIF,
DOGIE

maw: . CRAW, CROP, GULLET,
THROAT, STOMACH

mawkish: . . . . VAPID,
SICKENING, DISGUSTING,
NAUSEATING, SENTIMENTAL

maxilla: . . . . JAW(BONE)

maxim: . . SAW, RULE, ADAGE,
AXIOM, GNOME, MORAL,
MOTTO, SAYING, TRUISM,
PRECEPT, PROVERB, APHORISM,
DOCTRINE, PRINCIPLE

maximum: . . . . MOST, PEAK,
LIMIT, EXTREME, HIGHEST,
LARGEST, GREATEST

may: . . CAN, MIGHT, SHALL,
POSSIBLE

maybe: . . PERHAPS, POSSIBLY,
PERCHANCE, POSSIBILITY,
UNCERTAINTY

maze: . . . . . . DAZE, AMAZE,
CONFUSE, STUPEFY, BEWILDER,
CONFOUND, LABYRINTH

mazer: . . CUP, BOWL, GOBLET

meadow: . . . . . . LEA, MEAD,
FIELD, PASTURE, GRASSLAND

meager: . ARID, BARE, LANK,
LEAN, POOR, SLIM, THIN,
GAUNT, SCANT, SPARE,
BARREN, JEJUNE, NARROW,
SCANTY, SCARCE, SPARSE,
TENUOUS, SPARING,
INADEQUATE, EMACIATED

meal: . . . CHOW, FARE, FEED,
FOOD, MASH, MESS, FARINA,
FEAST, FLOUR, GRIST, LUNCH,
SNACK, DINNER, REPAST,
SUPPER, BANQUET, POTLUCK,
BREAKFAST, COLLATION

mean: . . . . LOW, BASE, LEAN,
NORM, POOR, NASTY, PETTY,
CRUEL, SNIDE, SORRY, ABJECT,
COMMON, DENOTE, HUMBLE,
INTEND, MEDIUM, MIDDLE,
PALTRY, SORDID, AVERAGE,
CAITIFF, IGNOBLE, PITIFUL,
PURPORT, PURPOSE, MISERLY,
SIGNIFY, VICIOUS, PENURIOUS

meander: .... ROAM, TURN, WIND, AMBLE, RAMBLE, WANDER

meaning: ... SENSE, IMPORT, INTENT, SPIRIT, BEARING, PURPORT, PURPOSE, INTENTION, DESIGNATION, SIGNIFICANCE

means: ... WAY, COST, TOOL, AGENT, AGENCY, METHOD, RICHES, WEALTH, AVERAGES, RESOURCES, INSTRUMENT, WHEREWITHAL

meantime: .... INTERIM, INTERVAL, WHILST

measure: ... LAW, ROD, FOOT, GAGE, INCH, METE, MILE, RULE, SPAN, STEP, TAPE, TIME, YARD, CLOCK, GAUGE, GIRTH, LITER, METER, RULER, SCALE, DEGREE, BUSHEL, APPRAISE, CALIPER, STATUTE, CALCULATE, CRITERION, STANDARD

meat: .... HAM, BEEF, CHOP, GIST, LAMB, PORK, VEAL, BACON, FLESH, STEAK, TRIPE, MUTTON, SAUSAGE, VENISON, HAMBURGER

meatus: ..... DUCT, CANAL, OPENING, PASSAGE, FORAMEN

mechanic: .... ARTISAN, WORKMAN, OPERATOR, ARTIFICER, CRAFTSMAN, REPAIRMAN, OPERATIVE

mechanical: .... AUTOMATIC, INVOLUNTARY, PERFUNCTORY, SPONTANEOUS, STEREOTYPED

medal: ...... DISK, BADGE, PLAQUE, DECORATION, MEDALLION

meddle: . PRY, NOSE, SNOOP, DABBLE, FINGER, MONKEY, TAMPER, INTRUDE, INTERFERE, INTERVENE, INTERLOPE

media: .. (also see **medium**) PRESS, RADIO, MAGAZINES, NEWSPAPERS, PERIODICALS, TELEVISION

medial: ... MIDDLE, AVERAGE, ORDINARY

median: .... MEAN, MEDIAL, AVERAGE, MIDDLE, CENTRAL

mediate: .... REFEREE, ARBITRATE, INTERCEDE, INTERPOSE, INTERVENE, CONCILIATE

mediator: .... ARBITER, REFEREE, GO-BETWEEN, INTERCESSOR, ARBITRATOR, INTERMEDIARY

medic: ... CLOVER, DOCTOR, INTERN, RESIDENT, CORPSMAN, SURGEON, PHYSICIAN

medicinal: .. IATRIC, CURING, HEALING, CURATIVE, SALUTARY, RELIVING

medicine: .... DRUG, TONIC, PHYSIC, REMEDY

mediocre: .... MEAN, SOSO, COMMON, MEDIUM, AVERAGE, INFERIOR, ORDINARY, MIDDLING, INDIFFERENT

meditate: .... MULL, MUSE, PORE, BROOD, STUDY, THINK, WEIGH, PONDER, REFLECT, REASON, COGITATE CONSIDER, DELIBERATE, CONTEMPLATE, RUMINATE

mediterranean: .... INLAND, MIDLAND, LANDLOCKED

medium: ... MEDIA, MEAN(S), MIDST, ORGAN, DEGREE, MEDIAL, AVERAGE, CHANNEL, PSYCHIC, MEDIATOR, INSTRUMENT, ENVIRONMENT

medley: .... OLIO, JUMBLE, FARRAGO, MELANGE, MIXTURE, MINGLING, POTPOURRI, HODGEPODGE

medulla: .... PITH, MARROW, ESSENCE, SUMMARY

meed: .... GIFT, BRIBE, REWARD, RECOMPENSE

meek: .... MILD, LOWLY, DOCILE, GENTLE, PACIFIC, MODERATE, YIELDING, SPINELESS, LAMBLIKE, SUBMISSIVE

meet: ... FIT, SIT, FACE, JOIN, EQUAL, OCCUR, MATCH, TOUCH, TRYST, BATTLE, COMBAT, CONFER, GATHER, PROPER, SEEMLY, CONTACT, CONVENE, FITTING, FULFILL, ASSEMBLE, CONFRONT, SUITABLE, INTERSECT, CONGREGATE, RENDEZVOUS

meeting: .. BEE, DATE, TRYST, RALLY, UNION, CAUCUS, HUDDLE, SESSION, ADJACENT, ASSEMBLY, CONCLAVE, CONGRESS, JUNCTION, CONFERENCE, SYMPOSIUM, RENDEZVOUS, CONVOCATION

melancholia: ...... GLOOM, ATHYMIA, DEPRESSION

melancholy: .... SAD, BLUE, DULL, GLUM, DREAR, DISMAL, SOMBER, SORROW, GLOOMY, DOLEFUL, PENSIVE, SADNESS, UNHAPPY, DOWNCAST, DEJECTION, DEPRESSION, DISCONSOLATE

melange: ...... see **medley**

meld: .. UNITE, BLEND, MERGE

melee: ... ROW, FRAY, RIOT, BRAWL, FIGHT, MIX-UP, AFFRAY, FRACAS, HASSLE, RUMBLE, RUCKUS, SCUFFLE, SKIRMISH, FREE-FOR-ALL

mellow: ... AGED, RICH, RIPE, SOFT, RIPEN, TIPSY, MATURE, RENDER

melodious: .... ARIOSE, DULCET, LYRICAL, MUSICAL, TUNEFUL, CANOROUS, HARMONIOUS

melodramatic: ... DRAMATIC, EMOTIONAL, HISTRIONIC, SENSATIONAL

melody: ... AIR, LAY, ARIA, SONG, TUNE, MUSIC, THEME, STRAIN, ARIETTA, HARMONY

melon: .... MUSK, PEPO, GOURD, WATER, CASABA, PAPAYA, PERSIAN, HONEYDEW, CANTALOUP(E)

melt: .... RUN, FLOW, FLUX, FUSE, THAW, SMELT, RENDER, SOFTEN, VANISH, DWINDLE, LIQUEFY, DISSOLVE

member: ... ARM, LEG, LIMB, PART, ORGAN, FELLOW, SECTION, DISTRICT, AFFILIATE

memento: ... RELIC, TOKEN, TROPHY, KEEPSAKE, REMINDER, REMEMBRANCE

memoir: .. RECORD, REPORT, HISTORY MEMORIAL, BIOGRAPHY, MONOGRAPH, NARRATIVE, REMINISCENCE

memorabilia: .... ANA

memorable: ...... NOTABLE, SPECIAL, REMARKABLE, EXTRAORDINARY

memorandum: .. . BILL, CHIT, NOTE, STUB, BRIEF, AGENDA, MINUTES, TICKLER, NOTATION, REMINDER

memorial: ... RELIC, MEMOIR, RECORD, SHRINE, STATUE, TROPHY, MONUMENT, RECOLLECTION, COMMEMORATIVE

memory: ...... MIND, ROTE, RETENTION, REMINISCENCE, REMEMBRANCE, RECOLLECTION, RETROSPECTION

menace: .. PERIL, DENOUNCE, JEOPARDY, THREAT(EN), FULMINATE

menage: .... CLUB, SOCIETY, DOMICILE, HOUSEHOLD, HOUSEKEEPING

mend: ..... FIX, SEW, DARN, HEAL, HELP, KNIT, AMEND, PATCH, BETTER, COBBLE, REPAIR, IMPROVE, RESTORE, AMELIORATE, CONVALESCE

mendacity: ..... LIE, LYING DECEIT, UNTRUTH, FALSEHOOD

medicant: .... MONK, FAKIR, BEGGAR

menial: ..... BASE, SORDID, VARLET, SERVILE, SERVANT,

DOMESTIC, DEGRADING,
UNDERLING

mental: . . . . PHRENIC,
INTELLECTUAL, INTELLIGENT

mentality: . . . . MIND, SENSE,
ACUMEN, REASON, ATTITUDE,
INTELLECT, DISPOSITION,
RATIONALITY, INTELLIGENCE

mention: . . CITE, HINT, NAME,
REFER, SPEAK, ALLUDE,
RECORD, SPECIFY, ALLUSION,
CITATION, STATEMENT,
REFERENCE

mentor: . . . COACH, ADVISER,
TEACHER, MONITOR,
COUNSELOR

mephitic: . . . FOUL, DEADLY,
NOXIOUS, POISONOUS

mephitis: . . . . ODER, SMELL,
STENCH, MIASMA

mercantile: . . . . . . TRADING,
COMMERCIAL

mercenary: . . HIRED, VENAL,
GREEDY, SORDID, COVETOUS,
HIRELING

merchandise: . . . . . WARE(S),
GOODS, COMMODITIES

merchant: . . . . COSTER,
DEALER, SELLER, SUTLER,
TRADER, VENDER, PURVEYOR,
TRADESMAN, SHOPKEEPER,
STOREKEEPER

merciful: . . BENIGN, SPARING,
BENIGNANT, FORGIVING,
CHARITABLE

merciless: . . . . GRIM, CRUEL,
SAVAGE, PITILESS, HEARTLESS,
RELENTLOUS

mercurial: . . . SWIFT, CLEVER,
LIVELY, SHREWD, FICKLE,
CHANGING, VOLATILE,
INCONSTANT

mercy: . . . . . . PITY, GRACE,
LENITY, CHARITY, QUARTER,
HUMANITY, CLEMENCY,
KINDNESS, LENIENCY,
TOLERANCE, COMPASSION,
FORGIVENESS

mere: . . . . SEA, BARE, LAKE,
ONLY, POOL, POND, PURE,
SOLE, BOUND, LIMIT, SHEER,
ENTIRE, SIMPLE, ABSOLUTE,
BOUNDARY

merely: . . . ALSO, JUST, ONLY,
QUITE, PURELY, SIMPLY

merge: . . . . MIX, FUSE, JOIN,
MELD, MELT, UNITE, BLEND,
ABSORB, MINGLE, COMBINE,
COALESCE, AMALGAMATE

meridian: . . . . APEX, NOON,
ZENITH, MIDDAY, CULMINATION

merit: . . EARN, MEED, VALUE,
WORTH, DESERT, REWARD,
DESERVE, EXCELLENCE

merriment: . . . . . FUN, GLEE,
MIRTH, GAIETY, FROLIC,
AMUSEMENT, DIVERSION

merry: . . . GAY, AIRY, GLAD,
JOLLY, HAPPY, BLITHE, JOCOSE,
FESTIVE, JOVIAL, JOYOUS,
CHEERFUL, MIRTHFUL,
HILARIOUS

mesa: . . . . . BUTTE, PLATEAU,
TABLELAND

mescal: . . . . AGAVE, CACTUS,
LIQUOR, PEYOTE

mesh: . . . . NET, WEB, SNARE,
TISSUE, TANGLE, ENGAGE,
NETTING, NETWORK,
ENTANGLE, INTERLOCK

mesmeric: . . . . . . MAGNETIC,
HYPNOTIC

mesne: . . . . MIDDLE,
INTERVENING, INTERMEDIATE

mess: . . . ROW, CHOW, FOOD,
HASH, MEAL, MUSS, BATCH,
BOTCH, DIRTY, BUNGLE,
DABBLE, JUMBLE, LITTER,
MEDDLE, MUDDLE, RUMPLE,
PUTTER, CRUMPLE, MIXTURE,
DISARRAY, DISORDER,
HODGEPODGE

message: . . . . . . LINE, MEMO,
NEWS, NOTE, WIRE, WORD,
CABLE, BREVET, LETTER,
REPORT, MISSIVE, MEMORANDA,
COMMUNICATION

messenger: . . . PAGE, ENVOY, HERALD, LEGATE, NUNCIO, APOSTLE, COURIER, PROPHET, HARBINGER, AMBASSADOR
of the gods: . . . MERCURY, HERMES

messy: . . . . . DIRTY, UNTIDY

metal: . . . . ORE, TIN, GOLD, IRON, LEAD, ZINC, COBALT, COPPER, PEWTER, RADIUM, SILVER, LITHIUM, BULLION, MERCURY, POTASSIUM, URANIUM, ALUMINUM
alloy: . . . . . BRASS, STEEL, BRONZE

metamorphose: . . . CHANGE, MUTATE, TRANSFORM, TRANSMUTE

metamorphosis: . . . CHANGE, MUTATION, METASTASIS, TRANSFORMATION

metaphor: . . . TROPE, SIMILE, ALLEGORY, COMPARISON

metaphorical: . . FIGURATIVE

metaphysical: . . . . . SUBTLE, ABSTRACT, ABSTRUSE

metastasis: . . . METABOLISM, TRANSFORMATION

mete: . . . DOLE, GIVE, ALLOT, AWARD, BOUND, LIMIT, MEASURE, ALLOCATE, APPORTION, BOUNDARY, DISTRIBUTE

meteoric: . . SWIFT, DAZZLING

meteor: . . . . . BOLIS, COMET, FIREBALL

meteorite: . . . . . . AEROLITH, AEROLITE, SIDERITE

meter: . . BEAT, TIME, VERSE, RHYTHM, CADENCE, MEASURE(R)

methane: . . . . . . PARAFFIN, HYDROCARBON

method: . . . . . . WAY, FORM, MODE, RULE, MEANS, STYLE, USAGE, COURSE, MANNER, SYSTEM, FASHION, FORMULA, PROCESS, PROCEDURE, TECHNIQUE

methodical: . . . . EXACT, FORMAL, SEVERE, PRECISE, ORDERLY, SYSTEMATIC

meticulous: . . . . NEAT, PRIM, FUSSY, CAREFUL, FINICAL, FASTIDIOUS, SCRUPULOUS

metier: . . . . LINE, FORTE, TRADE, CALLING, BUSINESS, SPECIALTY, OCCUPATION, PROFESSION

metropolis: . . . . . SEE, CITY, SEAT, CENTER, CAPITAL

metropolitan: . . . . . . CHIEF, URBAN, BISHOPS, LEADING, PRINCIPAL

mettle: . . . . . . FIRE, ARDOR, NERVE, PLUCK, SPUNK, GINGER, SPIRIT, BRAVERY, COURAGE, FORTITUDE

mew: . . . . DEN, BARN, CAGE, COOP, GULL, MOLT, SHED, CHANGE, GARAGE, STABLE, CONCEAL, CONFINE, ENCLOSE, ENCLOSURE
cat's: . . . . . MEOW, MIAU, MIAOW

mewl: . . . CRY, MEW, WHINE, SQUALL, WHIMPER

mezzanine: . . . . STORY, BALCONY, ENTRESOL

miasma: . . . . METHANE, MALARIA

mica: . . TALE, GLIST, BIOTITE, NACRITE, SILICATE, MINERAL, ISINGLASS, MUSCOVITE, LEPIDOLITE

mickle: . . . . . . MUCH, GREAT

microbe: . . . . . GERM, VIRUS, BACILLUS, ORGANISM, BACTERIUM

microcosm: . . . . WORLD, VILLAGE, UNIVERSE, COMMUNITY

microorganism(s): . . . GERM, VIRUS, AMOEBA, AEROBIA, PROTOZOA, BACTERIA, SPIROCHETE

microscopic: . . . . . . SMALL, MINUTE

microspores: . . . . . . POLLEN

middle: . . . . HUB, MID, MEAN, MESNE, MIDST, WAIST, CENTER, MEDIAN, MEDIAL, MESIAL, AVERAGE, CENTRAL

middleman: . . . . AGENT, BROKER, DEALER, TRADER, RETAILER, GO-BETWEEN, INTERMEDIARY

midge: . . FLY, GNAT, MIDGET, INSECT, BANTAM, DWARF, PUNKIE

midget: . . . . . MIDGE, DWARF, SMALL, MINIATURE

midshipman: . . . . PLEBE, CADET, REEFER, MIDDY

midst: . . . . see **medium**, **middle**

mien: . . . AIR, LOOK, ASPECT, MANNER, BEARING, CONDUCT, ATTITUDE, BEHAVIOR, CARRIAGE, DEMEANOR, APPEARANCE

might: . . . . . FORCE, POWER, VIGOR, ABILITY, STRENGTH

mighty: . . . BIG, HUGE, VAST, VERY, GREAT, POTENT, STRONG, ENORMOUS, FORCEFUL, POWERFUL, PUISSANT, VIGOROUS, EXTREMELY

mignon: . . . SMALL, DAINTY, PETITE, DELICATE

migrate: . . . . . FLEE, MOVE, TREK, COLONIZE, TRANSFER

migration: . . EXODUS, FLIGHT

migratory: . . . . ROVING, NOMADIC, WANDERING, PEREGRINE

mild: . . . CALM, EASY, MEEK, SOFT, TAME, BLAND, GENTLE, PLACID, CLEMENT, LENIENT, TEMPERATE, MODERATE

mildew: . . . . . MOLD, RUST, BLIGHT, FUNGUS

milestone: . . . STELE, EVENT, MARKER, PILLAR, LANDMARK

milieu: . . . . AMBIENCE, ENVIRON(MENT), SURROUNDINGS

militant: . . . . MARTIAL, SOLDIER, WARLIKE, FIGHTING, COMBATIVE, AGGRESSIVE

military: . . . (also see **army**) MARTIAL, SOLDIERS

milk: . . . LAC, SUCK, BLEED, DRAIN, NURSE, ELICIT, KUMISS, KOUMIS(S), SUCKLE, EXTRACT, LACTOSE

mill: . . CRUSH, GRIND, SHAPE, FINISH, POWDER, THRASH, FACTORY, MACHINE, TRANSFORM

millennium: . . . . . . UTOPIA, PARADISE

millstone: . . . . BURDEN, GRINDER, ALBATROSS, AFFLICTION

mime: . . . APE, COPY, CLOWN, FARCE, MIMIC, JESTER, BUFFOON, IMITATE

mimesis: . . . . MIMICRY, IMITATION

mimic: . . MIME, COPY, MOCK, PARROT, COPYING, IMITATE, IMITATIVE, SIMULATE(D)

minaret: . . . . . LAMP, TOWER

minatory: . . . . . . MENACING

mince: . . . . CUT, DICE, CHOP, HASH, SUBDIVIDE

mind: . . . CARE, HEED, MOOD, OBEY, TEND, WILL, BRAIN, WATCH, MEMORY, PSYCHE, REASON, REGARD, OPINION, PURPOSE, INTELLECT, MENTALITY, REMEMBRANCE, INTELLIGENCE, RECOLLECTION

mindful: . . AWARE, CAREFUL, HEEDFUL, ATTENTIVE

mine: . . DIG, PIT, SAP, HOLE, DELVE, CAVITY, SOURCE, TUNNEL, COLLIERY, EXCAVATE, EXPLOSIVE, EXCAVATION

miner: . . . . DIGGER, SAPPER, PITMAN, COLLIER

mingle: .... MIX, FUSE, JOIN, BLEND, MERGE, UNITE, HUDDLE, COMBINE, COMPOST, COALESCE, COMPOUND, AMALGAMATE, CONSOLIDATE

miniature: ..... COPY, TINY, SMALL, LITTLE, MODEL, MINUTE, PAINTING, PORTRAIT, DIMINUTIVE

minim: ... JOT, DASH, DROP, MINNOW, MINUTE, TINIEST, SMALLEST, MINATURE

minimize: .... REDUCE, DETRACT, LESSEN, BELITTLE, DISPARAGE, DEPRECIATE

minimum: .. LEAST, LOWEST, SMALLEST

minion: ...... IDOL, NEAT, DAINTY, PRETTY, DARLING, DELICATE, FAVORITE, FOLLOWER, MISTRESS, PARAMOUR, UNDERLING

of the law: .... POLICEMAN

minister: ..... TEND, AGENT, CATER, SERVE, ATTEND, CLERIC, CURATE, PANDER, PARSON, PASTOR, SUPPLY, VIZIER, FURNISH, PROVIDE, SERVANT, PREACHER, SHEPHERD, REVEREND, DIPLOMAT, CLERGYMAN, AMBASSADOR

minor: .. LESS, PETIT, PETTY, YOUTH, INFANT, LESSER, SLIGHT, SMALLER, INFERIOR, SUBORDINATE, UNDER-AGE

minster: .... CHURCH, CATHEDRAL, MONASTERY

minstrel: ...... BARD, POET, SINGER, BLACKFACE, JONGLEUR, GLEEMAN, MUSICIAN, TROUBADOUR, ENTERTAINER

mint: ... COIN, HERB, PLANT, STAMP, CREATE, INVENT, FABRICATE

plant: ..... SAGE, BASIL, THYME, CATNIP, HYSSOP, MENTHA, RAMONA, DITTANY, OREGANO, BERGAMOT, LAVENDER, MARJORAM

minus: .... LACK, LESS, DEFECT, DEVOID, LACKING, WITHOUT, NEGATIVE, SUBTRACT, DEFICIENCY

minuscule: ... TINY, PETTY, SMALL, MINUTE, DIMINUTIVE, INSIGNIFICANT

minute: .... JOT, WEE, MITE, NOTE, TIME, TINY, PETTY, SMALL, ATOMIC, LITTLE, MOMENT, SLIGHT, INSTANT, DETAILED, MINUSCLE, MICROSCOPIC

minutiae: . DETAILS, TRIFLES, PARTICULARS

miracle: .... FEAT, MARVEL, WONDER, PHENOMENON

miraculous: .... UNNATURAL, MARVELOUS, WONDERFUL, SUPERNATURAL

mirage: ... VISION, CHIMERA, ILLUSION, DELUSION, PHENOMENON, REFRACTION

mire: .... BOG, MUD, MUCK, OOZE, SLEW, SLUE, MARSH, SLUSH, STALL, SWAMP, SLOUGH, SLUDGE

mirror: .. REFLECT, CRYSTAL, SPECULUM, GIRANDOLE, (LOOKING)GLASS

mirth: .... FUN, JOY, GLEE, CHEER, GAIETY, LEVITY, JOLLITY, HILARITY, LAUGHTER, FESTIVITY

misadventure: .... see misfortune

miscarriage: ...... MISHAP, FAILURE, MISTAKE, ABORTION, MISCHANCE

miscarry: ...... ERR, FAIL, ABORT, FOUNDER

miscellaneous: ..... MIXED, SUNDRY, VARIED, ASSORTED

miscellany: .... OLIO, MELANGE, MIXTURE, POTPOURRI, HODGEPODGE

mischief: . . . . . HARM, HURT, PRANK, TRICK, WRACK, DAMAGE, INJURY, DEVILTRY
maker: . . IMP, WAG, PEST, DEVIL, KNAVE, ROGUE, SCAMP, HELLION, PRANKSTER

mischievous: . . . . SLY, ARCH, ELFIN, PESKY, IMPISH, NAUGHTY, PRANKISH, DEVILISH, ROGUISH

miscreant: . . . . . . RASCAL, VILLAIN, INFIDEL, CRIMINAL, HERETIC, SCOUNDREL

miscue: . . . MISS, SLIP, ERROR, MISTAKE

misdeed: . . . . . . SIN, CRIME, FAULT, OFFENSE

misdemeanor: . . SIN, CRIME, FAULT, DELICT, OFFENSE, MISCONDUCT

mise: . . LEVY, PACT, GRANT, TREATY, IMMUNITY, AGREEMENT

miserable: . . . . ABJECT, FORLORN, UNHAPPY, PITIABLE, WRETCHED, DESPICABLE, DISCOMFORT

miserly: . . . . . MEAN, CLOSE, TIGHT, GREEDY, STINGY, COVETOUS, GRASPING, NIGGARD(LY), PENURIOUS

misery: . . . WOE, ACHE, PAIN, AGONY, GRIEF, SORROW, ANGUISH, POVERTY, SADNESS, SQUALOR, CALAMITY, DISTRESS, ADVERSITY, PRIVATION, SUFFERING, AFFLICTION, DEPRESSION

misfortune: . . . . WOE, DOLE, HARM, GRIEF, MISERY, MISHAP, ILL-LUCK, REVERSE, TROUBLE, ACCIDENT, CALAMITY, CASUALTY, DISASTER, ADVERSITY, MISCHANCE, AFFLICTION, CATASTROPHE, MISADVENTURE

misgiving: . . . . FEAR, DOUBT, QUALM, ANXIETY, APPREHENSION, SCRUPLE

mishap: . . . . see **misfortune**

misinform: . . . . LIE, MISREPRESENT

mislead: . . . . . . DUPE, FOOL, DELUDE, DECEIVE

mismanage: . . . . . . BUNGLE, BOTCH

misrepresent: . . . . LIE, DECEIVE, DISTORT, GARBLE

miss: . . . . . ERR, FAIL, GIRL, LACK, LASS, LOSE, MUFF, OMIT, SKIP, SLIP, AVOID, LAPSE, MISCUE, FAILURE, MISTRESS, OVERLOOK

misshapen: . . . . UGLY, MALFORMED, DEFORMED, DISTORTED

missile: . . . . . SHOT, ARROW, LANCE, SHAFT, SHELL, SPEAR, BULLET, WEAPON, ROCKET, GRENADE, PROJECTILE, BOOMERANG

missing: . . . . LOST, ABSENT, LACKING

mission: . . CHARGE, ERRAND, EMBASSY, COMMISSION, DELEGATION

missive: . . . . . NOTE, BILLET, LETTER, MESSAGE, EPISTLE, MISSILE, DOCUMENT

misstep: . . SLIP, TRIP, ERROR, FAUX PAS

mist: . . . . . DIM, FOG, BLUR, DAMP, FILM, HAZE, SMOG, SMUR, SOUP, BRUME, CLOUD, MISLE, VAPOR, SEREIN, MIZZLE, SHADOW, OBSCURITY, GAUZE
rain like: . . . . DRIZZLE

mistake: . . . ERR, BULL, SLIP, BONER, FAULT, FOLLY, MISCUE, ERROR, RENEGE, BLUNDER

mistaken: . . . . WRONG, ERRONEOUS, INCORRECT

mister: . . . . DON, SIR, HERR, SENOR, SIGNOR, MONSIEUR

mistreat: . . . ABUSE, VIOLATE

mistrust: . . DOUBT, SUSPICION
misunderstanding: . . . .
BREACH, QUARREL, IMBROGLIO
misuse: . . . ABUSE, MISTREAT,
PERVERT, MALTREAT
mite: . . . . . BIT, ATOM, TICK,
SPECK, ATOMY, SPIDER,
ACARID, ACARUS, MINUTE,
SMIDGE, CHIGGER, ARACHNID
miter: . . . . BELT, TIARA,
GIRDLE, HEADDRESS,
HEADBAND
mitigate: . . . . . BALM, BATE,
COOL, EASE, ABATE, ALLAY,
REMIT, SLAKE, LESSEN, PACIFY,
TEMPER, SOFTEN, APPEASE,
ASSUAGE, MOLLIFY, RELIEVE,
DIMINISH, MODERATE,
EXTENUATE
mittimus: . . WRIT, WARRANT,
DISCHARGE, DISMISSAL
mix: . . . . . . (also see **merge,**
mingle) ALLOY, BLEND, CROSS,
KNEAD, JUMBLE, MUDDLE,
BLUNDER, CONFUSE, SHUFFLE,
COALESCE, COMPOUND,
CONFOUND
mixture: . . . . . . HASH, OLIO,
BLEND, MELANGE, MEDLEY,
AMALGAM, COMPOUND,
HODGEPODGE, FARRAGO,
POTPOURRI, (MISH)MASH
moan: . . . CRY, WAIL, GROAN,
BEWAIL, LAMENT, GRIEVE,
DEPLORE, WHIMPER, COMPLAIN
moat: . . LAKE, POND, FOSS(E),
DITCH, TRENCH
mob: . . . CREW, GANG, HERD,
MASS, CROWD, DROVE, FLOCK,
GROUP, CLIQUE, RABBLE,
THRONG, RIFFRAFF, MULTITUDE
mobile: . . . . . FLUID, FICKLE,
MOVABLE, VARIABLE,
FLEXIBLE, CHANGEABLE
moccasin: . . . . . . PAC, PACK,
SHAKE, LOAFER, SLIPPER,
LARRIGAN, FLOWER,
COTTONMOUTH

mock: . . . . . APE, DEFY, GIBE,
JAPE, JEER, LEER, FLEER,
FLOUT, MIMIC, SCOFF, SNEER,
TAUNT, DERIDE, RIDICULE,
IMITATE, IMITATION,
COUNTERFEIT
mode: . . . . . CUT, FAD, WAY,
ORDER, VOGUE, STYLE,
CUSTOM, MANNER, METHOD,
SYSTEM, FASHION, CONVENTION
model: . . . SIT, FORM, MOLD,
POSE, TYPE, IDEAL, MOCK-UP,
SHAPE, DESIGN, SITTER,
EXAMPLE, FASHION, MANIKIN,
PARAGON, PATTERN, TEMPLET,
EXEMPLAR, PARADIGM,
SPECIMAN, STANDARD,
ARCHETYPE, FACSIMILE,
MINIATURE, PROTOTYPE,
MANNEQUIN
moderate: . . . . BATE, CALM,
EASE, EASY, EVEN, MILD,
ABATE, LOWER, SOBER,
FRUGAL, GENTLE, LESSEN,
SOFTEN, TEMPER, CONTROL,
PRESIDE, DECREASE, DIMINISH,
ALLEVIATE, MITIGATE,
TEMPERATE
moderation: . . . . . CONTROL,
RESTRAINT, ABSTINENCE,
MITIGATION, TEMPERANCE
modern: . . . . NEO, NEW,
LATEST, RECENT NEOTERIC,
UP-TO-DATE
modernize: . . . . . . RETOOL,
UPDATE, RENOVATE
modest: . . . COY, SHY, PRIM,
DECENT, DEMURE, HUMBLE,
BASHFUL, DECOROUS,
RESERVED, RETIRING,
VERECUND, UNASSUMING
modicum: . . . . BIT, AMOUNT,
PORTION
modify: . . . EDIT, TONE, VARY,
ALTER, AMEND, LIMIT,
CHANGE, TEMPER, ASSUAGE,
QUALIFY, MITIGATE, MODERATE
modish: . . . . CHIC, STYLISH,
FASHIONABLE

modulate: ... TONE, CHANGE, ADJUST, ADAPT, INTONE, ATTUNE, INFLECT

modus: ...... WAY, MEANS, MANNER, METHOD

mogul: ...... LORD, NABOB, RULER, MAGNATE, AUTOCRAT, MONGOLIAN, LOCOMOTIVE

Mohammed: ..... PROPHET, MAHOMET, MAHOUND, MUHAMMAD

birthplace: ...... MECCA

burial place: .... MEDINA

religion founded: ...... MOSLEM, ISLAM

moiety: .... HALF, PART, SHARE, PORTION

moil: .... MIRE, SOIL, SPOT, TIRE, TOIL, LABOR, TAINT, WEARY, DEFILE, TORMENT, TROUBLE, TURMOIL, DRUDGE(RY), VEXATION, CONFUSION

moist: ... WET, DANK, DAMP, HUMID, RAINY, CLAMMY, IRRIGUOUS

moisten: .. DIP, WET, BATHE, (BE)DEW, LEACH, DAMPEN, IRRIGATE, SPRINKLE

with oil: .... EMBROCATE

moisture: .. DEW, FOG, DRIP, DROP, MIST, HUMOR, VAPOR, WATER, LIQUID, HUMIDITY

molar: .... TOOTH, GRINDER, CHOPPER

molasses: .... SIRUP, SYRUP, THERIACA, TREACLE, BLACKSTRAP

mold: .... DIE, CAST, FORM, SOIL, FRAME, FUNGUS, HUMUS, KNEAD, SHAPE, MATRIX, MILDEW, FASHION, MOULAGE, PATTERN

molder: ...... ROT, DECAY, CRUMBLE

molding: ...... BEAD, BEAK, CYMA, OGEE, CONGE, SPLAY, TALON, TORUS, BAQUET, FASCIA, NEBULE, REGLET, LISTEL, FILLET, BEADING, REEDING, SHAPING, CORNICE

moldy: ..... FUSTY, HOARY, MUCID, MUSTY, STALE

mole: ..... PIER, PILE, JETTY, QUAY, BURROW, RODENT, MAMMAL, BARRIER, EXCAVATE, STARNOSE, BREAKWATER

molecule: .... PARTICLE

component: ...... ATOM

molest: ..... ANNOY, TEASE, ASSAIL, BOTHER, HARASS, PESTER, DISTURB, TROUBLE

mollify: .... CALM, EASE, ALLAY, PACIFY, SOFTEN, SOOTHE, TEMPER, APPEASE, PLACATE, MITIGATE, CONCILIATE

mollusk: ..... CLAM, SNAIL, SQUID, HELIC, WHELK, CHITON, COCKLE, LIMPET, MUREX, TRITON, ABALONE, OCTOPUS, OYSTER, SCALLOP, NAUTILUS, PTEROPOD, CUTTLEFISH, WENTLETRAP

molt: .... MEW, SHED, CAST(OFF), EXUVIATE

molten: .. MELTED, LIQUEFIED

rock: .... LAVA, MAGMA

moment: .. SEC, TICK, FLASH, JIFFY, POINT, TRICE, MINUTE SECOND, INSTANT, TWINKLING, IMPORT(ANCE), CONSEQUENCE

momentarily: ...... SOON, SHORTLY

momentary: ..... PASSING, TRANSIENT, TRANSITORY

momentous: ...... GRAVE, FATEFUL, SERIOUS, WEIGHTY, EVENTFUL, IMPORTANT, PONDEROUS, INFLUENTIAL

momentum: ...... FORCE, POWER, SPEED, IMPETUS

monad: .. ATOM, UNIT, DIETY, ELEMENT, RADICAL, PARTICLE, ZOOSPORE, MICROCOSM, MONATOMIC

monarch: .... REI, REX, ROI, CZAR, KING, SHAH, TSAR,

RULER, DESPOT, KAISER, EMPEROR, AUTOCRAT, BUTTERFLY, POTENTATE, SOVEREIGN

monastery: . . ABBEY, FRIARY, PRIORY, COVENT, HOSPICE, MINSTER, NUNNERY, CLOISTER, LAMASERY, SANCTUARY, HERMITAGE

monastic: . . . . MONK, FRIAR, OBLATE, ASCETIC, MONKISH, RECLUSE, ABBATIAL, CENOBITE, MONACHAL

haircut: . . . . . . TONSURE

life: . . . . CLOISTER

monde: . . . . GLOBE, MOUND, WORLD, CIRCLE, SOCIETY

monetary: . . . . . . FINANCIAL PECUNIARY

money: . . . WAD, BILL, CASH, COIN, JACK, JAKE, LOOT, BRASS, BREAD, CLINK, DOUGH, FUNDS, LUCRE, BOODLE, CHANGE, MAZUMA, SPENCE, SILVER, TENDER, WAMPUM, WEALTH, LETTUCE, CURRENCY

mongrel: . . CUR, DOG, MUTT, HYBRID, BASTARD

monition: . . ORDER, ADVICE, NOTICE, CAUTION, SUMMONS, WARNING, CITATION

monitor: . . . CHECK, MENTOR, LIZARD, WARSHIP, IRONCLAD, REMINDER, RECEIVER, INSTIGATOR

monk: . . FRA, LAMA, CLERK, FRIAR, PADRE, PRIOR, CENOBITE, MONASTIC, ANCHORITE

monkey: . . . . . . FOOL, PLAY, BURRO, MEDDLE, SIMIAN, TAMPER, TRIFLE, PRIMATE, INTERFERE

monkeyshine: . . . . . . JOKE, PRANK, TRICK, MISCHIEF

monogram: . . . . CIPHER, SKETCH, INITIALS, LETTERS

monograph: . . . . . . PAPER, MEMOIR, THESIS, TREATISE

monolith: . . PILLAR, OBELISK, COLUMN, MENHIR, MEGALITH, MONUMENT

monologue: . . . . . SOLILOQUY

monomania: . . . . . . CRAZE, CRANK, OBSESSION, SINGLE-MINDED

monopoly: . . . . POOL, GRANT, RIGHT, TRUST, CARTEL, CORNER, CHARTER, CONTROL, SYNDICATE

monotonous: . . DEAD, DRAB, DULL, FLAT, DREARY, HUMDRUM, TEDIOUS, UNIFORM, TIRESOME, UNVARIED, WEARISOME, REPETITIVE

monotony: . . . . TEDIUM

monster: . . . . (also see **beast**) GILA, HUGE, OGRE, FREAK, GIANT, SPHINX, UNICORN, CENTAUR, ENORMOUS

monstrous: . . . . HUGE, VAST, HIDEOUS, IMMENSE, TITANIC, COLOSSAL, DEFORMED, ENORMOUS, GIGANTIC, HORRIBLE, ATROCIOUS, OUTRAGEOUS, PRODIGIOUS, STUPENDOUS, TREMENDOUS

monument: . . . TOMB, CAIRN, STELE, EFFIGY, MENHIR, SHRINE, STATUTE, TABLET, OBELISK, CENOTAPH, CROMLECH, MEMORIAL, GRAVESTONE, PANTHEON, MAUSOLEUM

mood: . . . TUNE, VEIN, WHIM, HUMOR, MORALE, TEMPER, CAPRICE, FEELING, SPIRITS, ATMOSPHERE, DISPOSITION

moody: . . . . GLUM, GLOOMY, GRUMPY, SULLEN, PENSIVE, BROODING, DEPRESSED

moon: . . . ORB, LUNA, LUNAR, SELENIC, SATELLITE, LUMINARY

moor: . . . . . BOG, FEN, DOCK, FELL, HEATH, LANDE, MARSH, SWAMP, ANCHOR, FASTEN, SECURE, MOSLEM, MUSLIM

moot: . . . . . DIG, PLEA, TELL, ARGUE, PLEAD, DEBATE, DISCUSS, MEETING, ARGUMENT, ASSEMBLY, DISPUTED, DEBATABLE

mop: . . . RUB, SWAB, WASH, WIPE, CLEAN, MALKIN, MERKIN, GRIMACE

mope: . . . POUT, SULK, BROOD

moppet: . . . TOT, BABY, DOLL, GIRL, TIKE, CHILD, TODDLER, YOUNGSTER

mora: . . . . . . DELAY, STOOL, DEFAULT, FOOTSTOOL, POSTPONEMENT

moral: . . . . GOOD, PURE, MAXIM, CHASTE, ETHICAL, UPRIGHT, VIRTUOUS, HONORABLE, RIGHTEOUS

morale: . . HOPE, MOOD, ZEAL, SPIRIT, TEMPER, CONDITION, CONFIDENCE

morals: . . . . ETHICS

morass: . . . BOG, FEN, QUAG, MARSH, SWAMP, QUAGMIRE

morbid: . . . . . SICK, GRISLY, DISEASED, GRUESOME, HORRIBLE, UNHEALTHY, PATHOLOGICAL, APPREHENSIVE

mordant: . . . . . ACID, KEEN, SHARP, ACRID, BITING, BURNING, CAUSTIC, PUNGENT, CUTTING, SARCASTIC, CORROSIVE

more: . . . ALSO, PLUS, AGAIN, EXTRA, CUSTOM, MANNER, GREATER, FURTHER, ADDITIONAL

moreover: . . . . . AND, ALSO, THEN, BESIDES, LIKEWISE, FURTHER

mores: . . . . CUSTOMS, FOLKWAYS, CONVENTIONS

morgue: . . . . LIBRARY, MORTUARY

moribund: . . DYING, EFFETE, DECADENT, DECAYING, TERMINATED

morning: . . . . . EOS, DAWN, MORN, MATIN, AURORA, MORROW, SUNRISE, DAYBREAK

moron: . . . . . . FOOL, AMENT, IDIOT, STUPID, DULLARD, NITWIT, IMBECILE

morose: . . . . . . BLUE, DOUR, GLUM, SOUR, SULKY, SURLY, GLOOMY, SULLEN, UNHAPPY

morro: . . HILL, BLUFF, POINT, CASTLE, HEADLAND

morsel: . . . . . BIT, ORT, BITE, DISH, CRUMB, PIECE, SCRAP, SNACK, TIDBIT, MORCEAU

mort: . . DEAD, LARD, DEATH, FATAL, DEADLY, GREASE

mortal: . . . . DIRE, BEING, FATAL, HUMAN, DEADLY, LETHAL, PERSON, CAPITAL, EXTREME, GREVIOUS, IMPLACABLE

mortar: . . . . BOWL, COMPO, PUTTY, CANNON, PLASTER, CEMENT, PETARD

mortgage: . . . . BOND, DEED, LIEN, PLEDGE, WADSET, ENCUMBRANCE

mortician: . . . . UNDERTAKER

mortification: . . . . . SHAME, CHAGRIN, GANGRENE, HUMILIATION, EMBARRASMENT

mortify: . . . . ABASE, ABASH, DECAY, SHAME, HUMBLE, OFFEND, HUMILIATE, EMBARRASS

mortuary: . . . . . CREMATORY, SEPULCHER, CINERARIUM

mosaic: . . . . . . TILED, TILES, INLAY, COLLAGE, ORMOLU

mosey: . . . . AMBLE, DEPART, RAMBLE, STROLL, WANDER, SHUFFLE(ALONG)

Moslem: . . (also see **Muslim**) BERBER, PATHAN, PAYNIM, ISLAMIC, SARACEN, MOSLEMITE, MUSSULMAN, MOHAMMEDAN

mosque: . . . . MOSK, CAABA, CHURCH, DARGAH, KAABEH, MASJID, SHRINE, TEMPLE
tower: . . . JAMI, MINARET

moss: . . BOG, SWAMP, LICHEN

most: . . . . BEST, CHIEF, MAXIMUM, GREATEST, MAJORITY, PRINCIPAL

mostly: . . . CHIEFLY, USUALLY

mote: . . . . . DOT, HILL, IOTA, ATOMY, SPECK, TRIFLE, PARTICLE

mother: . . . . . DAM, AMMA, DAME, MAMA, WOMB, DREGS, MATER, NURSE, FOSTER, MATRON, ORIGIN, PARENT, NUTURE, MATRIARCH

motif: . . . . IDEA, THEME, SUBJECT, FEATURE

motion: . . . . MOVE, GESTURE, IMPULSE, PROPOSE, SUGGEST, MOVEMENT, PROPOSAL, SUGGESTION

motion picture: . . . . . FILM, SHOW, FLICK, MOVIE, TALKY, CARTOON, CINEMA, FLICKER, PHOTOPLAY

motionless: . . . DEAD, INERT, RIGID, STILL, BECALMED, IMMOBILE, STAGNANT, QUIESCENT

motivate: . . . . MOVE, IMPEL, INCITE, INDUCE, INSPIRE, INFLUENCE, INSTIGATE, STIMULATE

motive: . . . . GOAL, SPUR, CAUSE, OBJECT, REASON, IMPULSE, PURPOSE, STIMULUS, OBJECTIVE, IMPELLENT, INCENTIVE, INDUCEMENT

motley: . . . . MIXED, DIVERSE, MOTTLED, PIEBALD, VARIGATED, HETEROGENEOUS

motor: . . . . . AUTO, ENGINE, TURBINE, MACHINE

mottled: . . . . . . PIED, PINTO, MOTLEY, DAPPLED, PIEBALD, SPOTTED, VARIEGATED

motto: . . . . . ADAGE, AXIOM, GNOME, MAXIM, DEVICE, SAYING, SLOGAN, PRECEPT, APHORISM

moue: . . . . FACE, POUT, GRIMACE

mould: . . . . see **mold**

mound: . . . . DAM, TEE, BANK, DENE, DUNE, HEAP, HILL, HUMP, PILE, TERP, CAIRN, GLOBE, KNOLL, STACK, BARROW, BULWORK, HUMMOCK, RAMPART, TUMULUS, EMBANKMENT

mount: . . . . FIX, GLUE, HILL, PONY, POST, RISE, CLIMB, HORSE, PASTE, STEED, ASCEND, ESCALATE, INCREASE, PROMONTARY, MOUNTAIN

mountaineer: . . . . . CLIMBER, SHERPA, ALPINIST, HILLBILLY, ALPESTRIAN

mountebank: . . GULL, CHEAT, QUACK, EMPIRIC, IMPOSTOR, CHARLATAN, PRETENDER

mourn: . . . RUE, DOLE, LONG, SIGH, WEEP, BEMOAN, GRIEVE, LAMENT, (BE)WAIL, SORROW, DEPLORE

mournful: . . . . . SAD, BLACK, WOEFUL, DOLEFUL, PITIFUL, FUNEREAL, GREVIOUS, SORROWFUL, LAMENTABLE, LUGUBRIOUS, MELANCHOLY, LACRIMOSE

mouse: . . GIRL, HUNT, KNOT, BRUISE, BLACK EYE, RODENT

mouth: . . . . . OS, GAB, MUG, SAY, LIPS, FRONT, STOMA, CAVITY, RICTUS, DECLAIM, OPENING, ORIFICE, STOMATA, ENTRANCE, GRIMACE
of the: . . . ORAL, BUCCAL, RICTAL, PALATAL, STOMATIC, OSCULAR
part: . . . . . LIP, TONGUE, UVULA, VELUM, PALATE, PHARYNX

river: . . . . . DELTA, FIRTH,
ESTUARY

mouthpiece: . . REED, BOCAL,
NOZZLE, LAWYER, ATTORNEY,
SPOKESMAN

mouton: . . . . . . FUR, WOOL,
SHEEPSKIN

movable: . . . . LOOSE, FICKLE,
MOBILE, MOTILE, PORTABLE

move: . . . . . GO, ACT, GOAD,
PLAY, PUSH, SPUR, STIR,
BUDGE, CAUSE, CARRY, IMPEL,
ROUSE, SHIFT, START, SWEEP,
AFFECT, AROUSE, EXCITE,
INCITE, INDUCE, KINDLE,
PROMPT, ACTUATE, ADVANCE,
AGITATE, ANIMATE, INSPIRE,
MIGRATE, PROPOSE, PROVOKE,
EMIGRATE, EVACUATE,
MOTIVATE, TRANSFER,
INSTIGATE, STIMULATE

along: . . . MOSEY, SCRAM,
SASHAY, MAUNDER

back: . . . . . EBB, RECEDE,
RETREAT, REGRESS

back and forth: . . . WAG,
FLAP, ROCK, TACK, DODGE,
WEAVE, TEETER, WABBLE,
SEESAW, WIGWAG, ZIGZAG,
SHUTTLE, OSCILATE

forward: . . . . EDGE, NOSE,
DRIVE, FORGE, PROGRESS,
ADVANCE

furtively: . . . . LURK, SLIP,
CREEP, SNEAK, SLINK,
SKULK

heavily: . . . LUG, LUMBER,
TRUDGE, WALLOP

movement: . ACTION, TEMPO,
TREND, MOTION, RHYTHM

movie: . . see **motion picture**

moving: . . MOTILE, CURRENT,
AMBULANT, PATHETIC,
POIGNANT, STIRRING,
IMPELLING, TOUCHING,
TRANSIENT, AMBULATORY

mow: . . BIN, CUT, LAY, CLIP,
HEAP, LOFT, MASS, MATH, PILE,
REAP, RICK, STACK, SCYTHE,
SICKLE, DESTROY, GRIMACE,
HAYLOFT, HAYSTACK

much: . . LOTS, MANY, GREAT,
HEAPS, SCADS, ALMOST,
MICKLE, NEARLY, GREATLY,
ABUNDANT, MULTITUDE

mucid: . . . . MUSTY, MOLDY,
SLIMY, MUCOUS

mucilage: . . . ARABIN, PASTE,
GLUE, GUM, PASTE, CEMENT,
ADHESIVE

muck: . . . DIRT, DUNG, MESS,
MIRE, FILTH, SLIME, WASTE,
MANURE, REFUSE, FERTILIZER

mucous: . . . . . MOIST, SLIMY,
VISCOUS, BLENNOID

mud: . . . . DIRT, GORE, MIRE,
MUCK, OOZE, LIBEL, SLIME,
SLUSH, SLUDGE, MURGEON,
SLANDER

muddle: . . MIX, DAZE, HASH,
MESS, ADDLE, SNAFU, JUMBLE,
BUNGLE, CONFUSE, FLUSTER,
PERPLEX, BEFUDDLE,
BEWILDER, FLOUNDER

muddy: . . . DULL, MIRY, RILE,
ROIL, DIRTY, VAGUE, ROILY,
SLUDGY, CLOUDY, SLOPPY,
TURBID, OBSCURE, CONFUSED,
SPATTERED

muezzin: . . . . CRIER

call: . . . . ADAN, AZAN

place: . . . . MINARET

muff: . . . FUR, FLUB, BOTCH,
ERROR, BUNGLE, FUMBLE

muffin: . . . COB, GEM, BREAD,
SCONE, CRUMPET, POPOVER

muffle: . . . GAG, DAMP, DULL,
MUTE, WRAP, DAMPEN,
DEADEN, SHROUD, STIFLE,
SILENCE

muffler: . . . . . MUTE, SCARF,
BAFFLE, SILENCER

mug: . . . . CUP, DUPE, FACE,
FOOL, TOBY, MOUTH, MUNGO,
STEIN, NOGGIN, SEIDEL,
ASSAULT, GRIMACE, TANKARD,
PHOTOGRAPH

muggins: .... DOMINO, DUPE, CARD GAME, FOOL

muggy: ..... HUMID, SULTRY

mulch: ..... COVER, STRAW, LITTER, COMPOST, SAWDUST

mulct: .. FINE, BILK, CHEAT, DEFRAUD, AMERCE, FLEECE, DECEIVE, PENALIZE

mule: .... MUTE, HINNY, HYBRID, TRACTOR, SLIPPER, LOCOMOTIVE

mulish: .... BALKY, SULLEN, STERILE, PERVERSE, STUBBORN, OBSTINATE, PIGHEADED

mull: .. MUSE, CRUSH, GRIND, SPICE, THINK, FLAVOR, MUSLIN, PONDER, POWDER, SQUEEZE, SWEETEN, COGITATE, CONSIDER, PULVERIZE

multifarious: .... MANY, VARIED, DIVERSE, MANIFOLD

multiple: .... MANY, PLURAL, MANIFOLD, NUMEROUS

multiply: ... BREED, SPREAD, AMPLIFY, AUGMENT, MAGNIFY, INCREASE, REPRODUCE

multitude: ..... MOB, ARMY, HOST, MANY, MASS, MUCH, RUCK, CROWD, DROVE, FLOCK, HORDE, SWARM, GALAXY, LEGION, MYRIAD, THRONG

multitudinous: ...... MANY, NUMEROUS, MANIFOLD

mumble: ..... CHEW, MUMP, MUTTER, MURMUR, GRUMBLE

mummer: .... MIME, ACTOR, GUISER, PLAYER, MASKER, MASQUER, PARADER

mummify: .... DRY, SHRIVEL

mummy: .... RELIC, CORPSE, CADAVER, CARCASS

mump: .... BEG, CHEAT, MUMBLE, MUTTER, GRIMACE

munch: .... EAT, CHEW, CHAMP, GROWSE

mundane: .... EARTHLY, PROSAIC, SECULAR, TERRENE, WORLDLY, TEMPORAL, TERRESTIAL

munificent: .... AMPLE, LAVISH, LIBERAL, GENEROUS, BOUNTIFUL, BENEVOLENT

muniment: ...... RECORD, DEFENSE, DOCUMENT, EVIDENCE, VALUABLES, FORTIFICATION

murder: ...... KILL, SLAY, DEATH, BUTCHER, CARNAGE, KILLING, HOMICIDE, SLAUGHTER, ASSASSINATE

parent's: .... MATRICIDE, PATRICIDE

murky: .. DIM, DARK, BLACK, DENSE, FOGGY, MISTY, THICK, GLOOMY, OBSCURE

murmur: ..... HUM, CURR, PURL, PURR, BABBLE, MUMBLE, MUTTER, GRUMBLE, WHISPER, COMPLAIN

muscle: ..... THEW, BRAWN, BICEPS, SINEW, TERES, LACERT, RECTUS, TENSOR, TISSUE, DILATOR, ERECTOR, LEVATOR, ROTATOR, EXTENSOR, STRENGTH, SPHINCTER

muscular: ... THEWY, BURLY, BRAWNY, ROBUST, SINEWY, STRONG, TOROSE, ATHLETIC

muse: ...... MULL, DREAM, THINK, PONDER, REFLECT, GODDESS, MEDITATE, COGITATE, CONSIDER, RUMINATE, MEDITATION

museum: ..... GALLERY, REPOSITORY

custodian: ..... CURATOR

mush: .... CUT, PAP, ATOLE, CRUSH, GRUEL, TRAVEL, CONFUSE, JOURNEY, FLATTERY, PORRIDGE, SENTIMENTALITY

mushroom: .. GROW, AGARIC, FUNGUS, SPREAD, MORIL, MOREL, AMIANITA, TOADSTOOL, CHAMPIGNON, CHANTERELLE

mushy: .... SOFT, WEAK, GUSHY, THICK, EFFUSIVE, SENTIMENTAL

music: . . . . (also see special section **Musical Terms**) AIR, LAY, ODE, TUNE, CHORAL, LYRICAL, MELODY, MELODIC, MELODIOUS, HARMONY, HARMONIC, HARMONIOUS, RHYTHM, RHYTHMIC

musical: . . . . . . MELODIOUS, LYRIC(AL), CANOROUS

musical composition: . . (also see special section **Musical Terms**) GLEE, OPUS, CENTO, ETUDE, FUGUE, OPERA, MOTET, RONDO, BALLAD, MINUET, SONATA, CANTATA, CHANSON, PRELUDE, SCHERZO, VIRELAI, BERCEUSE, CONCERTO, NOCTURNE, ORATORIO, SERENATA, SERENADE, SONATINA, SYMPHONY, BAGATELLE, CABALETTA, CAPRICCIO, INTERLUDE, INTERMEZZO, HUMORESQUE

musing: . . . . REVERIE, MEDITATION, REFLECTION, CONTEMPLATION

muskeg: . . . . . . BOG, MARSH

muskellunge: . . . . PIKE

musket: . . . . . HAWK, FUSIL, FALCON, DRAGOON, FIREARM, FLINTLOCK

muskmelon: . . . . . ATIMON, MANGO, CASABA, CANTALOUPE

Muslim: . . . . . (see **Moslem**)

muss: . . . . see **mess**

mussel: . . . . . UNIO, MOLLUSK

Mussulman: . . (see **Moslem**)

must: . . . ALBA, MOLD, MUSK, SAPA, STUM, WINE, JUICE, OUGHT, SHALL, MILDEW, REFUSE, ESSENTIAL, NECESSARY, OBLIGATION

mustang: . . . . PONY, PINTO, HORSE, BRONCO

muster: . . . CALL, LEVY, LIST, ROLL, GATHER, ROSTER, SUMMON, COLLECT, MARSHAL, ASSEMBLE, ACCUMULATE, CONGREGATE

musty: . . DULL, RANK, SOUR, FETID, FUSTY, HOARY, MOLDY, MUCID, STALE, TRITE, RANCID, SMELLY, SPOILED, ANTIQUATED

mutable: . . . . FICKLE, VARIABLE, VOLATILE, INCONSTANT, CHANGEABLE, VACILLATING

mutate: . . . . . VARY, ALTER, CHANGE, MODIFY

mutation: . . . . CHANGE, REVOLT, EVOLUTION, REVOLUTION, SALTATION

mute: . . . MUM, DUMB, SURD, DEADEN, MUFFLE, SILENT, MUFFLER, SILENCER, VOICELESS, SPEECHLESS, INARTICULATE

mutilate: . . . . . . MAR, HACK, MAIM, DAMAGE, DEFACE, DEFORM, MANGLE, CRIPPLE, DESTROY, DISFIGURE, DISMEMBER

mutinous: . . . . . . SEDITIOUS, REBELLIOUS, REFRACTORY, DISOBEDIENT, INSUBORDINATE

mutiny: . . . . . RISE, REVOLT, STRIFE, INSURRECTION, REBELLION

mutt: . . CUR, DOG, MONGREL

mutter: . . . GROWL, MUMBLE, GRUMBLE, COMPLAIN, MURMUR

mutual: . . . JOINT, COMMON, RECIPROCAL

muzzle: . . GAG, GRUB, NOSE, ROOT, SNOUT, MUFFLE, RESTRAIN, SILENCE

myopic: . . . . PURBLIND, NEARSIGHTED, SHORTSIGHTED

myriad: . . . . . . COUNTLESS, MULTITUDE, INNUMERABLE

mysterious: . . . . DIM, DARK, RUNIC, WEIRD, ARCANE, MYSTIC, OCCULT, SECRET, CRYPTIC, ABSTRUSE, ESOTERIC, ENIGMATIC, INSCRUTABLE, INEXPLICABLE

mystery: . . . . . RUNE, CRAFT, ENIGMA, PUZZLE, RIDDLE,

SECRET, ARCANUM, WHODUNIT, CONUNDRUM

mystic: . . SEER, YOGA, YOGI, EPOPT, RUNIC, OCCULT, ORPHIC, SECRET, SUFIST, CRYPTIC, EPOPTIC, OBSCURE, ESOTERIC, SYMBOLIC, ENIGMATIC, CABALISTIC, MYSTERIOUS

mystical: . . . . DARK, OCCULT, SECRET, SYMBOLIC, SPIRITUAL, ENIGMATIC, MYSTERIOUS

mystify: . . . . . HOAX, BEFOG, MUDDLE, PUZZLE, BECLOUD, CONFUSE, PERPLEX, BEWILDER, BEFUDDLE, BAMBOOZLE, OBFUSCATE

myth: . . . SAGA, TALE, FABLE, FANCY, STORY, LEGEND, PARABLE

mythical: . . . . . IMAGINARY, LEGENDARY, FICTITIOUS

N

N: *Greek:* . . . . NU
Hebrew: . . . . NUN

nab: . . . GRAB, SNAG, CATCH, SEIZE, ARREST, SNATCH, CAPTURE, APPREHEND

nacelle: . . . BASKET, SHELTER, FUSELAGE, COMPARTMENT

nacre: . . SHELLFISH, MOTHER-OF-PEARL

nadir: . . . DEPTHS, LOW POINT

nag: . . TIT, FRET, PONY, RIDE, TWIT, ANNOY, HORSE, SCOLD, SHREW, TEASE, BADGER, BERATE, BOTHER, HARASS, HECKLE, HECTOR, PESTER, PLAGUE, HENPECK, HARANGUE

naga, nag: . . COBRA, SNAKE

nagger: . . . . . SCOLD, SHREW, VIRAGO, TERMAGANT

naiad: . . . . . NYMPH, MUSSEL

naif: . . . . NAIVE, ARTLESS

nail: . . . FIX, PEG, PIN, BRAD, CLAW, SPAD, STUD, TACK, AFFIX, CATCH, SPIKE, SPRIG, CLINCH, FASTEN, HAMMER, SECURE, TENTER, UNGUIS, UNGULA, CAPTURE

naive: . . . . . . FRANK, SIMPLE, ARTLESS, CHILDISH, INNOCENT, CHILDLIKE, GUILELESS, INGENUOUS

naked: . . BARE, NUDE, OPEN, PLAIN, EXPOSED, UNCLOTHED, UNCOVERED

namby-pamby: . . . . . SILLY, VAPID, INSIPID, WISHY-WASHY

name: . . . . DUB, CALL, CITE, TERM, CLAIM, COUNT, NOMEN, STYLE, TITLE, LABEL, SELECT, APPOINT, ENTITLE, EPITHET, MENTION, MONIKER, CHRISTEN, IDENTIFY, COGNOMEN, NOMINATE, DESIGNATE, REPUTATION, APPELLATION

assumed: . . . . ALIAS, ANONYM, INCOGNITO, PSEUDONYM, SOBRIQUET, NOM DE PLUME

nameless: . . . . BASTARD, OBSCURE, ANONYMOUS, UNKNOWN, UNIDENTIFIED

namely: . . . . VIZ, TO WIT, FAMOUS, SILICET, EXPRESSLY, VIDELICET, ESPECIALLY

nanny: . . . . . . GOAT, NURSE

naos: . . . . . . CELLA, TEMPLE

nap: . . . . . NOD, DOZE, FUZZ, LINT, PILE, SHAG, WINK, FLUFF, SLEEP, STEAL, SIESTA, SNOOZE

nape: . . . . PALL, SCRAG, SCRUFF, NUCHA, NUQUE

napery: . . . . . LINEN, DOILIES, NAPKINS, DAMASK

napkin: . . . . BIB, DOILY, TOWEL, DIAPER, NAPERY, KERCHIEF, SERVIETTE

nappy: . . . ALE, DISH, HAIRY, WOOLLY, DOWNY, LIQUOR, FOAMING

narcotic: . . . . (also see **marijuna**) BANG, DOPE, JUNK, DRUG, BHANG, ETHER, OPIUM,

HEROIN, OPIATE, ANODYNE,
COCAINE, CODEINE, HASHISH,
HYNOTIC, MORPHINE, SEDATIVE,
SOPORIFIC

nark: . . . . SPY, VEX, ANNOY,
INFORMER, IRRITATE,
STOOL PIGEON

narrate: . . . . . TELL, STATE,
DETAIL, RECITE, RECOUNT,
RELATE, REPORT, DESCRIBE

narrow: . . . . . MEAN, CLOSE,
LIMIT, SCANT, TAPER, BIASED,
MEAGER, STRAIT, STRICT,
BIGOTED, LIMITED, CONDENSE,
CONTRACT, CONSTRICT,
HIDEBOUND, PREJUDICED,
RESTRICTED, CONTRACT

narrows: . . . . STRAIT, SOUND

narthex: . . . PORCH, PORTICO,
VESTIBULE

nasal: . . . . . . RHINAL, NARINE

nascency: . . . BIRTH, ORIGIN,
GENESIS, BEGINNING,
FORMATION

nasty: . . . MEAN, FOUL, UGLY,
FILTHY, DIRTY, HARMFUL,
OBSCENE, MALICIOUS,
OFFENSIVE, DISGUSTING

natal: . . . . . INNATE, INBORN,
NATIVE, CONGENITAL

natant: . . AFLOAT, SWIMMING,
FLOATING

natatorium: . . . . BATH, POOL

nation: . . HOST, RACE, CASTE,
CLASS, STATE, PEOPLE,
COUNTRY

national: . . CITIZEN, FEDERAL

native: . . . . SON, NATAL,
INBORN, INNATE, NORMAL,
CITIZEN, ENDEMIC, NATURAL,
DOMESTIC, INHERENT,
ORIGINAL, ENCHORIC,
RESIDENT, ABORIGINE,
CONGENITAL, INDIGENOUS

natty: . . . . CHIC, NEAT, TIDY,
TRIM, SMART, SHARP, SPRUCE,
FASTIDIOUS

natural: . BORN, EASY, REAL,
WILD, COMMON, CRETIN,

INBORN, INBRED, INNATE,
NATIVE, NORMAL, IHERENT,
ORDINARY, PRIMITIVE,
CONGENITAL, UNPOSED

ability: . . . . GIFT, GENIUS,
KNACK, TALENT, FLAIR,
APTITUDE

naturalize: . . . . ADOPT,
ACCUSTOM, ACCLIMATE,
ACCLIMATIZE, DOMESTICATE,
FAMILIARIZE

nature: . . . KIND, SORT, TYPE,
ESSENCE, CHARACTER

naughty: . . . . BAD, EVIL,
IMPISH, WRONG, WICKED,
OBSCENE, IMPROPER,
DISOBEDIENT, MISCHIEVOUS

nausea: . . . . . . PALL, QUALM,
DISGUST, SICKNESS, QUEASINESS

nauseating: . . . . NASTY,
LOATHSOME, SICKENING,
DISGUSTING, DISTASTEFUL

nautical: . . . NAVAL, MARINE,
OCEANIC, MARITIME

nautilus: . . . . MOLLUSK,
ARGONAUT

naval: . . . . NAUTICAL

navel: . . . . UMBILICUS

navigate: . . . . . . SAIL, STEER,
CRUISE, DIRECT, MANAGE,
OPERATE

navvy: . . . . LABORER

navy: . . . . FLEET, WARSHIPS,
SEA FORCE

nawab: . . . . see nabob

Nazi: . . . . FASCIST, HITLERITE

near: . . BY, KIN, DEAR, NIGH,
ABOUT, ANENT, CLOSE, HANDY,
ALMOST, AROUND, BESIDE,
NARROW, STINGY, SIMILAR,
THRIFTY, VICINAL, ADJACENT,
APPROACH, INTIMATE

nearest: . . . . NEXT, CLOSEST

nearly: . . . . ABOUT, ALMOST

neat: . . . . NET, CHIC, PRIM,
PURE, SNUG, TIDY, TAUT, TRIM,
CLEAN, NATTY, ADROIT,
DAPPER, NATTY, ORDERLY,
SPIFFY, SPRUCE, SOIGNE,
UNMIXED

neb: ... NIB, TIP, BEAK, BILL, SNOUT, NOSE

nebulous: .... HAZY, FOGGY, MISTY, VAGUE, CLOUDY, UNCLEAR, OBSCURE, INDEFINITE, INDISTINCT

necessarily: ...... PERFORCE

necessary: .... MUST, PRIVY, VITAL, TOILET, NEEDFUL, ESSENTIAL, MANDATORY, REQUISITE, REQUIRED

necessitate: ...... COMPEL, ENTAIL, REQUIRE, OBLIGE

necessity: .... FATE, COMPULSION, NEED, WANT

neck: .... PET, CAPE, CRAG, KISS, SPOON, CARESS, CERVIX, COLLUM, FONDLE, GULLET, STRAIT, CHANNEL, EMBRACE, ISTHMUS

necklace: .... ROPE, BEADS, CHAIN, NOOSE, COLLAR, LOCKET, TORQUE, STRAND, BALDRIC, CHAPLET, RIVERIERE, CARCANET, LAVALIER

necktie: ...... BOW, BAND, ASCOT, SCARF, CRAVAT, CHOKER, FOULARD, FOUR-IN-HAND

necromancy: ... ART, MAGIC, SORCERY

necropolis: ..... CEMETERY, GRAVEYARD

necropsy: ... AUTOPSY, POST MORTEM

nectar: .... DRINK, HONEY, AMBROSIA, BEVERAGE

need: .. LACK, WANT, CRAVE, DESIRE, POVERTY, REQUIRE, EXIGENCY, EMERGENCY, NECESSITY, REQUISITE

needle: .. GOAD, PROD, PRICK, TEASE, HECKLE, PROVOKE, POINTER, INDICATOR

needlework: ...... SEWING, SAMPLER, TATTING, KNITTING, HEMSTITCH, EMBROIDERY, CROCHETING

needy: ... POOR, DESTITUTE, INDIGENT, PENNILESS

nefarious: .... WICKED, VICIOUS, HEINOUS, HORRIBLE, INFAMOUS, ATROCIOUS

negate: ...... DENY, VOID, ANNUL, REFUTE, NULLIFY, COUNTERACT, NEUTRALIZE

negation: ... EMPTY, DENIAL, REFUSAL, NULLITY, NONENTITY, ANNULMENT

negative: .... NO, NAY, NOR, NOT, FILM, VETO, MINUS, NEVER

neglect: .... FAIL, OMIT, SLIP, SHIRK, FORGET, IGNORE, SLIGHT, DEFAULT, FAILURE, OMISSION, OVERLOOK, OVERSIGHT, DISREGARD

neglectful: .... LAX, REMISS, DERELICT, CARELESS, HEEDLESS

negligee: ..... ROBE, GOWN, PEIGNOR, NIGHTGOWN

negligible: .... TRIFLING, TRIVIAL

negotiate: .... DEAL, TREAT, BARGAIN, DICKER, DISCUSS, PARLEY, TRANSACT

neighborhood: ...... AREA, VENUE, LOCALE, REGION, SECTION, DISTRICT, PURLIEU, VICINAGE, VICINITY, LOCALITY, PRECINCT, COMMUNITY, TERRITORY

nemesis: ... BANE, AVENGER, GODDESS, RETRIBUTION

neophyte: ... TYRO, NOVICE, AMATEUR, CONVERT, BEGINNER, PROSELYTE

neoteric: ...... NEW, LATE, MODERN, RECENT

nepotism: ...... PATRONAGE, FAVORITISM

Nero: ..... DESPOT, TYRANT, EMPEROR, FIDDLER

nerve: .... GALL, GRIT, GUTS, CHEEK, PLUCK, SINEW, SPUNK, APLOMB, DARING, COURAGE, AUDACITY, BOLDNESS,

TEMERITY, COOLNESS,
STRENGTH, BRAZENNESS,
RESOLUTION

nerves: . . . . FIT, JITTERS,
HYSTERIA

nervous: . . . . . EDGY, JUMPY,
TENSE, TIMID, TOUCHY,
JITTERY, FEARFUL, FIDGETY,
TIMOROUS, EXCITABLE,
SENSITIVE, HIGHSTRUNG

nescient: . . . . INFIDEL,
AGNOSTIC, IGNORANT

ness: . . . . . CAPE, HEADLAND,
PROMONTORY

nest: . . . . . . DEN, WEB, AERY,
DRAY, HOME, NIDE, ABODE,
AERIE, EYRIE, HAUNT, NIDUS,
HOTBED, RESORT, LODGING,
RETREAT, RESIDENCE

nestle: . . . . . PET, SNUGGLE,
SHELTER, CUDDLE, NUZZLE,
SETTLE

nestling: . . BABY, BIRD, EYAS,
POULT, SQUAB, OWLET,
EAGLET, FLEDGLING

nestor: . . . . . SAGE, ADVISER,
WISE MAN, COUNSELOR

net: . . GIN, WEB, CAUL, GAIN,
LACE, LAWN, MESH, NEAT,
PURE, TRAP, TRIM, WEIR,
CLEAN, CLEAR, GAUZE, SEIZE,
SNARE, TULLE, YIELD, COBWEB,
ENTRAP, PROFIT, ENSNARE,
RETICLE, BALANCE, LEFT-OVER

nether: . . . . . DOWN, LOWER,
UNDER, DOWNWARD

nettle: . . . . VEX, FRET, WEED,
ANNOY, PEEVE, PIQUE, STING,
RUFFLE, PROVOKE, IRRITATE

network: . . . . . . WEB, LACE,
MESH, RETE, PLEXUS, RESEAU,
RETICULUM

neuter: . . GENDER, ASEXUAL,
NEITHER, SEXLESS

neutral: . . . . ALOOF,
COLORLESS, INDEFINITE,
INDIFFERENT, NONPARTISAN

neutralize: . . . . ANNUL,
ABOLISH, BALANCE, NULLIFY,

VITIATE, FRUSTRATE,
COUNTERACT

neve: . . . . . ICE, SNOW, FIRN,
GLACIER

nevertheless: . . . . BUT, YET,
STILL, HOWEVER, HOWSOEVER

nevus: . . . . . MOLE, TUMOR,
SPILOMA, BIRTHMARK

new: . . . . . NEO, LATE, FRESH,
GREEN, NOVEL, MODERN,
RECENT, UNUSED, NEOTERIC,
ORIGINAL, DIFFERENT

newcomer: . . . . . . SETTLER,
IMMIGRANT, TENDERFOOT

newel: . . . . POST

news: . . . . . . WORD, NOTICE,
REPORT, TIDINGS,
INFORMATION, INSTRUCTION,
INTELLIGENCE

newsman: . . . . CUB, SCRIBE,
REPORTER, JOURNALIST,
COLUMNIST

newspaper: . . . DAILY, PAPER,
SHEET, GAZETTE, JOURNAL,
TABLOID, NEWSPRINT,
PUBLICATION

newsstand: . . BOOTH, KIOSK,
STALL

next: . . THEN, AFTER, BESIDE,
CLOSEST, ENSUING, NEAREST,
ADJOINING, FOLLOWING,
PROXIMATE, CONTIGUOUS

nexus: . . . . TIE, LINK,
CONNECTION

nib: . . . . . . PEN, BEAK, BILL,
POINT, PRONG

nibble: . . . . . EAT, NIP, BITE,
GNAW, KNAP, MORSEL, BROWSE

nice: . . . . . FINE, GOOD, NEAT,
DAINTY, MINUTE, PRETTY,
SUBTLE, ELEGANT, FINICAL,
PRECISE, REFINED, DELICATE,
PLEASANT, AGREEABLE,
EXQUISITE, FASTIDIOUS

niche: . . . APSE, NOOK, SLOT,
ALCOVE, RECESS, CORNER

nick: . . . . . CAT, CHIP, SLIT,
CHEAT, NOTCH, SCORE, TALLY,

TRICK, ARREST, RECORD, DEFRAUD, INDENTION

nickname: ...... AGNAME, AGNOMEN, MONIKER, COGNOMEN, MONICKER, SO(U)BRIQUET

nide, nidus: .... NEST

nieve: .... FIST, HAND

nifty: ...... GOOD, SMART, STYLISH

niggard: .... CHURL, MISER, SKINFLINT, CURMUDGEON

niggardly: .... MEAN, CLOSE, MISERLY, SCANTY, STINGY, AVARICIOUS, CLOSEFISTED

nigh: .... AT, NEAR, CLOSE, ALMOST, NEARLY, ADJACENT

night: .... DARK(NESS), EVENING

nightfall: .... EVE, DUSK, TWILIGHT

nightstick: .... CLUB, TRUNCHEON

nihil: .... NOTHING

nil: ... NULL, ZERO, NOTHING

nimble: ...... DEFT, SPRAY, AGILE, ALERT, FLEET, LIGHT, QUICK, ADROIT, CLEVER, LISSOM, LIVELY, VOLANT, DEXTEROUS

nimbus: .... AURA, HALO, CLOUD, VAPOR, GLORIA, AUREOLE, ATMOSPHERE

nimiety: .... EXCESS, REDUNDANCY

nincompoop: ... BOOB, FOOL, DOLT, NITWIT, IDIOT, MORON, NINNY, SIMPLETON, JACKASS

nip: ... CUT, SIP, BITE, CLIP, DRAM, TANG, CHECK, CLAMP, DRINK, FROST, PINCH, SEVER, STEAL, BLIGHT, SNATCH, TIPPLE, SQUEEZE

nipper: ... BOY, LAD, CLAW, BITER, PLIERS, URCHIN, PINCERS, FORCEPS, TWEEZERS, HANDCUFFS

nippy: ...... BRISK, SHARP, BITING, NIMBLE

nisus: .... EFFORT, IMPULSE, ENDEAVOR

nit: ...... EGG, NUT, INSECT, SPECK

nitrate: ...... SALT, ESTER, NITER, SALTPETER, FERTILIZER

nitwit: ... see nimcompoop

niveous: .. SNOWY, SNOWLIKE

nob: .... HEAD, JACK

nobble: ..... CHEAT, BRIBE, STEAL, SWINDLE

noble: .... FINE, GOOD, PEER, PURE, GRAND, GREAT, LOFTY, AUGUST, HEROIC, KINGLY, EXALTED, STATELY, SUBLIME, ELEVATED, MAJESTIC, DIGNIFIED, PATRICIAN, BLUEBLOOD

nobleman: .... DON, DUKE, EARL, LORD, PEER, BARON, COUNT, THANE, PRINCE, HIDALGO, MARQUIS, ARISTOCRAT

noblewoman: .... LADY, PEERESS, DUCHESS, CONTESSA, COUNTESS, MARQUISE

nobody: .. NONE, NONENTITY

nocent: ... GUILTY, HARMFUL, NOXIOUS, CRIMINAL, INJURIOUS

nocturnal: .. NIGHT, NIGHTLY

nocuous: .... NOXIOUS, HARMFUL

nod: ..... BOW, BECK, BEND, DOZE, BECKON, DROWSE, NUTATE

node: ... BOW, BUMP, KNOB, KNOT, LUMP, JOINT, NODULE, DILEMMA, GRANULE, SWELLING, TUBERCLE

noel: .... CAROL, CHRISTMAS

noesis: .... PERCEPTION, COGNITION

nog: ...... ALE, PIN, BRICK, BLOCK

noggin: ... CUP, MUG, HEAD, PATE

noise: .. (also see sound) DIN, BRUIT, CLAMOR, (UP)ROAR, RACKET, STRIDOR, HUBBUB

noiseless: . . . . QUIET, STILL, SILENT, TACIT, CATLIKE

noisome: . . (also see **noxious**) FOUL, FETID, STINKING, HARMFUL, OFFENSIVE, MALODOROUS

noisy: . . . . . LOUD, BLATANT, STREPENT, CLAMOROUS, TURBULENT, BOISTEROUS

nom de plume: . . PEN NAME, PSEUDONYM

nomad: . . . . . GYPSY, ROVER, TRAMP, ROAMER, WANDERER, ITINERANT

nomadic: . . . . . . ITINERANT

nomenclature: . . . . . . NAME, GLOSSARY, REGISTER, DICTIONARY, VOCABULARY, APPELATION, DESIGNATION

nominal: . . . . SMALL, SLIGHT, TOKEN, TITULAR, TRIVIAL

nominate: . . . . CALL, NAME, SLATE, APPOINT, PROPOSE, SPECIFY, DESIGNATE

nominee: . . . . APPOINTEE, CANDIDATE

nonage: . . . . MINORITY, IMMATURITY

nonbeliever: . . . . PAGAN, INFIDEL, ATHEIST, AGNOSTIC

nonchalant: . . COOL, CASUAL, CARELESS, INDIFFERENT, INSOUCIANT

nonconformist: . . . . REBEL, HERETIC, DISSENTER, RECUSANT, DISSIDENT, BOHEMIAN

none: . . . NARY, NO ONE, NOT ANY, NOTHING

nonentity: . . . ZERO, NOBODY, CIPHER, NOTHING

nonesuch: . . . . APPLE, MODEL, PARAGON, MATCHLESS, NONPAREIL, UNEQUALLED

nonpareil: . . BEST, PARAGON, PERFECT, SUPREME, NONESUCH, PEERLESS, UNRIVALED

nonplus: . . . . BLANK, STUMP, PERPLEX, PUZZLE, CONFUSE, MYSTIFY, CONFOUND, EMBARRASS

nonsense: . . BAH, ROT, BLAH, BOSH, BULL, BUNK, FLAM, TOSH, FUDGE, HOOEY, BILGE, BUMKUM, DRIVEL, HOKUM, BLARNEY, BLATHER, BUNCOME, BALONEY, INANITY, TWADDLE, RUBBISH, FALDEROL, FLIMFLAM, TOMMYROT, TRUMPERY, ABSURDITY, FANDANGLE, FRIVOLITY, BALDERDASH, FLAPDOODLE, RIGAMAROLE, TOM FOOLERY, FOOLISHNESS

nonsensical: . . . . . ABSURD, INANE, SILLY, FOOLISH, RIDICULOUS

nonstop: . . . . . . MARATHON, CONTINUOUS

noodle: . . HEAD, FOOL, PATE, PASTA

nook: . . . . DEN, COVE, GLEN, HOLE, ANGLE, NICHE, ALCOVE, CORNER, CRANNY, RECESS, CREVICE, RETREAT

noon: . . . . MIDDAY, MERIDAN

noose: . . . LOOP, TRAP, BIGHT, SNARE, ENTRAP, HALTER, LARIAT, ENSNARE, EXECUTE

norm: . . RULE, TYPE, GAUGE, MODEL, AVERAGE, PATTERN, STANDARD, TEMPLATE

normal: . . USUAL, AVERAGE, NATURAL, REGULAR, ORDINARY, STANDARD, TYPICAL

Norseman: . . . . VIKING

nose: . . NEB, PRY, SPY, BEAK, CONK, SCENT, SMELL, SNIFF, SNOOP, SNOUT, SPOUT, DETECT, DEFEAT, MUFFLE, MUZZLE, NOZZLE, SEARCH, DISCOVER, INFORMER

nos(e)y: . . CURIOUS, PRYING, INQUISITIVE

nostalgia: . . . . LONGING, MELANCHOLY, HOMESICKNESS

nostril: . . . . NARE

nostrum: . . . . REMEDY, PANACEA

not: . . . . NAY, NOR, NOUGHT, NEITHER, NEGATION, NEGATIVE, NOTHINGNESS

notable: . . FABLED, FAMOUS, SIGNAL, EMINENT, STORIED, HISTORIC, STRIKING, MEMORABLE

notarize: . . . ATTEST, CERTIFY

notary: . . . . OFFICIAL, OBSERVER, SCRIVENER

notch: . . . . . . CUT, GAP, JAG, DENT, MARK, NICK, STEP, SCORE, TALLY, CROTCH, DEFILE, DEGREE, INDENT, RECORD, CRENATE, SERRATE, INDENTURE

notched: . . . EROSE, CRENATE, SERRATE, DENTATE

note: . . IOU, JOT, SEE, BILL, CHIT, FAME, HEED, MARK, MEMO, TONE, TUNE, LABEL, BILLET, LETTER, NOTICE, RECORD, REGARD, REMARK, RENOWN, REPORT, COMMENT, MESSAGE, MISSIVE, OBSERVE

noted: . . . . FAMOUS, EMINENT, RENOWNED, CELEBRATED, ILLUSTROUS

noteworthy: . . . . . NOTABLE, SPECIAL, EMINENT, OUTSTANDING

nothing: . . . NIL, FREE, NONE, ZERO, AUGHT, NIHIL, NAUGHT, NOUGHT, TRIFLE

notice: . . . . . AD, SEE, ESPY, HEED, MARK, NEWS, NOTE, SIGN, ADVICE, BILLET, REGARD, ARTICLE, BILLING, DISCERN, OBSERVE, WARNING, APPRISAL, CITATION

notify: . . . CITE, PAGE, TELL, WARN, ADVISE, INFORM, APPRISE, DECLARE, ACQUAINT

notion: . . IDEA, VIEW, WHIM, CURIO, FANCY, IMAGE, BELIEF, DESIRE, THEORY, INKLING, OPINION, THOUGHT

notoriety: . . . ECLAT, REPUTE, PUBLICITY, REPUTATION

notorious: . . ARRANT, FAMED, FAMOUS, INFAMOUS, WELL KNOWN

Notre Dame: . . . OUR LADY, CATHEDRAL

notwithstanding: . THO, YET, EVEN, MAUGER, MAUGRE, DESPITE, HOWEVER, ALTHOUGH, NEVERTHELESS

nougat: . . . . CANDY, CONFECTION

nought: . . . . . . ZERO, CIPHER, USELESS, NOTHING, WORTHLESS

noun: . . . NAME, SUBSTANTIVE

nourish: . . . . . FEED, GROW, BREED, NURSE, FOSTER, CHERISH, SUPPORT, SUSTAIN, DEVELOP, CULTIVATE

nourishing: . . . . ALIBLE, NUTRIENT, NUTRITIOUS, ALIMENTAL, ALIMENTARY

nous: . . . . . . MIND, REASON, INTELLECT

novel: . . . NEW, RARE, FRESH, STORY, RECENT, FICTION, ROMANCE, STRANGE, UNUSUAL, ORIGINAL, UNCOMMON

novelty: . . . . . FAD, CHANGE, TRINKET, WRINKLE, GIMCRACK, INNOVATION, BRIC-A-BRAC

novice: . TIRO, TYRO, ROOKY, ROOKIE, AMATEUR, CONVERT, ACOLYTE, BEGINNER, NEOPHYTE, TENDERFOOT, APPRENTICE, GREENHORN

now: . . . . HERE, TODAY, PRESENT, AT ONCE, FORTHWITH, IMMEDIATELY

noxious: . ILL, EVIL, NOCENT, BANEFUL, NOISOME, HARMFUL, VIRULENT, MEPHITIC, MIASMIC, MIASMAL, PERNICIOUS

nozzle: . NOSE, VENT, SNOUT, SPOUT

nuance: . . SHADE, VARIATION

nub: . . . . . CORE, CRUX, GIST, KNOB, SNAG, LUMP

nubilous: ... FOGGY, MISTY, VAGUE, CLOUDY, OBSCURE, INDEFINITE, VAPOROUS

nucleus: ..... CORE, FOCUS, UMBRA, KERNEL, CENTER

nude: ...... BARE, NAKED, STRIPPED, UNCLOTHED

nudge: .... JOG, POKE, PUSH, PROD, ELBOW, JOSTLE

nudist: .... ADAMITE, GYMNOSOPHIST

nugatory: ... VAIN, TRIVIAL, INVALID, TRIFLING, FRUSTRATE, INEFFECTUAL

nugget: .. HUNK, LUMP, MASS, SLUG

nuisance: ..... BANE, BORE, PEST, PLAGUE, TROUBLE, ANNOYANCE

null: .... NIL, VOID, INVALID, NONEXISTENT

nullah: .... RAVINE, GORGE, GULLY

nullify: .. NULL, UNDO, VOID, CANCEL, ANNUL, NEGATE, REPEAL, OVERRIDE, ABOLISH, ABROGATE, FRUSTRATE, INVALIDATE

numb: .... DEADEN, STUPID, TORPID, STUPEFY, HELPLESS, INSENSIBLE, UNFEELING

number: ...... SUM, DATA, MANY, HOST, COUNT, DIGIT, SCORE, TOTAL, BUNDLE, FIGURE, MYRIAD, COMPUTE, DECIMAL, SEVERAL, QUANTITY, FRACTION, AGGREGATE, CALCULATE, MULTITUDE

numerous: ... LOTS, MANY, MYRIAD, COPIOUS, CROWDED, ABUNDANT, MANIFOLD, MULTIPLE, PLENTIFUL

nun: ...... SISTER, VESTAL, VOTARY

nuncio: .. LEGATE, DELEGATE, AMBASSADOR

nunnery: .... ABBEY, PRIORY, CONVENT, CLOISTER

nuptial(s): .... BRIDAL, MARITAL, WEDDING, HYMENEAL, MARRIAGE, MATRIMONIAL

nurse: . . AMAH, AYAH, CARE, FEED, REAR, TEND, MAMMY, NANNY, ATTEND, CRADLE, FOSTER, SUCKLE, NOURISH, NUTURE

nuture: . . FEED, FOOD, REAR, NURSE, TRAIN, FOSTER, CHERISH, EDUCATE, NOURISH, NUTRIMENT

nut: .... BURR, COCO, COLA, CORE, KOLA, ACORN, BETEL, CRANK, FRUIT, HAZEL, PECAN, PINON, ALMOND, BRAZIL, CASHEW, LICHEE, LITCHI, KERNEL, PEANUT, WALNUT, FILBERT, HICKORY, PROBLEM, BEECHNUT, CHESTNUT, ECCENTRIC

nutmeg: ...... MACE, SPICE

nutria: .... FUR, COYPU, RODENT

nutrient: ...... NUTRITIOUS, NOURISHING

nutriment: . FOOD, ALIMENT, NOURISHMENT

nuts, nutty: .. GAGA, BUGGY, CRAZY, QUEER, SPICY, AMOROUS, FOOLISH, PIQUANT, DEMENTED, UNBALANCED, ENTHUSIASTIC

nuzzle: .. RUB, PUSH, NESTLE, SNUGGLE

nymph: ..... AEGLE, LARVA, NAIAD, SIREN, OREAD, SYLPH, WOMAN, MAIDEN, NEREID, GODDESS, HAMADRYAD

O

O: *Greek*.......... OMEGA, OMICRON

oaf: .... (also see **fool**) BOOR, DOLT, LOUT, RUBE, DUNCE, IDIOT, RUSTIC, SIMPLETON

oar: ... ROW, BLADE, PROPEL, ROWER, SCULL, SWEEP, PADDLE

oasis: . . . . . OJO, SPA, WADI, WADY, SPRING, DOUMA,

oast: . . . . KILN, OVEN

oath: . VOW, CURSE, PLEDGE, PLIGHT, AFFIDAVIT, EXPLETIVE, PROFANITY, SWEARWORD

obclude: . . . . HIDE

obdurate: . . . . . FIRM, HARD, ADAMANT, STUBBORN, OBSTINATE, INFLEXIBLE, IMMOVABLE

obeah: . . . . . CHARM, FETISH, VOODOO, TALISMAN, WITCHCRAFT

obedience: . . . . DOCILITY, COMPLIANCE, CONFORMITY, SUBMISSION

obedient: . DOCILE, DUTIFUL, MINDFUL, YIELDING, AMENABLE, TRACTABLE, COMPLIANT

obeisance: . . BOW, HOMAGE, CONGE(E), CURTSY, FEALTY, SALAAM, DEFERENCE, REVERENCE, GENUFLECTION

obelisk: . . . . . PYLON, SHAFT, DAGGER, OBELUS, PILLAR, NEEDLE, MONUMENT

obese: . . FAT, PLUMP, PUDGY, PURSY, FLESHY, ROTUND, PORTLY, ADIPOSE, LIPAROUS, CORPULENT

obey: . . . HEAR, MIND, HEED, SUBMIT, COMPLY, FOLLOW, EXECUTE

obfuscate: . . . . DIM, DARKEN, CONFUSE, OBSCURE, PERPLEX, STUPEFY, BEWILDER

obi: . . SASH, CHARM, OBEAH, FETISH, MAGIC, GIRDLE, TALISMAN

object: . . . . AIM, END, GOAL, ITEM, MIND, ARGUE, CAVIL, DEMUR, THING, DESIGN, INTENT, MOTIVE, OPPOSE, TARGET, DISSENT, PROTEST, PURPOSE, QUARREL, CHALLANGE

objection: . . . BUT, PROTEST, QUARREL, DEMURRER, EXCEPTION, OPPOSITION

objective: . . AIM, END, FAIR, GOAL, REAL, ACTUAL, MOTIVE, REALTY, TARGET, PURPOSE, DETACHED, INTENTION, IMPERSONAL

objet d'art: . . . VASE, CURIO, BIBELOT, FIGURINE

objurgate: . . . ABUSE, CHIDE, REBUKE, REPROVE, BERATE, UPBRAID, EXECRATE

oblate: . . . . NUN, MONK, ASCETIC, MONASTIC

obligate: . . . . OWE, BIND

obligation: . . . . VOW, BOND, DEBT, DUTY, LOAN, MUST, OATH, ONUS, PLEDGE, BURDEN, PROMISE, CONTRACT, AGREEMENT, LIABILITY

obligatory: . . . . . . BINDING, BOUNDEN, FORCIBLE, REQUIRED, MANDATORY

oblige: . . . . . . PAWN, FORCE, COMPEL, PLEASE, GRATIFY, MORTGAGE, CONSTRAIN, NECESSITATE

obliging: . . . . HELPFUL, AMIABLE, AGREEABLE, COURTEOUS

oblique: . AWRY, BIAS, CANT, SKEW, ASKEW, CROSS, SLANT, ASLANT, ASKANCE, CROOKED, INCLINED, INDIRECT, SIDEWAYS, SLANTING

obliterate: . . . . . BLOT, RAZE, ANNUL, ERASE, CANCEL, DELETE, EFFACE, SPONGE, EXPUNGE, DESTROY, ANNIHILATE

oblivion: . . . . LETHE, PARDON, AMNESTY, FORGETFULNESS

oblivious: . . . . . . HEEDLESS, FORGETFUL

oblong: . . . . ELONGATED, ELLIPTICAL, RECTANGULAR

obloquy: .... ABUSE, ODIUM, INFAMY, CALUMNY, CENSURE, DISGRACE, DISHONOR

obnoxious: .... FOUL, VILE, HORRID, ODIOUS, HATEFUL, UNPLEASANT, OFFENSIVE, REPULSIVE

obscene: . RAW, FOUL, LEWD, BAWDY, GROSS, NASTY, COARSE, FILTHY, SMUTTY, VULGAR, PROFANE, INDECENT, NAUGHTY, OFFENSIVE, REPULSIVE, PORNOGRAPHIC

obscure: ... DIM, FOG, BLUR, DARK, HAZY, FAINT, FOGGY, MURKY, VAGUE, CLOUDY, DARKEN, GLOOMY, REMOTE, CONFUSE, CRYPTIC, ECLIPSE, SHADOWY, UNKNOWN, ABSTRUSE, DISGUISE, NAMELESS, NEBULOUS, NUBILOUS, AMBIGUOUS, OBFUSCATE, ENIGMATIC, RECONDITE, OVERSHADOW

obsequious: ...... DEVOTED, DUTIFUL, FAWNING, SERVILE, SLAVISH, OBEDIENT, TOADYISH, COMPLIANT, SUBMISSIVE

observance: .... FORM, RITE, RULE, CUSTOM, CEREMONY, PRACTICE

observant: .... ALERT, CAREFUL, MINDFUL, WATCHFUL, PERCEPTIVE, ATTENTIVE

observation: ... HEED, NOTE, ESPIAL, REMARK, COMMENT, ASSERTION

observe: .... EYE, SEE, SPY, ESPY, HEED, LOOK, NOTE, OBEY, ABIDE, STUDY, WATCH, BEHOLD, FOLLOW, NOTICE, REGARD, REMARK, DISCERN, COMMENT, RESPECT, WITNESS, PERCEIVE, CELEBRATE

observer: ...... AUDIENCE, ONLOOKER, LOOKOUT, WATCHER, BYSTANDER, SPECTATOR

obsess: ..... BESET, HAUNT, HARASS, PREOCCUPY

obsession: ... CRAZE, MANIA, HANG-UP, PASSION, IDEE FIXE, FIXATION

obsolete: ...... OLD, DATED, PASSE, ANCIENT, ARCHAIC, OUTDATED, DISCARDED, OUTMODED, ANTIQUATED

obstacle: ... BAR, DAM, LET, SNAG, BLOCK, HITCH, HURDLE, BARRIER, IMPEDIMENT, HINDRANCE, DIFFICULTY

obstetrician: .. ACCOUCHEUR

obstinate: ...... SET, DOUR, BALKY, TOUGH, DOGGED, MULISH, ONERY, WILLFUL, OBDURATE, PERVERSE, STUBBORN, HARDHEADED, PIGHEADED, BULLHEADED, UNBENDING, INFLEXIBLE, PERSISTENT

obstreperous: ...... NOISY, UNRULY, BOISTEROUS, VOCIFEROUS

obstruct: .. BAR, DAM, CLOG, BESET, BLOCK, CHECK, CHOKE, DELAY, IMPEDE, HINDER, HAMPER, OPPOSE, RETARD, OCCLUDE, BARRICADE

obstruction: .. SNAG, HITCH, BARRIER, EMBOLISM, FILIBUSTER, OBSTACLE, IMPEDIMENT, HINDRANCE

obtain: .... GET, WIN, EARN, FANG, GAIN, REAP, CADGE, REACH, ATTAIN, DERIVE, SECURE, ACHIEVE, ACQUIRE, CAPTURE, PROCURE, PREVAIL, RECEIVE

obtrude: ..... EJECT, EXPEL, IMPOSE

obturate: ..... CLOSE, PLUG

obtuse: .. DIM, DULL, BLUNT, DENSE, STUPID

obverse: ..... FACE, FRONT, CONVERSE, COUNTERPART

obviate: .... PREVENT, PRECLUDE, FORESTALL

obvious: . . . . CLEAR, GROSS, OVERT, PLAIN, PATENT, EVIDENT, GLARING, VISIBLE, APPARENT, DISTINCT, MANIFEST, PALPABLE

occasion: . . . . . TIME, CAUSE, EVENT, NONCE, CEREMONY, EXIGENCY, FUNCTION, INCIDENT, CONDITION, HAPPENING

occasional: . . . . ODD, RARE, ORRA, STRAY, CASUAL, SPORADIC, IRREGULAR, INFREQUENT

occlude: . . . . . CLOSE, SHUT, BLOCK, ABSORB, OBSTRUCT

occult: . . . . MAGIC, HIDDEN, MYSTIC, SECRET, VOODOO, CRYPTIC, ESOTERIC, CONCEALED, RECONDITE, MYSTERIOUS

occupancy: . TENANCY, TERM

occupant: . INMATE, TENANT, CITIZEN, DWELLER, HABITANT, INHABITANT

occupation: . . . . . JOB, TOIL, WORK, CRAFT, TRADE, CAREER, MEITER, TENURE, CALLING, PURSUIT, BUSINESS, FUNCTION, VOCATION, EMPLOYMENT, PROFESSION

occupied: . . . . . BUSY, RAPT, ENGROSSED

occupy: . . . . . SIT, USE, FILL, HOLD, TAKE, ABSORB, EMPLOY, ENGAGE, TENANT, ENGROSS, FULFILL, PERVADE, POSSESS, INTEREST

occur: . . . . . BE, COME, MEET, PASS, EXIST, APPEAR, ARRIVE, BETIDE, BEFALL, HAPPEN

occurrence: . . . CASE, EVENT, EPISODE, INCIDENT, OCCASION, ENCOUNTER, HAPPENING

ocean: . . (also see **sea**) DEEP, MAIN, BRINE, EXPANSE, ARCTIC, INDIAN, PACIFIC, ATLANTIC, ANTARCTIC

ocelot: . . . . . . CAT, LEOPARD

octave: . . . . . EIGHT, EIGHTH

octopus: . . . . . SQUID, POLYP, POULPE, OCTOPOD, DEVILFISH, MOLLUSK

octoroon: . . . METIS, MESTEE, MUSTEE

octuple: . . . . EIGHTFOLD

ocular: . . . . LENS, OPTIC, VISUAL, EYESIGHT

odd: . . . . . FELL, LEFT, LONE, ORRA, RARE, DROLL, EXTRA, FUNNY, QUEER, WEIRD, QUAINT, UNEVEN, AZYGOUS, BIZARRE, CURIOUS, STRANGE, UNUSUAL, FREAKISH, PECULIAR, SINGULAR, UNPAIRED, ECCENTRIC, INCIDENTAL, OCCASIONAL

oddment: . . . . SCRAP, LEFTOVER, REMNANT

odds: . . . DISPUTE, QUARREL, VARIANCE, ADVANTAGE, DISSENSION

ode: . . . POEM, HYMN, PSALM, CANTICLE

odeon, odeum: . . . . . HALL, GALLERY, THEATRE

odious: . . FOUL, VILE, LOATH, HATEFUL, HEINOUS, INFAMOUS, ABHORRENT, INVIDIOUS, OBNOXIOUS, REPUGNANT, OFFENSIVE, DISGUSTING, REPULSIVE, DETESTABLE

odium: . . . . INFAMY, STIGMA, DISFAVOR, DISGRACE, ANTIPATHY, APPROBIUM

odor: . . . FUME, NOSE, TANG, AROMA, SCENT, SMELL, STINK, BREATH, FLAVOR, STENCH, BOUQUET, ESSENCE, PERFUME, FRAGRANCE

odorous: . . FETID, AROMATIC, REDOLENT, FRAGRANT

of: . . . . . . BY, FROM, ABOUT, HAVING, THROUGH, CONCERNING

off: . . . . . AGEE, AWAY, DOFF, GONE, ERROR, ASIDE, WRONG,

ABSENT, REMOTE, DISTANT,
FURTHER, REMOVED

offend: . . . . SIN, VEX, HURT,
MIFF, ABUSE, ANGER, ANNOY,
GRATE, PIQUE, SHOCK, WRONG,
GRIEVE, INSULT, AFFRONT,
MORTIFY, OUTRAGE, SLIGHT,
VIOLATE, DISPLEASE

offense: . . SIN, CRIME, ERROR,
FAULT, DELICT, FELONY,
MISDEED, OUTRAGE, UMBRAGE,
TRESPASS, INDIGNITY,
AGRESSION, RESENTMENT,
MISDEMEANOR, TRANSGRESSION

offensive: . . . . . FOUL, UGLY,
FETID, ATTACK, COARSE,
HORRID, FULSOME, HATEFUL,
ODIOUS, NOISOME, LOATHSOME,
OBNOXIOUS, REPULSIVE,
AGGRESSIVE, DISGUSTING

offer: . . . . BID, ADDUCE,
ALLEGE, TENDER, ADVANCE,
COMMEND, PRESENT, PROFFER,
PROPOSE, SUGGEST, OVERTURE,
VOLUNTEER

offering: . . . . GIFT, CORBAN,
PRESENT, TRIBUTE, OBLATION,
SACRIFICE, CONTRIBUTION

offhand: . . . . CURT, CASUAL,
BRUSQUE, INFORMAL,
SLAPDASH, EXTEMPORE,
IMPROMPTU, IMPROVISED

office: . . . . DUTY, POST, ROLE,
STAFF, BUREAU, SERVICE,
FUNCTION, POSITION, BALIWICK,
SINECURE, SITUATION

official: . . . . FORMAL,
EXECUTIVE, AUTHORIZED,
BUREAUCRAT

officiate: . . . . . ACT, PRESIDE,
PERFORM

officious: . . . . FORMAL,
ARROGANT, IMPUDENT,
PUSHING, OBLIGING,
PRAGMATIC, MEDDLESOME,
EFFICACIOUS, GRATUITOUS

offset: . . . . . . SPUR, CONTRA,
BRANCH, BALANCE,
COMPENSATE, COMPLEMENT

offshoot: . . . . ISSUE, BOUGH,
SICON, BRANCH, SPROUT

offspring: . . . . . . FRY, SEED,
BROOD, FRUIT, ISSUE, SICON,
RESULT, OUTCOME, PRODUCE,
PRODUCT, PROGENY, CHILDREN,
GENITURE, DESCENDENT

often: . . COMMON, FREQUENT,
REPEATED, FREQUENTLY,
CONTINUALLY

ogee: . . . . see **molding**

ogle: . . . . . EYE, GAZE, LEER,
STARE, EXAMINE

ogre: . . . . . . DEMON, GIANT,
TYRANT, MONSTER

oil: . . FAT, BALM, FUEL, LUBE,
TUNG, BRIBE, OLEUM, ACEITE,
ANOINT, ASURUM, GREASE,
LANOLIN, LUBRICATE,
LUBRICANT, PAINTING,
PETROLEUM

oilseed: . . . . . TIN, BEN, TEEL,
SESAME, LINSEED, RAPESEED,
CASTORBEAN, COTTONSEED

oily: . . . . . FAT, GLIB, BLAND,
SLEEK, SLICK, SOAPY, SUAVE,
GREASY, OLEOSE, SMOOTH,
PINGUID, SLIPPERY, UNCTUOUS,
SEBACEOUS, OLEAGINOUS

ointment: . . . . BALM, NARD,
SALVE, BALSAM, POMADE,
UNGUENT, CALAMINE,
INUNCTION

okra: . . . . POD, PLANT, SOUP,
BENDY, GUMBO

old: . . . . AGED, AULD, GRAY,
YORE, WISE, WORN, DATED,
HOARY, PASSE, STALE,
FORMER, INFIRM, MATURE,
SENILE, SHABBY, ANTIQUE,
ARCHAIC, ANCIENT, MEDIEVAL,
OBSOLETE, ANTIQUATED

oleaginous: . . OILY, GREASY,
UNCTUOUS

oleo: . . . . SPREAD, MARGARINE

oleoresin: . . . ANIME, ELEMI,
TOLUS, BALSAM, TURPENTINE

olfaction: . . . . OSMESIS,
SMELLING

olfactory organ: . . . . . . NOSE

olio: . . MESS, STEW, MEDLEY, MELANGE, MIXTURE, MISHMASH, POTPOURRI, HODGEPODGE, MISCELLANY

olive: . . TREE, OLEA, RELISH, WREATH, APPETISER

olla: . . . JAR, JUG, POT, STEW

ollapodrida: . . . HASH, STEW, OLIO, OLLA, MEDLEY, ASSORTMENT, HODGEPODGE, MISCELLANY

ology: . . . . ISM, SCIENCE

Olympian: . . . . . . EXALTED, GODLIKE, MAJESTIC, CELESTIAL

Olympus: . . . . SKY, MOUNT, HEAVEN

omega: . . . . END, LAST

omen: . . BODE, SIGN, AUGUR, FREET, TOKEN, AUGURY, AUSPICE, PORTENT, PRESAGE, WARNING, PRECURSOR, INDICATION, PREMONITION

ominous: . . . . . . DOUR, GRIM, GRAVE, DISMAL, FATEFUL, SINISTER, MENACING, PROPHETIC, PORTENTOUS, THREATENING

omission: . . . . . CUT, ERROR, DEFAULT, FAILURE, NEGLECT, EXCLUSION, OVERSIGHT

omit: . . . . CUT, DELE, DROP, MISS, SKIP, SLIP, ELIDE, CANCEL, DELETE, EXCEPT, FORGET, IGNORE, DISCARD, NEGLECT, OVERLOOK, DISREGARD, PRETERMIT

omnipotent: . . . GOD, DIETY, GREAT, ARRANT, MIGHTY, ALMIGHTY, POWERFUL, UNEQUALED, ALL-POWERFUL

omnipresent: . . . . IMMANENT, UBIQUITOUS

omniscient: . . . . WISE, LEARNED, POWERFUL, ALL-KNOWING, EVERPRESENT

on: . . . . ATOP, UPON, ABOVE, ABOUT, AHEAD, ALONG, ANENT, WITHIN, FORWARD, CONCERNING

onager: . . . . . . ASS, DONKEY, CATAPULT

once: . . . . . ANES, ONE TIME, FORMER(LY), QUONDAM, ERST(WHILE), WHENEVER

once-over: . . . . GLANCE, SURVEY, SCRUTINY

oncoming: . . . . . IMPENDING, APPROACH(ING)

one: . . . AN, ACE, UNA, SAME, SOLE, SOME, UNAL, UNIT, ALONE, UNITY, PERSON, SINGLE, UNIQUE, UNITED, NUMERAL, PRONOUN, UNBROKEN, UNDIVIDED, INDIVIDUAL

one-sided: . . . ROUT, BIASED, UNEVEN, UNFAIR, UNJUST, BIGOTED, PARTIAL, EX PARTE, PREJUDICED, UNILATERAL

oneness: . . UNITY, CONCORD, IDENTITY, SAMENESS

onerous: . . . . HARD, HEAVY, ARDUOUS, EXACTING, DIFFICULT, LABORIOUS, OPPRESSIVE, BURDENSOME

onion: . . BOLL, BULB, CEPA, LEEK, CHIVE, CIBOL, PEARL, BERMUDA, SHALLOT, ESCHALOT, SCALLION

onlooker: . . . . WITNESS, AUDIENCE, BEHOLDER, SPECTATOR, BYSTANDER, RUBBERNECK

only: . . . . . BUT, JUST, LONE, MERE, SOLE, BARELY, MERELY, SIMPLY, SINGLY, SOLELY, EXCEPTING, EXCLUSIVELY

onset: . . . DASH, RUSH, START, ASSAULT, ATTACK, CHARGE, ATTEMPT, BEGINNING, ONSLAUGHT

onto: . . . . ATOP, AWARE, COGNIZANT, CONVERSANT

onus: . . . . DUTY, LOAD, BURDEN, CHARGE, OBLIGATION, RESPONSIBILITY

onward: .... AHEAD, ALONG, FORTH, FORWARD, ADVANCING

oodles: ...... HEAPS, LOTS, MANY, SCADS, SLEWS, ABUNDANCE

oolong: .... TEA

oomiak: ..... BOAT, UNIAK, KAYAK, CANOE

oomph: ..... VIGOR, ENERGY

ooze: . BOG, MUD, SOP, DRIP, FLOW, LEAK, MIRE, SEEP, EXUDE, GLEET, BLEED, MARSH, SLIME, SWEAT, SLUDGE, TRANSUDE, PERMEATE, PERCOLATE, EXUDATE, SEDIMENT

opalescent: ..... IRIDESCENT

opaque: ..... DARK, DULL, STUPID, OBSCURE, OBTUSE

open: .... AJAR, FREE, PARE, UNDO, AGAPE, BEGIN, CLEAR, FRANK, OVERT, PLAIN, START, UNTIE, CANDID, DIRECT, EXPOSE, HONEST, PATENT, PUBLIC, UNBOLT, UNFOLD, UNFURL, UNLOCK, UNSEAL, ARTLESS, OBVIOUS, SINCERE, APPARENT, COMMENCE, DISCLOSE, INITIATE, MANIFEST, UNFASTEN, ORIGINATE, GENEROUS, AVAILABLE

opening: .... OS, GAP, BORE, DOOR, GATE, HOLE, PASS, PORE, RIFT, SLIT, SLOT, VENT, CLEFT, DEBUT, MOUTH, START, AVENUE, BREACH, CHANCE, GAMBIT, HIATUS, OUTLET, PORTAL, CREVICE, FISSURE, ORIFICE, VACANCY, APERTURE, OVERTURE, OPPORTUNITY, INAUGURATION

operate: ... ACT, MAN, RUN, TEND, WORK, AFFECT, EFFECT, CONDUCT, MANAGE, MANIPULATE

operation: ... DEED, ACTION, AGENCY, PROCESS, PROJECT, CREATION, FUNCTION, ACTUATION, PROCEDURE, PRODUCTION

operative: ..... SPY, HAND, ARTIST, WORKER, ARTISAN, MECHANIC, EFFECTIVE, DETECTIVE

operator: ... AGENT, QUACK, DEALER, MANAGER, SURGEON, CONDUCTOR

operculum: ...... LID, FLAP

operose: ... BUSY, DILIGENT, LABORIOUS, INDUSTRIOUS

ophidian: .. ASP, EEL, SNAKE, CONGER, REPTILE, SERPENT

opinion: ...... IDEA, VIEW, GUESS, TENET, ADVICE, BELIEF, DICTUM, ESTEEM, NOTION, REPUTE, CONCEPT, THOUGHT, DECISION, ESTIMATE, CONSENSUS, CONVICTION, SENTIMENT, JUDGMENT, IMPRESSION, EVALUATION, PERSUASION

opium: .... DRUG, NARCOTIC

opponent: ..... FOE, ENEMY, ADVERSARY, ASSAILANT, ANTAGONIST

opportune: . READY, TIMELY, APROPOS, SUITABLE, FAVORABLE, WELL-TIMED, AUSPICIOUS, CONVENIENT, PROPITIOUS, SEASONABLE

opportunity: ..... CHANCE, OPENING, OCCASION, ADVANTAGE, POSSIBILITY, CIRCUMSTANCE

oppose: ..... PIT, VIE, BUCK, COPE, DARE, DEFY, FACE, MEET, STEM, ARGUE, BLOCK, CHECK, CROSS, FIGHT, REBEL, REBUT, REPEL, COMBAT, OBJECT, OPPUGN, RESIST, CONTEST, CONTER, CONFRONT, OBSTRUCT, WITHSTAND

opposed: .... ANTI, ADVERSE, AGAINST, HOSTILE

opposite: .... ANENT, POLAR, ACROSS, AVERSE, FACING, ADVERSE, COUNTER, INVERSE,

REVERSE, VIS-A-VIS,
CONTRARY, ANTIPODE
oppress: . . . . . LOAD, CRUSH,
GRIND, WEIGH, WRONG,
BURDEN, EXTORT, HARASS,
RAVISH, SUBDUE, AFFLICT,
REPRESS, TRAMPLE, DISTRESS,
SUPPRESS, PERSECUTE,
TYRANNIZE
oppressive: . . . HARD, CLOSE,
HARSH, HEAVY, SEVERE,
ONEROUS, RIGOROUS,
TYRANNICAL
opprobrium: . . . . . . ABUSE,
ODIUM, SHAME, SCORN,
INFAMY, INSULT, CALUMNY,
OFFENSE, SCANDAL, DISGRACE,
DISHONOR, REPROACH
oppugn: . . . OPPOSE, DISPUTE
opt: . . . . CULL, PICK, ELECT,
CHOOSE, SELECT, DECIDE
optic: . . EYE, OCULAR, VISUAL
optimistic: . . . ROSY, JOYOUS,
HOPEFUL, ROSEATE,
EXPECTANT, SANGUINE
option: . . CHOICE, PRIVILEGE,
ALTERNATIVE
optional: . . . . ELECTIVE,
VOLUNTARY
opulent: . . FAT, RICH, AMPLE,
LAVISH, PROFUSE, WEALTHY,
ABUNDANT, AFFLUENT,
LUXURIANT
opus: . . . . . . WORK, OPERA,
SYMPHONY, COMPOSITION
oracle: . . . . . . SEER, AUGUR
oracular: . . . . . OTIC, VATIC,
ORPHIC, PROPHETIC,
MYSTERIOUS
oral: . . . . ALOUD, VOCAL,
VERBAL, STOMATIC, SPOKEN,
UTTERED
orange: . . . . . MOCK, CITRUS,
TANGERINE, MANDARIN
orate: . . . . . . MOUTH, PLEAD,
SPEAK, SPIEL, SPOUT, ADDRESS,
DECLAIM, LECTURE,
HARANGUE, DISCOURSE,

PERORATE, SPEECHIFY,
FILIBUSTER
oratory: . CHAPEL, CHANTRY,
ELOCUTION
orb: . . . . . . EYE, SUN, BALL,
MOON, STAR, EARTH, GLOBE,
CIRCLE, PLANET, SPHERE,
CIRCUIT
orbit: . . . . PATH, TRACK,
SOCKET, CIRCUIT, ELLIPSE
orchestra: . . . . BAND, GROUP,
PARQUET, ENSEMBLE
orchestral section: . . . WIND,
WOOD, BRASS, STRING,
TIMPANY, PERCUSSION
ordain: . . . . . . DEEM, ALLOT,
ENACT, ORDER, DECREE,
ADJUDGE, APPOINT, COMMAND,
DESTINE, INSTALL, PREPARE,
ESTABLISH, PRESCRIBE
ordeal: . . . TRIAL, HARDSHIP,
EXPERIENCE, TRIBULATION
order: . . . . . BAN, BID, BOON,
FIAT, FORM, RANK, RULE,
WILL, ALIGN, ARRAY, CLASS,
EDICT, GENUS, GRADE,
CHARGE, COSMOS, DECREE,
DEGREE, DEMAND, DIRECT,
ENJOIN, MANAGE, METHOD,
ORDAIN, POLICE, SERIES,
SYSTEM, ADJUDGE, ARRANGE,
BIDDING, COMMAND, MANDATE,
PRESCRIPT, PRESCRIBE,
DIRECTION, INSTRUCT(ION)
orderly: . . AIDE, NEAT, TIDY,
TRIM, REGULAR, DECOROUS,
OBEDIENT, PEACEABLY,
SYSTEMATIC, ATTENDANT,
METHODICAL, WELL-BEHAVED
ordinance: . . . . . LAW, FIAT,
RITE, EDICT, ASSIZE, DECREE,
CONTROL, STATUTE
ordinary: . . . PLAIN, USUAL,
COMMON, NORMAL, TAVERN,
MEDIAL, AVERAGE, MILL-RUN,
NATURAL, PROSAIC, REGULAR,
ROUTINE, VULGATE, EVERYDAY,
HABITUAL, MEDIOCRE,
CUSTOMARY, COMMONPLACE

ordnance: . . . GUNS, ARMOR, MISSLES, WEAPONS, ARTILLERY, TORPEDOES, AMMUNITION
piece: . . CANNON, MORTAR
ordure: . . . . . . DUNG, FILTH, MANURE
ore: . . . . . . METAL, MINERAL
oread: . . . . . NYMPH, NAIAD
organ: . . . . . . PIPE, MEANS, BARREL, MEDIUM, MELODEON, HARMONICA, HARMONIUM, HURDY-GURDY, INSTRUMENT, PERIODICAL
organic: . . INBORN, NATURAL, INHERENT, FUNDAMENTAL, INSTRUMENTAL, CONSTITUTIONAL
organism: . . ANIMAL, PLANT, AEROBE, MONAD, MONAS
organization: . . . CLUB, FIRM, CADRE, GUILD, SETUP, UNION, OUTFIT, SOCIETY, ASSOCIATION, CORPORATION
organize: . . . FORM, SET UP, INSTITUTE, ARRANGE, SYSTEMATIZE
orgy: . . . LARK, BASH, BINGE, SPREE, REVELRY, CAROUSAL
orient: . . ASIA, EAST, ADAPT, ADJUST, FAREAST
oriental: . . . . ASIAN, PEARL, BRIGHT, RISING, SHINING, LUSTROUS, PELLUCID, EASTERN, ASIATIC, CHINESE, JAPANESE
orifice: . . HOLE, PORE, VENT, INLET, MOUTH, STOMA, CAVITY, OUTLET, CHIMNEY, OPENING, OSTIOLE, APERTURE, SPIRACLE
origin: . . . . NEE, GERM, RISE, ROOT, SEED, BIRTH, CAUSE, START, NATURE, PARENT, SOURCE, GENESIS, LINEAGE, ANCESTRY, NASCENCE, BEGINNING, PARENTAGE, EXTRACTION
original: . . . . . . NEW, FIRST, NOVEL, NATIVE, PRIMAL, INITIAL, PRIMARY, EARLIEST, PRISTINE, AUTHENTIC, INVENTIVE, ABORIGINAL
originate: . . . . ARISE, BEGIN, BREED, CAUSE, FOUND, START, DEVISE, CREATE, INVENT, EMANATE, PRODUCE, COMMENCE, CONTRIVE, DISOVER, GENERATE, INITIATE, ESTABLISH, INSTITUTE
orison: . . . PRAYER, SPEECH
orle: . . . . . . BORDE, FILLET, WREATH, BEARING, CHAPLET
ormolu: . . . . . . GILT, GOLD, ALLOY, VARNISH
ornament: . . . . (also see **decoration**) FOB, PIN, ETCH, TOOL, TRIM, ADORN, CHASE, INLAY, AMULET, BEDAUB, BEDECK, BROOCH, EMBOSS, ENRICH, ENGRAVE, GARNISH, SPANGLE, TRINKET, DECORATE, LAVALIER, ADORNMENT
ornamental: . . . . . . FANCY, ELEGANT, DECORATIVE
ornate: . . . . . . FINE, FANCY, SHOWY, FLORID, AUREATE, BAROQUE, FLOWERY, ELABORATE, FLAMBOYANT
ornery: . . . . . . MEAN, TESTY, MULISH, CRABBED, IRRITABLE, OBSTINATE, ORDINARY, STUBBORN, QUARRELSOME, CANTANKEROUS
orotund: . . . . . FULL, CLEAR, SHOWY, MELLOW, STRONG, POMPOUS, RESONANT, BOMBASTIC
orphan: . . WAIF, FOUNDLING
orphic: . . . . MYSTIC, OCCULT, ORACULAR
orra: . . . . ODD, EXTRA, OCCASIONAL, UNEMPLOYED
ort: . . . BIT, CRUMB, SCRAP, MORSEL, REFUSE, FRAGMENT, LEFTOVER, REMNANT
orthodox: . . . . PROPER, CANONIC, CORRECT, ACCEPTED, STANDARD, CONVENTIONAL

os: . . . BONE, ESKER, MOUTH, OPENING

oscillate: . . . . . . WAG, ROCK, SWAY, VARY, WAVE, SWING, WAVER, WEAVE, VIBRATE, LIBRATE, FLUCTUATE, VACILLATE

oscitant: . . . . DULL, DROWSY, GAPING, SLEEPY, STUPID, YAWNING, CARELESS, SLUGGISH, APATHETIC

osseous: . . . . . BONE, BONY, OSTEAL, OSSIFEROUS

ossicle: . . . . . . BONE, INCUS, STAPES, BONELET, MALLEUS, EARBONE

ossuary: . . . . . . URN, TOMB, VAULT, RECEPTACLE

osteal: . . . . . BONY, OSSEOUS

ostensible: . . . . . . SEEMING, APPARENT, SPECIOUS, PRETENDED, PROFESSED

ostentation: . . . SHOW, POMP, ECLAT, FLARE, GLOSS, PARADE, DISPLAY, PAGEANT, FLOURISH, PRETENSE, SPLURGE, SHOWINESS, SPECTACLE, EXHIBITION

ostentatious: . . ARTY, LOUD, GANDY, SHOWY, OBVIOUS, POMPOUS, ELABORATE, FLAUNTING, PRETENTIOUS

ostiole: . . . . . . PORE, STOMA, ORIFICE, OPENING

osteoma: . . . . TUMOR

ostracize: . . . . . BAR, SNUB, EXILE, BANISH, REJECT, EXCLUDE, BLACKBALL, PROSCRIBE, EXPATRIATE

otalgia: . . . . EARACHE

other: . . . . ELSE, MORE, FORMER, FURTHER, DISTINCT, DIFFERENT, ADDITIONAL

otherwise: . . . . . ELSE, ALIAS, ALITER, DIFFERENTLY

otic: . . . . . AURAL, AUDITORY

otiose: . . . IDLE, LAZY, VAIN, FUTILE, STERILE, USELESS, INACTIVE, INDOLENT, REPOSING, UNEMPLOYED

otologist: . . . . AURIST

ottoman: . . . . . . POUF, SEAT, TURK, COUCH, DIVAN, FABRIC, (FOOT)STOOL

oubliette: . . . . DUNGEON

ouch: . . . . . . ADORN, BEZEL, CLASP, BROOCH, BUCKLE, FIBULA, ORNAMENT, EXCLAMATION

ought: . MUST, ZERO, CIPHER, NAUGHT, SHOULD, BEHOOVE, ANYTHING

oust: . . . EXPEL, EJECT, EVICT, BANISH, BOUNCE, REMOVE, DISMISS, DISPOSSESS

out: . AWAY, FORTH, ABSENT, BEGONE, ISSUED, EXTERNAL, PUBLISHED

outage: . . . . . VENT, OUTLET, SUSPENSION, INTERRUPTION

outbreak: . . . . . RASH, RIOT, BURST, RUCKUS, TUMULT, ERUPTION, OCCURRENCE, INSURRECTION

outbuilding: . . . BARN, SHED, PRIVY, GARAGE, BACKHOUSE

outburst: . . . . . GALE, GUST, RAGE, TIFF, BLAST, FLARE, STORM, BLOWUP, TIRADE, FLAREUP, TANTRUM, TORRENT, ERUPTION, EXPLOSION

outcast: . . . . . EXILE, LEPER, PARIAH, WRETCH, REJECTED, EXPATRIATE

outclass: . . . . . BEST, EXCEL, SURPASS

outcome: . . . . . . FATE, ISSUE, EFFECT, RESULT, UPSHOT, SEQUEL, EMANATE, AFTERMATH, CONSEQUENCE

outcry: . . . HUE, BAWL, YELL, ALARM, NOISE, SHOUT, CLAMOR, PROTEST, OBJECTION

outdo: . . . . CAP, EXCEL, DEFEAT, EXCEED, SURPASS

outer: . . . . ALIEN, ECTAL, UTTER, FOREIGN, OUTSIDE,

EXTERNAL, EXTERIOR, EXTRANEOUS, COAT, HUSK, SHELL, CRUST, RIND, WRAP, COCOON

outfit: .... KIT, RIG, GANG, GARB, GEAR, SUIT, TEAM, UNIT, EQUIP, ATTIRE, FURNISH, EQUIPMENT, CAPARISON, ORGANIZATION, PARAPHERNALIA

outflank: ... EVADE, OUTWIT, THWART

outflow: .... DRAIN, EFFLUX

outgoing: ...... SOCIABLE, GREGARIOUS

outgrowth: .... RESULT, OFFSHOOT, EMERGENCE

outlandish: .. ALIEN, ABSURD, EXOTIC, BIZARRE, FOREIGN, STRANGE, UNCOUTH, PECULIAR, FANTASTIC

outlaw: .... BAN, EXILE, BANDIT, BANISH, FUGITIVE, CRIMINAL, PROHIBIT, BRIGAND, PROSCRIBE, DESPERADO, HIGHWAYMAN

outlay: ..... COST, EXPENSE, EXPEDITURE, DISBURSEMENT

outlet: ... EXIT, VENT, ISSUE, AGENCY, EGRESS, ESCAPE, MARKET, OPENING, PASSAGE

outline: .. MAP, DRAW, PLAN, BRIEF, CHART, DRAFT, FRAME, SHAPE, TRACE, DESIGN, SCHEMA, SKETCH, CONTOUR, PROFILE, SUMMARY, DESCRIBE, SYNOPSIS, DELINEATE

outlook: ..... VIEW, VISTA, ASPECT, PROSPECT, PERCEPTION, EXPECTATION

outmoded: .. DATED, PASSE, ANTIQUE, OBSOLETE

output: ..... POWER, YIELD, ENERGY, PRODUCT(ION)

outrage: .... ABUSE, INSULT, OFFEND, RAVISH, AFFRONT, OFFENSE, SCANDAL, VIOLATE, ATROCITY

outrageous: ...... HEINOUS, OBSCENE, FLAGRANT, SHOCKING, ATROCIOUS, MONSTROUS, EXORBITANT

outre: ... BIZARRE, STRANGE, ECCENTRIC

outright: .... TOTAL, WHOLE, DIRECT, OPENLY, COMPLETE, ENTIRELY

outset: ... START, BEGINNING

outsider: .. ALIEN, STRANGER, NON-MEMBER, FOREIGNER

outspoken: .... BOLD, FREE, OPEN, BLUNT, FRANK, CANDID, EXPLICIT, UNRESERVED

outstanding: ...... FAMED, NOTED, FAMOUS, MARKED, UNPAID, EMINENT, NOTABLE, PRINCIPAL, PROMINENT, UNSETTLED, PROJECTING, CONSPICUOUS, EXCEPTIONAL

outstrip: .... CAP, TOP, WIN, BEST, LEAD, PASS, EXCEL, EXCEED, SURPASS

outward: .... ECTAD, OUTER, OVERT, VISIBLE, APPARENT

outwit: ... FOX, BALK, BEST, FOIL, BLOCK, CHECK, BAFFLE, THWART, FRUSTRATE, OUTSMART, OVERCOME, CIRCUMVENT

oval: ..... ELLIPSE, STADIUM, EGG-SHAPED, ELLIPSOIDAL, ELLIPTIC(AL)

ovation: .... APPLAUSE, PLAUDIT, EXULTATION

oven: .... KILN, LEER, OAST, BAKER, FURNACE

overage: ... EXCESS, SURPLUS

overbearing: ...... PROUD, HAUGHTY, ARROGANT, CAVALIER, SNOBBISH, IMPERIOUS, DISDAINFUL, DOMINEERING

overcast: ... DIM, SEW, DARK, DULL, CLOUDY, DARKEN, GLOOMY, LOWERING

overcharge: ... GYP, EXCISE, GOUGE, HOLD UP

overcome: .. GET, WIN, BEAT, BEST, CRUSH, DEFEAT, EXCEED, MASTER, SUBDUE, CONQUER, CONFUTE, CONVINCE, OVERWHELM, SURMOUNT, VANQUISH

overdue: ..... LATE, TARDY, ARREARS, BELATED, DELAYED

overflow: ..... SLOP, TEEM, VENT, FLOOD, SPATE, SPILL, DELUGE, OUTLET, ALLUVION, INUNDATE

overhang: ..... JUT, BEETLE, PROJECT, SUSPEND

overhaul: .... REPAIR, EXAMINE, OVERTAKE, RENOVATE

overhead: ... ABOVE, ALOFT, COSTS, EXPENSE

overjoyed: .... ELATED, JUBILANT, DELIGHTED

overlapping: .... OBVOLUTE, IMBRICATE, EQUITANT

overlay: .... CAP, LAP, CEIL, COAT, PARE, COVER, GLAZE, PLATE, SPREAD, VENEER, ENCRUST, COVERING, SUPERIMPOSE

overlook: . MISS, OMIT, SKIP, FORGO, EXCUSE, FORGET, IGNORE, MANAGE, ABSOLVE, CONDONE, INSPECT, NEGLECT, DISREGARD

overman: ... CHIEF, LEADER, ARBITER, FOREMAN, REFEREE, OVERSEER, ARBITRATOR

overnice: ... FUSSY, PRECISE, FINICKY, FASTIDIOUS

overpower: .... AWE, BEAT, ROUT, CRUSH, DEFEAT, MASTER, SUBDUE, CONQUER, CONTROL, CONVINCE, VANQUISH

override: .... VETO, DEFEAT, NULLIFY

overrule: ..... VETO, ANNUL, ABROGATE, COUNTERMAND

overrun: .... CRUSH, INFEST, SWARM, RAVAGE, SPREAD, DESTROY

oversee: .... STEER, WATCH, SURVEY, EXAMINE, INSPECT, SUPERVISE, SUPERINTEND

overseer: ..... BOSS, REEVE, CENSOR, BALIFF, FOREMAN, MANAGER, STEWARD, INSPECTOR, SUPERVISOR, TASKMASTER, SUPERINTENDENT

overshadow: ... DIM, COVER, DWARF, DARKEN, OBSCURE, ECLIPSE, DOMINATE

overshoot: .... EXCEED

oversight: .... CARE, ERROR, LAPSE, SLIP(UP), BLUNDER, CONTROL, MISTAKE, OMISSION, DIRECTION

overt: .... OPEN, PUBLIC, PATENT, OBVIOUS, APPARENT, MANIFEST, OBSERVABLE

overthrow: ...... END, TIP, DOWN, HURL, RAZE, ROUT, RUIN, FLING, UPSET, WORST, DEFEAT, DEPOSE, TOPPLE, UNSEAT, OVERCOME, CONQUER, DESTROY, VANQUISH

overture: .. OFFER, OPENING, PRELUDE, APERTURE, PROPOSAL, PROPOSITION

overturn: .. TIP, CAVE, COUP, UPSET, TOPPLE, CAPSIZE, DESTROY, PERVERT, REVERSE, SUBVERT

overwhelm: .. BURY, AMAZE, CRUSH, DEFEAT, SWAMP, DELUGE, ENGULF, CONQUER, ASTONISH, INUNDATE

ovoid: .. OVATE, EGG-SHAPED, OVIFORM

ovule: .. EGG, SEED, EMBRYO, GEMMULE

ovum: .... EGG, SEED, SPORE

owing: .... DUE, UNPAID

own: ... AVOW, HAVE, HOLD, ADMIT, CONCEDE, CONFESS, POSSESS, RECOGNIZE, ACKNOWLEDGE

ownership: . . . . TITLE, TENANCY, DOMINIUM, POSSESSION, PROPRIETORSHIP

ox: . . . . . . YAK, ANOA, BEEF, MUSK, ZEBU, BISON, STEER, BOVINE, BANTENG, BUFFALO, BULLOCK

oxford: . . . . . . SHOE, CLOTH, COLLEGE, COTTON, BROGAN, UNIVERSITY

oxidize: . . . . . RUST, CALCINE

oxter: . . . . ARM, ARMPIT

oxygen: . . . . AIR, GAS, OZONE

oxygenate: . . . . . . AERATE, OXIDIZE

oyster: . . BIVALVE, SCALLOP, MOLLUSK, BLUEPOINT

ozone: . . . . . . AIR, OXYGEN

P

P: *Greek:* . . . . PI, RHO
Hebrew: . . . . PEH

pabulum: . . . FOOD, CEREAL, ALIMENT, SUPPORT, SUSTENANCE

pace: . . . . CLIP, GAIT, LOPE, RATE, STEP, TROT, WALK, AMBLE, SPEED, TEMPO, TREAD, CANTER, GALLOP, SPRINT, STRIDE, DOGTROT

pachyderm: . . . . . ELEPHANT, RHINO(CEROS), HIPPO(TAMUS)

pacific: . . CALM, MEEK, MILD, OCEAN, IRENIC, PLACID, SERENE, TRANQUIL, PEACEFUL

pacifer: . . . SOP, RING, NIPPLE, APPEASER

pacify: . . CALM, EASE, LULL, ABATE, ALLAY, QUIET, STILL, SOOTHE, APPEASE, ASSUAGE, PLACATE, MOLLIFY, MITIGATE, ALLEVIATE, RECONCILE, PROPITIATE, CONCILATE

pack: . . . WAD, BALE, CRAM, DECK, GANG, LOAD, MASS, STOW, TAMP, CROWD, FLOCK, GROUP, HORDE, PRESS, TRUSS,

BUNDLE, BURDEN, DUFFLE, EMBALE, ENCASE, FARDEL, KNAPSACK

package: . . . BOX, PAD, BALE, CASE, BUNDLE, CARTON, PACKET, PARCEL

pact: . . . . . . MISE, CARTEL, TREATY, BARGAIN, COMPACT, ALLIANCE, CONTRACT, COVENANT, AGREEMENT

pad: . . . . MAT, WAD, WAY, FOOT, PATH, ROAD, WALK, QUILT, STUFF, BUFFER, PILLOW, SADDLE, TABLET, TRUDGE, BOLSTER, CUSHION, FOOTFALL, HIGHWAYMAN

paddle: . . . . BAT, OAR, ROW, WADE, SCULL, SPANK, DABBLE, TODDLE, PROPEL, RACKET

paddock: . LOT, FROG, PARK, TOAD, FIELD, SLEDGE, ENCLOSURE

padlock: . . . . LOCK, FASTEN, CLOSING, FASTENER

padre: . . . . . MONK, CLERIC, FATHER, PRIEST, CHAPLAIN

padrone: . . MASTER, PATRON, LANDLOARD, INNKEEPER

paean: . . ODE, HYMN, SONG, PRAISE

pagan: . . . . ETHNIC, PAYNIM, INFIDEL, HEATHEN, IDOLATOR, UNBELIEVER

page: . . . . BOY, CALL, LEAF, FOLIO, SHEET, RECORD, SUMMON, FOOTBOY, SERVANT, HENCHMAN, ATTENDANT, MESSENGER

pageant: . . . . POMP, SHOW, PARADE, TABLEAU, SPECTACLE, EXHIBITION, PROCESSION

paid: . . SETTLED, DISBURSED, DISCHARGED

pail: . . . . CAN, BOWIE, SKEEL, STOUP, BUCKET, PIGGIN, VESSEL, CANNIKIN

pain: . . . ACHE, AGRA, CARE, HARM, HURT, PANG, AGONY, CRAMP, GRIEF, STING, THROE,

WOUND, GRIEVE, TWINGE,
ANGUISH, PENALTY, TORTURE,
TRAVAIL, TROUBLE, DISTRESS,
SUFFERING

painful: . . . . . . ACHY, SORE,
IRKSOME, EXACTING,
DIFFICULT, LABORIOUS

painkiller: . . . . OPIATE,
ANODYNE, ASPIRIN, NARCOTIC,
ANALGESIC, PAREGORIC,
ANESTHESIA

pains: . . . . . . CARE, EFFORT,
TROUBLE, EXERTION

painstaking: . . . . . CAREFUL,
DILIGENT, EXACTING,
ASSIDUOUS, ELABORATE,
LABORIOUS

paint: . . . COAT, DAUB, GAUD,
LIMN, ADORN, COLOR, FUCUS,
ROUGE, STAIN, DEPICT,
ENAMEL, PORTRAY, PICTURE,
PIGMENT, PRETEND, STIPPLE,
DECORATE, LIPSTICK

painter: . . . ARTIST, ARTISTE,
COUGAR, PANTHER, DECORATOR

painting: . . . . . . OIL, MURAL,
CANVAS, IMPASTO, PORTRAIT,
LANDSCAPE, WATERCOLOR

genre: . . . . . . ABSTRACT,
CUBIST, ORIENTAL,
SURREALISTIC,
IMPRESSIONISTIC

pair: . . . . . . DUO, TWO, CASE,
DIAD, DUAD, DUET, DYAD,
MATE, SPAN, TEAM, YOKE,
BRACE, MATCH, UNITE, COUPLE

pal: . . . ALLY, CHUM, BUDDY,
CRONY, FRIEND, COMRADE,
PARTNER, ASSOCIATE,
COMPANION

palace: . . . . . COURT, SERAI,
CASTLE, ALCAZAR, EDIFICE,
MANSION, PRETORIUM

palatable: . . . . SAPID, TASTY,
SAVORY, PLEASING,
AGREEABLE, DELICIOUS,
TOOTHSOME

palate: . . . . . TASTE, LIKING,
RELISH, VELUM, UVULA

palatial: . . . LARGE, ORNATE,
STATELY, MAGNIFICENT

palaver: . . . . . . CHAT, TALK,
DEBATE, PARLEY, CHATTER,
WHEEDLE, CAJOLERY,
FLATTER(Y), CONFERENCE,
CONVERSATION

pale: . . . . . DIM, WAN, ASHY,
FADE, GREY, PALL, ASHEN,
BLEAK, FENCE, LIVID, LURID,
STAKE, STICK, WHITE, ANEMIC,
BLANCH, CHALKY, FEEBLE,
PALLID, PICKET, SALLOW,
WHITEN, GHASTLY

paleness: . . . . PALLOR

palestra: . . . . SCHOOL,
GYMNASIUM

paling: . . . . . . PALE, FENCE,
STAKE, PICKET, FENCING,
ENCLOSURE

palisade: . . . . . CLIFF, FENCE,
STAKE, BARRIER, ENCLOSE,
FORTIFY, ESPALIER, SURROUND

pall: . . . . BORE, CLOY, PALE,
SATE, CLOAK, CLOTH, QUALM,
MANTLE, NAUSEA, DISGUST,
SATIATE, COVERING

pallet: . . . . . . BED, COT, PAD,
PATE, PAWL, COUCH, QUILT,
BLANKET, MATTRESS,
PLATFORM

palliate: . . . . . . EASE, HIDE,
SALVE, CLOAK, COVER,
EXCUSE, LESSEN, SOFTEN,
SOOTHE, TEMPER, CONCEAL,
SHELTER, MITIGATE,
ALLEVIATE, EXTENUATE,
EXCULPATE

pallid: . . . WAN, ASHY, PALE,
BLEAK, FAINT, WHITE,
SHALLOW, GHASTLY,
COLORLESS

palm: . . . COCO, DATE, TREE,
HIDE, ROYAL, THENAR,
TROPHY, CONCEAL, VICTORY,
TRIUMPH

palmate: . . . . . FLAT, BROAD,
LOBED, WEBBED, WEB-FOOTED

palpable: .... RANK, PLAIN, PATENT, AUDIBLE, EVIDENT, OBVIOUS, TACTILE, APPARENT, MANIFEST, TANGIBLE, NOTICEABLE

palpitation: .... BEAT, PANT, THROB, FLICKER, FLUTTER, PULSATION, QUIVERING, TREMBLING, SALTATION

palsied: ... SHAKY, SHAKING, PARALYZED, TOTTERING, TREMBLING

palter: ... FIB, LIE, BABBLE, HAGGLE, TRIFLE, QUIBBLE, CHATTER, EQUIVOCATE, PREVARICATE

paltry: .. BALD, BARE, BASE, MEAN, PUNY, VILE, PETTY, SMALL, FLIMSY, TRASHY, PITIFUL, RUBBISH, TRIVIAL, PICAYUNE, TRIFLING, WORTHLESS, DESPICABLE

paludal: ... BOGGY, MARSHY

pampas: .... PLAINS

pamper: .. PET, BABY, CRAM, GLUT, HUMOR, SPOIL, CARESS, CODDLE, COSHER, COSSET, FONDLE, GRATIFY, INDULGE, SATIATE

pamphlet: .. TRACT, FOLDER, BOOKLET, LEAFLET, TREATISE, BROCHURE, CATALOG(UE)

pan: .... DISH, WASH, BASIN, ROAST, UNITE, VESSEL, ROTATE, CRANIUM, SKILLET, GRIDDLE, (ICE)FLOE, SUBSOIL, RIDICULE, CRITICIZE

panacea: .... CURE, EXLIXIR, REMEDY, CURE-ALL, HEAL-ALL, NOSTRUM, MEDICINE, CATHOLICON

panache: ... PLUME, APLOMB, FLAMBOYANCE

Panama: .... HAT, GULF, CANAL, DARIEN, ISTHMUS

pancake: .. BLINTZE, FRITTER, HOTCAKE, FLAPJACK, GRIDDLECAKE

panda: ..... WAH, BEARCAT

pandemic: .... GENERAL, PREVALENT

pandemonium: ..... HELL, CHAOS, NOISE, TUMULT, UPROAR, DISORDER, CONFUSION

pander: .... PIMP, CATER, PROCURER, GO-BETWEEN

pane: ..... GLASS, SECTION, RONDEL

panegyric: .. ELOGE, EULOGY, PRAISE, ORATION, ECOMIUM, TRIBUTE, LAUDATION

panel: .... JURY, GROUP, SADDLE, VENIRE, DECORATE

pang: .. ACHE, PAIN, AGONY, SPASM, THROE, TWINGE, ANGUISH, PAROXYSM

panic: ... FEAR, FRAY, FUNK, ALARM, CHAOS, SCARE, BUTTON, FRIGHT, TERROR, STAMPEDE

panorama: ... VIEW, SCENE, SWEEP, VISTA, PICTURE, SCENERY

pant: ... BLOW, GASP, HUFF, PUFF, HEAVE, THROB, YEARN, PALPITATE, PULSATE

pantheon: ... TOMB, TEMPLE

panther: .. CAT, PARD, PUMA, COUGAR, JAGUAR, LEOPARD

pantry: .... AMBRY, CLOSET, EWRY, LARDER, SPENCE, BUTTERY, CUPBOARD

pants: .... JEANS, LEVIS, SLACKS, KNICKERS, TROUSERS, DRAWERS

pap: .... MASH, PULP, TEAT, NIPPLE, EMULSION

papal: ...... (also see **Pope**) APOSTOLIC, PONTIFICAL

papaya: .... PA(W)PAW

paper: ..... DAILY, ESSAY, SCRIP, SHEET, THEME, TRACT, CARTEL, REPORT, THESIS, JOURNAL, WRITING, DOCUMENT, TREATISE, MONOGRAPH, PERIODICAL, EXAMINATION, DISSERTATION

papule: .... BLISTER, PIMPLE

par: . . . . . . EQUAL, NORMAL, AVERAGE, STANDARD

parable: . . . . . MYTH, TALE, FABLE, STORY, ALLEGORY, APOLOGUE, SIMILITUDE

parade: . . . . . . POMP, SHOW, WALK, MARCH, STRUT, FLAUNT, REVIEW, STROLL, CORTEGE, DISPLAY, EXHIBIT, CEREMONY, CAVALCADE, PROCESSION, PROMENADE

paradigm: . . . . MODEL, PATTERN, EXAMPLE

Paradise: . . . . EDEN, BLISS, HEAVEN, UTOPIA, ELYSIUM

paragon: . . . . . . GEM, TYPE, IDEAL, MODEL, PATTERN, DIAMOND, NONPARIEL

parakeet: . . BUDGIE, PARROT, LOVEBIRD, PARAQUET, BUDGERIGAR

parallel: . . . . . EVEN, EQUAL, MATCH, ANALOGUE, COLLATERAL, COUNTERPART

parallelogram: . . . . . RHOMB, OBLONG, SQUARE, RHOMBOID, RECTANGLE

paralysis: . . . CRAMP, PALSY, POLIO, PTOSIS, STROKE, PARESIS, PARAPLEGIA, HEMIPLEGIA

paramount: . . ABOVE, CHIEF, RULER, CAPITAL, SUPREME, DOMINANT, SUPERIOR, PRE-EMINENT

paramour: . . LEMAN, LOVER, MINION, MISTRESS, SWEETHEART, INAMORATA

parapet: . . WALL, BULWARK, RAILING, RAMPART, BREASTWORK

paraphernalia: . . . . . . GEAR, OUTFIT, APPARATUS, BELONGINGS, TRAPPINGS, EQUIPMENT, FURNISHINGS

parasite: . . . . . . BUG, MOSS, DRONE, LEECH, LICHEN, TOADY, VIRUS, FUNGUS, HANGER-ON, MOOCHER,

SPONGE(R), MISTLETOE, SYCOPHANT

parasol: . . . . UMBRELLA, SUNSHADE, BUMBERSHOOT

parcel: . . . LOT, DEAL, METE, PACK, PART, PLAT, BUNCH, GROUP, PIECE, BUNDLE, DIVIDE, PACKET, PACKAGE, PORTION, DISTRIBUTE

parch: . . . DRY, BURN, HEAT, SEAR, ROAST, TOAST, SCORCH, SHRIVEL

parched: . . . DRY, ARID, SERE, FIERY, TORRID, THIRSTY, ANHYDROUS

parchment: . . . . SCROLL, VELLUM, DIPLOMA, PAPYRUS, SHEEPSKIN

pardon: . . . . MERCY, REMIT, SPARE, ASSOIL, EXCUSE, ABSOLVE, AMNESTY, CONDONE, FORGIVE, OVERLOOK, REPRIEVE, TOLERATE, EXCULPATE, REMISSION, ABSOLUTION, INDULGENCE

pare: . . . . . CUT, CHIP, PEEL, SKIN, TRIM, SHAVE, SKIVE, REDUCE, REMOVE, RESECT, CURTAIL, WHITTLE, DIMINISH

paregoric: . . . . . . ANODYNE, SOOTHING, SEDATIVE

parent: . . . . DAME, SIRE, MATER, PATER, AUTHOR, FATHER, MOTHER, ORIGIN, SOURCE, GENITOR, ANCESTOR, FOREFATHER, PROGENITOR

parentage: . . BIRTH, FAMILY, ORIGIN, ANCESTRY, PATERNITY, EXTRACTION

pariah: . . . . EXILE, OUTCAST, LEPER, WRETCH

parish: . . . . . CONGREGATION

parity: . . . . . PAR, ANALOGY, EQUALITY, SIMILARITY

park: . . . . . . STOP, SQUARE, COMMONS, PADDOCK, STADIUM, PLAYGROUND

parlance: .... TALK, IDIOM, DICTION, SPEECH, DISCOURSE, LANGUAGE

parlay: ...... BET, WAGER, EXPLOIT

parley: ...... TALK, SPEAK, TREAT, UTTER, WAGER, CONFER, POWWOW, DISCUSS, PALAVER, CONVERSE, DISCOURSE, NEGOTIATE, CONFERENCE

parliament: .. DIET, COUNCIL, CONGRESS, LEGISLATURE

parlous: ..... KEEN, RISKY, CLEVER, SHREWD, CUNNING, PERILOUS, DANGEROUS

parochial: .... NARROW, LIMITED, PROVINCIAL

parody: ..... SKIT, SATIRE, TRAVESTY, BURLESQUE, IMITATION, CARICATURE

parole: ..... ORAL, PLEDGE, PROMISE

paroxysm: ...... FIT, PANG, AGONY, SPASM, THROE, ATTACK, OUTBURST, CONVULSION

parrot: ... ARA, COPY, ECHO, JAKO, LORY, ARARA, BUDGIE, MACAW, MIMIC, POLLY, REPEAT, IMITATE, COCKATOO, LORIKEET, LOVEBIRD, PARAKEET, COCKATEEL

parry: .. FEND, VOID, WARD, AVOID, BLOCK, EVADE, THWART, DEFLECT, EVASION

parse: .. ANALYZE, DIAGRAM, CONSTRUE

parsimonious: ...... MEAN, NEAR, CLOSE, SCANT, SPARE, FRUGAL, NARROW, SKIMPY, STINGY, MISERLY, SPARING, COVETOUS, GRASPING, MERCENARY, NIGGARDLY, PENURIOUS

parson: .... RECTOR, PASTOR, MINISTER, PREACHER, CLERGYMAN

parsonage: .... MANSE, RECTORY

part: ... DEAL, DOLE, DUTY, ROLE, SOME, LEAVE, PIECE, QUOTA, SEVER, SHARE, SPLIT, BEHALF, CLEAVE, DEPART, DETAIL, DIVIDE, MEMBER, SUNDER, ELEMENT, PORTION, SECTION, SEGMENT, DIVISION, ESTRANGE, FRACTION, FRAGMENT, SEPARATE

partake: ...... EAT, SHARE, DIVIDE, PARTICIPATE

partial: ...... PART, BIASED, UNFAIR, COLORED, PARTWAY, INCLINED, ONE-SIDED, PARTISAN, FRACTIONAL, INCOMPLETE, PREJUDICED

participant: .... PARTY, PLAYER, PARTISAN, ACCOMPLICE, PARTAKER

participate: ..... JOIN, SIDE, ENTER, SHARE, COMPETE, PARTAKE, COOPERATE

particle: ..... BIT, DOT, JOT, ATOM, IOTA, MITE, MOTE, WHIT, FLECK, GRAIN, SHRED, SPECK, SMIDGE, TITTLE, GRANULE, SMIDGIN, MOLECULE, SCINTILLA

particular: .... ITEM, NICE, FUSSY, THING, DETAIL, ARTICLE, CAREFUL, CORRECT, FINICAL, PRECISE, SPECIAL, UNUSUAL, ACCURATE, CONCRETE, DETAILED, DISTINCT, ESPECIAL, EXACTING, ITEMIZED, SPECIFIC, FASTIDIOUS

partisan: ...... PIKE, STAFF, BIASED, ZEALOT, DEVOTEE, FANATIC, HALBERD, ADHERENT, FOLLOWER, STALWART, GUERRILLA

partite: .... PARTED, DIVIDED

partition: .... WALL, ALLOT, DIVIDE, SCREEN, SEPTUM, DIVIDER, ENCLOSE, PORTION, CLEAVAGE, DIVISION,

SEVERANCE, DISTRIBUTE, APPORTION

partner: . . PAL, ALLY, HALF, MATE, WIFE, SHARER, COMRADE, CONSORT, HUSBAND, TEAMMATE, ASSOCIATE, COLLEAGUE, COMPANION, ACCOMPLICE

parturition: . . . . LABOR, TRAVAIL, DELIVERY, CHILDBIRTH

party: . . . . TEA, BASH, CLAN, SECT, SIDE, CABAL, GROUP, CLIQUE, FIESTA, PERSON, SOCIAL, SOIREE, COMPANY, FACTION, SHINDIG, CAROUSAL, GATHERING

pass: . . GO, END, GAP, ABRA, COVE, GHAT, HAND, LANE, MOVE, ENACT, GORGE, LAPSE, OCCUR, RELAY, CONVEY, DEFILE, DEPART, ELAPSE, EXCEED, HAPPEN, PERMIT, STRAIT, TICKET, APPROVE, DEVOLVE, PROCEED, OUTSTRIP

passable: . . . . . . FAIR, SOSO, ADEQUATE, TOLERABLE

passage: . . . GAT, WAY, ADIT, DOOR, DUCT, EXIT, FLUE, FORD, GATE, HALL, LANE, PATH, RACE, RAMP, ROAD, SLIP, VENT, AISLE, ALLEY, CANAL, ENTRY, GOING, GORGE, ACCESS, ARCADE, ATRIUM, AVENUE, BURROW, COURSE, DEFILE, EGRESS, STRAIT, TRAVEL, TUNNEL, VOYAGE, CHANNEL, GANGWAY, JOURNEY, OPENING, TRANSIT, CORRIDOR, CROSSING, MIGRATION

passe: . . . . AGED, PAST, OBSOLETE, OUTMODED, ANTIQUATED, OUT-OF-DATE

passenger: . . . . FARE, RIDER, TRAVELER

passing: . . . DEATH, CASUAL, CURSORY, ELAPSING, FLEETING, DEPARTING, EXCEEDING, TRANSIENT, MOMENTARY

passion: . . . . IRE, JOY, FIRE, FURY, HATE, HEAT, LOVE, LUST, RAGE, ZEAL, AGONY, ANGER, ARDOR, GRIEF, DESIRE, FERVOR, EMOTION, FEELING

passionate: . . . . FERVID, ARDENT, AMOROUS, FLAMING, FERVENT, INTENSE, TORRID, FRENETIC

passive: . . . . . INERT, QUIET, STOIC, STOLID, INACTIVE, PATIENT, DORMANT, APATHETIC

past: . . . . . . BY, AGO, GONE, OVER, YORE, AFTER, AGONE, ENDED, SINCE, BEHIND, BEYOND, BYGONE, FOREGONE, COMPLETED

paste: . . . . . . HIT, PAP, BEAT, BLOW, GLUE, MASH, PATE, CANDY, CREAM, DOUGH, FALSE, PUNCH, STICK, ATTACH, BATTER, FASTEN, STRASS, FILLING, MUCILAGE, ADHESIVE, IMITATION

pastel: . . DYE, TINT, CRAYON, DRAWING, PICTURE

pasticcio: . . . . OLIO, CENTO, MEDLEY, JUMBLE, POTPOURRI, PASTICHE, HODGE PODGE

pastille: . . TABLET, LOZENGE

pastime: . . . . GAME, HOBBY, SPORT, DIVERSION, RECREATION, AMUSEMENT

pastor: . . . . . ANGEL, RABBI, CURATE, KEEPER, PARSON, PRIEST, RECTOR, DOMINIE, GUARDIAN, MINISTER, SHEPHERD, CLERGYMAN

pastoral: . . . . POEM, DRAMA, RURAL, CROSIER, RUSTIC, BUCOLIC, IDYLLIC, ROMANCE

pastry: . . . . PIE, CAKE, FLAN, TART, ECLAIR, TORTE, STRUDEL, POPOVER, DOUGHNUT, NAPOLEON, TURNOVER

pat: . . . . APT, DAB, FIT, TAP, FIXED, TOUCH, CARESS, SOOTHE, STRIKE, STROKE,

TIMELY, APROPOS, SUITABLE, OPPORTUNE

patch: .... BIT, DARN, MEND, PLOT, RAMP, CLUMP, COVER, PIECE, SCRAP, BLOTCH, COBBLE, DOLLOP, PARCEL, REPAIR, REVAMP, SOLDER, REMNANT, COVERING, DRESSING, RECONCILE

patchwork: .. CENTO, QUILT, JUMBLE, MOSAIC, SCRAPS, FRAGMENTS, HODGE PODGE

pate: ...... PIE, TOP, HEAD, CROWN, PASTE, PASTY, PATTY, NOGGIN

patella: .... PAN, DISH, VASE, ROTULA, KNEECAP, KNEEPAN

paten: .... AREA, DISC, DISH, DISK, HOST, PLATE, PATINA, VESSEL

patent: .... ARCA, OPEN, OVERT, PLAIN, TITLE, EVIDENT, LICENSE, OBVIOUS, APPARENT, ENDURING, MANIFEST, FRANCHISE

paternity: .. FATHER, ORIGIN, PARENTAGE, FATHERHOOD, AUTHORSHIP

path: ..... PAT, RUT, WAY, FARE, LANE, LINE, ROAD, WALK, ALLEY, BYWAY, ORBIT, ROUTE, TRACK, TRAIL, COURSE, GROOVE, FOOTWAY

pathetic: ..... SAD, MOVING, PITIFUL, STIRRING

pathogen: .... GERM, VIRUS, MICROBE

pathos: .... SUFFERING, POIGNANCY

patience: ... CALM, STOICISM, COMPOSURE, ENDURANCE, FORTITUDE, FORBEARANCE, RESIGNATION

patient: .... CASE, MEEK, STEADY, INVALID, FORBEARING, TOLERANT

patina: ...... FILM, PLATE, PATEN, CRUST, COATING, VERDIGRIS

patio: .... TERRACE, COURT(YARD)

patois: .... CREOLE, SPEECH, DIALECT

patriarch: .. ELDER, FATHER, BISHOP, ANCIENT, VENERABLE

patrician: .... NOBLE, ARISTOCRAT(IC)

patrimony: ..... ANCESTRY, HERITAGE, INHERITANCE

patriot: .... CHAUVINIST, NATIONALIST, COMPATRIATE

patrol: ..... GUARD, SCOUT, WATCH, PROTECT, RECONNOITER

patrolman: ... COP, GUARD, INSPECTOR, POLICEMAN

patron: ..... BUYER, GUEST, SAINT, CLIENT, SPONSOR, ADVOCATE, CHAMPION, PADRONE, CUSTOMER, DEFENDER, GUARDIAN, BENEFACTOR, PROTECTOR, SUPPORTER

patronage: .. AEGIS, FAVOR, CUSTOM, AUSPICES, SUPPORT, BUSINESS, SPONSORSHIP, CLIENTELE, ASSISTANCE

patten: .. BASE, CLOG, FOOT, SHOE, SKATE, STAND, STILT, SANDAL, SUPPORT, OVERSHOE

patter: .. TALK, CANT, LINGO, JARGON, CHATTER, GURGLE

pattern: ..... FORM, NORM, PLAN, DRAFT, GUIDE, IDEAL, MODEL, DESIGN, FORMAT, SAMPLE, EXAMPLE, DIAGRAM, PROJECT, STENCIL, PARADIGM, SPECIMAN, TEMPLATE, ARCHETYPE

paucity: .... LACK, DEARTH, FEWNESS, SCARCITY

paunch: .... BELLY, RUMEN, ABDOMEN, STOMACH, POT BELLY

pauper: .. BEGGAR, INDIGENT

pause: ... HALT, LULL, REST, STOP, WAIT, ABIDE, BREAK, CEASE, DELAY, DEMUR, DWELL,

HOVER, TARRY, BREACH,
BREATH, FALTER, RESPITE,
BREATHER, HESITATE,
HESITATION, CESSATION

pave: . . . . LAY, PATH, STUD,
TILE, COVER, FLOOR, COBBLE,
SMOOTH, OVERLAY, PREPARE,
ASPHALT, MACADAM

pavid: . . . . . . TIMID, AFRAID,
FEARFUL

pavilion: . . . . . . FLAG, TENT,
KIOSK, CANOPY, ENSIGN,
LITTER, AURICLE, GALLERY,
MARQUEE, COVERING

paw: . . . . . . PUD, TOE, FOOT,
GAUM, HAND, MAUL, PATY,
TOUCH, FATHER, HANDLE,
FLIPPER, FOREFOOT

pawl: . . . . . COG, DOG, BOLT,
TENT, TRIP, CATCH, CLICK,
DETENT, PALLET, TRIPPER,
TONGUE, RATCHET

pawn: . . . DUPE, GAGE, HOCK,
SOAK, TOOL, STAKE, WAGER,
LUMBER, PLEDGE, PIGNUS,
COUNTER, HOSTAGE, PEACOCK,
GUARANTY, CHESSMAN

pawpaw: . . . . PAPAYA

pay: . . FEE, TIP, ANTE, MEET,
RENT, WAGE, REMIT, DEFRAY,
REWARD, SALARY, SETTLE,
IMBURSE, REQUITE, SATISFY,
STIPEND, TRIBUTE, INDEMNIFY,
REIMBURSE, COMPENSATE,
LIQUIDATE, REMUNERATE,
RECOMPENSE

payable: . . . . . DUE, OWING,
OUTSTANDING

payment: . . . FEE, TAX, BILL,
DUES, FINE, LEVY, TOLL, PRICE,
PLEDGE, REBATE, RETURN,
REWARD, TARIFF, ALIMONY,
ANNUITY, CUSTOMS, PENSION,
STIPEND, TUITION, REMITTANCE

paynim: . . PAGAN, HEATHEN,
MOSLEM, INFIDEL

payoff: . . FIX, BRIBE, CLIMAX,
RECKONING, SETTLEMENT

peace: . . . CALM, EASE, REST,
AMITY, GRITH, QUIET, REPOSE,
SHALOM, CONCORD, HARMONY,
SECURITY, SERENITY,
TRANQUILITY

peaceable: . . GENTLE, IRENIC,
PACIFIC, SOLOMON

peacock: . . . . . . MAO, PAVO,
PAON, PAWN

peak: . . . . . ALP, TOP, ACME,
APEX, FADE, CREST, CROWN,
DROOP, HEIGHT, SHRINK,
SUMMIT, EPITOME, MAXIMUM,
AIGUILLE, PINNACLE,
PROMONTORY

peal: . . . . . CLAP, RING, TOLL,
CHIME, RESOUND, SUMMONS,
THUNDER, CARILLON

pearl: . . . GEM, BEAD, NACRE,
ONION, OLIVET, BOUTON,
ORIENT, MARGARITE

peasant: . BOOR, HIND, PEON,
RYOT, SERF, CHURL, KNAVE,
COTTAR, FARMER, FELLAH,
RUSTIC, VILLEIN

pebble: . . . . . SCREE, STONE,
GRAVEL, QUARTZ

peccadillo: . . . . FAULT,
OFFENSE, MISCHIEF

peccant: . . . MORBID, SINNER,
SINFUL, SINNING, CORRUPT,
INCORRECT, UNHEALTHY

peck: . . DAB, DOT, NAG, NIP,
CARP, KISS, PICK, HARASS,
NIBBLE

peculate: . . . . STEAL, MISUSE,
EMBEZZLE, APPROPRIATE

peculiar: . . . . . ODD, QUEER,
UNIQUE, SCREWY, CURIOUS,
STRANGE, SPECIAL, UNUSUAL,
SINGULAR, ECCENTRIC,
EXCLUSIVE, PARTICULAR,
DISTINCTIVE

peculiarity: . . . KINK, QUIRK,
TRAIT, TWIST, ODDITY,
ATTRIBUTE, IDIOSYNCRACY

pecuniary: . . . . . FINANCIAL,
MONETARY

pedagogue: . . . . TUTOR,
PEDANT, DOMINIE, TEACHER
pedal: . . . . TREADLE,
(FOOT)LEVER
pedant: . . . . . TUTOR, PURIST,
TEACHER, SCHOLAR,
EDUCATOR, PEDAGOGUE
pedantic: . . . . BOOKISH,
ACADEMIC, DIDACTIC,
MORALISTIC
peddle: . . HAWK, SELL, VEND,
CADGE
peddler: . . . FAKER, BROKER,
COSTER, DUFFER, HAWKER,
SELLER, CAMELOT, CHAPMAN,
PACKMAN, HUCKSTER,
PITCHMAN
pedestal: . . . . . BASE, PILLAR,
PODIUM, SUPPORT, FOUNDATION
pedestrian: . . . DULL, SLOW,
HOOFER, WALKER, FOOTMAN,
PROSAIC, COMMONPLACE
pedigree: . . . . STEMMA,
DESCENT, LINEAGE, ANCESTRY,
GENEALOGY, BLOODLINE
peek: . . . . LOOK, PEEP, PEER,
GLANCE
peel: . . . . BARK, FLAY, HULL,
PARE, RIND, SHED, SKIN, TRIM,
STAKE, STRIP, SHOVEL, TOWER,
UNDRESS, PALISADE, STOCKADE
peep: . . . . . PRY, SPY, LOOK,
PEEK, PEER, PULE, CHEEP,
CHIRP, SNOOP, TWEET, GLANCE,
GLIMPSE
peer: . . . . PRY, DUKE, EARL,
GAZE, LOOK, LORD, MATE,
PEEP, BARON, EQUAL, NOBLE,
RIVAL, STARE, SQUINT,
COMPEER, COMRADE, MARQUIS,
PALADIN, NOBLEMAN,
SUPERIOR, VISCOUNT
peerage: . . . . RANK, DIGNITY,
NOBILITY
peeress: . . . LADY, DUCHESS,
BARONESS, MARQUISE
peerless: . . . . . . MATCHLESS,
NONPAREIL, UNRIVALED,
SUPERLATIVE

peeve: . . . . IRE, GRUDGE,
NETTLE, IRRITATE,
ANNOY(ANCE)
peevish: . . . . . SOUR, TECHY,
TESTY, CRUSTY, GRUMPY,
SULLEN, TOUCHY, CRABBED,
FRETFUL, WASPISH, CAPTIOUS,
CHOLERIC, CROTCHED,
PETULANT, FRACTIOUS,
IMPATIENT, IRASCIBLE,
SPLENETIC, IRRITABLE,
QUERULOUS
peg: . . . . FIX, HOB, NOG, PIN,
BOLT, PLUG, STEP, CLEAT,
DOWEL, PERCH, PITON, PRONG,
SPILL, STAKE, THOLE, MARKER,
SUPPORT, FASTENER
peignor: . . . GOWN, KIMONO,
WRAPPER, NEGLIGEE,
HOUSECOAT, DRESSING GOWN
pelage: . . . . FUR, HAIR, PELT
pelagic: . . MARINE, OCEANIC,
ACQUATIC
pelf: . . . . ROB, GAIN, BOOTY,
LUCRE, MONEY, SPOIL, TRASH,
PILFER, REFUSE, RICHES,
WEALTH, RUBBISH
pellet: . . . . WAD, PILL, BALL,
SHOT, STONE, BULLET, PILULE,
GRANULE
pellicle: . . . FILM, SCUM, SKIN,
CRUST, CUTICLE, MEMBRANE
pellucid: . . . . CLEAR, SHEER,
BRIGHT, LIMPID, CRYSTAL,
TRANSPARENT
pelota: . . . . JAI ALAI
pelt: . . . . . FUR, BEAT, BLOW,
CAST, DASH, FELL, HIDE, HURL,
PELL, SKIN, HURRY, STONE,
POUND, GALLOP, HASTEN,
PELAGE, PEPPER, REFUSE,
STRIKE, RAWHIDE, RUBBISH
pelvic: . . . . ILIAC, PUBIC
pen: . . COT, STY, BOLT, CAGE,
COTE, COOP, FOLD, JAIL, YARD,
CRAWL, HUTCH, KRAAL, QUILL,
WRITE, CORRAL, FASTEN,
INDITE, RECORD, STYLUS,

COMPOSE, CONFINE, FOUNTAIN, BALLPOINT, ENCLOSURE

penal: . . . . PUNITIVE

penalize: . . . . . . FINE, PUNISH

penalty: . . . FINE, LOSS, PAIN, MULCT, AMERCE, FORFEIT, HARDSHIP, FORFEITURE, HANDICAP, PUNISHMENT

penance: . . . . SORROW, REMORSE, ATONEMENT, PENITENCE, SUFFERING, CONTRITION, REPENTANCE, PUNISHMENT

penchant: . . . . BENT, FLAIR, TASTE, LIKING, FONDNESS, LEANING, INCLINATION

pendant: . . . . BOB, FOB, JAG, TAIL, AIGLET, TASSEL, EARRING, PENSILE, GIRANDOLE, LAVALIER(E)

pendent: . . . . HANGING, PENDING, PENSILE, SUSPENDED, UNDECIDED, PENDULOUS

pending: . . . . UNTIL, DURING, UNDECIDED

pendulous: . . . . . . HANGING, SWINGING

penetrate: . . . . . BORE, DIVE, GORE, STAB, BREAK, ENTER, IMBUE, REACH, FATHOM, PIERCE, DISCERN, PERVADE, PERMEATE, INSINUATE, PERFORATE, UNDERSTOOD

penetrating: . . ACUTE, DEEP, KEEN, SHARP, ASTUTE, SHREWD, SHRILL, SUBTLE, PUNGENT, INCISIVE, SAGACIOUS

penetration: . . . . . ACUMEN, INSIGHT, INTRUSION

peninsula: . . . . NECK, PENILE, CHERSONESE

penitence: . . . . RUE, REGRET, REMORSE, ATTRITION, CONTRITION, REPENTANCE

penetint: . . SORRY, CONTRITE, REPENTANT, REMORSEFUL

penitentiary: . . . . . JUG, PEN, JAIL, STIR, TENCH, PRISON, BIG-HOUSE

penman: . . . AUTHOR, SCRIBE, WRITER, CHIROGRAPHER, CALLIGRAPHER

pennant: . . . . . FLAG, ROGER, CORNET, ENSIGN, BANNER, BURGEE, PENNON, STREAMER

penniless: . . . . POOR, FLAT, BROKE, NEEDY, BANKRUPT, INSOLVENT, IMPECUNIOUS

pennon: . . . . . . FLAG, WING, BANNER, PINION, PENNANT, FEATHER

pensile: . . HANGING, PENDENT

pension: . . . . PAYMENT, STIPEND, SUBSIDY, TRIBUTE, GRATUITY, ALLOWANCE

pensive: . . . SOBER, DREAMY, MUSING, WISTFUL, MEDITATIVE, REFLECTIVE, THOUGHTFUL

pent: . . . . . CAGED, PENNED, CONFINED, ENCLOSED

Pentateuch: . . . . LAW, BIBLE, TORA(H)

penurious: . . . MEAN, POOR, BARREN, SCANTY, STINGY, MISERLY, WANTING, INDIGENT, DESTITUTE, AVARICIOUS

penury: . . . . BEGGARY, POVERTY, INDIGENCE, PRIVATION

peon: . . . PAWN, SERF, SLAVE, THRALL, LABORER, FOOTMAN, PEASANT

people: . . . (also see **person**) KIN, FOLK, HERD, PAIS, RACE, DEMOS, LAITY, TRIBE, PUBLIC, STOCK, GENTRY, NATION, MASSES, PERSONS, MORTALS, NATION, CITIZENS, HUMANS, POPULATE, INHABITANTS

pep: . . GO, VIM, DASH, SNAP, VERVE, VIGOR, ENERGY, GINGER

peplum: . . . . SHAWL, SKIRT, KERCHIEF, OVERSKIRT

pepo: . . . . . MELON, SQUASH, GOURD, PUMPKIN, CUCUMBER

pepper: . . . . HOT, RED, BEAT, KAVA, PELT, BETEL, GREEN,

SWEET, SPICE, STRAFE, RIDDLE,
CAYENNE, PIMIENTO, CHILIES,
TABASCO, SPRINKLE,
CONDIMENT
peppery: . . . . . . HOT, FIERY,
TESTY, SPICY, SHARP, PIQUANT,
PUNGENT, CHOLERIC, IRRITABLE
per: . . . . BY, EACH, THROUGH
per se: . . . ITSELF, DIRECTLY,
ESSENTIALLY, INTRINSICALLY
peradventure: . . . . . MAYBE,
CHANCE, MAYHAP, PERHAPS,
POSSIBLY
perambulate: . . . . WALK,
RAMBLE, STROLL, TRAVERSE
perambulator: . . . . . . PRAM,
BUGGY, BABY-CARRIAGE
perceive: . . . SEE, FEEL, HEAR,
KNOW, NOTE, SCENT, SENSE,
GRASP, SMELL, TASTE, TOUCH,
BEHOLD, NOTICE, DISCERN,
OBSERVE, RECOGNIZE,
COMPREHEND, UNDERSTAND
percentage: . . . PART, SHARE,
PORTION
perceptible: . . . . . . TACTILE,
VISIBLE, SENSIBLE, PALPABLE,
TANGIBLE, APPRECIABLE,
DISCERNIBLE
perception: . . . . GRASP,
INSIGHT, ACUMEN, NOESIS,
SENSATION, COGNITION
perch: . . BAR, PEG, ROD, SIT,
FISH, POLE, SEAT, LIGHT,
ROOST, RUFFE, ALIGHT, SETTLE,
SAUGER, PERCOID
perchance: . . . . MAYBE,
MAYHAP, POSSIBLY, PERHAPS
percolate: . . . . BREW, OOZE,
PERK, SIFT, EXUDE, LEACH,
FILTER, DRAIN, STRAIN,
PERMEATE
percussion: . . IMPACT, SHOCK
instrument: . BELL, DRUM,
GONG, TRAP, PIANO,
CYMBALS, MARACA,
MARIMBA, TRIANGLE,
XYLOPHONE, TAMBOURINE,
GLOCKENSPIEL

perdition: . . . . . HELL, LOSS,
RUIN, DAMNATION,
DESTRUCTION
perdu(e): . . . . HIDDEN,
CONCEALED
peregrinate: . . . . . TRAVEL,
WANDER, JOURNEY, SOJOURN,
TRAVERSE
peregrine: . . . . HAWK, ALIEN,
EXOTIC, FALCON, FOREIGN,
PILGRAM, STRANGE,
MIGRATORY
peremptory: . . FINAL, UTTER,
EXPRESS, DECISIVE, DOGMATIC,
IMPERIOUS, ABSOLUTE,
ARBITRARY
perennial: . . . . LASTING,
ENDURING, CONTINUAL,
PERMANENT, PERPETUAL
perfect: . . . . ALL, FILL, FINE,
HOLY, PURE, EXACT, IDEAL,
RIGHT, MODEL, SHEER, UTTER,
WHOLE, ENTIRE, FINISH,
REFINE, POLISH, CONCOCT,
CORRECT, PRECISE, ABSOLUTE,
ACCURATE, COMPLETE,
FLAWLESS, FAULTLESS,
CONSUMMATE, IMMACULATE
perfection: . . . ACME, IDEAL,
FULNESS, PARAGON, PRECISION,
MATURITY
perfidious: . . . . FALSE,
DISLOYAL, DISHONEST,
FAITHLESS, TRAITOROUS,
TREACHEROUS
perfidy: . . . . TREASON,
BETRAYAL, TREACHERY,
INFIDELITY
perforate: . . . . BORE, DRILL,
PUNCH, PIERCE, RIDDLE,
PENETRATE
perform: . . . . DO, ACT, FILL,
PLAY, ENACT, EXERT, EXECUTE,
FULFILL, EFFECT, RENDER,
ACHIEVE, EXHIBIT, FURNISH,
TRANSACT, ACCOMPLISH,
PERPETRATE
performance: . . . ACT, DEED,
FEAT, SHOW, WORK, STUNT,

ACTING, BENEFIT, CONCERT, EXPLOIT, MATINEE, FUNCTION, DISCHARGE, EXECUTION, EXHIBITION, RENDITION

perfume: ...... ATAR, NOSE, AROMA, ATTAR, CENSE, MYRRH, SCENT, SMELL, FLAVOR, BOUQUET, ESSENCE, INCENSE, FRAGRANCE

perfunctory: .... CARELESS, MECHANICAL, INDIFFERENT, SUPERFICIAL

pergola: .... ARBOR, BOWER, TRELLIS, BALCONY, COLONNADE

perhaps: ..... HAPS, MAYBE, HAPPEN, MAYHAP, DOUBTFUL, PERCHANCE, POSSIBLY, PROBABLY

peril: . RISK, CRISIS, HAZARD, DANGER, MENACE, IMPERIL, JEOPARDY, ADVENTURE

perimeter: .... RIM, OUTLINE, BORDER, BOUNDARY, PERIPHERY, CIRCUMFERENCE

period: ..... AGE, DOT, END, EON, ERA, AEON, SPAN, STOP, TERM, TIME, CLOSE, CYCLE, EPOCH, POINT, STAGE, SPELL, DECADE, SEASON, DURATION, INTERVAL, CONCLUSION, TERMINATION

periodic: .... ERAL, ANNUAL, ESTESIAN, REGULAR, RECURRENT, INTERMITTENT

periodical: . DAILY, ANNUAL, REVIEW, ETESIAN, GAZETTE, PICTORIAL, JOURNAL, TABLOID, BULLETIN, MAGAZINE, NEWSPAPER, NEWSLETTER

peripatetic: ..... RAMBLING, ITINERANT, WANDERING

peripheral: .. OUTER, DISTAL, DISTANT, CONFINED, EXTERNAL

periphery: ... LIP, RIM, BRIM, EDGE, AMBIT, LIMIT, AREOLA, BORDER, OUTSIDE, ENVIRONS, PERIMETER, CIRCUMFERENCE

perish: .... DIE, END, FADE, FALL, RUIN, DEPART, EXPIRE, SUCCUMB

peristyle: .... COURT, COLONNADE

periwig: ... PERUKE, TOUPEE

periwinkle: ... SHELL, SNAIL, MUSSEL, MYRTLE

perjure: .... LIE, FORSWEAR

permanent: .. FIXED, STABLE, ABIDING, DURABLE, LASTING, CONSTANT, ENDURING, CONTINUAL, PERPETUAL, PERENNIAL

permeable: ...... POROUS, PERVIOUS

permeate: ..... FILL, IMBUE, DRENCH, DIFFUSE, PERVADE, SATURATE, PERCOLATE, PENETRATE

permission: .. GRACE, LEAVE, LICENSE, CONSENT

permit: .... LET, LEVE, PASS, ADMIT, ALLOW, FAVOR, GRACE, GRANT, LEAVE, ENTREE, SUFFER, CONSENT, SANCTION, LICENSE, WARRANT, TOLERATE, AUTHORIZE

permutation: ..... CHANGE, ALTERATION, INTERCHANGE

pernicious: ..... BAD, EVIL, FATAL, DEADLY, MALIGN, WICKED, BALEFUL, BANEFUL, HARMFUL, NOISOME, VICIOUS, NOXIOUS, RUINOUS, VILLAINOUS, DELETERIOUS

perorate: . ORATE, DECLAIM, HARANGUE

perpendicular: .... SINE, ERECT, PLUMB, SHEER, APOTHEM, UPRIGHT, BINORMAL, VERTICAL

perpetrate: ... DO, COMMIT, EFFECT, PERFORM

perpetual: .... ENDLESS, ETERNAL, LASTING, CONSTANT, UNENDING, CONTINUAL, INCESSANT, PERENNIAL, PERMANENT, EVERLASTING

perpetuate: . . . . : . CONTINUE, MAINTAIN, PRESERVE
perplex: . . . . STUMP, AMAZE, BAFFLE, BOGGLE, HAMPER, HARASS, HOBBLE, MUDDLE, PUZZLE, CONFUSE, MYSTIFY, NONPLUS, BEWILDER, CONFOUND, DISTRACT, DISTRESS, FLUMMOX, BAMBOOZLE, OBFUSCATE
perquisite: . . . . . . FEE, TIP, BONUS, INCOME, ADJUNCT, APPANAGE, GRATUITY, ACCESSORY, PEROGATIVE
persecute: . . . . BAIT, ANNOY, HARRY, HOUND, WRACK, WRONG, HARASS, AFFLICT, OPPRESS, TORMENT, TORTURE
perseverance: . . . . GRIT, PATIENCE, TENACITY, PERSISTENCE, PERTINACITY, ASSIDUITY, DILIGENCE, ENDURANCE, INSISTENCE
persevere: . . ENDURE, PERSIST
Persia: . . . . IRAN
persiflage: . . . . BANTER, BADINAGE, RAILLERY
persist: . . . . . . LAST, INSIST, ENDURE, REMAIN, PERSEVERE, CONTINUE
persistent: . . . HARD, GRITTY, DOGGED, DURABLE, CONSTANT, ENDURING, FREQUENT, OBDURATE, RESOLUTE, TENACIOUS, STUBBORN, CONTINUED, RELENTLESS
persnickety: . . . . FUSSY, FASTIDIOUS
person: . . . . . (also see **man, people**) EGG, GUY, ONE, BODY, CHAP, SELF, SOUL, BEING, CHILD, HUMAN, WIGHT, WOMEN, ENTITY, FELLOW, INDIVIDUAL
personable: . . . . . . COMELY, SHAPELY, HANDSOME, ATTRACTIVE

personal: . . . OWN, PRIVATE, INTIMATE, CORPORAL, INDIVIDUAL
personality: . . . . . EGO, SELF, PRESENCE, CHARACTER, DISPOSITION, INDIVIDUALITY
personate: . . . . SEE IMPERSONATE
personify: . . . . EMBODY, REPRESENT, IMPERSONATE
personnel: . . . . CREW, STAFF, WORKERS, EMPLOYEES
perspective: . . . . VISTA, OUTLOOK, VIEWPOINT
perspicacious: . . . . . . KEEN, ACUTE, SHREWD, PERCEPTIVE
perspicacity: . . . . . ACUMEN, INSIGHT
perspicuous: . CLEAR, LUCID, PLAIN, MANIFEST, CONSPICUOUS
perspire: . . . . . SWEAT, EGEST
persuade: . . . . . WIN, COAX, GAIN, SWAY, URGE, ENTICE, INDUCE, ENTREAT, CONVINCE
persuasion: . . . . BELIEF, OPINION, CONVICTION
persuasive: . . . . . . COGENT, ELOQUENT, CONVINCING
pert: . . . . FLIP, BOLD, ALERT, BRASH, BRISK, COCKY, QUICK, SASSY, SAUCY, SMART, CLEVER, COMELY, DAPPER, FRISKY, LIVELY, FORWARD, IMPUDENT, INSOLENT
pertain: . . BELONG, RELATE, CONCERN, ACCESSORY
pertinacious: . . . . . DOGGED, STUBBORN, OBSTINATE, TENACIOUS, DETERMINED
pertinent: . . . . APT, FIT, PROPER, TIMELY, APROPOS, RELEVANT, GERMANE, RELATIVE, APPLICABLE
perturb: . . . . UPSET, WORRY, RUFFLE, AGITATE, CONFUSE, DISTURB, TROUBLE, DISTRESS, DISCOMPOSE, DISCONCERT
peruke: . . WIG, HAIR, PERIWIG

peruse: . . . . SCAN, READ, STUDY, SURVEY, EXAMINE, INSPECT, SCRUTINIZE

pervade: . . . . . . FILL, BATHE, IMBUE, DIFFUSE, OCCUPY, PERMEATE, PENETRATE

perverse: . . . AWRY, DIVERS, WICKED, WIFUL, CONTRARY, DIFFICULT, FRACTIOUS, CONTENTIOUS, UNTOWARD

pervert: . . . . . . RUIN, SKEW, WARP, ABUSE, DEBASE, DIVERT, MISUSE, CONTORT, CORRUPT, DEPRAVE, DISTORT, MISLEAD, VITIATE, MISDIRECT

pervious: . . . . . PERMEABLE, ACCESSIBLE, PENETRABLE

pesky: . . . . ANNOYING, BOTHERSOME, MISCHIEVOUS, TROUBLESOME

pessimism: . . . . GLOOM, DESPAIR

pessimistic: . . . . . . GLOOMY, ALARMED, WORRIED, CYNICAL

pest: . . . . . IMP, BANE, WEED, MOUSE, INSECT, PLAGUE, VERMIN, EPIDEMIC, NUISANCE

pester: . . . . . DUN, NAG, RIB, VEX, ANNOY, DEVIL, HARRY, TEASE, WORRY, HECTOR, BADGER, HARASS, BOTHER, MOLEST, TROUBLE, AGGRAVATE

pestilence: . . . . PLAGUE, DISEASE, SCOURGE, EPIDEMIC

pet: . . . . . . CAT, DOG, COAX, DEAR, HUFF, NECK, SULK, TIFF, HUMOR, QUIET, SPOIL, CARESS, CODDLE, COSSET, CUDDLE, DARLING, DANDLE, FONDLE, PAMPER, STROKE, INDULGE, FAVORITE

petcock: . . . . VALVE, FAUCET

peter: . . . FADE, FAIL, WANE, CEASE, DWINDLE, EXHAUST, DIMINISH

petit: . . MEAN, PETTY, MINOR, SMALL, LITTLE, INSIGNIFICANT

petite: . . . . TRIM, SMALL, DEMURE, DIMINUTIVE

petition: . . . . ASK, BEG, SUE, BILL, BOON, PLEA, PRAY, SUIT, WISH, APPLY, PLEAD, APPEAL, PRAYER, ENTREAT, IMPLORE, REQUEST, SOLICIT, ENTREATY, SUPPLICATE

petrify: . . . . . . STUN, NUMB, HARDEN, DEADEN, TERRIFY, FOSSILIZE

petroleum: . . . . OIL, ILLUMINANT, PROPELANT

product: . . . . WAX, COKE, ETHYL, PITCH, BUTANE, PETROL, ALCOHOL, BITUMEN, NAPHTHA, GASOLINE, KEROSENE, BENZENE, PARAFFIN

petty: . . . BASE, MEAN, PUNY, MINOR, SMALL, PALTRY, TRIVIAL, CHILDISH, PICAYUNE, FRIVOLOUS, SUBORDINATE, UNIMPORTANT

petulant: . . . . CROSS, HUFFY, SAUCY, SHORT, TESTY, SULLEN, WILFUL, FRETFUL, PEEVISH, CONTRARY, PERVERSE, IMPATIENT, IRASCIBLE, HOITY-TOITY, IRRITABLE

pew: . . . . . DESK, SEAT, SLIP, STALL, BENCH

phantasm: . . DREAM, FANCY, GHOST, VAPOR, SPECTER, DELUSION

phantom: . . . . IDOL, GHOST, IMAGE, SHADE, SPIRIT, VISION, SPECTER, ILLUSION, (E)IDOLON, FANTASY, APPARITION

pharos: . . . . CLOAK, BEACON, LANTERN, CHANDELIER, LIGHTHOUSE

phase: . . PART, SIDE, ANGLE, FACET, STAGE, ASPECT

phenomenon: . . . . . EVENT, UNUSUAL

phial: . . . . CUP, BOWL, VIAL, BOTTLE, VESSEL

philanthropic: . . . . HUMANE, CHARITABLE, ALTRUISTIC, BENEVOLENT

philippic: . . . . TIRADE, DIATRIBE, SCREED, ORATION, INVECTIVE, HARANGUE

philosophy: . . YOGA, EGOISM, MONISM, DUALISM, STOICISM, ESOTERICS, EMPIRICISM, ESTHETICS, PRAGMATISM

philter: . . . . . POTION, CHARM

phlegmatic: . . . CALM, COOL, DULL, SLOW, INERT, WATERY, VISCOUS, COMPOSED, SLUGGISH, APATHETIC, IMPASSIVE

phlogistic: . . . FIERY, HEATED, BURNING, FLAMING, IMPASSIONED, INFLAMMATORY

phobia: . . . . . . FEAR, AGORA, HATRED

phony: . . . . . . FAKE, SHAM, BOGUS, FALSE, SPURIOUS, IMPOSTER, CHARLATAN, FICTITIOUS, COUNTERFEIT

photograph: . . . . MUG, PIX, FILM, SHOT, SNAP, STILL, PRINT, PICTURE, TINTYPE, LIKENESS, PORTRAIT, SNAPSHOT

phrase: . . . . . . TERM, WORD, IDIOM, STATE, CLAUSE, CLICHE, SLOGAN, DICTION, EPIGRAM, THOUGHT, LOCUTION, EXPRESSION

phraseology: . . . . . DIALECT, WORDING, DICTION, EXPRESSION, PARLANCE

phrenetic: . . . WILD, INSANE, EXCITED, FANATIC, FRENETIC, DELIRIOUS

phrenic: . . . . MENTAL

phylactery: . . . . CHARM, AMULET, TALISMAN

phyletic: . . . . RACIAL

physic: . . . PURGE, APERIENT, LAXATIVE, CATHARTIC, PURGATIVE

physical: . . . SOMAL, BODILY, NATURAL, SOMATIC, MATERIAL, CORPOREAL

physician: . . . . . DOC, MEDIC, QUACK, DOCTOR, INTERN, HEALER, MEDICO, CONSULTANT, PRACTITIONER

physiognomy: . . MUG, FACE, PORTRAIT, COUNTENANCE

physique: . . . BODY, FIGURE, STRENGTH, APPEARANCE, CONSTITUTION

piano: . . . . . GRAND, SOFTLY, SPINET, CLAVICAL, UPRIGHT, CLAVICHORD, HARPSICHORD

piazza: . . . . PORCH, SQUARE, ARCADE, GALLERY, PORTICO, VERANDA(H)

picaroon: . . . ROGUE, THIEF, BANDIT, PIRATE, RASCAL, BRIGAND, ADVENTURER

picayune: . . . . MEAN, CHEAP, PETTY, SMALL, LITTLE, PALTRY, TRIVIAL

pick: . . . . CULL, GAFF, PIKE, ELECT, ELITE, GLEAN, PROBE, PLUCK, CHOICE, CHOOSE, GATHER, PICKAX, SELECT, MATTOCK, PLECTRUM

picket: . . . . PEG, PALE, POST, FENCE, GUARD, STAKE, FASTEN, PALING, TETHER, ENCLOSE, FORTIFY

pickings: . . . SCRAPS, SPOILS

pickle: . . . . FIX, JAM, ALEC, CORN, DILL, MESS, ACHAR, BRINE, SOUSE, CAPERS, CHUTNEY, GHERKIN, VITRIOL, MARINATE, PREDICAMENT

pickled: . . . DRUNK, SOUSED, INTOXICATED

pickpocket: . . . . . DIP, HOOK, PRIG, THIEF, CUTPURSE

picnic: . . . . JUNKET, OUTING, COOKOUT, BARBEQUE, CLAMBAKE

pictorial: . . . . GRAPHIC, VIVID

picture: . . . (also see **motion picture**) OIL, COPY, ICON, IDEA, IMAGE, PHOTO, PRINT, SCENE, SLIDE, STILL, VINET, CRAYON, DEPICT, CANVAS, PASTEL, ETCHING, EXPLAIN, IMAGINE, PORTRAY, PROFILE,

REFLECT, TABLEAU, DESCRIBE,
LIKENESS, PAINTING, PORTRAIT,
VIGNETTE, LANDSCAPE,
MINIATURE, ILLUSTRATE,
PHOTOGRAPH, WATERCOLOR

picturesque: .... VIVID,
QUAINT, SCENIC, GRAPHIC,
IDYLLIC, STRIKING

piddle: .... TOY, PICK, PLAY,
TRIFLE, DAWDLE, PUTTER

piddling: .. PALTRY, TRIVIAL,
USELESS, INSIGNIFICANT

pie: ..... MESS, PATE, TART,
CHAOS, GRAFT, PASTY, PATTY,
JUMBLE, PASTRY, MIXTURE,
COBBLER, DESSERT, TURNOVER

piebald: ..... PIED, HORSE,
MIXED, MOTLEY, PINTO,
CALICO, MOTTLED, DAPPLED

piece: .. BIT, EKE, CHIP, COIN,
HUNK, JOIN, MEND, PART,
STUB, UNIT, CHUNK, CRUMB,
FLAKE, PATCH, SCRAP, SHRED,
SLICE, STRIP, CANTLE, MORSEL,
PARCEL, SLIVER, FIREARM,
PORTION, SECTION, SEGMENT,
SPLINTER, FRAGMENT,
FRACTION

pie: .... see **piebald**

pier: ..... DOCK, MOLE, PILE,
QUAY, SLIP, JETTY, WHARF,
SUPPORT, BUTTRESS, PILASTER,
LANDING, BREAKWATER

pierce: .. BORE, GORE, STAB,
DRILL, ENTER, GOUGE, GRIDE,
LANCE, PRICK, PROBE, PUNCH,
SPEAR, SPIKE, STICK, STING,
CLEAVE, IMPALE, RIDDLE,
THRUST, DISCERN, PENETRATE,
PUNCTURE, LANCINATE

piercing: .. FELL, HIGH, KEEN,
CLEAR, SHARP, SHRILL,
INCISIVE, CUTTING, PUNGENT

pig: . HAM, HOG, SOW, BOAR,
PORK, BACON, INGOT, SHOAT,
SHOTE, SWINE, FARROW,
PORKER, CASTING, GLUTTON

pigboat: .... SUBMARINE

pigeon: ... BIRD, DOVE, DUPE,
GULL, DECOY, PLUCK, SQUAB,
FLEECE, POUTER, FANTAIL,
JACOBIN, TUMBLER

piggish: ... FILTHY, GREEDY,
SELFISH, GLUTTONOUS

pigheaded: ..... PERVERSE,
STUBBORN, OBSTINATE

pigment: ...... DYE, COLOR,
PAINT, COLORANT

pigmy: .... see **pygmy**

pignus: ..... PAWN, PLEDGE

pigtail: ..... QUEUE, BRAID

pike: .... FISH, LUCE, PICK,
ROAD, POINT, SPIKE, TOWER,
BEACON, PICKAX, SUMMIT,
HIGHWAY, TOLL-ROAD,
SPEARHEAD, PICKEREL

piker: ... COWARD, GAMBLER,
QUITTER, SHIRKER, VAGRANT,
TIGHTWAD, CHEAPSKATE

pilaster: ...... ANTA, PIER,
COLUMN

pilchard: .... SARDINE,
HERRING, FUMADO

pile: ..... NAP, BANK, LEAP,
MASS, MOLE, PIER, RICK, SHAG,
AMASS, CROWD, SPILE, STACK,
HOARD, STAKE, PILLAR,
FORTUNE, BUTTRESS,
ACCUMULATE

pilfer: .... ROB, HOOK, LOOT,
TAKE, FILCH, SNEAK, STEAL,
SWIPE, SNITCH, THIEVE,
PURLOIN, SCROUNGE

pilgrim: .... CRUSADER,
TRAVELER, WAYFARER,
SOJOURNER, WANDERER

pilgrimage: .... HADJ, TRIP,
JOURNEY

pill: ... BALL, BOLUS, CREEK,
DRAGEE, PELLET, PILULE,
CAPSULE, GRANULE, PLACEBO

pillage: .. FLAY, LOOT, PREY,
SACK, BOOTY, FORAY, RIFLE,
SPOIL, STRIP, MARAUD, RAPINE,
RAVAGE, DESPOIL, PLUNDER,
DEVASTATE

pillar: . . . . . LAT, PIER, PILE, POST, PYLON, SHAFT, STELE, COLUMN, OBELISK, SUPPORT, MONUMENT, PILASTER

pillory: . . . . . YOKE, STOCKS, CANGUE, EXPOSE, GIBBET

pillow: . . . . PAD, BLOCK, BOLSTER, HEADREST, CUSHION, SUPPORT

pilose: . . . . . HAIRY, HIRSUTE

pilot: . . . ACE, LEAD, FLYER, GUIDE, STEER, LEADER, AVIATOR, CONDUCT, CHAPLAIN, DIRECTOR, GOVENOR, HELMSMAN, PREACHER

pilule: . . . . PILL

pimento: . . . . PAPRIKA, ALLSPICE

pimple: . . BLOB, FLAW, POCK, PAPULE, WHEAL, PUSTULE, CARBUNCLE

pin: . . . FIX, NOG, PEG, BOLT, JOIN, LILL, NAIL, TACK, AFFIX, BADGE, DOWEL, RIVET, STAKE, BROOCH, COTTER, FASTEN, SECURE, SKEWER, TOGGLE, TRIFLE, SPINDLE, FASTENER, ORNAMENT

pinafore: . . . . SLIP, TIER, APRON, DRESS, SMOCK, SUNDRESS

pince nez: . . . . . EYEGLASSES, LORGNON

pincer: . . . . . CHELA, PLIERS, TONGS, TENAIL, NIPPER, GRIPPER, TWEEZER, FORCEPS

pinch: . . . . . . NIP, ROB, BITE, RAID, CRAMP, FILCH, GRIPE, STEAL, TWEAK, ARREST, CRISIS, SNATCH, SNITCH, CONFINE, SQUEEZE, CONTRACT, DISTRESS, EMERGENCY

pine: . . . . FIR, ACHE, LONG, MOPE, TREE, CEDAR, DROOP, CONIFER, KAURY, KAURI, PINON, WASTE, YEARN, BALSAM, GRIEVE, LAMENT, SPRUCE, WITHER, DWINDLE, LANGUISH, EVERGREEN, PONDEROSA

pineapple: . . . . . BOMB, PINA, ANANA, GRENADE, ORNAMENT

pinquid: . . FAT, OILY, FATTY, FERTILE, GREASY, UNCTUOUS

pinion: . . . . . PIN, TIE, BIND, GEAR, WING, QUILL, CONFINE, DISABLE, FEATHER, SHACKLE, PENNANT, COGWHEEL

pink: . . . . CUT, ROSY, STAB, TINT, COLOR, CORAL, PRICK, FLOWER, PIERCE, SALMON, BLOSSOM, RADICAL

pinnacle: . . TOP, ACME, APEX, PEAK, CREST, CROWN, SPIRE, FINIAL, SUMMIT

pinpoint: . . . . AIM, DOT, FIX, EXACT, LOCATE, PRECISE

pintle: . . . . . . BOLT, HINGE, DOWEL,

pinto: . . . PIED, PONY, HORSE, CALICO, MOTTLED, PAINTED, PIEBALD, SPOTTED

pioneer: . . . . MINER, PAVER, DIGGER, PLANTER, SETTLER, COLONIST, EXPLORER

pious: . . GOOD, HOLY, GODLY, SACRED, DEVOUT, SAINTLY, FAITHFUL, RELIGIOUS

pip: . . HIT, PEEP, SEED, SPOT, CHEEP, CHIRP

pipe: . . . . OAT, CASK, DUET, FIFE, FLUE, LEAD, MAIN, REED, TUBE, BRIAR, CANAL, DRAIN, SPOUT, HOOKAH, LEADER, OUTLET, TUBULE, CALUMET, CONDUIT, FISTULA, WHISTLE

piping: . . . . EDGING, TUBING

piquant: . . . . . . RACY, TART, SALTY, SHARP, SPICY, TASTY, BITING, PEPPERY, PUNGENT, POIGNANT, PROVOCATIVE, STIMULATING

pique: . . FRET, GOAD, ANNOY, PEEVE, SPITE, COTTON, EXCITE, FABRIC, GRUDGE, MALICE, NETTLE, OFFEND, OFFENSE, PROVOKE, UMBRAGE, IRRITATE,

VEXATION, ANNOYANCE, RESENTMENT

pirate: . . . . ROVER, ROBBER, BRIGAND, CORSAIR, MARAUDER, SEAWOLF, PICAROON, PREDATOR, BUCANEER, FREEBOOTER, PRIVATEER

literary: . . . . . PLAGIARIST

pistol: . . . . . DAG, GAT, GUN, ROD, BARKER, BUFFER, HEATER, FIREARM, REVOLVER, AUTOMATIC, DERRINGER

pit: . . . . . . BUTT, FOSS, HELL, HOLE, MINE, POOL, SEED, SUMP, TRAP, WELL, ABYSS, ARENA, CHASM, DELFT, FOSSA, FOVEA, GRAVE, SHAFT, SNARE, STONE, CAVERN, CAVITY, HOLLOW, OPPOSE, POCKMARK, EXCAVATION

pitch: . . DIP, KEY, TAR, CANT, CAST, HURL, ROLL, REEL, SEND, TONE, TOSS, SWAY, FLING, HEAVE, LUNGE, LURCH, ERECT, RESIN, THROW, ENCAMP, PLUNGE, TOTTER, ASPHALT, BITUMEN, ALCHITRAN

pitcher: . . . JAR, JUG, EWER, OLLA, TOBY, CARAFE, HEAVER, HURLER, TOSSER, CONTAINER, BALLPLAYER

piteous: . . . MOVING, PITIFUL, PATHETIC, TOUCHING

pitfall: . . LURE, TRAP, SNARE, DANGER, DIFFICULTY

pith: . . . . . NUB, CORE, CRUX, GIST, MEAT, PULP, FORCE, VIGOR, KERNAL, MARROW, ESSENCE, MEDULIA, SUBSTANCE

pithy: . . . . . . CRISP, MEATY, TERSE, COMPACT, CONCISE, FORCEFUL, LACONIC, SENTENTIOUS

pitiful: . . . . SAD, MEAN, WOEFUL, FORLORN, PATHETIC, MISERABLE, SORROWFUL, DESPICABLE, LAMENTABLE

pittance: . . BIT, ALMS, DOLE, GIFT, MITE, TRIFLE, ALLOWANCE

pitted: . . FOVEATE, OPPOSED, SCARRED, POCKMARKED

pity: . . . . RUTH, MERCY, PATHOS, CLEMENCY, SYMPATHY, COMPASSION, CONDOLENCE, TENDERNESS, COMMISERATE

pivot: . . TURN, HINGE, SWING, WHEEL, PINTLE, SWIVEL

pivotal: . . . POLAR, CENTRAL, CRUCIAL, CARDINAL

pixy: . . . . ELF, FAIRY, SPRITE

placard: . . . BILL, POST, SIGN, POSTER

placate: . . . . . CALM, QUIET, PACIFY, SOOTHE, APPEASE, MOLLIFY, COCILIATE

place: . . . . . . LAY, PUT, SET, AREA, LIEU, POST, ROOM, SEAT, SITE, SPOT, COURT, LOCUS, PLANT, ROOM, SITUS, SPACE, STEAD, LOCALE, LOCATE, REGION, SQUARE, DEPOSIT, DISPOSE, SITUATE, DWELLING, LOCATION, POSITION, RESIDENCE, SITUATION

placid: . . CALM, EVEN, MILD, QUIET, GENTLE, SERENE, TRANQUIL, PEACEFUL, IMPASSIVE, UNRUFFLED

plagiarism: . . . . CRIB, THEFT, PIRACY

plague: . . . . DUN, POX, VEX, FRET, PEST, ANNOY, HARRY, TEASE, WORRY, HARASS, HECTOR, PESTER, WANION, SCOURGE, TORMENT, CALAMITY, EPIDEMIC, IRRITATE, NUISANCE, AFFLICTION, PESTILENCE, INFESTATION

plain: . . . BALD, BARE, EVEN, FAIR, FLAT, MERE, MOOR, OPEN, BLUNT, CLEAR, FRANK, GROSS, HEATH, HOMEY, LLANO, VELDT, LEVEL, CAMPO,

COARSE, HOMELY, HUMBLE,
MEADOW, PAMPAS, PATENT,
SIMPLE, TUNDRA, EVIDENT,
LEGIBLE, OBVIOUS, PRAIRIE,
SAVANNAH, APPARENT,
DISTINCT, UNADORNED,
CAMPAGNA, PALPABLE

plaintiff: . . . . . SUER, SUITOR,
ACCUSER, RECOVERER,
COMPLAINANT

plaintive: . . . SAD, WISTFUL,
MOURNFUL, REPINING,
LAMENTFUL, SORROWFUL,
MELANCHOLY

plait: . . . . . PLY, FOLD, KNIT,
BRAID, CRIMP, PLEAT, QUEUE,
TRESS, WEAVE, GATHER,
PLEACH, WIMPLE, PIGTAIL

plan: . . . . . AIM, MAP, IDEA,
PLAT, PLOT, DRAFT, ETTLE,
FRAME, BUDGET, DESIGN,
DEVISE, INTEND, LAYOUT,
METHOD, POLICY, SCHEMA,
SCHEME, SKETCH, SYSTEM,
ARRANGE, DIAGRAM, DRAWING,
OUTLINE, PROGRAM, PROJECT,
PURPOSE, CONSPIRE, CONTRIVE,
SCHEDULE, CALCULATE

plane: . . . EVEN, FLAT, SOAR,
GLIDE, LEVEL, SMOOTH,
AIRFOIL, SURFACE

planet: . ORB, MARS, EARTH,
ORBIT, PLUTO, VENUS,
SATURN, SPHERE, URANUS,
JUPITER, MERCURY, NEPTUNE,
ASTEROID

planetarium: . . . . . . ORRERY

plank: . DECK, SLAB, BOARD,
SLATE, LUMBER, TIMBER,
PLANCHER, PRINCIPLE

plant: . . . . . (also see Special
Section, **Plants**) FIX, SET,
SOW, BUSH, FERN, HERB, MILL,
RAPE, ROOT, SEED, SLIP, TREE,
WORT, BERRY, DECOY, FOUND,
FRUIT, GRAIN, SHOOT, WORKS,
ANNUAL, CLOVER, FLOWER,
LEGUME, CREEPER, CUTTING,
FACTORY, BUILDING, BUSINESS,

ESTABLISH, PERENNIAL,
SUCCULENT, VEGETABLE

plantation: . . FARM, ESTATE,
COLONY, HACIENDA

planter: . . . SOWER, FARMER,
GROWER, SEEDER, PIONEER,
SETTLER, COLONIST

plaque: . . . . PIN, BADGE,
MEDAL, BROOCH, TABLET

plaster: . . . . . DAUB, COVER,
GROUT, SALVE, SMEAR,
MORTAR, OVERLAY, PARGET,
STUCCO

plastic: . . . . . SOFT, DUCTILE,
FICTILE, PLIABLE, FLEXIBLE,
FORMATIVE

plat: . . . . . . LOT, MAP, FLAT,
PLAN, BRAID, CHART, LEVEL,
PLAIN, PLAIT

plate: . . . . COAT, DISC, DISH,
DISK, GRID, TILE, ARMOR,
FACIA, PATEN, SCUTE, LAMINA,
PATINA, PLATEN, VENEER,
PLATTER, OVERLAY, LAMELLA

plateau: . DISH, MESA, PUNA,
SEIR, FIELD, HAMADA, PLAQUE,
SALVER, UPLANDS, TABLELAND,
ALTIPLANO

platen: . . . . ROLLER

platform: . . . . BANK, BEMA,
DAIS, DECK, PLAN, BENCH,
DOLLY, FLOOR, STAGE,
PODIUM, PULPIT, PALLET,
ESTRADE, PROGRAM, ROSTRUM,
BALCONY, GALLERY

platitude: . . CLICHE, TRUISM,
BROMIDE, DULLNESS,
TRITENESS, COMMONPLACE

platter: . . . . DISH, PLATE,
RECORD, SALVER, (HOME)BASE,
TRENCHER

plaudit: . . . . . CLAP, PRAISE,
OVATION, APPLAUSE,
APPROVAL, ENCOMIUM

plausible: . . . . SPECIOUS,
CREDIBLE, OSTENSIBLE

play: . ACT, BET, FUN, GAME,
MOVE, ROMP, CHARM, DALLY,
FRISK, DRAMA, ENACT, FLIRT,

SPORT, CAVORT, FROLIC, GAMBLE, GAMBOL, TRIFLE, DISPORT, EXECUTE, PERFORM, AMUSEMENT, DIVERSION, RECREATION

player: . . CAST, STAR, ACTOR, LEADER, MUMMER, GAMBLER, GAMESTER, THESPIAN, PERFORMER, COMPETITOR, CONTESTANT

playful: . . . . MERRY, FRISKY, JOCOSE, JOKING, WANTON, JOCULAR, HUMOROUS, SPORTIVE, SKITTISH, KITTENISH

playing field: . . . PARK, OVAL, ARENA, DIAMOND

plaza: . . . . . MARKET, SQUARE

plea: . . . . SUE, SUIT, EXCUSE, APPEAL, ANSWER, PRAYER, SOLICIT, REQUEST, ENTREATY, ARGUMENT, PETITION, ALLEGATION, SUPPLICATION

plead: . . . . BEG, SUE, ARGUE, APPEAL, ALLEGE, ASSERT, BESEECH, IMPLORE, ENTREAT, SOLICIT, ADVOCATE, PETITION, IMPORTUNE, SUPPLICATE

pleasant: . . GAY, FINE, GOOD, NICE, MERRY, SWEET, GENIAL, AMIABLE, AMUSING, JOCULAR, WINSOME, GRACIOUS, HUMOROUS, ENJOYABLE, AGREEABLE

please: . . . SUIT, WILL, WISH, AGREE, AMUSE, ELATE, HUMOR, APPEASE, CONTENT, GRATIFY, INDULGE, DELIGHT, SATISFY, GLADDEN, PLACATE

pleasing: . . . NICE, PLEASANT, FETCHING, AGREEABLE, ATTRACTIVE, DELECTABLE

pleasure: . . . FUN, JOY, EASE, WILL, WISH, MIRTH, SPORT, GRACE, CHOICE, GAIETY, LIKING, RELISH, DELIGHT, GLADNESS, HILARITY, AMUSEMENT, ENJOYMENT, HAPPINESS

pleat: . . . . FOLD, KILT, PLAIT, SHIRR, BRAID, PLICATE, RUFFLE

plebeian: . . . . COMMON, COARSE, VULGAR, ILLBRED, LOWBORN, ORDINARY

plebiscite: . . . VOTE, DECREE, MANDATE, REFERENDUM

pledge: . . . BET, VOW, BOND, GAGE, HAND, HEST, HOCK, OATH, PAWN, SEAL, WAGE, WORD, SWEAR, TOAST, TOKEN, TROTH, ASSURE, COMMIT, ENGAGE, PAROLE, PLIGHT, BETROTH, DEPOSIT, EARNEST, PROMISE, CONTRACT, GUARANTY, MORTGAGE, ASSURANCE

plenary: . . . . . FULL, ENTIRE, PERFECT, ABSOLUTE, COMPLETE

plenipotentiary: . . . . ENVOY, MINISTER, AMBASSADOR

plenteous: . . . . COPIOUS, ABUNDANT

plentiful: . . FULL, RICH, RIFE, AMPLE, GALORE, COPIOUS, FERTILE, LIBERAL, OPULENT, PROFUSE, REPLETE, ABUNDANT, FRUITFUL, GENEROUS, PROLIFIC, BOUNTIFUL

plenty: . . . . . . ENOW, HEAP, AMPLE, ENOUGH, COPIOUS, FULLNESS, OPULENCE, ABUNDANCE, AFFLUENCE

plethora: . . . . . GLUT, EXCESS, FULLNESS, REPLETION

plexus: . . . . RETE, RETIN, TANGLE, NETWORK

pliable: . . . EASY, LIMP, SOFT, LITHE, LIMBER, PLIANT, SUPPLE, DUCTILE, FLACID, PLASTIC, TENSILE, FLEXIBLE, MALLEABLE

plight: . . . . RISK, STATE, ENGAGE, PLEDGE, STATUS, BETROTH, PROMISE, POSITION, SITUATION, CONDITION, DIFFICULTY

plod: ... GRUB, PLUG, SLOG, STEP, TOIL, WALK, WORK, DRUDGE, TRUDGE

plop: .... DROP, PLUMP

plot: .... LOT, MAP, DRAW, LAND, PLAN, PLAT, CABAL, CHART, DRAFT, DESIGN, DEVISE, PATCH, SCHEME, SECRET, COMPACT, CONNIVE, DIAGRAM, OUTLINE, CONSPIRE, CONTRIVE, ENGINEER, INTRIGUE, SCENARIO, MACHINATE, CONSPIRACY

plow, plough: ... DIG, FARM, LIST, MOLE, ROVE, TILL, BREAK, FURROW, CULTIVATE

ploy: ... BEND, JOKE, SPORT, TRICK, FROLIC, PASTIME, ESCAPADE, MANEUVER, STRATEGY, STRATAGEM

pluck: ..... ROB, TUG, GRIT, GUTS, JERK, PICK, PULL, TEAR, CHEEK, NERVE, SPUNK, STRIP, STRUM, TWANG, DARING, FINGER, FLEECE, GATHER, SNATCH, SPIRIT, TWEEZE, BRAVERY, COURAGE, DEPLUME, PLUNDER, SWINDLE, GAMENESS, ENDURANCE, FORTITUDE

plug: . NAG, PEG, TAP, BUNG, CALK, CORK, PLOD, SLOG, BOOST, CAULK, ESTOP, SHOOT, PITCH, SPILE, DOSSIL, DOTTLE, SPIGOT, TAMPON, STOPPER, TAMPION, ADVERTISE, PUBLICISE

plumage: .... DOWN, DRESS, HACKLE, FEATHERS, ADORNMENT

plumb: ...... BUNG, DELVE, PROBE, SOLVE, SOUND, FATHOM, PLUNGE, WHOLLY, EXPLORE, PLUMMET, ABSOLUTE, COMPLETE, ENTIRELY, VERTICAL

plume: ...... DOWN, TUFT, CREST, EGRET, PREEN, PRUNE, AIGRET, FEATHER, PANACHE, AIGRETTE, MARABOU

plummet: ..... DROP, FALL, LEAD, PLUMB, WEIGHT

plump: ... FAT, DROP, FALL, PLOP, SINK, TIDY, BUXOM, OBESE, PLUNK, STOUT, CHUBBY, FLESHY, PORTLY, ROTUND, BLUNTLY, DISTEND, ROLY-POLY

plunder: ... GUT, ROB, LOOT, PELF, PREY, RAID, SACK, SWAG, BOOTY, HARRY, RIFLE, SPOIL, STEAL, STRIP, BOODLE, MARAUD, PILFER, RAPINE, RAVAGE, RAVISH, DESPOIL, PILLAGE, RANSACK, DEPREDATE, DEVASTATE

plunge: ...... BEG, DIG, DIP, DIVE, DUCK, DUMP, DUNK, SINK, DOUSE, DOWSE, FLING, LUNGE, MERSE, PLUMB, SOUSE, GAMBLE, THRUST, IMMERSE, SUBMERGE

plunger: .... DIVER, PISTON, DASHER, GAMBLER, SPECULATOR

plunk: .. BLOW, DROP, FLOP, SINK, THUD, PLUCK, PLUMP, SOUND, STRUM, THROW, TWANG

plurality: .... MAJORITY

plus: ..... ADD, MORE, OVER, EXTRA, EXCESS, ADDITION, POSITIVE

plush: .. OPULENT, LUXURIOUS

ply: ..... WEB, BEND, FOLD, MOLD, URGE, WORK, BESET, LAYER, PLAIT, WIELD, HANDLE, TRAVEL, BELABOR, SHUTTLE, EXERCISE, IMPORTUNE

poach: ... MIX, BOIL, COOK, STAB, STIR, DRIVE, FORCE, SHIRR, SPEAR, STEAL, STEAM, PIERCE, TRAMPLE, ENCROACH, TRESPASS

pock: .... PIT, SCAR, PIMPLE, PUSTULE

pocket: ..... BAG, BIN, FOB, SAC, POKE, SACK, POUCH,

CAVITY, CONCEAL, CONFINE, ENCLOSE

pocketbook: .... BAG, FOB, POKE, POUCH, PURSE, WALLET, BILLFOLD, HANDBAG

pod: ... BAG, BUR, COD, SAC, ARIL, BOLL, BURR, HULL, CAROB, POUCH, SHELL, SHUCK, FLOCK, SCHOOL, COCOON, LEGUME, CAPSULE, SEEDCASE

podesta: .... JUDGE, MAYOR, GOVENOR, OFFICIAL, MAGISTRATE

podium: ...... BASE, DIAS, PEDESTAL, PLATFORM

poem: ..... ODE, EPIC, RIME, SONG, CANTO, DITTY, ELEGY, LYRIC, VERSE; BALLAD, EPOPEE, EULOGY, IAMBIC, JINGLE, SONNET, SESTINA, VIRELAY, SOLILOQUY

poet: .. BARD, ODIST, LYRIST, RHYMER, DREAMER, ELEGIST, METRIST, IDYLLIST

poetic: .... LYRIC, DREAMY, ROMANTIC, BEAUTIFUL, IMAGINATIVE

pogrom: .... ATTACK, MASSACRE, SLAUGHTER

poi: .... TARO, FOOD, PASTE

poignant: ..... KEEN, TART, ACUTE, SHARP, BITING, MOVING, CUTTING, PIQUANT, POINTED, PUNGENT, TOUCHING, PRICKING

poind: .... SELL, SEIZE, IMPOUND, DISTRAINT

point: ... AIM, DOT, JOT, NIB, TIP, APEX, BARB, CAPE, CRUX, FOCI, GIST, HORN, PEAK, POLE, SHOW, SPOT, ANGLE, FOCUS, ISSUE, PRONG, SPECK, TAPER, ALLUDE, DEGREE, DIRECT, PERIOD, EMPHASIS, INDICATE

pointed: .... ACUTE, PIKED, SHARP, TERSE, MARKED, PEAKED, PICKED, ACTUATE, CONCISE, CONICAL, INCISIVE, PIERCING, STINGING

pointer: .... ARM, DOG, TIP, CLUE, DIAL, HAND, HINT, VANE, WAND, INDEX, ARROW, SETTER, GNOMON, INDICES, INDICATOR, RETRIEVER

pointless: .... DULL, BLUNT, INANE, SILLY, VAPID, STUPID, INSIPID, SENSELESS

poise: ..... HOVER, APLOMB, BALANCE, BEARING, LIBERATE, SUPPORT, SUSPEND, CALMNESS, CARRIAGE, MAINTAIN, EQUIPOISE, STABILITY, EQUILIBRIUM

poison: .. BANE, DRUG, GALL, TAINT, TOXIN, VENOM, VIRUS, INFECT, MIASMA, ARSENIC, CORRUPT, HEMLOCK, PERVERT, VITIATE, PTOMAINE, TOXICANT

poisonous: ... TOXIC, VIROSE, NOXIOUS, VENOMOUS, VIRULENT, VIPERINE, MEPHITIC, MALIGNANT

poke: .. BAG, DIG, DUB, HAT, JAB, JOG, PRY, BLOW, PROD, PUSH, GOAD, ROOT, SACK, NUDGE, PROBE, PUNCH, PURSE, BONNET, DAWDLE, LOITER, MEDDLE, POCKET, PUTTER, THRUST, WALLET, INTRUDE, POCKETBOOK

poker: ... ROD, CHIP, DART, DRAW, GAME, STUD

pole: ..... BAR, ROD, AXIS, BOOM, MAST, POST, PROP, SPAR, WAND, CABER, SHAFT, STUFF, STAKE, STILT, THILL, TOTEM

polemic: .... MOOT, DEBATABLE, ARGUMENT, DISPUTATION, CONTROVERSIAL

polestar: ... GUIDE, POLARIS, LODESTAR, NORTH STAR

police: .... GUARD, WATCH, GOVERN, PATROL, PROTECT, CARABINIERI, CONSTABULARY

policeman: .. COP, PIG, BULL, DICK, BOBBY, COPPER, MINION, PEELER, GUMSHOE, OFFICER,

FLATFOOT, TROOPER, CONSTABLE, PATROLMAN, GENDARME

policy: . . . PLAN, CONTRACT, DIPLOMACY, PRINCIPLE, PLATFORM

polish: . . RUB, BUFF, GLAZE, GLOSS, GRIND, SCOUR, SHEEN, SHINE, SLICK, FINISH, LUSTER, REFINE, SMOOTH, BURNISH, CULTURE, BRIGHTEN, CIVILIZE, LEVIGATE, REFINEMENT

polished: . . . . . FINE, SLEEK, POLITE, SUAVE, GLOSSY, POLITE, REFINED, URBANE

polishing material: . . . WAX, SAND, EMERY, PUMICE, RABAT, ABRASIVE

polite: . . . . CIVIL, SUAVE, GENTLE, URBANE, CORRECT, COURTLY, GALLANT, GENTEEL, REFINED, CULTURED, GRACIOUS, MANNERLY, POLISHED, COURTEOUS

politic: . . . . . . WISE, SUAVE, SHREWD, PRUDENT, TACTFUL, EXPEDIENT, SAGACIOUS, DIPLOMATIC

politician: . . . . HEELER, POLITICO, SCHEMER, SENATOR, INTRIGUER, STATESMAN, CONGRESSMAN

poll: . . . . . . CUT, CLIP, CROP, HEAD, LIST, TRIM, VOTE, COUNT, JUROR, SHAVE, SHEAR, FLEECE, SURVEY, CANVASS, DESPOIL, LISTING, COUNTING, REGISTER, ENUMERATE

pollute: . . FOUL, SOIL, DIRTY, SMEAR, SULLY, TAINT, BEFOUL, DEFILE, CORRUPT, PROFANE, VIOLATE, CONTAMINATE

poltergeist: . . . GHOST, SPIRIT

poltroon: . CAD, IDLE, LAZY, COWARD, CRAVEN, DASTARD, SLUGGARD

polygon: . . . . NGON, SQUARE, DECAGON, NONAGON, OCTAGON, PENTAGON, TRIANGLE, HEXAGON, ISAGON, TETRAGON

Polynesian: . . . ATI, MALAY, MAORI, SAMOAN, TONGAN, TAHITIAN, KANAKA, HAWAIIAN, NUKUORO

pomade: . . SALVE, UNGUENT, OINTMENT, COSMETIC, POMATUM

pommel: . . BAT, BEAT, KNOB, HANDLE

pomp: . . . . . . SHOW, STATE, PARADE, CORTEGE, DISPLAY, PAGEANT, CEREMONY, GRANDEUR, SPLENDOR, PAGEANTRY, SPECTACLE

pompous: . . . . . BIG, TUMID, TURGID, BLOATED, FUSTIAN, ORUTUND, STATELY, STILTED, BOMBASTIC, GRANDIOSE, MAGNIFIC, HIGHFALUTIN, PRETENTIOUS

pond: . . . . DAM, DELF, DIKE, LAKE, MERE, POOL, TARN, LAGOON, SALINA, LAGUNE

ponder: . MULL, MUSE, PORE, BROOD, WEIGH, REASON, REFLECT, APPRAISE, COGITATE, CONSIDER, EVALUATE, PERPEND, MEDITATE, RUMINATE

ponderous: . . . DULL, BULKY, GRAVE, HEAVY, AWKWARD, LABORED, MASSIVE, WEIGHTY, UNWEILDY, IMPORTANT

poniard: . . DAGGER, STILETTO

pontiff: . . . . . . POPE, BISHOP

pontifical: . . . . PAPAL, POMPOUS, EPISCOPAL

pontoon: . . . . . BOAT, BARGE, FLOAT, BRIDGE, VESSEL, CAISSON

pony: . . . . . COB, NAG, CRIB, GLASS, HORSE, LIQUOR, BRONCO, CAYUSE, SHELTY, SHELTIE

pool: . . CAR, PIT, POT, CARR, DIKE, GAME, LINN, LOCH, MERE, POND, TANK, FUNDS, KITTY, PLASH, STAKE, TRUST,

CARTEL, PUDDLE, COMBINE,
BILLIARDS, MONOPOLY

poor: . . . . . BAD, ILL, BASE,
LEAN, MEAN, CHEAP, DINKY,
NEEDY, SEEDY, ABJECT,
BARREN, HUMBLE, PALTRY,
SCANTY, SHABBY, DESTITUTE,
INFERIOR, INDIGENT,
PENNILESS, IMPERFECT,
PENURIOUS

Pope: . . . . . (also see **Papal**)
RAFF, VICAR, BISHOP, PRIEST,
PUFFIN, SHRIKE, PONTIFF,
PATRIARCH

poppycock: . . . . . ROT, BOSH,
NONSENSE, BALONEY

populace: . . . . . MOB, MASS,
DEMOS, PEOPLE, MASSES

popular: . . . . LAY, COMMON,
SIMPLE, DEMOTIC, FAVORED,
ACCEPTED, FAVORITE,
PREVALENT, VULGATE,
ENCHORIAL, EXOTERIC

populate: . OCCUPY, INHABIT,
PEOPLE

porcelain: . . . . MING, CHINA,
SPODE, LIMOGES, DRESDEN,
CELADON, SEVRES, HAVILAND,
WEDGEWOOD

porch: . . . . . . STOA, LANAI,
PLAZA, STOOP, LOGGIA,
PARVIS, PIAZZA, BALCONY,
PORTICO, GALILEE, GALLERY,
TERRACE, VERANDA

pore: . . . CON, READ, STOMA,
STUDY, PONDER, OPENING,
ORIFICE, OSTIOLE, MEDITATE,
FORAMEN, CHANNEL

pork: . . . . . . HAM, PIG, HOG,
BACON, MONEY, SWINE,
SAUSAGE

pornographic: . . . . . . LEWD,
OBSCENE, LICENTIOUS,
SALACIOUS

porridge: . . . . MUSH, SAMP,
ATOLE, BROSE, GROUT, GRUEL,
BURGOO, OATMEAL, POTTAGE,
POLENTA, STIRABOUT

port: . . . . GATE, LEFT, WINE,
CARRY, HAVEN, HARBOR,
REFUGE, SHELTER, GATEWAY,
ANCHORAGE

portable:. . MOBILE, MOVABLE

portal: . . ARCH, DOOR, GATE,
DOORWAY, GATEWAY,
POSTERN, ENTRANCE

portend: . . . . . BODE, WARN,
AUGUR, DIVINE, FORBODE,
PRESAGE, FORESHADOW,
PROPHESY

portent: . . . . . . OMEN, SIGN,
EVENT, PRODIGY, MARVEL,
WARNING, MEANING

portentous: . . . DIRE, FATAL,
GRAVE, SOLEMN, FATEFUL,
OMINOUS, SINISTER,
SIGNIFICANT

porter: . . ALE, BEER, CARRY,
HAMAL, STOUT, REDCAP,
BALIFF, JANITOR, CARRIER,
CONCIERGE, GATEKEEPER,
DOORMAN

portico: . . . . see **porch**

portion: . . . . BIT, CUT, DAB,
LOT, DEAL, DOLE, PART,
ALLOT, ALLOW, DIVVY,
DOWER, ENDOW, QUOTA,
RATIO, DIVIDE, MOIETY,
PARCEL, RATION, DESTINY,
HELPING, SECTION, SEGMENT,
SERVING, QUANTITY

portly: . . FAT, OBESE, STOUT

portrait: . . . . IMAGE, EFFIGY,
PICTURE, LIKENESS

portray: . ACT, DRAW, FORM,
LIMN, MIME, SHOW, ENACT,
IMAGE, PAINT, DEPICT,
FASHION, PICTURE, DESCRIBE,
PERSONATE, DELINEATE,
REPRESENT

pose: . . . . . SET, SIT, MODEL,
PLACE, BAFFLE, PUZZLE,
STANCE, PROPOSE, POSTURE,
MANNERISM, PRETENSE,
PROPOUND, ATTITUDE

posh: . . . . . SMART, SPRUCE,
SWANKY, ELEGANT, LUXURIOUS

posit: ..... AFFIRM, ASSERT, ASSUME, SITUATE, POSTULATE

position: ..... JOB, LIE, SET, POSE, POST, RANK, SITE, LOCUS, PLACE, SITUS, STAND, BILLET, ESTATE, LOCALE, OFFICE, PLIGHT, STANCE, STATUS, CALLING, POSTURE, STATION, ATTITUDE, SITUATION, LOCATION

positive: ...... PLUS, SURE, ACTUAL, EXPRESS, PRECISE, ASSURED, CERTAIN, ABSOLUTE, COMPLETE, CONSTANT, EMPHATIC, EXPLICIT, SPECIFIC, ASSERTIVE, CONFIDENT

possess: ...... OWN, HAVE, REACH, OCCUPY, INHABIT, DOMINATE, MAINTAIN

possessed: ... MAD, CRAZED, CHARMED, DEMONIAC

possession: ... AVER, HOLD, SEISIN, WEALTH, CONTROL, MASTERY, PROPERTY, OWNERSHIP

possible: ..... MAY, LIKELY, FEASIBLE, PROBABLE, POTENTIAL, CONTINGENT, PRACTICABLE

possibly: ... MAYBE, PERHAPS

post: .. JOB, SET, DOLE, FORT, MAIL, POLE, RIDE, SEND, NEWEL, PLACE, STAKE, ASSIGN, COLUMN, INFORM, OFFICE, PILLAR, MARKER, DISPATCH, BOLLARD, STATION, COURIER, POSITION, GARRISON

poster: .... BILL, SIGN, AFFICHE, PLACARD, STICKER, BILLBOARD

posterior: ..... BACK, HIND, REAR, BEHIND, RETRAL, DORSAL, BUTTOCK, HINDER, SUBSEQUENT

posterity: .. FUTURE, SEQUEL, DESCENDANTS

postern: .. DOOR, EXIT, GATE, BACKDOOR, BACKGATE, ENTRANCE

postiche: ..... WIG, SWITCH, TOUPEE, ARTIFICIAL, PRETENSE, IMITATION

postpone: ..... STAY, WAIT, DEFER, DELAY, REMIT, TABLE, REMAND, SHELVE, ADJOURN, PIGEONHOLE

postulant: ...... APPLICANT, CANDIDATE, PETITIONER

postulate: .... CLAIM, POSIT, AXIOM, THESIS, ASSUME, DEMAND, PRESUME, PREMISE, REQUIRE, HYPOTHESIS

posture: .... POSE, STANCE, BEARING, POSITION, ATTITUDE, CARRIAGE

pot: .. BAG, PAN, URN, POOL, OLLA, CRUSE, KITTY, SHOOT, ALUDEL, KETTLE, SECURE, VESSEL, PIPKIN, CALDRON, JARDINIERE

potage: ...... SOUP, BROTH

potassium: .. ALUM, POTASH

potation: .... DRAM, DRAFT, DRINK, LIQUOR, SPIRITS, BEVERAGE

potato: .... OCA, YAM, SPUD, TUBER, IDAHO, TATER

potency: .... FORCE, MIGHT, POWER, VIGOR, ENERGY, EFFICACY, STRENGTH, VITALITY, FERTILITY

potent: ..... ABLE, COGENT, MIGHTY, STRONG, POWERFUL, VIRULENT, EFFECTIVE

potentate: ..... AMIR, EMIR, MOGUL, RULER, MONARCH, SOVEREIGN

potential: . LATENT, MIGHTY, POSSIBLE, UNREALIZED, INFLUENTIAL, UNDEVELOPED

pother: .... ADO, ROW, FUSS, STIR, WORRY, UPROAR, BUSTLE, BOTHER, HARASS, TROUBLE

pothouse: ..... INN, TAVERN

potiche: .... JAR, VASE

potion: .. BREW, DOSE, DRUG, DRAFT, DRINK, DRAUGHT, PHILTER, NEPENTHE

potpourri: . . . . . OLIO, STEW, MEDLEY, MIXTURE, ANTHOLOGY, MISCELLANY

pottage: . . . . . . SOUP, STEW, PORRIDGE

pottery: . . . . . WARE, CHINA, DELFT, CERAMICS, DELFTWARE, STONEWARE, EARTHENWARE

pouch: . . . . BAG, COD, POD, SAC, CYST, SACK, BURSA, PURSE, POCKET, SPORRAN, SPLEUCHAN

poultry: . . . . . FOWL, DUCKS, GEESE, PIGEONS, TURKEYS, CHICKENS, PHEASANTS

pounce: . . NAB, CLAW, LEAP, STAB, POUND, STAMP, SWOOP, TALON, SPRING

pound: . . . PEN, BEAT, BRAY, MAUL, QUID, TAMP, UNIT, CRUSH, KNOCK, THROB, THUMP, HAMMER, WEIGHT, CONFUSE, PULVERIZE, ENCLOSURE, MALLEATE

pour: . . . EMIT, FLOW, GUSH, RAIN, TEEM, TIDE, VENT, WELL, DRAIN, EMPTY, ISSUE, SPOUT, AFFUSE, DECANT, EFFUSE, STREAM, SWARM, DISCHARGE

poverty: . . . . . . LACK, NEED, WANT, DEARTH, PENURY, PAUCITY, SCARCITY, INDIGENCE

powder: . . . . . . DUST, TALC, BORON, CRUSH, FLOUR, POLLEN, POUNCE, COSMETIC, SPRINKLE, PULVERIZE

power: . . . . VIS, IRON, SWAY, FORCE, MIGHT, STEAM, VIGOR, WIELD, EMPIRE, ENERGY, THRONE, ABILITY, COMMAND, CONTROL, POTENCY, CAPACITY, EFFICACY, STRENGTH, AUTHORITY, INFLUENCE

powerful: . . . . . ABLE, STOUT, BRAWNY, COGENT, POTENT, MIGHTY, STRONG, EFFECTIVE, EFFECTUAL

powerless: . . . WEAK, FEEBLE, UNABLE, IMPOTENT

practical: . . . UTILE, ACTUAL, USABLE, USEFUL, WORKING, FEASIBLE, POSSIBLE, WORKABLE, PRAGMATIC

practice: . . . . . DO, PLY, TRY, USE, APPLY, CANON, CAUSE, DRILL, HABIT, TRADE, TRAIN, USAGE, WORKOUT, CUSTOM, PERFORM, EXERCISE, PRAXIS, REHEARSE

pragmatic: . . . . . . SKILLED, DOGMATIC, EMPIRICAL, PRACTICAL, OFFICIOUS, SYSTEMATIC

prairie: . . . . . CAMAS, LLANO, PLAIN, PAMPAS, STEPPE, SAVANNA, GRASSLAND

praise: . . LAUD, TOUT, BLESS, EXALT, EXTOL, GLORY, HONOR, KUDOS, ACCLAIM, APPLAUD, COMMEND, GLORIFY, PLAUDIT, TRIBUTE, APPLAUSE, PANEGYRIC, EULOGIZE, ENCOMIUM, COMPLIMENT

prance: . . . . . CAPER, DANCE, STRUT, CAVORT, FROLIC, SWAGGER

prank: . . . DIDO, HOAX, JAPE, JOKE, LARK, ANTIC, CAPER, TRICK, FROLIC, GAMBOL, MISCHIEF, ESCAPADE

prate: . . . . . . GAB, YAP, BLAB, CARP, CHAT, BOAST, CHATTER, TATTLE, PRATTLE, BABBLE, TWADDLE, HARANGUE

praxis: . . . ACTION, CUSTOM, PRACTICE

pray: . . . ASK, BEG, BID, SUE, APPEAL, INVOKE, REQUEST, ENTREAT, IMPLORE, BESEECH, APPEAL, PETITION, SUPPLICATE

prayer: . . . AVE, BEAD, BOON, PLEA, SUIT, GRACE, MATIN, APPEAL, ORISON, LITANY, REQUEST, ENTREATY, PETITION, NOVENA

preach: . . . . TEACH, EXHORT, INFORM, LECTURE, ADVOCATE,

INSTRUCT, PROCLAIM, SERMONIZE

preacher: . PARSON, RECTOR, MINISTER, CLERGYMAN, EVANGELIST, PREDICANT, PULPITEER

preamble: . . . . PREFACE

precarious: . . . . RISKY, DUBIOUS, INSECURE, PERILOUS, UNSTABLE, DANGEROUS, HAZARDOUS, UNCERTAIN

precede: . . . . . . HEAD, LEAD, USHER, FORERUN, PREDATE, ANTECEDE, INTRODUCE

precedent: . . . MODEL, USAGE, EXAMPLE, DECISION, STANDARD

precept: . . LAW, RULE, TORA, WRIT, ADAGE, AXIOM, BRIEF, MAXIM, ORDER, SUTRA, TORAH, DICTUM, COMMAND, MANDATE, DOCTRINE, APHORISM, PRINCIPLE

precinct(s): . . AMBIT, BOUND, BOUNDRY, DISTRICT, ENVIRONS, ENCLOSURE, NEIGHBORHOOD

precious: . . . . . . DEAR, RARE, LOVED, COSTLY, BELOVED, ARRANT, VALUABLE

precipice: . . . . . CRAG, DROP, LINN, BLUFF, BRINK, CLIFF, STEEP, DECLIVITY

precipitate: . . . . FALL, HURL, RASH, HASTY, HEADY, SPEED, THROW, ABRUPT, HASTEN, SUDDEN, TUMBLE, HEADLONG, CONDENSE, SETTLING, IMPETUOUS, IMPULSIVE

precipitation: . . . DEW, HAIL, MIST, RAIN, RUSH, SNOW, HASTE, SLEET, DOWNPOUR

precipitous: . . . RASH, HASTY, SHEER, STEEP

precis: . . . . DIGEST, RESUME, SYNOPSIS, ABSTRACT, SUMMARY

precise: . . . EVEN, NICE, PRIM, EXACT, FORMAL, MINUTE, STRICT, PRISSY, CERTAIN, CORRECT, FINICKY, LITERAL,

ACCURATE, DEFINITE, EXPLICIT, FAULTLESS, PARTICULAR

preclude: . . . . . . BAR, STOP, AVERT, CLOSE, DEBAR, ESTOP, FORBID, PREVENT, HINDER, INHIBIT, IMPEDE, FORECLOSE

precursor: . . . OMEN, HERALD, ANCESTOR, HARBINGER, MESSENGER, FORERUNNER, FOREFATHER

predatory: . . . . . . PREYING, ROBBING, PILLAGING, PIRATICAL, RAPACIOUS, PLUNDERING, PREDACIOUS

predestine: . . . DOOM, FATE, DEGREE, ORDAIN, DESTINE, DETERMINE, PREORDAIN

predetermine: . . . . BIAS, DECREE, DESTINE, PREDICT, FORECAST, PREJUDICE

predicament: . . . . . FIX, JAM, HOLE, PASS, SPOT, STEW, PICKLE, PLIGHT, SCRAPE, DILEMMA, QUANDARY, SITUATION

predict: . . . . . DOPE, OMEN, AUGUR, DIVINE, FOREBODE, PRESAGE, PORTEND, FORETELL, PROPHESY, FORECAST, PROGNOSTICATE

prediction: . . . . . FORECAST, PROPHECY

predilection: . . . BENT, BIAS, TASTE, LIKING, FONDNESS, LEANING, TENDENCY, PREJUDICE, PARTIALITY, PROPENSITY, PREFERENCE

predisposed: . . . . . . PRONE, BIASED, PARTIAL, INCLINED, PREJUDICED

predominant: . . . . . RULING, REIGNING, SUPERIOR, ASCENDENT

preempt: . . . . . SEIZE, USURP, ESTABLISH, MONOPOLIZE, APPROPRIATE

preface: . . . . BEGIN, FRONT, START, PROEM, PRECEDE, PRELUDE, PREAMBLE,

FOREWORD, FRONTISPIECE,
INTRODUCTION
prefer: ... OPT, LIKE, ELECT,
FAVOR, DESIRE, RATHER,
CHOOSE, SELECT
pregnable: .... VULNERABLE
pregnancy: .... CYESIS,
FETATION, GESTATION
pregnant: .. HEAVY, GRAVID,
FERTILE, TEEMING, WEIGHTY,
ENCEINTE, FRUITFUL, PROLIFIC,
EXPECTING, ABOUNDING,
GESTATING, POTENTIAL
prejudice: ..... BENT, BIAS,
HARM, HURT, DAMAGE,
HATRED, IMPAIR, BIGOTRY,
IMPERIL, OPINION, PARTIALITY
prelate: ...... HEAD, CHIEF,
BISHOP, PRIEST, PRIMATE,
CARDINAL, SUPERIOR
preliminary: .... PRIOR,
PREFACE, PREVIOUS,
PREFACTORY, THRESHOLD,
ANTECEDENT
prelude: .. PROEM, DESCANT,
PREFACE, OPENING, OVERTURE
premature: .. EARLY, UNRIPE,
IMMATURE, UNTIMELY,
PRECOCIOUS, INOPPORTUNE
premise: ... BASIS, PREFACE,
GROUND, POSTULATE,
ASSUMPTION, PROPOSITION
premium: ...... FEE, AGIO,
BONUS, PRIZE, BOUNTY,
REWARD, LAGNAPPE,
RECOMPENSE
premonition: .... OMEN,
HUNCH, WARNING, FOREBODING
preoccupation: .. OBESSION,
FIXATION
preoccupied: ... LOST, RAPT,
ABSENT, FILLED, ABSORBED,
ENGROSSED
prepare: ..... ARM, FIT, FIX,
GET, SET, EDIT, GIRD, MAKE,
PAVE, ADAPT, ALERT, COACH,
CURRY, EQUIP, FRAME, GROOM,
PRIME, READY, TRAIN, ADJUST,
DEVISE, ARRANGE, CONCOCT,

CONFECT, FURNISH, PROVIDE,
QUALIFY, ACCUSTOM,
REHEARSE
preponderant: .. ASCENDANT,
DOMINANT
preposition: ..... AT, BY, IN,
ON, TO, UP, BUT, FOR, OFF,
OUT, FROM, INTO, ONTO, OVER,
UNTO, UPON, WITH, ABOUT,
AFTER
preposterous: .... ABSURD,
SCREWY, FOOLISH, SENSELESS,
RIDICULOUS, IRRATIONAL,
NONSENSICAL
prerogative: .... RIGHT,
PRIORITY, PRIVILEGE,
PRECEDENCE
presage: ..... BODE, OMEN,
SIGN, AUGUR, TOKEN,
PORTEND, WARNING, PREDICT,
PORTENT, FORETELL,
HARBINGER, PREDICTION
prescience: ..... FORESIGHT
prescribe: ..... SET, ALLOT,
GUIDE, LIMIT, ORDER, DEFINE,
DIRECT, ORDAIN, OUTLAW,
COMMAND, DICTATE
prescription: .... RECIPE
presence: ...... WIT, MIEN,
BEING, GHOST, SPIRIT,
BEARING, COMPANY, DIGNITY,
SPECTRE, ASSEMBLY,
ATTENDANCE, APPEARANCE
present: .. NOW, BOON, GIFT,
GIVE, HERE, SHOW, GRANT,
NONCE, OFFER, READY, TODAY,
CONFER, DONATE, RENDER,
BESTOW, TENDER, DISPLAY,
EXHIBIT, LARGESS, PERFORM,
DONATION, GRATUITY,
LAGNAPPE
presentment: ...... HUNCH,
FOREBODING, PREMONITION
presently: ..... NOW, ANON,
SOON, SHORTLY, DIRECTLY,
NOWADAYS
preserve: .. CAN, DRY, JAM,
CORN, CURE, KEEP, SALT,
SAVE, GUARD, JELLY, SPARE,

STORE, SMOKE, DEFEND, PICKLE, RETAIN, SECURE, SHIELD, UPHOLD, PROTECT, SUSTAIN, CONSERVE, MAINTAIN, SAFEGUARD, PERPETUATE

preside: . . DIRECT, CONTROL, MODERATE, CONDUCT, REGULATE

President, U.S.: . . . . SEE SPECIAL SECTION

press: . . . . HUG, BALE, BIND, CRAM, IRON, MASH, PUSH, SPUR, URGE, CHEST, CROWD, CRUSH, DRIVE, FORCE, KNEAD, WEDGE, WRING, COMPEL, ROLLER, SMOOTH, SQUASH, THRONG, EMBRACE, ENTREAT, SQUEEZE, WARDROBE, NEWSPAPER, JOURNALISTS

pressing: . . URGENT, EXIGENT, EXACTING, IMPERATIVE

pressure: . . . . . HEAT, PUSH, FORCE, DURESS, STRESS, SQUEEZE, DEMANDS, URGENCY, EXIGENCY, CONSTRAINT

prestige: . . . FAME, RENOWN, INFLUENCE, IMPORTANCE, REPUTATION

presume: . . . . DARE, GUESS, IMPOSE, ASSUME, DARESAY, VENTURE, SUPPOSE, CONJECTURE

presumption: . . . . TEMERITY, INFERENCE

presumptuous: . . . . . BOLD, FORWARD, ARROGANT, ASSUMING, FAMILIAR, IMPUDENT, INSOLENT, AUDACIOUS

pretend: . . ACT, POSE, SEEM, SHAM, CLAIM, FEIGN, AFFECT, ALLEGE, ASSUME, PROFESS, SIMULATE, DISSEMBLE

pretender: . . . . FAKE, SHAM, SNOB, FAKER, QUACK, IMPOSTER, CLAIMANT, ASPIRANT, DECEIVER, CHARLATAN, MOUNTEBANK, FOURFLUSHER

pretense: . . . ACT, AIR, BRAG, FLAM, RUSE, SHAM, SHOW, CLOAK, COVER, FEINT, GUISE, TRICK, EXCUSE, FICTION, PRETEXT, ARTIFICE, DECEPTION

pretentious: . . ARTY, GAUDY, SHOWY, POMPOUS, AFFECTED, ASSUMING, OSTENTATIOUS

pretermit: . . . OMIT, IGNORE, NEGLECT, OVERLOOK

pretext: . . . . PRETENSE

pretty: . . . CUTE, FAIR, NICE, BONNY, BONNIE, COMELY, BEAUTIFUL, ATTRACTIVE

prevail: . . . . WIN, REIGN, INDUCE, OBTAIN, PERSIST, DOMINATE, TRIUMPH, SUCCEED, PERSUADE

prevalent: . . . RIFE, COMMON, CURRENT, GENERAL, RAMPANT, PANDEMIC, REGNANT, EXTENSIVE, PREVAILING, WIDESPREAD

prevaricate: . . . . . FIB, LIE, EVADE, QUIBBLE, PALTER, EQUIVOCATE

prevent: . . . BAR, GAG, BIND, SAVE, STOP, WARN, AVERT, DEBAR, DETER, ESTOP, HINDER, IMPEDE, BLOCK, DEFEND, RESIST, THWART, OBVIATE, PRECLUDE, PROHIBIT, RESTRAIN, FORESTALL, FRUSTRATE

previous: . . ERE, FORE, PAST, PRIOR, SUPRA, BEFORE, BYGONE, FORMER, EARLIER, FOREGOING, PRECEDING

prey: . . . . ROB, FEED, PRIZE, BOOTY, RAVEN, SEIZE, SPOIL, VICTIM, QUARRY, CAPTURE, PLUNDER

price: . . . . . FEE, COST, FARE, HIRE, RATE, VALUE, WORTH, CHARGE, RANSOM, REWARD, EXPENSE, EVALUATE, ESTIMATE

prick: . . . . DOT, GOAD, PINK, PROD, SPUR, STAB, BRIAR, POINT, QUALM, SMART, SPINE,

STING, THORN, INCITE, NETTLE,
PIERCE, SKEWER, TINGLE,
BRAMBLE, PUNCTURE

pride: ...... GLORY, PIQUE,
VALOR, ESTEEM, EGOISM,
SPIRIT, VANITY, CONCEIT,
DISDAIN, ELATION, HAUTEUR,
RESPECT, ARROGANCE,
VAINGLORY, SELF-ESTEEM

prig: .... FOP, DANDY, FILCH,
PLEAD, PRUDE, STEAL, THIEF,
HAGGLE, PILFER, PURIST,
BARGAIN, PICKPOCKET

prim: .... NEAT, NICE, STIFF,
DEMURE, FORMAL, PROPER,
PRISSY, CORRECT, PECISE,
MODEST, PRUDISH, PRIGGISH

primary: ..... MAIN, CHIEF,
FIRST, CAPITAL, CENTRAL,
INITIAL, ULTIMATE, ORIGINAL,
PRINCIPAL, ELEMENTAL,
ELEMENTARY, PREEMINENT

primate: .. APE, MAN, LEMUR,
ORANG, BISHOP, GIBBON,
MONKEY, GORILLA,
ORANGUTAN, ANTHROPOID,
ARCHBISHOP

prime: ... PICK, SIZE, FIRST,
COACH, CHOICE, CREAM,
PREPARE, EXCELLENT,
UNDERCOAT

primitive: .... WILD, BASIC,
CRUDE, FIRST, ROUGH, SIMPLE,
ANCIENT, ARCHAIC, BARBARIC,
ORIGINAL

primp: ..... ADORN, DRESS,
PREEN, PRINK, PRUNE

prince: .... BEY, RAS, AMIR,
EMIR, RAJA, RULER, DESPOT,
MONARCH, PRINCIPE,
POTENTATE, SOVERIGN

princely: .... NOBLE, REGAL,
ROYAL, LAVISH, LIBERAL,
MUNIFICENT

principal: ...... TOP, ARCH,
HEAD, HIGH, LEAD, MAIN,
CHIEF, FIRST, MAJOR, PRIME,
CAPITAL, CHATTEL, LEADING,
PREMIER, PRIMARY, STELLAR,

CARDINAL, DOMINANT,
FOREMOST

principle: ..... LAW, IDEAL,
RULE, AXIOM, CANON, MAXIM,
TENET, DICTUM, ESSENCE,
PRECEPT, THEOREM, DOCTRINE,
POSTULATE

prink: ...... DECK, ADORN,
DRESS, PRIMP, PREEN, PRUNE

print: ... COPY, FILM, ISSUE,
STAMP, FABRIC, EDITION,
ENGRAVE, ETCHING, IMPRESS,
PUBLISH, PICTURE, NEGATIVE,
ENGRAVING, IMPRESSION

prior: .. EX, ERE, FORE, PAST,
BEFORE, FORMER, EARLIER,
ANTERIOR, PREVIOUS,
ANTECEDENT

priority: .... POSITION,
PRIVILEGE, PRECEDENCE,
SUPERIORITY

priory: ... ABBEY, NUNNERY,
CLOISTER, MONASTERY,
SANCTUARY

prison: .. CAN, GIB, JUG, PEN,
BRIG, CAGE, CELL, GAOL,
HELL, HOLE, KEEP, QUOD,
ROCK, STIR, CLINK, COOLER,
LOCKUP, DUNGEON,
CALABOOSE, HOOSEGOW,
BRIDEWELL, BASTILLE,
PENITENTIARY

prisoner: ...... CON, LIFER,
INMATE, CAITIFF, CAPTIVE,
CONVICT, CULPRIT, JAILBIRD

prissy: ...... PRIM, FUSSY,
FINICKY, PRECISE, PRUDISH

pristine: ...... NEW, PURE,
EARLY, FIRST, FRESH, PRIMARY,
UNSPOILED, ORIGINAL,
PRIMITIVE

privacy: .... RETREAT,
SECRECY, SOLITUDE, SECLUSION

private: ... CLOSET, COVERT,
SECRET, SOLDIER, ESOTERIC,
PERSONAL, INTIMATE,
SECLUDED, SOLITARY,
CONFIDENTIAL

privilege: . . . . . . LAW, USE, FAVOR, GRACE, GRANT, RIGHT, PATENT, CHARTER, LIBERTY, EASEMENT, IMMUNITY, ADVANTAGE, EXEMPTION, FRANCHISE, PEROGATIVE

privy: . . . . JAKES, STOOL, CLOACA, HIDDEN, SECRET, TOILET, FURTIVE, LATRINE, PRIVATE, INTIMATE, OUTHOUSE, NECESSARY

prize: . . . . CUP, PRY, AWARD, BACON, BOOTY, LEVER, MEDAL, PURSE, STAKE, VALUE, ESTEEM, REWARD, TROPHY, CAPTURE, PREMIUM, TREASURE

probability: . . ODDS, CHANCE, LIKELIHOOD, CREDIBILITY

probable: . . . . LIKELY, POSSIBLE, CREDIBLE, FEASIBLE

probation: . . . . . TEST, TRIAL, TESTING, PAROLE

probe: . . . . . . TEST, GROPE, SOUND, PIERCE, SEARCH, EXPLORE, STYLET, EXAMINE, PENETRATE, INSTRUMENT, SCRUTINIZE, INVESTIGATE

probity: . . . . HONEST, INTEGRITY, RECTITUDE, UPRIGHTNESS

problem: . . . . . . NUT, CRUX, KNOT, TASK, POSER, ENIGMA, PUZZLE, RIDDLE, DILEMMA, QUESTION, DIFFICULTY

problematical: . . . DOUBTFUL, AMBIGUOUS, EQUIVOCAL, UNCERTAIN, QUESTIONABLE

proboscis: . . . . NOSE, SNOUT, TRUNK

procedure: . . . . TACTIC, METHOD, PROCESS, PROGRAM, ROUTINE

proceed: . . . GO, FARE, MOVE, PASS, ARISE, ISSUE, MARCH, ADVANCE, CONTINUE, PROGRESS

proceeding(s): . . ACTA, ACTS, STEPS, DOINGS, AFFAIR, COURSE, CONDUCT, MEASURE, PROCEDURE, TRANSACTIONS

proceeds: . . . . LOOT, BOOTY, ISSUE, PROFITS, INCOME, RETURN

process: . . COOK, SUIT, WRIT, ORDER, COURSE, MANNER, METHOD, NOTICE, SYSTEM, ADVANCE, PROGRESS, OPERATION, PROCEDURE

procession: . . . FILE, MARCH, TRAIN, LITANY, PARADE, RETINUE, CORTEGE, PAGEANT, CAVALCADE

proclaim: . . BID, CRY, CALL, TOUT, BLARE, CLAIM, VOICE, BLAZON, HERALD, PREACH, DECLARE, DIVULGE, PUBLISH, ENOUNCE, TRUMPET, ANNOUNCE

proclamation: . . . BAN, FIAT, BANNS, EDICT, UKASE, NOTICE, MANIFESTO

proclivity: . . . BENT, TALENT, LEANING, PROPENSITY, DISPOSITION, INCLINATION

procrastinate: . . . . . DEFER, DELAY, DILLY DALLY, STALL, POSTPONE

procreate: . . . . . SIRE, BEGET, PRODUCE, ENGENDER, GENERATE

procure: . . . GET, FIND, GAIN, BRING, EFFECT, OBTAIN, SECURE, ACQUIRE

prod: . . EGG, DIG, JAB, GOAD, POKE, URGE, ROUSE, DRIVE, INCITE, THRUST

prodigal: . . . . FLUSH, LAVISH, LIBERAL, PROFUSE, WASTEFUL, WASTREL, SPENDER, ABUNDANT, GENEROUS, PROFLIGATE, SPENDTHRIFT

prodigious: . . . HUGE, GIANT, AMAZING, IMMENSE, ENORMOUS, GIGANTIC,, MARVELOUS, WONDERFUL

prodigy: . . . . . . OMEN, SIGN, WONDER, MARVEL

produce: . . . DO, BEAR, FORM, MAKE, SHOW, BEGET, BREED, CAUSE, ISSUE, SHAPE, STAGE,

YIELD, CREATE, FRUITS, EXHIBIT, ENGENDER, GENERATE, FABRICATE, VEGETABLES, MANUFACTURE

product: . . . . . . CROP, ITEM, FRUIT, YIELD, RESULT, OFFSPRING, OUTGROWTH

productive: . . . RICH, ACTIVE, FECUND, FERTILE, PROLIFIC, CREATIVE, FRUITFUL, FRUCTUOUS

proem: . . PREFACE, PRELUDE, FOREWARD, OVERTURE, PREAMBLE, INTRODUCTION

profane: . . . . . FOUL, ABUSE, DEBASE, DEFILE, UNHOLY, VULGAR, WICKED, IMPIOUS, OBSCENE, UNGODLY, VIOLATE, DESECRATE, IRREVERENT, BLASPHEME

profess: . . . . . OWN, AVOW, ADMIT, CLAIM, AFFIRM, ALLEGE, CONFESS, DECLARE, PROCLAIM

profession: . . . . ART, CRAFT, FAITH, FORTE, TRADE, AVOWAL, CAREER, METIER, CALLING, PURSUIT, FUNCTION, VOCATION, EMPLOYMENT, OCCUPATION

proffer: . . . BID, GIVE, HAND, OFFER, EXTEND, TENDER, PRESENT

proficient: . . . . . . APT, DEFT, ADEPT, EXPERT, VERSED, SKILLED, EFFECTIVE

profile: . . . . . FORM, FIGURE, CONTOUR, DRAWING, OUTLINE, SKETCH, SILHOUETTE

profit: . . . . . NET, PAY, BOOT, GAIN, AVAIL, LUCRE, RETURN, ACCOUNT, BENEFIT, REVENUE, INCREASE, ADVANTAGE

profligate: . . . . CORRUPT, SPENDER, WASTREL, DEPRAVED, FLAGRANT, WASTEFUL, DISSOLUTE

profound: . . . . . DEEP, SAGE, WISE, ABYSS, HEAVY, ABSMAL, INTENSE, ABSTRUSE, SAGACIOUS

profuse: . . . . LUSH, GALORE, HEARTY, LAVISH, COPIOUS, LIBERAL, ABUNDANT, PRODIGAL, GENEROUS, BOUNTIFUL, EXUBERANT, PLENTIFUL

prog: . . . . FORAGE, PLUNDER

progeny: . . . . . . RACE, SEED, BREED, BROOD, ISSUE, SCION, SHOOT, FAMILY, STRAIN, OFFSPRING, CHILDREN

prognosticate: . . . . . . BODE, AUGUR, DIVINE, PORTEND, PREDICT, FOREBODE, FORETELL, PROPHESY

program: . . . . . CARD, LIST, PLAN, SHOW, AGENDA, NOTICE, CATALOG, OUTLINE, BULLETIN, SCHEDULE, SYLLABUS, PROSPECTUS

progress: . . . . . FARE, FLOW, GROW, MARCH, COURSE, GROWTH, MOTION, ADVANCE, DEVELOP, HEADWAY, IMPROVE, DEVELOPMENT

prohibit: . . . BAN, BAR, STOP, TABU, VETO, DEBAR, ESTOP, TABOO, ENJOIN, FORBID, HINDER, OUTLAW, DISALLOW

project: . . . JUT, LAP, ABUT, IDEA, PLAN, SEND, TASK, SHOOT, DESIGN, DEVICE, SCHEME, PATTERN, PROBLEM, PROTRUDE, PROPOSAL, INTENTION, ENTERPRISE

projectile: . . . . BOMB, DART, ROCK, SHOT, SPEAR, ARROW, SHELL, BULLET, ROCKET, MISSILE, JAVELIN, TORPEDO, SHRAPNEL

projection: . . . . . ARM, CAM, EAR, ELL, FIN, HUB, JAG, LUG, NOB, TOE, APSE, BARB, FANG, LOBE, BULGE, LEDGE, SOCLE, TOOTH, TORUS, DORMER, CORNICE, PROTRUSION

proletarian:... MEAN, RUDE, COARSE, VULGAR, WORKER, LABORER

prolific: .. FECUND, FERTILE, TEEMING, FRUITFUL, ABOUNDING, PRODUCTIVE

prolix: .... WORDY, DIFFUSE, PROSAIC, TEDIOUS, VERBOSE, TIRESOME, PROLONGED, LONG-WINDED, DISCURSIVE, PROTACTED

prolong: .... DEFER, NURSE, EXTEND, STRETCH, CONTINUE, LENGTHEN, PROTRACT

promenade:.... BALL, DECK, HALL, MALL, WALK, PRADO, AVENUE, MARINA, PARADE, STROLL, ALAMEDA, GALLERY, BOARDWALK, ESPLANADE

prominent: .... CHIEF, MARKED, SIGNAL, EMINENT, NOTABLE, OBVIOUS, SALIENT, MANIFEST, CELEBRATED, CONSPICUOUS

promise:...... VOW, OATH, SURE, WORD, AGREE, GRANT ASSURE, ENGAGE, PAROLE, PLEDGE, PLIGHT, BETROTH, CONTRACT, COVENANT, ASSUARANCE, GUARANTEE

promote:....... AID, HELP, BOOST, NURSE, RAISE, SPEED, BETTER, FOSTER, PREFER, ADVANCE, ELEVATE, FURTHER, PATRONIZE

prompt: ... CUE, EGG, LEAD, MOVE, URGE, YARE, ALERT, QUICK, READY, ADVISE, ASSIST, NIMBLE, REMIND, INSPIRE, ANIMATE

promulgate: ..... DECLARE, PUBLISH, ANNOUNCE, PROCLAIM, ADVERTISE

prone: .... APT, BENT, FLAT, SUPINE, ADDICTED, DISPOSED, INCLINED, RECUMBENT, PROSTRATE

prong: .... NIB, PEG, FANG, FORK, HORN, TINE, POINT, TOOTH, BRANCH

pronounce: ... PASS, SPEAK, UTTER, AFFIRM, DECLARE, ENOUNCE, ANNOUNCE, ENUNCIATE, ARTICULATE

pronto:... AT ONCE, QUICKLY

proof:.. TEST, TRIAL, RESULT, EXHIBIT, OUTCOME, ARGUMENT, EVIDENCE, TESTIMONY

prop: ... LEG, STAY, BRACE, SHORE, STAFF, STILT, CRUTCH, FULCRUM, SUPPORT, SUSTAIN, BUTTRESS, STRENGTHEN

propagate: ... RAISE, BREED, DIFFUSE, SPREAD, ENGENDER, GENERATE, INCREASE, MULTIPLY, CIRCULATE, DISSEMINATE

propel: ... GUN, ROW, MOVE, POLE, PUSH, SEND, URGE, DRIVE, FLICK, FORCE, IMPEL, SHOVE, PROJECT

propeller: ... FAN, FIN, OAR, VANE, BLADE, ROTOR, DRIVER, PADDLE

propensity: ..... YEN, BENT, BIAS, FLAIR, APTNESS, AVIDITY, APPETITE, TENDENCY, PENCHANT, PROCLIVITY, INCLINATION

proper:..... DUE, FIT, FAIR, GOOD, MEET, PRIM, RIGHT, CHASTE, DECENT, HONEST, MODEST, SEDATE, SEEMLY, CORRECT, FITTING, ACCURATE, DECOROUS, SUITABLE

property: .... ALOD, GEAR, ASSET, GOODS, MANOR, DOMAIN, ESTATE, REALTY, WEALTH, CHATTEL, HOLDINGS, ATTRIBUTE, HOMESTEAD, OWNERSHIP, POSSESSIONS

prophecy:....... ORACLE, UTTERANCE, FORECAST, PREDICTION, FORETELLING

prophesy: . . . AUGUR, DIVINE, PRESAGE, PREDICT, FORETELL, FORECAST

prophet: . . . . SEER, LEADER, MANTIS, ORACLE, AUGURER, DIVINER, TEACHER, PRESAGER, SOOTHSAYER, VACINATOR

prophetic: . . VATIC, MANTIC, FATEFUL, VATICAL, ORACULAR, PRESCIENT, PREDICTIVE

propinquity: . . . . . KINSHIP, NEARNESS, AFFINITY, VICINITY, PROXIMITY

propitiate: . . . ATONE, PACIFY, APPEASE, EXPIATE, SATISFY, CONCILIATE

propitious: . . HAPPY, LUCKY, BENIGN, BENIGNANT, OPPORTUNE, PROMISING, FAVORABLE, AUSPICIOUS

proponent: . . . . . . BACKER, PROPOSER, ADVOCATE, STALWART

proportion: . . . . PART, RATE, QUOTA, RATIO, SHARE, PORTION, RELATION, DIMENSION, BALANCE, SYMMETRY

proposal: . BID, MOVE, PLAN, OFFER, DESIGN, FEELER, MOTION, SCHEME, TENDER, PROJECT, OVERTURE, SUGGESTION

propose: . . . . . . GIVE, MOOT, MOVE, STATE, ALLEGE, DESIGN, PROPOUND, NOMINATE

proposition: . . PLAN, AXIOM, OFFER, AFFAIR, THEORY, PREMISE, PROJECT, THEOREM, OFFERING, PROPOSAL

propound: . . . . . POSE, POSIT, STATE, PROPOSE

prosaic: . DRAB, DULL, FLAT, PROLIX, STOLID, HUMDRUM, INSIPID, TEDIOUS, TIRESOME, LITERAL, UNPOETIC

proscribe: . . . . . BAN, TABU, EXILE, TABOO, BANISH, FORBID, OUTLAW, PROHIBIT, INTERDICT

prosecute: . . . . . . SUE, URGE, CARRY, CHASE, ACCUSE, CHARGE, FOLLOW, INDICT, PURSUE, ENFORCE, CONTINUE

prospect: . . . . . HOPE, VIEW, BUYER, SCENE, VISTA, ASPECT, OUTLOOK, SEARCH, CUSTOMER, APPLICANT, CANDIDATE

prospective: . . . . . . LIKELY, FUTURE

prosper: . . . . . . WAX, FARE, SPEED, THRIVE, BLOSSOM, SUCCEED, FLOURISH

prosperity: . BOOM, WEALTH, FORTUNE, SUCCESS, BONANZA

prostrate: . . . . . FELL, FLAT, PRONE, FALLEN, SUPINE, DEJECTED, OVERCOME, COLLAPSED, FLATTENED, RECUMBENT

protagonist: . . . . FOE, HERO, STAR, ENEMY, RIVAL, CONTENDER

protect: . . . . . . ARM, SAVE, GUARD, SHIELD, DEFEND, INSURE, SHELTER, PRESERVE

protector: . . GUARD, KEEPER, PATRON, SHIELD, GUARDIAN, DEFENDER, CUSTODIAN

protest: . . . . . . BEEF, KICK, DEMUR, AFFIRM, ASSERT, HOLLER, OBJECT, OUTCRY, SQUAWK, CONTEST, DECLARE, DISSENT, COMPLAIN, COMPLAINT, OBJECTION

prototype: . . . . MODEL, EMBLEM, PATTERN, ORIGINAL, ARCHETYPE

protract: . . . . DEFER, DELAY, EXTEND, STRETCH, PROLONG, CONTINUE, ELONGATE, LENGTHEN

protrude: . . . . . JUT, BULGE, PROJECT, EXTRUDE, INTERFERE, EXSERT

protuberance: ... NUB, EAR, WEN, BOLL, BULB, BUMP, HUMP, KNOB, KNOT, LOBE, LUMP, NODE, SNAG, UMBO, BULGE, BUNCH, INION, TORUS, VENTER, SWELLING

proud: .... (also see **pride**) ARROGANT, HAUGHTY, SPIRITED, STATELY, IMPOSING, IMPRESSIVE, OVERBEARING

prove: ... TRY, AVER, TEST, DEBUNK, REFUTE, VERIFY, CONFIRM, PROBATE, IDENTIFY, ASCERTAIN, ESTABLISH, DEMONSTRATE

provenance: ...... ORIGIN, SOURCE, DERIVATION

provender: .... HAY, CORN, FEED, FOOD, OATS, FODDER, FORAGE, PROVISIONS

proverb: ..... SAW, ADAGE, AXIOM, MAXIM, MOTTO, BYWORD, ENIGMA, SAYING, PARABLE, ALLEGORY, APHORISM

provide: ..... CATER, EQUIP, STOCK, YIELD, AFFORD, PURVEY, RATION, RENDER, SUPPLY, FURNISH, STIPULATE

provident: ... WISE, FRUGAL, SAVING, CAREFUL, PRUDENT, THRIFTY, CAUTIOUS, DISCREET, ECONOMICAL

providential: ...... LUCKY, FORTUNATE

province: .... AREA, RANGE, REALM, SHIRE, TRACT, COLONY, DOMAIN, REGION, SPHERE, COUNTRY, DISTRICT, DIVISION, BALIWICK, TERRITORY

provincial: ... RUDE, CRUDE, LOCAL, NARROW, RUSTIC, INSULAR, LIMITED, PAROCHIAL, UNCULTURED

provision: ..... FARE, FOOD, BOARD, STOCK, STORE, CLAUSE, SUPPLY, PROVISO, VICTUALS, CONDITION

provisional: ...... INTERIM, PROVISORY, TENTATIVE, TEMPORARY, CONTINGENT

provisions: ... CATE, CHOW, FARE, FOOD, BOARD, TERMS, FORAGE, LARDER, STOCKS, STORES, VIANDS, RATIONS, GROCERIES

proviso: .. CLAUSE, ARTICLE, CAUTION, CONDITION, STIPULATION

provoke: .. VEX, BAIT, GOAD, MOVE, SPUR, STIR, ANGER, ANNOY, CAUSE, EVOKE, PIQUE, TEASE, AROUSE, EXCITE, HARASS, INCITE, NEEDLE, NETTLE, AFFRONT, INCENSE, IRRITATE, AGGRAVATE, EXASPERATE

provost: ..... HEAD, CHIEF, JAILER, KEEPER, PREFECT, DIRECTOR, OFFICIAL

prowess: .... VALOR, SKILL, ABILITY, COURAGE

prowl: ...... LURK, ROAM, SKULK, RAMBLE, WANDER

proximity: ...... NEARNESS, VICINAGE, VICINITY, ADJACENCE, CLOSENESS, CONTIGUITY, PROPINQUITY

proxy: ..... AGENT, POWER, DEPUTY, PROCTOR, FUNCTION, SUBSTITUTE

prude: .... PRIG

prudent: ...... SAGE, WISE, CANNY, CHARY, FRUGAL, CAREFUL, SENSIBLE, DISCREET, CAUTIOUS, PROVIDENT, SAGACIOUS, ECONOMICAL

prudish: ..... PRIM, PRISSY, PRIGGISH, OVERMODEST

prune: ..... CUT, LOP, CLIP, PLUM, SHED, TRIM, FRUIT, PREEN, PURGE, SHEAR

prurient: .... LEWD, ITCHING, LONGING, LUSTFUL, LASCIVIOUS

pry: ...... SPY, GAZE, LIFT, LOOK, MOVE, NOSE, PEEK, PEEP, PEER, JIMMY, LEVER,

PRIZE, RAISE, SNOOP,
CROWBAR, INSPECT

prying: . . . . . . NOSY, NOSEY,
SNOOPING, CURIOUS,
INQUISITIVE

psalm: . . ODE, HYMN, POEM,
SONG, LAUD, VENITE,
CANTATE, INTROIT, CANTICLE,
MISERERE

pseudo: . . . . . . FAKE, MOCK,
SHAM, BOGUS, FALSE, FEIGNED,
SPURIOUS, PRETENDED,
COUNTERFEIT

pseudonym: . . . . . (also see
nickname) ALIAS, ANONYM,
NOM DE PLUME

psyche: . . MIND, SOUL, SPIRIT

psychiatrist: . . . . . . SHRINK,
ANALYST, ALIENIST

psychotic: . . . . MAD, CRAZY,
INSANE, NEUROTIC, DISORDERED

pub: . . . . . BAR, INN, TAVERN

public: . . INN, OPEN, COVERT,
STATE, PEOPLE, COMMON,
COMMUNAL, COMMUNITY

publication: . . . BOOK, PAPER,
ANNALS, DIGEST, ARTICLE,
BOOKLET, PHAMPHLET,
CIRCULAR, MAGAZINE,
BULLETIN, JOURNAL,
PERIODICAL

publicity: . . . . AIR, BUILDUP,
NOTICE, RECLAME, PUFFERY,
PROMOTION, ADVERTISING,
INFORMATION

publish: . . . AIR, EDIT, VENT,
ISSUE, NOISE, PUBLISH,
BLAZON, DEFAME, EXPOSE,
DIFFUSE, DIVULGE, RELEASE,
ANNOUNCE, PROCLAIM,
PROMULGATE

puck: . . . . . . ELF, IMP, DISK,
SPRITE, (HOB)GOBLIN

pucker: . . FOLD, KNOT, POUT,
TUCK, BULGE, PURSE, CREASE,
COCKLE, SMOCK, WRINKLE,
CONTRACT

pudding: . . . . . . HOY, DUFF,
MUSH, SAGO, BURGOO, HAGGIS,

CUSTARD, DESSERT, SAUSAGE,
ROLY-POLY

pudgy: . . . . FAT, PLUMP,
DUMPY, BULGING, ROLY-POLY

puerile: . . . . . . WEAK, SILLY,
YOUNG, BABYISH, FOOLISH,
TRIVIAL, CHILDISH, IMMATURE,
JUVENILE, UNWORTHY,
INFANTILE

puff: . . . . . PAD, BLOW, FLAM,
GUST, PANT, POUF, WAIF,
WAFT, FLUFF, WHIFF, PRAISE,
BREATH, DISTEND, INFLATE,
SWELL(ING)

pugilist: . . LUG, PUG, BOXER,
BATTLER, BRUSIER, FIGHTER,
RINGSTER

pugnacious: . . . . . . WARLIKE,
FIGHTING, BELLICOSE,
QUARRELSOME, AGGRESSIVE,
COMBATIVE, BELLIGERENT,
CONTENTIOUS

puisne: . . . . . . PUNY, JUDGE,
PETTY, FEEBLE, JUNIOR,
SUBSEQUENT, SUBORDINATE

puissant: . . MIGHTY, STRONG,
POTENT, POWERFUL, FORCEFUL

pulchritude: . . . . . . GRACE,
BEAUTY, COMELINESS,
EXCELLENCE, LOVELINESS

pule: . . . . CRY, PEEP, CHEEP,
WHINE, WHIMPER

pull: . . . . . TOW, TUG, CLAW,
DRAG, DRAW, HALE, HAUL,
JERK, MOVE, YANK, HEAVE,
PLUCK, ATTRACT, INFLUENCE

pulley: . . . . WHEEL, TACKLE,
SHEAVE

pullulate: . . . . . BUD, TEEM,
BREED, GERMINATE

pulp: . . . . . PAP, PITH, MASS,
CHYME, MAGMA, POMACE

pulpit: . . AMBO, BEMA, DESK,
CHAIR, STAGE, LECTERN,
ROSTRUM, PLATFORM, MINISTRY

pulsate: . BEAT, MOVE, PANT,
THROB, QUIVER, VIBRATE

pulse: . . . . BEAT, THROB,
FEELING, SPHYGMUS

pulverize: . . . . BRAY, MEAL, MILL, MULL, CRUSH, GRIND, POUND, POWDER, ATOMIZE, DEMOLISH, LEVIGATE, TRITURATE

puma: . . . . . . CAT, COUGAR, PANTHER, (MOUNTAIN)LION, CATAMOUNT

pumice: . . POLISH, ABRASIVE

pummel: . . . . . BEAT, MAUL, BATTER, HAMMER

pump: . . . GIN, RAM, DRAW, JACK, QUIZ, SHOE, INFLATE, QUESTION

punch: . . . . . ADE, BOP, BOX, JAB, BLOW, POKE, PROD, DOWSE, DRINK, FORCE, PASTE, STAMP, PIERCE, STRIKE, BUFFET, PUNCTURE, PERFORATE

puncheon: . . AWL, DIE, CASK, POST, STUD, PUNCH, STAMP, TIMBER

punctilious: . . . PRIM, EXACT, FORMAL, PROPER, STRICT, CAREFUL, CORRECT, PRECISE, SCRUPULOUS

punctuation mark: . . . . DOT, DASH, COLON, COMMA, QUOTE, HYPHEN, PERIOD, BRACKETS, ELLIPSIS, SEMICOLON, APOSTROPHE, PARENTHESIS

puncture: . . . . . BITE, HOLE, STAB, VENT, PRICK, WOUND, PIERCE, PERFORATE

pundit: . . . . . SAGE, SAVANT, SCHOLAR, TEACHER

pungent: . . . . . . KEEN, RACY, TART, ACRID, ACUTE, SALTY, SHARP, SPICY, TANGY, BITING, BITTER, CAUSTIC, PEPPERY, PIQUANT, AROMATIC, POIGNANT, STINGING, EXPRESSIVE

punish: . . . BEAT, FINE, WHIP, ABUSE, SCOLD, SMITE, SPANK, STRAP, WREAK, AMERCE, AVENGE, CHASTEN, CORRECT, SCOURGE, CHASTISE,

CASTIGATE, PENALIZE, DISCIPLINE

punitive: . . . . PENAL, PUNISHING, VINDICTIVE

punt: . . BOAT, KICK, PROPEL, GAMBLE

puny: . . WEAK, FRAIL, PETTY, SMALL, FEEBLE, PUISNE, SICKLY, SLIGHT, INFERIOR

pupil: . . TYRO, CADET, PLEBE, LEARNER, SCHOLAR, DISCIPLE, TRAINEE, STUDENT, NEOPHYTE

puppet: . . BABY, DOLL, DUPE, PAWN, TOOL, MARIONETTE

purchase: . . . . . BUY, ACATE, ORDER, OBTAIN, ACQUIRE, BARGAIN, EMPTION, ACQUISITION

purdah: . . . SCREEN, CURTAIN

pure: . . . FINE, GOOD, MERE, NEAT, TRUE, CLEAN, CLEAR, FRESH, MORAL, SHEER, UTTER, CANDID, CHASTE, SIMPLE, VESTAL, VIRGIN, PERFECT, SINCERE, SINLESS, UNMIXED, ABSOLUTE, COMPLETE, INNOCENT, VIRTUOUS

purgative: . . . JALAP, PHYSIC, LAXATIVE, APERIENT, CATHARTIC

purge: . . . RID, FLUX, CLEAR, PHYSIC, PURIFY, REMOVE, DETERGE, CLEANSE, ABSTERGE, EXORCISE

purify: . . . . . CLEAN, CLEAR, PURGE, FILTER, REFINE, BAPTIZE, CLARIFY, CLEANSE, DISTILL, DEPURATE, SANCTIFY

purl: . . . . RIB, EDDY, KNOT, LOOP, FRILL, SWIRL, PEARL, MURMUR, RIPPLE, PURFLE, STITCH

purlieu: . . HAUNT, ENVIRONS, HANGOUT, NEIGHBORHOOD

purloin: . . . . . . CRIB, STEAL, FILCH, SWIPE, PILFER, ABSTRACT, PLAGARIZE

purple: . . . . . . PLUM, GRAPE, LILAC, MAUVE, REGAL, ROYAL,

MAROON, ORNATE, AMARANTH,
IMPERIAL, LAVENDER,
AMETHYST

purport: ...... GIST, MEAN,
CLAIM, DRIFT, SENSE, TENOR,
EFFECT, IMPORT, INTENT,
OBJECT, MEANING, PROFESS,
INTENTION, SUBSTANCE

purpose: .... AIM, END, USE,
BENT, GOAL, MEAN, PLAN,
SAKE, DESIGN, INTEND, INTENT,
MOTIVE, MISSION, INTENTION,
OBJECTIVE

purse: .... BAG, KNIT, POKE,
BURSE, MONEY, POUCH, PRIZE,
PUCKER, WALLET, HANDBAG,
FINANCES, BILLFOLD,
TREASURY, EXCHEQUER,
POCKETBOOK

purser: ... BURSAR, CASHIER,
PAYMASTER, TREASURER

pursue: ... DOG, RUN, HUNT,
SEEK, CHASE, HOUND, STALK,
TRAIL, FOLLOW, PROCEED,
CONTINUE, PROSECUTE

pursuit: .... CHASE, QUEST,
CALLING, OCCUPATION

pursy: .. FAT, OBESE, PUDGY,
PUFFY, SWOLLEN

purvey: .... TAX, CATER,
SUPPLY, FURNISH, PROCURE,
PROVIDE, PROVISION

push: ... POLE, PROD, URGE,
BOOST, CROWD, DRIVE, ELBOW,
FORCE, IMPEL, NUDGE, PRESS,
SHOVE, CLIQUE, EFFORT,
ENERGY, EXPAND, EXTEND,
HUSTLE, JOSTLE, PROPEL,
THRUST, ADVANCE, PROMOTE

pusillanimous: .... TAME,
TIMID, AFRAID, COWARDLY,
IRRESOLUTE, FAINTHEARTED

pustule: ...... BLOB, BURL,
BLAIN, WHEAL, BLOTCH,
PIMPLE, BLISTER, ERUPTION,
SWELLING

put: ... (also see **place**) LAY,
SET, CAST, PUSH, URGE, APPLY,
DRIVE, FORCE, IMPEL, IMPOSE,

PLACE, STATE, WAGER,
ATTACH, BESTOW, THRUST,
DEPOSIT, EXPRESS

away: ...... KILL, STOW,
STORE, MURDER, CONSUME

down: .... CRUSH, QUASH,
HUMBLE, RECORD,
DEGRADE, DEPRESS,
SUPPRESS

forward: ... SHOW, OFFER,
PRESENT, PROPOSE, PUBLISH

off: ... FOB, DOFF, DEFER,
DELAY, EVADE, STALL,
TABLE, DIVERT, SHELVE,
DISCARD, POSTPONE

out: .... IRK, VEX, OUST,
ANGER, ANNOY, DOUSE,
EJECT, EVICT, EXILE, EXPEL,
BANISH, DEPORT, QUENCH,
DISMISS, PUBLISH,
DISPLACE, DISTRESS,
INCOMMODE, DISCOMPOSE,
DISCONCERT, EXTINGUISH

up: .... CAN, POST, ERECT,
SHOW, BUILD, LODGE,
CONSTRUCT

up with: .... BEAR, TAKE,
BROOK, STAND, ENDURE,
STOMACH, TOLERATE

putrefy: ...... ROT, DECAY,
FESTER, CORRUPT, DECOMPOSE,
DISINTEGRATE

putrid: ...... FOUL, ROTTEN,
DECAYED, NOISOME, VICIOUS,
DEPRAVED, STINKING,
PUTRESCENT, DISAGREEABLE

puttee: ...... SPAT, GAITER,
PUTTY, LEGGING

puzzle: ..... POSER, REBUS,
STICK, STUMP, BAFFLE,
ENIGMA, RIDDLE, ANAGRAM,
CHARADE, CONFUSE, MYSTERY,
MYSTIFY, NONPLUS, PARADOX,
PERPLEX, ACROSTIC, BEWILDER,
INTRIGUE, QUESTION,
CONUNDRUM, DUM(B)FOUND

puzzling: .. ODD, EQUIVOCAL,
ENIGMATIC

pygmy: . . . . ELF, PIXY, RUNT, ATOMY, DWARF, GNOME, MINIM, SHORT

pylon: . . . . . . POST, TOWER, MARKER, PYRAMID, GATEWAY, MONUMENT

pyramid: . . . . HEAP, BUILD, ACCRUE, INCREASE

pyre: . . . . BIER, PILE

pyrene: . . . . PIP, SEED, STONE

pyretic: . . . . FEVERISH

pyromaniac: . . . . . FIREBUG, ARSONIST, INCENDIARY

pyrotechnics: . . . . FIREWORKS

python: . . . . BOA, SNAKE, SERPENT, ANACONDA

pythonic: . . HUGE, INSPIRED, ORACULAR, MONSTROUS, PROPHETIC

Q

Q: *Greek:* . . . . KAPPA

quack: . CRY, FAKER, FRAUD, CROCUS, IMPOSTER, CHARLATAN, PRETENDER, MOUNTEBANK, DEMAGOGUE

quad: . . . JAIL, QUOD, BLOCK, CAMPUS, PERSON, PRISON,

quake: . . . . . SHAKE, WAVER, QUIVER, SHIVER, TREMOR, SHUDDER, TREMBLE, VIBRATE

qualification: . . . . . ABILITY, APTITUDE, CONDITION, KNOWLEDGE, REQUISITE, CAPABILITY, COMPETENCE, EXPERIENCE

qualified: . . . . . . FIT, ABLE, ELGIBLE, COMPETENT, LIMITED

qualify: . . . FIT, PASS, ADAPT, EQUIP, LIMIT, ENABLE, MODIFY, SOFTEN, TEMPER, ASSUAGE, ENTITLE, PREPARE, DESCRIBE, MITIGATE, MODERATE, RESTRAIN, RESTRICT

quality: . . AURA, COST, RANK, RATE, SORT, TONE, CLASS, SIBLING, QUADRAT, QUANDRANGLE

quadragesimal: . . . . FORTY, LENTEN

quadrangle: . . . . . . COURT, SQUARE, COURTYARD, TETRAGON

quadrant: . . . . ARC, FOURTH, SEXTANT, ALTIMETER, INSTRUMENT

quadrate: . . . . SUIT, AGREE, IDEAL, SQUARE, CONFORM, PERFECT, QUARTER, BALANCED, RECTANGLE, CORRESPOND

quadroon: . . . . HYBRID, MULATTO

quadrumane: . . . . . . APE, MONKEY, BABOON, GORILLA, PRIMATE, CHIMPANZEE

quadruped: . . . . . . MAMMAL, FOURLEGGED

quaggy: . . . . . . MIRY, SOFT, BOGGY

quagmire: . . . . . . BOG, FEN, MARSH, SWAMP, MORASS

quail: . . . BIRD, WILT, COLIN, COWER, SHAKE, CRINGE, FLINCH, RECOIL, SHRINK, BOBWHITE, PARTRIDGE

quaint: . . . . . ADD, ANTIQUE, CURIOUS, STRANGE, UNUSUAL, FANCIFUL, PECULIAR, SINGULAR GRADE, POWER, TASTE, TRAIT, NATURE, STATUS, VIRTUE, CALIBER, CAPACITY, NOBILITY, FEATURE, PROPERTY, ATTRIBUTE, CHARACTER, EXCELLENCE

qualm: . . . . . DOUBT, SPASM, ATTACK, NAUSEA, REGRET, TWINGE, SCRUPLE, FAINTNESS, UNEASINESS, MISGIVING, COMPUNCTION

quandry: . . . . . . FIX, PASS, PICKLE, STRAIT, DILEMMA, NONPLUS, PREDICAMENT

quant: . . . . . . POLE, PROPEL

quantity: . . . . (also see **amount**) any, bit, jag, jog, lot, sum, atom, bulk, dash,

dose, dram, drop, iota, lick,
lots, mass, much, raft, slew,
unit, batch, bunch, grist,
hoard, scads, stack, store,
amount, degree, extent,
morsel, number, weight,
average, modicum, portion,
allowance

quantum: . . . UNIT, AMOUNT,
PORTION, QUANTITY

quarantine: . . BAN, EXCLUDE,
ISOLATE, RESTRAIN

quarrel: . . ROW, FEUD, FUSS,
SPAT, TIFF, BRAWL, BROIL,
BRUSH, CAVIL, FLITE, SCENE,
SCRAP, AFFRAY, BICKER,
BREACH, CHISEL, DEBATE,
FRACAS, HASSLE, JANGLE,
STRIFE, CONTEND, DISPUTE,
RHUBARB, RUCTION, WRANGLE,
ARGUMENT, SQUABBLE,
ALTERCATION, CONTROVERSY

quarrelsome: . . . . . HOSTILE,
BRAWLING, CHOLERIC,
PETULANT, BELLICOSE,
IRASCIBLE, IRRITABLE,
LITIGIOUS, BELLIGERENT,
PUGNACIOUS, CONTENTIOUS

quarry: . . . . . . GAME, PREY,
CHASE, LATOMY, OBJECT,
RAVINE, VICTIM, EXCAVATE

quarter: . . . . . . COIN, SPAN,
HOUSE, LODGE, MERCY, TRACT,
ASSIGN, BILLET, CANTON,
HARBOR, SHELTER, FOURTH,
DISTRICT, CLEMENCY

quarters: . . . ABODE, CAMP,
ROOM, BILLETS, LODGING,
SHELTER, BARRACKS,
DORMITORY

quash: . . DROP, VOID, ABATE,
ANNUL, CRUSH, QUELL,
CANCEL, ABOLISH, ABROGATE,
SUPPRESS

quaver: . . . . . . SHAKE, TRILL,
TREMBLE, TREMOLO, VIBRATE

quay: . . . . KEY, DOCK, MOLE,
PIER, LEVEE, WHARF, LANDING

queasy: . . . . TIMID, DELICATE,
QUALMISH, TICKLISH,
TROUBLED, NAUSEATED,
UNCERTAIN, UNSETTLED,
FASTITIOUS

queer: . . . ODD, RUM, COMIC,
DROLL, FAINT, FUNNY, GIDDY,
SPOIL, WEIRD, ERRATIC,
UNUSUAL, BIZARRE, STRANGE,
ABNORMAL, PECULIAR,
SINGULAR, ECCENTRIC

quell: . . . . END, CALM, COOL,
DAMP, KILL, ALLAY, CHECK,
CRUSH, QUASH, QUIET, STILL,
PACIFY, REDUCE, SOOTHE,
STANCH, STIFLE, SUBDUE,
ASSAUGE, REPRESS, SUPPRESS

quench: . . . . . COOL, DOUSE,
SLAKE, SATISFY, EXTINGUISH

querulous: . . . . . . FRETFUL,
PEEVISH, WHINING, PETULANT

query: . . . . ASK, DOUBT,
DEMAND, INQUIRE, INQUIRY,
QUESTION, CHALLENGE

quest: . . . . HUNT, SEEK,
SEARCH, EXAMINE, JOURNEY,
PURSUIT

question: . . . ASK, POSE, QUIZ,
DOUBT, GRILL, ISSUE, POINT,
QUERY, APPOSE, DEBATE,
RIDDLE, DISPUTE, INQUIRE,
INQUIRY, PROBLEM,
INTERROGATE

questionable: . . MOOT, FISHY,
SHADY, DUBIOUS, SUSPECT,
DOUBTFUL, EQUIVOCAL,
UNCERTAIN, DEBATABLE,
SUSPICIOUS

queue: . . . . CUE, FILE, LINE,
BRAID, PLAIT, TRESS, PIGTAIL

quibble: . . . PUN, CARP, QUIP,
CAVIL, CHEAT, EVADE, BAFFLE,
EVASION, EQUIVOCATE

quick: . . . . . APT, DEFT, FAST,
FLIT, LIVE, SPRY, YARE,
ACUTE, AGILE, ALERT, ALIVE,
BRISK, FLEET, RAPID, READY,
SHARP, SWIFT, ABRUPT,
LIVELY, NIMBLE, PROMPT,

SNAPPY, SPEEDY, SUDDEN, VOLANT

quicken: ...... STIR, WHET, HURRY, SPEED, AROUSE, EXCITE, HASTEN, INCITE, REVIVE, ANIMATE, ENLIVEN, PROVOKE, EXPIDITE, STIMULATE, ACCELERATE

quickly: . ANON, FAST, SOON, PRESTO, PRONTO, RAPIDLY, SPEEDILY

quid: ... CUD, PLUG, POUND, SOVEREIGN

quiescent: .... STILL, QUIET, LATENT, STATIC, DORMANT, RESTING, INACTIVE, SLEEPING, MOTIONLESS

quiet: .... COY, MUM, CALM, DEAD, EASE, HUSH, LULL, MILD, REST, TAME, ALLAY, INERT, PEACE, STILL, HUSHED, PACIFY, PLACID, SECRET, SEDATE, SERENE, SILENT, SMOOTH, SOOTHE, STATIC, COMPOSE, SILENCE, STILLNESS

quilt: .... PAD, SEW, DUVET, EIDER, CADDOW, PALLET, STITCH, BLANKET, COVERLET, BEDCOVER, COMFORTER, PATCHWORK

quip: . MOT, PUN, GIBE, JEST, JOKE, SALLY, TAUNT, QUIBBLE, WITTICISM, WISECRACK

quirk: .. KINK, TURN, KNACK, TRAIT, TWIST, STRIKE, STROKE, ODDITY, CAPRICE, DEVIATION, PECULIARITY

quit: ...... RID, FREE, STOP, AVOID, CEASE, CLEAR, LEAVE, REPAY, ACQUIT, DEPART, DESIST, RESIGN, RETIRE, VACATE, ABANDON, FORSAKE, RELEASE, RELIEVE, ABDICATE, RENOUNCE

quitclaim: .. ACQUIT, RELEASE

quite: ... ALL, VERY, STARK, TRULY, ENOUGH, REALLY, TOTALLY, UTTERLY, ENTIRELY, WHOLELY, COMPLETELY

quiver: ...... CASE, QUAKE, SHAKE, TRILL, ARROWS, NIMBLE, SHEATH, SHIVER, TREMOR, FLUTTER, SHUDDER, TREMBLE, VIBRATE

quixotic: .. ABSURD, UTOPIAN, ROMANTIC, VISIONARY, CHIVALROUS, IDEALISTIC

quiz: ... ASK, EXAM, HOAX, JOKE, TEST, PROBE, EXAMINE, QUESTION, EXAMINATION

quizzical: ... ODD, COMICAL, AMUSING, PERPLEXED

quod: .... JUG, JAIL, COURT, PRISON

quoin: .. COIN, LOCK, BLOCK, CORNER, KEYSTONE

quoit: ... DISC, RING, DISCUS, RINGER

quondam: .. ONCE, ONETIME, FORMER, ERSTWHILE

quorum: .. GROUP, COMPANY, COUNCIL, MAJORITY

quota: ...... PART, SHARE, DIVIDE, RATING, DIVIDEND, ALLOTMENT, PROPORTION

quotation: .. PRICE, CITATION, EXCERPT, EXTRACT

quote: ... CITE, NAME, NOTE, REFER, ADDUCE, ALLEGE, ALLUDE, REPEAT, EXCERPT, EXTRACT, REFERENCE

quoth: ...... SAID, SPOKE

quotidian: .. DAILY, TRIVIAL, EVERYDAY, ORDINARY

quotient: .... RESULT

R

R: *Greek:* .... RHO
  Hebrew: .... RESH

rabato: ...... RUFF, COLLAR

rabbet: ...... JOINT, REBATE

rabbi: ...... LORD, AMORA, MASTER, TEACHER

rabbit: .... BUN, DOE, BUCK, CONY, HARE, BUNNY, COWARD, NOVICE, RODENT

rabble: . . . MOB, HERD, RAFF, CROWD, RAGTAG, DOGGERY, CANAILLE, RIFFRAFF

rabid: . . . . MAD, RAGING, FRANTIC, FURIOUS, VIOLENT, ZEALOUS, FRENZIED, FANATICAL, ENTHUSIASTIC

rabies: . . . LYSSA, MADNESS, HYDROPHOBIA

race: . . . . . RUN, DASH, FOLK, HERD, KIND, LINE, ROOT, RUSH, SORT, STEM, BLOOD, BREED, CASTE, CLASS, HURRY, RELAY, SPEED, STOCK, TRIBE, FAMILY, GROOVE, HASTEN, HURDLE, PEOPLE, SPRINT, STIRPS, STRAIN, CHANNEL, CONTEND, CONTEST, LINEAGE, REGATTA, RUNNING, MARATHON, PEDIGREE

division: . . . . . . NEGROID, CAUCASIAN, MONOGOLOID

racecourse: . . . . OVAL, TURF, TRACK, ARENA, CIRCUS, COURSE, RACEWAY, HIPPODROME

racer: . . CRAB, MILER, SNAKE, HOTROD, RUNNER, SERPENT, SPRINTER, TRACKMAN, BLACKSNAKE

raceway: . . CANAL, CHANNEL, FISHWAY, MILLRACE

rachis: . . . . STEM, SPINE, BACKBONE

rachitis: . . . . RICKETS

rack: . . . BAR, FLY, GIN, JIB, CRIB, GAIT, PACE, PATH, SKIN, BRAKE, FLAKE, FRAME, HORSE, STAND, TRACE, TRACK, COURSE, GANTRY, HARASS, STRAIN, WRENCH, AGONIZE, GRATING, OPPRESS, PATHWAY, STRETCH, TORMENT, UPHEAVAL, TORTURE, WRECKAGE

racket: . . . BAT, DIN, BABEL, NOISE, TRICK, CLAMOR, HUBBUB, OUTCRY, PADDLE, UPROAR, SCHEME, CLANGOR, CLATTER, REVELRY, SNOWSHOE

raconteur: . . . . . . NARRATOR, STORY TELLER

racy: . . BRISK, FRESH, SMART, SPICY, SWIFT, LIVELY, RISQUE, PIQUANT, PUNGENT, INDECENT, SPIRITED, STIRRING, VIGOROUS

raddle: . . ROD, BEAT, COLOR, OCHER, TWIST, CUDGEL, THRASH, INTERWEAVE

radiance: . . . . BEAM, GLOW, GLARE, GLEAM, GLORY, LIGHT, SHEEN, SHINE, LUSTER, GLITTER, GLOWING, SHINING, SPLENDOR, BRIGHTNESS

radiant: . . . AGLOW, BRIGHT, BEAMING, RESPLENDENT

radiate: . EMIT, CAST, BEAM, SHINE, SPREAD, DIFFUSE, EMANATE

radical: . . RED, ROOT, BASAL, BASIC, REBEL, ULTRA, DRASTIC, EXTREME, FORWARD, FIREBRAND, LEFTIST, ORGANIC, SUPPORT, CARDINAL, COMPLETE, EXTREMIST

radio: . . . . SET, PORTABLE, WIRELESS, BROADCAST, SHORTWAVE, TRANSISTOR, WALKIE-TALKIE

radius: . . . KEN, RAY, ORBIT, RANGE, SPOKE, SWEEP, EXTENT, LENGTH

radix: . . . . BASE, ROOT, RADICAL, ETYMON

raff: . . . HEAP, RAKE, TRASH, HUDDLE, JUMBLE, LITTER, RABBLE, RUBBISH, RIFFRAFF

raffish: . . . . . . LOW, CHEAP, FLASHY, TAWDRY, VULGAR, UNKEMPT, WORTHLESS, DISREPUTABLE

raffle: . . . . . JUMBLE, REFUSE, TANGLE, DRAWING, LOTTERY, RUBBISH, SERRATE

raft: . . . . . CRIB, FLUE, HEAP, SPAR, BALSA, BARGE, FLOAT, CATAMARAN, COLLECTION

rag: . . JAG, RIB, JOSH, MOCK,
RAIL, RATE, TUNE, DANCE,
SCOLD, SCRAP, SLATE, SHRED,
TEASE, HARASS, RUMPUS,
TATTER, UPROAR, QUARREL,
REMNANT

rage: . FAD, IRE, BEEF, FUME,
FURY, RANT, RAVE, ANGER,
CHAFE, CRAZE, FUROR, MANIA,
STORM, VOGUE, WRATH,
FERVOR, FRENZY, FURORE,
SPREAD, TEMPER, EMOTION,
FASHION

ragged: . . . . . HARSH, ROUGH,
FRAYED, JAGGED, SHABBY,
SHAGGY, UNEVEN, RAMPAGE,
UNKEMPT, STRIDENT,
TATTERED, DEFECTIVE,
IMPERFECT, IRREGULAR

raging: . . . . . RABID, FIERCE,
FERVENT, RAMPANT,
FEROCIOUS, RAMPAGING

raglan: . . . . TOPCOAT,
OVERCOAT

ragout: . . . . HASH, STEW,
SALMI, GOULASH, HARICOT,
TUCKET

raid: . . . . FORAY, ATTACK
FORAGE, HARASS, INROAD,
INVADE, MARAUD, SORTIE,
ASSAULT, INVASION, INCURSION

rail: . . . . . BAR, BIRD, COOT,
RANT, RATE, SLAT, SORA,
ABUSE, CHIDE, GUARD, FENCE,
HERON, PLANK, SCOFF, SCOLD,
BERATE, REVILE, MUDHEN,
COMPLAIN

railing: . . . . BAR, FENCE,
BARRIER, PARAPET, BANISTER,
ESPALIER, GUARDRAIL,
BALUSTRADE

raillery: . . . SATIRE, BANTER,
BADINAGE, RIDICULE,
PERSIFLAGE

railroad: . . HERD, LINE, PUSH,
RUSH, HURRY, TRACK,
TANSPORT

bridge: . . . . TRESTLE,
VIADUCT

car: . . . . . COACH, DINER,
PARLOR, COAL-CAR,
CABOOSE, SLEEPER,
SMOKER, PULLMAN,
GONDOLA

raiment: . . . . see **dress**

rain: . . . . . FALL, MIST, POUR,
STORM, DELUGE, SEREIN,
SHOWER, DRIZZLE, DOWNPOUR,
SPRINKLE, CLOUDBURST

rainbow: . . . . . . IRIS, ARC(H)

raincoat: . . SLICKER, PONCHO,
ULSTER, TRENCH COAT,
MACKINTOSH

raise: . . . BUOY, GROW, HEFT,
HIKE, LEVY, LIFT, REAR, RISE,
STIR, BOOST, BREED, ELATE,
ERECT, EXALT, HEAVE, HOIST,
AROUSE, ASCEND, AWAKEN,
EXCITE, GATHER, INCITE,
MUSTER, OBTAIN, UPLIFT,
ADVANCE, COLLECT, ELEVATE,
PROCURE, PRODUCE, PROMOTE,
HEIGHTEN, INCREASE,
CULTIVATE, PROPAGATE

rake: . . . COMB, PATH, ROUE,
TRIP, GLEAN, SCOUR, TRACK,
GATHER, LECHER, SCRAPE,
COLLECT, SCRATCH, LOTHARIO,
DEBAUCHEE

rally: . . . . MEET, ROUSE,
AROUSE, ATTACK, BANTER,
REVIVE, RECOVER, RESURGE,
COLLECT, GATHERING,
ASSEMBLY, RECUPERATE

ram: . . . . HIT, TUP, BUTT,
CRAM, TAMP, AIRES, CRASH,
DRIVE, POUND, PRESS, SHEEP,
STUFF, BATTER, STRIKE,
COLLIDE, BULLDOZE

ramble: . GAD, ROAM, ROVE,
WALK, JAUNT, PROWL, RANGE,
SPREAD, STROLL, TRAVEL,
WANDER, MEANDER, SAUNTER,
EXCURSION

rambunctious: . . . . . . WILD,
UNRULY, BOISTEROUS,
DISORDERLY

ramification: . . ARM, RAMUS, BRANCH, RESULT, SPREAD, DIVISION, OFFSHOOT, DIVERGENCE

ramp: . . . BANK, RAGE, REAR, RUSH, WALK, CRAWL, SLOPE, STAND, STORM, UNRULY, INCLINE, SWINDLE, GRADIENT, HELICLINE, PASSAGE, ROADWAY

rampage: . . . . . RAGE, RUSH, WILD, OUTBREAK

rampant: . . . . RIFE, FIERCE, VIOLENT, UNCHECKED, WIDESPREAD

rampart: . . . . WALL, MOUND, REDAN, BARRIER, BULWARK, RAVELIN, PARAPET, EMBANKMENT

ramshackle: . . . . . . LOOSE, SHAKY, RICKETY, DISORDERLY, RUN-DOWN

ranch: . CASA, FARM, GRAZE, ACREAGE, SCRATCH, ESTANCIA, HACIENDA, PLANTATION

rancid: . . . . . . RANK, SOUR, MUSTY, STALE, SMELLY, STINKING, SPOILED

rancor: . . . . IRE, GALL, HATE, SPITE, ENMITY, MALICE, HATRED, ANIMOSITY, HOSTILITY

rand: . . . EDGE, RIDGE, STRIP, BORDER, MARGIN

random: . . . STRAY, CASUAL, CHANCE, AIMLESS, DESULTORY, HIT-OR-MISS, HAPHAZARD, ACCIDENTAL

randy: . . . . CRUDE, COARSE, BEGGAR, VULGAR, LUSTFUL, DISORDERLY

range: . . . KEN, ROW, AREA, FARM, LINE, RANK, ROVE, ROAM, ALIGN, CLASS, FIELD, GAMUT, ORDER, REACH, SCOPE, SPACE, STOVE, STRAY, EXTENT, RAMBLE, SERIES, SPHERE, STROLL, WANDER, EXPLORE, HABITAT, SAUNTER, GRASSLAND

rank: . . . . . ROW, FILE, LINE, RATE, SORT, TIER, ARRAY, CASTE, CLASS, GRADE, ORDER, RANGE, ARRANT, COARSE, DEGREE, RANCID, RATING, SERIES, STATUS, CALIBER, COPIOUS, EXTREME, FERTILE, GLARING, QUALITY, SMELLY, STATION, ABUNDANT, CLASSIFY, DIVISION, EMINENCE, POSITION, INDECENT, FLAGRANT, STANDING, LUXURIANT, OFFENSIVE

rankle: . . . . . GALL, FESTER, INFLAME, IRRITATE

ransack: . . . . . . LOOT, SACK, RIFLE, STEAL, SEARCH, PILLAGE, RUMMAGE

ransom: . . . . . . BUY, PRICE, RESCUE, REDEEM, EXPIATE, BLOODMONEY

rant: . . . FUME, RAGE, RAIL, RAVE, BOAST, SCOLD, SPOUT, DECLAIM, TIRADE, BLUSTER, HARANGUE

rap: . . . BOP, HIT, TAP, BLOW, CUFF, KNAP, BLAME, CLOUT, KNOCK, STEAL, SNATCH, STRIKE, THWACK, SENTENCE, CRITICIZE, PUNISHMENT

rapacious: . . . . GREEDY, COVETOUS, GRASPING, RAVENOUS, AVARICIOUS, VORACIOUS

rape: . . . . COLE, FILE, PULP, ABUSE, DEFILE, RAVISH, TURNIP, DISPOIL, VIOLATE, PLUNDER, ASSAULT, CABBAGE

rapid: . . FAST, CHUTE, FLEET, QUICK, SWIFT, ABRUPT, SPEEDY

rapidity: . . . . HASTE, SPEED, CELERITY, VELOCITY

rapport: . . . . ACCORD, HARMONY, AFFINITY, AGREEMENT, RELATIONSHIP

rapt: . . . . DEEP, INTENT, ABSORBED, ECSTATIC, ENCHANTED, ENGROSSED

rapture: . . . . BLISS, DELIGHT, ECSTASY, RHAPSODY,

HAPPINESS, TRANSPORT,
EXULTATION

rare: .... ODD, FINE, GOOD,
THIN, CHOICE, SCARCE,
SELDOM, UNIQUE, ANTIQUE,
CURIOUS, EXTREME, SPECIAL,
TENUOUS, UNUSUAL,
UNCOMMON, UNDERDONE,
INFREQUENT

rascal: ... CAD, IMP, GYPSY,
KNAVE, ROUGE, SCAMP,
VARLET, MISCREANT,
SCOUNDREL, SCALAWAG,
SCAPEGRACE

rash: .. BOLD, WILD, BRASH,
HASTY, HIVES, DARING,
ECZEMA, UNWARY, WANTON,
FOOLISH, CARELESS, RECKLESS,
ERUPTION, FOOLHARDY

rashness: .. FOLLY, TEMERITY

rasp: .... RUB, FILE, ERUCT,
GRATE, ABRADE, SCRAPE,
IRRITATE

rat: ..... RODENT, VERMIN,
BETRAYER, DESERTER,
INFORMER, RENEGADE,
SQUEALER, STOOL-PIGEON

ratchet: ..... PAWL, CLICK,
CATCH, WHEEL, DETENT,
BOBBIN

rate: .. FEE, TAX, FARE, PACE,
RANK, BLAME, CHIDE, GRADE,
PRICE, CLASS, RATIO, SCOLD,
SCORE, VALUE, ASSESS,
CHARGE, ESTEEM, RECKON,
REGARD, TARIFF, CENSURE,
CHASTEN, DESERVE, REPROVE,
APPRAISE, CLASSIFY, ESTIMATE,
EVALUATE, PROPORTION

rather: ..... PRIOR, BEFORE,
CHOICE, SOONER, EARLIER,
SOMEWHAT, CERTAINLY,
PREFERABLY

ratify:.. PASS, SEAL, AFFIRM,
VERIFY, APPROVE, CONFIRM,
ENDORSE, SANCTION,
AUTHORIZE

rating: ...... RANK, CLASS,
GRADE, SCORE, MARK, REBUKE,

ESTIMATE, SCOLDING,
STANDING, REPRIMAND,
EVALUATION

ratio: ... RATE, SINE, QUOTA,
SHARE, COSINE, DEGREE,
AVERAGE, PORTION, RELATION,
QUOTIENT, PERCENTAGE,
PROPORTION

ration: .. DOLE, FOOD, METE,
ALLOT, SHARE, DIVIDE,
PORTION, ALLOWANCE,
ALLOTMENT, DISTRIBUTE

rational: ..... SANE, LUCID,
SOBER, SOUND, LOGICAL,
SENSIBLE, REASONABLE

rationale: ... BASIS, REASON

rattan: .. CANE, PALM, REED,
SEGA, WICKER

rattle:.. RALE, STUN, ADDLE,
ANNOY, CLACK, NOISE, UPSET,
RACKET, UPROAR, AGITATE,
CHATTER, CLAPPER, CLATTER,
FLUSTER, MARACAS,
CREPITATE, DISCONCERT

raucous: ..... LOUD, HARSH,
NOISY, ROUGH, COARSE,
HOARSE, BRAYING, RASPING,
STRIDENT

ravage:... LOOT, PREY, RUIN,
SACK, HARRY, HAVOC, SPOIL,
WASTE, FORAGE, DESPOIL,
DESTROY, PILLAGE, PLUNDER,
VIOLATE, DESOLATE,
DEVASTATE

rave: ... RAGE, RANT, ROAR,
STORM, BLUSTER, HARANGUE

ravel: .... RUN, FRAY, RAIL,
UNDO, SNARL, SLEAVE,
TANGLE, UNWIND, INVOLVE,
UNTWIST, ENTANGLE, SEPARATE

ravenous: .. GREEDY, HUNGY,
LUPINE, VORACIOUS, RAPACIOUS

ravine: ... DELL, GILL, LINN,
SIKE, WADI, WADY, CHINE,
DITCH, FLUME, GORGE, GULCH,
GULLY, STRID, ARROYO,
CANYON, CLOUGH, COULEE,
NULLAH, BARRANCA

raving: . . RAGING, FRENZIED, DELIRIOUS, INCOHERENT, IRRATIONAL

ravish: . . ROB, RAPE, ABUSE, CHARM, SEIZE, DEFILE, SNATCH, DELIGHT, DESPOIL, ENCHANT, PLUNDER, DEFLOWER, CAPTIVATE, ENRAPTURE

raw: . . . . COLD, DAMP, NUDE, RAVE, SORE, BAWDY, BLEAK, CRUDE, GREEN, HARSH, NAKED, CHILLY, UNFAIR, NATURAL, OBSCENE, UNCOOKED, INDECENT

rawboned: . . . LEAN, GAUNT

ray: . . . . BEAM, BETA, FLAIR, GLEEM, LASER, LIGHT, MANTA, PETAL, SHINE, SKATE, TRACE, GLANCE, STREAK, STRIPE, VISION

raze: . . . RUIN, TEAR, ERASE, LEVEL, SHAVE, EFFACE, SCRAPE, DESTROY, SCRATCH, DEMOLISH, DISMANTLE, DEPREDATE, OBLITERATE

razz: . . SASS, CHAFF, TEASE, BANTER, DERIDE, HECKLE, RIDICULE

re: . . . . ABOUT, ANENT, CONCERNING, REGARDING

reach: . . . COME, GAIN, SEEK, SPAN, GRASP, RANGE, SCOPE, AFFECT, ARRIVE, ATTAIN, EXTEND, EXTENT, STRIVE, ACHIEVE, EXPANSE, STRETCH, PENETRATE, ACCOMPLISH

react: . . . RESPOND, REDOUND

reaction: . . . . . KICK, START, ANSWER, REFLEX, RESPONSE, TROPISM, INFLUENCE, IMPRESSION

read: . . . . CON, PORE, SCAN, SKIN, TELL, STUDY, ADVISE, BROWSE, PERUSE, RELATE, FORSEE, INTERPRET, CONSTRUE, FORETELL, UNDERSTAND, DECIPHER

reader: . . . . . BOOK, LECTOR, PRIMER, RECITER, LECTURER, PERUSER, INSTRUCTOR

readily: . . . EASILY, QUICKLY, WILLINGLY

readiness: . . EASE, FREEDOM, ALACRITY, FACILITY, VOLITION, DEXTERITY, EAGERNESS, QUICKNESS, PROMPTNESS

reading: . . LESSON, LECTION, PERUSAL, LECTURE, RECITAL, COLLATION, RECORD(ING)

ready: . . APT, FIT, SET, FREE, HERE, OPEN, RIPE, WARE, YARE, ALERT, EAGER, HANDY, QUICK, ACTIVE, PROMPT, LIKELY, WILLING, PREPARED, INCLINED, AVAILABLE, AGREEABLE

real: . . . . . COIN, VERY, TRUE, BEING, ACTUAL, CERTAIN, FACTUAL, GENUINE, LITERAL, SINCERE, CONCRETE, TANGIBLE, AUTHENTIC

real estate: . . . ALLOD, LAND, REALTY, FREEHOLD, PROPERTY

realistic: . . . VIVID, LIFELIKE, PRACTICAL

reality: . . . . . . FACT, VERITY, TRUTH

realize: . . . GET, GAIN, KNOW, SENSE, EFFECT, OBTAIN, ACHIEVE, ACQUIRE, FULFILL, COMPLETE, CONCEIVE, UNDERSTAND, APPREHEND, ACCOMPLISH

really: . . . . . QUITE, TRULY, INDEED, ACTUALLY

realm: . . . . . LAND, BOURN, CLIME, BOURNE, CIRCLE, DOMAIN, EMPIRE, REGION, SPHERE, COUNTRY, DEMESME, KINGDOM, TERRENE, DIVISION, DOMINION, PROVINCE, TERRITORY

ream: . . BORE, DRAW, BEVEL, WIDEN, ENLARGE, STRETCH, ENLARGE

reanimate: . . RALLY, RENEW, REVIVE, RESUSCITATE

reap: . . . . CUT, MOW, CROP, GAIN, RAKE, GLEAN, GARNER, GATHER, ACQUIRE, COLLECT, HARVEST

rear: . . . . . AFT, END, BACK, BUCK, GROW, LAST, LIFT, RISE, TAIL, ABAFT, BREED, BUILD, ERECT, NURSE, RAISE, STERN, TRAIN, BEHIND, FOSTER, SUCKLE, ARRIERE, EDUCATE, ELEVATE, NUTURE, CONSTRUCT, POSTERIOR

reason: . . . . MIND, NOUS, ARGUE, BASIS, BRAIN, CAUSE, LOGIC, LOGOS, SENSE, THINK, GROUND, MOTIVE, PONDER, SANITY, DISCUSS, JUSTIFY, MEANING, ARGUMENT, INTELLECT, RATIONALE, RATIOCINATE, EXPLANATION

reasonable: . . . . . FAIR, JUST, SANE, LOGICAL, FEASIBLE, RATIONAL, SENSIBLE, EQUITABLE, INEXPENSIVE

reata: . . ROPE, LASSO, LARIAT

reave: . . . ROB, TEAR, BURST, SEIZE, SPLIT, PILLAGE

rebate: . . . . LESSEN, REDUCE, REFUND, WEAKEN, DIMINISH, DISCOUNT, KICKBACK, RAKE-OFF, DEDUCTION, REDUCTION

rebel: . . DEFY, RISE, OPPOSE, RESIST, REVOLT, MUTINEER, RENEGADE, DISSENTER, DISSIDENT

rebellion: . MUTINY, REVOLT, DEFIANCE, SEDITION, UPRISING, RESISTANCE, REVOLUTION, INSURGENCE, INSURRECTION

rebound: . . . . ECHO, CAROM, BOUNCE, CARROM, RECOIL, RESILE, RETURN, SPRING, REFLECT, RESOUND, RICOCHET, BOOMERANG, REVERBERATE

rebuff: . . SLAP, SNUB, CHECK, CHIDE, REPEL, SCOLD, SPURN, REFUSE, REPULSE, REJECT

rebuke: . . . BEAT, SLAP, SNUB, BLAME, CHIDE, SCOLD, BERATE, DERIDE, CENSURE, LECTURE, REPROOF, REPROVE, UPBRAID, ADMONISH, REPRIMAND, REPREHEND

rebut: . . . . . . REPLY, OPPOSE, REBUFF, REFUTE, DISPROVE, CONTRADICT

recalcitrant: . . . . . . REBEL, UNRULY, DEFIANT, OBSTINATE, RESISTANT, REBELLIOUS, REFRACTORY

recall: . . . . ANNUL, CANCEL, ENCORE, REMIND, REPEAL, REVIVE, REVOKE, ABOLISH, RESCIND, RETRACT, REMEMBER, WITHDRAW, RECOLLECT, REMINISCE

recant: . . . . ABJURE, REVOKE, ABANDON, DISAVOW, RETRACT, WITHDRAW, RENOUNCE

recapitulate: . . . SUM, ESSAY, REPEAT, REVIEW, RESTATE, REITERATE, SUMMARIZE

recede: . . . . . . EBB, DEPART, RETIRE, DEVIATE, RETREAT, WITHDRAW, RETROGRADE

receipt: . . . . STUB, TAKE, BINDER, RECIPE, FORMULA, QUITTANCE, ACQUITTANCE

receivable: . . . . DUE

receive: . . . GET, HOLD, TAKE, ADMIT, ADOPT, GREET, ACCEPT, ASSUME, OBTAIN, ACQUIRE, PROCURE

receiver: . . . . . HOST, FENCE, BAILEE, PORTER, CATCHER, TRUSTEE, TREASURER, COLLECTOR, RECIPIENT, RECEPTIONIST

recent: . . NEW, LATE, FRESH, MODERN, CURRENT, NEOTERIC

receptacle: . . BIN, BOX, CAN, CUP, PAN, POT, TUB, URN, VAT, CASE, CELL, CRIB, FONT, PAIL, TRAY, VASE, WELL, TANK, BASIN, CHEST, TORUS, BASKET, BOTTLE, BUCKET, CARTON,

HAMPER, HOPPER, TROUGH,
VESSEL, CISTERN, HUMIDOR,
PITCHER, CANISTER, CONTAINER

reception: . . . . . TEA, LEVEE,
PARTY, DURBAR, SOIREE,
ACCUEIL, OVATION, WELCOME,
GREETING, ADMITTANCE

recess: . . . BAY, APSE, CAVE,
COVE, GROT, HOLE, NOOK,
CLEFT, CRYPT, NICHE, SINUS,
ALCOVE, CLOSET, GROTTO,
BREAK, HOLLOW, RETIRE,
ADJOURN, CONCEAL, RETREAT,
SECLUDE, INTERVAL, VACATION

recession: . SLUMP, RECEDING

recipe: . . FORMULA, REMEDY,
RECEIPT, PRESCRIPTION

reciprocal: . . . . . . MUTUAL,
ALTERNATE, CONVERTIBLE

reciprocate: . . . . . . REPAY,
RETURN, EXCHANGE,
ALTERNATE, RECOMPENSE

recital: . . SAGA, TALE, STORY,
REPORT, ACCOUNT, CONCERT,
PROGRAM, MUSICALE,
NARRATION, STATEMENT,
REPETITION

recite: . . . SAY, TELL, CHANT,
SPOUT, DECLAIM, INTONE,
RELATE, RECOUNT, NARRATE,
ENUMERATE

reckless: . . . . . . BOLD, RASH,
MADCAP, WANTON, HEEDLESS,
CARELESS, AUDACIUOS,
BODACIOUS, DAREDEVIL,
IMPRUDENT

reckon: . . DATE, DEEM, RATE,
TELL, AUDIT, COUNT, THINK,
JUDGE, FIGURE, IMPUTE,
NUMBER, REGARD, REPUTE,
ACCOUNT, ASCRIBE, COMPUTE,
CONSIDER, SUPPOSE, ESTIMATE,
CALCULATE, ENUMERATE

reclaim: . . . . . . SAVE, TAME,
TRAIN, RANSOM, RECALL,
REDEEM, REFORM, REPAIR,
RESCUE, REVOKE, RECOVER,
· RESTORE, SALVAGE,
REGENERATE

recline: . . . . . . LAY, LIE, SIT,
LEAN, LOLL, REST, REPOSE

reclining: . . . LYING, SUPINE,
LEANING, LOLLING, RESTING,
REPOSING, RECUMBENT

recluse: . . . . NUN, MONK,
HERMIT, SECRET, EREMITE,
SOLITAIRE, SOLITARY,
ANCHORITE, ANCHORESS

recognizance: . BOND, RANK,
BADGE, TOKEN, AVOWAL,
PLEDGE, SYMBOL, OBLIGATION

recognize: . . KEN, OWN, SEE,
KNOW, NOTE, SPOT, ADMIT,
GREET, ACCEPT, RECALL,
SALUTE, CONSENT, CORRECT,
RECOVER, IDENTIFY, PERCEIVE,
APPREHEND

recoil: . . . SHY, KICK, COWER,
QUAIL, WINCE, FLINCH, RESILE,
SHRINK, REBOUND, RETREAT,
REVERSE, WITHDRAW

recollect: . . . . RECALL,
REMEMBER

recommend: . . . PLUG, TOUT,
REFER, ADVISE, COMMIT,
COMMEND, CONSIGN, COUNSEL,
ENTRUST, ADVOCATE

recompense: . . . . . FEE, PAY,
REPAY, AMENDS, BOUNTY,
REWARD, SALARY, REQUITE,
INDEMNIFY, REIMBURSE,
REPAYMENT, COMPENSATE,
REMUNERATE

reconcile: . . . AGREE, ATONE,
ADJUST, PACIFY, SETTLE,
SQUARE, EXPIATE, RESTORE,
REUNITE, HARMONIZE

recondite: . . . . DEEP, HIDDEN,
MYSTIC, OBSCURE, ABSTRUSE,
PROFOUND

reconnaisance: . . . . . SURVEY

reconnoiter: . . . SPY, SCOUT,
SURVEY, EXPLORE, EXAMINE

record: . . . . LOG, TAB, ACTA,
BOOK, FILE, MEMO, NOTE,
POST, ROLL, TAPE, ANNAL,
CHART, ENTER, ENTRY, SCORE,
AGENDA, ENROLL, REPORT,

ACCOUNT, ARCHIVE, DOSSIER, HISTORY, JOURNAL, REGISTER, CHRONICLE

recount: ..... TELL, RECITE, RECKON, RELATE, REPEAT, ACCOUNT, NARRATE, DESCRIBE, ENUMERATE

recoup: .... RECOVER, INDEMNIFY, REIMBURSE, COMPENSATE, RECUPERATE

recover: ..... GET, AMEND, RALLY, UPSET, OBTAIN, RECOUP, REFORM, RESCUE, RETAKE, RECLAIM, RESTORE, SALVAGE, OVERCOME, RETRIVE, REPOSSESS, CONVALESCE, RECUPERATE

recreant: ... FALSE, COWARD, CRAVEN, YELLOW, TRAITOR, COWARDLY, DESERTER, DISLOYAL, UNFAITHFUL

recreation: ... PLAY, DANCE, HOBBY, SPORT, PICNIC, RENEWAL, PASTIME, AMUSEMENT, AVOCATION, DIVERSION, RELAXATION

recrement: ... SCUM, DREGS, DROSS, SPUME, WASTE, REFUSE

recruit: ..... BOOT, ROOKY, GATHER, MUSTER, ROOKIE, SUPPLY, DRAFTEE, PRIVATE, REFRESH, SOLDIER, ENLISTEE, INDUCTEE, REINFORCE, REPLENISH, CONSCRIPT

rectangle: .... OBLONG, SQUARE, QUADRATE

rectify: ..... AMEND, RIGHT, ADJUST, BETTER, PURIFY, REFINE, REMEDY, CORRECT, DISTILL

rectitude: .. EQUITY, VIRTUE, HONESTY, INTEGRITY

rector: ...... HEAD, CHIEF, RULER, LEADER, PRIEST, PROCTOR, MINISTER

recumbent: .... IDLE, LYING, PRONE, RESTING, LEANING, REPOSING, RECLINING

recuperate: ... HEAL, RALLY, RECOUP, REGAIN, RECOVER, REIMBURSE, CONVALESCE

recur: ..... ADVERT, REPEAT, RETURN, REARISE, REAPPEAR

red: ... ROSY, RUBY, COLOR, CORAL, FIERY, ROSET, RUDDY, CHERRY, DANGER, GARNET, CRIMSON, GLOWING, LEFTIST, RADICAL, RUSSIAN, SCARLET, BLUSHING, INFLAMED, RUBICUND, ANARCHIST, BLOODSHOT, BOLSHEVIK, COMMUNIST, VERMILLION

redact: ..... EDIT, DRAFT, FRAME, REDUCE, REVISE

redden: ...... BLUSH, FLUSH

rede: .... SAW, PLAN, TALE, TELL, STORY, ADVISE, RELATE, SCHEME, COUNSEL, EXPLAIN, NARRATE, PROVERB

redeem: ..... SAVE, ATONE, RANSOM, REGAIN, RESCUE, FULFILL, RECLAIM, RECOVER, RESTORE, LIBERATE

redolence: ... ODOR, AROMA, SCENT, SMELL, PERFUME, FRAGRANCE

redouble: . REECHO, REFOLD, REPEAT, RETRACE, INCREASE

redoubt: ..... BREASTWORK, STRONGHOLD

redoubtable: ...... DREAD, FEARSOME, FORMIDABLE

redound: .... REACT, RECOIL, RETURN, CONDUCE, REVERBERATE

redress: ... AMEND, EMEND, ADJUST, RELIEF, REMEDY, CORRECT, RELIEVE, COMPENSATE, REPARATION

reduce: ... CUT, BATE, BUST, DIET, EASE, PARE, THIN, ABUSE, ABATE, ANNUL, BREAK, LEVEL, LOWER, SCALE, SLASH, CHANGE, DEBASE, DEMOTE, DERATE, DILUTE, HUMBLE, LESSEN, REFINE, SUBDUE, WEAKEN, ABRIDGE, COMMUTE,

CURTAIL, DEGRADE, DEPLETE, WHITTLE, CONDENSE, CONTRACT, DECREASE, DIMINISH, DISCOUNT, MINIMIZE, DEPRECIATE

redundancy: .... VERBIAGE, PLETHORA, VERBOSITY, NIMIETY, PLEONASM, TAUTOLOGY

redundant: .... WORDY, LAVISH, PROLIX, COPIOUS, VERBOSE, EXCESSIVE, PLEONASTIC, REPETITIOUS

reecho: .... RESOUND, RESONATE

reed: .... PIPE, SLEY, STEM, GRASS, STALK, RATTAN, BULRUSH

reef: .. BAR, CAY, KEY, LODE, VEIN, ATOLL, LEDGE, SHELF, SHOAL, RIDGE, SHORTEN

reefer: ..... COAT, JACKET, OYSTER, CIGARETTE, MIDSHIPMAN

reek: ... EMIT, FUME, VENT, EXUDE, SMELL, SMOKE, STEAM, STINK, VAPOR, EXHALE, STENCH

reel: ..... DRUM, ROLL, SPIN, SWAY, WIND, DANCE, LURCH, SPOOL SWIFT, SWING, WAVER, WHIRL, WINCE, BOBBIN, TEETER, TOTTER, STAGGER, WINDLESS

reeve: .... PASS, SLIP, WIND, TWIST, PUCKER, THREAD, BALIFF, STEWARD, WRINKLE, OVERSEER, SHEEPFOLD

refection: .... FOOD, DRINK, REPAST, LUNCH, REFRESHMENT

refer: ... CITE, SEND, RECUR, POINT, ADVERT, ALLUDE, ASSIGN, CHARGE, COMMIT, DIRECT, IMPUTE, RELATE, RETURN, SUBMIT, ASCRIBE, CONSULT, MENTION, SPECIFY, IDENTIFY, ATTRIBUTE

referee: ..... JUDGE, DECIDE, UMPIRE, ARBITER, MEDIATOR, ARBITRATOR

reference: .. QUOTE, ASPECT, REGARD, MENTION, RELEVANCE, CONNECTION, PERTINENCE, ALLUSION, TESTIMONAL

book: ... ATLAS, MANUAL, ALMANAC, HANDBOOK, SYLLABUS, THESAURUS, DICTIONARY, ENCYCLOPEDIA

referendum: .... VOTE, MANDATE, PLEBISCITE

refine: ..... SMELT, FILTER, FINISH, CLARIFY, CLEANSE, IMPROVE, PERFECT, SEPARATE, ELABORATE

refined: ..... CIVIL, POLITE, URBANE, COURTLY, ELEGANT, GENTEEL, DELICATE, GRACEFUL, COURTEOUS

refinement: .... POLISH, FINESSE, GENTILITY, DELICACY, ELEGANCE

reflect: ...... ECHO, MUSE, IMAGE, THINK, DIVERT, MIRROR, PONDER, DEFLECT, COGITATE, CONSIDER, MEDITATE, RUMINATE, DELIBERATE

reflection: .... IDEA, BLAME, IMAGE, MUSING, REFLEX, THOUGHT, LIKENESS, DISCREDIT, COGITATION, MEDITATION

reflective: .... PENSIVE

reform: ..... MEND, AMEND, PRUNE, RENEW, BETTER, PUNISH, REPAIR, REVISE, CENSURE, CORRECT, IMPROVE, RECLAIM, RECTIFY, REHABILITATE

refractory: ...... UNRULY, RESTIVE, CONTRARY, PERVERSE, STUBBORN, OBSTINATE, REBELLIOUS

refrain: .. BOB, CURB, SHUN, SONG, AVOID, CEASE, CHECK,

refresh: . . . . . . COOL, REST,
BATHE, CHEER, RENEW, SLACK,
REVISE, REVIVE, ENLIVEN,
HEARTEN, RESTORE, RECREATE,
RENOVATE, REPLENISH,
INVIGORATE

refreshment: . . . . . . DRINK,
SNACK, REFECTION

refuge: . . HOME, PORT, ROCK,
HAVEN, ASYLUM, COVERT,
HARBOR, RESORT, CITADEL,
RETREAT, SHELTER, SANCTUARY

refugee: . . . . EXILE, EMIGRE,
EVACUEE, ESCAPEE, FUGITIVE

refulgent: . . . . BRIGHT,
RADIANT, SHINING, GLOWING

refund: . . . . REPAY, REBATE,
REIMBURSE, REPAYMENT

refurbish: . . . RENEW, POLISH,
REVAMP, FRESHEN, RENOVATE

refuse: . . . NAY, NILL, BALK,
DENY, DIRT, JUNK, SCUM,
VETO, CHAFF, OFFAL, REPEL,
SCRAP, TRASH, WASTE, DEBRIS,
EJECTA, FORBID, LITTER,
NAYSAY, REBUFF, REJECT,
DECLINE, GARBAGE, RUBBISH,
REPULSE

refute: . . . . . . DENY, REBUT,
ASSOIL, CONFUTE, DISPROVE,
CONTRADICT

regain: . . . RECOUP, RECOVER

regal: . . . . KINGLY, STATELY,
IMPERIAL, MAJESTIC

regale: . . . . . FEAST, TREAT,
ENTERTAIN

regalia: . . . FINERY, EMBLEMS,
SYMBOLS, COSTUMES, INSIGNIA,
DECORATIONS

regard: . . . . CON, EYE, CARE,
DEEM, GAZE, HEED, HOLD,
LOOK, MIND, NOTE, SAKE,
VIEW, HONOR, THINK, TREAT,
WATCH, ADMIRE, ASPECT,
BEHOLD, ESTEEM, GLANCE,

FORGO, VERSE, CHORUS,
PHRASE, ABSTAIN, FORBEAR,
RESPONSE, RESTRAIN,
WITHHOLD

NOTICE, REPUTE, REVERE,
CONCERN, OBSERVE, RESPECT,
CONSIDER, INTEREST,
AFFECTION, ATTENTION,
REFERENCE

regarding: . . . . . RE, ABOUT,
CONCERNING

regent: . . . RULER, GOVERNOR

regimen: . . . . . . DIET, RULE,
SYSTEM, GOVERNMENT

region: . . AREA, BELT, ZONE,
CLIME, PLACE, REALM, SPACE,
TRACT, LOCALE, SHPERE,
CLIMATE, COUNTRY, DEMESME,
KINGDOM, DIVISION, LATITUDE,
PROVINCE, VICINITY, TERRITORY

regional: . . LOCAL, SECTIONAL

register: . . . . . . LIST, ROLL,
ANNAL, DIARY, ENTER, ENTRY,
METER, SLATE, AGENDA,
DOCKET, ENLIST, ENROLL,
RECORD, ROSTER, ASCRIBE,
CERTIFY, LICENSE, CALENDAR,
SCHEDULE

regnant: . . RULING, REIGNING,
DOMINENT, PREVALENT

regress: . . . . RETURN,
RETROGRADE

regret: . . . RUE, MISS, GRIEF,
MOURN, SORRY, LAMENT,
REPENT, REPINE, SORROW,
DEPLORE, REMORSE,
PENITENCE, REPENTENCE

regular: . . . . . EVEN, EXACT,
USUAL, NORMAL, PROPER,
STATED, STEADY, STABLE,
CORRECT, ORDERLY, UNIFORM,
CONSTANT, HABITUAL,
ORDINARY, CUSTOMARY

regulate: . . . SET, PACE, RULE,
TIME, GUIDE, ORDER, ADJUST,
DIRECT, GOVERN, ARRANGE,
CONDUCT, CONTROL, CORRECT,
RECTIFY, MODULATE

regulation: . . . . LAW, RULE,
BYLAW, CANON, REGIMEN,
STATUTE, ORDINANCE

regulator: . . . . VALVE,
GOVERNOR

rehearse: .... DRILL, TRAIN, RECITE, REPEAT, PRACTICE

reign: .. RULE, SWAY, POWER, REALM, EMPIRE, GOVERN, REGIME, KINGDOM, PREVAIL, DOMINATE, DOMINION

reimburse: .... PAY, REPAY, DEFRAY, RECOUP, REFUND, REPLACE, INDEMNIFY, COMPENSATE, RECOMPENSE

rein: .... CURB, SLOW, STOP, TURN, CHECK, GUIDE, LEASH, STRAP, BRIDLE, DIRECT, GOVERN, CONTROL, REPRESS, RESTRAIN, HINDRANCE

reinstate: .. REVEST, RESTORE

reiterate: ... HARP, REPEAT, REHEARSE, RECAPITULATE

reject: .. DEFY, SNUB, VETO, EJECT, REPEL, SCORN, SPURN, VOMIT, ABJURE, DISOWN, REBUFF, REFUSE, DECLINE, DISCARD, DISMISS, FORSAKE, ABNEGATE, BLACKBALL, OSTRACIZE, DISAPPROVE

rejoice: ..... CHEER, ELATE, EXULT, GLORY, DELIGHT, GLADDEN, JUBILATE, EXHILARATE

rejoin: .... REPLY, ANSWER, RESPOND, REUNITE

relapse: ... FALL, SINK, SLIP, SETBACK, BACKSLIDE

relate: ...... REFER, STATE, ALLUDE, DETAIL, RECITE, REPORT, CONNECT, DECLARE, NARRATE, PERTAIN, RECOUNT, DESCRIBE, ASSOCIATE, CORRELATE

related: .. KIN, AKIN, ALLIED, COGNATE, GERMANE, KINDRED, AFFILIATE, CONNECTED, APPROPRIATE

relation: .... SIB, RATIO, DEGREE, FAMILY, STATUS, ACCOUNT, BEARING, KINSHIP, RECITAL, AFFINITY, RELATIVE, CONNECTION

relative: . KIN, SIB, KINDRED, KINSMAN, SIBLING, RELATION, RELEVANT, CONNECTED, PERTINENT

relax: .... EASE, OPEN, REST, ABATE, REMIT, DIVERT, LESSEN, LOOSEN, REDUCE, SOFTEN, UNBEND, RELEASE, RELIEVE, SLACKEN, MITIGATE

relaxation: .... REPOSE, DETENTE, RECREATION, AMUSEMENT, DIVERSION

relay: ... POST, RACE, SHIFT, REMOUNT, RELEASE, FORWARD, STATION, TRANSMIT

release: ... BAIL, DROP, FREE, TRIP, UNDO, VENT, CLEAR, RELAY, REMIT, UNTIE, ACQUIT, DEMISE, EXEMPT, LOOSEN, PAROLE, RELIEF, REMISE, SPRING, WAIVER, ABSOLVE, DELIVER, FREEDOM, PUBLISH, RELIEVE, UNLEASH, LIBERATE, UNFASTEN, ACQUITTAL, DISCHARGE, QUITCLAIM

relegate: .... EXILE, ASSIGN, BANISH, COMMIT, DEPORT, REMOVE, CONSIGN

relent: ...... MELT, ABATE, THAW, YIELD, SOFTEN, ABANDON, MOLLIFY, SLACKEN

relentless: ..... GRIM, HARD, HARSH, STERN, STRICT, PITILESS, RIGOROUS, IMMOVABLE, MERCILESS

relevant: ..... APT, TIMELY, APROPOS, GERMANE, APPOSITE, CONNECTED, PERTINENT, RELATED, APPLICABLE

reliable: ..... TRUE, TRIED, HONEST, STEADY, TESTED, TRUSTY, CERTAIN, AUTHENTIC, DEPENDABLE

relic: . CURIO, RUIN, MUMMY, REMAIN, ANTIQUE, MEMENTO, REMNANT, RESIDUE, SOUVENIR

relief: .... AID, ALMS, BOOT, DOLE, EASING, SUCCOR, REMEDY, RELEASE

relieve: . . . . . AID, RID, EASE, FREE, HELP, ABATE, ALLAY, RAISE, SLAKE, SPARE, SPELL, ASSIST, LESSEN, REDUCE, REMEDY, REMOVE, SUCCOR, ASSUAGE, COMFORT, LIGHTEN, SUPPORT, SUSTAIN, DIMINISH, MITIGATE, ALLEVIATE

religion: . CULT, SECT, PIETY, FAITH, BELIEF, VOODOO, WORSHIP

religious: . . . HOLY, GODLY, PIOUS, DEVOUT, DIVINE, FERVENT, ZEALOUS, FAITHFUL, SPIRITUAL

relinquish: . . . . CEDE, DROP, QUIT, DEMIT, LEAVE, WAIVE, YIELD, DESERT, FOREGO, REMISE, RESIGN, ABANDON, RELEASE, ABDICATE, RENOUNCE, SURRENDER

relish: . . . . LIKE, TANG, ZEST, ANCHOR, ENJOY, GUSTO, SAUCE, SAVOR, TASTE, CANAPE, FLAVOR, DELIGHT, APPETIZER, PLEASURE

relucent: . . . BRIGHT, RADIENT

reluct: . . . . . FIGHT, REVOLT

reluctant: . . . . LOTH, LOATH, AVERSE, ADVERSE, GRUDGING, HESITANT, OPPOSING, RESISTING, UNWILLING

rely: . . . . BANK, BASE, HOLD, HOPE, LEAN, REST, COUNT, TRUST, CLEAVE, DEPEND, EXPECT, RECKON, BELIEVE

remain: . . BIDE, LAST, REST, STAY, WAIT, ABIDE, DWELL, STAND, TARRY, ENDURE, LINGER, RESIDE, PERSIST, CONTINUE

remainder: . . . . REST, STUB, STUMP, BALANCE, REMNANT, RESIDUE, SURPLUS, RESIDUAL, LEAVINGS, RESIDUUM, LEFTOVERS

remains: . . . . . DUST, ASHES, RELIC, RUINS, TRACE, CORPSE, FOSSIL, REMNANT, FRAGMENT, CADAVER, VESTIGES

remand: . . . RETURN, COMMIT

remark: . . SAY, NOTE, WORD, STATE, NOTICE, REGARD, COMMENT, DESCANT, EXPRESS, OBSERVE, INDICATE, SARCASM, ASPERSION, COMMENTARY

remarkable: . UNCO, SIGNAL, NOTABLE, STRANGE, UNUSUAL, EGREGIOUS, WONDERFUL, EXCEPTIONAL

remedy: . . AID, BALM, BOOT, CURE, DRUG, HEAL, HELP, AMEND, SALVE, ELIXIR, RELIEF, REPAIR, RECIPE, ARCANUM, CORRECT, NOSTRUM, PANACEA, REDRESS, RECTIFY, RELIEVE, ANTIDOTE, MEDICINE, TREATMENT

remember: . . . . RECALL, RECORD, REMIND, REWARD, MENTION, RECOLLECT, REMINISCE, COMMEMORATE

remembrance: . . . . GIFT, TOKEN, MEMORY, NOTICE, TROPHY, MEMENTO, MENTION, KEEPSAKE, MEMORIAL, SOUVENIR

reminder: . . . . . . CUE, HING, MEMO, NOTE, MEMENTO, TICKLER, SOUVENIR

remiss: . . LAX, LAZY, SLACK, TARDY, LANGUID, CARELESS, DERELICT, DILATORY, NEGLIGENT

remit: . . . PAY, SEND, RELAX, CANCEL, EXCUSE, PARDON, RETURN, SUBMIT, ABSOLVE, FORGIVE, RELEASE, SLACKEN

remnant: . . see **remainder**, **remains**

remonstrate: . . . . . . ARGUE, PLEAD, OBJECT, PROTEST, COMPLAIN

remorse: . . RUE, PITY, GRIEF, QUALM, REGRET, SORROW, PENANCE, PENITENCE, REPENTENT, CONTRITION

remote: . . . . FAR, OFF, AFAR, COOL, ALOOF, FAINT, VAGUE, SLIGHT, DISTANT, FARAWAY, FOREIGN, REMOVED, SECLUDED, ABSTRACTED

remove: . . . RID, DOFF, FIRE, FREE, KILL, OUST, PARE, RAZE, SACK, VOID, ERASE, EJECT, EVICT, EXPEL, CANCEL, CONVEY, DEDUCT, DELETE, DEPOSE, DISBAR, RECALL, RETIRE, UPROOT, DISMISS, EXTRACT, ABSTRACT, DISPLACE, TRANSFER, ELIMINATE, ASSASSINATE

remuneration: . . . . PAY, WAGES, SALARY, REWARD, PAYMENT, STIPEND, EMOLUMENT, RECOMPENSE, COMPENSATION

renaissance: . . . . . REBIRTH, REVIVAL, RENASCENCE

rend: . . CUT, RIP, PULL, RIVE, SLIT, TEAR, BREAK, BURST, SEVER, SPLIT, WREST, BREACH, CLEAVE, DIVIDE, REMOVE, SUNDER, RUPTURE, FRACTURE, LACERATE, SEPARATE

render: . . DO, ACT, PAY, TRY, GIVE, MAKE, MELT, PLAY, TREAT, YIELD, DEPICT, RECITE, RETURN, SUBMIT, DELIVER, EXTRACT, FURNISH, INFLICT, PERFORM, PRESENT, TRANSMIT, INTERPRET, SURRENDER, TRANSLATE, CONTRIBUTE

rendezvous: . . . . DATE, MEET, PLACE, TRYST, HANGOUT, MEETING, RETREAT, ASSEMBLE, GATHERING, APPOINTMENT

rendition: . . . . VERSION, DELIVERY, SURRENDER, DELIVERANCE, PERFORMANCE

renegade: . . . . . RAT, REBEL, TRAITOR, APOSTATE, DESERTER, FUGITIVE, TURNCOAT

renege: . . . . . . DENY, WELSH, REFUSE, REVOKE, DECLINE, RENOUNCE

renew: . . (also see **renovate**) EXTEND, REFILL, REPAIR, REPEAT, RESUME, REVAMP, REVIVE, FRESHEN, REBUILD, REFRESH, RESTORE, RENOVATE, REPLENISH, INVIGORATE, REGENERATE, REJUVENATE

renounce: . . . . . CEDE, DEFY, DENY, CEASE, WAIVE, ABJURE, DESERT, DISOWN, FOREGO, RECANT, REJECT, RENEGE, REPEAL, RESIGN, ABANDON, DISAVOW, FORSAKE, RETRACT, ABDICATE, ABNEGATE, DISCLAIM, FORSWEAR, RELINQUISH

renovate: . . (also see **renew**) REDO, ALTER, CLEAN, PURITY, REVIVE, CLEANSE, FURBISH, REPLACE, RESTORE

renown: . . . . . . FAME, NOTE, NAME, ECLAT, GLORY, KUDOS, ACCLAIM, EMINENCE, CELEBRITY, REPUTATION

renowned: . . . . KNOWN, FAMOUS

rent: . . . . GAP, LET, RIP, HIRE, HOLE, TOLL, CHINK, CLEFT, CRACK, LEASE, SPLIT, BREACH, ENGAGE, INCOME, RETURN, SCHISM, FISSURE, OPENING, REVENUE, RUPTURE

repair: . . . . . GO, FIX, DARN, HEAL, MEND, AMEND, PATCH, PIECE, RENEW, REMEDY, RETURN, REVAMP, REVIVE, RESTORE, CORRECT, REBUILD, RENOVATE

reparation: . . BOTE, AMENDS, REPAIRS, DAMAGES, REDRESS, ATONEMENT, INDEMNITY, RECOMPENSE

repatriate: . . . . RETURN

repay: . . . . AVENGE, PROFIT, PUNISH, REFUND, RETURN, REWARD, REQUITE, REIMBURSE, RETALIATE, RECOMPENSE

repeal: . . . . AMEND, ANNUL, EMEND, CANCEL, RECALL,

REVOKE, ABOLISH, RESCIND, RETRACT, REVERSE, ABROGATE, RENOUNCE, WITHDRAW, REVOCATION

repeat: .... BIS, CITE, ECHO, DITTO, QUOTE, RECAP, RECUR, ENCORE, PARROT, RECITE, RETELL, ITERATE, RECOUNT, RESTATE, DUPLICATE, REITERATE

repel: ... BEAT, STOP, CHECK, FORCE, SPURN, COMBAT, DEFEND, OPPOSE, REBUFF, REFUSE, REJECT, RESIST, DECLINE, REPULSE, VANQUISH

repellent: .... GRIM, HARSH, REPUGNANT, REPULSIVE, WATERPROOF

repent: ...... RUE, GRIEVE, REGRET, CREEPING, CRAWLING

repercussion: .... ECHO, RECOIL, REBOUND, REACTION

repertory: ..... LIST, INDEX, STOCK, COLLECTION, STOREHOUSE

repetition: ...... BIS, COPY, ECHO, ROTE, REPLICA, REHEARSAL, RECITATION, RECURRENCE

repine: ...... FRET, MOURN, LAMENT, COMPLAIN

replace: .. RELIEVE, RETURN, RESTORE, SUCCEED, SUPPLANT

replete: .. FAT, FULL, FILLED, STUFFED

replica: ...... COPY, IMAGE, CARBON, LIKENESS, FACSIMILE, REPRODUCTION

replicate: ... FOLD, REPEAT, MANIFOLD, DUPLICATE

reply: ..... REBUT, ANSWER, REJOIN, RETORT, RETURN, RESPOND, RETRACT, RIPOSTE, REPARTEE, RESPONSE, REJOINDER, COMEBACK

report: ... SAY, TALK, TELL, WORD, BRUIT, RUMOR, STATE, STORY, CAHIER, DIGEST, RELATE, REPEAT, RETURN,

GOSSIP, ACCOUNT, HEARSAY, HANSARD, NARRATE, SUMMARY, ANNOUNCE, BULLETIN, DENOUNCE, DESCRIBE, BROADCAST

repose: .. LAY, LIE, SET, SEE, CALM, EASE, RELY, REST, PEACE, PLACE, QUIET, SLEEP, CONFIDE, DEPOSIT, RECLINE, ENTRUST, SERENITY

repository: .... BOX, BANK, FILE, SAFE, CHEST, VAULT, CLOSET, MUSEUM, ARSENAL, CAPSULE, GRANERY, MAGAZINE, TREASURY

reprehend: .. WARN, BLAME, CHIDE, REBUKE, REPROVE, CENSURE, ADMONISH

represent: ..... ACT, SHOW, ENACT, DENOTE, DEPICT, TYPIFY, EXHIBIT, PICTURE, PORTRAY, PRODUCE, PROFESS, DESCRIBE, SIMULATE, EXEMPLIFY, SYMBOLIZE

represenation: ... MAP, ICON, IDOL, IKON, CHART, GRAPH, IMAGE, MODEL, AVOWAL, SAMPLE, ACCOUNT, DIAGRAM, MIMESIS, LIKENESS, PORTRAYAL, ALLEGORY, ALLEGATION

representative: .... AGENT, ENVOY, PROXY, CONSUL, DEPUTY, LEGATE, TYPICAL, DELEGATE, SALESMAN, AMBASSADOR

repress: .. CURB, HUSH, REIN, STOP, CHECK, CHOKE, CRUSH, QUELL, BRIDLE, DEADEN, STIFLE, SUBDUE, RESTRAIN, SUPPRESS, WITHHOLD, CONSTRAIN

reprieve: .... DEFER, DELAY, GRACE, ESCAPE, RESPITE, SUSPEND, POSTPONE

reprimand: ... BAWL, CHIDE, SCOLD, REBUFF, REBUKE, CENSURE, CHASTEN, REPOOF, REPROVE

reproach: . . . BLAME, CHIDE, SHAME, ACCUSE, REBUKE, REVILE, STIGMA, CENSURE, CONDEMN, REPROVE, UPBRAID, DISGRACE

reprobate: . . . . HARD, RAKE, ROUE, RASCAL, CONDEMN, CORRUPT, VICIOUS, CASTAWAY, DENOUNCE, DEPRAVED, HARDENED, REPREHEND, SCOUNDREL

reproduce: . . . COPY, DRAW, REPEAT, IMITATE, MULTIPLY, DUPLICATE, PROPAGATE

reproduction: . . . . . . COPY, FISSION, REPLICA, LIKENESS, PHOTOCOPY, COUNTERPART

reproof: . . . . see **reprimand**

reprove: . . . . see **reprimand**

reptant: . . . . CREEPING, CRAWLING

reptile: . . . . . WORM, SNAKE, LIZARD, TURTLE, SAURIAN, DINOSAUR, TORTISE, ALLIGATOR, CROCODILE

republic: . . . . STATE, DEMOCRACY, COMMONWEAL, GOVERNMENT, COMMONWEALTH

repudiate: . . . DENY, ABJURE, DISOWN, RECANT, REJECT, DISAVOW, DISCARD, DIVORCE, RETRACT, ABROGATE, DISCLAIM, RENOUNCE, DISAFFIRM

repugnance: . . . . . . ODIUM, ENMITY, HATRED, DISGUST, AVERSION, DISTASTE, LOATHING, ANTIPATHY, REPULSION, ABHORRENCE

repugnant: . . . . . . HATEFUL, INIMICAL, OFFENSIVE, REPELLENT, DISAGREEABLE

repulse: . . . . see **repel**

repulsion: . . . . DISLIKE, AVERSION, DISTASTE, REPUGNANCE

repulsive: . . . . . EVIL, UGLY, VILE, LOATH, COARSE, ODIOUS, HATEFUL, LOATHSOME, REVOLTING, DISGUSTING, OFFENSIVE, DISTASTEFUL

repute: . . . . . . FAME, ODOR, HONOR, ESTEEM, REGARD, RESPECT, CHARACTER

request: . . . . ASK, BEG, SUE, PLEA, PRAY, SUIT, APPLY, ORDER, APPEAL, DEMAND, INVITE, ENTREAT, SOLICIT, PETITION

require: . . . . . NEED, EXACT, FORCE, ORDER, COMPEL, DEMAND, ENJOIN, ENTAIL, EXPECT, OBLIGE

requirement: . . . DUTY, NEED, IMPOSITION

requisite: . . . . NEED, CONDITION, ESSENTIAL, REQUIRED

requite: . . . . . . PAY, ATONE, REPAY, ACQUIT, AVENGE, RETURN, REWARD, REVENGE, RETALIATE, COMPENSATE

rescind: . . . . . VOID, ANNUL, CANCEL, REVOKE, RECALL, REPEAL, ABOLISH, ABROGATE

rescue: . . . . FREE, SAVE, RANSOM, DELIVER, REDEEM, SUCCOR, RECLAIM, RELEASE, LIBERATE, EXTRICATE

research: . . STUDY, INQUIRY, EXAMINATION

resemblance: . . . . . . IMAGE, SIMILE, LIKENESS, SIMILARITY

resentment: . . . . . IRE, GALL, HUFF, ANGER, PIQUE, SPITE, ENMITY, GRUDGE, MALICE, RANCOR, SPLEEN, DUDGEON, UMBRAGE, OFFENSE, ACRIMONY

reserve: . CASH, FUND, KEEP, SAVE, SPARE, STOCK, STORE, ASSETS, RETAIN, BACKLOG, CAUTION, EARMARK, MODESTY, SHYNESS, SILENCE, SURPLUS, PRESERVE, WITHHOLD, RESTRAINT, RETENTION, RETICENCE

reserved: . . . . . SHY, QUIET, STAID, TAKEN, SEDATE,

DISTANT, CAUTIOUS, TACITURN,
RETICENT, RETIRING

reservoir: ..... VAT, POND,
POOL, SUMP, TANK, BASIN,
STORE, SUPPLY, CISTERN

reside: .. LIVE, ROOM, STAY,
ABIDE, DWELL, LODGE,
REMAIN, SETTLE, INHABIT,
SOJOURN

residence: ..... HOME, SEAT,
ABODE, HOUSE, MANSE, VILLA,
HABITAT, MANSION, DOMICILE,
DWELLING, APARTMENT

resident: ... LESSEE, TENANT,
CITIZEN, HABITANT, INHERENT,
OCCUPANT

residue: .. ASH, DREG, LEES,
MARC, REST, SILT, SLAG,
ASHES, DREGS, CINDER,
EXCESS, SLUDGE, SORDES,
BALANCE, REMAINS, REMNANT,
LEAVINGS, SEDIMENT,
REMAINDER

resign: . QUIT, DEMIT, REMIT,
YIELD, SUBMIT, ABANDON,
CONSIGN, DELIVER, ABDICATE,
RENOUNCE, SURRENDER,
RELINQUISH

resile: .... RECEDE, RETURN,
REBOUND, RETRACT, RETREAT

resilient: .. SUPPLE, BUOYANT,
ELASTIC, SPRINGY, FLEXIBLE,
BOUNCING, STRETCHY

resin: ..... LAC, GUM, TAR,
ALOE, BALM, AMBER, ANIME,
COPAL, GUGAL, MYRRH, PITCH,
ROSIN, BALSAM, MASTIC,
EXUDATE, LADANUM, SHELLAC

resist: ... BUCK, DEFY, FEND,
FIGHT, REBEL, REPEL, COMBAT,
DEFEAT, DEFEND, IMPUGN,
OPPOSE, CONTEST, PREVENT,
FRUSTRATE, WITHSTAND

resistance: .... DEFENSE,
HOSTILITY, DEFIANCE,
OPPOSITION

resolute: ...... BOLD, GRIM,
FIXED, POSITIVE, RESOLVED,
STALWART, DETERMINED

resolution: .... VOW, GRIT,
HEART, NERVE, PURPOSE,
RESOLVE, VERDICT, ANALYSIS,
BACKBONE, DECISION,
FIRMNESS, PROPOSAL,
STRENGTH, CERTAINTY,
FORTITUDE

resolve: ...... FREE, RELAX,
DECIDE, ANSWER, DISPEL,
INFORM, LOOSEN, REDUCE,
SETTLE, APPOINT, ANALYZE,
DISPOSE, EXPLAIN, LIQUEFY,
UNRAVEL, CONCLUDE, ANALYZE

resonant: .... RINGING,
SONOROUS, REECHOING,
VIBRANT, OROTUND

resound: ...... ECHO, PEAL,
EXTOL, RING, BOOM, VIBRATE,
REVERBERATE

resource(s): .. FUNDS, MEANS,
MONEY, ASSETS, STOCKS,
STORES, WEALTH, CAPITAL,
RESERVES, SUPPLIES, EXPEDIENT

respect: ...... AWE, DEFER,
HONOR, VALUE, ADMIRE,
ESTEEM, REGARD, REVERE,
OBSERVE, TRIBUTE, VENERATE

respectable: .... GOOD,
DECENT, HONEST, PROPER,
REPUTABLE

respite: .. LULL, REST, DELAY,
PAUSE, RECESS, LESIURE,
INTERVAL, REPRIVE, SURCEASE

resplendent: ...... BRIGHT,
BLAZING, RADIANT, SHINING,
DAZZLING, GLORIOUS,
GORGEOUS, SPLENDID,
BRILLANT

respond: .... (also see **reply**,
report) ECHO, FEEL, REACT,
WRITE, ANSWER, REJOIN,
RETORT, RETURN, CORRESPOND

responsible: .... LIABLE,
RELIABLE, REPUTABLE,
DEPENDABLE, ACCOUNTABLE

responsibility: . DUTY, ONUS,
BURDEN, LIABILITY,
OBLIGATION

rest: . . . . . . (also see **repose**)
CALM, EASE, LEAN, PROP,
RELY, SEAT, STAY, STOP,
ABIDE, PAUSE, PEACE, RELAX,
SLEEP, STAND, DEPEND, DESIST,
SETTLE, OTHERS, BALANCE,
LEISURE, REFRESH, REMAINS,
REMNANT, RESIDUE, RESPITE,
SUPPORT, SURPLUS, VACATION,
REMAINDER

restful: . . . . QUIET, PEACEFUL

restive: . . . . BALKY, UNEASY,
UNRULY, NERVOUS, FIDGETY,
RESTLESS, FRETFUL, IMPATIENT

restless: . . RESTIVE, UNEASY,
FRETFUL, AGITATED

restore: . . . . CURE, HEAL,
MEND, ATONE, RENEW, REPAY,
RIGHT, REPAIR, RETURN,
REVIVE, REBUILD, RECOVER,
REPLACE, RENOVATE,
REINSTATE, RECONSTRUCT

restrain: . . . BAR, DAM, BIND,
CALM, CURB, HOLD, REIN,
STAY, STOP, CHAIN, DETER,
LIMIT, ARREST, BRIDLE,
DETAIN, FETTER, FORBID,
TETHER, INHIBIT, SUPPRESS

restrict: . . . . . BAR, CRAMP,
LIMIT, CONFINE

result: . . . END, SUM, ENSUE,
FRUIT, ISSUE, SCORE, TOTAL,
EFFECT, UPSHOT, ANSWER,
OUTCOME, AFTERMATH,
EVENTUATE

resume: . . . RENEW, REOPEN,
REVIEW, PRECIS, EPITOME,
SUMMARY, ABSTRACT,
CONTINUE

resuscitate: . . . . REVIVE

retain: . . . HIRE, HOLD, KEEP,
SAVE, ADHERE, EMPLOY,
CONTAIN, RESERVE

retaliate: . . . REPAY, AVENGE,
PUNISH, REQUITE, REVENGE

retard: . . . . . . SLOW, BRAKE,
DEFER, DELAY, DETER,
DEADEN, DETAIN, HINDER,
IMPEDE, OBSTRUCT, POSTPONE

retention: . . . . MEMORY,
HOLDING, KEEPING, LEARNING

reticent: . . . SILENT, SPARING,
DISCREET, RESERVED, RETIRING,
TACITURN, SECRETIVE

reticule: . . . . . . (HAND)BAG,
POCKET, RETICLE

retinue: . . . . . BAND, CREW,
ROUT, SUITE, TRAIN, MEINY,
ESCORT, CORTEGE, ENTOURAGE,
RETAINERS

retire: . . . . EBB, REST, LEAVE,
DEPART, RECEDE, RECESS,
REMOVE, PENSION, RETREAT,
WITHDRAW

retired: . . . ABED, SECLUDED,
ASLEEP, EMERITUS

retiring: . . . . . . SHY, TIMID,
MODEST, RESERVED

retort: . QUIP, REPLY, SALLY,
REPARTEE, WITTICISM, RIPOSTE,
REJOIN(DER)

retract: . . . . ABJURE, CANCEL,
RECALL, RECANT, REMOVE,
REPEAL, REVOKE, DISAVOW,
RESCIND, RETREAT, WITHDRAW

retreat: . . . DEN, CAVE, LAIR,
NEST, NOOK, ARBOR, BOWER,
STUDY, ASYLUM, HARBOR,
RECEDE, RECESS, REFUGE,
RETIRE, HIDEOUT, SANCTUM,
SHELTER, WITHDRAW

retrench: . CUT, OMIT, PARE,
DELETE, LESSEN, CURTAIL,
REDUCE, DECREASE, DIMINISH,
CUT-DOWN, ECONOMIZE

retribution: . . . PAY, RETURN,
REQUITAL, NEMESIS, REWARD,
REVENGE, VENGENCE

retrieve: . . RECALL, RECOVER,
RESTORE, REGAIN, REVIVE

retrograde: . . SLOW, RECEDE,
DECLINE, REGRESS, REVERSE,
INVERSE

retrogress: . . . . . . DECLINE,
FALLBACK, DEGENERATE

return: . . . . . RECUR, REMIT,
REPAY, REPLY, YIELD, ANSWER,
PROFIT, REVERT, RESPOND,

**REPLACE, REQUITE, REELECT, REPORT, RESTORE, RESPONSE, REVENUE, REVERSE

revamp:** ..... REDO, PATCH
reveal: .. BARE, JAMB, OPEN, SHOW, TELL, BETRAY, EXPOSE, IMPART, UNVEIL, EXHIBIT, DIVULGE, DISCLOSE, DISPLAY, UNCOVER, MANIFEST
revel: .... JOY, ORGY, SPREE, CAROUSE, DELIGHT, ROISTER, CAROUSAL, FESTIVITY
revelation: .... DISCLOSURE
revenge: ... AVENGE, TALION, REQUITE, RETALIATE, VENGEANCE
revenue: ..... RENT, YIELD, INCOME, PROFIT, RETURN, FINANCE, INTEREST
reverberate: ... ECHO, RING, REECHO, REFLECT, RESOUND, REBOUND
revere: ...... LOVE, ADORE, HONOR, ADMIRE, ESTEEM, RESPECT, VENERATE, WORSHIP
reverie: .... DREAM, MUSING, VISION, FANTASY
reverse: .... ANNUL, UPSET, DEFEAT, INVERT, REPEAL, REVOKE, ABOLISH, BACKUP, BACKSET, CONVERT, SUBVERT, CONTRARY, CONVERSE, DISASTER, OPPOSITE
revert: ... ADVERT, RETURN, ESCHEAT, REVERSE, BACKSLIDE
review: ...... EDIT, RECAP, PARADE, REPORT, RESUME, REVUE, ACCOUNT INSPECT, CEREMONY, CRITIQUE, CRITICISM
revile: .... RAIL, ABUSE, BLAME, SCOLD, DEBASE, MALIGN, VILIFY, ASPERSE, REPROACH
revise: ...... EDIT, ALTER, AMEND, CHANGE, REDACT, CORRECT, IMPROVE, REWRITE
revival: ... RECALL, REBIRTH, RENEWAL, RENAISSANCE

revive: ..... RALLY, RENEW, ROUSE, RETURN, ENLIVEN, FRESHEN, RECOVER, REFRESH, RESURGE, RESTORE, REAWAKEN, REKINDLE, REANIMATE, RESURRECT, RESUSCITATE
revoke: ..... ADEEM, ANNUL, RENIG, ABJURE, CANCEL, RECALL, RECANT, RENEGE, REPEAL, ABOLISH, RESCIND, RETRACT, REVERSE, ABROGATE, WITHDRAW
revolt: .... REBEL, MUTINY, OFFEND, DISGUST, RENOUNCE, SEDITION, UPRISING, REBELLION
revolting: ... UGLY, HORRID, HATEFUL, HIDEOUS, SHOCKING, OFFENSIVE, LOATHSOME, REPELLANT, REPULSIVE
revolution: .... GYRE, TURN, CYCLE, CIRCUIT, UPRISING, ROTATION, REBELLION
revolve: .. ROLL, SPIN, TURN, RECUR, ORBIT, SWING, TWIRL, WHEEL, WHIRL, CIRCLE, GYRATE, ROTATE, AGITATE
revulsion: .... AVERSION
reward: ..... FEE, PAY, TIP, AWARD, BONUS, MERIT, MEDAL, PRIZE, WAGES, YIELD, BOUNTY, PROFIT, RETURN, SALARY, TROPHY, GUERDON, PREMIUM
rewrite: ...... EDIT, REVISE
rex: .... KING
rheum: ..... COLD, RHINITIS, CATARRH
rhinal: .... NASAL
rhomb: .... PARALLELOGRAM
rhubarb: ... ERROR, HASSLE, MISTAKE, ARGUMENT, PIEPLANT, DISCUSSION
rhythm: .. BEAT, LILT, TIME, METER, PULSE, SWING, TEMPO, CADENCE, MEASURE
rhythmic: .... POETIC, METRICAL, RECURRENT
ria: .... BAY, CREEK, INLET

rialto: . . . . . . MART, BRIDGE, MARKET, EXCHANGE

riant: . . . . GAY, BLITHE, CHEERFUL, LAUGHING, SMILING

riata: . . ROPE, LASSO, LARIAT

rib: . . . . . BONE, HAIR, STAY, VEIN, TWIT, COSTA, RIDGE, TEASE

ribald: . . . . . . LOW, COARSE, VULGAR, OBSCENE, OFFENSIVE

ribbed: . . . . COSTATE, RIDGED

ribbon: . . . BOW, BAND, TAPE, BADGE, BRAID, SHRED, STRIP, CORDON, DECORATION

rice: . . . GRAIN, PILAF, PILAU, CEREAL, PADDY

rich: . . . . FAT, DEAR, AMPLE, ABSURD, COSTLY, CREAMY, GREASY, POTENT, COPIOUS, FERTILE, MONEYED, OPULENT, WEALTHY, ABUNDANT, AFFLUENT, VALUABLE, WELL-TO-DO, LUXURIOUS, ABOUNDING

rickety: . . . . . WEAK, SHAKY, FEEBLE, SENILE

ricochet: . . . . . SKIP, CAROM, BOUNCE, GLANCE, REBOUND

rid: . . . FREE, CLEAR, EMPTY, ASSOIL, REMOVE, RESCUE, DELIVER, RELIEVE, DISPATCH, LIBERATE, ERADICATE

riddle: . CRUX, REBUS, SIEVE, ENIGMA, PEPPER, PUZZLE, MYSTERY, PROBLEM, CONUNDRUM, PERFORATE

ride: . . . BAIT, DRIVE, FLOAT, MOTOR, MOUNT, TEASE, HARASS, JOURNEY, TORMENT

rider: . . . . FARE, JOKER, CLAUSE, COWBOY, JOCKEY, ADDITION, HORSEMAN, PASSENGER, AMENDMENT, EQUESTRIAN

ridge: . . . . . RIB, TOP, BACK, BANK, DUNE, RAND, REEF, RING, RUGA, SEAM, SPUR, WALE, WAVE, WELT, ARETE, CHINE, COSTA, CREST, SPINE, STRIA, WRINKLE, HOGBACK, ELEVATION, RAZORBACK

ridicule: . . . PAN, GIBE, JEER, JEST, MOCK, RAZZ, TWIT, CHAFF, ROAST, SCOFF, SNEER, TAUNT, DERIDE, EXPOSE, SATIRE, LAMPOON, SARCASM, DERISION

ridiculous: . . . . . . ABSURD, AMUSING, FOOLISH, FARCICAL, GROTESQUE, LUDICROUS, IRRATIONAL, OUTRAGEOUS

rife: . . . . . . BRIEF, CURRENT, REPLETE, ABUNDANT, NUMEROUS, PLENTIFUL, PREVALENT, PREVAILING, WIDESPREAD

riffraff: . . . MOB, RAFF, SCUM, TRASH, RABBLE, REFUSE, RUBBISH

rifle: . . . . . . ARM, GUN, ROB, REEVE, STEAL, FURROW, GROOVE, WEAPON, CARBINE, PILLAGE, PLUNDER, RANSACK, CHASSEPOT

rift: . . . . GAP, FLAW, BREAK, CHASM, CLEFT, CRACK, SPLIT, BREACH, CLEAVE, DIVIDE, BLEMISH, FISSURE, OPENING, DIVISION

rig: . . . FIT, FIX, CART, FOOL, GEAR, HOAX, DRESS, EQUIP, RIFLE, TRICK, ATTIRE, CLOTHE, OUTFIT, TACKLE, ARRANGE, COSTUME, ACCOUTER, CARRIAGE, APPARATUS, EQUIPMENT, MANIPULATE

right: . . . . . FIT, FAIR, GOOD, REAL, SANE, TRUE, DROIT, SOUND, TITLE, EQUITY, LAWFUL, NORMAL, PATENT, PROPER, CORRECT, FITTING, GENUINE, DEXTRAL, LICENSE, RECTIFY, REDRESS, EASEMENT, STRAIGHT, VIRTUOUS, SUITABLE, EQUITABLE, FRANCHISE

righteous: . . . . GOOD, HOLY, JUST, GODLY, MORAL, PIOUS,

DEVOUT, SINLESS, UPRIGHT,
VIRTUOUS

rigid: .... SET, FIRM, HARD,
TAUT, FIXED, STERN, STIFF,
TENSE, SEVERE, STRAIT,
STRICT, RIGOROUS, AUSTERE,
IMMOVABLE, STRINGENT,
UNBENDING, INFLEXIBLE

rigor: .. ASPERITY, HARDSHIP,
RIGIDITY, SEVERITY,
AUSTERITY, HARSHNESS,
STIFFNESS, DIFFICULTY

rigorous: ..... RIGID, STERN,
STIFF, HARSH, STRICT, DRASTIC,
PRECISE, ACCURATE

rile: ..... REX, ROIL, ANGER,
ANNOY, UPSET, AGITATE,
IRRITATE

rill: .. BROOK, CREEK, DITCH,
TRENCH, VALLEY, FURROW,
GROOVE

rim: ...... LIP, BANK, BRIM,
EDGE, RING, BRINK, VERGE,
BORDER, FLANGE, MARGIN,
BOUNDRY, PERIMETER

rind: ... BARK, HUSK, PEEL,
SKIN, CRUST, CORTEX, EPICARP,
PEELING

ring: ... CUT, RIM, SET, BAIL,
BAND, DING, GYRE, HALO,
HOOP, LINK, PEAL, TOLL,
ARENA, BEZEL, CHIME, CLANG,
GROUP, KNELL, BORDER,
CIRCLE, CLIQUE, COLLAR,
CORONA, GASKET, GIRDLE,
TERRET, ANNULET, CIRCLET,
GROMMET, RESOUND,
BRACELET, ENCIRCLE,
SURROUND, RESOUND, SIGNAL,
CIRQUE

ringlet: .. CURL, TRESS, LOCK

rinse: .. WASH, LAVE, DOUSE,
SLUICE, CLEANSE

riot: .... DIN, ORGY, BRAWL,
MELEE, REVEL, AFFRAY,
BELAM, CLAMOR, TUMULT,
UPROAR, HUBBUB, DISPUTE,
DISORDER, UPRISING,
COMMOTION, DONNY BROOK

riotous: .... LOUD, WILD,
NOISY, WANTON, BOISTEROUS,
DISSOLUTE, LUXURIANT,
DISORDERLY

rip: ..... REND, RENT, RIVE,
TEAR, SPLIT, SUNDER,
LACERATE

ripe: .... ADULT, READY,
MATURE, MELLOW, COMPLETE,
DEVELOPED, FULL-GROWN

ripost(e): .... REPLY, RETORT,
THRUST, RETURN, REPARTEE

ripple: ... LAP, CURL, PURL,
RIFT, WAVE, CRINKLE,
WAVELET, WRINKLE, UNDULATE

rise: .... FLOW, HILL, GROW,
LOOM, REAR, SOAR, WELL,
ARISE, CLIMB, ISSUE, OCCUR,
MOUNT, REBEL, STAND, SURGE,
SWELL, TOWER, ASCEND,
ASCENT, EMERGE, GROWTH,
REVOLT, THRIVE, ADVANCE,
ELEVATE, PROSPER

risible: ... FUNNY, AMUSING,
LUDICROUS, LAUGHABLE

risk: ... DARE, PERIL, STAKE,
CHANCE, DANGER, GAMBLE,
HAZARD, PLIGHT, PLUNGE,
VENTURE, JEOPARDY

risque: ... RACY, RISKY, OFF-
COLOR, SCABROUS, AUDACIOUS

rite: .. CULT, FORM, AUGURY,
NOVENA, PRAYER, LITURGY,
CEREMONY

ritzy: .. POSH, TONY, CLASSY,
MODISH, ELEGANT, LUXURIOUS

rivage: ...... BANK, SHORE,
COAST

rival: ...... FOE, VIE, PEER,
EQUAL, MATCH, COMPETE,
EMULATE, FEUDING, OPPONENT,
ADVERSARY, COMPETITOR

rive: .. RIP, REND, RENT, RIFT,
TEAR, CLEFT, SHORE, SPLIT,
CLEAVE, SUNDER, THRUST,
LACERATE

river: ..... BAYOU, WADDY,
STREAM, CHANNEL

rivet: .... BOLT, FASTEN

rivulet: . . . . . RILL, ARROYO, BROOK, STREAM, RUNLET

road: . . . . WAY, ITER, PATH, ROUTE, AVENUE, COURSE, STREET, ESTRADA, HIGHWAY, PASSAGE, RAILWAY, MACADAM, CAUSEWAY, CUL-DE-SAC, PAVEMENT

roam: . . . . . ERR, GAD, ROIL, ROVE, PROWL, RANGE, RAMBLE, STROLL, TRAVEL, WANDER, MEANDER, STRAGGLE, GALLIVANT

roar: . . . . . DIN, BELL, ROLL, BOOM, BRAY, CLAP, YELL, GROWL, BELLOW, RUMBLE, THUNDER, LAUGHTER, SHOUTING

roast: . . . . PAN, BAKE, HEAT, RAZZ, BROIL, GRILL, PARCH, RIDICULE, CRITICISE, BARBECUE

rob: . . . . . . COP, CLIP, FLAY, LOOT, PELF, TAKE, FILCH, PINCH, REAVE, RIFLE, STEAL, STRIP, BURGLE, HIJACK, PILFER, RAVISH, SNATCH, THIEVE, DESPOIL, PILLAGE, PLUNDER, PLAGIARIZE

robber: . . . . . . YEGG, THIEF, BANDIT, PIRATE, BRIGAND, FOOTPAD, BANDIDO, LADRONE, MARAUDER, BUCCANEER

robe: . . . . . . (also see **dress, gown**) TOGA, WRAP, ARRAY, CAMIS, CLOAK, COVER, SIMAR, TUNIC, CAFTAN, CHIMER, CLOTHE, DOLMAN, KIMONO, MANTLE, COSTUME, GARMENT, VESTMENT

robot: . . . . GOLEM, ANDROID, AUTOMATION

robust: . . . . . . HALE, HARDY, HUSKY, LUSTY, ROUGH, SOUND, STOUT, WALLY, BRAWNY, HEARTY, RUGGED, STRONG, STURDY, HEALTHY, ATHLETIC MUSCULAR, VIGOROUS

rock: . . . . ORE, CRAG, PEAK, REEF, REEL, ROLL, SWAY, AGATE, CANDY, CLIFF, FLINT, SCREE, SHAKE, SHALE, SLATE, STONE, BASALT, GRAVEL, PEBBLE, REFUGE, SILICA, TETTER, TOTTER, DIAMOND, GRANITE, SUPPORT, TREMBLE, VIBRATE, OSCILLATE

rocker: . . . . . CHAIR, SKATE, CRADLE

rocky: . HARD, WEAK, DIZZY, SHAKY, STONY, CRAGGY, UNSTEADY

rococo: . . FLORID, TASTELESS, BAROQUE

rod: . . . BAR, GAT, GUN, GUY, RIB, AXLE, BOLT, CANE, LATH, POLE, PROD, SPIT, TWIG, WAND, ARROW, BATON, BOARD, PERCH, SHAFT, SPOKE, STAFF, STICK, STRIP, FERULE, PISTOL, PISTON, SKEWER, SWITCH, TOGGLE, MEASURE, SCEPTER, SPINDLE, REVOLVER

rodent: . . . RAT, CAVY, CONY, HARE, MOLE, PIKA, VOLE, MOUSE, AGOUTI, BEAVER, GERBIL, GOPHER, MARMOT, MURINE, RABBIT, WEASEL, HAMSTER, MUSKRAT, LEPORIDE, SQUIRREL, PORCUPINE, CHINCHILLA, CHIPMUNK

roe: . . OVA, MILT, PEA, DEER, CORAL, SPAWN, CAVIAR, (FISH)EGGS

rogue: . . . IMP, KITE, CHEAT, CRANK, GYPSY, KNAVE, SCAMP, SHARK, TRAMP, BEGGAR, RASCAL, HELLION, VAGRANT, VILLAIN, PICAROON, SCAPEGRACE, SCOUNDREL, VAGABOND

roil: . . IRK, VEX, FOUL, RILE, ROMP, STIR, ANGER, ANNOY, MUDDY, RUFFLE, DISTURB, DISPLEASE, IRRITATE

roister: . . . . . . BRAG, BULLY, REVEL, SPREE, SWAGGER

role: . . . . . . BIT, CAST, DUTY, PART, OFFICE, BUSINESS, FUNCTION, CHARACTER

roll: . . BUN, ROB, CAKE, COIL, LIST, PEAL, SWAY, TURN, WIND, WRAP, BAGEL, FRISK, LURCH, TRILL, WHEEL, BUNDLE, ENFOLD, ENWRAP, ROSTER, ROTATE, SCROLL, SPIRAL, TUMBLE, BISCUIT, BRIOCHE, REVOLVE, TRUNDLE, REGISTER, DRUM BEAT

roller: . . BAND, WAVE, SKATE, WHEEL, CANARY, CASTER, PIGEON, PLATEN, BANDAGE, BREAKER, TUMBLER, CYLINDER

rollick: . . . . . . ROMP, CAPER, FRISK, FROLIC, GAMBOL

rollicking: . . . . GAY, JOVIAL, LIVELY, CAREFREE, HILARIOUS

roly-poly: . . . PUDGY, DUMPY, ROUND, PORTLY, ROTUND, PUDDING

romaine: . . . . . COS, LETTUCE

romance: . . . . WOO, COURT, DREAM, NOVEL, STORY, AFFAIR, FANTASY, FICTION, EXAGGERATE

romantic: . . POETIC, UNREAL, FANCIFUL, QUIXOTIC, IMAGINARY, FABULOUS, VISIONARY, IDEALISTIC, SENTIMENTAL

romp: . . . PLAY, ROIL, FROLIC, ROLLICK

rondure: . . . . CIRCLE, SPHERE

rood: . . . . . . CROSS, CRUCIFIX

roof: . . . . TOP, DOME, COVER, PALATE, THATCH, SHELTER, CUPOLA, GAMBREL

rook: . . BIRD, CROW, CHEAT, RAVEN, STEAL, CASTLE, DEFRAUD, SWINDLE(R)

room: . . . . DEN, CELL, HALL, LODGE, PLACE, SALON, SCOPE, SPACE, STUDY, ATRIUM, CLOSET, LEEWAY, RESIDE, SALOON, BOUDOIR, CHAMBER,

CUBICLE, EXPANSE, GALLERY, LODGING, QUARTER, ROTUNDA

roomy: . . . . . AMPLE, BROAD, SPACY, SPACIOUS, CAPACIOUS, COMMODIOUS

rooster: . . . . COCK, CHANTICLEER

root: . . . . . DIG, BASE, CORE, GRUB, ROUT, BASIS, CHEER, GROUT, RADIX, SHOUT, BOTTOM, ORIGIN, SOURCE, RADICAL, RHIZOME, BEGINNING, FOUNDATION

rope: . . GUY, TIE, TOW, BIND, CORD, HEMP, LINE, STAY, CABLE, LASSO, LONGE, RIATA, SHEET, FASTEN, HALTER, HAWSER, LARIAT, MARLIN, HALYARD, PAINTER

rosary: . . . . BEADS, GARDEN, CHAPLET, GARLAND

rose: . . . (also see **rise**) FLUSH, FLOWER, PERFUME, NOZZLE, RAMBLER, HELLEBORE

rosin: . . . . see **resin**

roster: . . . LIST, ROLL, SLATE

rostrum: . . . . . . BEAK, DIAS, SNOUT, STAGE, PULPIT, LECTERN, TRIBUNE, PLATFORM, PROBISCUS

rosy: . . . RED, PINK, RUDDY, BRIGHT, FLORID, FLUSHED, BLUSHING, FAVORABLE, PROMISING, RUBICUND

rot: . . . . . . RET, BOSH, JOKE, DECAY, SPOIL, TRASH, FESTER, CORRUPT, PUTREFY, RUBBISH, TWADDLE, NONSENSE, DECOMPOSE

rota: . . . . LIST, ROLL, COURT, ROUTINE, ROUND, ROSTER, REGISTER

rotate: . . . PASS, ROLL, SPIN, TURN, TWIRL, WHEEL, WHIRL, GYRATE, REVOLVE, TRUNDLE, ALTERNATE

rote: . . LIST, LEARN, CUSTOM, MEMORY, REPEAT, SYSTEM, ROUTINE, PRACTICE,

AUTOMATIC, REPETITION,
MECHANICAL

rotten: .... BAD, EVIL, FOUL,
RANK, ADDLE, FETID, NASTY,
PUTRID, CARRION, CORRUPT,
DECAYED, SPOILED, TAINTED,
UNSOUND, DEPRAVED,
OFFENSIVE, PUTREFIED,
DECOMPOSED, PUTRESCENT

rotund: ..... OBESE, PLUMP,
ROUND, STOUT, CHUBBY,
PORTLY, ROLYPOLY, SONOROUS

roue: .... RAKE, LIBERTINE,
DEBAUCHEE, RAKEHELL

rough: . HARD, RUDE, BRUTE,
CRUDE, GRUFF, HARSH, HUSKY,
LUMPY, ROWDY, STERN, SURLY,
UNCUT, ABRUPT, BROKEN,
CHOPPY, COARSE, CRAGGY,
HOARSE, JAGGED, RAGGED,
RUGGED, SEVERE, SHAGGY,
STORMY, UNEVEN, AUSTERE,
BOORISH, BRUSQUE, INEXACT,
JARRING, RAUCOUS, UNPLANED,
IMPERFECT, TURBULENT,
RIOTOUS, VIOLENT, AGRESTIC

round: .. BEAT, BOUT, FULL,
RUNG, TOUR, GROUP, PLUMP,
CIRCLE, CURVED, COURSE,
PERIOD, ROTUND, BULBOUS,
CIRCUIT, CIRCULAR, GLOBULAR,
ROLYPOLY, SPHERICAL

roundabout: ...... DANCE,
DETOUR, JACKET, DEVIOUS,
CIRCULAR, INDIRECT,
TORTUOUS, CIRCUITOUS

rounded: ..... OVAL, OVATE,
CONVEX, ROTUND, FUSIFORM,
GIBBOUS, CIRCULAR

rouse: ... CALL, HAUL, MOVE,
STIR, WAKE, WHET, ALARM,
AWAKE, RAISE, RALLY, ROUST,
AROUSE, BESTIR, EXCITE,
FOMENT, REVIVE, ACTUATE,
AGITATE, ANIMATE, DISTURB,
ENLIVEN, STIMULATE, REVILE

rout: .... MOB, BAND, BEAT,
FUSS, ROAR, ROOT, CROWD,
SCOOP, SHOUT, SHORE,

BELLOW, CLAMOR, DEFEAT,
FLIGHT, RABBLE, ROUST,
SEARCH, THRONG, TUMULT,
UPROAR, DEBACLE, REPULSE,
RETREAT, RUMMAGE, DISPERSE,
STAMPEDE, VANQUISH

route: ..... RUN, WAY, LINE,
PATH, ROAD, MARCH, TRAIL,
COURSE, SKYWAY, CIRCUIT,
JOURNEY, ITINERARY

routine: .. RUT, ROTA, ROTE,
GRIND, HABIT, ROUND, COURSE,
SYSTEM, REGULAR, HUMDRUM,
CUSTOMARY

rover: ..... GO, GAD, MOVE,
PART, ROAM, PROWL, RANGE,
STRAY, PIERCE, RAMBLE,
STROLL, WANDER

row: ..... OAR, BANK, FILE,
FUSS, LINE, LIST, RANK, SPAT,
TIER, BRAWL, BROIL, NOISE,
CLAMOR, PADDLE, PROPEL,
RUCKUS, DISPUTE, QUARREL,
ARGUMENT, SQUABBLE,
COMMOTION

rowboat: ... COG, GIG, DORY,
CANOE, COBLE, SCULL, SKIFF,
SHELL, CAIQUE, GALLEY,
WHERRY, GONDOLA

rowdy: ...... RUDE, TOUGH,
NOISY, HOOD(LUM), PLUG-
UGLY, LARRIKIN,
ROUGH(NECK), BOISTEROUS

royal: .. RIAL, NOBLE, REGAL,
AUGUST, KINGLY, STATELY,
IMPERIAL, MAJESTIC, PRINCELY,
SPLENDID, SOVEREIGN,
MAGNIFICENT

rub: ..... BUFF, FRET, RASP,
SAND, WEAR, WIPE, CHAFE,
GRATE, GRIND, SCOUR, SMEAR,
ABRADE, POLISH, SCRAPE,
SMOOTH, STROKE, BURNISH,
MASSAGE, FRICTION, IRRITATE

rubber: .. GUM, PARA, BAND,
LATEX, CAUCHO, ERASER,
EBONITE, ELASTIC, GUAYULE,
MASSEUR, MASSEUSE,

OVERSHOE, VULCANITE,
CAOUTCHOUC

rubbish: . . DUST, JUNK, RAFF,
DROSS, OFFAL, TRIPE, TRASH,
WASTE, DEBRIS, GARBLE,
LITTER, REFUSE, RUBBLE,
BAGGAGE, RUMMAGE,
NONSENSE, TRUMPERY

rube: . . . HICK, JAKE, YOKEL,
RUSTIC, BUMPKIN, HAYSEED,
COUNTRYMAN

rubicund: . . . . . . RED, ROSY,
RUBY, RUDDY, FLORID,
FLUSHED, REDDISH, REDNESS

ruche: . . . . FRILL, TRIMMING

ruck: . . . . RUT, FOLD, HEAP,
MASS, PILE, RAKE, RICK,
COWER, CROWD, STACK,
CREASE, PUCKER, CRUMPLE,
WRINKLE

ruckus: . . . ADO, ROW, FRAY,
BRAWL, MELEE, HASSLE,
RUMPUS, UPROAR, RUNCTION,
CONFUSION

rudder: . . . . . . HELM, TILLER

ruddy: . . RED, ROSY, FLORID,
TANNED, FLUSHED, REDDISH,
RUBICUND

rude: . . . BOLD, CURT, BLUFF,
CRUDE, GROSS, GRUFF, HARSH,
ROUGH, SAUCY, ROWDY,
CLUMSY, COARSE, RUSTIC,
SEVERE, VULGAR, BOORISH,
LOUTISH, UNCIVIL, UNCOUTH,
CHURLISH, HOMESPUN,
IMPOLITE, IMPUDENT,
INSOLENT, INSULTING

rudimentary: . . . . . . INITIAL,
ELEMENTAL, VESTIGIAL,
INCHOATE, ELEMENTARY,
FUNDAMENTAL

rue: . . . PITY, GRIEF, MOURN,
BEWAIL, GRIEVE, LAMENT,
REGRET, REPENT, SORROW,
DEPLORE, REMORSE, PENITENT,
REPENTENCE

ruff: . . . PERCH, PLAIT, REEVE,
STAMP, TRUMP, COLLAR,
FRAISE, HACKLE, PIGEON,

RABATO, RUFFLE, SUNFISH,
DRUMBEAT, SANDPIPER

ruffian: . . . . . GOON, THUG,
BULLY, ROWDY, TOUGH, PLUG-
UGLY, HIGHBINDER, HOODLUM,
HOOLIGAN, GANGSTER,
CUTTHROAT

ruffle: . . . . . VEX, FRET, ROIL,
ANNOY, CRIMP, FRILL, JABOT,
PLEAT, SHAKE, RIFFLE, RIPPLE,
TOUSLE, AGITATE, DERANGE,
DISTURB, FLOUNCE, SHUFFLE,
WRINKLE, DISHEVEL,
DRUMBEAT, FURBELOW

rug: . . MAT, AFGAN, CARPET,
FRIEZE, RUNNER, TOUPEE,
BLANKET, DRUGGET, LAPPROBE,
FOOTCLOTH, COVERING

ruga: . . . . . . FOLD, CREASE,
WRINKLE, MEMBRANE

rugby: . . . . FOOTBALL

rugged: . . . . . . HARD, RUDE,
HARDY, HARSH, ROUGH,
CRAGGY, ROBUST, SEVERE,
STORMY, STRONG, STURDY,
UNEVEN, AUSTERE, WRINKLED,
IRREGULAR

ruin: . . . BANE, BUST, DASH,
DOOM, FALL, HARM, LOSS,
BLAST, BREAK, DECAY, HAVOC,
SPOIL, WRECK, BEGGAR,
BLIGHT, DAMAGE, DEFEAT,
DIDDLE, PERISH, RAVAGE,
DECAYED, DESPOIL, DESTROY,
PERVERT, SUBVERT, BANKRUPT,
CALAMITY, DEMOLISH,
DESOLATE, DISASTER,
DOWNFALL, WRECK(AGE)

rule: . . . . . LAW, LINE, NORM,
SWAY, BYLAW, CANON, GUIDE,
MAXIM, ORDER, REIGN, DECIDE,
DECREE, DIRECT, GOVERN,
MANAGE, METHOD, REGIME,
COMMAND, CONDUCT,
CONTROL, PRECEPT, PREVAIL,
REGIMEN, DECISION, DOMINEER,
REGULATE, STANDARD,
CRITERION, REGULATION

ruler: . . . . AMIR, CZAR, EMIR, KING, LORD, SHAH, TSAR, TZAR, AMEER, EMEER, PRIOR, QUEEN, RAJAH, DESPOT, FERULE, GERENT, PRINCE, REGENT, SULTAN, TYRANT, EMPEROR, MONARCH, AUTOCRAT, GOVERNOR, POTENTATE, SOVERIGN

rumble: . . . . GROWL, MELEE, RUMOR, REPORT, RIPPLE, UPROAR, GRUMBLE, COMPLAINT, FREE-FOR-ALL, DISTURBANCE

rumen: . . . . . . CUD, GULLET, PAUNCH, STOMACH

ruminant: . . OX, YAK, DEER, GOAT, BISON, CAMEL, LLAMA, MOOSE, OKAPI, SHEEP, ALPACA, CATTLE, VICUNA, BUFFALO, CHEWING, GIRAFFE, ANTELOPE, MEDITATIVE

ruminate: . . . . CHEW, MULL, MUSE, THINK, WEIGH, PONDER, REFECT, COGITATE, CONSIDER, MEDITATE

rummage: . . . . . SALE, GRUB, GATHER, LITTER, SEARCH, COLLECT, DERANGE, EXAMINE, RANSACK, RUBBISH

rumor: . . . BUZZ, TALK, TELL, WORD, BRUIT, STORY, CLAMOR, GOSSIP, MURMUR, REPORT, SPREAD, UPROAR, HEARSAY, WHISPER, GRAPEVINE, SCUTTLEBUTT

rumple: . . . . MUSS, CREASE, TOUSLE, CRIMPLE, CRUMPLE, WRINKLE, DISHEVEL

rumpus: . . . see **row, ruckus**

run: . . . . GO, HIE, PLY, DART, DASH, FLOW, GAIT, HUNT, LEAK, LOPE, POUR, RACE, SCUD, TRIP, TROT, HURRY, ROUTE, SCOOT, SPEED, COURSE, EXTEND, GALLOP, GOVERN, HASTEN, MANAGE, OUTPUT, PURSUE, SCURRY, SPRINT, CONDUCT, JOURNEY, OPERATE, SCAMPER, SMUGGLE, CONTINUE, FUNCTION, STAMPEDE

run away: . . . . . BOLT, FLEE, ELOPE, DECAMP, DESERT, ESCAPE, ABSCOND

runaway: . . . . ESCAPEE, DESERTER, FUGITIVE, RUNAGATE

rundle: . . BALL, DRUM, RUNG, STEP, CIRCLE, SPHERE

rundlet: . . . . . CASK, BARREL

rung: . . . . ROD, STEP, SPOKE, STAFF, STAIR, STAKE, TREAD, RUNDLE, CROSSBAR

runnel: . . . . . BROOK, CREEK, RIVULET, RUNLET, CHANNEL

runner: . . . RUG, SKI, AGENT, BLADE, MILER, RACER, RAVEL, SCARF, SKATE, STOLON, COURIER, OPERATOR, SMUGGLER, MESSENGER

running: . . LINEAR, CURRENT, CURSIVE, MELTING, FLOWING, CREEPING, CLIMBING, CONTINUOUS

runt: . . CHIT, DWARF, PYGMY

runway: . . . . . . PATH, RAMP, CHUTE, STRIP, TRACK, GROOVE, TROUGH, CHANNEL, AIRSTRIP

rupture: . . . . . . REND, RENT, BREAK, BURST, SPLIT, BREACH, HERNIA, RUCTION, FRACTURE, DISRUPTION

rural: . . . . RUSTIC, BUCOLIC, COUNTRY, GEOPONIC, PASTORAL, AGRESTIC, ARCADIAN

ruse: . . HOAX, WILE, DODGE, FEINT, FRAUD, TRICK, DECEIT, ARTIFICE, STRATEGEM, SUBTERFUGE

rush: . . . . DART, DASH, GUST, RACE, REED, ROUT, REAR, DRIVE, HASTE, HURRY, PRESS, SALLY, SPATE, SPEED, STRAW, SURGE, ATTACK, CHARGE, HASTEN, HURTLE, HUSTLE, ASSAULT, BULRUSH, CATTAIL,

HIGHTAIL, TORRENT, STAMPEDE, ONSLAUGHT

rusk: . . CAKE, BREAD, CRISP, TOAST, BISCUIT, ZWIEBACK

rust: . . . . ERODE, OXIDE, AERUGO, BLIGHT, CANKER, FUNGUS, PATINA, CORRODE, EROSION, OXIDIZE, CORROSION, OXIDATION, VERDIGRIS

rustic: . . . BOOR, CLOD, HICK, HIND, JAKE, RUBE, RUDE, CHURL, PLAIN, ROUGH, RURAL, YOKEL, COARSE, SIMPLE, SYLVAN, ARTLESS, BOORISH, BUCOLIC, BUMPKIN, HAYSEED, PEASANT, AGRESTIC, PASTORAL, Arcadian

rustler: . . . . . THIEF, ROBBER

rut: . . . . DITCH, TRACK, GROOVE, FURROW, ROUTINE

ruthless: . . . CRUEL, SAVAGE, PITILESS, FEROCIOUS

rye: . . . . RIE, GRAIN, GRASS, CEREAL, WHISKY, GENTLEMAN

ryot: . . . . . FARMER, TENANT, PEASANT

S

S: *Greek:* . . . . SIGMA
Hebrew: . . . . SIN

sabotage: . . . . DESTROY, UNDERMINE, VADALIZE, DESTRUCTION

sac: . . BAG, POD, CYST, SACK, SAUK, BURSA, POUCH, CAVITY, INDIAN, VESICLE

saccharine: . . SWEET, SIRUPY, SUGARY

sack: . . . . . BAG, BED, BASE, LOOT, POKE, RUIN, GUNNY, POUCH, PURSE, WASTE, BURLAP, JACKET, RAVISH, WALLET, DISMISS, PILLAGE, PLUNDER, DESOLATE, DISCHARGE

sacrament: . . MASS, SYMBOL, BAPTISM, PENANCE, MATRIMONY, EUCHARIST, COMMUNION, CONFIRMATION

sacrarium: . . . . CHAPEL, CHANCEL, SHRINE, SANCTUARY

sacred: . . . . . . HOLY, DIVINE, BLESSED, HALLOWED, VENERATED, INVIOLATE, SACROSANCT, INVIOLABLE, CONSECRATED

sacrifice: . . . . . . HOST, COST, LOSS, HOMAGE, VICTIM, IMMOLATE, OFFERING, OBLATION

sacrilege: . . . . . BLASPHEMY, DESECRATION, PROFANATION

sacrilegious: . . . . . PROFANE, IRREVERENT, BLASPHEMOUS

sacrosanct: . . . HOLY, DIVINE, SACRED, INVIOLABLE

sad: . . . . . BAD, BLUE, DARK, SORRY, DISMAL, DREARY, GLOOMY, SOMBER, TRISTE, WOEFUL, UNHAPPY, DEJECTED, DOLEFUL, DOLOROUS, DOWNCAST, MOURNFUL, SORROWFUL

saddle: . . . PAD, LOAD, SEAT, RIDGE, ENCUMBER
part: . . . . . HORN, PANEL, GIRTH, POMMEL, CINCH, STIRRUP, CANTLE, LATIGO

sadness: . . . . BLUES, DUMPS, DOLAR, PATHOS

safari: . . . . HUNT, TREK, JOURNEY, EXPEDITION, CARAVAN

safe: . . . . BOX, SURE, CHEST, VAULT, COFFER, SECURE, UNHARMED, STRONGBOX, DEPOSITORY

safeguard: . . . PASS, CONVOY, GUARD, ESCORT, DEFEND, PROTECT

safety: . . . . SECURITY

sag: . . . . BEND, FLAG, HANG, SINK, WILT, CURVE, DRIFT, DROOP, SLUMP, SETTLE, DECLINE

saga: . . . . EPIC, EDDA, TALE, MYTH, STORY, LEGEND

sagacious: . . . . . SAGE, WISE, ACUTE, QUICK, ASTUTE, SAPIENT, SHREWD, DISCERNING, PERCEPTIVE

sagacity: . . ACUMEN, WISDOM, SAPIENCE

sage: . . . . HERB, MINT, SEER, WISE, GRAVE, NESTOR, SCHOLAR, SAPIENT, SHREWD, SOLEMN, LEARNED

sail: . . FLY, KITE, SCUD, SKIM, SOAR, FLOAT, GLIDE, SHEET, CANVAS, CRUISE, DEPART, EMBARK, VOYAGE, NAVIGATE

kind of: . . . . . . JIB, MAIN, ROYAL, LATEEN, MIZZEN, BALLOON, SPANKER, SPINNAKER

sailboat: . . . . . BARK, DHOW, YAWL, KETCH, SKIFF, SLOOP, SMACK, YACHT, CAIQUE, BARQUE, CARAVEL

sailor: . . . . . GOB, TAR, JACK, SALT, LASCAR, NAVYMAN, SEADOG, SHIPMAN, SEAMAN, BLUEJACKET

saint: . . . (see **patron**) HOLY, SANTA, SACRED, BLESSED, HALLOW, BEATIFY, CANONIZE, ENSHRINE

saintly: . . . . . . HOLY, PIOUS, DEVOUT, ANGELIC

sake: . . END, CAUSE, BEHALF, BENEFIT, MOTIVE, REGARD, ACCOUNT, CONCERN, PURPOSE

salaam: . . . . . . BOW, SALUTE, OBEISANCE, GREETING

salacious: . . LEWD, OBSCENE, LUSTFUL, SCABROUS

salary: . . . . FEE, PAY, WAGE, REWARD, STIPEND, EMOLUMENT, RECOMPENSE, COMPENSATION

sale: . . . DEAL, VEND, BARTER, MARKET, AUCTION, BARGAIN, SELLING, RUMMAGE, TRANSFER, VENDITION

sales talk: . . . . . LINE, SPIEL, PATTER, PITCH

salesman: . . . AGENT, CLERK, HAWKER, SUTLER, VENDOR, DRUMMER, PEDDLER, SOLICITOR

salient: . . TRENCH, CAPERING, LEAPING, NOTICEABLE, PROMINENT, CONSPICUOUS

salina: . . LAKE, POND, MARSH

saline: . TEAR, BRINE, SALTY, MARINAL, BRACKISH

sallow: . . WAN, PALE, PASTY, MUDDY, OSIER, PALLID, PARLOUS, WILLOW

sally: . . . . . JEST, LEAP, QUIP, ISSUE, ATTACK, SORTIE, RETORT, JAUNT, EXCURSION, WITTICISM, RIPOSTE, OUTBREAK

salon: . . . HALL, ROOM, SHOP, SHOW, LEVEE, GALLERY, RECEPTION

saloon: . . BAR, DIVE, COACH, TAVERN, BARROOM, CANTINA, GINMILL, GROGSHOP, DRAMSHOP, GROGGERY, HONKY-TONK

salt: . . SAL, TAR, WIT, ALUM, BORAX, BRINE, ESTER, SALIC, HUMOR, SHARP, WITTY, ALKALI, FLAVOR, SAILOR, SALINE, SEASON, PIQUANT, PICRATE

saltant: . . LEAPING, DANCING, JUMPING

salubrious: . . . . . SALUTARY, HEALTHFUL, WHOLESOME, BENEFICIAL

salutary: . . . . GOOD, BENIGN, HEALTHY, SALUBRIOUS, HEALTHFUL, BENEFICIAL, WHOLESOME

salutation: . . . . . . AVE, BOW, HAIL, ALOHA, HELLO, HOWDY, SALAAM, SALUTE, GREETING, WELCOME

salute: . . . . . BOW, NOD, TIP, HAIL, KISS, GREET, SALVO, CURTSY, WELCOME

salvage: . . . . . SAVE, RESCUE

salvation: . . . . RESCUE, REDEMPTION, PRESERVATION

salve: . . . . . . BALM, ANOINT, LOTION, SOOTHE, PLASTER, POMADE, ASSUAGE, UNGUENT, DEMULCENT, SMOOTH, OINTMENT

salver: . . . . . . TRAY, WAITER

salvo: . . . . . EXCUSE, SALUTE, VOLLEY, PRETEXT, EVASION, BROADSIDE, EXCEPTION, FUSILLADE

same: . . . ID, ILK, IBID, IDEM, LIKE, DITTO, ALIKE, EQUAL, SIMILAR, IDENTICAL

Samoan: . . . . . . POLYNESIAN

samovar: . . . . URN, TEAPOT

samp: . . GRITS, MEAL, MUSH, CEREAL, HOMINY, PORRIDGE

sample: . . . TRY, TEST, TASTE, SWATCH, EXAMPLE, PATTERN, SPECIMEN

sanatory: . . . . HEALING, CURATIVE, HEALTHFUL

sanctify: . . . . BLESS, PURIFY, HALLOW, DEDICATE, CONSECRATE

sanctimonious: . . . . . . HOLY, PIOUS, DEVOUT, SACRED, SAINTLY

sanction: . . LAW, AMEN, FIAT, ALLOW, ASSENT, DECREE, PERMIT, RATIFY, APPROVE, CONFIRM, ENDORSE, SUPPORT, ACCREDIT, APPROVAL, AUTHORIZE, ENCOURAGE, IMPRIMATURE

sanctuary: . . . BEMA, FANE, ABBEY, HAVEN, ASYLUM, CHAPEL, CHURCH, REFUGE, SHRINE, TEMPLE, SHELTER, CONVENT, RETREAT, SANCTUM, CLOISTER, HALIDOME, MONASTERY, RESERVATION

sanctum: . . . . . . DEN, STUDY, ADYTUM, OFFICE, SANCTUARY

sand: . . . DUNE, GRIT, BEACH, NERVE, ABRADE, DESERT, POLISH, SMOOTH, COURAGE

sandal: . . . . CLOG, SHOE, TALARIA, SLIPPER, HUARACHE

sandbar: . . DUNE, REEF, SPIT, BEACH, SHELF, SHOAL

sandy: . . . GRITTY, ARENOSE, SHIFTING, SABULOUS, ARENACEOUS

sane: . . WISE, LUCID, SOBER, SOUND, NORMAL, SAPIENT, RATIONAL, SENSIBLE, REASONABLE

sang froid: . . . . POISE, CALMNESS, COOLNESS, COMPOSURE, INSOUCIANCE

sanguine: . . . . RED, RUDDY, HOPEFUL, CHEERFUL, CONFIDENT, OPTIMISTIC

sanitary: . . . . HYGIENIC

sans: . . . . WITHOUT

sap: . . DIG, LAC, DUPE, FOOL, MILK, DRAIN, FLUID, JUICE, LATEX, VIGOR, ENERGY, TRENCH, WEAKEN, EXHAUST, VITALITY, UNDERMINE, DEBILITATE

sapid: . . . . . TASTY, SAVORY, TASTEFUL, PALATABLE

sapience: . . . . WISDOM, SAGACITY

sapient: . . SAGE, SANE, WISE, SHREWD, KNOWING, SAGACIOUS, DISCERNING

sapor: . . . . . . TANG, SAVOR, TASTE, FLAVOR, RELISH

sapper: . . . . . MINER, DIGGER

sappy: . . . . . INANE, JUICY, MOIST, PLUMP, SILLY, FATUOUS, FOOLISH

sarcasm: . . . . JEER, GIBE, IRONY, TAUNT, SATIRE, REBUKE, MOCKERY, RIDICULE

sarcastic: . . . . DRY, BITING, IRONIC, CUTTING, CAUSTIC, MORDANT, SARDONIC, VITRIOLIC

sarcophagus: . . TOMB, COFFIN

sardonic: . . . . DERISIVE, SARCASTIC

sash: . . . . OBI, BAND, BELT, TOBE, FRAME, SCARF, GIRDLE,

CASEMENT, WAISTBAND,
CUMMERBUND

Satan: . DEIL, NICK, DEMON,
DEVIL, EBLIS, FIEND, BELIAL,
LUCIFER, TEMPTER, MEPHISTO

satanic: . . . . . EVIL, WICKED,
INFERNAL, DIABOLICAL

satchel: . . . . BAG, CASE, GRIP,
VALISE

sate: . . . . . CLOY, CRAM, FILL,
GLUT, GORGE, STUFF, GRATIFY,
SATIATE, SATISFY, SURFEIT

satellite: . . . . . LUNA, MOON,
PLANET, FOLLOWER,
DEPENDENT

satiate: . . . . see **sate**

satire: . . . . WIT, IRONY,
PARODY, LAMPOON, MOCKERY,
SARCASM, RIDICULE

satisfaction: . . . . EASE, GREE,
AMENDS, CONTENT, PAYMENT,
PLEASURE, ATONEMENT,
RECOMPENSE, REPARATION

satisfy: . . . PAY, CLOY, FEED,
FILL, MEET, SATE, SUIT,
ATONE, REPAY, SERVE, SLAKE,
SOLVE, ANSWER, PLEASE,
SUPPLY, APPEASE, ASSUAGE,
CONTENT, EXPIATE, FULFILL,
GRATIFY, SATIATE, SUFFICE,
SURFEIT, CONVINCE

saturate: . . . . SOP, WET, FILL,
GLUT, SOAK, IMBUE, SOUSE,
STEEP, DRENCH, SEETHE,
INGRAIN, SATIATE, PERMEATE,
IMPREGNATE

saturnine: . . . . DULL, GLUM,
GRAVE, HEAVY, GLOOMY,
MOROSE, SULLEN, TACITURN

satyr: . . . FAUN, IDOL, DIETY,
LECHER, BUTTERFLY

sauce: . . . . . DIP, SOY, CHILI,
CURRY, FLAVOR, RELISH,
SEASON, MORNAY, DRESSING,
SOUBISE, TABASCO, MATELOTE,
VELOUTE, WORCHESTER

saucy: . . . ARCH, BOLD, PERT,
RUDE, BRASH, FRESH, SASSY,
COCKY, PERKY, FLIPPANT,

MALAPERT, IMPUDENT,
INSOLENT, IMPERTINENT

saunter: . . . . . . IDLE, ROAM,
ROVE, WALK, AMBLE, DAWDLE,
LOITER, POTTER, RAMBLE,
STROLL, WANDER

saurian: . . . LIZARD, REPTILE,
CROCODILE, DINOSAUR,
ALLIGATOR

sausage: . . . SALAMI, WEINER,
BALOGNA, BALONEY, SAVELOY,
FRANKFURTER, BRATWURST,
LIVERWURST

savage: . . . FELL, GRIM, WILD,
BRUTE, CRUDE, CRUEL, FERAL,
BRUTAL, FERINE, FIERCE,
BESTIAL, BRUTISH, FURIOUS,
RUGGED, UNTAMED, RUTHLESS,
FEROCIOUS, BARBARIAN,
BARBAROUS, PRIMATIVE

savanna(h): . . . . PLAIN,
GRASSLAND

savant: . . . . SAGE, SCHOLAR,
PUNDIT

save: . . . BUT, KEEP, AMASS,
GUARD, HOARD, SALVE, SPARE,
STORE, DEFEND, EXCEPT,
REDEEM, RESCUE, RETAIN,
SCRIMP, UNLESS, HUSBAND,
PROTECT, RESERVE, SALVAGE,
CONSERVE, PRESERVE

saving: . . . . EXCEPT, FRUGAL,
THRIFTY

savoir-faire: . . . . TACT,
ADROITNESS, DIPLOMACY

savor: . . . ODOR, ZEST, SAPOR,
SCENT, SMACK, TASTE, SMELL,
AROMA, TINGE, SEASON,
FLAVOR, RELISH

savory: . . . . . . SALTY, SAPID,
TASTY, YUMMY, PIQUANT,
PLEASING, AGREEABLE,
PALATABLE, APPETIZING

saw: . . . . (also see **see**) CUT,
ADAGE, AXIOM, MAXIM,
MOTTO, SAYING, CLICHE,
PROVERB, APHORISM

sawyer: . . . BEETLE, LOGMAN,
LUMBERMAN, WOODCUTTER

say: .... AVER, DEEM, TELL, MOUTH, SPEAK, STATE, UTTER, ADVISE, ALLEGE, ASSERT, CHANCE, RECITE, RELATE, REMARK, REPEAT, REPORT, DECLARE, EXPRESS, ITERATE, ANNOUNCE, INDICATE

saying: .... see saw

scab: ...... CRUST, MANGE, ESCHAR, BLACKLEG, SCOUNDREL, STRIKEBREAKER

scabbard: .... CASE, SHEATH(E), HOLSTER, PILCHER

scabrous: ... MANGY, SCALY, RISQUE, SALACIOUS

scaffold: ...... CAGE, LOFT, EASEL, GIBBET, GALLOWS, PLATFORM

scale: .... CUP, BOWL, FILM, HUSK, PEEL, RATE, RULE, SHED, SIZE, CLIMB, FLAKE, GAMUT, WEIGH, ASCEND, LAMINA, VESSEL, WEIGHT, BALANCE, CLAMBER, COATING, LAMELLA, MEASURE, ESCALADE, GRADATION

scallion: ..... LEEK, ONION, SHALLOT

scallop: .. PINK, QUIN, CRENA, NOTCH, CRENATE, MOLLUSK, CRENULATION

scalp: .... ROB, SKIN, CHEAT, DEFEAT, TROPHY

scaly: .... LOW, BASE, MEAN, SCURFY, SCABBY, MANGY, LEPROSE, SQUAMATE

scamp: .... IMP, ROUGE, RASCAL, SCALAWAG, SCOUNDREL, SCAPEGRACE, SPALPEEN

scamper: .. RUN, RACE, SCUD, SPEED, HASTEN SCURRY, BRATTLE, SKITTER, SKEDADDLE

scan: .. EYE, STUDY, WATCH, PERUSE, SURVEY, EXAMINE, OBSERVE, ANALYZE, SCRUTINIZE

scandal: .... ODIUM, SHAME, GOSSIP, CALUMNY, DISGRACE, OUTRAGE, SLANDER, IGNOMINY

scandalize: . SHOCK, OFFEND, OUTRAGE, MALIGN

scandalous: ..... LIBELOUS, SHOCKING, SHAMEFUL, OFFENSIVE

Scandinavian: ...... DANE, LAPP, NORSE, SWEDE, NORDIC, NORSEMAN, ICELANDER, NORWEGIAN

scant: ... FEW, LEAN, CHARY, SHORT, STINT, MEAGER, HARROW, SCRIMP, SLIGHT, SPARSE, LIMITED, SPARING, INADEQUATE

scantling: .... BEAM, STUD, TIMBER

scanty: ..... CLOSE, SHORT, SMALL, SPARE, MEAGER, SPARSE, SCARCE, LIMITED, SPARING, EXIGUOUS, INSUFFICIENT

scapegoat: ..... BUTT, DUPE, PATSY, VICTIM

scapegrace: .. ROGUE, SCAMP, RASCAL, SCALAWAG

scar: .... MAR, MARK, ROCK, SEAM, SLIT, CLIFF, DEFACE, BLEMISH, CICATRIX, CICATRICE, POCKMARK, DISFIGURE

scarab: .... CHARM, BEETLE

scarce: . DEAR, RARE, SCANT, SHORT, MEAGER, SCANTY, SPARSE, UNCOMMON, INFREQUENT

scarcely: ... BARELY, HARDLY

scarcity: ...... LACK, NEED, WANT, DEARTH, FAMINE, RARITY, POVERTY, PAUCITY, SHORTAGE

scare: ... AWE, FEAR, ALARM, DREAD, PANIC, FRIGHT, STARTLE, TERRIFY, FRIGHTEN

scarf: ..... BOA, TIE, BAND, SARI, SASH, WRAP, ASCOT, COVER, SHAWL, STOLE, CRAVAT, TAPULO, TIPPET,

MUFFLER, NECKTIE, FOULARD,
KERCHIEF, MANTILLA,
BABUSHKA, NECKERCHIEF
scarp: .... SLOPE, DECLIVITY
scathing: ... BITING, SEVERE,
MORDANT, BLASTING, SEARING,
SCORCHING, WITHERING
scatter: ... SOW, DEAL, ROUT,
SHED, FLING, SPRAY, STREW,
DISPEL, LITTER, SHOWER,
RADIATE, SPRINKLE, DISPERSE,
DISSIPATE
scatterbrained: .... GIDDY,
FLIGHTY, FRIVOLOUS
scattered: . SPARSE, ERRATIC,
SPORADIC, STREWN, IRREGULAR
scenario: ..... PLOT, SCRIPT,
OUTLINE, LIBRETTO,
CONTINUITY
scend: .... HEAVE, PITCH
scene: ..... ACT, SITE, VIEW,
SIGHT, VISTA, LOCALE,
DIORAMA, DISPLAY, EPISODE,
PICTURE, QUARREL, TABLEAU,
SETTING, LANDSCAPE,
SPECTACLE
scenic: .... DRAMATIC,
PANORAMIC, THEATRICAL,
PICTURESQUE
scent: ... CLUE, NOSE, ODOR,
AROMA, SAVOR, SMELL, SNIFF,
SPOOR, TRACK, BREATH,
FLAVOR, BOUQUET, ESSENCE,
PERFUME, EFFLUVIA,
FRAGRANCE
scepter: ...... ROD, MACE,
BATON, STAFF, WAND,
EMBLEM, FERULA, TRIDENT
schedule: . ... BOOK, CARD,
LIST, PLAN, TIME, SLATE,
TABLE, AGENDA, TARIFF,
ROUTINE, CALENDAR, REGISTER,
CATALOG(UE), INVENTORY,
TIMETABLE
schema: ..... PLAN, FIGURE,
OUTLINE, DIAGRAM
scheme: ... AIM, GIN, WEB,
PLAN, PLOT, ANGLE, CABAL,
DRAFT, TABLE, DESIGN,

DEVICE, DEVISE, FIGURE,
RACKET, CONCOCT, DIAGRAM,
SYSTEM, PROJECT, OUTLINE,
PURPOSE, CONSPIRE, INTRIGUE
scheming: .. CRAFTY, TRICKY
schism: ... RENT, SECT, SPLIT,
BREACH, DIVISION, SECESSION,
SEPARATION
scholar: .... PUPIL, PEDANT,
PUNDIT, SAVANT, STUDENT,
LEARNER, CLASSICIST,
ACADEMICIAN
scholarly: .... ERUDITE,
LEARNED, STUDIOUS,
SCHOLASTIC
school: .. CULT, SECT, DRILL,
ECOLE, FLOCK, GROUP, LYCEE,
TRAIN, TEACH, LYCEUM,
MANEGE, COLLEGE, CONVENT,
EDUCATE, ACADEMY, SEMINAR,
INSTRUCT, SEMINARY,
CULTIVATE, UNIVERSITY,
INSTITUTION
science: ...... ART, SKILL,
OLOGY, TECHNICS,
TECHNOLOGY
scintilla: .. BIT, ATOM, IOATA,
WHIT, SPARK, TRACE, PARTICLE
scintillate: ... FLASH, GLEAM,
GITTER, SPARKLE, TWINKLE
scion: ..... BUD, SON, HEIR,
SLIP, TWIG, SHOOT, SPRIG,
SPROUT, OFFSHOOT, OFFSPRING,
DESCENDANT
scoff: .. GIB, GIRD, JEER, JIBE,
LEER, MOCK, RAIL, FLEER,
FLOUT, SNEER, TAUNT, DERIDE,
RIDICULE
scold: ..... JAW, NAG, YAP,
RAIL, RANT, RATE, ABUSE,
CHIDE, DERIDE, (BE)RATE,
REPROVE, REBUKE, UPBRAID,
REVILE, CHASTISE, LAMBASTE
sconce: ... HUT, FORT, HEAD,
SHED, COVER, SKULL, BRAINS,
HELMET, SCREEN, BRACKET,
BULWARK, FORTIFY, LANTERN,
SHELTER, ENTRENCH

scoop: . . . . . DIG, BAIL, BEAT, LADE, GOUGE, LADLE, SPOON, BUCKET, DIPPER, DREDGE, SHOVEL, TROWEL, EXCAVATE

scoot: . . DART, SCUD, SHOOT, BEGONE, DECAMP, SCURRY, SKEDADDLE

scope: . . . AREA, GOAL, ROOM, AMBIT, RANGE, REACH, THEME, DOMAIN, EXTENT, IMPORT, LENGTH, OBJECT, SPHERE, TARGET, DISTANCE, LATITUDE

scorch: . . BURN, CHAR, FLAY, SEAR, SKIN, PARCH, SCORE, SINGE, STING, TOAST, SCATHE, WITHER, BLISTER, SCRATCH, SHRIVEL

score: . . . . . . CUT, RUN, TAB, DEBT, GOAL, LINE, MARK, RATE, CHALK, COUNT, JUDGE, NOTCH, SCOLD, SLASH, TALLY, ABRADE, FURROW, GRUDGE, NUMBER, RECORD, SCOTCH, RATING, TWENTY, WEIGHT, ACCOUNT, SCRATCH, UPBRAID, CRITICIZE

scoria: . . . . AA, LAVA, SLAG, DROSS, REFUSE

scorn: . . . JEER, MOCK, SCOFF, SPURN, DERIDE, REJECT, SLIGHT, CONDEMN, CONTEMN, DESPISE, DISDAIN, CONTEMPT, DERISION

scornful: . . ALOOF, HAUGHTY, STUCKUP, ARROGANT, INSOLENT, DISDAINFUL

scot: . . . . TAX, LEVY, ASSESS

Scot: . . . GAIL, PICT, KILTIE, CALENDONIA, HIGHLANDER

scotch: . . CUT, STOP, BLOCK, CHECK, CRUSH, NOTCH, SCORE, WEDGE, HINDER, STIFLE, STINGY, WHISKY, SCRATCH, FRUSTRATE

scoundrel: . . . . . CAD, SCAB, CHEAT, KNAVE, ROGUE, SCAMP, RASCAL, VARLET, BEGGAR, VILLAIN, MISCREANT, REPROBATE, BLACKGUARD

scour: . . . . RUB, BEAT, RAKE, SAND, WASH, CLEAN, FLUSH, PURGE, SCRUB, POLISH, PUNISH, SCRAPE, SEARCH, CLEANSE, FURBISH, BRIGHTEN

scourge: . . . . BANE, FLAY, FLOG, LASH, WHIP, HARRY, SLASH, PLAGUE, PUNISH, SWITCH, AFFLICT, TORMENT, CHASTISE, AFFLICTION, DISCIPLINE

scout: . . . . . GUY, SPY, CHAP, JEER, LOOK, SCOFF, WATCH, FELLOW, SEARCH, EXPLORE, LOOKOUT, OBSERVE, EMISSARY, RIDICULE, TENDERFOOT, RECONNOITER

scow: . . . . BOAT, BARGE, FLATBOAT, LIGHTER

scowl: . . . . LOUR, MOUE, FROWN, GLARE, (G)LOWER, GRIMACE

scraggly: . . . ROUGH, JAGGED, RAGGED, UNKEMPT, IRREGULAR

scraggy: . BONY, LEAN, THIN, ROUGH, WEEDY, RUGGED, SKINNY

scram: . . . LAM, SCAT, SHOO, BEAT IT, VAMO(O)SE

scramble: . . . . . MIX, CLIMB, CROWD, JOSTLE, SPREAD, STRIVE, CLAMBER, SCUFFLE

scrap: . . BIT, END, ORT, RAG, CHIP, JUNK, FIGHT, GRAIN, PIECE, SHRED, WASTE, MORSEL, REFUSE, DISCARD, ODDMENT, QUARREL, REMNANT, LEFTOVER, ARGUMENT, FRAGMENT, FRACTION

scrape: . . . . BOW, HOE, ROW, RUB, RAKE, RASP, SCUD, ERASE, GRATE, GRAZE, GRIDE, SCOUR, SCUFF, SHAVE, ABRADE, DREDGE, GATHER, SCRATCH, DIFFICULTY, PREDICAMENT

scratch: . . . . DIG, MAR, RUB, CLAW, LINE, MARK, RAKE, CHAFE, ERASE, GRATE, SCORE,

WOUND, CANCEL, FURROW,
GATHER, INJURY, SCOTCH,
SCRAPE, SCRAWL, EXPUNGE,
SCORIFY, INCISION, SCRIBBLE

scrawny: ...... LEAN, THIN,
SCRAGGY, RAWBONED

scream: .. CRY, WAIL, YELL,
YOWL, SHRIEK, SQUALL

scree: ...... STONE, TALUS,
PEBBLE, RUBBLE

screech: ...... see **scream**

screen: .. CAGE, HIDE, MASK,
MESH, SIFT, VEIL, BLIND,
CLOAK, COVER, GRILL, SHADE,
SIEVE, FILTER, GRILLE,
PURDAH, SCONCE SHIELD,
SHROUD, CONCEAL, CURTAIN,
PROTECT, SECLUDE, SHELTER,
PARTITION

screw: ... KEY, TURN, WIND,
WORM, CHEAT, GUARD, MISER,
TWIST, GIMLET, SALARY,
SPIRAL, DISTORT, SQUEEZE,
TIGHTEN, PROPELLER

screwball: ...... NUT, SAP,
CRANK, DIPPY, FANATIC,
CRACKPOT, DUMBBELL,
BLOCKHEAD, ECCENTRIC,
PECULIAR, IRRATIONAL
IMPRACTICAL

scribble: .... DASH, SCRAWL,
WRITE, DOODLE

scribe: .... CLERK, WRITER,
AUTHOR, COPIER, NOTARY,
PENMAN, DRAFTSMAN,
SECRETARY, SCRIVENER,
JOURNALIST

scrimmage: .. PLAY, BATTLE,
MELEE, FIGHT, TUSSLE,
AFFRAY, PRACTICE

scrimp: .... SAVE, STINT,
SKIMP, SCANTY, ECONOMIZE

scrip: .. BAG, LIST, SATCHEL,
WALLET, WRITING, CERTIFICATE

script: . LIBRETTO, SCENARIO,
PENMANSHIP, HANDWRITING

scripture(s): .. TEXT, WORD,
WRIT, BIBLE, KORAN, TORAH,
SUTRA, ITALA, VULGATE,
ALCORAN

scrofulous: ...... CORRUPT,
DEGENERATE

scroll: .. LIST, ROLL, RECORD,
SPIRAL, VOLUTE, SCHEDULE

scrounge: ... CADGE, STEAL,
PILFER, SEARCH, SPONGE

scrub: .... MOP, RUB, MEAN,
POOR, RANT, WASH, CLEAN,
SCOUR, SMALL, BRUSH,
PALTRY, CLEANSE, INFERIOR

scruple: .... DEMUR, DOUBT,
QUALM, MISGIVING

scrupulous: .... EXACT,
HONEST, PROPER, STRICT,
UPRIGHT, CAREFUL, PRECISE,
CORRECT, FINICAL, ACCURATE,
PUNCTILIOUS

scrutinize: ... CON, EYE, PRY,
SCAN, SIFT, PROBE, INSPECT,
EXAMINE, OBSERVE

scud: ..... FLY, RUN, BLOW,
SKIM, GLIDE

scuff: ...... BRUSH, GRAZE,
TOUCH, BUFFET, SCRAPE,
SHUFFLE, SLIPPER

scuffle: ..... FRAY, BRAWL,
FIGHT, MELEE, AFFRAY,
TUSSLE, SHUFFLE, STRUGGLE

scull: ... OAR, BOAT, SHELL,
PROPEL, PADDLE, WHERRY,
ROWBOAT

scum: .... FOAM, SCUD, SILT,
SKIM, DROSS, FROTH, SPUME,
RABBLE, REFUSE, SCORIA,
PELLICLE

scurrilous: .... LOW, FOUL,
VILE, GROSS, COARSE, RIBALD,
VULGAR, ABUSIVE, INDECENT,
INSULTING, OFFENSIVE

scurry: .... HIE, RUN, DART,
RACE, SCOOT, FLURRY,
HASTEN, SCAMPER, SCUTTLE,
HIGHTAIL, SKEDADDLE

scuttle: .... HOD, RUN, SINK,
VETO, SCOOT, BASKET,
BUCKET, SCOTCH, SCURRY,
SCAMPER, SHOVEL, HATCHWAY

scuttlebut:. . . RUMOR, GOSSIP

sea: . . . . DEEP, MAIN, MARE, WAVE, SWELL, OCEAN

arm:. . . . BAY, GULF, LOCH, BAYOU, FIRTH, FIORD, INLET, LOUGH, ESTUARY

seal: . . . . CAP, FIX, SET, WAX, BIND, BULL, SHUT, SIGN, BULLA, CLOSE, SIGIL, STAMP, TOKEN, WAFER, ATTEST, CACHET, CLINCH, FASTEN, PLEDGE, RATIFY, SECURE, SIGNET, CONFINE, CONFIRM, INITIAL, GUARANTY, VALIDATE, GUARANTEE

seam: . . . . . SEW, FOLD, JOIN, LINE, MARK, PURL, SCAR, CLEFT, JOINT, LAYER, RIDGE, STRIP, UNITE, GROOVE, STREAK, SUTURE, CREVICE, FISSURE, WRINKLE, JUNCTURE

seaman: . . . . see **sailor**

seance: . . . MEETING, SESSION, SITTING

sear:. . . (also see **sere**) BURN, MARK, SCAR, BRAND, BROWN, PARCH, SINGE, BRAISE, DEADEN, HARDEN, SCATHE, SCORCH, WITHER, CAUTERIZE

search: . . COMB, GRUB, HUNT, LOOK, NOSE, ROUT, SEEK, DELVE, FRISK, GROPE, PROBE, QUEST, BREVIT, FERRET, FORAGE, PIERCE, SURVEY, CANVASS, EXAMINE, EXPLORE, INQUIRE, INSPECT, RANSACK, RUMMAGE, SCROUNGE, SCRUTINY

season: . . . . AGE, DRY, CORN, CURE, FALL, SALT, TIDE, TIME, DEVIL, IMBUE, INURE, RIPEN, SAVOR, SPICE, TINGE, AUTUMN, FLAVOR, MATURE, SPRING, SUMMER, TEMPER, WINTER, WEATHER, ACCUSTOM, MARINATE, HABITUATE, ACCLIMATE

seasonable: . . . . TIMELY, APROPOS, SUITABLE, OPPORTUNE, APPROPRIATE

seasonal: . . . . PERIODIC

seat: . . FIX, PEW, APSE, FORM, HOLD, HOME, SITE, SOFA, BENCH, CENTER, CHAIR, FLOOR, PLACE, STOOL, PERCH, USHER, ROOST, LOCATE, SEDILE, SETTEE, SETTLE, THRONE, CAPITAL, INSTALL, OTTOMAN, SEDILLA, SITUATE, STATION, TABORET, BLEACHER, BUTTOCKS, LOCATION

sebaceous: . . . . OILY, FATTY. **SECEDE:** . . WITHDRAW, SEPARATE

seclude: . . BAR, DENY, HIDE, EXPEL, REMOVE, RETIRE, SCREEN, EXCLUDE, ISOLATE IMMURE, PROTECT, RETREAT, SEPARATE, WITHDRAW, SEGREGATE, SEQUESTER

secluded: . . . ALOOF, APART, REMOTE, SECRET, PRIVATE, HERMITIC, ISOLATED, SOLITARY

second: . . . AID, ABET, BACK, ECHO, JIFFY, TRICE, ASSIST, ATTEND, BACKER, HANDLE, MOMENT, ANOTHER, CONFIRM, ENDORSE, FURTHER, INSTANT, SUPPORT, SUSTAIN, INFERIOR, ASSISTANT, IMPERFECT, RUNNER-UP

secret: . . DARK, HIDE, BLIND, CABAL, CLOSE, INNER, PRIVY, ARCANE, CLOSET, COVERT, HIDDEN, OCCULT, ARCANUM, CRYPTIC, FURTIVE, MYSTERY, PRIVATE, UNKNOWN, ESOTERIC, INTIMATE, STEALTHY, CONCEALED, UNDERHAND, CLANDESTINE

secretary: . . . . . DESK, CLERK, ESCRITOIRE, AMANUENSIS

secrete: . . BURY, HIDE, OOZE, STOW, STASH, CACHE, EXUDE, CONCEAL

secretion: . . GUM, SAP, BILE, MILK, JUICE, LATEX, MUCUS, RESIN, SUDOR, SWEAT, SALIVA, EXUDATION

sect: . . . . CLAN, CULT, CLASS, GROUP, ORDER, PARTY, SCHOOL, FACTION, SECTION, FOLLOWING, DENOMINATION

sectarian: . . . . BIGOTED, HERETIC, APOSTATE, DISSENTER

section: . . PANE, PART, PIECE, SLICE, PORTION, SEGMENT, DIVISION

secular: . . LAY, LAIC, CIVIL, CARNAL, VULGAR, EARTHLY, PROFANE, WORDLY, TEMPORAL

secure: . . . . . BUY, GET, TIE, BAIL, BIND, BOLT, FAST, FIRM, GIRD, MOOR, NAIL, SAFE, SURE, BELAY, CHAIN, GUARD, TRICE, TRUSS, ANCHOR, ASSURE, CLINCH, ENSURE, FASTEN, OBTAIN, STABLE, ACQUIRE, CERTAIN, PROCURE, PROTECT, CONFIDENT

security: . . . . . . BAIL, BOND, GAGE, GRITH, GUARD, PLEDGE, SAFETY, SURETY, DEFENSE, HOSTAGE, SHELTER, GUARANTY, WARRANTY, INSURANCE, COLLATERAL, SAFEGUARD, GUARANTEE

sedate: . . CALM, COOL, DRUG, GRAVE, QUIET, SOBER, STAID, DEMURE, PROPER, SERENE, SERIOUS, SETTLED, COMPOSED, DECOROUS, DIGNIFIED, TRANQUILIZE

sediment: . . LEE, OOZE, SILT, DREGS, DRAFT, GROUT, MAGMA, WASTE, BOTTOM, REFUSE, SLUDGE, DEPOSIT, GROUNDS

sedition: . . . REVOLT, STRIFE, TUMULT, REBELLION, TREASON

seduce: . . . . . LURE, CHARM, DECOY, TEMPT, ALLURE, ENTICE, CORRUPT, DEBAUCH, INVEIGLE, PERSUADE

sedulous: . . BUSY, DILIGENT, UNTIRING, ASSIDUOUS, LABORIOUS, PERSISTENT

sedum: . . . . STONECROP

see: . . SPY, ESPY, IBID, LOOK, MEET, SCRY, SEAT, VIEW, VISIT, ATTEND, BEHOLD, DESCRY, DETECT, ESCORT, NOTICE, OFFICE, THRONE, DIOCESE, DISCERN, EXAMINE, INSPECT, OBSERVE, WITNESS, DISCOVER, PERCEIVE, VISUALIZE, COMPREHEND

seed: . . . . EGG, PEA, PIP, PIT, SOW, BEAN, GERM, MILT, ACORN, GRAIN, OVULE, SPERM, SPORE, STOCK, KERNAL, ORIGIN, SOURCE, PROGENY, ANCESTRY, BEGINNING, OFFSPRING

seedy: . . . . . . WORN, TACKY, SHABBY, SCRUFFY

seek: . . . . . BEG, SUE, WOO, HUNT, COURT, ESSAY, PROBE, QUEST, SCOUT, TRACE, ASPIRE, FOLLOW, PURSUE, SEARCH, ATTEMPT, BESEECH, ENTREAT, EXPLORE, INQUIRE, REQUEST, SOLICIT, ENDEAVOR, IMPORTUNE, INVESTIGATE

seem: . . . . LOOK, FEIGN, APPEAR, PRETEND, MANIFEST

seemly: . . . . FIT, FAIR, MEET, COMELY, DECENT, PROPER, SUITED, FITTING, DECOROUS, GRACEFUL, SUITABLE

seep: . . LEAK, OOZE, EXUDE, PERCOLATE, PERMEATE, INFILTRATE

seer: . . . . SAGE, AUGUR, MYSTIC, ORACLE, DIVINER, PROPHET, PREDICTOR, FORECASTER, SOOTHSAYER, CLAIRVOYANT

seesaw: . . . . TEETER, TOTTER, ALTENATE, CROSSRUFF, VACILLATE

seethe: ... BOIL, STEW, TEEM, STEEP, BUBBLE, SIMMER, FERMENT, SATURATE

segment: ...... PART, PIECE, DIVIDE, SECTOR, PORTION, SECTION, DIVISION, FRAGMENT, SEPARATE

segregate: .... PART, SEVER, DIVIDE, SELECT, ISOLATE, SECLUDE, CLASSIFY, SEPARATE

seize: .. BAG, COP, NAB, NET, BIND, BITE, CLAW, GRAB, GRIP, HOOK, PREY, TAKE, TRAP, ANNEX, CATCH, GRASP, USURP, WREST, ARREST, ATTACH, CLINCH, CLUTCH, COLLAR, FASTEN, SNATCH, CAPTURE, GRAPNEL, ARROGATE, APPREHEND, CONFISCATE

seldom: ..... RARE, RARELY, INFREQUENT, INFREQUENTLY

select: .... OPT, CULL, DRAW, NAME, PICK, WALE, ELECT, ELITE, ASSIGN, CHOICE, CHOOSE, CHOSEN, PICKED, PREFER, EXCELLENT, EXCLUSIVE, SEGREGATE

self: ..... EGO, OWN, SAME, BEING, PERSONAL, PERSONALITY

assurance: .... POISE, APLOMB, COMPOSURE, CONFIDENCE

centered: ...... SELFISH, EGOCENTRIC, INDEPENDENT

conceit: .. PRIDE, VANITY, EGOTISM

confident: ...... POISED, ASSURED, COCKSURE

conscious: .... SHY, TIMID

esteem: ... PRIDE, VANITY, EGOISM, EGOTISM

evident: .... CLEAR, OBVIOUS, AXIOMATIC

government: .. AUTONOMY, INDEPENDENCE

possessed: .. COOL, CALM, COMPOSED, UNDISTURBED

satisfied: .... SMUG, COMPLACENT

sell: ..... BILK, CANT, DEAL, DUMP, DUPE, GULL, HAWK, HOAX, VEND, CHEAT, TRADE, TRICK, BARTER, BETRAY, MARKET, PEDDLE, RETAIL, AUCTION, BARGAIN, DECEIVE, DISPOSE, CONVINCE, PERSUADE, TRANSFER, NEGOTIATE, WHOLESALE

seller: ... VENDOR, PEDDLER, DEALER, SELLER, SUTLER, TRADER, VENDOR, PEDDLER, RETAILER, SALESMAN, TRADESMAN

semblance: ... COPY, FORM, LOOK, GUISE, IMAGE, ASPECT, FIGURE, PRETEXT, LIKENESS, PRETENSE, APPEARANCE, SIMILARITY

seminary: .... SCHOOL, ACADEMY, COLLEGE, INSTITUTION

send: .... MAIL, SHIP, IMPEL, ISSUE, RELAY, REMIT, CONVEY, DEPUTE, PROPEL, ADDRESS, CONSIGN, DELIVER, FORWARD, INFLICT, PROJECT, DISPATCH, TRANSMIT

senile: ... OLD, AGED, WEAK, DOTTY, DOTARD, INFIRM, ELDERLY, DECREPIT, DODDERING

senior: ...... DEAN, ELDER, OLDER, STUDENT, SUPERIOR

seniority: .... AGE, STATUS, QUALITY, PRIORITY, PRECEDENCE

sensation: ..... HIT, SENSE, EMOTION, FEELING, INTEREST, EXPERIENCE, EXCITEMENT, PERCEPTION

sensational: .... LURID, DRAMATIC, EXCITING, SHOCKING, STARTLING, THRILLING

sense: ..... SEE, FELL, HEAR, MIND, SIGHT, SMELL, TASTE, TOUCH, IMPORT, INTUIT, REASON, SANITY, WISDOM,

FEELING, MEANING, JUDGMENT, PERCEIVE, PRUDENCE, SAPIENCE
organ: ... EAR, EYE, NOSE, SKIN, NERVE, FEELER, TONGUE, ANTENNA, RECEPTOR

senseless: ..... MAD, DUMB, BLIND, INANE, INEPT, ABSURD, STUPID, UNWISE, WANTON, FOOLISH, IDIOTIC, INSENSATE, UNFEELING, HALF-WITTED, IRRATIONAL, UNCONSCIOUS

sensible: ...... SANE, WISE, AWARE, PRUDENT, RATIONAL, REASONABLE

sensitive: ...... RAW, SORE, ACUTE, ALIVE, TENSE, TENDER, TOUCHY, DELICATE, RECEPTIVE, RESPONSIVE

sensual: ..... LEWD, ALIVE, CARNAL, COARSE, FLESHY, LUSTFUL, WORLDLY, SEDUCTIVE, VOLUPTUOUS

sentence: ..... RAP, DOOM, DECIDE, DECREE, SAYING, ADJUDGE, CONDEMN, OPINION, PASSAGE, PROVERB, DECISION, JUDGMENT, STATEMENT

sententious: ... PITHY, SHORT, TERSE, COMPACT, CONCISE, POINTED

sentient: .... ALIVE, LIVING, FEELING, SENSIBLE, CONSCIOUS

sentiment: ...... EMOTION, FEELING, MEANING, OPINION, ATTITUDE, SENSATION

sentimental: ...... GUSHY, MUSHY, MAUDLIN, MAWKISH, SCHMALZ, ROMANTIC, IDEALISTIC

sentinel: ... GUARD, WATCH, PICKET, SENTRY, SOLDIER, LOOKOUT, WATCHMAN

separate: ...... CULL, DEAL, FREE, PART, REND, RIFT, SHED, SIFT, SLAY, SORT, ALONE, ALOOF, APART, ASIDE, SEVER, SPACE, SPLIT, STRIP, BREACH, CLEAVE, DECIDE, DEDUCT,

DEPART, DETACH, DIVIDE, REMOVE, SECEDE, SECERN, SUNDER, WINNOW, ANALYZE, DISJOIN, DISPART, DIVERSE, ISOLATE, ABSTRACT, ALIENATE, DETACHED, DISPERSE, DISTINCT, DISCRETE, SOLITARY, DISENGAGE, SEGREGATE, DISCONNECT

separation: ... GULF, BREAK, SCHISM, DIVORCE, PARTITION, SECESSION

septic: .... PUTRID, ROTTEN, INFECTIVE

septum: ... WALL, PARTITION

sepulcher: .... BURY, TOMB, CRYPT, GRAVE, INTER, VAULT, ENTOMB, MONUMENT, REPOSITORY

sepulchral: .... DISMAL, GLOOMY, FUNEREAL, TOMBLIKE

sequel: .... NEXT, ISSUE, EFFECT, RESULT, UPSHOT, OUTCOME, AFTERMATH, CONCLUSION

sequence: ...... RUN, SET, GAMUT, ORDER, COURSE, SERIES, SEQUEL, STRAIGHT, SUCCESSION

sequester: .... SEIZE, ENISLE, ISOLATE, SECLUDE, SEPARATE, SEGREGATE, CONFISCATE

sequestered: ...... ALONE, LONELY, SEIZED, PRIVATE, RECLUSE, REMOVED, RETIRED, ISOLATED, SECLUDED, SOLITARY, SEPARATED, WITHDRAWN, CLOISTERED, SEGREGATED, CONFISCATED

seraglio: .... SERAI, HAREM, PALACE, ZENANA

serape: ..... CLOAK, SHAWL, BLANKET

seraph: ...... ANGEL, PURE, CHERUB

seraphic: .... ANGELIC

sere: ..... DRY, WAX, WORN, DRIED, PARCHED, SEVERAL,

VARIOUS, SCORCHED, SEPARATE, WITHERED

serene: . . . . . . CALM, COOL, CLEAR, QUIET, BRIGHT, PLACID, SEDATE, STEADY, PACIFIC, EQUABLE, TRANQUIL, IMPASSIVE, COMPOSED

serf: . . . . ESNE, PEON, CHURL, HELOT, SLAVE, THRALL, VASSAL, BONDMAN, VILLEIN, PEASANT

series: . . . . SET, LIST, CHAIN, GAMUT, COURSE, CATEGORY, SEQUENCE, GRADATION, SUCCESSION

serious: . . . DEEP, GRIM, KEEN, GRAVE, HEAVY, SOBER, STAID, SEDATE, SEVERE, SOLEMN, AUSTERE, EARNEST, WEIGHTY, SINCERE, CRITICAL, IMPORTANT, MOMENTOUS

sermon: . . . . TALK, HOMILY, SPEECH, ADDRESS, LECTURE, DISCOURSE

serous: . . . . . . THIN, WATERY

serpent: . . . . see snake

serpentine: . . . WILY, SNAKY, COILED, SINUOUS, TURNING, WINDING, CUNNING, CIRCUITOUS

serried: . . . . DENSE, MASSED, PACKED, COMPACT, CROWDED

servant: . . . . . AMAH, COOK, ESNE, HELP, HIND, MAID, PAGE, GILLY, GROOM, NURSE, SLAVE, VALET, BATMAN, BUTLER, FLUNKY, GARCON, GILLIE, HELPER, LACKEY, MENIAL, VARLET, VASSAL, DOMESTIC

serve: . . . . . ACT, AID, ABET, GIVE, HELP, PASS, TEND, WAIT, CATER, LADLE, ANSWER, ASSIST, ATTEND, SUPPLY, SUCCOR, ADVANCE, DELIVER, FORWARD, FURTHER, SATISFY, FUNCTION, MINISTER, OFFICIATE, DISTRIBUTE

service: . . . . USE, MASS, RITE, WORK, FAVOR, WAGES, FEALTY, HOMAGE, REPAIR, SUPPLY, SLAVERY, UTILITY, MINISTRY, RECOMPENSE, EMPLOYMENT

serviceable: . . . . USEFUL, USABLE, DURABLE, HELPFUL, LASTING, BENEFICIAL

servile: . . BASE, BOND, MEAN, TAME, ABJECT, MENIAL, SORDID, FAWNING, SLAVISH, CRINGING, DEPENDENT, PARASITIC, TRUCKLING, OBSEQUIOUS

servitude: . . YOKE, BONDAGE, PEONAGE, SERFDOM, SERVICE, SLAVERY, SENTENCE, CAPTIVITY

session: . . . . . TERM, SEANCE, MEETING, SITTING, ASSEMBLY

set: . . . . . FIX, GEL, KIT, LAY, PUT, SIT, BENT, CLAN, CLUB, COCK, CREW, GANG, LAID, POST, SEAT, WANE, ALIGN, BATCH, BROOD, EMBED, FIXED, GROUP, IMBED, PLACE, PLANT, READY, RIGID, ADJUST, CEMENT, CIRCLE, CLIQUE, DEFINE, HARDEN, IMPOSE, IMPOST, ORDAIN, RECORD, SERIES, SETTLE, ARRANGE, CONGEAL, COTERIE, DEPOSIT, STATION, STIFFEN, SCENERY, IMMOBILE, REGULATE, RESOLUTE, SOLIDIFY, COAGULATE, DESIGNATE, DETERMINE, ESTABLISH, IMMOVABLE, OBSTINATE, PRESCRIBE, STABILIZE, ASSORTMENT, COLLECTION

apart: . . . ELECT, EXEMPT, ISOLATE, RESERVE, SEGREGATE

aside: . . . . . VOID, ANNUL, DEFER, QUASH, TABLE, EXCEPT, REJECT, DISCARD, DISMISS, EARMARK, EXCLUDE, RESERVE, OVERRULE, SEPARATE

setback: . . . . . LOSS, UPSET, RELAPSE, REVERSE, REVERSAL

settee: . . . SEAT, SOFA, BENCH, DIVAN, LOUNGE

setting: . . . EGGS, TRAP, PAVE, DECOR, SCENE, SHARE, LOCALE, MILIEU, SCENERY, MOUNTING, BACKGROUND, ENVIRONMENT

settle: . . . END, FIX, PAY, SAG, SET, CALM, FIRM, REST, ROUT, SEAT, SINK, SOFA, AGREE, AUDIT, CLEAR, COUCH, LODGE, ORDER, PERCH, PLANT, QUIET, SOLVE, ACCORD, ADJUST, ASSIGN, DECIDE, LOCATE, SECURE, SOOTHE, APPOINT, ARRANGE, CLARIFY, CONFIRM, CONFORM, DEPOSIT, DISPOSE, PROVIDE, RESOLVE, SUBSIDE, COLONIZE, CONCLUDE, ENSCONCE, REGULATE, DESIGNATE, DETERMINE, ESTABLISH, LIQUIDATE, ADJUDICATE

settled: . . FAST, FIXED, STAID, SEDATE, VESTED, CERTAIN, DECIDED, PEOPLED, DECOROUS, SEDENTARY, STEADFAST, CONSISTENT, DETERMINED, UNCHANGING, ESTABLISHED

settlement: . . CAMP, COLONY, HAMLET, PAYMENT, VILLAGE, DECISION, DISPOSAL, FIXATION, SEDIMENT, COMMUNITY, ADJUSTMENT, CONCLUSION, ARRANGEMENT

settler: . . . BOOMER, SOONER, PLANTER, PIONEER, COLONIST, EMIGRANT, IMMIGRANT, HOMESTEADER

sever: . . . . CUT, PART, REND, SLIT, BREAK, BREACH, CLEAVE, DEPART, DETACH, DIVIDE, SUNDER, DISJOIN, DISPART, DIVORCE, DISUNITE, SEPARATE, DISMEMBER, SEGREGATE, DISCONNECT

several: . . . . FEW, SOME, DIVERS, SUNDRY, DIVERSE, VARIOUS, DISTINCT, PECULIAR, SEPARATE, DIFFERENT

severe: . . . BAD, DOUR, HARD, KEEN, ACUTE, CRUEL, GRAVE, GRUFF, HARSH, RIGID, ROUGH, SHARP, STARK, STERN, STIFF, SEDATE, SOLEMN, STRICT, UNKIND, ASCETIC, AUSTERE, CAUSTIC, CRUCIAL, DRASTIC, EXTREME, INTENSE, SERIOUS, VIOLENT, EXACTING, RIGOROUS, DIFFICULT, STRINGENT

sew: . . . . . BIND, DARN, JOIN, MEND, SEAM, TACK, BASTE, SMOCK, GUILT, UNITE, FASTEN, STITCH, SUTURE

sewer: . . . . PIPE, DRAIN, GUTTER, CONDUIT, SEAMSTRESS

sexton: . . . . VERGER, SACRIST(AN), GRAVEDIGGER

sexual: . . . . . GAMIC, CARNAL
continence: . . . . CHASTITY
inclination: . . . . . . LIBIDO

shabby: . . OLD, BASE, MEAN, WORN, DINGY, SEEDY, DOWDY, PALTRY, RAGGED, RATTY, TACKY, UNKEMPT, THREADBARE, DISGRACEFUL

shack: . . HUT, CABIN, HOVEL, SHANTY

shackle: . . . TIE, BAND, BIND, BOND, CURB, GIRD, GYVE, IRON, BILBO, CHAIN, FETTER, HAMPER, HINDER, HOBBLE, PINION, SECURE, CONFINE, MANACLE, TRAMMEL, LEG-IRON, RESTRAIN

shade: . . . . DIM, HUE, DARK, DULL, TINT, TONE, VEIL, COLOR, COVER, TINGE, TRACE, UMBRA, AWNING, CANOPY, DARKEN, DEGREE, NUANCE, SCREEN, SHADOW, SHIELD, CURTAIN, OBSCURE, PROTECT, SHUTTER, UMBRAGE, VESTIGE

shaded walk: . . . . MALL, ARBOR, ARCADE, ALAMEDA, CLOISTER

shading:. . . . . TRACE
UMBER, UMBRA, FOLLOW,
SHROUD, REMNANT, VESTIGE
shady: . DUBIOUS, DOUBTFUL,
SHADOWY, UMBROUS,
DISHONEST, UNDERHANDED
shaft: . . BAR, PIT, RAY, ROD,
AXLE, BEAM, BOLT, FLUE,
HOLE, POLE, STEM, ARBOR,
ARROW, IRONY, LANCE, SHANK,
SPEAR, SPIRE, STALK, THILL,
TRUNK, COLUMN, HANDLE,
PILLAR, TONGUE, CHIMNEY,
CONDUIT, FLAGPOLE, JAVELIN,
MISSLE, OBELISK, SPINDLE
shag: . . . . . MAT, NAP, HAIR,
MANE, MASS, WOOL, FIBER,
REFUSE, TOBACCO, CORMORANT
shaggy: . . . . . BUSHY, FURRY,
HAIRY, NAPPY, ROUGH,
HIRSUTE, SCRUBBY, UNKEMPT,
STRAGGLY
shake: . . JAR, JOG, RID, WAG,
FREE, JOLT, MOVE, ROCK, STIR,
SWAY, TOSS, WAVE, CHURN,
DRINK, QUAKE, SHOCK, SWING,
QUAVER, QUIVER, RATTLE,
SHIVER, TREMOR, WOBBLE,
AGITATE, DISTURB, FLUSTER,
TREMBLE, UNNERVE, VIBRATE,
BRANDISH, CONVULSE,
DISLODGE, EARTHQUAKE
shaky: . . . . . . WEAK, DICKY,
DOTTY, QUAKY, GROGGY,
INFIRM, WOBBLY, RICKETY,
UNSOUND, INSECURE,
TOTTERING, TREMBLING,
TREMULOUS, UNCERTAIN,
UNRELIABLE
shall: . . . . MAY, MUST, WILL,
WOULD, OBLIGED
shallop: . . . . . BOAT, DINGHY
shallot: . . . . . . BULB, ONION,
SCALLION, ESCHALOT
shallow: . . . . WEAK, SHOAL,
FLIMSY, SLIGHT, CURSORY,

FAKE, EBB
CHEAT, FALSE, FEIGN, FRAUD,
PHONY, TRICK, DECEIT,
DELUDE, HUMBUG, DECEIVE,
FORGERY, PRETENSE,
DECEPTION, IMITATION,
ARTIFICIAL, COUNTERFEIT
shaman: . . . . MONK, PRIEST,
CONJURER, MEDICINE MAN
shame: . . FIE, ABASE, ABASH,
BEMEAN, DEGRADE, MORTIFY,
DISGRACE, DISHONOR,
EMBARRASS, HUMILIATE
shameful: . . . . BASE, MEAN,
GROSS, IGNOBILE, IMPROPER,
INDECENT, DEGRADING,
DISHONEST, SCANDALOUS,
DISGRACEFUL, OFFENSIVE
shameless: . . . . BRAZEN,
IMMODEST, IMPUDENT,
ABANDONED
shanghai: . . . . . DRUG, SHIP,
KIDNAP
Shangri-la: . . . . UTOPIA,
PARADISE
shank: . . . LEG, GAMB, SHIN,
STEM, GAMBE, KNIFE, LADLE,
SHAFT
shanty: . . . . see shack
shape: . . . . FIT, HEW, BEND,
CAST, FORM, MAKE, MOLD,
PLAN, TRIM, BLOCK, BUILD,
CARVE, FRAME, GUISE, MODEL,
MOULD, STATE, CREATE,
DESIGN, DEVISE, FIGURE,
ARRANGE, CONFORM, CONTOUR,
FASHION, PHANTON, POSTURE,
WHITTLE, CONTRIVE, CONDITION
shapely: . . . . . . NEAT, TRIM,
SVELT, COMELY
share: . . BIT, CUT, LOT, DEAL,
DOLE, HAND, PART, DIVVY,
QUOTA, RATIO, STAKE, CLEAVE,
DIVIDE, IMPART, MOIETY,
RATION, PARTAKE, PORTION,
DIVIDEND, DIVISION,

ALLOTMENT, ALLOWANCE,
APPORTION, DISTRIBUTE

shark: . GATA, HAYE, MAKO,
TOPE, CHEAT, EXPERT,
LAWYER, USURER, DOGFISH,
SHARPER, SPONGER, MANEATER,
PARASITE, SWINDLER,
THRESHER, PORBEAGLE,
SHOVELHEAD, HAMMERHEAD

sharp: . . . ACID, COLD, FELL,
GLEG, KEEN, SOUR, ACERB,
ACRID, ACUTE, ADEPT, ALERT,
BRISK, CRISP, EDGED, HARSH,
NIPPY, SALTY, SMART, STEEP,
TANGY, WITTY, ABRUPT,
ACUATE, ASTUTE, BARBED,
BITING, BITTER, CLEVER,
CRAFTY, EXPERT, PEAKED,
SEVERE, SHREWD, SHRILL,
CAUSTIC, CUNNING, CUTTING,
GRATING, INTENSE, PIQUANT,
POINTED, PUNGENT, DISTINCT,
HANDSOME, INCISIVE, PIERCING,
SAGACIOUS, TENCHANT,
VITRIOLIC

sharpen: . . . . . . EDGE, HONE,
WHET, STROP, GRIND,
ENHANCE, INTENSIFY

sharpshooter: . . . . . . SHOT,
SNIPER, RIFLEMAN, MARKSMAN

shatter: . . . . . BLOW, DASH,
BLAST, BREAK, BURST, CRASH,
SMASH, WRECK, BATTER,
SHIVER, DESTROY, DISABLE,
SPLINTER

shave: . . . . CUT, PARE, TRIM,
GRAZE, PLANE, SHEAR, SKIVE,
SCRAPE, TONSURE, WHITTLE

shawl: . . . . . MAUD, WRAP,
MANTA, SERAPE, PEPLOS,
TALLITH, MUFFLER, PAISLEY

shay: . . . . . CHAISE, BUGGY,
CARRIAGE

sheaf: . . . . BALE, BUNCH,
BUNDLE, CLUSTER

shear: . . . . . CUT, CLIP, CROP,
REAP, SNIP, TRIM, CARVE,
PRUNE, SEVER, SHAVE, STRIP,
CLEAVE, DIVEST, FLEECE,

REMOVE, DEPRIVE, SCISSOR,
WHITTLE

sheath: . . . . COT, BOOT, CASE,
DRESS, OCREA, THECA, STALL,
SLEEVE, SPATHE, COVERING,
ENVELOPE, CAPSULE, SCABBARD

shebang: . . . . . DEAL, THING,
AFFAIR, MATTER, OUTFIT,
CONCERN, BUSINESS,
CONTRIVANCE

shed: . . . . . . CUT, HUT, BYRE,
CAST, COTE, DROP, EMIT,
HULL, MOLT, PART, PEEL,
BOOTH, CABIN, HOVEL, REPEL,
SCALE, DIVIDE, EFFUSE,
HANGAR, IMPART, LEAN-TO,
SLOUGH, COTTAGE, DIFFUSE,
EMANATE, RADIATE, DISCARD,
SCATTER, SHELTER, DISPERSE,
OUTHOUSE, SEPARATE,
SPRINKLE

sheen: . . . . . . GLEAM, GLOSS,
SHINE, BRIGHT, GLOSSY,
LUSTER, POLISH, GLISTEN,
GLITTER, RADIANT, SHIMMER,
SHINING, LUSTROUS

sheep: . . . . SHA, ARUI, OVINE,
URIAL, AOUDAD, ARGALI,
MERINO, OORIAL, WETHER,
BIGHORN, CARACUL, CHEVIOT,
KARAKUL, MOUFLON,
RUMINANT, BLACKFACE,
BROADTAIL

sheepfold: . . . COT, PEN, REE,
COTE, KRAAL

sheeplike: . . . . MEEK, OVINE,
TIMID, DOCILE

sheer: . . . . FINE, MERE, PURE,
VEER, THIN, TURN, CLEAR,
STARK, STEEP, UTTER, ABRUPT,
SWERVE, DEVIATE, UNMIXED,
ABSOLUTE, DIAPHANOUS,
TRANSPARENT

sheet: . . . . PAGE, ROPE, SAIL,
LINEN, PAPER, PLATE, SHROUD,
EXPANSE, NEWSPAPER

shelf: . . . BANK, BERM, REEF,
SILL, BERME, LEDGE, SHOAL,

MANTEL, BEDROCK, GRADINE, RETABLE, SANDBAR, STRATUM

shell: . . . . POD, BOAT, BOMB, HULL, HUSK, TEST, CONCH, COVER, COWRY, CRUST, MONEY, MUREX, SHARD, SHUCK, DUGOUT, LORICA, STRAFE, ABALONE, BOMBARD, CAPSULE, GRENADE, MISSILE, MOLLUSK, CARAPACE, COVERING, EXTERIOR, CARTRIDGE, PROJECTILE

shellac(k): . . . . . LACK, BEAT, DRUB, RESIN, VARNISH, LACQUER

shellacking: . . . . DEFEAT, BEATING, WHIPPING

shellfish: . . . . . CLAM, CRAB, NACRE, COCKLE, LIMPET, SHRIMP, LOBSTER, MOLLUSK, SCALLOP, ABALONE, BARNACLE, CRUSTACEAN

shelter: . . . (also see asylum, house, shack, shed) LEE, ABRI, BARN, CAMP, PORT, ROOF, TENT, BIELD, BOWER, CLOAK, COVER, HAVEN, BURROW, COVERT, HARBOR, HOSTEL, SCONCE, SCREEN, SHIELD, TRENCH, FOXHOLE, HOSPICE, RETREAT, TRAILER, SANCTUARY, PROTECTION

shelve: . . . . . DEFER, LEDGE, SHELF, TABLE, MANTEL, RETIRE, PROJECT, OVERHANG, PLATFORM, PIGEONHOLE

shenanigan: . . . . TRICK, FOOLERY, MISCHIEF, NONSENSE, TRICKERY

Sheol: . . . . HELL, HADES, UNDERWORLD

shepherd: . . . . . HERD, LEAD, TEND, DRIVE, GUARD, WATCH, ATTEND, GATHER, HERDER, LEADER, PASTOR, GUARDIAN, MINISTER

sheriff: . . . . . REEVE, GRIEVE, BALIFF, OFFICER

shibboleth: . . TEST, SLOGAN, PASSWORD, CRITERION, WATCHWORD

shield: . . . . ECU, EGIS, HIDE, AEGIS, ARMOR, AVERT, CLOAK, COVER, GUARD, SHADE, TARGE, CANOPY, DEFEND, SCREEN, BUCKLER, CONCEAL, DEFENSE, PREVENT, PROTECT, SHELTER, TESTUDO, PROTECTOR

shift: . . . . . RID, DEAL, FEND, HAUL, MOVE, QUIT, STIR, TURN, VEER, AVOID, DODGE, EVADE, FEINT, HOURS, SHUNT, SLIDE, CHANGE, PERIOD, SWITCH, CHEMISE, DEVIATE, DISPOSE, EVASION, REPLACE, SHUFFLE, EXCHANGE, TRANSFER, ASSIGNMENT

shifty: . . . . FICKLE, TRICKY, DEVIOUS, EVASIVE, FURTIVE, CHANGEABLE

shill: . . . . ACCOMPLICE, CONFEDERATE

shillelagh: . . . CLUB, CUDGEL

shilly-shally: . . . . . . HEDGE, WAVER, TRIFLE, HESITATE, VACILLATE

shimmer: . . . . FLASH, LIGHT, GLIMMER, GLISTEN

shimmy: . . . . DANCE, SHAKE, QUIVER, CHEMISE, TREMBLE, VIBRATE

shine: . . . RAY, BEAM, GLOW, BLAZE, EXCEL, GLEAM, LIGHT, GLINT, GLOSS, SHEEN, LUSTER, POLISH, FLICKER, GLISTEN, GLITTER, RADIATE, TWINKLE

shingle: . . . . CLIP, SHIM, SIGN, SLAT, SIDING, HAIRCUT, ROOFING, SIGNBOARD

shining: . . . AGLOW, GLARY, LUCID, NITID, BRIGHT, GLOSSY, LUCENT, BEAMING, EMINENT, GLOWING, RADIANT, GLEAMING, LUSTROUS

ship: . . . . . BOAT, BRIG, SEND, HULK, LINER, YACHT, TARTAN, VESSEL, CLIPPER, TANKER,

GALLEON, AIRCRAFT, DISPATCH, TRANSPORT, FREIGHTER

shirk:... DUCK, FUNK, SHUN, AVOID, DODGE, EVADE, SKULK, SLACK, DESERT, MALINGER, GOLDBRICK

shirker:.. DODGER, EVADER, LOAFER, TRUANT, SLACKER

shirt:.... TEE, POLO, SARK, DRESS, PARKA, SPORT, CAMISE, JERSEY, SKIVVY, CHEMISE

shiver:..... CHILL, QUAKE, SHAKE, BREAK, QUIVER, TREMOR, TWITCH, FLICKER, SHATTER, TREMBLE, SPLINTER, VIBRATE, SHUDDER, FRAGMENT

shoal:.... BAR, BANK, MASS, REEF, SPIT, CROWD, SCHOOL, THRONG, SHALLOW, MULTITUDE

shock:... JAR, BLOW, HEAP, JOLT, PILE, STUN, APPAL, BRUNT, SCARE, SHAKE, FRIGHT, IMPACT, OFFEND, SHAGGY, STROKE, TRAUMA, ASTOUND, DISGUST, HORRIFY, STARTLE, TERRIFY, PARALYZE, COLLISION, CONCUSSION

shoddy:..... POOR, CHEAP, SHABBY, INFERIOR

shoe:.... CUE, BOOT, CLOG, FLAT, MULE, PUMP, SABOT, BROGAN, BROUGE, GAITER, GALOSH, LOAFER, OXFORD, PATTEN, SANDAL, SLIPPER, SNEAKER, MOCCASIN, FOOTWEAR, CLODHOPPER

shoo:....... MOVE, SCAT, GET OUT, SCRAM

shoot:.. BUD, FIRE, POT, ROD, CAST, CHIT, DART, EMIT, FILM, FIRE, GROW, HURL, MOVE, PLUG, PUSH, TWIG, CHUTE, DRIVE, EJECT, SCION, SNIPE, SPEAR, SPOUT, SPRAY, SPRIG, SPURT, THROW, TUBER, UTTER, WOUND, INJECT, PROPEL, SPROUT, STOLON, STRIKE, TWINGE, BURGEON, PROJECT, DISCHARGE

shop:..... STORE, MARKET, PRISON, BOTEGA, FACTORY, BOUTIQUE

shore:... BANK, EDGE, LAND, PROP, SAND, BEACH, BRINK, COAST, RIVAGE, STRAND, SEASIDE, SUPPORT, WATERSIDE

short:.... LOW, CURT, RUDE, BLUFF, BRIEF, BRUSK, CRISP, HARSH, SCANT, TERSE, ABRUPT, SCANTY, SCARCE, BRIEFLY, BRUSQUE, CONCISE, CURTAIL, FRIABLE, LACKING, SUMMARY, SUCCINCT

shortage:..... LACK, NEED, DEFICIT, DEFICIENCY, INSUFFICIENCY

shortcoming:.. FLAW, FAULT, DEFECT, FAILURE, DEFICIENCY, INADEQUACY

shorten:.... BOB, CUT, LOP, CLIP, DOCK, REEF, CHECK, ELIDE, REEVE, LESSEN, REDUCE, ABRIDGE, CURTAIL, DEPRIVE, CONDENSE, CONTRACT, DECREASE, DIMINISH, ABBREVIATE

shortly:..... ANON, SOON, RUDELY, QUICKLY, PRESENTLY

shortsighted:....... DULL, MYOPIC, OBTUSE, NEARSIGHTED

shorty:............. RUNT

shot:... (also see **shoot**) POP, TRY, DOSE, BLANK, DRINK, GUESS, PHOTO, RANGE, REACH, SALLY, SCOPE, SHELL, TIRED, WEARY, BULLET, PELLET, ATTEMPT, FLECKED, MISSILE, MARKSMAN, PROJECTILE

shoulder:.... BERM, EDGE, LIFT, PUSH, TAKE, ASSUME, CARRY, RAISE, AXILA

blade:......... SCAPULA

shout:..... BOO, CRY, HUE, BAWL, CALL, HOOT, ROAR, ROOT, YELL, YELP, CHEER, WHOOP, CLAMOR, HALLOO, HOLLER, HURRAH, OUTCRY, ACCLAIM

shove: . . . . JOG, BUNT, CAST, PUSH, DRIVE, EJECT, NUDGE, SHUNT, HUSTLE, JOSTLE, PROPEL, THRUST

shovel: . . . . VAN, PALE, PEEL, SCOOP, SPADE, THRUST

shovelhead: . . . . SHARK, CATFISH, STURGEON

show: . . . . DASH, FAIR, LEAD, POMP, COACH, FARCE, GUIDE, MOVIE, PROVE, REVUE, SIGHT, TEACH, TRAIN, APPEAR, BLAZON, CINEMA, CIRCUS, DENOTE, DIRECT, ESCORT, EVINCE, EXPOSE, FLAUNT, INFORM, PARADE, REVEAL, UNVEIL, DISPLAY, DIVULGE, EXHIBIT, EXPLAIN, PAGEANT, PERFORM, PRESENT, PRETENSE, CEREMONY, DISCLOSE, FLOURISH, INDICATE, INSTRUCT, MANIFEST, BURLESQUE

shower: . . BATH, HAIL, POUR, RAIN, WASH, BATHE, PARTY, SLEET, SPRAY, WATER, DELUGE, PEPPER, DRIZZLE, SCATTER, SPRINKLE, RAINFALL

showy: . . . . . . ARTY, LOUD, GAUDY, FLASHY, GARISH, ORNATE, SWANKY, DASHING, POMPOUS, GORGEOUS, STRIKING, FLAMBOYANT, PRETENTIOUS, OSTENTATIOUS

shred: . . . BIT, CUT, JAG, RAG, FELL, SNIP, TEAR, WISP, GRATE, PIECE, SCRAP, SEVER, SHARD, STRIP, DIVIDE, SLIVER, TATTER, FRAZZLE, VESTIGE, FRAGMENT, PARTICLE

shrew: . NAG, CURSE, HARPY, SCOLD, VIXEN, MAMMAL, VIRAGO, SORICINE, TERMAGANT

shrewd: . . SLY, CAGY, FOXY, KEEN, SAGE, WILY, ACUTE, CANNY, SHARP, SMART, ARTFUL, ASTUTE, CLEVER, CRAFTY, SUBTLE, CUNNING, POLITIC, SAPIENT, SAGACIOUS

shriek: . . CRY, YELL, HOLLER, OUTCRY, SCREAM, SCREECH

shrift: . . . . ABSOLUTION, CONFESSION, DISCLOSURE

shrill: . . . HIGH, KEEN, ACUTE, SHARP, BITING, SHRIEK, SCREECH, PIERCING, STRIDENT, HIGH-PITCHED, PENETRATING

shrimp: . . . . . . KID, DWARF, SHAVER, STRIPLING, CRUSTACEAN

shrine: . . . . . . TOMB, ALTAR, CHAPEL, DAGOBA, GROTTO, HALLOW, TEMPLE, CANONIZE, RELIQUARY, TABERNACLE

shrink: . . SHY, FUNK, SHUN, WANE, COWER, QUAIL, RIVEL, WIZEN, BLENCH, CRINGE, FLINCH, HUDDLE, RECOIL, RETIRE, WITHER, ATROPHY, DWINDLE, SHRIVEL, CONDENSE, CONTRACT, DECREASE, CONSTRICT, DEPRECIATE

shrinking: . . . . . SHY, TIMID, AFRAID, DIFFIDENT

shrive: . . . . . . FREE, PURGE, PARDON, ABSOLVE

shrivel: . . . . . . CURL, PARCH, RIVEL, WIZEN, SHRINK, WITHER, WRINKLE, MUMMIFY

shroud: . . . HIDE, PALL, TRIM, VEIL, ARRAY, CLOAK, COVER, DRESS, SHADE, SHEET, CLOTHE, SCREEN, SHADOW, CONCEAL, CURTAIN, ENVELOP, FOLIAGE, GARMENT, PLUMAGE, CEREMENT, CLOTHING, COVERING

shrub: . . TOD, BUSH, GORSE, HEDGE, PLANT, PUNCH, CUDGEL, PRIVET, BRAMBLE, HEATHER, BEVERAGE, CHAPARRAL

shuck: . . POD, HUSK, SHELL, REMOVE, DISCARD

shudder: . . . . QUAKE, SHAKE, SHIVER, TREMOR, TREMBLE

shuffle: . . . . MIX, GAIT, PLOD, DANCE, SHIFT, SCUFF, TRICK,

JUMBLE, REMOVE, RIFFLE,
SCLAFF, DECEIVE, EVASION,
QUIBBLE, SCUFFLE, SHAMBLE,
ARTIFICE

shun: . . . . . . AVERT, AVOID,
DODGE, EVADE, ESCHEW,
FORBEAR, REFRAIN, FOREBEAR

shunt: . . . . . . SHIFT, SHOVE,
DIVERT, REMOVE, SWITCH,
RECHANNEL, SIDETRACK

shut: . . . . . BAN, BAR, CLOSE,
SLAM, CLIMAX, FASTEN,
FORBID, CONFINE, EXCLUDE,
SECURED, PROHIBIT, OSTRACIZE

shutter: . . . . . BLIND, SLIDE,
COVER, SCREEN, JALOUSIE,
PERSIENNE

shy: . . . . . . COY, MIM, BALK,
JUMP, SHUN, WARY, ALOOF,
AVOID, CHARY, SCANT, SHORT,
START, THROW, TIMID,
DEMURE, MODEST, RECOIL,
SHRINK, BASHFUL, LACKING,
HESITANT, DIFFIDENT,
RESERVED, RETIRING,
RELUCTANT

sib: . . . KIN, ALLIED, SISTER,
BROTHER, KINDRED, RELATED,
SIBLING, RELATIVE

sibling: . . . . KIN, SISTER,
BROTHER

sibyl: . . . . . WITCH, SEERESS,
ORACLE, SORCERESS,
FORTUNETELLER

sibylline: . . . . OCCULT,
ORACULAR, AMBIGUOS,
EQUIVOCAL, PROPHETIC

sic: . . SO, SEEK, SUCH, THUS,
URGE, CHASE, ATTACK, INCITE

sick: . . BAD, ILL, WAN, ABED,
WEAK, BADLY, FED-UP, UNFIT,
WEARY, AILING, UNWELL,
UNSOUND, IMPAIRED,
DEPRESSED, DISGUSTED,
NAUSEATED, SURFEITED,
UNHEALTHY, INDISPOSED

person: . . . . INVALID,
PATIENT

sickness: . . MALADY, NAUSEA,
AILMENT, DISEASE, ILLNESS,
DISTEMPER, INFIRMITY,
WEARINESS

side: . . . . . EDGE, FACE, LINE,
PART, TEAM, WALL, AGREE,
FACET, FLANK, PARTY, PHASE,
PLACE, SHORE, SLOPE, WIDTH,
ASPECT, BORDER, MARGIN,
FACTION, LATERAL, SUPPORT,
SURFACE, POSITION, OUTSKIRTS,
COLLATERAL

sideboard: . . . . BUFFET,
CREDENZA, CUPBOARD

sideslip: . . . . . . SKID, SLIDE

sidestep: . . . . . DUCK, AVOID,
EVADE

sidetrack: . . . . TURN, AVERT,
SHUNT, DIVERT, SIDING,
SWITCH

sidle: . . EDGE, SKEW, LOITER,
SAUNTER

siege: . . . . SEE, RANK, SEAT,
BENCH, BESET, PLACE, PRIVY,
ATTACK, THRONE, SITTING,
STATION, BLOCKADE,
BELEAGUER

siesta: . . . . . NAP, REST, SLEEP

sieve: . . . . SIFT, BASKET,
BOLTER, FILTER, RIDDLE,
SCREEN, SIFTER, STRAIN,
CHAFFER, CRIBBLE, COLANDER,
SEPARATE, STRAINER

sift: . . . . . BOLT, CULL, SEEK,
SIEVE, WEIGH, DREDGE, FILTER,
RIDDLE, SCREEN, SEARCH,
STRAIN, WINNOW, EXAMINE,
INSPECT, SEPARATE

sigh: . . . . . SOB, SOUF, MOAN,
MOURN, SOUGH, YEARN,
GRIEVE, LAMENT, SUSPIRE

sight: . . . . . AIM, EYE, BEAD,
ESPY, GAZE, LOOK, SHOW,
VIEW, SCENE, ASPECT, BEHOLD,
DESCRY, GLANCE, VISION,
DISCERN, DISPLAY, GLIMPSE,
PICTURE, SPECTACLE

sign(s): . . . . . AD, CUE, NOD,
HIRE, MARK, NOTE, OMEN,

BADGE, IMAGE, INDEX, SPOOR,
TOKEN, TRACE, BANNER,
BEACON, BECKON, EMBLEM,
ENSIGN, MOTION, NOTICE,
POSTER, SYMBOL, ENDORSE,
GESTURE, INDICIA, INSIGNE,
PICTURE, PORTENT, VESTIGE,
WARNING, SYMPTOM,
EVIDENCE, PASSWORD,
STANDARD, SUBSCRIBE,
INDICATION, ADVERTISEMENT

signal: . . . CUE, BUZZ, FLAG,
SIGN, WARN, ALARM, BUZZER,
ENSIGN, NOTIFY, BETOKEN,
EMINENT, NOTABLE, PRESAGE,
SIGNIFY, STRIKING, PROMINENT,
REMARKABLE, COMMUNICATE

signature: . . . . . SEAL, HAND,
MARK, NAME, SIGIL,
AUTOGRAPH

signet: . . MARK, SEAL, SIGIL,
STAMP

significance: . . . . . . IMPORT,
MOMENT, MEANING, PURPORT

significant: . . . . GRAVE,
OMINOUS, WEIGHTY,
IMPORTANT, MOMENTOUS,
MEANINGFUL, PORTENTOUS

signify: . . . . . . BODE, MEAN,
SHOW, AUGUR, IMPLY, DENOTE,
IMPORT, BETOKEN, INDICATE,
INTIMATE, MANIFEST

silage: . . . . . . FEED, FODDER

silence: . . . GAG, HUSH, LULL,
MUTE, CHOKE, QUIET, STILL,
MUFFLE, REPRESS, SECRECY,
SUPPRESS, THROTTLE,
STILLNESS

silent: . . . MUM, DUMB, MUTE,
QUIET, STILL, TACIT, WHIST,
INACTIVE, RESERVED,
RETICENT, TACITURN,
NOISELESS, SECRETIVE,
SPEECHLESS

silhouette: . . . . OUTLINE,
PORTRAIT

silica: . . . MICA, SAND, FLINT,
SILEX, QUARTZ, MINERAL

silk: . . . GROS, CAFFA, CHINA,
CREPE, MOIRE, PEKIN, SATIN,
SURAH, TABBY, TULLE, VOILE,
FAILLE, MADRAS, MANTUA,
PONGEE, SAMITE, SENDAL,
VELOUR, ALAMODE, SANSET,
TAFETTA, SARCENET,
SHANTUNG, CHARMEUSE
coarse: . . TUSSAH, TUSSAR,
TUSSER

silken: . . . FINE, SOFT, SLEEK,
SUAVE, GENTLE, GLOSSY,
SMOOTH, ELEGANT, DELICATE,
LUSTROUS, LUXURIOUS

silkworm: . . ER(A), TUSSA(H),
TUSSER, BOMBYX, TUSSORE

sill: . . . BEAM, SEAT, BENCH,
FRAME, LEDGE, TIMBER,
THRESHOLD

silly: . . . . . MAD, DAFT, FOND,
FOOL, SIMP, ANILE, BARMY,
DAFFY, DAZED, GOOFY, INANE,
KOOKY, SAPPY, ABSURD,
CUCKOO, STUPID, UNWISE,
ASININE, FATUOUS, FOOLISH,
WITLESS, CHILDISH, IMBECILE,
PUERILE, LUDICROUS,
SLAP-HAPPY

silt: . SCUM, DREGS, DEPOSIT,
MORAINE, RESIDUE, SEDIMENT,
ALLUVIUM

silver: . . . . COIN, MONEY,
PLATE, SYCEE, ARGENT,
BULLION, ARGENTUM,
LUSTROUS, PRECIOUS,
STERLING, TABLEWARE
tongued: . . . . . . ORATOR,
ELOQUENT

simar: . . . . . . ROBE, JACKET

simian: . . . . . . APE, MONKEY

similar: . . . . SIB, AKIN, LIKE,
SUCH, ALIKE, AGNATE,
EVENLY, UNIFORM, ANALOGIC,
PARALLEL, SEMBLANCE,
ANALOGOUS, RESEMBLING

similitude: . . . IMAGE, SIMILE,
ANALOGY, PARABLE,
ALLEGORY, LIKENESS,

FACSIMILE, SEMBLANCE,
SIMILARITY

simmer: ...... BOIL, STEW,
BRAISE, SEETHE

down: .... COOL, SUBSIDE

simper: ..... MINCE, SMIRK,
SMILE, WHIMPER

simple: .. BALD, BARE, DULL,
EASY, MERE, POOR, PURE,
REAL, SNAP, TRUE, LOWLY,
GREEN, NAIVE, NAKED, PLAIN,
COMMON, HOMELY, HUMBLE,
RUSTIC, SEVERE, SINGLE,
STUPID, ARTLESS, AUSTERE,
IDYLLIC, NATURAL, SINCERE,
SPARTAN, UNMIXED,
ABSOLUTE, GULLIBLE,
HOMEMADE, IGNORANT,
INNOCENT, ORDINARY,
ELEMENTAL, PRIMITIVE,
UNADORNED, ELEMENTARY

simpleton: .. ASS, DAW, OAF,
SAP, BOOB, DOLT, FOOL, GABY,
GAWK, GOWK, LOUT, ZANY,
BOBBY, DUNCE, GOOSE, IDIOT,
NINNY, NODDY, MORON,
DIMWIT, GANDER, NITWIT,
GOMERAL, IMBECILE,
NUMSKULL, NINCOMPOOP

simplify: .... CLARIFY,
EXPOUND, ELUCIDATE,
INTERPRET

simply: .... JUST, ONLY,
MERELY

simulate: ... ACT, APE, FAKE,
MOCK, SHAM, FEIGN, AFFECT,
ASSUME, IMITATE, PRETEND,
PERSONATE, COUNTERFEIT

simulation: .... FEINT,
PRETENSE, FEIGNING,
HYPOCRISY

sin: . ERR, DEBT, ENVY, EVIL,
LUST, VICE, ANGER, BLAME,
CRIME, ERROR, FAULT, FOLLY,
GREED, GUILT, PRIDE, SLOTH,
WRONG, FELONY, OFFENSE,
VIOLATE, GLUTTONY, INIQUITY,
TRESPASS, DEVIATION,

PECCADILLO, TRANSGRESS,
WICKEDNESS, MISDEMEANOR

since: .. AS, AGO, FOR, NOW,
ERGO, GONE, PAST, SITH,
AFTER, HENCE, LATER,
ALREADY, BECAUSE, WHEREAS,
INASMUCH, AFTERWARD,
THEREFORE, THEREUPON,
CONSIDERING

sincere: ... OPEN, PURE, REAL,
TRUE, FRANK, CANDID,
DEVOUT, HONEST, CORRECT,
EARNEST, GENUINE, UPRIGHT,
FAITHFUL, TRUTHFUL,
VIRTUOUS, AUTHENTIC,
HEARTFELT, UNFEIGNED,
VERACIOUS, UNAFFECTED

sinciput: .... FOREHEAD

sinecure: .... PIPE, SNAP,
CINCH, GRAVY, OFFICE

sinew(s): .... FORCE, SNARE,
MUSCLE, TENDON

sinewy: .... FIRM, WIRY,
TOUGH, BRAWNY, ROBUST,
STRONG, STRINGY, MUSCULAR,
POWERFUL

sinful: ... BAD, EVIL, WICKED,
IMMORAL, PECCANT, UNGODLY,
VICIOUS, INIQUITOUS

sing: ..... HUM, CANT, LILT,
CAROL, CHANT, CROON, YODEL,
BETRAY, INTONE, SQUEAL,
WARBLE, CONFESS, DESCANT,
ROULADE

singe: ... BURN, CHAR, SEAR,
SCORCH

singer: .. ALTO, BARD, BIRD,
BASS, DIVA, POET, BASSO,
TENOR, ARTIST, CANTOR,
ARTISTE, CHANTER, CAROLER,
CROONER, SOLOIST, SOPRANO,
YODELER, BARITONE,
MINSTREL, VOCALIST,
CHANTEUSE, CHORISTER,
CONTRALTO, DESCANTER,
CANTATRICE

single: .... ACE, ONE, LONE,
ONLY, SOLE, SOLO, UNIT,
ALONE, UNWED, UNIQUE,

SEPARATE, SINGULAR,
SOLITARY, UNMARRIED,
INDIVIDUAL, PARTICULAR

singly: . ONCE, SOLO, ALONE,
MERELY, UNAIDED

singular: . . ODD, EACH, RARE,
SOLE, QUEER, SINGLE, UNIQUE,
PRIVATE, STRANGE, UNUSUAL,
ISOLATED, PECULIAR,
SEPARATE, UNCOMMON,
ECCENTRIC, INDIVIDUAL

sinister: . . DARK, EVIL, GRIM,
LEFT, WICKED, ADVERSE,
BALEFUL, CORRUPT, OMINOUS,
MALICIOUS, UNDERHAND,
DISASTROUS, PORTENTOUS

sink: . . . . BOG, DIP, EBB, SAG,
BOWL, CAVE, DROP, FAIL,
FALL, RUIN, WANE, BASIN,
DRAIN, DROOP, EMBOG, LOWER,
SEWER, SLOPE, SLUMP, DEBASE,
RECEDE, PLUNGE, SETTLE,
DECLINE, DEPRESS, DESCEND,
IMMERSE, SUBSIDE, DECREASE,
DIMINISH, SUBMERGE

sinuous: . . . . WAVY, SNAKY,
BENDING, CROOKED, CURVING,
DEVIOUS, WINDING, SLITHERY,
INTRICATE, CIRCUITOUS,
SERPENTINE

sinus: . . . . BAY, BEND, FOLD,
CURVE, ANTRUM, CAVITY,
HOLLOW, RECESS, CHANNEL,
DEPRESSION

sir: . . . . . LORD, TITLE, SAHIB,
SENOR, KNIGHT, MASTER,
EFFENDI, SEIGNOR, MONSIEUR,
GENTLEMAN

sire: . . . BEGET, (FORE)FATHER

siren: . . . . VAMP, WITCH,
NYMPH, ENCHANTRESS,
CHARMER, LORELEI, FOGHORN,
MERMAID, WHISTLE

sirocco: . . . . WIND

sissy: . . . . GIRLISH, MILKSOP,
PANTYWAIST

sister: . . . . NUN, SIB, SIS,
NURSE, SOROR, SIBLING

sit: . . . . . . MEET, POSE, REST,
SEAT, BROOD, DWELL, PERCH,
PRESS, ROOST, SQUAT, OCCUPY,
REMAIN, CONVENE

on: . . . . REBUKE, REPRESS,
SQUELCH, SUPPRESS,
REPRIMAND

site: . . . . . RUIN, SEAT, SPOT,
PLACE, SCENE, STEAD, VENUE,
LOCALE, LOCATION, POSITION,
LOCATION

sitting: . . . . . . SEAT, PLACE,
CLUTCH, POSING, SEANCE,
SEATED, SEDENT, MEETING,
SESSION

situate: . . . PUT, SEAT, PLACE,
POSIT, LOCATE, STATION

situation: . . JOB, CASE, NEED,
POST, SEAT, SITE, BERTH,
PLACE, STATE, LOCALE,
PLIGHT, SCRAPE, STRAIT,
DILEMMA, STATION, LOCALITY,
LOCATION, POSITION,
QUANDRY, CONDITION,
EMERGENCY, PREDICAMENT

situs: . . . . PLACE, LOCATION,
POSITION

sizable: . . BIG, HUGE, LARGE,
SUBSTANTIAL

size: . . . . AREA, BORE, BULK,
MASS, GLAZE, GRADE, ADJUST,
AMOUNT, EXTENT, VOLUME,
STIFFEN, CLASSIFY, DIMENSION,
MAGNITUDE

sizzling: . . . . . . HOT, TORRID

skate: . . . . . RAY, FISH, PLUG,
SHOE, SKID, GLIDE, HORSE,
ROCKER

blade: . . . . RUNNER

skating arena: . . . . RINK

skean: . . . . SWORD, DAGGER

skedaddle: . . . FLEE, SCOOT,
DECAMP, SCURRY, SCAMPER

skein: . . . RAP, HANK, MESH,
WIND, FLOCK, FLIGHT, SLEEVE,
THIMBLE

skeleton: . . . . . . PAST, ATOMY,
BONES, CORAL, FRAME,
MUMMY, SKETCH, CARCASS,

OUTLINE, REMAINS, FRAMEWORK

skeptic: . . . . CYNIC, DOUBTER, INFIDEL, AGNOSTIC, DISBELIEVER

skeptical: . . . . DUBIOUS, DOUBTING, FAITHLESS, QUESTIONING

sketch: . . . . JOT, MAP, DRAW, PLAN, PLAY, SKIT, DRAFT, PAINT, STORY, TRACE, APERCU, DESIGN, CARTOON, DRAWING, OUTLINE, DESCRIBE, DELINEATE, SUMMARIZE

skew: . . . AWRY, SLIP, TURN, AVOID, SLANT, SIDLE, TWIST, ESCAPE, ESCHEW, GLANCE, SQUINT, SWERVE, BLUNDER, DISTORT, OBLIQUE, DEVIATE, PERVERT

skewer: . . . . . PIN, ROD, SPIT, TRUSS, FASTEN, BROACH, PIERCE, BROCHETTE

skid: . . . . . BAR, CURB, DRAG, HOOK, RAIL, SCUD, SLIP, TRIG, BRAKE, CHECK, SLIDE, FENDER, RUNNER, TIMBER, SUPPORT, PLATFORM, SIDESLIP

skill: . . . . . ART, GIFT, CRAFT, KNACK, TALENT, ABILITY, APTNESS, CUNNING, FINESSE, MASTERY, SCIENCE, KNOW-HOW, PROWRESS, CAPACITY, DEFTNESS, FACILITY, ADEPTNESS, EXPERTISE, DEXTERITY, CAPABILITY, PROFICIENCY

skillful: . . . . APT, ABLE, DEFT, ADEPT, HANDY, ADROIT, CLEVER, EXPERT, HABILE, CAPABLE, DEXTROUS, INGENIOUS, PROFICIENT, ACCOMPLISHED

skim: . . . . . . CUT, FLIT, SAIL, SCUD, SCUM, SKIP, CLEAR, GLIDE, GRAZE, STUDY, THROW, GLANCE

skimp: . . . MEAGER, SCANTY, SCRIMP, ECONOMIZE

skimpy: . . . . CHARY, SPARE, SCANTY, STINGY, NIGGARDLY, PARSIMONIOUS

skin: . . . . BARK, COAT, DERM, FELL, FILM, FLAY, HIDE, PARE, PEEL, PELT, RIND, SCUM, CHEAT, CUTIS, DERMA, FRAUD, LAYER, SCALP, SHELL, STRIP, CALLUS, FLEECE, SCRAPE, CUTICLE, DEFRAUD, PLATING, SURFACE, SWINDLE, COVERING, MEMBRANE, PELLICLE, EPIDERMIS, INTEGUMENT

skinflint: . . . MISER, NIGGARD, TIGHTWAD

skinny: . . BONY, LEAN, THIN, SCANT, SCRAGGY, EMACIATED

skip: . . DAP, HOP, GAIT, JUMP, LEAP, MISS, OMIT, TRIP, BOUND, CAPER, ELIDE, FRISK, LEAVE, SCOUT, VAULT, DECAMP, ESCAPE, GAMBOL, SPRING, ABSCOND, SKITTER, RICOCHET

skipper: . . . SAURY, MASTER, CAPTAIN, BUTTERFLY

skirmish: . . . BRUSH, FIGHT, MELEE, ACTION, AFFRAY, BATTLE, BICKER, COMBAT, CONTEST, CONFLICT, FLOURISH, ENCOUNTER

skirt: . . . . . RIM, EDGE, FLAP, GIRL, WOMAN, BORDER, FRINGE, KIRTLE, DRINDL, PANNIER, HOBBLE, PETTICOAT, PERIPHERY

skit: . . . . . . ACT, GIBE, GIRL, HOAX, JEER, JEST, PLAY, CAPER, REVUE, STORY, TRICK, PARODY, SKETCH, RIDICULE, SLAPSTICK

skitter: . . . PASS, SKIM, SKIP, GLIDE, SCAMPER, SCATTER, SPRINKLE

skittish: . . COY, SHY, JUMPY, FICKLE, LIVELY, NERVOUS, PLAYFUL, RESTIVE, SPIRITED, EXCITABLE, FRIVOLOUS, CAPRICIOUS

skittle(s): ...... PIN, PLAY, BOWLS, NINEPINS

skive: .... DART, PARE, SKIM, SHAVE

skivvy: ...... UNDERWEAR, UNDERSHIRT

skulk: .. HIDE, LURK, DODGE, EVADE, HEDGE, MICHE, PROWL, SHIRK, SLINK, SNEAK, MALINGER

skull: ... BEAN, HEAD, MIND, BRAIN, SCONCE, CRANIUM, BRAINPAN

skullcap: ..... COIF, CALOT, BEANIE, PILEUS, CALOTTE, CAPELINE, YARMULKE, ZUCCHETTO

skunk: .... BEAT, POLECAT, STINKER, BETRAYER

sky: .. BLUE, ETHER, WELKIN, CELESTIAL, HEAVENS, EMPYREAN, FIRMAMENT

skylark: ..... PLAY, FROLIC

skylight: .. DORMER, WINDOW

skyline: .... HORIZON

slab: ... TILE, CHUNK, DALLE, PIECE, SLICE, STELE, TABLET

slack: ..... LAX, DULL, IDLE, LAZE, LULL, SLOW, SOFT, WEAK, LOOSE, RELAX, SHIRK, SLAKE, TARDY, ABATED, LOOSEN, REMISS, CARELESS, DILATORY, INACTIVE, LISTLESS, RELAXED, SLUGGISH, DISSOLUTE, NEGLIGENT

slacken: ...... EASE, SLOW, ABATE, DELAY, LET UP, RELAX, LOOSEN, REDUCE, RELENT, RETARD, DECREASE, MODERATE

slacker: ...... SPIV, IDLER, LOAFER, TRUANT, SHIRKER

slag: .. LAVA, DROSS, WASTE, CINDER, REFUSE, SCORIA

slake: .... WET, COOL, SATE, ABATE, ALLAY, LESSEN, QUENCH, REDUCE, APPEASE, HYDRATE, RELIEVE, SATISFY, DECREASE, MITIGATE, MODERATE

slam: ..... HIT, PAN, BANG, BEAT, CUFF, DASH, SHUT, VOLE, CLASH, CLOSE, THROW, IMPACT, CRITICIZE

slander: ...... MUD, LIBEL, SMEAR, SHAME, DEFAME, MALIGN, REVILE, VILIFY, ASPERSE, BLACKEN, SCANDAL, CALUMNY, TRADUCE, DEROGATE, MALEDICTION

slang: .. CANT, ARGOT, LINGO, JARGON, PATOIS, VULGAR, DIALECT

slant: ..... TIP, BEND, BIAS, CANT, HEEL, SKEW, TILT, ANGLE, BEVEL, POINT, SLOPE, BIASED, GLANCE, INCLINE, OPINION, ATTITUDE

slanting: ...... BIAS, SKEW, ASKEW, ATILT, ASLANT, ASLOPE, ATHWART, CROOKED, OBLIQUE

slap: .. HIT, RAP, LAP, BEAT, BLOW, CLAP, CUFF, SNUB, SPAT, SMACK, SPANK, WHACK, BUFFET, INSULT, REBUFF, SLIGHT, STRIKE, THWACK

slapdash: . HASTY, OFFHAND, CARELESS, IMPETUOUS, HAPHAZARD

slash: .... CUT, GASH, LASH, SLIT, CRACK, WOUND, ATTACK, LESSEN, REDUCE, STRIKE, STRIPE, CENSURE, SCOURGE, CRITICIZE

slat: .. BAR, RIB, BEAT, FLAP, HURL, LATH, SLAB, SLAP, TOSS, SPLIT, STRIP, THROW, PUMMEL, SPLINE, STRIKE

slate: .... LIST, ROCK, TILE, ABUSE, COLOR, PLANK, SCOLD, BALLOT, BERATE, ENROLL, PUNISH, RECORD, ROSTER, TABLET, TICKET, THRASH, CENSURE, ROOFING, NOMINATE, REGISTER, SCHEDULE, CRITICIZE

slattern: ...... DRAB, SLUT, IDLER, SLOPPY, TRIFLER, TROLLOP, CARELESS, SLOVENLY

slaughter: . . . (also see **slay**) KILL, MURDER, POGROM, BUTCHER, CARNAGE, KILLING, BUTCHERY, HECATOMB, MASSACRE

slaughterhouse: . . ABATTOIR, BUTCHERY

slave: . . . BOND, ESHE, PEON, SERF, TOIL, HELOT, THANE, ADDICT, DRUDGE, THRALL, RASSAL, BONDMAN, CAPTIVE, CHATTEL, SERVANT

slaver: . . . . . DROOL, SMEAR, DRIVEL, SALIVA, SLOBBER, HUMBUG, NONSENSE

slavery: . BONDAGE, SERVICE, DRUDGERY, CAPTIVITY, SERVITUDE, SERFDOM, HELOTRY, THRALLDOM

slavish: . . . . LOW, BASE, ABJECT, MENIAL, SERVILE

slay: . . . . (also see **slaughter**) KILL, MURDER, BUTCHER, DESTROY, EXECUTE, ANNHILATE, ASSASSINATE, EXTERMINATE

sleazy: . . . . THIN, FLIMSY, TAWDRY

sled: . . . . LUGE, PUNG, TODE, JUMPER, SLEIGH, SLEDGE, BOBSLED, COASTER, TRAVOIS, VEHICLE, TOBOGGAN

sledge: . DRAY, SLED, BREAK, HAMMER, HURDLE, SLEIGH, STRIKE

sleek: . . OILY, GLOSSY, SHINY, SLICK, SMART, SUAVE, FINISH, POLISH, SMOOTH, SOIGNE, POLISHED

sleep: . . . . . NAP, NOD, DOSS, DOZE, REST, DEATH, SUPOR, DROWSE, REPOSE, SIESTA, SNOOZE, STUPOR, SHUTEYE, SLUMBER

sleepiness: . . . . DROWSINESS, SOMNOLENCE

sleeping: . . . . ABED, LATENT, DORMANT, INACTIVE, QUIESCENT

place: . . . . BED, COT, PAD, BUNK, DOSS, FLOP, BERTH, COUCH, PALLET, CUBICLE, LODGING, DORMITORY

sleepy: . . DULL, DOZY, TIRED, DROWSY, SLUGGISH, SOPOROSE, LETHARGIC, SOMNOLENT

sleeve: . . . . ARM, GIGOT, ARMLET

sleigh: . . . . . (also see **sled**) PUNG, CUTTER, CARIOLE, TOBOGGAN

sleight: . . . . . KNACK, SKILL, TRICK, AGILITY, CONJURE, CUNNING, ARTIFICE, DEFTNESS, TRICKERY, DEXTERITY, QUICKNESS, STRATAGEM

slender: . LANK, LEAN, SLIM, THIN, FRAIL, GAUNT, LITHE, PETIT, REEDY, SMALL, SVELT, SYLPH, WISPY, LISSOM, MEAGER, SLIGHT, SVELT, WILLOWY, GRACILE, TENUOUS

sleuth: . . . . . . TEC, TRACER, TRACKER, TRAILER, DETECTIVE, OPERATIVE, HAWKSHAW, PRIVATE EYE, INVESTIGATOR

slew: . . . . LOT, SLUE, TURN, TWIST, SWAMP, SLOUGH

slice: . . . . . CUT, SAW, CHIP, GASH, HUNK, PART, SLAB, CARVE, CHUNK, LAYER, PIECE, SHAVE, SKIVE, CANTLE, DIVIDE, RASHER, SLIVER, PORTION, SEPARATE, SPLINTER

slick: . . . . FINE, NEAT, OILY, TIDY, PREEN, SLEEK, SMART, SUAVE, ADROIT, CLEVER, CRAFTY, GLOSSY, POLISH, SMOOTH, SMARTEN, SLIPPERY, UNCTUOUS, EXCELLENT, INGENIOUS

slicker: . . . . . . DUDE, CHEAT, GAMBLER

slide: . . . . SKID, SLED, SLEW, SLIP, SLUE, CHUTE, COAST, GLIDE, INCLINE, SLITHER, GLISSADE, AVALANCHE

slight: . . . . CUT, SLAP, SNUB, SLIM, THIN, FRAIL, LIGHT, FAINT, MINOR, SCANT, SCORN, SMALL, FLIMSY, IGNORE, MEAGER, SCANTY, DISTAIN, FRAGILE, NEGLECT, NOMINAL, SHALLOW, TENUOUS, SLENDER, TRIVIAL, CARELESS, DELICATE, DISREGARD, INDIGNITY

slightest: . . . . LEAST

slim: . . . . see **slender**

slime: . . . MUD, GORE, MUCK, OOZE, GLEET, MUCUOUS, SLUDGE, SEDIMENT

slimy: . . . . VILE, FILTHY, VULGAR, VISCID, VISCOUS, GLUTINOUS, OFFENSIVE, REPULSIVE, DISGUSTING

sling: . . . CAST, HURL, DRINK, FLING, THROW, BANDAGE

slink: . LURK, CRAWL, CREEP, SNEAK, SKULK, STEAL

slip: . . ERR, FALL, OMIT, PIER, SHED, SKID, SLUE, TRIP, CHUTE, ELUDE, ERROR, FAULT, BONER, GAFFE, GLIDE, LAPSE, LEASH, SCION, SLIDE, MISCUE, TUMBLE, BLUNDER, FAUX PAS, MISSTEP, MISTAKE, NEGLECT, SLITHER, OVERSIGHT, PETTICOAT

slipper: . . . . MULE, SHOE, MOYLE, SCUFF, STEP-IN, SANDAL

slippery: . . . . . . EELY, GLIB, SLICK, SLIMY, CRAFTY, GREASY, SHIFTY, TRICKY, ELUSIVE, EVASIVE, UNSTABLE, DECEITFUL, UNCERTAIN, UNRELIABLE

shipshod: . . . . SLOPPY, CARELESS, SLOVENLY, DISORDERLY, WISHY-WASHY

slit: . . . . . CUT, GASH, NICK, RENT, TEAR, SLASH, SPLIT, CLEAVE, FISSURE, OPENING, APERATURE, INCISION

slither: . . . SLIP, SLIDE, GLIDE

sliver: . . . CUT, FIBER, SHRED, SLICE, SPLIT, STRAND, FRAGMENT, SPLINTER

slobber: . . . . DROOL, SLAVER

slog: . . . . . PLOD, SLUG, TOIL

slogan: . . . . MOTTO, SHIBBOLETH, CATCHWORD

slop: . . . . MUD, GUSH, MASH, SNOW, SLUSH, SPILL, SLOSH, SWILL, WASTE, REFUSE, SPLASH

slope: . . . . . . DIP, BANK, BRAE, BROW, CANT, HANG, RAMP, RISE, TILT, BEVEL, SCARP, SLANT, TALUS, GRADE, SPLAY, ASCENT, GLACIS, DESCENT, INCLINE, TERRACE, GRADIENT, HILLSIDE, ACCLIVITY, DECLIVITY

sloppy: . . . . MESSY, MUDDY, SLUSHY, UNTIDY, SPLASHY, CARELESS, SLIPSHOD, SLOVENLY

slot: . . . . CUT, TRACK, TRAIL, GROOVE, HOLLOW, KEYWAY, OPENING, APERATURE, DEPRESSION

sloth: . . . . IDLE, LAZY, SLOW, ANIMAL, INERTIA, NEGLECT, IDLENESS, LAZINESS, SLOWNESS, EDENTATE, INDOLENCE

slough: . . . . BOG, MUD, MIRE, MOLT, OOZE, PLOD, SHED, SLEW, SLUE, BAYOU, INLET, MARSH, SWAMP, CHANNEL, DISCARD

slovenly: . . . . LAZY, DOWDY, MESSY, BLOWZY, FROUSY, GRUBBY, SLOPPY, UNTIDY, UNKEMPT, CARELESS, SLIPSHOD, NEGLIGENT, DISORDERLY

slow: . . . . LAX, DULL, LATE, POKY, DELAY, POKEY, SLACK, TARDY, BORING, HAMPER, HINDER, RETARD, STOLID, STUPID, GRADUAL, LAGGARD, SLACKEN, DILATORY, DIMINISH, SLUGGISH, LEISURELY, UNHURRIED, DECELERATE, DELIBERATE

sludge: . . . . ICE, MUD, MIRE, OOZE, SLEET, SLUSH, WASTE, DEPOSIT, SEDIMENT

slue: . . . . SLEW, TURN, VEER, PIVOT, SWING, TWIST, SLOUGH

slug: . . . . . HIT, BLOW, SLOW, SWAT, DELAY, DRINK, SNAIL, TOKEN, BULLET, NUGGET, PELLET, STRIKE, MOLLUSK, TREPANG, CATERPILLAR, GASTROPOD

sluggard: . . . . LAZY, DRONE, IDLER, LOAFER

sluggish: . . . . . . DULL, LAZY, LOGY, SLOW, FAINT, HEAVY, INERT, DROWSY, LEADEN, TORPID, LANGUID, INACTIVE, INDOLENT STAGNANT, LETHARGIC, TARDIGRADE

sluice: . . . . GASH, PIPE, RACE, FLUME, BREACH, STREAM, TROUGH, CHANNEL, LAUNDER, OPENING, IRRIGATE, FLOODGATE

slum: . . . . . BARRIO, GHETTO

slumber: . . . . . COMA, DOZE, SLEEP, DROWSE, REPOSE

slump: . . . SAG, FALL, DROP, SINK, SLIP, SETTLE, DECLINE, COLLAPSE, RECESSION, DEPRECIATE, DEPRESSION

slur: . . . BLOT, BLUR, DECRY, ELIDE, GLIDE, SLIDE, SMEAR, STAIN, SULLY, INSULT, MACULE, SLIGHT, SMIRCH, STIGMA, ASPERSE, BLEMISH, CALUMNY, TRADUCE, BESMIRCH, DISGRACE, INNUENDO, ASPERSION, CRITICIZE, DISCREDIT, DISPARAGE

slush: . . . . MUD, MIRE, PULP, SLOP, WASH, GROUT, DRIVEL, SPLASH

slut: . . . . DRAB, JADE, BITCH, FILTH, QUEAN, HARLOT, TROLLOP, SLATTERN

sly: . . . . CAGEY, FOXY, WILY, ARTFUL, CLEVER, CRAFTY, SECRET, SHREWD, SLINKY, SNEAKY, SUBTLE, TRICKY, CUNNING, FURTIVE, SNEAKING, INSIDIOUS, SECRETIVE

smack: . . . . BIT, HIT, BLOW, BOAT, BUSS, MISS, SLAP, TANG, SAVOR, SLOOP, TASTE, TRACE, WHACK, CUTTER, FLAVOR, STRIKE, THWACK, VESSEL, VESTIGE, SAILBOAT

small: . . DAB, LIL, LOW, TOT, WEE, PUNY, RUNT, THIN, TINY, WHIT, WISP, DINKY, MINIM, MINOR, PETTY, SCANT, TEENY, ATOMIC, GRUBBY, HUMBLE, LITTLE, BANTAM, MIGNON, MINUTE, MODEST, PETITE, TRIVIAL, MINIATURE, MINUSCULE

smallest: . . . . LEAST, MINIM, TINIEST

smart: . . . . APT, CHIC, NEAT, POSH, TRIG, WILY, WISE, ACUTE, ALERT, BRISK, CLEAN, NATTY, NIFTY, SHARP, SLICK, STING, WITTY, ASTUTE, CLEVER, DAPPER, SHREWD, SPRUCE, SUFFER, SWANKY, CAPABLE, DASHING, STYLISH

smash: . . . HIT, BASH, BLOW, DASH, ROUT, RUIN, BREAK, CRASH, CRUSH, STAVE, WRECK, DEFEAT, DESTROY, SHATTER, SUCCESS, COLLAPSE, COLLISION, BANKRUPTCY

smear: . . . . DAB, RUB, BLUR, DAUB, SOIL, SPOT, STAIN, SULLY, BEDAUB, BLOTCH, DEFAME, DEFEAT, DEFILE, GREASE, MALIGN, SMIRCH, SMUDGE, SPREAD, PLASTER, SLANDER

smell: . . . FOUL, NOSE, ODOR, OLID, REEK, AROMA, FLAIR, SCENT, SENSE, SNIFF, TRACE, WHIFF, STINK, BREATH, FLAVOR, STENCH, PERFUME, FRAGRANCE

smile: . . BEAM, GRIN, LAUGH, SMIRK, SNEER, SIMPER, GRIMACE

smirch: .. BLOT, SOIL, DIRTY, SMEAR, STAIN, SULLY, TAINT, BLOTCH, SMUDGE, SMUTCH, BLACKEN, BLEMISH, TARNISH, DISCOLOR, DISHONOR

smirk: .. GRIN, LEER, SMILE, SIMPER, GRIMACE

smite: ..... HIT, CUFF, KILL, SLAP, SLAY, SWAT, BLAST, ATTACK, DEFEAT, ENAMOR, HAMMER, STRIKE, AFFLICT, CHASTEN, DESTROY, DISTRESS

smithereens: .. BITS, PIECES, FRAGMENTS

smitten: ...... AFFECTED, STRICKEN, AFFLICTED, ENAMORED

smock: ...... KAMIS, SHIFT, FROCK, CAMISE, CHEMISE

smog: .... MIST, SMAZE

smoke: .. FLOC, FUME, FUNK, HAZE, MIST, SMOG, SMAZE, SMUDGE, VAPOR, CIGAR(ETTE)

smokestack: .... FLUE, PIPE, FUNNEL, CHIMNEY

smooth: . BALD, CALM, EASE, EASY, EVEN, GLIB, IRON, MILD, PAVE, OILY, SAND, SOFT, BLAND, GLAZE, GLOZE, GRIND, LEVEL, PLANE, PREEN, PRESS, QUIET, SILKY, SLEEK, SLICK, SUAVE, CREAMY, FLUENT, GLASSY, GLOSSY, MANGLE, POLISH, REFINE, SERENE, URBANE, AMIABLE, EQUABLE, FLATTEN, PLASTER, GLABROUS, VELVETY, POLISHED, SOOTHING, UNRUFFLED

smother: .... CHOKE, STIFLE, WELTER, OVERLIE, SMOLDER, SUPRESS, SUFFOCATE

smudge: .... see **smirch**

smug: .... NEAT, PRIG, TIDY, TRIM, CLEAN, SMART, SUAVE, SPRUCE, CORRECT, CONFIDENT, COMPLACENT

smuggler: ..... GUNRUNNER, BOOTLEGGER, (RUM)RUNNER

smut: .... BUNT, SOOT, SPOT, GRIME, STAIN, SULLY, TAINT, BLIGHT, FUNGUS, SMUDGE, OBSCENITY

smutty: .... DIRTY, OBSCENE

snack: ... BIT, BITE, LUNCH, QUICK, TASTE, MORSEL, REPAST, TIFFIN, CANAPE, PORTION

snafu: .... MIX-UP, BOOBOO, MUDDLE, DISORDER, CONFUSION

snag: ..... NUB, TEAR, TINE, TRIM, BREAK, CATCH, HITCH, POINT, STUMP, TOOTH, HAZARD, OBSTACLE, HINDRANCE

snail: .. SLUG, WILK, DRONE, HELIX, WHELK, TRITON, WINKLE, MOLLUSK, SLUGGARD, ESCARGOT, GASTROPOD

snake: .... ASP, BOA, BOMA, CURL, DRAG, SKID, WIND, WORM, ABOMA, ADDER, COBRA, CRAWL, KRAIT, MAMBA, RACER, VIPER, PYTHON, RATTLER, REPTILE, SERPENT, ANACONDA, MOCCASIN, OPHIDIAN, BLACKSNAKE, BUSHMASTER, COPPERHEAD, SIDEWINDER, COTTONHEAD

snaky: ... SLY, EVIL, WAVY, SINUOUS, ANGUINE, WINDING, PERFIDIOUS, SERPENTINE

snap: ..... BITE, CLIP, EASY, FLIP, KNAP, SHUT, BREAK, CATCH, CINCH, CLOSE, CRACK, FLICK, GRASP, SPELL, VIGOR, WAFER, COOKIE, ENERGY, FILLIP, SIMPLE, SNATCH, CRACKLE, FASTENER, SINECURE

snappish: .... EDGY, RUDE, TART, SHORT, TESTY, CROSS, UNCIVIL, IRRITABLE, IRASCIBLE

snappy: ...... TRIM, BRISK, CROSS, QUICK, SHARP, SMART, SUDDEN, PUNGENT, STYLISH

snare: ... GIN, NET, PIT, WEB, LURE, MESH, TRAP, BENET,

CATCH, GRASP, NOOSE,
AMBUSH, COBWEB, ENTRAP,
TANGLE, PITFALL, DRAGNET,
ENTANGLE

snarl: . . . . GIN, GIRN, GNAR,
KNOT, CATCH, GNARL, GROWL,
SCOLD, TANGLE, GRUMBLE,
COMPLAIN, ENTANGLE,
CONFUSION, COMPLICATE

snatch: . . . . BIT, NAB, GRAB,
SNAP, TAKE, TRAP, CATCH,
GRASP, PLUCK, SEIZE, SNARE,
SPELL, SWIPE, WREST, KIDNAP,
REMOVE, FRAGMENT

sneak: . LURK, FILCH, SKULK,
SLINK, SNOOP, STEAL,
COWARD, PILFER

sneaking: . . . . SLY, HIDDEN,
SECRET, FURTIVE, COWARDLY

sneer: . . . . GIBE, GRIM, JEER,
MOCK, FLEER, FLOUT, SCOFF,
SCORN, SMILE, SNORT,
GRIMACE, RIDICULE

snell: . . . . GUT, HARD, KEEN,
ACUTE, EAGER, HARSH, QUICK,
SHARP, SMART, SNOOD,
CLEVER, LEADER, SEVERE,
CAUSTIC, PUNGENT

snicker: . . . . LAUGH, NEIGH,
SNEER, SNIRL, TEHEE, GIGGLE,
NICKER, TITTER, SNIGGER

snide: . . . . . LOW, SLY, BASE,
MEAN, TRICKY, INFERIOR,
MALICIOUS

sniff: . . NOSE, SCENT, SMELL,
SNORT, SNUFF, DETECT,
INHALE, PERCEIVE

snigger: . . . . . . see snicker

snip: . . . BIT, CUT, CLIP, CURB,
SNAP, CHECK, NOTCH, PIECE,
SHEAR, SHRED, SNATCH,
FRAGMENT, PARTICLE

snitch: . . . . . . TELL, CATCH,
PEACH, PINCH, STEAL, THIEF,
INFORM, PILFER, SNATCH,
SQUEAL, INFORMER

snivel: . . . CRY, CANT, FRET,
SNIFF, SNUFFLE, COMPLAIN

snobbish: . . . RITZY, SNOOTY,
UPPITY, UPPISH, HIGH-HAT,
STUCK-UP

snoop: . . . PRY, LOOK, LURK,
NOSE, PEEK, PEEP, PROWL,
SKULK, SNEAK, BUSYBODY

snooty: . . . PROUD, HAUGHTY,
SNOBBISH, HOITY-TOITY

snooze: . . . . see sleep

snort: . . . NIP, LAUGH, DRINK,
SNIFF, SNORT, SNUFF

snout: . . . . NEB, BEAK, NOSE,
SPOUT, TRUNK, NOZZLE,
MUZZLE, ROSTRUM

snowy: . . . . . . PURE, NIVAL,
WHITE, BRUMAL, WINTRY,
NIVEOUS, SPOTLESS

snub: . . CUT, CHECK, SCORN,
IGNORE, REBUFF, SLIGHT,
TAUTEN, AFFRONT, REPRESS,
RESTRAIN, HIGH-HAT

snuff: . . ODOR, PINCH, SCENT,
SMELL, SNIFF, SNORT, DOUSE,
INHALE, EXTINGUISH

snug: . . . COZY, NEAT, SAFE,
TAUT, TIDY, TRIM, WARM,
QUIET, TIGHT, SECURE,
COMPACT, COMFORTABLE

snuggle: . . . NESTLE, CUDDLE

so: . . SIC, ERGO, THEN, THUS,
TRUE, VERY, HENCE, BECAUSE,
THEREFORE, LIKEWISE,
ACCORDINGLY

soak: . . . DIP, HIT, RET, SOG,
SOP, SOT, WET, BLOW, OOZE,
DRINK, IMBUE, SOUSE, STEEP,
DRENCH, IMBIBE, IMBRUE,
STEEP, DRUNKARD, MACERATE,
PERMEATE, SATURATE

soaked: . . . . . . WET, SOGGY,
SODDEN

soap: . . . . SAPO, MONEY,
LATHER, CASTILE, FLATTER,
CLEANSER, DETERGENT

soapy: . . . . . . OILY, SAUVE,
SMOOTH, SAPONIC, LATHERED,
UNCTUOUS

soar: . . FLY, LIFT, RISE, SAIL,
FLOAT, GLIDE, HOVER, PLANE,

TOWER, ASPIRE, ASCEND, TRANSCEND

sob: . . . . . CRY, WAIL, WEEP, BOOHOO, WHIMPER

sober: . . . CALM, COOL, SANE, GRAVE, PLAIN, QUIET, STAID, SEDATE, SEVERE, SIMPLE, SOLEMN, SOMBER, STEADY, SUBDUE, EARNEST, SERIOUS, DECOROUS, ABSTINENT, TEMPERATE

sobriety: . . . . GRAVITY, RESTRAINT, SOLEMNITY, ABSTINENCE, SEDATENESS, TEMPERANCE, MODERATION

sobriquet: . . . . NAME, ALIAS, EPITHET, NICKNAME, APPELLATION

sociable: . . . . AFFABLE, AMINABLE, FRIENDLY, OUTGOING, INFORMAL, AGREEABLE, GREGARIOUS

social: . . . . . BEE, TEA, STAG, PARTY, SMOKER, SOIREE, SHINDIG, AGREEABLE, CONVIVIAL, GATHERING, GREGARIOUS

socialist: . . . RED, ANARCHIST, COMMUNIST, BOLSHEVIST, NATIONALIST

society: . . . . (also see **organization**) BUND, CLAN, GILD, GUILD, ORDER, UNION, MENAGE, ACADEMY, COMPANY, ALLIANCE, COMMUNITY, ASSOCIATION

sociology: . . . . DEMOTICS

sock: . . . . HIT, BEAT, BLOW, SHOE, ANKLET, COMEDY, SANDAL, STRIKE, WALLOP, STOCKING, PLOWSHARE

sod: . . . . . DIRT, PEAT, SOIL, TURF, DELFT, DIVOT, EARTH, GLEBE, SWARD

sodality: . . . . UNION, UNITY, FELLOWSHIP, FATERNITY

sodden: . . . . . DRUNK, HEAVY, MOIST, SOGGY, BOILED,

DULLED, SOAKED, STEWED, STUPID, STEEPED, SATURATED

sofa: . . . . COUCH, DIVAN, LOUNGE, SETTEE, DAYBED, DAVENPORT, CHESTERFIELD

soft: . . . . . LOW, EASY, FINE, LIMP, MILD, WEAK, BLAND, CUSHY, DOWNY, FAINT, MUSHY, FLABBY, FLUFFY, GENTLE, PLACID, SILKEN, SMOOTH, TENDER, CLEMENT, DUCTILE, LENIENT, LIGHTLY, QUIETLY, SQUASHY, SUBDUED, VELVETY, FEMININE, FLEXIBLE, TRANQUIL, TEMPERATE, TRACTABLE

soften: . . . RET, EASE, MELT, ALLAY, RELAX, STEEP, YIELD, ANNEAL, GENTLE, LOOSEN, PACIFY, RELENT, SOOTHE, SUBDUE, TEMPER, APPEASE, ASSUAGE, MOLLIFY, ENERVATE, MACERATE, MITIGATE, MODERATE, ALLEVIATE, MELIORATE

soggy: . . . WET, DAMP, HEAVY, SOAKED, SODDEN, WATERY, SATURATED

soigne: . . TIDY, NEAT, SLEEK, WELL-GROOMED

soil: . . . . . SOD, BLOT, BLUR, CLAY, DAUB, DIRT, LAND, LOAM, MARL, SPOT, DIRTY, EARTH, FILTH, GLEBE, GUMBO, GRIME, LOESS, SMEAR, STAIN, SULLY, DEFILE, GROUND, REFUSE, SEWAGE, SMIRCH, SMUDGE, BEGRIME, CORRUPT, POLLUTE, TARNISH, ALLUVIUM, DISGRACE, CONTAMINATE

sojourn: . . BIDE, REST, STAY, ABIDE, DELAY, DWELL, LODGE, TARRY, VISIT, RESIDE, TRAVEL

solace: . . . . . ALLAY, AMUSE, CHEER, RELIEF, SOOTHE, ASSUAGE, COMFORT, CONSOLE, ALLEVIATE, DIVERSION

solar: . . . . HELIACAL

solder: . . . BOND, FUSE, JOIN, MEND, BRAZE, PATCH, UNITE, CEMENT

sole: . . ONE, DISH, FISH, FOOT, LONE, MERE, ONLY, ALONE, FLOUR, PLATE, SLADE, BOTTOM, ENTIRE, SINGLE, UNIQUE, FLATFISH, HALIBUT, SOLITARY, UNSHARED, EXCLUSIVE

solecism: . . . . . BARBARISM, DEVIATION, IMPROPRIETY

solely: . . . ALL, ONLY, ALONE, MERELY, SINGLY, ENTIRELY, EXCLUSIVELY

solemn: . . . . . . SAD, GRAVE, SOBER, AUGUST, DEVOUT, FORMAL, GLOOMY, RITUAL, SACRED, SEVERE, SOMBER, EARNEST, SERIOUS, STATELY, FUNEREAL, DIGNIFIED

solemnity: . . . . . . GRAVITY, CEREMONY, FORMALITY

solicit: . . . . ASK, BEG, BID, WOO, PLEA, SEEK, APPLY, COURT, CRAVE, MOOCH, TEMPT, ENTICE, INVITE, BESEECH, CANVASS, ENTREAT, IMPLORE, REQUEST, CAMPAIGN, PETITION, IMPORTUNE, PANHANDLE, SUPPLICATE

solicitude: . . . . . CARE, EASE, FEAR, HEED, ANXIETY, CONCERN, CAREFULNESS, APPREHENSION

solid: . . . CONE, CUBE, FIRM, FULL, HARD, DENSE, MASSY, SOUND, STIFF, THICK, STABLE, STRONG, BEDROCK, COMPACT, MASSIVE, UNIFORM, GENUINE, CONSTANT, RELIABLE, STERLING, UNBROKEN

solidify: . . . GEL, SET, CAKE, JELL, CEMENT, HARDEN, COMPACT, CONGEAL, CONCRETE, COAGULATE, CONSOLIDATE

solidity: . . . . FIRMNESS, HARDNESS, SOLIDNESS, STABILITY

solioquy: . . POEM, DISCOURSE, MONOLOGUE

solitare: . . . . . . GEM, GAME, HERMIT, LONELY, DIAMOND, RECLUSE, PATIENCE

solitary: . . . . . . LONE, SOLE, ALONE, ONLY, HERMIT, LONELY, REMOTE, SINGLE, DESOLATE, LONESOME, INDIVIDUAL, CONFINEMENT

solitude: . . . . PRIVACY, ISOLATION, SECLUSION, REMOTENESS

solon: . . . . . SAGE, SENATOR, WISEMAN, LAWGIVER, LAWMAKER, LEGISLATOR

solution: . . . . . . KEY, BREAK, ANSWER, ANALYSIS, DISCHARGE, EXPLANATION

solve: . . . . FATHOM, UNFOLD, EXPLAIN, RESOLVE, UNRAVEL, INTERPRET, DETERMINE

somatic: . . BODILY, PARIETAL, PHYSICAL, CORPOREAL

somber: . . SAD, DARK, DULL, DUSKY, GRAVE, SOBER, DISMAL, GLOOMY, SEVERE, SOLEMN, AUSTERE, DEPRESSED

some: . . . . . ANY, BUT, PART, ABOUT, PORTION, SEVERAL

sometime: . . . . . . LATE, ONCE, FORMER, ERST(WHILE)

somnolent: . . . . SLEEPY, DROWSY

son: . . . . HEIR, CHILD, SCION, NATIVE, DISCIPLE, PROGENY, OFFSPRING, DESCENDANT

song: . . . . . LAY, ODE, ARIA, CANT, DIRGE, ELEGY, HYMN, POEM, RUNE, TUNE, BLUES, CANTO, CAROL, CHANT, DITTY, LYRIC, MUSIC, PSALM, VERSE, ANTHEM, BALLAD, CHANTY, MELODY, POETRY, SONNET, LULLABY, VESPERS, CANTICLE

sonority: . . . . . . RESONANCE

sonorous: . . . . RINGING, IMPOSING, RESONANT, IMPRESSIVE

soon: . . . . ERE, ANON, ENOW, EARLY, LATER, QUICK, SPEEDY, PRONTO, BETIME, ERELONG, QUICKLY, READILY, SHORTLY, DIRECTLY, SPEEDILY, PRESENTLY

soot: . . . COOM, SMUT, COLLY, CROCK, GRIME, SMOKE, BISTRE, CARBON, BLACKEN, LAMPBLACK

sooth: . . . . FACT, REAL, SOFT, SWEET, TRULY, TRUTH, COMFORT, GENUINE, PRESENT, REALITY, PLEASING, PLEASURE, TRUTHFUL, DELIGHTFUL

soothe: . . . PET, CALM, EASE, LULL, ALLAY, QUIET, SALVE, PACIFY, SOLACE, STROKE, APPEASE, ASSUAGE, COMFORT, MOLLIFY, PLACATE, RELIEVE, MITIGATE, PALLIATE, ALLEVIATE

soothing: . . EASING, CALMING, LENITIVE

soothsay: . . . . PREDICT, FORETELL

soothsayer: . . . SEER, AUGUR, MANTIS, AUGUER, ORACLE, DIVINER, PROPHET, HARUSPEX

sooty: . . DARK, DUSKY, BLACK

sop: . . . . DUNK, GIFT, LUMP, MESS, OOZE, SOAK, BRIBE, CLOUD, CLUMP, STEEP, SATURATE, CONCESSION

sophisticate: . . ALTER, SPOIL, DEBASE, CORRUPT, FALSIFY, MISLEAD, ADULTERATE

sophisticated: . . . HEP, WISE, BLASE, SUBTLE, REFINED, WORLDLY, ADULTERATED

sophistry: . . . . DECEIT, FALLACY, ARGUMENT, TRICKERY, CHICANERY, DECEPTION

sopor: . . . . . . SLEEP, STUPOR, LETHARGY

soporific: . DROWSY, OPIATE, HYPNOTIC, NARCOTIC, SOMNIFIC

soppy: . . . . WET, RAINY, SOAKED, MAWKISH, SENTIMENTAL

sorcerer: . . . . MAGI, MAGUS, WIZARD, WARLOCK, MAGICIAN, CONJURER, CHALDEAN

sorceress: . . . . SYBIL, WITCH, CIRCE, LAMIA, MEDEA

sorcery: . . ART, OBE, MAGIC, OBEAH, SPELL, FETISH, VOODOO, WITCHCRAFT, THEURGY, SORTILEGE, DIABLERIE, DIABOLISM, NECROMANSY, CONJURATION

sordid: . . . LOW, BASE, MEAN, VILE, DIRTY, GROSS, FILTHY, IGNOBLE, SELFISH, SQUALID, GRUESOME, WRETCHED, MERCENARY, DESPICABLE

sore: . . . . BOIL, PAIN, ANGRY, BLAIN, GRIEF, ULCER, VEXED, WOUND, BITTER, BRUISE, FESTER, LESION, TENDER, TOUCHY, ACHING, ANNOYED, PAINFUL, PUSTULE, ABRASION, INFLAMED, OFFENDED, IRRITATED, RESENTFUL, SENSITIVE

sorehead: . . . LOSER, GRIPER, MALCONTENT

sorely: . . . . GREATLY, SEVERELY, URGENTLY, EXTREMELY, GRIEVOUSLY

sorrow: . . . . RUE, WOE, BALE, CARE, DOLE, LOSS, DOLAR, GRIEF, MOURN, GRIEVE, LAMENT, MISERY, REGRET, ANGUISH, SADNESS, TROUBLE, CALAMITY, DISTRESS, ADVERSITY

sorry: . . . . BAD, SAD, MEAN, POOR, DISMAL, REGRET, REPENT, PITIFUL, CONTRITE, GRIEVOUS, INFERIOR, WRETCHED, MISERABLE, REGRETFUL, REMORSEFUL

sort: .. ILK, LOT, CULL, KIND, RACE, RANK, SIFT, TYPE, ALLOT, BATCH, BREED, CLASS, GENUS, GRADE, GROUP, ORDER, ASSIGN, CHOOSE, GENDER, MANNER, NATURE, SELECT, ARRANGE, QUALITY, SPECIES, VARIETY, CLASSIFY, SEPARATE, CHARACTER

sortie: .. RAID, SALLY, FORAY

sortilege: .... SORCERY, PROPHECY, DIVINATION

sot: . TOPER, SOUSE, RUMMY, INEBRIATE, DRUNKARD

sough: . SIGH, MOAN, CHANT, DITCH, DRAIN, RUMOR, MURMER, RUSTLE, BREATHE, MOANING, WHISTLE

soul: ... AME, ANIMA, ATMAN, FORCE, HEART, ESPRIT, PNEUMA, SPIRIT, COURAGE, ESSENCE, EMBODIMENT

sound: ..... CRY, DIN, HUM, FIRM, GOOD, HAIL, HONK, PURL, SAFE, SANE, TEST, TONE, TRIG, TRUE, ALARM, AUDIO, BLARE, CLANG, INLET, NOISE, PLUMB, PROBE, SOLID, VALID, WHOLE, BEDLAM, CLAMOR, APPEAR, FATHOM, HONEST, HUBBUB, INTACT, RACKET, ROBUST, SECURE, STABLE, STRAIT, STRONG, STURDY, TUMULT, UPROAR, CLANGOR, CLATTER, HEALTHY, MEASURE, RELIABLE, STRIDOR, UNDAMAGED

soundless: .... MUTE, QUIET, STILL, SILENT, ASONANT

soup: ..... BROTH, GUMBO, PUREE, BISQUE, BORSHT, BURGOO, BORSCHT, POTTAGE, CHOWDER, BOUILLON, CONNSOMME, GAZPACHO, MINESTRONE

sour: .... WRY, ACID, DOUR, GRIM, TART, ACERB, ACRID, CROSS, GRUFF, ACETIC, ACIDIC, BITTER, MOROSE, RANCID, SULLEN, ACETOSE, ACETOUS, CRABBED, ACERBATE, ACIDULOUS, ASTRINGENT

source: .. FONT, GERM, HEAD, RISE, ROOT, SEED, FOUNT, ORIGIN, PARENT, SPRING, FOUNTAIN, BEGINNING, HEADSPRING, WELLSPRING

souse: ... DUCK SOAK, WASH, BATHE, BRINE, DRENCH, PICKLE, PLUNGE, SWOOP, THWACK IMMERSE, TIPPLER, DRUNKARD, SATURATE, SUBMERGE

soused: ...... DRUNK, TIPSY

soutane: .... TUNIC, CLOAK, CASSOCK

souvenir: .... CURIO, RELIC, SCRAP, KEEPSAKE, REMINDER, MOMENTO

sovereign: ..... KING, CHIEF, LIEGE, ROYAL, RULER, PRINCE, POUND, EMPEROR, HIGHEST, MONARCH, SUPREME, GREATEST, REIGNING, SUPERIOR

sovereignty: .. RULE, SWAY, REALM, DIADEM, EMPERY, EMPIRE, DYNASTY, MAJESTY, ROYALTY, SCEPTRE, THRONE, DOMINION, SUPREMACY

sow: ...... HOG, PIG, SEED, DITCH, DRAIN, DRILL, PLANT, STREW, SWINE, SLUICE, SPREAD, CHANNEL, SCATTER, DISPERSE, BROADCAST, PROPAGATE, DISSEMINATE

spa: .. BATH, OASIS, RESORT, SPRING

space: .... GAP, AREA, PATH, ROOM, VOID, WALK, AMBIT, RANGE, TRACK, COURSE, DIVIDE, EXTENT, REGION, ARRANGE, EXPANSE, CAPACITY, DISTANCE, DURATION, INTERVAL, RESERVATION

spacious: ..... VAST, AMPLE, BROAD, GREAT, LARGE, ROOMY, CAPACIOUS, EXPANSIVE, EXTENSIVE

spade: . . . . DIG, SAM, SPUD, GRAFT, SCOOP, SHOVEL

spalpeen: . . . . BOY, SCAMP, RASCAL

span: . . . . PAIR, ROPE, SWIM, TEAM, TIME, COVER, CROSS, REACH, SEIZE, BRIDGE, EXTEND, PERIOD, QUARTER, SPREAD, MEASURE, STRETCH, DISTANCE, DURATION

spangle: . . . ADORN, GLEAM, PLATE, AIGLET, SEQUIN, GLISTEN, GLITTER, SPARKLE, SPRINKLE

Spaniard: . . LATIN, ESPANOL, IBERIAN, CASTILIAN

spank: . . . CUFF, SLAP, WHIP, SMACK, PADDLE, STRIKE, CHASTISE

spanking: . . . . BRISK, FRESH, LARGE, RAPID, LIVELY, STRONG, DASHING, VIGOROUS

spanner: . . . . WRENCH

spar: . . . . . BAR, BOX, ROD, BEAM, BOLT, BOOM, GAFF, MAST, POLE, RUNG, SHUT, YARD, CLOSE, FIGHT, LUNGE, SPRIT, BARITE, BICKER, CHARGE, FASTEN, RAFTER, STRIKE, TIMBER, DISPUTE, ENCLOSE, WRANGLE, YARDARM

spare: . . . . FREE, LEAN, PART, SAVE, SLIM, THIN, AVOID, EXTRA, FAVOR, GAUNT, LANKY, STINT, DESIST, ENDURE, FRUGAL, MEAGER, SCANTY, FORBEAR, LEISURE, REFRAIN, RELIEVE, RESERVE, PRESERVE, TOLERATE

sparge: . . . . . SPRAY, SPLASH, SPRINKLE

sparing: . . . SCANT, FRUGAL, MEAGER, SAVING, SCANTY, CAREFUL, LIMITED, THRIFTY, MERCIFUL, STINTING, SCRIMPING

spark: . . . ARC, WOO, BEAU, COURT, FLASH, GRAIN, LOVER, TRACE, KINDLE, PARTICLE, ACTIVATE, SCINTILLA, SWEETHEART

sparkle: . . . . . BLINK, FLASH, GLEAM, GLINT, SHINE, SPARK, DIFFUSE, GLITTER, GLISTEN, RADIATE, REFLECT, SCATTER, DISPERSE, SPRINKLE, VIVACITY, CORUSCATE, EFFERVESCE, BRILLIANCE, SCINTILLATE

sparkling: . . BRIGHT, LIVELY, STARRY, SHINING, ANIMATED, FLASHING, GLEAMING, BRILLIANT, TWINKLING, GLITTERING, EFFERVESCENT

sparse: . . . . . . THIN, SCANT, MEAGER

spartan: . . . . BRAVE, HARDY, FRUGAL, HEROIC, SEVERE, LACONIC, STOICAL, WARLIKE, UNDAUNTED, COURAGEOUS

spasm: . . . . . . FIT, TIC, GRIP, KINK, PANG, CRAMP, CRICK, THROE, CHOREA, CONVULSION

spasmodic: . . . . FITFUL, SUDDEN, INTERMITTENT

spat: . . . . . . ROW, FUSS, TIFF, EJECT, SPAWN, GAITER, OYSTER, SPLASH, DISPUTE, LEGGING, QUARREL

spate: . . . GUSH, RAIN, FLOOD, DELUGE, FRESHET, OUTFLOW, TORRENT, DOWNPOUR, OUTPOURING, RAINSTORM, INUNDATION, WATERSPOUT

spatter: . . SOIL, SPOT, SPRAY, SPURT, DEFAME, SPLASH, SCATTER, SPRINKLE

spawn: . . . ROE, EGGS, GERM, SEED, SPAT, DEPOSIT, PRODUCE, GENERATE

spay: . . . . . GELD, CASTRATE, STERILIZE

speak: . . . SAY, CARP, CHAT, HAIL, RANT, RAVE, TALK, TELL, EXTOL, ORATE, UTTER, MENTION, REVEAL, ADDRESS, DECLAIM, DECLARE, EXPRESS, CONVERSE, HARANGUE,

PROCLAIM, DISCOURSE, PRONOUNCE, ARTICULATE

spear: . . . . . GAD, ROD, DART, GAFF, PIKE, REED, STAB, BLADE, LANCE, SHAFT, SHOOT, STALK, IMPALE, PIERCE, STRIKE, FEATHER, HARPOON, JAVELIN, MISSILE, TRIDENT, PENETRATE

spearhead: . . . . VAN, GAFF, LEAD, VANGUARD

special: . . DEAR, RARE, CHIEF, EXTRA, UNIQUE, LIMITED, UNUSUAL, FAVORITE, INTIMATE, PECULIAR, PERSONAL, SPECIFIC, UNCOMMON, INDIVIDUAL, PARTICULAR, RESTRICTED, DISTINCTIVE

specialty: . . . . . LINE, FORTE, SKILL, MEITER, APTITUDE

specie: . . CASH, COIN, MONEY

species: . . . KIND, RACE, SORT, TYPE, BREED, CLASS, GENRE, VARIETY, CATEGORY

specific: . . . EXACT, PRECISE, CONCRETE, DEFINITE, EXPLICIT, PECULIAR, PARTICULAR, RESTRICTED

specify: . . . . NAME, TELL, ALLOT, STATE, ASSIGN, DEFINE, DETAIL, MENTION, DESCRIBE, DESIGNATE, STIPULATE

specimen: . . . MODEL, RELIC, TOKEN, SAMPLE, SWATCH, EXAMPLE, PATTERN

specious: . . . . . GAY, SHOWY, GLOSSY, HOLLOW, COLORED, PLAUSIBLE, OSTENSIBLE, HYPROCRITICAL

speck: . . . BIT, DOT, JOT, NIT, BLOT, IOTA, MARK, MITE, MOTE, SPOT, WHIT, FLECK, STAIN, BLEMISH, PARTICLE

speckle: . . . . . . DOT, FLECK, MOTTLE, DAPPLE, MACULATE

spectacle: . . . . SHOW, VIEW, MODEL, SCENE, SIGHT, DISPLAY, DIORAMA, PAGENT, PANORAMA, EXHIBITION

spectator: . . . . WITNESS, ONLOOKER, BEHOLDER, KIBITZER, WATCHER, OBSERVER, LOOKER-ON

specter: . . . . . BOGY, GHOST, SPOOK, SPIRIT, WRAITH, SHADOW, BUG A BOO, PHANTOM, PHANTASM, APPARITION

spectral: . . . . EERY, SPOOKY, GHOSTLY, PHANTOM

speculate: . . . GUESS, THINK, GAMBLE, PONDER, WONDER, CONSIDER, MEDITATE, RUMINATE, THEORIZE, CONJECTURE, DELIBERATE, CONTEMPLATE

sped: . RAN, RACED, DARTED, DASHED, GALLOPED, HASTENED, ACCELERATED

speech: . . . LIP, TALK, IDIOM, VOICE, SLANG, DILOGY, SERMON, TIRADE, ADDRESS, DIALECT, ORATION, EPILOGUE, HARANGUE, LANGUAGE, EXPRESSION, UTTERANCE, DECLAMATION

speechless: . . . MUM, DUMB, MUTE, SILENT, VOICELESS, TONGUE-TIED, APHONIC, APHASIC

speed: . . . FLY, HIE, RIP, RATE, RACE, RUSH, TEAR, HASTE, HURRY, HASTEN, CELERITY, DISPATCH, EXPEDITE, RAPIDITY, VELOCITY, QUICKNESS, SWIFTNESS, ACCELERATE

speedily: . . . . . . FAST, SOON, APACE, QUICKLY, RAPIDLY, PROMPTLY, POSTHASTE

speedy: . . . . . . FAST, APACE, FLEET, SWIFT, RAPID, QUICK, PROMPT

spell: . . BAR, FIT, HEX, FORM, LATH, MEAN, RUNG, SAVE, TALE, TELL, TURN, CHARM, CURSE, MAGIC, SPARE, SPEAK, STORY, UTTER, IMPORT, PERIOD, RELATE, RELIEF,

TRANCE, BEWITCH, COMPOSE, RELIEVE, SIGNIFY, SORCERY

spellbind: . . . HOLD, CHARM, ENCHANT, ENTRANCE, FASCINATE

spend: . . . . RUN, USE, FLOW, GIVE, LOSE, PASS, EXERT, WASTE, BESTOW, DEVOTE, ELAPSE, EXPEND, LAVISH, CONSUME EXHAUST, FATIGUE, PERFORM, DISBURSE, SQUANDER, DISSIPATE

spendthrift: . . . . . . WASTER, WASTREL, ROUNDER, PRODIGAL, WASTEFUL, PROFLIGATE, SQUANDERER

spent: . . . . BEAT, PAID, USED, WORN, TIRED, WEARY, EFFETE, FAGGED, CONSUMED, EXHAUSTED, SQUANDERED

sperm: . . MILT, SEED, SEMEN, WHALE

spew: . . . SPUE, OOZE, EJECT, EXUDE, VOMIT, EXTRUDE, SCATTER, DISGORGE

sphacelate: . . . . . DECAYED, MORTIFY, WITHERED, MORTIFIED

sphere: . . . . ORB, SKY, BALL, RANK, STAR, AMBIT, ARENA, CLASS, FIELD, GLOBE, ORBIT, ORDER, RANGE, REALM, SCOPE, DOMAIN, PLANET, CIRCUIT, COMPASS, RONDURE, THEATRE, PROVINCE

spherical: . . . ORBIC, OVOID, ROUND, ROTUND, GLOBATE, GLOBOID, GLOBOSE, GLOBULAR

sphinx: . . . . . MOTH, RIDDLE, ENIGMA, MONSTER, PROPHET

spice: . . DASH, ODOR, AROMA, TASTE, FLAVOR, RELISH, SEASON, PERFUME, VARIETY, ADMIXTURE, CONDIMENT, SEASONING, APPEARANCE
kind of: . . . . . DILL, MACE, MINT, MULL, SAGE, ANISE, BASIL, CAPER, CHILI, CLOVE, CUMIN, CURRY, POPPY, THYME, BORAGE, BURNET, CELERY, CHIVES, CLOVES, GINGER, NUTMEG, PEPPER, SAVORY, SESAME, SORREL, STACTE, TAMARA, CANELLA, CARAWAY, CAYENNE, CHERVIL, FENNEL, MUSTARD, OREGENO, PAPRIKA, PARSLEY, PIMENTO, SAFFRON, ALLSPICE, CARDAMON, CINNAMON, MARJORAM, ROSEMARY, TARAGON, TUMERIC, CORIANDER, SASSAFRASS, SPEARMINT

spicule: . . DART, NAIL, SPIKE, SPINE, ACTINE, PRICKLE, SCLERITE

spicy: . . . . HOT, KEEN, RACY, JUICY, RISQUE, GINGERY, PEPPRY, PIQUANT, PUNGENT, AROMATIC, FRAGRANT

spider: . . . . TRIPOD, TRIVET, SKILLET, ARACHNID, (FRYING)PAN, TARANTULA

spiel: . . . . TALK, SPEECH

spiffy: . . . . NEAT, SMART, SPRUCE

spigot: . . . . . . PEG, PIN, TAP, COCK, PLUG, SPILE, SPOUT, VALVE, FAUCET

spike: . . . . GAD, BROB, FOIL, NAIL, FINE, UMBO, AMENT, BLOCK, PITON, PRONG, SPINE, ANTLER, EARLET, FINISH, IMPALE, PIERCE, SPADIX, THWART, MACKEREL, FRUSTRATE

spile: . . PIN, ROD, TAP, BUNG, PLUG, RULE, TUBE, SPILL, SPOUT, STAKE, SPIGOT, SPLINTER

spill: . . . PEG, PIN, ROD, DISK, FALL, FLOW, PLUG, SPILE, SPOIL, SPOOL, WASTE, REVEAL, TUMBLE, DESTROY, DIVULGE, SCATTER, OVERFLOW, SPLINTER

spin: . . . . . BIRL, BURL, GYRE, REEL, TURN, SWIRL, TWIRL, TWIST, WEAVE, WHIRL, GYRATE, ROTATE, REVOLVE

spindle: . . . . PIN, ROD, AXIS, AXLE, STEM, ARBOR, SHAFT, STALK, DISTAFF, TRIBLET, MANDREL

spine: . . . RAY, BACK, CHINE, RIDGE, QUILL, SPIKE, THORN, CHAETA, NEEDLE, RACHIS, SPIRIT, COURAGE, PRICKLE, SPICULE, BACKBONE, VERTEBRAE

spinet: . PIANO, HARPSICHORD

spinnaker: . . . . SAIL

spinner: . . TOP, LURE, SPOON, SPIDER, WEAVER, NARRATOR, SILKWORM

spinney: . . . . COPSE, GROVE, THICKET

spinning: . . . . ROTARY, REELING, WHIRLING, REVOLVING

spiny: . . . . . HISPID, THORNY, PRICKLY, SPINOSE, ACICULAR, ACANTHOID

spiracle: . . . . . . HOLE, PORE, VENT, ORIFICE, BLOWHOLE, AIR HOLE

spiral: . . COIL, CURL, CURVE, HELIX, COILING, CURVING, HELICAL, WINDING, CIRCLING, HELCOID, CORKSCREW

spire: . . . . COIL, CURL, PEAK, STALK, SHAFT, TOWER, WHORL, FLECHE, SPIRAL, SPROUT, STEEPLE

spirit: . . . . . PEP, VIM, ELAN, FIRE, LIFE, MIND, MOOD, SOUL, WILL, WIND, ANGEL, ARDOR, BOGEY, ETHOS, FAIRY, GHOST, HAUNT, HEART, METAL, PLUCK, SPOOK, SPUNK, VERVE, VIGOR, ENERGY, GINGER, METTLE, MORALE, BANSHEE, BRAVERY, COURAGE, VIVACITY, APPARITION, ENTHUSIASM

spirited: . . . . BRISK, EAGER, FIERY, PERKY, ACTIVE, ARDENT, LIVELY, SPUNKY, DASHING, ANIMATED, VIGOROUS, ENERGETIC, SPRIGHTLY

spiritless: . . . . COLD, DEAD, DULL, MEEK, VAPID, DEJECTED, LISTLESS, DEPRESSED, LACKADAISICAL

spiritual: . . . . . . HOLY, PURE, SONG, DEVOUT, DIVINE, SACRED

spit: . . FIX, ROD, EMIT, RAIN, REEF, SNOW, EJECT, SHOAL, STICK, SWORD, DAGGER, IMPALE, SALIVA, BROACH, SKEWER, SPUTUM, SPINDLE, SPITTLE, SANDBANK, EXPECTORATE

spite: . . . . VEX, HATE, HURT, ANNOY, PIQUE, VENOM, ENMITY, GRUDGE, HATRED, MALICE, RANCOR, SPLEEN, THWART, DISLIKE, ILL-WILL, MORTIFY, DISGRACE, ANIMOSITY

spiteful: . . . . MEAN, CATTY, SNIDE, VIPERINE, VIPEROUS, MALICIOUS, SPLENETIC, VENOMOUS, VINDICTIVE

splash: . . . LAP, DASH, DAUB, SPOT, BATHE, SPRAY, BLOTCH, DABBLE, SPARGE, SPRINKLE, SPLATTER, SPLOTCH, SPATTER

splatter: . . . . . DAB, SPLASH, SPATTER, SPRINKLE

splay: . . AWRY, FLAN, BEVEL, SLANT, SLOPE, CLUMSY, EXPAND, SPREAD, AWKWARD, SLOPING, UNGAINLY, DISLOCATE, SPREADING

spleen: . . . FIRE, MILT, MOOD, WHIM, ANGER, ORGAN, SPITE, MALICE, DISLIKE, MELANCHOLY

splendid: . . . . . . FINE, GOOD, GRAND, REGAL, SHOWY, BRIGHT, SUBERB, RIPPING, SUBLIME, LUSTROUS,

GORGEOUS, GLORIOUS,
BRILLIANT, EXCELLENT

splendor: .... POMP, ECLAT,
GLORY, SHEEN, BRIGHT,
LUSTER, GLITTER, GRANDEUR,
RADIANCE, BRILLIANCE

splenetic: . SULLEN, PEEVISH,
SPITEFUL, IRRITABLE,
MALICIOUS

splice: ... WED, JOIN, MARRY,
UNITE, INTERWEAVE

splint: ...... LATH, BRACE,
PLATE, FASTEN, CONFINE

splinter: ...... CHIP, REND,
BREAK, SLICE, SMASH, SPLIT,
FASTEN, SHIVER, SLIVER,
CONFINE, FLINDER, SHATTER,
FRAGMENT

split: ... CHAP, REND, RENT,
RIVE, TEAR, BREAK, BURST,
CLEFT, CRACK, REAVE, RIVEN,
SHARE, WEDGE, BISECT,
BOTTLE, BREACH, BROKEN,
CLEAVE, CLOVEN, DIVIDE,
SCHISM, SLIVER, SUNDER,
FISSURE, RUPTURE, SHATTER,
FRAGMENT, SEPARATE,
SPLINTER

splotch: .. DAB, BLOT, DAUP,
SPOT, SMEAR, STAIN, BLOTCH,
SPLASH

splurge: .. EFFORT, DISPLAY,
OSTENTATION

spoil: ..... MAR, ROB, ROT,
LOOT, MESS, PREY, RUIN,
SACK, SWAG, BOOTY, DECAY,
PRIZE, STRIP, TAINT, WASTE,
CODDLE, DAMAGE, DEFACE,
IMPAIR, INJURE, PAMPER,
PERISH, RAVAGE, CORRUPT,
DESTROY, INDULGE, PILLAGE,
PLUNDER, VIOLATE, VITIATE

spoke: ..... PIN, BAR, GRIP,
RUNG, ROUND, STAKE, STICK,
HANDHOLD

spoken: .... ORAL, SAID,
VOCAL, UTTERED

spoliate: ..... ROB, DESPOIL,
PILLAGE, PLUNDER

sponge: .. BUM, CAKE, SWAB,
WIPE, ASCON, CADGE, ERASE,
MOOCH, CLEANSE, PUDDING,
SCRUNGE, PARASITE, SCROUNGE

spongy: ... ELASTIC, POROUS,
ABSORBENT

sponsor: ... ANGEL, BACKER,
PATRON, SURETY, GODFATHER,
INTRODUCE

sponsorship: ... EGIS, AEGIS,
AUSPICES

spontaneous: ... FREE, WILD,
CARELESS, AUTOMATIC,
IMPULSIVE, INSTINCTIVE

spoof: .... FOOL, HOAX, JOKE,
TRICK, DECEIVE, SWINDLE,
NONSENSE

spook: ..... GHOST, HAUNT,
SPIRIT, WRAITH, SPECTER,
APPARITION

spooky: ..... EERIE, WEIRD,
GHOSTLY, UNCANNY, SPECTRAL

spool: .. REEL, WIND, BOBBIN,
BROACH, SPINDLE, CYLINDER

spoon: .. PET, NECK, LADLE,
SCOOP, CARESS, SHOVEL

spoonfed: ...... CODDLED,
PAMPERED

spoony: .... SILLY, FOOLISH,
AMOROUS, SENTIMENTAL

spoor: ..... SCENT, TRACE,
TRAIL, TRACK

sporadic: ..... IRREGULAR,
OCCASIONAL, DESULTORY

spore: .. GERM, SEED, ZYGOTE

sport: .... FUN, GAME, JEST,
JOKE, MOCK, PLAY, ROMP,
WEAR, DALLY, FREAK, FROLIC,
MUTANT, CONTEST, PASTIME,
DIVERSION, AMUSEMENT,
RECREATION

site: ... GYM, GRID, OVAL,
POOL, RING, RINK, ARENA,
COURT, FIELD, GREEN,
LINKS, TRACK, COURSE,
DIAMOND, STADIUM,
COLISEUM, HIPPODROME

sporty: ..... LOUD, FLASHY,
SHOWY

spot: . . . BIT, DAB, DOT, BLOT, BLUR, FLAW, JAM, MARK, SITE, BLAZE, FLECK, MACLE, NEVUS, PATCH, PLACE, POINT, SPECK, STAIN, SULLY, TAINT, BLOTCH, DEFECT, DETECT, LOCATE, MACULA, BLEMISH, FRECKLE, SPLOTCH, HANDICAP, LOCALITY, LOCATION, MACULATE, POSITION, RECOGNIZE

spotless: . . . . . PURE, CLEAN, SNOWY, BLAMELESS, UNSULLIED, IMMACULATE, UMBLEMISHED

spotted: . . . . . PIED, CALICO, ESPIED, NOTED, MARKED, DAPPLED, MOTTLED, MACULATE, NOTICED, STAINED, SULLIED, BLEMISHED

spotty: . . UNEVEN, IRREGULAR

spousal: . . . . WEDLOCK, CEREMONY, MARRIAGE, NUPITALS

spouse: . . MATE, WIFE, BRIDE, CONSORT, HUSBAND, PARTNER, COMPANION, BRIDEGROOM

spout: . . . . . . JET, JUT, FLOW, GUSH, PAWN, PIPE, RANT, EJECT, ISSUE, ORATE, SHOOT, SHOUT, SPEAK, SPILE, SPURT, UTTER, NOZZLE, RECITE, SPIGOT, SQUIRT, STREAM, CONDUIT, DECLAIM, PAWNSHOP, DISCHARGE

sprawl: . . . LIE, LOLL, CRAWL, SPREAD, SCRAMBLE

spray: . . . . . JET, MIST, TWIG, BOUGH, SHOOT, SPRIG, SPUME, BRANCH, SHOWER, SPARGE, SPREAD, ATOMIZE, BOUQUET, SCATTER, SPRINKLE, DISCHARGE

spread: . . . . . FAN, JAM, TED, OLEO, MEAL, SPAN, BRUIT, COVER, FLARE, JELLY, FEAST, SMEAR, SPLAY, STREW, WIDEN, BUTTER, DIALATE, EXPAND, EXTEND, EXTENT, RAMIFY, UNFOLD, UNFURL, BROADEN, DIFFUSE, DISTEND, DIVERGE, ENLARGE, EXHIBIT, EXPANSE, OVERLAY, PROLONG, PUBLISH, RADIATE, SCATTER, STRETCH, DIFFUSE, DISPENSE, DISPERSE, INCREASE, MULTIPLY, PERMEATE, BROADCAST, CIRCULATE, PROPAGATE, DISTRIBUTE, DISSEMINATE

spree: . . . . . BAT, JAG, BOUT, BUST, LARK, ORGY, ROMP, TEAR, TOOT, BINGE, REVEL, BENDER, BUSTER, FROLIC, DEBAUCH, WASSIL, CAROUSAL

sprig: . . . . BRAD, NAIL, TRIM, TWIG, BOUGH, SCION, SHOOT, SPRAY, YOUTH, BRANCH, TENDRIL

sprightly: . . GAY, TID, PERT, AGILE, BRISK, ACTIVE, BLITHE, LIVELY, JAUNTY, BUOYANT, CHIPPER, QUICKLY, ANIMATED, VIGOROUS

spring: . . AIN, FLY, HOP, SPA, BOLT, DART, FONT, HEAD, JUMP, LEAP, RISE, STEM, WARP, WELL, ARISE, BOUND, ISSUE, SHOOT, SPURT, VAULT, BOUNCE, EMERGE, SEASON, SOURCE, THERME, FOUNTAIN

springe: . . . . . . TRAP, SNARE

springing back: . . . ELASTIC, RESILIENT, RENASCENT

springy: . . . . . WET, SPONGY, ELASTIC, FLEXIBLE, RESILANT

sprinkle: . . . DEG, DOT, WET, DUST, RAIN, SPOT, FLOUR, SPRAY, STREW, WATER, DABBLE, DREDGE, SPARGE, SPLASH, SHOWER, DRIZZLE, SCATTER, SPATTER, DISPERSE

sprint: . . . RUN, DASH, RACE

sprinter: . . . RACER, DASHER, RUNNER, ATHLETE, TRACKMAN

sprite: . . ELF, FAY, HOB, IMP, NIS, NIX, ELVE, PIXY, ARIEL, FAIRY, GENIE, GHOST, GNOME, PIXIE, GOBLIN, BROWNIE, HOBGOBLIN, APPARITION

sprout: . . . . BUD, SON, CION, CHIT, GERM, GROW, SCION, SHOOT, SPIRE, SPRIG, GROWTH, RATOON, BURGEON, GERMINATE

spruce: . . NEAT, POSH, SMUG, TRIG, TRIM, LARCH, NATTY, SMART, DAPPER, CONIFER, EPINETTE

spry: . . AGILE, BRISK, QUICK, SMART, ACTIVE, CLEVER, NIMBLE, VIGOROUS

spud: . . . . DIG, DRILL, KNIFE, SPADE, DAGGER, PADDLE, POTATO, REAMER, SHOVEL, PROJECTION

spume: . . . . . . FOAM, SCUM, FROTH

spunk: . . GRIT, PUNK, FLAME, NERVE, PLUCK, SPARK, KINDLE, METTLE, STARCH, SPIRIT, TINDER, COURAGE

spunky: . . . . GAME, BRAVE, PLUCKY, SPIRITED, COURAGEOUS

spur: . . . . EGG, GAFF, GOAD, MOVE, PROD, URGE, ARETE, BRACE, DRIVE, HURRY, IMPEL, PRESS, PRICK, RIDGE, ROWEL, STRUT, AROUSE, CALCAR, EXCITE, FOMENT, GRIFFE, HASTEN, INCITE, MOTIVE, SIDING, STIMULUS, INCENTIVE

spurious: . . . . FAKE, SHAM, BOGUS, FALSE, PHONY, SNIDE, FORCED, FORGED, BASTARD, ARTIFICIAL, FRAUDULENT, COUNTERFEIT

spurn: . . DASH, KICK, SCORN, REBUFF, REFUSE, REJECT, STRIKE, CONTEMN, DECLINE, DISDAIN

spurt: . . . . JET, DART, GUSH, BURST, EXPEL, SHOOT, SPOUT, SQUIRT, STREAM, INCREASE

spy: . . . PRY, EYE, SEE, ESPY, FINK, KEEK, NOSE, NOTE, AGENT, SCOUT, SNEAK, SNOOP, WATCH, BEHOLD, DESCRY, DETECT, SEARCH, DISCERN, EXAMINE, INSPECT, OBSERVE, SNOOPER, DISCOVER, INFORMER, PERCEIVE

spying: . . . . ESPIONAGE

squab: . SOFA, COUCH, PIPER, PLUMP, SHORT, THICK, PIGEON, CUSHION

squabble: . . . . . ROW, MUSS, SPAT, BRAWL, BICKER, HASSLE, CONTEND, DISPUTE, QUARREL, WRANGLE

squalid: . . . . . FOUL, MEAN, POOR, DIRTY, MANGY, FILTHY, SORDID, UNCLEAN, MISERABLE, REPULSIVE

squall: . . . CRY, GALE, GUST, WAUL, WAWL, STORM, FLURRY, SCREAM, SHOWER, SQUAWK, DISPUTE, TROUBLE, WINDSTORM

squalor: . . MUD, DIRT, FILTH, FILTHINESS

squander: . . . SPEND, WASTE, LAVISH, CONSUME, DEBAUCH, DISPEND, SCATTER, DISPERSE, MISSPEND

square: . . . EVEN, FAIR, PARK, RULE, TRUE, AGREE, EXACT, PLAZA, TALLY, HONEST, SETTLE, COMMONS, QUADRATE, BALANCED, RECONCILE

squash: . . . BEAT, FALL, PEPO, STOP, CRUSH, GOURD, PRESS, QUELL, SPORT, SQUISH, FLATTEN, PUMPKIN, SILENCE, SQUEEZE, SQUELCH, SUPPRESS

squat: . . . . . SIT, FALL, SINK, DUMPY, PUDGY, TUBBY, STOOP, CROUCH, SETTLE, STUBBY, THICKSET

squatter: . . . NESTER, SETTLER

squawk: . . . . CRY, KICK, PROTEST, COMPLAIN

squeak: . . . . CRY, CREAK

squeal: . . CRY, BLAB, SING, BETRAY, INFORM, PROTEST, COMPLAIN

squeamish: . . . SHY, DAINTY, MODEST, QUEASY, FINICAL, PRUDISH, QUALMISH,

RELUCTANT, SENSITIVE,
FASTIDIOUS

squeeze: .... EKE, HUG, JAM,
NIP, CROWD, CRUSH, FORCE,
PINCH, PRESS, WRING, CORNER,
EXTORT, SQUASH, THRUST,
EXTRACT, OPPRESS, SCRUNCH,
COMPRESS, CONDENSE,
PRESSURE, CONSTRICT

squelch: .... CRUSH, QUASH,
QUELL, KIBOSH, REBUKE,
SQUASH, SUBDUE, SILENCE,
SUPPRESS

squid: ... MOLLUSK, OCTOPUS,
CALAMARY, CUTTLEFISH

squilla: ..... PRAWN, SHRIMP

squint: .. CAST, PEER, SKEW,
GLANCE, STRABISMUS

squire: .... DONZEL, ESCORT,
GALLANT, HENCHMAN,
SERVITOR, ACCOMPANY,
ATTENDANT, GENTLEMAN,
ARMOR-BEARER

squirm: ... WRITHE, WIGGLE,
WRIGGLE

squirt: ... JET, SPURT, SPIRT,
SHOOT, STREAM

stab: .. JAB, TRY, GORE, PINK,
SPIT, DRIVE, KNIVE, LUNGE,
PRICK, PUNCH, WOUND, PIERCE,
STRIKE, STROKE, THRUST,
ATTEMPT, PUNCTURE,
PENETRATE

stability: ... POISE, BALANCE,
FIRMNESS, CONSTANCY,
PERMANENCE, STABLENESS,
STEADINESS

stable: ... BARN, FAST, FIRM,
SHED, SURE, FIXED, SOLID,
SOUND, STALL, HANGAR,
SECURE, STEADY, STRONG,
STURDY, DURABLE, LASTING,
CONSTANT, STEADFAST,
ENDURING, PADDOCK

stableman: .... GROOM,
HOLSTER, CURRIER

stack: .... HEAP, PILE, RICK,
RUCK, STOW, TIER, GROUP,

MOUND, SHOCK, CHIMNEY,
CONDUIT

staddle: .. ROW, BASE, CANE,
TREE, FRAME, STAFF, SWATH,
CRUTCH, SUPPORT

stadium: ..... BOWL, PARK,
OVAL, ARENA, STAGE,
COLISEUM

staff: ..... BAR, GAD, ROD,
CANE, CLUB, MACE, POLE,
PROD, WAND, AIDES, BATON,
CROOK, LANCE, SPEAR, STAVE,
STICK, VERGE, CUDGEL,
CROISER, RETINUE, SCEPTER,
SUPPORT, CADUCEUS,
PERSONNEL, TRUNCHEON,
ALPENSTOCK

stage: .... ERA, DAIS, DOCK,
STEP, SHOW, TIER, BOARD,
COACH, DRAMA, FLOOR,
GRADE, LEVEL, PHASE, STAIR,
STORY, DEGREE, DISPLAY,
EXHIBIT, PRESENT, PRODUCE,
ROSTRUM, STADIUM, THEATER,
PLATFORM, SCAFFOLD,
GRADATION

stagger: . REEL, ROCK, STUN,
SWAY, LURCH, SHAKE, WAVER,
HOBBLE, TOTTER, STARTLE,
TREMBLE, VIBRATE,
OVERWHELM, UNSETTLE

stagnant: ..... DULL, FOUL,
INERT, STALE, STILL, TORPID,
STANDING, SLUGGISH,
MOTIONLESS

staid: ... SET, FIXED, GRAVE,
SOBER, SEDATE, STEADY,
SERIOUS, DECOROUS

stain: .... DYE, BLOT, BLUR,
SOIL, SPOT, TINT, IMBUE,
PAINT, SMEAR, SPOT, SULLY,
TAINT, TINGE, BLOTCH,
SMIRCH, SMUDGE, MACULA,
STIGMA, BLEMISH, CORRUPT,
SPLOTCH, TARNISH, DISCOLOR,
DISHONOR, MACULATE,
TINCTURE

stair: ... STEP, STAGE, STILE,
DEGREE

stake: . . . BET, PEG, PIN, POT, SET, ANTE, PALE, PILE, POLE, POOL, POST, RISK, HITCH, SPILE, STICK, WAGER, GAMBLE, HAZARD, PICKET, TETHER, INTEREST, FINANCE

stale: . . . . OLD, FLAT, HOAR, BANAL, CORNY, FUSTY, MOLDY, MUSTY, TRITE, VAPID, INSIPID, STAGNANT, TASTELESS, HACKNEYED

stalemate: . . . . . . TIE, DRAW, CHECK, IMPASSE, DEADLOCK, STANDSTILL

stalk: . . . . AXIS, HUNT, STEM, HAULM, SCAPE, SPEAR, STIPE, STRAW, PURSUE, RATOON, PEDICEL, PETIOLE

stall: . . . BIN, COT, PEW, CRIB, LOGE, SEAT, BOOTH, CHECK, DELAY, HEDGE, STAND, MANGER, STABLE, STATION, ENCLOSURE, TEMPORIZE, DILLY-DALLY, COMPARTMENT

stalwart: . . . . . FIRM, BRAVE, STOUT, BRAWNY, ROBUST, STRONG, STURDY, VALIANT, RESOLUTE, SUPPORTER

stamina: . . . . . . GUTS, GRIT, VIGOR, BACKBONE, CAPACITY, STRENGTH, ENDURANCE

stammer: . . . . . HEM, HACK, FALTER, STUMBLE, STUTTER, HESITATE

stamp: . . . DIE, FORM, MARK, SEAL, SIGN, TAMP, TOOL, BRAND, CRUSH, POUND, PRESS, PRINT, CACHET, SIGNET, IMPRESS, IMPRINT, INDICIA, POSTAGE, STICKER

stampede: . . . . . BOLT, ROUT, RUSH, PANIC, FLIGHT, DEBACLE

stance: . . . . . POSE, POSTURE, STATION, POSITION

stanch: . . . FIRM, STEM, STOP, TRUE, ALLAY, CHECK, CLOSE, LOYAL, QUELL, QUENCH, STEADY, STRONG, TRUSTY, CONSTANT, FAITHFUL,

RESOLUTE, STEADFAST, EXTINGUISH, UNWAVERING, WATERTIGHT

stanchion: . . . . . BAR, BEAM, POST, PROP, BRACE, SUPPORT, UPRIGHT

stand: . . . . . SET, BEAR, EASE, FACE, HALT, HOLD, LAST, RACK, STOP, ABIDE, ARISE, BOOTH, CEASE, EASEL, ERECT, PAUSE, STALL, TABLE, ENDURE, PODIUM, REMAIN, RESIST, TRIPOD, TRIVET, OPINION, STATION, SUPPORT, TABORET, ATTITUDE, MAINTAIN, TOLERATE

standard: . . . . . . PAR, FLAG, NORM, CANON, GRADE, GAUGE, IDEAL, LEVEL, MODEL, BANNER, COLORS, ENSIGN, NORMAL, SAMPLE, CLASSIC, EXAMPLE, PATTERN, REGULAR, TYPICAL, UNIFORM, ACCEPTED, GONFALON, ORDINARY, ORTHODOX, CRITERION, YARDSTICK

standing: . . . . RANK, BEING, ERECT, FIXED, STABLE, STANCE, STATUS, LASTING, STATANT, STATION, UPRIGHT, LOCATION, POSITION, PRESTIGE, STAGNANT, PERMANENT, REPUTATION

standstill: . . . . . HALT, REST, STOP, CESSATION, DEADLOCK, STALEMATE

stanza: . . . . . ENVOI, STAVE, VERSE, STROPE, STROPHE, DISTICH, DIVISION

staple: . . . CLIP, SALT, CHIEF, FIBER, FLOUR, SUGAR, PRINCIPAL, COMMODITY

star: . . . . . . ACE, SUN, HERO, LEAD, NOVA, ACTOR, BADGE, EXCEL, SHINE, ACTRESS, HEROINE, LEADING, INGENUE, STELLAR, ASTERISK, CHAMPION, LUMINARY, PRINCIPAL

starch: ... VIM, ARUM, SAGO, TARO, VIGOR, AMYLUM, STRONG, CASSAVA, STIFFEN, GLYCOGEN, STRENGTH, ARROWROOT, FORMALITY, STIFFNESS, CARBOHYDRATE

stare: ... GAPE, GAUP, GAWK, GAZE, LOOK, OGLE, PEER, GLARE, GLOWER, GOGGLE

stark: ... BARE, FIRM, HARD, PURE, BLEAK, HARSH, RIGID, ROUGH, SHEER, STERN, STIFF, UTTER, BARREN, SEVERE, WHOLLY, VIOLENT, ABSOLUTE, DESOLATE, ENTIRELY, STRIPPED, UNADORNED

starry: .... ASTRAL, BRIGHT, SHINING, STELLAR, SIDEREAL, STELLATE, SPARKLING

start: ... RUN, SHY, JERK, JUMP, LEAD, OPEN, BEGIN, ENTER, ONSET, ROUSE, SALLY, SHOCK, WINCE, FLINCH, FRIGHT, LAUNCH, OUTSET, TWITCH, COMMENCE, INCEPTION, ORIGINATE

startle: ..... ALARM, ROUSE, SCARE, SHOCK, START, EXCITE, AFFRIGHT, FRIGHTEN, SURPRISE, ELECTRIFY, GALVANIZE

starve: ...... FAST, FAMISH, HUNGER

stash: .. HIDE, STORE, CACHE, HOARD, SECRETE

state: .... SAY, AVER, ETAT, MODE, MOOD, POMP, RANK, TELL, STYLE, UTTER, AFFIRM, ALLEGE, ASSERT, AVOUCH, EMPIRE, NATION, POLITY, RECITE, RELATE, REPORT, STATUS, THRONE, COUNTRY, DECLARE, DIGNITY, EXPRESS, NARRATE, SPECIFY, CEREMONY, POSITION, CONDITION, SITUATION

stately: ..... GRAND, LOFTY, REGAL, ROYAL, AUGUST, FORMAL, COURTLY, IMPERIAL, IMPOSING, MAJESTIC, DIGNIFIED

statement: ..... BILL, AUDIT, DICTUM, PRECIS, REMARK, REPORT, RESUME, ACCOUNT, ADDRESS, ARTICLE, INVOICE, PREFACE, RECITAL, SUMMARY, ABSTRACT, ASSERTION, AVERMENT, BULLETIN, SENTENCE, AFFADAVIT, MANIFESTO, NARRATIVE, TESTIMONY, ALLEGATION, COMMUNIQUE, DEPOSITION, EXPRESSION, DECLARATION

static: ... RESTING, INACTIVE, QUIESCENT, STATIONARY

station: .... FIX, SET, CAMP, POST, RANK, SEAT, SPOT, STOP, BERTH, DEPOT, FIELD, PLACE, ASSIGN, DEGREE, REGION, STANCE, STATUS, APPOINT, HABITAT, POSTURE, POSITION, LOCATION, TERMINUS, TERMINAL

stationary: ..... SET, FAST, FIXED, STABLE, STATIC, IMMOBILE, MOVELESS, IMMOVABLE, SENDENTARY

stationery: . INK, PEN, BOOK, LINEN, PAPER, PENCIL, ENVELOPE, PAPETERIE

statue: ... BUST, ICON, IKON, NUDE, IMAGE, BRONZE, EFFIGY, CARVING, FIGURINE, LIKENESS, MONUMENT, SCULPTURE

base: .. PLINTH, PEDESTAL

gigantic: ...... COLOSSUS

statuesque: ...... STATELY, GRACEFUL

stature: .... HEIGHT

status: ...... RANK, STATE, ASPECT, POSITION, RELATION, STANDING, CONDITION

statute: .... ACT, LAW, RULE, EDICT, ASSIZE, DECREE, ENACTMENT, ORDINANCE, REGULATION

staunch: .... see **stanch**

stave: .... BAR, RUNG, SLAT, STAP, BREAK, KNOCK, STAFF,

STICK, CUDGEL, VERSES,
STANZA, PUNCTURE

stay: . . . DAM, GUY, RIB, BIDE,
HALT, HOLD, KEEP, LIVE, PROP,
REST, ROPE, STEM, STOP, TACK,
WAIT, ABIDE, AWAIT, BRACE,
CABLE, CEASE, CHECK, DELAY,
DWELL, PAUSE, QUELL, STAND,
TARRY, ARREST, DETAIN,
FASTEN, LINGER, REMAIN,
RESIDE, SECURE, REFRAIN,
SOJOURN, SUPPORT, SUSTAIN,
CONTINUE, RESTRAIN,
CESSATION

staying power: . . . . STAMINA,
ENDURANCE

stead: . . . . FARM, HELP, LIEU,
SITE, SPOT, PLACE, ASSIST,
REPLACE, SERVICE, SUPPORT,
LOCALITY

steadfast: . . . . . FAST, FIRM,
TRUE, FIXED, STABLE, STANCH,
STEADY, CERTAIN, STAUNCH,
CONSTANT, FAITHFUL,
RESOLUTE, IMMOVABLE

steady: . . CALM, EVEN, FIRM,
FIXED, SOBER, STAID, STABLE,
STURDY, ASSURED, EQUABLE,
REGULAR, UNIFORM,
CONSTANT, DILIGENT,
FAITHFUL, RELIABLE,
RESOLUTE, STEADFAST

steal: . . BAG, COP, NIM, RAP,
ROB, CRIB, GLOM, HOOK, LIFT,
LOOT, PRIG, TAKE, CREEP,
FILCH, PINCH, POACH, STALK,
SWIPE, ABDUCT, BURGLE,
DIVERT, KIDNAP, PILFER,
PINCH, PIRATE, RUSTLE,
SNITCH, THIEVE, PURLOIN,
EMBEZZLE, PECULATE,
PLAGIARIZE

stealthy: . . . . . SLY, ARTFUL,
SECRET, FELINE, SNEAKY,
CUNNING, FURTIVE,
CLANDESTINE, SURREPTITIOUS

steam: . . . GAS, BOIL, FUME,
REEK, FORCE, POWER, SMOKE,
VAPOR, ENERGY, VAPORIZE

steamer: . . . . . . BOAT, SHIP,
LINER, VESSEL, STEAMSHIP

steed: . . . . HORSE, CHARGER,
COURSER, STALLION

steel: . . . . BAR, RAIL, INURE,
METAL, DAMASK, HARDEN,
TOLEDO, TOUGHEN, BESSEMER,
STRENGTHEN

steep: . . . . . RET, SOP, BATH,
BREW, SOAK, STEW, TALL,
BATHE, IMBUE, LOFTY, SHARP,
SHEER, ABRUPT, DRENCH,
DECOCT, IMBRUE, INFUSE,
SEETHE, EXTRACT, EXTREME,
IMMERSE, ELEVATED,
MACERATE, SATURATE,
EXCESSIVE, PRECIPICE,
PRECIPITOUS

steeple: . . . . . SPIRE, TOWER,
BELFRY, CUPOLA, FLECHE,
MINARET, PINNACLE

steer: . . . OX, CON, TIP, YAK,
BEEF, CONN, HELM, LEAD,
STOT, GUIDE, PILOT, BOVINE,
CATTLE, DIRECT, GOVERN,
MANAGE, BULLOCK, CONTROL

steering gear: . . . . . . HELM,
WHEEL, RUDDER, TILLER

steersman: . . . . PILOT,
HELMSMAN, WHEELER,
COX(SWAIN), NAVIGATOR

steeve: . . PACK, SPAR, STOW,
STORE, STUFF, DERRICK

stein: . . . . MUG, TOBY

steinbok: . . . . ANTELOPE

stela, stele: . . . SLAB, PILLAR,
HEADSTONE, MONUMENT,
GRAVESTONE

stellar: . . . . . CHIEF, ASTRAL,
STARRY, LEADING, SIDEREAL,
STARLIKE, STELLATE, PRINCIPAL

stem: . . . . . BOW, DAM, RAM,
AXIS, BASE, BODY, BOLE,
CANE, CULM, HALT, HOLD,
PROW, RACE, REED, RISE,
ROOT, STOP, ARISE, CHECK,
HAULM, SHAFT, STALK, STIPE,
STOCK, TRUNK, BRANCH,
DERIVE, OPPOSE SPRING,

STANCH, LINEAGE, PETIOLE, PEDICLE, PEDUNCLE, ANCESTRY, RESTRAIN

stench: . ODOR, REEK, FETOR, SMELL, STINK, FOETOR

stentorian: . . . . LOUD

step: . . . . . STY, WAY, GAIT, PACE, PLOD, RANK, REST, RUNG, WALK, CRUSH, DANCE, GRADE, LEDGE, LEVEL, PLANE, ROUND, SHELF, STAGE, STAIR, STRUT, TREAD, ACTION, DEGREE, SQUASH, STRIDE, ADVANCE, IMPRINT, MEASURE, FOOTFALL, FOOTHOLD, FOOTPRINT

steppe: . . . . . PLAIN, PRARIE, WASTELAND

stereotyped: . . . . TRITE, HACKNEYED

sterile: . . . DRY, ARID, DEAD, GELD, BARREN, EFFETE, OTIOSE, ASEPTIC, USELESS, IMPOTENT, FRUITLESS, INFERTILE, UNFRUITFUL, INEFFECTIVE

sterilize: . . . . . . GELD, SPAY, DISINFECT, CASTRATE, EMASCULATE

sterling: . . . PENNY, GENUINE, EXCELLENT

stern: . . . . AFT, BACK, DOUR, FIRM, GRIM, HARD, REAR, ABAFT, HARSH, ROUGH, GLOOMY, SEVERE, STRICT, AUSTERE, EXACTING, UNBENDING, FORBIDDING

sternum: . . . . . . BREASTBONE

sternutation: . . . . . . SNEEZE, SNEEZING

stevedore: . . . . DOCKER, LUMPER, LOADER, STOWER, LONGSHOREMAN

stew: . . . . BOIL, COOK, DISH, FRET, HASH, MESS, OLIO, CURRY, IMBUE, STEEP, WORRY, BURGOO, POTPIE, RAGOUT, SEETHE, SIMMER, HARICOT, GOULASH, SWELTER,

MULLIGAN, POTPOURRI, HODGEPODGE, HOTCHPOTCH

steward: . . . REEVE, BUTLER, FACTOR, WAITER, BALIFF, CURATOR, MANAGER, OFFICER, PROCTOR, CUSTODIAN, SENESCHAL

stewed: . . . . DRUNK, INEBRIATED, INTOXICATED

stick: . . BAT, BOW, CUE, GAD, GUM, PUT, ROD, SET, CANE, CLUB, FIFE, GLUE, MAST, POGO, POKE, POLE, STAB, TWIG, WAND, AFFIX, BATON, CHEAT, CLING, FAGOT, FLUTE, MOUNT, PLACE, PRICK, SHOOT, STAFF, STAVE, ADHERE, ATTACH, BAFFLE, CEMENT, CLEAVE, COHERE, CUDGEL, ENDURE, FASTEN, FERULE, IMPALE, PADDLE, PIERCE, PUZZLE, RAMMER, STRIKE, THRUST, CONFINE, DEFRAUD, BLUDGEON, CLARINET, HESITATE, PUNCTURE, TOLERATE

sticker: . . . . . . BURR, KNIFE, LABEL, POSER, THORN, POSTER, PUZZLE, WEAPON, BRAMBLE

sticky: . . . . . GLUEY, GOOEY, GUMMY, HUMID, MESSY, TACKY, CLAMMY, VISCID, VISCOUS, ADHESIVE, GLUTINOUS

stiff: . . . . . FIRM, HARD, HIGH, HOBO, TAUT, WIRY, FIXED, HARSH, RIGID, TENSE, TIGHT, TRAMP, CLUMSY, FORMAL, PROPER, SEVERE, STANCH, STRONG, STURDY, WOODEN, AWKARD, CADAVER, PRECISE, EXACTING, RESOLUTE, RIGOROUS, STARCHED, STUBBORN, DIFFICULT, LABORIOUS, OBSTINATE, UNBENDING, INFLEXIBLE

stiffen: . . . . SET, BRACE, BENUMB, HARDEN, STARCH, TAUTEN, THICKEN, INSPISSATE

stifle: . . . GAG, STOP, CHECK, CHOKE, MUFFLE, QUENCH,

SCOTCH, REPRESS, SMOTHER, STRANGLE, SUPPRESS, THROTTLE, SUFFOCATE, EXTINGUISH

stigma: . . BLOT, MARK, SCAR, SPOT, BRAND, CLOUD, ODIUM, STAIN, TINT, DEFECT, BLEMISH

stile: . . . . STEP(S)

still: . . . BUT, MUM, THO, YET, ALSO, CALM, EVEN, EVER, HUSH, LULL, STOP, ALLAY, CHECK, INERT, PHOTO, QUIET, ALWAYS, HUSHED, PACIFY, PLACID, SERENE, SILENT, SOOTHE, WITHAL, ALEMBIC, APPEASE, HOWEVER, SILENCE, SUBDUED, INACTIVE, RESTRAIN, SUPPRESS, TRANQUIL, NOISELESS, STATIONARY, DISTILLERY, MOTIONLESS

stillness: . . . . . HUSH, PEACE, QUIET, SILENCE, CALMNESS, QUIETUDE

stilted: . FORMAL, AWKWARD, POMPOUS, AFFECTED, BOMBASTIC, PEDANTIC

stimulate: . . FUN, JOG, GOAD, MOVE, SPUR, STIR, URGE, WHET, ELATE, IMPEL, ROUSE, STING, AROUSE, EXCITE, FILLIP, INCITE, ANIMATE, ENLIVEN, INSPIRE, PROVOKE, QUICKEN, IRRITATE, MOTIVATE, GALVANIZE, INSTIGATE, EXHILARATE, INVIGORATE

stimulus: . . . . , GOAD, PROD, SPUR, DRIVE, STING, FILLIP, MOTIVE, IMPULSE, IMPETUS, INCENTIVE

sting: . . . . BITE, DUPE, GOAD, PAIN, CHEAT, PRICK, SHAFT, SMART, WOUND, IMPALE, NETTLE, PIERCE, STIMULI, IRRITATE, STIMULUS, STIMULATE

stinging: . . . . NIPPY, BITING, BITTER, CAUSTIC, PIQUANT, PUNGENT, PIERCING, IRRITATING

stingy: . . . . . . MEAN, NEAR, CHEAP, CLOSE, SHARP, TIGHT, GREEDY, MEAGER, SCANTY, MISERLY, SKIMPING, STINTING, NIGGARD, SELFISH, NIGGARDLY, PENURIOUS

stink: . . ODOR, REEK, SMELL, STENCH

stinking: . . . . . . FOUL, RANK, DRUNK, FETID, MUSTY, PUTRID, RANCID, SMELLY, NOISOME, OFFENSIVE, BAD-SMELLING, MALODOROUS

stint: . . . BOUT, DUTY, TASK, CHORE, LIMIT, SCANT, SPARE, STUNT, ASSIGN, DIVIDE, SCRIMP, CONFINE, QUANTITY, RESTRAIN, RESTRICT, ECONOMIZE, ASSIGNMENT, LIMITATION

stipe: . STEM, STALK, PETIOLE

stipend: . . . FEE, PAY, WAGE, INCOME, SALARY, PAYMENT, PREBEND, PENSION, ALLOWANCE

stipulate: . . AGREE, DEMAND, ARRANGE, BARGAIN, PROVIDE, REQUIRE, SPECIFY

stipulation: . . ITEM, CLAUSE, DETAIL, ARTICLE, BARGAIN, PROVISO, CONTRACT, COVENANT, AGREEMENT, CONDITION, PROVISION

stir: . . . ADO, FAN, MIX, FUSS, JAIL, MOVE, PLOW, POKE, RILE, ROIL, TO-DO, BUDGE, CHURN, RALLY, ROUSE, ROUST, SHAKE, STOKE, WAKEN, AROUSE, AWAKEN, BUSTLE, EXCITE, FLURRY, HUBBUB, INCITE, MOTION, MUDDLE, PRISON, TUMULT, AGITATE, ANIMATE, DISTURB, INFLAME, PROVOKE, TROUBLE, DISPLACE, MOVEMENT, COMMOTION, STIMULATE

stirk: . . . COW, BULL, HEIFER, BULLOCK

stirps: . . . . . . RACE, STOCK, FAMILY

stirring: . . . . BUSY, ACTIVE, MOVING, ROUSING, EXCITING, INSPIRING

stitch: . . . . . . BIT, HEM, SEW, ACHE, PAIN, PURL, TACK, BASTE, CRICK, PICOT, QUILT, UNITE, FASTEN, PIERCE, SUTURE, EMBROIDER

stoa: . . . . WALK, PORTICO

stoat: . . . . . ERMINE, WEASEL

stock: . . . BAND, BOND, BUTT, RACE, STEM, BLOOD, BREED, GOODS, STAKE, STICK, STORE, TRITE, TRUNK, ASSETS, CRAVAT, HANDLE, STRAIN, SUPPLY, STIRPS, CAPITAL, DESCENT, LINEAGE, PROVIDE, RHIZOME, ANCESTRY, ORDINARY, INVENTORY, REPERTORY

stockade: . . . . . PEN, ETAPE, POUND, CORRAL, KENNEL, BARRIER, ENCLOSURE

stock exchange: . . . . BOURSE

stocking: . . . . . . HOSE, SOCK, NYLON, HOSIERY

stockpile: . . . STORE, SUPPLY, HOARD, RESERVE

stocky: . . . . . STOUT, PLUMP, STUBBY, CHUNKY, STURDY, STUBBED, THICKSET

stodgy: . . . . . . DULL, BULKY, THICK, LUMPISH, TEDIOUS

stoic: . . . . . PORCH, ASCETIC, PATIENT, SPARTAN, IMPASSIVE

stolid: . . . DULL, FIRM, SLOW, BEEFY, STUPID, WOODEN, PASSIVE, IMPASSIVE, PHLEGMATIC

stolon: . . . RUNNER, RHIZOME

stoma: . . . . . . PORE, MOUTH, ORIFICE, OPENING

stomach: . . GUT, MAW, BEAR, CRAW, CROP, BELLY, BROOK, RUMEN, DESIRE, ENDURE, PAUNCH, ABDOMEN, GIZZARD, APPETITE, TOLERATE

stone: . . . . . . GEM, PIT, PELT, ROCK, BLOCK, BRICK, LAPIS, COBBLE, PEBBLE, MARBLE, BOULDER, DIAMOND, DORNICK, PETRIFY, MEMORIAL, MONUMENT

precious: . . . . GEM, OPAL, RUBY, BERYL, PEARL, TOPAZ, GARNET, JASPER, LAZULI, DIAMOND, EMERALD, AMETHYST, SAPPHIRE, TIGEREYE

semi-precious: . . . . JADE, ONYX, SARD, AGATE, CORAL, LUPIS, OLIVIN, ZIRCON, PERIDOT, TOURMALINE

stoneware: . GRES, CERAMIC, POTTERY, EARTHENWARE

stony: . . . COLD, HARD, FIXED, RIGID, ADAMANT, OBDURATE, PITILESS, PETRIFIED, PETROUS, PETROSAL, INEXORABLE

stooge: . . FOIL, TOOL, PAWN, DUMMY, ASSISTANT, UNDERLING

stool: . . SEAT, BENCH, CHAIR, PRIVY, STUMP, GROWTH, COMMODE, TABORET, OTTOMAN, FOOTREST

stool pigeon: . . . . . . SPY, DECOY, NARK, PEACHER, BETRAYER, INFORMER

stoop: . . . . BOW, BEND, LEAN, LOUT, DEIGN, LOWER, PORCH, SWOOP, YIELD, CROUCH, VERANDAH, CONDESCEND

stop: . . . . . . BAR, DAM, END, BUNG, CLOG, DROP, HALT, PLUG, QUIT, STAY, STEM, WHOA, AVAST, BELAY, BLOCK, BREAK, CEASE, CHECK, CHOKE, CLOSE, DELAY, PAUSE, POINT, REPEL, STALL, TARRY, ALIGHT, ANCHOR, ARREST, DEFEAT, DESIST, DETAIN, FINISH, PERIOD, SCOTCH, STANCH, PREVENT, SOJOURN, STAUNCH,

SUSPEND, PROHIBIT, INTERCEPT, SUPPRESS

stopcock: ... VALVE, FAUCET

stopgap: .... RESORT, EXPEDIENT, MAKESHIFT, SUBSTITUTE

storage place: ... BIN, BARN, CAVE, CRIB, LOFT, SHED, SILO, ATTIC, CACHE, DEPOT, HUTCH, CELLAR, CLOSET, ARSENAL, GRANARY, BASEMENT, CUPBOARD, ELEVATOR, MAGAZINE, BLOOD BANK, RESERVOIR, WAREHOUSE

store: ... FUND, HOLD, MASS, SAVE, SHOP, STOW, AMASS, CACHE, HOARD, LAY-UP, STOCK, GARNER, OUTLET, SUPPLY, COLLECT, DEPOSIT, FURNISH, HUSBAND, PROVIDE, RESERVE, RESTORE, BOUTIQUE, EMPORIUM, ACCUMULATE, COMMISSARY

storied: .... FAMOUS, LEGENDARY

storm: .. FUME, GALE, GUST, HAIL, RAGE, RAIN, RANT, RAVE, SNOW, WIND, STOUR, ATTACK, TUMULT, ASSAULT, CYCLONE, RAMPAGE, TEMPEST, TORNADO, TROUBLE, TYPHOON, CALAMITY, ERUPTION, OUTBURST, UPHEAVAL, HURRICANE, CLOUDBURST

stormy: ..... WILD, RAGING, VIOLENT, INCLEMENT

story: ...... FIB, LIE, MYTH, PLOT, REDE, TALE, YARN, ETAGE, FABLE, FLOOR, RUMOR, LEGEND, RECORD, REPORT, ACCOUNT, ARTICLE, DISPATCH, EPISODE, PARABLE, ANECDOTE, FALSEHOOD, HAPPENING, NARRATION, NARRATIVE

stound: ... ACHE, PAIN, PANG, STUN, GRIEF, SHOCK, SMART, THROB, BRUISE, SORROW, TWINGE, STUPEFY, ASTONISH

stoup: ..... CUP, CASK, PAIL, BASIN, BUCKET, FLAGON, VESSEL, MEASURE, TANKARD

stour: .... GALE, ROUGH, STORM, COMBAT, STRIFE, TUMULT, ASSAULT, TURMOIL

stout: ..... ALE, FAT, BEER, BOCK, BOLD, FIRM, BRAVE, BURLY, HARDY, HUSKY, OBESE, PLUMP, SOLID, TOUGH, FLESHY, PORTER, PORTLY, ROBUST, ROTUND, STABLE, STANCH, STOCKY, STRONG, STURDY, DEFIANT, ENDURING, RESOLUTE, STALWART, THICKSET, CORPULENT, COURAGEOUS

stove: ... ETNA, KILN, OVEN, GRATE, PLATE, RANGE, HEATER, GRIDDLE, FURNACE

stow: ... CRAM, HIDE, HOLD, MASS, PACK, CROWD, LODGE, PLACE, STOCK, STORE, COMMIT, STEEVE, ARRANGE, CONTAIN, SECRETE

strabismus: .... SQUINT, CROSS-EYE

straddle: .... HEDGE, OPTION, SPRAWL, ASTRIDE, BRACKET, NONCOMMITAL

strafe: ...... RAKE, SHELL, BOMBARD, CASTIGATE

straggle: ..... ROVE, STRAY, TRAIL, WANDER, RAMBLE, MEANDER

straight: ...... NEAT, PURE, ERECT, FRANK, LEVEL, PLAIN, RIGID, CANDID, DIRECT, HONEST, SINCERE, STRETCH, THROUGH, UNMIXED, UPRIGHT, ALIGNED, ACCURATE, RELIABLE, SEQUENCE, UNBROKEN, CONTINUOUS

strain: .... TAX, TRY, HEFT, KIND, LINE, PULL, RACE, SIFT, SORT, TONE, TUNE, VEIN, BREED, CLASS, EXERT, FORCE, HEAVE, PRESS, SHADE, SIEVE, STOCK, BURDEN, EFFORT, EXTEND, FAMILY, FILTER,

INJURE, MELODY, SPRAIN, STRAND, STRESS, STRIVE

strained: . . . . . TAUT, TENSE, FORCED, INTENSE, WEAKENED, WRENCHED, DISTORTED

strainer: . . . . . . SILE, SIEVE, STRUM, TAMIS, FILTER, SIFTER, COLANDER

strait: . . . AREA, NECK, PASS, PHARE, TIGHT, NARROW, CHANNEL, ISTHMUS

laced: . . . . STIFF, SEVERE, STRICT, STUFFY, PRIGGISH, STUBBORN, OBSTINATE, PURITANIC

straits: . . . . . . PINCH, RIGOR, NARROWS, POVERTY, DISTRESS, DIFFICULTY

strand: . . BANK, QUAY, ROPE, WIRE, BEACH, FIBER, SHORE, WHARF, GROUND, GUTTER, MAROON, STREAM, STRING, THREAD, CHANNEL, CURRENT, FILAMENT, NECKLACE

strange: . . ODD, FELL, RARE, UNCO, ALIEN, EERIE, FREMD, NOVEL, OUTRE, QUEER, EXOTIC, QUAINT, CURIOUS, ERRATIC, FOREIGN, UNCANNY, UNKNOWN, UNUSUAL, ABNORMAL, PECULIAR, SINGULAR, UNCOMMON, ECCENTRIC, UNNATURAL

stranger: . . . . . . GOY, ALIEN, GUEST, EMIGRE, VISITOR, EMIGRANT, INTRUDER, NEWCOMER, OUTSIDER, FOREIGNER, OUTLANDER, TRAMONTANE

strangle: . . . . . . KILL, SLAY, CHOKE, STIFFLE, GAROTTE, REPRESS, SMOTHER, SUPPRESS, THROTTLE, SUFFOCATE

strap: . . . . . TAB, TIE, BAND, BELT, BIND, REIN, WHIP, LEASH, STRIP, STROP, THONG, FASTEN, HALTER, PUNISH, SECURE, LANIARD, LANYARD, SHARPEN, CHASTISE

strapping: . . . . ROBUST, STRONG, WELL-BUILT

strategem: . . . . . COUP, PLOY, RUSE, WILE, CHEAT, FRAUD, TRICK, DEVICE, SCHEME, TACTIC, FINESSE, ARTIFICE, MANEUVER, CHICANERY, DECEPTION

strategy: . . . . PLAN, TACTICS, ARTIFICE, INTRIGUE, MANEUVER

stratum: . . . . . . BED, LAYER, LEVEL, SECTION, DIVISION

straw: . . . . . HAT, CULM, PIPE, RUSH, STEM, CHAFF, RAFIA, STALK, FESCUE, LITTER, TRIFLE, FLAXEN, FODDER, YELLOWISH

stray: . . . . ERR, LOST, ROAM, ROVE, WAIF, RANGE, CASUAL, ERRANT, RANDOM, SWERVE, WANDER, DEVIATE, DIGRESS, MEANDER, SAUNTER, DETACHED, ISOLATED, MAVERICK, STRAGGLE, STRAGGLER, UNRELATED, INCIDENTAL

streak: . . . LINE, TEAR, VEIN, FLECK, FREAK, HURRY, LAYER, LINED, SMEAR, SPELL, STRIA, TRACE, TRAIT, MOTTLE, STRAIN, STRIPE, STRATUM, STRIPED

stream: . . . RUN, BECK, BURN, FLOW, FLUX, GUSH, KILL, RILL, POUR, RUSH, BAYOU, BOURN, BROOK, CREEK, FLOSS, FLUME, ISSUE, RIVER, TREND, ARROYO, BOURNE, COURSE, RUNNEL, CHANNEL, CURRENT, RIVULET, TORRENT

streamer: . . JET, FLAG, STRIP, BANNER, GUIDON, RIBBON, PENDANT, PENNANT, BANDEROL, HEADLINE

street: . . . . . . RUE, VIA, WAY, LANE, ROAD, CALLE, COURT, PLACE, AVENUE, HIGHWAY, ROADWAY, STRASSE,

CONTRADA, BOULEVARD, THOROUGHFARE

strength: . . ARM, BEEF, IRON, BRAWN, FORCE, MIGHT, POWER, SINEW, VIGOR, ENERGY, POTENCY, STAMINA, CAPACITY, FIRMNESS, SOLIDITY, ENDURANCE

strengthen: . . . . BACK, PROP, BRACE, FORTIFY

strenuous: . . . HARD, ARDENT, SEVERE, ARDUOUS, ZEALOUS, VIGOROUS

stress: . . . . . . FORCE, LABOR, ACCENT, STRAIN, AFFLICT, AMPLIFY, OVERTAX, TENSION, URGENCY, DISTRESS, EMPHASIS, EXERTION, PRESSURE, EMPHASIZE

stretch: . . . EKE, HANG, SPAN, WALK, REACH, SPACE, SWEEP, TRACT, COURSE, DIALATE, EXPAND, EXTEND, SPREAD, STRAIN, DISTEND, ENLARGE, EXPANSE, TENSION, ELONGATE, EXAGGERATE

strew: . . . . . LITTER, SPREAD, DIFFUSE, SCATTER, SPRINKLE, BROADCAST, DISSEMINATE

stria: . . . BAND, LINE, RIDGE, FILLET, FURROW, GROOVE, HOLLOW, STREAK, STRIPE, CHANNEL

stricken: . . STRUCK, SMITTEN, WOUNDED, AFFLICTED

strict: . . . . HARD, CLOSE, EXACT, HARSH, RIGID, STERN, TIGHT, ENTIRE, NARROW, SEVERE, ASCETIC, AUSTERE, BINDING, CORRECT, PRECISE, ABSOLUTE, ACCURATE, LIMITING, VIGOROUS, STRAIGHT, PURITANIC, STRINGENT, INFLEXIBLE, SCRUPULOUS, PUNCTILIOUS

stricture: . . . . BINDING, CENSURE, CLOSING, STENOSIS, CRITICISM, CONTRACTION

stride: . . . LOPE, PACE, STEP, WALK, STALK, ADVANCE, STRADDLE

strides: . . . . PROGRESS, ADVANCEMENT

strident: . . . . HARSH, SHRILL, GRATING, RAUCOUS

strife: . . . . FEUD, FIGHT, COMBAT, DEBATE, CONTEST, DISCORD, QUARREL, CONFLICT, STRUGGLE, CONTENTION

strigil: . . . . FLUTING

strike: . . . . . BAT, BOX, COP, DAB, HEW, HIT, LAM, PAT, RAM, RAP, TAP, WAP, BAFF, BANG, BASH, BEAN, BEAT, BIFF, BUMP, BUNT, COUP, CUFF, DASH, DAUB, FLOG, LASH, PELT, ROUT, SLAP, SLUG, SWAT, CLASH, CLOUT, FIGHT, FILCH, IMPEL, KNOCK, POUND, PUNCH, SLASH, SMEAR, SMITE, SPANK, SWIPE, WHANG, ASSAIL, ATTACK, ATTAIN, BUFFET, HAMMER, IGNITE, PUNISH, AFFLICT, COLLIDE, IMPINGE, IMPRESS, HAULDOWN, STRUGGLE, DISMANTLE

against: . . . BUMP, CRASH, COLLIDE

demonstrator: . . . . PICKET

dumb: . . . . . STUN, AMAZE, ASTOUND

out: . . . FAN, DELE, ELIDE, ERASE, CANCEL, DELETE, EXPUNGE, ELIMINATE

strikebreaker: . . . RAT, FINK, GOON, SCAB, BLACKLEG

striker: . . . . BAT, SCAB, BATMAN, BATTER, HAMMER, HELPER, HITTER, MALLET, CLAPPER, HARPOONER

striking: . . . . VIVID, SALIENT, STUNNING, ARRESTING, EFFECTIVE, REMARKABLE, CONSPICUOUS

string: . . BAND, CORD, FOOL, HANG, HOAX, JOSH, LACE, LINE, ROPE, CHAIN, JOLLY,

STRIP, TWINE, CATGUT, SERIES, THREAD, CONDITION

stringed instrument:. . . UKE, HARP, KOTO, LUTE, LYRE, BANJO, CELLO, PIANO, REBEC, VIOLA, FIDDLE, GUITAR, SPINET, VIOLIN, ZITHER, CITHARA, CITHERN, CITTERN, SAMISEN, UKELELE, DULCIMER, MANDOLIN, CLAVICHORD, HARPSICORD

stringent: . . . . HARD, RIGID, TENSE, TIGHT, SEVERE, STRICT, BINDING, EXTREME

stringy:. . . . . . LONG, ROPY, GLUEY, SINEWY, VISCID, FIBROUS, VISCOUS

strip: . . . . . . ROB, TAG, TAB, BAND, BARE, BELT, DOFF, FLAY, HULL, HUSK, LATH, PEEL, SKIN, TEAR, CLEAR, PLUCK, SHRED, SPOIL, SWATH, BATTEN, BORDER, DENUDE, DIVEST, EXPOSE, FLENSE, REDUCE, REMOVE, RUNWAY, SWATHE, BANDAGE, BEREAVE, DEPRIVE, DISROBE, PILLAGE, PLUNDER, UNCOVER, UNDRESS, DISARRAY, DISMANTLE, DISPOSSES

stripe: . . . BAR, BAND, BELT, KIND, LASH, LINE, MARK, SORT, TYPE, WALE, WEAL, WELT, ZONE, STRIA, BORDER, STREAK, STRIKE, STROKE, CHEVRON, LINEATE, PATTERN, DIVISION

striped:. . . BANDED, BARRED, LINEATE, STRIATE, ZONATE, VITTATE, STREAKED

stripped:. . . . . . BARE, NUDE, PICKED, SHORN, DENUDED, DEPRIVED, DIVESTED

strive:. . . AIM, TRY, TUG, VIE, COPE, SEEK, TOIL, FIGHT, LABOR, BATTLE, RESIST, STRAIN, COMPETE, CONTEND, EMULATE, STRUGGLE, ENDEAVOR

stroke: . . BAT, FIT, HEW, HIT, PAT, PET, RUB, BEAT, BLOW, COUP, DASH, FLIP, HURL, LASH, MARK, MILK, SHOT, WHET, FLUKE, ICTUS, KNOCK, POWER, PULSE, ROWER, CARESS, FONDLE, IMPACT, SOOTHE, STRIPE, SEIZURE, SHARPEN, INFLUENCE

stroll: . . ROVE, ROAM, WALK, MOSEY, RANGE, STRAY, TRAMP, RAMBLE, WANDER, SAUNTER, PROMENADE

strong: . . . . FIT, ABLE, BOLD, FIRM, FORT, HALE, HARD, RANK, WIRY, EAGER, FRESH, GREAT, GROSS, HARDY, HEAVY, LARGE, LUSTY, SOLID, SOUND, STOUT, TOUGH, ACTIVE, ARDENT, BRAWNY, MIGHTY, POTENT, ROBUST, SINEWY, STABLE, STRICT, STURDY, VIRILE, DURABLE, FERTILE, INTENSE, VIOLENT, ZEALOUS, ATHELETIC, FLAGRANT, FORCEFUL, MUSCULAR, POWERFUL, PUISSANT, RIGOROUS, STALWART, VEHEMENT, VIGOROUS

strongbox: . . . . CASE, SAFE, CHEST, VAULT, COFFER

stronghold: . . . . FORT, KEEP, AERIE, TOWER, CASTLE, CITADEL, REDOUBT, FASTNESS, FORTRESS

struck: . . . . . . SMIT, SMOTE, SMITTEN, PUNISHED, SHUTDOWN

structure: . . . . . DAM, FORM, FRAME, BRIDGE, FORMAT, MAKE-UP, EDIFICE, TEXTURE, BUILDING, FORMATION, ARRANGEMENT, COMPOSITION

struggle: . . . . TRY, TUG, VIE, COPE, FIGHT, HEAVE, LABOR, BATTLE, COMBAT, EFFORT, STRIFE, STRIKE, STRIVE, THROES, TUSSLE, CONTEND, CONTEST, SCUFFLE, WARFARE, WRESTLE, CONFLICT,

ENDEAVOR, EXERTION,
SCRAMBLE, CONTENTION,
DIFFICULTY

strumpet: . . WENCH, HARLOT,
COCOTTE, HARRIDAN,
PROSTITUTE

strut: . . . . BRAG, GAIT, STEP,
WALK, BRACE, BULGE, SWELL,
PARADE, THRUST, DISTEND,
STIFFEN, STRETCH, SUPPORT,
SWAGGER, PROTRUDE

stub: . . . . PEN, BUTT, DOLT,
CRUSH, DRIVE, SQUAT, STUMP,
COUPON, STOCKY, UPROOT,
FEATHER, REMNANT, THICKSET,
EXTIRPATE

stubborn: . . . . . SET, FIXED,
HARDY, HARSH, ROUGH,
TOUGH, COARSE, DOGGED,
MULISH, ONERY, STURDY,
FROWARD, WILLFUL,
OBDURATE, PERVERSE,
RESOLUTE, DIFFICULT,
OBSTINATE, BULLHEADED,
DETERMINED, HARDHEADED,
INFLEXIBLE, REFRACTORY,
UNYIELDING

stuckup: . . . VAIN, HAUGHTY,
ARROGANT, SNOBBISH,
CONCEITED

stud: . . DOT, PIN, ROD, BOSS,
KNOB, POST, STEM, STUB,
ADORN, BRACE, STUMP,
AIGLET, BUTTON, PILLAR,
SUPPORT, STALLION,
STUDHORSE

student: . . . . . COED, CADET,
PLEBE, PUPIL, LEARNER,
SCHOLAR, TRAINEE, DISCIPLE,
COLLEGIAN, MIDSHIPMAN

studies: . . . . . ARTS, SCIENCE,
HUMANITIES, EDUCATION,
SCHOOLING

studio: . . ATELIER, BOTTEGA,
WORKSHOP

study: . . . . . CON, DEN, BONE,
CRAM, MUSE, PORE, READ,
ROOM, SCAN, ESSAY, WEIGH,
PERUSE, PONDER, ANALYZE,

CANVASS, EXAMINE, CONSIDER,
MEDITATE, SCRUTINIZE,
CONTEMPLATE

stuff: . . . . . PAD, RAM, WAD,
CRAM, FILL, JUNK, PACK, PLUG,
CROWD, FORCE, FABRIC,
MATTER, REFUSE, STIFLE,
SUPPLY, THINGS, BOMBAST,
ELEMENT, ESSENCE, FILLING,
MIXTURE, SATIATE, MATERIAL,
NONSENSE, OVERLOAD,
SUBSTANCE

stuffy: . . DULL, PRIM, CLOSE,
STODGY, STRAIT-LACED

stumble: . . . ERR, FALL, SLIP,
TRIP, LURCH, FALTER, HAPPEN,
OFFEND, BLUNDER, FAILURE,
FOUNDER, STAGGER, FLOUNDER

stumbling block: . . . .
OBSTACLE, HINDRANCE,
IMPEDIMENT

stump: . . . . LOP, BUTT, FOIL,
GRUB, SNAG, STUB, BLOCK,
BAFFLE, CORNER, PUZZLE,
THWART, TRAVEL, CANVASS,
NONPLUS, PERPLEX, ROSTRUM,
STUMBLE, PLATFORM

stun: . . BOWL, DAZE, AMAZE,
DAUNT, DIZZY, SHOCK, APPALL,
BENUMB, DEADEN, ASTOUND,
STUPEFY, ASTONISH, BEWILDER,
DUMBFOUND, OVERWHELM

stunning: . . . . STYLISH,
DAZZLING, BEAUTIFUL,
REMARKABLE

stunt: . . . ACT, FEAT, BLUNT,
CHECK, CRAMP, DWARF, TRICK,
HINDER, CURTAIL, UNDERSIZED

stupefacient: . . . . DRUG,
NARCOTIC

stupefy: . . SOT, DAZE, DOPE,
DRUG, DULL, NUMB, PALL,
STUN, AMAZE, BESOT, BLUNT,
DAUNT, SHOCK, BEDAZE,
BENUMB, MUDDLE, ASTOUND,
CONFUSE, ASTONISH,
BEWILDER, CONFOUND,
OBFUSCATE

stupendous: . . . . GREAT, AMAZING, IMMENSE, ENORMOUS, MONSTROUS, WONDERFUL, ASTOUNDING, ASTONISHING, OVERWHELMING

stupid: . . DULL, DUMB, SLOW, CRASS, DAZED, DENSE, DIZZY, DOPEY, INANE, INEPT, BORING, OBTUSE, SILLY, SIMPLE, TORPID, ASININE, FATUOUS, FOOLISH, STUNNED, TOMFOOL, VACUOUS, WITLESS, BACKWARD, RETARDED, SLUGGISH, BRAINLESS, INSENSATE, INSIPIENT, SENSELESS, IRRATIONAL *person:* . . ASS, SAP, CLOD, COOT, DOLT, DOPE, FOOL, JERK, LOON, DUNCE, GOOSE, IDIOT, MORON, NINNY, DULLARD, FATHEAD, NUMSKULL, BLOCKHEAD

stupor: . . FOG, COMA, SOPOR, TORPOR, TRANCE, NARCOSIS, LETHARGY

sturdy: . . . . . GID, SET, FIRM, HARDY, SOUND, STERN, STIFF, STOUT, BRAWNY, ROBUST, RUGGED, STABLE, STEADY, STRONG, RESOLUTE, STALWART, STUBBORN, VIGOROUS, DETERMINED

sty: . PEN, HAW, BOIL, STEPS, STILE, SWELLING, ENCLOSURE

style: . . . AIR, FAD, PEN, PIN, TON, CALL, GARB, KIND, MAKE, MADE, NAME, SORT, TERM, TYPE, BRAND, GENRE, VOGUE, DESIGN, FORMAT, MANNER, METHOD, NEEDLE, STYLUS, ALAMODE, ENTITLE, FASHION, VARIETY, DEMEANOR, DESIGNATE, TECHNIQUE

stylet: . . . . . . ORGAN, PROBE, DAGGER, LANCET, POINARD, STILETTO, APPENDAGE

stylish: . . CHIC, TONY, NIFTY, NOBBY, SMART, CLASSY, DRESSY, JAUNTY, MODISH, SPIFFY, SWANKY, ALAMODE, DASHING, FASHIONABLE

stylus: . . . . PEN, NEEDLE

stymie, stymy: . . BALK, FOIL, BLOCK, HINDER, IMPEDE, OBSTRUCT

suave: . . . EASY, OILY, SMUG, BLAND, SOAPY, POLITE, SMOOTH, URBANE, COURTLY, GRACIOUS, PLEASANT, POLISHED, UNCTUOUS

subdue: . COW, BEND, CALM, TAME, ALLAY, BREAK, CHARM, CRUSH, DAUNT, LOWER, QUELL, SOBER, BRIDLE, DISARM, EVINCE, MASTER, REDUCE, SOFTEN, STEADY, CONQUER, CONTROL, REPRESS, SQUELCH, VANQUISH, OVERCOME, SUBJUGATE, OVERPOWER

subject: . . . . . . TEXT, BASIS, CAUSE, NOUN, LIEGE, MOTIF, THEME, TOPIC, LIABLE, MATTER, MOTIVE, REASON, SUBMIT, VASSAL, ARTICLE, CITIZEN, EXPOSED, SERVANT, INCIDENT, INFERIOR, OBEDIENT, DEPENDENT, SUBJUGATE, SUBSTANCE, CONTINGENT

subjoin: . . . . . . ADD, AFFIX, ANNEX, APPEND, ATTACH

subjugate: . . . TAME, MASTER, REDUCE, CONQUER, VANQUISH, OVERCOME

sublime: . . . . . HIGH, GRAND, GREAT, LOFTY, NOBLE, PURIFY, REFINE, EXALTED, SUPREME, EMPYREAL, HEAVENLY, MAJESTIC, SPLENDID

submarine: . . . . . SUB, TUB, DIVER, U-BOAT, PERISCOPE, SUBMERSIBLE

submerge: . . . . . . DIP, BURY, DIVE, HIDE, SINK, SOUSE, SWAMP, WHELM, DELUGE, DRENCH, ENGULF, PLUNGE, INUNDATE, SUPPRESS

submission: . . . . . MEEKNESS, OBEDIENCE, SURRENDER, RESIGNATION

submissive: . . . MEEK, TAME, DOCILE, HUMBLE, PASSIVE, SERVILE, OBEDIENT, YIELDING, COMPLIANT

submit: . . . BOW, BEND, OBEY, ABIDE, AGREE, DEFER, HEALD, STOOP, YIELD, ASSENT, COMPLY, RESIGN, SUDUE, SUFFER, PROPOSE, SUCCUMB, ACQUIESCE, SURRENDER

subordinate: . . AIDE, MINOR, UNDER, SUBDUE, CONTROL, INFERIOR, OBEDIENT, SERVIENT, ANCILLARY, ASSISTANT, AUXILIARY, DEPENDENT, SECONDARY, UNDERLING

suborn: . . . . . . BRIBE, EQUIP, INCITE, INDUCE, CORRUPT, FURNISH, PROCURE, PROVIDE, INSTIGATE

subpoena: . . . WRIT, SUMMON

subrogate: . . . . . SUBSTITUTE

subrosa: . . . . SECRETLY

subscribe: . . . . SIGN, AGREE, FAVOR, ASSENT, ATTEST, PLEDGE, CONSENT, SUPPORT, SANCTION

subsequently: . . . . . AFTER, LATER, SINCE, AFTERWARD, THEREAFTER

subservient: . . . . . SERVILE, ACCESSORY, OBSEQUIOUS, SUBMISSIVE

subside: . . EBB, BATE, FALL, LULL, SINK, WANE, ABATE, CEASE, LOWER, SETTLE, DESCEND, FLATTEN, RELAPSE, DECREASE, WITHDRAW

subsidiary: . . . . . . RESERVE, ACCESSORY, TRIBUTARY, AUXILIARY, COLLATERAL, SUPPLEMENTARY

subsidy: . . . AID, GIFT, HELP, BONUS, GRANT, BOUNTY, PENSION, SUPPORT, ASSISTANCE, SUBVENTION

subsist: . . . . BE, FARE, FEED, LIVE, STAY, ABIDE, EXIST, REMAIN, SUPPORT, CONTINUE, MAINTAIN

subsistence: . . BEING, LIVING, ALLOWANCE, SUBSTANCE, PROVISIONS, LIVELIHOOD

substance: . . . . . SUM, BODY, CORE, GIST, MASS, MEAT, PITH, BASIS, METAL, STUFF, GROUND, IMPORT, MATTER, REALTY, SPIRIT, WEALTH, ALIMENT, ESSENCE, MATERIAL, MEANING, REALITY, PURPORT, HARDNESS, SOLIDITY, AFFLUENCE, RESOURCES

substantial: . . . . FIRM, REAL, TRUE, AMPLE, LARGE, SOLID, SOUND, STOUT, ACTUAL, STABLE, STRONG, STURDY, WEALTHY, TANGIBLE, CORPOREAL, IMPORTANT

substantiate: . . . . . . PROVE, ASSURE, EMBODY, VERIFY, CONFIRM, ESTABLISH, CORROBORATE

substantive: . . . NOUN, SOILD, ACTUAL, ENTITY, PRONOUN, ESSENTIAL

substitute: . . . . VICE, EXTRA, PROXY, VICAR, DEPUTY, FILL-IN, ERSATZ, RINGER, COMMUTE, REPLACE, EXCHANGE, MAKE-SHIFT, ALTERNATE, SUPPLANT, SUBROGATE, SURROGATE

subterfuge: . . . RUSE, BLIND, TRICK, DEVISE, ESCAPE, REFUGE, EVASION, ARTIFICE, PRETENSE, DECEPTION

subterranean: . . . . . . CAVE, CAVERN, HIDDEN, SECRET, UNDERGROUND

subtile: . . . . see **subtle**

subtitle: . . . . SUBHEAD

subtle: . . . . SLY, DEFT, FINE, KEEN, RARE, THIN, NICE, WILY, ACUTE, ARTFUL, CLEVER, CRAFTY, SHREWD, CUNNING, ELUSIVE, REFINED, TENUOUS,

ABSTRUSE, DELICATE,
SKILLFUL, DESIGNING,
INGENIOUS, INTRICATE

subtract: .... MINUS, LESSEN,
DEDUCT, REMOVE, DETRACT,
WITHDRAW, WITHHOLD

suburb: .. TOWN, OUTSKIRT,
BARRIO, ENVIRON, PERIPHERY

subvention: ..... AID, HELP,
GRANT, SUBSIDY, SUPPORT,
ENDOWMENT, ASSISTANCE

subvert: .. SAP, RUIN, UPSET,
CORRUPT, DESTROY, PERVERT,
ALIENATE, OVERTURN,
OVERTHROW, UNDERMINE

subway: ..... TUBE, METRO,
TUNNEL, UNDERGROUND

succeed: .. WIN, FARE, ENSUE,
OCCUR, ATTAIN, FOLLOW,
HAPPEN, THRIVE, ACHIEVE,
ASCEND, INHERIT, PREVAIL,
PROSPER, REPLACE, FLOURISH,
SUPPLANT, SUPERSEDE,
ACCOMPLISH

success: .... HIT, FORTUNE,
TRIUMPH, VICTORY

succession: ..... ROW, RUN,
COURSE, SERIES, DYNASTY,
SEQUENCE, GRADATION

successive: ... CONSECUTIVE

succinct: ..... CURT, BRIEF,
PITHY, SHORT, TERSE,
COMPACT, CONCISE, LACONIC

succor: ... AID, ABET, CURE,
HELP, ASSIST, REFUGE, RELIEF,
RESCUE, COMFORT, DELIVER,
PROVIDE, SUSTAIN, BEFRIEND,
MITIGATE, ALLEVIATE,
ASSISTANCE

succulent: ..... ALOE, LUSH,
FRESH, JUICY, TASTY, CACTUS,
TENDER

succumb: . DIE, FALL, YIELD,
PERISH, SUBMIT

such: ..... AS, SO, SIC, KIND,
LIKE, SOME, CERTAIN, SIMILAR

suck: .... SIP, DRAW, SWIG,
BLEED, DRAFT, DRAIN, DRINK,
NURSE, ABSORB, INBIBE,
INHALE, CONSUME, EXTRACT

sucker: ... DUPE, LEECH, ALL-
DAY, VICTIM, LOLLIPOP

suckle: .. FEED, REAR, NURSE,
FOSTER, LACTATE, NOURISH

sucrose: .... SUGAR,
SACCHAROSE

suction: .. INTAKE, DRAWING,
LIFTING

sud: .... FOAM, BUBBLE,
LATHER

sudden: ...... RUSH, SOON,
EARLY, HASTY, SHORT, SWIFT,
ABRUPT, SPEEDY, HEADLONG,
METEORIC, IMPETUOUS,
IMPROMPTU, UNEXPECTED,
PRECIPITATE

sudor: .... SWEAT,
PERSPIRATION

sue: .... BEG, WOO, SEEK,
URGE, CHASE, COURT, APPEAL,
PLEAD, FOLLOW, BESEECH,
ENTREAT, REQUEST, SOLICIT,
CONTINUE, LITIGATE, PETITION,
PROSECUTE

suffer: .... LET, BEAR, BIDE,
DREE, ADMIT, ALLOW, ENDURE,
GRIEVE, PERMIT, SUBMIT,
AGONIZE, UNDERGO, TOLERATE,
EXPERIENCE

sufferance: ... PAIN, MISERY,
CONSENT, RESPITE, PATIENCE,
SANCTION, PASSIVITY,
TOLERATION

suffering: .. ILL, BALE, LOSS,
PAIN, AGONY, AILING, INJURY,
DISTRESS, SICKNESS,
ADVERSITY, AFFLICTION,
TRIBULATION

suffice: .... DO, SERVE,
ANSWER, APPEASE, CONTENT,
SATISFY

sufficient: ... DUE, FIT, ABLE,
ENOW, GOOD, AMPLE, ENOUGH,
PLENTY, ABUNDANT,
ADEQUATE, COMPETENT,
EFFECTIVE, EFFICIENT,
QUALIFIED

suffocate: .... KILL, CHOKE, STIFLE, DESTROY, SMOTHER, STRANGLE, SUPPRESS, THROTTLE, ASPHYXIATE, EXTINGUISH

suffrage: ... AID, HELP, VOTE, RIGHT, VOICE, ASSENT, BALLOT, PRAYER, VOTING, WITNESS, PETITION, FRANCHISE, TESTIMONY

suffuse: .. FILL, POUR, BATHE, COLOR, DIFFUSE, OVERSPREAD

sugar: ..... GUR, OSE, BEET, CANE, CANDY, MAPLE, FUCOSE, GULOSE, HEXOSE, KETOSE, CARMEL, CHITOSE, FONDANT, GLUCOSE, LACTOSE, MALTOSE, SUCROSE, SWEETEN, TETROSE, DEXTROSE, FRUCTOSE, LEVULOSE, MUSCAVADO, SACCHAROSE

substitute: .... SACCHARIN

suggest: ...... HINT, MOVE, IMPLY, ALLUDE, BROACH, PROMPT, CONNOTE, INSPIRE, PROPOSE, INDICATE, INTIMATE, INSINUATE

suggestion: .... HINT, IDEA, TINGE, TOUCH, TRACE, ADVICE, INKLING, SOUPCON, PROPOSAL, COMPLAINT, ACCUSATION, INTIMATION, INDICATION

suit: ...... CASE, KIND, PLEA, SORT, ADAPT, AGREE, APPLY, CLASS, GROUP, HABIT, MATCH, ORDER, ACCORD, ADJUST, ANSWER, APPEAL, ASSORT, ATTIRE, OUTFIT, PLEASE, SERIES, WOOING, ARRANGE, CLOTHES, CONFORM, COSTUME, REQUEST, SATISFY, UNIFORM, COURTING, ENTREATY, PETITION, SEQUENCE, HARMONIZE

suitable: .... APT, DUE, FIT, ABLE, MEET, RIGHT, COMELY, PROPER, APROPOS, FITTING, SEEMING, ADEQUATE, BECOMING, ELIGIBLE, MATCHING, COMPETENT, CONGRUOUS, COMPATIBLE, CONSISTENT, APPROPRIATE

suite: ... SET, GROUP, STAFF, TRAIN, SERIES, RETINUE, APARTMENT

suitor: ..... BEAU, WOOER, ADMIRER, PETITIONER

sulcate: .. FLUTED, GROOVED, FURROWED

sulfur: .... BRIMSTONE

sulfuric acid: ...... VITRIOL

sulk: ... MOPE, POUT, GROUCH

sulky: .... GIG, CART, GLUM, GLOOMY, SULLEN, CARRIAGE

sullen: .. DOUR, DULL, GLUM, SOUR, BLACK, CROSS, MOODY, POUTY, SULKY, SURLY, DISMAL, GLOOMY, MOROSE, SOMBER, BALEFUL, LOWERING

sully: ... BLOT, BLUR, FOUL, SOIL, CLOUD, DIRTY, SMEAR, STAIN, TAINT, DARKEN, DEFILE, SMIRCH, BLACKEN, BLEMISH, CORRUPT, POLLUTE, TARNISH, BESMIRCH

sultry: .. HOT, CLOSE, FIERY, HUMID, LURID, MUGGY, TORRID, SENSUAL, TROPICAL, OPPRESSIVE, PASSIONATE, SWELTERING

sum: ...... ADD, END, GIST, COUNT, GROSS, ISSUE, TOTAL, WHOLE, AMOUNT, NUMBER, RESULT, INTEGER, ADDITION, ENTIRETY, PERORATE, QUANTITY, AGGREGATE, CALCULATE, MAGNITUDE, SUBSTANCE

summary: ...... SUM, GIST, BRIEF, RECAP, SHORT, DIGEST, PRECIS, RESUME, CONCISE, EPITOME, EXTRACT, RUN-DOWN, ABSTRACT, SUCCINCT, SYLLABUS, SYNOPSIS, CONDENSED, COMPENDIUM, ABRIDGEMENT

summit: .... (also see **mountain, peak**) CAP, TIP,

TOP, ACME, APEX, KNAP, ROOF, CREST, CROWN, RIDGE, CLIMAX, HEIGHT, VERTEX, ZENITH, PINNACLE

summon: . . BID, CALL, CITE, PAGE, EVOKE, RALLY, ROUSE, ACCITE, APPEAL, AROUSE, COMPEL, DEMAND, GATHER, MUSTER, COLLECT, COMMAND, CONJURE, CONVENE, CONVOKE, SUPOENA

summons: . . . . . CALL, WRIT, VENIRE, COMMAND, MONITION, WARNING, CITATION

sump: . . MUD, OIL, PIT, POOL, PUMP, TANK, WELL, DRAIN, PUDDLE, CISTERN, CESSPOOL, RESERVOIR

sumptuous: . . . RICH, GRAND, COSTLY, DELUXE, LAVISH, SUPERB, SPLENDID, EXPENSIVE, LUXURIOUS

sun: . . ORB, SOL, TAN, TITAN, LUMINARY

darkening: . . . . . . ECLIPSE
halo: . . . . CORONA
orbit/path: . . . . . . ECLIPTIC
pertaining to: . . . . SOLAR, HELIACAL
room/porch: . . . SOLARIUM
shadow: . . . . UMBRA

sunder: . . . . RIP, PART, REND, RIVE, BREAK, SEVER, SPLIT, CLEAVE, DIVIDE, DISJOIN, DISRUPT, DIVORCE, SEPARATE

sundry: . . . . DIVERS, DIVERSE, SEVERAL, VARIOUS, DISTINCT, FREQUENT, MANIFOLD, NUMEROUS, SEPARATE, DIFFERENT, DISUNITED, MISCELLANEOUS

sunny: . GAY, WARM, CLEAR, HAPPY, BRIGHT, GOLDEN, CHEERFUL, SPARKLING, VIVACIOUS, CHEERFUL

sunshade: . . VISOR, AWNING, PARASOL, UMBRELLA

sup: . . EAT, SIP, DINE, DRINK, FEAST

super: . . . . . . ACTOR, EXTRA, JANITOR, EXCELLENT, FIRST-RATE

superabundance: . . . FLOOD, EXCESS, PLETHORA

superannuate: . . . . . RETIRE, OUTLAST, OBSOLETE, OUT-OF-DATE

superannuated: . . . . . AGED, ANILE, PASSE, RETIRED, OBSOLETE, OUTDATED, ANTIQUATED

superb: . . FINE, RICH, GRAND, NOBLE, ELEGANT, STATELY, MAJESTIC, SPLENDID, EXCELLENT, LUXURIOUS

supercilious: . . . . . . LOFTY, PROUD, SNOOTY, UPPISH, HAUGHTY, ARROGANT, SCORNFUL, SNOBBISH, ARBITRARY, OVERBEARING

superficial: . . . GLIB, HASTY, CASUAL, FLIMSY, SLIGHT, SHALLOW, CURSORY, EXTERNAL, SKIN-DEEP

superfluous: . . OVER, EXTRA, SPARE, DE TROP, OTIOSE, SURPLUS, USELESS, NEEDLESS, EXCESSIVE, REDUNDANT

superintend: . . BOSS, GUIDE, DIRECT, MANAGE, CONTROL, INSPECT, OVERSEE, SUPERVISE, ADMINISTER

superior: . . . . . . BOSS, FINE, HEAD, OVER, ABOVE, UPPER, BETTER, HIGHER, SENIOR, GREATER, HAUGHTY, RANKING, ARROGANT, ASSUMING, DOMINANT, ELEVATED, MASTERLY, EXCELLENT, PREEMINENT

superlative: . . . . ACME, BEST, PEAK, ULTRA, UTMOST, EXTREME, SUPREME, PEERLESS, EXCESSIVE, EXAGGERATED

supernal: . . . . DIVINE, HEAVENLY, CELESTIAL, ETHEREAL

supernatural: . . . . . MAGIC,
DIVINE, OCCULT, MARVELOUS,
UNEARTHLY, MIRACULOUS

superscribe: . . . . . . WRITE,
DIRECT, ADDRESS, ENGRAVE

supersede: . . . . REPLACE,
SUCCEED, DISPLACE, OVERRIDE,
SUPPLANT

supervene: . ENSUE, FOLLOW,
HAPPEN, SUPERSEDE

supervise: . . . . . BOSS, EDIT,
CHECK, DIRECT, GOVERN,
MANAGE, PERUSE, REVISE,
CONDUCT, CORRECT, INSPECT,
OVERSEE

supervisor: . . . . . . CENSOR,
FOREMAN, PROCTOR, DIRECTOR,
OVERSEER, MANAGER

supine: . . . . . . INERT, PRONE,
ABJECT, DROWSY, PASSIVE,
UNALERT, INACTIVE, INDOLENT,
LISTLESS, SLUGGISH, NEGLIGENT

supplant: . . . . OUST, UPSET,
USURP, FOLLOW, REMOVE,
UPROOT, REPLACE, SUCCEED,
DISPLACE, EXTIRPATE,
OVERTHROW, SUPERSEDE

supple: . . . SLY, AGILE, LITHE,
LIMBER, LISSOM, NIMBLE,
PLIANT, CUNNING, ELASTIC,
PLIABLE, SERVILE, FLEXIBLE,
YIELDING, ADAPTABLE,
COMPLIANT, RESILIENT,
RESPONSIVE

supplement: . . ADD, CODICIL,
ADDENDUM, ADDITION,
APPENDIX, ACCESSORY

supplicate: . . . . . BEG, SUE,
PRAY, PLEAD, APPEAL, INVOKE,
BESEECH, ENTREAT, IMPLORE,
REQUEST, SOLICIT, PETITION,
IMPORTUNE

supply: . . . . . AID, FIT, FEED,
FILL, FUND, GIVE, HELP,
CACHE, CATER, EQUIP, HOARD,
RELAY, STOCK, STORE, YIELD,
AFFORD, PURVEY, SUCCOR,
FURNISH, NOURISH, PLENISH,

PROVIDE, REPLACE, RESERVE,
SATISFY, PROVISION, REPLENISH

support: . . . AID, ARM, GUY,
LEG, PEG, RIB, ABET, BACK,
BASE, BEAM, BEAR, HELP,
KEEP, LIMB, PROP, STAY,
BOOST, BRACE, CARRY, CHEER,
EASEL, FAVOR, HINGE, SHORE,
SLING, STAFF, STRUT, TRUSS,
ANCHOR, BEHALF, DEFEND,
ENDURE, LINTEL, PILLAR,
SECOND, SHIELD, SPLINT,
SUFFER, TRIPOD, TRIVET,
UPHOLD, VERIFY, BOLSTER,
COMFORT, CONFIRM, ENDORSE,
ESPOUSE, FULCRUM, NOURISH,
NUTURE, PROTECT, SUSTAIN,
TRELLIS, TRESTLE, APPROVAL,
BEFRIEND, BUTTRESS,
EVIDENCE, MAINTAIN,
PEDESTAL, SANCTION,
SKELETON, ENCOURAGE,
REINFORCE, STANCHION,
ASSISTANCE

supporter: . . . . . . FAN, ALLY,
BACKER, PATRON, ROOTER,
SECOND, ABETTOR, BOOSTER,
FOUNDER, ADHERENT,
ADVOCATE, FOLLOWER,
HENCHMAN, PARTISAN,
AUXILIARY

suppose: . . . . . DEEM, TROW,
WEEN, IMPLY, JUDGE, OPINE,
THINK, ASSUME, EXPECT,
BELIEVE, RECKON, IMAGINE,
OPINION, PRESUME, SURMISE,
SUSPECT, CONCEIVE,
CONCLUDE, CONSIDER,
CONJECTURE

supposition: . . . IF, NOTION,
THEORY, POSTULATE,
CONJECTURE, HYPOTHESIS

suppress: . HIDE, KEEP, KILL,
STOP, CHECK, CHOKE, CRUSH,
QUASH, QUELL, ARREST,
BRIDLE, CENSOR, RETARD,
STIFLE, SUBDUE, CONCEAL,
DESTROY, EXCLUDE, PREVENT,
REPRESS, SILENCE, SMOTHER,

SQUELCH, PROHIBIT, RESTRAIN, THROTTLE, WITHHOLD, INTERDICT, OVERPOWER, OVERTHROW, EXTINGUISH

supremacy: . . SWAY, POWER, CONTROL, MASTERY, DOMINION, AUTHORITY, AUTOCRACY, DOMINANCE, INFLUENCE

supreme: . . . . . LAST, CHIEF, FINAL, UTMOST, CRUCIAL, HIGHEST, FOREMOST, GREATEST, PEERLESS, ULTIMATE, PARAMOUNT, PREEMINENT

surcease: . . END, REST, STAY, STOP, DEFER, DELAY, DESIST, RELIEF, RESPITE, SUSPEND, POSTPONE, CESSATION

surcingle: . . . . . BAND, BELT, GIRDLE

surd: . . RADICAL, VOICELESS, IRRATIONAL

sure: . . . . FAST, FIRM, SAFE, TRUE, SECURE, STABLE, STEADY, STRONG, ASSURED, CERTAIN, ENDURING, POSITIVE, RELIABLE, UNERRING, AUTHENTIC, CONFIDENT, CONVINCED, STEADFAST, UNDOUBTED, UNFAILING, DEPENDABLE, INFALLIBLE

surely: . . . . . . YES, REALLY, CERTAINLY

surety: . . . . BAIL, BOND, PLEDGE, HOSTAGE, SPONSOR, SECURITY, ASSURANCE, CERTAINTY, GUARANTEE, GUARANTOR

surf: . . FOAM, WAVES, SPRAY, SWELLS, BREAKERS

surface: . AREA, FACE, PAVE, SIDE, SKIN, FACET, PLANE, FACING, FINISH, PATINA, OBVERSE, OUTSIDE, REVERSE, EXTERIOR, SUPERFICIAL

surfeit: . . CLOY, FEED, GLUT, JADE, SATE, EXCESS, SUPPLY, REPLETE, SATIATE, SATIETY, SATISFY, SATIATION, DISCOMFORT

surfeited: . . . . . SICK, BLASE, FED-UP, SATED, COMPLETE

surge: . . . . RISE, RUSH, TIDE, WAVE, HEAVE, SWELL, BILLOW, ROLLING, SWEEPING, SWELLING

surly: . . GLUM, RUDE, BLUFF, CROSS, GRUFF, SULKY, ABRUPT, CRUSTY, GRUMPY, MOROSE, SULLEN, BOORISH, CRABBED, HAUGHTY, UNCIVIL, ARROGANT, CHURLISH, GROWLING, ILL-NATURED, INTRACTABLE

surmise: . . . . . DEEM, GUESS, INFER, OPINE, TRACE, IMAGINE, PRESUME, SUPPOSE, SUSPECT, ALLEGATION, CONCLUSION, CONJECTURE

surmount: . . TOP, PASS, RISE, CLIMB, CROWN, EXCEL, ASCEND, EXCEED, HURDLE, SUBDUE, CONQUER, SURPASS, OVERCOME, NEGOTIATE, TRANSCEND

surname: . . . . BYNAME, AGNOMEN, COGNOMEN, APPELATION

surpass: . . . CAP, TOP, BEAT, BEST, EXCEL, OUTDO, BETTER, EXCEED, ECLIPSE, OUTRANK, OUTCLASS, OUTREACH, OUTSTRIP, SURMOUNT, TRANSCEND

surplus: . . . . . . OVER, REST, EXTRA, SPARE, EXCESS, OVERAGE, BACKLOG, RESERVE

surprise: . . . AWE, CAP, JOLT, ALARM, AMAZE, CATCH, SEIZE, SHOCK, DETECT, STRIKE, WONDER, ASTOUND, CAPTURE, PERPLEX, STARTLE, ASTONISH, BEWILDER, CONFOUND, DUMFOUND, OVERCOME

surrender: . . . . CEDE, FALL, GIVE, REMIT, YIELD, REMISE, RESIGN, TENDER, SUBMIT, WAIVER, ABANDON, CESSION, CONCEDE, DELIVER, FORSAKE,

REMITTAL, ABDICATION, CAPITULATE, RELINQUISH, SUBMISSION

surreptituous: . . . . SLY, SECRET, BOOTLEG, FURTIVE, SNEAKY, STEALTHY, UNDERHAND, CLANDESTINE

surrogate: . . JUDGE, DEPUTY, DELEGATE, SUBROGATE, SUBSTITUTE

surround: . . BAR, HEM, BELT, GIRD, RING, BESET, EMBAY, FLOOD, CIRCLE, CORRAL, ENCASE, ENRING, INVEST, BESEIGE, EMBOSOM, ENCLOSE, ENVELOP, ENVIRON, ENCIRCLE, INUNDATE, BELEAGUER, ENCOMPASS

surrounding: . . . . . . ABOUT, MIDST, MILIEU, AMBIENT, CONTEXT, SETTING, AMBIANCE, ENTOURAGE, ENVIRONMENT

surveillance: . . SPY, WATCH, OBSERVATION

survey: . . . POLL, SCAN, VIEW, STUDY, REGARD, REVIEW, SEARCH, EXAMINE, INSPECT, CANVASS, CONSIDER, TRAVERSE, DELINEATE, DETERMINE, SCRUTINIZE

survive: . OUTLAST, OUTLIVE, WEATHER

susceptible: . . . . EASY, OPEN, SOFT, LIABLE, EXPOSED, SUBJECT, ALLERGIC, RECEPTIVE, SENSITIVE, RESPONSIVE, VULNERABLE

suscitate: . . . ROUSE, EXCITE, ANIMATE, STIMULATE

suspect: . . . . . FEAR, DOUBT, GUESS, DUBIOUS, IMAGINE, INKLING, PRESUME SUPPOSE, SURMISE, CONCEIVE, DISTRUST, MISTRUST, DISCREDIT, DISBELIEVE, INTIMATION

suspend: . . BAR, HALT, HANG, OUST, CEASE, DEBAR, DEFER, DEMUR, EXPEL, DANGLE, RECESS, ADJOURN, EXCLUDE,

INTERMIT, POSTPONE, WITHHOLD

suspended: . . HUNG, LATENT, ABEYANT, HANGING, PENDENT, PENSILE, INACTIVE, INOPERATIVE

suspension: . . . STOP, DELAY, RECESS, TRUCE, ABEYANCE, BUOYANCE, STOPPAGE, PENDANCY, ARMISTICE, CEASE-FIRE, PROBATION, REMISSION

suspicion: . . . . . FEAR, HINT, DOUBT, HUNCH, TOUCH, TRACE, INKLING, DISTRUST, MISTRUST, MISGIVING, INTIMATION, SUGGESTION, UNEASINESS

suspicious: . . . FISHY, LEERY, DOUBTFUL, EQUIVOCAL, SKEPTICAL

sustain: . . ABET, BACK, BEAR, BUOY, FEED, HELP, PROP, CARRY, ASSIST, ENDURE, FOSTER, SUCCOR, SUFFER, SUPPLY, UPHOLD, COMFORT, CONFIRM, CONSOLE, NOURISH, PROVIDE, SUPPORT, BEFRIEND, MAINTAIN, ENCOURAGE, WITHSTAND

sustenance: . . . FOOD, MEAT, BREAD, VIAND, LIVING, UPKEEP, ALIMENT, SUPPORT, NUTRITION, PROVISION

susurrant: . . . . . . RUSTLING, MURMURING, WHISPERING

suttee: . . . . SUICIDE, IMMOLATION

suture: . . . SEW, LINE, SEAM, STITCH, JUNCTION, ARTHROSIS

svelte: . . . . SLIM, LITHE, LISSOM(E), SLENDER, GRACEFUL

swab: . . . . MOB, LOUT, WIPE, BRUSH, CLEAN, SPONGE, MEDICATE

swaddle: . . . . . . BIND, WRAP, SWATHE

swag: . . SAG, TIP, LIST, LOOT, SWAY, BOOTY, LURCH, SWING, BUNDLE, PLUNDER

swagger: . . . . . BRAG, BLUFF, BOAST, BULLY, STRUT, SWELL, PRANCE, RUFFLE, BLUSTER, QUARREL, ROISTER

swain: . . . . . LOVER, YOUTH, RUSTIC, SUITOR, ADMIRER, GALLANT, PEASANT, SERVANT, SHEPHERD

swallow: . . . . . EAT, SIP, SUP, BEAR, BIRD, BOLT, GULP, TERN, DRINK, MERGE, SWIFT, ABSORB, ENGULF, IMBIBE, INGEST, MARTIN, RECANT, THROAT, BELIEVE, CONSUME, ENGORGE, RETRACT, SUPPRESS, TOLERATE

swamp: . . . . BOG, FEN, MOOR, MUCK, SINK, SLUE, FLOOD, MARSH, DELUGE, ENGULF, MORASS, SLOUGH, INUNDATE, OVERCOME, QUAGMIRE, SUBMERGE, OVERWHELM

swanky: . . . . . POSH, PLUSH, SHOWY, STYLISH

swap: . . . . . TRADE, BARTER, EXCHANGE

sward: . . . SOD, LAWN, TURF

swarm: . . . HIVE, NEST, SHIN, TEEM, CLOUD, CROWD, FLOCK, GROUP, HORDE, MOUNT, ABOUND, INVEST, THRONG, MIGRATE, OVERRUN, ASSEMBLE, MULTITUDE, CONGREGATE

swart(hy): . . . . . DUN, DARK, DUSKY, DISMAL, GLOOMY

swat: . BAT, HIT, RAP, BLOW, CLOUT, STRIKE

swath: . . ROW, STRIP, TRACK, STROKE, WINDROW

swathe: . . BAND, BIND, WRAP, ENFOLD, BANDAGE, ENVELOP, SWADDLE, SURROUND, WRAPPING

sway: . . . REEL, ROCK, RULE, VEER, FORCE, GUIDE, LURCH, POWER, SHAKE, SWING, WAVER, WIELD, DIRECT, DIVERT, GOVERN, SWERVE, TOTTER, CONTROL, DEFLECT, DOMINION, INFLUENCE, FLUCTUATE, OSCILLATE, VACILLATE

swear: . . . VOW, BIND, CUSS, CURSE, UTTER, ADJURE, AFFIRM, ASSERT, DEPOSE, PLEDGE, DECLARE, PROMISE, EXECRATE, BLASPHEME

sweat: . . . EMIT, HEAT, OOZE, WORK, BLEED, EXUDE, LABOR, SUDOR, DRUDGE, FLEECE, LATHER, EXCRETE, EXPLOIT, EXTRACT, FERMENT, SWELTER, CONDENSE, EXERCISE, OVERWORK, PERSPIRE, TRANSUDE, PERSPIRATION

sweep: . . . OAR, DRAG, DUST, LINE, RAKE, BROOM, BRUSH, CLEAN, CLEAR, DRIVE, RANGE, SCOPE, SCOUR, STRIP, SURGE, SWATH, TRAIL, EXTEND, REMOVE, CONTOUR, STRETCH, TRAVERSE

sweeping: . . . . . . EXTENSIVE

sweet: . . . . . BONNY, CANDY, HONEY, FRESH, DULCET, GENTLE, LOVELY, NECTAR, PRETTY, SUGARY, SYRUPY, BELOVED, CARMEL, DARLING, MUSICAL, WINNING, FETCHING, FRAGRANT, LUSCIOUS, PLEASANT, AGREEABLE, MELODIOUS, CONFECTION, HARMONIOUS

sweetheart: . . . . BEAU, DEAR, DOLL, GILL, JILL, LASS, LOVE, AMOUR, FLAME, LEMAN, LOVER, STEADY, LADYLOVE, TRUELOVE

sweetmeat: . . CAKE, CANDY, GOODY, COMFIT, DRAGEE, PASTRY, NOUGAT, CARMEL, DESSERT, CONSERVE, MARZIPAN, PRESERVE, SUGARPLUM, CONFECTION

swell: . . FOP, HOB, SEA, BELL, BULK, GROW, HUFF, RISE, SURF, TOFF, WAVE, BLOAT, BULGE, GRAND, GREAT, HEAVE, SURGE, BILLOW, DILATE,

EXPAND, EXTEND, PUFF-UP,
TIPTOP, TUMEFY, AUGMENT,
DISTEND, ENLARGE, INFLATE,
INCREASE, EXCELLENT,
INTUMESCE

swelling: . . STY, BLEB, BUBO,
BUMP, LUMP, NODE, PUFF,
BLAIN, BULGE, BUNCH, EDEMA,
TUMOR, GATHER, GOITER,
GROWTH, ROLLER, GIBBOUS,
TURGENT, TUMESCENT

swelter: . . . . . HEAT, ROAST,
SWEAT, PERSPIRE

sweltering: . . . HOT, SULTRY

swerve: . . SKEW, TURN, VEER,
SHEER, SHIFT, STRAY, YIELD,
CAREEN, DEVIATE, DEFLECT,
DIGRESS

swift: . . . BIRD, FAST, FLEET,
HASTY, QUICK, RAPID, PROMPT,
SPEEDY

swiftness: . . . HASTE, SPEED,
CELERITY, VELOCITY

swill: . . . . FILL, GULP, SLOP,
WASH, DRINK, FLOOD, QUAFF,
RINSE, WASTE, DRENCH,
GUZZLE, REFUSE, GARBAGE,
HOGWASH

swimming: . . . . FILLED,
NATANT, FLOODED, VERTIGO,
DIZZINESS

act of: . . . . NATATION

pool: . . . . TANK,
NATATORIUM

swindle: . . . CON, GYP, BILK,
CLIP, DUPE, FAKE, ROOK, SKIN,
BUNCO, BUNKO, CHEAT, COZEN,
FOIST, FRAUD, GOUGE, SPOOF,
TRICK, FLEECE, DIDDLE,
DEFRAUD, FLIM FLAM

swindler: . FOB, GYP, HAWK,
CHEAT, CROOK, ROGUE, SHARK,
CONMAN, FORGER, SHAVER,
COZNER, SHARPER, SKINNER

swine: . . . . . . HOG, PIG, SOW,
BOAR, PECCARY, PORCINE

swing: . . . HANG, LILT, SLEW,
SWAY, WHIP, SHAKE, TREND,
WAVER, DANGLE, RHYTHM,
STROKE, SWITCH, FLUTTER,
SUSPEND, TRAPEZE, VIBRATE,
BRANDISH, UNDULATE,
FLUCTUATE, OSCILLATE

swipe: . . . . . CUT, HIT, BLOW,
GLOM, LEVER, STEAL, PILFER,
SNATCH, STRIKE

swirl: . . CURL, EDDY, CURVE,
TWIST, WHIRL, WHORL

swish: . . . CANE, FLOG, LASH,
WHIP, SMART, RUSTLE, STRIKE,
STYLISH

switch: . . . ROD, BEAT, FLOG,
LASH, TURN, TWIG, WAND,
WHIP, SHIFT, SHUNT, STICK,
SWING, CHANGE, DIVERT,
STRIKE, TOGGLE, SCOURGE,
HICKORY, EXCHANGE,
TRANSFER

swollen: . . . . . BLOW, TUMID,
EDEMIC, TURGID, BLOATED,
BULBOUS, BULGING POMPOUS,
TURGENT, ENLARGED,
INFLATED, VARICOSE,
DISTENDED, INCREASED,
TUMESCENT

swoon: . . . FIT, FAINT, SPELL,
ATTACK, ECTASY, SYNCOPE

swoop: . . CUT, SEIZE, SWEEP,
POUNCE, DESCENT, DESCEND

sword: . . . DIRK, EPEE, FOIL,
BILBO, BLADE, ESTOC, KURI,
SABER, SKEAN, CREESE,
DAMASK, PARANG, RAPIER,
TOLEDO, CUTLASS, CLAYMORE,
DAMASCUS, SCIMITAR

sworn: . . . BOUND, DEVOTED,
PLEDGED, AFFIRMED,
ATTESTED, PROMISED,
CONFIRMED

sybarite: . . . . EPICURE,
SENSUALIST, VOLUPTUARY

sycophant: . . . . TOADY,
FLUNKY, FAWNING, SPANIEL,
YES-MAN, PARASITE, HANGER-
ON, TOADEATER, FLATTERER,
BOOTLICKER

syllabus: . . . . OUTLINE, SUMMARY, ABSTRACT, SYNOPSIS

syllogism: . . . . LOGIC, ARGUMENT, REASONING

sylph: . . . . . ELF, FAY, FAIRY, UNDINE

sylphlike: . . . . LISSOME, SLENDER, GRACEFUL

sylvan: . . . . RUSTIC, WOODED

symbol: . . (also see **emblem**) ICON, IKON, MARK, SIGN, WORD, BADGE, CREST, CROSS, IMAGE, TOKEN, TOTEM, ENSIGN, FIGURE, LETTER, DIAGRAM, CHARACTER, TRADEMARK

symbolize: . . AGREE, CONCUR, TYPIFY, BETOKEN, EXPRESS, SIGNIFY, REPRESENT

symmetrical: . . . . . REGULAR, SPHERAL, BALANCED

symmetry: . . . . . HARMONY, BALANCE, CONGRUITY, CONFORMITY, PROPORTION

sympathetic: . . . . SOFT, HUMANE, TENDER, CONDOLENT, CONGENIAL, SENSITIVE, AGREEABLE

sympathize: . . . . . CONDOLE, COMMISERATE

sympathy: . . . PITY, ACCORD, LIKING, HARMONY, AFFINITY, INTEREST, AGREEMENT, COMPASSION, CONDOLENCE

symphony: . . . . MUSIC, CONCORD, HARMONY

symposium: . . . . TALK, DIALOGUE, CONFERENCE, DISCUSSION

symptom: . . . . SIGN, FEVER, WARNING, INDICATION

synagogue: . . . SHUL, GROUP, TEMPLE, BUILDING, CONGREGATION

synchronize: . . . . ARRANGE, REGULATE, COORDINATE

syncope: . . . . FAINT, SWOON, ELISION, CESSATION

syndic: . . . . . AGENT, JUDGE, MAYOR, MANAGER, OFFICER, TRUSTEE, ADVOCATE, OFFICIAL, MAGISTRATE

syndicate: . . . CHAIN, GROUP, TRUST, CARTEL, COUNCIL, MONOPOLY, COMMITTEE, ASSOCIATION

synod: . . . . . . BODY, COURT, COUNCIL, MEETING, ASSEMBLY, CONVENTION

synopsis: . . . . . . GIST, PLAN, BRIEF, DIGEST, RESUME, SUMMARY, ABSTRACT

syntax: . . . . ORDER, SYSTEM, STRUCTURE, ARRANGEMENT

synthetic: . SHAM, ARTIFICIAL

syringe: . . . . INJECTOR

syrinx: . . . . PANPIPE

syrup: . KARO, SAPA, MAPLE, ORGEAT, GLUCOSE, TREACLE, SORGHUM, MOLASSES

system: . . . ISM, CODE, CULT, GROUP, ORDER, CIRCLE, METHOD, REGIME, SCHEMA, REGIMEN, RELIGION, UNIVERSE, PROCEDURE, REGULARITY, ARRANGEMENT

systematic: . . . . NEAT, ORDERLY, REGULAR, ORGANIZED, METHODICAL

systematize: . . . . . . ADJUST, ARRANGE, CATALOG, ORGANIZE

T

T: *Greek:* . . . . TAU
Hebrew: . . . . . TAU, TAV, TAW, TETH

taa: . . . . PAGODA

tab: . . PAN, BILL, FLAP, LOOP, AGLET, CHECK, INDEX, LABEL, SCORE, STRAP, STRIP, AIGLET, RECORD, ACCOUNT, LATCHET, APPENDAGE, RECKONING

tabard: . . . . INN, CAPE, COAT, CLOAK, JACKET, MANTLE, PENDANT

tabasco: . . . . SAUCE

tabby: . . . CAT, GOWN, SILK, DRESS, MOIRE, FABRIC, GOSSIP, MOREEN, PADDING, TAFFETA, BRINDLED

taberna: . . HUT, SHED, SHOP, TENT, BOOTH, TAVERN, SHELTER

tabernacle: . . . TENT, ABODE, HOVEL, NICHE, CHURCH, RECESS, RESIDE, SUPPORT, DWELLING, SANCTUARY, STRUCTURE, HABITATION

tabes: . . . . ATROPHY, EMACIATION, CONSUMPTION, TUBERCULOSIS

tabescent: . . . . WASTING, WITHERING

table: . . . . FARE, FEED, FOOD, LIST, SLAB, BENCH, BOARD, DEFER, INDEX, PANEL, PLATE, RECORD, REPAST, SHELVE, TABLET, LISTING, SURFACE, POSTPONE, SCHEDULE, TABULATE, FURNITURE, COMPILATION

tableau: . . . . SCENE, PICTURE

tableland: . . . MESA, PUNA, KAR(R)OO, PLATEAU

tablet: . . . . PAD, PILL, SLAB, FACIA, PANEL, SLATE, STELE, TROCHE, LOZENGE

tabloid: . . . . SHORT, TROCHE, CONDENSED, NEWSPAPER

taboo: . . . BAN, TABU, DEBAR, VERBOTEN, PROHIBITED, FORBID(DEN)

tabor: . . . . . DRUM, TIMBREL, AT(T)ABAL, TABOURET

taboret: . . . . . DRUM, SEAT, STAND, STOOL, TABOR

tabu: . . . . see taboo

tabulate: . . . . LIST, ARRANGE

tache: . . . HOOK, SPOT, CLASP, FAULT, HABIT, STAIN, ATTACH, BUCKLE, BLEMISH, TARNISH

tacit: . . . . STILL, SILENT, IMPLIED, IMPLICIT, UNSPOKEN, SOUNDLESS, UNDERSTOOD

taciturn: . . SILENT, RETICENT, RESERVED, SATURNINE

tack: . . ADD, PIN, SEW, BEAT, BRAD, CLAP, FOOD, GEAR, HAUL, JIBE, JOIN, LINK, NAIL, ROPE, TRIM, BASTE, CATCH, RIDER, SPELL, TRYING, UNITE, ATTACH, COURSE, FASTEN, METHOD, SECURE, STITCH, TACKLE, ZIGZAG, CLOTHES, CONNECT, CONTRACT, AGREEMENT, FASTENING

tackle: . . . . CAT, RIG, ARMS, FOOD, GEAR, LUFF, DRINK, SEIZE, STUFF, GRASP, ATTACH, COLLAR, SECURE, GRAPPLE, HARNESS, RIGGING, WEAPONS, WINDLESS, APPARATUS, EQUIPMENT, UNDERTAKE

tacky: . . . . . . DOWDY, SEEDY, SHABBY, STICKY, UNTIDY, ADHESIVE, SLOVENLY

tact: . . . . POISE, TOUCH, STROKE, FEELING, FINESSE, DELICACY, DIPLOMACY, ADROITNESS, CLEVERNESS, DISCRETION, SAVOIR-FAIRE

tactics: . . . . . PLOY, METHOD, SYSTEM, STRATEGY, MANEUVERS, STRATEGM

tactless: . . . . . RUDE, BRASH, GAUCHE, IMPOLITE

tad: . . . . CHILD, YOUNGSTER

tadpole: . . . . POLLIWOG

tag: . . DOG, END, TAB, FLAP, GAME, JOIN, LOCK, TAIL, AGLET, LABEL, SHRED, STRIP, TALLY, TOUCH, AIGLET, APPEND, ATTACH, FASTEN, FOLLOW, RABBLE, REFRAIN, REMNANT

tail: . . . BUN, CUE, END, TAG, BACK, BUNT, BUSH, FLEE, HIND, LAST, REAR, SCUT, QUEUE, FOLLOW, SHADOW, SWITCH, PENDANT, RETINUE, BUTTOCKS, APPENDAGE, EXTREMITY

tailing: . . . . . WASTE, REFUSE

tailless: . . . . ACAUDAL,
ANUROUS, ACAUDATE
tailor: . . . . . FIT, SNIP, STYLE,
DRAPER, SARTOR, FASHION,
BUSHELMAN, CLOTHIER
taint: . . . . . DYE, HUE, EVIL,
SPOT, CLOUD, COLOR, IMBUE,
SPOIL, STAIN, SULLY, TINGE,
TOUCH, TRACE, DEFILE, INFECT,
POISON, STIGMA, BLEMISH,
CORRUPT, DEBAUCH, DEPRAVE,
POLLUTE, DISGRACE,
IMPREGNATE, INFECT(ION),
CONTAMINATE
take: . . . BUY, EAT, GET, HIT,
USE, WIN, GLOM, GRIP, HAUL,
LEAD, RENT, TRAP, ADOPT,
AVAIL, CARRY, CATCH, CHARM,
CHEAT, DRINK, GRASP, INFER,
LEASE, SEIZE, SNARE, STEAL,
ABSORB, ACCEPT, ARREST,
ASSUME, ATTACH, ATTACK,
BORROW, CHOOSE, CONVEY,
DEDUCE, DEDUCT, DERIVE,
ENDURE, ENGAGE, OBTAIN,
OCCUPY, PROFIT, REMOVE,
SECURE, SELECT, ACQUIRE,
ASSUME, CAPTURE, CONDUCT,
EXTRACT, PRESUME, RECEIVE,
ABSTRACT, PROCEEDS,
RECEIPTS, SUBTRACT,
APPREHEND, APPROPRIATE
by force: . . . GRAB, CATCH,
SEIZE, USURP, WREST,
SNATCH, CAPTURE,
COMMANDEER
down: . . . . NOTE, RECORD
exception: . . . . . . DEMUR
in: . . FURL, ADMIT, ANNEX,
CHEAT, FENCE, TRICK,
VISIT, ESCORT, DECEIVE,
EMBRACE, ENCLOSE,
INCLUDE, RECEIVE,
CONTRACT, COMPREHEND,
UNDERSTAND
off: . . DOFF, FLEE, BEGIN,
LEAVE, MIMIC, START,
DEDUCT, DEPART, REMOVE,

DISCOUNT, SUBTRACT,
WITHDRAW, BURLESQUE
offense: . . . . RESENT
on: . . . . . . HIRE, ASSUME,
EMPLOY, ENGAGE, OPPOSE,
TACKLE, RECEIVE,
UNDERTAKE
out: . . . COPY, DELE, OMIT,
ELIDE, DEDUCT, DELETE,
EFFACE, ESCORT, REMOVE,
EXTRACT, SCRATCH,
EXPUNGE, ABSTRACT,
SEPARATE, ELIMINATE
place: . . . OCCUR, HAPPEN,
SUPERVENE
taken aback: . . . . STARTLED,
SURPRISED, DUMBFOUNDED
taking: . . . CAPTURE, SEIZING,
WINNING, ALLURING,
CATCHING, ENGAGING,
GRASPING, RAPACIOUS,
ATTRACTIVE, CONTAGIOUS,
INFECTIOUS
takings: . . PROFITS, RECEIPTS
tale: . . . . . AGALITE, POWDER,
TALCUM, STEATITE, SOAPSTONE
tale: . . . . . LIE, MYTH, SAGA,
REDE, YARN, FABLE, STORY,
TALLY, TOTAL, GOSSIP,
LEGEND, REPORT, ACCOUNT,
FICTION, PARABLE, RECITAL,
ANECDOTE, FALSEHOOD,
NARRATIVE
talent: . GIFT, DOWRY, FLAIR,
KNACK, MONEY, SKILL, GENIUS,
POWERS, RICHES, WEALTH,
ABILITY, FACULTY, FEATURE,
APTITUDE, CAPACITY,
ATTRIBUTE
talented: . . . . . ABLE, SMART,
CLEVER, GIFTED
talesman: . . . . JUROR
talion: . . . . REVENGE,
PUNISHMENT, RETALIATION
talisman: . . . . . OBI, CHARM,
OBEAH, AMULET, FETISH,
GRIGRI, SCARAB
talk: . . . . . . JAW, YAP, BLAT,
CARP, CHAT, CHIN, PARLE,

PRATE, RUMOR, SPEAK, UTTER, CONFER, DEBATE, GABBLE, GOSSIP, REASON, PARLEY, REPORT, SPEECH, ADDRESS, CHATTER, CONSULT, DISCUSS, LECTURE, MEETING, PALAVER, CHITCHAT, CONVERSE, DISCOURSE, CONFERENCE, DISCUSSION, CONVERSATION

back: . . . . SASS, RETORT, RIPOSTE, COMEBACK, REPARTEE, REJOINDER

foolish: . . GAB, GAS, BOSH, BULL, BUNK, PRATE, BABBLE, DRIVEL, TATTLE, BLABBER, BLATHER, CHATTER, PRATTLE, TWADDLE, BUNCOMBE, FAPDOODLE, POPPYCOCK

talkative: . . . . GLIB, GABBY, GASSY, CHATTY, FLUENT, VEBOSE, VOLUBLE, GARRULOUS, LOQUACIOUS

tall: . . . . HIGH, LANK, LONG, GRAND, GREAT, LANKY, LARGE, LOFTY, RANGY, STEEP, SKYHIGH, TOWERING, HIGHFLOWN, INCREDIBLE, EXAGGERATED

tallow: . . FAT, SUET, GREASE, STEARIN

tally: . . . . . . RUN, TAB, TAG, GOAL, JIBE, MARK, MATE, SUIT, AGREE, CHECK, COUNT, GRADE, LABEL, MATCH, NOTCH, SCORE, ACCORD, RECKON, RECORD, SQUARE, ACCOUNT, COMPARE, ESTIMATE, REGISTER, AGREEMENT, RECKONING, CORRESPOND

talon: . . . CLAW, HEEL, FANG, NAIL, HALLUX, POUNCE, MOLDING

talus: . . . . . . ANKLE, SCREE, SLOPE, DEBRIS, ANKLEBONE, KNUCKLEBONE

tambour: . . . . . . CUP, DESK, DRUM, TABORET, EMBROIDERY

tambourine: . . DRUM, DAIRA, TABOR, TIMBREL

tame: . . . . BUST, DULL, MILD, BREAK, DAUNT, PRUNE, DOCILE, GENTLE, HUMBLE, SOFTEN, SUBDUE, CRUSHED, SERVILE, CIVILIZE, HARMLESS, TRACTABLE, DOMESTICATE

tameness: . . . . DOCILITY, GENTLENESS, MANSUETUDE

tamp: . . . RAM, PACK, POUND, THUMP

tamper: . . . FIX, FOOL, PLOT, ALTER, BRIBE, CHANGE, DABBLE, MEDDLE, SCHEME, TINKER, CORRUPT, MACHINE, INFLUENCE, INTERFERE

tampion: . . . . . . BUNG, PLUG, COVER, STOPPER

tan: . . . . . DUN, TAW, BARK, BEAT, BLUFF, ECRU, FLOG, WHIP, BEIGE, BROWN, TAWNY, TOAST, BRONZE, TANNIN, THRASH, SUNBURN

tang: . . . . BUTT, FANG, FOIL, ODOR, PANG, TINE, ZEST, KNIFE, PRICK, PRONG, STING, TASTE, TINGE, TOUCH, TRACE, FLAVOR, PIERCE

tangent: . . . . TOUCHING, ADJACENT

tangible: . . . . REAL, ACTUAL, TACTILE, DEFINITE, PALPABLE, TOUCHABLE, PERCEPTIBLE

tangle: . . . MAT, KINK, KNOT, MESH, TRAP, GNARL, RAVEL, SNARE, SNARL, MIX-UP, WEAVE, ENTRAP, MUDDLE, SLEAVE, EMBROIL, INVOLVE, INTERTWINE

tank: . . . . VAT, LAKE, POND, POOL, BASIN, BOILER, BUNKER, CISTERN, AQUARIUM, CONTAINER, RESERVOIR

tankard: . . CUP, MUG, STOUP, POTTLE

tantalize: . . . TAUNT, TEASE, HARASS, BEWITCH, TORMENT, TITILLATE

tantamount: ...... EQUAL, IDENTICAL, EQUIVALENT

tantara: .... BLAST, BLARE, FANFARE, FLOURISH

tantrum: .... FIT, PET, HUFF, RAGE, RAVE, OUTBURST

tap: .... BAR, PAT, RAP, TIT, BEAT, COCK, CORK, DRAW, FLIP, HOLE, OPEN, PIPE, PLUG, BREAK, KNOCK, SPILE, DRAFT, VALVE, BROACH, FAUCET, SPIGOT, STRIKE, CONNECT, STOPPER

tape: ..... TIE, BAND, BIND, SCALE, STRIP, RIBBON, SECURE, BANDAGE, BINDING

taper: ... REAM, WANE, WICK, LIGHT, POINT, CANDLE, LESSEN, NARROW, TROWEL, CONICAL, DWINDLE, DECREASE, DIMINISH

tapered: ... CONOID, TERETE, CONICAL

tapestry: ..... ARRAS, TAPIS, DOSSER, GOBELIN

taphouse: ... BAR, PUB, INN, SALOON, TAVERN

tapir: ... DANTA, ANTEATER, UNGULATE

tapis: .... BAND, HIDE, SASH, CARPET, HANGING, TAPESTRY

tappet: .... CAM, LEVER

taproom: .... see **taphouse**

tar: ..... GOB, BREA, SALT, BLACK, PITCH, CRESOL, SAILOR, SEAMAN, BLACKEN, MARINER, ALCHITRAN, BLUEJACKET

tarboosh: .... CAP, FEZ

tardy: ..... LAG, LAX, LATE, SLOW, DELAY, SLACK, REMISS, RETARD, BELATED, OVERDUE, DELAYED

tare: .. WEED, VETCH, WEIGH, LEAKAGE, ALLOWANCE, DEDUCTION

target: ... AIM, BUTT, GOAL, MARK, SIGHT, OBJECT, BULLSEYE, OBJECTIVE

tariff: ..... TAX, DUTY, LIST, RATE, SCALE, CHARGE, SYSTEM, TRIBUTE, SCHEDULE

tarn: .... LAKE, LOCH, POOL

tarnish: .. DIM, BLOT, DULL, SOIL, SPOT, CLOUD, DIRTY, SPOIL, STAIN, SULLY, TAINT, DARKEN, DEFILE, SMIRCH, ASPERSE, BLEMISH, OBSCURE, BESMIRCH, DISCOLOR

tarry: ..... LAG, BIDE, LOLL, REST, STAY, STOP, WAIT, ABIDE, AWAIT, DALLY, DEFER, DELAY, DWELL, LODGE, PAUSE, ARREST, LINGER, LOITER, REMAIN, SOJOURN

tarsus: ...... HOCK, ANKLE

tart: .... PIE, ACID, FLAN, KEEN, SOUR, ACUTE, HUSSY, SHARP, TRAMP, PASTRY, SEVERE, WANTON, CAUSTIC, CUTTING, PIQUANT, PUNGENT, FRUITPIE, TURNOVER, ACIDULOUS

tartan: .... SHIP, PLAID, HIGHLANDER

task: ...... JOB, TAX, DUTY, ONUS, TEST, TOIL, WORK, CHORE, LABOR, STINT, STUDY, BURDEN, IMPOST, LESSON, STRAIN, DRUDGERY, ASSIGNMENT

tassel: .... TUFT, ADORN, FRINGE, TERCEL, ZIZITH, PENDANT, CORNSILK

taste: ... BIT, EAT, SIP, TRY, BENT, GUST, HINT, TANG, TEST, DRINK, FLAIR, GUSTO, SAPOR, SAVOR, SPICE, TOUCH, TRACE, DEGUST, FLAVOR, LIKING, PALATE, RELISH, SAMPLE, ELEGANCE, EXPERIENCE, PREFERENCE

tasteful: ..... NEAT, TASTY, ELEGANT, REFINED

tasteless: .... DULL, FLAT, SAPID, STALE, VAPID, INSIPID, SAVORLESS, INARTISTIC

tasty: ...... SAPID, SAVORY, PALATAL, LUSCIOUS, PALATABLE, TOOTHSOME, FLAVORFUL, DELICIOUS

tatter: . . . . . TAG, RAG, TEAR, SCRAP, SHRED

tattered: . . . . TORN, JAGGED, RAGGED, SHAGGY

tattle: . . . BLAB, CHAT, TALK, TELL, PEACH, PRATE, GOSSIP, CHATTER

taunt: . . . . DARE, GIBE, JEER, JEST, JIBE, MOCK, TALL, TWIT, FLEER, SCOFF, SNEER, TEASE, TEMPT, DERIDE, NEEDLE, PROVOKE, RIDICULE, REPROACH

taut: . . . . EDGY, FIRM, NEAT, SNUG, TIDY, TRIM, RIGID, STIFF, TENSE, TIGHT, SEVERE, STRICT, NERVOUS

tavern: . . . . . BAR, INN, PUB, BISTRO, HOSTEL, SALOON, TAPROOM, ALEHOUSE, TAPHOUSE, ROADHOUSE, ORDINARY

tawdry: . . . . CHEAP, GAUDY, SHOWY, SLEAZY, RAFFISH

tawny: . . . . . . TAN, BROWN, DUSKY, OLIVE, SWART, TANNED, RUBIATE

tax: . . . . . CESS, DUTY, FINE, LEVY, RATE, SCAT, SESS, SCOT, TASK, TOLL, ABUSE, EXACT, ORDER, SCATT, STINT, TITHE, VALUE, ACCUSE, ASSESS, BURDEN, CHARGE, DEMAND, EXCISE, IMPOSE, IMPOST, STRAIN, TARIFF, LICENSE, TRIBUTE

tea: . . . . PARTY, REPAST, BEVERAGE, FUNCTION, COLLATION, DECOCTION, RECEPTION

teach: . . . . DRILL, SHOW, COACH, EDIFY, ENDUE, GUIDE, TRAIN, TUTOR, DIRECT, LESSON, PREACH, SCHOOL, APPRISE, CONDUCT, EDUCATE, INSTRUCT, ENLIGHTEN, DISCIPLINE

teacher: . . . . GURU, COACH, GUIDE, RABBI, TUTOR, DOCENT, DOCTOR, MENTOR, MULLAH, PEDANT, PUNDIT, TRAINER, EDUCATOR, PREACHER, PROFESSOR, INSTRUCTOR, PEDAGOG(UE), PRECEPTOR

teaching: . . MORAL, PRECEPT, DOCTRINE, DISCIPLINE, TUTELAGE, PEDAGOGY, INSTRUCTION

team: . . . CREW, GANG, JOIN, PAIR, RACE, SPAN, SQUAD, YOKE, BROOD, CHAIN, FLOCK, GROUP, COUPLE, VARSITY

teamster: . . CARTER, DRIVER, CARRIER

tear: . . . JAG, RIP, RUN, CLAW, PULL, RAGE, REND, RENT, RIVE, SNAG, WEEP, REAVE, SPLIT, SPREE, CLEAVE, DAMAGE, DIVIDE, TATTER, WRENCH, DISRUPT, LACERATE

tearful: . . . . . . SAD, CRYING, WATERY, SNIVELY, WEEPING, LAC(H)RYMOSE

tease: . . . BEG, GUY, IRK, KID, NAG, RAG, RIB, VEX, CARD, COAX, COMB, FRET, MOCK, RAZZ, RIDE, TWIT, ANNOY, CHEVY, DEVIL, TAUNT, BADGER, BOTHER, HARASS, HECKLE, HECTOR, MOLEST, NEEDLE, PESTER, PLAGUE, DISTURB, PROVOKE, TORMENT, IRRITATE, AGGRAVATE, TANTALIZE, IMPORTUNE

technique: . . . ART, METHOD, PROCEDURE

techy: . . . . TOUCHY, VEXING, FRETFUL, PEEVISH, IRRITABLE, SENSITIVE

tedious: . . DRY, DEAD, DULL, LONG, SLOW, PROSY, DREARY, BORING, TIRESOME, HUMDRUM, IRKSOME, PROSAIC, WEARISOME, MONOTONOUS

tedium: . . . ENNUI, BOREDOM, DOLDRUM, MONOTONY

teem: . . . . FILL, GUSH, POUR, RAIN, SWIM, BRING, DRAIN, EMPTY, FETCH, SWARM,

ABOUND, SEETHE, PRODUCE, ABUNDANT, CONCEIVE

teeming: . . . . . FULL, AGUSH, POURING, REPLETE, CROWDING, PROLIFIC, ABOUNDING, OVERFLOWING

teeny: . . . . WEE, TINY, SMALL

teepee: . . . . LODGE, WIGWAM

teeter: . . . . . . ROCK, SWAY, WAVER, JIGGLE, QUIVER, SEESAW, WOBBLE, ROCKING, TREMBLE, VACILLATE

teeth: . . . . . . (also see **tooth**) TINES, MOLARS, CANINES, CUSPIDS, GRINDERS, INCISORS
decay: . . . . CARIES
deposit: . . . . TARTAR
false: . . PLATE, DENTURES
hard part: . . . . . . IVORY, DENTIN(E)

teetotaler: . . . DRY, NONUSER, NON-DRINKER, ABSTAINER, REFRAINER

teetotalism: . . . . ABSTINENCE, TEMPERANCE

tegmen: . . . . COVER, PLATE, COVERING, TEGUMENT

tegument: . . . . . COAT, HIDE, SKIN, COVER, SHELL, TESTA, TEGMEN

telegram: . . . . WIRE, CABLE, MESSAGE

telephone: . . . . . BUZZ, CALL, DIAL, PHONE, RING(UP)

telescope: . . . . . . JAM, TUBE, GLASS, SHORTEN, COLLAPSE, CONDENSE, SIMPLIFY, SPYGLASS

telescopic: . . . . . . FARSEEING

television: . . . . . . TV, TUBE, VIDEO, TELLY

tell: . . . BID, RAT, SAY, CHAT, DEEM, HILL, TALK, COUNT, MOUND, ORDER, SPEAK, STATE, UTTER, VALUE, DIRECT, IMPART, INFORM, NUMBER, RECITE, RELATE, REPEAT, REPORT, REVEAL, TATTLE, ACCOUNT, COMMAND, DIVULGE, MENTION, NARRATE, RECOUNT, REQUEST, ANNOUNCE, DISCLOSE

teller: . . . . . CLERK, CASHIER, INFORMER, NARRATOR

telling: . . . . VALID, COGENT, FORCEFUL, STRIKING, EFFECTIVE, PERTINENT, CONVINCING

telltale: . . . . TATTLER, BETRAYER, INFORMER, INDICATOR

telson: . . . SOMITE, SEGMENT

temblor: . . . . TREMOR, (EARTH)QUAKE

temerarious: . . RASH, NERVE, CHANCE, HEEDLESS, RECKLESS, VENTUROUS

temerity: . . . . . GALL, CHEEK, NERVE, AUDACITY, RASHNESS, BOLDNESS, EFFRONTRY

temper: . . . . . FIT, IRE, PET, BATE, CURB, MEAN, MOOD, NEAL, RAGE, TONE, ADAPT, ANGER, BLEND, HUMOR, ADJUST, ANNEAL, ATTUNE, DANDER, DIRECT, HARDEN, MANAGE, MODIFY, REDUCE, SEASON, SOFTEN, SOOTHE, SPIRIT, STEADY, ASSAUGE, CONTROL, MOLLIFY, TOUGHEN, MITIGATE, MODERATE, MODULATE, REGULATE, RESTRAIN, TANTRUM, DISPOSITION, COMPOSURE

temperament: . . . . . . MOOD, HUMOR, NATURE, CLIMATE, EMOTION, ADJUSTMENT, DISPOSITION

temperance: . . . . SOBRIETY, MODERATION, ABSTIENCE

temperate: . . . . CALM, COOL, MILD, SOBER, SOFTEN, MODERATE, ABSTEMIOUS, RESTRAINED

tempest: . . . . . . GALE, WIND, STORM, TUMULT, TURMOIL, AGITATION, COMMOTION

tempestuous: . . . . . . GUSTY, STORMY, VIOLENT, TURBULENT

temple: . . FANE, NAOS, RATH, CELLA, EDILE, RATHA, CHURCH,

PAGODA, MOSQUE, BASILICA, SANCTUARY, TABERNACLE

tempo: ... BEAT, PACE, RATE, TIME, SPEED, RHYTHM

temporal: ..... LAIC, CIVIL, CARNAL, EARTHLY, WORLDLY, SECULAR, MUNDANE, TRANSIENT, TRANSITORY

temporary: .... ACTING, TIMELY, INTERIM, SECULAR, TOPICAL, EPHEMERAL, TRANSITORY, PROVISIONAL

temporize: .. DELAY, HEDGE, STALL, HUMOR, YIELD, PARLEY, SOOTHE, NEGOTIATE

tempt: ... TRY, LEAD, LURE, TEST, DECOY, TAUNT, ALLURE, ENTICE, INDUCE, SEDUCE, ATTRACT, PROVOKE, PERSUADE

tempting: ...... ALLURING, SEDUCTIVE, ATTRACTIVE

temptress: ..... EVE, VAMP, SIREN, CIRCE, DELILAH, LORELEI, ENCHANTRESS

tenacious: .. ROUGH, CLINGY, DOGGED, STICKY, VISCOUS, ADHESIVE, STICKING, STUBBORN, RETENTIVE, PERSISTENT

tenancy: ... ESTATE, TENURE, HOLDING, OCCUPANCY, POSSESSION

tenant: ... HOLDER, INMATE, LEASER, LESSEE, OCCUPY, RENTER, VASSAL, DWELLER, RESIDENT, VILLEIN, OCCUPANT, INHABITANT

tend: ... CARE, LEAD, MIND, WORK, AWAIT, GUARD, NURSE, OFFER, SERVE, TREAT, WATCH, ATTEND, DIRECT, EXPECT, FOSTER, LISTEN, MANAGE, SUPPLY, HEARKEN, INCLINE, OVERSEE, PROVIDE, OPERATE, MINISTER, CULTIVATE

tendency: .. SET, BENT, BIAS, TIDE, DRIFT, DRIVE, TENOR, TREND, COURSE, BEARING, LEANING, DIRECTION,

PRONENESS, PROCLIVITY, PROPENSITY, INCLINATION, DISPOSITION

tender: .... BID, BOAT, KIND, MILD, SHIP, SOFT, SORE, WARM, WEAK, FRAIL, LIGHT, OFFER, YOUNG, FEEBLE, GENTLE, HUMANE, LOVING, TOUCHY, VESSEL, CAREFUL, FRAGILE, PRESENT, PROFFER, TENUOUS, DELICATE, IMMATURE, MERCIFUL, PROPOSAL, TICKLISH, SENSITIVE, SUCCULENT, SOFTHEARTED

tenderness: .... LOVE, PITY, KINDNESS, SOFTNESS, SYMPATHY, WEAKNESS, AFFECTION, COMPASSION, GENTLENESS

tendon: ...... BAND, CORD, THEW, NERVE, SINEW, TISSUE, LEADER, MUSCLE, HAMSTRING

tendril: .. BINE, CURL, CLASP, SPRIG, BRANCH, RINGLET, STIPULE

tenebrous: ..... SAD, DARK, DUSKY, GLOOMY, OBSCURE, DARKNESS

tenet: ... ISM, VIEW, CANON, CREED, DOGMA, MAXIM, BELIEF, DECREE, OPINION, DOCTRINE, PRINCIPLE

tenfold: ... DENARY, DECUPLE

tenor: ... DRIFT, GIST, DRIFT, TREND, COURSE, INTENT, NATURE, SINGER, PURPORT, MEANING, TENDENCY

tense: .... FLEX, RAPT, TAUT, TIME, DRAWN, RIGID, STIFF, TIGHT, INTENT, TAUTEN, INTENSE, ELECTRIC, STRAINED, STRETCHED

tensile: .... PLIANT, PLASTIC, DUCTILE, FLEXIBLE, TENSIBLE

tension: ... STRAIN, STRESS, CLOSURE, PRESSURE

tent: ... CAMP, YURT, LODGE, TEPEE, BIGTOP, ENCAMP,

TEEPEE, WIGWAM, MARQUEE,
SHELTER

tentacle: . . . . . PALP, FEELER,
TENDRIL, ANTENNA

tentative: . . . . . TEMPORARY,
PROVISIONAL

tenterhooks: . . . . TENSE,
STRAIN, ANXIOUS, SUSPENSE

tenuity: . . RARITY, POVERTY,
DELICACY, FINENESS,
RARENESS, THINNESS,
FAINTNESS, INDIGENCE

tenuous: . . FINE, RARE, SLIM,
THIN, SLIGHT, FLIMSY, SUBTLE,
SLENDER, DELICATE, ETHEREAL

tenure: . . . . . . TERM, LEASE,
MANNER, SOCAGE, HOLDING,
CONDITION, INCUMBENCY

tepee, tee pee: . . . . . . TENT,
LODGE, WIGWAM

tepid: . . . . (LUKE)WARM

teratoid: . . . . MONSTER,
MONSTROUS

tercel: . . . HAWK, PEREGRINE

tercet: . . . . TRIPLET

tergal: . . . . . BACK, DORSAL

tergiversate: . . . LIE, EVADE,
HEDGE, APOSTATIZE,
EQUIVOCATE

tergum: . . . . BACK

term: . . . NAME, TIME, WORD,
BOUND, LIMIT, PERIOD,
TENURE, ARTICLE, SESSION,
SEMESTER, DURATION,
EXPRESSION

termagant: . . . . SHREW,
HELLCAT, VIXEN, AMAZON,
FURIOUS, HELLCAT, SCOLDING

terminal: . . . . . . END, LAST,
ANODE, DEPOT, FINAL, LIMIT,
FINISH, CATHODE, CLOSING,
STATION, ULTIMATE,
ELECTRODE, EXTREMITY

terminate: . . . . . . END, CALL,
HALT, STOP, CEASE, CLOSE,
LIMIT, EXPIRE, FINISH, RESULT,
ACHIEVE, CONFINE, COMPLETE,
CONCLUDE

termination: . . END, BOUND,
CLOSE, LIMIT, ENDING, EXPIRY,

FINALE, FINISH, PERIOD,
RESULT, UPSHOT, OUTCOME,
BOUNDRY, DECISION,
EXTREMITY, COMPLETION,
CONCLUSION, EXPIRATION

terms: . . . . AGREEMENT,
CONDITIONS, PROVISIONS,
LIMITATIONS, STIPULATIONS

ternary: . . . . . THIRD, TRIAD,
TREBLE, TRIPLE, TRINITY,
THREEFOLD

terrace: . BANK, DIAS, MESA,
STEP, BENCH, PATIO, GALLERY,
PLATEAU, PORTICO, BALCONY,
PLATFORM, COLONNADE

terrain: . . . TRACT, GROUND,
MILIEU, REGION, ENVIRONMENT

terrapin: . . . . EMYD, TURTLE

terrestrial: . . . . . . LAYMAN,
MORTAL, MUNDANE, WORLDLY,
PLANETARY, EARTHLY

terrible: . . . . . DIRE, AWFUL,
LURID, SEVERE, TRAGIC,
EXTREME, FEARFUL, GHASTLY,
HIDEOUS, INTENSE, PAINFUL,
DREADFUL, ATROCIOUS,
FRIGHTFUL

terribly: . . VERY, EXTREMELY

terrific: . . . GREAT, EXTREME,
DREADFUL, EXCITING,
TERRIBLE, APPALLING,
EXCELLENT, FRIGHTFUL,
TREMENDOUS

terrify: . . AWE, COW, ALARM,
APPAL, DAUNT, HAUNT, SCARE,
SHOCK, APPALL, DISMAY,
FRIGHTEN

terrifying: . . . . HORRID,
HIDEOUS, DREADFUL, TERRIBLE

territory: . . . . AREA, LAND,
FIELD, SCOPE, STATE, TRACT,
EXTENT, GROUND, REGION,
SPHERE, COUNTRY, PORTION,
DISTRICT, ENVIRONS, PROVINCE,
TERRENE, DOMAIN

terror: . . . AWE, FEAR, PEST,
ALARM, DREAD, PANIC,
DISMAY, FRIGHT, HORROR

terse: ... CURT, NEAT, BRIEF, CRISP, PITHY, ABRUPT, COMPACT, CONCISE, LACONIC, POINTED, REFINED, POLISHED, SUCCINCT

tessellate: ..... TILE, INLAY, MOSAIC, CHECKER

test: ..... TRY, EXAM, FEEL, ASSAY, CHECK, PROOF, PROVE, SHELL, TASTE, TRIAL, ORDEAL, SAMPLE, TRYOUT, APPROVE, EXAMINE, STANDARD, CRITERION, DETERMINE, EXPERIMENT

testa: ..... SHELL, COATING, COVERING, TEGUMENT, INTEGUMENT

testament: .. WILL, COVENANT

testator: .. LEGATOR, WITNESS

testifier: .... WITNESS, DEPONENT

testify: .... AFFIRM, ATTEST, DEPONE, DEPOSE, SWEAR, DECLARE, PROFESS, INDICATE, MANIFEST

testimonial: ... SIGN, TOKEN, TRIBUTE, WARRANT, EVIDENCE, CERTIFICATE, REFERENCE, COMPLIMENT

testimony: ... PROOF, ATTEST, AVOWAL, WITNESS, EVIDENCE, DEPOSITION, DECLARATION

testy: .... TOUCHY, PEEVISH, PEPPERY, WASPISH, IRRITABLE, SENSITIVE

tetanus: . LOCKJAW, TRISMUS

tetched: ... LOCO, DEMENTED

tetchy: .... see testy

tete-a-tete: .... SEAT, SOFA, CHAT, CONVERSATION

tether: .... TIE, BAND, ROPE, CABLE, CHAIN, LEASH, LIMIT, FASTEN, LARIAT, PICKET, CONFINE, RESTRAIN

tetragon: .... SQUARE, RHOMBUS, QUADRANGLE

tetter: ..... ECZEMA, HERPES, LICHEN

Teuton(ic): .... DUTCH, ENGLISH, GOTHIC, NORDIC, GERMAN(IC), SCANDINAVIAN

tew: ..... VEX, BEAT, FUSS, PULL, KNEAD, TEASE, INCITE, STRIVE, TUYERE, FATIGUE, STRUGGLE

tewel: .... BORE, HOLE, PIPE, TOOL, VENT, FUNNEL, TUYERE, CHIMNEY

text: ... BOOK, THEME, TOPIC, PASSAGE, SUBJECT, WORDING

textile: ...... FLAX, WOOL, CLOTH, LINEN, WOVEN, FABRIC, COTTON, DRAPERY, MERCERY

texture: . WEB, WALE, WARP, WOOF, GRAIN, WEAVE, FABRIC, TISSUE, STRUCTURE, COMPOSITION

thane: .... CHURL, FREEMAN, SERVANT, WARRIOR

thankless: ..... UNGRATEFUL
person: .... INGRATE

thatch: ... HAIR, NIPA, PALM, GRASS, REEDS, STRAW, RUSHES, ROOF(ING)

thaumaturgy: ...... MAGIC

thaw: .. EASE, MELT, RELENT, SOFTEN, UNBEND, LIQUEFY, DISSOLVE

theater: ... ARENA, DRAMA, HOUSE, STAGE, BOARDS, MOVIEHOUSE, PLAYHOUSE

theatrical: ... SHOWY, STAGY, SCENIC, POMPOUS, AFFECTED, DRAMATIC, ARTIFICIAL, HISTRIONIC

theca: .. SAC, CASE, COCOON, CAPSULE

theft: .... PIRACY, LARCENY, ROBBERY, BURGLARY, THIEVERY, PLAGIARISM

theme: .. BASE, TEXT, ESSAY, MOTIF, TOPIC, MATTER, THESES, THESIS, DISCOURSE, COMPOSITION

then: .... NEXT, ALORS, BESIDES, FORMERLY, MOREOVER, THEREFORE

thence: . . AWAY, ELSEWHERE, THEREFORE, THEREFROM

theologian: . . ARIUS, DIVINE, AQUINAS, LUTHER, CALVIN, ORIGEN

theoretical: . . . . IDEAL, ABSTRACT, ACADEMIC, SPECULATIVE, HYPOTHETICAL

theorize: . . . . GUESS, POSTULATE, SPECULATE

theory: . . . . ISM, IDEA, LAW, PLAN, GUESS, SCHEME, THESIS, FORMULA, DOCTRINE, PRINCIPLE, CONJECTURE, HYPOTHESIS

therapeutic: . . . . . CURATIVE

therapy: . . CURE, TREATMENT

there: . . . AT, YON, TOWARD, YONDER, THITHER

thereafter: . . . . SINCE, AFTERWARD, ACCORDINGLY, THENCEFORTH

therefore: . . . . AS, SO, ERGO, THEN, THUS, HENCE, SINCE, THENCE, ACCORDINGLY, CONSEQUENTLY

thermal: . . . . . . HOT, WARM

thermometer, type of: . . . . . CELSIUS, REAUMUR, CENTIGRADE, FAHRENHEIT

thesaurus: . . . . LEXICON, TREASURY, DICTIONARY, STOREHOUSE

thesis: . . . . ESSAY, POINT, THEME, THEORY, PREMISE, TREATISE, POSTULATE, MONOGRAPH, ASSUMPTION, PROPOSITION, DISSERTATION

Thespian: . . ACTOR, PLAYER, ACTRESS, TRAGEDIAN, PERFORMER

thetic: . . . . POSITIVE, ARBITRARY, PRESCRIBED

theurgy: . . . . MAGIC

thew: . . FORM, MODE, HABIT, POWER, SINEW, TRAIT, CUSTOM, MANNER, MUSCLE, VIRTUE, QUALITY, STRENGTH, DISCIPLINE, RESOLUTION

thews: . . . SINEWS, MUSCLES

thewy: . . SINEWY, MUSCULAR

thick: . . . . FAT, DULL, HAZY, BROAD, BURLY, CLOSE, CRASS, DENSE, GROSS, HEAVY, HUSKY, PLUMP, SOLID, COARSE, OBTUSE, SHAGGY, STUPID, TURBID, COMPACT, CROWDED, MUFFLED, VISCOUS, ABUNDANT, FRIENDLY, GUTTURAL, INTIMATE, PROFOUND, LUXURIANT, INDISTINCT

thicken: . . GEL, CLOT, CURD, CLOUD, CROWD, FLOCK, CURDLE, DEEPEN, HARDEN, CONGEAL, STIFFEN, CONDENSE, SOLIDIFY, COAGULATE, INSPISSATE

thicket: . . . TOD, BOSK, BUSH, RONE, SHAW, BRAKE, CLUMP, COPSE, BRUSH, GROVE, HEDGE, BOSCAGE, COPPICE, SPINNEY, BRUSHWOOD, CHAPARRAL, UNDERBRUSH

thickhead: . . . . FOOL, DUNCE, IDIOT

thickness: . . . . . PLY, LAYER, SHEET, STRATUM, DIAMETER, DENSENESS, DIMENSION

thickset: . . . . STUB, BEEFY, SQUAT, STOUT, STOCKY, CHUNKY, STUBBY

thief: . . . . BANDIT, HOOKER, LOOTER, RASCAL, ROBBER, BRIGAND, BURGLAR, FILCHER, STEALER, GANGSTER, LARCENER, PILFERER, PICKPOCKET, PLAGARIST, SHOPLIFTER

thigh: . . HAM, HOCK, FEMUR, FLANK

thin: . . . . BONY, FINE, LANK, LEAN, PALE, RARE, SLIM, WEAK, FAINT, GAUNT, LANKY, SCANT, SHEER, SPARE, WIZEN, DILUTE, FLIMSY, MEAGER, PAPERY, REDUCE, SCANTY, SCARCE, SKINNY, SLIGHT, SLINKY, SPARSE, WATERY,

WEAKEN, SCRAWNY, SLENDER, TENUOUS, HAIRLINE, EMACIATED

thing: . . . . . ACT, RES, DEED, FACT, IDEA, ITEM, ASSET, BEING, CAUSE, CHOSE, EVENT, POINT, AFFAIR, DETAIL, ENTITY, MATTER, NOTION, OBJECT, REASON, TRIFLE, ARTICLE, INCIDENT, PROPERTY, HAPPENING

think: . . . DEEM, MULL, MUSE, TROW, WEAN, BROOD, JUDGE, OPINE, ESTEEM, EXPECT, IDEATE, INVENT, PONDER, REASON, RECALL, RECKON, SCHEME, BELIEVE, CONCOCT, IMAGINE, REFLECT, SUPPOSE, SURMISE, COGITATE, CONCEIVE, CONSIDER, MEDITATE, RUMINATE, CALCULATE, CEREBRATE, DETERMINE, RECOLLECT, SPECULATE, CONJECTURE, DELIBERATE, CONTEMPLATE

thinness: . . . RARITY, TENUITY

third: . . . TERNARY, TERTIARY

thirl: . . . . . . PIERCE, THRILL

thirst: . . . . . . LONG, CRAVE, DESIRE, DRYNESS, ARIDITY, CRAVING, LONGING

thither: . . . . . . YON, HENCE, THERE, YONDER, THEREAT

thole: . . . PEG, PIN, OARLOCK

thong: . . . LACE, LASH, REIN, RIEM, LASSO, LEASH, STRAP, STRIP, LANYARD, WHIPLASH

thorax: . . . . CHEST

thorn: . . . GOAD, TREE, BRIAR, BRIER, SPINE, WORRY, NETTLE, BRAMBLE, PRICKLE, VEXATION

thorny: . . . . . . SHARP, SPINY, SPINAL, BRAMBLY, BRISTLY, PRICKLY, SPINATE, SPINOSE

thorough: . . . . . DEEP, FULL, ARRANT, ABSOLUTE, ACCURATE, COMPLETE, FINISHED, DOWNRIGHT, INTENSIVE, OUT-AND-OUT, EXHAUSTIVE

thoroughbred: . . . . . HORSE, CULTURED, HIGHBORN, WELL-BRED, PEDIGREED, BLUEBLOOD

thoroughfare: . . . . . . ROAD, ALLEY, AVENUE, STREET, HIGHWAY, PASSAGE, TRANSIT, CONCOURSE, BOULEVARD

though: . . . . HOWEVER, NEVERTHELESS

thought: . . . . . . CARE, HEED, HOPE, IDEA, MIND, VIEW, DEEMED, OPINED, CONCEPT, JUDGING, OPINION, REASONING, INTELLECT, COGITATION, MEDITATION

thoughtful: . . KIND, CAREFUL, HEEDFUL, MINDFUL, PENSIVE, PRUDENT, SERIOUS, ATTENTIVE, DESIGNING, REGARDFUL, REFLECTIVE

thoughtless: . . . RASH, STUPID, REMISS, CARELESS, HEEDLESS, RECKLESS, UNTHINKING

thrall: . . . . SERF, SLAVE, BONDAGE, BONDMAN, CAPTIVE, SLAVERY, SUBJECT, ENTHRALL, SUFFERING, SUBJUGATED

thralldom: . . . . . BONDAGE, SLAVERY, SERVITUDE

thrash: . . . . LAM, TAN, BEAT, CANE, DRUB, FLOG, HIDE, LACE, LASH, ROUT, SAIL, WHIP, BASTE, FLAIL, POUND, SWING, WHANG, WHALE, DEFEAT, LARRUP, THRESH, THWACK, WALLOP, BELABOR, TROUNCE, LAMBASTE, VANQUISH

thread: . . . RAY, CORD, LINE, VEIN, YARN, FIBER, FILUM, INKLE, LINEN, LISLE, REEVE, WEAVE, STRAND, STRATA, STRING, STRATUM, FILAMENT, FINENESS, RAVELING

threadbare: . . WORN, SEEDY, STALE, TRITE, FRAYED, RAGGED, SHABBY

thready: . . . . . . THIN, WEAK,
STRINGY, FIBROUS
threap: . . . . . . URGE, ARGUE,
CHIDE, SCOLD, ASSERT,
HAGGLE, INSIST, DISPUTE,
QUARREL, COMPLAIN
threat: . . . . . . URGE, WARN,
BLUFF, CHIDE, CROWD, PERIL,
COMPEL, MENACE, BLUSTER,
OPPRESS, PORTEND, TROUBLE,
WARNING, COMPULSION
threatening: . . BIG, SULLEN,
OMINOUS, MINACIOUS,
MENACING, IMPENDING,
FORMIDABLE
three: . . . TREY, TRIO, TRIAD,
TRIAS, TRINITY
threefold: . . . TRINE, TREBLE,
TRIPLE, THRICE, TRINAL,
TRIPLEX, TRIPARTITE
thresh: . . BEAT, FLOG, FLAIL,
THRASH
out: . . . . ARGUE, DEBATE,
DISCUSS
threshold: . . EVE, GATE, SILL,
LIMEN, OUTSET, DOORSILL,
ENTRANCE, BEGINNING
thrice: . . . VERY, THREEFOLD
thrift: . . . . ECONOMY,
FRUGALITY, HUSBANDRY
thrifty: . . . . . . NEAR, SMALL,
FRUGAL, SAVING, CAREFUL,
SPARING, PROVIDENT,
ECONOMICAL
thrill: . . KICK, ELATE, FLUSH,
THIRL, EXCITE, QUIVER,
TREMOR, TREMBLE, VIBRATE,
ELECTRIFY, EXHILARATE
thrilling: . . . . ELECTRIC,
EXCITING, THROBBING,
VIBRATING
thrive: . . WAX, GAIN, GROW,
ADDLE, BATTEN, FATTEN,
IMPROVE, PROSPER, SUCCEED,
FLOURISH, INCREASE
throat: . . MAW, CRAG, CROP,
LANE, TUBE, GORGE, FAUCES,
GROOVE, GULLET, CHANNEL,
ORIFICE, WEASAND, THROTTLE

throaty: . HOARSE, GUTTERAL
throb: . . . ACHE, BEAT, DRUM,
PANT, PUMP, POUND, PULSE,
THUMP, PULSATE, VIBRATE,
PALPITATE, PULSATION
throe: . . . PAIN, PANG, RACK,
AGONY, SPASM, EFFORT,
ANGUISH
thrombus: . . . . . CLOT, FIBRIN
throne: . . . . SEE, APSE, SEAT,
CHAIR, POWER, RULER,
CATHEDRA, SOVEREIGN(TY)
throng: . . CREW, HOST, PUSH,
ROUT, CROWD, HORDE, PRESS,
SWARM, BUSTLE, STRESS,
CONFUSION, MULTITUDE
throttle: . . GAG, GUN, CHECK,
CHOKE, VALVE, THROAT,
COMPRESS, GAROTTE, SILENCE,
STRANGLE, SUPPRESS,
SUFFOCATE, ACCELERATOR
through, thru: . . . . BY, PER,
VIA, DONE, OVER, AMONG,
ENDED, ACROSS, FINISHED,
COMPLETED
throw: . . . . LOB, SHY, CAST,
DASH, HURL, PELT, RACK,
SHED, TOSS, CHUCK, CHUNK,
CRANK, FLICK, FLING, HEAVE,
IMPEL, PITCH, SLING, START,
TWIST, UPSET, WHIRL, DEFEAT,
INJECT, SPREAD, SPRING,
THRUST, WRENCH, DISCARD,
PROJECT, CATAPULT
away: . . . WASTE, REFUSE,
REJECT, DISCARD,
SQUANDER
out: . . EMIT, OUST, EGEST,
EJECT, EVICT, EXPEL,
UTTER, BOUNCE, REJECT,
DISCARD, EXCRETE,
PROJECT, ELIMINATE
over: . . . . JILT, ABANDON
overboard: . . . . JETTISON
together: . . . . . . COLLECT,
ASSEMBLE
up: . . . PUKE, SPEW, DEMIT,
RETCH, VOMIT, REJECT,
REGORGE, RELINQUISH

throwback: . . CHECK, DELAY, REPEL, REFUSE, REJECT, RETORT, REVERSAL, ATAVISM

thrown: . . . . CAST, HURLED, PITCHED, UNSEATED

thrust: . . . . JAB, POKE, PROP, PUSH, STAB, TILT, DRIVE, FORCE, IMPEL, LUNGE, PRESS, SHOVE, ATTACK, PIERCE, RIPOST, ASSAULT, INTRUDE, INTERJECT, INTERPOSE

thud: . . . . BLOW, THUMP

thug: . . . . . . GOON, ROUGH, TOUGH, DACOIT, GUNMAN, MUGGER, GORILLA, RUFFIAN, ASSASSIN, GANGSTER, CUTTHROAT, STRANGLER

thumb: . . . . . . DIGIT, POLLEX

thump: . . . HIT, BEAT, BUMP, DRUB, THUD, WHIP, KNOCK, POUND, THROB, BOUNCE, CUDGEL, THRASH, POMMEL

thunder: . . . . . . CLAP, PEAL, RAGE, ROLL, ROAR, CRASH, RUMBLE, FULMINATE

thurible: . . . . CENSER

thus: . SO, SIC, ERGO, HENCE, THEREFORE

thwack: . RAP, SLAP, KNOCK, SMACK, WHACK, DEFEAT, STRIKE

thwart: . . . BALK, FOIL, SEAT, BENCH, CLASS, CROSS, PARRY, BAFFLE, DEFEAT, HINDER, OPPOSE, OUTWIT, RESIST, OBLIQUE, PREVENT, OBSTRUCT, FRUSTRATE

thymus: . . . . GLAND, SWEETBREAD

thyroid disease: . . . . GOITER, CRETINISM

tiara: . . . . . CROWN, DIADEM, CORONET, HEADRESS

tibia: . . . . . . FLUTE, CNEMIS, SHIN(BONE)

tic: . . . . JERK, SPASM, TWITCH

tick: . . DOT, TAG, TAP, CASE, DASH, MARK, MITE, NOTE, PEST, CLICK, CHECK, COUNT, COVER, SPECK, ACARID, CREDIT, INSECT, JIGGER, MOMENT, RECORD, SECOND, INSTANT, CHIGGER, PARASITE, ARACHNID

ticket: . . . . TAG, CARD, PASS, SLIP, CHECK, DUCAT, LABEL, SCORE, SLATE, TOKEN, BALLOT, PERMIT, DOCKET, LICENSE, VOUCHER, WARRANT, CARDBOARD

tickle: . . . . STIR, AMUSE, EXCITE, PLEASE, THRILL, TINGLE, DELIGHT, GRATIFY, TITILIATE

tickler: . . . PUZZLE, REMINDER

ticklish: . . . . RISKY, FICKLE, QUEASY, TOUCHY, CRITICAL, DELICATE, UNSTABLE, UNCERTAIN, PRECARIOUS

tidbit: . . . . . GOODY, MORSEL, GOSSIP, CANAPE

tide: . . EBB, RIP, FLOW, NEAP, TIME, CARRY, DRIFT, DRIVE, FLOOD, SURGE, MOMENT, PERIOD, SEASON, SPRING, STREAM, CURRENT, OCCASION

tidings: . . . . . . NEWS, WORD, EVENT, GOSPEL, REPORT, ACCOUNT, EVANGEL, MESSAGE, INFORMATION

tidy: . . . . GOOD, NEAT, TAUT, TRIG, TRIM, CLEAN, GREAT, GROOM, LARGE, COMELY, SPRUCE, ORDERLY, SHIPSHAPE, CONSIDERABLE

tie: . . . . . ROD, BAND, BEAM, BOND, CORD, DRAW, JOIN, KNOT, LACE, LASH, LINK, MOOR, ROPE, ASCOT, BRACE, CHAIN, EQUAL, HITCH, MARRY, NEXUS, TRUSS, UNION, UNITE, ATTACH, COUPLE, CRAVAT, FASTEN, STRING, TETHER, CONFINE, CONNECT, RESTRICT, STANDOFF, CONSTRAIN, STALEMATE, FOUR-IN-HAND

tier: .... ROW, BANK, RANK, LAYER, STACK, STORY, DEGREE, ARRANGE, PINAFORE

tiff: .... HUFF, MIFF, MOOD, SPAT, DRAFT, DRINK, HUMOR, LUNCH, LIQUOR, QUARREL, ARGUMENT

tiffin: .. TEA, LUNCH, SNACK, EATING

tiger: .. CAT, FELINE, JAGUAR, LEOPARD, CARNIVORE, SABERTOOTH

tigerish: .... CRUEL, FIERCE, FEROCIOUS

tight: .... FAST, FIRM, HARD, HELD, NEAT, SNUG, TIDY, TRIM, TAUT, BOUND, CHEAP, CLOSE, DENSE, DRUNK, FIXED, SOLID, TENSE, TIPSY, PACKED, SEVERE, STEADY, STINGY, STRICT, COMPACT, CONCISE, MISERLY, EXACTING, NIGGARDLY

tightlipped: .... TERSE, SECRETIVE, TACITURN

tightwad: .... MISER, PIKER, SKINFLINT, NIGGARD

tile: ... BRICK, DRAIN, PLATE, SLATE, PANTILE, TESSERA, TEGULA, CERAMIC

till: ..... SOW, FARM, PLOW, UNTO, LABOR, UNTIL, CASKET, DRAWER, REGISTER, PREPARE, CULTIVATE

tiller: ... BAR, HELM, LEVER, STICK, FARMER, CULTIVATOR, PLOWMAN

tilt: . TIP, CANT, DUEL, HEEL, LEAN, LIST, FIGHT, JOUST, PITCH, SLANT, SLOPE, AWNING, CANOPY, OPPOSE, SEESAW, CONTEST, INCLINE, TOURNAMENT

timbral: ..... KETTLEDRUM

timber: .... LOG, RIB, BEAM, WOOD, TREE, TREES, FOREST, LUMBER, SUPPORT

timbre: .... TONE

timbrel: .... TABOR, TAMBOURINE

time: ..... AGE, DAY, ERA, DATE, HOUR, TERM, WEEK, YEAR, CLOCK, EPOCH, MONTH, TEMPO, TENSE, WATCH, MINUTE, MOMENT, PERIOD, SEASON, SECOND, INSTANT, INTERVAL, OCCASION, DURATION

timely: .... PROMPT, OPPORTUNE, PERTINENT, SEASONABLE

timetable: ...... SCHEDULE

timid: .. SHY, MOUSY, PAVID, AFRAID, BASHFUL, FEARFUL, NERVOUS, CHICKEN, RESERVED, RETIRING, TIMOROUS

timorous: ..... SHY, TIMID, FEARFUL, TREPID

tin: ...... BOX, CAN, PAN, LATTEN, STANNUM, PRESERVE, CONTAINER

tincture: ..... CAST, TINT, COLOR, IMBUE, SHADE, TAINT, TINGE, TRACE, ELIXIR, VESTIGE

tine: ... FORK, PRONG, SPIKE, TOOTH, ANTLER, HARROW, TYND

tinge: .... DYE, TINT, COLOR, IMBUE, SAVOR, SHADE, STAIN, TAINT, TOUCH, TRACE, FLAVOR, TINCTURE

tingle: ..... NIP, DIRL, RING, STING, THIRL, DINDLE, PRICKLE

tinker: .. FUSS, MEND, WORK, CAIRD, PATCH, MENDER, POTTER, PUTTER, REPAIR, BUNGLER, SILVERSIDES, MACKEREL

tinsel: ...... SHAM, SHOWY, GAUDY, TAWDRY

tint: ..... DYE, HUE, BLUSH, COLOR, SHADE, STAIN, TINGE, TRACE

tiny: ... WEE, SMALL, TEENY, ATOMIC, MINUTE, MINUSCLE, MINIATURE, DIMINUTIVE

tip: . . . . CAP, CUE, END, FEE, NEB, TAP, TOE, TOP, APEX, CANT, CLUE, HEEL, HINT, KEEL, LEAN, LIST, TILT, VAIL, CROWN, SLANT, SPIRE, STEER, UPSET, CAREEN, SUMMIT, TOPPLE, GRATUITY, CUMSHAW, BAKSHISH

tippet: . . . . BOA, FUR, CAPE, HOOD, SCARF, AMICE, ALMUCE, LIRIPIPE

tipple: . BIB, NIP, SIP, DRINK, LIQUOR

tippler: . . SOT, SOUSE, TOPER, DRINKER

tipsy: . . HIGH, AWRY, DRUNK, CROOKED, LOADED, GROGGY, INTOXICATED

tiptop: . . . BEST, FIRST-RATE, SHIPSHAPE

tirade: . . . . . SPATE, SPEECH, CENSURE, DIATRIBE, HARANGUE, PHILIPPIC

tire: . . . . . FAG, LAG, BAND, BORE, CLOY, HOOP, JADE, PALL, WEARY, CASING, EXHAUST, FATIGUE

tired: . . . . . . BLOWN, JADED, SPENT, WEARY, SLEEPY, FATIGUED

tiresome: . . . . . DRY, DULL, BORING, DREARY, PROSAIC, TEDIOUS, FATIGUING

tissue: . . . . GUM, WEB, FIBER, MESH, TELA, GAUZE, CLOTH, PAPER, WEAVE, RIBBON, GRISTLE, NETWORK

tit: . . NAG, TAP, BIRD, BLOW, GIRL, JADE, TEAT, NIPPLE, BREAST, HORSE

titanic: . . . . . . HUGE, GREAT, IMMENSE, COLOSSAL, GIGANTIC

tithe: . . . . TAX, LEVY, TENTH

titillate: . . . EXCITE, TICKLE, TANTALIZE, STIMULATE

title: . . . DEED, NAME, CLAIM, RIGHT, ASSIGN, LEGEND, NOTICE, RECORD, ASCRIBE, CAPTION, EPITHET, HEADING,

DOCUMENT, MUNIMENT, APPELLATION, DESIGNATION

titter: . . . . . LAUGH, GIGGLE, SNICKER

tittle: . . . . . . DOT, JOT, IOTA, WHIT, POINT, TILDE, ACCENT, PARTICLE

titular: . . . . NOMINAL

tizzy: . . . . SNIT, DITHER, ANXIETY, EXCITEMENT

to: . . . . . . TILL, UNTO, WITH, UNTIL, TOWARD, FORWARD, THITHER

do: . . . . STIR, FUSS, COMMOTION

the point: . . . . APT, GERMANE, RELATED, RELEVANT, PERTINENT

toady: . . . . . . FAWN, FLUNKY, LACKEY, TRUCKLE, PARASITE, FLATTERER, SYCOPHANT, LICKSPITTLE

toast: . . . . DRY, TAN, WARM, BROWN, DRINK, MELBA, SKOAL, PLEDGE, PROSIT, SALUTE, PROPOSE, COMPLIMENT

tobacco: . . . . . . PLUG, QUID, WEED, CIGAR, SMOKE, SNUFF, CHEWING, CIGARETTE

toboggan: . . . . SLED, CHUTE, COASTER, DECLINE

toby: . . . . JUG, MUG, CIGAR, STEIN, PITCHER

tocsin: . . . . . . BELL, ALARM

today: . . NOW, HERE, PRESENT

toddle: . . . . . WALK, STROLL, WADDLE, TOTTER, SAUNTER

toe: . . . . . PAW, TIP, DIGIT

tog(s): . . . DUDS, COAT, DRESS, CLOTHES, GARMENT

toga: . . . ROBE, GOWN, TUNIC

together: . . . . . . MIX, ALONG, CHAIN, UNION, UNISON, CONCERT, HARMONY, ENSEMBLE, ASSOCIATED

toggle: . . . . PIN, ROD, BOLT, COTTER

toil: . . . . DRAG, PLOD, PULL, SLOG, TASK, WORK, LABOR,

SLAVE, SNARE, DRUDGE,
EFFORT, STRIFE, CONTEND,
TRAVAIL, STRUGGLE

toilet: ...... CLOTH, DRESS,
ATTIRE, COSTUME, BATHROOM,
GROOMING, COMMODE,
LAVATORY

toilsome: ... HARD, ARDUOUS,
LABORIOUS

token: .... GIFT, OMEN, SIGN,
SLUG, BADGE, CHECK, INDEX,
MEDAL, AMULET, EMBLEM,
PLEDGE, SIGNAL, SYMBOL,
MEMENTO, SIGNIFY, EVIDENCE,
KEEPSAKE, SOUVENIR,
INDICATION

tolerable: ..... FAIR, SO-SO,
BEARABLE, PASSABLE,
ENDURABLE

tolerably: .... FAIRLY,
MODERATELY

tolerance: .... MARGIN,
ALLOWANCE, ENDURANCE,
VARIATION

tolerate: ..... BEAR, ABIDE,
ALLOW, BROOK, STAND,
ENDURE, PERMIT, SUFFER

toll: .... TAX, DRAW, DUTY,
PEAL, RING, KNELL, SOUND,
CHARGE, CUSTOM, EXCISE,
IMPOST, ASSESSMENT,
EXACTION

tomato: ..... FRUIT, WOMAN,
LOVEAPPLE

tomb: .. CIST, CRYPT, GRAVE,
VAULT, BURIAL, CASKET,
OSSUARY, CATACOMB,
CENOTAPH, MONUMENT,
SEPULCHER, MAUSOLEUM

tombstone: .... STELE,
MONUMENT

tome: ...... BOOK, VOLUME

tomfoolery: ..... NONSENSE,
SILLINESS

tommyrot: ...... RUBBISH,
NONSENSE, SILLINESS

tomorrow: ...... MANANA

ton: .... LOTS, MODE, STYLE,
VOGUE, FASHION

tone: .... HUE, KEY, MOOD,
NOTE, TINT, PITCH, SOUND,
STYLE, MODIFY, TEMPER,
TIMBRE, QUALITY, COLORING,
MITIGATE, MODULATE,
ATMOSPHERE

tongs: ..... CLAMP, FORCEPS,
PINCERS

tongue: ... TAB, FLAP, IDIOM,
LINGUA, SPEECH, DIALECT

bell's: .... CLAPPER

lashing: ...... REPROOF,
SCOLDING, REPRIMAND

tonic: ..... BRACER, ELIXER,
FILLIP, PICKUP, BRACING,
MEDICINE, ROBORANT,
STIMULANT, INVIGORATING

tony: ..... SMART, STYLISH,
LUXURIOUS

too: ..... AND, ALSO, VERY,
OVERLY, BESIDES, AS WELL,
LIKEWISE, EXTREMELY

tool: ...... MEANS, DEVICE,
GADGET, UTENSIL, IMPLEMENT,
APPLIANCE, INSTRUMENT

boring: ...... AWL, BIT,
AUGER, DRILL, GIMLET,
TREPAN

carpenter's: .... AXE, BIT,
SAW, RASP, AUGER, BEVEL,
LEVEL, PLANE, CHISEL,
GIMLET, HAMMER, PLIERS,
SQUARE, HATCHET

cobbler's: .... AWL,
HAMMER

engraver's: ...... BURIN

garden: ..... HOE, RAKE,
EDGER, MOWER, SPADE,
SHEARS, SHOVEL, TROWEL

mason's: .... CHISEL

tooth: .. (also see **teeth**) COG,
JAG, PEG, FANG, SNAG, TINE,
TUSH, TUSK, IVORY, MOLAR,
POINT, PRONG, CUSPID,
GRINDER, INCISOR, PROJECTION,
APPETITE

toothache: ..... ODONTALGIA

toothed: .. DENTED, DENTATE,
SERRATED

toothsome: . TASTY, SAVORY, DELICIOUS

top: . . . . ACE, CAP, LID, TIP, TOY, ACME, APEX, CROP, HEAD, LEAD, PEAK, PICK, ROOF, COVER, CREAM, CREST, CROWN, EQUAL, EXCEL, OUTDO, PRUNE, RIDGE, UPSET, BETTER, EXCEED, FINIAL, SUMMIT, VERTEX, ZENITH, HIGHEST, SURPASS, FOREMOST, PINNACLE, UPPERMOST

topee: . . . . CAP, HAT, HELMET

toper: . . SOT, SOUSE, RUMMY, BOOZER, TOSSPOT, DRUNKARD

topic: . . . . ITEM, TEXT, ISSUE, THEME, REASON, HEADING, SUBJECT, ARGUMENT

topical: . . LOCAL, TEMPORARY

topknot: . . HAIR, HEAD, TUFT, CREST, HEADDRESS

topple: . . . . . TIP, FALL, TILT, UPSET, TOTTER, TUMBLE, OVERTURN, OVERTHROW

tops: . . . . A-ONE, ACES, BEST, SUPREME

topsy-turvy: . . . . CONFUSED, INVERTED, DISORDERLY

toque: . . . . HAT, BONNET, HEADDRESS

tor: . . . . . CRAG, HILL, PEAK, MOUND, PINNACLE

tora(h): . . . . LAW, TETEL, PRECEPT, PENTATEUCH

torch: . . . LAMP, LINK, BLAZE, BRAND, CRESSET, FLAMBEAU, FLASHLIGHT

torment: . . . . RIB, VEX, BAIT, PAIN, RACK, AGONY, ANNOY, CHEVY, DEVIL, HARRY, TEASE, WRACK, BADGER, HARASS, HECTOR, MISERY, PESTER, PLAGUE, AGITATE, ANGUISH, BEDEVIL, HAGRIDE, TORTURE, TRAVAIL, DISTRESS, SUFFERING, TANTALIZE

torn: . . . REFT, RENT, RIVEN, RIPPED, TATTERED, LACERATED

tornado: . . . . SQUALL, CYCLONE, THUNDER, TWISTER, HURRICANE, WHIRLWIND

toro: . . . . . . BULL, COWFISH

torose: . . BRAWNY, BULGING, SWOLLEN, KNOBBED, MUSCULAR, CYLINDRICAL

torpedo: . . RAY, MINE, RUIN, WRECK, ATTACK, DAMAGE, GUNMAN, DESTROY, EXPLODE, FIREWORK, GANGSTER, PARALYZE, SABOTAGE, NUMBFISH, CRAMPFISH, PROJECTILE

torpid: . DULL, NUMB, INERT, STUPID, DORMANT, SLUGGISH, APATHETIC, LETHARGIC

torpor: . . . . . . COMA, SLEEP, APATHY, STUPOR, LETHARGY

torque: . . . . . . CHAIN, TWIST, COLLAR, NECKLACE

torrefy: . . . . DRY, PARCH, ROAST, SCORCH

torrent: . . . . . RUSH, FLOOD, SPATE, STREAM, RUSHING, ROARING, DOWNPOUR

torrid: . . . HOT, ARID, DRIED, ARDENT, SULTRY, BURNING, PARCHED, ZEALOUS, TROPICAL, SCORCHING, PASSIONATE

tortoise: . . TURTLE, TERRAPIN

tortuous: . . SPIRAL, CROOKED, DEVIOUS, SINUATE, SINUOUS, WINDING, CIRCUITOUS

torture: . . . . . . PAIN, RACK, AGONY, TWIST, PUNISH, WRENCH, ANGUISH, DISTORT, TORMENT, DISTRESS, AFFLICTION, THIRD DEGREE

toss: . . LOB, CAST, FLIP, HIKE, HURL, SNAP, CHUCK, FLICK, FLING, HEAVE, PITCH, THROW, BUFFET, CHANCE, FILLIP, AGITATE

tosspot: . . . . see **toper**

tot: . . . . . ADD, CHILD, TOTAL, DRINK, TODDLER

total: . . . . . ADD, ALL, SUM, GROSS, UTTER, WHOLE,

AMOUNT, ENTIRE, ABSOLUTE,
COMPLETE, ENTIRETY,
OUTRIGHT, AGGREGATE
totality: . . . . ENTIRETY
totally: . . . . QUITE, WHOLLY,
ENTIRELY, COMPLETELY
tote: . . . . . . LUG, TOT, BEAR,
HAUL, LOAD, CARRY, COUNT,
TOTAL, RECKON, TRANSPORT
totter: . . . REEL, ROCK, SWAY,
PITCH, SHAKE, SWING, WAVER,
FALTER, QUIVER, SEESAW,
STAGGER, TODDLE
tottering: . . SHAKY, GROGGY,
RICKETY, SHAKING, UNSTEADY,
WAVERING, FALTERING,
CHANGEABLE
touch: . . DAB, PAT, RAP, TAG,
TAP, ABUT, FEEL, MEET, TINT,
TASTE, TINGE, TRACE, TRAIT,
ADJOIN, AFFECT, BORDER,
BORROW, FINGER, HANDLE,
MOLEST, STROKE, CONTACT,
IMPINGE, MENTION, PALPATE
touched: . . . . MOVED,
AFFECTED, DEMENTED
touching: . . . . MOVING,
CONTACT, MEETING, TANGENT,
ADJACENT, PATHETIC,
AFFECTING, CONJOINED,
CONTACTING, CONTIGUOUS
touchy: . . . . . . SORE, CROSS,
HUFFY, RISKY, TESTY, PEEVISH,
TICKLISH, IRRITABLE,
SENSITIVE, IRASCIBLE,
PRECARIOUS
tough: . . . . THUG, WIRY,
HARDY, RIGID, ROUGH, STIFF,
ROBUST, SINEWY, STICKY,
STRONG, RUFFIAN, VISCOUS,
COHESIVE, ENDURING
HARDENED, STUBBORN,
VIGOROUS, DIFFICULT,
GLUTINOUS, OBSTINATE,
HARDBOILED
toughen: . . . INURE, ANNEAL,
ENDURE, TEMPER
toupee: . . RUG, WIG, PERUKE,
PERIWIG, HAIRPIECE

tour: . . . . . GO, TRIP, COVER,
DRIVE, RANGE, ROUND, SHIFT,
COURSE, TRAVEL, CIRCUIT,
JOURNEY, EXCURSION
tourist: . . . . TRIPPER,
SIGHTSEER, TRAVELER
tournament: . . . OPEN, TILT,
JOUST, TRIAL, BATTLE,
CONTEST, TOURNEY,
COMPETITION
tourney: . . . . . . TOURNAMENT
tousle: . . MUSS, PULL, TEAR,
TOUSE, RUFFLE, RUMPLE,
DISHEVEL
tout: . . . SPY, TIP, PEER, PUFF,
THIEF, PRAISE, LOOKOUT,
SOLICIT, TIPSTER, INFORMER,
PROCLAIM, SOLICITOR,
BALLYHOO, RECOMMEND
tow: . . . . . TEW, TUG, DRAG,
DRAW, HAUL, LEAD, PULL,
ROPE, BARGE, FIBER, HAWSER,
TUGBOAT
toward: . . BY, NEAR, ABOUT,
ANENT, COMING, FACING,
ONWARD, FORWARD
towel: . . . . DRY, RUB, CLOTH,
WIPER, DIAPER, NAPKIN,
HANDCLOTH, SERVIETTE
tower: . . . REAR, RISE, SILO,
SOAR, PYLON, SPIRE, BELFRY,
CASTLE, DONJON, PAGODA,
PRISON, TURRET, BASTILE,
BULWARK, CITADEL, ELEVATE,
MINARET, STEEPLE, ZIKKURAT,
CAMPANILE
towering: . . . . . HIGH, TALL,
GREAT, LOFTY, EMINENT
town: . . BURG, CITY, BOURG,
BURGH, HAMLET, PARISH,
PODUNK, PUEBLO, BOROUGH,
VILLAGE, METROPOLIS
townsman: . . . . . CIT(IZEN),
OPPIDAN, RESIDENT,
INHABITANT
toxic: . . . . POISONOUS
toxin: . . . . . . VENOM, POISON
toy: . . . . . . PET, FOOL, PLAY,
WHIM, ANTIC, DALLY, FANCY,

FLIRT, SPORT, BAUBLE, FINGER,
GEWGAW, TRIFLE, CAPRICE,
PASTIME, TRINKET, FLIRTING,
GIMCRACK, TEETOTUM,
PLAYTHING

trace: ... CLEW, CLUE, COPY,
DRAW, HINT, MARK, PATH,
SEEK, SIGN, STEP, TANG,
PROBE, SHADE, TINGE, TOUCH,
TRACK, TRAIL, DEDUCE,
DERIVE, DETECT, FOLLOW,
LOCATE, OUTLINE, REMNANT,
UNCOVER, VESTIGE, DISCOVER,
ASCERTAIN, DELINEATE,
ESTABLISH, SCINTILLA

trachea: .... DUCT, WINDPIPE

track: .... RUT, WAY, DRAW,
HUNT, LINE, MARK, OVAL,
PATH, RAIL, ROAD, SLOT, SPUR,
WAKE, ROUTE, SCENT, SPOOR,
TRACE, TRAIL, TREAD, COURSE,
FOLLOW, PURSUE, TRAVEL,
CIRCUIT, VESTIGE, SPEEDWAY,
ASCERTAIN, FOOTPRINT

tracker: .... TAIL, HUNTER,
HOUND, DETECTIVE

tract: .. AREA, ZONE, RANGE,
ESTATE, EXTENT, REGION,
COUNTRY, EXPANSE, LEAFLET,
STRETCH, BROCHURE, DISTRICT,
PAMPHLET, TREATISE,
TERRITORY

tractable: ... EASY, DOCILE,
GENTLE, PLIANT, DUCTILE,
AMENABLE, FLEXIBLE,
OBEDIANT, WORKABLE,
ADAPTABLE, COMPLIANT,
MALLEABLE

tractile: ... PLIANT, DUCTILE,
TENSILE

traction: .. POWER, DRAWING,
PULLING, FRICTION

trade: .... BUY, DEAL, SELL,
SWAP, WORK, CRAFT, ACTION,
BARTER, MEITER, BARGAIN,
CALLING, PURSUIT, TRAFFIC,
BUSINESS, CLIENTELE,
EXCHANGE, OCCUPATION,
COMMERCE, CUSTOMERS

association: ...... GUILD,
CARTEL, SYNDICATE

center: ...... PIT, MART,
MARKET, EXCHANGE

trademark: .... BRAND

trader: ...... SHIP, DEALER,
MONGER, SELLER, SUTLER,
MERCHANT, STOREKEEPER

tradesman: .... BUYER,
ARTISAN, WORKMAN,
HUCKSTER, MERCHANT,
CRAFTSMAN, STOREKEEPER

tradition: ..... CODE, LORE,
USAGE, BELIEF, CUSTOM,
LEGEND, PRACTICE,
CONVENTION

traduce: ..... SLUR, ABUSE,
DEBASE, DEFAME, MALIGN,
REVILE, ASPERSE, BLACKEN,
DETRACT, PEVERT, SLANDER,
DISGRACE

traffic: .. BUY, SELL, TRADE,
BARTER, MARKET, BUSINESS,
DEALING, COMMERCE,
EXCHANGE, INTERCOURSE

tragedy: .... PLAY, DRAMA,
MISERY, CALAMITY, DISASTER,
CATASTROPHE

tragic: ... SAD, DIRE, FATAL,
MOURNFUL, PATHETIC,
TERRIBLE, CALAMITOUS

trail: ..... LAG, TAG, DRAG,
HANG, HEEL, HUNT, PATH,
SLOT, TAIL, WAKE, BLAZE,
HOUND, ROUTE, SCENT, SPOOR,
TRACE, TRACK, COURSE,
FOLLOW, TRAIPSE, FOOTPATH,
STRAGGLE

trailer: .... VAN, TAIL, VINE,
WAGON, TRACER, TRACKER

train: ..... AIM, ROW, LEAD,
LINE, LURE, REAR, TAIL,
COACH, DECOY, DRILL, GROOM,
GUIDE, SUITE, TEACH, TRACE,
DIRECT, SCHOOL, SERIES,
CARAVAN, CONDUCT, CORTEGE,
EDUCATE, PREPARE, RETINUE,
ACCUSTOM, INSTRUCT,

REHEARSE, SEQUENCE,
CONDITION, PROCESSION
kind: ..... FLIER, LOCAL,
SPECIAL, EXPRESS, FREIGHT,
LIMITED, MONORAIL
trainee: ..... PUPIL, NOVICE,
APPRENTICE, NOVITIATE
trainer: ..... COACH, TAMER,
TEACHER, HANDLER,
INSTRUCTOR
traipse: .... GAD, WALK,
TRAMP, TRAIL, TRUDGE,
WANDER
trait: ... FEATURE, QUALITY,
MANNERISM, PECULIARITY,
CHARACTERISTIC
traitor: .... APOSTATE,
RECREANT, RENEGADE
traject: ...... CAST, THROW
trajectory: ..... ARC, PATH
trammel: ...... NET, LOCK,
CHECK, FASTEN, FETTER,
HAMPER, HINDER, IMPEDE,
CONFINE, POTHOOK, PREVENT,
SHACKLE, RESTRAIN,
INSTRUMENT, POTHOOK,
SHACKLE
tramp: ... BUM, HIKE, HOBO,
HOOF, PLOD, TART, VAMP,
WALK, CLUMP, JAUNT,
RAMBLE, TRAVEL, TRUDGE,
WANDER, STEAMER, TRAIPSE,
VAGRANT, VAGABOND,
EXCURSION, PROSTITUTE
trample: ...... FOIL, HURT,
CRUSH, TREAD, INJURE,
DESTROY, VIOLATE
trance: . COMA, DAZE, SPELL,
STUPOR, ECTASY, STUPOR,
HYPNOSIS, CATALEPSY
tranquil: ..... CALM, COOL,
EVEN, MILD, QUIET, STILL,
GENTLE, PLACID, SERENE,
STEADY, PACIFIC, RESTFUL,
COMPOSED, PEACEFUL
tranquility: ... POISE, PEACE,
QUIET, SERENITY
tranquilize: .... LULL, CALM,
QUIET, ALLAY, OPIATE, SETTLE,

SOOTHE, APPEASE, ASSUAGE,
SEDATIVE, ALLEVIATE
transact: ..... DEAL, TREAT,
CONDUCT, PERFORM,
COMPLETE, TRANSFER,
NEGOTIATE
transaction: .... DEAL, SALE,
ACTION, AFFAIR, BARGAIN,
BUSINESS, PROCEEDING,
PROPOSITION
transcend: ... CLIMB, EXCEL,
RAISE, EXCEED, ELEVATE,
SURPASS, OUTSTRIP, OVERSTEP,
SURMOUNT
transcipt(ion): ...... COPY,
RECORD, DUPLICATE,
REPRODUCTION
transfer: ...... CEDE, DEED,
MOVE, PASS, SALE, CARRY,
GRANT, SHIFT, ASSIGN,
CHANGE, CONVEY, DEMISE,
REMOVE, SWITCH, DISPOSE,
ALIENATE, TRANSPORT,
TRANSFUSE
transfix: .... FIX, PIN, NAIL,
SPEAR, STICK, FASTEN, IMPALE,
PIERCE, IMMOBILIZE
transform: ... TURN, ALTER,
CHANGE, CONVERT,
TRANSMUTE, TRANSFIGURE,
METAMORPHOSE
transfuse: ... IMBUE, INSTILL,
TRANSFER
transgress: ...... ERR, SIN,
BREAK, OFFEND, DISOBEY,
VIOLATE, INFRACT, OVERSTEP,
TRESPASS
transient: .... FUGITIVE,
EPHEMERAL, INTINERANT,
MIGRATORY, MOMENTARY,
TEMPORARY, FLEETING
transit: .... RAPID, CHANGE,
PASSAGE, THEODOLITE,
CONVEYANCE
transition: .... PHASE, SHIFT,
CHANGE, PASSAGE, PASSING,
TRANSFER, CONVERSION

transitory: . . . . BRIEF,
FLEETING, EPHEMERAL,
TEMPORARY, MOMENTARY
translate: . . . READ, CHANGE,
DECODE, REMOVE, RENDER,
CONVERT, CONSTRUE,
DECIPHER, TRANSFER,
PARAPHRASE, INTERPRET
translation: . . . . PONY,
VERSION, PARAPHRASE,
RENDITION, INTERPRETATION
translucent: . . CLEAR, LIMPID,
PELLUCID, TRANSPARENT
transmit: . . . . . EMIT, HAND,
SEND, CARRY, RELAY, CONVEY,
RENDER, CONDUCT, FORWARD,
COMMUNICATE
transmute: . . . . . . CHANGE,
CONVERT
transom: . . . . . SLAT, TRAVE,
LINTEL, LOUVER, CROSSPIECE
transparent: . . OPEN, CLEAR,
FRANK, GAUZY, LUCID, SHEER,
CANDID, LIMPID, LUCENT,
HYALINE, HYALOID, OBVIOUS,
PELLUCID, TRANSLUCENT,
DIAPHANOUS
transpire: . . . PASS, HAPPEN,
OCCUR
transplant: . . . . GRAFT,
RESETTLE, RELOCATE
transport: . . . . . BEAR, BOAT,
HAUL, MOVE, SEND, SHIP,
TOTE, BRING, CARRY, FERRY,
TRUCK, CONVEY, ECTASY,
PASSION, PORTAGE, RUPTURE,
SMUGGLE, AIRPLANE,
ENTRANCE, ENRAPTURE
transpose: . . . SHIFT, CHANGE,
INVERT, CONVERT, REVERSE,
EXCHANGE, REARRANGE,
INTERCHANGE
transverse: . . . . BAR, OVER,
PASS, RUNG, CROSS, ROUTE,
ACROSS, STRIPE, BARRIER,
OBLIQUE, CROSSBEAM,
CROSSWISE, CROSSPIECE
trap: . . BAG, GET, GIN, NET,
PIT, CAGE, LURE, NAIL, WEIR,

BUGGY, CATCH, MOUTH,
SHARE, TRICK, AMBUSH,
ENMESH, CAPTURE, ENSNARE,
LUGGAGE, PITFALL, CARRIAGE
trappings: . . . . . DUDS, GEAR,
HARNESS, COVERING,
ORNAMENT, REGALIA,
CAPARISON, ADORNMENTS
traps: . . . . . . BELLS, DRUMS,
CYMBALS
trash: . . . JUNK, RAFF, TRIPE,
WASTE, BUSHWA, COLLAR,
DEBRIS, HALTER, HINDER,
RABBLE, REFUSE, RETARD,
RUBBLE, BLATHER, RUBBISH,
NONSENSE, RESTRAIN,
RIFFRAFF, BALDERDASH
trashy: . . . . WORTHLESS
trauma: . . . SHOCK, WOUND,
INJURY
travail: . . . PAIN, PANG, TASK,
TOIL, WORK, AGONY, LABOR,
EFFORT, ANGUISH, TORMENT,
TROUBLE, EXERTION, SUFFERING
trave: . . . . CROSSBEAM
travel: . . MOVE, MUSH, POST,
RIDE, TOUR, TREK, TRIP, WALK,
WEND, COAST, ORBIT,
COMMUTE, JOURNEY, MIGRATE,
PASSAGE, PROCEED, SOJOURN,
TRAFFIC, TRAVERSE
traveler: . . . NOMAD, TRAMP,
VIATOR, PILGRIM, TOURIST,
VOYAGER, WANDERER,
WAYFARER, ITINERANT
traverse: . . . . . . DENY, FORD,
PASS, CROSS, PIVOT, SWIVEL,
COURSE, CROSSPIECE
travesty: . . . PARODY, SATIRE,
MOCKERY, BURLESQUE,
CARICATURE
trawl: . . . . . NET, FISH, LINE,
DRAGNET
tray: . . . . HOD, TILL, SERVER,
SALVER, COASTER
treacherous: . . . . FALSE,
FICKLE, DISLOYAL, INSECURE,
PLOTTING, UNSTABLE,
FAITHLESS, DECEITFUL,

treachery: . . . . DECEIT,
PERFIDY, TREASON, UNTRUTH,
BETRAYAL
INSIDIOUS, PERFIDIOUS,
UNRELIABLE
treacle: . . . . . CURE, REMEDY,
MOLASSES, ANTIDOTE
tread: . . . RUT, MARK, RUNG,
STEP, WALK, CRUSH, PRESS,
STAIR, STAMP, TRACK, TRAIL,
COURSE, CRUNCH, SUBDUE,
CONQUER, REPRESS, TRAMPLE,
FOOTFALL, FOOTPRINT
treadle: . . . . . . LEVER, PEDAL
treason: . . . . PERFIDY,
BETRAYAL, SEDITION,
TREACHERY
treasure: . . . . CACHE, HOARD,
PRIZE, STORE, TROVE, VALUE,
RICHES, WEALTH, CHERISH,
FINANCE
treasurer: . . BURSAR, PURSER,
CASHIER, CURATOR, GUARDIAN
treasury: . . . . . . FISC, FUND,
VAULT, CHEST, HOARD,
COFFER, BURSARY, EXCHEQUER,
REPOSITORY
treat: . . . . USE, DEAL, DOSE,
ARGUE, DUTCH, FEAST, TOUCH,
CONFER, DOCTOR, GOVERN,
HANDLE, PARLEY, REGALE,
REGARD, REPAST, BARGAIN,
DELIGHT, DISCUSS, CONSIDER,
TRANSACT, NEGOTIATE,
ENTERTAIN
badly: . . . . . SNUB, ABUSE,
SCORN, INSULT, ILL-USE
tenderly: . . . PET, CODDLE,
PAMPER
treatise: . . . . ESSAY, PAPER,
TRACT, THESIS, ACCOUNT,
BROCHURE, DISCOURSE,
MONOGRAPH, COMMENTARY,
DISSERTATION
treatment: . . . . . . USE, CARE,
USAGE, THERAPY, HANDLING,
APPROACH, MANAGEMENT
treaty: . . . . . PACT, ARTICLE,
COMPACT, CONCORD, ENTENTE,
ALLIANCE, CONTRACT,
COVENANT, AGREEMENT,
CONCORDAT
treble: . . . . SHRILL, TRIPLE,
SOPRANO, THREEFOLD
tree: . . . . . POLE, POST, TRAP,
WOOD, ARBOR, CATCH, SHAFT,
STAFF, STAKE, STICK, CORNER,
CUDGEL, GIBBET, TIMBER,
CAPTURE, GALLOWS, HATRACK,
SAPLING, COATRACK,
COSTUMER, SEEDLING,
GENEALOGY
kind, common: . . . . . ASH,
ELM, FIG, FIR, GUM, LIN,
OAK, YEW, COCO, PALM,
PINE, TEAK, ALDER, ASPEN,
BALSA, BEECH, BIRCH,
CAROB, CEDAR, ELDER,
GINKO, HAZEL, LARCH,
MAPLE, OLIVE, PECAN,
PINON, SUMAC, TULIP,
ACACIA, ALMOND, BALSAM,
BANYAN, CASHEW, CITRON,
LAUREL, LINDEN, LOCUST,
MIMOSA, MYRTLE, POPLAR,
SPRUCE, TUPELO, WALNUT,
WILLOW, CATALPA,
CONIFER, CYPRESS,
DOGWOOD, HEMLOCK,
HICKORY, JUNIPER,
REDWOOD, SEQUOIA,
ALLSPICE, BASSWOOD,
BAYBERRY, CHESTNUT,
GUMWOOD, IRONWOOD,
MAGNOLIA, MAHOGANY,
MANGROVE, MULBERRY,
SYCAMORE, TAMARACK,
PERSIMMON, SASSAFRAS,
COTTONWOOD, EUCALYPTUS,
SANDALWOOD
balsam: . . . . . FIR, TOLU,
TORCHWOOD
bark: . . . . . . ROSS, TAPA,
CORTEX
conebearing: . . . FIR, YEW,
PINE, ALDER, CEDAR,
LARCH, CONIFER, SPRUCE

evergreen: ..... FIR, YEW,
PINE, CAROB, CEDAR,
CLOVE, HOLLY, LARCH,
LEMON, OLIVE, BALSAM,
ORANGE, SPRUCE, CONIFER,
HEMLOCK, JUNIPER,
EUCALYPTUS

exudation: .... GUM, LAC,
SAP, TAR, COPAL, LATEX,
RESIN, ROSIN, BALATA,
BALSAM

flowering: ... TITI, AGATI,
TITIS, CHERRY, MIMOSA,
REDBUD, CATALPA,
DOGWOOD, CLEASTER,
MAGNOLIA, OLEASTER

fruit: ... FIG, DATE, LIME,
PEAR, PLUM, APPLE, LEMON,
MANGO, OLIVE, PAPAW,
PEACH, ALMOND, BANANA,
CHERRY, LITCHI, ORANGE,
PAPAYA, PAWPAW, APRICOT,
AVOCADO, COCONUT,
TANGELO, TANGERINE,
GRAPEFRUIT, PERSIMMON

group: .... BOSK, ARBOR,
COPSE, GROVE, SCRUB,
WOODS, FOREST, TIMBER,
COPPICE, ORCHARD

part: . BARK, BOLE, BURL,
KNOT, LEAF, ROOT, TWIG,
SHAFT, SPRAY, SPRIG,
BOUGH, TRUNK, BRANCH

trefoil: .. CLOVER, SHAMROCK

trek: ...... MARCH, TRAVEL,
JOURNEY, MIGRATION,
EXPEDITION

trellis: ..... ARBOR, BOWER,
LATTICE, PERGOLA, ESPALIER

tremble: .... QUAKE, SHAKE,
QUAVER, QUIVER, SHIVER,
TOTTER, TREMOR, WOBBLE,
FLICKER, VIBRATE, SHUDDER

tremendous: ... BIG, AWFUL,
GIANT, GREAT, LARGE,
AMAZING, DREADFUL,
ENORMOUS, HORRIBLE,
POWERFUL, TERRIFIC,
FRIGHTFUL, MOMENTOUS,
MONSTROUS

tremor: .... QUAKE, QUIVER,
SHIVER, THRILL, SHAKING,
TREMBLE, VIBRATION

tremulous: .. ASPEN, SHAKY,
TIMID, FEARFUL, NERVOUS,
PALSIED, QUAVERY, WAVERING,
QUAVERING, QUIVERING

trench: .... CUT, SAP, BURY,
GASH, MOAT, CARVE, DITCH,
FOSSE, SLASH, SLICE, FURROW,
GROOVE, GUTTER

trenchant: .... KEEN, ACUTE,
SHARP, BITING, CUTTING,
CLEAR-CUT, FORCEFUL,
INCISIVE, PENETRATING

trencher: .. BOARD, DIGGER,
SAPPER, PLATTER

trencherman: .... SPONGER,
PARASITE, GLUTTON, HANGER-
ON

trend: .... RUN, BEND, BENT,
TONE, VEIN, DRIFT, SWING,
TENOR, COURSE, MOVEMENT,
TENDENCY

trepidation: ... FEAR, ALARM,
DREAD, DISMAY, TREMOR,
AGITATION

trespass: ...... SIN, POACH,
BREACH, INVADE, OFFEND,
INTRUDE, OFFENSE, INFRINGE,
ENCROACH, INFRACTION,
TRANSGRESS

tress: ... CURL, LOCK, PLAIT,
BRAID, QUEUE, PIGTAIL,
RINGLET

triad: .... THREE, TRINE,
TRIUNE, TRINITY

trial: .... BOUT, CASE, TEST,
ASSAY, ESSAY, GRIEF, PROOF,
EFFORT, ORDEAL, SAMPLE,
ATTEMPT, CONTEST, HEARING,
INQUEST, INQUIRY, ENDEAVOR,
HARDSHIP, PROBATION,
AFFLICTION, EXPERIMENT

triangle: .... DELTA, TRIGON,
SCALENE, ISOSCELES

398

tribe: . . . BAND, CLAN, KIND, RACE, CLASS, GROUP, FAMILY

tribulation: . . . WOE, AGONY, TRIAL, MISERY, SORROW, DISTRESS

tribunal: . . . . . . ROTA, SEAT, BENCH, COURT, FORUM, ASSEMBLY

tribune: . . . . . DIAS, THRONE, PLATFORM, MAGISTRATE

tributary: . . . RIVER, STREAM, FEEDER, SUBJECT, AUXILIARY, SUBSIDARY

tribute: . . . . FEE, TAX, DUES, DUTY, GIFT, LEVY, GRANT, EULOGY, HOMAGE, IMPOST, PRAISE, TARIFF, OVATION, PAYMENT, RESPECT, OFFERING

trice: . . . . . TIE, BIND, GIRD, LASH, JIFFY, MOMENT, SECURE, INSTANT, SECOND, TWINKLING

trick: . . FOB, FOX, FUB, GAG, TOY, BILK, DIDO, DUPE, FLAM, FOOL, GAFF, GULL, HOAX, JAPE, JEST, JOKE, NICK, RUSE, TRAP, WILE, CATCH, CHEAT, CULLY, FRAUD, GUILE, KNACK, PRANK, SHIFT, STUNT, DODGE, DELUDE, ENTRAP, HUMBUG, TRIFLE, DECEIVE, DEFRAUD, GIMMICK, SLEIGHT, SWINDLE, ARTIFICE, FLIM FLAM, HOODWINK, BAMBOOZLE, DECEPTION, CHICANERY, STRATEGEM

trickle: . . . DRIP, DROP, FLOW, SEEP, EXUDE, DISTILL, DRIBBLE

trickster: . . CHEAT, RASCAL, SLICKER, MAGICIAN, PRANKSTER, SWINDLER

tricky: . . . . SLY, SMART, ARTFUL, CATCHY, CRAFTY, DEVIOUS, TICKLISH, DECEITFUL, INTRICATE, DECEPTIVE

trident: . . . . SPEAR

tried: . . . . . PROVED, SELECT, TESTED, FAITHFUL, RELIABLE

trifle: . . BIT, TOY, DOIT, JEST, MOCK, MOTE, PLAY, DALLY, FLIRT, BAUBLE, DABBLE, DAWDLE, DELUDE, DIDDLE, DOODLE, FIDDLE, FIDGET, GEWGAW, LITTLE, PALTER, POTTER, DECEIVE, DESSERT, GIMCRACK, FALDERAL

trifling: . . . . . . IDLE, INANE, PETTY, FUTILE, LITTLE, PALTRY, PEANUTS, SHALLOW, TRIVIAL, PIDDLING, FRIVOLOUS

trifoliate: . . TERNATE, THREE-LEAFED

trifolium: . . . . CLOVER, TREFOIL, SHAMROCK

trig: . . FIT, CHIC, CRAM, FILL, FIRM, FULL, NEAT, PRIM, PROP, TIDY, TRIM, WELL, BRISK, CHOKE, DANDY, NATTY, SMART, SOUND, STIFF, STUFF, WEDGE, ACTIVE, LIVELY, SPRUCE, STRONG, PRECISE, SUPPORT, METHODICAL

trigger: . . . . FIRE, TRIP, INITIATE, LAUNCH

trigon: . . HARP, LYRE, TRINE, TRIANGLE

trigonometric function: . . . . . SINE, COSINE, SECANT, TANGENT

trill: . . . . FLOW, ROLL, TURN, TWIRL, QUAVER, WARBLE, MORDENT, VIBRATE, VIBRATO, TREMOLO

trim: . BOB, CUT, LOP, BEAT, CHIC, CLIP, CROP, DECK, DOCK, EDGE, FINE, FIRM, NEAT, PARE, SNUG, TAUT, TIDY, TRIG, ADORN, CHEAT, CHIDE, DRESS, EQUIP, NATTY, NIFTY, PREEN, PRUNE, SHAVE, SHEAR, SCOLD, ADJUST, DAPPER, DEFEAT, MODIFY, SPRUCE, THRASH, BALANCE, FURNISH, ORDERLY, DECORATE, ORNAMENT, EMBELLISH, SHIPSHAPE

trimming: . . . . . GIMP, LACE, BRAID, RUCHE, DEFEAT, FRIEZE, FRINGE, BEATING, EDGING, PIPING, RUCHING, FURBELOW,

ORNAMENT, RICKRACK, DECORATION

trinal: . . . TRIPLE, THREEFOLD

trine: . . . . . MARCH, TRIAD, TRIGON, TRIPLE, TRIUNE, TRINITY, THREEFOLD, FAVORABLE

trinket: . . . TOY, GAUD, RING, BIJOU, JEWEL, BANGLE, BAUBLE, GEWGAW, TRIFLE, BIBELOT, JEWELRY, GIMCRACK, KICKSHAW, ORNAMENT, KNICKKNACK

trip: . . ERR, HIKE, SKIP, SLIP, SPIN, TILT, TOUR, CAPER, CATCH, ERROR, JAUNT, LAPSE, TREAD, CRUISE, FALTER, OUTING, TUMBLE, VOYAGE, BLUNDER, JOURNEY, MISSTEP, MISTAKE, RELEASE, STUMBLE, EXCURSION

tripe: . . . . . TRASH, RUBBISH

triple: . . . . TRIAD, TRINE, TREBLE, TRINAL, TERNARY, THREEFOLD, TRIPLICATE

tripod: . . CAT, EASEL, STAND, SPIDER, TRIPOS, TRIVET

trite: . . . . . . WORN, BANAL, CORNY, MUSTY, STOCK, STALE, VAPID, CLICHE, COMMON, JEJUNE, BROMIDE, HACKNEYED, THREADBARE, COMMONPLACE

triturate: . . . . . RUB, CRUSH, GRIND, PULVERIZE

triumph: . . . . . . WIN, GAIN, EXULT, GLORY, DEFEAT, CONQUER, PREVAIL, REJOICE, SUCCESS, VICTORY, EXULTATION

trivet: . . . . . STAND, SPIDER, TRIPOD

trivial: . . . . . BANAL, INANE, PETTY, SMALL, TRITE, FLIMSY, LITTLE, PALTRY, SLIGHT, NOMINAL, ORDINARY, TRIFLING, FRIVOLOUS, UNIMPORTANT

troche: . . . . PASTIL, ROTULA, TABLET, LOZENGE, PASTILLE, COUGH DROP

troll: . . . . . IMP, FISH, LURE, REEL, ROLL, SING, SPIN, TURN, CATCH, CHANT, DWARF, GIANT, GNOME, SPOON, REVOLVE

trolley: . . . . . . CART, TRAM, STREETCAR

trollop: . . . . SLUT, SLATTERN, PROSTITUTE

trommel: . . . . SIEVE, SCREEN

troop: . . . . LOT, ARMY, BAND, CROWD, FLOCK, GROUP, TROUPE, BATTERY, CAVALRY, COMPANY, SOLDIERS

trooper: . SOLDIER, MOUNTIE, POLICEMAN, CAVALRYMAN

trophy: . . . . CUP, PALM, AWARD, MEDAL, PRIZE, LAUREL, REWARD, SPOILS, MEMENTO, MEMORIAL

tropical: . . . . . . HOT, WARM, TORRID, SULTRY

trot: . . . . . . JOG, RUN, GAIT, HURRY, CANTER, HASTEN

troth: . . . . . . FAITH, PLEDGE

troubadour: . . POET, SINGER, MINSTREL, MUSICIAN, BALLADEER, JONGLEUR

trouble: . ADO, AIL, IRK, ILL, VEX, WOE, CARE, FUSS, HARM, PAIN, SORE, STIR, ANGER, ANNOY, GRIEF, TEASE, WORRY, BOTHER, EFFORT, HARASS, MISHAP, MOLEST, PESTER, PLAGUE, OBSESS, SORROW, AFFLICT, AGITATE, ANXIETY, CONCERN, DISEASE, DISTURB, AILMENT, ILLNESS, PERTURB, TRAVAIL, CALAMITY, DISORDER, DISTRESS, ADVERSITY, INCOMMODE

troublemaker: . . IMP, GOSSIP, AGITATOR, PROVOCATEUR

trough: . . . . BIN, HOD, BOSH, BOWL, TANK, BASIN, DRAIN, CHUTE, FLUME, GUTTER, SLUICE, VALLEY, MANGER, CHANNEL, CONDUIT

trounce: . . . . BEAT, FLOG,
CUDGEL, DEFEAT, PUNISH,
THRASH

troupe: . . . . . . BAND, GROUP,
COMPANY

trousers: . . . . . JEANS, PANTS,
SKILTS, SLACKS, BREECHES,
CULOTTES, PANTALOONS

truant: . . . . IDLE, STRAY,
ERRANT, SHIRKER, SLACKER,
VAGRANT, SHIFTLESS

truce: . . . . . PAUSE, RESPITE,
ARMISTICE, CEASEFIRE,
CESSATION

truck: . . . . VAN, DEAL, DRAY,
LORRY, TRADE, TRASH,
BARROW, BARTER, CAMION,
PEDDLE, BARGAIN, RUBBISH,
TRUNDLE, EXCHANGE,
NEGOTIATE, TRANSPORT

truckle: . . . . FAWN, TOADY,
WHEEL, CASTER, CHEESE,
CRINGE, SUBMIT, YIELD,
TRUNDLE

truculent: . . . . MEAN, RUDE,
CRUEL, HARSH, FIERCE,
SAVAGE, RUTHLESS,
FEROCIOUS, BELLIGERENT

trudge: . . . PAD, PLOD, SLOG,
WALK, TRAMP, TRAIPSE

true: . . . . . JUST, PURE, REAL,
ALIGN, ALINE, EXACT, LEVEL,
LOYAL, PLUMB, RIGHT, VALID,
ACTUAL, HONEST, LAWFUL,
PROPER, STANCH, CERTAIN,
CORRECT, FACTUAL, GENUINE,
PRECISE, SINCERE, STAUNCH,
ACCURATE, BONAFIDE,
CONSTANT, FAITHFUL,
RELIABLE, UNERRING,
AUTHENTIC, STEADFAST

truffle: . . . . FUNGUS,
MUSHROOM, EARTHNUT

truism: . . . . . . FACT, AXIOM,
PLATITUDE

truly: . . . . . . QUITE, INDEED,
REALLY, ACTUALLY,
FAITHFULLY

trumpery: . . . FRAUD, SHOWY,
TRASH, DECEIT, PALTRY,
RUBBISH, NONSENSE, TRICKERY

trumpet: . . . . . HORN, BLARE,
FUNNEL, CLARION, PROCLAIM

truncate: . . . . . CUT, LOP, TRIM,
LESSEN, SHORTEN

truncheon: . . . CLUB, MACE,
STEM, STAFF, BATON, CUDGEL

trundle: . . BED, CART, ROLL,
TRUCK, WHEEL, BARROW,
CASTER

trunk: . . . BOX, BODY, BOLE,
PIPE, STEM, TUBE, CHEST,
SNOUT, TORSO, COFFER,
THORAX, BAGGAGE, PROBOSCIS,
COMPARTMENT

truss: . . . . . TIE, BIND, FURL,
GIRD, PACK, PROP, BRACE,
BUNDLE, FASTEN, PACKAGE,
SUPPORT, TIGHTEN

trust: . . . CARE, DUTY, HOPE,
RELY, TASK, FAITH, BELIEF,
CARTEL, CHARGE, CREDIT,
DEPEND, BELIEVE, CONFIDE,
CUSTODY, KEEPING, LOYALTY,
MONOPOLY, RELIANCE,
SECURITY, FIDUCIARY,
CONFIDENCE

trustee: . . . . GARNISHEE,
CUSTODIAN

trustworthy: . . . SAFE, TRIED,
HONEST, TESTED, RELIABLE,
STA(U)NCH

truth: . . . . FACT, VERITY,
HONESTY, REALITY, ACCURACY,
FIDELITY, VERACITY,
ACTUALITY, INTEGRITY

truthful: . . HONEST, CORRECT,
VERACIOUS

try: . . . . STAB, TEST, ANNOY,
ASSAY, ESSAY, PROVE, TRIAL,
CHOOSE, HARASS, REFINE,
SAMPLE, SCREEN, SELECT,
STRIVE, ADJUDGE, AFFLICT,
ATTEMPT, CONTEST, EXTRACT,
SUBJECT, TORMENT, VENTURE,
AUDITION, ENDEAVOR,

IRRITATE, STRUGGLE,
UNDERTAKE, EXPERIMENT

trying: ... SEVERE, IRKSOME,
PAINFUL, ANNOYING

tryout: .... TEST, TRIAL,
AUDITION

tryst: ..... DATE, MEETING,
ENGAGEMENT, RENDEZVOUS

tub: ...... (also see **barrel,
cistern, vat, vessel**) HOD, VAT,
BATH, BOAT, CASK, TRAM,
BARGE, KEEVE, SKEEL,
BUCKET, FIRKIN, KEELER,
VESSEL, CISTERN, HOGSHEAD,
CONTAINER

tube: ... DUCT, FLUE, HOSE,
PIPE, CHUTE, BARREL, SIPHON,
SUBWAY, TUNNEL, CANNULA,
CONDUIT, FISTULA, PIPETTE,
CYLINDER, TELESCOPE

tuber:..... OCA, YAM, BEET,
BULB, CORM, EDDO, ROOT,
TARO, JALAP, ONION, SALEP,
MANIOC, POTATO, CASSAVA,
RHIZOME

tubercle:........ NODULE,
PROJECTION

tuberculosis: ..... PHTHISIS,
CONSUMPTION

tuck: . JAM, LAP, TAP, CRAM,
FOLD, POKE, WRAP, COVER,
PINCH, PLEAT, RUCHE, STUFF,
SWORD, GATHER, PUCKER,
RAPIER, TIGHTEN

tuft: .. COMA, BEARD, BUNCH,
CLUMP, CREST, PLUME,
COMOSE, GOATEE, POMPON,
TASSEL, CLUSTER, TOPKNOT

tug: .... TOW, DRAG, DRAW,
HAUL, PULL, TOIL, YANK,
EXERT, LABOR, STRAIN, STRIVE,
TUSSLE, CONTEND, WRESTLE,
STRUGGLE

tuition:.... FEE, CARE, COST,
WATCH, CHARGE, CUSTODY,
TEACHING, PROTECTION,
INSTRUCTION

tumble:... FALL, FLOP, LEAP,
ROLL, TRIP, PITCH, SPILL,
WHIRL, RUMPLE, SPRING,
TOUSLE, COLLAPSE, DISORDER,
OVERTHROW, HANDSPRING,
SOMERSAULT

tumbler:.. DOG, CART, DOVE,
GLASS, PIGEON, ROLLER,
ACROBAT, GYMNAST

tumbrel:..... (DUMP)CART,
WAGON, CAISSON

tumefy:...... PUFF, SWELL

tumid: ... TURGID, BLOATED,
BULGING, FUSTIAN POMPOUS,
SWOLLEN, BURSTING,
ENLARGED, INFLATED,
BOMBASTIC, DISTENDED

tumor: ... WEN, YAW, CYST,
GUMMA, PILES, CANCER,
GLIOMA, LIPOMA, ANGIOMA,
NEUROMA, ADENOMA,
SARCOMA, PAPILLA, BLASTOMA,
GANGLION, HEPATOMA,
NEOPLASM, PAPILOMA,
SWELLING, SCIRRHUS,
TERATOMA, CARCINOMA,
GRANULOMA, HEMORRHOID

type: .... BENIGN,
MALIGNANT

tumult:.... DIN, MOB, FUSS,
RIOT, STIR, BABEL, BRAWL,
BROIL, BABBLE, BEDLAM,
HUBBUB, UPROAR, FERMENT,
TEMPEST, TURMOIL, DISORDER,
OUTBREAK, UPRISING

tumultous: ...... RIOTOUS,
TURBULENT

tun: ...... TUB, VAT, CASK

tundra:.. PLAIN, WASTELAND

tune: ..... AIR, ARIA, LILT,
SONG, TONE, MELODY,
HARMONY, CONCORD,
AGREEMENT, ADJUSTMENT

tunic: .... COAT, JAMA, JUPE,
ROBE, TOGA, FROCK, GIPON,
JUPON, BASQUE, CHITON,
KIRTLE

tunnel: .... DIG, SAP, BORE,
FLUE, TUBE, BURROW, SUBWAY

turban:..... CAP, FEZ, HAT,
MANDIL, HEADDRESS

turbid: . . . . . . DARK, DULL,
DENSE, MUDDY, ROILY,
CLOUDY, MUDDLED, POLLUTED
turbulence: . . . . . . TUMULT,
UPROAR, FERMENT, RIOTING,
DISORDER, COMMOTION
turbulent: . . . . WILD, ROUGH,
STORMY, UNRULY, FURIOUS,
VIOLENT, AGITATED
turf: . . . . . SOD, PEAT, DIVOT,
GRASS, SWARD, TRACK
turgid: . . . TUMID, BLOATED,
POMPOUS, SWOLLEN, INFLATED,
BOMBASTIC
turkey: . . . . TOM, POULT,
BUSTARD, FAILURE, GOBBLER
turmoil: . . . ADO, DIN, UPSET,
WORRY, HUBBUB, TUMULT,
UNREST, UPROAR, WELTER,
FERMENT, QUARREL, TEMPEST,
AGITATION, COMMOTION,
CONFUSION
turn: . . . . . BOW, LAP, BEND,
BENT, CANT, PLOW, ROLL,
SLEW, SLUE, SPIN, VEER,
ALTER, AVERT, BLUNT, CRAMP,
CROOK, CURVE, HINGE, PIVOT,
QUIRK, REPEL, SCREW, TREND,
WHIRL, WHEEL, CHANGE,
DIRECT, DIVERT, GYRATE,
INVERT, ROTATE, SWERVE,
SWITCH, SWIVEL, VOLUTE,
ZIGZAG, CONVERT, DEVIATE,
REVERSE, REVOLVE, EXCHANGE,
PERSUADE, PIROUETTE,
TRANSFORM
aside: . . . . . . FEND, VEER,
BRUSH, SHUNT, DETOUR,
DIVERT, SWERVE, BLANCH,
DEFLECT
away: . . . . . SHOO, AVERT,
AVOID, EVADE, REPEL,
SHUNT, DIVERT, DECLINE,
DEFLECT, DEVIATE, DISMISS,
DIVERGE, SWERVE,
ESTRANGE
back: . . . . . . FOLD, REPEL,
RETURN, REVERT, EVOLUTE,
REPULSE, RETRACE

down: . . . . . . FOLD, VETO,
SPURN, INVERT, REFUSE,
REJECT, DECLINE
loose: . . . . FREE, RELEASE,
LIBERATE
out: . . OUST, TRIG, ARRAY,
EVERT, EXPEL, OUTFIT,
OUTPUT, ABANDON,
BECOME, DISMISS, PRODUCE,
EQUIPAGE, DISCHARGE,
GATHERING, ATTENDANCE
over: . KEEL, TART, SPILL,
UPSET, INVERT, PONDER,
REFORM, EVOLUTE, CAPSIZE,
DELEGATE, TRANSFER,
RELINQUISH
turncoat: . . . . TRAITOR,
DESERTER, RENEGADE,
APOSTATE
turner: . . . . ACROBAT,
TUMBLER, GYMNAST
turning: . . ROTARY, FLEXION,
WINDING, TWISTING,
REVOLUTION
point: . . . . . CRUX, HINGE,
PIVOT, CRISIS, CLIMAX,
SOLSTICE
turnkey: . . . . SCREW, JAILER,
WARDER
turret: . . . TOWER, BARTIZAN,
GUNHOUSE
turtle: . . . . REPTILE, SNAPPER,
TERRAPIN, TORTOISE
tush, tusk: . . . FANG, IVORY,
TOOTH, CANINE
tusker: . . . BOAR, ELEPHANT,
WALRUS, WARTHOG, NARWHAL,
PECCARY
tussle: . . . . . FIGHT, CONTEND,
CONTEST, GRAPPLE, WRESTLE,
SCUFFLE, STRUGGLE
tussock: . . . . . TUFT, BUNCH,
CLUMP, HASSOCK, THICKET
tutelage: . . . . CARE, NUTURE,
TEACHING, PROTECTION,
INSTRUCTION, GUARDIANSHIP
tutor: . . . . . . COACH, DRILL,
GUIDE, TEACH, TRAIN, MASTER,
MENTOR, SCHOOL, PEDAGOG,

TEACHER, GUARDIAN,
INSTRUCT, PRECEPTOR,
DISCIPLINE, INSTRUCTOR

tuyere: ... TEW, PIPE, TEWEL,
NOZZLE

twaddle: ...... ROT, BUNK,
PRATE, BABBLE, DRIVEL,
FUSTIAN, PRATTLE, NONSENSE

tweak: ..... PINCH, PLUCK,
TWIST, TWITCH

tweet: .. PEEP, CHIRP, CHIRRUP

tweeter: ..... LOUDSPEAKER

twibill: ... CHISEL, MATTOCK,
(BATTLE)AX

twice: .... BIS, DOUBLY, TWO
TIMES

twig: .... ROD, SLIP, BOUGH,
SCION, SHOOT, SPRAY, SPRIG,
BRANCH, SWITCH

twilight: .... EVE, DUSK,
GLOAM, EVENTIDE, EVENFALL,
GLOAMING, CREPUSCLE

twin: .... TWO, DUAL, PAIR,
GEMEL, DOUBLE, COUPLE,
PAIRED, TWOFOLD, DIDYMOUS

twine: ... COIL, CORD, TURN,
WARP, WRAP, BRAID, SNARL,
TWIST, ENLACE, STRING,
THREAD, WREATHE, ENCIRCLE,
INTERLACE, INTERWEAVE

twinge: ... ACHE, PAIN, PANG,
QUALM, SHOOT, TWEAK,
TWITCH

twinkle: ..... WINK, BLINK,
FLASH, GLEAM, GLINT, SHINE,
FLICKER, FLUTTER, GLIMMER,
GLITTER, SPARKLE, SCINTILLATE

twinkling: .... WINK, FLASH,
GLEAM, TRICE, MOMENT,
INSTANT

twirl: .... COIL, CURL, SPIN,
TURN, TWIST, WHIRL, GYRATE,
ROTATE, REVOLVE, FLOURISH,
ROTATION

twist: ..... TIC, BEND, COIL,
CURL, SKEW, SLEW, SLUE, SPIN,
TURN, WARP, WIND, CRINK,
CROOK, CURVE, GNARL, QUIRK,
REEVE, SCREW, SNARL, SWIRL,

TWEAK, TWINE, TWIRL, WREST,
WRICK, WRING, ENLACE,
SPIRAL, SQUIRM, THREAD,
WRENCH, WRITHE, CONFUSE,
CONTORT, REVOLVE

twisted: ...... WRY, SKEW,
AWRY, WARPED, TORTILE,
CONTORTED

twit: ...... RIB, GIBE, JOSH,
BLAME, CHIRP, TAUNT, TEASE,
UPBRAID, REPROACH, RIDICULE

twitch: ..... TIC, TUG, JERK,
PICK, PULL, YANK, PLUCK,
TWEAK, SNATCH, TWINGE,
VELLICATE

twitter: ..... CHIRP, GIGGLE,
TITTER, CHATTER, FLUTTER,
CHIRRUP, TREMBLE, CHIRPING

two: ..... DUO, BOTH, DUET,
PAIR, BRACE, TWAIN, COUPLE,
TWINS

twofold: ..... DUAL, BINAL,
DUPLE(X), BINARY, DOUBLE,
BIFARIOUS, DUPLICATE

tycoon: .... BARON, MOGUL,
MAGNATE, FINANCIER

tympan: .. DRUM, MEMBRANE

tympanum: ...... EARDRUM

tympany: ...... BOMBAST,
CONCEIT, INFLATION,
DISTENTION

type: ... FONT, FORM, KIND,
SIGN, SORT, BREED, CLASS,
GENRE, GROUP, MODEL, ORDER,
STAMP, TOKEN, EMBLEM,
NATURE, SYMBOL, EXAMPLE,
IMPRESS, PARAGON, PATTERN,
SPECIES, VARIETY, CLASSIFY,
CHARACTER

measure: ... EM, EN, POINT

case: ..... UPPER, LOWER

kind: .... ITALIC, ROMAN,
BOLDFACE, CONDENSED

size, style: ... PICA, ELITE,
AGATE, ROMAN, MINION,
BREVIER, NONPAREIL

typewriter, part: ..... KEY,
PLATEN, ROLLER, SPACER,
CARRIAGE, TABULATOR

typhoon: . . . . . . WIND, STORM, CYCLONE, HURRICANE

typical: . . . . NORMAL, REGULATOR, SYMBOLIC, CHARACTERISTIC

typify: . . . . EMBODY, EXEMPLIFY, REPRESENT, SYMBOLIZE

tyrannical: . . CRUEL, HARSH, UNJUST, DESPOTIC, ARBITRARY, IMPERIOUS, OPPRESSIVE

tyranny: . . . RIGOR, CRUELTY, SEVERITY, DESPOTISM, HARSHNESS

tyrant: . . DESPOT, OPPRESSOR

tyro: . . . . . . PUPIL, NOVICE, AMATEUR, BEGINNER, NEOPHYTE, APPRENTICE

tzigane: . . . . GYPSY

U

U-boat: . . . . SUBMARINE

uberous: . . . . COPIOUS, ABUNDANT, FRUITFUL

ubiquitous: . . . EVERYWHERE, OMNIPRESENT

ubiquity: . . . . OMNIPRESENCE

ugly: . . . BAD, VILE, AWFUL, CROSS, CRANKY, HOMELY, CRABBED, HIDEOUS, OMINOUS, GRUESOME, HORRIBLE, TERRIBLE, UNGAINLY, UNLOVELY, DANGEROUS, FRIGHTFUL, LOATHSOME, OFFENSIVE, REPULSIVE, UNSIGHTLY, ILL-NATURED, UNPLEASANT, ILL-TEMPERED, THREATENING

uitlander: . . . . . FOREIGNER, OUTLANDER

ukase: . . . . . EDICT, ORDER, DECREE, COMMAND

ulcer: . . . . NOMA, SORE, CANKER, CHANCRE

ulcerate: . . . . FESTER

ule: . . . . CAUCHO

ulna: . . . . . . BONE, CUBITUS

ulster: . . . . OVERCOAT

ulterior: . . . LATER, FUTURE, HIDDEN, FURTHER, SUBSEQUENT, SUCCEEDING, UNDISCLOSED, UNREVEALED

ultimate: . . END, LAST, FINAL, REMOTE, EXTREME, PRIMARY, MAXIMUM, FARTHEST, EVENTUAL, CONCLUSIVE

ultimatum: . . . . ORDER, LAST OFFER, DEMAND

ultra: . . . BEYOND, EXTREME, FORWARD, EXCESSIVE, RADICAL, EXTREMIST, AVANT GARDE

ulu: . . . . KNIFE

ululate: . . . . BAY, CRY, HOOT, HOWL, PULE, WAIL, YELP, LAMENT, SCREECH

umber: . . . . BROWN, SHADE, DARKEN, SHADOW, PROTECT, PIGMENT, GRAYLING, UMBRETTE

umbilicus: . . . . NAVEL

umbles: . . . . ENTRAILS

umbra: . . . . FISH, GHOST, SHADE, SHADOW, PHANTOM, VESTIGE

umbrage: . . DOUBT, PIQUE, SHADE, TRACE, OFFEND, SHADOW, FOLIAGE, OFFENSE, PRETEXT, SHELTER, SUSPICION, PROTECTION, RESENTMENT

umbrella: . . GAMP, COVER, BLIND, GUARD, SHADE, CANOPY, CHATTA, SCREEN, PARASOL, SHELTER, SUNSHADE, BUMBERSHOOT

umiak: . . . . . . BOAT, CANOE, KAYAK

umpire: . . . . JUDGE, DECIDE, ARBITER, REFEREE, DAYSMAN, SUPERVISE, ARBITRATOR

unable: . . CANNOT, HELPLESS, IMPOTENT, INCAPABLE, INCOMPETENT, UNQUALIFIED

unaccented: . . . . ATONIC, STRESSLESS

unaccompanied: . . . . . BARE, SOLO, ALONE

unaccustomed: . . . . . . NEW, STRANGE, UNFAMILIAR

unadorned: . . . PLAIN, STARK, BALD, BARE, NAKED, PLAIN, STARK, AUSTERE

unadulterated: . . . . . . NEAT, PURE, CLEAN, HONEST, GENUINE, SINCERE, UNMIXED, IMMUTABLE

unaffected: . . . . NAIF, REAL, NAIVE, PLAIN, RUSTIC, SIMPLE, ARTLESS, GENUINE, NATURAL, SINCERE, UNMOVED, UNBIASED, INGENUOUS

unalloyed: . . . PURE, GENUINE, UNMIXED

unanimous: . . SOLID, UNITED, CONSENSUS

unappeasable: . . IMPLACABLE

unapproachable: . . . ALOOF, DISTANT, INACCESSIBLE

unarmed: . . . . BARE, DEFENSELESS

unassuming: . . SHY, MODEST, NATURAL, RETIRING, DIFFIDENT

unattached: . . . FREE, LONE, LOOSE, SINGLE, UNMARRIED, INDEPENDENT

unavailing: . . . . FUTILE, GAINLESS

unavoidable: . . . . INEVITABLE

unaware: . . . . UNWARY, HEEDLESS, IGNORANT, THOUGHTLESS

unbalanced: . . . . . UNEVEN, DERANGED, LOPSIDED, ONE-SIDED

unbecoming: . . . . IMPROPER, UNSEEMLY, UNWORTHY, INDECOROUS

unbelief: . . . . . . SKEPTICISM, AGNOSTICISM, INCREDULITY

unbelievable: . . . . FANTASTIC, INCREDIBLE

unbeliever: . . . . PAGAN, ATHEIST, DOUBTER, SKEPTIC, AGNOSTIC, HERETIC, INFIDEL, MISCREANT, FREETHINKER

unbend: . . . . . . REST, THAW, YIELD, RELENT, RELAX, SLACKEN, STRAIGHTEN

unbending: . . . . . SET, FIRM, RIGID, STIFF, STERN, OBDURATE, RESOLUTE, ADAMANT

unbiased: . . . . . . FAIR, JUST, DETACHED, OBJECTIVE, IMPARTIAL

unbind: . . . . . . FREE, UNDO, UNTIE, DETACH, LOOSEN, RELEASE, UNFASTEN

unbleached: . . ECRU, BEIGE, NATURAL

unblemished: . . PURE, CLEAN, SPOTLESS, STAINLESS

unbolt: . . . . . . OPEN, UNBAR, UNPIN, UNLOCK, UNFASTEN

unbosom: . . . . . TELL, REVEAL

unbounded: . . . . OPEN, LIMITLESS, UNCHECKED, UNLIMITED, MEASURELESS

unbridled: . . . . FREE, LOOSE, VIOLENT, DISSOLUTE, UNCHECKED, LICENTIOUS

unbroken: . . . . . . ONE, FLAT, WHOLE, ENTIRE, INTACT, UNTAMED, UNPLOWED, CONTINUAL, UNDIVIDED, UNSUBDUED, CONTINUOUS

unburden: . . . . . . RID, EASE, EMPTY, UNLOAD, RELIEVE

uncalled for: . . IMPERTINENT, GRATUITOUS, UNNECESSARY

uncanny: . . . . . EERY, EERIE, SCARY, UNCO, WEIRD, SPOOKY, STRANGE, UNNATURAL, MYSTERIOUS

unceasing: . . . . ENDLESS, ETERNAL, CONTINUAL, INCESSANT, PERPETUAL, CONTINUOUS, EVERLASTING

unceremonious: . . . . . CURT, BLUFF, BLUNT, ABRUPT, FAMILIAR, INFORMAL

uncertain: . . . HAZY, VAGUE, CHANCY, FITFUL, QUEASY, DUBIOUS, DOUBTFUL,

VARIABLE, AMBIGUOUS,
HAZARDOUS, UNDECIDED,
INDEFINITE, PRECARIOUS

uncertainty: ..... GAMBLE,
HAZARD, WONDER, DUBIETY,
SUSPENSE, SKEPTICISM

unchecked: ..... FREE, RIFE,
LOOSE, RAMPANT

uncivil: ..... RUDE, BLUFF,
IMPOLITE, BARBAROUS,
INDECOROUS

uncivilized: .... RUDE, WILD,
FERAL, BRUTAL, SAVAGE,
BARBARIC, PRIMITIVE

unclean: ...... FOUL, VILE,
BLACK, DIRTY, FILTHY,
IMPURE, DEFILED, LEPROUS,
OBSCENE, POLLUTED, SQUALID,
UNCHASTE

unclose: ..... OPEN, REVEAL

unclothe: .. STRIP, UNDRESS,
UNCOVER

unclothed: ..... BARE, NUDE,
NAKED

unco: ...... GREAT, WEIRD,
FOREIGN, STRANGE, NOTABLE,
UNCANNY, UNKNOWN

uncoil: .... UNWIND

uncombed: ...... UNKEMPT

uncommitted: ...... FREE,
UNPLEDGED

uncommon: .... ODD, RARE,
NOVEL, CHOICE, EXOTIC,
SCARCE, UNIQUE, SPECIAL,
STRANGE, UNUSUAL,
INFREQUENT, REMARKABLE,
EXCEPTIONAL

uncommunicative: .. SILENT,
RESERVED, RETICENT, TACITURN

uncomplicated: ..... EASY,
PLAIN, SIMPLE

uncompromising: ..... SET,
FIRM, RIGID, STERN, STRICT,
ADAMANT, UNBENDING,
DETERMINED, INFLEXIBLE,
UNYIELDING

unconcerned: .. COOL, EASY,
ALOOF, CARELESS, DETACHED,

APATHETIC, INSOUCIANT,
INDIFFERENT

unconditional: ...... FREE,
TOTAL, ABSOLUTE, EXPLICIT

unconfined: ..... LAX, FREE,
LOOSE, UNCAGED, BOUNDLESS,
LIMITLESS

unconfirmed: ..... RUMOR,
GOSSIP, REPORT, HEARSAY

unconnected: ..... ABRUPT,
DETACHED, DISCRETE,
RAMBLING, SEPARATE,
INCOHERENT

unconquerable: .. INVINCIBLE

unconscious: .... OUT, ASLEEP,
BLOTTO, TORPID, STUNNED,
UNAWARE, COMOTOSE,
IGNORANT, INANIMATE,
MINDLESS, UNWITTING,
INSENSIBLE

state: .... COMA, SWOON,
TRANCE, SYNCOPE,
HYPNOSIS, NARCOSIS

unconstrained: . EASY, FREE,
LOOSE, NATURAL, FAMILIAR,
UNFETTERED, SPONTANEOUS

uncontrolled: ... FREE, WILD,
LOOSE, IRREGULAR,
UNMANAGED, HYSTERICAL,
LICENTIOUS, UNFETTERED,
UNGOVERNED

unconventional: .... REBEL,
OUTRE, CASUAL, DEVIOUS,
BOHEMIAN, UNUSUAL,
INFORMAL

uncouple: .. LOOSE, RELEASE,
DIVORCE, UNFASTEN,
DISCONNECT

uncouth: ..... RUDE, CRUDE,
GAUCHE, CLUMSY, VULGAR,
AWKWARD, BOORISH, LOUTISH,
UNGAINLY, UNREFINED,
UNCULTURED

person: ..... OAF, BOOR,
LOUT, YOKEL, RUSTIC,
BUM(P)KIN

uncover: ...... DOFF, OPEN,
DENUDE, DETECT, DIVEST,
EXPOSE, REMOVE, REVEAL,

UNVEIL, DISPLAY, DIVULGE, UNDRAPE, UNEARTH, DISCLOSE, DISCOVER

uncovered: . . . . BALD, BARE, NUDE, OPEN, NAKED, EXPOSED, BAREHEADED

unction: . . . . OIL, UNGUENT, OINTMENT

give extreme: . . . . . ANELE

unctuous: . . . . . . FAT, OILY, FATTY, SLEEK, SOAPY, SUAVE, FERVID, GREASY, PINQUID, PLASTIC, SMOOTH, OLEAGINOUS

uncultivated: . . . ARID, WILD, FERAL, COARSE, DESERT, FALLOW, VIRGIN, UNCOUTH, BARBAROUS

uncultured: . . RUDE, COARSE, ARTLESS, BOORISH, ILL-BRED, UNREFINED

undaunted: . . . BOLD, BRAVE, INTREPID, FEARLESS, CONFIDENT, COURAGEOUS, UNDISMAYED

undecided: . . . . MOOT, HESITANT, PENDANT, PENDING, DOUBTFUL, WAVERING, UNCERTAIN, UNSETTLED, IRRESOLUTE, UNRESOLVED

undemonstrative: . . . . CALM, COLD, COOL, QUIET, RESERVED, RESTRAINED

undeniable: . . . . TRUE, CERTAIN, IRREFUTABLE

under: . . . . BELOW, LOWER, NEATH, NETHER, BENEATH, UNDERNEATH

underage: . . . . MINOR, IMMATURE

undercover man: . . . . . SPY, AGENT, SLEUTH, DETECTIVE, COUNTERSPY

underdone: . . . . RARE

underestimate: . . . MINIMIZE, UNDERRATE, UNDERVALUE

undergo: . . . . . . BEAR, PASS, ENDURE, SUFFER, SUSTAIN, EXPERIENCE

underground: . . . . . SECRET, HIDDEN, BENEATH, UNDERCOVER

burial place: . . . . CRYPT, CATACOMB

dweller: . GNOME, DWARF, TROLL

fungus: . . . . TRUFFLE, EARTHNUT

passage: . . . . . SAP, TUBE, SEWER, TUNNEL, BURROW

railway: . . . TUBE, METRO, SUBWAY

worker: . . MINER, MUCKER, PITMAN, SAPPER, SANDHOG

underhand: . . . SLY, COVERT, SECRET, CLANDESTINE

underhanded: . . SLY, MEAN, SHADY, SNEAKY, TRICKY, UNFAIR, DECEITFUL, FRAUDULENT

underline: . . . MARK, STRESS, EMPHASIZE

underling: . . . AIDE, MENIAL, MINION, INFERIOR, SUBALTERN, SUBORDINATE

underlying: . . . . BASIC, OBSCURE, CARDINAL, FUNDAMENTAL

undermine: . . . . SAP, DRAIN, IMPAIR, ERODE, WEAKEN, SUBVERT, ENFEEBLE, EXCAVATE

underpin, underprop: . . . . . PROP, UPHOLD, JUSTIFY, SUPPORT, MAINTAIN

underrate: . . . . DECRY, BELITTLE, UNDERVALUE

underscore: . . . . STRESS, EMPHASIZE, ITALICIZE

undersized: . . . PUNY, RUNTY, SMALL, SCRUBBY

understand: . GET, KEN, SEE, KNOW, GRASP, INFER, SAVEY, SAVVY, SENSE, ASSUME, FOLLOW, REASON, DISCERN, REALIZE, PERCEIVE, APPREHEND, APPRECIATE, COMPREHEND

understanding: . . . . . IDEA, AMITY, BRAIN, SENSE, ACCORD,

HUMANE, KINDLY, TREATY,
COMPACT, CONCEPT, EMPATHY,
ENTENTE, KNOWING,
CONTRACT, JUDGMENT,
SYMPATHY, AGREEMENT,
KNOWLEDGE, ACCEPTANCE,
DISCERNMENT

understood: . . CLEAR, LUCID,
TACIT, SENSED, AGREED,
ASSUMED, IMPLIED, IMPLICIT,
PRESUMED

undertake: . . . . TRY, DARE,
OFFER, SEIZE, ACCEPT, ASSUME,
ENGAGE, PLEDGE, TACKLE,
ATTEMPT, EXECUTE, PERFORM,
PROMISE, CONTRACT,
COVENANT, ENDEAVOR,
VOLUNTEER

undertaking: . . . . JOB, TASK,
CHARGE, PLEDGE, CALLING,
PROJECT, PROMISE, VENTURE,
ADVENTURE, ENTERPRISE,
GUARANTEE, PROPOSITION

undertow: . . . EDDY, VORTEX,
CURRENT, RIPTIDE

underwater *ship:* . . . U-BOAT,
PIGBOAT, SUBMARINE

apparatus: . . . . . . SCUBA,
CAISSON, SNORKEL,
BATHYSPHERE

underwear: . . . . SLIP, PANTY,
SCANTY, SHORTS, UNDIES,
STEPINS, FLANNELS, LINGERIE,
SKIVVIES

underworld: . . HELL, HADES,
SHEOL, EREBUS, GANGLAND,
ANTIPODES

underwrite: . . . . . . INSURE,
ASSURE, ASSUME, FINANCE,
SPONSOR, SUBSCRIBE

undetermined: . . . . . VAGUE,
DUBIOUS, DOUBTFUL,
EQUIVOCAL

undeveloped: . . . . . . CRUDE,
LATENT, IMMATURE

undiluted: . . . . . NEAT, PURE,
SHEER, STRAIGHT

undine: . . . . . SYLPH, NYMPH,
SEAMAID

undisciplined: . . . . . . WILD,
UNRULY, WANTON, UNTRAINED

undisguised: . . . BALD, OPEN,
OVERT, FRANK, BAREFACED

undivided: . . . . ONE, TOTAL,
WHOLE, ENTIRE, INTACT,
COMPLETE, UNBROKEN,
CONTINUOUS

undo: . . . OPEN, RUIN, ANNUL,
LOOSE, SOLVE, BETRAY,
CANCEL, DEFEAT, UNWRAP,
DESTROY, DISJOIN, NULLIFY,
RELEASE, UNCOVER, UNRAVEL,
UNFASTEN, DISCONNECT,
INVALIDATE

undomesticated: . . . . . WILD,
FERAL, UNTAMED

undone: . . RAW, UNFINISHED

undoubtedly: . . . . SURE,
CERTAINLY, ADMITTEDLY,
INDUBITABLY

undraped: . . . . . BARE, NUDE

undress: . . . . . . DOFF, STRIP,
DIVEST, DISROBE, UNCLOTHE,
DISHABILLE

undue: . . . . EXTREME,
IMPROPER, EXCESSIVE,
INORDINATE, EXORBITANT

undulate: . . . . ROLL, WAVE,
SWING, BILLOW, RIPPLE,
FLUCTUATE

undulation: . . WAVE, HEAVE,
SWELL, SURGE, RIPPLE,
PULSATION

unduly: . . . . UNJUSTLY,
IMPROPERLY, EXCESSIVELY

undying: . . . . ABIDING,
AGELESS, ENDLESS, ETERNAL,
IMMORTAL, CONTINUAL,
DEATHLESS

unearth: . . . . . . DIG, LEARN,
EXHUME, EXPOSE, UNCOVER,
DISCLOSE, DISCOVER

unearthly: . . . . . EERY, EERIE,
WEIRD, GHOSTLY, UNCANNY,
TERRIFIC, APPALLING,
FANTASTIC, MYSTERIOUS

uneasiness: . . . . WORRY,
UNREST, ANXIETY, MALAISE,

DISQUITE, DISCOMFORT,
DISCONTENT

uneasy: . . . . ANXIOUS,
AWKWARD, FIDGETY, FRETFUL,
NERVOUS, RESTIVE, RESTLESS,
CONCERNED, PERTURBED,
UNSETTLED

uneducated: . . . . IGNORANT,
ILLITERATE, UNLETTERED,
UNLEARNED, UNSCHOOLED

unemotional: . . COLD, STONY,
STOLID, STOLICAL, APATHETIC,
PHLEGMATIC

unemployed: . . IDLE, OTIOSE,
INACTIVE

unending: . . . . ENDLESS,
ETERNAL, UNDYING, TIMELESS,
CEASELESS, CONTINUOUS

unenthusiastic: . . . . . COOL,
COLD, APATHETIC,
PHLEGMATIC, INDIFFERENT

unequal: . . . UNEVEN, UNFAIR,
UNJUST, VARIABLE, DISPARATE,
IRREGULAR, INADEQUATE,
FLUCTUATING

unequalled: . . . . . . SUPREME,
PEERLESS, MATCHLESS,
NONPAREIL, UNRIVALED

unequivocal: . . CLEAR, PLAIN,
SINCERE, DEFINITE, EXPLICIT,
CERTAINLY

unerring: . . . . . SURE, TRUE,
EXACT, CERTAIN, ACCURATE,
INERRANT, UNFAILING,
INFALLIBLE

uneven: . . . . . . ODD, EROSE,
ROUGH, RUGGED, UNFAIR,
UNJUST, UNLIKE, RAGGED,
SPOTTY, CROOKED, UNEQUAL,
VARYING, IRREGULAR,
LOPSIDED, ILL-MATCHED,
FLUCTUATING

unexceptional: . . . UNUSUAL,
REGULAR, COMMON, ORDINARY

unexciting: . . . . DULL, DEAD,
TAME, VAPID, BORING, PROSAIC

unexpected: . . . . . . ABRUPT,
SUDDEN, UNFORSEEN

unexpired: . . . ALIVE, VALID,
ACTIVE, OPERATIVE

unfailing: . . . SURE, CERTAIN,
RELIABLE, UNERRING,
INFALLIBLE, UNFLAGGING

unfair: . . . . . FOUL, WRONG,
BIASED, UNJUST, WRONGFUL,
PARTIAL, DISHONEST,
UNETHICAL

unfaithful: . . . . . . UNTRUE,
INFIDEL, TRATIOR, DERELICT,
DISLOYAL, TURNCOAT,
DISHONEST, TRAITOROUS

unfaltering: . . . TRUE, BRAVE,
STEADY

unfamiliar: . . NEW, STRANGE,
UNKNOWN, UNACCUSTOMED

unfasten: . . . . . FREE, OPEN,
UNDO, LOOSE, UNBAR, UNFIX,
UNTIE, DETACH, LOOSEN,
UNLOCK, UNTETHER

unfavorable: . . . . . BAD, ILL,
FOUL, AVERSE, ADVERSE,
CONTRARY, INIMICAL

unfeeling: . . . . DULL, HARD,
NUMB, CRUEL, HARSH, STERN,
STONY, BRUTAL, STOLID,
CALLOUS, OBDURATE,
APATHETIC, HEARTLESS,
INSENSATE, INSENSITIVE,
INSENSIBLE

unfit: . . . . BAD, SICK, INAPT,
INEPT, FAULTY, DISABLED,
INEDIBLE, IMPROPER,
UNSUITABLE

unfix: . . . . . DETACH, LOOSEN

unflattering: . . . . . . FRANK,
BLUNT, CANDID, DEROGATORY,
UNBECOMING

unfledged: . . . . GREEN,
CALLOW, IMMATURE

unflinching: . FIRM, STANCH,
RESOLUTE, STEADFAST

unfold: . . . . . OPEN, DEPLOY,
EVOLVE, EXPAND, FLOWER,
DISPLAY, DIVULGE, RELEASE,
DISCLOSE

unforeseen: . . . . . . CASUAL, SUDDEN, UNEXPECTED, ACCIDENTAL

unfortunate: . . . . ILL, POOR, DISMAL, WRETCH, HAPLESS, UNLUCKY, LUCKLESS, WRETCHED

unfounded: . . . . IDLE, BASELESS, CHIMERICAL, GROUNDLESS

unfrequented: . . . . LONELY, ISOLATED, SOLITARY

unfriendly: . . . . COLD, COOL, REMOTE, ASOCIAL, HOSTILE, INIMICAL, UNSOCIAL, ANTAGONISTIC

unfruitful: . . . . BARREN, STERILE, USELESS, INFERTILE

unfurl: . . . . . OPEN, EXPAND, UNFOLD, SPREAD, UNROLL

ungainly: . . . UGLY, LANKY, CLUMSY, AWKWARD, BOORISH, UNCOUTH

ungenerous: . MEAN, HARSH, HASTY, STINGY, MISERLY

ungodly: . . . SINFUL, WICKED, IMPIOUS, DREADFUL

ungovernable: . . . . . . WILD, UNRULY, UNBRIDLED, DISORDERLY, REBELLIOUS

ungracious: . . . . RUDE, IMPOLITE, CHURLISH, AWKWARD, OFFENSIVE

ungual: . . NAIL, HOOF, CLAW, TALON

unguent: . . . . . BALM, SALVE, CHRISM, POMADE, OINTMENT, LUBRICANT

ungulate: . . . COW, HOG, PIG, DEER, HORSE, TAPIR, CATTLE, HOOFED, ELEPHANT, RHINOCEROS

unhandy: . . . . CLUMSY, AWKWARD

unhappy: . . . . . . SAD, BLUE, MOROSE, DISMAL, UNLUCKY, DEJECTED, ILL-FATED, WRETCHED, MISERABLE, SORROWFUL

unharmed: . . . SAFE, UNHURT

unhealthy: . . . . . . ILL, SICK, SICKLY, MORBID

unheeding: . DEAF, CARELESS

unholy: . . . . IMPURE, WICKED, IMPIOUS, PROFANE, DREADFUL, SHOCKING

unhorse: . . . . . SPILL, UPSET, DISLODGE, OVERTHROW

unhurried: . . . . EASY, SLOW, DELIBERATE

uniform: . . EVEN, FLAT, SUIT, EQUAL, LEVEL, LIVERY, OUTFIT, STEADY, EQUABLE, REGULAR, CONSTANT, STANDARD, CONTINUAL, UNVARYING, CONSISTENT

unify: . . . . . . WELD, MERGE, UNITE, COALESCE, CORRELATE, INTEGRATE, CONSOLIDATE

unilateral: . . . . . . ONE-SIDED

unimaginative: . . . . . . DULL, LITERAL, PROSAIC, ORDINARY

unimpeachable: . . . . CLEAN, RELIABLE, BLAMELESS, FAULTLESS

unimportant: . . . . . . MINOR, PETTY, SMALL, LITTLE, PALTRY, TRIVIAL, NEGLIGIBLE

uninhabited: . . . . . . EMPTY, VACANT, DESERTED, DESOLATE, TENANTLESS

unintelligent: . . . . DUMB, OBTUSE, STUPID, UNWISE, FOOLISH, IGNORANT, SENSELESS, IRRATIONAL

unintentional: . . UNWITTING, ACCIDENTAL, INADVERTANT

uninteresting: . . DRY, DRAB, DULL, FLAT, STALE, BORING, JEJUNE, PROLIX, STUPID, HUMDRUM, INSIPID, PROSAIC, TEDIOUS, VERBOSE, TIRESOME, COLORLESS, UNEXCITING

union: . . ONE, BLOC, ARTEL, UNITY, CARTEL, COPULA, FUSION, LEAGUE, MERGER, AMALGAM, CONCORD, CONTACT, ETENTE, LIASON,

MEETING, SOCIETY, ALLIANCE,
JUNCTION, MARRIAGE,
COALITION, SYNDICATE,
COHERENCE, CONNECTION,
FEDERATION, ASSOCIATION,
CONFEDERATION, CONJUNCTION
business:....... CARTEL,
SYNDICATE
jack: .... FLAG
political:........ BLOC,
COALITION
trade:..... GUILD, HANSE
unique:.... ODD, ONE, RARE,
SOLE, ALONE, SINGLE,
NOTABLE, SPECIAL, UNUSUAL,
PECULIAR, SINGULAR,
MATCHLESS
unison:.... UNION, ACCORD,
CONCORD, HARMONY,
AGREEMENT, CONSONANT,
IDENTICAL, UNANIMITY,
CONCORDANT
unit:...... ACE, ONE, ITEM,
DIGIT, GROUP, MONAD, PIECE,
WHOLE, ENTITY, STANDARD,
INDIVIDUAL
unite:.. ADD, SEW, TIE, WED,
ALLY, BAND, BIND, FUSE, JOIN,
KNIT, LINK, MELD, PAIR, WELD,
AFFIX, ANNEX, BLEND, GRAFT,
HITCH, MARRY, MERGE, PIECE,
RALLY, ATTACH, CEMENT,
COHERE, COUPLE, MINGLE,
SOLDER, SPLICE, COMBINE,
CONJOIN, CONNECT, CONSORT,
ASSEMBLE, COALESCE,
FEDERATE, AFFILIATE,
AGGREGATE, ASSOCIATE,
AMALGAMATE, CONSOLIDATE
united:...... ONE, AGREED,
JOINED, COMBINED,
CONJUGATE, CORPORATE
unity:....... ONE, ACCORD,
CONCORD, HARMONY, ONENESS,
ALLIANCE, AGREEMENT,
SINGLENESS, SOLIDARITY
universal:..... ALL, TOTAL,
WHOLE, COMMON, COSMIC,
ENTIRE, GLOBAL, GENERAL,

GENERIC, CATHOLIC,
CONSTANT, PANDEMIC,
ECUMENIC(AL)
universe:.... EARTH, MONAD,
WORLD, COSMOS, NATURE,
SYSTEM, CREATION,
MACROCOSM
unjust:..... CRUEL, UNFAIR,
BIASED, PARTIAL, WRONGFUL
unkempt:... CRUDE, MESSY,
ROUGH, FROWZY, SHABBY,
SHAGGY, UNTIDY, RUFFLED,
SQUALID, TOUSLED, SLOVENLY,
UNCOMBED
unkind:.... CRUEL, HARSH,
ROUGH, STERN, SEVERE,
WICKED
unknown:.. UNCO, STRANGE,
OBSCURE, ANONYMOUS,
INCOGNITO
unlace:...... UNDO, UNTIE,
LOOSEN, UNFASTEN
unlawful:....... BASTARD,
ILLICIT, ILLEGAL, ILLEGITIMATE
goods:.... CONTRABAND
hunting:...... POACHING
importation:.. SMUGGLING
intrusion:..... TRESPASS
liquor:.:...... BOOTLEG
unlearned:..... IGNORANT,
ILLITERATE, UNTAUGHT,
UNSCHOOLED, UNEDUCATED
unleash:..... FREE, LOOSE,
RELEASE
unleavened:...... AZYMOUS
unless:...... SAVE, EXCEPT
unlettered:..... IGNORANT,
ILLITERATE, UNEDUCATED
unlike:... UNEVEN, DIVERSE,
DIFFERENT, DISSIMILAR
unlikely:.......... UNFIT,
IMPROBABLE
unlimited:.......... VAST,
BOUNDLESS, UNDEFINED,
UNIVERSAL
unload:.. RID, DUMP, EMPTY,
REMOVE, DISCARD, LIGHTEN,
RELIEVE, UNBURDEN,
LIQUIDATE

unlock: . . . . . . OPEN, REVEAL

unloose: . . . . . UNDO, UNTIE,
RELEASE

unlucky: . . . . BAD, ILL,
HAPLESS, ILLFATED,
ILLSTARRED, ILLOMENED

unmannerly: . . . . . . RUDE,
BOORISH, UNCIVIL, IMPOLITE,
DISCOURTEOUS

unmarried: . . LONE, UNWED,
CHASTE, CELIBATE

in law: . . . . SOLE

man: . . . . CELIBATE,
BACHELOR

woman: . . . . . . MAIDEN,
SPINSTER

unmask: . . . EXPOSE, REVEAL,
UNCLOAK, DISCLOSE

unmelodious: . . . . DISSONANT

unmerciful: . . . . CRUEL,
PITILESS, RUTHLESS

unmindful: . . . . . CARELESS,
NEEDLESS, FORGETFUL,
NEGLIGENT

unmistakable: . . . . . . OPEN,
CLEAR, PLAIN, PATENT,
EVIDENT, OBVIOUS, APPARENT,
DEFINITE

unmitigated: . . . . . . SHEER,
ARRANT, ABSOLUTE, CLEARCUT,
UNMODIFIED

unmoved: . . . . CALM, COOL,
FIRM, STONY, ADAMANT,
OBDURATE, STUBBORN,
UNSHAKEN, APATHETIC,
INSENSATE, UNAFFECTED

unnatural: . . . ERRY, EERIE,
STRANGE, UNCANNY,
ABNORMAL, AFFECTED,
IRREGULAR, ARTIFICIAL

unnerve: . . . . SHAKE, SHOCK,
UNMAN

unoccupied: . . IDLE, EMPTY,
VACANT, UNEMPLOYED

unofficial: . . . . PRIVATE,
INFORMAL

unorganized: . . . . . . MESSY,
CHAOTIC, DISORDERLY

unostentatious: . . . . . QUIET,
MODEST, RESTRAINED

unpaid: . . . . . . DUE, OWING,
ARREAR, UNREVENGED

unparalled: . . . . ALONE,
UNIQUE, UNEQUAL, PEERLESS,
MATCHLESS, INIMITABLE

unpleasant: . . . . . . IRKSOME,
OFFENSIVE, ABOMINABLE,
UNGRACIOUS, DISTASTEFUL,
DISAGREEABLE

unpleasantness: . . . . . SPAT,
QUARREL

unplowed: . . . . LEA, FALLOW,
UNTILLED

unpolished: . . CRUDE, ROUGH,
COARSE, AGRESTIC, BARBAROUS

unprecedented: . . . . . . NEW,
NOVEL

unpredictable: . . . . CASUAL,
CAPRICIOUS

unprejudiced: . . . . FAIR,
IMPARTIAL, UNBIASED

unpremediated: . . . CASUAL,
EXTEMPORE, ACCIDENTAL,
SPONTANEOUS

unprincipled: . . . IMMORAL,
PERFIDIOUS, UNSCRUPULOUS

unproductive: . . ARID, DEAD,
BARREN, STERILE, UNFRUITFUL

unpropitious: . . . . EVIL,
ADVERSE, UNTIMELY,
INOPPORTUNE

unprotected: . . . . . EXPOSED,
HELPLESS, UNGUARDED

unqualified: . . BARE, SHEER,
UNFIT, ENTIRE, UNABLE,
ABSOLUTE, COMPLETE,
DEFINITE, CATEGORIC,
INCAPABLE, INCOMPETENT

unquestionable: . . . CERTAIN,
DECIDED, EVIDENT, IMPLICIT,
POSITIVE

unravel: . . . . . UNDO, FEAZE,
SOLVE, UNTANGLE, SEPARATE

unreal: . . . . FALSE, FANCIED,
FANCIFUL, ILLUSORY,
SPURIOUS, IMAGINARY,
PRETENDED, VISIONARY,
ARTIFICIAL, FICTITIOUS,
IMAGINARY

unreasonable: . . MAD, INANE, UNDUE, ABSURD, EXCESSIVE, SENSELESS, IRRATIONAL, EXORBITANT

unrefined: . . . . . RAW, LOUD, RUDE, CRASS, CRUDE, GROSS, COARSE, VULGAR, UNCOUTH

unrelaxed: . . . . TAUT, TENSE

unrelenting: . . . GRIM, HARD, CRUEL, STERN, SEVERE, ADAMANT, MERCILESS, INEXORABLE, INFLEXIBLE, UNYIELDING

unremitting: . . BUSY, HARD, NONSTOP, ASSIDUOUS, CONTINUAL, INCESSANT, PERSISTENT

unreserved: . . . FREE, FRANK, CANDID, OUTSPOKEN, FRIENDLY, UNLIMITED

unrest: . . . . ALARM, MOTION, FERMENT, DISQUIET, AGITATION, COMMOTION

unrestrained: . . FREE, WILD, LOOSE, WANTON, RIOTOUS, ABANDONED, DISSOLUTE, EXPANSIVE

unrevealed: . . . . HIDDEN, LATENT, MASKED, COVERED, CONCEALED

unripe: . . . GREEN, IMMATURE

unrivaled: . . . . . . PEERLESS, MATCHLESS, NONPAREIL

unruffled: . . . . CALM, COOL, PLACID, POISED, SERENE, SMOOTH, UNFAZED

unruly: . . . . WILD, LAWLESS, RESTIVE, RIOTOUS, FRACTIOUS, DISORDERLY

unsafe: . . EXPOSED, INSECURE, PERILOUS, DANGEROUS, HAZARDOUS, UNRELIABLE

unsavory: . . . . INSIPID, TASTELESS, OFFENSIVE, UNPLEASANT, DISAGREEABLE

unscramble: . SOLVE, CLEAR, UNRAVEL, STRAIGHTEN

unscrupulous: . . DISHONEST, MISCREANT, UNPRINCIPLED

unseasonable: . . . . . UNRIPE, UNTIMELY, PREMATURE, INOPPORTUNE

unseal: . . . . . . OPEN, DISCLOSE

unseat: . . . . . OUST, REMOVE, UNHORSE, DISLODGE, OVERTHROW

unseemly: . . . . UNDUE, IMPROPER, INDECENT, UNWORTHY, INDECOROUS, UNBECOMING

unseen: . . . . INVISIBLE, UNNOTICED, UNOBSERVED

unsettle: . . . UPSET, DERANGE, DISTURB, DISORDER, DISPLACE, DISQUIET, DISTRESS, DISARRANGE, DISCOMPOSE

unsettled: . . MOOT, DUBIOUS, RESTLESS, UNSTABLE, AMBIGUOUS, DESULTORY, ITINERANT, UNCERTAIN, PRECARIOUS

unsightly: . . UGLY, UNGAINLY

unskilled: . . . . RUDE, GREEN, INEPT, CLUMSY, AWKWARD

unsophisticated: . . . . . . NAIF, PURE, FRANK, NAIVE, CALLOW, SIMPLE, ARTLESS, INNOCENT, INGENIOUS

unsound: . . . . . . EVIL, SICK, WEAK, CRAZY, DOTTY, FALSE, FRAIL, RISKY, SHAKY, ADDLED, FLAWED, HOLLOW, ROTTEN, DECAYED, DISEASED, IMPAIRED, INSECURE, DEFECTIVE, IMPERFECT, TOTTERING

unsparing: . . . . LAVISH, LIBERAL, PROFUSE

unspeakable: . . . . BAD, VILE, WICKED, HEINOUS, INEFFABLE

unspoken: . . . TACIT, SILENT, UNSAID, INEFFABLE

unstable: . . . . LOOSE, SANDY, FICKLE, FITFUL, LABILE, ASTATIC, ERRATIC, FLIGHTY, PLASTIC, INSECURE, TICKLISH, UNSTEADY, VARIABLE, FAITHLESS, IRREGULAR,

UNSETTLED, CHANGEABLE, INCONSTANT

unsteady: ... DIZZY, SHAKY, FICKLE, GROGGY, WOBBLY, ERRATIC, QUAVERY, RICKETY, UNSOUND, WAYWARD, UNSTABLE, VARIABLE, WAVERING, DESULTORY, IRREGULAR, UNCERTAIN, CAPRICIOUS, INCONSTANT

unsubstantial: .. AIRY, SLIM, FILMY, LIGHT, FLIMSY, PAPERY, SLIGHT, UNREAL, NOMINAL, SHADOWY, FILIGREE, VISIONARY, IMMATERIAL

unsuccessful: ...... LOSING, FAILING, UNLUCKY, ABORTIVE, FRUITLESS, DISASTROUS, INEFFECTUAL

unsuitable: ... INAPT, UNFIT

untamed: .... WILD, FERAL, FERINE, UNRULY

untended: ...... UNCARED, NEGLECTED

unthinking: .. RASH, CASUAL, CARELESS, HEEDLESS, IMPETUOUS, THOUGHTLESS

untidy: .... DOWDY, MESSY, MUSSY, SLOPPY, CARELESS, LITTERED, SLOVENLY, UNKEMPT, SLIPSHOD, DISHEVELED, DISORDERED
person: ... SLOB, SLOVEN, SLATTERN

untie: ... FREE, UNDO, LOOSE, UNBIND, UNFASTEN

until: .. TO, TIL, TILL, UNTO, BEFORE, PENDING

untimely: ..... PREMATURE, INOPPORTUNE

untiring: .. BUSY, SEDULOUS, TIRELESS, INDEFATIGABLE

unto: .... TIL, UNTIL

untold: ... VAST, COUNTLESS, BOUNDLESS, UNRELATED, UNIFORMED, UNREVEALED, INCALCULABLE, INDESCRIBABLE

untouched: ... PURE, INTACT, VIRGIN, PRISTINE

untoward: ...... UNRULY, UNLUCKY, IMPROPER, PERVERSE, STUBBORN, UNSEEMLY, VEXATIOUS, INDECOROUS, UNGRACEFUL, UNFORTUNATE

untrained: ..... RAW, WILD, GREEN, AWKWARD, UNTAMED, UNSCHOOLED, UNSKILLED, AMETEURISH

untrue: ..... FALSE, WRONG, DISLOYAL, ERRONEOUS, FAITHLESS, INCORRECT, FALLACIOUS, UNFAITHFUL

untruth: ... FIB, LIE, FABLE, FALSEHOOD, CANARD, MENDACITY, FABRICATION

untutored: .. NAIVE, SIMPLE, ARTLESS, IGNORANT, UNTAUGHT, UNLEARNED, ILLITERATE

untwine: .... UNTIE, UNROLL, UNRAVEL

untwist: .... FREE, OPEN, RAVEL, UNRAVEL, UNTWINE, SEPARATE, STRAIGHTEN, DISENTANGLE

unusual: ...... ODD, RARE, NOVEL, OUTRE, QUEER, WEIRD, QUAINT, UNIQUE, STRANGE, ABNORMAL, UNCOMMON, SINGULAR, DIFFERENT, ECCENTRIC

unvarnished: .. BALD, PLAIN, SIMPLE, LITERAL, UNGLAZED, UNADORNED

unvarying: .... DRONE, UNIFORM, CONSTANT, MONOTONE

unveil: .... REVEAL, UNMASK, UNCOVER, DISCLOSE

unvoiced: .... SURD, TACIT, SECRET, UNUTTERED

unwarranted: ..... UNDUE, UNJUSTIFIED

unwary: ... RASH, UNAWARE, CARELESS

unwavering: ... FIRM, SOLID, STABLE, CONSTANT, STEADFAST

unwearied: . . . . BUSY, TIRELESS, ASSIDUOUS

unwelcome: . . . . NONGRATA, UNWANTED, INTRUDING, INTRUSIVE

unwholesome: . . . . EVIL, IMPURE, CORRUPT, HARMFUL, NOISOME, NOXIOUS, UNCLEAN, UNHEALTHY, DISTASTEFUL

unwieldy: . . BULKY, CLUMSY, AWKWARD, HULKING, UNGAINLY, PONDEROUS, CUMBERSOME

unwilling: . . . . LOTH, LOATH, AVERSE, RELUCTANT

unwind: . . . RAVEL, UNCOIL, UNREEL, UNROLL, UNTANGLE

unwise: . . . . . INANE, SIMPLE, FOOLISH, UNSOUND, WITLESS, TACTLESS, BRAINLESS, IMPOLITIC, IMPRUDENT, SENSELESS, IRRATIONAL

unwitting: . . . . . . INNOCENT, ACCIDENTAL, UNCONSCIOUS

unwonted: . . . RARE, UNUSED, UNUSUAL, UNCOMMON, INFREQUENT

unworthy: . . . . BENEATH, SHAMEFUL, UNSEEMLY, DESPICABLE, UNDESERVED, UNDESERVING

unwrinkled: . . . . . . SMOOTH

unwritten: . . . ORAL, BLANK, VOCAL, VERBAL
law: . . CUSTOM, TRADITION

unyielding: . . . . . SET, FAST, FIRM, GRIM, HARD, IRON, RIGID, STERN, STIFF, STONY, FROZEN, STEELY, ADAMANT, OBDURATE, STUBBORN, INELASTIC, OBSTINATE, UNBENDING, DETERMINED, INEXORABLE

up: . . . . . BUSY, OVER, RISE, ABOVE, ALOFT, ASTIR, RAISE, ACTIVE, SUCCESS
and-coming: . . PROMISING
and down: . . . . ERECT, UNEVEN, UPRIGHT,

VERTICAL, IRREGULAR, UNDULATING
in arms: . . . ANGRY, IRATE
to date: . . . NEW, MODERN, STYLISH, FASHIONABLE

upbraid: . . . . . TWIT, ABUSE, BLAME, CHIDE, SCOLD, SCORE, ACCUSE, REBUKE, CENSURE, REPROVE, REPROACH

upbringing: . . . . . BREEDING, TRAINING

upend: . . . . INVERT

upgrade: . . . . . RAISE, SLOPE, ASCENT, INCLINE, INCREASE, PROMOTION

upheaval: . . STORM, REVOLT, AGITATION, CATACLYSM, COMMOTION, CONVULSION

uphill: . . . . . RISING, TIRING, ASCENDING, DIFFICULT, LABORIOUS

uphold: . . . AID, ABET, BACK, BEAR, FAVOR, RAISE, DEFEND, SECOND, CONFIRM, SUPPORT, SUSTAIN, CONSERVE, MAINTAIN, ENCOURAGE

upkeep: . . . . . COST, REPAIR, SUPPORT, MAINTAIN, MAINTENANCE

uplift: . . . . ERECT, RAISE, TOWER, ELEVATE, IMPROVE, UPHEAVAL, ELEVATION

upon: . . . . . . ON, OER, OVER, ATOP, ABOUT, ABOVE, TOUCHING, CONCERNING

upper: . . BUNK, OVER, VAMP, ABOVE, BERTH, HIGHER, SUPERIOR
air: . . . . . . ETHER, OZONE
case: . . . . CAPITAL
class: . . . . . ELITE, SENIOR
hand: . . . LEAD, MASTERY, ADVANTAGE

uppermost: . . . . FIRST, DOMINANT

uppish/uppity: . . . . . PROUD, HAUGHTY, SNOBBISH, ARROGANT

upright: . . GOOD, JUST, TRUE, ERECT, MORAL, PIANO, RIGHT,

HONEST, SQUARE, SINCERE, STRAIGHT, VERTICAL, VIRTUOUS, HONORABLE

uprising: . . . . . RIOT, ASCENT, MUTINY, PUTSCH, REVOLT, ASCENDING, COMMOTION, REBELLION

uproar: . . . . DIN, RIOT, ROUT, BABEL, BRAWL, NOISE, BEDLAM, BUSTLE, CLAMOR, FRACAS, HUBBUB, RACKET, RUCKUS, TUMULT, FERMENT, TURMOIL, OUTBREAK, BROUHAHA, COMMOTION, DISTURBANCE

uproot: . . . DIG, GRUB, STUB, SUPPLANT, ERADICATE, EXTIRPATE, EXTERMINATE

upset: . . . . . IRK, COUP, KEEL, RILE, DEFEAT, TOPPLE, CAPSIZE, CONFUSE, DISTURB, PERVERT, QUARREL, REVERSE, SUBVERT, DISORDER, DISTRESS, OVERTURN, DISCOMFIT, EMBARRASS, OVERTHROW, PERTURBED

upshot: . . . . . . END, RESULT, SEQUEL, OUTCOME, CONCLUSION

upstage: . . . . . SNUB, ALOOF, OFFISH, SNOOTY, BACKWARD, OUTSHINE, SNOBBISH, CONCEITED

upstart: . . . . SNOB, PARVENU

upsurge: . . BOOM, INCREASE, INFLATION

upward: . . . . . MORE, OVER, ABOVE, LOFTY, AIRWARD, SKYWARD, INCREASE, ASCENDING

uranic: . . . . CELESTIAL, HEAVENLY

urban: . . . . . CIVIC, OPPIDAN

urbane: . . . . . CIVIL, SUAVE, POLITE, SMOOTH, AFFABLE, ELEGANT, REFINED, POLISHED, COURTEIOUS

urchin: . . . . . BOY, ELF, IMP, TAD, ARAB, BRAT, CHILD, GAMIN, HEDGEHOG, YOUNGSTER

uredo: . . . HIVES, URTICARIA

urge: . . DUN, EGG, PLY, SUE, YEN, COAX, GOAD, PROD, PUSH, SPUR, DRIVE, FORCE, HURRY, IMPEL, PLEAD, PRESS, ALLEGE, COMPEL, DEMAND, EXCITE, EXHORT, INCITE, INDUCE, INSIST, ANIMATE, ENTREAT, IMPULSE, PROVOKE, SOLICIT, ADVOCATE, PERSUADE, IMPORTUNE, INFLUENCE, STIMULATE

urgency: . . . . . NEED, HASTE, HURRY, CRISIS, STRESS, EXIGENCY, PRESSURE, INSISTENCE

urgent: . . . . . . HOT, GRAVE, EXIGENT, CRITICAL, PRESSING, IMPORTANT, INSISTENT

urn: . . . . . JAR, BURY, EWER, KIST, VASE, GRAVE, STEEN, VESSEL, OSSUARY, PITCHER, SAMOVAR, CONTAINER, JARDINIERE

shaped: . . . . . . URCEOLATE

urticaria: . . . . HIVES, UREDO

usable: . . . . FIT, AVAILABLE, PRACTICAL, CONVENIENT, FUNCTIONAL

usage: . . WONT, HABIT, IDIOM, CUSTOM, METHOD, CONDUCT, MANNERS, UTILITY, BEHAVIOR, PRACTICE, TREATMENT, CONVENTION

use: . . . . . TRY, HIRE, WONT, APPLY, AVAIL, HABIT, SPEND, TREAT, VALUE, WIELD, CUSTOM, EMPLOY, EXPEND, OCCUPY, BENEFIT, CONSUME, EXHAUST, PURPOSE, SERVICE, UTILTY, ACCUSTOM, EXERCISE, FUNCTION, PRACTICE, HABITUATE, TREATMENT

as example: . . . . CITE

up: . . . . TIRE, SPEND, EXPEND, CONSUME, DEPLETE, EXHAUST, EAROUT

wastefully: . . . . . FRITTER, SQUANDER, DISSIPATE

used: . . . . SECONDHAND

useful: . . . . . . GOOD, UTILE, HELPFUL, PRACTICAL, BENEFICIAL, PROFITABLE, SERVICEABLE

useless: . . IDLE, VAIN, FUTILE, OTIOSE, INUTILE, HOPELESS, NEEDLESS, FRUITLESS, WORTHLESS, INEFFECTUAL

usher: . . . . LEAD, GUIDE, ESCORT, HERALD, CONDUCT, FORERUN, PRECEDE, INTRODUCE, PERCURSOR, DOORKEEPER

usual: . . . COMMON, NORMAL, WONTED, AVERAGE, GENERAL, REGULAR, TYPICAL, FREQUENT, HABITUAL, ORDINARY, ORTHODOX, CUSTOMARY, ACCUSTOMED, PREVAILING

usurer: . . . SHARK, SHYLOCK, VAMPIRE, MONEYLENDER

usurp: . . . . TAKE, SEIZE, ASSUME, ACCROACH, ARROGATE

utensil: . . . . POT, PAN, TOOL, SIEVE, GRATER, VESSEL, SKILLET, COLLANDER, IMPLEMENT

uterus: . . . . . WOMB, MATRIX

utile: . . . USEFUL, PRACTICAL, PROFITABLE

utilitarian: . . PLAIN, USEFUL, ECONOMIC, PRACTICAL, FUNCTIONAL

utility: . . USE, AVAIL, PROFIT, BENEFIT, SERVICE

utilize: . . . . . . USE, EMPLOY

utmost: . . . . END, BEST, LAST, FINAL, EXTREME, MAXIMUM, FARTHEST, GREATEST, REMOTEST, UTTERMOST

Utopia: . . SHANGRI-LA, EDEN

Utopian: . . . IDEAL, EDENIC, IDEALIST, VISIONARY, CHIMERICAL

utricle: . . . . . . SAC, VESICLE

utter: . . . . SAY, BLAT, EMIT, GASP, PRAY, RAIL, RANK, TELL, VENT, BLURT, DRAWL, FINAL, ISSUE, SHEER, SPEAK, SPILL, SPOUT, STARK, STATE, TOTAL, VOICE, ASSERT, BROACH, ENTIRE, MUMBLE, REVEAL, WARBLE, DIVULGE, EXPRESS, EXTREME, ITERATE, ABSOLUTE, COMPLETE, DISCLOSE, ENUNCIATE, PRONOUNCE, ARTICULATE

utterance: . . . . GAB, ORDER, DICTUM, SPEECH, REQUEST, COMMAND, EFFUSION, QUESTION, STATEMENT, EXPRESSION

utterly: . . . . . FULLY, STARK, TOTALLY, ENTIRELY, ABSOLUTELY, COMPLETELY

uttermost: . . . FINAL, UTMOST, EXTREME, OUTMOST

uxorial: . . . . WIFELY

V

V: *Greek:* . . . . UPSILON
Hebrew: . . . . VAV
shaped cut: . . . . . . NOTCH
shaped piece: . . . . PIE, WEDGE
symbol: . . . . VICTORY

vacancy: . . . . . . GAP, BLANK, BREAK, CHASM, SPACE, CAVITY, HOLLOW, INTERIM, OPENING, VACUITY, EMPTINESS, INTERSTICE

vacant: . . . FREE, IDLE, OPEN, VOID, BLANK, EMPTY, BARREN, DEVOID, HOLLOW, LONELY, LACKING, LEISURE, VACUOUS, WANTING, UNFILLED, DISENGAGED, UNOCCUPIED, UNTENANTED

vacate: . . QUIT, VOID, ANNUL, EMPTY, LEAVE, ABANDON, ABOLISH, ABDICATE, ABROGATE, EVACUATE

vacation: . . . . . REST, LEAVE, SPELL, OUTING, RECESS, HOLIDAY, LEISURE, RESPITE, FURLOUGH

vaccinate: . . . . . . INOCULATE

vaccine: . . . . . SERA, SERUM, VIRUS

vaccillate: . . . SWAY, WAVER, FALTER, SEESAW, TEETER, TOTTER, FLUTTER, STAGGER, HESITATE, FLUCTUATE

vacuity: . . . . VOID, VACUUM, INANITY, VACANCY, EMPTINESS

vacuous: . . DULL, IDLE, VOID, BLANK, EMPTY, INANE, STUPID, UNFILLED, SENSELESS

vacuum: . . . . VOID

vagabond: . . . . . BUM, VAG, HOBO, ROVER, SCAMP, TRAMP, RASCAL, TRUANT, DRIFTER, NOMADIC, VAGRANT, WAYWARD, BOHEMIAN, DRIFTING, WANDERER, ITINERANT, SHIFTLESS, WANDERING

vagary: . . . . . ROAM, WHIM, CAPER, FANCY, FREAK, JAUNT, STRAY, TRICK, BREACH, NOTION, ODDITY, RAMBLE, WHIMSY, CAPRICE, RAMBLING, DEPARTURE, WANDERING, DIGRESSION

vagrant: . . . . . see **vagabond**

vague: . . . DIM, DARK, HAZY, LOOSE, MISTY, OBSCURE, SHADOWY, SKETCHY, UNFIXED, VAGRANT, CONFUSED, NEBULOUS, VAGABOND, AMBIGUOUS, UNCERTAIN, WANDERING, INDEFINITE, INDISTINCT, INTANGIBLE

vain: . . . IDLE, SMUG, EMPTY, PETTY, PROUD, FUTILE, HOLLOW, OTIOSE, SNOOTY, FOOLISH, STUCKUP, USELESS, CONCEITED, FRUITLESS, UNAVAILING

valance: . . . DRAPE, CURTAIN, DRAPERY, HANGING

vale: . . . . DALE, DEAN, DELL, GLEN, ADIEU, GLADE, DINGLE, VALLEY, FAREWELL

valediction: . . . . ADIEU, GOODBY, ADDRESS, FAREWELL

valedictory: . . . . . . ORATION

valentine: . . . . . CARD, GIFT, LOVE, GREETING, SWEETHEART

valet: . . . . DRESSER, ATTENDANT, MANSERVANT

valiant: . . . . . . BOLD, BRAVE, HEROIC, STRONG, STURDY, INTREPID, STALWART

valid: . . GOOD, TRUE, LEGAL, SOUND, COGENT, LAWFUL, BINDING, TELLING, FORCIBLE, AUTHENTIC

validate: . . . . . SEAL, AFFIRM, CONFIRM, ESTABLISH, AUTHORIZE

valise: . . . . . BAG, CASE, GRIP, SATCHEL, BAGGAGE, SUITCASE

valley: . . . DIP, DALE, DEAN, DELL, GLEN, VALE, WADI, BASIN, GORGE, GULLY, SWALE, WADDY, CANADA, CANYON, COMBE, COOMB, COULEE, GULCH, DINGLE, HOLLOW, RAVINE, TROUGH, DEPRESSION

valor: . . . . . . ARETE, MERIT, VALUE, WORTH, VIRTUE, BRAVERY, COURAGE, HEROISM, PROWRESS, VALUATION, DISTINCTION

valuable: . . . . . DEAR, ASSET, COSTLY, USEFUL, WORTHY, PRECIOUS, EXCELLENT, IMPORTANT, TREASURED, WORTHWHILE

value: . . . . USE, COST, RATE, CHEAP, PRICE, PRIZE, WORTH, ASSESS, ASSIZE, EQUITY, ESTEEM, EXTEND, ACCOUNT, APPRIZE, AVERAGE, CHERISH, COMPUTE, RESPECT, UTILITY,

APPRISE, ESTIMATE, EVALUATE, TREASURE, INVENTORY, APPRECIATE, IMPORTANCE

valve: . . . . TAP, COCK, GATE, DAMPER, FAUCET, OUTLET, PISTON, SPIGOT, PETCOCK, SHUTOFF, STOPCOCK, THROTTLE, FLOODGATE

vamoose: . . GO, LAM, SCUT, LEAVE, SCRAM, DECAMP, DEPART, SKIDDOO

vamp: . . . . . . PATCH, REPAIR, SEDUCE, BEGUILE, CONCOCT, FABRICATE, IMPROVISE

vampire: . . . . . . BAT, SIREN, LAMIA, ALUKAH, USURER, SEDUCER, BLACKMAILER, BLOODSUCKER, EXTORTIONER

van: . . . . . FORE, LEAD, SAIL, WING, FRONT, LORRY, TRUCK, WAGON, CARAVAN, FOURGON, VEHICLE, FOREWARD, FOREFRONT

vandal: . . . . . HUN, SARACEN, HOOLIGAN, PLUNDERER

vandalize: . . . . MAR, TRASH, DEFACE

vandyke: . . . BEARD, COLLAR, GOATEE, ARTIST

vane: . . . . ARM, WEB, WING, BLADE, FEATHER, VEXILLUM, WEATHERCOCK

vanguard: . . . . FRONT

vanish: . . . . FADE, MELT, CLEAR, SCATTER, DISSOLVE, EVANESCE, DISAPPEAR

vanity: . . . . . . PRIDE, EGOISM, CONCEIT, EGOTISM, FUTILITY, IDLENESS, VAINGLORY

vanquish: . . GET, WIN, BEAT, BEST, LICK, ROUT, EXPEL, FLOOR, DEFEAT, EXPUGN, MASTER, SUBDUE, CONFUTE, CONQUER, OVERCOME, SUPPRESS, SURMOUNT, OVERTHROW, SUBJUGATE

vantage: . . . . . GAIN, COIGN, CHANCE, PROFIT, ADVANTAGE, PERQUISITE

vapid: . . . . DRY, DULL, FLAT, PALL, INANE, STALE, TRITE, JEJUNE, INSIPID, LIFELESS, POINTLESS, TASTLESS, FLAVORLESS, SPIRITLESS, UNEXCITING

vapor: . . . GAS, BRAG, FUME, HAZE, MIST, REEK, SMOG, BOAST, BRUME, CLOUD, SMOKE, STEAM, BREATH, NIMBUS, EXHAUST, HALITUS, BLUSTER, CONTRAIL

vaporous: . . . FUNNY, FOGGY, MISTY, HALITOUS, FLEETING

vaquero: . . . . COWBOY

variable: . . . . FLUX, CHOPPY, FICKLE, FITFUL, PROTEAN, MUTABLE, ROLLING, UNEQUAL, VARIANT, VARYING, ABERRANT, FLOATING, UNSTABLE, UNSTEADY, VOLATILE, IRREGULAR, UNCERTAIN, CAPRICIOUS, CHANGEABLE, FLUCTUATING

variation: . . . . TURN, ERROR, SHADE, CHANGE, SWITCH, CYCLING, HETERISM, MUTATION, DEVIATION, TOLERANCE

varicolored: . . . . . MOTLEY, MOTTLED, DIVERSIFIED

varicose: . . . VARIS, SWOLLEN, DILATED, ENLARGED

varied: . . . DAEDAL, SEVERAL, VARIANT, VARIOUS, MANIFOLD, VARIGATED

variegate: . . . . . . DIVERSIFY

variegated: . . . . PIED, SHOT, DAEDAL, MOTLEY, DAPPLED, FLECKED, MOTTLED, PIEBALD, SPECKLED

variety: . . . . KIND, SORT, BREED, CLASS, COLOR, SPECIES, DIVERSITY, DIFFERENCE

variola: . . . . SMALLPOX

various: . . . . . . MANY, DIVERS, SUNDRY, DIVERSE, SEVERAL, MANIFOLD, DIFFERENT

varlet: . . BOY, PAGE, KNAVE, RASCAL, COISTREL, SCOUNDREL

varnish: . . . . . SPAR, GLOSS, JAPAN, ENAMEL, LACQUER, SHELLAC(K), EMBELLISH

vary: . . . . ALTER, SHIFT, CHANGE, DIFFER, MODIFY, SWERVE, DEVIATE, DISSENT, DIVERGE, DISAGREE, ALTERNATE, DIVERSIFY, FLUCTUATE, OSCILLATE

vas: . . . . DUCT, VESSEL

vase: . . . . . JAR, URN, VASO, ASKOS, TAZZA, CRATER, DEINOS, KRATER, AMPHORA, POTICHE, JARDINIERE

vassal: . . . ESNE, SERF, LIEGE, SLAVE, VARLET, BONDMAN, SUBJECT, SERVANT

vast: . . . HUG, BROAD, GREAT, LARGE, COSMIC, UNTOLD, IMMENSE, OCEANIC, COLOSSAL, ENORMOUS, GIGANTIC, BOUNDLESS, EXTENSIVE, ENORMOUS

vat: . . (also see **barrel, tub, vessel**) BAC, FAT, PIT, TUB, TUN, BACK, BECK, CASK, COOM, GYLE, KEEL, KIER, TANK, COOMB, KEEVE, KIEVE, BARREL, KETTLE, VESSEL, CALDRON, CISTERN

vatic: . . INSPIRED, PROPHETIC

vaticinate: . . . . . . FORETELL, PREDICT, PROPHESY

vaticinator: . . SEER, ORACLE, PROPHET

vaudeville: . . . . REVUE, BURLESQUE, VARIETY(SHOW)

vault: . . . . . BOX, PIT, ARCH, CAVE, COPE, COVE, DOME, JUMP, LEAP, OVER, ROOF, SAFE, TOMB, BOUND CROFT, CRYPT, CURVE, EMBOW, CAVERN, CELLAR, CRATER, CUPOLA, DONJON, GROTTO, HURDLE, SPRING, CEILING, CHAMBER, DUNGEON, OSSUARY, CATACOMB, DEPOSITORY

vaunt: . . . . . . BRAG, CROW, BOAST, ROOSE, AVAUNT, BLUSTER, GLORIFY, FLOURISH

veer: . CUT, DIP, YAW, SLEW, SLUE, SWAY, TACK, TURN, ALTER, SHEER, SHIFT, BROACH, CAREEN, CHANGE, SWERVE, DEVIATE, DIGRESS

vegetable: . . PEA, YAM, BEAN, BEET, CORN, KALE, LEEK, OKRA, SASS, SOYA, CHARD, ONION, PLANT, CARROT, CELERY, ENDIVE, LENTIL, LEGUME, PEPPER, POTATO, RADISH, SQUASH, TOMATO, TURNIP, CABBAGE, LETTUCE, PARSLEY, PARSNIP, PEASCOD, RHUBARB, SPINACH, BROCCOLI, CUCUMBER, EGGPLANT, RUTABAGA, ARTICHOKE, CAULIFLOWER

vegetation: . . . . . . GROWTH, VERDURE, VERDANT, GREENERY

vehement: . . . . HOT, ANGRY, EAGER, FIERY, KEEN, LOUD, YEDER, ARDENT, FERVID, FIERCE, FLASHY, HEATED, RAGING, STRONG, ANIMOSE, ANIMOUS, FERVENT, FURIOUS, INTENSE, VIOLENT, FORCEFUL, PASSIONATE

vehicle: . . . . . ARK, BUS, CAB, CAR, VAN, AUTO, CART, JEEP, SHAY, SLED, TAXI, WAIN, ARABA, BRAKE, BREAK, BUGGY, DILLY, LORRY, SEDAN, SULKY, TRAIN, TRUCK, WAGON, BARROW, CAMPER, CHARET, DIESEL, HANSOM, HEARSE, JITNEY, LANDAU, SLEDGE, SLEIGH, SURREY, TROIKA, CHARIOT, BICYCLE, CRUISER, ICEBOAT, MACHINE, MINIBUS, OMNIBUS, CARRIAGE, AMBULANCE, BUCKBOARD, AUTOMOBILE, CONVEYANCE, MOTORCYCLE, SNOWMOBILE, STAGECOACH,

veil: . . . . . DIM, CAUL, FILM, HIDE, MASK, WRAP, CLOAK, COVER, ORALE, SHADE, VELUM, BUMBLE, MASQUE, SCREEN, SHADOW, SHROUD, SOFTEN, CONCEAL, CURTAIN, CALYPTRA, DISGUISE, HEADRAIL, MANTILLA

vein: . . . . . . BED, RIB, DASH, LODE, MOOD, SEAM, VENA, WAVE, REEF, COSTA, LEDGE, SHADE, SMACK, TINGE, TOUCH, TREND, BLOOD, TENOR, CAVITY, STRAIN, STREAK, VESSEL, CHANNEL, CREVICE, FISSURE, JUGULAR, STRATUM

veld(t): . . . MEADOW, PLAINS, GRASSLAND

velleity: . . . . . . HOPE, WISH, DESIRE, VOLITION

vellicate: . . . . . PULL, PINCH, PLUCK, TWITCH, TITILATE

velocipede: . . . . . . BICYCLE, TRICYCLE, HANDCAR

velocity: . . . . . . PACE, RATE, SPEED, CELERITY, RAPIDITY, QUICKNESS, SWIFTNESS

velum: . . . . . VEIL, AWNING, PALATE

velvet: . . . . . . GAIN, PROFIT, VELOUR, SURPLUS, WINNINGS

velvety: . . . . . SOFT, SMOOTH, MELLOW

venal: . . . . VENOUS, CORRUPT, VENDIBLE, MERCENARY

vend: . . . . SELL, HAWK, MARKET, PEDDLE, PUBLISH, TRANSFER

vendetta: . . . . FEUD

vendible: . . . . VENAL, SAL(E)ABLE, MERCENARY, MARKETABLE

vendor: . . . SELLER, ALIENOR, MERCHANT, RETAILER, SALESMAN

veneer: . . . LAC, BURL, COAT, FACE, SHOW, GLAZE, GLOSS, JAPAN, LAYER, PLATE, ENAMEL, OVERLAY, COATING, FACING, VARNISH

venerable: . . . . . OLD, AGED, SAGE, HOARY, AUGUST, ANCIENT, ANTIQUE, CLASSIC, SACRED, PATRIARCH

venerate: . . . . FEAR, ADORE, REVERE, HALLOW, WORSHIP

veneration: . . . . AWE, FEAR, ESTEEM, HOMAGE, RESPECT, WORSHIP, DEVOTION, ADORATION, REVERENCE

venery: . . . . CHASE, HUNTING

vengeance: . . . . WRACK, WREAK, WRECK, AVENGE, WANION, REVENGE, REPRISAL, REQUITAL

vengeful: . . . . SPITEFUL, VINDICTIVE

venial: . . . . TRIVIAL, ALLOWABLE, EXCUSABLE, TOLERABLE, PARDONABLE

venom: . . BANE, GALL, SPITE, VIRUS, MALICE, POISON

venomous: . . TOXIC, ATTERN, DEADLY, SNAKEY, BANEFUL, NOXIOUS, SPITEFUL, VIPERINE, VIRULENT, MALICIOUS, MALIGNANT, POISONOUS

vent: . . . . DRAW, EMIT, EXIT, FLUE, HOLE, SLIT, EJECT, ISSUE, ESCAPE, OUTLET, FISSURE, OPENING, ORIFICE, PASSAGE, RELEASE, APERATURE, DISGORGE, EMISSION, DISCHARGE

ventilate: . . . . AIR, FAN, AERATE, EXPOSE, EXPRESS

ventilation: . . . . . . AERAGE, AIRING, BREATHING

ventilator: . . . . FAN, LOUVER, BLOWER

ventral: . . . BELLY, STERNAL, ABDOMINAL

venture: . . . TRY, DARE, RISK, WAGE, BRAVE, ESSAY, STAKE, WAGER, CHANCE, FLYER, FEELER, HAZARD, FLUTTER, ATTEMPT, TRESPASS, ADVENTURE, SPECULATE, ENTERPRISE

venturesome:... BOLD, RASH, RISKY, DARING, PARLOUS, FEARLESS, HEEDLESS, RECKLESS, TEMEROUS, AUDACIOUS, FOOLHARDY

veracious:... TRUE, HONEST, SINCERE, VERIDIC, FAITHFUL, ACCURATE, TRUTHFUL

veracity:.. TRUTH, HONESTY, ACCURACY, PRECISION, SINCERITY

veranda(h):.. LANAI, PORCH, STOEP, STOOP, LOGGIA, PIAZZA, BALCONY, GALLERY, PORTICO

verbal:...... ORAL, VOCAL, WORDY, SPOKEN, TALKATIVE, ARTICULATE

verbatim:... EXACT, DIRECT, VERBAL, ORALLY, LITERAL

verbiage:.. TALK, CHATTER, FUSTIAN, PROLIXITY, WORDINESS

verbose:... WINDY, WORDY, PROLIX, DIFFUSE, WORDISH, REDUNDANT

verboten:.... TABU, TABOO, FORBIDDEN

verdant:...... RAW, FRESH, GREEN, VIRID, IMMATURE, INNOCENT

verdict:..... WORD, ASSIZE, FINDING, OPINION, DECISION, JUDGMENT, DECISION

verdure:........ GREENERY, GREENNESS, VIRIDITY

verecund:.... SHY, MODEST, BASHFUL

verge:... LIP, RIM, ROD, TOP, EDGE, WAND, BOUND, BRINK, LIMIT, MARGE, POINT, RANGE, SCOPE, SHAFT, STAFF, STICK, TOUCH, BORDER, MARGIN, BOUNDRY, YARDLAND, EXTREMITY

verify:.. AVER, BACK, TEST, AUDIT, CHECK, PROVE, AFFIRM, ATTEST, SECOND, CERTIFY, CONFIRM, SUPPORT, MAINTAIN, ESTABLISH

verily:.... YEA, YES, AMEN, TRULY, CERTES, INDEED, PARDIE, REALLY, CERTAINLY

veritable:..... REAL, TRUE, ACTUAL, GOSPEL, HONEST, PROPER, GENUINE, AUTHENTIC

veritas:........... TRUTH

verity:...... FACT, TRUTH, REALITY

vermiform:.... LONG, THIN, SLENDER, WORM-LIKE, WORM-SHAPED

vermin:.. LICE, MICE, PEST, RATS, FILTH, FLEAS, FLIES, BEDBUGS, RODENTS, VARMINT, WEASEL

vernacular:... IDIOM, LINGO, COMMON, JARGON, PATOIS, VULGAR, DIALECT

vernal:...... MILD, WARM, FRESH, YOUNG, YOUTHFUL, SPRINGLIKE

versatile:... HANDY, FICKLE, MOBILE, FLEXILE, VARIABLE, MANY-SIDED, TALENTED

verse:.... EPIC, LINE, POEM, RIME, SONG, TURN, BLANK, METER, METRE, STAVE, STICH, RHYME, JINGLE, SONNET, STANZA, DIMETER, STICHOS, TRIPODY, DOGGEREL, LIMERICK

versed:..... ADEPT, BESEEN, ERUDITE, LEARNED, TURNED, SKILLED, FAMILIAR, PRACTICED, PROFICIENT

version:.. EDITION, TURNING, ACCOUNT, RENDITION, TRANSLATION

versus:... VS., CON, AGAINST

vertebra:.... AXIS, ATLAS, DORSAL, LUMBAR, SACRAL, SPONDYL

vertebrate:... FISH, REPTILE, MAMMAL, BACKBONED

vertex:.. TOP, APEX, CROWN, SUMMIT, ZENITH

vertical:.... APEAK, ERECT, PLUMB, SHEER, ABRUPT,

HEIGHT, SUMMIT, UPRIGHT,
PERPENDICULAR

verticil: . . . . WHORL

vertiginous: . . . DIZZY, GIDDY,
WHIRLING

vertigo: . . . . DINUS, MEGRIM,
DIZZINESS, GIDDINESS

verve: . . . . PEP, DASH, ELAN,
ARDOR, VIGOR, BOUNCE,
SPIRIT, ENERGY, VIVACITY,
ENTHUSIASM

very: . . . SO, TOO, BIG, EVEN,
FELL, FULL, REAL, SAME, TRES,
TRUE, UNCO, ASSI, AWFUL,
MOLTO, QUITE, SUPER, TRULY,
UTTER, ACTUAL, MIGHTY,
PROPER, REALLY, DIMOLTO,
EXACTLY, GENUINE, GREATLY,
PRECISE, ABSOLUTE, COMPLETE,
ESPECIAL, PECULIAR, RIGHTFUL,
STRANGE, TRUTHFUL,
EXTREMELY, IDENTICAL

vesicle: . . . . SAC, BLEB, CELL,
CYST, BULLA, VESSEL, CAVITY,
BLISTER, BLADDER, UTRICLE

vesper: . . EVE, STAR, VENUS,
EVENING, EVENTIDE, HESPERUS

vespers: . . PRAYER, SERVICE,
EVENSONG

vessel: . CAN, COG, CUP, JAR,
KIT, MUG, PAN, POT, TUB, URN,
VAS, VAT, BARK, BELL, BOAT,
BOWL, BRIG, CASK, DISH,
DRUM, DUCT, EWER, FONT,
JUNK, OLLA, SHIP, TANK, TUBE,
VASE, VEIN, YAWL, AORTA,
BARGE, BASIN, BLOOD, CANAL,
CANOE, COGUE, CRAFT, CROCK,
CRUET, FLASK, GLASS, LAVER,
LINER, PHIAL, STEIN, ARTERY,
BARREL, BOILER, BOTTLE,
BUCKET, COFFIN, COOTIE,
CRATER, FLAGON, FIRKIN,
FLAGON, GALLEY, GOBLET,
KETTLE, KRATER, LATEEN,
PACKET, PATERA, RETORT,
SITULA, BALLOON, CISTERN,
CLIPPER, CRESSET, FRIGATE,
GABBARD, GABBART, PINNACE,

PITCHER, STEAMER, TANKARD,
TUMBLER, TRACHEA, UTENSIL,
YETLING, CANNIKAN, CRUCIBLE,
DECANTER, GALLEON,
SCHOONER, RECEPTACLE

vest: . . DRESS, ENDOW, GILET,
ACCRUE, BOLERO, CLOTHE,
INVEST, JACKET, JERKIN,
WESKIT, EMPOWER, GARMENT,
WAISTCOAT, UNDERSHIRT

vestal: . NUN, PURE, CHASTE,
VIRGIN(AL)

vestibule: . . . . HALL, ENTRY,
FOYER, LOBBY, PORCH,
ATRIUM, NARTEX, PASSAGE,
ANTEROOM, ENTRANCE

vestige: . . . . BIT, TAG, MARK,
SIGN, RELIC, SHRED, SMACK,
SPARK, TRACE, TRACK, UMBRA,
SHADOW, REMAINS, LEFTOVER,
TINCTURE

vestment: . . . (also see **dress**)
GARB, GEAR, GOWN, ROBE,
COTTA, ROCHET, GARMENT,
CLOTHING, COVERING,
HABILIMENT

ecclesiastic: . . ALB, ALBA,
COPE, ALBAE, AMICE,
EPHOD, FANON, MITER,
ORALE, STOLE, LAPPET,
PALIUM, SACCOS, CASSOCK,
MANIPLE, TUNICLE,
CHASUBLE, DALMATIC,
SURPLICE

ecclesiastic: . . . . ALB,
SURPLICE, CHASUBLE

vet(eran): . . . . OLDSTER,
TROUPER, EMERITUS,
HARDENED, OLDTIMER,
SEASONED, EXPERIENCED

veterinarian: . . . . . . LEECH,
DOCTOR, FARRIER

veto: . . . . . NIX, KILL, FORBID,
KIBOSH, DISALLOW, PROHIBIT,
DISAPPROVE

vex: . . . IRE, IRK, TEW, CARK,
CHAW, FASH, GALL, MIFF, RILE,
ROIL, ANGER, ANNOY, CHAFE,
HARRY, SPITE, TEASE, WORRY,

WRACK, BOTHER, HARASS,
MADDEN, MOLEST, NEEDLE,
NETTLE, OFFEND, PLAGUE,
AFFLICT, AGITATE, DISTURB,
PROVOKE, TORMENT, TROUBLE,
IRRITATE, ACERBATE,
INFURIATE

vexatious: .... MEAN, SORE,
NASTY, PESKY, ACHING,
ANNOYING, IRKSOME,
CUMBROUS, UNTOWARD,
IRRITABLE, PESTILENT,
TROUBLESOME

viaduct: ... BRIDGE, TRESTLE

vial: .. AMPUL, CRUET, PHIAL,
AMPULE, BOTTLE, CASTER,
AMPOULE

viand: .... DIET, DISH, FARE,
FOOD, EDIBLE, VICTUALS,
PROVISIONS

viator: .... TRAVELER,
WAYFARER

vibrant: ..... ALIVE, RINGY,
QUIVERING, RESONANT,
SONOROUS, VIGOROUS,
ENERGETIC

vibrate: ... JAR, WAG, BEAT,
DIRL, ROCK, TIRL, WHIR,
PULSE, QUAKE, SHAKE, SWING,
THROB, TRILL, WAVER,
LAUNCH, QUAVER, DINDLE,
QUIVER, SHIVER, THRILL,
SHIMMY, RESOUND, RESONATE,
TREMBLE, FLUTTER,
FLUCTUATE, OSCILLATE,
VACILLATE

vibration: . DINGLE, QUAVER,
QUIVER, THRILL, TREMOR,
FLUTTER, TEMBLOR, TREMELO,
FREMITUS, OSCILLATION,
VACILLATION

vicar: ..... PROXY, DEPUTY,
PRIEST, MINISTER, CLERGYMAN,
SUBSTITUTE, VICEGERENT

vice: .. SIN, EVIL, GRIP, HOLD,
CRIME, FAULT, FORCE, GRASP,
PROXY, STEAD, TAINT, DEFECT,
BLEMISH, FAILING, INSTEAD,
SQUEEZE, WEAKNESS, INIQUITY,

DEPRAVITY, ADDICTION,
CORRUPTION, SUBSTITUTE,
WICKEDNESS

vicegerent: .. VICAR, DEPUTY

viceroy: .... NABOB, NAZIM,
EXARCH, REGENT, SATRAP,
PROVOST, BUTTERFLY,
VICEGERENT

vicinity: . REGION, ENVIRONS,
NEARNESS, PROXIMITY,
NEIGHBORHOOD

vicious: ..... BAD, ILL, EVIL,
FOUL, MEAN, UGLY, VILE,
WICKED, IMMORAL, NOXIOUS,
DEBASING, DEPRAVED,
SPITEFUL, DANGEROUS,
DEFECTIVE, DISSOLUTE,
MALICIOUS, MALIGNANT,
NEFARIOUS, MONSTROUS

vicissitude: ...... CHANGE,
MUTATION

victim: .. DUPE, GOAT, GULL,
LAMB, MARK, PREY, QUARRY,
SUCKER

victor: ... CAPTOR, WINNER,
BANGSTER, UNBEATEN,
CONQUEROR

victory: .... WIN, PALM,
LAUREL, MASTERY, SUCCESS,
TRIUMPH, CONQUEST,
SUPREMACY

victual(s): ...... EAT, FEED,
FOOD, GRUB, VIANDS, VITTLES,
PROVISIONS, NOURISHMENT

vie: ..... RUN, COPE, RIVAL,
OPPOSE, STRIVE, COMPETE,
CONTEND, CONTEST, EMULATE,
STRUGGLE

view: ... AIM, EYE, KEN, SEE,
VUE, GOAL, LOOK, SCAN,
SCAPE, SCENE, SIGHT, SLANT,
VISTA, WATCH, ADMIRE,
ASPECT, BEHOLD, BELIEF,
NOTION, OBJECT, REGARD,
SURVEY, VISION, EXAMINE,
GLIMPSE, INSPECT, OPINION,
PICTURE, PROFILE, WITNESS,
ATTITUDE, PANORAMA,
PROSPECT

vigil: .. EVE, WAKE, WATCH, GUARD

vigilant: ..... AGOG, WARY, ALERT, AWARE, AWAKE, CHARY, SHARP, CAREFUL, WAKEFUL, CAUTIOUS, WATCHFUL, ATTENTIVE

vigor: .. PEP, SAP, VIM, DASH, SNAP, ZEAL, ARDOR, DRIVE, FLUSH, FORCE, VERVE, POWER, ENERGY, HEALTH, SPRING, STARCH, IMPETUS, POTENCY, STAMINA, STRENGTH, VITALITY, INTENSITY

vigorous: ..... HALE, SPRY, EAGER, HARDY, LUSTY, HEARTY, LIVELY, ROBUST, STRONG, STURDY, CORDIAL, ATHELETIC, FORCEFUL, MUSCULAR, ENERGETIC, STRENUOUS

Viking: ...... ERIC, PIRATE, ROVER, NORSEMAN

vile: ...... BAD, LOW, BASE, FOUL, MEAN, RANK, CHEAP, SLIMY, ABJECT, COARSE, FILTHY, IMPURE, ODIOUS, SINFUL, SORDID, SCURVY, WICKED, BESTIAL, CORRUPT, DEBASED, IGNOBILE, VICIOUS, DEPRAVED, LOATHSOME, NEFARIOUS, OBNOXIOUS, OFFENSIVE, REPULSIVE

vilify: .. ABUSE, LIBEL, STAIN, DEFAME, MALIGN, REVILE, ASPERSE, BLACKEN, CHEAPEN, DEGRADE, SLANDER, TRADUCE, BELITTLE, DISGRACE, DISHONOR, DISPARGE, CALUMNIATE, DEPRECIATE

village: .... GAV, MIR, REW, BURG, DORP, HOME, KAIK, STAD, WICK, BOURG, KRAAL, THORP, TOWN, VICUS, BARRIO, BUSTEE, CASTLE, HAMLET, PUEBLO, THORPE, BOROUGH, CASERIO, CLACHAN, VILLAKIN, SETTLEMENT

villain: .. LOUT, SERF, CHURL, DEMON, DEVIL, FELON, KNAVE, ROUGE, SCAMP, RASCAL, SCELERAT, CRIMINAL, MISCREANT, SCOUNDREL

villainous: ...... BAD, LOW, BASE, EVIL, MEAN, VILE, VULGAR, WICKED, CRIMINAL, DEPRAVED, FLAGRANT, WRETCHED, DASTARDLY, FELONIOUS, DETESTABLE

villainy: .. CRIME, KNAVERY, DEPRAVITY

villatic: ..... RURAL, RUSTIC

villein: ... CARL, ESNE, SERF, CHURL, COTTER, TENANT, PEASANT, BONDMAN

vim: .. PEP, ZIP, ELAN, FORCE, VIGOR, ENERGY, GINGER, SPIRIT, STRENGTH

vindicate: .... FREE, CLEAR, RIGHT, ACQUIT, ASSERT, AVENGE, DEFEND, EXCUSE, UPHOLD, ABSOLVE, DERAIGN, JUSTIFY, PROPUGN, REVENGE, SUPPORT, SUSTAIN, MAINTAIN, EXCULPATE, EXONERATE

vindictive: .... HOSTILE, PUNITIVE, SPITEFUL, VENGEFUL, MALICIOUS

vinegar: .. VIM, ACID, EISEL, ACETUM, ALEGAR

bottle: .. CRUET, CASTER, CASTOR

dregs: .... MOTHER

preserve in: ..... PICKLE, MARINATE

vinegary: .. SOUR, ACETOSE, CRABBED, ILL-TEMPERED

vintage: .. OLD, CROP, WINE, CUVEE, MODEL, CHOICE, ARCHAIC, CLASSIC, OUTMODED

violate: .... ERR, SIN, FLAW, RAPE, ABUSE, BREAK, FORCE, SPOIL, WRONG, BETRAY, BROACH, DEFILE, DEFOUL, INJURE, INSULT, INVADE, OFFEND, RAVISH, CORRUPT, DEBAUCH, DISOBEY, DISTURB,

FALSIFY, INFRACT, OUTRAGE,
POLLUTE, PROFANE, TRESPASS,
DEFLOWER, DISHONOR,
INFRINGE, MISTREAT,
DESECRATE

violation: ... CRIME, ERROR,
BREACH, INFRACTION,
DESECRATION

violence: ...... FURY, RAGE,
FORCE, STORM, BENSIL,
FERVOR, HUBRIS, ASSAULT,
BENSAIL, STRESS, OUTRAGE,
FEROCITY, SEVERITY,
DESECRATION

violent: ... HOT, HIGH, LOUD,
WILD, ACUTE, FIERY, GREAT,
HEADY, HEFTY, RABID, ROUGH,
SHARP, VIVID, FIERCE, MANIAC,
MIGHTY, RAGING, SAVAGE,
SEVERE, STORMY, STRONG,
DRASTIC, EXTREME, FURIOUS,
HOTSPUR, INTENSE, RAMMISH,
RAMPANT, TEARING, FLAGRANT,
FORCEFUL, FORCIBLE,
FRENETIC, MANIACAL,
VEHEMENT, PHRENETIC,
TURBULENT

violin: .... ALTO, BASS, VIOL,
CELLO, VIOLA, FIDDLE

VIP: .... BIGSHOT, NOTABLE,
TOPBRASS, CELEBRITY

viper: .. ASP, ADDER, SNAKE,
REPTILE, CERASTES,
BUSHMASTER, FER-DE-LANCE,
COPPERHEAD, RATTLESNAKE

viperous: .... SPITEFUL,
VENOMOUS, MALICIOUS

virago: ...... FURY, RANDY,
SCOLD, VIXEN, AMAZON,
BELDAM, HELLCAT, TERMAGANT

virgin: ... NEW, NUN, MAID,
PURE, FIRST, FRESH, CHASTE,
MAIDEN, MODEST, VESTAL,
INITIAL, MADONNA, SPINSTER,
UNALLOYED, UNDEFILED,
UNSULLIED, UNTOUCHED

virginal: ..... PURE, INTACT,
SPINET, MAIDENLY,
HARPSICHORD

viridity: .. YOUTH, VERDURE,
VERDANCY, FRESHNESS,
GREENNESS

virile: ...... MALE, MACHO,
MANLY, FORCEFUL, POWERFUL,
VIGOROUS, MASCULINE,
MASTERFUL

virtual: ... IMPLICIT, LITERAL,
PRACTICAL

virtually: .... BUT, ALMOST,
NEARLY, MORALLY,
PRACTICALLY, LITERALLY

virtue: ...... THEW, ARETE,
GRACE, MERIT, VALOR,
BOUNTY, PURITY, CHARITY,
PROBITY, QUALITY, CHASTITY,
EFFICACY, GOODNESS,
MORALITY, EXCELLENCE

virtues: ...... HOPE, FAITH,
CHARITY, JUSTICE, PRUDENCE,
FORTITUDE, TEMPERANCE

virtuoso: ... ARTIST, EXPERT,
SAVANT, MAESTRO, AESTHETE,
ESTHETIC, CONNOISSEUR

virtuous: ...... GOOD, PURE,
BRAVE, MORAL, PIOUS,
CHASTE, HONEST, MODEST,
GODDARD, UPRIGHT, VALIANT,
VALOROUS, RIGHTEOUS

virulent: ..... RANK, ACRID,
RABID, BITTER, MALIGN,
POTENT, HOSTILE, NOXIOUS,
SPITEFUL, DEADLY, VENOMOUS,
MALIGNANT, INFECTIOUS

virus: ..... VENOM, POISON,
VACCINE, PATHOGEN

vis: ... FORCE, POWER, VIGOR,
STRENGTH

a-vis: ...... SEAT, SOFA,
CARRIAGE, OPPOSITE,
FACE TO FACE

visage: ... MAP, FACE, LOOK,
SHOW, IMAGE, ASPECT,
PORTRAIT, APPEARANCE,
COUNTENANCE

viscera: ...... GUTS, VITALS,
ENTRAILS, INNARDS, INTESTINES

viscid: .... GUMMY, STICKY,
SIRUPY, VISCOUS

viscous: .. LIMY, ROPY, SISY, GLUEY, GOBBY, GUMMY, PASTY, TARRY, THICK, MUCOUS, VISCID, STICKY, SYRUPY

vise: ... DIAL, CLAM, CLAMP, CRAMP, WINCH

visible: ..... SEEN, EXTANT, VISUAL, EVIDENT, GLARING, OBVIOUS, APPARENT, MANIFEST, CONSPICUOUS, PERCEPTIBLE, DISCERNIBLE

vision: ...... EYE, DREAM, FANCY, IMAGE, SIGHT, BEAUTY, MIRAGE, SEEING, FANTASY, IMAGINE, PICTURE

defect: .. ANOPIA, MYOPIA, DIPLOPIA

visionary: ...... FEY, AERY, AIRY, WILD, IDEAL, UNREAL, DREAMER, FANTAST, LAPUTAN, UTOPIAN, ACADEMIC, DELUSIVE, IDEALIST, QUIXOTIC, ROMANTIC, FANTASTIC, ILLUSIONIST, IMAGINARY, IMPRACTICAL

visit: .... DO, GAM, SEE, VIS, CALL, CHAT, STAY, APPLY, HAUNT, ASSAIL, ATTEND, AFFLICT, FREQUENT, INFLICT, INSPECT, SOJOURN, CONVERSE, INSPECTION

visitation: ...... DISASTER, AFFLICTION

visitor: .... GUEST, CALLER, COMPANY, VISITANT

visor: .. BRIM, MASK, VIZARD, EYE-SHADE

vista: .... VIEW, SCENE, OUTLOOK, PANORAMA, PROSPECT, PERSPECTIVE

visual: ..... OPTIC, OCULAR, SCOPIC, VISIBLE, OPTICAL, PERCEPTIBLE

visualize: ..... SEE, FANCY, IDEATE, IMAGINE, PICTURE, CONCEIVE, ENVISAGE, IMAGINE

vita: .... LIFE

vital: .... KEY, LIVE, BASIC, CHIEF, FATAL, DEADLY, LIVELY, LIVING, MORTAL, MOVING, VIABLE, ANIMATE, CAPITAL, EXIGENT, VIGOROUS, ELEMENTAL, ENERGETIC, ESSENTIAL, IMPORTANT, NECESSARY, REQUISITE, IMPERATIVE

fluid: ...... SAP, BLOOD, LYMPH

organ: .... HEART, LUNG, LIVER

vitality: ..... SAP, VIM, LIFE, ZEST, ZING, GUSTO, JUICE, OOMPH, PULSE, PUNCH, VIGOR, BIOSIS, BREATH, ENERGY, POISON, HEALTH, PIZAZZ, STARCH, STRENGTH

vitalize: .... ACTIVATE, ENERGIZE, ANIMATE

vitellus: .... YOLK

vitiate: .. BEAT, BEND, SPOIL, TAINT, DEBASE, CANCEL, IMPAIR, POISON, WEAKEN, CORRUPT, DEPRAVE, PERVERT, POLLUTE, ADULTERATE, INVALIDATE

vitreous: .. GLASSY, HYALINE, HYALOID

vitrify: ...... BAKE, GLAZE

vitriolic: .... SHARP, BITING, BITTER, CAUSTIC, MORDANT, SCATHING, VIRULENT, SARCASTIC

vituperate: ... RAIL, ABUSE, CURSE, SCOLD, BERATE, REVILE, CENSURE

vivacious: ...... GAY, AIRY, PERT, BRISK, CRISP, MERRY, ACTIVE, BREEZY, BRIGHT, LIVELY, BUOYANT, ZESTFUL, ANIMATED, SPIRITED, SPORTIVE, SPRIGHTLY

vivacity: .. BRIO, FIRE, DASH, ELAN, ARDOR, VERVE, VIGOR, GAIETY, GAYNESS, SPARKLE, LIVELINESS, ANIMATION

vivid: . . . . DEEP, KEEN, LIVE, RICH, CLEAR, FRESH, LURID, SHARP, ACTIVE, BRIGHT, LIVELY, STRONG, EIDETIC, FLAMING, GLOWING, GRAPHIC, INTENSE, COLORFUL, DISTINCT, DRAMATIC, STRIKING, BRILLIANT

vivify: . . . . ENDUE, FOMENT, REVIVE, ANIMATE, ENLIVEN, QUICKEN, INVIGORATE

vixen: . . . . . FOX, NAG, BARD, FURY, SCOLD, SHREW, VIRAGO, HELLCAT, TERMAGANT

viz: . . . . . TO-WIT, NAMELY, VIDELICET

vizard: . . . . . . MASK, VISOR, DISGUISE

vocabulary: . . . . WORDS, DICTION, LEXICON, GLOSSARY, WORDBOOK, DICTIONARY

vocal: . . SUNG, ORAL, VOWEL, FLUENT, VERBAL, SONANT, SPOKEN, UTTERED, VOICED, ELOQUENT, ARTICULATE

vocation: . . . . . CALL, WORK, TRADE, CAREER, MEITER, CALLING, BUSINESS, FOLLOWING, EMPLOYMENT, OCCUPATION, PROFESSION

vociferate: . . . . . CRY, BAWL, ROAR, SHOUT, UTTER, ASSERT, BELLOW, CLAMOR

vociferation: . . . . . CLAMOR, OUTCRY

vociferous: . . . LOUD, NOISY, BAWLING, BLATANT, BRAWLING, STRIDENT, TURBULENT, CLAMOROUS, BOISTEROUS

vogue: . . . . . CUT, FAD, TON, CHIC, MODE, RAGE, TURN, STYLE, CUSTOM, FASHION, PRACTICE, POPULARITY

voice: . . . . . SAY, VOX, EMIT, GIVE, HARP, VOTE, RUMOR, UTTER, CHOOSE, REPORT, SPEECH, STEVEN, TOUNGE, DIVULGE, EXPRESS, OPINION, ANNOUNCE, PROCLAIM, ARTICULATE

voiced: . . . . SONANT

voiceless: . . . . MUM, DUMB, MUTE, SURD, ATONIC, FLATED, SILENT, APHONIC, SPIRATE, APHONOUS, SPEECHLESS

void: . . . . . GAP, FREE, IDLE, LACK, MUTE, NULL, VAIN, WANT, ABYSS, ANNUL, BLANK, EJECT, EMPTY, LEAVE, SPACE, CANCEL, HOLLOW, REMOVE, VACANT, VACATE, VACUUM, INVALID, LACKING, NULLIFY, OPENING, USELESS, VACUITY, WANTING, EVACUATE, DISCHARGE, EMPTINESS, UNOCCUPIED

volant: . . . . . . AGILE, LIGHT, QUICK, FLYING, NIMBLE

volatile: . . . . . AIRY, ETHER, LIGHT, FICKLE, FLYING, LIVELY, VOLAGE, BUOYANT, ELASTIC, FLIGHTY, GASEOUS, MUTABLE, FLEETING, FUGITIVE, VAPOROUS, MERCURICAL, TRANSIENT, CAPRICIOUS

volition: . . . . . WILL, CHOICE, INTENT, VELLITY

volley: . . . . . BURST, CROWD, SALVO, FLIGHT, BARRAGE, COMPANY, PLATOON, FUSILLADE

voluble: . . . . . GLIB, WORDY, FLUENT, GARRULOUS, TAKATIVE, LOQUACIOUS

volume: . . . . . BOOK, BULK, MASS, SIZE, TOME, AMOUNT, CONTENT, CUBAGE, SCROLL, CAPACITY, DOCUMENT, FULLNESS, LOUDNESS, QUANTITY, STRENGTH, CUBATURE, AGGREGATE

of sound unit: . . . DECIBEL

voluminous: . . FULL, BULKY, LARGE

voluntary: . . . . FREE, FREELY, WILLFUL, WILLING, ELECTIVE, FREEWILL, UNFORCED,

OPTIONAL, WILLINGLY,
DELIBERATE, INTENTIONAL

volunteer: ... OFFER, ENLIST,
PROFFER, WORKER

voluptuary: .... SYBARITE,
HEDONIST, SENSUALIST

voluptuous: .... LYDIAN,
SULTRY, SENSUAL, LUSCIOUS,
SENSUOUS

volute: ...... TURN, HELIX,
WHORL, SCROLL, CILLERY,
SPIRALED

volution: ...... COIL, TURN,
TWIST, WHORL, ROLLING,
REVOLVING

vomit: .. BARF, BOKE, BOLK,
PUKE, SPEW, SPUE, BRAKE,
HEAVE, REACH, RETCH,
EMETIC, REJECT, REGORGE,
DISGORGE, REGURGITATE

vomiting: .... BOKE, EMESIS

voodoo: .. HEX, OBI, CHARM,
MAGIC, OBEAH, FETISH,
HOODOO, SORCERER,
WITCHCRAFT

voracious: .. EAGER, GREEDY,
HUNGRY, BULIMIC, ESURIANT,
EDACIOUS, RAVENOUS,
INSATIABLE, RAPACIOUS

voracity: ... GREED, BULIMIA,
EDACITY, RAPACITY

vortex: .. APEX, EDDY, GYRE,
SWIRL, WHIRL, TORNADO,
WHIRLPOOL, WHIRLWIND

votary: ... FAN, NUN, MONK,
ZEALOT, CELIBATE, DEVOTEE,
ADHERENT, FOLLOWER

vote: .. NO, AYE, CON, NAY,
PRO, YES, ANTI, POLL, ELECT,
GRACE, GRANT, ASSIGN,
BALLOT, CHOICE, DECLARE,
OPINION, SUFFRAGE,
PLEBISCITE, REFERENDUM,
FRANCHISE

voter: .... POLLER, ELECTOR,
BALLOTER, CHOOSER,
ASSENTOR, CONSTIUENT

vouch: .. VOW, AVER, BACK,
AFFIRM, ALLEGE, ASSURE,

ATTEST, SECOND, CERTIFY,
CONFIRM, DECLARE, ENDORSE,
RESOLVE, SPONSOR, SUPPORT,
WARRANT, ACCREDIT,
MAINTAIN, GUARANTEE

voucher: .... CHIT, COUPON,
TICKET, RECEIPT, WARRANT,
DEBENTURE

vouchsafe: ..... GIVE, SEND,
DEIGN, GRANT, YIELD, ASSURE,
BESTOW, BETEEM, CONCEDE,
GUARANTEE

vow: ...... LAY, VUM, BIND,
OATH, VOTE, SWEAR, BEHEST,
BEHIGHT, DEVOTE, PLEDGE,
DECLARE, PROMISE, DEDICATE,
ASSERTION

vox: .... VOICE

voyage: ...... TRIP, CRUISE,
TRAVEL, EXCURSION, JOURNEY,
PASSAGE

vs.: .... VERSUS

vulcanite: .. EBONITE, RUBBER

vulgar: .. LOW, LEWD, LOUD,
RUDE, CRUDE, GROSS, COARSE,
COMMON, SLANGY, BOORISH,
LOW-BRED, OBSCENE, POPULAR,
PROFANE, CHURLISH,
ORDINARY, PLEBEIAN,
UNREFINED

vulnerable: .. WEAK, NAKED,
LIABLE, EXPOSED, PREGNABLE,
UNTENABLE, ASSAILABLE,
DEFENSELESS, SUSCEPTIBLE

vulpine: .... SLY, FOXY,
ARTFUL, CLEVER, CRAFTY,
TRICKY, CUNNING, ALOPECOID

vulture: ..... PAPA, AREND,
GRAPE, GRIPE, GRIPH, URUBU,
CONDOR, FALCON, GRIPHE,
GRIFFIN, AASVOGEL, ZOPILOTE,
GALLINAZO

vum: .... VOW

W

wabble: ...... see **wobble**

wacky: ...... ODD, QUEER,
CRAZY, INSANE, MENTAL,

SCREWY, ERRATIC, ECCENTRIC,
IRRATIONAL

wad:. . . BAT, BET, GAG, PAD,
CRAM, HEAP, LINE, LUMP,
MASS, PLUG, ROLL, TUFT,
MONEY, STUFF, BUNDLE,
PLEDGE, WEALTH, BANKROLL,
COMPRESS

waddle: . . . . WAG, WOBBLE,
TODDLE

waddy: . . . PEG, BEAT, CANE,
CLUB, STICK, COWBOY

wade:. . . FORD, SLOG, SLOSH,
PADDLE, PROCEED, STRUGGLE

wader: . . . BOOT, COOT, IBIS,
RAIL, CRANE, EGRET, HERON,
SNIPE, STORK, SANDPIPER

wadi: . . . . OASIS, RIVER,
RAVINE, STREAM, VALLEY,
CHANNEL, WATERCOURSE

wafer: . . . CAKE, DISK, RING,
SEAL, SNAP, CANDY, MATZOH,
BISCUIT, CRACKER

waff: . . . . WAG, FLAP, GUST,
ODOR, PUFF, WAVE, GHOST,
WHIFF, PALTRY, WRAITH,
FLUTTER, GLIMPSE, INFERIOR,
LOW-BORN, SOLITARY,
VAGABOND

waffle: . . . . . . CAKE, WAFER

waft: . . . . BLOW, FLAG, GUST,
ORDOR, PUFF, WAVE, WING,
CARRY, DRIFT, FLOAT, TASTE,
WHIFF, BECKON, BREATH,
DIRECT, PROPEL, SIGNAL,
GLIMPSE, TRANSPORT

wag:. . . . . . NOD, WIT, CARD,
MOVE, SWAY, WAVE, JOKER,
ROGUE, SHAKE, SWING,
BECKON, SIGNAL, JESTER,
VIBRATE, FARCEUR, PUNSTER,
WAGGLE, WIGGLE, BRANDISH,
FLOURISH, JOKESTER,
OSCILLATE

wage: . . FEE, PAY, WAR, HIRE,
LEVY, BRIBE, FIGHT, INCUR,
EMPLOY, ENGAGE, REWARD,
SALARY, CONDUCT, CONTEND,

STIPEND, EMOLUMENT,
RECOMPENSE

wager: . . BET, BID, LAY, PUT,
VIE, ANTE, GAGE, RISK, PRIZE,
SPORT, STAKE, GAMBLE,
HAZARD, IMPONE, PARLAY,
PLEDGE, VENTURE

waggery: . . . WIT, JEST, JOKE,
FOOLERY

waggish: . . . . . ARCH, DROLL,
MERRY, JOCOSE, JESTING,
JOCULAR, PARLOUS, PLAYFUL,
ROGUISH, HUMOROUS, SPORTIVE

waggle: . . . . WAG, TOTTER,
WADDLE, WOBBLE

wagon: . . . . CAR, VAN, CART,
DRAY, TRAM, WAIN, BUGGY,
DILLY, LORRY, TRUCK,
CAMION, TELEGA, CAISSON,
CHARIOT, COASTER, FOURGON,
VEHICLE, SCHOONER, TRAILER,
TUMBREL, TUMBRIL

waif: . ARAB, GAMIN, STRAY,
VAGRANT, HOMELESS,
FOUNDLING

wail: . . . . . . CRY, SOB, BAWL,
HOWL, MOAN, WAUL, WAWL,
WEEP, YOWL, MOURN,
BEMOAN, BEWAIL, GRIEVE,
LAMENT, DEPLORE, ULULATE,
COMPLAINT, CATERWAUL

wain: . . . . . . CART, WAGON,
CHARIOT

wainscot: . . . . CEIL, LINING,
CEILING, PANELING, PARTITION,
WALLBOARD

waist: . . BELT, SHIRT, GIRDLE,
BODICE, BLOUSE, BASQUE,
MIDDLE, CORSAGE, CAMISOLE,
UNDERSHIRT

waistband: . . . . . OBI, BELT,
SASH, GIRDLE, CINCTURE

waistcloth: . . . . . . SARONG,
PAREUS, LAVA-LAVA

waistcoat: . . . . VEST, BENJY,
GILET, JACKET, JERKIN, WESKIT

wait: . . . . BIDE, PARK, REST,
STAY, STOP, TEND, CATER,
COURT, DALLY, DEFER, DELAY,

SERVE, TARRY, WATCH,
AMBUSH, ATTEND, ESCORT,
EXPECT, LINGER, REMAIN,
HESITATE, POSTPONE

waiter: . . . . . TRAY, CARHOP,
GARCON, SALVER, SERVER,
MESSBOY, SERVANT, STEWARD,
WATCHER, WATCHMAN,
ATTENDANT

waive: . . CAST, ABEY, DEFER,
FORGO, LEAVE, YIELD, DESERT,
FOREGO, REFUSE, REJECT,
VACATE, ABANDON, DECLINE,
FORBEAR, FORSAKE, POSTPONE,
RENOUNCE, RELINQUISH

wake: . . . CALL, STIR, ALERT,
REVEL, ROUSE, TRACK, TRAIL,
VIGIL, WAKEN, WATCH,
AROUSE, AWAKEN, REVIVE,
FEATHER

wakeful: . . ALERT, RESTLESS,
VIGILANT, SLEEPLESS,
WATCHFUL

wale: . . . . RIB, BEST, BLOW,
FLOG, MARK, PICK, WEAL,
WELT, RIDGE, WHEAL, CHOICE,
CHOOSE, SELECT, STROKE,
STREAK, STRIPE, TEXTURE,
TIMBER

walk: . . . . . MOG, PAD, FOOT,
GAIT, HIKE, HOOF, LIMP, MALL,
PACE, PATH, PLOD, RAMP,
REEL, ROAM, STEP, STOA,
WADE, ALLEE, ALLEY, AMBLE,
LEAVE, MARCH, MINCE, SLOSH,
STRAY, STRUT, STUMP, TRAIL,
TRAMP, TREAD, TROOP,
ARCADE, HOBBLE, LUMBER,
PAESEAR, PRANCE, RAMBLE,
SASHAY, STRIDE, STROLL,
TIPTOE, TODDLE, TRUDGE,
WANDER, ALAMEDA, SAUNTER,
SHUFFLE, SWAGGER, TRAIPSE,
AMBULATE, FRESCADE,
TRAVERSE, ESPLANADE,
PROMENADE, PERAMBULATE,
PEREGRINATE

walker: . . . . AMBULANT,
STROLLER, PEDESTRIAN

walking: . . . . . . AMBULANT,
GRADIENT, PEDESTRIAN

walkout: . . . . STRIKE

wall: . . DAM, CURB, DIKE, HA-
HA, FENCE, LEVEE, REDAN,
SCARP, BAILEY, ESCARP,
PARIES, PODIUM, SCREEN,
SEPTUM, BARRIER, BASTION,
CURTAIN, DEFENSE, ENCLOSE
PARAPET, RAMPART,
BULKHEAD, BARRICADE,
PARTITION, REVETMENT,
BREAKWATER, EMBANKMENT

wallaby: . . . . KANGAROO

wallet: . . . BAG, PACK, POKE,
SACK, PURSE, SCRIP, BUDGET,
BILLFOLD, KNAPSACK,
POCKETBOOK

wallop: . . BEAT, BLOW, FLOG,
LICK, SLUG, SOCK, WHIP,
WHOP, PASTE, POUND, DEFEAT,
IMPACT, STRIKE, THRASH,
TROUNCE, LAMBASTE

wallow: . . . . PIT, FADE, MIRE,
SLOSH, GROVEL, HOLLOW,
PUDDLE, TROUGH, WELTER,
WITHER, MUDHOLE, FLOUNDER,
LUXURIATE

wally: . . . TOY, FINE, STURDY,
STRONG, PLEASING, SPLENDID,
EXCELLENT, FIRSTRATE

waltz: . . . . . . DANCE, MUSIC,
VALSE, BOSTON, VIENNA

wampum: . . . . PEAG, BEADS,
MONEY, SEWAN, ROANOKE

wamus: . . . JACKET, CARDIGAN

wan: . . . . . DIM, FADE, PALE,
SICK, ASHEN, FAINT, WHITE,
DISMAL, FEEBLE, GLOOMY,
PALLID, PALLOR, PEAKED,
SICKLY, GHASTLY, LANGUID,
COLORLESS

wand: . . . . ROD, MACE, POLE,
TWIG, BATON, SHOOT, STAFF,
STICK, VERGE, SWITCH,
WATTLE, POINTER, RHABDOS,
SCEPTER, CADUCEUS

wander: . . . BUM, ERR, GAD,
HAIK, HAKE, MAZE, RAVE,

ROAM, ROIL, ROVE, WALK,
DRIFT, KNOCK, PROWL, RANGE,
STRAY, TRAIK, CRUISE,
DANDER, RAMBLE, STROLL,
TRAVEL, DEVIATE, DIGRESS,
MEANDER, SAUNTER, TRAIPSE,
DIVAGATE, STRAGGLE,
TRAVERSE, PEREGRINATE

wanderer: . . . . ARAB, HOBO,
WAIF, GYPSY, NOMAD, ROVER,
TRAMP, BEDOUIN, MIGRANT,
PILGRIM, RAMBLER, VAGRANT,
FUGITIVE, VAGABOND,
ITINERANT

wandering: . . . . VAGUE,
ARRANT, ASTRAY, ERRANT,
ROVING, DEVIOUS, ERRATIC,
JOURNEY, NOMADIC, ODESSEY,
VAGRANT, WINDING,
ABERRANT, RAMBLING,
CIRCUITOUS, INCOHERENT

wandle: . . . . . AGILE, LITHE,
SUPPLE

wane: . . . GO, EBB, FAIL, SINK,
ABATE, DECAY, PETER, REPINE,
DECLINE, DWINDLE, SUBSIDE,
DECREASE, DIMINISH

wangle: . . GET, FAKE, SHAKE,
ADJUST, CHANGE, JUGGLE,
OBTAIN, WIGGLE, FALSIFY,
FINAGLE, WRIGGLE, WHEEDLE,
CONTRIVE, MANIPULATE

want: . . . . GAP, HOLE, LACK,
LIKE, MISS, NEED, PINE, VOID,
WISH, CRAVE, FAULT, BESOIN,
CHOOSE, DEARTH, DESIRE,
HUNGER, PENURY, PLIGHT,
ABSENCE, BEGGARY, BLEMISH,
CRAVING, LACKING, MISSING,
POVERTY, REQUIRE, VACANCY,
EXIGENCY, SCARCITY,
SHORTAGE, DEFICIENT,
INDIGENCE, NECESSITY,
PRIVATION

wanton: . . . . . LEWD, RASH,
TART, WILD, DALLY, MERRY,
TRAMP, FRISKY, FROLIC,
GIGLET, HARLOT, LAVISH,
TRIFLE, UNRULY, FULSOME,

HAGGARD, IMMORAL, LUSTFUL,
PLAYFUL, SENSUAL, WAYWARD,
FLAGRANT, INHUMANE,
PLAYSOME, PRODIGAL,
RECKLESS, SENSELESS,
SPITEFUL, SPORTIVE,
UNCHASTE, DISSOLUTE,
LUXURIANT, MALICIOUS,
EXTRAVAGANT

war: . . . . FEUD, STRIFE,
CONFLICT, HOSTILITY,
BELLIGERENCE

warble: . . . . . . SING, CAROL,
CHANT, CHIRL, CHIRM, SHAKE,
TRILL, YODEL, VIBRATE

ward: . . . . CARE, FEND, JAIL,
RULE, AVERT, GUARD, PARRY,
REPEL, WATCH, CHARGE,
DEFEND, GOVERN, PRISON,
SHIELD, CUSTODY, DEFENSE,
KEEPING, PROTECT, DISTRICT

warden: . . . GUARD, DISDAR,
JAILER, JAILOR, KEEPER,
RANGER, REGENT, SEXTON,
ALCAIDE, TRUSTEE, TURNKEY,
WATCHMAN, CUSTODIAN,
GATEKEEPER, GUARDIAN,
CONSTABLE

wardrobe: . . . . CLOSET,
VESTRY, CLOTHES, APPAREL,
ARMOIRE, CABINET, CHAMBER,
TROUSEAU

ware: . . . . . . AWARE, CHINA,
DISHES, GOODS, READY, SPEND,
STUFF, CAREFUL, FABRICS,
HEEDFUL, POTTERY, PRUDENT,
SEAWEED, PRODUCTS,
SQUANDER, VIGILANT,
CONSCIOUS, COMMODITIES,
MERCHANDISE

warehouse: . . . . HONG, SILO,
DEPOT, ETAPE, STORE, BODEGA,
GODOWN, CAMARIN, ELEVATOR,
ENTREPOT, MAGAZINE

warfare: . . . . see war

warlike: . HOSTILE, MARTIAL,
MILITANT, MILTARY,
BELLICOSE, BELLIGERENT

warlock: . . . WITCH, WIZARD, SORCERER, CONJURER, MAGICIAN

warm: . . (also see **hot**) AVID, BASK, BEEK, HEAT, KEEN, KIND, MILD, ANGRY, CALID, CHAFE, EAGER, FIREY, FRESH, SUNNY, TEPID, TOAST, ARDENT, DEVOUT, GENIAL, HEARTY, HEATED, KINDLY, LIVELY, LOVING, TENDER, TOASTY, AMOROUS, CLEMENT, CORDIAL, FERVANT, GLOWING, SINCERE, THERMAL, ZEALOUS, FRIENDLY, GENEROUS, SANGUINE, VEHEMENT, IRRITATED

warmth: . . . . . . ELAN, ZEST, ARDOR, FERVOR, ENTHUSIASM

warn: . . FLAG, REDE, ALARM, ALERT, ADVISE, INFORM, NOTIFY, SIGNAL, APPRISE, APPRIZE, CAUTION, COUNSEL, PORTEND, ADMONISH, THREATEN, REPREHEND

warning: . . . . . OMEN, ALARM, KNELL, SIREN, BEACON, AUGURY, BEWARE, CAVEAT, SIGNAL, TIPOFF, TOCSIN, PORTENT PRESAGE

warp: . . . . . MUD, WEB, WRY, BEND, BIAS, CAST, LINE, ROPE, SILT, SWAY, TURN, WARF, ANGLE, CROOK, QUIRK, TWINE, TWIST, WEAVE, BUCKLE, DEFORM, SWERVE, CONTORT, DEFLECT, DISTORT, PERVERT, SEDIMENT, ABERRATION, INTERTWINE

warrant: . . . . . WRIT, BERAT, GUARD, ORDER, RIGHT, VOUCH, ASSERT, BREVET, ENSURE, INSURE, PARDON, PERMIT, PLEVIN, SAFETY, BEHIGHT, JUSTIFY, PROMISE, PRECEPT, PROTECT, VOUCHER, GUARANTY, MITTIMUS, SANCTION, AUTHORIZE, GUARANTEE, AUTHORIZATION

warren: . . . . . . SLUM, HUTCH, RABBITRY, TENEMENT

warrior: . . . . . HERO, BRAVE, AMAZON, FIGHTER, SOLDIER, CHAMPION, COMBATANT

wart: . . . . TUMOR, SYCOMA, VERRUCA, KERATOSIS, PAPILLOMA

wary: . . SHY, ALERT, CAGEY, CANNY, CHARY, LEERY, CAREFUL, GUARDED, PRUDENT, CAUTIOUS, DISCREET, SKITTISH, WATCHFUL, VIGILANT, SUSPICIOUS

wash: . . LAP, MUD, PAN, TUB, LAVE, SILT, SLOP, SOAP, SUDS, BATHE, CLEAN, CLEAR, DRIFT, ELUTE, FLOAT, FLUSH, LEACH, RINSE, SCOUR, SCRUB, SLOSH, SOUSE, SWILL, BUDDLE, CRADLE, DEBRIS, PURIFY, SLUICE, CLEANSE, LAUNDER, SHAMPOO, ABLUTION, ALLUVIUM

basin/bowel: . . . . LAVER, LAVABO, LAVATORY

washout: . . . . . FLOP, GULCH, GULLY, FIASCO, FAILURE

waspish: . . . TESTY, FRETFUL, PEVISH, SLENDER, CHOLERIC, PETULANT, SNAPPISH, SPITEFUL, IRASCIBLE, IRRITABLE, BAD-TEMPERED

wassail: . . . . . LARK, ORGY, ROMP, DRINK, REVEL, TOAST, FROLIC, PLEDGE, CAROUSE, REVELRY, CAROUSAL, FESTIVITY

waste: . . . . . . EAT, ROT, GOB, FAIL, IDLE, JUNK, LOSS, PINE, RAZE, RUIN, SACK, WEAR, CHAFF, DECAY, DWINE, HAVOC, SCRAP, SPILL, SPOIL, BARREN, BEZZLE, DESERT, DEBRIS, DEVOUR, MOLDER, RAVAGE, REFUSE, ATHROPHY, CONSUME, CORRODE, DESTROY, DWINDLE, EXHAUST, FRITTER, GARBAGE, RUBBISH, DECREASE, DEMOLISH, DESOLATE,

ENFEEBLE, LEFTOVER,
MACERATE, SQUANDER,
DEVASTATE, DISSIPATE,
EMACIATE, EXCRETION,
WILDERNESS
time: ...... IDLE, LOAF,
LOITER, DAWDLE, FIDDLE,
DIDDLE
wasted: ... GUANT, HAGGARD,
DECREPIT, EMACIATED
wasteful: .. LAVISH, PROFUSE,
PRODIGAL, SPENDFUL,
SPENDTHRIFT, EXTRAVAGANT
wasteland: .... FEN, MOOR,
MARSH, SWAMP, WILDS,
DESERT, MORASS, TUNDRA,
STEPPE, BADLANDS
wastrel: .... PRODIGAL,
SPENDTHRIFT
watch: .. EYE, SPY, SEE, TAB,
ESPY, GLOM, HEED, KEEP,
LOOK, MARK, MIND, TEND,
VIEW, WAIT, WAKE, WARD,
AWAIT, CLOCK, GUARD, SCOUT,
TIMER, VIGIL, BEHOLD,
DEFEND, FOLLOW, PATROL,
POLICE, REGARD, SENTRY,
SHADOW, TICKER, BIVOUAC,
LOOKOUT, OBSERVE, OVERSEE,
HOROLOGE, SCRUTINY,
SENTINEL, TIMEPIECE
watcher: .. SPY, TAIL, SCOUT,
SHADOW, SPOTTER, LOOKOUT,
OBSERVOR, WATCHMAN
watchful: .... WARY, ALERT,
VIGILANT, OPEN-EYED,
CAUTIOUS, OBSERVANT,
ATTENTIVE
watchmaker: ... HOROLOGIST
watchman: .. GUARD, SCOUT,
SENTRY, SENTINEL, WARDER,
WARDEN, LOOKOUT,
DOORKEEPER
watchword: .... MOTTO,
SLOGAN, SIGNAL, BATTLECRY,
SHIBBOLETH, PASSWORD
water: .... EAU, WET, AGUA,
AQUA, BATH, BRIM, BROO,
BURN, LAKE, POND, POOL,

TIDE, WAVE, BRINE, FLUID,
FLUME, LAVER, LOUGH, LYMPH,
RIVER, SPRAY, TEARS, DILUTE,
LIQUID, SALIVA, STREAM,
MOISTEN, CALENDAR,
BEVERAGE, IRRIGATE, SPRINKLE
barrier: .... DAM, BOOM,
DIKE, DYKE, MOLE, REEF,
WEIR, EMBANKMENT
body: ... BAY, SEA, GULF,
LAKE, MEAR, POND, POOL,
WELL, FIORD, OASIS,
OCEAN, LAGOON, STRAIT,
CISTERN, SPRINGS,
RESERVOIR
bottle: ... OLLA, CARAFE,
DECANTER
course: ...... RUN, DIKE,
DYKE, RACE, WADI, WADY,
BROOK, CANAL, CHUTE,
CREEK, DITCH, DRAIN,
FLUME, GORGE, GULLY,
RIVER, ARROYO, CANYON,
GUTTER, NULLAH, RAVINE,
SLUICE, STREAM, CHANNEL,
CULVERT, TRINKET,
BARRANCA, RACEWAY,
AQUEDUCT
pipe: . DUCT, HOSE, MAIN,
TUBE, DRAIN, HOOKAH,
CULVERT, AQUEDUCT,
NARGILEH
waterbuck: .. ANTELOPE, KOB
watercraft: .. see **boat, ship**
waterfall: .. LIN, FOSS, LINN,
CHUTE, FORCE, CASCADE,
CHIGNON, CATARACT
watering place: .. SPA, POOL,
WELL, OASIS, RESORT, SPRING
waterless: ...... DRY, ARID,
BARREN, ANHYDROUS
watery: ... WET, THIN, WEAK,
FLUID, SAMMY, SOGGY,
WASHY, BLASHY, SEROUS,
SOAKED, AQUEOUS, HYDROUS,
TEARFUL, WEEPING, HUMOROUS
wattle: ... ROD, GILL, JOWL,
TWIG, WAND, BOREE, COOBA,
FENCE, STICK, TWIST, ACACIA,

COOBAH, DEWLAP, HURDLE,
LAPPET, CARUNCLE,
FRAMEWORK
wave: ..... FAN, SEA, WAG,
BECK, BORE, CURL, FLAG,
FLAP, SURF, SWAY, WAFF,
WAFT, BLESS, CRIMP, CURVE,
EAGER, EAGRE, FLOAT, FLOOD,
RIDGE, SHAKE, SURGE, SWELL,
SWING, BECKON, BILLOW,
COMBER, FLAUNT, MARCEL,
RIPPLE, ROLLER, SEESAW,
SIGNAL, BREAKER, FLICKER,
FLUTTER, VIBRATE, BRANDISH,
FLOURISH, UNDULATE,
WHITECAP, FLUCTUATE,
PERMANENT, VIBRATION,
UNDULATION
waver: .... REEL, SWAY,
QUAKE, SWING, CHANGE,
FALTER, QUAVER, SWERVE,
TEETER, TOTTER, FLICKER,
FLUTTER, STAGGER, TREMBLE,
VIBRATE, HESITATE,
FLUCTUATE, OSCILLATE,
VACILLATE
wavering: ... WEAK, FICKLE,
DUBIOUS, LAMBENT, DOUBTFUL,
FLEXUOUS, UNSTEADY,
DESULTORY, PENDULOUS,
IRRESOLUTE
wavy: .... CRISP, CURLY,
MOIRE, SNAKY, UNDEE, FLYING,
REPAND, UNDATE, BILLOWY,
SINUATE, SINUOUS, WIGGLY,
BUCKLED, CURVING, ROLLING,
UNDULATE, UNDULANT
wax: .... CERA, CERE, CODE,
GROW, PELA, BECOME, CERATE,
CERESIN, CERUMEN, INCREASE,
PARAFFIN
way: ...... VIA, FORE, GAIT,
LANE, MODE, PACE, PATH,
PLAN, ROAD, WONT, ALLEY,
GOING, HABIT, MILKY, ROUTE,
SPACE, STEPS, STYLE, TRACK,
ACCESS, ARCADE, AVENUE,
CAREER, CHEMIN, COURSE,
DETOUR, DEVICE, MANNER,

METHOD, SCHEME, STREET,
CHANNEL, FASHION, HIGHWAY,
OPENING, PASSAGE, APPROACH,
CAUSEWAY, CONTRADA,
DIRECTION, PROCEDURE
waybill: .... MANIFEST
wayfarer: . VIATOR, PILGRIM,
TRAVELER
waylay: ..... AWAIT, BELAY,
BESET, BLOCK, AMBUSH,
FORELAY, OBSTRUCT, SURPRISE,
AMBUSCADE
wayward: .... UNRULY,
ERRATIC, NAUGHTY, VAGRANT,
WILLFUL, CONTRARY,
PERVERSE, STUBBORN,
UNSTEADY, IRREGULAR,
HEADSTRONG
weak: .... DIM, WAN, PUNY,
SOFT, THIN, ANILE, BAUCH,
CRIMP, DICKY, FAINT, FRAIL,
SEELY, SLACK, WASHY,
WAUGH, WEARY, YOUNG,
DEBILE, DILUTE, DOTISH,
EFFETE, FEEBLE, FLABBY,
FLAGGY, FLIMSY, FOIBLE,
INFIRM, LIMBER, SICKLY,
TENDER, UNSURE, UNWISE,
WATERY, BRITTLE, DWAIBLE,
FLACCID, FRAGILE, INSIPID,
INVALID, PUERILE, CHILDISH,
DECREPIT, DELICATE, FECKLESS,
FEMININE, HELPLESS,
IMPOTENT, CHILDLIKE,
ENFEEBLED, POWERLESS,
SPINELESS, INADEQUATE,
VULNERABLE
weaken: .. SAP, FLAG, DAMP,
HURT, THIN, TIRE, ABATE,
ALLAY, BLUNT, BREAK, DELAY,
WATER, APPALL, DEADEN,
DEFEAT, DILUTE, IMPAIR,
LESSEN, REBATE, REDUCE,
SICKEN, SOFTEN, CORRODE,
CORRUPT, CRIPPLE, DECLINE,
DEPRESS, DISABLE, EXHAUST,
MOLLIFY, UNNERVE, VITIATE,
DIMINISH, ENERVATE,
ENFEEBLE, ATTENUATE,

UNDERMINE, DEBILITATE, DEMORALIZE

weakling: . . . . SISSY, SOFTIE, CRYBABY, PANTYWAIST

weakness: . . . FLAW, ATONY, CRACK, FAULT, FOLLY, DEFECT, FOIBLE, LIKING, ACRATIA, AILMENT, FAILING, FISSURE, FRAILTY, LANGUOR, ASTHENIA, DEBILITY, DELICACY, FONDNESS, INABILITY, INFIRMITY, ATTENUATION

weal: . . . LINE, MARK, WALE, WELT, RIDGE, STATE, WHEAL, CHOICE, RICHES, STRIPE, WEALTH, WELFARE, HAPPINESS, WELL-BEING

wealth: . . GEAR, GOLD, GOOD, WEAL, MEANS, MONEY, WORTH, ASSETS, MAMMON, RICHES, TALENT, CAPITAL, FORTUNE, WELFARE, OPULENCE, PROPERTY, TREASURE, ABUNDANCE, AFFLUENCE

wealthy: . . . FAT, FULL, RICH, AMPLE, PURSY, LOADED, MONEYED, OPULENT, AFFLUENT, WELL-TO-DO, PROSPEROUS

weapon: . . . ARM, BOW, GUN, BEAK, BOLA, BOLO, CLAW, CLUB, DART, DIRK, EPEE, FOIL, HORN, MACE, PIKE, ARROW, BOLAS, KNIFE, LANCE, RIFLE, SABER, SPEAR, SWORD, TALON, VOUGE, CANNON, DAGGER, GLAIVE, MORTAR, PISTOL, RAPIER, BAZOOKA, CARBINE, FIREARM, GISARME, HALBERD, HARPOON, JAVELIN, MACHETE, MISSLE, ARQUEBUS, CATAPULT, CROSSBOW, REVOLVER, STILLETO, TOMAHAWK, DERRINGER, SLINGSHOT, BLUNDERBUSS

wear: . . . . . DON, RUB, FRAY, FRET, TIRE, CHAFE, ERODE, GRIND, SPORT, WEARY, ABRADE, ATTIRE, ENDURE, IMPAIR, APPAREL, CLOTHES, CONSUME, CORRODE, EXHAUST, FATIGUE, FRAZZLE, DIMINISH, DETERIORATE

wearied: . . . . . TIRED, JADED, FAGGED, POOPED, FATIGUED, EXHAUSTED

weariness: . . . ENNUI, TEDIUM, FATIGUE, BOREDOM, VEXATION, LASSITUDE

wearisome: . . . . DRY, DULL, HARD, SLOW, BORING, DISMAL, DREARY, PROLIX, TIRING, IRKSOME, TEDIOUS, TIRESOME, TOILSOME, FATIGUING, LABORIOUS, VEXATIOUS, MONOTONOUS

weary: . . . . . FAG, IRK, SAD, BORE, CLOY, JADE, PALL, POOP, PUNY, TIRE, WEAK, WORN, ANNOY, BORED, CURSE, SPENT, TIRED, ABRADE, HARASS, PLAGUE, SICKLY, TUCKER, WEAKEN, EXHAUST, FATIGUE, IRKSOME, TEDIOUS, WORNOUT, FATIGUED, TIRESOME, TUCKERED, WRETCHED, SURFEITED

weasand: . GULLET, THROAT, TRACHEA, WINDPIPE

weasel: . . . . CANE, VARE, SNEAK, STOAT, ERMINE, FERRET, VERMIN, EQUIVOCATE

weather: . . . DRY, SKY, HAIL, RAIN, SNOW, WIND, SLEET, STORM, SEASON, CLIMATE, SURVIVE

weathered: . . . . FADED, TANNED, BRONZED, GNARLED, STAINED, BLEACHED, HARDENED, SURVIVED, TOUGHENED

weave: . . . MAT, DARN, JOIN, KNIT, LACE, SPIN, WIND, BRAID, PLAIT, TWIST, TWINE, DEVISE, CANILLE, ENTWINE, FASHION, CONTRIVE, FABRICATE, INTERLACE, INTERWIND

web:.. MAT, NET, PLY, CAUL,
MAZE, TELA, TRAP, WARP,
WEFT, SNARE, FABRIC, TISSUE,
ENSNARE, NETWORK, TEXTURE,
ENTANGLE, GOSSAMER,
MEMBRANE, VEXILLUM

webbed:.. RINGED, PALMATE

wed:..... JOIN, WIVE, BRIDE,
ELOPE, MARRY, UNITE, JOINED,
PLEDGE, ESPOUSE, SPLICED

wedding:.... BRIDAL, SPLICE,
NUPITAL, CEREMONY,
ESPOUSAL, MARRIAGE

wedge:..... JAM, KEY, VEE,
CLUB, PLUG, SHIM, SHOE, TRIG,
CHOCK, CLEAT, COIGN, QUOIN,
SLICE, SPLIT, CLEAVE, COTTER,
SECTOR, SCOTCH, SEPARATE,
TRIANGLE, VOUSSOIR

shaped:....... CUNEAL,
SPHENIC, CUNEATED,
SPHENOID, CUNEIFORM

wedlock:....... MARRIAGE,
MATRIMONY

wee:... TINY, BITTY, EARLY,
SMALL, TEENY, LITTLE,
MINUTE, YOUNG, DIMINUTIVE

weed:...... BUR, HOE, RID,
CHOP, CULL, DOCK, GARB,
LOCO, MILK, TARE, CIGAR,
COCKLE, DRESS, NETTLE,
REMOVE, SPURGE, CLOTHES,
GARMENT, THISTLE, TOBACCO,
CLOTHING, PLANTAIN,
PURSLANE, DANDELION,
ERADICATE

week:......... SENNIGHT,
HEBDOMAD

weekday:......... FERIA

weekly:....... PERIODICAL,
HEBDOMADAL, PUBLICATION

ween:....... HOPE, THINK,
EXPECT, BELIEVE, SUPPOSE,
IMAGINE, CONCEIVE

weep:..... CRY, SOB, BAWL,
OOZE, TEAR, WAIL, EXUDE,
MOURN, BEWAIL

weft:.... WEB, FILM, WARP,
WOOF, YARN, FILLING

weigh:.... BEAR, HEFT, LIFT,
TARE, HEAVE, HOIST, POISE,
RAISE, BURDEN, PONDER,
REGARD, ANALYZE, BALANCE,
EXAMINE, MEASURE, PORTION,
REFLECT, CONSIDER,
EVALUATE, MEDITATE,
APPORTION

weighing device:.... SCALE,
TRONE, BALANCE

weight:.... NET, TON, DRAM,
GRAM, HEFT, LOAD, CARAT,
GRAIN, OUNCE, POUND, POWER,
SCALE, VALUE, BURDEN,
CHARGE, IMPORT, MOMENT,
STRESS, BALLAST, GRAVITY,
PLUMMET, QUARTER, TONNAGE,
EMPHASIS, ENCUMBER,
PRESSURE, PRESTIGE,
AUTHORITY, HEAVINESS,
INFLUENCE, IMPORTANCE

weighty:.... BULKY, HEAVY,
HEAFTY, LARGE, OBESE, SOLID,
SEVERE, SOLEMN, MASSIVE,
ONEROUS, SERIOUS, GRIEVOUS,
POWERFUL, CORPULENT,
MOMENTOUS, PONDEROUS,
BURDENSOME, CUMBERSOME,
OPPRESSIVE

weir:..... DAM, PEN, TRAP,
FENCE, GARTH, LEVEE,
BARRIER, MILLDAM

weird:... ODD, EERIE, EERY,
UNCO, WILD, QUEER, SCARY,
CREEPY, SPOOKY, CURIOUS,
GHOSTLY, MACABRE, STRANGE,
UNCANNY, UNUSUAL,
ELDRITCH, UNEARTHLY,
MYSTERIOUS

welcome:.... HAIL, ADOPT,
CHEER, GREET, INVITE,
ACCLAIM, EMBRACE, RECEIVE,
BIENVENU(E), GREETING,
PLEASANT, AGREEABLE,
DESIRABLE, ACCEPTABLE,
SALUTATION

weld:.. JOIN, UNITE, SOLDER,
CONSOLIDATE

welfare: ... WEAL, WEALTH, BLESSING, WELLBEING, PROSPERITY

welkin: .. AIR, SKY, HEAVENS, ATMOSPHERE

well: ... FIT, PIT, FINE, FLOW, GOOD, GUSH, HALE, HOLE, SUMP, TRIG, FOUNT, GREAT, SHAFT, GUSHER, HEARTY, PROPER, SPRING, CISTERN, HEALTHY, ARTESIAN, EXPERTLY, FOUNTAIN

balanced: .. SANE, POISED, SENSIBLE

being: ...... GOOD, WEAL, WELFARE, HAPPINESS, PROSPERITY

groomed: .. NEAT, CLEAN, SLEEK, SLICK, SOIGNE

heeled: .. RICH, WEALTHY, MONEYED, PROSPEROUS

known: .... FAMOUS, EMINENT, PROMINENT, FAMILIAR, NOTORIOUS

timed: .... TIMELY, OPPORTUNE, AUSPICIOUS, SEASONABLE

Welsh: ... CELT(IC), CYMRIC, CAMBRIAN

welsher: . CHEAT, DEADBEAT, SWINDLER

welt: .... BEAT, MARK, LASH, WALE, W(H)EAL, RIDGE, STRIPE, THRASH

welter: ... REEL, ROLL, TOSS, WILT, GROVEL, TUMBLE, SOAKED, WALLOW, WITHER, WRITHE, SMOTHER, STAGGER, TURMOIL, CONFUSION

wen: .... CYST, MOLE, RUNE, TALPA, TUMOR, GOITER

wench: ... DELL, DILL, DOXY, DRAB, GILL, GIRL, MAID, GOUGE, HUSSY, WHORE, WOMAN, MAIDEN, WANTON, SERVANT, STRUMPET

wend: ..... GO, BOW, FARE, PASS, BETAKE, DEPART, TRAVEL, JOURNEY, PROCEED

West: .. FRONTIER, OCCIDENT

wet: .. DEW, DIP, SOP, DAMP, DANK, DEWY, LASH, RAIN, SOAK, BATHE, FOGGY, HUMID, JUICE, JUICY, LEACH, MISTY, MOIST, MUSHY, RAINY, SOGGY, SOPPY, SWEAT, WRONG, CLASHY, DAMPEN, DRENCH, HUMECT, IMBRUE, MARSHY, SHOWER, SOAKED, SODDEN, SPONGY, WATERY, MOISTEN, SOPPING, SPLASHY, DAMPENED, IRRIGATE, MISTAKEN, MOISTURE, SPRINKLE, MISGUIDED

blanket: ...... KILLJOY, SPOILSPORT

wether: .. RAM, WOOL, SHEEP

whack: ..... HIT, LAM, TRY, BANG, BEAT, BELT, BLOW, SLAP, SHARE, THUMP, WHANG, SMACK, STRIKE, STROKE, THWACK, CHANCE, ATTEMPT, PORTION, ALLOWANCE

whacky: .... WILD, FOOLISH, MADCAP, ECCENTRIC

whale: ..... HIT, SEI, BEAT, BLUE, CETE, DRUB, LASH, ORCA, WHIP, WHOP, POGGY, SPERM, WHACK, BALEEN, BELUGA, BLOWER, KILLER, STRIKE, THRASH, BOWHEAD, DOLPHIN, FINBACK, GRAMPUS, RIPSACK, SPOUTER, CHACHALOT, CETACEAN, HARDHEAD, HUMPBACK, PORPOISE, BLACKFISH

whalebone: .... BALEEN

whang: .. BANG, BEAT, BLOW, STRIKE, WHACK, THRASH

wharf: ... DOCK, PIER, SLIP, QUAI, QUAY, BERTH, JETTY, LANDING

wheal: . MARK, WALE, WEAL, WELT, STRIPE, PIMPLE, PUSTULE

wheat: ..... CORN, DURRA, DURUM, GRAIN, SPELT, TRIGO, CEREAL, STAPLE, TURKEY, EINKORN, SEMOULE

coat: . . . . BRAN
cracked: . . . . GROATS
disease: . . . . BUNT, RUST,
SMUT, AECIA, ERGOT,
AECIUM
wheedle: . . COG, CANT, COAX,
CARNY, JOLLY, WHINE,
BANTER, CAJOLE, CARNEY,
WANGLE, BLARNEY, FLATTER,
PERSUADE, SCROUNGE,
INFLUENCE
wheel: . . . . BUR, CAM, COG,
BIKE, DISK, GEAR, HELM, ROLL,
TURN, NORIA, PIVOT, ROTOR,
ROWEL, SKEIF, SKIVE, TRUCK,
CASTER, CIRCLE, PULLEY,
ROLLER, ROTATE, RUNDLE,
SHEAVE, BICYCLE, CHUKKER,
PEDRAIL, REVOLVE, TRUNDLE,
ROTATION, REVOLUTION
wheeze: . . GAG, JOKE, GASP,
HOOSE, HOOZE, TRICK
whelk: . . . . . ACNE, SNAIL,
MUREX, PAPULE, PIMPLE,
PUSTULE, WINKLE, GASTROPOD
whelp: . . . . . CUB, DOG, PUP,
SON, CHIT, FAWN, CHILD,
PUPPY, YOUTH
when: . . . . . AS, TIME, UNTIL,
WHILE, MOMENT, WHEREAS,
ALTHOUGH
whenever: . . . . ANYTIME
where: . . . . . PLACE, THERE,
WITHER, LOCATION
whereabouts: . . . . . . LOCATION
whereas: . . . AS, SINCE, WHILE
wherefore: . . . WHY, CAUSE,
REASON, THEREFORE,
ACCORDINGLY
wherefrom: . . . . WHENCE
wherewithal: . . CASH, MEANS,
MONEY, RESOURCES
wherry: . . . . SCULL, BARGE,
LIGHTER, ROWBOAT, VEHICLE
whet: . . HONE, GRIND, ROUSE,
STROP, EXCITE, SHARPEN,
STIMULATE
whether: . . IF, WHERE, EITHER
whetstone: . . . BURR, BUHR,
HONE, SHARPENER

which: . . . . . AS, THE, WHO,
THAT, WHOM, WHATEVER
whiff: . . . . FAN, BLOW, GUFF,
GUST, HINT, ODOR, PUFF,
WAFT, EXPEL, FLUFF, SMELL,
SMOKE, BREATH, EXHALE,
INHALE, INSTANT
whiffle: . . BLOW, EMIT, SWAY,
TURN, VEER, WAVE, EXPEL,
SHAME, SHIFT, CHANGE,
THICKER, FLUTTER, SCATTER,
DISPERSE, VACCILATE
while: . . . . AS, YET, TILL,
UNTIL, WHENAS, WHEREAS
whilom: . . . . . . ONCE, PAST,
FORMER(LY), EARST(WHILE)
whim: . . . . . . FAD, GIG, IDEA,
KINK, MOOD, CRANK, FANCY,
HUMOR, QUIRK, MEGRIM,
NOTION, VAGARY, WHIMSY,
CAPRICE, CROCHET, CAPPRICCO
whimper: . CRY, SOB, MEWL,
MOAN, PULE, WEEP, WHINE,
SIMPER, MURMUR, YAMMER,
GRIZZLE, SNIFFLE, SNUFFLE
whimsical: . . . ODD, DROLL,
QUEER, COCKLE, QUAINT,
FANCIFUL, BIZZARO, FREAKISH,
ECCENTRIC, HUMOROUS,
FANTASTIC, CAPRICIOUS
whimsy: . . . . see **whim**
whine: . . . WOW, CANT, GIRN,
MEWL, MOAN, PEWL, YARM,
BLEAT, CROON, SNIVEL,
YAMMER, WHIMPER, COMPLAIN
whinny: . . . . . HINNY, NEIGH
whip: . . CAT, GAD, ROD, TAN,
BEAT, CANE, CAST, CROP,
FLAP, FLAY, FLOG, GOAD,
HIDE, LACE, LASH, LICK, URGE,
WALE, ABUSE, BIRCH, CRACK,
FLAIL, FLICK, IMPEL, KNOUT,
OUTDO, QUIRT, SLASH, SPANK,
STRAP, SWING, SWISH, WHALE,
WHISK, DEFEAT, INCITE,
LARRUP, PUNISH, STRIKE,
SWINGE, SWITCH, THRASH,
BELABOR, CHICOTE, CONQUER,
COWHIDE, KURBASH, LAMBAST,

RAWHIDE, SCOURGE, SJAMBOK,
DISCIPLINE, FLAGELLATE

whippersnapper: . . . SQUIRT,
UPSTART

whir: . . . . . FLY, BIRR, BURR,
BUZZ, WHIZ, SWIRL, BUSTLE,
REVOLVE, VIBRATE,
COMMOTION

whirl: . . . EDDY, GYRE, REEL,
RUSH, SPIN, STIR, TIRL, TURN,
DRILL, GIDDY, SWIRL, TWIRL,
TWIST, WALTZ, BUSTLE,
CIRCLE, GYRATE, HURTLE,
ROTATE, SWINGE, TUMULT,
UPROAR, VORTEX, REVOLVE,
TURMOIL, COMMOTION,
PIROUETTE

whirlpool: . . . . . EDDY, GULF,
SUCK, WEEL, GORCE, SWIRL,
VORTEX, SUCKHOLE,
MAELSTROM

whirlwind: . . . . OE, VORTEX,
CYCLONE, TORNADO,
HURRICANE, MAELSTROM,
TOURBILLION

whiskers: . . BEARD, GOUTEE,
STUBBLE, MUSTACHE,
SIDEBURNS, MUTTONCHOPS

whisk(e)y: . . . . . RYE, BOND,
CORN, IRISH, HOOCH, POTEEN,
REDEYE, ROTGUT, SCOTCH,
BOURBON, BUSTHEAD,
FIREWATER, POPSKULL,
MOONSHINE, MOUNTAIN DEW

whisper: . . . . . . BUZZ, HINT,
RUMOR, TRACE, BREEZE,
BREATH, MURMUR

whist: . . . GAME, HUSH, MORT,
MUTE, CARDS, QUIET, STILL,
SILENT, SILENCE

whistle: . . . BLOW, PIPE, TOOT,
SIREN, HOOTER, FOGHORN

whit: . BIT, JOT, ATOM, DOIT,
HATE, IOTA, SPECK, TITTLE,
PARTICLE

white: . . . WAN, ASHY, BAWN,
PALE, LILY, PURE, ASHEN,
BLOND, HOARY, IVORY,
SNOWY, ALBINO, ARGENT,

BLANCH, CHALKY, HONEST,
PALLID, SILVER, SILVERY,
INNOCENT, SPOTLESS,
CAUCASIAN

whitecap: . . . . WAVE

whiten: . . . . . . PALE, CHALK,
BLANCH, BLEACH, ETIOLATE

whitewash: . . . . PARGET,
CONCEAL, PLASTER

whither: . . . . . BLOW, GUST,
HURL, RUSH, HURRY, SHAKE,
THROW, WHERE, FLURRY,
BLUSTER, TREMBLE, WHEREVER

whitlow: . . . . FELON, AGNAIL,
FETLOW

whittle: . . CUT, PARE, CARVE,
KNIFE, SHAPE, SHAVE, SHAWL,
MANTLE, REDUCE, REMOVE,
BLANKET

whiz(z): . . HUM, BUZZ, HISS,
PIRR, WHIR, HURRY, SPEED,
CORKER, EXPERT, BARGAIN

whoa: . . . . HALT, STOP

whole: . . . . AIL, SUM, FULL,
HALE, SOLE, TOTO, UNIT,
GROSS, SOLID, SOUND, TOTAL,
UNCUT, ENTIRE, HEALED,
INTACT, INTEGER, PERFECT,
ABSOLUTE, COMPLETE,
ENSEMBLE, ENTIRELY,
ENTIRETY, UNBROKEN,
UNANIMOUS, UNDIVIDED

wholesale: . . . . . BULK, LOTS,
GROSS, MASSIVE, SWEEPING,
EXTENSIVE

wholesome: . . . GOOD, CLEAN,
SOUND, BENIGN, ROBUST,
HEALTHY, PRUDENT, CURATIVE,
HALESOME, REMEDIAL,
SALUTORY, VIGOROUS,
BENEFICIAL, PROPITIOUS,
SALUBRIOUS

wholly: . . ALL, ONLY, FULLY,
QUITE, STARK, ALGATE,
PURELY, SOLELY, SOUNDLY,
TOTALLY, ENTIRELY,
ALTOGETHER

whoop: . . . CRY, CALL, HOOT,
YELL, CHEER, SHOUT

whooping cough: . . PERTUSSIS

whop: . . . . WAP, BEAT, BLOW, BUMP, FLOP, THUD, KNOCK, THUMP, STRIKE, STROKE, THRASH

whorl: . TURN, CYCLE, SPIRE, SWIRL, WHIRL, VOLUTE, WREATH, GYRATION, VERTICIL, VOLUTION

why: . . . . HOW, QUI, ENIGMA, FORWHY, WHEREFORE

wick: . . . . . BAD, BAY, BEND, EVIL, FARM, TOWN, ANGLE, CREEK, DAIRY, CORNER, HAMLET, BOROUGH, VILLAGE, FARMSTEAD

wicked: . . . BAD, DARK, EVIL, FOUL, LEWD, VILE, WRONG, GUILTY, HORRID, SINFUL, UNHOLY, UNJUST, BEASTLY, GODLESS, HEINOUS, HELLISH, IMMORAL, IMPIOUS, NAUGHTY, NOXIOUS, PROFANE, UNGODLY, VICIOUS, CRIMINAL, DEPRAVED, DEVILISH, DIABOLIC, FELONOUS, FIENDISH, FLAGRANT, INDECENT, PERVERSE, ATROCIOUS, MALACIOUS, NEFARIOUS, PERNICIOUS

wicker: . . . . . . TWIG, OSIER, WITHE, WILLOW

wicket: . . ARCH, DOOR, GATE, HOOP, HATCH, STUMP, WINDOW, OPENING

wickiup: . . . . . . HUT, TEPEE, SHELTER, WIGWAM

wide: . . . . . . AMPLE, BROAD, LARGE, LOOSE, ROOMY, OPENED, EXPANDED, SPACIOUS, CAPACIOUS, EXTENSIVE

widely: . . FAR, AFAR, BROAD, ABROAD, GREATLY, LARGELY

widen: . . . . REAM, DIALATE, EXPAND, EXTEND, SPREAD, AMPLIFY, BROADEN, ENLARGE

widespread: . . RIFE, DIFFUSE, GENERAL, POPULAR, RAMPANT, CATHOLIC, EXTENDED, PANDEMIC, SWEEPING, EXTENSIVE, PERVASIVE, PREVALENT, UNIVERSAL

widow: . . . . . DAME, WIDDY, MATRON, RELICT, DOWAGER, BEREAVED

width: . . . . GIRTH, BREADTH, BROADNESS, WIDENESS, LATITUDE

wield: . . . . . PLY, RUN, BEAR, COPE, DEAL, RULE, APPLY, EXERT, POWER, SWING, DIRECT, EMPLOY, GOVERN, BRANDISH, EXERCISE, DETERMINE, MANIPULATE

wife: . . . . UX, HEN, RIB, MRS, FEME, FERE, FRAU, FROW, MAMA, MATE, UXOR, BRIDE, GAMMER, MISSIS, MISSUS, MATRON, SQUAW, WAHINE, CONSORT, PARTNER, HELPMATE, HELPMATE, MISTRESS

wig: . . . . . . RUG, GIZZ, TETE, JUDGE, SCOLD, PERUKE, REBUKE, TOUPEE, CENSURE, PERIWIG

wiggle: . . . . . . WAG, SHAKE, JIGGLE, WAGGLE, WANGLE, WOBBLE, STAGGER, WRIGGLE

wigwag: . . . . . . CODE, SIGNAL

wigwam: . . . . . . TIPI, LODGE, TEPEE, TEEPEE, WICKIUP

wild: . . . . . MAD, REE, DAFT, FAST, GAGA, CRAZY, FERAL, ROUGH, WASTE, DESERT, FERINE, FIERCE, LAVISH, MADCAP, RAMAGE, SAVAGE, STORMY, UNRULY, BESERK, BESTIAL, ERRATIC, FRANTIC, NATURAL, RIOTOUS, UNTAMED, ABERRANT, AGRESTAL, BARBARIC, CHIMERIC, DESOLATE, FAROUCHE, FRENETIC, HELLICAT, RECKLESS, UNTILLED, BARBAROUS, DISTURBED, FEROCIOUS, PHRENETIC, PRIMITIVE, TURBULENT, UNBRIDLED, BOISTEROUS, DISORDERLY, LICENTIOUS

wildcat: . . . . BALU, EYRA, LYNX, MARGAY, OCELOT, SERVAL, PANTHER

wildebeest: . . GNU, ANTELOPE

wilderness: . . . BUSH, WASTE, DESERT, FOREST, JUNGLE, STEPPE, TUNDRA, SOLITUDE, BADLANDS, BOONDOCKS, WASTELAND

wildness: . . . FERITY, RAMAGE, FEROCITY, SAVAGERY

wile: . . . . . ART, LURE, RUSE, CHARM, FRAUD, GUILE, TRICK, ALLURE, DECEIT, ENTICE, BEGUILE, ARTIFICE, TRICKERY, STRATAGEM

will: . . . . . . EGO, MAY, WISH, SHALL, POWER, CHOICE, CHOOSE, DECREE, DESIRE, DEVISE, LEGATE, LIKING, PREFER, COMMAND, AMBITION, APPETITE, BEQUEATH, PLEASURE, VOLITION, INTENTION, TESTAMENT

addition to: . . . . . CODICIL

handwritten: . HOLOGRAPH

having made a: . . TESTATE

having no: . . . . INTESTATE

maker: . . . . DEVISOR, TESTATOR

willful: . . . . . . RASH, HEADY, FEISTY, WAYWARD, STUBBORN, CAMSTEARY, OBSTINATE, HEADSTRONG

willies: . . . . CREEPS, JITTERS, NERVOUSNESS

willing: . . . . APT, BAIN, FAIN, GLAD, LIEF, PRONE, READY, MINDED, CONTENT, TENDING, DESIROUS, DISPOSED, UNFORCED, AGREEABLE, CONSENTING, VOLITIONAL

willingly: . . . . . . FAIN, LIEF, FREELY, GLADLY, READILY

willow: . . ITEA, OSIER, SALIX, SALLOW, TEASER

twig: . . . . OSTER, WITHE, SALLOW

willowy: . . . . . LITHE, SVELT, PLIANT, SLENDER, FLEXIBLE

wilt: . . . . . . EBB, SAG, DROP, FADE, FLAG, DROOP, WITHER, SHRIVEL, LANGUISH, COLLAPSE

wily: . . . . SLY, FOXY, CANNY, SLICK, SMART, ARTFUL, ASTUTE, CLEVER, CRAFTY, SHREWD, SUBTLE, TRICKY, CUNNING, POLITIC, INSIDIOUS

wimble: . . . . AWL, BORE, AUGER, BRACE, BRISK, ACTIVE, GIMLET, LIVELY, NIMBLE, PIERCE, PENETRATE

wimple: . BEND, FOLD, TURN, VEIL, WIND, CURVE, TWIST, GORGET, RIPPLE, MEANDER, HEADDRESS

win: . . . . BAG, COP, GET, HIT, EARN, GAIN, LICK, TAKE, CHARM, SCORE, SWEEP, ATTAIN, CLINCH, DEFEAT, OBTAIN, SECURE, ACHIEVE, ACQUIRE, CAPTURE, CONQUER, PREVAIL, SUCCEED, TRIUMPH, VANQUISH, CAPTIVATE, OVERCOME, ACCOMPLISH

wince: . . . . . . REEL, START, CRINGE, FLINCH, RECOIL, SHRINK, GRIMACE

winch: . . JACK, REEL, CRANK, HOIST, ROLLER, WHIMSY, WINDLASS

wind: . . . . . . AIR, BIRR, BISE, BORA, COIL, CURL, FLAW, GALE, GUST, KONA, PUFF, REEL, WEND, WRAP, BLAST, CRANK, CURVE, EURUS, FOEHN, NOSER, SPOOL, STORM, TRADE, TWINE, TWIST, WEAVE, BOREAS, BOUGHT, BREATH, BREEZE, BUSTER, GIBLEH, SAMIEL, SIMOON, SILMOON, SQUALL, ZEPHYR, CHINOOK, CYCLONE, ENTWINE, ESTESIAN, GREGALE, KHAMAIN, MEANDER, MISTRAL, MONSOON, PAMPERO, REVOLVE, SIROCCO, TEMPEST, TORNADO, TYPHOON, WULLIWA,

BLIZZARD, LEVANTER,
HURRICANE, NOREASTER
gauge: . . . . VANE,
ANEMOMETER
instrument: . . . SAX, FIFE,
HORN, OBOE, REED, TUBA,
BUGLE, FLUTE, ORGAN,
CORONET, BASSOON,
HAUTBOY, OCARINA,
SACKPUT, CLARINET,
TROMBONE, HARMONICA,
SAXOPHONE
windfall: . . . . . . BOON, VAIL,
GRAVY, BONANZA, FORTUNE,
BUCKSHEE
winding: . . . . . MAZY, WILY,
CRANK, AMBAGE, DETOUR,
SCREWY, SPIRAL, TRICKY,
TWISTY, COILING, CRINKLE,
DEVIOUS, MEANDER, SINUOUS,
SNAKING, WRIGGLY, RAMBLING,
TORTUOUS, TWISTING,
DECEITFUL, INTRICATE,
MEANDROUS, CIRCUITOUS,
SERPENTINE
windlass: . . . . . CRAB, REEL,
HOIST, WINCH, CAPSTAN
window: . . . . BAY, PORT,
GABLE, GLAZE, ORIEL,
DORMER, GRILLE, LANCET,
WICKET, BALCONE, FENETRE,
LUCARNE, LUTHERN, MIRADOR,
OPENING, ORIFICE, TRANSOM,
APERTURE, CASEMENT,
FENESTER, FANLIGHT, SKYLIGHT
windpipe: . ARTERY, GULLET,
THROAT, WEASAND, TRACHEA,
THROTTLE, ESOPHAGUS
windrow: . . SWATH, FURROW
windy: . . . . . . AIRY, BLOWY,
EMPTY, GUSTY, HUFFY,
BREEZY, STORMY, GUSTFUL,
POMPOUS, VERBOSE, BOASTFUL,
AEOLISTIC, BOMBASTIC,
BOISTEROUS
wine: . . . . . VIN, ASTI, BRUT,
PORT, ROSE, MEDOC, RHINE,
SOAVE, TOKAY, CANARY,
CLARET, SHERRY, CATAWBA,

CHABLIS, CHATEAU, CHIANTI,
MADEIRA, MARGAUX,
MARSALA, VINTAGE, MOSELLE,
BORDEAUX, BURGUNDY,
DUBONNET, MUSCADEL,
MUSCATEL, RIESLING,
SAUTERNE, VERMOUTH,
CHAMPAGNE, ZINFANDEL,
BEAUJOLAIS
wing: . . ALA, ARM, BAY, ELL,
FAN, FIN, FLY, OAR, RIB, VAN,
LIMB, SAIL, ALULA, ANNEX,
FLANK, PINNA, VOLET, WOUND,
FLIGHT, HASTEN, PENNON,
PINION, FLUTTER
winged: . . . . . . AILE, ALAR,
ALATE, LOFTY, RAPID, SWIFT,
ALATED, PENNATE, WOUNDED,
ELEVATED, FEATHERED
wingless: . . . . APTERAL,
APTEROUS
wink: . . . . . BAT, NAP, HINT,
BLINK, FLASH, GLEAM, PRINK,
SLEEP, SIGNAL, CONNIVE,
FLICKER, INSTANT, NICTATE,
SLUMBER, SPARKLE, TWINKLE
winner: . . . . EARNER, VICTOR,
FACEMAN, SLEEPER, BANGSTER,
CONQUEROR
winning: . . . . . GAIN, SWEET,
PROFIT, TAKING, VICTORY,
WINSOME, CHARMING,
ATTRACTIVE
winnow: . . FAN, BEAT, FLAP,
SIFT, DIGHT, SIEVE, ASSORT,
DELETE, REMOVE, SELECT,
ANALYZE, EXAMINE, SCATTER,
DISPERSE, SEPARATE,
ELIMINATE
winsome: . . . . GAY, BONNY,
MERRY, SWEET, BLITHE,
BONNIE, WINNING, CHARMING,
CHEERFUL, ENGAGING,
PLEASANT, AGREEABLE,
ATTRACTIVE
winter: . . . . . . FROST, SNOW,
SEASON, HIBERNATE
wintry: . . . ICY, AGED, COLD,
SNOWY, WHITE, BOREAL,

FRIGID, HIEMAL, STORMY, BRUMOUS, CHILLING, HIBERNAL

wipe: . . . . . DRY, MOP, RUB, BEAT, BLOW, DRUB, DUST, GIBE, KILL, JEER, SWAB, CLEAN, DIGHT, ERASE, STAIN, SWIPE, TOWEL, CANCEL, DEFEAT, EFFACE, REMOVE, SPONGE, STRIKE, STROKE, ABOLISH, CLEANSE, EXHAUST, SQUEEGEE, ELIMINATE, ERADICATE, LIQUIDATE, ANNIHILATE, OBLITERATE, EXTERMINATE

wiper: . . . . TOWEL, DUSTER, NAPKIN, DISHRAG, TRIPPET

wire: . . . . GUY, COIL, CABLE, STAPLE, FASTEN, STRAND, FILAMENT, TELEGRAM, TELEGRAPH, CABLEGRAM

wireless: . . . . RADIO

wiry: . . LEAN, THIN, HARDY, STIFF, TOUGH, KNOTTY, SINEWY, STRINGY, STRONG, THREADY

wisdom: . . . . WIT, LORE, SAVVY, SENSE, ADVICE, POLICY, JUDGMENT, PRUDENCE, SAPIENCE, SAGACITY, LEARNING, ERUDITION, KNOWLEDGE

wise: . . . . . HEP, DEEP, SAGE, SANE, WARY, AWARE, CANNY, SMART, SOUND, ADVISE, CRAFTY, DIRECT, INFORM, SHREWD, VERSED, CUNNING, ERUDITE EXPLAIN, HEEDFUL, KNOWING, LEARNED, POLITIC, PRUDENT, SAPIENT, DISCREET, INFORMED, PERSUADE, PROFOUND, SENSIBLE, COGNIZANT, EXPEDIENT, JUDICIOUS, PROVIDENT, SAGACIOUS, DISCERNING, OMNISCIENT, INTELLIGENT

wisecrack: . . . . . . GAG, GIBE, JOKE, QUIP

wish: . . . . . BID, CARE, HOPE, LONG, VOTE, WANT, WILL, COVET, CRAVE, DREAM, YEARN, BEHEST, DESIRE, INVOKE, LONGING, PROPOSE, REQUEST, PETITION, YEARNING, ASPIRATION

wishbone: . . . . . FURCULUM, FOURCHETTE

wishy-washy: . . . PALE, THIN, WEAK, BLAND, TEPID, VAPID, FEEBLE, TRASHY, WATERY, INSIPID, SLOVENLY, SLIPSHOD, NAMBY-PAMBY

wisp: . TATE, BROOM, BRUSH, BUNCH, SCRAP, SHRED, TORCH, TWIST, WHISK, BUNDLE, PARCEL, RUMPLE, WREATH, CRUMPLE, HANDFUL, FRAGMENT

wispy: . . . . . . FILMY, FRAIL, SLIGHT, SLENDER

wistful: . . . INTENT, LONGING, PENSIVE, WISHFUL, MOURNFUL, YEARNING, ATTENTIVE, NOSTALGIC

wit: . . . . WAG, KNOW, MIND, BRAIN, HUMOR, IRONY, LEARN, SENSE, THINK, ACUMEN, ESPRIT, NAMELY, REASON, SANITY, SATIRE, WISDOM, CUNNING, FACULTY, PUNSTER, SARCASM, WARLOCK, COMEDIAN, HUMORIST, REPARTEE, INTELLECT

witch: . . . HAG, HEX, CHARM, CRONE, HARPY, LAMIA, SIREN, SYBIL, CUMMER, KIMMER, WIZARD, ENCHANT, CARLINE, HELLCAT, FASCINATE, SORCERESS, ENCHANTRESS

witchcraft: . . CHARM, MAGIC, ABEAH, SORCERY, WIZARDRY

with: . . . BY, CUM, MID, MIT, AVEC, NEAR, ALONG, AMONG, AGAINST, ALONGSIDE

withdraw: . . GO, DROP, QUIT, TAKE, VOID, WEAN, AVOID, ABSENT, DEPART, DESERT, DETACH, FLINCH, RECALL, RECANT, RECEDE, REMOVE, RETIRE, REVOKE, SECEDE,

SHRINK, ABSCOND, DECLINE, DESCEND, DETRACT, EXTRACT, FORSAKE, PULLOUT, REFRAIN, REGRESS, RETRACT, RETREAT, SCRATCH, SECLUDE, SUBDUCE, SUBSIDE, ABSTRACT, ALIENATE, DEROGATE, EVACUATE, RENOUNCE, SEPARATE, SUBTRACT, DISENGAGE, SEQUESTER, RELINQUISH, RETROGRADE

withe: . . . ROPE, TWIG, OSIER, BRANCH, WILLOW, WICKER

wither: . . . . . AGE, DIE, DRY, FADE, PINE, WILT, DECAY, WIZEN, SHRINK, WEAKEN, SHRIVEL, WRINKLE, LANGUISH

withhold: . . . . CURB, DENY, HIDE, KEEP, STOP, CHECK, DESIST, DETAIN, REFUSE, RETAIN, ABSTAIN, BOYCOTT, FORBEAR, REFRAIN, REPRESS, RESERVE, POSTPONE, RESTRAIN, SUBTRACT

within: . . . IN, ON, BEN, INLY, INTO, AMONG, INNER, INTRA, DURING, HEREIN, INSIDE, INDOORS, ENCLOSED, INCLUDED, INWARDLY

without: . . . EX, BOUT, FREE, SANS, SINE, MINUS, BERIFT, BEYOND, LACKING, OUTSIDE, WANTING, OUTDOORS, OUTWARDLY, EXTERNALLY

withstand: . . . . . BEAR, BIDE, DEFY, ABIDE, COMBAT, ENDURE, OPPOSE, RESIST, CONTAIN, GAINSAY, CONFRONT, CONTEST, FORBEAR, CONTRADICT, CONTROVERT

witless: . . . . . . MAD, CRAZY, GROSS, SILLY, INSANE, STUPID, FATUOUS, FOOLISH, HEEDLESS, BRAINLESS, SLAPHAPPY

witness: . SEE, PROOF, TESTE, ATTEST, BEHOLD, MARTYR, RECORD, OBSERVE, TESTIFY, EVIDENCE, OBSERVER,

ONLOOKER, SPECTATOR, TESTIFIER

witticism: . . MOT, PUN, GIBE, JEER, JEST, JOKE, QUIP, SALLY, WISECRACK

witty: . . . . GASH, WILY, WISE, COMIC, DROLL, SHARP, SMART, BRIGHT, CLEVER, FACETE, JOCOSE, JOCUND, AMUSING, COMICAL, JOCULAR, KNOWING, HUMOROUS, FACETIOUS, INTELLIGENT

wizard: . . MAGE, SAGE, SEER, FIEND, WITCH, EXPERT, GENIUS, PELLAR, SHAMAN, MAGICAL, PRODIGY, WARLOCK, CHARMING, CONJURER, MAGICIAN, SORCERER

wizen: . . . . . . DRY, WITHER, SHRIVEL

wobble: . . . . SHAKE, WAVER, QUAVER, TREMBLE, WADDLE, SHIMMY, VACILLATE

woe: . . . . . BALE, BANE, PAIN, DOLOR, GRIEF, MISERY, SORROW, TROUBLE, CALAMITY, DISASTER, DISTRESS, DEJECTION, AFFLICTION, DESOLATION, MISFORTUNE

wolf: . . GLUT, LOBE, CANINE, CHANCO, COYOTE, MASHER, LADYKILLER, PHILANDERER

wolfish: . . . . RAVENOUS, RAPACIOUS

woman: . . . . DAM, GIN, HER, SHE, BINT, BABE, BABY, DAME, DONA, FRAU, FROW, JANE, JILL, LADY, MAID, MAMA, WIFE, BEGUM, BIDDY, BROAD, CHICK, DOLLY, DONNA, FEMME, FRAIL, MADAM, MUJER, QUEAN, SKIRT, SMOCK, SQUAW, TOOTS, VIXEN, AMAZON, CALICO, CUMMER, DOMIA, FEMALE, KIMMER, MATRON, MULIER, SENORA, SISTER, VIRAGO, WAHINE, CARLINE, DISTAFF, SIGNORA, FRAULEIN, DAUGHTER,

MISTRESS, SENORITA, PETTICOAT, SWEETHEART

attractive: . . . DISH, DOLL, PERI, BELLE, DOLLY, FILLY, HOURI, PIN-UP, SIREN, SYLPH, VENUS, BEAUTY, EYEFUL, LOOKER, VISION, CHARMER, STUNNER, VAMPIRE

kept: . . . . MISTRESS, CONCUBINE, DEMIMODAINE

lewd, loose: . . . BAG, BIM, TIB, DRAB, FLAP, JADE, JILT, SLUT, TART, BIMBO, BITCH, HUSSY, QUEAN, TROLL, WENCH, CHIPPY, GIGLET, HARLOT, MALKIN, WANTON, FLAPPER, COCOTTE, BAGGAGE, JEZEBEL, TROLLOP, COURTESAN

bad-tempered, objectionable: . CAT, GAD, HAG, NAG, SOW, BIDDY, BITCH, FAGOT, FRUMP, HARPY, HUSSY, SCOLD, SHREW, VIXEN, WITCH, FAGGOT, GORGON, HOYDEN, VIRAGO, HELLCAT, BATTLE-AX, FISHWIFE, HARRIDAN, SPITFIRE, GRIMALKIN, TERMAGANT

chaste, single: . . . VESTAL, VIRGIN, MISTRESS, SPINSTER

old, elderly: . . . GIB, HAG, HEN, BABA, DAME, TROT, CRONE, FAGOT, FRUMP, WITCH, BELDAM, MATRON, CARLIN(E), GAMMER, GRANNY, DOWAGER, HARRIDAN, GRANDDAM, SPINSTER, CAILLEACH

slang: . . . . . . BABE, DISH, DOVE, JILL, BIMBO, BROAD, CHICK, SKIRT, FLOSSY, SQUAW, TOOTS, BAGGAGE, FLOSSIE, TOMATO

slovenly, unattractive: . . . . BAG, DOG, SOW, DRAB,

SLUT, BEAST, CRONE, DOWDY, FRUMP, MALKIN, WITCH, BELDAME, TROLLOP, FLEABAG

young (also see girl): . . . . BIT, TIB, BIRD, BURD, CHIT, DELL, DOLL, LASS, PUSS, MINX, TART, CHICK, FILLY, FLUFF, NYMPH, TRULL, WENCH, DAMSEL, HEIFER, LASSIE, SHEILA, SUBDEB, CHICKEN, DAMOZEL, DAUGHTER

womb: . . . . BELLY, CRADLE, MATRIX, UTERUS, VENTER

wombat: . . . . BADGER, MARSUPIAL

wonder: . . AWE, MUSE, SIGN, UNCO, ADMIRE, ESTEEM, MARVEL, CURIOUS, MIRACLE, PRODIGY, STRANGE, SURPRISE, AMAZEMENT

wont: . . . USE, HABIT, USAGE, USUAL, CUSTOM, INCLINED, PRACTICE, ACCUSTOMED

woo: . . . . . . BEG, SUE, COAX, SEEK, SUIT, COURT, SPARK, SPOON, ASSAIL, INVITE, ADDRESS, BESEECH, ENTREAT, SOLICIT, IMPORTUNE

wood: . . . (also see tree) HAG, KEG, KIP, BOIS, BOSK, BOWL, CASK, HOLT, CAHUY, GROVE, HURST, STICK, TREES, XYLEM, FOREST, LUMBER, TIMBER, COPPICE

woodcutter: . . . . . . AXEMAN, LOGGER, SAWYER, CHOPPER, LUMBERJACK, LUMBERMAN

wooded: . . . BOSKY, SYLVAN, FORESTED

wooden: . . . . . . DRY, DULL, OAKEN, STIFF, TREEN, CLUMSY, STOLID, AWKWARD, DEADPAN, LIFELESS, SPIRITLESS, INSENSITIVE

woodland: . . GROVE, FOREST, TIMBERLAND

clearing: . . . . GLADE

woodsman: . . . . SCOUT,
HUNTER, RANGER, TRAPPER,
FORESTER, VOYAGEUR,
WOODCUTTER

woodwind: . . . OBOE, FLUTE,
BASSOON, PICCOLO, CLARINET,
SAXOPHONE

woody: . . . . BOSKY, SYLVAN,
XYLOID, LIGNOSE, LIGNEOUS

wooer: . . . . . . BEAU, LOVER,
SUITOR, COURTIER

woof: . . . . ABB, BARK, WEFT,
CLOTH, WEAVE, FABRIC,
FILLING, TEXTURE

wool: . . . . FUR, HAIR, LANA,
LAMB, PILE, SHAG, YARN
LLAMA, SHEEP, ALPACA,
ANGORA, GREASE, JERSEY,
MERINO, MOHAIR, TWEED,
FLEECE, FLANNEL, CASHMERE,
CLOTHING, MORTLING,
BROADCLOTH

woolly: . . . . FLEECY, LANOSE,
LANATE, FLOCCOSE, PERONATE,
FLOCCULENT

woozy: . . . . . . SICK, DRUNK,
SHAKY, TIGHT, BLURRY,
TREMBLY, MUDDLED,
BEFUDDLED

word: . . . NEWS, TALK, TERM,
ADAGE, HONOR, MAXIM,
MOTTO, ORDER, PAROL,
RUMOR, ASSENT, AVOWAL,
PLEDGE, REMARK, REPORT,
SAYING, SIGNAL, SPEECH,
ACCOUNT, ADJUNCT,
COMMAND, COMMENT, DICTION,
MESSAGE, PROMISE, PROVERB,
TIDINGS, ACROSTIC,
COMPOUND, LOCUTION,
DIRECTION, STATEMENT,
EXPRESSION, AFFIRMATION,
DECLARATION, INFORMATION
book: . . LEXICON, SPELLER,
LIBRETTO, THESAURUS,
DICTIONARY
figurative: . . . . TROPE,
SIMILE, METONYM,
METAPHOR

for word: . . . . . EXACTLY,
LITERAL, VERBATIM
of opposite meaning: . . . . .
ANTONYM
of similar meaning: . . . . . .
SYNONYM
*same pronunciation,
different meaning:* . . . .
HOMONYM, HOMOPHONE
*same spelling, different
meaning:* . . . . HETERONYM,
HOMOGRAPH

wordiness: . . . . . PLEONASM,
PROLIXITY, VERBIAGE,
VERBOSITY

wording: . . . . DICTION,
PHRASING, EXPRESSION,
PHRASEOLOGY

words: . . . . . . TEXT, LYRICS,
DISPUTE, QUARREL, LIBRETTO

wordy: . . . . . WINDY, PROLIX,
DIFFUSE, VERBOSE,
GARRULOUS, REDUNDANT

work: . . . DO, ACT, JOB, PLY,
DUTY, FEND, MOVE, OPUS,
PLAN, TASK, TEND, TILL, TOIL,
WORM, CHORE, CRAFT, DRAFT,
ERGON, EXERT, GRAFT, GRIND,
KNEAD, LABOR, PRESS, SOLVE,
STINT, TRADE, ARBEIT, DESIGN,
EFFECT, EFFORT, HUSTLE,
RESULT, STRIVE, BELABOR,
CALLING, EXECUTE, EXPLOIT,
EVOLVE, OPERATE, MISSION,
PATTERN, PERFORM, PURSUIT,
TRAVAIL, ACTIVITY, BUSINESS,
CREATION, DRUDGERY,
EXERCISE, EXECUTION,
EXERTION, FUNCTION,
INDUSTRY, STRUGGLE,
EMPLOYMENT, OCCUPATION,
PROFESSION, ACHIEVEMENT
assignment: . . . JOB, BEAT,
DUTY, CHORE, TASK, SHIFT,
STINT, TRICK, MISSION
avoid: . . . . SHIRK, SKULK,
GOLDBRICK, MALINGER,
BOONDOGGLE

group: . . . . CREW, GANG, TEAM, CORPS, DETAIL, SHIFT, STAFF, PERSONNEL

hard: . . . TEW, PLY, CHAR, GRUB, MOIL, MUCK, PLOD, PLUG, SLOG, TOIL, GRIND, LABOR, SWEAT, DRUDGE, EFFORT, HUSTLE, TRAVAIL, SLAVERY, DRUDGERY

workable: . . . . RIPE, YOUNG, MELLOW, PLIANT, FEASIBLE, PRACTICAL

workaday: . . DRUB, PROSAIC, HUMDRUM, ORDINARY, COMMONPLACE

worker: . DOER, HAND, HELP, HIND, SCAB, CLERK, NAVVY, SLAVE, EARNER, HELPER, TOILER, ARTISAN, EMPLOYE, LABORER, OPERATOR, SERVANT, DOMESTIC, ARTIFICER, CREATOR, CRAFTSMAN, OPERATIVE, WAGE-EARNER, BREADWINNER

working: . . . . . BUSY, ALERT, GOING, ACTIVE, RUNNING, EMPLOYED, OPERATING, OPERATIVE

world: . ORB, EARTH, GLOBE, REALM, COSMOS, DOMAIN, PUBLIC, KINGDOM, MANKIND, CREATION, HUMANITY, UNIVERSE

worldly: . . . . . LAY, CARNAL, EARTHY, EARTHLY, MUNDANE, PROFANE, SECULAR, SENSUAL, TERRENE, TEMPORAL, TERRESTIAL

worm: . . BOB, EEL, ESS, LOA, GRUB, NAID, NAIS, NEMA, LARVA, LEECH, SNAKE, TINEA, MAGGOT, PALOLO, TEREDO, WRETCH, ANNELID, ASCARID, REPTILE, SAGITTA, SERPENT, TAGTAIL, WRIGGLE, CERCARIA, HELMINTH, NEMATODE, NEMERTINA

worn, worn-out: . . . . . OLD, SERE, USED, EROSE, TIRED, JADED, PASSE, SEEDY, SPENT, STALE, TRITE, ERODED, EFFETE, FRAYED, RAGGED, SHABBY, ABRADED, ATTRITE, HAGGARD, CONSUMED, DECREPIT, FRAZZLED, OBSOLETE, WEAKENED, ENFEEBLED, EXHAUSTED, HACKNEYED, BEDRAGGLED, THREADBARE

worried: . . UNEASY, ANXIOUS, CONCERNED, CAREWORN

worry: . . . . DOG, NAG, VEX, BAIT, CARE, CARK, FAZE, FRET, FUSS, HARE, MOIL, STEW, ANNOY, CHOKE, GALLY, HARRY, HURRY, SHAKE, TEASE, TOUSE, BADGER, BOTHER, FIDGET, HARASS, HATTER, HECTOR, PESTER, PLAGUE, POTHER, ANXIETY, CHAGRIN, CONCERN, DISTURB, PERTURB, TORMENT, TROUBLE, DISTRESS, STRANGLE, UNEASYNESS

worship: . . . . . . CULT, FAME, LOVE, ADORE, DEIFY, DULIA, HONOR, CREDIT, HOMAGE, PRAISE, RENOWN, REPUTE, REVERE, IDOLISM, IDOLIZE, IMAGERY, LITURGY, BLESSING, DEVOTION, HIERURGY, IDOLATRY, VENERATE, ADORATION, REVERENCE, ADMIRATION, VENERATION

worshipper: . . . . . ADORER, VOTARY, DEVOTEE, DISCIPLE, ADMIRER, IDOLIST, IDOLATER, VENERATOR

worst: . . . . BEAT, BEST, LAST, OUTDO, DEFEAT, POOREST, DISCOMFIT, OVERTHROW

worsted: . . . . . GARN, WOOL, SERGE, ETAMINE, WHIPCORD, GABARDINE

worth: . . . . . . MERIT, PRICE, VALUE, BOUNTY, DESERT, ESTEEM, REGARD, RICHES, VIRTUE, WEALTH, DIGNITY, WORSHIP, SPLENDOR,

EMINENCE, DESERVING,
EXCELLENCE, IMPORTANCE

worthless: . . BAD, BUM, LOW,
BASE, EVIL, IDLE, VAIN, BILGE,
BLANK, DREGS, INANE, LOSEL,
LOUSY, SCRAP, TRIPE, ABJECT,
CHEESY, CRUMMY, DROSSY,
FUTILE, HOLLOW, MEASLY,
NAUGHT, PALTRY, PIDDLE,
PUTRID, ROTTEN, TRASHY,
FUSTIAN, NOTHING, RUBBISH,
USELESS, FECKLESS,
NUGATORY, TRIFLING,
WRETCHED, FRIVOLOUS,
VALUELESS

worthy: . DEAR, FAIR, GOOD,
NOBLE, PIOUS, CONDIGN,
ELIGIBLE, LAUDABLE,
MERITING, VALUABLE,
COMPETENT, DESERVING,
ESTIMABLE, QUALIFIED,
MERITORIOUS

would: . . . . . . WANT, WISH,
COULD, SHOULD

wound: . . . CUT, BITE, CLAW,
GASH, GORE, HARM, HURT,
MAIM, PAIN, SCAR, SORE, STAB,
FEAR, WING, BLOOD, BREAK,
GANCH, KNIFE, SHOOT, STICK,
STING, BREACH, BRUISE,
CREASE, DAMAGE, GRIEVE,
HARROW, INJURE, INJURY,
LESION, OFFEND, PIERCE,
TRAUMA, AFFLICT, ATTAINT,
BATTERY, BLISTER, SCRATCH,
DISTRESS, INCISION, LACERATE,
PUNCTURE, LACERATION

woven: . . . . . LACY, BROCHE,
BROCADE, DAMASSE

wrack: . . . KELP, RACK, RUIN,
TRASH, WRECK, AVENGE,
CLOUDS, DEFEAT, DESTROY,
SEAWEED, TORMENT,
CALAMITY, DOWNFALL,
WRECKAGE, OVERTHROW,
SHIPWRECK

wraith: . . . . . . WAFT, FETCH,
GHOST, SPOOK, SHADOW,
SPECTER, SPECTRE, APPARITION

wrangle: . . (also see **quarrel**)
RAG, ROW, MOIL, SPAR, TIFT,
ARGUE, BRAWL, CHIDE,
BICKER, DEBATE, HAGGLE,
HASSLE, CONTEND, DISPUTE,
SQUABBLE, ALTERCATION,
CONTROVERSY

wrangler: . . . . ARGUER,
COWBOY, DEBATER,
HERDSMAN, DEFENDER,
OPPONENT, DISPUTANT,
ANTAGONIST

wrap: . . . . . HAP, WAP, BIND,
CERE, COIL, FOLD, FURL, HIDE,
ROLL, TUCK, WIND, CLASP,
CLOAK, COVER, MANTA, NUBIA,
TWINE, AFGHAN, CLOTHE,
DOLMAN, ENFOLD, INVEST,
MUFFLE, SHROUD, SWATHE,
BLANKET, CONCEAL, ENCLOSE,
ENVELOP, PACKAGE, SWADDLE,
ENSHROUD, ENSWATHE,
SURROUND

wrapper: . . . GOWN, APRON,
COVER, SHAWL, SMOCK,
FARDEL, JACKET, VESTURE,
OVERALL, COVERING, GALABIA,
GALABEAH

wrath: . . . . IRE, FURY, RAGE,
ANGER, CHOLER, FELONY,
PASSION, VIOLENCE

wreak: . . . . . CAUSE, EXACT,
AVENGE, EXPEND, PUNISH,
GRATIFY, INDULGE, INFLICT,
REVENGE

wreath: . . LEI, ORLE, CROWN,
OLIVE, TORSE, WHORL,
ANADEM, CORONA, CRANTS,
LAUREL, SPIREA, CHAPLET,
CORONAL, CORONET, CROWNAL,
FESTOON, GARLAND, WRINKLE

wreathe: . . BIND, COIL, ROLL,
TURN, WIND, TWINE, TWIST,
WRING, WRENCH, WRITHE,
CONTORT, ENTWINE, ENVELOP,
INTWIST, INVOLVE, ENCIRCLE,
SURROUND

wreck: . . HULK, RAZE, RUIN,
BLAST, CRASH, RUINS, SMASH,

TRASH, WRACK, DAMAGE,
DEFEAT, DESPOIL, THWART,
DESTROY, DISABLE, FOUNDER,
SHATTER, TORPEDO, DEMOLISH,
DERELICT, SABOTAGE,
SHAMBLES, OVERTHROW,
DESTRUCTION

wreckage: . . WRACK, FINDAL,
JETSAM, FLOTSAM

wrench: . . . JERK, PIPE, PULL,
RACK, TEAR, TOOL, TURN,
CRICK, CRINK, FORCE, TWIST,
WREST, WRING, INJURY,
MONKEY, SPRAIN, STRAIN,
TWINGE, CRESCENT, DISTORT,
SPANNER, STILLSON,
DISTORTION

wrest: . . REND, RUSE, EXACT,
FORCE, FRAUD, SEIZE, STRIP,
TRICK, TWIST, USURP, WRING,
ELICIT, EXTORT, SNATCH,
WRENCH, EXTRACT, WRESTLE

wrestle: . . . . . TUG, RASSLE,
SQUIRM, STRIVE, TUSSLE,
WRAXLE, WRITHE, CONTEND,
GRAPPLE, SCUFFLE, STRUGGLE

wrestler: . . . . MATMAN,
MAULER, GRAPPLER

wretch: . . . BUM, DOG, WORM,
EXILE, LOSER, MISER, SLAVE,
BEGGAR, PAUPER, PARIAH,
CAITIFF, HILDING, OUTCAST,
SCROYLE, DERELICT,
RECREANT, SCULLION,
MISCREANT, POLTROON

wretched: . . SAD, BASE, EVIL,
FOUL, LEWD, LORN, MEAN,
POOR, DAWNY, SORRY, ABJECT,
DISMAL, MEAGER, PALTRY,
SHABBY, SICKLY, SORDID,
WOEFUL, ABYSMAL, BALEFUL,
CAITIFF, FORLORN, PITIFUL,
SQUALID, UNHAPPY, DEJECTED,
GRIEVOUS, INFERIOR,
AFFLICTED, EXECRABLE,
MISERABLE

wriggle: . . FRIG, LASH, TURN,
WIND, DODGE, EVADE, SLIDE,
SNAKE, TWIST, SQUIRM,

WIDDLE, WIGGLE, WINTLE,
WRITHE, MEANDER, TWIDDLE,
WRESTLE, SQUIGGLE,
EQUIVOCATE

wring: . . . . . . RACK, DRAIN,
EXACT, PRESS, SCREW, TWIST,
WREST, ELICIT, EXTORT,
SQUIRM, WRENCH, EXTRACT,
OPPRESS, SQUEEZE, TORMENT,
TORTURE, WRESTLE, COMPRESS,
STRUGGLE

wrinkle: . . . FAD, RUT, FOLD,
IDEA, KNIT, LIRK, RUCK, RUGA,
SEAM, BREAK, CRIMP, FANCY,
FAULT, REEVE, RIDGE, RIVEL,
TWIST, BUCKLE, COCKLE,
CREASE, FURROW, PUCKER,
RIMPLE, RUMPLE, CRIMPLE,
CRINKLE, CRUMPLE, FRUMPLE,
NOVELTY, SHRIVEL, CONTRACT,
CORRUGATE

wrinkled: . . . LINED, RUGATE,
RUGGED, RUGOSE, SEAMED,
COCKLED, ROUCHED, SAVOYED,
CRUMPLED, FURROWED,
PUCKERED, RUGULOSE,
WRIZZLED

wrist: . . . . ULNA, JOINT,
CARPUS, CARPAL(E)

wristband: . . . CUFF, BRACER

wristlet: . . . . . BAND, STRAP,
BRACELET, HANDCUFF

writ: . . . BREVE, BRIEF, TALES,
CAPIAS, ELEGIT, EXTENT,
PLAINT, VENIRE, DETINUE,
EXIGENT, PRECEPT, PROCESS,
SUMMONS, WARRANT,
DETAINER, DOCUMENT,
MANDAMUS, MITTIMUS,
REPLEVIN, SUPOENA,
WARRANTY, INJUNCTION,
INSTRUMENT

write: . . INK, JOT, PEN, DASH,
SIGN, DRAFT, DIRECT, ENFACE,
INDITE, RECORD, REPORT,
SCRAWL, SCRIBE, SCRIVE,
SKETCH, COMPOSE, DICTATE,
ENGROSS, SCRATCH, INSCRIBE,

SCRIBBLE, EXPATIATE,
LUCUBRATE
writer: . . . (also see **author**)
BARD, COPY, HACK, POET,
CLERK, GHOST, ODIST, CRITIC,
GLOZER, LAWYER, NOTARY,
PENMAN, RHYMER, SCRIBE,
ANALYST, COPYIST, ESSAYER,
GLOSSER, HYMNIST, PENSTER,
COMPOSER, DIDACTIC,
HUMORIST, LYRICIST, NOVELIST,
PREFACER, REPORTER,
REVIEWER, SCRIPTOR,
ANNOTATOR, COLUMNIST,
DRAMATIST, SCRIBBLER,
SCRIVENER, AMANUENSIS,
CHRONICLER, JOURNALIST,
PLAGARIST, BIOGRAPHER
writhe: . . BEND, CURL, TURN,
WIND, TWIRL, TWIST, WREST,
WRING, SCREEN, SQUIRM,
AGONIZE, CONTORT, SHRIVEL,
WRESTLE, WRIGGLE,
CONVOLVE, CONVOLUTE,
INSINUATE
writing: . . . . . BOOK, POEM,
WRIT, DIARY, CRAFT, ESSAY,
LIBEL, PROSE, VERSE, GOSSIP,
LETTER, SCRIPT, ARTICLE,
EPISTLE, CONTRACT,
DOCUMENT, PAMPHLET,
TREATISE, MONOGRAPH
wrong: . . BAD, ILL, OFF, OUT,
SIN, AWRY, EVIL, HARM, HURT,
TORT, ABUSE, AGLEY, AMISS,
CRIME, ERROR, FALSE, GRIEF,
MALUM, UNFIT, ASTRAY,
BLOOEY, FAULTY, INJURE,
INJURY, MALIGN, OFFEND,
SEDUCE, SINFUL, UNFAIR,
UNJUST, UNTRUE, WICKED,
ABUSIVE, CROOKED, DEFRAUD,
IMMORAL, MISDEED, NAUGHTY,
VIOLATE, AGGRIEVE,
COCKEYED, DISHONOR,
IMPROPER, INIQUITY,
MISTAKEN, PERVERSE,
ERRONEOUS, INCORRECT,
INJURIOUS, INJUSTICE,
VIOLATION, INACCURATE,
INIQUITOUS, MISCONDUCT,
MALFEASANCE, MISFEASANCE
wroth: . . . . . ANGRY, IRATE,
IREFUL, INCENSED, WRATHFUL,
TURBULENT
wrought: . . . . MADE, EAGER,
TENSE, BEATEN, FORMED,
SHAPED, WORKED, CREATED,
EXCITED, DECORATED,
HAMMERED, DISTURBED,
FASHIONED, STIMULATED
wry: . . . . . BEND, BIAS, SOUR,
TURN, ASKEW, AVERT, TWIST,
WRONG, WRING, SWERVE,
WARPED, WRITHE, CONTORT,
CROOKED, DEFLECT, DEVIATE,
DISTORT, TWISTED, CONTRARY,
PERVERSE, DISTORTED

X

X: . . . . . TEN, MARK, CROSS,
ERROR, MISTAKE, SIGNATURE
Greek: XI
xanthic: . . . . YELLOW,
YELLOWISH
Xanthippe: . . SCOLD, SHREW,
NAGGER, VIRAGO, TERMAGANT
xanthous: . . . . YELLOW
Xavier, saint: . . . . FRANCIS
xebec: . . . BOAT, SHIP, VESSEL,
CHEBEC
xenium: . . . . GIFT, PRESENT,
DELICACY
xeno: . . . . GUEST
Xeres: . . . . . . WINE, JEREZ,
SHERRY
xerophilous plant/animal: . . .
CAMEL, CACTUS, XEROPHYTE
xerotic: . . . . DRY, SEC
xiphoid: . . ENSIFORM, SWORD-
SHAPED
Xmas: . . . . YULE(TIDE),
CHRISTMAS
Xtian: . . . . CHRISTIAN
xurel: . . . . SCAD, SAUREL
xylem: . . . WOOD, HADROM(E)

xyloid: . . . . WOODY, LIGNEUS
xylonite: . . . . CELLULOID
xylophone: . . REGAL, SARON,
BALAFO, GAMBANG, GAMELON,
MARIMBA, GAMELANG,
GIGELIRA, STICCADO
xyst, xystos, xystus: . . STOA,
WALK, PORCH, PORTICO,
TERRACE
xyster: . . . . . (BONE)SCRAPER

Y

Y: *Greek:* . . . . UPSILON
Hebrew: . . . . YOD(H)
yabber: . . . . . TALK, GIBBER,
JABBER, CHATTER
yacht: . . . . BOAT, RACE, SAIL,
SHIP, CRAFT, SONDER,
CRUISE(R)
basin: . . . . MARINA
flag: . . . . BURGEE
tender: . . . . DINGHY
yaffle: . . ARMFUL, HANDFUL,
WOODPECKER
yahoo: . . . . . . LOUT, BRUTE,
CLOWN, ROWDY, BUMPKIN
Yahwe(h): . . . GOD, JEHOVAH
yak: . . . . OX, GAG, JOKE,
LAUGH, SARLAK, BUFFALO
yakka: . . . . . . WORK, LABOR
Yale: . . . . ELI, LOCK,
UNIVERSITY
yam: . . HOI, UBE, UBI, LIMA,
ROOT, TUGUI, IGNAME, BONITA,
(SWEET)POTATO
yamen: . . . . . COURT, OFFICE,
MANSION, RESIDENCE
yammer: . . CRY, WAIL, YELL,
CRAVE, SCOLD, SHOUT, WHINE,
YEARN, CLAMOR, DESIRE,
LAMENT, CHATTER, GRUMBLE,
WHIMPER, COMPLAIN
yank: . . . BLOW, FLOG, JERK,
PULL, HOICK, BUFFET, TWITCH
Yank, Yankee: . AMERICAN,
NORTHERNER

yap: . . GAB, YIP, BARK, TALK,
YAWP, MOUTH, ROWDY, SCOLD,
JABBER, WAFFLE, BUMPKIN,
CHATTER, HOODLUM
Yaqui: . . . . . . RIVER, INDIAN
yard: . . . ROD, LAWN, QUAD,
SPAR, COURT, GARTH, PATIO,
STAFF, STICK, CONFINE,
GROUNDS, CURTILAGE,
ENCLOSURE, PLAYGROUND
yare: . BRISK, EAGER, QUICK,
READY, ACTIVE, LIVELY,
NIMBLE, PROMPT
yarn: . . . . ABB, GARN, SLUB,
TALE, FIBER, INKLE, STORY,
ANGORA, BOUCLE, CADDIS,
CREWEL, FLORET, MERINO,
SAXONY, SPINEL, THREAD,
CADDICE, EISWOOL, GENAPPE,
SCHAPPE, ROUNDING,
FINGERING
ball: . . . . CLEW, CLUE
knot: . . . . BURL
quantity: . . . . . COP, LEA,
CLEW, CLUE, HANK, HASP,
SKEIN, SPANGLE, SPINDLE
yardstick: . . . . . . STANDARD,
CRITERION
yashmak: . . . . VEIL
yatag(h)an: . . . KNIFE, SABER
yaud: . . . . JADE, MARE
yaupon: . . . HOLLY, CASSINE,
CASSENA
yaw: . . . . GAPE, TURN, VEER,
LURCH, SHEER, BROACH,
SWERVE, DEVIATE
yawl: . . BOAT, HOWL, DANDY,
KETCH, SCREAM, VESSEL,
SAILBOAT
yawn: . . . . GAP, GAPE, YAUP,
YAWP, CHASM, OPENING,
OSCITATE
cause, usually: . . . . ENNUI,
FATIGUE, BOREDOM,
TEDIUM, DULLNESS,
DROWSINESS
yawp: . . . . . . BAY, CRY, YAP,
BAWL, GAPE, YELP, YAWN,
STARE, SQUAWK, COMPLAIN

yclept: .... NAMED, CALLED, KNOWN (AS)

ye: ...... YOU, THEE, THOU

yea(h): ... JA, YA, AYE, YES, INDEED, TRULY, ASSENT, REALLY, VERILY

yeanling: .... KID, LAMB, NEWBORN

year: .... AGE, TIME, ANNO, ANNUS

designating a: .... LEAP, LUNAR, SOLAR, FISCAL, NATURAL, CALENDAR, SIDEREAL, TROPICAL, ASTRONOMICAL

yearbook: .. ANNAL, ANNUAL, SERIAL, ALMANAC

yearling: .... COLT, LEVERET, HORNOTINE

yearly: .. ETESIAN, ANNUALLY

yearn: .... BEG, YEN, ACHE, BURN, LONG, PINE, SIGH, CRAVE, ASPIRE, DESIRE, GRIEVE, HANKER, YAMMER

yeast: .... BEE, BEES, BARM, FOAM, RISE, FROTH, SPUME, LEAVEN, RISING, FERMENT

yeasty: ..... LIGHT, FROTHY, TRIVIAL, RESTLESS, FRIVOLOUS, UNSETTLED

yegg: ...... THIEF, ROBBER, BURGLAR, CRIMINAL, SAFECRACKER

yell: ...... CRY, RAH, CALL, GOWL, HOWL, ROAR, YARM, YOWL, CHEER, SHOUT, TIGER, WHOOP, OUTCRY, BELLOW, HOLLER, SCREAM, SHRIEK, YAMMER

yellow: .. BUFF, ECRU, GOLD, GULL, SERE, YOLK, ALOMA, AMBER, BLAKE, BLOND, FAVEL, LEMON, OCHRE, SANDY, BANANA, BUTTER, FLAVIC, FLAVID, FLAXEN, GOLDEN, JONQUIL, XANTHIC, COWARDLY, MUSTARD, SAFFRON, RECREANT, XANTHOUS, FLAVICANT, JAUNDICED

bird: .. CANARY, MELINE, ORIOLE, WARBLER, GOLDFINCH

yellowhammer: .. BIRD, YITE, VERDIN, FLICKER, WOODPECKER

yellowlegs: ..... SANDPIPER

yelp: ... CRY, YAP, YIP, BARK, BRAG, YAWP, BOAST, SHOUT, SHRIEK, SQUAWK, SQUEAL, ULULATE, COMPLAIN, CRITICIZE

yen: .... see **yearn**

yeoman: .. CLERK, RETAINER, MANSERVANT, ASSISTANT, FREEHOLDER

yes: .. AY, DA, IS, JA, SI, YA, AYE, ISS, OUI, YAW, YEH, YEP, YUP, YEAH, TRULY, AGREE, ASSENT, AGREEMENT, ASSUREDLY

yet: .. AND, BUT, NOW, ALSO, EVEN, STILL, ALGATE(S), THOUGH, BESIDES, FINALLY, FURTHER, HOWEVER, HITHERTO, EVENTUALLY

yeti: ... MONSTER, SNOWMAN

yew: .... TREE, CONIFER, EVERGREEN

Yiddish: .... JEWISH, LANGUAGE

synagogue: .... SHUL

yield: ..... BOW, NET, PAY, BEAR, BEND, CEDE, CESS, CROP, FALL, FOLD, GIVE, OBEY, QUIT, VAIL, WAGE, ADDLE, ADMIT, AGREE, ALLOW, AVALE, DEFER, BUDGE, GRANT, HEALD, HIELD, LEAVE, STOOP, WAIVE, ACCEDE, BUCKLE, COMPLY, IMPART, OUTPUT, PROFIT, RELENT, RENDER, RETURN, SOFTEN, SUBMIT, SUPPLY, SWERVE, ABANDON, CONCEDE, CONSENT, DELIVER, FURNISH, HARVEST, KNUCKLE, PRODUCE, PRODUCT, REVENUE, SUCCUMB, ACQUIESCE, SURRENDER, CAPITULATE, RELINQUISH

yill: .... ALE

yip: .... see **yelp**

yodel: . . . CALL, SING, CAROL, SHOUT, WARBLE, REFRAIN

yogi: . . YOGA, FAKIR, FAKEER, MYSTIC, SWAMI, ASCETIC

yoke: . . . . . BOW, TIE, BAIL, BOND, DRAG, JOIN, LINK, PAIR, SPAN, TEAM, BANGY, MARRY, BANGHY, CANGUE, COUPLE, HALTER, INSPAN, BONDAGE, ENSLAVE, HARNESS, OPPRESS, SLAVERY, RESTRAIN, SERVITUDE

yokefellow: . . . . MATE, WIFE, SPOUSE, PARTNER, ASSOCIATE, HUSBAND

yokel: . . . . OAF, BOOR, CLOD, HICK, JAKE, LOUT, RUBE, FARMER, OBTUSE, RUSTIC, BUMPKIN, HAYSEED, ABDERITE, GULLIBLE, COUNTRYMAN

yolk: . . . . CENTER, YELLOW, ESSENCE, VITELLUS

yon(der): . . . . AWAY, THAT, THERE, THOSE, BEYOND, DISTANT, FARTHER, FURTHER, THITHER

yore: . ELD, PAST, LONG AGO

young: . . FRY, TYRO, BROOD, FETUS, FRESH, GREEN, YOUTH, FOETUS, JUNIOR, LITTER, CHILDISH, IMMATURE, JUVENILE, YOUTHFUL, OFFSPRING, ADOLESCENT

animal: . . . CUB, KID, PUP, CALF, COLT, FAWN, FOAL, JOEY, LAMB, CHICK, PUPPY, SHOAT, WHELP, KITTEN, FLEDGLING, SUCKLING

youngster: . . . (also see **child**) BOY, IMP, KID, LAD, TAD, TOT, BABY, GIRL, LASS, TIKE, YOUTH, MOPPET, SHAVER, URCHIN, BANTLING, SPALPEEN

youth: . . BUD, CHAP, CHABO, FILLY, MINOR, SWAIN, WHELP, HOYDEN, MASTER, SQUIRT, CALLANT, EPHEBOS, GOSSOON, JUVENAL, PUBERTY, SAPLING, JUVENILE, TEENAGER, STRIPLING, YOUNGSTER, ADOLESCENT, ADOLESCENCE

youthful: . . . . . NEW, EARLY, FRESH, GREEN, YOUNG, ACTIVE, JUNIOR, MAIDEN, VERNAL, VIRGIN, PUERILE, IMMATURE, JUVENILE, VIGOROUS

yow: . . . . GREAT, OUCH, WONDERFUL

yowl: . . . . CRY, HOWL, WAIL, YELL, YELP

yucca: . . LILY, PITA, PALMA, SOAPWEED

yule: . . . . NOEL, XMAS, CHRISTMAS, CHRISTMASTIDE

Z

Z: . . . .
Greek: . . . . ZETA
Hebrew: . . . . ZAYIN

zac: . . . . GOAT, IBEX

zacate, zacaton: . . . . . . HAY, GRASS, FORAGE

zany: . . DOLT, FOOL, CLOWN, CRAZY, DOTTY, NUTTY, TOADY, BUFFOON, IDIOTIC, CLOWNISH, SCREWBALL, SIMPLETON

zarf: . . . CUP, STAND, HOLDER

zeal: . . . . ELAN, FIRE, ARDOR, FLAME, HEART, SPIRIT, VERVE, DESIRE, FERVOR, WARMTH, PASSION, DEVOTION, INTEREST, EAGERNESS, ENTHUSIASM, FANTATICISM

zealot: . . . . FAN, BIGOT, VOTARY, DEVOTEE, FANATIC, PARTISAN, VOTARESS, ENTHUSIAST

zealous: . . . . . . HOT, RABID, ARDENT, FERVID, DEVOTED, EARNEST, EMULOUS, FERVENT, FORWARD, JEALOUS, FRENETIC, VIGOROUS, RELIGIOUS, PERFERVID, PHRENETIC, ENTHUSIASTIC

zebec(k): . . . . BOAT, SHIP

zebra: . . . . DAUW

extinct: . . . . QUAGGA

zebu: . . . . BRAHMA, BRAMIN

zecchin(o): . . . COIN, SEQUIN

zenana: . . HAREM, SERAGLIO

zenith: . . . TOP, ACME, APEX,
PEAK, VERTEX, HEIGHT,
SUMMIT, CULMINATION

zeppelin: . . . BLIMP, DIRIGIBLE

zero: . . . . . NIL, NUL, NULL,
EMPTY, CIPHER, (N)AUGHT,
(N)OUGHT, NOTHING, NULLITY,
SCRATCH

zest: . . . . PEP, VIM, ZIP, BRIO,
ELAN, TANG, ZEAL, ZING,
GUSTO, SAVOR, TASTE,
ENERGY, FLAVOR, RELISH,
STINGO, VITALITY, PIQUANCY,
ENJOYMENT, ENTHUSIASM

zestful: . . RACY, SAPID, SPICY,
BREEZY, HEARTY, PIQUANT,
PUNGENT

Zeus: . . . . ALASTOR, JUPITER

ziggurat: . . . TOWER, PYRAMID

zigzag: . . . . TACK, TURN,
ANGLE, CRANK, WEAVE,
BROKEN, INDENT, CRANKLE,
STAGGER, FLEXUOUS, TRAVERSE

zimarra: . . CLOAK, CASSOCK,
SOUTANE

zinc: . . . . ADAMINE, SPELTER,
TUTENAQUE, GALVANIZE

zing: . . . . see zest

zingara, zingaro: . . . . GYPSY

Zion: . . . . . . HILL, HEAVEN,
ISRAEL, UTOPIA

zip: . . . . see zest

zipper: . . . . FASTENER

zippy: . . . . . . BRISK, TANGY,
SNAPPY, ENERGETIC

zircon: . . . AZORITE, JACINTH

zither: . . KOTO, LYRE, ROTA,
VINA, CITHARA, AUTOHARP

zizith: . . . . FRINGES, TASSELS

zodiac: . . . . CIRCLE, GIRDLE,
BALDRIC

sign: . . LEO, RAM, BULL,
CRAB, FISH, GOAT, LION,
ARIES, LIBRA, SCALE,
TWINS, VIRGO, ARCHER,
CANCER, GEMINI, PISCES,
TAURUS, SCORPIO,
AQUARIUS, CAPRICORN,
SAGITTARIUS

zone: . . . AREA, BAND, BEAM,
BELT, CLIME, PATH, STRIP,
LAYER, TRACT, CIRCLE,
COURSE, GIRDLE, REGION,
CLIMATE, CIRCUIT, CINCTURE

zoo: . . VIVARIUM, MENAGERIE

zooid: . . . . CORAL, POLYPITE,
HYDRANTH

zoophyte: . . CORAL, SPONGE,
HYDROID, RETEPORE

zoril(a): . . . SKUNK, WEASEL,
POLECAT, MARIPUT

zoster: . . . . . . BELT, GIRDLE

zuccetto: . . . . CALOTTE,
SOLIDEO, SKULLCAP

zucchini: . . . GOURD, SQUASH

zuisin: . . . . . DUCK, WIDGEON

Zulu: . . . . BANTU, KAFFIR,
ISLAND, MATABELE

Zuni: . . . . . INDIAN, PUEBLO

zwieback: . . . . RUSK, TOAST

zygote: . . OOSPERM, OOSPORE,
SPORANT

zymase: . . . YEAST, ENZYME,
FERMENT

zymone: . . . . GLUTEN

THE UNITED STATES

For each of the states, this section gives the capital, principal cities or towns, major lakes, rivers, etc. State nicknames and state birds, flowers, and trees are also given.

Alabama:
Capital: Montgomery
Cities: Anniston, Birmingham, Decatur, Mobile, Selma
Lake: Martin
Mountain: Lookout, Raccoon
Nickname: Cotton State
River: Coosa, Mobile, Tennessee, Mississippi
State Bird: Yellowhammer
State Flower: Camellia
State Tree: Longleaf pine

Alaska:
Capital: Juneau
Cities: Anchorage, Fairbanks, Nome, Sitka
Islands: Adak, Atka, Attu, Kodiak, Aleutians, Priblofs
Mountain: McKinley
River: Yukon, Copper, Tanana
State Bird: Ptarmigan
State Flower: Forget-me-not
State Tree: Spruce

Arizona:
Capital: Phoenix
Cities: Yuma, Tempe, Tucson, Nogales, Flagstaff
Desert: Painted
Nickname: Apache, Ocotillo
River: Gila, Colorado
State Bird: Cactus Wren
State Flower: Sagugaro, Cactus
State Tree: Paloverde

Arkansas:
Capital: Little Rock
Cities: Fort Smith

Mountains: Ozark
Nickname: Wonder State, Bear State
State Bird: Mockingbird
State Flower: Apple Blossom
State Tree: Shortleaf pine

California:
Capital: Sacramento
Cities: San Francisco, Los Angeles, San Diego, San Jose, Long Beach, Oakland, Lodi, Carmel, Covina, Eureka, Fresno, Pomona, Alameda, Burbank, Altadena, Berkeley, Pasadena
Desert: Mojave, Colorado
Mountain: Muir, Lassen, Shasta, Whitney
Nickname: Golden State
Park: Sequoia, Yosemite
State Bird: Quail
State Flower: Poppy
State Tree: Redwood
Valley: Napa

Colorado:
Capital: Denver
Cities: Pueblo, Boulder, Greely, Colorado Springs
Mountain: Oso, Long's, Pike's, Elbert, Arapahoe
Nickname: Centennial State
Park: Estes
River: Yampa, Dolores, Gunnison, Colorado
State Flower: Columbine
State Tree: Spruce

Connecticut:
  Capital: Hartford
  Cities: Danbury, Meridian,
    Bridgeport, New Haven,
    Waterbury
  Nickname: Nutmeg State
  River: Housatonic
  State Bird: Robin
  State Flower: Laurel
  State Tree: Oak

Delaware:
  Capital: Dover
  Cities: Lewes, Newark,
    Chester, Elsmere,
    Wilmington
  Nickname: First, Diamond
  State Bird: Bluehen
  State Flower: Peach
  State Tree: Holly

District of Columbia:
  River: Potomac

Florida:
  Capital: Tallahassee
  Cities: Miami, Ocala,
    Tampa, Orlando,
    Pompano, Sarasota,
    Pensacola, Jacksonville
  Lake: Kissimmee,
    Okeechobee
  Nickname: Sunshine State
  State Bird: Mockingbird
  State Tree: Palmetto
  Wetlands: Everglades

Georgia:
  Capital: Atlanta
  Cities: Macon, Augusta,
    Columbus, Decatur,
    Marietta, Savannah
  Mountain: Kenneshaw
  Nickname: Peach State
  State Bird: Thrasher
  State Tree: Live Oak

Hawaii:
  Capital: Honolulu
  Cities: Hilo, Kailua

  Beach: Waikiki
  Islands: Maui, Oahu, Kauai,
    Lanai, Hawaii, Niihau,
    Molokai, Kahoolawe
  Nickname: Aloha
  State Bird: Goose
  State Flower: Hibiscus
  State Tree: Candlenut
  Volcano: Kilauea, Mauna
    Kea, Mauna Loa

Idaho:
  Capital: Boise
  Cities: DuBois, Moscow,
    Nampa, Pocatello, Twin
    Falls
  Nickname: Gem State,
    Potato State
  River: Columbia, Snake
  State Bird: Bluebird
  State Flower: Syringa
  State Gem: Garnet

Illinois:
  Capital: Springfield
  Cities: Alton, Cairo, Elgin,
    Pekin, Joliet, Peoria,
    Moline, Skokie, Urbana,
    Chicago, Decatur,
    Rockford
  Lake: Michigan
  Nickname: Prairie
  River: Ohio, Rock, Wabash,
    Sangamon
  State Bird: Cardinal
  State Flower: Violet
  State Tree: Oak

Indiana:
  Capital: Indianapolis
  Cities: Gary, Peru, Angola,
    Goshen, Kokomo,
    Muncie, Wabash,
    Evansville
  Lake: Manitou, Michigan
  Nickname: Hoosier
  River: Ohio, Wabash,
    White, Tippecanoe
  State Bird: Cardinal

State Flower: Peony
State Tree: Tulip

Iowa:
  Capital: Des Moines
  Cities: Ames, Sioux,
    Clinton, Dubuque,
    Waterloo, Davenport,
    Cedar Rapids
  Nickname: Hawkeye
  River: Cedar, Skunk,
    Missouri
  State Bird: Goldfinch
  State Flower: Wild Rose
  State Tree: Oak

Kansas:
  Capital: Topeka
  Cities: Dodge, Salina,
    Topeka, Abilene, Wichita
  Nickname: Jayhawker,
    Sunflower
  River: Saline, Arkansas,
    Missouri
  State Bird: Meadowlark
  State Flower: Sunflower
  State Tree: Cottonwood

Kentucky:
  Capital: Frankfort
  Cities: Berea, Harlan,
    Paducah, Covington,
    Lexington, Owensboro
  Lake: Cumberland
  Nickname: Bluegrass
  River: Ohio, Salt
  State Bird: Cardinal
  State Flower: Goldenrod
  State Tree: Tulip

Louisiana:
  Capital: Baton Rouge
  Cities: Monroe, Bogalusa,
    Shreveport, New Orleans
  County: Parish
  Dialect: Creole
  Nickname: Sugar, Creole,
    Pelican
  River: Amite, Sabine,
    Mississippi

Stream: Bayou
State Bird: Pelican
State Flower: Magnolia
State Tree: Cypress

Maine:
  Capital: Augusta
  Cities: Bath, Auburn,
    Bangor, Lewiston,
    Portland
  Lake: Moose, Sebago
  Mountain: Katahdin
  Nickname: Lumber, Pinetree
  River: Saco, Kennebee
  State Bird: Chickadee
  State Flower: Pinecone
  State Tree/Symbol: Pine

Maryland:
  Capital: Annapolis
  Cities: Aberdeen, Bethesda,
    Baltimore
  Founder: Calvert
  Nickname: Cockcade,
    Oldline
  River: Chester, Potomac
  State Bird: Oriole
  State Tree: Oak

Massachusetts:
  Capital: Boston
  Cities: Lynn, Salem,
    Lowell, Quincy, Revere,
    Holyoke, Plymouth,
    Cambridge, Worcester,
    Springfield
  Island: Nantucket
  Mountain: Tom, Taconic,
    Berkshire
  Nickname: Bay State
  Pond: Walden
  River: Charles
  State Bird: Chickadee
  State Flower: Arbutus,
    Mayflower
  State Tree: Elm

Michigan:
  Capital: Lansing
  Cities: Flint, Adrian,
    Warren, Detroit, Lansing,

Pontiac, Saginaw, Ann
Arbor, Dearborn,
Muskegon, Marquette,
Kalamazoo, Grand Rapids
Lake: Huron, Ontario,
Michigan, Superior
Nickname: Wolverine
River: Cass, Huron
Strait: Mackinac
State Bird: Robin
State Flower: Apple
Blossom
State Fish: Trout

Minnesota:
Capital: St. Paul
Cities: Ely, Duluth,
Winoma, Bemidji,
Hibbing, Mankato,
Rochester, Minneapolis
Lake: Itasca, Superior
Mountain: Eagle, Mesabi
Nickname: Gopher
River: Mississippi, St. Croix
State Bird: Loon
State Tree: Red Pine

Mississippi:
Capital: Jackson
Cities: Biloxi, Natchez,
Gulfport, Meridian,
Hattiesburg
Nickname: Bayou, Magnolia
River: Pearl, Yazoo, Big
Black, Mississippi
State Bird: Mockingbird
State Flower: Magnolia
State Tree: Magnolia

Missouri:
Capital: Jefferson City
Cities: Joplin, Sedalia, St.
Louis, Hannibal, Kansas
City
Mountains: Ozarks
Nickname: Show me,
Bullion
State Bird: Bluebird
State Flower: Hawthorn

State Tree: Dogwood

Montana:
Capital: Helena
Cities: Butte, Billings,
Missoula, Great Falls
Lake: Flathead, Medicine
Mountain: Bitterroot, Lewis,
Cabinet, Big Belt
Nickname: Big Sky
Park: Glacier
River: Teton, Littlehorn,
Missouri
State Bird: Meadowlark
State Flower: Bitterroot

Nebraska:
Capital: Lincoln
Cities: Omaha, Fremont,
Hastings
Nickname: Cornhusker
River: Platte, Elkhorn
State Bird: Meadowlark
State Flower: Goldenrod
State Tree: Elm

Nevada:
Capital: Carson City
Cities: Elko, Reno, Las
Vegas
Lake: Tahoe
Nickname: Silver
State Bird: Bluebird
State Flower: Sagebrush
State Tree: Pinon, Aspen

New Hampshire:
Capital: Concord
Cities: Dover, Keene,
Exeter, Nashua,
Manchester
Lake: Sunapee
Mountain: White, Mt.
Washington
Nickname: Granite State
River: Saco, Merrimack
State Bird: Finch
State Flower: Lilac
State Tree: Birch

New Jersey:
Capital: Trenton
Cities: Camden, Newark,
Rahway, Bayonne,
Hoboken, Passaic,
Trenton, Elizabeth,
Paterson, Secaucus,
Hackensack
Nickname: Garden State
River: Passaic, Raritan,
Ramapo
State Bird: Goldfinch
State Flower: Violet
State Tree: Red Oak

New Mexico:
Capital: Santa Fe
Cities: Hobbs, Clovis,
Gallup, Carlsbad,
Roswell, Albuquerque
Cavern: Carlsbad
Mountain: Wheeler
Nickname: Yucca, Sunshine
River: Gila, Pecos,
Cimmarron
State Bird: Roadrunner
State Flower: Yucca
State Tree: Pinon

New York:
Capital: Albany
Cities: Rye, Rome, Troy,
Utica, Elmira, Ithaca,
Buffalo, Saratoga,
Syracuse, Yonkers,
Rochester
City Boroughs: Bronx,
Kings, Queens, Brooklyn,
Richmond, Manhattan
Island: Fire, Long, Ellis,
Staten, Liberty, Shelter,
Governors, Manhattan
Lake: Erie, Cayuga, George,
Oneida, Placid, Seneca,
Ontario, Saranac, Success
Mountains: Catskill,
Appalachian, Adirondack,
Taconic
Nickname: Empire

River: Harlem, Hudson,
Mohawk, Niagara,
Genesee
State Bird: Bluebird
State Flower: Rose
State Tree: Sugar Maple

North Carolina:
Capital: Raleigh
Cities: Durham, Shelby,
Raleigh, Gastonia,
Charlotte, Greensboro
Cape: Fear, Hatteras,
Lookout
Nickname: Tarheel State
River: Tar, Neuse, Peedee,
Roanoke
State Bird: Cardinal
State Flower: Dogwood
State Tree: Pine

North Dakota:
Capital: Bismark
Cities: Minot, Fargo,
Jamestown, Grand Forks
Mountain: White Butte
Nickname: Flickertail, Sioux
River: Missouri
State Bird: Meadowlark
State Flower: Pairie Rose
State Tree: Elm

Ohio:
Capital: Columbus
Cities: Akron, Canton,
Dayton, Toledo,
Sandusky, Cincinnati,
Cleveland, Youngstown
Lake: Erie
Nickname: Buckeye State
River: Miami, Scioto, Ohio
State Bird: Cardinal
State Flower: Carnation
State Tree: Buckeye

Oklahoma:
Capital: Oklahoma City
Cities: Ada, Enid, Miami,
Tulsa, Lawton, Stillwell,
Muskogee

Nickname: Sooner State
River: Red, Arkansas,
Canadian, Cimarron
State Flower: Mistletoe
State Tree: Redbud

Oregon:
Capital: Salem
Cities: Eugene, Astoria,
Medford, Coquille,
Portland, Corvallis
Dam: Bonneville
Mountain: Hood, Cascades,
Wilson
Nickname: Beaver State
River: Snake, Columbia,
Kalamath, Willamette
State Bird: Meadowlark
State Flower: Grape
State Tree: Fir

Pennsylvania:
Capital: Harrisburg
Cities: Erie, York, Scranton,
Altoona, Lancaster,
Allentown, Pittsburgh,
Philadelphia, Gettysburg
Mountain: Pocono,
Allegheny, Appalachian
Nickname: Keystone State
River: Ohio, Allegheny,
Delaware, Monongahela,
Susquehanna
Sect: Amish
State Bird: Grouse
State Flower: Laurel
State Tree: Hemlock

Rhode Island:
Capital: Providence
Cities: Bristol, Newport,
Warwick, Cranston,
Pawtucket
Founder: Roger Williams
River: Pawtuxet, Blackstone
State Flower: Violet
State Tree: Maple

South Carolina:
Capital: Columbia
Cities: Aiken, Greenville,
Charleston, Spartanburg

Fort: Sumter
Island: Hilton Head
Lake: Catawba, Moultrie
Mountain: Blue Ridge,
Sassafras
River: Peedee, Saluda,
Santee, Catawba,
Savannah
State Bird: Wren
State Flower: Jasmine
State Tree: Palmetto

South Dakota:
Capital: Pierre
Cities: Huron, Yankton,
Aberdeen, Deadwood,
Rapid City, Sioux Falls
Monument: Rushmore
Mountain: Black Hills
Nickname: Coyote
River: James, Missouri,
Vermillion, Big Sioux
State Bird: Phesant
State Flower: Pasque
State Tree: Spruce

Tennessee:
Capital: Nashville
Cities: Memphis, Jackson,
Pulaski, Knoxville,
Chattanooga
Dam: Norris, Wilson,
Wheeler
Mountain: Lookout,
Appalachian, Cumberland,
Smoky
Nickname: Volunteer State
Park: Shiloh
River: Cumberland,
Tennessee, Mississippi
State Bird: Mockingbird
State Flower: Iris
State Tree: Poplar

Texas:
Capital: Austin
Cities: Waco, Tyler, Dallas,
El Paso, Laredo, Odessa,
Abilene, Houston,

Lubbock, Amarillo, Fort
Worth, Galveston, San
Antonio, Corpus Christi
Fortress: Alamo
Nickname: Lone Star
River: Red, Pecos, Brazos,
Neches, Nueces, Rio
Grande
State Bird: Mockingbird
State Flower: Bluebonnet
State Tree: Pecan

Utah:
Capital: Salt Lake City
Cities: Logan, Ogden, Provo
Lake: Salt, Swan, Utah,
Sevier
Mountain: Kings, Uinta,
Peale, Wasateh
Nickname: Beehive State
Park: Zion
River: Weber, Jordan
Sevier, Colorado
State Bird: Seagull
State Flower: Sego Lily
State Tree: Spruce

Vermont:
Capital: Montpelier
Cities: Barre, Stowe,
Rutland, Bennington,
Burlington
Lake: Champlain
Mountain: Green, Taconic
Nickname: Green Mountain
State Bird: Thrush
State Flower: Clover
State Tree: Maple

Virginia:
Capital: Richmond
Cities: Norfolk, Pulaski,
Roanoke, Portsmouth,
Newport News, Virginia
Beach, Williamsburg
Mount: Vernon
Mountain: Appalachian,
Alleghany, Blue Ridge

Nickname: Old Dominion,
Mother of Presidents
River: James, Potomac,
Rapidan
State Bird: Cardinal
State Flower: Dogwood
State Tree: Dogwood

Washington:
Capital: Olympia
Cities: Tacoma, Yakima,
Everett, Rainier, Seattle,
Spokane, Aberdeen
Dam: Coulee
Mountain: Logan, Olympus,
Rainier, Cascade,
Olympic
Nickname: Chinook
River: Snake, Yakima,
Columbia
State Bird: Goldfinch
State Tree: Hemlock

West Virginia:
Capital: Charleston
Cities: Weirton, Wheeling,
Huntington
Mountain: Alleghany
Nickname: Mountain
River: Elk, Ohio, Potomac
State Bird: Cardinal
State Flower: Rhododendron
State Tree: Maple

Wisconsin:
Capital: Madison
Cities: Beloit, Racine,
Sparta, Ashland, Kenosha,
Oshkosh, La Crosse,
Milwaukee
Lake: Michigan, Winnebago
Nickname: Badger State
River: Fox, Black, Rock,
Chippewa
State Bird: Robin
State Fish: Musky
State Flower: Violet
State Tree: Maple

Wyoming:
  Capital: Cheyenne
  Cities: Cody, Laramie,
    Jackson, Rawlins,
    Sheridan
  Cavern: Shoshone
  Mountain: Moran, Teton,
    Laramie, Gannet Peak

Nickname: Equality
Park: Yellowstone
River: Snake, Teton, Platte,
  Big Horn
State Bird: Meadowlark
State Flower: Paintbrush
State Tree: Cottonwood

CANADA

Bay: James, Hudson, Ungara, Georgian
Capital: Ottawa
Island: Read, Banks, Bylot, Coats, Devon, Sable, Baffin, Mansel,
  Victoria, Anticosti, Vancouver
Lake: Bear, Cree, Cras, Seul, Garry, Rainy, Slave,Teslin, Louise,
  Simcoe, Abitibi, DuBawnt, Nipigon, Kootenay
Measure: ton, minor, perch, point, arpent, roture, chainon
Mountain: Gold, Logan, Robson, Cascade, Rockies, St. Elias,
  Notre Dame, Tremblant, Laurentian
Park: Yoho, Banff, Acadia, Jasper
River: Hay, Red, Back, Leaf, Peace, Slave, Yukon, Albany, Fraser,
  Nelson, Ottawa, Skeena, Thelon, Saquenay, Athabasca,
  Churchill, Mackenzie, Richelieu, St. Lawrence, Saskatche-
  wan
Symbol: Maple leaf
Territory: Yukon, Northwest

PROVINCES

The capital of each province is followed by a (c.).

Quebec: *Cit.:* Quebec City (c.), Hull, Sorel, Laval, Verdun, La
  Prarie; *Cape:* Gaspe; *Riv.:* Saguenay
Alberta: *Cit.:* Edmonton (c.), Calgary, Red Deer, Lethbridge,
  Medicine Hat; *Lake:* Banff, Jasper, Waterton; *Riv.:* Bow, Old-
  man, Wapiti, Athabasca
Ontario: *Cit.:* Toronto (c.), Emo, Galt, London, Ottawa, Windsor,
  Hamilton, Kingston, Kitchener; *Lake:* Simcoe, Oswego; *Canal:*
  Trent, Rideau
Manitoba: *Cit.:* Winnepeg (c.), Carman, Brandon, Dauphin, Kil-
  larney; *Riv.:* Red, Seal, Swan, Nelson, Pembina, Churchill,
  Saskatchewan
Nova Scotia (Acadia): *Cit.:* Halifax (c.), Truro, Pictou, Sydney,
  Arichat, Baddeck, Dartmouth; *Bay:* Fundy; *Strait:* Canso
New Brunswick: *Cit.:* Fredericton (c.), Burton, Moncton, Ba-
  thurst, Gagetown; *Mtn.:* Carleton
Newfoundland: *Cit.:* St. Johns (c.), Gander, Howley, Wabana,
  Cornerbrook; *Airport:* Gander; *Cape:* Ray, Race, Bauld; *Riv.:*
  Gander, Humber, Exploits

Saskatchewan: *Cit.:* Regina (c.), Climax, Estevan, Moosejaw, Rosetown, Saskatoon; *Lake:* Rouge, Reindeer, Athabaska, Churchill; *Riv.:* Wood, Moose, Souris, Frenchman
British Columbia: *Cit.:* Victoria (c.), Kelowna, Kamloops, Vancouver; *Mtn.:* Coast, Cariboo, Cascade, Purcell, Selkirk, Monashee; *Riv.:* Nass, Peace, Fraser, Skeena, Stikine
Prince Edward Island: *Cit.:* Charlottetown (c.), Abney, Souris, Tignish, Montague, Georgetown; *Bay:* Rollas, Edgmont, Orwell, Malpeque

COUNTRIES OF THE WORLD

This section contains the names of all the countries in the world together with their chief cities and rivers, the language or languages spoken in each, and the currency used. The capital of each country is listed together with the cities but is followed by (c.). For United States and Canada, see special sections.

Afghanistan: *Cit.:* Kabul (c.), Herat, Kunduz, Ghazni, Kandahar; *Riv.:* Kabul, Helamand; *Lang.:* Dari, Pahsto, Pushtu, Balochi, Baluchi; *Curr.:* Pul, Abbasi, Amania, Afghani
Albania: *Cit.:* Tirana, Tirane (c.), Berat, Avlona, Durres, Durazzo, Koritza, Scutari; *Riv.:* Arta, Drin; *Lang.:* Cham, Gheg, Tosk; *Curr.:* Lek, Frane, Quintar
Algeria: *Cit.:* Algiers (c.), Bone, Oran, Blida, Media, Annaba, Tlemcen, Constantine; *Lang.:* French, Arabic, Berber; *Curr.:* Algerian dinar
Angola: *Cit.:* Luanda (c.), Buengela, Mossamedes, Lobito; *Lang.:* Bantu, Kimbundu, Portuguese; *Curr.:* Macuta, Macute
Argentina: *Cit.:* Buenos Aires (c.), Azul, Goya, Puan, Bahia, Lanus, Salta, Parana, La Plata, Cordoba, Mendoza, Rosario, Tucuman; *Riv.:* Negro, Plata, Grande, Parana, Salado, Paraguay; *Lang.:* Spanish; *Curr.:* Peso, Centavo, Argentino
Armenia: *Cit.:* Erivan (c.), Erzurum, Trabzon, Yerevan; *Riv.:* Kur, Aras, Cyrus, Halys, Araxes, Tigris, Euphrates; *Lang.:* Armen, Gomer
Australia: *Cit.:* Canberra (c.), Perth, Darwin, Hobart, Sydney, Geelong, Adelaide, Brisbane, Hamilton, Toowomba, Melbourne, Newcastle; *Riv.:* Murray, Darling, Murrumidgee, Lachlan, Victoria; *Lang.:* English; *Curr.:* Australian dollar, Dump, Pound, Shilling
Austria: *Cit.:* Wein (c.), Vienna (c.), Graz, Linz, Salzburg, Innsbruck, Klagenfurt; *Riv.:* Inn, Mur, Drau, Elbe, Enns, Raab, Danube; *Lang.:* German; *Curr.:* Ducat, Krone, Florin, Heller, Zehner, Groschen, Schilling
Bahamas: *Cit.:* Nassau (c.), Freeport; *Islands:* Abaco, Exuma, Andros, Bimini, Eleuthera; *Lang.:* English; *Curr.:* Bahaman dollar

Bangladesh: *Cit.:* Dacca (c.), Chittagong, Chalna, Khulna; *Riv.:* Brahmaputra, Ganges; *Lang.:* Bengali, English; *Curr.:* Bangladesh rupee, Taka

Barbados: *Cit.:* Bridgetown (c.); *Native:* Bim; *Lang.:* English; *Curr.:* East Caribbean dollar

Belgium: *Cit.:* Brusels (c.), Antwerp, Mons, Charleroi, Namur, Liège, Ghent, Ypres, Ostend, Bruges, Verviers; *Riv.:* Lys, Dyle, Maas, Meuse, Scheldt; *Lang.:* Dutch, French, Walloon; *Curr.:* Belga, Franc, Centime

Bhutan: *Cit.:* Thimbu (c.), Punakha, Tashi Cho Dzong; *Lang.:* Dzongkha; *Curr.:* Indian rupee, Paisa

Bolivia: *Cit.:* La Paz (c.), Sucre (c.), Oruru, Potosi; *Riv.:* Beni, Orton, Mamore, Guapore, Paraguay; *Lang.:* Spnaish, Aymara, Quecha; *Curr.:* Tomin, Bolivar, Centavo, Boliviano

Botswana: *Cit.:* Gaborone (c.), Kayne, Serowe; *Lang.:* English, Bantu, Click, Tswana, Khoisan, Setswana; *Curr.:* South African rand

Brazil: *Cit.:* Brasilia (c.), Rio, Lapa, Para, Bahia, Belem, Cera, Natal, Manaos, Santos, Campinas, San Paulo, Porto Alegre, Rio de Janeiro; *Riv.:* Apa, Negro, Amazon, Paraiba do Sul, São Francisco, Paraguay, Parana, Uruguay; *Lang.:* Portuguese; *Curr.:* Reis, Conto, Dobra, Milreis, Cruzeiro

Bulgaria: *Cit.:* Sofia (c.), Ruse, Byclu, Stara, Varna, Bleven, Burgas, Plevna, Shumen, Shumla, Sliver, Slivno, Widden, Zagora, Plovdiv, Sistova, Trinova, Rustchuk; *Riv.:* Danube, Iskar, Mesta, Marica, Maritsa; *Lang.:* Bulgarian, Turkish; *Curr.:* Lev, Lew, Stotinka

Burma: *Cit.:* Rangoon (c.), Ava, Pegu, Akyah, Prome, Lashio, Mandalay; *Riv.:* Salwin, Sutang, Salween, Sittang, Chindwin, Irrawaddy; *Lang.:* Wa, Lai, Chin, Pegu, Kachin, English; *Curr.:* Kyat

Burundi: *Cit.:* Bujumbura (c.), Ngozi, Bururi, Kitega, Muyinga; *Riv.:* Kagera, Ruvubu, Ruzizi; *Lang.:* French, tribal languages; *Curr.:* Burundi franc

Cambodia (Khmer Republic): *Cit.:* P(h)nompenh (c.), Ream, Kampot, Pursat, Kohnieh, Rovieng, Samrong; *Riv.:* Bassac, Mekong, Porong, Sehkong; *Lang.:* Khmer, French; *Curr.:* Riel, Puttan, Piaster

Cameroon: *Cit.:* Yaounde (c.), Douala; *Lang.:* French, English, tribal languages; *Curr.:* CFA franc

Canada (see **Special Section**)

Canary Islands: *Cit.:* Santa Cruz (c.), Laguna, Arrecife, Valverde; *Islands:* Roca, Clara, Ferro, Lobos, Palma, Gomero, Inferno, Graciosa, Rocca, Tenerife, Lanzarote

Cape Verde Islands: *Cit.:* Praia (c.); *Islands:* Sal, Fago; *Lang.:* Portuguese; *Curr.:* Escudo (Portuguese)

Central African Republic: *Cit.:* Bangui (c.), Obo, Birao, Kembe, Ngoto; *Riv.:* Ubangi, Shari, Bomu, Kotto, Sangha; *Lang.:* French, tribal languages; *Curr.:* CFA franc

Chad: *Cit.:* Fort-Lamy (c.); *Riv.:* Shari, Logone, Bahr el Ghazal; *Lang.:* French, Arabic, tribal languages; *Curr.:* CFA franc

Chile: *Cit.:* Santiago (c.), Arauco, Serena, Caldera, Copiapo, Coquimbo, Santiago, Valparaiso, Concepcion; *Riv.:* Loa, Itata, Maipu, Maule, Bio Bio, Copiaco, Valdivia; *Lang.:* Spanish; *Curr.:* Peso, Libra, Condor, Escudo

China: *Cit.:* Peking (c.), Macao, Canton, Mukden, Harbin, Nanking, Suchow, Shanghai, Tientsin, Chungking; *Riv.:* Yangtze, Yellow,West, Pai; *Lang.:* Wu, Shan, Mandarin, Cantonese; *Curr.:* Pu, Cash, Cent, Mace, Tael, Tiao, Yuan, Chiao, Sycee, Dollar

Colombia: *Cit.:* Bogota (c.), Cali, Neiva, Pasto, Tunja, Cucuta, Ibaque, Quibdo, Leticia, Popayan, Medellin, Cartagena; *Riv.:* Sinu, Tomo, Cauca, Atrato, Amazon, Magdalena; *Lang.:* Spanish; *Curr.:* Peso, Real, Condor, Peseta, Centavo

Comoro Islands: *Cit.:* Moroni (c.); *Islands:* Mwali, Moheli, Nzwani, Anjouan, Njazidja; *Lang.:* Arabic; *Curr.:* CFA franc

Congo: *Cit.:* Brazzaville (c.), Pointe-Noire, Dolisie; *Riv.:* Congo, Niari, Ubangi, Ogowel; *Lang.:* French, Bantu, Swahili, Lingala, Kongo; *Curr.:* CFA franc

Costa Rica: *Cit.:* San Jose (c.), Limon, Heredia, Alajuela, Puntarenas; *Lang.:* Spanish; *Curr.:* Colon, Centimo

Crete: *Cit.:* Canea (c.), Hag, Khora, Khania, Kisamo, Retino, Kasteli, Heraclion; *Lang.:* Minoan

Cuba: *Cit.:* Havana (c.), Palmira, Mantanzas, Santiago, Guantanamo; *Riv.:* Zaza, Cauto; *Lang.:* Spanish; *Curr.:* Peso, Centavo, Cuarenta

Cyprus: *Cit.:* Nicosia (c.), Larnaca, Limassol, Famagusta; *Lang.:* Turkish, English; *Curr.:* Cyprus pound, Para, Piaster

Czechoslovakia: *Cit.:* Prague (c.), Praha (c.), Brno, Eger, Tuzla, Aussig, Budweis, Teplitz, Ostrava; *Riv.:* Elbe, Vltava, Oder, Vistula, Morava, Danube; *Lang.:* Czech, Slovak, German, Hungarian, Ukrainian, Polish; *Curr.:* Ducat, Haler, Heller, Crown, Koruna

Dahomey: *Cit.:* Porto Novo (c.), Kandi, Abomey, Cotonou; *Riv.:* Niger; *Lang.:* Sudani, French; *Curr.:* CFA franc

Denmark: *Cit.:* Copenhagen (c.), Aarhus, Odense, Aalborg, Horsens, Randers; *Riv.:* Asa, Holm, Stor, Guden, Lonborg; *Lang.:* Danish; *Curr.:* Ora, Ore, Krone

Dominican Republic: *Cit.:* Santo Domingo (c.), Santiago, San Cristobal, La Vega, San Pedro de Marcoris, La Romana, Puerto Plata; *Islands:* Beata, Saona, Altovelo, Catalina, Hispanola; *Riv.:* Yuna, Ozama; *Lang.:* Spanish; *Curr.:* Oro, Peso

Equador: *Cit.:* Quito (c.), Loja, Guano, Mocha, Ambato, Cuenca, Ibarra, Pujili, Tulcan, Guayaquil; *Islands:* Galapagos; *Riv.:* Napo, Tigre, Pastaza, Guayas, Esmeraldas; *Lang.:* Spanish; *Curr.:* Sucre, Condor, Centavo

Egypt: *Cit.:* Cairo (c.), Aswan, Sais, Gizeh, Luxor, Tanis, Abydos, Armant, Thebes, Alexandria; *Riv.:* Nile; *Lang.:* Arabic;

Curr.: Fils, Dinar, Girsh, Pound, Dirham, Guinea, Junahy, Piaster, Milleme

El Salvador: *Cit.:* San Salvador (c.), Santa Ana, San Miguel, Cutuco, Acajutla; *Lang.:* Spanish; *Curr.:* Peso, Colon, Centavo

England: See United Kingdom

Estonia: *Cit.:* Tallinn (c.), Narva, Parnu, Reval, Tartu; *Riv.:* Ema, Narva, Parnu, Kasari; *Lang.:* Russian, Tartu; *Curr.:* Sent, Kroon Estmark

Ethiopia: *Cit.:* Addis Ababa (c.), Gore, Aduwa, Aksum, Assab, Harar, Asmara, Gondar, Gambela, Diredawa; *Riv.:* Omo, Baro, Abbi, Takkaze; *Lang.:* Amharic, English, Geez, Tigre, Somali; *Curr.:* Besa, Birr, Amole, Girsh, Dollar, Talari, Ashrafi, Piaster

Fiji: *Cit:* Suva (c.), Mau, Momi, Nandi, Etumba, Sagara

Finland: *Cit.:* Helsinki (c.), Aba, Abo, Vasa, Turku, Tampere; *Riv.:* Kemi, Oulu, Kymi, Kokemäki, Vuoksi; *Lang.:* Avar, Lapp, Ugric, Magyar, Ostyak, Tarast, Samoyed, Estonian; *Curr.:* Penni, Markka

France: *Cit.:* Paris (c.), Nice, Brest, Havre, Lyons, Reims, Tours, Vichy, Calais, Nantes, Sevres, Orleans, Bordeaux, Toulouse, Marseille; *Anthem:* Marseillaise; *Riv.:* Loire, Rhone, Saone, Seine, Garonne; *Curr.:* Ecu, Sol, Sou, Gros, Agnel, Blanc, Blank, Franc, Obole, Livre, Denier, Dizain, Teston, Centime, Testoon, Cavalier, Napoleon

Gabon: *Cit.:* Libreville (c.), Port Gentil; *Lang.:* French, tribal languages; *Curr.:* CFA franc

Gambia: *Cit.:* Banjul (c.); *Riv.:* Gambia; *Lang.:* English, Jola, Wolof, Fulani, Malinke; *Curr.:* Pound, Dalasi, Butut

Germany: *Cit.:* Bonn (c.), Berlin (c.), Essen, Bremen, Munich, Cologne, Dresden, Hamburg, Leipzig, Potsdam, Dortmund, Nuremberg, Stuttgart, Wiesbaden, Dusseldorf, Heidelburg; *Riv.:* Elbe, Oder, Ruhr, Rhine, Saale, Spree, Danube; *Lang.:* Deutsch; *Curr.:* Mark, Kronen, Thaler, Pfennig, Groschen

Ghana: *Cit.:* Accra (c.), Takoradi; *Riv.:* Volta; *Lang.:* Ga, Ewe, Twi, Fanti, Hausa, Dagbani, Dagomba; *Curr.:* Cedi, Pesewa

Greece: *Cit.:* Athens (c.), Volos, Candia, Delphi, Patras, Corinth, Larissa, Piraenus, Salonika; *Riv.:* Vardar, Peneus, Achelous, Alpheus; *Lang.:* Greek; *Curr.:* Obol, Hecte, Diobol, Lepton, Stater, Drachma, Diobolon

Greenland:*Cit.:* Godthaab (c.), Etah, Thule, Umanak; *Air Base:* Thule; *Native:* Ita; *Discoverer:* Eric; *Bay:* Baffin

Guatemala: *Cit.:* Guatemala City (c.), Coban, Salama, Livingston, Zacapa, Puerto Barrios; *Riv.:* Dulce, San Jose, Montagua; *Lang.:* Spanish, Indian dialects; *Curr.:* Peso, Centavo, Quetzal

Guinea: *Cit.:* Conakry (c.), Bata, Kankan; *Riv.:* Gambia, Niger, Senegal; *Lang.:* French, tribal languages; *Curr.:* Guinea franc

Guyana: *Cit.:* Georgetown (c.); *Riv.:* Essequibo, Demerara, Berbice; *Lang.:* English; *Curr.:* Guyana dollar

Haiti: *Cit.:* Port-au-Prince (c.), Cap-Haitien, Les Cayes; *Riv.:* Artibonite; *Lang.:* French, Creole; *Curr.:* Gourde

Honduras: *Cit.:* Tegucigalpa (c.), Yoro, Gracias; *Riv.:* Uloa, Aguan, Negro; *Lang.:* Spanish, Indian dialects; *Curr.:* Peso, Centavo, Lempira

Hong Kong: *Cit.:* Victoria (c.), Kowloon; *Curr.:* Cent, Dollar

Hungary: *Cit.:* Budapest (c.), Ozd, Gyor, Pecs, Erlau, Szeged, Debrecen, Szegedin, Kecskemet; *Riv.:* Raab, Sajo, Drave, Maros, Tiza, Danube, Poprad, Theiss, Zagyva, Vistula; *Lang.:* Magyar, Hungarian; *Curr.:* Gara, Balas, Pengo, Filler, Forint, Korona

Iceland: *Cit.:* Reikjavik, Reykjavik (c.); *Riv.:* Jokulsal, Thjorsa, Hvita; *Lang.:* Norse; *Curr.:* Aurar, Eyrir, Krona

India: *Cit.:* New Delhi (c.), Calcutta, Bombay, Delhi, Jaipur, Madras, Rangoon, Mandalay, Lucknow, Hyderabad, Ahmedabad; *Riv.:* Tapti, Ganges, Mahanadi, Godavari, Krishna, Cauvery, Irawadi, Irrawaddy; *Lang.:* Urdu, Hindu, English, Tamil, Teluga, Sanskrit, Malayalam, Kanarese, Bengali, Assamese, Oriya, Marathi, Gujarati, Punjabi, Sindhi, Kashmiri; *Curr.:* Lac, Pie, Anna, Dawm, Fels, Hoon, Lakh, Pice, Tara, Abidi, Crore, Paisa, Rupee

Indonesia: *Cit.:* Djarkarta (c.), Surubaja, Jakarta, Bandung; *Islands:* Bali, Java, Timor, Flores, Lombok, Madoera, Sumatra, New Guinea; *Lang.:* Bahasa, Malayan; *Curr.:* Rupiah

Iran: *Cit.:* Teheran (c.), Amol, Resht, Kasvin, Kerman, Meshed, Shiraz, Tabriz, Hamaden, Ispahan, Tabrees; *Riv.:* Karun, Atrek, Safid, Tigris, Karkhek, Euphrates; *Lang.:* Zend, Pahlavi, Kurdish, Azerbaijani; *Curr.:* Pul, Asar, Cran, Lari, Rial, Bisti, Daric, Dinar, Larin, Shahi, Toman, Stater, Ashrafi, Kasbeke, Pahlavi

Iraq: *Cit.:* Baghdad (c.), Mosul, Kirkuk, Basra; *Riv.:* Zab, Tigris, Euphrates; *Lang.:* Arabic, Kurdish; *Curr.:* Dinar

Ireland: *Cit.:* Tara, Dublin (c.), Cork, Adare, Lurgan, Limerick, Tralee, Tipperary; *Riv.:* Shannon, Barrow, Suir, Blackwater; *Lang.:* English, Gaelic; *Curr.:* Rap, Real, Irish pound

Israel: *Cit.:* Jerusalem (c.), Haifa, Jaffa, Joppa, Tel Aviv, Beersheba; *Riv.:* Jordan, Yarkon, Kishon; *Lang.:* Hebrew, Arabic, English; *Curr.:* Agora, Pound, Shekel

Italy: *Cit.:* Rome (c.), Milan, Naples, Turin, Genoa, Palermo, Bologna, Florence, Catania, Venice, Bari, Trieste, Messina, Verona, Padua, Pompeii, Sorrento; *Riv.:* Po, Arno, Adige, Piave, Tiber; *Lang.:* Italian; *Curr.:* Lira, Tari, Grano, Paoli, Soldo, Ducato, Sequin, Teston(e), Zecchino, Centisimo

Ivory Coast: *Cit.:* Abidjan (c.), Bouake; *Riv.:* Komoe, Bandama, Sassandra; *Lang.:* French, Dioula, tribal languages; *Curr.:* CFA franc

Jamaica: *Cit.:* Kingston (c.); *Lang.:* English; *Curr.:* Jamaican pound

Japan: *Cit.:* Tokyo (c.), Kobe, Kyoto, Osaka, Nagoya, Sasebo, Okayama, Nagasaki, Yokohama, Hiroshima; *Volcano:* Fujiyama; *Lang.:* Japanese; *Curr.:* Bu, Rin, Sen, Yen, Oban, Koban, Obang, Tempo, Ichebu, Itzebu, Kobang

Jordan: *Cit.:* Amman (c.), Aquaba, Jericho; *Riv.:* Jordan, Yarmuk; *Lang.:* Arabic; *Curr.:* Jordan dinar

Kenya: *Cit.:* Nairobi (c.), Mombasa, Kilidini; *Riv.:* Tana; *Lang.:* English, Swahili, Luo, Kikuyu; *Curr.:* East African shilling.

Khmer Republic: see Cambodia

Korea, North: *Cit.:* Pyongyang (c.), Wonsan; *Riv.:* Nam, Yalu, Taedong; *Lang.:* Korean; *Curr.:* Jun, Won, Hwan

Korea, South: *Cit.:* Seoul (c.), Taegu, Pusan, Inchon; *Riv.:* Han, Naktong; *Lang.:* Korean; *Curr.:* Won, Hwan

Kuwait: *Cit.:* Kuwait (c.), Hawalli; *Lang.:* Arabic; *Curr.:* Kuwait dinar

Laos: *Cit.:* Vientiane (admin. c.), Luang Prabang (royal c.); *Riv.:* Mekong; *Lang.:* Laotian, French; *Curr.:* Kip

Latvia: *Cit.:* Riga (c.), Libau, Dvinsk, Libava, Dunaberg, Daugavpils; *Riv.:* Aa, Ogre; *Lang.:* Latvian, Russian; *Curr.:* Lat, Rublis, Kapeika

Lebanon: *Cit.:* Beirut (c.), Tripoli, Zahle, Saida, Tyre; *Riv.:* Orontes, Litani; *Lang.:* Arabic, French, English; *Curr.:* Livre, Piastre, Pound

Lesotho: *Cit.:* Masero (c.); *Riv.:* Orange, Caledon; *Lang.:* English, Sotho, Sesotho; *Curr.:* South African rand

Liberia: *Cit.:* Monrovia (c.), Buchanan, Marshall; *Riv.:* Manna, Cavalla, St. Paul; *Lang.:* English, tribal languages; *Curr.:* Liberian dollar, U.S. dollar

Libya: *Cit.:* Tripoli (c.), Benghazi, Sebba, Tobruk; *Lang.:* Arabic, Italian; *Curr.:* Libyan pound, Dirham

Lichtenstein: *Cit.:* Vaduz (c.); *Riv.:* Rhine; *Castle:* Gutemburg; *Lang.:* German; *Curr.:* Swiss franc

Lithuania: *Cit.:* Vilna (c.), Memel; *Riv.:* Neman; *Lang.:* Latvian, Russian; *Curr.:* Lit, Litas, Marka, Centas, Fennig, Ostmark

Luxembourg: *Cit.:* Luxembourg (c.); *Riv.:* Moselle; *Lang.:* French, Letzeburgesch, German; *Curr.:* Luxembourg franc

Madagascar: *Cit.:* Antananarivo (c.), Mojanga; *Riv.:* Kopa, Mania, Sofia; *Lang.:* Various; *Curr.:* CFA pound

Malawi: *Cit.:* Lilongwe (c.), Zomba, Blantyre-Limbe; *Lang.:* Yeo, Centu, Bantu, English; *Curr.:* Pound, Kwacha, Tambla

Malaysia: *Cit.:* Kuala Lumpur (c.), Penang (George Town); *Riv.:* Pahang, Perak; *Lang.:* Malay, English, Tagalog, Chinese, Tamil; *Curr.:* Malaysian dollar, Tra, Trah

Maldive Islands: *Cit.:* Male (c.); *Lang.:* Maldivian (Sinhalese), Arabic; *Curr.:* Rupee

Mali: *Cit.:* Bamako (c.), Kayes, Segou; *Riv.:* Niger, Senegal; *Lang.:* French, tribal languages; *Curr.:* Mali franc

Malta: *Cit.:* Valetta (c.); *Islands:* Gozo, Comio; *Lang.:* Maltese, English; *Curr.:* Maltese pound, Grain, Grano

Mauritania: *Cit.:* Nouakchott (c.), Port-Etienne; *Riv.:* Senegal; *Lang.:* Arabic, tribal languages, French; *Curr.:* CFA franc, Ouguiya

Mexico: *Cit.:* Mexico City (c.), Guadalajara, Monterrey, Puebla, Merida, Torreon, San Luis, Potosi, Leon, Cuidad Juarez, Veracruz, Tampico, Mexicali; *Riv.:* Rio Grande, Panuco, Santiago-Lerma, Nazas, Balsas, Fuerte, Casas Grandes; *Lang.:* Spanish, Indian dialects; *Curr.:* Peso, Adobe, Azteca, Centavo, Piaster

Monaco: *Cit.:* Monaco (c.); *Riv.:* ; *Lang.:* French; *Curr.:* Monegasque franc

Mongolia: *Cit.:* Ulan Bator (c.), Darkhan, Choibalsan, Kobdo, Sukhe Bator; *Riv.:* Ongin, Baidarik, Kerulen, Selenge, Orhon, Dzhabhan; *Desert:* Gobi; *Lang.:* Mongolian, Russian; *Curr.:* Tugrik, Mungo

Montenegro: *Cit.:* Cetinje (c.), Niksic; *Riv.:* Ibar, Drina, Moraca; *Curr.:* Para, Florin, Perpera

Morocco: *Cit.:* Rabat (c.), Casablanca, Tangier, Fez, Marrakesh, Meknes, Oujda, Tetuan; *Lang.:* Arabic, Berber, French; *Curr.:* Okia, Rial, Okieh, Dirham, Mouzouna

Mozambique: *Cit.:* Maputo (c.), Lourenco, Marques, Beira; *Riv.:* Limpopo, Rovuma, Zambezi, Savi; *Lang.:* Native languages, Portuguese; *Curr.:* Escudo (Portuguese), Metical

Nepal: *Cit.:* Katmandu (c.), Palan, Bhatgaon; *Riv.:* Kali, Karnali, Gandak, Kosi; *Mtn.:* Everest; *Lang.:* Nepali, Newari, Photia; *Curr.:* Nepalese rupee, Mohar

Netherlands: *Cit.:* Amsterdam (legal c.), The Hague (actual c.), Rotterdam, Utrecht, Haarlem, Eindhoven, Groningen, Tilburg; *Riv.:* Rhine, Scheldt, Maas; *Lang.:* Dutch; *Curr.:* Cent, Doit, Ryder, Florin, Gulden, Stiver, Duckaton, Escalin, Guilder

New Guinea: *Cit.:* Port Moresby (c.), Rabaul; *Island Group:* Solomons; *Riv.:* Fly, Sepik, Amberno

New Zealand: *Cit.:* Wellington (c.), Auckland, Christchurch, Dunedin, Hutt; *Riv.:* Waikato, Wanganui, Rangitikei, Manawatu, Clutha, Waitaki; *Lang.:* English; *Curr.:* New Zealand dollar

Nicaragua: *Cit.:* Managua (c.), Leon, Granada; *Riv.:* Coco, Tuma, Rio Grande, Escondido, San Juan; *Lang.:* Spanish; *Curr.:* Peso, Centavo, Cordoba

Niger: *Cit.:* Niamey (c.), Zinder; *Riv.:* Niger; *Lang.:* French, tribal languages; *Curr.:* CFA franc

Nigeria: *Cit.:* Lagos (c.), Kano, Ibadan, Ogbomosho; *Riv.:* Niger, Benue; *Lang.:* English, tribal languages, Arabic; *Curr.:* Nigerian pound, Kobo, Naira

Norway: *Cit.:* Oslo (c.), Bergen, Trondheim, Stavanger, Drammen, Kristiansand, Skien; *Riv.:* Ena, Tana, Lougen, Glomma; *Lang.:* Norwegian; *Curr.:* Ore, Krone

Oman: *Cit.:* Muscat (c.), Matrah, Salalah; *Lang.:* Arabic, Indian dialects; *Curr.:* Persian Gulf rupee, Ghazi

Pakistan: *Cit.:* Islamabad (c.), Karachi, Lyallpur, Lahore, Hyderabad, Multan, Rawalpindi, Gujranwala, Pesawar; *Riv.:* Indus, Jhelum, Chenab, Sutlej; *Lang.:* Urdu, English, Punjabi, Pushtu, Sindhi, Baluchi, Bengali; *Curr.:* Pakistani rupee, Anna

Panama: *Cit.:* Panama City (c.), Colon, Balboa, Cristobal; *Riv.:* Chagres, Chepo, Tuira; *Lang.:* Spanish; *Curr.:* Balboa

Paraguay: *Cit.:* Asuncion (c.), Concepcion, Encarnacion, Villarrica; *Riv.:* Paraguay, Parana, Pilcomayo; *Lang.:* Spanish, Guarani; *Curr.:* Peso, Guarani

Peru: *Cit.:* Lima (c.), Callao, Arequipa, Cuzco, Iquitos, Chiclayo, Trujillo, Ica, Chimbote, Huancayo; *Riv.:* Maranon, Huallaga, Ucayali, Apurimac, Urubamba; *Lang.:* Spanish, Aymara, Quechua; *Curr.:* Sol, Libra, Dinero, Centavo

Philippines: *Cit.:* Manila (c.), Quezon City (c.), Cebu, Iliolo, Davao, Cavite, Basilan; *Islands:* Cebu, Batan, Leyte, Luzon, Panay, Midora, Palawan, Mindanao; *Riv.:* Agusan, Cagayan; *Lang.:* Moro,Bicol, Ibanag, Ilocano, Visayan, Tagalog, English, Spanish; *Curr.:* Peso, Peseta, Centavo, Sentimo

Poland: *Cit.:* Warsaw (c.), Lodz, Cracow, Poznan, Wroclaw, Gdansk, Szczecin, Katowice; *Riv.:* Bug, San, Oder, Warta, Vistula, Philica, Dniester; *Lang.:* Polish; *Curr.:* Ducat, Grosz, Marka, Zolty, Fennig, Halerz, Korona

Portugal: *Cit.:* Lisbon (c.), Ovar, Braga, Oporto, Setubal, Coimbra; *Riv.:* Tagus, Douro, Guadiana; *Lang.:* Portuguese; *Curr.:* Rei, Peca, Real, Conto, Coroa, Dobra, Indio, Escudo, Marcuta, Pataca, Testao, Vintem, Centavo, Crusado, Moidore, Equipaga

Puerto Rico: *Cit.:* San Juan (c.), Ponce, Dorado, Arecibo, Mayaguez; *Riv.:* Camuy, Tanama; *Lang.:* English, Spanish; *Curr.:* Dollar

Qatar: *Cit.:* Doha (c.), Dukhan, Umm Sa'id; *Lang.:* Arabic; *Curr.:* Riyal

Rhodesia: see **Zimbabwe**

Rumania: *Cit.:* Bucharest (c.), Cluj, Timisoara, Ploesti, Braila, Constanta; *Riv.:* Alt, Olt, Jiul, Prut, Danube; *Lang.:* Rumanian, Hungarian, Turkish, German; *Curr.:* Ban, Lei, Leu, Ley

Russia: *Cit.:* Moscow (c.), Kiev, Omsk, Orel, Kasan, Minsk, Pensa, Pskov, Odessa, Rostov, Sartov, Ivanovo, Rybinsk, Orenburg, Smolensk, Taganrog, Vladimir, Petrograd, Sevastopol, Vladivostok; *Republics:* Uzbek, Kazakh, Kirgiz, Latvia,Armenia, Estonia, Georgia, Tadzhik, Turkmen, Ukraine, Moldvia, Lithuania, Byelorussia, Azerbaidzhan; *Riv.:* Orel, Ural, Volga, Dnieper; *Mtn. Rge.:* Alai, Ural, Caucaus; *Lang.:* Russian; *Curr.:* Altin, Kopec, Ruble, Grivna, Kopeck

Rwanda: *Cit.:* Kigali (c.), Butare, Nyanza; *Lang.:* French, Kirundi, Swahili; *Curr.:* Franc

San Marino: *Cit.:* San Marino (c.); *Mount:* Titano; *Lang.:* Italian; *Curr.:* Italian lira

Sardinia: *Cit.:* Cagliari (c.), Nuoro, Sassari, Thatari; *Riv.:* Mannu, Tirosa, Samassi; *Lang.:* Catalan; *Curr.:* Carline

Saudi Arabia: *Cit.:* Riyadh (c.), Mecca (c.), Jidda, Medina; *Desert:* Nefud; *Lang.:* Arabic; *Curr.:* Riyal, Halala

Scotland: *Cit.:* Edinburgh (c.), Leith, Perth, Dundee, Glasgow, Aberdeen, Stirling, Inverness, St. Andrews; *Riv.:* Ayr, Dee, Spey, Afton, Clyde, Tweed, Deveron; *Islands:* Orkney, Hebrides, Shetland; *Curr.:* Demy, Bodle, Groat, Plack, Rider, Bawbee

Senegal: *Cit.:* Dakar (c.), Saint-Louis, Kaolack, Thies, Diourbel; *Riv.:* Senegal, Gambia, Saloum, Casamance; *Lang.:* Tribal languages, French; *Curr.:* CFA franc

Sicily: *Cit.:* Palermo (c.), Enna, Noto, Ragusa, Catania, Marsala, Messina, Trapani; *Riv.:* Salso, Belice, Simeto, Platani; *Volcano:* Etna, Aetna; *Lang.:* Italian; *Curr.:* Lira

Sierra Leone: *Cit.:* Freetown (c.); *Lang.:* Krio, Mende, Temne, English; *Curr.:* Leone

Singapore: *Cit.:* Singapore (c.); *Riv.:* Sungei, Seletar; *Lang.:* English, Chinese, Malay, Tamil; *Curr.:* Singapore dollar

Somalia: *Cit.:* Mogadishu (c.), Berbera, Hargeisa, Merca, Kismayu; *Riv.:* Juba, Nogal, Webi Shebeli; *Lang.:* Somali, Italian, Arabic, English; *Curr.:* Besa, Somali shilling

South Africa: *Cit.:* Pretoria (admin. c.), Cape Town (legis. c.), Bloemfontein (judic. c.), Johannesburg, Durban, Port Elizabeth, Germiston, Benoni, Springs, East London; *Riv.:* Orange, Vaal, Caledon; *Lang.:* English, Afrikaans, Bantu, Hindi, Tamil, Telegu, Bujarati; *Curr.:* Cent, Rand, Pound, Florin

Spain: *Cit.:* Madrid (c.), Cadiz, Toledo, Barcelona, Valencia, Seville, Cordova, Granada; *Riv.:* Ebro, Douro, Tagus, Guadiana, Guadaliquivir; *Lang.:* Spanish, Catalan, Galician, Basque; *Curr.:* Dobla, Cuarto, Doblon, Pesata, Alfonso, Centimo, Piaster, Cuartino

Sri Lanka: *Cit.:* Colombo (c.), Jaffna, Kandy, Galle; *Lang.:* Sinhalese,Tamil, English; *Curr.:* Sri Lanka rupee, Cent

Sudan: *Cit.:* Khartoum (c.), Port Sudan, Omdurman; *Riv.:* White Nile, Blue Nile, Nile; *Lang.:* Arabic, English, Ga, Ewe, Ibo, Kru, Efik, Mole, Tshi, Yoruba, Mandingo; *Curr.:* Sudanese pound

Swaziland: *Cit.:* Mbabane (c.), Manzini; *Riv.:* Usutu, Komati; *Lang.:* English, Swazi, Siswati; *Curr.:* South African rand

Sweden: *Cit.:* Stockholm (c.), Goteborg, Malmo, Norrkoping, Halsingborg, Orebro, Uppsala, Vasteras, Boras, Linkoping; *Riv.:* Ljusne, Indal, Angerman, Lule, Tornea; *Lang.:* Swedish, Lapp; *Curr.:* Ore, Krona, Skilling

Switzerland: *Cit.:* Bern (c.), Zurich, Basel, Geneva, Lausanne, St. Gall, Winterthur, Lucerne; *Riv.:* Rhine, Aar, Rhone, Inn; *Lang.:* German, French, Italian, Romansh; *Curr.:* Franc, Rappe, Rappen, Angster, Centime, Duplone, Blaffert

Syria: *Cit.:* Damascus (c.), Aleppo, Latakia, Homs, Hama; *Riv.:* Euphrates, Jordan, Orontes; *Lang.:* Arabic, Kurdish, Armenian, Turkish, Circassian;; *Curr.:* Syrian pound, Talent, Piaster

Taiwan (Republic of China): *Cit.:* Taipei (c.), Kaohsiung, Tainan, Taichung; *Riv.:* ; *Lang.:* Chinese; *Curr.:* Taiwan dollar

Tanzania: *Cit.:* Dar es Salaam (c.), Tanga, Moshi, Kigoma, Lindi, Zanzibar; *Riv.:* Pangani, Rufiji, Lukuledi, Ruvuma; *Lang.:* Swahili, English, Bantu, Arabic; *Curr.:* Tanzanian shilling

Thailand: *Cit.:* Bangkok (c.), Nakhon, Ayutthaya, Chiangmai; *Riv.:* Mekong, Chao Phraya; *Lang.:* Thai, Chinese; *Curr.:* At, Att, Baht, Fuang, Tical, Pynung, Salung, Satang

Tibet: *Cit.:* Lassa (c.), Lhasa (c.), Karak, Gartok, Totling; *Riv.:* Song, Indus, Salween; *Lang.:* Bodskad; *Curr.:* Tanga

Togo: *Cit.:* Lome (c.); *Riv.:* Mono; *Lang.:* French, tribal languages; *Curr.:* CFA franc

Tonga (Friendly Islands): *Cit.:* Nuku'alofa (c.); *Islands:* Ono, Tofu, Vavau, Haapai; *Lang.:* Tonganese; *Curr.:* Tongan pound, Paanga, Seniti

Trinidad and Tobago: *Cit.:* Port of Spain (c.), Toco, Arima, San Fernando, Scarborough; *Riv.:* Caroni, Ortoire; *Lang.:* English, Indian and Chinese dialects; *Curr.:* Trinidad and Tobago dollar

Tunisia: *Cit.:* Tunis (c.), Bizerte, Sousse, Sfax, Gabes, Kairouan; *Riv.:* Medjerda; *Lang.:* Arabic, French, Italian; *Curr.:* Dinar

Turkey: *Cit.:* Ankara (c.), Istanbul, Izmir, Adana, Bursa, Ankara, Edessa; *Riv.:* Tigris, Euphrates, Kizil, Irmak; *Lang.:* Turkish, Kurdish, Arabic; *Curr.:* Lira, Para, Akcha, Asper, Attun, Rebia, Acheh, Sequin, Zequin, Altilik, Beshlik, Pataque, Piaster, Medjidie, Zecchino

Uganda: *Cit.:* Kampala (c.), Entebbe, Jinja, Mbale; *Riv.:* White Nile; *Lang.:* English, Ateso,Ganda, Luganda, Swahili; *Curr.:* Uganda shilling

Union of Soviet Socialist Republics: see **Russia.**

United Arab Emirates: *Cit.:* Abu Dhabi (c.), Dubai, Ajman, Ras al-Khaimah, Sharjah, Umm al-Qaiwan, Fujairah; *Lang.:* Arabic; *Curr.:* UAE dirham

United Kingdom of Great Britain and Northern Ireland: *Cit.:* London (c.), Birmingham, Leeds, Sheffield, Manchester, Liverpool, Clydebank, Glasgow, Edinburgh, Dundee, Bristol, Belfast, Londonderry, Bangor, Lurgan, Ballymena, Lisburn, Portadown; *Riv.:* Spey, Avon, Dee, Tay, Forth, Tweed, Tyne, Ouse, Trent, Thames, Severn, Clyde; *Lang.:* English, Welsh, Gaelic; *Curr.:* pound

United States of America: (see **Special Section**).

Upper Volta: *Cit.:* Ouagadougou (c.); *Lang.:* French, Bobo, Lobi, Samo, Mande, Mossi; *Curr.:* CFA franc

Uruguay: *Cit.:* Montevideo (c.), Salto, Rivera, Mercedes, Paysandu; *Riv.:* Rio de la Plata, Uruguay, Rio Negro; *Lang.:* Spanish; *Curr.:* Peso, Centesimo

Venezuela: *Cit.:* Caracas (c.), Maracaibo, Barquisimeto, Valencia, Maracay; *Riv.:* Orinoco; *Lang.:* Spanish; *Curr.:* Real, Medio, Fuerte, Bolivar, Centimo, Morocato

Vietnam, North: *Cit.:* Hanoi (c.), Haiphong; *Riv.:* Da, Chu, Chay; *Gulf:* Tonkin; *Lang.:* Vietnamese, Chinese, French; *Curr.:* Dong

Vietnam, South: *Cit.:* Saigon (c.), Hue, Dalat, Da Nang; *Riv.:* Ba, Song, Mekong, Dongnai; *Lang.:* French, Chinese, Cham, Khmer, Rhade; *Curr.:* Piastre

Western Samoa: *Cit.:* Apia (c.); *Islands:* Upolu, Manono, Savaii, Apolima; *Lang.:* Samoan (Polynesian), English; *Curr.:* Tala

Yemen: *Cit.:* Sana(a) (c.), Taiz, Moka, Damar, Hodeida, Moucha; *Lang.:* Arabic; *Curr.:* Riyal

Yugoslavia: *Cit.:* Belgrade (c.), Nis, Agram, Morava, Mostar, Prilep, Skopje, Vardar, Zagreb, Monastir, Sarajevo, Subotica; *Riv.:* Danube, Drava, Neretva, Morava; *Lang.:* Slovene, Macedonian, Serbo Croatian; *Curr.:* Para, Dinar

Zaire (Congo): *Cit.:* Kinshasa (c.); *Riv.:* Congo, Ubangi, Aruwimi; *Lang.:* French, Kikongo, Lingala, Swahili, Tshiluba; *Curr.:* Zaire

Zambia: *Cit.:* Lusaka (c.), Ndola, Kitwe, Luanshya; *Riv.:* Zambesi, Kafue, Luangwa, Luapula; *Lang.:* Bantu, English, Tonga, Afrikaans; *Curr.:* Ngwee, Kwacha

U.S. PRESIDENTS

The presidents are listed in order according to the years of their term. Following the president's name the following abbreviations are used to indicate other important information: *Wf.*—Wife; *Par.*—Party; *V.P.*—Vice-President; *St.*—State of birth; *Tm.*—Term of office.

1. WASHINGTON, George; *Wf.*—Martha Dandridge Custis; *Par.*—Fed.; *V.P.*—Adams; *St.*—VA; *Tm.*—1789–1797
2. ADAMS, John; *Wf.*—Abigal Smith; *Par.*—Fed.; *V.P.*—Jefferson; *St.*—MA; *Tm.*—1797–1801
3. JEFFERSON, Thomas; *Wf.*—Martha Wayles Skelton; *Par.*—Dem.-Rep.; *V.P.*—Burr, Clinton; *St.*—VA; *Tm.*—1801–1809
4. MADISON, James; *Wf.*—Dorothea Payne Todd "Dolley"; *Par.*—Dem.-Rep.; *V.P.*—Clinton, Gerry; *St.*—VA; *Tm.*—1809–1817
5. MONROE, James; *Wf.*—Elizabeth Kortright; *Par.*—Dem.-Rep.; *V.P.*—Tompkins; *St.*—VA; *Tm.*—1817–1825
6. ADAMS, John Quincy; *Wf.*—Louise Catherine Johnson; *Par.*—Dem.Rep.; *V.P.*—Calhoun; *St.*—MA; *Tm.*—1825–1829
7. JACKSON, Andrew; *Wf.*—Rachel Donelson Robards; *Par.*—Dem.; *V.P.*—Calhoun, Van Buren; *St.*—SC; *Tm.*—1829–1837
8. VAN BUREN, Martin; *Wf.*—Hannah Hoes; *Par.*—Dem.; *V.P.*—Johnson; *St.*—NY; *Tm.*—1837–1841

9. HARRISON, William Henry; *Wf.*—Anna Symmes; *Par.*—Whig; *V.P.*—Tyler; *St.*—VA; *Tm.*—1841

10. TYLER, John; *Wf.*—Letitia Christian and Julia Gardiner; *Par.*—Dem.; *V.P.*—; *St.*—VA; *Tm.*—1841–1845

11. POLK, James Knox; *Wf.*—Sarah Childress; *Par.*—Dem.; *V.P.*—Dallas; *St.*—NC; *Tm.*—1845–1849

12. TAYLOR, Zachary; *Wf.*—Margaret Smith; *Par.*—Whig; *V.P.*—Fillmore; *St.*—VA; *Tm.*—1849–1850

13. FILLMORE, Millard; *Wf.*—Abigail Powers and Caroline Carmichael McIntosh; *Par.*—Whig; *V.P.*—; *St.*—NY; *Tm.*—1850–1853

14. PIERCE, Franklin; *Wf.*—Jane Mears Appleton; *Par.*—Dem.; *V.P.*—King; *St.*—NH; *Tm.*—1853–1857

15. BUCHANAN, James; *Wf.*—; *Par.*—Dem.; *V.P.*—Breckenridge; *St.*—PA; *Tm.*—1857–1861

16. LINCOLN, Abraham; *Wf.*—Mary Todd; *Par.*—Rep.; *V.P.*—Hamlin, Johnson; *St.*—KY; *Tm.*—1861–1865

17. JOHNSON, Andrew; *Wf.*—Eliza McCardle; *Par.*—Dem.; *V.P.*—; *St.*—NC; *Tm.*—1865–1869

18. GRANT, Ulysses Simpson; *Wf.*—Julia Dent; *Par.*—Rep.; *V.P.*—Colfax, Wilson; *St.*—OH; *Tm.*—1869–1877

19. HAYES, Rutherford Birchard; *Wf.*—Lucy Ware Webb; *Par.*—Rep.; *V.P.*—Wheeler; *St.*—OH; *Tm.*—1877–1881

20. GARFIELD, James Abram; *Wf.*—Lucretia Rudolph; *Par.*—Rep.; *V.P.*—Arthur; *St.*—OH; *Tm.*—1881

21. ARTHUR, Chester Alan; *Wf.*—Ellen Lewis Herndon; *Par.*—Rep.; *V.P.*—; *St.*—VT; *Tm.*—1881–1885

22. CLEVELAND, Stephen Grover; *Wf.*—Frances Folsom; *Par.*—Dem.; *V.P.*—Hendricks; *St.*—NJ; *Tm.*—1885–1889

23. HARRISON, Benjamin; *Wf.*—Caroline Lavinia Scott and Mary Scott Lord Dimmick; *Par.*—Rep.; *V.P.*—Morton; *St.*—OH; *Tm.*—1889–1893

24. CLEVELAND, Stephen Grover; *Wf.*—Frances Folsom; *Par.*—Dem.; *V.P.*—Stevenson; *St.*—NJ; *Tm.*—1893–1897

25. MC KINLEY, William; *Wf.*—Ida Saxton; *Par.*—Rep.; *V.P.*—Hobart, Roosevelt; *St.*—OH; *Tm.*—1897–1901

26. ROOSEVELT, Theodore; *Wf.*—Alice Hathaway Lee and Edith Kermit Carow; *Par.*—Rep.; *V.P.*—Fairbanks; *St.*—NY; *Tm.*—1901–1909

27. TAFT, William Howard; *Wf.*—Helen Herron; *Par.*—Rep.; *V.P.*—Sherman; *St.*—OH; *Tm.*—1909–1913

28. WILSON, Thomas Woodrow; *Wf.*—Ellen Louise Axson and Edith Bolling Galt; *Par.*—Dem.; *V.P.*—Marshall; *St.*—VA; *Tm.*—1913–1921

29. HARDING, Warren Gamaliel; *Wf.*—Florence Kling De Wolfe; *Par.*—Rep.; *V.P.*—Coolidge; *St.*—OH; *Tm.*—1921–1923

30. COOLIDGE, John Calvin; *Wf.*—Grace Anna Goodhue; *Par.*—Rep.; *V.P.*—Dawes; *St.*—VT; *Tm.*—1923–1929

31. HOOVER, Herbert Clark; *Wf.*—Lou Henry; *Par.*—Rep.; *V.P.*—Curtis; *St.*—IA; *Tm.*—1929–1933

32. ROOSEVELT, Franklin Delano; *Wf.*—Anna Eleanor Roosevelt; *Par.*—Dem.; *V.P.*—Garner, Wallace Truman; *St.*—NY; *Tm.*—1933–1945
33. TRUMAN, Harry S.; *Wf.*—Elizabeth (Bess) Wallace; *Par.*—Dem.; *V.P.*—Barkley; *St.*—MO; *Tm.*—1945–1953
34. EISENHOWER, Dwight David; *Wf.*—Mamie Geneva Doud; *Par.*—Rep.; *V.P.*—Nixon; *St.*—TX; *Tm.*—1953–1961
35. KENNEDY, John Fitzgerald; *Wf.*—Jacqueline Lee Bouvier; *Par.*—Dem.; *V.P.*—Johnson; *St.*—MA; *Tm.*—1961–1963
36. JOHNSON, Lyndon Baines; *Wf.*—Claudia Alta Taylor "Lady Bird"; *Par.*—Dem.; *V.P.*—Humphrey; *St.*—TX; *Tm.*—1963–1968
37. NIXON, Richard Milhous; *Wf.*—Thelma Catherine Patricia Ryan "Pat"; *Par.*—Rep.; *V.P.*—Agnew, Ford; *St.*—CA; *Tm.*—1968–1974
38. FORD, Gerald Rudolph; *Wf.*—Elizabeth Bloomer Warren "Betty"; *Par.*—Rep.; *V.P.*—Rockefeller; *St.*—NE; *Tm.*—1974–1977
39. CARTER, James Earl, Jr.; *Wf.*—Rosalynn Smith; *Par.*—Dem.; *V.P.*—Mondale; *St.*—GA; *Tm.*—1977–1981
40. REAGAN, Ronald Wilson; *Wf.*—Anne Frances Robbins Davis "Nancy"; *Par.*—Rep.; *V.P.*—Bush; *St.*—IL; *Tm.*—1981–1989
41. BUSH, George Herbert; *Wf.*—Barbara Pierce; *Par.*—Rep.; *V.P.*—Quale; *St.*—TX; *Tm.*—1989–

BIRDS

Extinct Birds: moa, dodo, jibi, kiwi, mamo, rukh, offbird

3 LETTERS

ani, auk, daw, emu, ioa, iwa, jay, nun, owl, pie, roa, tit, tui

4 LETTERS

avis, benu, chat, coot, crow, dove, duck, gull, hawk, ibis, jack, kagu, kite, knot, lark, loon, mamo, moho, myna, osel, quit, rhea, rook, ruff, skua, sora, swan, tern, tody, wren

5 LETTERS

baker, brant, chuck, clear, crane, eagle, egret, elant, finch, glead, goose, grebe, heron, hobby, jalep, junco, laird, liver, merle, mynah, ousel, ouzel, pewit, quail, raven, robin, snipe, stilt, stork, swift, terek, towee, tureo, twite, vireo

6 LETTERS

argala, avocet, budgie, bulbul, canary, condor, cuckoo, curlew, darter, dickey, dipper, driver, drongo, ducker, dunlin, falcon, finger, fulmar, gannet, grouse, guinea, hoopee, hooter, jacana, jaeger, linnet, magpie, marten, mocker, oriole, oscine, osprey, parrot, peewee, petrel, pigeon, phoebe, plover, puffin, shrike, silvan, sylvan, thrush, toucan, trogan, turnix, verdin, yawper

7 LETTERS

antbird, apertix, babbler, bittern, bluejay, bunting, bustard, buzzard, catbird, chirper, cotinga, courlan, flapper, flicker, fligger, goshawk, grackle, hornero, humming, hurgila, incomer, irrisor, jacamar, jackdaw, kestrel, kinglet, lapwing, minivet, mocking, ortolan, ostrich, peacock, pelican, penguin, redwing, skylark, sparrow, sunbird, swallow, tanager, tinamou, titlark, tomfool, trochil, vulture, warbler, waxwing, waybung

8 LETTERS

accentor, airplane, amadavat, annotine, blackcap, blackneb, bluebird, boatbill, bobolink, bobwhite, cardinal, carinate, chicadee, cockatoo, cocorico, drepanic, fernbird, firebird, firetail, flamingo, grayling, grosbeak, gruiform, ibisbill, killdeer, kingbird, lobefoot, longspur, lyrebird, nuthatch, oxpecker, palmiped, pheasant, plumiped, poorwill, preacher, puffbird, redstart, saltator, starling, swamphen, tapacolo, thrasher, throstle, titmouse, umbrette, whinchat, woodchat, woodcock, yearbird

9 LETTERS

albatross, blackbird, blackcock, brambling, bullfinch, cassowary, cockyolly, crossbill, coachwhip, cormorant, didappers, goldfinch, merganser, partridge, peregrine, phalarope, sandpiper, solitaire

10 LETTERS

bufflehead, kingfisher, kookaburra, meadowlark, roadrunner, sanderling, shearwater, tropicbird, turtledove, woodpecker

11 LETTERS

lammergeier, nightingale

PLANTS
Garden Plants — Flowering Plants

4 LETTERS

arum
fern
iris
ixia
lily
pink
rose
sego

5 LETTERS

aster
avens
calla
canna
daisy
gowan
hosta
lilac
lotus
pansy
pense
peony
phlox
poppy
sedum
stock
tulip
vetch
viola
vinca
yucca
zamia

6 LETTERS

allium
asalia
azalea
balsam
bellis

bletia
clivia
cosmos
crocus
dahlia
lupine
olivia
orchid
oxalis
violet
spirea
yarrow
zinnia

7 LETTERS

aconite
agathea
allyssum
amaranth
anchusa
anemone
arbutus
astible
begonia
celosia
clarkia
cowslip
freesia
gazania
gentian
gerbera
godetia
jasmine
jonquil
lobelia
monarda
muscari
pavonia
petunia
primula
rhodora
statice

verbena

8 LETTERS

acanthus
ageratum
arctotis
bluebell
caladium
camellia
clematis
cyclamen
daffodil
dianthus
foxglove
gardenia
geranium
gloxinia
harebell
hepatica
hyacinth
larkspur
lavender
marigold
myosotis
plantain
primrose
scabiosa
sparaxis
sweet pea
tithonia
watsonia

9 LETTERS

amaryllis
blettilla
buttercup
calendula
campanula
candytuft
carnation
centaurea

cinararia
columbine
coreopsis
digitalis
gladiolus
goldenrod
hollyhock
hydrangea
impatiens
linararia

monkshood
narcissus
nicotiana
penstemon
portulaca
snowdrops

10 LETTERS

coneflower
delphinium

gaillardia
gypsophila
heliotrope
marguerite
pincushion
poinsettia
ranunculus
snapdragon

Medicinal Plants

3 LETTERS

hop
oak

4 LETTERS

aloe
dill
flax
lime
sage

5 LETTERS

buchu
elder
erica
guaco
jalap
peony
poppy
senna
tansy

6 LETTERS

arnica
carrot

catnep
catnip
fennel
garlic
ipecac
kousso
laurel
nettle
simple

7 LETTERS

aconite
boneset
calamus
camphor
caraway
catechu
copaiba
ephedra
gentian
hemlock
henbane
juniper
lobelia
muellin
mustard
parsley
rhubarb
saffron

8 LETTERS

barberry
camomile
crowfoot
foxglove
licorice
plantain
rosemary
valerian
wormwood

9 LETTERS

asparagus
bearberry
buckthorn
chamomile
colchicum
coltsfoot
dandelion
monkshead

10 LETTERS

assafetida
penny royal
peppermint
stavesacre

Poisonous Plants

atis, loco, datura, aconite, amanita, henbane, calfkill, locoweed,
oleander

MUSICAL TERMS

1 Letter

A: ORCHESTRA TUNED TO

2 Letters

AI: IN THE STYLE OF
IN: INTO

3 Letters

AIR: SHORT TUNE OR MELODY
BAR: VERTICLE LINE DIVIDING THE STAFF
CON: WITH
ECO: ECHO
IRA: ANGER
PIU: MORE

4 Letters

ALLA: IN THE STYLE OF
APRE: HARSH
ARIA: AN AIR, TUNE, A SONG
BEAT: UNIT OF RHYTHM
CHEF (D'ORCHESTRA): CONDUCTOR
CLEF: CHARACTER ON THE STAFF
CODA: PASSAGE ENDING A MOVEMENT
DEUT: TWO VOICES
DEUX: FOR TWO HANDS
ECHO: ECHO, REPEAT
FINE: END
FINO: AS FAR UP; UP TO
FLAT: CHARACTER ON THE STAFF
GLEE: ENGLISH COMPOSITION FOR 3 OR MORE VOICES
HOLD: PROLONGATION OF A NOTE
HYMN: SONG OF PRAISE
JOTA: NATIONAL SPANISH DANCE
LENO: FAINT; QUIET

LIED: GERMAN SONG
LOCO: PLACE
POCO: LITTLE
REEL: LIVELY DANCE
REST: PAUSE BETWEEN TWO NOTES
SANS: WITHOUT
SINO: AS FAR AS; UP TO
SOLO: SINGLE VOICE
SONO: SOUND; TONE
TACE: BE SILENT
TEMA: THEME
TUNE: A SIMPLE SONG
VAMP: IMPROVISE AN ACCOMPANIMENT
VIVO: LIVELY; BRISKLY
VOCE: VOICE

5 Letters

CANTO: MELODY OR CHANT
CHANT: SHORT SACRED SONG
CHORD: A HARMONY OF 2 OR MORE TONES
CLOSE: CADENZA ENDING A SECTION OR PIECE
BATON: CONDUCTOR'S WAND
BOCCA: MOUTHPIECE
CANON: CONTRAPUNTAL COMPOSITION
DIRGE: FUNERAL HYMN
DOLCE: SWEET; SOFT
ELEGY: MELANCHOLY COMPOSITION
FLING: SCOTTISH DANCE
FOLIA: SPANISH DANCE
FUGUE: A FLIGHT
GLIDE: CARRYING A TONE FROM ONE NOTE TO THE NEXT
IL PIU: THE MOST
JALEO: SPANISH DANCE
LARGO: SLOW AND STATELY
LENTO: SLOW, BUT NOT DRAGGING
MESTO: SAD; MELANCHOLY

METER, METRE: Symmetrical Grouping of Musical Notes
MEZZO: Half
MINIM: Half-note
MOLTO: Very; much
PAUSA: Rest; pause
PAVAN: Italian-Spanish dance
PEZZO: Piece
PIANO: Soft; softly
PIECE: Musical composition
PITCH: Position of a tone in a musical scale
POLKA: Bohemian dance
SAMBA: Brazilian dance
SCALE: Series of notes which form any major or minor key
SEGNO: A sign
SENZA: Without
SHARP: Character on the staff
SOAVE: Suavely; flowingly
TANGO: Argentine dance
TANTO: As much; so much
TARDO: Slow; lingering
TEMPO: Rate of speed
VALSE: Waltz

6 Letters

ADAGIO: A slow movement
AL FINE: To the end
ANTHEM: Sacred vocal music
A TEMPO: At the preceding rate of speed
BALLAD: A short song
BOLERO: Spanish dance
CHIARO: Clear; pure
COMODO: Leisurely; easily
CON IRA: Wrathfully
DA CAPO: From the beginning
DECISO: With decision

DI GALA: Gaily; merrily
ENCORE: Repeat; again
FACILE: Easy; fluent
FEBILE: Feeble; weak
FEROCE: Wildly
FINALE: Last movement
FLORID: Embellished with runs; ornamental
GIUSTO: Proper
INFINO: As far as; up to
INTIMO: Heartfelt; fervent
JARABE: Mexican dance
LEGATO: Slurred; no break between notes
LITANY: Song of supplication
MINUET: Early French dance
PAVANA: Italian-Spanish dance
PRESTO: Great rapidity
RUBATO: Flexible melody
SEMPRE: Always; throughout
VELOCE: Acceleration
VIVACE: Lively; animated

7 Letters

AGILITA: Vivacity
AGITATO: Agitated
ALLEGRO: Lively or rapid
ALLONGE: Prolonged
AMABILE: Sweet and tender
ANDANDO: Easy and flowing
ANDANTE: Moderately slow
ANIMATO: Vivaciously
ANIMOSO: Spirited
BOROCCO: Eccentric
CADENCE: Rhythm
CADENZA: Elaborate ending passage
CALMATO: Calmly
CAMPANA: Bell

CONTATA: Vocal work with instrumental accompaniment

CANTATO: Singingly

CANZONE: Folk song

CHANSON: Song

CLAVIER: Keyboard

COMPASS: Range of a voice

CON BRIO: Spiritedly

CON MOTO: Energetic movement

DECIBEL: Intensity of sound

DELFRIO: Frenzy, excitement

DI MOLTO: Very; extremely

DOLENTE: Sad

DOMINANT: Fifth note of a scale

FERMATA: A hold, pause, or interruption

FERVIDO: Fervent; vehement

FERVOSO: Agitated style

GAVOTTE: Old English dance

GENTILE: Gracefully

GIOCOSO: Humorously

GIOJOSO: Blithe; joyful

HANACCA: Moravian dance

HAUTBOY: Oboe

INTRADA: Short introduction; prelude

INTROIT: Antiphonal chant

MAESTRO: Master; conductor

MARCATO: With distinctness and emphasis

MAZURKA: Polish dance

MORDENT: Two or more grace notes

PASSAGE: Section of a composition

PENSOSO: Pensive; thoughtful

PIETOSO: Pitifully; movingly

PICCOLO: Small or little

PLACIDO: Smooth; placid

POI A POI: By degrees

ROBUSTO: Firmly and boldly

RUSTICO: Rural; rustic

SCHERZO: Vivacious movement

SERIOSO: In a grave style

8 Letters

A BALLATA: In singing style

AFFABILE: Sweetly and gracefully

BEL CANTO: Beautiful song

BERCEUSE: Lullaby

CALMANDO: Growing calm

CANTICLE: Sacred chant

CARILLON: Chime

CAVATINA: Short aria

CHACONNE: Spanish dance

CON AMORE: Lovingly

DAL SEGNO: From the sign

DELICATO: In a delicate style

DIAPASON: Octave

DIATONIC: Natural scale

DISCRETO: Comparatively subdued

DOLCIATO: Softer; calmer

DOLOROSA: Sorrowfully

ECCLESIA: Church

ELEGANTE: Gracefully

ENFATICO: With emphasis

FANDANGO: Spanish dance

FANTASIA: Caprice

FERVENTE: Ardently; fervently

FROLICH: Joyous; gay

HABABERA: Cuban contradance

LARGANDO: Growing broader

LEGGIERO: Light; DELICATE

LENTANDO: Growing SLOWER

LIBRETTO: Words of an OPERA

MADRIGAL: Elaborate VOCAL SETTING OF A LYRIC POEM

MAESTOSO: Majestic; STATELY

MODULATE: Transition OF A KEY

NOCTURNE: A dreamy SERENADE PLAYED AT NIGHT

OSTINATO: Continuous GROUP OF NOTES

PARLANDO: Declamatory STYLE

RHAPSODY: A free, ECSTATIC COMPOSITION

RIGAUDON: Lively French DANCE

RIGOROSO: Exact, strict TIME

RISOLUTO: In a decided STYLE

RITENUTO: Detained; SLOWER

SARABAND: Saracens DANCE WITH CASTANETS

SEMPLIS: In a natural STYLE

SERENADE: Night music

SOGGETTO: Subject; THEME

UNA CORDA: Soft pedal

VIGOROSO: Vigorously

9 Letters

A CAPPELLA: Unaccompanied

ANDANTINO: A little SLOWER THAN ANDANTE

ANTIPHONE: Alternate SINGING

BAGATELLE: A short, EASY PIECE OF MUSIC

BARCAROLE: Venetian BOAT-SONG

BELLICOSO: In a warlike STYLE

BERGOMASK: Clownlike DANCE

CANTABILE: In a singing STYLE

CAPRICCIO: In a CAPRICIOUS STYLE

CHROMATIC: Proceeding BY HALF-STEPS

CON DOLORE: Expressing GRIEF

CON FRETTA: Hurriedly

CON RABBIA: With frenzy

FARANDOLE: Circle dance

GLISSANDO: With a SLIDING MOVE

GRANDIOSO: Grand; noble

IMPROMPTU: An EXTEMPORANEOUS PRODUCTION

LACRIMOSO: Tearful

MALAGUENA: Spanish FOLK MUSIC

PIZZICATO: Pinched; PLUCKED

POCO A POCO: Little by LITTLE

POLONAISE: Polish dance

SOTTO VOCE: In an OVERTONE

TROPPO, NON: Not too MUCH

10 Letters

ACCELERADO: Livier; FASTER

ACCIDENTAL: Chromatic SIGN NOT IN KEY-SIGNATURE

ALLA MARCIA: In march STYLE

ALLARGANDO: Growing SLOWER

ALLEGRETTO: Light and Cheerful

BERGERETTE: Pastoral Song

COMPANELLA: Small Bell

CLAVICHORD: Forerunner of a Piano

CON ANIMATO: With Spirit

CON AUDACIA: Boldly

CONCERTINA: Smaller than an Accordian

CON FERVORE: Fervently

CON GRAVITA: Slowly; Seriously

DISSONANCE: Discord

IMPRESARIO: Conductor of Opera and Concerts; Manager

LARGAMENTA: Broadly

LENTAMENTE: Slowly

NACHTMUSIK: Serenade

RECITATIVE: Declamatory in opera

RINFORZO: Reinforcement

RITARDANDO: Growing Slower

SENTIMENTO: With Feeling

SYNCOPATED: Jazz

TARANTELLA: Italian Dance

NOTED COMPOSERS

3 Letters

ABT, Franz
BAX, Arnold
CUI, Cesar
KEY, Francis Scott
LOW, Joseph

4 Letters

ADAM, Adolphe
ARNE, Thomas
BACH, Johann Sebastian
BACH, Karl
BERG, Alban
BULL, John
BYRD, William
CAGE, John
DUNN, James
FOSS, Lukas
GADE, Niels
IVES, Charles
KERN, Jerome
LALO, Edouard
ORFF, Carl
PERI, Jacopo
RAFF, Joachim
RIES, Franz
RINK, Johann
ROSE, Billy

WOLF, Hugo

5 Letters

AUBER, Daniel-Francois-Esprit
BALFE, Michael
BIZET, Georges
BLOCH, Ernest
BOHM, Carl
BRUCH, Max
CESTI, Marc'Antonio
DENZA, Luigi
DUKAS, Paul
ELGAR, Edward
FALLA, Manuel de
FAURE, Gabriel-Urbain
FOOTE, Arthur
FRIML, Rudolf
GLUCK, Christoph
GRIEG, Edvard
GROFE, Ferde
HAYDN, Franz
HEINS, Carl
HOLST, Gustav
IBERT, Jacques
ISAAK, Heinrich
LEHAR, Franz
LISZT, Franz
LOEWE, Carl

LULLY, JEAN-BAPTISTE
MOORE, DOUGLAS
NEVIN, ETHELBERT
O'HARA, GEOFFREY
PAINE, JOHN KNOWLES
RAVEL, MAURICE
REGER, MAX
SATIE, ERIK
SOUSA, JOHN PHILIP
STILL, WILLIAM GRANT
SUPPE, FRANZ VON
VERDI, GIUSEPPE
WATTS, WINTER
WEBER, CARL MARIA
WEILL, KURT
WIDOR, CHARLES MARIE

MOZART, WOLFGANG
    AMADEUS
PIERNE, HENRI GABRIEL
PLEYEL, IGNAZ
PORTER, COLE
RAMEAU, JEAN PHILIPPE
ROGERS, JAMES
ROGERS, RICHARD
SCHUTZ, HEINRICH
STRAUS, OSKAR
TAYLOR, DEEMS
THOMAS, AMBROISE
VECCHI, ORAZIO
VITALI, GIOVANNI
WAGNER, RICHARD
WALTON, WILLIAM
WEBERN, ANTON

6 Letters

BARBER, SAMUEL
BARTOK, BELA
BERLIN, IRVING
BOULEZ, PIERRE
BRAHMS, JOHANNES
CADMAN, CHARLES
CARTER, ELLIOTT
CHAVEZ, CARLOS
CHOPIN, FREDERIC
DUPARC, HENRI
DVORAK, ANTONIN
ENESCO, GEORGES
FLOTOW, FRIEDRICH VON
FOSTER, STEPHEN
FRANCK, CESAR
GLINKA, MIKHAIL
GOUNOD, CHARLES
HALEVY, JACQUES
HANDEL, GEORGE
    FREDERICK
HARRIS, VICTOR
HILLER, FERDINAND
JOPLIN, SCOTT
KODALY, ZOLTAN
KRENEK, ERNST
KUHLAU, FRIEDRICH
LIADOV, ANATOL
MAHLER, GUSTAV
MORLEY, THOMAS

7 Letters

ALBENIZ, ISAAC
ALLEGRI, GREGORIO
ARENSKY, ANTON
BABBITT, MILTON
BELLINI, VINCENZO
BERLIOZ, HECTOR
BORODIN, ALEXANDER
BRITTEN, BENJAMIN
CACCINI, GIULIO
CAVALLI, FRANCESCO
COPLAND, AARON
CORELLI, ARCANGELO
DEBUSSY, CLAUDE
DELIBES, LEO
DES PREZ, JOAQUIN
GIBBONS, ORLANDO
GRIFFES, CHARLES
HASSLER, HANS
HERBERT, VICTOR
JANACEK, LEOS
LA FORGE, FRANK
LECUONA, ERNESTO
LE JEUNE, CLAUDE
MANCINI, HENRY
MARTINU, BOHUSLAV
MENOTTI, GIAN CARLO
MILHAUD, DARIUS
NICOLAI, OTTO
OBRECHT, JAKOB

OKEGHEM, Johannes
PHILIPP, Isidor
POULENC, Francis
PUCCINI, Giacomo
PURCELL, Henry
RIEGGER, Wallingford
RODGERS, Richard
ROMBERG, Sigmund
ROSSINI, Gioacchino
SCHUMAN, William
SINDING, Christian
SMETANA, Bedrich
STRAUSS, Johann
STRAUSS, Richard
THOMSON, Virgil
VIVALDI, Antonio
WEELKES, Thomas
YOUMANS, Vincent

8 Letters

ARCADELT, Jacob
BARTLETT, Homer
BRUCKNER, Anton
CHAUSSON, Ernest
CLEMENTI, Muzio
COUPERIN, Francois
DIABELLI, Anton
GABRIELI, Andrea
GERSHWIN, George
GIORDANO, Umberto
GOLDMARK, Karl
GRANADOS, Enrique

HONEGGER, Arthur
JOMMELLI, Niccolo
KREISLER, Fritz
LOEFFLER, Charles
LORTZING, Albert
MASCAGNI, Pietro
MASSENET, Jules
PAGANINI, Nicola
PALMGREN, Selim
PICCINNI, Nicola
PIZZETTI, Ildebrando
RESPIGHI, Ottorino
ROSSINI, Gioacchino
SCHUBERT, Franz
SCHUMANN, Robert
SIBELIUS, Jean
SPONTINI, Gasparo
SULLIVAN, Arthur
THOMPSON, Randall
WOODWARD, Herbert

9 Letters

BERNSTEIN, Leonard
HINDEMITH, Paul
MACDOWELL, Edward
OFFENBACH, Jacques
STOKOWSKI, Leopold

10 Letters

PADEREWSKI, Ignaz
RUBINSTEIN, Anton

FAMOUS PEN NAMES

Francois Arouet: VOLTAIRE

Henri Beyle: STENDHAL

Eric Arthur Blair: GEORGE ORWELL

Anne Bronte: ACTON BELL

Charlotte Bronte: CURRER BELL

Emily Bront: ELLIS BELL

Charles Browne: ARTEMUS WARD

Agatha Christie: MARY WESTMACOTT

Samuel Clemens: MARK TWAIN

David Cornwell: JOHN LECARRE

Charles Dickens: BOZ

Charles Dodgson: LEWIS CARROLL

Amandine Dupin: GEORGE SAND

Mary Ann Evans: GEORGE ELIOT

Benjamin Franklin: POOR RICHARD

Charles Lamb: ELIA

David Locke: PETROLEUM NASBY

Edna St. Vincent Millay: NANCY BOYD

H. H. Munro: SAKI

Alexi Peshkov: MAXIM GORKI

Jean Baptiste Poquelin: MOLIERE

William S. Porter: O. HENRY

Louise de la Ramee: OUIDA

Jacques Thibault: ANATOLE FRANCE

Louis Viaud: PIERRE LOTI

MYTHOLOGY

Gods (Deities), Goddesses, Mythical Places and Names

The following lists principally include mythological names of Babylonian, Egyptian, Greek, Norse, and Roman mythlogical Gods, persons, and places. However, Assyrian, Celtic, Hindu, and English folklore names are also included.

2 LETTERS

Ai
Ba
Ea
Er
Ge
Io
Ka
Ma (or Maat)
Nu
Ra
Re
Su
Ve
Zu

3 LETTERS

Abu (or Anu)
Akh
Ara
Ate
Aya
Ban
Bau
Bel
Bes
Dis
Eir
Eos
Geb
Hea
Hel
Ino

Ira
Keb
Ler
Lua
Lug
Min
Nun
Nut
Nox (or Nyx)
Ops
Oro
Pan
Pax
Ran
Seb
Set
Shu
Sif
Sin
Sol
Sri
Tat
Tem (or Tum)
Tiu (or Tiw)
Tyr
Ull
Uma
Urd
Utu
Vac
Van
Vor
Zio

4 LETTERS

Aani
Acis
Adad (or Adda, Addu)
Agni
Akal
Aias
Amon
Amor
Amun
Anat
Anax
Apet (or Anta)
Apsu
Ares
Argo
Arne
Askr
Asur
Atli
Atmu
Atys
Auge
Aura
Baal
Bana
Bast
Besa
Bran
Buto
Clio
Coel
Deva (or Dewa)

Dian	Nona	Circe
Dido	Norn	Comus
Dike (or Dice)	Odin	Cotys
Echo	Ossa	Creon
Enki	Otus	Cupid
Enyo	Rama	Dagan
Enzu	Rhea	Dagda
Erda	Saga	Damia
Eris	Sati	Danae
Eros	Seth	Diana
Faun	Siva	Dione
Frey	Spes	Dirce
Gaea (or Gaia)	Styx	Donar
Geri	Tari	Doris
Gula	Thor	Dyaus
Gwyn	Troy	Dylan
Hebe	Tyrr	Eneas
Hela	Upis	Epona
Hera	Utug	Erato
Hero	Vayu	Etana
Hler	Vili	Eurus
Hora	Wate	Fates
Hoth	Yama	Fauna
Inti	Ymir (or Ymer)	Fides
Iris	Zeus	Flora
Irra		Fomor
Isis	**5 LETTERS**	Freki
Jove		Freya
Juno	Aegir	Frigg
Kali	Aegis	Galli
Kama	Aesir	Girru
Khem	Aeson	Hadad
Kore	Aikos	Hades
Leda	Alcis	Helen
Leto	Altis	Helle
Lleu (or Llew)	Amata	Herse
Loki	Ammon	Hoder
Lugh	Anath	Hodur
Luna	Argus	Horae
Maat	Arion	Horus
Maia	Aruru	Hotei
Mara	Assur	Hothr
Mars	Atlas	Hours
Ment	Attis	Hydra
Mors	Bhaga	Hylas
Nabu (or Nebo)	Brage (or Bragi)	Hymen
Natt (or Nott)	Cacus	Irene
Nike	Ceres	Istar
Nina	Chaos	Ixion

Janus
Jason
Jorth
Khnum
Komos
Laius
Lares
Manes
Marut
Medea
Mentu
Midas
Mimir
Minos
Momus
Montu
Moria
Morta
Muses
Nanna
Nerid
Ninib
Niobe
Nisus
Notus
Nusku
Orcus
Orion
Parca
Paris
Picus
Pluto
Priam
Remus
Rudra
Salus
Samas
Satyr
Sebek
Sedna
Seker
Sibyl
Silen
Siris
Sobek
Surya
Terra
Thoth
Tyche

Urash
Ushas
Uther
Vanir
Venus
Vesta
Wotan (or Wodan,
  Woden)

6 LETTERS

Acamas
Admete (or Admeta)
Adonis
Aeacus (or Aikos)
Aeetes
Aegeus
Aegina
Aeneas
Aengus
Aeolus
Aerope
Agenor
Aglaia
Alecto
Althea
Amenti
Amycus
Annona
Anubis (Inpu
  Hermanubis)
Anunit
Apollo
Arthur (King
  Arthur)
Asgard
Athena (Pallas
  Athene)
Atreus
Augeas
Aurora
Auster
Baldur (Balder)
Babbar
Baucis
Boreas
Brahma
Cadmus
Castor

Charon
Chiron
Clotho
Clytie
Cronus
Cybele
Danaus
Daphne
Decuma
Deimos
Delphi
Dryads
Eecatl
Eirene
Elaine
Erebus
Europa
Evadne
Faunus
Formax
Freyja
Furies
Gawain
Genius
Graces
Haemon
Hathor
Hecate
Hector
Hecuba
Helios
Hermes
Hestia
Hygeia
Icarus
Isolde (and
  Tristram)
Ishtar
Kahemu
Klotho
Kubera (or Kuvera)
Kyrene
Latona
Levana
Lucina
Matris
Matuta
Maumet
Medusa

Mentor
Merlin
Modred (or
Mordred)
Moirai (or Moerae)
Naiads
Nannar
Nereus
Nessus
Nestor
Nymphs
Oenone
Oreads
Osiris
Pallas (or Pallas
Athene)
Panisk
Parcae
Peleus
Pelias
Pelion
Pelops
Peneus
Perkun
Peroun
Plutus
Pollux
Psyche
Pyrrha
Python
Saturn
Satyrs
Scylla
Selena
Semele
Shango
Sibyls
Sirens
Skanda
Sokari
Somnus
Sphinx
Stheno
Tanith
Tellus
Tereus
Teshup
Tethys
Thalia

Themis
Thetis
Thisbe
Titans
Tithon
Tityos
Tlaloc
Triton
Turnus
Uranie
Uranus
Vacuna
Vishnu
Vivien
Vulcan
Zethus

7 LETTERS

Abderos
Acarnan
Acestes
Achates
Acheron
Actaeon
Admetus
Alcmene (or
Alcmena)
Alcmeon
Alfadur
Alpheus
Amazons
Amphion
Amymone
Anahita
Ancaeus
Antaeus
Antiope
Arachne
Ariadne
Artemis
Astarte
Asteria
Astraea
Atlanta
Atlamas
Atropos
Aumakua
Avernus

Bacchus
Bellona
Branwen
Briseis
Busiris
Calaeno
Calchas
Calydon
Calypso
Camelot
Camenae
Camilla
Camulus
Cecrops
Centaur
Chloris
Clymene
Cotytto
Curetes
Cyclops
Daidale
Damkina
Danaids
Daphnis
Demeter
Demurge
Diomede
Electra
Elysion
Epigoni
Eunomia
Euryale
Euterpe
Evander
Forsete
Fortuna
Galahad (Sir)
Galatea
Glaucus
Gorgons
Gwydion
Harpies
Helenus
Helicon
Hurakan
Hyponos
Imhotep
Incubus
Jocasta

Jupiter
Jurojin
Khepera
Krishna
Kuretes
Kwannon
Laertes
Lakshmi
Laocoon
Leander
Maenads
Marsyas
Megaera
Mercury
Mexitli
Midgard
Minerva
Mordred
Nemesis
Nephele
Neptune
Nereids
Nerthus
Ninurta
Oceanus
Oedipus
Olympus
Omphale
Orestes
Orpheus
Ouranos
Pandora
Perchta
Perseus
Phaedra
Phaeton
Phoebus
Phrixus
Priapus
Proteus
Pylades
Pyramus
Pyrrhus
Romulus
Serapis
Shamash
Silenus
Taranis
Theseus

Ulysses

8 LETTERS

Achelous
Achilles
Aconteus
Acrisius
Adrastus
Aegyptus
Alcestis
Alcionus
Alcithoe
Ambrosia
Amaethon
Anaxibia
Anchises
Antigone
Arethusa
Astyanax
Atalanta
Atlantis
Briareos
Brunhild
Caduceus
Calliope
Callisto
Capaneus
Castalia
Centaurs
Centeotl
Cerberus
Charites
Chimaera
Cyclopes
Daedalus
Dardanus
Deianira
Dionysus
Dioscuri
Endymion
Enyalius
Eteocles
Eurydice
Eurynome
Fomorion
Ganymede
Heracles
Hercules

Hormonia
Hyperion
Justitia
Juventas
Keraunia
Kerberos
Lachesis
Laodamia
Laomedon
Libitina
Lapithae
Meleager
Menelaus
Minotaur
Morpheus
Nausicaa
Ningirsu
Oceanids
Odysseus
Oenomaus
Oenopion
Paladium
Palaemon
Parjanya
Pasiphae
Pasithea (or Aglaia)
Phaethon
Penelope
Pentheus
Philemon
Pleiades
Poseidon
Quirinus
Ragnarok
Sangreal
Sarpedon
Sisyphus
Tantalus
Tartarus
Thanatos
Thyestes
Tiresias
Tithonus
Tonatiuh
Tristram (and
  Isolde)
Va'etudo
Valt. 'la
Valky. ?

Zephyrus

9 LETTERS

Aegisthus
Agamemnon
Alcathous
Amaltheia
Androcles
Andromeda
Aphrodite
Argonauts
Aristaeus
Asklepios
Autolycus
Cassandra
Charybdis
Chryseies
Deucalion
Eumenides
Eurytheus
Excalibur
Guinevere
Hippolyte
Holy Grail
Hymenaeus (or
  Hymen)
Kassandra
Labyrinth
Launcelot (Sir)
Melpomene
Mnemosyne

Narcissus
Parnassus
Palamedes
Parmassus
Patroclus
Polynices
Pygmalion
Siegfried
Telegonus
Tisiphone
Trojan War
Tyndareus
Zernebock

10 LETTERS

Acheliodes
Amphiaraus
Amphitrite
Amphitryon
Amphoteros
Andromache
Antilochus
Ascalaphos
Bacchantes
Bucephalus
Cassiopeia
Cornucopia
Euphrosyne
Hamadryads
Hephaistos
Hesperides

Hippocrine
Iphigeneia
King Arthur
Niebelungs
Persephone
Polydeuces
Polyhymnia
Polyphemus
Prometheus
Proserpina
Telemachus

11 LETTERS

Aescalapius
Bacchanalia
Bellerophon
Hyancinthos
Neoptolemus (or
  Pyrrhus)
Penthesilea
Round Table
Terpsichore

12 LETTERS

Clytemnestra
Golden Fleece
Hypermnestra
Pallas Athene
Rhadamanthus

BIBLICAL NAMES, PLACES, PERSONS

Books (in order)

OLD TESTAMENT

1 GENESIS
2 EXODUS
3 LEVITICUS
4 NUMBERS
5 DEUTERONOMY
6 JOSHUA
7 JUDGES
8 RUTH
9 SAMUEL 1
10 SAMUEL 2
11 KINGS 1
12 KINGS 2
13 CHRONICLES 1
14 CHRONICLES 2
15 EZRA
16 NEHEMIAH
17 ESTHER
18 JOB
19 PSALMS

20 PROVERBS
21 ECCLESIASTES
22 SONG OF SOLOMON
23 ISAIAH
24 JEREMIAH
25 LAMENTATIONS
26 EZEKIEL
27 DANIEL
28 HOSEA
29 JOEL
30 AMOS
31 OBADIAH
32 JONAH
33 MICAH
34 NAHUM
35 HABAKKUK
36 ZEPHANIAH
37 HAGGAI
38 ZECHARIAH
39 MALACHI

NEW TESTAMENT

1 MATTHEW
2 MARK
3 LUKE
4 JOHN
5 THE ACTS
6 ROMANS
7 CORINTHIANS 1
8 CORINTHIANS 2
9 GALATIANS
10 EPHESIANS
11 PHILIPPIANS
12 COLOSSIANS
13 THESSALONIANS 1

14 THESSALONIANS 2
15 TIMOTHY 1
16 TIMOTHY 2
17 TITUS
18 PHILEMON
19 HEBREWS
20 JAMES
21 PETER 1
22 PETER 2
23 JOHN 1
24 JOHN 2
25 JOHN 3
26 JUDE
27 REVELATION

Biblical Kings/Rulers: OG,
ASA, GOG, IRA, IVA,
AGAG, AHAB, AHAZ,
AMON, BERA, ELAH,
JEHU, OMRI, REBA, SAUL,
DAVID, HEROD, HIRAM,
JORAM, NADAB, REZIN,
ZIMRI, BIRSHA, HEZION,
JAPHIA, JOSHUA, JOTHAM,
JEHORAM, SOLOMON

Biblical Patriarchs: JOB, REU,
ADAM, ENOS, NOAH,
SETH, SHEM, ABRAM,
ISAAC, JACOB, JARED,
NAHOR, PELEG, TERAH,
LAMECH

Biblical Peoples/Tribes: DAN,
GOG, AMON, ANAK,
ARAD, CUSH, EMIN,
MOAB, PHUD, PHUT,
SEBA, AMMON, ARKITE,
HAMITE, HIVITE, KENITE,
SEMITE, SHELAH, SINITE,
AMORITE, DODANIN,
EDOMITE, HITTITE,
LEHABIM, MOABITE,
REPHAIM

Biblical Places
City: DAN, AVEN, CANA,
ELON, GATH, GAZA,
NAIN, ZOAR, BABEL,
EKRON, JOPPA, SODOM,
BETHEL, HEBRON,
JERICHO, BABYLON,
GOMORRAH, NAZARETH,
JERUSALEM
Country: PUL, ARAM,
EDOM, ENON, GATH,
MOAB, SEBA, SEIR,
SHEBA, AMMON, CANAAN,

CHALDEA, GALILEE,
SAMARIA
Hill: ZION
Kingdom: ELAM, MOAB,
SHEBA, JUDEA, JUDAH,
ISRAEL, SAMARIA,
CHALDEAE
Mountain: HOR, EBAL,
NAIN, NEBO, PEOR, SEIR,
SINA, ZION, HOREB,
SINAI, TABOR, ARARAT,
GILEAD, OLIVET, PISGAH
River: ZAB, NILE, ABANA,
ARNON, KISHON, JORDAN

Biblical Prophets: AMOS,
EZRA, JOEL, HOSEA,
JONAH, MICAH, MOSES,
DANIEL, NAHUM, ELIJAH,
ELISHA, ISAIAH, EZEKIEL,
JEREMIAH

Biblical Men: OG, ARA, ELI,
GOG, HAM, LOT, URI,
ABEL, AMOS, BOAZ,
CAIN, CUSH, EBAL, ENOS,
ESAU, HETH, IRAD, JOAB,
LEVI, MOAB, OBED,
OMAR, OREB, SETH,
AARON, ABIAH, ADAM,
ANNAS, CALEB, ENOCH,
HIRAM, ISAAC, JACOB,
JAMES, NAHOR, URIAH,
SAMSON, ANANIAS,
ISHMAEL

Biblical Women: EVE, LEAH,
MARY, RUTH, DINAH,
HAGAR, JULIA, JUNIA,
LYDIA, MERAB, NAOMI,
PHOEBE, SARAH, DORCAS,
ESTHER, HANNAH,
MIRIAM, RACHEL,
SALOME, VASHTI,
ABIGAIL, TABITHA

ALPHABETS

ARABIC

1. alif
2. ba
3. ta
4. sa
5. jim
6. ha
7. kha
8. dal
9. zal
10. ra
11. za
12. sin
13. shin
14. sad
15. dad
16. ta
17. ain
18. ghain
19. fa
20. qaf
21. kaf
22. lam
23. min
24. nun
25. ha
26. waw
27. ya

GREEK

1. alpha
2. beta
3. gamma
4. delta
5. epsilon
6. zeta
7. eta
8. theta
9. iota
10. kappa
11. lambda
12. mu
13. nu
14. xi
15. omicron
16. pi
17. rho
18. sigma
19. tau
20. upsilon
21. phi
22. chi
23. psi
24. omega

HEBREW

1. aleph
2. beth
3. gimmel
4. daleth
5. he
6. vav
7. zayin
8. kheth
9. teth
10. yod
11. kaph
12. lamed
13. mem
14. nun
15. samekh
16. ayin
17. pe
18. tsadi
19. koph
20. resh
21. sin
22. dhin
23. tav

CHEMICAL ELEMENTS AND THEIR ABBREVIATIONS

ACTINIUM, Ac
ALUMINUM, Al
AMERICIUM, Am
ANTIMONY, Sb
ARGON, Ar
ARSENIC, As
ASTATINE, At
BARIUM, Ba
BERKELIUM, Bk
BERYLLIUM, Be
BISMUTH, Bi
BORON, B
BROMINE, Br
CADMIUM, Cd
CALCIUM, Ca
CALIFORNIUM, Cf
CARBON, C
CERIUM, Ce
CESIUM, Cs
CHLORINE, Cl
CHROMIUM, Cr
COBALT, Co
COPPER, Cu
CURIUM, Cm
DYSPROSIUM, Dy
EINSTEINIUM, Es
ERBIUM, Er
EUROPIUM, Eu
FERMIUM, Fm
FLOURINE, F
FRANCIUM, Fr
GADOLINIUM, Gd
GALLIUM, Ga
GERMANIUM, Ge
GOLD, Au
HAFNIUM, Hf
HELIUM, He
HOLMIUM, Ho
HYDROGEN, H
INDIUM, In
IODINE, I
IRIDIUM, Ir
IRON, Fe
KRYPTON, Kr
LANTHANUM, La

LAWRENCIUM, Lw
LEAD, Pb
LITHIUM, Li
LUTENIUM, Lu
MAGNESIUM, Mg
MANGANESE, Mn
MEDELEVIUM, Md
MERCURY, Hg
MOLYBDENUM, Mo
NEODYMIUM, Nd
NEON, Ne
NEPTUNIUM, Np
NICKEL, Ni
NIOBIUM, Nb
NITROGEN, N
NOBELIUM, No
OSMIUM, Os
OXYGEN, O
PALLADIUM, Pd
PHOSPHORUS, P
PLATINUM, Pt
PLUTONIUM, Pu
POLENIUM, Po
POTASSIUM, K
PRASEODYMIUM, Pr
PROMETHIUM, Pm
PROTACTINIUM, Pa
RADIUM, Ra
RADON, Rn
RHENIUM, Re
RHODIUM, Rh
RUBIDIUM, Rb
RUTHENIUM, Ru
SAMARIUM, Sm
SCANDIUM, Sc
SELENIUM, Se
SILICON, Si
SILVER, Ag
SODIUM, Na
STRONTIUM, Sr
SULFUR, S
TANTALUM, Ta
TECHNETIUM, Tc
TELLURIUM, Te
TERBIUM, Tb

THALLIUM, Tl
THORIUM, Th
THULIUM, Tm
TIN, Sn
TITANIUM, Ti
TUNGSTEN, W

URANIUM, U
VANADIUM, V
XENON, Xe
YTTERBIUM, Yb
YTTRIUM, Y
ZINC, Zn
ZIRCONIUM, Zr

GEOLOGIC TIME

Cambrian: EARLIEST PERIOD OF THE PALEOZOIC ERA.

Carboniferous: PERIOD PRECEDING THE PERMIAN PERIOD OF THE PALEOZOIC ERA.

Cenozoic: MOST RECENT ERA.

Cretaceous: MOST RECENT PERIOD OF THE MESOZOIC ERA.

Devonian: PERIOD PRECEDING THE PERMIAN PERIOD OF THE PALEOZOIC ERA.

Eocene: EPOCH OF THE TERTIARY PERIOD OF THE CENOZOIC ERA.

Jurassic: INTERMEDIATE PERIOD OF THE MESOZOIC ERA.

Mesozoic: ERA PRECEDING THE CENOZOIC.

Miocene: EPOCH OF THE TERTIARY PERIOD OF THE CENOZOIC ERA.

Mississippian: MORE DISTANT OF THE CARBONIFEROUS PERIODS OF THE PALEOZOIC ERA.

Oligocene: EPOCH OF THE TERTIARY PERIOD OF THE CENOZOIC ERA.

Ordovician: PERIOD PRECEDING THE CARBONIFEROUS PERIOD OF THE PALEOZOIC ERA.

Paleocene: EPOCH OF THE TERTIARY PERIOD OF THE CENOZOIC ERA.

Paleozoic: ERA PRECEDING THE MESOZOIC ERA.

Pennsylvanian: MORE RECENT OF THE CARBONIFEROUS PERIODS OF THE PALEOZOIC ERA.

Permian: MOST RECENT PERIOD OF THE PALEOZOIC ERA.

Pleistocene: EPOCH OF THE QUATERNARY PERIOD OF THE CENOZOIC ERA.

Precambrian: EARLIEST ERA OF GEOLOGIC TIME, PRECEDING THE PALEOZOIC ERA.

Quaternary: MORE RECENT PERIOD OF THE CENOZOIC ERA.

Recent: EPOCH OF THE QUATERNARY PERIOD AND THE CENOZOIC ERA.

Tertiary: OLDER PERIOD OF THE CENOZOIC ERA.

Triassic: MOST DISTANT PERIOD OF THE MESOZOIC ERA.

Penguin Group (USA) Online

What will you be reading tomorrow?

Tom Clancy, Patricia Cornwell, W.E.B. Griffin,
Nora Roberts, William Gibson, Robin Cook,
Brian Jacques, Catherine Coulter, Stephen King,
Dean Koontz, Ken Follett, Clive Cussler,
Eric Jerome Dickey, John Sandford,
Terry McMillan, Sue Monk Kidd, Amy Tan,
John Berendt…

You'll find them all at
penguin.com

*Read excerpts and newsletters,
find tour schedules and reading group guides,
and enter contests.*

Subscribe to Penguin Group (USA) newsletters
and get an exclusive inside look
at exciting new titles and the authors you love
long before everyone else does.

PENGUIN GROUP (USA)
us.penguingroup.com

M224G1107